GW01018407

Computation and Modelling in Insurance and Finance

Scientific computing is as critical for the analysis of risk in insurance and finance as are mathematics and statistics, and it should be taught jointly with them. This book offers such an integrated approach at an introductory level and provides readers with much of what is needed in practice, including how simulation programs are designed, used and reused (with modifications) as situations change. Complex problems with risk from many sources are discussed, as is the sensitivity of conclusions on assumptions and historical data.

The tools of modelling and simulation are outlined in Part I with special emphasis on the Monte Carlo method and its use. Part II deals with general insurance and Part III with life insurance and financial risk. Algorithms that can be implemented on any programming platform are spread throughout, and a program library written in R is included. Numerous figures and experiments with R code illustrate the text.

The author's non-technical approach is ideal for graduate students, the only prerequisites being introductory courses in calculus and linear algebra, probability and statistics. The book will also be useful for actuaries and other analysts in the industry looking to update their skills.

ERIK BØLVIKEN, with broad experience as an applied statistician, holds the Chair of Actuarial Science at the University of Oslo and was for many years a partner in Gabler and Partners, Oslo.

INTERNATIONAL SERIES ON ACTUARIAL SCIENCE

The *International Series on Actuarial Science*, published by Cambridge University Press in conjunction with the Institute and Faculty of Actuaries, contains textbooks for students taking courses in or related to actuarial science, as well as more advanced works designed for continuing professional development or for describing and synthesizing research. The series is a vehicle for publishing books that reflect changes and developments in the curriculum, that encourage the introduction of courses on actuarial science in universities, and that show how actuarial science can be used in all areas where there is long-term financial risk.

A complete list of books in the series can be found at www.cambridge.org/statistics. Recent titles include the following:

Solutions Manual for Actuarial Mathematics for Life Contingent Risks (2nd Edition)
David C.M. Dickson, Mary R. Hardy & Howard R. Waters

Actuarial Mathematics for Life Contingent Risks (2nd Edition)
David C.M. Dickson, Mary R. Hardy & Howard R. Waters

Risk Modelling in General Insurance
Roger J. Gray & Susan M. Pitts

Financial Enterprise Risk Management
Paul Sweeting

Regression Modeling with Actuarial and Financial Applications
Edward W. Frees

Predictive Modeling Applications in Actuarial Science, Volume I: Predictive Modeling Techniques
Edited by Edward W. Frees, Richard A. Derrig & Glenn Meyers

Nonlife Actuarial Models
Yiu-Kuen Tse

Generalized Linear Models for Insurance Data
Piet De Jong & Gillian Z. Heller

COMPUTATION AND MODELLING IN INSURANCE AND FINANCE

ERIK BØLVIKEN
University of Oslo

CAMBRIDGE
UNIVERSITY PRESS

University Printing House, Cambridge CB2 8BS, United Kingdom

Published in the United States of America by Cambridge University Press, New York

Cambridge University Press is part of the University of Cambridge.

It furthers the University's mission by disseminating knowledge in the pursuit of education, learning and research at the highest international levels of excellence.

www.cambridge.org
Information on this title: www.cambridge.org/9780521830485

First published 2014

Printing in the United Kingdom by TJ International Ltd. Padstow Cornwall

A catalogue record for this publication is available from the British Library

Library of Congress Cataloguing in Publication data
Bølviken, Erik.
Computation and modelling in insurance and finance / Erik Bølviken.
pages cm
Includes bibliographical references and index.
ISBN 978-0-521-83048-5 (Hardback)
1. Insurance–Mathematical models. 2. Finance–Mathematical models. I. Title.
HG8781.B675 2014
368′.01–dc23 2013045316

ISBN 978-0-521-83048-5 Hardback

Contents

Preface

The book is organized as a broad introduction to concepts, models and computational techniques in Part I and with general insurance and life insurance/financial risk in Parts II and III. The latter are largely self-contained and can probably be read on their own. Each part may be used as a basis for a university course; we do that in Oslo. Computation is more strongly emphasized than in traditional textbooks. Stochastic models are defined in the way they are simulated in the computer and examined through numerical experiments. This cuts down on the mathematics and enables students to reach 'advanced' models quickly. Numerical experimentation is also a way to illustrate risk concepts and to indicate the impact of assumptions that are often somewhat arbitrary. One of the aims of this book is to teach how the computer is put to work effectively.

Other issues are error in risk assessments and the use of historical data, each of which are tasks for statistics. Many of the models and distributions are presented with simple fitting procedures, and there is an entire chapter on error analysis and on the difference between risk under the underlying, real model and the one we actually use. Such error is in my opinion often treated too lightly: we should be very much aware of the distinction between the complex, random mechanisms in real life and our simplified model versions with deviating parameters. In a nebulous and ever-changing world modelling should be kept simple and limited to the essential.

The reader must be familiar with elementary calculus, probability and matrix algebra (the last two being reviewed in appendices) and should preferably have some programming experience. These apart, the book is self-contained with concepts and methods developed from scratch. The text is equipped with algorithms written in pseudo-code that can be programmed on any platform whereas the exercises make use of the open-source R software which permits Monte Carlo simulation of quite complex problems through a handful of commands. People can teach themselves the tricks of R programming by following the instructions in the exercises (my recommendation), but it is also possible to use the associated R library passively. The exercises vary from the theoretical to the numerical. There is a good deal of experimentation and model comparison.

I am grateful to my editor at Cambridge University Press, David Tranah, for proposing the project and for following the work with infinite patience over a much longer period than originally envisaged. Montserrat Guillen provided a stimulating environment at The University of Barcelona where some parts were written. Ragnar Norberg at London School of Economics was kind enough to go through an earlier version of the entire manuscript. My friends at Gabler in Oslo, above all Christian Fotland and Arve Moe have been a source of inspiration. Jostein Sørvoll, former head of the same company, taught me some of the practical sides of insurance as did Torbjørn Jakobsen for finance and Nils Haavardsson for insurance. I also thank Morten Folkeson and Steinar Holm for providing some of the historical data. Many of the exercises were checked by my students Eirik Sagstuen and Rebecca Wiborg.

Erik Bølviken
Oslo, December 2013

1
Introduction

1.1 A view on the evaluation of risk

1.1.1 The role of mathematics

How is evaluation of risk influenced by modern computing? Consider the way we use mathematics, first as a vendor of models of complicated risk processes. These models are usually stochastic. They are in general insurance probability distributions of claim numbers and losses and in life insurance and finance, stochastic processes describing lifecycles and investment returns. Mathematics is from this point of view a *language*, a way risk is expressed, and it is a language we must master. Otherwise statements of risk cannot be related to reality, it would be impossible to say what conclusions mean in any precise manner and nor could analyses be presented effectively to clients. Actuarial science is in this sense almost untouched by modern computational facilities. The basic concepts and models remain what they were, notwithstanding, of course, the strong growth of risk products throughout the last decades. This development may have had something to do with computers, but not much with computing per se.

However, mathematics is also *deductions* with precise conclusions derived from precise assumptions through the rules of logic. That is the way mathematics is taught at school and university. It is here that computing enters applied mathematical disciplines like actuarial science. More and more of these deductions are implemented in computers and carried out there. This has been going on for decades. It leans on an endless growth in computing power, a true technological revolution opening up simpler and more general computational methods which require less of users.

1.1.2 Risk methodology

An example of such an all-purpose computational technique is **stochastic simulation**. Simplified versions of processes taking place in real life are then reproduced

The world of risk	*In the computer*	*Sources for $\widehat{M}$:*
		Historical experience
$M \rightarrow X$	$\widehat{M} \rightarrow X^*$	*The implied market view*
	$\uparrow$	*Deductions from no-arbitrage*
	Assumed mechanism	*Judgement, physical modelling*

Figure 1.1 The working process: Main steps in risk evaluation.

in the computer. Risk in finance and insurance is future uncertain gains and losses, designated in this book by letters such as X and Y. Typical examples are compensations for claims in general insurance, pension schemes interrupted upon death in life insurance and future values of shares and bonds in finance. There are also secondary (or derived) products where values and payoffs are channelled through contract clauses set up in advance. Such agreements are known as **derivatives** in finance and **reinsurance** in insurance.

The mathematical approach, unanimously accepted today, is through probabilities with risks X and Y seen as **random variables**. We shall know their values eventually (after the event), but for planning and control and to price risk-taking activities we need them in advance and must fall back on their probabilities. This leads to a working process such as the one depicted in Figure 1.1. The real world on the left is an enormously complicated mechanism (denoted M) that yields a future X.

We shall never know M, though our paradigm is that it does exist as a well-defined stochastic mechanism. Since it is beyond reach, a simplified version $\widehat{M}$ is constructed in its place and used to study X. Its expected value is used for valuation and the percentiles for control, and unlike in engineering we are rarely concerned with predicting a specific value. Note that everything falls apart if $\widehat{M}$ deviates too strongly from the true mechanism M. This issue of **error** is a serious one indeed. Chapter 7 is an introduction.

What there is to go on when $\widehat{M}$ is constructed is listed on the right in Figure 1.1. Learning from the past is an obvious source (but not all of it is relevant). In finance, current asset prices bring market opinion about the future. This so-called **implied view** is introduced briefly in Section 1.4, and there will be more in Part III. Then there is the theory of **arbitrage**, where riskless financial income is assumed impossible. The innocent-looking no-arbitrage condition has wide implications, which are discussed in Chapter 14. In practice, some personal judgement behind $\widehat{M}$ is often present, but this is not for general argument, and nor shall we go into the physical modelling used in large-claims insurance where hurricanes, earthquakes or floods are imitated in the computer. This book is about how $\widehat{M}$ is constructed from the first three sources (historical data above all), how it is implemented in the computer and how the computer model is used to determine the probability distribution of X. Note that $\widehat{M}$ is inevitably linked to the past even though perceived trends and changes may have been built into it, and there is no way of knowing how well it captures a future which sometimes extends over decades. While this doesn't make the mathematical approach powerless, it does suggest simple and transparent models and a humble attitude towards it all.

1.1.3 The computer model

The real risk variable X will materialize only once. The economic result of a financial investment in a particular year is a unique event, as is the aggregated claim against an insurance portfolio during a certain period of time. With the computer model, that is different. Once it has been set up it can be played as many times as we please. Let $X_1^*, \dots, X_m^*$ be realizations of X revealing which values are likely and which are not, and how bad things might be if we are unlucky. The * will be used to distinguish computer simulations from real variables and m will always denote the number of simulations.

The method portrayed on the left of Figure 1.1 is known as the **Monte Carlo** method or **stochastic simulation**. It belongs to the realm of numerical integration; see Evans and Schwarz (2000) for a summary of this important branch of numerical mathematics. Monte Carlo integration dates back a long way. It is computationally slow, but other numerical methods (that might do the job faster) often require more expertise and get bogged down for high-dimensional integrals, which are precisely what we often need in practice. The Monte Carlo method is unique in handling many variables well.

What is the significance of numerical speed anyway? Does it really matter that some specialized technique (demanding more time and know-how to implement) is (say) one hundred times faster when the one we use only takes a second? If the procedure for some reason is to be repeated in a loop thousands of times, it would matter. Often, however, slow Monte Carlo is quite enough, and, indeed, the practical limit to its use is moving steadily as computers become more and more powerful. How far have we got? The author's portable computer from 2006 (with T60p processor) took three seconds to produce ten million Pareto draws through Algorithm 2.13 implemented in Fortran. This is an insurance portfolio of 1000 claims simulated 10 000 times! Generating the normal is even faster, and if speed is a priority, try the table methods in Section 4.2.

One of the aims of this book is to demonstrate how these opportunities are utilized. Principal issues are how simulations programs are designed, how they are modified to deal with related (but different) problems and how different programs are merged to handle situations of increasing complexity with several risk factors contributing jointly. The versatility and usefulness of Monte Carlo is indicated in

Section 1.5 (and in Chapter 3 too). By mastering it you are well equipped to deal with much that comes your way and avoid getting stuck when pre-programmed software doesn't have what you need. What platform should you go for? Algorithms in this book are written in a pseudo-code that goes with everything. Excel and Visual Basic are standard in the industry and may be used even for simulation. Much higher speed is obtained with C, Pascal or Fortran, and in the opinion of this author people are well advised to learn software like those. There are other possibilities as well, and the open-source R-package is used with the exercises. Much can be achieved with a platform you know!

1.2 Insurance risk: Basic concepts

1.2.1 Introduction

Property or **general insurance** is economic responsibility for incidents such as fires or accidents passed on (entirely or in part) to an insurer against a fee. The contract, known as a **policy**, releases indemnities (**claims**) when such events occur. A central quantity is the total claim X amassed during a certain period of time (typically a year). Often $X = 0$ (no events), but on rare occasions X is huge. An insurance company copes whatever happens, if properly run. It has a **portfolio** of many such risks and only a few of them materialize. But this raises the issue of controlling the total uncertainty, which is a major theme in general insurance.

Life insurance is also built up from random payments X. **Term insurance**, where beneficiaries receive compensation upon the death of the policy holder, is similar to property insurance in that unexpected events lead to payoffs. **Pension schemes** are the opposite. Now the payments go on as long as the insured is alive, and they are likely, not rare. Yet the basic approach remains the same, with random variables X expressing the uncertainty involved.

1.2.2 Pricing insurance risk

Transfers of risk through X do not take place for free. The fee (or **premium**), charged in advance, depends on the market conditions, but the expectation is a guideline. Introduce

$$\pi^{\text{pu}} = E(X), \tag{1.1}$$

which is known as the **pure premium** and defines a break-even situation. A company receiving π^{pu} for its services will, in the absence of all overhead cost and all financial income, neither earn nor lose in the long run. This is a consequence of the law of large numbers in probability theory; see Appendix A.2.

Such a pricing strategy is (of course) out of the question, and companies add **loadings** γ on top of π^{pu}. The premium charged is then

$$\pi = (1+\gamma)\pi^{\text{pu}}, \tag{1.2}$$

and we may regard $\gamma\pi^{\text{pu}}$ as the cost of risk. It is influenced thoroughly by the market situation, and in many branches of insurance is known to exhibit strong fluctuations; see Section 11.5 for a simple model. There have been attempts to determine γ from theoretical arguments, see Young (2004) for a review, but these efforts are not used much in practice and will not be considered.

The loading concept separates the market side from the insurance process itself, but another issue is whether the pure premium is known. Stochastic models for X always depend on unknown quantities such as parameters or probability distributions. They are determined from experience or even assessed informally if historical data are lacking, and there is a crucial distinction between the true π^{pu} with perfect knowledge of the underlying situation and the $\hat{\pi}^{\text{pu}}$ used for analysis and decisions. The discrepancy between what we seek and what we get is a fundamental issue of **error** that is present everywhere (see Figure 1.1), and there is special notation for it. A parameter or quantity with a ^ such as $\hat{\psi}$ means an estimate or an assessment of an underlying, unknown ψ. Chapter 7 offers a general discussion of errors and how they are confronted.

1.2.3 Portfolios and solvency

A second major theme in insurance is **control**. Companies are obliged to set aside funds to cover future obligations, and this is even a major theme in the *legal* definition of insurance. A company carries responsibility for many policies. It will lose on some and gain on others. In property insurance policies without accidents are profitable, those with large claims are not. Long lives in pension schemes lead to losses, short ones to gains. *At the portfolio level, gains and losses average out.* This is the beauty of a large agent handling many risks simultaneously.

Suppose a portfolio consists of J policies with claims $X_1, \dots, X_J$. The total claim is then

$$\mathcal{X} = X_1 + \cdots + X_J, \tag{1.3}$$

where calligraphic letters like $\mathcal{X}$ will be used for quantities at the portfolio level. We are certainly interested in $E(\mathcal{X})$, but equally important is its distribution. Regulators demand sufficient funds to cover $\mathcal{X}$ with high probability. The mathematical formulation is in terms of a percentile q_ϵ, which is the solution of the equation

$$\Pr(\mathcal{X} > q_\epsilon) = \epsilon \tag{1.4}$$

where ϵ is a small number (for example 1%). The amount q_ϵ is known as the **solvency capital** or **reserve**. Percentiles are used in finance too and are then often called value at risk (or **VaR** for short). As elsewhere, the true q_ϵ we seek is not the same as the estimated $\hat{q}_\epsilon$ we get.

1.2.4 Risk ceding and reinsurance

Risk is ceded from ordinary policy holders to companies, but companies do the same thing between themselves. This is known as **reinsurance**, and the ceding company is known as the **cedent**. The rationale *could* be the same; i.e., that a financially weaker agent is passing risk to a stronger one. In reality even the largest companies do this to diversify risk, and financially the cedent may be as strong as the reinsurer. There is now a chain of responsibilities that can be depicted as follows:

original clients	$\longrightarrow$	cedent	$\longrightarrow$	reinsurer
$\mathcal{X}$ *(primary)*		$\mathcal{X}^{\text{ce}} = \mathcal{X} - \mathcal{X}^{\text{re}}$		$\mathcal{X}^{\text{re}}$ *(derived)*

The original risk $\mathcal{X}$ is split between cedent and reinsurer through two separate relationships, where the cedent part $\mathcal{X}^{\text{ce}}$ is net and the difference between two cash flows. Of course $\mathcal{X}^{\text{re}} \leq \mathcal{X}$; i.e., the responsibility of the reinsurer is always *less* than the original claim. Note the calligraphic style that applies to portfolios. There may in practice be several rounds of such cedings in complicated networks extending around the globe. One reinsurer may go to a second reinsurer, and so on. Modern methods provide the means to analyse risk taken by an agent who is far away from the primary source. Ceding and reinsurance are tools used by managers to tune portfolios to a desired risk profile.

1.3 Financial risk: Basic concepts

1.3.1 Introduction

Gone are the days when insurance liabilities were insulated from assets and insurance companies carried all the financial risk themselves. One trend is ceding to customers. In countries like the USA and Britain, insurance products with financial risk integrated have been sold for decades under names such as unit link or universal life. The rationale is that clients receive higher expected financial income in exchange for carrying more risk. Pension plans today are increasingly **contributed benefits** (CB), where financial risk rests with individuals. There is also much interest in investment strategies tailored to given liabilities and how they distribute over time. This is known as **asset liability management** (ALM) and is discussed in

Chapter 15. The present section and the next one review the main concepts of finance.

1.3.2 Rates of interest

An ordinary bank deposit v_0 grows to $(1 + r)v_0$ at the end of one period and to $(1 + r)^K v_0$ after K of them. Here r, the **rate of interest**, depends on the length of the period. Suppose interest is compounded over K segments, each of length $1/K$, so that the total time is one. If interest per segment is r/K, the value of the account becomes

$$\left(1 + \frac{r}{K}\right)^K v_0 \to e^r v_0, \quad \text{as} \quad K \to \infty,$$

after one of the most famous limits of mathematics. Interest earnings may therefore be cited as

$$rv_0 \quad \text{or} \quad (e^r - 1)v_0,$$

depending on whether we include 'interest on interest'. The second form implies continuous compounding of interest and higher earnings ($e^r - 1 > r$ if $r > 0$), and now $(e^r)^k = e^{rk}$ takes over from $(1 + r)^k$. It doesn't really matter which form we choose, since they can be made equivalent by adjusting r.

1.3.3 Financial returns

Let V_0 be the value of a financial asset at the start of a period and V_1 the value at the end of it. The relative gain

$$R = \frac{V_1 - V_0}{V_0} \tag{1.5}$$

is known as the **return** on the asset. Solving for V_1 yields

$$V_1 = (1 + R)V_0, \tag{1.6}$$

with RV_0, the financial income. Clearly R acts like interest, but there is more to it than that. Interest is a fixed benefit offered by a bank (or an issuer of a very secure bond) in return for making a deposit and is risk free. Shares of company stock, in contrast, are fraught with risk. They may go up (R positive) or down (R negative). When dealing with such assets, V_1 (and hence R) is determined by the market, whereas with ordinary interest r is given and V_1 follows.

The return R is the more general concept and is a random variable with a probability distribution. Take the randomness away, and we are back to a fixed rate of interest r. As r depends on the time between V_0 and V_1, so does the distribution of

R; as will appear many times in this book. Whether the rate of interest r really *is* risk free is not as obvious as it seems. True, you do get a fixed share of your deposit as a reward, but that does not tell its worth in **real** terms when price increases are taken into account. Indeed, over longer time horizons risk due to inflation may be huge and even reduce the real value of cash deposits and bonds. Saving money with a bank at a fixed rate of interest may also bring **opportunity cost** if the market rate after a while exceeds what you get. These issues are discussed and integrated with other sources of risk in Part III.

1.3.4 Log-returns

Economics and finance have often constructed stochastic models for R directly. An alternative is the **log-return**

$$X = \log(1 + R), \tag{1.7}$$

which by (1.5) can be written $X = \log(V_1) - \log(V_0)$; i.e., as a difference of logarithms. The modern theory of financial derivatives (Section 3.5 and Chapter 14) is based on X. Actually, X and R do not necessarily deviate that strongly since the Taylor series of $\log(1 + R)$ is

$$X = R - \frac{R^2}{2} + \frac{R^3}{3} + \cdots,$$

where R (a fairly small number) dominates so that $X \doteq R$, at least over short periods. It follows that the distributions of R and X must be rather similar (see Section 2.4), but this is not to say that the discrepancy is unimportant. It depends on the amount of random variation present, and the longer the time horizon the more X deviates from R; see Section 5.4 for an illustration.

1.3.5 Financial portfolios

Investments are often spread over many assets as **baskets** or financial **portfolios**. By intuition this must reduce risk; see Section 5.3, where the issue is discussed. A central quantity is the portfolio return, denoted $\mathcal{R}$ (in calligraphic style). Its relationship to the individual returns R_j of the assets is as follows. Let $V_{10}, \ldots, V_{J0}$ be investments in J assets. The portfolio value is then

$$\mathcal{V}_0 = \sum_{j=1}^{J} V_{j0} \quad \text{growing at the end of the period to} \quad \mathcal{V}_1 = \sum_{j=1}^{J} (1 + R_j) V_{j0}.$$

Subtract $\mathcal{V}_0$ from $\mathcal{V}_1$ and divide by $\mathcal{V}_0$, and you get the portfolio return

$$\mathcal{R} = \sum_{j=1}^{J} w_j R_j \quad \text{where } w_j = \frac{V_{0j}}{\mathcal{V}_0}. \tag{1.8}$$

Here w_j is the **weight** on asset j and

$$w_1 + \cdots + w_J = 1. \tag{1.9}$$

Financial weights define the distribution on individual assets and will, in this book, usually be normalized so that they sum to 1.

The mathematics allow negative w_j. With bank deposits this corresponds to borrowing. It is also possible with shares, known as **short selling**. A loss due to a negative development is then carried by somebody else. The mechanism is as follows. A short contract with a buyer is to sell shares at the end of the period at an agreed price. At that point we shall have to buy at market price, gaining if it is lower than our agreement, losing if not. Short contracts may be an instrument to lower risk (see Section 5.3) and require **liquidity**; i.e., assets that are traded regularly.

1.4 Risk over time

1.4.1 Introduction

A huge number of problems in finance and insurance have time as one of the central ingredients, and this requires additional quantities and concepts. Many of these are introduced below. The emphasis is on finance, where the number of such quantities is both more plentiful and more complex than in insurance. Time itself is worth a comment. In this book it will be run on equidistant sequences, either

$$\underset{\textit{time scale for evaluation}}{T_k = kT} \qquad \text{or} \qquad \underset{\textit{time scale for modelling}}{t_k = kh} \tag{1.10}$$

for $k = 0, 1, \ldots$ On the left, T is an accounting period (e.g., year, quarter, month) or the time to expiry of a bond or an option. Financial returns R_k, portfolio values $\mathcal{V}_k$ and insurance liabilities $\mathcal{X}_k$ are followed over T_k. The present is always at $T_0 = 0$, whereas $k > 0$ is the future which requires stochastic models to portray what is likely and what is not. *Negative* time will sometimes be used for past values.

The time scale h is used for modelling. It may coincide with T, but it may well be smaller so that $T = Kh$ for $K > 1$. How models on different time scales are related is important; see Section 5.7, where this issue is discussed. There is also much scope for very short time increments where $h \to 0$ (so that $K = T/h \to \infty$). This is known as **continuous-time modelling** and is above all a trick to find simple mathematical solutions. Parameters or variables are then often cited as **intensities**, which are quantities per time unit. An example is interest rates, which will on several occasions be designated rh with r an intensity and not a rate as in Section 1.3. Claim frequencies in property insurance (Chapter 8) and mortalities in life insurance (Chapter 12) are other examples of using intensities for modelling. This section is concerned with the macro time scale T only.

1.4.2 Accumulation of values

If v_0 is the original value of a financial asset, by $T_K = KT$ it is worth

$$V_K = (1 + R_1)(1 + R_2)\cdots(1 + R_K)V_0 = (1 + R_{0:K})v_0,$$

where $R_1, \dots, R_K$ are the returns. This defines $R_{0:K}$ on the right as the K**-step** return

$$\underbrace{R_{0:K} = (1 + R_1)\cdots(1 + R_K) - 1}_{\textit{ordinary returns}} \quad \text{and also} \quad \underbrace{X_{0:K} = X_1 + \cdots + X_K}_{\textit{log-returns}}, \tag{1.11}$$

where $X_k = \log(1 + R_k)$ and $X_{0:K} = \log(1 + R_{0:K})$. The log-returns on the right are accumulated by adding them. Interest is a special case (an important one!) and grows from $T_0 = 0$ to T_K according to

$$r_{0:K} = (1 + r_1)(1 + r_2)\cdots(1 + r_K) - 1, \tag{1.12}$$

where $r_1, \dots, r_K$ are the future rates. This reduces to $r_{0:K} = (1 + r)^K - 1$ if all $r_k = r$, but in practice r_k will float in a way that is unknown at $T_0 = 0$.

Often V_K aggregates economic and financial activity beyond the initial investment v_0. Let B_k be income or expenses that surface at time T_k, and suppose the financial income or loss coming from the sequence $B_1, \dots, B_K$ is the same as for the original asset. The total value at T_K is then the sum

$$V_K = (1 + R_{0:K})v_0 + \sum_{k=1}^{K}(1 + R_{k:K})B_k, \tag{1.13}$$

where $R_{k:K} = (1 + R_{k+1})\cdots(1 + R_K) - 1$ with $R_{K:K} = 0$. Later in this section $B_1, \dots, B_K$ will be a fixed cash flow, but further on (for example in Section 3.6) there will be huge uncertainty as to what their values are going to be, with additional random variation on top of the financial uncertainty.

1.4.3 Forward rates of interest

Future interest rates like r_k or $r_{0:K}$ are hopeless to predict from mathematical models (you will see why in Section 6.4), but there is also a market view that conveys the so-called **implied rates**. Consider an asset of value v_0 that will be traded at time T_K for a price $V_0(K)$ agreed today. Such contracts are called **forwards** and define inherent rates of interest $r_0(0\colon K)$ through

$$V_0(K) = \{1 + r_0(0\colon K)\}v_0 \quad \text{or} \quad r_0(0\colon K) = \frac{V_0(K)}{v_0} - 1. \tag{1.14}$$

Note the difference from (1.12) where $r_{0:K}$ is uncertain, whereas now $V_0(K)$ and hence $r_0(0\colon K)$ is fixed by the contract and known at $T_0 = 0$. Forward rates can in practice be deduced from many different sources, and the results are virtually identical. Otherwise there would have been market inconsistencies opening up money-earning schemes with no risk attached; more on this in Chapter 14.

We are often interested in breaking the rate $r_0(0\colon K)$ down into its average value $\bar{r}_0(0\colon K)$ per period. The natural definition is

$$1 + r_0(0\colon K) = \{1 + \bar{r}_0(0\colon K)\}^K \quad \text{or} \quad \bar{r}_0(0\colon K) = \{1 + r_0(0\colon K)\}^{1/K} - 1, \tag{1.15}$$

and as K is varied, the sequence $\bar{r}_0(0\colon K)$ traces out the **interest-rate curve** or **yield curve**, which is published daily in the financial press.

1.4.4 Present and fair values

What is the value today of receiving B_1 at time T_1? Surely it must be $B_1/(1 + r)$, which grows to precisely B_1 when interest is added. More generally, B_k at T_k is under constant rate of interest worth $B_k/(1+r)^k$, today, which motivates the **present value** (PV) as the value of a payment stream $B_0, \dots, B_K$ through

$$\text{PV} = \sum_{k=0}^{K} d_k B_k \quad \text{where} \quad d_k = \frac{1}{(1 + r)^k}. \tag{1.16}$$

This is a popular criterion in all spheres of economic life and used for assets and liabilities alike. It applies even when $B_0, \dots, B_K$ are stochastic (then the present value is too). Individual payments may be both positive and negative.

The quantities $d_k = 1/(1 + r)^k$ (or $d_k = e^{-rk}$ if interest is continuously compounded) are known as **discount factors**; they devaluate or discount future income. In life insurance, r is called the **technical rate**. The value to use isn't obvious, least of all with payment streams lasting decades ahead. Market discounting is an alternative. The coefficient d_k in (1.16) is then replaced by

$$d_k = \frac{1}{\{1 + \bar{r}_0(0\colon k)\}^k} = \frac{1}{1 + r_0(0\colon k)} \quad \text{or} \quad d_k = P_0(0\colon k), \tag{1.17}$$

where $P_0(0\colon k)$ comes from the bond market; see below. Instead of choosing the technical rate r administratively, the market view is used. The resulting valuation, known as **fair value**, holds obvious attraction, but also the disadvantage that such discount sequences fluctuate randomly, bringing uncertainty even if there was none at the start; see Section 15.3.

1.4.5 Bonds and yields

Governments and private companies raise capital by issuing **bonds**. In return for money received upfront, the issuer makes fixed payments to bond holders at certain points in time $T_0, \ldots, T_K$. The last one at T_K is a big one and known as the **face** of the bond. Earlier payments can be seen as interest on a loan that size, but it is simplest to define a bond as a fixed cash flow. How long it lasts varies enormously, from a year or less up to half a century or even longer. Bonds have a huge second-hand market and are traded regularly.

Should bonds be valued through present or fair values? Actually it is the other way around. The present value is *given* by what the market is willing to pay, and the rate of interest determined by the resulting equation. We are dealing with a fixed payment stream $B_0, \ldots, B_K$. Let V_0 be its market value at $T_0 = 0$. The **yield** y from buying the rights to the stream is then the solution of the equation

$$V_0 = \sum_{k=0}^{K} \frac{B_k}{(1+y)^k}. \tag{1.18}$$

With more than one payment a numerical method such as bisection is needed to determine y; see Appendix C.4.

A special case is the **zero-coupon** bond or **T-bond**, for which $B_0 = \cdots = B_{K-1} = 0$. It is **unit faced** if $B_K = 1$. Now the only transaction occurs at maturity T_K, and in a market operating rationally its yield y is the same as the forward rate of interest $\bar{r}_0(0\colon K)$. The price of unit-faced T-bonds will be denoted $P_0(0\colon K)$, which is what is charged today for the right to receive one money unit at T_K and relates to the forward rate of interest through

$$P_0(0\colon K) = \frac{1}{1 + r_0(0\colon K)} = \frac{1}{\{1 + \bar{r}_0(0\colon K)\}^K}. \tag{1.19}$$

Why? Because anything else would have allowed riskless financial income, which is incompatible with free markets. The prices $P_0(0\colon K)$ will be used a lot in Chapters 14 and 15.

1.4.6 Duration

The timing of bonds and other fixed payment streams is often measured through their **duration** $\mathcal{D}$. There are several versions which vary in detail. One possibility is

$$\mathcal{D} = \sum_{k=0}^{K} q_k T_k \quad \text{where} \quad q_k = \frac{B_k(1+r)^{-k}}{\sum_{i=0}^{K} B_i(1+r)^{-i}}. \tag{1.20}$$

The sequence $q_0, \ldots, q_K$ adds to one and is a probability distribution if all $B_k > 0$. Since q_k is proportional to the present value of the kth payment, $\mathcal{D}$ is formally an expectation that expresses how long the cash flow $B_0, \ldots, B_K$ is 'on average'.

For a zero-coupon bond maturing at $T_K = KT$, we have

$$q_K = 1 \quad \text{and} \quad q_k = 0, \quad \text{for} \quad k < K$$

so that $\mathcal{D} = T_K$, a sensible result! A bond with fixed coupon payments and a final (much larger) face has duration between $T_K/2$ and T_K.

1.4.7 Investment strategies

Long-term management of financial risk is usually concerned with different classes of assets which fluctuate jointly. Let $\mathcal{R}_k$ be the portfolio return in period k. The account $\{\mathcal{V}_k\}$ then evolves according to

$$\mathcal{V}_k = (1 + \mathcal{R}_k)\mathcal{V}_{k-1}, \quad k = 1, 2, \ldots, \tag{1.21}$$

where the link of $\mathcal{R}_k$ to the individual assets is through (1.8) as before. If R_{jk} is the return of asset j in period k, then

$$\mathcal{R}_k = \sum_{j=1}^{J} w_j R_{jk}, \tag{1.22}$$

and the weights $w_1, \ldots, w_J$ define the investment strategy. One way is to keep them fixed, as in (1.22) where they do not depend on k. This is not achieved automatically since individual investments meet with unequal success, which changes their relative value. Weights can only be kept fixed by buying and selling. Restructuring financial weights in such a way is known as **rebalancing**.

The opposite line is to let weights float freely. Mathematically this is more conveniently expressed through

$$\mathcal{V}_k = \sum_{j=1}^{J} V_{jk} \quad \text{where } V_{jk} = (1 + R_{jk})V_{jk-1}, \quad j = 1, \ldots, J,$$

emphasizing assets rather than returns. For more on investment strategies, consult Section 15.5.

1.5 Method: A unified beginning

1.5.1 Introduction

How to make the preceding quantities and concepts flourish? Stochastic models and Monte Carlo are needed! Here is an example introducting both. Let $X_1, X_2, \dots$ be an independent, random series driving $Y_1, Y_2, \dots$ through the recursion

$$Y_k = a_k Y_{k-1} + X_k, \quad k = 1, 2 \dots, \quad \text{starting at} \quad Y_0 = y_0 \tag{1.23}$$

which covers a number of important situations. The series $a_1, a_2, \dots$ may be fixed coefficients. Another possibility is $a_k = 1 + r$ where r is a rate of interest, and now $Y_1, Y_2, \dots$ are values of an account influenced by random input. A more advanced version is

$$\underset{\text{financial risk}}{a_k = 1 + \mathcal{R}_k} \quad \text{and} \quad \underset{\text{insurance risk}}{X_k = -\mathcal{X}_k,} \tag{1.24}$$

and two different sources of risk that might themselves demand extensive modelling and simulation are integrated. There will be more on this in Section 15.6. Here the target is a more modest one. A simple Monte Carlo algorithm and notation for such schemes will first be presented and then four simple examples. The aim is to introduce a general line of attack and indicate the power of Monte Carlo for problem solving, learning and communication.

1.5.2 Monte Carlo algorithms and notation

Let $Y_1, \dots, Y_K$ be the first K variables of the sequence (1.23). How they are simulated is indicated by the scheme in Algorithm 1.1 (a skeleton!), which is the first algorithm of the book. After initialization (Line 1) the random terms X_k^* are drawn (Line 3) and the new values Y_k^* found. All simulated variables are *-marked, a convention that will be followed everywhere. The backward arrow $\leftarrow$ signifies that the variable on the left is assigned the value on the right, more convenient notation than an ordinary equality sign. For example, when only the *last* value Y_K^* is wanted (as is frequent), statements like $Y^* \leftarrow aY^* + X^*$ simply overwrite Y^*, and values of the past are *not* stored in the computer. The % symbol will be used for inserting comments.

A huge number of simulation experiments in insurance and finance fit this scheme or some simple variation of it, which suggests a fairly stable pattern of Monte Carlo programming that can be lifted from one problem to another. Is K in Algorithm 1.1 random (as in Example 2 below)? Draw it prior to entering the loop on Line 2. Random a_k as in (1.24)? Similarly, remove it from the input list and generate it before computing Y_k^* on Line 4.

Algorithm 1.1 Basic recursion

```
Input: y_0, a_1, ..., a_k
Y*_0 ← y_0                                  %Initialization
%Draw K here if random
For k = 1, ..., K do
    Sample X*_k                             %Many possibilities
    Y*_k ← a_k Y*_{k-1} + X*_k              %New value
Return Y*_0, ..., Y*_K (or just Y*_K).
```

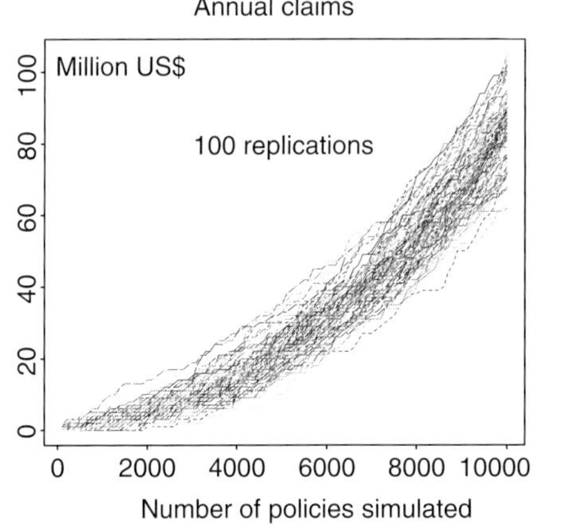

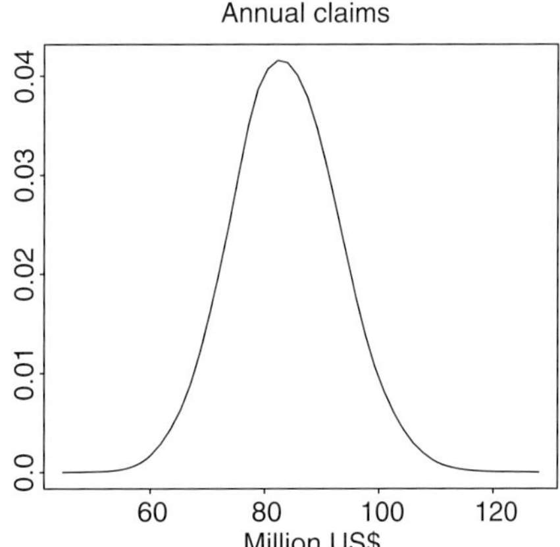

Figure 1.2 Simulations of term insurance. *Left*: 100 parallel runs through insurance portfolio. *Right*: Annual density function obtained from $m = 10\,000$ simulations.

1.5.3 Example: Term insurance

Consider J contracts where the death of policy holders releases one-time payments. How frequently this occurs is controlled by probabilities depending on age and sex of the individuals, which would be available on file. The situation is so simple that it is possible to examine portfolio liability and its uncertainty through mathematics (this is done in Section 3.4), but the point now is to use Monte Carlo. Let X_j be the payoff for policy j, either 0 when the policy holder survives or s_j when she (or he) does not. The stochastic model is

$$\Pr(X_j = 0) = p_j \quad \text{and} \quad \Pr(X_j = s_j) = 1 - p_j,$$

where p_j is the probability of survival. A simulation goes through the entire portfolio, reads policy information from file, draws those who die (whom we have to pay for) and adds all the payments together. In Algorithm 1.1 take $K = J$, $a_k = 1$ and X_j^* is either 0 or s_j; details in Section 3.4.

The example in Figure 1.2 shows annual expenses for $J = 10\,000$ policies for which $s_j = 1$ for all j (money unit: one million US$). All policy holders were

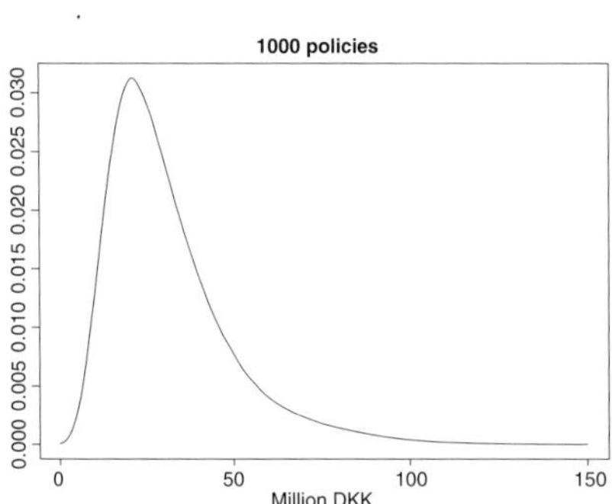

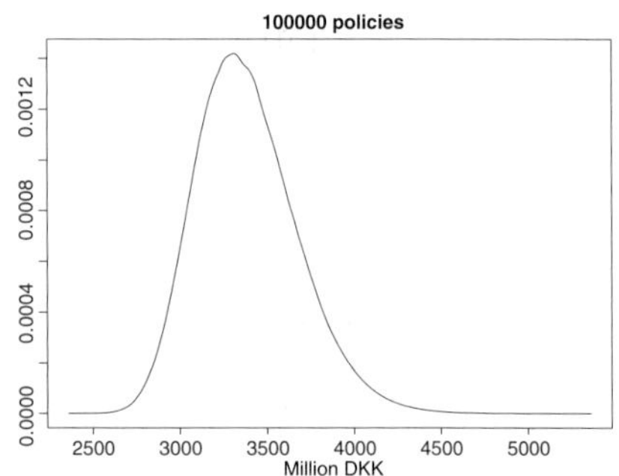

Figure 1.3 Density functions of the total claim against portfolio of fire risks (seven/eight Danish kroner (DKK) for one euro).

between 30 and 60 years, with survival probabilities and age distribution as specified in Section 3.4. One hundred parallel runs through the portfolio are plotted jointly on the left, showing how the simulations evolve. The curved shape has no significance. It is due to the age of the policy holders having been ordered on file so that the young ones with low death rates are examined first. What counts is the variation at the end, which is between 65 and 105 million. Another view is provided by the probability density function on the right, which has been estimated from the simulations by means of the kernel method in Section 2.2 (larger experiment needed). The Gaussian shape follows from the Lindeberg extension of the central limit theorem (Appendix A.4). Such risk is often ignored in life insurance, but in this example uncertainty isn't negligible.

1.5.4 Example: Property insurance

A classic model in property insurance is identical risks. Claims are then equally likely for everybody, and losses exhibit no systematic variation between individuals. The portfolio payout is

$$\mathcal{X} = Z_1 + \cdots + Z_{\mathcal{N}},$$

where $\mathcal{N}$ is the number of insurance incidents and $Z_1, Z_2, \ldots$ their cost. In Algorithm 1.1 $K = \mathcal{N}$ (and drawn prior to the loop), $a_k = 1$ and $X_k = Z_k$; consult Algorithm 3.1 for details.

The example in Figure 1.3 was run with annual claim frequency 1% per policy and a Poisson distribution for $\mathcal{N}$. Losses $Z_1, Z_2, \ldots$ were drawn from the empirical distribution function (Section 9.2) of the Danish fire data introduced in Section 9.6. The latter is a record of more than 2000 industrial fires, the largest going up to several hundred million Danish kroner (divide by seven or eight for euros, or ten for US dollars). Figure 1.3 shows the density function for the portfolio liabilities

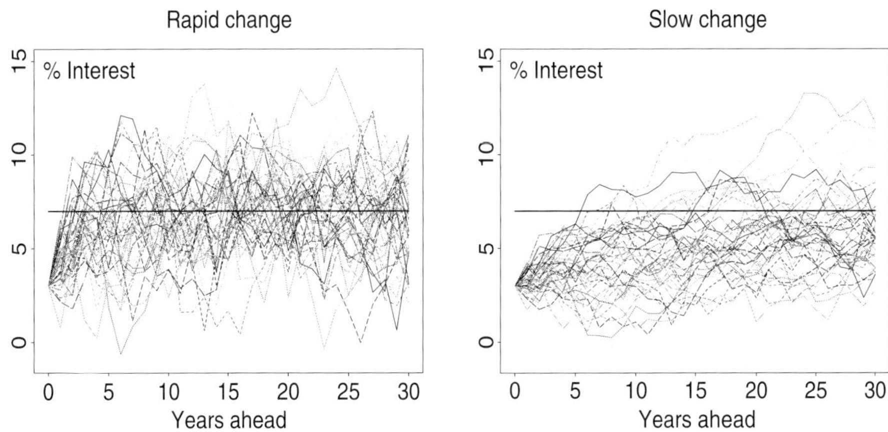

Figure 1.4 Simulations of the annual rate of interest from the Vasiček model.

of a 'small' portfolio ($J = 1000$) on the left and a 'large' one ($J = 100\,000$) on the right. The uncertainty is now much larger than in the first example. Note that the density function on the left is strongly skewed, but this asymmetry is straightened out as the portfolio grows, and the distribution becomes more Gaussian. The central limit theorem tells us this must be so.

1.5.5 Example: Reversion to mean

Monte Carlo is also a useful tool for examining the behaviour of stochastic models. One type concerns interest rates, equity volatilities, rates of inflation and exchange rates. All of these tend to fluctuate between certain, not clearly defined limits, and if they move too far out on either side, there are forces in the economy that pull them back again. This is known as **reversion to mean** and applies to a number of financial variables.

Interest rates are an important example. One of the most popular models, proposed by Vasiček (1977), is the recursion

$$r_k = Y_k + \xi \quad \text{where} \quad Y_k = aY_{k-1} + \sigma\varepsilon_k, \qquad k = 1, 2, \ldots, \tag{1.25}$$

starting at $Y_0 = r_0 - \xi$. Here ξ, a and σ are fixed parameters and $\{\varepsilon_k\}$ independent and identically distributed variables with mean 0 and standard deviation 1. The model is known as an autoregression of order 1 and is examined in Section 5.6. Here the objective is simulation, which is carried out by taking $a_k = a$ in Algorithm 1.1 and adding ξ to the output $Y_1^*, Y_2^* \ldots$ so that Monte Carlo interest rates $r_1^*, r_2^*, \ldots$ are produced.

Figure 1.4 shows simulated scenarios on an annual time scale under Gaussian models. The parameters are

$$\underbrace{r_0 = 3\%, \xi = 7\%, a = 0.70, \sigma = 0.016;}_{\text{'rapid' change}} \quad \underbrace{r_0 = 3\%, \xi = 7\%, a = 0.95, \sigma = 0.007}_{\text{'slow' change}}$$

both representing high-interest-rate regimes. The simulations start at $r_0 = 3\%$, much lower than the long-term average $\xi = 7\%$. That level is reached quickly on the left with all traces of *systematic* changes in patterns having gone after about 5 years. Phenomena of this kind are known as **stationary** and are discussed in Section 5.6. The same behaviour is observed with the second model on the right, but now the transient period until fluctuations stabilize is much longer, and after 25 years movements may still be slightly on the rise upwards. This is caused by the large value of a and is *not* realistic for interest rates in practice. Stationarity requires $-1 < a < 1$ and model behaviour changes completely outside this interval, as will emerge next.

1.5.6 Example: Equity over time

Stock prices $\{S_k\}$ are *not* mean reverting. They represent traded commodities, and had it been possible to identify systematic factors that drove them up and down, we would have been able to act upon them to earn money. But that opportunity would have been available to everybody, removing the forces we were utilizing and rendering the idea useless. Models for equity are for this reason very different from those for interest rates, and based on stochastically independent returns. A common specification is

$$R_k = e^{\xi+\sigma\varepsilon_k} - 1, \qquad k = 1, 2, \ldots, \tag{1.26}$$

where ε_k is a sequence of independent random variables with mean 0 and standard deviation 1. By definition $S_k = (1 + R_k)S_{k-1}$ so that

$$S_k = S_{k-1}e^{\xi+\sigma\varepsilon_k}, \quad k = 1, 2, \ldots, \qquad \text{starting at } S_0 = s_0. \tag{1.27}$$

This is known as a **geometric random walk** with $\log(S_k)$ following an ordinary random walk; see Section 5.5.

The behaviour of these models can be studied through Monte Carlo using Algorithm 1.1. Apply it to $Y_k = \log(S_k)$ (using $a_k = 1$ and $X_k = \xi + \sigma\varepsilon_k$) and convert the simulations by taking $S_k^* = e^{Y_k^*}$. The simulated scenarios in Figure 1.5 are monthly and apply to the k-step returns $R_{0:k}^* = S_k^*/S_0 - 1$ rather than the share price directly (the initial value $S_0 = s_0$ is then immaterial). Values for the parameters were:

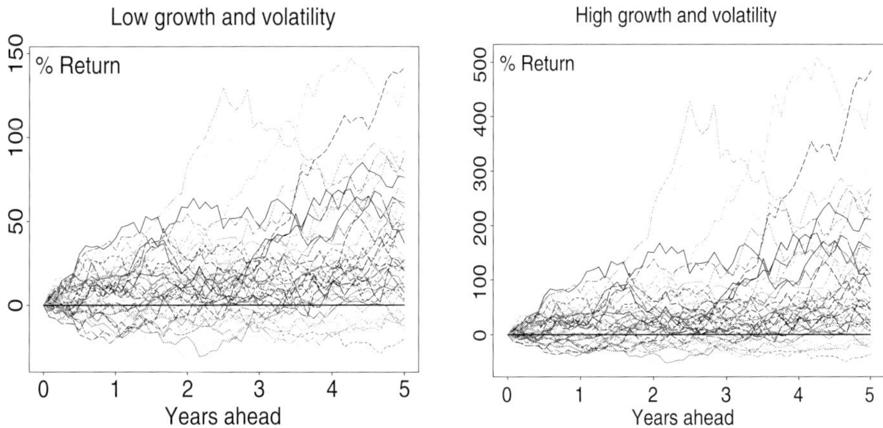

Figure 1.5 Simulations of accumulated equity return from geometric random walk (monthly time scale).

$$\underbrace{\xi = 0.4\%, \sigma = 4\%}_{\textit{low yield and risk}} \quad \text{and} \quad \underbrace{\xi = 0.8\%, \sigma = 8\%}_{\textit{high yield and risk}}$$

and the random terms ε_k in (1.27) are Gaussian. The potential for huge gain *and* huge loss is enormous.

After 5 years up to 50% of the original capital is lost in some of the scenarios on the right in Figure 1.5! Be aware that scales on the vertical axes differ so that the uncertainty of the first model scenario is around one-third of the other. The performance of equity is wild and unstable and quite different from money-market assets.

1.6 How the book is planned

1.6.1 Mathematical level

This is an elementary treatise, at least in terms of the mathematics used. No more than a bare necessity of ordinary and probabilistic calculus is demanded, and mathematical arguments rarely exceed calculations of means and variances. Whenever possible, models are presented the way they are simulated in the computer. This is an easier track to follow than probabilistic descriptions in terms of distributions (which quickly become complicated), and more advanced modelling can be reached faster. Exact density functions, whether for single or many variables, are required chiefly for maximum likelihood estimation of parameters anyway. Nor is it necessary to rely on artillery as heavy as stochastic analysis and Itô calculus to understand the basics of financial derivatives (see Chapter 14). The mathematics in this book is always in discrete time with modelling in continuous time as limits when the time increment $h \to 0$.

1.6.2 Organization

The main concepts of risk in insurance and finance were introduced above, and why stochastic simulation is such a unifying tool was indicated in Section 1.5. The latter is a forerunner of the entire Part I, where the Monte Carlo method and its potential are presented jointly with elementary models in insurance and finance. The idea is to get Monte Carlo settled early as a vehicle for analysis, learning and communication. Other major tools for risk studies are stochastic modelling of dependence (Chapters 5 and 6) and historical estimation and error (Chapter 7). Part I carries mathematical, statistical and computational methods from one application area to another, with examples from everywhere. The two other parts of the book deal with general insurance (Part II) and life insurance and financial risk (Part III). Their treatment is now systematic, with more complex models and situations. Algorithms will be presented as in Algorithm 1.1, which is written in a pseudo-code taken from Devroye (1986). Readers may implement them on a platform of their choice.

1.6.3 Exercises and R

The exercises contain many numerical studies where numbers are put to theory and key conditions are varied to provide insight into the sensitivity of results and how this issue is addressed. Implementation is possible on any platform, and the skeleton algorithms in the text should be of assistance. But the exercises have also been equiped with R-commands which draw on the open R-package. Originally conceived as software for statistical analysis under the name Splus, R has today also become an excellent tool for simulation schemes, though slower than C or Fortran. Most of what is in this book is suitable for R, and its vector and matrix tools combined with other facilities permit programming which is very compact indeed. The exercises have taken advantage of this, and the handful of R-commands necessary to carry them out are provided in the text. Alternatively, invoke the associated library of R-programs.

R runs on Linux, Windows and Mac compilers and can be downloaded from htttp://www.r-project.org, where you will find documentation too; for example, Venables and Smith (2010). A standard introduction to Splus in statistics is Venables and Ripley (2002).

1.6.4 Notational rules and conventions

In a book of this kind it is impossible to prevent some symbol overlap. Mathematical notation is introduced along the way, but it may be helpful to summarize a few conventions. Variables are capital Roman letters such as X and Y or calligraphic analogues $\mathcal{X}$ or $\mathcal{Y}$ for portfolios. Their values are lowercase letters x and y. Except for interest rates (see below), these rules are in force everywhere. Parameters are usually Greek letters α, β and so on with ε (and occasionally η) being reserved for the standard normal $N(0, 1)$ or sometimes just standardized variables with mean 0 and standard deviation 1. Time is always indexed by k as $t_k = kh$ or $T_k = kT$, where h is used for modelling and T for accounting. On many occasions h and T differ. We need to distinguish between the present at $k = 0$, where variables are known and the future at $k > 0$, where they are not. The past is occasionally represented by $k < 0$. Variables in real life, say X or Y, are *-marked as X^* or Y^* when simulated in the computer (though not in the R-programs in the exercises). *Very* important is the difference between random variables X realized under the true model M and their analogues $\hat{X}$ under $\widehat{M}$. There is a similar distinction between a true parameter α and its estimate $\hat{\alpha}$. If both prior estimation *and* Monte Carlo are involved, X is written $\hat{X}^*$. Vectors and matrices are set in bold face.

Financial return and money-market instruments require a host of symbols and rules of indexing. Simple ones like R_k and r_k apply to period k, whereas $R_{0:k}$ and $r_{0:k}$ define returns that accrue from 0 to k. A symbol like $\bar{r}_{0:k}$ designates the average rate of interest (or yield) per period up to k. All of $R_{0:k}$, $r_{0:k}$ and $\bar{r}_{0:k}$ only become known at time k and are very different from forward analogues like $r_0(0\colon k)$ and $\bar{r}_0(0\colon k)$ which are agreed between two parties at $k = 0$. Even more complex notation will be needed in Part III with (for example) $\bar{r}_k(K\colon J)$ being the rate of interest settled at time k of a forward contract running further ahead from K to J. The general rule is time as index and the contract period in parentheses.

1.7 Bibliographical notes

1.7.1 General work

For ideas on the practical side of the actuarial profession, try Szabo (2004). A general introduction to assets and liabilities is Booth *et al.* (1999), with management issues covered in Williams *et al.* (1998). Neither of these make much use of mathematics, but there is more of that in Panjer (1998), which is a collection of articles by different authors. The encyclopaedia edited by Teugels and Sundt (2004) is a broad review of actuarial science and its history, with more weight on mathematical than computational ideas. Entirely devoted to history, ancient included, are the ten volumes edited by Haberman and Sibbett (1995) and the landmark papers on pension insurance in Bodie and Davis (2000). Useful, elementary reviews of traditional life and property insurance mathematics are Gerber (1997), Promislow (2006) and Boland (2007). There are countless introductions to financial risk that take the material in Sections 1.3 and 1.4 much further. Mathematics is kept on a fairly elementary level in Copeland *et al.* (2005) and Hull (2006), the latest editions of two classics. An exceptionally clear outline of investment risk is Luenberger (1998); see also Danthine and Donaldson (2005). Maddala and Rao (1996) and Ruppert (2004) are reviews of the statistical side of financial modelling.

1.7.2 Monte Carlo

Simulation was established as a central method of science during the final decades of the twentieth century. The term means two different things and is, in applied physics and parts of engineering, often associated with numerical solutions of partial differential equations; see Langtangen (2003). Apart from powerful computers being needed in both cases, this has little to do with the version used here. Stochastic simulation (or Monte Carlo) is an enormously versatile technique. It was used to reconstruct global processes in Casti (1997) and networks of economic agents in Levy *et al.* (2000); see Bølviken (2004) for other references. Applications in the present book are less exotic, although there will be many extensions of the processes simulated in Section 1.5. Monte Carlo is well established in actuarial science, yet few textbooks apart from Daykin *et al.* (1994) integrate the technique deeply. This is different in financial economics, where a number of such books have been written. Elementary introductions are Vose (2008) and Chan and Wong (2006), with Lyuu (2002) being more advanced. In statistics, Gentle (2003), Robert and Casella (2004) and Ripley (2006) are reviews of Monte Carlo-based methodology, with Gentle *et al.* (2004) being a collection of articles over a broad spectrum of themes. Ross (2002) and Fishman (2001), (2006) are introductions to stochastic simulation in operations research.

PART I

TOOLS FOR RISK ANALYSIS

2

Getting started the Monte Carlo way

2.1 Introduction

The Monte Carlo way, what does it mean? More than how simulation experiments are set up and put to work; *how* models are presented is affected too. The main theme is still that of Section 1.5. Risk variables X may have many random sources, and it is often hard, or even impossible, to find their density function $f(x)$ or distribution function $F(x)$ through exact mathematics. This is true even when random mechanisms are simple to write down and fully known. It is here that Monte Carlo and computer simulations $X_1^*, \ldots, X_m^*$ come in and permit distributions to be *approximated*. How that is done and the error it brings about are discussed in Section 2.2.

The purpose of this chapter is to introduce a toolkit for much of Part I. This includes standard probability distributions and stochastic models to work with, and the fastest route to real problems is to define them the way they are simulated in the computer! The Gaussian-based modelling in Section 2.4 is an example of how quickly such tactics take us beyond the elementary. Add the distributions describing skewness in Section 2.5, and quite a number of risk problems are solvable as we see in the next chapter. Distributions are presented with simple (and fast) methods of sampling. You are not advised to, but you *can* skip them if you like (Section 2.3 in particular) and rely on pre-programmed software like R and Matlab or downloadable libraries associated with C and Fortran; see Press *et al.* (2007) for the latter. However, the study of sampling algorithms is excellent computer training, and pre-programmed software has its limitations. Not all the examples in this book would have been practical on such platforms, and something useful always seems to be missing. There will be more on the Monte Carlo technique in Chapter 4.

2.2 How simulations are used

2.2.1 *Introduction*

Risk analyses make use of expectations, standard deviations, percentiles and density functions. This section demonstrates how they are worked out from simulations $X_1^*, \dots, X_m^*$, what error this brings and how the sample size m is determined. We draw on statistics, using the same methods with the same error formulae as for historical data. The experiments below have useful things to say about error in ordinary statistical estimation too.

2.2.2 *Mean and standard deviation*

Let $\xi = E(X)$ be the expectation and $\sigma = \text{sd}(X)$ the standard deviation of X. Their Monte Carlo estimates are

$$\overline{X}^* = \frac{1}{m}(X_1^* + \cdots + X_m^*) \quad \text{and} \quad s^* = \sqrt{\frac{1}{m-1}\sum_{i=1}^{m}(X_i^* - \overline{X}^*)^2} \tag{2.1}$$

with the statistical properties for the mean being well known:

$$E(\overline{X}^* - \xi) = 0 \quad \text{and} \quad \text{sd}(\overline{X}^*) = \frac{\sigma}{\sqrt{m}}. \tag{2.2}$$

Monte Carlo estimates of ξ are unbiased, and their error may in theory be pushed below any level by raising m. An estimate of $\text{sd}(\overline{X}^*)$ is $s^*/\sqrt{m}$, where σ in the right of (2.2) has been replaced by s^*. This kind of uncertainty is often minor compared with other sources of error (see Chapter 7), but if $\overline{X}^*$ is used as the price of an asset or a transaction, high Monte Carlo accuracy may be necessary.

For s^* the statistical properties are approximately

$$E(s^* - \sigma) \doteq 0 \quad \text{and} \quad \text{sd}(s^*) \doteq \frac{\sigma}{\sqrt{2m}}\sqrt{1 + \kappa/2}, \tag{2.3}$$

where $\kappa = \text{kurt}(X)$ is the **kurtosis** of X (consult Appendix A.2 if kurtosis is unknown ground). For normal variables, $\kappa = 0$. These results may be less familiar than for the mean, but you will find them in Stuart and Ord (1987), p. 322. They are approximations and apply as $m \to \infty$. Large-sample results of this kind work excellently with Monte Carlo, where m is typically a big number.

2.2.3 *Example: Financial returns*

Let us examine $\overline{X}^*$ and s^* in a transparent situation where we don't need them. In Figure 2.1 they have been computed from m Gaussian simulations and plotted against m. The true values were $\xi = 0.5\%$ and $\sigma = 5\%$ (could be monthly returns

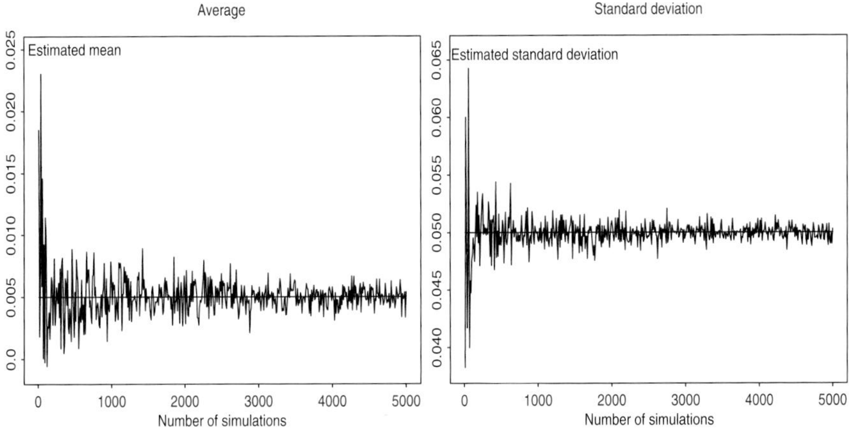

Figure 2.1 Average and standard deviation against the number of simulations for a Gaussian model with the underlying, exact values as straight lines.

from equity). All experiments were completely redone with new simulations for each m. That is why there is no smoothness in the curves as they jump around the true values.

The estimates tend to ξ and σ as $m \to \infty$. That we knew, but the experiment also tells us something else. *The mean is less accurately estimated than the standard deviation.* Suppose the simulations had been historical returns on equity. After 1000 months (about 80 years, a very long time) the relative error in the sample mean is still almost two-thirds of the true value! Errors that large make risk statements faulty and make the celebrated Markowitz theory of optimal investment in Section 5.3 much harder to use as a practical device. When financial derivatives are introduced in Section 3.5 (and in Chapter 14), it will emerge that the Black–Scholes–Merton theory removes these parameters from pricing formulae, doubtless one of the reasons for their success.

This is an elementary case that can be understood through exact mathematics. From the right-hand side of (2.2) and (2.3)

$$\frac{\mathrm{sd}(\overline{X}^*)}{\xi} = \frac{\sigma}{\xi}\frac{1}{\sqrt{m}} = \frac{10}{\sqrt{m}} \quad \text{and} \quad \frac{\mathrm{sd}(s^*)}{\sigma} \doteq \sqrt{1/2+\kappa/4}\,\frac{1}{\sqrt{m}} \doteq \frac{0.71}{\sqrt{m}}$$

after inserting $\xi = 0.005$, $\sigma = 0.05$ and $\kappa = 0$. Clearly $\overline{X}^*$ is much more uncertain than s^*. There is a general story here. First-order parameters (expectations and regression coefficients) are often harder to estimate accurately in finance than second-order ones (standard deviations and correlations); see Section 13.5, where this error pattern will be encountered with the celebrated Wilkie model.

2.2.4 Percentiles

The percentile q_ϵ is the solution of either of the equations

$$\underbrace{F(q_\epsilon) = 1 - \epsilon}_{upper} \quad \text{or} \quad \underbrace{F(q_\epsilon) = \epsilon}_{lower},$$

depending on whether the upper or the lower version is sought. With insurance risk it is typically the former, in finance the latter. Monte Carlo approximations q_ϵ^* are obtained by sorting the simulations, for example in descending order as $X_{(1)}^* \geq \cdots \geq X_{(m)}^*$. Then

$$\underbrace{q_\epsilon^* = X_{(\epsilon m)}^*}_{upper} \quad \text{or} \quad \underbrace{q_\epsilon^* = X_{((1-\epsilon)m)}^*}_{lower} \tag{2.4}$$

with error

$$E(q_\epsilon^* - q_\epsilon) \doteq 0 \quad \text{and} \quad \text{sd}(q_\epsilon^*) \doteq \frac{a_\epsilon}{\sqrt{m}}, \quad a_\epsilon = \frac{\sqrt{\epsilon(1-\epsilon)}}{f(q_\epsilon)} \tag{2.5}$$

which are again valid as $m \to \infty$; see Stuart and Ord (1987), p. 331. It is possible to evaluate $f(q_\epsilon)$ approximately through density estimation (see below) for a numerical value of a_ϵ.

The experiment in Figure 2.1 has been repeated in Figure 2.2 left for the upper 1% and 5% percentiles. Smaller ϵ seem to demand more simulations which is no more than common sense, but what about the distribution itself? A second experiment on the right in Figure 2.2 has been run with the t-distribution having two degrees of freedom. This is a model where large deviations occur much more frequently than under the normal (see Section 2.4), and errors are now magnified several times (look at the scale of the vertical axes). The result isn't accidental; consult Section 2.6, where there is a theoretical argument in support.

2.2.5 Density estimation

Another issue is how the density function $f(x)$ is visualized given simulations $X_1^*, \ldots, X_m^*$. Statistical software is available and works automatically, but it is still useful to have an idea of how such techniques operate, all the more so as there is a parameter to adjust. Many density functions in this book are drawn from simulations by means of the **Gaussian kernel** method. A smoothing parameter $h > 0$ is selected, and the estimate is the average of Gaussian density functions with standard deviation hs^* and centred at the m simulations X_i^*; i.e.,

$$f^*(x) = \frac{1}{m}\sum_{i=1}^{m} \frac{1}{hs^*}\varphi\left(\frac{x - X_i^*}{hs^*}\right) \quad \text{where} \quad \varphi(x) = \frac{1}{\sqrt{(2\pi}} e^{-x^2/2}. \tag{2.6}$$

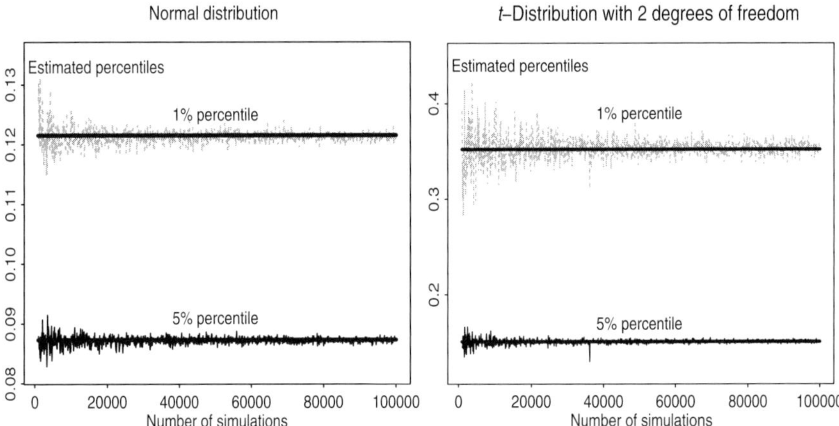

Figure 2.2 Estimated percentiles of simulated series against the number of simulations. *Note*: Scales of vertical axes differ.

As x is varied $f^*(x)$ traces out a curve which resembles the exact $f(x)$. Its statistical properties, derived in chapter 2 of Wand and Jones (1995), are if σ is the standard deviation of $f(x)$

$$E\{f^*(x) - f(x)\} \doteq \frac{1}{2}h^2\sigma^2\frac{d^2f(x)}{dx^2} \quad \text{and} \quad \text{sd}\{f^*(x)\} \doteq \frac{0.5311}{\sigma}\sqrt{\frac{f(x)}{hm}}. \tag{2.7}$$

The estimate is biased! The choice of h is a compromise between bias on the left (going *down* with h) and random variation on the right (going *up*). Software is usually equipped with a default value (which does not always work too well). In theory the choice depends on m, the 'best' value being proportional to the *fifth* root!

The curve $f^*(x)$ contains random bumps if h is too small. An example is shown in the left part of Figure 2.3, where the estimates come from $m = 1000$ simulations under the density function

$$f(x) = \frac{1}{2}x^2e^{-x}, \quad x > 0.$$

The curves become smoother when the value of h is raised on the right, but now bias tends to drag the estimates away from the true function. It may not matter too much if h is selected a little too low, and $h = 0.2$ might be a suitable choice in Figure 2.3. A sensible rule of thumb is to choose h in the range 0.05–0.30, but, as remarked above, it also depends on m. Kernels other than the Gaussian can be used; consult Scott (1992) or Wand and Jones (1995) for monographs on density estimation.

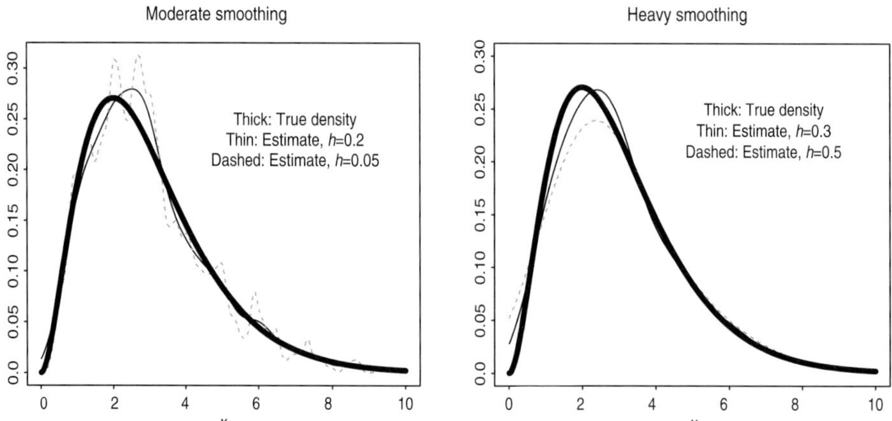

Figure 2.3 Kernel density estimates based on 1000 simulations from model in the text, shown as the thick solid line in both plots.

2.2.6 Monte Carlo error and selection of m

The discrepancy between a Monte Carlo approximation and its underlying, exact value is nearly always Gaussian as $m \to \infty$. For the sample mean this follows from the central limit theorem, and standard large-sample theory from statistics yields the result in most other cases; see Appendix A.4. A Monte Carlo evaluation ψ^* of some quantity ψ is therefore roughly Gaussian with mean ψ and standard deviation $a/\sqrt{m}$, where a is a constant. The result applies to all the examples above except the density estimate (there is still a theory, but the details are different; see Scott, 1992). Let a^* be an estimate of a obtained from the simulations (as explained above). The interval

$$\psi^* - 2\frac{a^*}{\sqrt{m}} < \psi < \psi^* + 2\frac{a^*}{\sqrt{m}} \tag{2.8}$$

then contains ψ with approximately 95% confidence. Here $a^* = s^*$ when ψ is the mean and $a^* = s^*\sqrt{1/2 + \kappa^*/4}$ when ψ is the standard deviation; see (2.2) and (2.3) right (for the kurtosis estimate κ^* consult Exercise 2.9).

Such results can also be used for design. Suppose the Monte Carlo standard deviation should be brought below some σ_0. The equation $a^*/\sqrt{m} = \sigma_0$, when solved for m, yields

$$m = \left(\frac{a^*}{\sigma_0}\right)^2 \tag{2.9}$$

which is the number of simulations required. For the idea to work you need the estimate a^*. Often the only way is to run a preliminary round of simulations, estimate a, determine m and complete the additional samples. The idea is much used with clinical studies in medicine! With some programming effort it is possible to automatize the process so that the computer takes care of it on its own. The selection of m is discussed further in Section 7.2.

2.3 How random variables are sampled

2.3.1 Introduction

The starting point is **uniform** random variables U for which all values between zero and one are equally likely. All platforms have built-in routines for drawing them; to see how they work, consult Section 4.6. Other random variables X are generated by manipulating uniforms, sometimes many independent ones $U_1, U_2, \dots$ are needed. The topic is, for the clever, full of ingenious tricks. Take the **Box–Muller** representation of Gaussian random variables; see Box and Muller (1958). If U_1 and U_2 are independent and uniform, then

$$\varepsilon_1 = \sqrt{-2\log(U_1)}\sin(2\pi U_2) \quad \text{and} \quad \varepsilon_2 = \sqrt{-2\log(U_1)}\cos(2\pi U_2) \tag{2.10}$$

are both $N(0, 1)$ and also independent; see Hörmann *et al.* (2004) for a proof. Not easy to guess, and there are many intriguing results of that kind. To get an overview, Devroye (1986) is still an excellent reference.

Many random variables are sampled through their representation in terms of other variables, but the issue in this section is the basic one of generating them given their distribution function $F(x)$ or density function $f(x)$. The three general methods presented below lead to fast samplers when applied smartly, but this is not a mandatory subject and may be skipped. Still, it takes little effort to learn the first method of inversion, which has links to the **copulas** of Section 6.7.

2.3.2 Inversion

Let $F(x)$ be a strictly increasing distribution function with inverse $x = F^{-1}(u)$ (which is the solution of the equation $F(x) = u$) and let

$$X = F^{-1}(U) \quad \text{or} \quad X = F^{-1}(1-U), \qquad U \sim \text{uniform}. \tag{2.11}$$

Consider the specification on the left for which $U = F(X)$. Note that

$$\Pr(X \leq x) = \Pr\{F(X) \leq F(x)\} = \Pr\{U \leq F(x)\} = F(x),$$

since $\Pr(U \leq u) = u$. In other words, X defined by (2.11) left has the distribution function $F(x)$, and we have a general sampling technique. The second version based on $1 - U$ is due to U and $1 - U$ having the same distribution. The situation is summarized in Algorithm 2.1, in which the solutions are known as an **antithetic**

Algorithm 2.1 Sampling by inversion

0 Input: The percentile function $F^{-1}(u)$
1 Draw $U^* \sim$ uniform
2 Return $X^* \leftarrow F^{-1}(U^*)$ or $X^* \leftarrow F^{-1}(1-U^*)$.

pair with a speed-enhancing potential to be discussed in Chapter 4. Whether Algorithm 2.1 is practical depends on the ease with which the percentile function $F^{-1}(u)$ can be computed. It works well for Gaussian variables, and there are a number of additional examples in Section 2.5.

2.3.3 Acceptance–rejection

Acceptance–rejection is a **random stopping** rule and much more subtle than inversion. The idea is to sample from a density function $g(x)$ of our choice. Simulations that do *not* meet a certain acceptance criterion A are discarded, and the rest will then come from the original density function $f(x)$. Magic? It works like this. Let $g(x|A)$ be the density function of the simulations kept. By Bayes' formula (consult Section 6.2 if necessary)

$$g(x|A) = \frac{\Pr(A|x)g(x)}{\Pr(A)}, \tag{2.12}$$

and we must specify $\Pr(A|x)$ – i.e., the probability that $X = x$ drawn from $g(x)$ is allowed to stand. Let M be a constant such that

$$M \geq \frac{f(x)}{g(x)}, \quad \text{for all } x, \tag{2.13}$$

and suppose X is accepted whenever a uniform random number U satisfies

$$U \leq \frac{f(x)}{Mg(x)}.$$

Note that the right-hand side is always less than one. Now

$$\Pr(A|x) = \Pr\left(U \leq \frac{f(x)}{Mg(x)}\right) = \frac{f(x)}{Mg(x)},$$

which in combination with (2.12) yields

$$g(x|A) = \frac{f(x)}{M\Pr(A)}.$$

The denominator must be one (otherwise $g(x|A)$ won't be a density function), and so

$$g(x|A) = f(x) \quad \text{and} \quad \Pr(A) = \frac{1}{M}. \tag{2.14}$$

Algorithm 2.2 Rejection–acceptance sampling

0 Input: $f(x)$, $g(x)$, M
1 Repeat
2 Draw $X^* \sim g(x)$
3 Draw $U^* \sim$ uniform
4 If $U^* \leq f(X^*)/Mg(X^*)$ then **stop** and return X^*.

We have indeed obtained the right distribution. In summary we have Algorithm 2.2.

The expected number of trials for one simulation is $1/\Pr(A)$ and hence M by (2.14) right. Good designs are those with low M.

2.3.4 Ratio of uniforms

This is another random stopping rule. It goes back to Kinderman and Monahan (1977) and requires $f(x)$ and $x^2 f(x)$ to be bounded functions. There are many examples of that type. Let a, b_- and b_+ be finite constants such that

$$\sqrt{f(x)} \leq a \quad \text{and} \quad b_- \leq x\sqrt{f(x)} \leq b_+ \quad \text{for all } x. \tag{2.15}$$

For maximum efficiency a and b_+ should be as small, and b_- as large, as possible. Let U_1 and U_2 be uniform random variables and define

$$V = aU_1 \quad \text{and} \quad X = \{b_- + (b_+ - b_-)U_2\}/V.$$

Suppose $V = v$ is fixed. Clearly $b_-/v < X < b_+/v$, and X is uniform over the interval $(b_-/v, b_+/v)$ with density function $f(x|v) = v/(b_+ - b_-)$ (if conditional and joint distributions are unfamiliar ground, consult Appendix A.3). Multiply by $f(v) = 1/a$ (the density function of V), and the joint density function of (X, V) appears as

$$f(x, v) = \frac{v}{a(b_+ - b_-)}, \quad 0 < v < a \quad \text{and} \quad \frac{b_-}{v} < x < \frac{b_+}{v}.$$

Let A be the event $V < \sqrt{f(X)}$ and write $f(x|A)$ for the density function of X given A. If A has occurred, then $XV > X\sqrt{f(X)} \geq b_-$ if $X < 0$ and $XV < X\sqrt{f(X)} \leq b_+$ if $X \geq 0$. It follows that A is inside the region where $f(x, v) > 0$, and the density function of X given A becomes

$$f(x|A) = p^{-1}\int_0^{\sqrt{f(x)}} \frac{v}{a(b_+ - b_-)}\,dv = \frac{p^{-1}}{2a(b_+ - b_-)}f(x) \quad \text{where} \quad p = \Pr(A).$$

But this only makes sense if $p^{-1} = 2a(b_+ - b_-)$ and $f(x|A) = f(x)$. In summary we have Algorithm 2.3.

Algorithm 2.3 Ratio of uniforms

0 Input: $f(x)$ and a, b_- and b_+ satisfying (2.15)
1 Repeat
2 Draw uniforms U_1^* and U_2^*
3 $V \leftarrow aU_1^*$ and $X^* \leftarrow \{b_- + (b_+ - b_-)U_2^*\}/V^*$
4 If $V^* < \sqrt{f(X^*)}$ then **stop** and return X^*.

The scheme is often able to deliver simple algorithms with high acceptance rate (see examples in Section 2.5). Normalization constants are not needed, and $f(x)$ may be replaced by any function proportional to it.

2.4 Making the Gaussian work

2.4.1 Introduction

The **Gaussian** (or **normal**) model is the most famous of all probability distributions, arguably the most important one too. It is familiar from introductory courses in statistics, yet built up from scratch below and is the first example of families of distributions being defined the way they are simulated in the computer. This allows topics like stochastic volatility, heavy tails and correlated variables to be introduced quickly, though their treatment here is only preliminary. *General*, dependent Gaussian variables require linear algebra and are dealt with in Chapter 5, which introduces time-dependent versions as well.

2.4.2 The normal family

Normal (or Gaussian) variables are linear functions of standard normal variables $N(0, 1)$ with distribution function

$$\Phi(x) = \int_{-\infty}^{x} \frac{1}{\sqrt{2\pi}} e^{-y^2/2} dy,$$

known as the Gaussian integral and often needed. Closed formulae do not exist, but there is an accurate approximation taken from Abramowitz and Stegun (1965) in Table 2.1. Symbols for $N(0, 1)$ variables in this book are ε and η.

The normal family of random variables is defined as

$$X = \xi + \sigma\varepsilon, \quad \varepsilon \sim N(0, 1), \tag{2.16}$$

where $\xi = E(X)$ and $\sigma = \text{sd}(X)$ are mean and standard deviation. A quick way to sample is through inversion. If $\Phi^{-1}(u)$ is the inverse of the Gaussian integral,

Table 2.1 Approximation to the normal integral $\Phi(x)$ when $x \geq 0$; use $\Phi(x) = 1 - \Phi(-x)$ for $x < 0$. The error is less than 1.5×10^{-7}.

$\Phi(x) = 1 - Q(z)\exp(-x^2/2)$ where		
$z = 1/(1 + c_0 x)$ and $Q(z) = z(c_1 + z(c_2 + z(c_3 + z(c_4 + zc_5))))$		
$c_0 = 0.2316419$	$c_1 = 0.127414796$	$c_2 = -0.142248368$
$c_3 = 0.710706870$	$c_4 = -0.7265760135$	$c_5 = 0.5307027145$

Algorithm 2.4 Gaussian generator

0 Input: ξ and σ
1 Generate $U^* \sim$ uniform
2 Return $X^* \leftarrow \xi + \sigma\Phi^{-1}(U^*)$. *%Or $\Phi^{-1}(U^*)$ replaced by ε^* generated by software directly*

then $\Phi^{-1}(U)$ is $N(0, 1)$ and Monte Carlo realizations from the normal family are generated as in Algorithm 2.4.

The prerequisite is that $\Phi^{-1}(u)$ is easy to compute, and there *are* fast methods available, for example the approximation in Table 2.2 developed by Odeh and Evans (1974) which is accurate to six (!) decimals. Even more accurate methods can be found in Jäckel (2002), who recommends Algorithm 2.4 for Gaussian sampling.

2.4.3 Modelling on logarithmic scale

Modelling on logarithmic scale is common. Examples within the realm of this book are

$$\underbrace{\log(1 + R) = \xi + \sigma\varepsilon}_{\text{return on equity}} \quad \text{and} \quad \underbrace{\log(Z) = \xi + \sigma\varepsilon}_{\text{claims in property insurance}} \tag{2.17}$$

where $\varepsilon \sim N(0, 1)$. The model is known as the **log-normal** family. It is the most common description of equity returns and also much used for losses in property insurance. Mean and standard deviation are

$$E(R) = e^{\xi+\sigma^2/2} - 1 \quad \text{and} \quad E(Z) = e^{\xi+\sigma^2/2}, \tag{2.18}$$

whereas

$$\text{sd}(R) \quad = \quad \text{sd}(Z) \quad = \quad E(Z)\sqrt{e^{\sigma^2} - 1}. \tag{2.19}$$

These formulae are among the most important ones in the entire theory of risk, and they will be used again and again. Sampling R and Z is easy: see Algorithm 2.5.

The shape of log-normal density functions is shown in Figure 2.4. There is a pronounced difference as σ is varied. The small value on the left is appropriate

Table 2.2 Approximation of Gaussian percentiles $\Phi^{-1}(u)$ for $u \geq 1/2$. Use $\Phi^{-1}(u) = -\Phi^{-1}(1-u)$ for $u < 1/2$. Accuracy: Six correct decimals

$$\phi^{-1}(u) = z + Q_1(z)/Q_2(z) \text{ where } z = \{-2\log(1-u)\}^{1/2} \text{ and}$$
$$Q_1(z) = c_0 + z(-1 + z(c_1 + z(c_2 + zc_3))),\ Q_2(z) = c_4 + z(c_5 + z(c_6 + z(c_7 + zc_8)))$$

$c_0 = -0.322232431088$	$c_1 = -0.342242088547$	$c_2 = -0.020423121024$
$c_3 = -0.0000453642210148$	$c_4 = 0.099348462606$	$c_5 = 0.58858157049$
$c_6 = 0.531103462366$	$c_7 = 0.10353775285$	$c_8 = 0.0038560700634$

Algorithm 2.5 Log-normal sampling

0 Input: ξ, σ
1 Draw $U^* \sim$ uniform and $\varepsilon^* \leftarrow \Phi^{-1}(U^*)$ *%Or ε^* directly*
2 Return $R^* \leftarrow e^{\xi+\sigma\varepsilon^*} - 1$ or $Z^* \leftarrow e^{\xi+\sigma\varepsilon^*}$.

for finance and yields a distribution resembling the normal. The strong skewness on the right where σ is large might be appropriate for large claims in property insurance.

2.4.4 Stochastic volatility

Financial risk is in many situations better described by making σ stochastic. A convenient specification is $\sigma = \xi_\sigma \sqrt{Z}$, where ξ_σ is a parameter and Z a random variable. Now (2.16) is extended to

$$X = \xi + \sigma\varepsilon \quad \text{with} \quad \sigma = \xi_\sigma \sqrt{Z}, \tag{2.20}$$

where Z and ε are independent. Note that $E(\varepsilon\sigma) = E(\varepsilon)E(\sigma) = 0$ so that $\xi = E(X)$ as before. We should be concerned with the scaling of Z. Two possibilities are $E(Z) = 1$ and $E(Z^2) = 1$, which make $\xi_\sigma = E(\sigma)$ and $\xi_\sigma^2 = E(\sigma^2)$ respectively. The **GARCH** models in Section 13.3 make use of the second version.

Standard deviation is known in finance as the **volatility**. Making it stochastic means that a very large Z may occur jointly with a very large or small ε, allowing X to fluctuate more strongly than when σ is fixed. The distribution has become **heavy tailed**. Such models have drawn much interest in finance, and dynamic versions where σ is linked to its earlier values will be introduced in Chapter 13.

Sampling is an extension of Algorithm 2.1; see Algorithm 2.6.

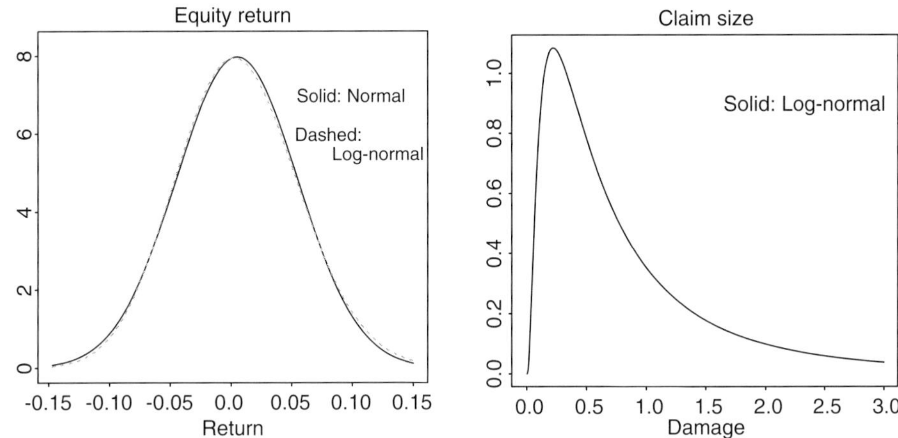

Figure 2.4 *Left*: Normal and log-normal density functions for $\xi = 0.005$, $\sigma = 0.05$. *Right*: Log-normal for $\xi = -0.5$, $\sigma = 1$.

Algorithm 2.6 Gaussian with stochastic volatility

0 Input: ξ, ξ_σ, model for Z
1 Draw Z^* and $\sigma^* \leftarrow \xi_\sigma \sqrt{Z^*}$ *%Many possibilities for Z^*; see text*
2 Generate $U^* \sim$ uniform.
3 Return $X^* \leftarrow \xi + \sigma^* \Phi^{-1}(U^*)$. *%Or $\Phi^{-1}(U^*)$ replaced by ε^* generated by software directly*

2.4.5 The *t*-family

The most common choice for Z in (2.20) is $Z = 1/G$, where G is a Gamma variable with mean 1 and shape α; see Section 2.5, where this distribution is introduced. The resulting model for X is

$$X = \xi + \xi_\sigma \frac{\varepsilon}{\sqrt{G}} \quad \text{where} \quad \varepsilon \sim N(0, 1), \tag{2.21}$$

which has mean and standard deviation

$$E(X) = \xi \quad \text{and} \quad \text{sd}(X) = \xi_\sigma \sqrt{\frac{\alpha}{\alpha - 1}}. \tag{2.22}$$

Finite mean requires $\alpha > 1/2$ (not visible in the mathematical expression) and finite standard deviation $\alpha > 1$.

The ratio $\varepsilon/\sqrt{G}$ follows the *t*-**distribution** with 2α **degrees of freedom** and converges to $N(0, 1)$ when $\alpha \to \infty$ (you will see why when the Gamma model is examined in Section 2.5). The density function resembles the normal with the same symmetric shape, and the extra parameter α often provides a better fit to financial data. Sampling may follow Algorithm 2.6 (use Algorithm 2.9 or 2.10 below

Algorithm 2.7 t-Generator for $\alpha > 1$

0 Input: $\xi, \xi_\sigma, \alpha, b = \xi_\sigma\sqrt{2\alpha}$ and $c = 1/\sqrt{2\alpha - 2}$
1 Repeat
2 Draw $\varepsilon^* \sim N(0,1)$ and $Y^* \leftarrow c\varepsilon^*$
3 If $|Y^*| < 1$, draw $U^* \sim$ uniform
and if $\log(U^*) \leq (\alpha - 1)\{\log(1 - Y^{*2}) + Y^{*2}\}$
stop and return $X^* \leftarrow \xi + bY^*/\sqrt{1 - Y^{*2}}$.

to generate Gamma), but higher speed is obtained by the acceptance–rejection procedure due to Marsaglia (1980) in Algorithm 2.7 which works for all $\alpha > 1$; see Section 2.6 for the proof. Acceptance is so rapid that a single trial is enough 80–90% of the time.

2.4.6 Dependent normal pairs

Many situations demand **correlated** variables. Gaussian versions are constructed by several linear representations of the form (2.16). A normal pair (X_1, X_2) is defined as

$$\begin{aligned} X_1 &= \xi_1 + \sigma_1\varepsilon_1 \\ X_2 &= \xi_2 + \sigma_2\varepsilon_2 \end{aligned} \quad \text{where} \quad \begin{aligned} \varepsilon_1 &= \eta_1 \\ \varepsilon_2 &= \rho\eta_1 + \sqrt{1-\rho^2}\,\eta_2 \end{aligned} \tag{2.23}$$

and a new feature is the submodel on the right based on independent $N(0,1)$ variables η_1 and η_2. Both ε_1 and ε_2 are $N(0,1)$ too, but they have now become **dependent** (or **covariating**) in a way controlled by ρ, which is the ordinary correlation coefficient (more on that in Chapter 5). Simulation is straightforward. Generate η_1^* and η_2^* by Gaussian sampling and insert them for η_1 and η_2 in (2.23); see Algorithm 2.8 later.

Normal pairs lead to the standard log-normal model for equity returns R_1 and R_2 through

$$R_1 = e^{X_1} - 1 \quad \text{and} \quad R_2 = e^{X_2} - 1,$$

where X_1 and X_2 are as above. Simulations of (R_1, R_2) based on $\xi_1 = \xi_2 = 0.5\%$ and $\sigma_1 = \sigma_2 = 5\%$ (monthly returns on equity) have been plotted in Figure 2.5 (upper row). The effect of varying ρ is pronounced, yet the variation for each variable individually is not affected at all.

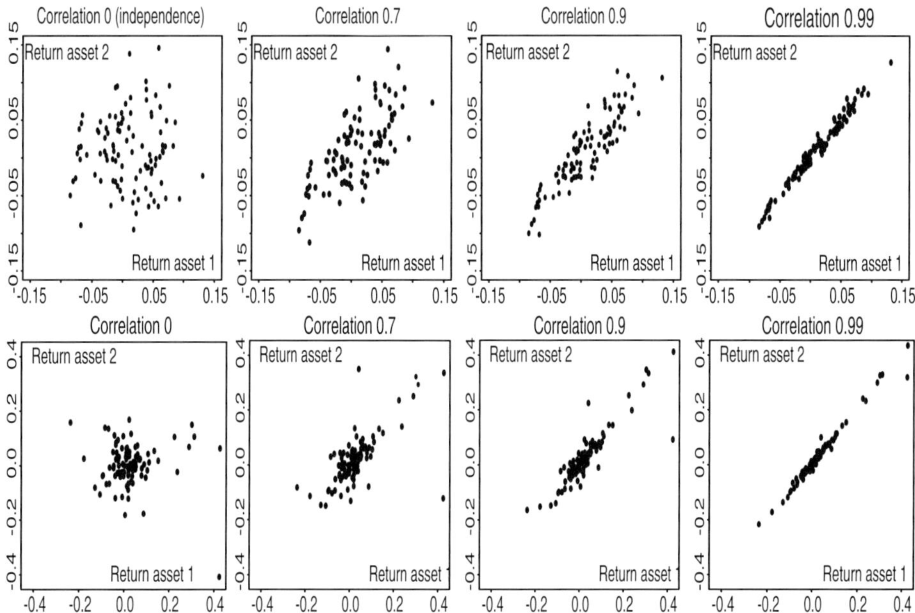

Figure 2.5 Joint plot of 100 pairs of simulated equity returns, the ordinary log-normal (*upper row*) with stochastic volatility added (*lower row*). *Note*: Axis scales differ between rows.

2.4.7 Dependence and heavy tails

Returns on equity investments may be *both* dependent and heavy tailed. Can that be handled? Easily! Combine (2.20) and (2.23), which leads to

$$\begin{aligned} X_1 &= \xi_1 + \sigma_1\eta_1 & & \sigma_1 = \xi_{\sigma 1}\sqrt{Z_1} \\ X_2 &= \xi_2 + \sigma_2(\rho\eta_1 + \sqrt{1-\rho^2}\,\eta_2) & \text{where} \quad & \sigma_2 = \xi_{\sigma 2}\sqrt{Z_2}. \end{aligned} \tag{2.24}$$

Here $\xi_{\sigma 1}$ and $\xi_{\sigma 2}$ are fixed parameters and Z_1 and Z_2 are *positive* random variables playing the same role as Z in (2.20). It is common to take $Z_1 = Z_2 = Z$, assuming fluctuations in σ_1 and σ_2 to be in perfect synchrony. This has no special justification, but it may lead to a joint density function of a 'nice' mathematical form. Not much is made of that in this book.

The effect on financial returns has been indicated in the lower row of Figure 2.5, where the model for the upper row was modified by introducing stochastic volatility. It was assumed that $Z_1 = Z_2$ was Gamma-distributed with shape $\alpha = 1$. Covariation emerges unchanged from the upper row, whereas uncertainty is much higher (axis scales are almost tripled).

Algorithm 2.8 Financial returns under equicorrelation

0 Input: $\xi_1,\ldots,\xi_J,\ \sigma_1,\ldots,\sigma_J,\ c_1=\sqrt{\rho},\ c_2=\sqrt{1-\rho}$
1 Generate $\eta_0^*\sim N(0,1)$ *%Common stochastic factor*
2 For $j=1,\ldots,J$ do
3 Generate $\eta^*\sim N(0,1)$
4 $\varepsilon^*\leftarrow c_1\eta_0^*+c_2\eta^*$ *%Randomness in jth return*
5 $R_j^*\leftarrow \exp(\xi_j+\sigma_j\varepsilon^*)-1$ *%Stochastic volatility: Draw Z^* and let $\sigma_j^*\leftarrow \xi_{\sigma j}\sqrt{Z^*}$; use it for σ_j*
6 Return $R_1^*,\ldots,R_J^*$.

2.4.8 Equicorrelation models

Many interacting Gaussian variables are common. Suppose

$$X_j=\xi_j+\sigma_j\varepsilon_j,\quad j=1,\ldots,J \tag{2.25}$$

where $\varepsilon_1,\ldots,\varepsilon_J$ are normal $N(0,1)$ and dependent. Their general form requires a dose of linear algebra and is dealt with in Section 5.4. A simple special case which will be used on several occasions is the **equicorrelation** model, under which

$$\varepsilon_j=\sqrt{\rho}\,\eta_0+\sqrt{1-\rho}\,\eta_j\quad j=1,\ldots,J. \tag{2.26}$$

Here $\eta_0,\eta_1,\ldots,\eta_J$ are independent and $N(0,1)$. All the ε_j are influenced by η_0, which is what makes them dependent. They have a common correlation coefficent ρ which must exceed $-1/(J-1)$; why is explained in Section 5.4. How correlated log-normal returns are generated under this model is summarized by the scheme in Algorithm 2.8. Heavy-tailed models are introduced through the comment on Line 5. Some of the exercises at the end of the chapter play with this algorithm.

2.5 Positive random variables

2.5.1 Introduction

The last issue of this start-up chapter is models for positive random variables. Their density functions start at the origin and can't be symmetric like the normal one unless there is some upper limit, which is rarely desirable to introduce. Many positive random variables are also **heavy tailed** in the sense that large deviations occur more often than under the normal; see Appendix A.2 for a definition. This is common in property insurance, where claims due to natural catastrophies or from accidents with industrial installations may be huge. The log-normal of the preceding section is one way of describing this kind of uncertainty, but there are many others.

2.5.2 The Gamma distribution

Very important is the **Gamma** family, for which the density function is

$$f(x) = \frac{(\alpha/\xi)^\alpha}{\Gamma(\alpha)} x^{\alpha-1} e^{-\alpha x/\xi}, \quad x > 0 \quad \text{where} \quad \Gamma(\alpha) = \int_0^\infty x^{\alpha-1} e^{-x}\, dx. \tag{2.27}$$

Here $\Gamma(\alpha)$ is the **Gamma** function, which is accurately evaluated by the approximation in Table 2.3; see Press *et al.* (2007). Growth is ultra-fast as α is raised, and it is often necessary to use logarithms to avoid computer overflow. The Gamma function coincides with the factorials when α is an integer, i.e., $\Gamma(n) = (n-1)!$.

Mean and standard deviation of Gamma variables are

$$E(X) = \xi \quad \text{and} \quad \text{sd}(X) = \xi/\sqrt{\alpha}. \tag{2.28}$$

The case $\xi = 1$ will be called the **standard** Gamma and denoted Gamma(α). In this book G is the usual symbol for it, and a general Gamma variable is defined as $X = \xi G$. It is good tactics to let the mean serve as one of the two parameters, though this differs from common usage (but see McCullagh and Nelder, 1989). Gamma distributions are much used as bricks in stochastic edifices, like the one behind the t-distribution in Section 2.4 (there are several other examples later on). Note that $\text{sd}(X) \to 0$ as $\alpha \to \infty$, removing all uncertainty. That's why the t-distribution becomes normal in the limit.

Sampling is not straightforward. There are no convenient stochastic representations to lean on, and the percentile function is complicated computationally with no fast and accurate approximations available. Inversion sampling is therefore unattractive, but there are several good acceptance–rejection methods. Those due to Best (1978) and Cheng and Feast (1979) are often cited. The ratio of uniforms seems at least as good. The scheme in Algorithm 2.9 (verified in Section 2.6) is simpler than a similar one in Kinderman and Monahan (1980), and as fast unless α is close to 1.

Algorithm 2.9 requires $\alpha > 1$. The case $\alpha \leq 1$ is handled by a result due to Stuart (1962). If $U \sim$ uniform, $Y \sim$ Gamma($1 + \alpha$) and U and Y are independent, then

$$X = (1 + \alpha^{-1}) Y U^{1/\alpha} \sim \text{Gamma}(\alpha);$$

see Section 2.6 for the proof. Computer commands are summarized in Algorithm 2.10.

Table 2.3 An approximation to the Gamma function (error less than 2×10^{-10}). Should be used on logarithmic form

$$\Gamma(x) \doteq \sqrt{2\pi}(x+4.5)^{x-0.5}e^{-(x+4.5)}C(x) \quad \text{where}$$

$$C(x) = a_0 + \frac{a_1}{x+1} + \frac{a_2}{(x+2)^2} + \frac{a_3}{(x+3)^3} + \frac{a_4}{(x+4)^4} + \frac{a_5}{(x+5)^5} + \frac{a_6}{(x+6)^6}$$

$$a_0 = 1.000000000190015 \quad a_1 = 76.18009172947146 \quad a_2 = -86.50532032941677$$

$$a_3 = 24.01409824083091 \quad a_4 = -1.231739572450155$$

$$a_5 = 0.1208650973866179\ 10^{-2} \quad a_6 = -0.5395239384953\ 10^{-5}$$

Algorithm 2.9 Gamma generator for $\alpha > 1$

0 Input: ξ, α, $g(y) = \{(1 + y/\sqrt{\alpha})/(1 - 1/\alpha)\}^{\alpha-1}e^{-y\sqrt{\alpha}-1}$
and $b_\pm = (y_\pm)\sqrt{g(y_\pm)}$ for $y_\pm = (2\sqrt{\alpha})^{-1} \pm \sqrt{2 + (4\alpha)^{-1}}$
1 Repeat
2 Sample $U_1^*, U_2^* \sim$ uniform
3 $Y^* \leftarrow \{b_- + (b_+ - b_-)U_2^*\}/U_1^*$
4 If $(U_1^*)^2 < g(Y^*)$ then **stop** and return $X^* \leftarrow \xi(1 + Y^*/\sqrt{\alpha})$.

The loop is repeated until the stop criterion is satisfied.

2.5.3 *The exponential distribution*

This is the special case $\alpha = 1$ of the Gamma family, and the density function is

$$f(x) = \frac{1}{\xi}e^{-x/\xi}, \quad x > 0. \tag{2.29}$$

The exponential distribution has ties to *all* other models of this section, and is worth singling out for that very reason. Mean and standard deviation follow from (2.28) and become

$$E(X) = \xi \quad \text{and} \quad \text{sd}(X) = \xi, \tag{2.30}$$

whereas the distribution and percentile functions are

$$F(x) = 1 - e^{-x/\xi} \quad \text{and} \quad F^{-1}(u) = -\xi\log(1-u)$$

which opens inversion (Algorithm 2.1) as a quick way of sampling; see Algorithm 2.11.

2.5.4 *The Weibull distribution*

The Weibull family (after a Swedish physicist) is related to the exponential through

$$X = \beta Y^{1/\alpha} \quad Y \text{ exponential with mean 1}, \tag{2.31}$$

Algorithm 2.10 Gamma generator for $\alpha \leq 1$

0 Input: ξ, α, $b = \xi(1 + \alpha^{-1})$
1 Sample $Y^* \sim$ Gamma$(1 + \alpha)$ *%Algorithm 2.9*
2 Sample $U^* \sim$ uniform
3 Return $X^* \leftarrow bY^*(U^*)^{1/\alpha}$.

Output X^* is Gamma distributed with mean ξ and shape α. Together Algorithms 2.9 and 2.10 provide quick sampling.

Algorithm 2.11 Exponential generator

0 Input: ξ
1 Draw $U^* \sim$ uniform
2 Return $X^* \leftarrow -\xi \log(U^*)$.

where α and β are positive parameters. Distribution and density function are

$$F(x) = 1 - e^{-(x/\beta)^\alpha} \quad \text{and} \quad f(x) = \frac{\alpha}{\beta}\left(\frac{x}{\beta}\right)^{\alpha-1} e^{-(x/\beta)^\alpha}, \qquad x > 0;$$

see Exercise 2.28. The representation (2.31) quickly yields

$$E(X) = \beta\Gamma(1 + 1/\alpha) \quad \text{and} \quad \text{sd}(X) = \beta\sqrt{\Gamma(1 + 2/\alpha) - \Gamma(1 + 1/\alpha)^2}, \tag{2.32}$$

where $\Gamma(x)$ is the Gamma function in Table 2.3. The Weibull distribution extends over the positive axis and is skewed to the right if $\alpha < 3.6$ and to the left if $\alpha > 3.6$. It resembles the normal when $\alpha = 3.6$; see Exercise 2.30. Simulation is easy from its definition and Algorithm 2.11; see Algorithm 2.12.

2.5.5 The Pareto distribution

Random variables with density function

$$f(x) = \frac{\alpha/\beta}{(1 + x/\beta)^{1+\alpha}}, \quad x > 0 \tag{2.33}$$

are **Pareto** distributed where again α and β are positive parameters. The model, which will be denoted Pareto(α,β), is *very* heavy tailed and is a popular choice for large claims in property insurance; more on that in Chapter 9. Mean and standard deviation are

$$E(X) = \frac{\beta}{\alpha - 1} \quad \text{and} \quad \text{sd}(X) = E(X)\sqrt{\frac{\alpha}{\alpha - 2}} \tag{2.34}$$

Algorithm 2.12 Weibull generator

0 Input: α, β
1 Sample $U^* \sim$ uniform
2 Return $X^* \leftarrow \beta(-\log U^*)^{1/\alpha}$.

Algorithm 2.13 Pareto generator

0 Input: α, β
1 Generate $U^* \sim$ uniform
2 Return $X^* \leftarrow \beta\{(U^*)^{-1/\alpha} - 1\}$.

which assume $\alpha > 1$ for the mean and $\alpha > 2$ for the standard deviation. They become infinite otherwise. Real phenomena with α between 1 and 2 (so that standard deviation doesn't exist) will be encountered in Chapter 7.

Suppose $\beta = (\alpha - 1)\xi$ is inserted into the Pareto density function. With ξ fixed

$$f(x) = \frac{\alpha}{\alpha - 1} \frac{\xi^{-1}}{\{1 + (x/\xi)/(\alpha - 1)\}^{1+\alpha}} \longrightarrow \frac{\xi^{-1}}{e^{x/\xi}} = \frac{1}{\xi} e^{-x/\xi} \quad \text{as} \quad \alpha \longrightarrow \infty,$$

and we have obtained the **exponential** distribution as a limiting member of the Pareto family. This is of some importance for extreme value methods; see Section 9.5.

The Pareto distribution function and its inverse are

$$F(x) = 1 - (1 + x/\beta)^{-\alpha}, \quad x > 0 \quad \text{and} \quad F^{-1}(u) = \beta\{(1 - u)^{-1/\alpha} - 1\}, \tag{2.35}$$

where the latter is found by solving the equation $F(x) = u$. The second version of the inversion algorithm yields the simple Pareto sampler in Algorithm 2.13.

2.5.6 The Poisson distribution

Suppose $X_1, X_2, \ldots$ are independent and exponentially distributed with mean 1. It can then be proved (see Section 2.6) that

$$\Pr(X_1 + \cdots + X_n < \lambda \leq X_1 + \cdots + X_{n+1}) = \frac{\lambda^n}{n!} e^{-\lambda} \tag{2.36}$$

for all $n \geq 0$ and all $\lambda > 0$. The **Poisson** probabilities on the right define the density function

$$\Pr(N = n) = \frac{\lambda^n}{n!} e^{-\lambda}, \quad n = 0, 1, \ldots \tag{2.37}$$

which is the central model for claim numbers in property insurance on which there is a lot to be said; see Chapter 8. Mean and standard deviation are

$$E(N) = \lambda \quad \text{and} \quad \text{sd}(N) = \sqrt{\lambda}, \tag{2.38}$$

Algorithm 2.14 Poisson generator

```
Input: λ
Y* ← 0
For n = 1, 2, ... do
    Draw U* ~ uniform and Y* ← Y* − log(U*)
    If Y* ≥ λ then
        stop and return N* ← n − 1.
```

and equal mean and variance is a characteristic property for the Poisson model. A simple sampler is provided by (2.36). It is then utilized that $X_j = -\log(U_j)$ is exponential if U_j is uniform, and the sum $X_1 + X_2 + \cdots$ is monitored until it exceeds λ; see Algorithm 2.14.

This is a **random stopping** rule, but of a different kind from those in Section 2.3. How long it takes for the sum of all $-\log(U^*)$ to exceed λ is counted and the number of trials minus one is returned. The method is inefficient for large λ, yet likely to be good enough for applications in property insurance; see Section 10.3. For large λ the more complicated acceptance–rejection method of Atkinson (1979) is better. Still another Poisson generator is presented in Section 4.2.

2.6 Mathematical arguments

2.6.1 Monte Carlo error and tails of distributions

The accuracy of Monte Carlo percentile estimation is determined by the coefficient a_ϵ in (2.5). Let $a_{1\epsilon}$ and $a_{2\epsilon}$ be its value for distribution functions $F_1(x)$ and $F_2(x)$ with density functions $f_1(x)$ and $f_2(x)$ and percentiles $q_{1\epsilon} = F_1^{-1}(1-\epsilon)$ and $q_{2\epsilon} = F_2^{-1}(1-\epsilon)$. Then from (2.5)

$$\frac{a_{2\epsilon}}{a_{1\epsilon}} = \frac{f_1(q_{1\epsilon})}{f_2(q_{2\epsilon})},$$

and we shall study this ratio as $\epsilon \to 0$. Note that

$$q_{2\epsilon} = F_2^{-1}(1-\epsilon) = F_2^{-1}\{F_1(q_{1\epsilon})\} \quad \text{so that} \quad \frac{q_{2\epsilon}}{q_{1\epsilon}} = \frac{F_2^{-1}\{F_1(q_{1\epsilon})\}}{q_{1\epsilon}},$$

which is a $0/0$ expression as $q_{1\epsilon} \to \infty$ with limit determined by the derivative of the numerator according to l'Hôpital's rule. Since $dF_2^{-1}(u)/du = 1/f_2\{F_2^{-1}(u)\}$, the chain rule yields

$$\frac{dF_2^{-1}\{F_1(q_{1\epsilon})\}}{dq_{1\epsilon}} = \frac{f_1(q_{1\epsilon})}{f_2\{F_2^{-1}\{F_1(q_{1\epsilon})\}\}} = \frac{f_1(q_{1\epsilon})}{f_2(q_{2\epsilon})} = \frac{a_{2\epsilon}}{a_{1\epsilon}},$$

and $a_{2\epsilon}/a_{1\epsilon}$ and $q_{2\epsilon}/q_{1\epsilon}$ have common limits as $q_{1\epsilon} \to \infty$ or equivalently as $\epsilon \to 0$. Suppose the second distribution has much larger percentiles than the first. The ratio $a_{2\epsilon}/a_{1\epsilon}$ is then much larger than 1, and the second model requires, for small ϵ, many more simulations for the same accuracy.

2.6.2 Algorithm 2.7 revisited

Let Y be a random variable with density function

$$f(y) = c_1(1 - y^2)^{\alpha-1}, \quad -1 < y < 1,$$

where c_1 is a normalization constant. Marsaglia's algorithm utilizes that $X = \sqrt{2\alpha}\,Y/\sqrt{1-Y^2}$ is t-distributed with 2α degrees of freedom; see Cook and Weisberg (1982). We may therefore sample Y instead of X, and an effective way is by acceptance–rejection through proposals from $g(y) = c_2 e^{-(\alpha-1)y^2}$ which is a zero-mean, normal density function with standard deviation $1/\sqrt{2\alpha-2}$. Note that

$$(1 - y^2)^{\alpha-1} \leq e^{-(\alpha-1)y^2} \quad \text{if} \quad -1 < y < 1,$$

which is verified by differentiating the logarithms. It follows that a proposal Y^* from the normal should be accepted if

$$U^* \leq \frac{(1 - Y^{*2})^{\alpha-1}}{e^{-(\alpha-1)Y^{*2}}},$$

which is Algorithm 2.7 when the criterion is rewritten in logarithmic form.

2.6.3 Algorithm 2.9 revisited

Suppose X is Gamma distributed with mean $\xi = \sqrt{\alpha}$ and shape α so that the density function is proportional to $x^{\alpha-1}e^{-\sqrt{\alpha}\,x}$. It is assumed that $\alpha > 1$. Let $Y = X - \sqrt{\alpha}$, which can be sampled effectively by a ratio of uniforms (Algorithm 2.3). Its density function is proportional to

$$f(y) = (y + \sqrt{\alpha})^{\alpha-1}e^{-\sqrt{\alpha}\,y}, \quad y > -\sqrt{\alpha},$$

and Algorithm 2.3 needs the maximum a of $\sqrt{f(y)}$ and the minimum and maximum b_- and b_+ of $y\sqrt{f(y)}$. Straightforward differentiation shows that $\sqrt{f(y)}$, has a maximum at $y = -1/\sqrt{\alpha}$ so that $a = (\sqrt{\alpha} - 1/\sqrt{\alpha})^{(\alpha-1)/2}e^{1/2}$, and after some tedious calculations it emerges that

$$\frac{dy\sqrt{f(y)}}{dy} = -\frac{\sqrt{\alpha}}{2}(y + \sqrt{\alpha})^{(\alpha-3)/2}e^{-\sqrt{\alpha}y/2}(y - y_-)(y - y_+)$$

where $y_\pm = (2\sqrt{\alpha})^{-1} \pm \sqrt{2 + (4\alpha)^{-1}}$. It is easy to see that $y_- > -\sqrt{\alpha}$ when $\alpha > 1$ so that $y\sqrt{f(y)}$ has minimum at y_- and maximum at y_+. Introduce

$$g(y) = \frac{f(y)}{a^2} = \frac{(y + \sqrt{\alpha})^{\alpha-1} e^{-\sqrt{\alpha}\,y}}{(\sqrt{\alpha} - 1/\sqrt{\alpha})^{\alpha-1} e^1} = \left(\frac{1 + y/\sqrt{\alpha}}{1 - 1/\alpha}\right)^{\alpha-1} e^{-\sqrt{\alpha}\,y-1},$$

which is the function in Algorithm 2.9. The ratio of uniforms scheme of Algorithm 2.3 for Y can now be organized as detailed in Algorithm 2.9, where the last statement transforms to a Gamma variable with mean ξ and shape α.

2.6.4 Algorithm 2.10 revisited

To establish Stuart's representation let $Z = YU^{1/\alpha}$ where $Y \sim \text{Gamma}(\alpha + 1)$ and U is uniform with Y and U independent. The conditional distribution function of Z given $Y = y$ is then

$$\Pr(Z \le z|y) = \Pr(yU^{1/\alpha} \le z) = \Pr(U \le (z/y)^\alpha) = (z/y)^\alpha, \quad 0 < z < y,$$

and elementary differentiation yields $f(z|y) = \alpha y^{-\alpha} z^{\alpha-1}$ for the density function. The joint $f(y, z)$ follows via multiplying by the density function of Y, which is $cy^\alpha e^{-(\alpha+1)y}$ for some constant c. Hence

$$f(y, z) = \alpha c z^{\alpha-1} e^{-(\alpha+1)y}, \quad 0 < z < y,$$

and the density function of Z becomes

$$f(z) = \int_z^\infty f(y, z)dy = \int_z^\infty \alpha c z^{\alpha-1} e^{-(\alpha+1)y} dy = \frac{\alpha c}{\alpha + 1} z^{\alpha-1} e^{-(\alpha+1)z},$$

which is a Gamma density. Taking $X = Z(\alpha + 1)/\alpha$ yields the standard Gamma distribution with mean 1 and shape α as in Algorithm 2.10.

2.6.5 Algorithm 2.14 revisited

Let $X_1, \ldots, X_{n+1}$ be stochastically independent with common density function $f(x) = e^{-x}$ for $x > 0$ and let $S_n = X_1 + \cdots + X_n$. The Poisson generator in Algorithm 2.14 is based on the probability

$$p_n(\lambda) = \Pr(S_n < \lambda \le S_n + X_{n+1})$$

which can be evaluated by conditioning on S_n. If its density function is $f_n(s)$, then

$$p_n(\lambda) = \int_0^\lambda \Pr(\lambda \le s + X_{n+1}|S_n = s) f_n(s)\, ds = \int_0^\lambda e^{-(\lambda-s)} f_n(s)\, ds.$$

But S_n is Gamma distributed with mean $\xi = n$ and shape $\alpha = n$; look up this result in Section 9.3 if it is unfamiliar. This means that $f_n(s) = s^{n-1}e^{-s}/(n-1)!$ and

$$p_n(\lambda) = \int_0^\lambda e^{-(\lambda-s)} s^{n-1} e^{-s}/(n-1)!\,ds = \frac{e^{-\lambda}}{(n-1)!}\int_0^\lambda s^{n-1}\,ds = \frac{\lambda^n}{n!}e^{-\lambda},$$

as was to be proved.

2.7 Bibliographical notes

2.7.1 *Statistics and distributions*

Parts of this chapter have drawn on results from statistics. Stuart and Ord (1987) is a broad, practical review which contains many of the central distributions. The non-parametric side of statistics is treated (for example) in Wasserman (2006), whereas Scott (1992) and Wand and Jones (1995) are specialist monographs on density estimation. The most common univariate distributions are reviewed in Johnson *et al.* (1994) (the continuous case), Johnson *et al.* (2005) (the discrete case) and Balakrishnan and Nevzorov (2003) (both types). Klugman *et al.* (2008) and Kleiber and Kotz (2003) are similar introductions in an actuarial and financial context; see also Panjer and Willmot (1992), Beirlant *et al.* (1996) and Klugman (2004) for treatments in general insurance. Gaussian models and stochastic volatility are discussed more thoroughly in Chapters 5 and 13, with references given in Sections 5.9 and 13.8.

2.7.2 *Sampling*

The classic reference on the sampling of non-uniform random variables is Devroye (1986), still eminently useful (most of these algorithms had been discovered by 1986). Gentle (2003) is a good alternative; see also Hörmann *et al.* (2004). Many of the models used in this book can be sampled by inversion, but Gamma, generalized Pareto and t-variables are exceptions. Algorithm 2.9 is believed to be new. Smart sampling methods for some of the central distributions in actuarial science are presented in Ahrens and Dieter (1974).

2.7.3 *Programming*

What platforms should you go for? High-level software packages are Splus or R (which is the same), MATLAB, Maple and Mathematica. All of them allow easy implementation with sampling generators for the most common distributions available as built-in routines. Much information is provided on their websites.[1] For textbooks consult Venables and Ripley (2002), Zivot and Wang (2003) or Krause and Olson (2005) (for R), Hunt *et al.* (2001) or Otto and Denier (2005) (MATLAB), Cornil and Testud (2001) or Dagpunar (2007) (Maple) and Wolfram (2003), Rose and Smith (2001), Landau (2005) or McMahon and Topa (2006) (Mathematica). Many problems are successful on these platforms, and you may even try Excel and Visual Basic (see Schneider, 2006). But if speed is needed, choose C, Fortran or Pascal. Most experiments in this book have been coded in Fortran90, and in most cases the computer time was a second or less. Introductions to these programming languages are Stoustrup (2013) and Harbison and Steele (2002) (for C), Ellis *et al.* (1994) and Chivers and Sleightholme (2006) (Fortran) and Savitch (1995) (Pascal). Parallel processing permits even higher speed, but this hasn't been used much in insurance and finance. Grama *et al.* (2003) is a general introduction (with examples from engineering and natural sciences); see also Nakano (2004) in the context of statistics. A Microsoft viewpoint is offered in Levy (2004).

2.8 Exercises

Section 2.2

Exercise 2.1 Let $R = e^{\xi+\sigma\varepsilon} - 1$ where $\varepsilon \sim N(0, 1)$.

(a) Write a program generating m simulations of R and compute their mean and standard deviation.

R-*commands*:

```
R=rlnorm(m,ξ,σ)-1; Mean=mean(R); Sd=sd(R).
```

(b) Run the program when $\xi = 0.005$ and $\sigma = 0.05$ using $m = 100$, 1000 and 10 000 simulations and compare with the exact $E(R) = e^{\xi+\sigma^2/2} - 1$ and $\text{sd}(R) = e^{\xi+\sigma^2/2}\sqrt{e^{\sigma^2} - 1}$.

(c) What does the experiment tell you about the chances of estimating ξ and σ from real historical returns?

Exercise 2.2 Distribution functions $F(x)$ and $G(x)$ are often compared by plotting their percentiles $F^{-1}(u)$ and $G^{-1}(u)$ against each other at $u = (i - 1/2)/n$ for $i = 1, \dots, n$. We shall apply this **Q–Q** technique to $R = \xi + \sigma\varepsilon$ and $R = e^{\xi+\sigma\varepsilon} - 1$ where $\varepsilon \sim N(0, 1)$.

(a) Argue that $\xi + \sigma\Phi^{-1}(u)$ and $e^{\xi+\sigma\Phi^{-1}(u)} - 1$ are the precentiles of the two models when $\Phi^{-1}(u)$ is the inverse Gaussian integral.

[1] http://www.r-project.org for R (and Splus), http://www.mathworks.com for MATLAB, http://www.maplesoft.com for Maple and http://www.wolfram.com for Mathematica.

(b) Write a program Q–Q plotting the two distributions.

R-*commands*:

```
u=(1:n-0.5)/n; qno=ξ+σ*qnorm(u); qln=exp(qno)-1;
plot(qno,qln).
```

(c) Run the program when $n = 1000$, $\xi = 0.005$ and $\sigma = 0.05$.

(d) Redo for $\sigma = 0.25$ and compare with the pattern in (c).

Exercise 2.3 Suppose $Y = a + bX$ where a and b are coefficients.

(a) If $F^{-1}(u)$ and $G^{-1}(u)$ are the percentiles of X and Y, argue that $G^{-1}(u) = a + bF^{-1}(u)$ so that the Q–Q plot is a straight line.

(b) Point out that changing the mean and standard deviation of a distribution shifts and rotates a Q–Q plot without affecting the shape.

Exercise 2.4 Q–Q plotting also works with Monte Carlo. Let $X^*_{(1)} \leq \cdots \leq X^*_{(m)}$ be ordered simulations under one model and $Y^*_{(1)} \leq \cdots \leq Y^*_{(m)}$ under another.

(a) Explain that Q–Q plotting implies $X^*_{(i)}$ being plotted against $Y^*_{(i)}$ for $i = 1, \ldots, m$.

(b) Write a program comparing normal and log-normal equity returns using simulations.

R-*commands*:

```
X=rnorm(m,ξ,σ); Y=rlnorm(m,ξ,σ)-1; plot(sort(X),sort(Y)).
```

(c) Run the program when $\xi = 0.005$ and $\sigma = 0.05$ using $m = 10\,000$ simulations.

(d) Redo when $\sigma = 0.25$ and argue that the conclusions are the same as in Exercise 2.2.

Exercise 2.5

(a) Generate $m = 1\,000\,000$ simulations of R in Exercise 2.1 when $\xi = 0.005$ and $\sigma = 0.05$ and plot the estimated density function.

R-*commands*:

```
R=rlnorm(m,ξ,σ)-1; plot(density(R)).
```

(b) Select the first 100 simulations in (a), use them to re-estimate the density function and enter it into the plot in (a).

R-*commands*:

```
d=density(R[1:100]); lines(d$x,d$y).
```

(c) Write a program redoing (a) and (b) with the second density estimate controlled by a smoothing parameter.

R-*commands*:

```
R=rlnorm(m,ξ,σ)-1; plot(density(R),ylim=c(0,10));
d=density(R[1:100],bw=0.015); lines(d$x,d$y).
```

(d) Experiment with the smoothing parameter.

R-*commands*:

Try `bw=0.005, 0.012, 0.018, 0.025`.

Exercise 2.6 Suppose m simulations are used to estimate the lower ϵ-percentile of R in Exercise 2.1.

(a) Write a program generating m_b such Monte Carlo evaluations.

R-*commands*:

```
X=rnorm(m*mb,ξ,σ); R=matrix(exp(X)-1,m,mb);
qε=apply(R,2,sort)[ε*m,].
```

(b) Run the program when $\xi = 0.005$, $\sigma = 0.05$, $m = 1000$, $\epsilon = 0.01$ and $m_b = 1000$, estimate/plot the density function of the Monte Carlo percentile and compare with the exact value.

R-*commands*:

```
plot(density(qε)); Exact=exp(ξ+σ*qnorm(ε))-1.
```

Exercise 2.7 Recall from (2.3) that $\mathrm{sd}(s^*) \doteq (\sigma/\sqrt{2m})\sqrt{1+\kappa/2}$, where κ is the kurtosis. Compute how much $\mathrm{sd}(s^*)$ is inflated when κ goes from 0 (Gaussian data) to 6 (which might be realistic for daily equity returns).

Exercise 2.8 The mathematical definition of kurtosis is $\kappa = E(X-\xi)^4/\sigma^4 - 3$ where $\xi = E(X)$ and $\sigma = \mathrm{sd}(X)$, and it has a simple interpretation under the stochastic volatility model (2.20); i.e., when $X = \xi + \xi_\sigma\sqrt{Z}\,\varepsilon$ with ε and Z independent and $\varepsilon \sim N(0,1)$.

(a) Show that $(X-\xi)^2 = \xi_\sigma^2 Z\varepsilon^2$ so that $\sigma^2 = E(X-\xi)^2 = \xi_\sigma^2 E(Z)$.
(b) Utilize $E(\varepsilon^4) = 3$ to deduce that $E(X-\xi)^4 = 3\xi_\sigma^4 E(Z^2)$.
(c) Use (a) and (b) to prove that $\kappa = 3\mathrm{var}(Z)/(EZ)^2$.
(d) Why is $\kappa = 0$ for normal variables? [*Comment*: Usually Z is scaled so that $E(Z) \doteq 1$, which makes $\kappa \doteq 3\mathrm{var}(Z)$.]

Exercise 2.9 A standard estimate of kurtosis κ given independent and identically distributed observations $x_1,\dots,x_n$ with mean and variance $\bar{x}$ and s^2 is

$$\hat{\kappa} = \frac{\hat{\nu}_4}{s^4} - 3 \quad \text{where} \quad \hat{\nu}_4 = \frac{1}{n}\sum_{i=1}^{n}(x_i-\bar{x})^4.$$

(a) Write a program simulating a log-normal sample $X_i = e^{\xi+\sigma\varepsilon_i}$ for $i = 1,\dots,n$, compute $\hat{\kappa}$ and compare with the exact $\kappa = e^{4\sigma^2} + 2e^{3\sigma^2} + 3e^{2\sigma^2} - 6$; see Johnson *et al.* (1994).

R-*commands*:

```
X=rlnorm(n,ξ,σ); X̄=mean(X); κ̂=mean((X-X̄)**4)/var(X)**2-3.
```

(b) Run the program under monthly equity return parameters $\xi = 0.005$ and $\sigma = 0.05$ when $n = 100$, $n = 10\,000$ and $n = 1\,000\,000$, compare with the exact κ and repeat a few times to get a feeling for the variability.
(c) Redo (b) when $\xi = 0$ and $\sigma = 1$ (could be losses in general insurance).
(d) Comment on the performance of this kurtosis estimate.

Section 2.3

Exercise 2.10 The Cauchy model has density and distribution function

$$f(x) = \frac{(\beta\pi)^{-1}}{1 + (x/\beta)^2} \quad \text{and} \quad F(x) = 1/2 + \text{atan}(x/\beta)/\pi$$

where $\beta > 0$ is a parameter.

(a) Show that $F^{-1}(u) = \beta \tan\{(u - 1/2)\pi\}$ and write down the inversion sampler.
(b) Implement a program generating m Cauchy-distributed variables and compute their average.
R-*commands*:
`U=runif(m); X=β*tan((U-0.5)*pi); Mean=mean(X)` or use
`X=rcauchy(m,scale=β)`.
(c) Run the program when $\beta = 1$ and $m = 100$, 1000, 10 000 and 100 000. [*Comment*: The pattern (or lack of it) is caused by the underlying expectation being infinite.]

Exercise 2.11 The distribution function $G(x)$ when X is confined to some sub-interval (a, b) differs from the original $F(x)$. Such **truncated** situations arise in property insurance and finance.

(a) Show that

$$G(x) = \frac{F(x) - F(a)}{F(b) - F(a)}, \qquad a < x < b.$$

[*Hint*: Use conditional probabilities (Section 6.2) and argue that $G(x) = \Pr(X \leq x|a < X < b)$, which is $\Pr(a < X < x)/\Pr(a < X < b)$.]
(b) Solve the equation $G(x) = u$ and show that $G^{-1}(u) = F^{-1}\{F(a)+[F(b)-F(a)]u\}$ which opens up inversion sampling of truncated models.

Exercise 2.12 Suppose we seek simulations of X above some threshold a.

(a) Use Exercise 2.11 to argue that it can be done through $X^* \leftarrow F^{-1}\{1 - p + pU^*\}$ where $p = 1 - F(a)$ and U^* is uniform.
(b) Write a program generating m simulations over the threshold when the original variable is $N(\xi, \sigma)$.

R-*commands*:

```
p=1-pnorm(a,ξ,σ); X=qnorm(1-p+p*runif(m),ξ,σ).
```

(c) Run the program when $m = 10\,000$, $\xi = 0$, $\sigma = 1$ and $a = 1, 2$ and 3 and compute mean and standard deviation.

R-*commands*:

```
Mean=mean(X); Sd=sd(X).
```

Exercise 2.13 Redo the preceding exercise for the log-normal $Y = e^X$; i.e., generate simulations above the threshold e^a when $a = 1$, 2 and 3 and compute mean and standard deviation now.

R-*commands*:

Take `X` from Exercise 2.12 and use `Y=exp(X); Mean=mean(Y); Sd=sd(Y).`

Exercise 2.14 Distributions truncated to an interval (a, b) can also be sampled by acceptance–rejection.

(a) Argue that this means that simulations X^* drawn from the original model are kept whenever $a < X^* < b$.

(b) Write a program generating m such simulations from $N(\xi, \sigma)$ when $b = \infty$ and compute the acceptance rate; i.e., the number of simulations kept divided by m.

R-*commands*:

```
X=rnorm(m,ξ,σ); X=X[X> a]; Acceptance=length(X)/m.
```

(c) Run the program when $m = 100\,000$, $\xi = 0$, $\sigma = 1$ and $a = 1$, 2 and 3 as in Exercise 2.12.

(d) Argue that the method is inferior to inversion when the latter is available; see also Exercise 4.3.

Exercise 2.15 This exercise constructs a sampler from Gamma(α) when $\alpha > 1$ by acceptance–rejection from the exponential. The density functions are then $f(x) = cx^{\alpha-1}e^{-\alpha x}$ and $g(x) = e^{-x}$ for $x > 0$.

(a) Show that $f(x)/g(x)$ attains its maximum at $x = 1$ and argue that

$$\frac{f(x)}{Mg(x)} = e^{(\alpha-1)(\log(x)-x+1)} \leq 1 \quad \text{if} \quad M = \frac{f(1)}{g(1)} = ce^{-\alpha+1}.$$

(b) Explain that an acceptance–rejection sampler inserts uniforms U_1^* and U_2^* into the scheme

$$X^* \leftarrow -\log(U_1^*) \quad \text{accepted if} \quad \log(U_2^*) < (\alpha - 1)(\log(X^*) - X^* + 1).$$

Exercise 2.16

(a) Write a program generating m simulations of Gamma(α) by means of the algorithm of the preceding exercise.

R-*commands*:

```
U1=runif(m); U2=runif(m); X=-log(U1);
X=X[log(U2)<(α-1)*(log(X)-X+1)].
```

(b) Run the program when $m = 100\,000$ and $\alpha = 2.5$, check that average and standard deviation are close to $E(X) = 1$ and $\text{sd}(X) = 1/\sqrt{2.5} \doteq 0.632$ and compute the acceptance rate.

R-*commands*:

```
Mean=mean(X); Sd=sd(X); Acceptance=length(X)/m.
```

The method is usable when $\alpha > 1$ isn't too large, though inferior to those in the text.

Exercise 2.17 To illustrate the ratio of uniform sampling, let $f(x) = e^{-x^2/2}$ with maximum at $x = 0$ so that $a = \sqrt{f(0)} = 1$ in Algorithm 2.3.

(a) Show that the minimum and maximum of $x\sqrt{f(x)}$ occurs at $x = -\sqrt{2}$ and $x = \sqrt{2}$, which means that $b_- = -\sqrt{2}e^{-1/2}$ and $b_+ = \sqrt{2}e^{-1/2}$ in Algorithm 2.3.

(b) Implement Algorithm 2.3 for the standard normal distribution.

R-*commands*:

```
b_=-sqrt(2)*exp(-0.5); b+=-b_; U1=runif(m);
U2=runif(m); X=(b_+(b+-b_)*U2)/U1;
X=X[U1<exp(-0.25*X*X)].
```

(c) Run the program for $m = 10\,000$, check that the mean and standard deviation of the simulated sample are close to 0 and 1 and compute the acceptance rate.

R-*commands*:

```
Mean=mean(X); Sd=sd(X); Acceptance=length(X)/m.
```

Section 2.4

Exercise 2.18 Suppose $X = \xi e^{-\sigma^2/2+\sigma\varepsilon}$ where $\varepsilon \sim N(0, 1)$.

(a) Draw $m = 10\,000$ simulations when $\xi = 1$ and $\sigma = 0.25$, compute their mean and plot the density function.

R-*commands*:

```
eps=rnorm(m); X=ξ*exp(-σ**2/2+σ*eps);
Mean=mean(X); plot(density(X)).
```

(b) Redo (a) when $\sigma = 0.5$ and $\sigma = 1$ and note how the density function changes while the mean doesn't.

Exercise 2.19 As model for financial returns, consider $R = e^{\xi+\xi_\sigma\sqrt{Z}\varepsilon} - 1$ where ε and Z are independent and $\varepsilon \sim N(0, 1)$. Suppose $Z = 1/G$ where $G \sim \text{Gamma}(\alpha)$.

(a) Argue that $\log(1 + R)$ is t-distributed.

(b) Write a program drawing m simulations of R.

R-*commands*:

```
eps=rnorm(m); G=rgamma(m,α)/α; R=exp(ξ + ξσ/sqrt(G)*eps)-1.
```

(c) Run the program when $m = 10\,000$, $\xi = 0.005$, $\xi_\sigma = 0.08$ and $\alpha = 10$ and estimate/plot the density function.

R-*commands*:

```
plot(density(R)).
```

Exercise 2.20 An alternative model for Z in Exercise 2.19 is $Z = e^{\tau^2/2+\tau\eta}$, where $\eta \sim N(0, 1)$ and $\tau \geq 0$ a parameter.

(a) Use the formulae for the mean and standard deviation of log-normal variables to argue that $E(1/Z) = 1$ and $\text{sd}(1/Z) = \sqrt{e^{\tau^2} - 1}$.

(b) Show that $1/Z$ has the same mean and variance as in Exercise 2.19 when $\tau = \sqrt{\log(1 + 1/\alpha)}$. [*Hint*: $\text{sd}(G) = 1/\sqrt{\alpha}$ when $G \sim \text{Gamma}(\alpha)$.]

(c) Write a program generating m simulations of $R_2 = e^{\xi+\xi_\sigma\sqrt{Z}\,\varepsilon} - 1$.

R-*commands*:

```
eps=rnorm(m); eta=rnorm(m); Z=exp(τ**2/2+τ*eta);
R2=exp(ξ + ξσ*sqrt(Z)*eps)-1.
```

(d) Run the program when $m = 10\,000$ with parameters as in Exercise 2.19 (meaning $\tau = \sqrt{\log(1 + 1/\alpha)}$) and estimate/plot the density function.

R-*commands*:

```
plot(density(R2)).
```

(e) Q–Q plot the simulations against those in Exercise 2.19 and comment.

R-*commands*:

With R from Exercise 2.19 use `plot(sort(R),sort(R2))`.

Exercise 2.21 Let $R_1 = e^{\xi+\sigma\varepsilon_1} - 1$ and $R_2 = e^{\xi+\sigma\varepsilon_2} - 1$ where $\varepsilon_1, \varepsilon_2 \sim N(0, 1)$ with $\rho = \text{cor}(\varepsilon_1, \varepsilon_2)$.

(a) Write a program generating m simulations of $(\varepsilon_1, \varepsilon_2)$.

R-*commands*:

```
eps=matrix(rnorm(2*m),m,2);
eps[,2]=ρ*eps[,1]+sqrt(1-ρ**2)*eps[,2].
```

(b) Add commands so that the portfolio return $\mathcal{R} = (R_1 + R_2)/2$ is simulated.

R-*commands*:

```
R=exp(ξ+σ*eps)-1; ℛ=0.5*(R[,1]+R[,2]).
```

(c) Draw $m = 100\,000$ simulations of $\mathcal{R}$ when $\xi = 0.05$, $\sigma = 0.25$ and $\rho = 0, 0.6$ and 0.9, compute each time the mean and standard deviation and compare their values.

R-*commands*:

`Mean=mean(`$\mathcal{R}$`); Sd=sd(`$\mathcal{R}$`).`

Exercise 2.22 Suppose the volatilities in Exercise 2.21 are stochastic so that $\sigma = \xi_\sigma/\sqrt{G}$ where $G \sim \text{Gamma}(\alpha)$.

(a) Write a program generating m simulations of $\mathcal{R}$ under this extended model.

R-*commands*:

Take `eps` from Exercise 2.21 and use σ`=`ξ_σ`/sqrt(rgamma(m,`α`)/`α`);`
R`=exp(`ξ`+`σ`*eps)-1;` $\mathcal{R}$`=0.5*(`R`[,1]+`R`[,2]).`

(b) Redo the experiment in Exercise 2.21(c) when $\alpha = 5$ and $\xi_\sigma = 0.25$ with the rest of the conditions as before, compute $E(\mathcal{R})$ and sd($\mathcal{R}$) from the simulations and compare with the results in Exercise 2.21.

R-*commands*:

`Mean=mean(`$\mathcal{R}$`); Sd=sd(`$\mathcal{R}$`).`

Exercise 2.23 Extend the model in Exercise 2.21 to J assets with returns $R_j = e^{\xi+\sigma\varepsilon_j} - 1$ where $\rho = \text{cor}(\varepsilon_i, \varepsilon_j)$ is the same for all pairs $i \neq j$.

(a) Write a program generating m simulations of $(\varepsilon_1, \ldots, \varepsilon_J)$.

R-*commands*:

`eps=matrix(rnorm((J+1)*m),m,J+1);`
`eps=sqrt(`ρ`)*eps[,1]+sqrt(1-`ρ`)*eps[,1:J+1].`

(b) Use (a) to simulate $\mathcal{R} = (R_1 + \cdots + R_J)/J$.

R-*commands*:

`R=exp(`ξ`+`σ`*eps)-1; R=apply(R,1,mean).`

(c) Draw $m = 10\,000$ simulations of $\mathcal{R}$ when $\xi = 0.05$, $\sigma = 0.25$ and $J = 5$ and $\rho = 0$, 0.6 and 0.9 and compare approximations of $E(\mathcal{R})$ and sd($\mathcal{R}$) with those in Exercise 2.21(c).

R-*commands*:

`Mean=mean(R); Sd=sd(R).`

Exercise 2.24 Models with stochastic correlations were proposed by Ball and Torus (2000). One construction is to start as in Exercise 2.21, but specify ρ as

$$\rho = \frac{(1+\rho_0)e^{\tau\eta} - (1-\rho_0)}{(1+\rho_0)e^{\tau\eta} + (1-\rho_0)} \quad \text{where} \quad \eta \sim N(0,1).$$

The parameters ρ_0 and τ satisfy $|\rho_0| < 1$ and $\tau \geq 0$.

(a) Argue that ρ_0 is the median of ρ and that $|\rho| < 1$. [*Hint*: The median appears when $\eta = 0$.]

(b) Simulate $(\varepsilon_1, \varepsilon_2)$ by extending the program in Exercise 2.21(a).

R-*commands*:

```
eps=matrix(rnorm(2*m),m,2); Z=exp(τ*rnorm(m));
ρ=((1+ρ0)*Z-(1-ρ0))/((1+ρ0)*Z+1-ρ0);
eps[,2]=ρ*eps[,1]+sqrt(1-ρ**2)*eps[,2].
```

(c) Simulate $\mathcal{R} = (R_1 + R_2)/2$.

R-*commands*:

As in Exercise 2.21(b).

(d) Draw $m = 10\,000$ simulations of $\mathcal{R}$ when $\xi = 0.05$ and $\sigma = 0.25$, $\rho_0 = 0.6$ and $\tau = 0.5$ and compute their mean and standard deviation.

R-*commands*:

```
Mean=mean(R); Sd=sd(R).
```

(e) Redo (d) when $\tau = 0$ and $\tau = 1$ and comment on the importance of stochastic correlation.

Section 2.5

Exercise 2.25 Gamma variables in this book are defined as $X = \xi G$ where G has mean 1 and shape α.

(a) Write a program generating m simulations of X.

R-*commands*:

```
G=rgamma(m,α)/α; X=ξ*G.
```

(b) Check that your program is correct by drawing $m = 10\,000$ simulations when $\xi = 10$ and $\alpha = 4$, compute their mean and standard deviation and compare with the exact values $E(X) = 10$ and $\text{sd}(X) = 5$.

R-*commands*:

```
Mean=mean(X); Sd=sd(X).
```

Exercise 2.26

(a) Write a program simulating Gamma variables over thresholds; i.e., if X is Gamma distributed, simulate $X - a$ given $X > a$.

R-*commands*:

```
X=ξ*rgamma(m,α)/α; X=X[X>a]-a.
```

(b) Run the program when $m = 100\,000$, $\xi = 10$, $\alpha = 4$ and $a = 5$, 15 and 25 and compute acceptance rate, mean and standard deviation of the simulations.

R-*commands*:

```
Acceptance=length(X)/m; Mean=mean(X); Sd=sd(X).
```

(c) Redo (b) when $\alpha = 1$ with the other parameters as before and notice how mean and standard deviation depend on a.

Exercise 2.27

(a) Modify the program in Exercise 2.26 so that it simulates Gamma variables truncated between a and b.

R-*commands*:

```
X=ξ*rgamma(m,α)/α; X=X[X>a&X<b].
```

(b) Run the program when $m = 100\,000$, $\xi = 10$, $\alpha = 4$, $a = 5$ and $b = 10$, 15 and 20, and compute acceptance rate, mean and standard deviation of the simulations.

R-*commands*:

As in Exercise 2.26(b).

(c) What is the intuition behind the standard deviations being smaller than $\xi/\sqrt{\alpha}$? See also Exercise 4.4.

Exercise 2.28 Consider the Weibull model $X = \beta Y^{1/\alpha}$ where Y is exponential with mean one and where α and β are positive parameters.

(a) Argue that the distribution function of X is

$$F(x) = \Pr(Y \leq (x/\beta)^{\alpha}) = 1 - e^{-(x/\beta)^{\alpha}}.$$

(b) Show that the Weibull sampler in Algorithm 2.12 is the inversion sampler.

Exercise 2.29 Let $\mathrm{med}(X) = F^{-1}(1/2)$ and $\mathrm{qd}(X) = F^{-1}(3/4) - F^{-1}(1/4)$ be the median and quartile difference of the Weibull distribution.

(a) Show that $\mathrm{med}(X) \doteq \beta 0.6931^{1/\alpha}$ and $\mathrm{qd}(X) \doteq \beta(1.3863^{1/\alpha} - 0.2877^{1/\alpha})$.

(b) Write a program generating m Weibull simulations.

R-*commands*:

`X=β*rexp(m)**(1/α)` or the intrinsic `X=rweibull(m,α,β)`.

(c) Run the program with $m = 100\,000$, $\alpha = 2$ and $\beta = 1$ and compute the sample median and sample quartile difference, which you compare with $\mathrm{med}(X) = 0.833$ and $\mathrm{qd}(X) = 0.641$.

R-*commands*:

```
X=sort(X); med=X[0.5*m]; qd=X[0.75*m]-X[0.25*m].
```

Exercise 2.30

(a) Generate $m = 10\,000$ simulations from the Weibull distribution when $\beta = 1$ and $\alpha = 2$, estimate the density function and plot it.

R-*commands*:

```
X=rweibull(m,α,β); plot(density(X,from=0)).
```

(b) Redo (a) when $\alpha = 3.6$ and $\alpha = 5$ and note the different shapes of the density function.

(c) Q–Q plot Weibull simulations against normal ones when $\alpha = 3.6$ and interpret the pattern.

R-*commands*:

With Weibull simulations as `X` use `Y=rnorm(m); plot(sort(X),sort(Y))`.

Exercise 2.31 The **Fréchet** model (used for losses in property insurance) has distribution function

$$F(x) = e^{-(x/\beta)^{-\alpha}}, \quad x > 0$$

where α and β are positive parameters.

(a) Show that $F^{-1}(u) = \beta\{-\log(u)\}^{-1/\alpha}$.

(b) Program the inversion sampler with m simulations.

R-*commands*:

```
U=runif(m); X=β*(-log(U))**(-1/α).
```

(c) Run the program when $m = 100\,000$, $\alpha = 2$ and $\beta = 1$ and check it by comparing the sample median and sample quartile difference with $\text{med}(X) = 1.201$ and $\text{qd}(X) = 1.015$.

R-*commands*:

As in Exercise 2.29(c).

Exercise 2.32 Another model for losses in property insurance is the **logistic** one, for which the distribution function is

$$F(x) = 1 - \frac{1+\alpha}{1+\alpha e^{x/\beta}}, \quad x > 0$$

where α and β are positive parameters.

(a) Show that $F^{-1}(u) = \beta \log\{(1 + u/\alpha)/(1 - u)\}$.

(b) Program the inversion sampler with m simulations.

R-*commands*:

```
U=runif(m); X=β*log((1+U/α)/(1-U)).
```

(c) Run the program when $m = 100\,000$, $\alpha = 2$ and $\beta = 1$ and compare the sample median and sample quartile difference with $\text{med}(X) = 0.916$ and $\text{qd}(X) = 1.299$.

R-*commands*:

As in Exercise 2.29(c).

Exercise 2.33 The **Burr** family is still another model that has been proposed for losses in property insurance. The distribution function is now

$$F(x) = 1 - \{1 + (x/\beta)^{\alpha_1}\}^{-\alpha_2}, \quad x > 0$$

where α_1, α_2 and β are positive parameters.

(a) Show that $F^{-1}(u) = \beta\{(1-u)^{-1/\alpha_2} - 1\}^{1/\alpha_1}$.

(b) Program the inversion sampler with m simulations.

R-*commands*:

```
U=runif(m); X=β*(U**(-1/α2)-1)**(1/α1).
```

(c) Run the program when $m = 100\,000$, $\alpha_1 = 2$, $\alpha_2 = 2$ and $\beta = 1$ and check it by comparing the sample median and sample quartile difference with med$(X) = 0.644$ and qd$(X) = 0.607$.

R-*commands*:

As in Exercise 2.29(c).

Exercise 2.34 Let $S = N_1 + N_2$ where N_1 and N_2 are independent and Poisson distributed with parameters λ_1 and λ_2 and let N be Poisson$(\lambda_1 + \lambda_2)$.

(a) Write a program generating m simulations of S and N.

R-*commands*:

```
S=rpois(m,λ1)+rpois(m,λ2); N=rpois(m,λ1+λ2).
```

(b) Run the program when $m = 1000$, $\lambda_1 = 4$ and $\lambda_2 = 7$ and compare the distributions of S and N through Q–Q plotting.

R-*commands*:

```
plot(sort(N),sort(S)).
```

The story is told in Section 8.2.

Exercise 2.35 Let $S = G_1 + G_2$ where $G_1 \sim$ Gamma(α), $G_2 \sim$ Gamma(α) with G_1 and G_2 independent and let $G \sim$ Gamma(2α).

(a) Write a program generating m simulations of S and G.

R-*commands*:

```
G1=rgamma(m,α)/α; G2=rgamma(m,α)/α; S=G1+G2;
G=rgamma(m,2*α)/(2*α).
```

(b) Run the program when $m = 1000$ and $\alpha = 2.5$ and compare the distributions of S and G through Q–Q plotting.

R-*commands*:

```
plot(sort(G),sort(S)).
```

Consult Section 9.3 for the full story.

3
Evaluating risk: A primer

3.1 Introduction

The hardest part of quantitative risk analysis is to find the stochastic models and judge their realism. This is discussed later. What is addressed now is how models are used once they are in place. Only a handful of probability distributions have been introduced, and yet a good deal can be achieved already. The present chapter is a *primer* introducing the main arenas and their first treatment computationally. We start with property insurance (an area of huge uncertainty) where core issues can be reached with very simple modelling. Life insurance is quickly reached too, but now something is very different. Once the stochastic model is given, there is little risk left! This doesn't rule out much uncertainty in the model itself, a topic discussed in Section 15.2. With financial risk there is again much randomness under the model assumed.

The target of this chapter is the general line. Many interesting points (demanding heavier modelling) are left out and dealt with later. A unifying theme is Monte Carlo as problem solver. By this we do *not* mean the computational technique which was treated in the preceding chapter (and in the next one too). What is on the agenda is the art of making the computer work for a purpose, how we arrange for it to chew away on computational obstacles and how it is utilized to get a feel for numbers. Monte Carlo is also an efficient way of handling the myriad of details in practical problems. Feed them into the computer and let simulation take over. Implementation is often straightforward, and existing programs might be reused with minor variations. The potential here is endless. Is there a new contract clause, say an exception from the exception? With mathematics new expressions are needed, and you may have to work them out anew, perhaps from scratch. But if you use simulations, there may be no more than an additional statement in the computer code. And often the mathematics becomes too unwieldy to be of much merit at all.

3.2 General insurance: Opening look

3.2.1 Introduction

Risk variables in general insurance are compensations, X, for damages or accidents to a policy holder for incidents during a certain period of time T (often 1 year). Let $\mathcal{X}$ be the same quantity for an entire portfolio of such contracts and consider the representations

$$\underset{\textit{policy level}}{X = Z_1 + \cdots + Z_N} \quad \text{and} \quad \underset{\textit{portfolio level, identical risks}}{\mathcal{X} = Z_1 + \cdots + Z_{\mathcal{N}}} \tag{3.1}$$

where N and $\mathcal{N}$ are the number of events and $Z_1, Z_2, \ldots$ what it costs to settle them. If N (or $\mathcal{N}$) is zero, then X (or $\mathcal{X}$) is zero too. The models for N and $\mathcal{N}$ depend on T.

For these descriptions to make sense, $Z_1, Z_2, \ldots$ must all follow the same probability distribution. That is plausible when dealing with a single policy. Surely an unlikely second event isn't on average any different from the first? Portfolios are often different. Claims depend on the object insured and the sum it is insured for, and we must go through the entire list of policies. Suppose there are J of them with claims $X_1, \ldots, X_J$. Then

$$\mathcal{X} = X_1 + \cdots + X_J \quad \text{where} \quad X_j = Z_{j1} + \cdots + Z_{jN_j}, \tag{3.2}$$

and claim numbers N_j and losses $Z_{j1}, Z_{j2}, \ldots$ may have models depending on j. If all Z_{ji} have a common distribution, then $\mathcal{X}$ in (3.2) collapses to $\mathcal{X}$ in (3.1) right by taking $\mathcal{N} = N_1 + \cdots + N_J$.

3.2.2 Enter contracts and their clauses

The preceding representations do not take into account the distinction between what an incident costs and what a policy holder receives. If the actual compensation is some function $H(z)$ of the total replacement value z, then (3.1) left changes to

$$X = H(Z_1) + \cdots + H(Z_N) \quad \text{where} \quad 0 \le H(z) \le z. \tag{3.3}$$

Note that $H(z)$ can't exceed the total cost z. A common type of contract is

$$H(z) = \begin{matrix} 0, & z \le a \\ z - a, & a < z \le a + b \\ b & z > a + b. \end{matrix} \tag{3.4}$$

Here a is a **deductible** subtracted from z (no reimbursement below it) and b a maximum insured sum per claim. These quantities typically vary over the portfolio so that $a = a_j$ and $b = b_j$ for policy j.

Reinsurance, introduced in Section 1.2, is handled mathematically in much the same way. The original risk is now shared between cedent and reinsurer through contracts that may apply to both individual policies/events *and* to the portfolio aggregate $\mathcal{X}$. Representations of the reinsurer part then become

$$\underbrace{X^{\text{re}} = H(Z_1) + \cdots + H(Z_N)}_{\textit{reinsurance per event}} \quad \text{or} \quad \underbrace{\mathcal{X}^{\text{re}} = H(\mathcal{X})}_{\textit{reinsurance on portfolio level}} \tag{3.5}$$

where $H(z)$ and $H(x)$ define the contracts, satisfying $0 \le H(z) \le z$ and $0 \le H(x) \le x$ as above. The example (3.4) is prominent in reinsurance too. It is now called a **layer** $a \times b$ contract and a is the **retention** limit of the cedent (who keeps all risk below it).

Reinsurance means that the cedent *net* responsibilities are $X^{\text{ce}} = X - X^{\text{re}}$ or $\mathcal{X}^{\text{ce}} = \mathcal{X} - \mathcal{X}^{\text{re}}$ instead of X and $\mathcal{X}$. Whether the point of view is cedent or reinsurer, there is a common theme in how we proceed. Claim numbers and losses are described by stochastic models. Their Monte Carlo realizations are generated in the computer, which is fed the detailed clauses of the payments under the contract. This agenda will be pursued in Section 3.3.

3.2.3 Stochastic modelling

A critical part of risk evaluation in general insurance is the uncertainty of the original claims. Much will be said on that issue in Part II, yet a number of problems can be attacked right away through the following introductory observations. Claim numbers, whether N (for policies) or $\mathcal{N}$ (for portfolios), are often well described by the Poisson distribution. Their parameters are

$$\underbrace{\lambda = \mu T}_{\textit{policy level}} \quad \text{and} \quad \underbrace{\lambda = J\mu T}_{\textit{portfolio level}} \tag{3.6}$$

where μ is the expected number of claims per policy per time unit. In automobile insurance $\mu = 5\%$ annually might be plausible (claims from one car in 20). This central parameter (known as an **intensity**) will be explored thoroughly in Chapter 8 and used as a vehicle for more advanced modelling.

There is also the loss Z per event, usually assumed to be stochastically independent of N. Modelling is almost always a question of pure experience. Common choices of distributions are Gamma, log-normal and Pareto, all introduced in the preceding chapter. A systematic study of claim size modelling is given in Chapter 9.

3.2.4 Risk diversification

The core idea of insurance is risk spread over many units. Insight into this issue can be obtained by very simple means if the policy risks $X_1, \ldots, X_J$ are stochastically independent. Mean and variance for the portfolio total are then

$$E(\mathcal{X}) = \pi_1 + \cdots + \pi_J \quad \text{and} \quad \text{var}(\mathcal{X}) = \sigma_1^2 + \cdots + \sigma_J^2,$$

where $\pi_j = E(X_j)$ and $\sigma_j = \text{sd}(X_j)$. Introduce

$$\overline{\pi} = \frac{1}{J}(\pi_1 + \cdots + \pi_J) \quad \text{and} \quad \overline{\sigma}^2 = \frac{1}{J}(\sigma_1^2 + \cdots + \sigma_J^2),$$

which are *average* expectation and variance. Then

$$E(\mathcal{X}) = J\overline{\pi} \quad \text{and} \quad \text{sd}(\mathcal{X}) = \sqrt{J}\overline{\sigma} \quad \text{so that} \quad \frac{\text{sd}(\mathcal{X})}{E(\mathcal{X})} = \frac{\overline{\sigma}/\overline{\pi}}{\sqrt{J}}, \tag{3.7}$$

and portfolio means and standard deviations depend on J and $\sqrt{J}$. The latter is much smaller, and as the number of policies grows, risk becomes unimportant. A precise argument rests on the law of large numbers in probability theory (Appendix A.4). As $J \to \infty$, both $\overline{\pi}$ and $\overline{\sigma}$ tend to their population means, and the ratio $\text{sd}(\mathcal{X})/E(\mathcal{X})$ in (3.7) approaches 0. In other words, *insurance risk can be diversified away through size*.

Are large portfolios, therefore, risk free? That's actually how we operate in life insurance and with pensions (Section 3.4), but it is never that simple. There is always uncertainty in underlying models, and, as we shall see in Section 6.3, risks in general insurance may well be dependent, which invalidates the formula for $\text{var}(\mathcal{X})$. The big insurers and reinsurers of this world handle hundreds of thousands of policies. Their portfolio risk isn't zero!

3.3 How Monte Carlo is put to work

3.3.1 Introduction

This section is a first demonstration of Monte Carlo as a problem solver. The arena is general insurance, where many problems relating to pricing and control can be worked out from simulated samples $\mathcal{X}_1^*, \ldots, \mathcal{X}_m^*$ of the portfolio payout $\mathcal{X}$. How they are generated is shown below through skeleton algorithms. Ideas for program validation are discussed too. A small portfolio of potentially large claims will be used for illustration. Let

$J = 100$,	$\mu T = 10\%$,	$Z \sim \text{Pareto}(\alpha,\beta)$ with $\alpha = 3,\ \beta = 2$
number of policies	*annual claim frequency*	*claim size distribution*

which means that the average number of incidents per year is $J\mu T = 10$ with the model for Z having mean and standard deviation $\xi = 1$ and $\sigma = \sqrt{3}$, say in million US$. The portfolio could be industrial installations insured through a small

Algorithm 3.1 Portfolio risk, identical policies

0 Input: $\lambda = J\mu T$, distribution of Z
1 $\mathcal{X}^* \leftarrow 0$
2 Generate $\mathcal{N}^*$ *%Often Poisson(λ) by means of Algorithm 2.14, alternative model in Chapter 8*
3 For $i = 1, \ldots, \mathcal{N}^*$ do
4 Draw Z^* *%Algorithms in Section 2.5, additional ones in Chapter 9*
5 $\mathcal{X}^* \leftarrow \mathcal{X}^* + Z^*$ *%Extension: Add $H(Z^*)$ instead; see Algorithm 3.3*
6 Return $\mathcal{X}^*$. *%With reinsurance $\mathcal{X}^{re} = H(\mathcal{X})$: Return $H(\mathcal{X}^*)$ instead*

Algorithm 3.2 Portfolio risk, heterogeneous case

0 Input: Information on all policies
1 $\mathcal{X}^* \leftarrow 0$
2 For $j = 1, \ldots, J$ do
3 Draw $\mathcal{X}_j^*$ *%Algorithm 3.1 for* **single policies**, *information from policy j read from file*
4 $\mathcal{X}^* \leftarrow \mathcal{X}^* + \mathcal{X}_j^*$
5 Return $\mathcal{X}^*$.

company such as a **captive**, which is set up by a mother firm to handle its insurance (often for reasons of taxation). Uncertainty from one year to the next is huge and easiest understood through Monte Carlo.

3.3.2 Skeleton algorithms

Monte Carlo implementation of portfolio risk in general insurance does not differ much from Algorithm 1.1. When risks are identical we get Algorithm 3.1 with straightforward logic. Start by drawing the number of claims $\mathcal{N}^*$ and then add the $\mathcal{N}^*$ losses. Sub-algorithms must be inserted on Lines 2 and 4. The study below employs Algorithm 2.14 (for Poisson distributions) and Algorithm 2.13 (Pareto). The number of commands is *not* high. Individual policies are covered by taking $J = 1$, and a second, outer loop now yields Algorithm 3.2, a version where policy risks vary.

This second algorithm goes through the entire portfolio, which could be a long loop, but modern computational facilities are up to it. Often most of the computer work is to draw the losses anyway with the same amount of work for both algorithms. How the setup is modified for reinsurance is explained below.

3.3.3 Checking the program

Does the program work as intended? Anyone who has attempted computer programming knows how easily errors creep in. Bug-detection techniques may belong to computer science but we shouldn't ignore them, and many situations offer tricks that can be used for control. In the present instance one way is to utilize the fact that

$$E(\mathcal{X}) = J\mu T\xi \quad \text{and} \quad \text{sd}(\mathcal{X}) = \sqrt{J\mu T(\xi^2 + \sigma^2)},$$

where $\xi = E(Z)$ and $\sigma = s(Z)$. This is valid when all risks are identical, as will be proved in Section 6.3. Though the simulations may have been meant for the percentiles of $\mathcal{X}$, we can always compute average and standard deviation and compare with the exact ones. Most implementation errors are then going to show up.

A test based on $m = 1000$ simulations gave the following results for the portfolio in Section 3.1:

Exact premium	Monte Carlo $\overline{\mathcal{X}}^*$	Exact standard deviation	Monte Carlo s^*
10	9.84 (0.22)	6.32	6.84 (0.77)

The number of simulations has been kept low on purpose. Are the discrepancies between the exact values and the Monte Carlo approximations within a plausible range? If not, there is error. Here both Monte Carlo assessments are within ± 2 standard deviations (in parentheses), and there is no sign of anything being wrong. Method: Estimated standard deviations are

$$\frac{s^*}{\sqrt{m}} \quad (\text{for } \overline{\mathcal{X}}^*) \quad \text{and} \quad \frac{s^*}{\sqrt{2m}}\sqrt{1+\kappa^*/2} \quad (\text{for } s^*);$$

see (2.2) and (2.3). The kurtosis κ^* (value: 48.6 here) can be taken from the simulations $\mathcal{X}_1^*, \ldots, \mathcal{X}_m^*$ as explained in Exercise 2.9. Insert $s^* = 6.84$, $\kappa^* = 48.6$ and $m = 1000$ and you get the values above. More simulations (easily affordable in this case) make the error analysis unecessary.

3.3.4 Computing the reserve

Simulations produce simple assessments of the reserve (no exact mathematical expressions now!). They must be ranked, say in descending order as

$$\mathcal{X}_{(1)}^* \geq \mathcal{X}_{(2)}^* \geq \cdots \geq \mathcal{X}_{(m)}^*,$$

and $\mathcal{X}_{(\epsilon m)}^*$ is used for the ϵ-percentile. How much Monte Carlo variation to expect is indicated in Table 3.1, with results from five repeated experiments. Uncertainty appears uncomfortably high when $m = 1000$, but is much dampened for $m = 10\,000$. Is your standard so strict that even the latter isn't good enough? Arguably even $m = 1000$ suffices in a case like the present one, where model parameters are almost certain to be hugely in error; see Chapter 7.

Table 3.1 Reserve for the Section 3.3 portfolio. No limit on responsibility

m	95% reserve Repeated experiments					99% reserve Repeated experiments				
1000	20.8	21.0	21.6	19.9	19.9	27.9	27.5	31.3	29.6	31.3
10 000	20.7	20.7	21.4	20.8	20.8	30.2	30.1	30.5	31.0	31.1

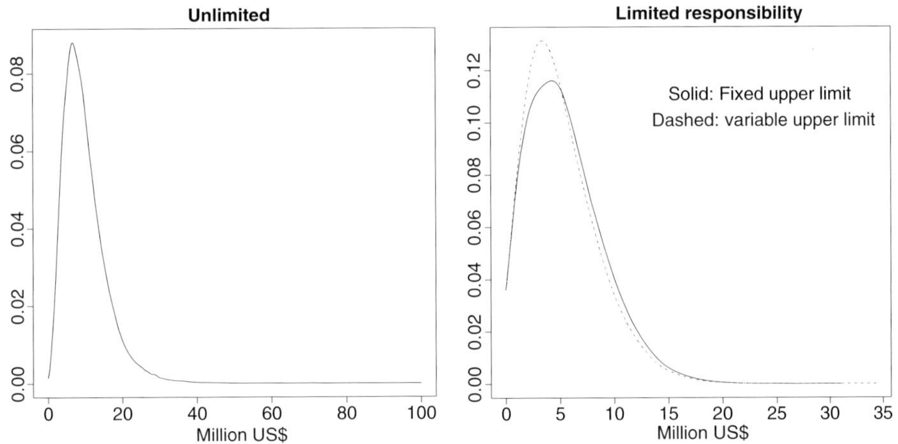

Figure 3.1 Density function of the total losses of the portfolio in Section 3.3 without (*left*) and with (*right*) limit on responsibility. *Note*: Scales on axes differ.

There seems to be a growing trend towards $\epsilon = 1\%$ as international standard. If adopted here, a company has to set aside around 30–31 (say million US$) as guarantee for its solvency, about three times as much as the average loss of the portfolio. But expenses *could* go higher. The probability density function of $\mathcal{X}$ has been plotted in Figure 3.1 left (using 100 000 simulations). Skewness is very pronounced, and variation stretches all the way up to 100 million. These high values are so rare that the solvency criterion does not capture them.

3.3.5 When responsibility is limited

The modification when compensations are $H(Z)$ instead of Z was indicated in Algorithm 3.1 through the comment on Line 5. Instead of the command $\mathcal{X}^* \leftarrow \mathcal{X}^* + Z^*$ use

$$\mathcal{X}^* \leftarrow \mathcal{X}^* + H^* \quad \text{where} \quad H^* \leftarrow H(Z^*),$$

and a sub-algorithm is needed to compute H^*. Under the payment function (3.4) this is Algorithm 3.3 with an easy logic. Start by subtracting the deductible a. If we

Algorithm 3.3 Deductible and maximum responsibility

0 Input: Z^* and limits a, b
1 $H^* \leftarrow Z^* - a$
2 If($H^* < 0$) then $H^* \leftarrow 0$
  else if $H^* > b$ then $H^* \leftarrow b$
3 Return H^*.

are now *below* zero or *above* the upper limit, the output is modified accordingly, and the original claim Z^* has been changed to the amount H^* actually reimbursed.

The effect on the reserve has been indicated by means of the following experiment. Let a be a common deductible and allow the upper limits of responsibility $b_1, \ldots, b_{100}$ to vary over the portfolio according to the scenarios

$$\underbrace{a = 0.5,\ b_1 = \cdots = b_{100} = 4;}_{\textit{Fixed-limit scenario}} \quad \underbrace{a = 0.5,\ b_1 = \cdots = b_{50} = 2,\ b_{51} = \cdots = b_{100} = 6.}_{\textit{Variable-limit scenario}}$$

On the left, all contracts are equal with maximum responsibility 4 times the average claim. On the right, the upper limit was either 2 or 6 with 4 kept as the average.

Running $m = 100\,000$ simulations under these scenarios leads to the following assessments of the reserve when the solvency level is varied:

90%	95%	99%	99.97%		90%	95%	99%	99.97%
10.2	12.0	15.6	21.9		9.7	11.5	15.2	21.7
Upper limits: Fixed					*Upper limits: Variable*			

The 99% reserves are now about 15 and halved compared with the unlimited case. It doesn't matter too much if the upper limit depends on policy. Estimated density functions of the total losses are plotted in Figure 3.1 right. The distribution is still skewed, but no longer with those super-heavy tails on the left.

3.3.6 Dealing with reinsurance

Reinsurance in terms of single events is computationally the same as the preceding example, but contracts that apply to the portfolio loss $\mathcal{X}$ must be handled differently. Now the reinsurer share is $\mathcal{X}^{\text{re}} = H(\mathcal{X})$, which is computed by applying Algorithm 3.3 to the output from Algorithm 3.1 or 3.2; see comments in Algorithm 3.1. There is no exact formula for the pure reinsurance premium, but we may use Monte Carlo. In mathematical terms the situation is

$$\pi^{\text{re}} = E\{H(\mathcal{X})\} \quad \text{approximated by} \quad \pi^{\text{re}*} = \frac{1}{m}\sum_{i=1}^{m} H(\mathcal{X}_i^*).$$

Table 3.2 Cedent reserve and pure reinsurance premium for the arrangement described in the text with unlimited reinsurance coverage

m = 1 00 0000 simulations

Retention limit (a)	0	10	20	30	40	50
99% cedent reserve	0	10	20	30	30.7	30.7
Reinsurance pure premium	10	2.23	0.39	0.11	0.041	0.021

Cedent net responsibility is $\mathcal{X}^{\text{ce}} = \mathcal{X} - H(\mathcal{X})$. If $C = \mathcal{X}^{\text{ce}}$ to ease notation, the cedent net reserve is approximately

$$C^*_{(m\epsilon)} \text{ where } C^*_{(1)} \geq C^*_2 \geq \cdots \geq C^*_m, \text{ sorted from } C^*_i = \mathcal{X}^*_i - H(\mathcal{X}^*_i),\ i = 1, \ldots, m$$

with the reinsurer reserve computed in the same way from $H(\mathcal{X}^*_1), \ldots, H(\mathcal{X}^*_m)$.

The portfolio of the preceding section with Pareto-distributed claims is used as illustration in Table 3.2. The original cedent responsibility was unlimited (not common in practice), and the reinsurer part $\mathcal{X}^{\text{re}} = \max(\mathcal{X} - a, 0)$. This makes reinsurance coverage unlimited too (again uncommon). Contracts of this particular type are known as **stop loss**. Table 3.2 shows the reinsurance premium and cedent net reserve (99%) as the retention limit a is varied. Note how the reserve of around 30 million is cut down to one-third (10 million) when the reinsurer covers all obligations above $a = 10$ million. The cost is 2.2 million in pure premium (and usually more). In practice, companies tailor the amount of reinsurance by balancing capital saved against extra cost.

3.4 Life insurance: A different story

3.4.1 Introduction

Liabilities in life and pension insurance are rarely handled as in the preceding section, and for good reason too. We shall now analyse what lies behind and indicate a general approach which will be developed in Chapter 12. Examples are common arrangements such as **life annuities** (fixed benefits for an individual) and **term insurance** (sum released when a policy holder dies). How long people live is a source of uncertainty. This is expressed mathematically through **life tables**, which are probabilities of survival given age.

3.4.2 Life insurance uncertainty

Consider J men and women on a pension, and suppose our interest lies in what they receive at the end of the coming period. This isn't completely known, since some of them will die, which makes their benefit stop. Let X_j be the payment for individual j. Then $X_j = s_j$ (a sum agreed) or $X_j = 0$ (death), and hence

$$\Pr(X_j = 0) = 1 - p_j \qquad \text{and} \qquad \Pr(X_j = s_j) = p_j$$

where p_j is the probability of survival. These are essentially Bernoulli variables with means and variances $\xi_j = E(X_j)$ and $\sigma_j^2 = \mathrm{var}(X_j)$ given as

$$\xi_j = p_j s_j \quad \text{and} \quad \sigma_j^2 = p_j(1 - p_j)s_j;$$

see Exercise 3.15 for details.

Suppose $X_1, \dots, X_J$ are independent. The total $\mathcal{X} = X_1 + \cdots + X_J$ for the portfolio may then be examined as in Section 3.2 through the averages $\bar{\xi}$ and $\bar{\sigma}^2$ of $\xi_1, \dots, \xi_J$ and $\sigma_1^2, \dots, \sigma_J^2$. To simplify the mathematics, suppose $s_j = s$ for everybody. The survival probabilities, which depend on the age and sex of the individuals, vary with j and we need

$$\bar{p} = \frac{1}{J}\sum_{j=1}^{J} p_j \quad \text{and} \quad \bar{\sigma}_p^2 = \frac{1}{J}\sum_{j=1}^{J}(p_j - \bar{p})^2 = \frac{1}{J}\left(\sum_{j=1}^{J} p_j^2\right) - \bar{p}^2;$$

verify the identity on the right yourself if it is unfamiliar. Clearly $\bar{\xi} = (\xi_1 + \cdots + \xi_J)/J = \bar{p}s$ and moreover

$$\bar{\sigma}^2 = \frac{1}{J}\sum_{j=1}^{J}\sigma_j^2 = \left(\frac{1}{J}\sum_{j=1}^{J} p_j(1 - p_j)\right)s^2 = \{\bar{p}(1 - \bar{p}) - \bar{\sigma}_p^2\}s^2$$

so that by (3.7)

$$\frac{\mathrm{sd}(\mathcal{X})}{E(\mathcal{X})} = \left(\frac{1/\bar{p} - 1 - (\bar{\sigma}_p/\bar{p})^2}{J}\right)^{1/2} \leq \left(\frac{1/\bar{p} - 1}{J}\right)^{1/2}. \tag{3.8}$$

How much is this? Try $\bar{p} = 0.99$, and the upper bound is 1% when $J = 100$ and 0.01% when $J = 1\,000\,000$. That isn't much, and usually only $E(\mathcal{X})$ is reported. Term insurance is handled by the same argument, but now payoffs follow deaths rather than survival, and $\bar{p}$ in (3.8) must be replaced by $1 - \bar{p}$. Uncertainty has become a good deal larger, although often ignored. Term insurance was simulated in Section 1.5.

3.4.3 *Life insurance mathematics*

Life insurance is concerned with the long-term perspective, and there is for each contract a sequence of payments $X_0, \dots, X_K$ at equidistant points in time. They may last for decades, and many arrangements allow the cash flow to go on until the recipient dies (K is then *infinite*). Valuation is traditionally by means of the expected present value

$$V_0 = \sum_{k=0}^{K} d^k E(X_k) \quad \text{where} \quad d = \frac{1}{1+r}. \tag{3.9}$$

Here r is known as the **technical rate of interest**. Why only the average matters was explained above. To calculate $E(X_k)$ we need **life tables**, which are probabilities ${}_kp_l$ of surviving the coming k periods for individuals at age l. There are different versions for men and women.

As an example, consider a defined benefit pension contract where a company receives contributions π until the retirement age l_r in return for paying a pension s afterwards until the recipient dies. If l_0 is the age at the beginning, the individual is in retirement when $l_0 + k \geq l_r$, and

$$E(X_k) = {}_kp_{l_0}(-\pi) \quad \text{if } k < l_r - l_0 \quad \text{and} \quad E(X_k) = {}_kp_{l_0}s \quad \text{if} \quad k \geq l_r - l_0.$$

Note the mathematical form, with payoffs multiplied by their probabilities, which is the essence of life insurance mathematics. Inserting into (3.9) yields

$$V_0 = \underbrace{-\pi \sum_{k=0}^{l_r-l_0-1} d^k {}_kp_{l_0}}_{\text{contributing stage}} + \underbrace{s \sum_{k=l_r-l_0}^{\infty} d^k {}_kp_{l_0}}_{\text{receiving stage}}. \tag{3.10}$$

Many traditional contracts are designed so that $V_0 = 0$, and π and s are then linked through the resulting equation, an idea known as **equivalence**. There is special actuarial notation for the sums in (3.10); consult Chapter 12.

Another quantity of interest is what it takes to support a future pension when future contributions are not taken into consideration. At age l_0 this **one-time premium** is

$$\pi_{l_0} = s \sum_{k=l_r-l_0}^{\infty} d^k {}_kp_{l_0}, \tag{3.11}$$

which an insurance company or pension scheme must book as an obligation. Adding these quantities over all policy holders defines the gross portfolio liability with future contributions *into* the scheme not counted.

3.4.4 Simulating pension schemes

The scope for Monte Carlo in life insurance may seem limited, but that is a bit premature. Simulation *is* a highly relevant tool when other aspects of risk are taken into account; see Chapter 15. But even in the present context with random effects largely unimportant it isn't such a bad idea to build simulation models to visualize

Algorithm 3.4 Present value of a pension cash flow

0 Input: $\{_1p_l\}$, $\{s_l\}$, initial age l_0, time ahead K
1 $\mathrm{PV}_0^* \leftarrow 0,\ d \leftarrow 1,\ l \leftarrow l_0$
2 For $k = 0, 1, \ldots, K$ do — *%Present value including K periods ahead*
3 $\quad \mathrm{PV}_0^* \leftarrow \mathrm{PV}_0^* + s_l d$ — *%Payment in advance*
4 $\quad$ Draw $U^* \sim$ uniform
5 $\quad$ If $(U^* > {_1p_l})$ **stop** and return PV_0^*. — *%Policy holder dead*
6 $\quad l \leftarrow l + 1$ and $d \leftarrow d/(1 + r)$ — *%Update and discount*

what happens. Let PV_0 be the present value of the actual payments $X_0, \ldots, X_K$ and suppose s_l is the payment at age l, for example $s_l = -\pi$ and $s_l = s$ for a defined benefit scheme. With l_0 the age at the beginning, PV_0 can be simulated as in Algorithm 3.4.

The algorithm goes through the life of the policy holder up to K periods ahead and tests (on Line 5) whether he (or she) dies. If so, everything stops. The cash flow is paid **in advance** at the beginning of each period, and the setup requires a slight change if it is **in arrears**. To simulate an entire portfolio, run the algorithm once for each policy holder and add the output.

3.4.5 Numerical example

How does the uncertainty of the present value depend on the time horizon ahead? The example in Figure 3.2 is for a portfolio of retired people between 60 and 93 years with age distribution laid out as in Section 15.2. Survival probabilities were

$$\log({_1p_l}) = -0.0009 - 0.000044e^{0.09076 \times l},$$

which might apply to males in a developed country with life expectancy of almost 75 years; see Section 12.3 for such computations. Additional assumptions were $s = 0.1$, $r = 3\%$ and $J = 100$ or $J = 1000$.

The portfolios are small since the idea is to emphasize that uncertainty due to how long people live is minor. Present values of payments up to K years ahead have been computed in Figure 3.2 and plotted against K. The curvature downwards is caused by the discounting (and also by mortalities increasing with age), but the main thing is the uncertainty, which is quite small on the right and somewhat larger on the left where the number of indviduals was only 100.

3.5 Financial risk: Derivatives as safety

3.5.1 Introduction

Financial risk can be reduced by spreading investments over different assets. Another way is through financial **derivatives** or **options**, which protect against

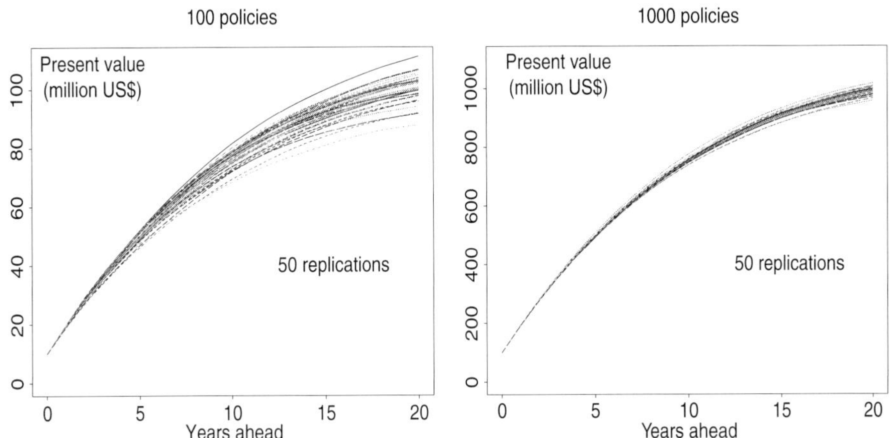

Figure 3.2 Simulated present values for portfolios of pension liabilities under the conditions in the text.

market movements generating loss. Numerous types of arrangements are in practical use (with the academic literature containing still more). The so-called **European** contracts (the only ones to be considered) release at a future date (known as the **expiry**) the amount

$$X = H(\mathcal{R})v_0, \tag{3.12}$$

where $\mathcal{R}$ is the return on a financial investment at that time, $H(r)$ a function containing the detailed payment clauses and v_0 the original value of the investment. Derivatives are secondary risk products, *derived* from primary ones, much like reinsurance is a secondary product in the insurance world.

Such rights to future compensation against unwelcome market development have to be paid for. This section is an introduction from a computational point of view. Only equity is considered. Derivatives in the money market (at least as important) are treated in Chapter 14, along with the mathematics (which is complicated).

3.5.2 Equity puts and calls

There are no limits on the number of functions $H(r)$ that could go into (3.12). Two of the most common are

$$\underbrace{X = \max(r_g - \mathcal{R}, 0)v_0}_{\textit{put option}} \quad \text{and} \quad \underbrace{X = \max(\mathcal{R} - r_g, 0)v_0}_{\textit{call option}}, \tag{3.13}$$

where r_g is fixed by the contract and v_0 is the initial value of the underlying asset. The **put** option on the left releases compensation whenever the return $\mathcal{R}$ falls below the floor r_g. This provides a **guaranteed return** in the sense that

$$(1 + \mathcal{R})v_0 + X = (1 + \mathcal{R})v_0 + \max(r_g - \mathcal{R}, 0)v_0 \geq (1 + r_g)v_0$$

and r_g is a minimum return on the investment (but only when the fee for the option is not counted). Many life insurance products are drawn up with such clauses. **Call** options on the right in (3.13) are the opposite. Now there is extra money if $\mathcal{R}$ exceeds r_g, and a borrower is protected against rising financial cost.

3.5.3 How equity options are valued

Derivatives are paid for upfront at time 0 when the contracts are set up. Possible valuations at that time for an option expiring at T are

$$\underbrace{\pi = e^{-rT}E(X)}_{\text{actuarial pricing}} \quad \text{or} \quad \underbrace{\pi = e^{-rT}E_Q(X)}_{\text{risk-neutral pricing}}, \tag{3.14}$$

where e^{-rT} is an ordinary discount. The central feature is the expected payoff. Why not **actuarial** pricing on the left? That's how we operate in insurance and reinsurance, but financial derivatives can be **hedged** in a way ordinary insurance cannot, and this makes a difference. Consider call options. Sellers of such contracts lose in a rising market when $\mathcal{R} > r_g$, but they may hold the underlying stock on the side and in this way offset the loss (at least partially). Their real risk must then be smaller than X itself, and $E(X)$ isn't a break-even price as in insurance.

The issue requires a big dose of mathematics. A series of fine-tuned, risk-reducing operations in Chapter 14 will lead to the so-called **risk-neutral** price in (3.14) right. It doesn't look that different from the other! Yet there *is* a crucial difference. The expectation is now calculated with respect to a special valuation model (usually denoted Q), which is as follows. Suppose the option $X = H(R)$ applies to a single equity asset with return R following the usual log-normal model. Mean and variance are then proportional to T (you'll see why in Section 5.7) so that $R = e^{\xi T + \sigma\sqrt{T}\varepsilon} - 1$ where $\varepsilon \sim N(0, 1)$. The Q-model turns out to be

$$R = e^{\xi_q T + \sigma\sqrt{T}\varepsilon} - 1 \quad \text{where} \quad \underbrace{\xi_q = r - \tfrac{1}{2}\sigma^2}_{Q\text{-model}}, \tag{3.15}$$

the same as the original except for ξ being replaced by ξ_q, which is determined by r and σ. Now

$$E_Q(R) = e^{\xi_q T + \sigma^2 T/2} - 1 = e^{rT} - 1$$

and the expected return of holding stock coincides under the Q-model with what you get from a bank account. What lies behind is a theoretical risk reduction so perfect that the option seller carries no risk at all! The theory is presented in Chapter 14.

3.5.4 The Black–Scholes formula

The put option in (3.13) has premium

$$\pi(v_0) = E_Q\{\max(r_g - R, 0)\}v_0 \quad \text{where} \quad R = e^{\xi_q T + \sigma\sqrt{T}\varepsilon} - 1$$

for which a closed formula is available. Indeed, if $\Phi(x)$ is the standard normal integral, then

$$\pi(v_0) = \{(1 + r_g)e^{-rT}\Phi(a) - \Phi(a - \sigma\sqrt{T})\}v_0 \tag{3.16}$$

where

$$a = \frac{\log(1 + r_g) - rT + \sigma^2 T/2}{\sigma\sqrt{T}}. \tag{3.17}$$

The result, verified in Section 3.7, is known as the **Black–Scholes** formula and is one of the most famous results in modern finance. Differentiate it with respect to σ, and it emerges that

$$\frac{\partial\pi(v_0)}{\partial\sigma} = \varphi(a - \sigma\sqrt{T})\sqrt{T}v_0 \quad \text{where} \quad \varphi(x) = \frac{1}{\sqrt{2\pi}}e^{-x^2/2}; \tag{3.18}$$

see Section 3.7 for verification. The expression is always positive. Higher uncertainty increases the cost of put options; certainly plausible, but it isn't a general result and other derivatives are different. For a similar pricing formula for calls, consult Exercise 3.28.

3.5.5 Options on portfolios

Valuation for derivatives that apply to several assets jointly is a direct extension of the one-asset case. The risk-neutral model, for J equity returns $R_1, \dots, R_J$ is now

$$R_j = e^{\xi_{qj}T + \sigma_j\sqrt{T}\varepsilon_j} - 1, \qquad \underset{Q\text{-model}}{\xi_{qj} = r - \tfrac{1}{2}\sigma_j^2}, \qquad \text{for } j = 1, \dots, J \tag{3.19}$$

where $\varepsilon_1, \dots, \varepsilon_J$ are $N(0, 1)$ and often correlated. Correlations and volatilities are inherited from the real model, whereas the original ξ_j are replaced by the risk-neutral analogues $\xi_{qj} = r - \sigma_j^2/2$. What is *not* the same as in the one-asset case is computation. Closed pricing formulae do not exist when $J > 1$, and Monte Carlo is the usual method.

The program in Algorithm 3.5 converts a correlated sample of standard normal Monte Carlo variables $\varepsilon_1^*, \dots, \varepsilon_J^*$ into the portfolio return $\mathcal{R}^*$ and a payoff X^*. If

Algorithm 3.5 Simulating equity options

0 Input: r, v_0 volatilities and correlations, asset weights $w_1, \dots, w_J$
1 Draw $\varepsilon_1^*, \dots, \varepsilon_J^*$ *%All $N(0, 1)$ and correlated, Algorithm 2.8 or as in Section 5.4*
2 $\mathcal{R}^* \leftarrow 0$
3 Repeat for $j = 1, \dots, J$
4 $\quad R^* \leftarrow \exp(rT - \sigma_j^2 T/2 + \sigma_j \sqrt{T}\varepsilon_j^*) - 1$ *%Return jth asset*
5 $\quad \mathcal{R}^* \leftarrow \mathcal{R}^* + w_j R^*$ *%Updating the portfolio return*
6 $X^* \leftarrow H(\mathcal{R}^*)v_0$ *%For put options: If $\mathcal{R}^* \geq r_g$ then $X^* \leftarrow 0$ else $X^* \leftarrow (r_g - \mathcal{R}^*)v_0$*
7 Return X^*.

$X_1^*, \dots, X_m^*$ are m replications, the option premium is approximately the discounted average

$$\pi^* = \frac{e^{-rT}}{m} \sum_{i=1}^{m} X_i^*.$$

This kind of simulation will also be needed in Chapter 15.

3.5.6 Are equity options expensive?

The minimum return on a put option cited above was *after* the premium had been paid, and the **effective** minimum is lower. When this expense is drawn from the original capital v_0, the balance sheet becomes

$$\underset{\textit{equity protected}}{\frac{v_0}{1+\pi(1)}} \quad + \quad \underset{\textit{option premium}}{\pi(1)\frac{v_0}{1+\pi(1)}} \quad = \quad \underset{\textit{original capital}}{v_0}$$

where $\pi(1)$ is the option premium per money unit. After the fee has been subtracted, the value of the equity is reduced to $v_0/\{1 + \pi(1)\}$ and at expiry the investor is guaranteed

$$\frac{v_0}{1+\pi(1)}(1 + r_g) = (1 + r_g')v_0 \quad \text{where} \quad r_g' = \frac{r_g - \pi(1)}{1 + \pi(1)} < r_g - \pi(1).$$

The effective minimum return is a little lower than $r_g - \pi(1)$.

How much is the option premium $\pi(1)$ eating up? It depends on the circumstances. Here is an example with $J = 4$ risky assets equally weighted as $w_1 = \cdots = w_4 = 0.25$. Their model is assumed log-normal and equicorrelated with common volatility. The annual guarantee $r_g = 7\%$ and the risk-free rate $r = 4\%$. Algorithm 3.5 gave the prices in Figure 3.3 left where $\pi(1)$ is plotted (%) against asset volatility for two different values of the correlation. Options are expensive! Annual

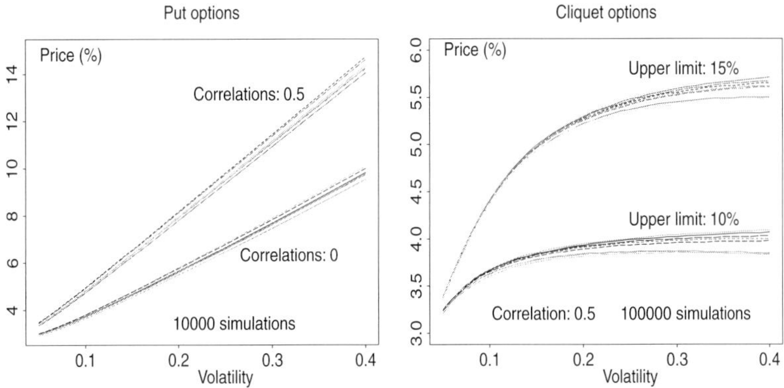

Figure 3.3 Prices of put options (*left*) and cliquet options (*right*), quoted as a percentage of the original holding. *Note*: Vertical axis scales differ.

volatilities of 25% (not unrealistic at all) would lead to a cost of 6–10%. High volatility and high correlation increase the uncertainty and make the price higher. Ten replications, each based on $m = 10\,000$ simulations, are plotted jointly[2] and indicate a Monte Carlo uncertainty that might in practice be found unacceptable for fixing the price.

One way to lower the cost is to allow the option seller to keep the top of the return. Such instruments, sometimes called **cliquet** options, have payoff

$$H(\mathcal{R}) = \begin{array}{ll} r_g - \mathcal{R}, & \mathcal{R} \leq r_g \\ 0, & r_g < \mathcal{R} \leq r_c \\ -(\mathcal{R} - r_c), & \mathcal{R} > r_c \end{array} \tag{3.20}$$

where the third line signals that any return above a ceiling r_c is kept by the option seller. The guarantee is still r_g, but this trick makes the instrument cheaper; see Figure 3.3 right where the underlying conditions are as before (with correlation between assets 0.5). When the ceiling is $r_c = 15\%$ and the volatility 25%, the price of the cliquet is close to half that of the put.

3.6 Risk over long terms

3.6.1 Introduction

Life insurance in Section 3.4 looked many years ahead and investments should too. Even general insurance where contracts are typically annual may benefit from a long-term view, for example to indicate the capital needed to support the scheme.

[2] Smoothness of the curves was achieved by using common random numbers; see Section 4.3.

We are now dealing with recursions like

$$\mathcal{Y}_k = \mathcal{Y}_{k-1} + \underset{\textit{financial income}}{\mathcal{R}_k\mathcal{Y}_{k-1}} + \underset{\textit{premium}}{\Pi_k} - \underset{\textit{overhead}}{\mathcal{O}_k} - \underset{\textit{claims}}{\mathcal{X}_k} \tag{3.21}$$

where financial income ($\mathcal{R}_k\mathcal{Y}_{k-1}$), premium income ($\Pi_k$), overhead cost ($\mathcal{O}_k$) and claims ($\mathcal{X}_k$) are integrated into net summaries ($\mathcal{Y}_k$) of the account. There might be additional terms as well, and claims and financial returns could be complex affairs with many sub-contributions. Another possibility is outstanding liabilities expiring later; see Section 11.6 (general insurance) and Chapter 12 (life and pension insurance) for this extension.

3.6.2 The ruin problem

A classic of actuarial science is conservative estimation of the inital capital $\mathcal{Y}_0 = v_0$ by requiring high probability of positive net assets $\mathcal{Y}_k$ at all times up to some terminating K. This leads to the **ruin** probability

$$p^{\text{ru}}(v_0) = \Pr(\underline{\mathcal{Y}} < 0 | Y_0 = v_0) \quad \text{where} \quad \underline{\mathcal{Y}} = \min(\mathcal{Y}_1, \dots, \mathcal{Y}_K). \tag{3.22}$$

The portfolio is bankrupt (out of money at some point) if $\underline{\mathcal{Y}} < 0$. That outcome shouldn't be a likely one.

The phrase 'ruin' is not to be taken too literally as companies (and regulators) are supposed to intervene long before that happens. Ruin probabilities are for planning. A common yardstick in academic literature is the equation

$$p^{\text{ru}}(v_0) = \epsilon \quad \text{with solution} \quad v_0 = v_{0\epsilon}, \tag{3.23}$$

and if $v_{0\epsilon}$ is put up at the beginning, the chance of net assets falling below zero during the next K periods is no more than ϵ. Solutions can in special cases be approximated by mathematical formulae; see Section 3.8 for references. Monte Carlo is usually easier and more accurate.

3.6.3 Cash flow simulations

The skeleton Algorithm 3.6 summarizes the steps behind a simulation of (3.21). It is a loop over k with sub-procedures generating financial returns (Line 3) and insurance liabilities (Line 4) which could be of all types. In the examples below premium income Π_k and overhead $\mathcal{O}_k$ are fixed, therefore not *-marked like the others (but see Section 11.5). An implicit assumption in Algorithm 3.6 is that insurance liabilities and financial returns are unrelated to each other and generated independently. Does that appear obvious? There are actually several situations where economic factors influence both and create links between them; see Chapter 15.

Algorithm 3.6 Integrating assets and liabilities

0 Input: Models for $\mathcal{R}_k$ and $\mathcal{X}_k$, sequences $\{\Pi_k\}$ and $\{O_k\}$
1 $\mathcal{Y}_0^* \leftarrow v_0$ and $\underline{\mathcal{Y}}^* \leftarrow v_0$ *%Initial cash and minimum*
2 For $k = 1, \dots, K$ do
3 Generate $\mathcal{R}^*$ *%Financial return in period k, simple possibility: Algorithm 2.8*
4 Generate $\mathcal{X}^*$ *%Liability in period k – life or non-life – simple possibilities: Algorithms 3.1 or 3.2*
5 $\mathcal{Y}_k^* \leftarrow (1 + \mathcal{R}^*)\mathcal{Y}_{k-1}^* + (\Pi_k - O_k) - \mathcal{X}^*$
6 If $\mathcal{Y}_k < \underline{\mathcal{Y}}^*$ then $\underline{\mathcal{Y}}^* \leftarrow \mathcal{Y}_k$ *%Updating the minimum*
7 Return $\mathcal{Y}_0^*, \dots, \mathcal{Y}_K^*$ and $\underline{\mathcal{Y}}^*$.

The algorithm returns a minimum value $\underline{\mathcal{Y}}^*$ over K periods. This has been built into the recursion (Line 6) by updating the preceding minimum whenever the current $\mathcal{Y}_k^*$ is smaller. Suppose m replications $\underline{\mathcal{Y}}_1^*, \dots, \underline{\mathcal{Y}}_m^*$ have been generated. The ruin probability is then approximated by

$$p^{\text{ru}*}(v_0) = \frac{1}{m}(I_1^* + \cdots + I_m^*) \quad \text{where} \quad I_i^* = \begin{array}{ll} 0 & \text{if } \underline{\mathcal{Y}}_i^* > 0 \\ 1 & \text{otherwise,} \end{array} \tag{3.24}$$

which is simply a count of how many times net assets have become negative at some point.

3.6.4 Solving the ruin equation

We would like to solve the equation $p^{\text{ru}*}(v_{0\epsilon}^*) = \epsilon$ so that $v_{0\epsilon}^*$ approximates the exact $v_{0\epsilon}$ in (3.23). Algorithm 3.6 provides a solution in the so-called **underwriter** situation without financial earnings. Many actuarial evaluations are of this type. Suppose Algorithm 3.6 is run with $\mathcal{R}^* = 0$ and with no initial capital, so that $v_0 = 0$. The account will now often go into minus (money is then borrowed for free), but we may still proceed and generate $\underline{\mathcal{Y}}_1^*, \dots, \underline{\mathcal{Y}}_m^*$ as m realizations of the minimum of $\mathcal{Y}_0, \dots, \mathcal{Y}_K$. Rank them in ascending order as $\underline{\mathcal{Y}}_{(1)}^* \leq \cdots \leq \underline{\mathcal{Y}}_{(m)}^*$. Then

$$v_{0\epsilon}^* = -\underline{\mathcal{Y}}_{(\epsilon m)}^* \quad \text{where} \quad v_{0\epsilon}^* \to v_{0\epsilon} \quad \text{as} \quad m \to \infty \tag{3.25}$$

which is fairly obvious; see Section 3.7 for a mathematical proof.

This method doesn't work when there is financial income, but there is another way. With $\mathcal{R}_{0:k} = (1 + \mathcal{R}_1) \cdots (1 + \mathcal{R}_k) - 1$ being the multi-step returns from Section 1.4, there is the representation

$$\mathcal{Y}_k = (1 + \mathcal{R}_{0:k})(v_0 - \mathcal{S}_k) \quad \text{where} \quad \mathcal{S}_k = \sum_{i=1}^{k} \frac{\mathcal{X}_i + O_i - \Pi_i}{1 + \mathcal{R}_{0:i}} \tag{3.26}$$

which is also verified in Section 3.7. The quantities $\mathcal{S}_k$ are sums of underwriter results up to time k when discounted back to time 0. This is exact algebra, and it doesn't matter if the discounts are uncertain. Hence, if $\mathcal{Y}_1, \dots, \mathcal{Y}_K$ are all positive, then v_0 exceeds all of $\mathcal{S}_1, \dots, \mathcal{S}_K$ and vice versa. The solution of the ruin equation can therefore be approximated by simulating $\mathcal{S}_1, \dots, \mathcal{S}_K$ and their maximum $\overline{\mathcal{S}} = \max(\mathcal{S}_1, \dots, \mathcal{S}_K)$. If $\overline{\mathcal{S}}_1^*, \dots, \overline{\mathcal{S}}_m^*$ are Monte Carlo realizations of $\overline{\mathcal{S}}$, then

$$v_{0\epsilon}^* = \overline{\mathcal{S}}_{(\epsilon m)}^* \quad \text{where} \quad \overline{\mathcal{S}}_{(1)}^* \geq \dots \geq \overline{\mathcal{S}}_{(m)}^*, \tag{3.27}$$

and again the approximation converges to the exact solution as $m \to \infty$. The method offers a solution to most ruin-type capital assessments. There are simple examples among the exercises and more advanced ones in Section 11.5.

3.6.5 *An underwriter example*

The first example is the portfolio in Section 3.3 with on average ten Pareto claims per year with parameters $\alpha = 3$ and $\beta = 2$ and with deductible and maximum responsibility $a = 0.5$ and $b = 4$ per incident. We saw in Section 3.3 that the 99% reserve is 15.6. The $m = 100$ simulated scenarios over $K = 10$ years in Figure 3.4 left were started from this value. Net premium income $\Pi_k - O_k$ was fixed at 6.0, which exceeds $E(\mathcal{X}_k)$ by around 10% and accounts for a slight average drift upwards. It is barely discernable, and the dominant feature is the enormous uncertainty. Earnings are sometimes huge (up to 100% and more over 10 years), but losses may be severe too (despite coverage being limited). These matters have now been learned in advance and might influence business strategy.

Solutions of the ruin equation using (3.25) with $m = 10\,000$ simulations are shown on the right in Figure 3.4 with ϵ varying between 0.5% and 25%. The impact of how long into the future we look is strong, with capital requirements three times as large (and more) when $K = 1$ is replaced by $K = 20$ years. Also note that the patterns seem to converge to a limiting value as K grows. The experiment made use of a technique known as **common random numbers** with the same simulations for all ϵ. This makes curves much smoother than they would have been otherwise. Common random numbers are discussed in Section 4.3.

3.6.6 *Financial income added*

How much do financial earnings influence the total uncertainty in a case like the preceding one? A first answer is offered on the left in Figure 3.5, where fixed annual returns $\mathcal{R} = 4\%$ have been added to the simulations in Figure 3.4 left. There is now a noticeable lift upwards. If the original capital is placed risk free at 4%, it has after

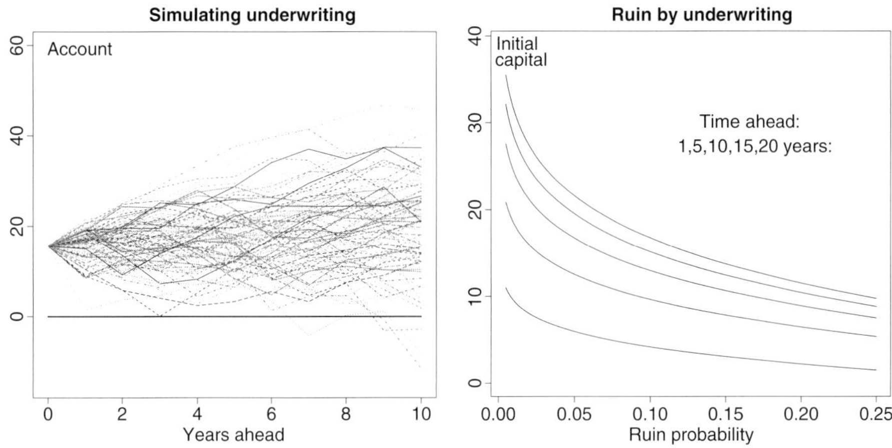

Figure 3.4 Underwriter results for the portfolio of Section 3.3. *Left*: One hundred simulated scenarios. *Right*: The solution of $v_{0\epsilon}$ of the ruin equation plotted against ϵ with the time horizon K varied between 1, 5, 10, 15 and 20 years.

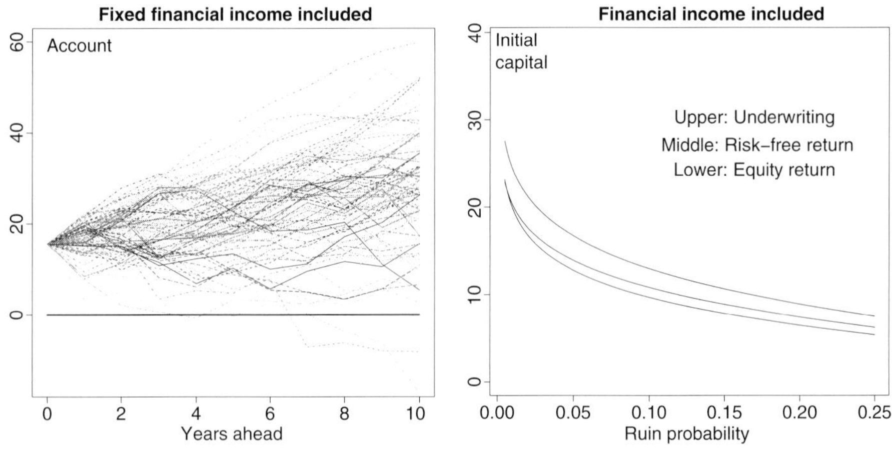

Figure 3.5 *Left*: Simulated portfolio returns (100 replications) with 4% fixed annual financial return added to those in Figure 3.4 left. *Right*: Solutions $v_{0\epsilon}$ of the ruin equation plotted against ϵ when $K = 10$ years and when financial income is varied.

10 years grown to $15 \times 1.04^{10} \doteq 22$, right in the middle of the heap. In practice there is not only financial income, but also financial risk.

This has been included on the right in Figure 3.5, where the ruin equation has been solved for the property insurance portfolio described earlier. It was now necessary to use the scheme in (3.26) and (3.27). The time horizon was $K = 10$ years, and the upper curve in Figure 3.5 which applies to pure underwriting is the same as the middle one in Figure 3.4 right. It is lowered, but not dramatically when a fixed return $\mathcal{R} = 4\%$ is added (middle curve) and a bit more when the financial income comes from an equity portfolio with 10% expected return (lower curve). The detailed assumptions behind the latter are four assets with log-normal returns $R_j = e^{\xi+\sigma\varepsilon_j} - 1$ where $\xi = 0.07531$, $\sigma = 0.2$, $\text{cor}(\varepsilon_i, \varepsilon_j) = 0.5$ for all $i \neq j$ and an equally weighted portfolio with return $\mathcal{R} = (R_1 + \cdots + R_4)/4$. It was simulated as explained in Section 2.4.

3.7 Mathematical arguments

3.7.1 The Black–Scholes formula

The premium for put options in terms of single assets is

$$\pi(v_0) = e^{-rT} E_Q\{\max(r_g - R, 0)\} v_0 \quad \text{where} \quad R = e^{\xi_q T + \sigma\sqrt{T}\varepsilon} - 1$$

for $\varepsilon \sim N(0, 1)$. There is a positive payoff if $R < r_g$ or equivalently if $\varepsilon < a$ where

$$a = \frac{\log(1 + r_g) - \xi_q T}{\sigma\sqrt{T}},$$

and the option premium becomes

$$\pi(v_0) = e^{-rT}\left(\int_{-\infty}^{a} (1 + r_g - e^{\xi_q T + \sigma\sqrt{T}x})\varphi(x)dx\right) v_0$$

where $\varphi(x) = (2\pi)^{-1/2}e^{-x^2/2}$. Splitting the integrand yields

$$\pi(v_0) = e^{-rT}\left((1 + r_g)\int_{-\infty}^{a} \varphi(x)dx - e^{\xi_q T}\int_{-\infty}^{a} e^{\sigma\sqrt{T}x}\varphi(x)dx\right) v_0$$

where the second integral on the right is

$$\int_{-\infty}^{a} e^{\sigma\sqrt{T}x}(2\pi)^{-1/2}e^{-x^2/2}dx = e^{\sigma^2 T/2}\int_{-\infty}^{a} (2\pi)^{-1/2}e^{-(x-\sigma\sqrt{T})^2/2}\,dx.$$

If $\Phi(x) = \int_{-\infty}^{x} \varphi(y)\,dy$ is the Gaussian integral, then

$$\pi(v_0) = e^{-rT}\{(1 + r_g)\Phi(a) - e^{\xi_q T + \sigma^2 T/2}\Phi(a - \sigma\sqrt{T})\}v_0,$$

and inserting $\xi_q = r - \sigma^2/2$ into this expression and into a yields the Black–Scholes formula (3.16).

3.7.2 The derivative with respect to σ

Differentiate $\pi(v_0) = \{(1 + r_g)e^{-rT}\Phi(a) - \Phi(a - \sigma\sqrt{T})\}v_0$ with respect to σ, and it emerges that

$$\frac{\partial\pi(v_0)}{\partial\sigma} = \{(1 + r_g)e^{-rT}\varphi(a) - \varphi(a - \sigma\sqrt{T})\}v_0\frac{\partial a}{\partial\sigma} + \varphi(a - \sigma\sqrt{T})\sqrt{T}\,v_0.$$

The first term on the right vanishes when $a = (\log(1 + r_g) - rT + \sigma^2 T/2)/(\sigma\sqrt{T})$ so that $\partial\pi(v_0)/\partial\sigma = \varphi(a - \sigma\sqrt{T})\sqrt{T}\,v_0$ as claimed in (3.18).

3.7.3 Solvency without financial earning

Let $\underline{\mathcal{Y}}(v_0)$ be the minimum value of the underwriter result over K periods when the initial capital is v_0 and let $\underline{\mathcal{Y}}_1^*, \dots, \underline{\mathcal{Y}}_m^*$ be simulations of $\underline{\mathcal{Y}}(0)$. Sort them in ascending order as $\underline{\mathcal{Y}}_{(1)}^* \leq \cdots \leq \underline{\mathcal{Y}}_{(m)}^*$ and note that $\underline{\mathcal{Y}}_{(\epsilon m)}^*$ is approximately the ϵ-percentile of $\underline{\mathcal{Y}}(0)$. There is no financial gain, and the minimum is therefore influenced by the initial capital through fixed shifts so that $\underline{\mathcal{Y}}(v_0) = \underline{\mathcal{Y}}(0) + v_0$. But then

$$\epsilon \doteq \Pr(\underline{\mathcal{Y}}(0) \leq \underline{\mathcal{Y}}_{(\epsilon m)}^*) = \Pr(\underline{\mathcal{Y}}(v_0) - v_0 \leq \underline{\mathcal{Y}}_{(\epsilon m)}^*)$$

which yields

$$\epsilon \doteq \Pr(\underline{\mathcal{Y}}(v_0) \leq 0) \quad \text{if} \quad v_0 = -\underline{\mathcal{Y}}_{(\epsilon m)}^*,$$

which was to be proved.

3.7.4 A representation of net assets

To prove the discount formula (3.26) go back to the accumulation rule (1.13) in Section 1.4 which says that $\mathcal{Y}_k$ as defined in (3.21) can be decomposed as

$$\mathcal{Y}_k = (1 + \mathcal{R}_{0:k})v_0 + \sum_{i=1}^{k}(1 + \mathcal{R}_{i:k})(\Pi_i - O_i - \mathcal{X}_i)$$

where $1 + \mathcal{R}_{i:k} = (1 + \mathcal{R}_{i+1}) \cdots (1 + \mathcal{R}_k)$. Note that $1 + \mathcal{R}_{i:k} = (1 + \mathcal{R}_{0:k})/(1 + \mathcal{R}_{0:i})$ which implies

$$\mathcal{Y}_k = (1 + \mathcal{R}_{0:k})\left(v_0 - \sum_{i=1}^{k}\frac{\mathcal{X}_i + O_i - \Pi_i}{1 + \mathcal{R}_{0:i}}\right),$$

the desired representation.

3.8 Bibliographical notes

3.8.1 General work

Property insurance, life insurance and financial derivatives are all treated in later parts of this book. If you seek simple mathematical introductions right away, try Straub (1997), Mikosch (2004) or Boland (2007) (property insurance), Gerber (1997) or Hardy (2003) (life insurance) and Roman (2004) or Benth (2004) (financial derivatives).

3.8.2 Monte Carlo and implementation

The main theme of the present chapter has been Monte Carlo as a problem solver. Introductory books emphasizing the role of the computer are scarce in insurance (Daykin *et al.*, 1994 is an exception), but there are more of them in finance, for example Shaw (1998), Benninga (2008) and Evans and Olson (2002). Coding and implementation is a fairly young scientific discipline, but old enough for reviews on how it's done to have started appearing in computer science. Hanson (1997) discusses program reuse and Baier and Katoen (2008) program verification with stochastic models included; see also Kaner *et al.* (1999). These are themes that may merit more attention than has been provided here. Section 3.3 gave examples of programs tested against known mathematical formulae for special cases. This is often a helpful technique.

3.8.3 Other numerical methods

Compound distributions of portfolio liabilities (Section 3.3) and ruin probabilities (Section 3.6) have often been tackled by methods other than Monte Carlo. Simple approximations coming from the central limit theorem and its Cornish–Fisher extension will be presented in Section 10.2. So-called **saddlepoint** approximations are another possibility (see Jensen, 1995). Very popular in certain quarters is the **Panjer** recursion which works with discrete claim size distributions. A continuous distribution is always *approximately* discrete (see Section 4.2), and the discretization is no limitation on practical use. The approach was popularized by Panjer (1981) following earlier work by Adelson (1966). Dickson (2005) and especially Sundt and Vernic (2009) are reviews. The original idea has been extended to cover ruin too; see Dickson (2005) for an outline, but financial risk is not included, and Panjer recursions lack the versatility of Monte Carlo.

3.9 Exercises

Section 3.2

Exercise 3.1 Let $\mathcal{X}$ be the portfolio loss when there are J identical risks. If the numbers of claims $\mathcal{N} \sim \text{Poisson}(J\mu T)$ and $\xi = E(Z)$ and $\sigma = \text{sd}(Z)$ are mean loss and standard deviation per incident, then $E(\mathcal{X}) = J\mu T\xi$ and $\text{var}(\mathcal{X}) = J\mu T(\sigma^2 + \xi^2)$ which will be proved in Section 6.3.

(a) Verify by means of these results that

$$\frac{\text{sd}(\mathcal{X})}{E(\mathcal{X})} = \sqrt{\frac{1 + \sigma^2/\xi^2}{J\mu T}}.$$

(b) In what sense are branches with rare events the most risky ones?

Exercise 3.2

(a) If Z in the previous exercise is Gamma distributed so that $\sigma = \xi/\sqrt{\alpha}$, show that $\text{sd}(\mathcal{X})/E(\mathcal{X}) = \sqrt{(1 + 1/\alpha)/(J\mu T)}$.
(b) The same question for the Pareto distribution for which $\sigma = \xi\sqrt{\alpha/(\alpha - 2)}$ for $\alpha > 2$ (Section 2.5); i.e., show that $\text{sd}(\mathcal{X})/E(\mathcal{X}) = \sqrt{2(\alpha - 1)/\{(\alpha - 2)J\mu T\}}$.
(c) Why are the ratios in (a) and (b) decreasing functions of α?

Exercise 3.3 Proportional reinsurance splits liabilities between cedent and reinsurer in fixed ratios. The reinsurer obligation is $Z^{\text{re}} = \gamma Z$ where $0 < \gamma < 1$ when the contract is per event.

(a) Argue that the same relationship $\mathcal{X}^{\text{re}} = \gamma\mathcal{X}$ applies at the portfolio level.
(b) Show that the relative risk $\text{sd}(\mathcal{X}^{\text{re}})/E(\mathcal{X}^{\text{re}})$ is independent of γ and the same as for the cedent.

Exercise 3.4 Let $Z^{\text{re}} = \max(Z - a, 0)$ for Pareto-distributed losses with parameters α and β.

(a) How do you compute the pure reinsurance premium by Monte Carlo when the number of claims is Poisson distributed with parameter $\lambda = \mu T$?
R-*commands*:
`U=runif(m); Z=β*(U**(-1/α)-1); Zre=pmax(Z-a,0);`
`πre=λ*mean(Zre)`; see also Section 10.6 for a formula.
(b) Compute the pure reinsurance premium for $a = 0$, 1, 4 and 6 when $\lambda = 10$, $\alpha = 3$ and $\beta = 2$ using $m = 100\,000$ simulations.
(c) Redo a couple of times to examine Monte Carlo uncertainty.

Exercise 3.5 Reinsurers transfer risk to other reinsurers. For contracts per event the situation is

$$\underset{\textit{cedent}}{Z} \longrightarrow \underset{\textit{first reinsurer}}{Z_1^{\text{re}} = H_1(Z)} \longrightarrow \underset{\textit{second reinsurer}}{Z_2^{\text{re}} = H_2(Z_1^{\text{re}})}.$$

Let $H_1(z) = \max(z - a, 0)$ and $H_2(z) = \gamma\max(z - b, 0)$ with other conditions as in Exercise 3.4.

(a) How do you compute the pure premium $\pi_2^{\rm re}$ of the second reinsurance?

R-*commands*:

```
U=runif(m); Z=β*(U**(-1/α)-1); Z₁ʳᵉ=pmax(Z-a,0);
Z₂ʳᵉ=γ*pmax(Z₁ʳᵉ-b,0); π₂ʳᵉ=λ*mean(Z₂ʳᵉ).
```

(b) Tabulate $\pi_2^{\rm re}$ for $b = 2$, 4 and 6 when $\gamma = 0.5$, $a = 1$, $\lambda = 10$, $\alpha = 3$ and $\beta = 2$ using $m = 100\,000$ simulations.

(c) Redo (b) for $a = 2$ and examine the impact on $\pi_2^{\rm re}$.

(d) Redo (b) and (c) a couple of times to get a feel for the simulation error.

Section 3.3

Exercise 3.6

(a) Implement Algorithm 3.1 so that m simulations of the portfolio loss $\mathcal{X}$ are generated when $Z = e^{\xi+\sigma\varepsilon}$ is log-normal and $\mathcal{N}$ Poisson distributed with parameter λ.

R-*commands*:

```
N=rpois(m,λ); X=1:m*0;
for (i in 1:m) {Z=rlnorm(N[i],ξ,σ); X[i]=sum(Z)}.
```

(b) Check the program when $\lambda = 10$, $\xi = 0$ and $\sigma = 1$ by computing the mean and standard deviation from $m = 10\,000$ simulations.

R-*commands*:

`Mean=mean(X); Sd=sd(X)` and compare with the exact $E(\mathcal{X}) = 16.487$ and $\mathrm{sd}(\mathcal{X}) = 8.596$.

Exercise 3.7

(a) If the program of the previous exercise passed the test, plot the density function of the simulations generated there.

R-*commands*:

```
plot(density(X)).
```

(b) Compute the 95% and 99% reserve and compare with $E(\mathcal{X})$.

R-*commands*:

```
ϵ=c(0.05,0.01); qϵ=sort(X)[(1 − ϵ)*m]; Mean=mean(X).
```

Exercise 3.8 Let $\lambda = 100$ in the Poisson/log-normal portfolio in Exercise 3.6 with $\xi = 0$ and $\sigma = 1$ as before.

(a) Generate $m = 10\,000$ simulations of $\mathcal{X}$, estimate/plot the density function and describe how it has changed from what it was in Exercise 3.7.

R-*commands*:

Exercise 3.7(a).

(b) Compute the 95% and 99% percentiles and point out that their ratios with $E(\mathcal{X})$ differ from what they were in Exercise 3.7.

R-*commands*:

Exercise 3.7(b).

Exercise 3.9

(a) Modify the program in Exercise 3.6 so that it applies to Gamma-distributed losses with mean ξ and shape α.

R-*commands*:

As in Exercise 3.6(a) except for `Z=ξ*rgamma(N[i],α)/α`.

(b) Check the program using $m = 10\,000$ simulations when $\lambda = 10$, $\xi = 1$ and $\alpha = 5$. [*Hint*: Use `Mean=mean(X); Sd=sd(X)` and compare with $E(\mathcal{X}) = 10$ and $\mathrm{sd}(\mathcal{X}) = 3.464$.]

(c) Plot the density function of $\mathcal{X}$ and compare with the one in Exercise 3.7.

R-*commands*:

`plot(density(X))`.

(d) Compute the 95% and 99% reserve and compare them with $E(\mathcal{X})$.

R-*commands*:

Exercise 3.7(b).

Exercise 3.10

(a) Write a program generating m simulations of log-normal losses $Z = e^{\xi+\sigma\varepsilon}$ converted to compensations H through a deductible a and a maximum insured sum b.

R-*commands*:

`Z=rlnorm(m,ξ,σ); H=pmin(pmax(Z-a,0),b)`.

(b) Run the program for $m = 100\,000$, $\xi = 0$, $\sigma = 1$, $a = 0$ and $b = 10\,000$ and compare the mean and standard deviation of the simulations with $E(Z) = 1.649$ and $\mathrm{sd}(Z) = 2.161$.

R-*commands*:

`Mean=mean(H); Sd=sd(H)`.

Exercise 3.11 Suppose the Gamma portfolio in Exercise 3.9 has been reinsured through an $a \times b$ contract per event.

(a) Write a program simulating the net loss of the cedent.

R-*commands*:

$\quad$ `N=rpois(m,`λ`); X=1:m*0;`
$\quad$ `for (i in 1:m) if(N[i] >0) {Z=`ξ`*rgamma(N[i],`α`)/`α`;`
$\quad$ Z^{re}`=pmin(pmax(Z-a,0),b); X[i]=sum(Z-`Z^{re}`)}.`

(b) Compute the 95% and 99% reserve when $b = 100$ and $a = 0.5, 1, 2, 100$ with $\lambda = 10$, $\xi = 1$ and $\alpha = 5$ and compare with the evaluations in Exercise 3.9.

R-*commands*:

For each value of a generate `X` and use ϵ`=c(0.05,0.01);` q_ϵ`=sort(X)[`$(1-\epsilon)$`*m].`

Exercise 3.12

(a) Modify the program in Exercise 3.11(a) so that reinsurer obligations are simulated instead.

R-*commands*:

The only change is `X[i]=sum(`Z^{re}`)` at the end.

(b) Compute the 95% and 99% reserve for the reinsurer under the four scenarios in Exercise 3.11.

R-*commands*:

As in Exercise 3.11(b).

(c) Use the simulations to approximate the re-insurance pure premia.

R-*commands*:

For each value of a generate `X` and use π^{re}`=mean(X).`

Exercise 3.13 Consider $a \times b$ reinsurance as in the previous exercises, but now applied to the total loss $\mathcal{X}$ and let the cedent portfolio be the log-normal one in Exercise 3.6.

(a) Compute the pure reinsurance premium for the parameters in Exercise 3.6 when $a = 15$ and $b = 25$ using $m = 100\,000$ simulations.

R-*commands*:

With X as in Exercise 3.6 use X^{re}`=pmin(pmax(X-a,0),b);` π^{re}`=mean(`X^{re}`).`

(b) Determine how much the 95% and 99% cedent reserve in Exercise 3.7(b) has been reduced.

R-*commands*:

ϵ`=c(0.05,0.01);` q_ϵ`=sort(X-`X^{re}`)[`$(1-\epsilon)$`*m].`

(c) Redo (b) for the reinsurer.

R-*commands*:

q_ϵ`=sort(`X^{re}`)[`ϵ`*m].`

Exercise 3.14 Redo Exercise 3.13 when $a = 25$ and $b = 35$.

(a) First recompute the pure reinsurance premium, then
(b) cedent reserves and
(c) reinsurer reserves and compare with the former results.

R-*commands*:

Those of Exercise 3.13.

Section 3.4

Exercise 3.15 Let $X = sB$ with s fixed and $\Pr(B = 1) = p = 1 - \Pr(B = 0)$.

(a) Argue that the model covers both term insurance (one-time payments upon the death of a policy holder) and single payments under a pension scheme.
(b) Show that

$$E(X) = ps \quad \text{and} \quad \text{var}(X) = p(1-p)s^2 \quad \text{so that} \quad \frac{\text{sd}(X)}{E(X)} = \sqrt{\frac{1}{p} - 1}.$$

(c) Use this to argue that uncertainty due to mortality is more important in term insurance than for pensions.

Exercise 3.16 Consider an insurance portfolio of J individuals with a sum s released each time someone dies.

(a) Calculate the standard deviation-to-mean ratio (3.8) when the mortality $p_j = 0.005$ for all individuals so that $\sigma_p = 0$.
(b) How large must J be for the ratio to be below 1%?
(c) Compute the same value for a pension portfolio.

Exercise 3.17 Let ${}_kp_{l_0}$ be the probability that a person of age l_0 survives the next k periods.

(a) Why is ${}_kp_{l_0} = p_{l_0}p_{l_0+1}\cdots p_{l_0+k-1}$ where $p_l = {}_1p_l$? [*Hint*: The individual must survive to age $l_0 + 1$, then to age $l_0 + 2$, and so on.]
(b) Write a program computing ${}_kp_{l_0}$ for $k = 0, 1, \ldots, K$ when $\log(p_l) = -\theta_0 - \theta_1 e^{\theta_2 l}$.

R-*commands*:

```
p=exp(-θ0-θ1*exp(θ2*l0:(l0+K-1))); kpl0=c(1,cumprod(p)).
```

(c) Run the program for $l_0 = 35$ and $K = 50$ when $\theta_0 = 0.0009$, $\theta_1 = 0.000044$ and $\theta_2 = 0.09076$ and plot ${}_kp_{35}$ against k.

R-*commands*:

```
plot(0:K,kpl0,''l'',ylim=c(0,1)).
```

(d) Rerun the program when $l_0 = 50$ and plot the new survival probabilities jointly with those in (c).

R-*commands*:

Compute ${}_kp_{l_0}$ and use `lines(0:K,`${}_kp_{l_0}$`)`.

(e) Add ${}_kp_{65}$ to the plot.

R-*commands*:

As in (d).

Exercise 3.18

(a) Write a program computing the one-time premium (3.11) when initial age and retirement are l_0 and l_r with $l_0 \leq l_r$ and the maximum age $l_e = 120$ years.

R-*commands*:

Generate ${}_kp_{l_0}$ as in Exercise 3.17 when K=l_e-l_0 and use

```
K=le-l0; Kr=lr-l0; dk=(1+r)**(-(0:K));
π=s*sum(dk[1+Kr:K]*kpl0[1+Kr:K]).
```

(b) Tabulate the one-time premium π_{l_0} when $s = 1$, $l_r = 65$, $r = 2\%$ and $l_0 = 20$, 35, 50 and 65 using the survival probabilities in Exercise 3.17.

(c) Redo (b) when $r = 4\%$ and examine how much the liabilities go down.

Exercise 3.19

(a) Write a program computing the one-time premium for an individual of age $l_0 \leq l_r$ when the retirement age l_r varies between l_{r1} and l_{r2}.

R-*commands*:

Take ${}_kp_{l_0}$ from Exercise 3.17 and use K=l_e-l_0; `dk=(1+r)**(-(0:K));`

```
a=dk[1:K]*kpl0[1:K]; π=array(0,K);
for (lr in lr1:lr2) π[lr]=s*sum(a[(1+lr-l0):K]).
```

(b) Run the program under the survival probabilities in Exercise 3.17 when $s = 1$, $l_0 = 45$, $l_{r1} = 55$, $l_{r2} = 70$, $l_e = 120$ and $r = 2\%$ and plot the results against l_r.

R-*commands*:

```
plot(lr1:lr2; π).
```

(c) Redo (b) when $l_0 = 35$ and plot the new results jointly with those in (b).

R-*commands*:

```
lines(lr1:lr2; π).
```

(d) Redo (b) and (c) when $r = 4\%$ and examine the change.

Exercise 3.20 Consider a portfolio of $\mathcal{N}_0$ individuals of the same sex and age l_0 with $\mathcal{N}_k$ the number alive at time k.

(a) Argue that the distribution of $\mathcal{N}_k$ given $\mathcal{N}_{k-1} = n$ is binomial with n trials and 'success' probability p_{l_0+k-1}.

(b) Write a program generating m simulations of the sequence $\mathcal{N}_1, \ldots, \mathcal{N}_K$.

R-*commands*:

Generate p as in Exercise 3.17(b) and use `N=matrix(`$\mathcal{N}_0$`,K+1,m);`
`for (k in 1:K) N[k+1,]=rbinom(m,N[k,],`p`[k])`.

(c) Run the program under the survival probabilities in Exercise 3.17 when $\mathcal{N}_0 = 1000$, $l_0 = 30$ and $K = 25$ using $m = 50$ and plot the percentage alive against time for the simulated sequences jointly.

R-*commands*:

`matplot(0:K,100*N/`$\mathcal{N}_0$`,''l'')`.

Exercise 3.21 Suppose the individuals of the preceding exercise have reached retirement age and draw the same pension s as long as they are alive.

(a) Argue that the payoff at time k is $\mathcal{X}_k = s\mathcal{N}_k$ and write a program simulating $\mathcal{X}_0, \ldots, \mathcal{X}_k$.

R-*commands*:

Generate `N` as in Exercise 3.20 and use `X=s*N`.

(b) Run the program when $\mathcal{N}_0 = 1000$, $l_0 = 65$, $s = 1$ and $K = 25$ using $m = 50$ and plot the simulated portfolio payoffs against k.

R-*commands*:

`matplot(0:K,X,''l'')`.

(c) Redo when $\mathcal{N}_0 = 10\,000$ and $100\,000$.

Exercise 3.22 Let the portfolio in Exercise 3.20 apply to term insurance so that the death of each policy holder releases a one-time payment s.

(a) Argue that the portfolio payoff at time k is $\mathcal{X}_k = s(\mathcal{N}_{k-1} - \mathcal{N}_k)$.

(b) Convert the simulations in Exercise 3.20 to simulations of $\mathcal{X}_1, \ldots, \mathcal{X}_K$.

R-*commands*:

`X=s*(N[1:K,]-N[1:K+1,])`.

(c) Simulate payoffs when $s = 1$ and $\mathcal{N}_0 = 1000$ and plot them jointly against time to visualize the uncertainty.

R-*commands*:

`matplot(1:K,X,''l'')`.

(c) Redo when $\mathcal{N}_0 = 10\,000$ and $100\,000$.

Section 3.5

Exercise 3.23

(a) Write a program computing the Black–Scholes price $\pi(v_0)$ for put options.

R-*commands*:

Look up (3.16) and (3.17) and use

```
sigT=sqrt(T)*σ; a=(log(1+r_g)-r*T+sigT**2/2)/sigT;
π=((1+r_g)*exp(-r*T)*pnorm(a)-pnorm(a-sigT))*v_0.
```

(b) Let $v_0 = 1$, $\sigma = 0.25$, $r = 0.03$ and $T = 1$ and examine how the premium depends on the guarantee by computing π when $r_g = -0.02, 0.0, \ldots, 0.10$.

Exercise 3.24 Many derivatives require Monte Carlo for their valuation. This exercise examines the accuracy for put options where exact answers are available. The premium is $\pi = e^{-rT} E_Q(X)$ where $X = \max(r_g - R, 0)v_0$ and $R = e^{rT-\sigma^2 T/2+\sigma\sqrt{T}\varepsilon} - 1$ for $\varepsilon \sim N(0,1)$.

(a) Write a program approximating π as the average of m simulations of X.

R-*commands*:

```
eps=rnorm(m); R=exp(r*T-σ**2*T/2+σ*sqrt(T)*eps)-1;
π=exp(-r*T)*mean(pmax(r_g-R,0))*v_0.
```

(b) Run the program when $\sigma = 0.25$, $r_g = 0.04$, $r = 0.03$, $v_0 = 1$ and $T = 1$ using $m = 10\,000$, $100\,000$ and $1\,000\,000$ simulations and repeat a few times to examine uncertainty. [*Comment*: The exact price in Exercise 3.23 is $\pi = 0.10464$.]

Exercise 3.25 A buyer of a put option expiring at T is guaranteed $v_0(1 + r_g)$ for equity worth $S_0 = v_0$ at time 0. Suppose the underlying stock is valued as S_1 at time $T_1 < T$.

(a) Argue that the put option at T_1 corresponds to a guarantee r_{g1} determined by the equation $(1 + r_{g1})S_1 = (1 + r_g)S_0$.

(b) Use the Black–Scholes formula (3.16) and (3.17) and write down a mathematical expression for the value of the option at T_1. [*Hint*: See Exercise 3.27.]

Exercise 3.26 The equity value S_1 and guarantee r_{g1} of the previous exercise are $R_1 = e^{\xi T_1+\sigma\sqrt{T_1}\varepsilon_1} - 1$, $S_1 = (1 + R_1)S_0$ and $r_{g1} = (1 + r_g)S_0/S_1 - 1$ where $\varepsilon_1 \sim N(0,1)$.

(a) Write a program generating m simulations of S_1 and r_{g1}.

R-*commands*:

```
eps=rnorm(m); R_1=exp(ξ*T_1+σ*sqrt(T_1)*eps)-1;
S_1=(1+R_1)*S_0; r_g1=(1+r_g)*S_0/S_1-1.
```

(b) Run the programs when $T = 1, \xi = 0.07, \sigma = 0.25, r_g = 0.04, r = 0.03, S_0 = 1$ and $T_1 = 0.5$ and plot the density function of r_{g1}. Use $m = 100\,000$.

R-*commands*:

plot(density(r_{g1})).

Exercise 3.27 The value of the option in Exercise 3.25 at time T_1 is

$$\pi_1 = \{(1 + r_{g1})e^{-rT_e}\Phi(a_1) - \Phi(a_1 - \sigma\sqrt{T_e})\}S_1$$

where

$$a_1 = \frac{\log(1 + r_{g1}) - rT_e + \sigma^2 T_e/2}{\sigma\sqrt{T_e}} \quad \text{and} \quad T_e = T - T_1.$$

(a) Extend the program of the preceding exercise so that it simulates π_1.

R-*commands*:

With r_{g1} and S_1 as in Exercise 3.26 use

$T_e = T - T_1$; b=σ* $\sqrt{T_e}$;

a_1=(log(1+r_{g1})-r*T_e+b**2/2)/b;

π_1=((1+r_{g1})*exp(-r*T_e)*pnorm(a_1)-pnorm(a_1-b))*S_1.

(b) Run the program under the conditions in Exercise 3.26 and plot the density function of π_1.

R-*commands*:

plot(density(π_1),from=0).

(c) Compare the distribution with the orginal option value $\pi = 0.10464$ from Exercise 3.23. [*Comment*: *Options are an uncertain business!*]

Exercise 3.28 Let $X_P = \max(r_g - \mathcal{R}, 0)v_0$ and $X_C = \max(\mathcal{R} - r_g, 0)v_0$ be the payoff for put and call options.

(a) Argue that $X_C - X_P = (R - r_g)v_0$ and when viewed as a derivative, priced as $e^{-rT}E_Q(X_C - X_P)$.
(b) Use this to deduce that option premia $\pi_P(v_0)$ and $\pi_C(v_0)$ for puts and calls are related through $\pi_C(v_0) - \pi_P(v_0) = e^{-rT}(E_Q(R) - r_g)v_0$ so that

$$\pi_C(v_0) = \pi_P(v_0) + \{1 - e^{-rT}(1 + r_g)\}v_0.$$

(c) Draw on the Black–Scholes formula (3.16) and prove that

$$\pi_C(v_0) = \{\Phi(-a + \sigma\sqrt{T}) - (1 + r_g)e^{-rT}\Phi(-a)\}v_0$$

where a is defined in (3.17). [*Hint*: Utilize that $\Phi(x) = 1 - \Phi(-x)$.]

Exercise 3.29 Let $X_P(r_g)$ and $X_C(r_g)$ be payoffs for put and call options with the guarantee made explicit in the notation and let $\pi_P(r_g)$ and $\pi_C(r_g)$ be their premia.

(a) Argue that the payoff (3.20) for cliquet options can be written $X = X_P(r_g) - X_C(r_c)$.

(b) Deduce that the premium for a cliquet becomes $\pi = \pi_P(r_g) - \pi_C(r_c)$ or

$$\pi = \pi_P(r_g) - \pi_P(r_c) - \{1 - e^{-rT}(1 + r_c)\}v_0.$$

[*Hint*: Use Exercise 3.28(b).]

(c) Compute the premium for the cliquet option when $T = 1$, $\sigma = 0.25$, $r_g = 0.04$, $r = 0.03$, $v_0 = 1$ and $r_c = 0.09, 0.12, 0.15$ and 0.50. Any comments?

R-*commands*:

Compute $\pi_P(r_g)$ and $\pi_P(r_c)$ through the commands in Exercise 3.23 and use
π=$\pi_P(r_g)$-$\pi_P(r_c)$-`(1-exp(-r*T)*(1+`r_c`))*`v_0.

Section 3.6

Exercise 3.30 Consider the underwriter process $\mathcal{Y}_k = \mathcal{Y}_{k-1} + \Pi - \mathcal{X}_k$ for $k = 1, \ldots, K$ where Π is net premium income (a constant) and $\mathcal{X}_1, \ldots, \mathcal{X}_K$ independent realizations of claims $\mathcal{X}$ against the Poisson/log-normal portfolio in Exercise 3.6.

(a) Write a program generating mK simulations of $\mathcal{X}$.

R-*commands*:

As in Exercise 3.6 with `m*K` in place of `m`.

(b) Generate m simulations of $\mathcal{Y}_1, \ldots, \mathcal{Y}_K$ when $\mathcal{Y}_0 = v_0$.

R-*commands*:

With X as the mK-vector in (a) use
`X=matrix(X,K,m); Y=`v_0`-apply(X-`Π`,2,cumsum)`.

(c) Run the program when $\lambda = 10$, $\xi = 0$, $\sigma = 1$, $\Pi = 18$, $v_0 = 35$, $K = 20$ and $m = 200$ and plot the underwriter results jointly against time.

R-*commands*:

Y`=rbind(rep(`v_0`,m),Y); matplot(0:K,`Y`,''l'')`.

(d) Repeat (c) when $\Pi = 16.4$ (close to the pure premium) and verify that the slight drift upwards has now disappeared.

Exercise 3.31

(a) Redo Exercise 3.30, but now with a portfolio 100 times larger so that $\lambda = 1000$. Start the simulations at $v_0 = 3500$ and make $\Pi = 1800$ so that the expected gain per policy is the same as before.

R-*commands*:

Those in Exercise 3.30.

(b) Why are the oscillations more peaceful than they were in Exercise 3.30?

Exercise 3.32

(a) Redo Exercise 3.30 one more time, now with different parameters $\xi = 0.455$ and $\sigma = 0.3$ for the losses, but with the rest of the conditions as before.

R-*commands*:

Those in Exercise 3.30.

(b) Why are the random oscillations smaller than in Exercise 3.30? [*Hint*: Mean loss per event is unchanged.]

Exercise 3.33

(a) Extend the program in Exercise 3.30 so that m simulations of the minimum of $\mathcal{Y}_1, \dots, \mathcal{Y}_K$ are returned.

R-*commands*:

Take `Y` from Exercise 3.30 and use `Ymin=apply(Y,2,min)`.

(b) Run the program in Exercise 3.30 from $v_0 = 0$ under the conditions there using $m = 10\,000$ simulations and compute the initial capital keeping the ruin probability at 5% and 1%.

R-*commands*:

$\epsilon = c(0.05, 0.01)$; $v_{0\epsilon}$`=-sort(Ymin)[`ϵ`*m]`.

(c) Redo (b) when $K = 10$ and $K = 5$ and compare the evaluations.

Exercise 3.34 Add financial income with constant return r to the recursion in Exercise 3.30 so that $\mathcal{Y}_k = (1+r)\mathcal{Y}_{k-1} + \Pi - \mathcal{X}_k$ for $k = 1, 2, \dots, K$.

(a) Write a program simulating the discounted underwriter results $\mathcal{S}_k = \sum_{i=1}^{k}(\mathcal{X}_i - \Pi)/(1+r)^i$; see (3.26).

R-*commands*:

With X as the matrix in Exercise 3.30(b) use

`rk=(1+r)**(1:K); B=(X-`Π`)/rk; S=apply(B,2,cumsum)`.

(b) Extend the program so that m simulations of $\mathcal{Y}_1, \dots, \mathcal{Y}_K$ are generated.

R-*commands*:

Use (3.26) which yields `Y=rk*(`v_0`-S)`.

(c) Run the programs in (a) and (b) under the conditions in Exercise 3.30 when $r = 0.04$, $\Pi = 18$, $K = 20$ and $m = 200$ and plot the net assets jointly against time.

R-*commands*:

Y`=rbind(rep(`v_0`,m),Y); matplot(0:K,`Y`,''l'')`.

(d) Compare the plot with that in Exercise 3.30(c) and judge the impact of financial earnings.

Exercise 3.35

(a) Redo the previous exercise under the loss model in Exercise 3.32.

R-*commands*:

Those of the previous exercise with different parameters.

(b) What about the significance of the financial earnings now?

Exercise 3.36

(a) Run the program in Exercise 3.34(a) under the same conditions except for $m =$ 10 000 and utilize (3.27) to compute the inital capital corresponding to 5% and 1% ruin.

R-*commands*:

$\epsilon = c(0.05, 0.01)$; `Smax=apply(S,2,max);`

$v_{0\epsilon}$`=sort(Smax)[(1-`ϵ`)*m].`

(b) How much has financial earnings lowered the capital compared with what it was in Exercise 3.33(b)?

(c) Redo (b) when $K = 10$ and $K = 5$ and compare with the assessments in Exercise 3.33(c).

4

Monte Carlo II: Improving technique

4.1 Introduction

With the exception of Section 4.2, and the first half of Section 4.3, the material of this chapter isn't much used elsewhere and can be skipped at first reading. Yet it would be regrettable in a book of this kind to stay solely with the very simplest of Monte Carlo. Specialist books in finance are Jäckel (2002), Glasserman (2004) and Dagpunar (2007). Most of their illustrations are from short-term finance and, it seems useful with a text more adapted to the needs of actuaries, with examples from general insurance too.

We shall start with **table look-up** methods in the next section. These are not always mentioned, yet they possess very useful qualities. They are general (can virtually always be used) and are ultra-fast once they are in place. With Poisson or multinomial sampling these are the methods of choice when there are *very* many repetitions. At the expense of some discretization error, continuous distributions can be handled too. The restriction of table methods is one of dimensionality. We must be able to break simulation down on independent variables or, at most, a handful of dependent ones. When that is impossible, **Markov chain Monte Carlo** is another general approach; see Section 4.8.

The other methods (Sections 4.3–4.6) are specifically geared towards speed enhancement, sometimes achieving drastic improvement. That is a prerequisite for their use, since they require more skill and take more time to implement. With everyday problems, technological progress pushes towards the simplest methods which (with the exception of Section 4.2) are not those of the present chapter. But when speed is needed, the ideas presented below might take you somewhere.

4.2 Table look-up methods

4.2.1 Introduction

Any continuous random variable X can be approximated by a discrete one. Outcomes are then among a given sequence $x_1, \dots, x_n$, and we pretend that the

Algorithm 4.1 Discrete uniform sampling

0 Input: $x_1, \ldots, x_n$
1 Sample $U^* \sim$ uniform
2 $i^* \leftarrow [1 + nU^*]$ *%Select random index*
3 Return $X^* \leftarrow x_{i^*}$.

distribution is

$$\Pr(X = x_i) = p_i$$

where $p_1 + \cdots + p_n = 1$. Passing from the continuous to the discrete brings numerical error, albeit a small one if the points are tight. How x_i and p_i are constructed is discussed below. Why bother with this crude approach? Answer: Because discrete distributions can be sampled *very* rapidly, leading to an efficient and general procedure which can be used with *any* distribution.

4.2.2 Uniform sampling

The simplest case is the **uniform** one for which $p_i = 1/n$. All outcomes are then equally likely. This situation arises when $x_1, \ldots, x_n$ are events from the past, say historical claims in property insurance or earlier returns of a financial portfolio. The uniform model assumes that everything seen before is equally likely to reappear in the future and has something to do with the **bootstrap** introduced in Chapter 7. Here the issue is the sampling which is outlined in Algorithm 4.1.

The scheme is easy to understand. On Line 2 the function $[x]$ is the largest integer $\leq x$. Note that

$$1 < 1 + nU^* < 1 + n$$

since $0 < U^* < 1$, and i^* is one of the integers $1, \ldots, n$, all equally likely to be selected. If the record consists of vectors $\mathbf{x}_1, \ldots, \mathbf{x}_n$, then $\mathbf{X}^* = \mathbf{x}_{i^*}$ is a vector too.

4.2.3 General discrete sampling

What about the non-uniform case? An obvious way is to draw U^* and return x_i if

$$p_1 + \cdots + p_{i-1} < U^* \leq p_1 + \cdots + p_i$$

which has the right probability p_i. The method can be regarded as a special case of inversion. It is also very inefficient, hopelessly slow for large n. **Guide tables** proposed by Chen and Asau (1974) offer a dramatic improvement. There is now a setup and a sampling phase. Let

$$P_j = p_1 + \cdots + p_j \quad \text{with} \quad P_0 = 0$$

Algorithm 4.2 Guide table setup

0 Input: $p_1, \ldots, p_n$, $P_0 \leftarrow 0$, $g_0 \leftarrow 1$
1 For $j = 1, \ldots, n$ do *%Computing and storing cumulative probabilities*
    $P_j \leftarrow P_{j-1} + p_j$
2 For $i = 1, \ldots, n$ do
3     $j \leftarrow g_{i-1} - 1$
4   Repeat $j \leftarrow j + 1$ until $P_j \geq i/n$ *%Smallest integer for which $P_j \geq i/n$*
5     $g_i \leftarrow j$ *%Correct index found*
6 Return: $P_0, \ldots, P_n$ and $g_1, \ldots, g_n$.

and introduce for $i = 1, \ldots, n$

$$g_i = \min\{j \geq 1 | P_j \geq i/n\}$$

which guides the table look-up. Note that g_i is the smallest integer j for which $P_j \geq i/n$ and that $1 \leq g_i \leq n$. The computation of these quantities is organized in Algorithm 4.2. On Line 4 the index j is raised until $P_j \geq i/n$, which makes $g_i = j$ the smallest integer satisfying this inequality.

The setup is carried out once before entering the sampling phase. Algorithm 4.3 summarizes the steps required. The loop on Line 3 proceeds until j^* has become the *smallest* integer for which $P_{j^*} \geq U^*$. Hence

$$\Pr(j^* = j) = \Pr(P_{j-1} < U^* \leq P_j) = P_j - P_{j-1} = p_j,$$

and x_j is returned with probability p_j. How much time are spent on finding j^*? Less than two trials are necessary on average! The algorithm tracks P_j down from $P_{g_{i^*}}$ to just below U^*, where g_{i^*} is the smallest integer for which $P_{g_{i^*}} \geq i^*/n$. Moreover, Line 2 in Algorithm 4.3 yields

$$i^* \leq 1 + nU^* \quad \text{so that} \quad U^* \geq \frac{i^* - 1}{n},$$

and it follows that no more than $1 + k_{i^*}$ attempts can be necessary on Line 3 where k_i is the number of P_j satisfying $(i-1)/n < P_j \leq i/n$. It follows that the expected number of trials is bounded from above by

$$E(1 + k_{i^*}) = \sum_{i=1}^{n} \Pr(i^* = i)(1 + k_i) = \frac{1}{n} \sum_{i=1}^{n} (1 + k_i) = 2$$

since $k_1 + \cdots + k_n = n$.

Algorithm 4.3 Guide table sampling

0 Input: $x_1, \ldots, x_n, P_1, \ldots, P_n, g_1, \ldots, g_n$
1 Sample $U^* \sim$ uniform
2 $i^* \leftarrow [1 + nU^*]$ and $j^* \leftarrow g_{i^*}$
3 Repeat $j^* \leftarrow j^* - 1$ while $P_{j^*-1} \geq U^*$ %*Stop reducing* j^* *when next* $P_{j^*-1} < U^*$
4 Return: $X^* \leftarrow x_{j^*}$.

4.2.4 Example: Poisson sampling

Algorithms 4.2 and 4.3 provide fast samplers for discrete distributions. Consider the Poisson model for which the guide table setup is

$$x_i = i - 1 \quad \text{and} \quad p_i = \frac{\lambda^{i-1}}{(i-1)!}e^{-\lambda} \quad \text{for} \quad i = 1, 2, \ldots, n$$

where n is selected to make the probabilities above p_n microscopic, say from 10^{-8} or 10^{-9} (no need to be modest!). You should *not* fall into the trap of using the Poisson density function for computation as this might easily bring underflow/overflow in the computer. Instead, implement the recursion

$$p_{i+1} = \frac{\lambda}{i}p_i \quad \text{for} \quad i = 1, 2, \ldots, n-1 \quad \text{starting at} \quad p_1 = e^{-\lambda}.$$

This is the fastest scheme anyway. It may for very large λ be necessary to convert the recursion to logarithms, run it on log-scale and take antilogarithms at the end.

The Poisson generator obtained from this procedure is much faster than the one in Algorithm 2.14 once the setup is completed. It also works better with the antitetic variables in Section 4.3. But when the Poisson parameter λ is changing all the time (a situation we shall encounter in Sections 8.3 and 11.3), the method is useless.

4.2.5 Making the continuous discrete

Table look-up is a useful method for continuous random variables. Discrete approximations are necessary, but the speed is insensitive to n, and we can afford finely meshed schemes to reduce numerical error. Let $f(x)$ be a density function over the positive axis or the entire real line with negligible probability (say 10^{-6} or smaller) above some constant A and below $-A$. Simple, equidistant discretizations over intervals $(0, A)$ and $(-A, A)$ are then

$$\underset{\textit{positive variables}}{x_i = \tfrac{i}{n+1}A} \qquad \text{and} \qquad \underset{\textit{variables over the entire real line}}{x_i = -A + \tfrac{2i}{n+1}A} \tag{4.1}$$

for $i = 1, \dots, n$ with corresponding probabilities

$$p_i = \frac{f(x_i)}{\sum_{j=1}^{n} f(x_j)}, \qquad i = 1, \dots, n. \tag{4.2}$$

If the distribution function $F(x)$ is simple to compute, an alternative is to skip Line 1 in Algorithm 4.2 and take $P_i = F(x_i)$ directly.

There are several points in favour of this approach. As long as the density $f(x)$ can be computed, $p_1, \dots, p_n$ can always be found and the inaccuracy in passing from the continuous to the discrete is overcome by raising n. The method is ultra-rapid when the setup phase (Algorithm 4.2) has been completed, and it beats the already efficient Gamma sampler (Algorithm 2.9) by a factor of five or six (against the faster Gaussian and Pareto samplers the gain was a less impressive 50% when tested). Other discretization schemes may be invented by using weights meant for numerical integration (see Appendix C.3), but this yields improvements only when the function to be simulated has smooth derivatives, and many important examples have not. The put option below is such a case.

Random vectors are easily tackled when they can be reduced to a sequence of independent drawings, but not when the discretization must apply to many variables jointly. True, grids such as (4.1) *can* be laid out in all directions, but the number of points grows rapidly with each new variable, and we can't handle more than a few. There is an example in Section 7.6.

4.2.6 Example: Put options

Stock options in terms of single assets provide a convenient test for table look-up since there is an exact formula to compare with. Consider a contract with payoff function

$$X = \max(r_g - R, 0) \quad \text{where} \quad R = e^{r - \sigma^2/2 + \sigma\varepsilon} - 1$$

and $\varepsilon \sim N(0, 1)$. How the premium of such a put option can be evaluated by Monte Carlo was dealt with in Section 3.5; see Algorithm 3.5. Now the objective is the accuracy of table look-up sampling. Consider the approximation

$$\varepsilon_i = -6 + \frac{2i}{n+1} 6, \quad \text{and} \quad p_i = \frac{e^{-\varepsilon_i^2/2}}{\sum_{j=1}^{n} e^{-\varepsilon_j^2/2}}, \qquad i = 1, \dots, n$$

which corresponds to $A = 6$ in (4.1), a suitable value since the chance of a standard normal random variable falling outside the interval $(-6, 6)$ is of order 10^{-9}.

Algorithm 3.5 was run with normal variables drawn from the preceding discrete approximation. Conditions and parameters selected were $r_g = 0$, $\sigma = 25\%$ and

$r = 7.125\%$, and the option expired after a year. Varying the number of points n gave the following results:

n	20	100	1000	10 000	Exact
Premium	6.58178%	6.55055%	6.55230%	6.55231%	6.55231%

Ten *billion* simulations were used, which is so many that there is virtually no Monte Carlo uncertainty, and errors are due to discretization only. Even $n = 100$ provides a fair approximation, but there is no need to keep n so low. With $n = 1000$ points the result is accurate to four decimals and with $n = 10\,000$ to five! The exact result is provided by the Black–Scholes formula (3.16) in Section 3.5.

4.3 Correlated sampling

4.3.1 Introduction

How simulations $X_1^*, \ldots, X_m^*$ are used to approximate the distribution of X and what error that brings about was discussed in Section 2.2. An independent sample was taken for granted. Why contemplate anything else? There are two related answers. First note that

$$\mathrm{var}(X_1^* + X_2^*) = \mathrm{var}(X_1^*) + \mathrm{var}(X_2^*) + 2\mathrm{cov}(X_1^*, X_2^*)$$

so that if

$$\sigma = \mathrm{sd}(X_1^*) = \mathrm{sd}(X_2^*) \quad \text{and} \quad \rho = \mathrm{cor}(X_1^*, X_2^*)$$

then

$$\mathrm{var}(X_1^* + X_2^*) = 2\sigma^2(1 + \rho). \tag{4.3}$$

For low variance the two simulations should be *negatively* correlated. This can be achieved through **antithetic** variables, as is introduced below.

There is a second, in a sense reverse, position. Suppose we want to compare quantities X_1^* and X_2^* coming from the same simulation program under different assumptions. Their standard deviations $\sigma_1 = \mathrm{sd}(X_1^*)$ and $\sigma_2 = \mathrm{sd}(X_2^*)$ differ, yet perhaps not by very much, so that we may assume $\sigma_1 \doteq \sigma_2 = \sigma$ (this is *not* essential). But then, similar to (4.3),

$$\mathrm{var}(X_2^* - X_1^*) \doteq 2\sigma^2(1 - \rho) \tag{4.4}$$

and now *positive* correlation is advantageous. Such designs are discussed first.

4.3.2 Common random numbers

Suppose $\boldsymbol{\theta}$ contains the input quantities to a simulation program, for example model parameters or contract clauses such as an interest rate guarantee or the maximum responsibility of an insurer. Monte Carlo simulations manipulate independent sequences of uniforms $U_1^*, U_2^*, \ldots$ in a way depending on $\boldsymbol{\theta}$. A formal mathematical representation is

$$X^* = H(U_1^*, U_2^*, \ldots; \boldsymbol{\theta}), \tag{4.5}$$

and the issue addressed is how experiments are planned when $\boldsymbol{\theta}$ (under our control) is varied. High correlation at different $\boldsymbol{\theta}$ is desirable when the issue is to examine how X^* and $\boldsymbol{\theta}$ are related, and a plausible step in that direction is to keep $U_1^*, U_2^*, \ldots$ fixed. The idea works with other variables than uniform ones; more on that below.

As a simple example consider the Pareto model of Section 2.5. There are two parameters β and α, and it will emerge in Chapter 7 that α is particularly difficult to pin down. Suppose we want to investigate the effect of varying it while keeping expectation $\xi = \beta/(\alpha - 1)$ fixed. Algorithm 2.13 yields the Pareto simulation

$$Z^* = \beta\{(U^*)^{-1/\alpha} - 1\} \quad \text{where} \quad \beta = \xi(\alpha - 1),$$

and although these realizations are enormously variable, Z^* is still a smooth function of α when U^* is fixed. Several of the displays in the second half of Chapter 3 made use of this technique. If m simulations are needed, start with the same uniform sample $U_1^*, \ldots, U_m^*$ and generate $Z_i^* = \beta\{(U_i^*)^{-1/\alpha} - 1\}$ for $i = 1, \ldots, m$ as α is varied.

The idea is known as **common random numbers**. Another name is **variate recycling** (same random variables being used repeatedly). Worthwile savings in computer time *may* result (see below), but more important is reduced Monte Carlo error for comparisons and smoothness in plots and displays. Common random numbers are also a sensible strategy when you want to optimize simulation output with respect to $\boldsymbol{\theta}$. The numerical methods in Appendix C.5 do not work properly with functions full of random Monte Carlo bumps. Actually, smooth displays are not guaranteed even when common random numbers *are* used. The approach works well with inversion (the Pareto sampler is a case in point), but not with random stopping rules such as rejection or ratio of uniform sampling; consult Figure 6.8 in Section 6.7 for an example. Now the number of trials depends on the underlying parameters, and when they are changed, discontinuities appear.

How are common random numbers implemented? It is easy when you code the entire thing yourself. Random drawings are then generated at the beginning and stored for later use. With pre-programmed software you must learn how the seed of the generator is manipulated; see Section 4.6.

4.3.3 Example from finance

The use of common random numbers does not necessarily force us all the way down to uniforms. A good illustration of alternative ways is Monte Carlo pricing of put options. The approximation is then

$$\pi^* = e^{-rT}\frac{1}{m}\sum_{i=1}^{m}\max(r_g - \mathcal{R}_i^*, 0), \tag{4.6}$$

where r_g is the guarantee and $\mathcal{R}_1^*, \dots, \mathcal{R}_m^*$ simulated portfolio returns. Under a risk-neutral log-normal model as in Section 3.6,

$$\mathcal{R}_i^* = \sum_{j=1}^{J} w_j R_{ji}^* \quad \text{where} \quad R_{ji}^* = e^{rT - \frac{1}{2}\sigma_j^2 T + \sigma_j\sqrt{T}\varepsilon_{ji}^*} - 1 \tag{4.7}$$

with $\varepsilon_{1i}^*, \dots, \varepsilon_{Ji}^*$ being $N(0,1)$ and correlated for each i. Suppose our interest lies in how the option price depends on the guarantee r_g. It is only necessary to store the portfolio returns $\mathcal{R}_1^*, \dots, \mathcal{R}_m^*$ and vary r_g. The resulting curve is smooth with small discontinuities in the derivative (they are of size e^{-rT}/m and appear at $r_g = \mathcal{R}_i^*$, $i = 1, \dots, m$). This is ultra-fast computationally and a much better picture to look at than when new returns are redrawn for each r_g.

What if our interest is the relationship between price and volatilities? The vectors $\varepsilon_{1i}^*, \dots, \varepsilon_{Ji}^*$ are then stored instead and the volatilities varied (that was how Figure 3.3 was constructed). We may go even further. Suppose the Gaussian model is the equicorrelated one so that

$$\varepsilon_{ji}^* = \sqrt{\rho}\,\eta_{0i}^* + \sqrt{1-\rho}\,\eta_{ji}^*, \quad j = 1, \dots, J; \tag{4.8}$$

see (2.26). If our aim is to study how ρ influences the option premium, the best procedure is to store all the simulated standard normals η_{ji}^*, vary ρ and proceed through (4.7) and (4.6).

4.3.4 Example from insurance

A second example is from property insurance. The policies are assumed identical, and each event is reinsured with retention limit a and unlimited coverage. Consider the cedent net reserve under Pareto-distributed losses. Monte Carlo approximations, developed in Section 3.3, are

$$q_\epsilon^* = \mathcal{X}_{(m\epsilon)}^* \quad \text{sorted descendingly from} \quad \mathcal{X}_1^*, \dots, \mathcal{X}_m^*$$

where under a Pareto model

$$\mathcal{X}_j^* = \sum_{i=1}^{\mathcal{N}_j^*}\min(Z_{ji}^*, a), \quad Z_{ji}^* = \beta\{(U_{ji}^*)^{-1/\alpha} - 1\}$$

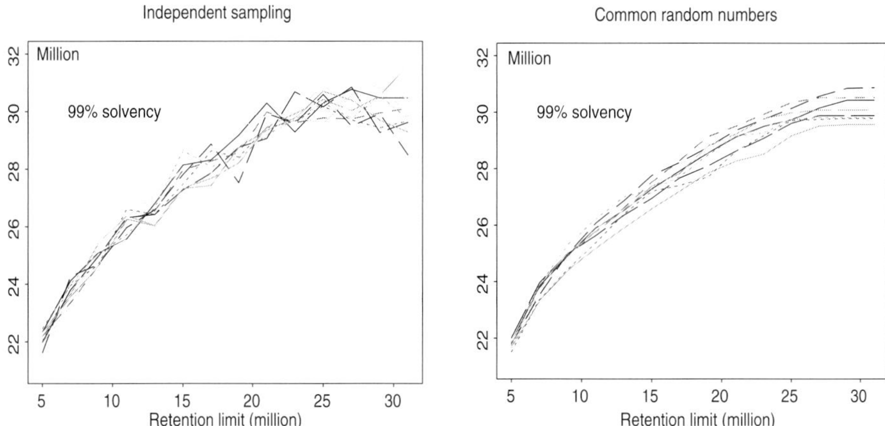

Figure 4.1 Capital requirement (99% solvency) under different limits of responsibility for the portfolio in Section 3.3 with $m = 10\,000$ simulations.

for $j = 1, \dots, m$ and $i = 1, 2, \dots, \mathcal{N}_j^*$. If we want to examine how the reserve depends on α, uniforms and claim numbers (U_{ij}^* and $\mathcal{N}_j^*$) are fixed and α varied.

Figure 4.1 examines the different issue of how the cedent reserve varies with the retention limit a. Now the Pareto variables Z_{ji}^* are stored along with $\mathcal{N}_1^*, \dots, \mathcal{N}_m^*$. The portfolio was that of Section 3.3 with $\lambda = 10$, $\alpha = 3$ and $\beta = 2$. Displays when random variables are redrawn for each value of a look like those in Figure 4.1 left. There are inelegant random jumps up and down, but they disappear when common random numbers are introduced on the right. Still, $m = 10\,000$ simulations are not enough to prevent visible discontinuities in the first derivatives. Ten replications convey the amount of simulation uncertainty involved.

4.3.5 Negative correlation: Antithetic designs

The purpose of common random numbers was to make simulations positively correlated. Antithetic designs take the reverse position. Now realizations $X_1^*, \dots, X_m^*$ are made *negatively* correlated to reduce Monte Carlo uncertainty in their average $\overline{X}^* = (X_1^* + \cdots + X_m^*)/m$. The idea, which was popularized by Hammersley and Morton (1956), applies pairwise. Suppose

$$\text{cor}(X_1^*, X_2^*) = \text{cor}(X_3^*, X_4^*) = \cdots = \text{cor}(X_{m-1}^*, X_m^*) = \rho \qquad (4.9)$$

with all other pairs uncorrelated (m is an even number). The variance of the average then becomes

$$\text{var}(\overline{X}^*) = \frac{\sigma^2}{m}(1 + \rho) \quad (m \text{ even}) \qquad (4.10)$$

which is verified in Section 4.7. Large and negative ρ bring useful cuts in Monte Carlo uncertainty.

Pairwise, negatively correlated simulations come from the observation that a uniform U^* has $U^\dagger = 1 - U^*$ as its **antithetic** twin. Both are uniforms and if one is large, the other must be small. Suppose a sequence of such pairs $(U_1^*, U_1^\dagger)$, $(U_2^*, U_2^\dagger)$, ... has been generated. The simulations

$$X^* = H(U_1^*, U_2^*, \dots) \quad \text{and} \quad X^\dagger = H(U_1^\dagger, U_2^\dagger, \dots)$$

are both equally valid, and we may hope that the negative correlation in the antithetic pairs carries over. The success of the idea is strongly dependent on the circumstances, as the following discussion shows. Even the detailed implementation matters.

4.3.6 *Examples of designs*

As with common random numbers we do not always have to go all the way back to the uniforms. For example, with $\Phi^{-1}(u)$ the Gaussian integral consider

$$\varepsilon^* = \Phi^{-1}(U^*) \quad \text{and} \quad \varepsilon^\dagger = \Phi^{-1}(1 - U^*) = -\Phi^{-1}(U^*) = -\varepsilon^*,$$

and $\varepsilon^\dagger = -\varepsilon^*$ is a second normal, perfectly negatively correlated with the first. This trick applies to any symmetric distribution and may also be used with vectors of correlated normals since $(\varepsilon_1^*, \dots, \varepsilon_J^*)$ and $(-\varepsilon_1^*, \dots, -\varepsilon_J^*)$ have the same joint distribution; see Section 5.4. In applications each member of the pair is inserted into certain non-linear functions, say $X^* = H(\varepsilon^*)$ and $X^\dagger = H(-\varepsilon^*)$. The example $H(\varepsilon) = (a + \varepsilon)^2$ is analysed in Exercise 4.8, where it is shown that

$$\operatorname{cor}(X^*, X^\dagger) = \frac{1 - 2a^2}{1 + 2a^2}$$

which depends strongly on a. The correlation approaches -1 for large a (making the antithetic trick work well) and exceeds zero for small a (worse than no gain). Antithetic sampling is *not* a method to be universally trusted.

Yet the approach is well established in computational finance (see Glasserman, 2004), but less so in insurance. Pareto and Poisson generators are examined in Table 4.1. The antithetic pair for the former is

$$Z^* = \beta\{(U^*)^{-1/\alpha} - 1\} \quad \text{and} \quad Z^\dagger = \beta\{(1 - U^*)^{-1/\alpha} - 1\},$$

and their correlation is shown in Table 4.1 for $\alpha > 2$ (it does not exist otherwise). Note the strong impact of α (for small α antithetic designs will not achieve much). The Poisson example illustrates another issue. Antithetic sampling works better with some implementations than others! The success of Algorithm 4.3 (guide table)

Table 4.1 Antithetic correlation for Pareto and Poisson generators

Behind Pareto: 10 million simulations. Behind Poisson: 1 million simulations

Pareto (inversion)			
$\alpha = 2.1$	$\alpha = 5$	$\alpha = 10$	$\alpha = 50$
−0.07	−0.43	−0.55	−0.63

Poisson, Algorithm 2.14				Poisson, Algorithm 4.3			
$\lambda = 1$	$\lambda = 10$	$\lambda = 50$	$\lambda = 100$	$\lambda = 1$	$\lambda = 10$	$\lambda = 50$	$\lambda = 100$
−0.58	−0.54	−0.59	−0.60	−0.74	−0.98	−0.996	−0.998

for large λ makes sense since Poisson variables are almost normal under such circumstances (Section 8.2), and the antithetic correlation must approach -1.

4.3.7 Antithetic design in property insurance

Option pricing with an antithetic design is examined in Section 4.5 (see Table 4.3), and we shall now study portfolio risk in property insurance. Let

$$\mathcal{X}^* = \sum_{i=1}^{\mathcal{N}^*} Z_i^* \quad \text{and} \quad \mathcal{X}^\dagger = \sum_{i=1}^{\mathcal{N}^\dagger} Z_i^\dagger \tag{4.11}$$

be antithetic simulations of claims $\mathcal{X}$ against a portfolio. How far down $\text{cor}(\mathcal{X}^*, \mathcal{X}^\dagger)$ is pushed depends on the generators; i.e., on

$$\rho_n = \text{cor}(\mathcal{N}^*, \mathcal{N}^\dagger) \quad \text{and} \quad \rho_z = \text{cor}(Z^*, Z^\dagger). \tag{4.12}$$

Let $\xi_z = E(Z)$ and $\sigma_z = \text{sd}(Z)$ be mean and standard deviation of the individual losses Z_i. Then

$$\text{cor}(\mathcal{X}^*, \mathcal{X}^\dagger) \geq \frac{\rho_n + \rho_z(\sigma_z/\xi_z)^2}{1 + (\sigma_z/\xi_z)^2} \quad \text{if} \quad \rho_z \leq 0, \tag{4.13}$$

which is proved in Section 4.7. Under no circumstances can the antithetic correlation in a portfolio simulation be pushed below the right-hand side of (4.13). The accuracy of the lower bound is a fair one, and it becomes exact as $\lambda \to \infty$ (Section 4.7 again). Try to insert values from Table 4.1, and you will discover that antithetic portfolio sampling may achieve something when you are concerned with quantities like $E\{H(\mathcal{X})\}$ for some function $H(x)$.

4.4 Importance sampling and rare events

4.4.1 Introduction

What is rare takes many simulations to evaluate. The probability p of some event is routinely estimated as the relative number of times it occurs in m simulations. Recall that the standard deviation of the estimate is the binomial $\sqrt{p(1-p)/m}$. Suppose we want it to be some fraction δ of the true value p. This yields for m the equation

$$\sqrt{\frac{p(1-p)}{m}} \doteq \sqrt{\frac{p}{m}} = \delta p \quad \text{or} \quad m = \frac{1}{\delta^2 p},$$

a huge number for rare events, for example a whopping one hundred million if $p = 0.01\%$ and $\delta = 1\%$.

A method of speeding these things up is **importance sampling**, an idea that goes back many decades. The setup creates an environment making rare events less rare, and is simple enough in theory, but it is a challenge to apply the method effectively in practice. Importance sampling is well established in computational finance; see Glasserman (2004), and here we shall try it on portfolio risk in property insurance.

4.4.2 The sampling method

Kick-off is the same as rejection sampling in Section 2.3. Instead of the original density function $f(x)$, simulations X_i^* come from an **importance** density function $g(x)$ of our choice. The error this induces is corrected by the **importance** weights

$$w_i^* = \frac{f(X_i^*)}{g(X_i^*)}, \qquad i = 1, \dots, m. \tag{4.14}$$

To see how they are used, consider the expectation

$$\psi = E\{\Psi(X)\} = \int_{-\infty}^{\infty} \Psi(x) f(x)\, dx \tag{4.15}$$

where $\Psi(x)$ is some function. The Monte Carlo **importance** estimate is then

$$\psi^* = \frac{1}{m} \sum_{i=1}^{m} w_i^* \Psi(X_i^*) \tag{4.16}$$

which is unbiased, i.e., $E(\psi^*) = \psi$. Its standard deviation is

$$\text{sd}(\psi^*) = \frac{\sigma}{\sqrt{m}} \quad \text{where} \quad \sigma^2 = \int_{-\infty}^{\infty} \frac{\Psi^2(x) f^2(x)}{g(x)}\, dx - \psi^2. \tag{4.17}$$

These results are verified in Section 4.7. By selecting $g(x)$ judiciously we hope to bring σ down.

4.4.3 Choice of importance distribution

Usually $g(x)$ is chosen so that it is positive in exactly the same region as $f(x)$. Otherwise the choice is free, albeit delicate. Bad selections improve matters little and unfortunate ones make them worse. If $\Psi(x) \geq 0$, the best way *in theory* is

$$g(x) = \psi^{-1}\Psi(x)f(x),$$

a density function by virtue of (4.15) which makes ψ the normalizing constant. To see why this is best, insert $g(x)$ into the integral defining σ^2 in (4.17) right. Then

$$\sigma^2 = \psi \int_{-\infty}^{\infty} \Psi(x)f(x)dx - \psi^2 = \psi^2 - \psi^2 = 0;$$

i.e., no simulation uncertainty at all!

That can't be a practical proposition, but it provides some guidance, and it suggests that the improvements could be huge if we are able to imitate the ideal choice. For example, suppose

$$\Psi(x) = I(x > a)$$

where $I(A)$ is the indicator function (1 if A is true and 0 otherwise). This means that $\psi = \Pr(X \geq a)$, and the 'optimum' result reveals that simulations exceeding a should be made more likely than they are. Good design is more than this. Usually X is a vector $\boldsymbol{X}$ of many variables leading to weights depending on many density functions multiplied together; see below. This is an unstable situation with small changes having a huge impact. Effective use of importance sampling requires insight.

4.4.4 Importance sampling in property insurance

The portfolio loss $\mathcal{X}$ in general insurance is often needed far out into the right tail, a situation for the importance sampler. Consider the ordinary Monte Carlo simulation

$$\mathcal{X}^* = H(Z_1^*) + \cdots + H(Z_{\mathcal{N}^*}^*)$$

where $\mathcal{N}^*$ is the count and $Z_1^*, Z_2^*, \ldots$ the claims (here assumed identical). We seek a setup that makes large losses more frequent than they are. Both claim numbers and claim size might be manipulated, but it is *not* a good idea to generate additional losses since much extra computer time would be needed to draw them.

A better way is to keep the distribution of $\mathcal{N}$ and change the density function of Z from $f(z)$ to $g(z)$. The probabilities of n claims of size $z_1, \ldots, z_n$ then become

$$\underbrace{\Pr(\mathcal{N} = n)f(z_1)\cdots f(z_n)}_{\text{true model}} \quad \text{and} \quad \underbrace{\Pr(\mathcal{N} = n)g(z_1)\cdots g(z_n)}_{\text{importance model}}.$$

Algorithm 4.4 Insurance portfolio importance sampler

0 Input: Model for $\mathcal{N}$, $f(z)$, $g(z)$
1 $\mathcal{X}^* \leftarrow 0$, $w^* \leftarrow 1$
2 Generate $\mathcal{N}^*$ *%As in Algorithm 3.1*
3 For $i = 1, \ldots, \mathcal{N}^*$ do
4 Draw Z^* *%From $g(z)$*
5 $\mathcal{X}^* \leftarrow \mathcal{X}^* + Z^*$ *%Or add $H(Z^*)$*
6 $w^* \leftarrow w^* f(Z^*)/g(Z^*)$. *%Importance weight revised*
7 Return $\mathcal{X}^*$ and w^*.

These are joint density functions, and their ratio defines the importance weights. Suppose $\mathcal{N}^* = n^*$ is the number of claims. The importance weight is then

$$w^* = \frac{f(Z_1^*)}{g(Z_1^*)} \cdots \frac{f(Z_{n^*}^*)}{g(Z_{n^*}^*)}$$

where $Z_1^*, \ldots, Z_{n^*}^*$ come from $g(z)$. Note that the distribution of $\mathcal{N}$ drops out since it is common to both models. The importance sampler for portfolio risk is summarized in Algorithm 4.4. It is an extension of that in Algorithm 3.1, with the importance weight on line 6 as a new feature. To use the algorithm the weight w^* is as important as $\mathcal{X}^*$. The output $(\mathcal{X}_1^*, w_1^*), \ldots, (\mathcal{X}_m^*, w_m^*)$ from m runs is then entered in the importance estimate (4.16).

4.4.5 Application: Reserves and reinsurance premia

One application is to reinsurance of the form $\mathcal{X}^{\text{re}} = H(\mathcal{X})$. Consider the standard $a \times b$ type in Section 3.2 for which

$$H(x) = \begin{array}{ll} 0, & x \le a \\ x - a, & a < x \le a + b \\ b, & x > a + b; \end{array}$$

see (3.4). If a is large, the ordinary Monte Carlo approximation of $E(\mathcal{X}^{\text{re}})$ requires many simulations, and importance sampling may offer relief. Computation of ordinary reserves is another example. Now we seek the solution of the equation

$$\Pr(\mathcal{X} \ge q_\epsilon) = \epsilon \quad \text{or approximately} \quad \frac{1}{m}\sum_{i=1}^{m} w_i^* I(\mathcal{X}_i^* \ge q_\epsilon^*) = \epsilon,$$

where the sum on the right is the importance estimate of the probability on the left, writing I for the indicator function returning 0 or 1. The approximate reserve q_ϵ^* is determined by sorting the simulations with the weights carried along; i.e.,

$$\begin{array}{ccc} \mathcal{X}_1^*, \dots, \mathcal{X}_m^* & \text{ranked as} & \mathcal{X}_{(1)}^* \geq \cdots \geq \mathcal{X}_{(m)}^* \\ w_1^*, \dots, w_m^* & \text{reordered as} & w_{[1]}^*, \dots, w_{[m]}^* \end{array}$$

so that $\mathcal{X}_{(i)}^*$ is attached the same weight $w_{[i]}^*$ as before. Numerical routines for such sorting are available in many software packages; see, for example, Press *et al.* (2007). This leads to

$$q_\epsilon^* = \mathcal{X}_{(i^*)}^* \quad \text{where} \quad i^* = \min\{i | w_{[1]}^* + \cdots + w_{[i]}^* \geq m\epsilon\} \tag{4.18}$$

and the weights of the largest simulations are added until they exceed $m\epsilon$; consult the exercises for R-programs.

4.4.6 Example: A Pareto portfolio

To illustrate how importance sampling is implemented, suppose $Z \sim \text{Pareto}(\alpha,\beta)$ and let the importance distribution be Pareto(α_1,β_1). Then

$$f(z) = \frac{\alpha/\beta}{(1 + z/\beta)^{1+\alpha}} \quad \text{and} \quad g(z) = \frac{\alpha_1/\beta_1}{(1 + z/\beta_1)^{1+\alpha_1}}$$

so that

$$\frac{f(z)}{g(z)} = \frac{\alpha\beta_1}{\alpha_1\beta} \cdot \frac{(1 + z/\beta_1)^{1+\alpha_1}}{(1 + z/\beta)^{1+\alpha}},$$

which defines the weight on Line 6 in Algorithm 4.4. The choice of α_1 and β_1 is a pragmatic one; i.e., find a pair that works! Some experimentation suggested that a possible choice could be

$$\alpha_1 = \frac{3}{4} + \frac{\alpha}{4} \quad \text{and} \quad \beta_1 = \frac{\beta}{2},$$

which performed well under many circumstances. If $\alpha > 1$, then $\alpha_1 < \alpha$ and $f(z)/g(z)$ is bounded as z is varied. The importance weights are then bounded too, and they should be! If they are not, look at the setup with suspicion; importance distributions should *not* have lighter tails than the true ones. The design of importance schemes is analysed theoretically in Asmussen and Glynn (2007), but the proposal is outside their recommendations.

Numerical experiments are shown in Table 4.2 for a Poisson/Pareto portfolio. The parameters were $\lambda = 10$, $\alpha = 3$ and $\beta = 2$ with unlimited cedent responsibility. Calculations of cedent reserve (no reinsurance) are on the left and reinsurance premia under $a \times b$ contracts on the aggregate $\mathcal{X}$ (with $b = 150$ and a varied) on the right. All evaluations (whether standard or importance) were based on $m = 10\,000$ simulations. To examine the simulation uncertainty, each experiment was repeated 1000 times and the Monte Carlo standard deviation estimated.

Table 4.2 Standard deviation (% of estimate) of Monte Carlo evaluations of ordinary reserves (*left*) and reinsurance premia (*right*) for a Pareto portfolio

1000 *replications for each round of simulations*

	Reserve (no reinsurance)			Reinsurance premium		
Conditions varied	95%	99%	99.97%	$a = 30$	$a = 50$	$a = 100$
Estimated values	21.0	30.6	73.8	0.105	0.025	0.0047
	Estimated standard deviation in % of estimate					
Ordinary Monte Carlo	1.12	2.29	5.0	17.4	48.7	13.7
Importance sampler	0.69	0.83	0.51	3.3	6.1	12.5

It is given as a percentage of the true values in the lower half of Table 4.2. Importance sampling *is* an improvement, but it ran about 50% slower and took more work to implement. Whether that is worthwhile may be open to question, but for the reinsurance example on the very right in Table 4.2 it would take $(137/12.5)^2 \doteq 1000$ as many simulations to obtain the same accuracy with ordinary Monte Carlo (the computer time would be 500 times longer). Usually there is more to gain by importance methods the rarer the events, as illustrated in Table 4.2.

4.5 Control variables

4.5.1 Introduction

Monte Carlo evaluation of $E(X)$ may benefit from the decomposition

$$E(X) = \underbrace{E(\tilde{X})}_{\textit{mathematics}} + \underbrace{E(X - \tilde{X})}_{\textit{sampling}} \tag{4.19}$$

where $\tilde{X}$ is a second random variable to be constructed. The idea is to sample $X - \tilde{X}$ instead of X and supply a mathematical formula for $E(\tilde{X})$. For this to be effective $\tilde{X}$ and X must correlate strongly to make the uncertainty of $X - \tilde{X}$ smaller than in X. More sophisticated versions of the scheme (4.19) are discussed in Jäckel (2002) and Glasserman (2004).

The effect of introducing such a **control variable** $\tilde{X}$ can be electric, but disadvantages are the same as with importance sampling. Implementation may be tricky and time-consuming, and new situations must be rethought from scratch. Good design requires $E(\tilde{X})$ to be tractable mathematically while $\tilde{X}$ and X are correlated, the stronger the better. The approach is successful with options on equity portfolios, and much of this section is concerned with this example.

4.5.2 The control method and reinsurance

Reinsurer premia provide simple examples of control schemes. Let $\mathcal{X}^{\rm re}$ and $\mathcal{X}^{\rm ce}$ be reinsurer and cedent (net) responsibility; see Section 3.2. Their sum $\mathcal{X}^{\rm re}+\mathcal{X}^{\rm ce}=\mathcal{X}$ is the total claim against the cedent portfolio with mean $E(\mathcal{X})=\lambda\xi_z$, where $\lambda=E(\mathcal{N})$ is the expected number of claims and $\xi_z=E(Z)$ the expected loss per claim; see Section 6.3. It follows that $\mathcal{X}$ may be used as a control variable for $\pi^{\rm re}=E(\mathcal{X}^{\rm re})$ since

$$E(\mathcal{X}^{\rm re})=E(\mathcal{X})+E(\mathcal{X}^{\rm re}-\mathcal{X})=\lambda\xi_z-E(\mathcal{X}^{\rm ce}),$$

and the expectations may be computed from simulations of either $\mathcal{X}^{\rm re}$ or $\mathcal{X}^{\rm ce}$ so that the one with the smallest variance can be chosen.

As an example, suppose $\mathcal{X}^{\rm re}=H(\mathcal{X})$ and let $\mathcal{X}_1^*,\dots,\mathcal{X}_m^*$ be simulations of $\mathcal{X}$. The Monte Carlo approximations of $\pi^{\rm re}$ and $\pi^{\rm ce}=E(\mathcal{X}^{\rm ce})$ are then linked through

$$\overline{\pi}^{\rm re*}=\lambda\xi_z-\overline{\pi}^{\rm ce*}\quad\text{where}\quad\overline{\pi}^{\rm ce*}=\frac{1}{m}\sum_{i=1}^{m}\{\mathcal{X}_i^*-H(\mathcal{X}_i^*)\},\tag{4.20}$$

which is a control scheme for $\pi^{\rm re}$. Which of $\mathcal{X}^{\rm ce}$ or $\mathcal{X}^{\rm re}$ it is best to simulate depends on the contract; consult the exercises for numerical illustrations.

4.5.3 Control scheme with equity options

Control variables are well established for Monte Carlo pricing of equity options (Glasserman, 2004). The payoff X has, under the risk-neutral model Q, the representation

$$X=H(\mathcal{R})\quad\text{where}\quad\mathcal{R}=\sum_{j=1}^{J}w_jR_j,\quad R_j=e^{rT-\sigma_j^2T/2+\sigma_j\sqrt{T}\varepsilon_j}-1$$

and $w_1+\cdots+w_J=1$; see (3.19) in Section 3.5. We seek $\pi=e^{-rT}E(\mathcal{X})$ when $\varepsilon_1,\dots,\varepsilon_J$ are $N(0,1)$ with correlations $\rho_{ij}=\text{cor}(\varepsilon_j,\varepsilon_j)$. Monte Carlo is needed when $J>1$.

A possible control variable is $\tilde{X}=H(\tilde{\mathcal{R}})$, where $\tilde{\mathcal{R}}$ is the return of a stock index constructed from the original assets with the idea of making $X-\tilde{X}$ small. The following scheme is motivated in Section 4.7. Let

$$\tilde{\mathcal{R}}=e^{\tilde{r}T-\frac{1}{2}\tilde{\sigma}^2T+\tilde{\sigma}\sqrt{T}\tilde{\varepsilon}}-1\quad\text{and}\quad\tilde{\varepsilon}=\frac{1}{\tilde{\sigma}}\sum_{j=1}^{J}w_j\sigma_j\varepsilon_j\tag{4.21}$$

where

$$\tilde{\sigma}^2=\sum_{i=1}^{J}\sum_{j=1}^{J}w_iw_j\sigma_i\sigma_j\rho_{ij}\quad\text{and}\quad\tilde{r}=r+\frac{1}{2}(\tilde{\sigma}^2-\sum_{j=1}^{J}w_j\sigma_j^2).\tag{4.22}$$

Algorithm 4.5 Control scheme for equity options

0 Input: T, r, $\sigma_1, \dots, \sigma_J$, $w_1, \dots, w_J$, ρ_{ij}, $\tilde{\sigma}$ and $\tilde{r}$ from (4.22)
1 $\mathcal{R}^* \leftarrow 0$, $Z^* \leftarrow 0$
2 Generate $\varepsilon_1^*, \dots, \varepsilon_J^*$ %**Correlated**, *Algorithm 2.8 or as in Section 5.4*
3 For $j = 1, \dots, J$ do
4 $\quad \mathcal{R}^* \leftarrow \mathcal{R}^* + w_j(e^{rT-\sigma_j^2T/2+\sigma_j\sqrt{T}\varepsilon_j^*} - 1)$ %*Asset j added to portfolio return*
5 $\quad Z^* \leftarrow Z^* + w_j\sigma_j\varepsilon_j^*$ %*Z^* simulation of $Z = \tilde{\sigma}\tilde{\varepsilon}$*
6 $\tilde{R}^* \leftarrow e^{\tilde{r}T-\tilde{\sigma}^2T/2+Z^*\sqrt{T}} - 1$ %*Return of the control asset*
7 $\tilde{X}^* \leftarrow H(\tilde{\mathcal{R}}^*)$ and $X^* \leftarrow H(\mathcal{R}^*)$ %*With put options: If $\mathcal{R}^* < r_g$ then $\tilde{X}^* \leftarrow r_g - \tilde{\mathcal{R}}^*$ else $\tilde{X}^* \leftarrow 0$, similar for X^**
8 Return $\tilde{X}^* - X^*$.

It follows from (A.21) in Table A.2 in Appendix A that $\tilde{\sigma} = \text{sd}(\sum_j w_j\sigma_j\varepsilon_j)$. Hence $\tilde{\varepsilon} \sim N(0,1)$, and $\tilde{\pi} = e^{-\tilde{r}T}E(\tilde{X})$ is an option price for which formulae like Black–Scholes are available when $\tilde{\sigma}$ and $\tilde{r}$ replace σ and r. This yields the control scheme

$$\pi = e^{(\tilde{r}-r)T}\tilde{\pi} + e^{-rT}E(X - \tilde{X}) \tag{4.23}$$

with implementation in Algorithm 4.5, which is Algorithm 3.5 with the control part added. The mean of m simulations of $\tilde{X} - X$ approximates $E(\tilde{X} - X)$ in (4.23).

4.5.4 Example: Put options

Consider a put option with guaranteed return r_g. With $\tilde{\sigma}$ and $\tilde{r}$ defined in (4.22), the Black–Scholes formula (3.16) yields

$$\tilde{\pi} = (1 + r_g)e^{-\tilde{r}T}\Phi(\tilde{a}) - \Phi(\tilde{a} - \tilde{\sigma}) \quad \text{where} \quad \tilde{a} = \frac{\log(1 + r_g) - \tilde{r}T + \tilde{\sigma}^2T/2}{\tilde{\sigma}\sqrt{T}}.$$

The control method in Table 4.3 has been tested on the equity portfolio of Section 3.5. There are four equicorrelated equities (correlations $\rho = 0.5$), common volatility (varied), the guaranteed rate $r_g = 7\%$ and the risk-free rate $r = 4\%$. Time to expiry was $T = 1$. Note that the Monte Carlo standard deviation reported in Table 4.1 is a percentage of the true option price. The experiments were carried out by *repeating* the Monte Carlo evaluations 1000 times and computing the standard deviation of these 1000 different evaluations.

Control schemes work! With little extra computational effort the Monte Carlo error is cut by factors ranging from 12 to 40. To achieve the same accuracy with ordinary Monte Carlo, the size of the experiments would have to go up by $12^2 \doteq 150$ or $40^2 = 1600$! Improvements are largest for small values of the volatility, a fact suggested by the mathematical argument in Section 4.7. The use of antithetic

Table 4.3 Standard deviation (% of estimate) when the price of a put option is Monte Carlo evaluated

1000 replications for each round of simulations

	1000 simulations used			10 000 simulations used		
Volatility (%)	10	20	30	10	20	30
True option price (%)	4.79	7.90	11.06	4.79	7.90	11.06
	Estimated standard deviation in % of true prices					
Ordinary Monte Carlo	3.76	3.78	3.75	1.11	1.18	1.17
Control variable	0.09	0.20	0.30	0.03	0.07	0.10
Antithetic variables	1.82	2.13	2.08	0.55	0.65	0.64

variables is added on the last line. This much simpler technique also shows worthwhile improvement over ordinary Monte Carlo. Consult the exercises to run experiments yourself.

4.6 Random numbers: Pseudo- and quasi-

4.6.1 Introduction

Uniform random numbers $U_1, U_2, \ldots$ are products of our software. Do we have to bother with their construction? The issue may look minor, yet many awful methods seem to have been employed in the past, see Ripley (2006) and Press *et al.* (2007). In a book on Monte Carlo techniques in finance, Jäckel (2002) urges users to check on the methods software vendors are using. Actually it is not such a bad idea to have some knowledge of this. Random numbers are not really random. With ordinary computers, how can they be? They *must* be created in some predetermined way, which violates randomness by definition. The point is that they *behave* as if they are, provided the design is a good one.

There is an additional reason for our interest. We saw in Chapter 2 that simulation error in ordinary Monte Carlo is proportional to $1/\sqrt{m}$. By employing so-called **quasi**-Monte Carlo methods this can in certain situations be pushed down to almost $1/m$, a much smaller number. In recent years this topic has attracted much interest in computational finance. One of the most popular and elegant schemes available will be introduced below.

4.6.2 Pseudo-random numbers

Among the most widely used methods for generating ordinary random numbers are the **linear congruential** ones. The numerical literature, such as Press *et al.* (2007), argues that these methods have stood the test if implemented properly. They are also simple. One of the *very* simplest is undoubtedly the integer recursion

$$I_j = aI_{j-1} \,(\text{mod } N), \quad j = 1, 2, \ldots \tag{4.24}$$

where a and N are integers. If you are not familiar with the modulus notation, (4.24) can also be written

$$I_j = aI_{j-1} - [aI_{j-1}/N]N.$$

Here $[x]$ is the largest integer $\leq x$, and the recursion operates by taking I_j as the remainder after subtracting from aI_{j-1} the largest integer having N as divisor. When N is a prime (an integer impossible to write as a product of other integers) and $0 < I_0 < N$, then $0 < I_j < N$ for all j and $U_j = I_j/N$ is a number between 0 and 1.

The sequence $U_1, U_2, \ldots$ behaves very much like an independent sequence of uniform drawings if a and N are chosen carefully. A good pair according to Press *et al.* (2007) is $a = 7^5 = 16\,807$ and $N = 2^{31} - 1 = 2\;147\;483\;647$. The choice is tested on the left in Figure 4.2. Each point has coordinates 'drawn' from this generator. They are spread out in a seemingly arbitrary fashion. Yet it is not difficult to imagine that methodology this simple has pitfalls! Notice that the entire sequence is foreseeable (hence the term **pseudo**-random). If it is rerun from the same start I_0, the very same sequence is obtained. Software usually offers a procedure to *select* I_0. This is useful with common random numbers (different simulations run from the same I_0) and when investigating Monte Carlo error (same experiment from different I_0).

4.6.3 Quasi-random numbers: Preliminaries

Quasi-random numbers are laid out in a more regular way than pseudo-random ones. Take a look at Figure 4.2 and the difference is evident. On the right (where $m = 100$ and $m = 1000$) the quasi-random points 'remember' earlier points and steadily fill in the unit quadrate better and better. Couldn't we simply use a completely regular grid, say a rectangular one, instead? Yes we could, but this approach becomes useless (requires too many points) in higher dimensions, and another disadvantage is that the number of simulations always has to be decided in advance. Quasi-Monte Carlo retains much of the flexibility of ordinary Monte Carlo, yet is within certain limits a good deal more accurate. The mathematics is quite sophisticated, and we shall have to be content with a cookbook presentation without proofs.

As with pseudo-Monte Carlo, integers remain the core of the technique, but now their **binary** representation is used. If that is unfamiliar ground, here is a crash course. Let N be an integer, at most $2^p - 1$, where p is the number of bits allocated to integers in the computer. Any such integer has a unique representation of the

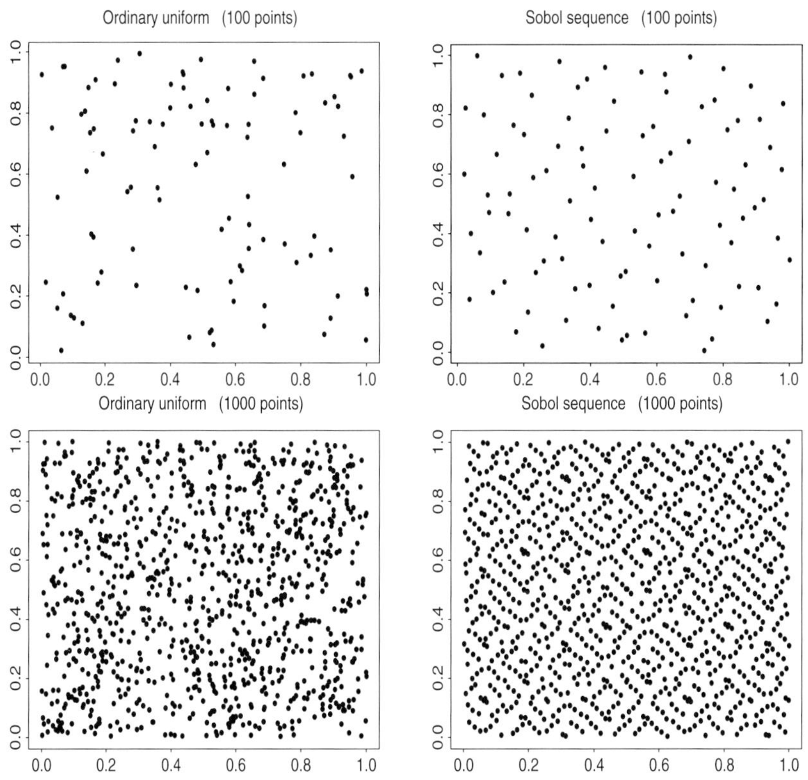

Figure 4.2 Ordinary uniform (*left*) and Sobol sequences (*right*) in two dimensions.

form

$$N = b_0 2^{p-1} + b_1 2^{p-2} + \cdots + b_{p-1}, \tag{4.25}$$

where $b_0, b_1, \ldots, b_{p-1}$ are **bits**; i.e., they are either zero or one. In the computer N is stored as the p-dimensional vector $(b_0, b_1, \ldots, b_{p-1})$. In the C language the default length is $p = 32$, meaning that integers up to $2^{32} - 1 = 4\ 294\ 967\ 295$ can be handled (larger numbers too if p is increased). We shall write

$$N = (b_0 b_1 \ldots b_{p-1})_2$$

to emphasize that we are dealing with a binary number system. Note that (4.25) is a representation in a well-defined mathematical sense. Different bit-sequences $b_0 b_1 \ldots b_{p-1}$ always yield different integers.

Quasi-Monte Carlo methods make use of the so-called **exclusive or** operation on bits. A shorthand name is **XOR** or $\oplus$. It is an intrinsic command in C and R can be carried out ultra-fast. Let N be the integer (4.25). Its XOR with $N' =$

Table 4.4 Coefficients of primitive, irreducible polynomials up to degree 5 (highest degree on the left) defining bit-sequences for Sobol numbers

Degree (d)	
1	(11)
2	(111)
3	(1101), (1011)
4	(11001), (10011)
5	(111101), (111011), (110111), (101111), (101001), (100101)

$(b'_0 b'_1 \ldots b'_{p-1})_2$ is then

$$N \oplus N' = (c_0 c_1 \ldots c_{p-1})_2 \quad \text{where} \quad c_i = \begin{cases} 0, & \text{if } b'_i = b_i \\ 1, & \text{if } b'_i \neq b_i. \end{cases} \tag{4.26}$$

In other words, exclusive or returns 0 for equal bits and 1 for unequal ones. For example,

$$N = 9 = (1001)_2 \quad \text{and} \quad N' = 12 = (1100)_2 \quad \text{yield} \quad N \oplus N' = (0101)_2 = 5.$$

The first and third bits (counted from the left) in N and N' have equal bits and lead to 0s in $N \oplus N'$, the two others are unequal and give 1.

4.6.4 Sobol sequences: Construction

The most popular of all quasi-random algorithms is arguably the Antonov–Saleev version of the Sobol sequence, for a lot of others consult Jäckel (2002). Sobol numbers have a setup and an execution phase. Setup starts from polynomials of the form

$$P(x) = x^d + a_1 x^{d-1} + \cdots + a_{d-1} x + a_d \quad \text{with} \quad a_d = 1,$$

where $a_1, \ldots, a_{d-1}$ are zero or one and $a_d = 1$. Such polynomials are in algebra called **primitive**. We are interested in the **irreducible** ones that can't be written as products of polynomials of lower order. These things are essential for the mathematics justifying the algorithms, but it need not concern us much (having dispensed with the mathematics already!). What *is* important is the polynomials at our disposal, or rather their coefficients. All possibilities up to degree 5 are listed in Table 4.4 with highest powers on the left. For example, the left polynomial of degree 3 is $x^3 + x^2 + 1$ and the one on the right is $x^3 + x + 1$. The number of different polynomials grows significantly with the degree d. More comprehensive tables are given in Press *et al.* (2007); see also Jäckel (2002).

A Sobol sequence is based on bits $a_1 a_2 \dots a_d$ of a primitive, irreducible polynomial of degree d. The bit of the leading power x^d (always one) doesn't count. For example if $d = 3$ in Table 4.4, the remaining bits are 101 and 011. The details of the next scheme follow Jäckel (2002). Choose d integers $v_1, \dots, v_d$ (considerable freedom here) and enter the recursion

$$v_j = \left[\frac{v_{j-d}}{2^d}\right] \oplus (a_1 v_{j-1}) \oplus \cdots \oplus (a_d v_{j-d}), \quad j = d+1, \dots, p. \tag{4.27}$$

The term $[v_{j-d}/2^d]$ is computed by shifting the $p - d$ *left*-most bits in v_{j-d} exactly d places to the right (so that they become the $p - d$ *right*-most ones) and filling the remaining d *left*-most bits with zeros. This integer is then XOR-operated with those of the preceding $v_{j-1}, \dots, v_{j-d}$ for which the corresponding bit a_j is one. Not easy to guess that this holds any interest! One possibility for the initial $v_1, \dots, v_d$ is

$$v_j = 2^{p-j}, \quad j = 1, \dots, d; \tag{4.28}$$

for other possibilities consult Jäckel (2002).

The integers $v_1, \dots, v_p$ now stored in the computer are known as the **direction** numbers and define the execution phase where integers $N_1, N_2, \dots$ are generated recursively through

$$\begin{aligned} j_k &= \text{position (from } \textit{right}\text{) of the right-most zero bit in } k, \\ N_{k+1} &= N_k \oplus v_{j_k}, \end{aligned} \qquad k = 0, 1, \dots, \tag{4.29}$$

starting at $N_0 = (00\dots0)_2$ (with p zeros). The quasi-random numbers are then

$$Q_k = \frac{N_k}{2^p}, \quad k = 1, 2, \dots, \tag{4.30}$$

which satisfy $0 < Q_k < 1$ for $k > 0$.

4.6.5 Higher dimension and random shifts

Applications often require quasi-random numbers in several directions jointly. A simulation using s different random numbers requires an s-dimensional version of (4.29). We then need s different sequences of direction numbers to yield s different sequences of integers. For direction i choose a primitive, irreducible bit-sequence $a_{i1}, \dots, a_{id_i}$ and generate direction numbers $v_{i1}, v_{i2}, \dots$ by means of (4.27). *Any* member of Table 4.4 will do (others too), but no two bit-sequences may be used twice (otherwise the quasi-random numbers become equal in two of the directions!). With the setup completed, enter the recursion

$$\begin{aligned} j_k &= \text{position (from } \textit{right}\text{) of the right-most zero bit in } k, \\ N_{ik+1} &= N_{ik} \oplus v_{ij_k}, \quad i = 1, \dots, s, \end{aligned} \qquad k = 0, 1, \dots,$$

starting at $N_{i0} = (00\dots0)_2$ for all i. There is now one recursion for each i with j_k being the same in all directions. This creates a coupling that is necessary for filling in quadrates and hypercubes regularly in all directions jointly. For the quasi-random numbers take

$$\mathbf{Q}_k = (Q_{1k}, \dots, Q_{sk}) \quad \text{where} \quad Q_{ik} = \frac{N_{ik}}{2^p}, \quad i = 1, \dots, s.$$

The test in Figure 4.2 was run for direction vectors constructed from $d = 1$ and $d = 2$.

Quasi-random numbers are not random, but **random shifts** make them. We then draw a *single* uniform s-vector $\mathbf{U}^* = (U_1^*, \dots, U_s^*)$ with $U_1^*, \dots, U_s^*$ being independent and uniform and change $\mathbf{Q}_k$ into

$$\mathbf{Q}_k^* = \mathbf{Q}_k + \mathbf{U}^* \pmod 1.$$

Is the notation unfamiliar? It simply means that each variable Q_{ik}^* is defined through

$$Q_{ik}^* = \begin{array}{lll} Q_{ik} + U_i^* & \text{if} & Q_{ik} + U_i^* < 1 \\ Q_{ik} + U_i^* - 1 & \text{if} & Q_{ik} + U_i^* \geq 1, \end{array}$$

ensuring values between zero and one. It is in fact easy to see that Q_{ik}^* is uniformly distributed. What is the point of the exercise? Answer: To retain the higher accuracy of quasi-randomness while forcing the estimates calculated to be unbiased if they would have been with ordinary Monte Carlo.

4.6.6 Quasi-random numbers: Accuracy

All algorithms in this book can be implemented with quasi-random numbers. Simply replace $U_1^*, \dots, U_s^*$ in ordinary Monte Carlo with $Q_{1k}, \dots, Q_{sk}$ or $Q_{1k}^*, \dots, Q_{sk}^*$. Theoretical performance is complicated material, but it *has* been established that error is at worst proportional to $\log(m)^s/m$, offering (for moderate s) huge improvements over the ordinary $1/\sqrt{m}$; see Glasserman (2004). But this is a conservative estimate, and the actual error could be much smaller. Indeed, successful applications for s up to several hundred and more have been reported. How well such methods work has also much to do with smoothness in how the random numbers are operated. Inversion sampling (usually smooth) is better suited than the rejection method with sharp discontinuity in how the random numbers are utilized. For the same reason percentiles go less well together with quasi-random sampling than do means and standard deviations.

With the latter, the Sobol sequences were outstanding when the experiments reported in Figure 2.1 were repeated. The model was (as before) normal with mean 0.005 and standard deviation 0.05, and Gaussian inversion was applied to

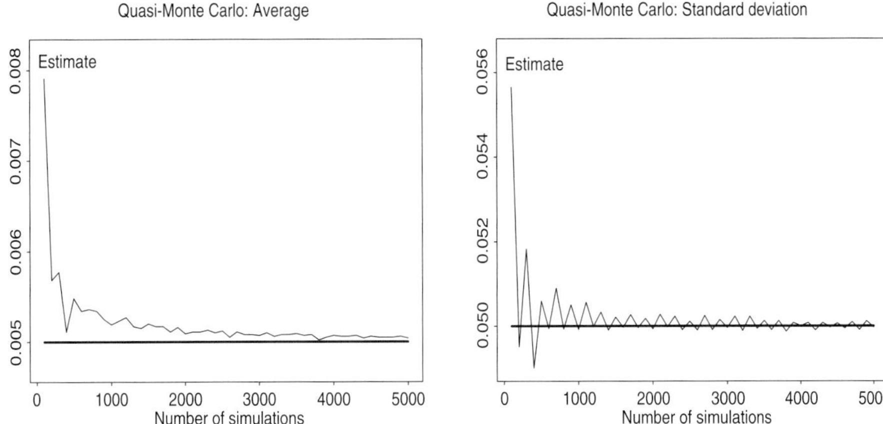

Figure 4.3 Sample mean and standard deviation against the number of quasi-Monte Carlo simulations to be compared with Figure 2.1.

the Sobol numbers. Sample means and standard deviations were computed for $m = 100, 200, \ldots$ up to $m = 5000$ and plotted against m in Figure 4.3. Direction numbers seesawed between those from $d = 1$ and those from $d = 2$ (it is this that causes the oscillating pattern to the right). If you compare with the plots in Figure 2.1, it emerges that the error has now become much smaller.

4.7 Mathematical arguments

4.7.1 *Efficiency of antithetic designs*

Let $X_1^*, \ldots, X_m^*$ be simulations with variance σ^2. For m even suppose $\mathrm{cor}(X_{2i-1}^*, X_{2i}^*) = \rho$ for $i = 1, \ldots, m/2$ with the rest of the pairs uncorrelated. The general variance formula for sums ((A.21) of Table A.2 in Appendix A.3) then yields

$$\mathrm{var}\left(\sum_{i=1}^{m} X_i^*\right) = m\sigma^2 + m\rho\sigma^2 = m\sigma^2(1+\rho)$$

since there are exactly $m/2$ correlated pairs. But for the mean $\overline{X}^* = (X_1^* + \cdots + X_m^*)/m$ it now follows that $\mathrm{var}(\overline{X}^*) = (\sigma^2/m)(1+\rho)$, which is (4.10).

4.7.2 *Antithetic variables and property insurance*

Let $(\mathcal{N}^*, \mathcal{N}^\dagger)$ and $(Z_i^*, Z_i^\dagger)$ for $i = 1, 2, \ldots$ be antithetic pairs so that

$$\mathcal{X}^* = \sum_{i=1}^{\mathcal{N}^*} Z_i^* \quad \text{and} \quad \mathcal{X}^\dagger = \sum_{i=1}^{\mathcal{N}^\dagger} Z_i^\dagger$$

are the antithetically simulated portfolio losses. Their conditional covariance given $(\mathcal{N}^*, \mathcal{N}^\dagger)$ is determined by the number of antithetic pairs. Indeed, the sums of covariance formula ((A.22) of Table A.2 in Appendix A.3) yield

$$\text{cov}(\mathcal{X}^*, \mathcal{X}^\dagger | \mathcal{N}^*, \mathcal{N}^\dagger) = \sum_{i=1}^{M} \text{cov}(Z_i^*, Z_i^\dagger) \quad \text{where} \quad M = \min(\mathcal{N}^*, \mathcal{N}^\dagger),$$

from which it follows that

$$\text{cov}(\mathcal{X}^*, \mathcal{X}^\dagger | \mathcal{N}^*, \mathcal{N}^\dagger) = M\rho_z\sigma_z^2$$

where $\rho_z = \text{cor}(Z_i^*, Z_i^\dagger)$ and $\sigma_z^2 = \text{var}(Z_i^*) = \text{var}(Z_i^\dagger)$. Moreover, if $\xi_z = E(Z_i^*) = E(Z_i^\dagger)$ then

$$E(\mathcal{X}^* | \mathcal{N}^*, \mathcal{N}^\dagger) = \mathcal{N}^*\xi_z \quad \text{and} \quad E(\mathcal{X}^\dagger | \mathcal{N}^*, \mathcal{N}^\dagger) = \mathcal{N}^\dagger\xi_z,$$

and the double rule for covariances ((A.26) of Table A.4 in Appendix A.3) yields

$$\text{cov}(\mathcal{X}^*, \mathcal{X}^\dagger) = E(M)\rho_z\sigma_z^2 + \text{cov}(\mathcal{N}^*\xi_z, \mathcal{N}^\dagger\xi_z) = E(M)\rho_z\sigma_z^2 + \text{cov}(\mathcal{N}^*, \mathcal{N}^\dagger)\xi_z^2.$$

Since $\lambda = \text{var}(\mathcal{N}^*) = \text{var}(\mathcal{N}^\dagger)$, we have

$$\text{cov}(\mathcal{N}^*, \mathcal{N}^\dagger) = \rho_n\lambda$$

where $\rho_n = \text{cor}(\mathcal{N}^*, \mathcal{N}^\dagger)$. Hence

$$\text{cov}(\mathcal{X}^*, \mathcal{X}^\dagger) = E(M)\rho_z\sigma_z^2 + \rho_n\lambda\xi_z^2$$

where

$$E(M) = E\{\min(\mathcal{N}^*, \mathcal{N}^\dagger)\} \le E(\mathcal{N}^*) = \lambda,$$

and, if $\rho_z \le 0$, then

$$\text{cov}(\mathcal{X}^*, \mathcal{X}^\dagger) \ge \lambda\rho_z\sigma_z^2 + \rho_n\lambda\xi_z^2 = \lambda(\rho_z\sigma_z^2 + \rho_n\xi_z^2).$$

Since $\text{var}(\mathcal{X}^*) = \text{var}(\mathcal{X}^\dagger) = \lambda(\xi_z^2 + \sigma_z^2)$ (which was used in Section 3.3 and is proved in Section 6.3), it follows that

$$\text{cor}(\mathcal{X}^*, \mathcal{X}^\dagger) \ge \frac{\lambda(\rho_z\sigma_z^2 + \rho_n\xi_z^2)}{\lambda(\xi_z^2 + \sigma_z^2)} = \frac{\rho_z + \rho_n(\xi_z/\sigma_z)^2}{1 + (\xi_z/\sigma_z)^2}$$

which is (4.13). As $\lambda \to \infty$, $E(M)/\lambda \to 1$ and the lower bound becomes an equality.

4.7.3 Importance sampling

To verify the statistical properties of the importance estimate (4.16), note that the expectation is

$$E(\psi^*) = E\{w_i^*\Psi(X_i^*)\} = E\left(\frac{f(X_i^*)}{g(X_i^*)}\Psi(X_i^*)\right) = \int_{-\infty}^{\infty}\frac{f(x)}{g(x)}\Psi(x)g(x)\,dx = \psi$$

since $g(x)$ cancels. The standard deviation (4.17) has the familiar form $\sigma/\sqrt{m}$ where

$$\sigma^2 = \text{var}\{w_i^*\Psi(X_i^*)\} = E\{(w_i^*)^2\Psi(X_i^*)^2\} - \psi^2,$$

and it follows that

$$\begin{aligned}\sigma^2 &= E\left(\frac{f(X_i^*)^2}{g(X_i^*)^2}\Psi(X_i^*)^2\right) - \psi^2 = \int_{-\infty}^{\infty}\frac{f(x)^2}{g(x)^2}\Psi(x)^2 g(x)\,dx - \psi^2\\ &= \int_{-\infty}^{\infty}\frac{\Psi(x)^2 f(x)^2}{g(x)}dx - \psi^2\end{aligned}$$

as claimed.

4.7.4 Control scheme for equity options

The sampling method for pricing basket equity options in Section 4.5 is now motivated. Start with the original returns

$$R_j = e^{rT-\sigma_j^2T/2+\sigma_j\sqrt{T}\varepsilon_j} - 1 = e^{rT}e^{-\sigma_j^2T/2+\sigma_j\sqrt{T}\varepsilon_j} - 1$$

and apply the approximation $e^x \doteq 1 + x$ with $x = -\sigma_j^2T/2 + \sigma_j\sqrt{T}\varepsilon_j$. This yields

$$R_j \doteq e^{rT}(1 - \sigma_j^2T/2 + \sigma_j\sqrt{T}\varepsilon_j) - 1 = e^{rT} - 1 + e^{rT}(-\sigma_j^2T/2 + \sigma_j\sqrt{T}\varepsilon_j).$$

It follows (since $w_1 + \cdots + w_J = 1$) that

$$\mathcal{R} = \sum_{j=1}^{J} w_jR_j \doteq e^{rT} - 1 + e^{rT}\sum_{j=1}^{J} w_j(-\sigma_j^2T/2 + \sigma_j\sqrt{T}\varepsilon_j)$$

or

$$\mathcal{R} \doteq e^{rT} - 1 + e^{rT}(-\overline{\sigma}^2T/2 + \tilde{\sigma}\sqrt{T}\tilde{\varepsilon})$$

where

$$\overline{\sigma}^2 = \sum_{j=1}^{J} w_j\sigma_j^2, \quad \tilde{\sigma}\tilde{\varepsilon} = \sum_{j=1}^{J} w_j\sigma_j\varepsilon_j.$$

But $\tilde{R}$ in (4.21) may be treated in the same way. After inserting $\tilde{r} = r + (\tilde{\sigma}^2 - \overline{\sigma}^2)/2$ then

$$\tilde{\mathcal{R}} = e^{\tilde{r}T - \tilde{\sigma}^2 T/2 + \tilde{\sigma}\sqrt{T}\tilde{\varepsilon}} - 1 = e^{rT - \overline{\sigma}^2 T/2 + \tilde{\sigma}\sqrt{T}\tilde{\varepsilon}} - 1 \doteq e^{rT} - 1 + e^{rT}(-\overline{\sigma}^2 T/2 + \tilde{\sigma}\sqrt{T}\tilde{\varepsilon})$$

and the linearizations of $\mathcal{R}$ and $\tilde{R}$ coincide.

The control scheme works when these approximations are accurate. This is for small volatilities, which lead to small exponents in the exponential functions with accurate linearizations that make $\tilde{\mathcal{R}} - \mathcal{R}$ small. The speed enhancement in Table 4.3 was most impressive for small volatilities.

4.8 Bibliographical notes

4.8.1 General work

Devroye (1986) is still an outstanding work on the generation of random variables with known distributions. Other useful, general books on stochastic simulation are Gentle (2003), Hörmann *et al.* (2004) and Ripley (2006). Jäckel (2002), Wasserman (2006), McLeish (2005) and Dagpunar (2007) are reviews from a financial point of view. Queues and networks are the principal applications in Rubinstein and Melamed (1998), while use in statistics is emphasized in Robert and Casella (2004) and Gentle *et al.* (2004). Theoretical analyses of simulation algorithms are developed in Asmussen and Glynn (2007) through probabilistic arguments. For additional elementary books, consult Section 1.7.

4.8.2 Special techniques

A prerequisite for table look-up is quick sampling of non-uniform, discrete probabilities. The guide table method due to Chen and Asau (1974) was used in Section 4.2; for other possibilities consult Devroye (1986) and Hörmann *et al.* (2004). Three of the other sections dealt with Monte Carlo variance reduction. A remarkably perceptive, early study is Hammersley and Handscomb (1964). Glasserman (2004) offers a thorough, more recent treatment with additional techniques that have not been included here. Antithetic variables (Section 4.3) go back at least to Hammersley and Morton (1956) and control variables (Section 4.5) to Fieller and Hartley (1954). Importance sampling (Section 4.4) is covered by a huge number of authors. Good expositions are found in Evans and Schwarz (2000), Glasserman (2004) and Ripley (2006). Design is analysed more deeply in Asmussen and Glynn (2007), and their theoretical study suggests exponential tilting for rare event simulation. In general insurance this means that losses are drawn from a density function of the form $g(z) = ce^{\theta z}f(z)$ for a suitable parameter θ instead of from the original $f(z)$. This may not work when the tails of $f(z)$ are

Algorithm 4.6 Metropolis–Hastings

0 Input: $f(\mathbf{x})$, $q(\mathbf{x}|\mathbf{y})$ and $\mathbf{X}^* \leftarrow \mathbf{x}_0$
1 Repeat
2 Draw $\mathbf{Y}^*$ from $q(\mathbf{y}|\mathbf{X}^*)$ and $P^* \leftarrow \min\left(\frac{q(\mathbf{X}^*|\mathbf{Y}^*)f(\mathbf{Y}^*)}{q(\mathbf{Y}^*|\mathbf{X}^*)f(\mathbf{X}^*)}, 1\right)$
3 Draw $\mathbf{U}^* \sim$ uniform and $\mathbf{X}^* \leftarrow \mathbf{Y}^*$ if $U^* < P^*$.

as heavy as for the Pareto model; see Asmussen and Kroese (2006) for such situations. Quasi-Monte Carlo is reviewed in Press *et al.* (2007) and from the point of view of computational finance in Jäckel (2002) and Glasserman (2004). The theoretical and mathematical side is covered in Niederreiter (1992).

4.8.3 Markov chain Monte Carlo

These algorithms (often designated **MCMC**) require powerful computers and have been gaining momentum. An entire scenario is through a single, recursive operation generated as the limit of a random sequence of vectors. The idea comes originally from statistical physics (Metropolis *et al.*, 1953) with a substantial improvement due to Hastings (1970). Although now developed much further, the early Metropolis–Hastings version remains the most common one, and Hastings' original article is still an excellent introduction. The method makes use of a family of *proposal* densities $q(\mathbf{x}|\mathbf{y})$ chosen quite freely. A simulation $\mathbf{X}^*$ from a given density function $f(\mathbf{x})$ is then obtained; see Algorithm 4.6.

Note that $\mathbf{X}^*$ does not always change during the iteration. The loop sets up a Markov process which is stopped when stationarity is reached. Not easy to guess that a simulated vector $\mathbf{X}^*$ from $f(\mathbf{x})$ then appears, but the proof is actually quite straightforward; see Ripley (2006). When to stop is a serious practical problem that has been researched extensively. There is also much to learn about design. Only ratios $f(\mathbf{Y}^*)/f(\mathbf{X}^*)$ count, which means that normalization constants drop out. This is often convenient and was crucial for the original applications by the Metropolis group.

4.8.4 High-dimensional systems

MCMC is meant for complex, high-dimensional stochastic systems of a kind encountered in statistical physics and in statistical problems in space and time. Some of the models in Sections 11.4 and 13.2 could have been fitted by MCMC. These methods are really means of last resort, and it is unlikely that they will ever play the role in actuarial science and finance that they do in (say) spatial statistics. Good references are Gilks *et al.* (1996), Liu (2001), Chib (2004), Robert and

Casella (2004), Ripley (2006) and even Hammersley and Handscomb (1964); consult also Gamerman and Lopes (2006) for Bayesian applications. Another iterative simulation method is **sequential** Monte Carlo as outlined in Doucet *et al.* (2001), which deals with complex simulation in time.

4.9 Exercises

Section 4.2

Exercise 4.1

(a) If $f(z) = 4ze^{-2z}$, $z > 0$, write a program setting up a discrete approximation over the interval $(0, b)$ with n points.

R-*commands*:

```
z=1:n*(b/(n+1)); p=z*exp(-2*z); p=p/sum(p).
```

(b) Compute the mean and standard deviation when $b = 10$ and $n = 1000$ and compare with the exact values $E(Z) = 1$ and $\text{sd}(Z) = 1/\sqrt{2}$.

R-*commands*:

```
Mean=sum(p*z); Sd=sqrt(sum(p*(z-Mean)**2)).
```

(c) Draw $m = 1000$ simulations from $f(z)$ and from the discrete approximation in (b) and compare through a Q–Q plot.

R-*commands*:

```
Ze=rgamma(m,2)/2; Za=sample(z,m,replace=T,prob=p);
qqplot(Ze,Za); lines(Za,Za).
```

Exercise 4.2 Let $\mathcal{X} = Z_1 + \cdots + Z_\mathcal{N}$ with $\mathcal{N}, Z_1, Z_2, \ldots$ independent, $\mathcal{N} \sim$ Poisson(λ) and $Z_1, Z_2, \ldots$ distributed as Z in Exercise 4.1.

(a) Use the program in Exercise 3.9 with $m = 10\,000$ simulations to compute the upper $\epsilon = 1\%$ percentile of $\mathcal{X}$ when $\lambda = 10$.

R-*commands*:

```
N=rpois(m,λ); X=1:m*0;
for (i in 1:m) {Z=rgamma(N[i],2)/2; X[i]=sum(Z)};
sort(X)[m*(1 − ϵ)].
```

(b) Redo for the approximation in Exercise 4.1(a).

R-*commands*:

Those in (a) with `Z=sample(z,N[i],replace=T,prob=p)` with z, p from Exercise 4.1.

(c) Redo (a) and (b) a few times and also for $\epsilon = 0.05$.

(d) Judge the quality of the discrete approximation.

Exercise 4.3

(a) Argue that a table look-up scheme for X inside (a, b) may be set up through

$$x_i = a + \frac{i(b-a)}{n+1}, \qquad p_i = \frac{f(x_i)}{\sum_{j=1}^n f(x_j)}, \qquad i = 1, \ldots, n$$

where $f(x)$ is the density function of X.

(b) Why may this be more efficient than drawing X from its original distribution and keeping those inside (a, b)?

Exercise 4.4

(a) Program a discrete approximation of X, given $a < X < b$, when $f(x) = cx^{\alpha-1}e^{-\alpha x/\xi}$.

R-*commands*:

```
x=a+1:n*(b-a)/(n+1); p=x**(α-1)*exp(-α*x/ξ); p=p/sum(p).
```

(b) Add commands computing $E(X - a|a < X < b)$ and $\text{sd}(X - a|a < X < b)$.

R-*commands*:

```
Mean=sum(p*(x-a)); Sd=sqrt(sum(p*(x-a-Mean)**2)).
```

(c) Tabulate these means and standard deviations for $\xi = 1$, $\alpha = 0.5$, $b = 50$, $n = 10\,000$ with a successively percentile 50, 75, 90, 99, 99.9, 99.99 and 99.999% of the original distribution.

R-*commands*:

With percentile $1 - \epsilon$ use `a=ξ*qgamma(1-ϵ,α)/α` prior to (a) and (b).

(d) Redo when $\alpha = 1$ and comment on the pattern.

Exercise 4.5

(a) Write a program drawing m samples from the discrete approximation in Exercise 4.4.

R-*commands*:

With `x` and `p` in Exercise 4.4(a) use `X=sample(x,m,replace=T,prob=p)`.

(b) Run the program when $\xi = 1$, $\alpha = 20$, $m = 10\,000$, $b = 50$ and $a = 0.5$, 1, 2 and 4 and each time Q–Q plot against the exponential distribution.

R-*commands*:

```
Y=rexp(m); qqplot(X,Y).
```

(c) What is the pattern as a is being raised? Consult Section 9.5 for the story.

Exercise 4.6 The **inverse Gaussian** distribution (possible model for volatility and insurance losses) has density function

$$f(x) = \sqrt{\frac{\theta}{2\pi x^3}} e^{-\theta(x-\xi)^2/(2\xi^2 x)}, \qquad x > 0$$

with $\xi, \theta > 0$. Sampling isn't immediate (nothing in R), but see Dagpunar (2007).

(a) Design a table look-up scheme with n points in $(0, b)$.

R-*commands*:

```
x=1:n*b/(n+1);
p=exp(-θ*(x-ξ)**2/(2*ξ**2*x))/x**1.5; p=p/sum(p).
```

(b) Plot the discrete density function when $\xi = 1$, $\theta = 1$, $b = 100$ and $n = 10\,000$, compute its mean and standard deviation and compare with the exact values $E(X) = \xi$ and $\mathrm{sd}(X) = \xi^{3/2}/\theta^{1/2}$.

R-*commands*:

```
plot(p,x); Mean=sum(p*x); Sd=sqrt(sum(p*(x-Mean)**2)).
```

(c) Redo when $\theta = 5$ and $b = 10$.

Exercise 4.7 Another distribution you won't find in R is the **extended Pareto** with density function

$$f(x) = c\frac{x^{\theta-1}}{(1+x)^{\alpha+\theta}}, \qquad x > 0$$

$\alpha, \theta > 0$ and c a constant. Mean and variance (when they exist) are $E(X) = \theta/(\alpha-1)$ and $\mathrm{var}(X) = (EX)^2(\alpha+\theta-1)/\{\theta(\alpha-2)\}$; see Section 9.4.

(a) Design a table look-up scheme with n points in $(0, b)$.

R-*commands*:

```
x=1:n*b/(n+1); p=x**(θ-1)/(1+x)**(α+θ); p=p/sum(p).
```

(b) Draw $m = 100\,000$ simulations when $\alpha = 5$, $\theta = 4$, $n = 10\,000$ and $b = 50$.

R-*commands*:

```
X=sample(x,m,replace=T,prob=p).
```

(c) Compute the mean and standard deviation of the simulations and compare with the exact values $E(X) = 1$ and $\mathrm{sd}(X) = 0.817$.

R-*commands*:

```
Mean=mean(X); Sd=sd(X).
```

Section 4.3

Exercise 4.8 Note that $X^* = (a+\varepsilon^*)^2$ and $X^\dagger = (a-\varepsilon^*)^2$ are antithetic simulations when $\varepsilon^* \sim N(0,1)$.

(a) Verify $E(X^*) = E(X^\dagger) = 1 + a^2$ and $\mathrm{var}(X^*) = \mathrm{var}(X^\dagger) = 2 + 4a^2$. [*Hint*: Utilize $\mathrm{var}(X^*) = E(a+\varepsilon^*)^4 - \{E(a+\varepsilon^*)^2\}^2$ and expand the powers. You will need $E(\varepsilon^{*4}) = 3$.]

(b) Also show that $\mathrm{cov}(X^*, X^\dagger) = 2 - 4a^2$ so that $\mathrm{cor}(X^*, X^\dagger) = (1-2a^2)/(1+2a^2)$.

(c) Discuss how this expression depends on a and the implications for antithetic sampling.

Exercise 4.9 The standard sampler for exponential variables is $X^* = -\log(U^*)$ with antithetic twin $X^\dagger = -\log(1 - U^*)$.

(a) Determine their correlation by Monte Carlo using $m = 100\,000$ simulations.

R-*commands*:

```
U=runif(m); Cor=cor(-log(U),-log(1-U)).
```

(b) How much will antithetic designs lower the standard deviation of Monte Carlo means for exponential variables? Compare with Table 4.1 for Pareto variables.

Exercise 4.10 Means of functions of log-normal variables in finance are often computed by Monte Carlo.

(a) Argue that antithetic designs yield pairs $X^* = e^{\xi+\sigma\varepsilon^*}$ and $X^\dagger = e^{\xi-\sigma\varepsilon^*}$ so that $X^*X^\dagger = e^{2\xi}$.

(b) Show that $\text{cor}(X^*, X^\dagger) = -e^{-\sigma^2}$. [*Hint*: Utilize that $X^*X^\dagger$ is fixed and that $E(X^*) = e^{\xi+\sigma^2/2}$, $\text{sd}(X^*) = e^{\xi+\sigma^2/2}\sqrt{e^{\sigma^2} - 1}$.]

(c) How does efficiency of antithetic sampling depend on σ?

Exercise 4.11 Consider the antithetic pair $X^* = \max(r_g - R^*, 0)$ and $X^\dagger = \max(r_g - R^\dagger, 0)$ where $R^* = e^{r-\sigma^2/2+\sigma\varepsilon^*} - 1$ and $R^\dagger = e^{r-\sigma^2/2-\sigma\varepsilon^*} - 1$ for $\varepsilon^* \sim N(0,1)$.

(a) Compute $\text{cor}(X^*, X^\dagger)$ using $m = 10\,000$ simulations when $r_g = 5\%$, $r = 4\%$ and $\sigma = 0.15$, 0.25 and 0.35.

R-*commands*:

```
ξq=r-σ**2/2; eps=rnorm(m); X*=pmax(1+rg-exp(ξq+σ*eps),0);
X†=pmax(1+rg-exp(ξq-σ*eps),0); Cor=cor(X*,X†).
```

(b) What is the potential of antithetic sampling when option premia are computed by Monte Carlo?

Exercise 4.12 With $\varepsilon_1^*, \ldots, \varepsilon_m^*$ simulations from $N(0,1)$, consider

$$\pi^* = \frac{e^{-r}}{m}\sum_{i=1}^{m}\max(r_g - R_i^*, 0) \quad \text{where} \quad R_i^* = e^{r-\sigma^2/2+\sigma\varepsilon_i^*} - 1, \quad i = 1, \ldots, m$$

which approximates the premium for a put option. Let $r = 4\%$ and $\sigma = 0.25$.

(a) Make $m_b = 10$ joint plots of π^* against r_g for $r_g = -2, -1, 0, \ldots, 6\%$ using $m = 10\,000$ simulations with $R_1^*, \ldots, R_m^*$ redrawn for each r_g.

R-*commands*:

```
ξq=r-σ^2/2; rg=(1:9-3)*0.01; π=matrix(0,9,mb);
for (i in 1:9) {eps=matrix(rnorm(mb*m),m,mb);
R=exp(ξq+σ*eps)-1;
π[i,]=exp(-r)*apply(pmax(rg[i]-R,0),2,mean)}; matplot(rg,π).
```

(b) Redo (a) when the simulated returns are kept fixed as r_g is varied.

R-*commands*:

Generate R prior to the loop in (a).

(c) Interpret the difference between the two plots.

Exercise 4.13 Let π^{re} be the reinsurance premium when $\mathcal{X}^{\text{re}} = \max(\mathcal{X}-a, 0)$ with the approximation

$$\pi^{\text{re}*} = \frac{1}{m}\sum_{i=1}^{m}\max(\mathcal{X}_i^* - a, 0)$$

where $\mathcal{X}_1^*, \ldots, \mathcal{X}_m^*$ are simulations of $\mathcal{X}$.

(a) Plot $\pi^{\text{re}*}$ against a for $a = 10, 11, \ldots, 20$ under the model in Exercise 4.2 when $m = 10\,000$ and $\mathcal{X}_1^*, \ldots, \mathcal{X}_m^*$ are kept fixed.

R-*commands*:

Draw `X` as in Exercise 4.2(a) and use `a=10:20; π^re=a; for (i in 1:11) π^re[i]=mean(pmax(X-a[i],0)); plot(a,π^re)`.

(b) Redo with $m = 1000$ and examine the discontinuities in the derivatives.

R-*commands*:

As in (a) with $m = 1000$.

Section 4.4

Exercise 4.14 Let $R_1^*, \ldots, R_m^*$ be simulations of the log-normal $R = e^{\xi+\sigma\varepsilon} - 1$ when ε is drawn from $N(\delta, 1)$ instead of $N(0, 1)$.

(a) Show that this yields importance weights $w_i^* = e^{-\delta\varepsilon_i^*+\delta^2/2}$ with $\varepsilon_i^* \sim N(\delta, 1)$.

(b) Write a program generating m_b sequences of such simulations and importance weights.

R-*commands*:

```
eps=matrix(rnorm(m*m_b),m,m_b)+δ; R=exp(ξ+σ*eps)-1;
w=exp(-δ*eps+δ**2/2).
```

(c) Run the program when $\xi = 0.05$, $\sigma = 0.20$, $\delta = -2$, $m = 10\,000$ and $m_b = 100$ and compute for $\epsilon = 0.01$ m_b approximations of the lower ϵ-percentile of R when $\varepsilon \sim N(\delta, 1)$.

R-*commands*:

```
q_ε=apply(R,2,sort)[ε*m,].
```

(d) Compare with the exact value −0.33984 under the correct distribution.

Exercise 4.15

(a) Convert the simulations in Exercise 4.14 to Monte Carlo estimates of the lower ϵ-percentile of the original distribution.

R-*commands*:

With `R` and w as in Exercise 4.14 use q_ϵ`=array(0,`m_b`);`
`for (i in 1:`m_b`){ind=sort.list(R[,i]); s=cumsum(w[ind,i]);`
`ii=length(s[s<m*`ϵ`]);` q_ϵ`[i]=R[ind[ii],i]}`.

(b) Run the program under the conditions in Exercise 4.14 when $\epsilon = 0.01$ and compute the mean and standard deviation of the $m_b = 100$ assessments of this percentile of R.

R-*commands*:

`Mean=mean(`q_ϵ`); Sd=sd(`q_ϵ`)`.

(c) Redo (b) when $\delta = 0, -1$ and -3 and determine when discrepancies from the true -0.33984 are smallest.

Exercise 4.16 Many theorists recommend as a measure of downside risk $C_\epsilon = E(R|R < q_\epsilon)$, known as the **conditional value at risk** (or CVaR).

(a) Argue that its importance estimate (4.16) is

$$C_\epsilon^* = \frac{1}{m\epsilon}(w_1^* R_1^* I_1^* + \cdots + w_m^* R_m^* I_m^*) \quad \text{where} \quad I_i^* = \begin{matrix} 0, & R_i^* \geq q_\epsilon \\ 1, & R_i < q_\epsilon. \end{matrix}$$

(b) Program an importance sampler using the setup in Exercise 4.14.

R-*commands*:

With `w` and `R` as in Exercise 4.14 use `I=R<` q_ϵ`;`
C_ϵ`=apply(w*R*I,2,mean)/`ϵ.

(c) Generate $m_b = 100$ evaluations of C_ϵ under the conditions in Exercise 4.15(a), compute their mean and standard deviation and compare with the exact value -0.38194.

R-*commands*:

`Mean=mean(`C_ϵ`); Sd=sd(`C_ϵ`)`.

(d) Redo for $\delta = 0, -1$ and -3 and determine the value minimizing Monte Carlo error.

Exercise 4.17 The preceding exercises were only for training, but consider the log-normal equicorrelation model

$$R_j = e^{\xi + \sigma(\sqrt{\rho}\epsilon_0 + \sqrt{1-\rho}\,\varepsilon_j)} - 1, \quad j = 1, \ldots, J$$

with $\varepsilon_0, \ldots, \varepsilon_J$ independent and $N(0, 1)$.

(a) If $\varepsilon_0, \ldots, \varepsilon_J$ are sampled from $N(\delta, 1)$, show that the importance weight is $w^* = e^{-\delta(\varepsilon_0^* + \cdots + \varepsilon_J^*) + (J+1)\delta^2/2}$.

(b) Write a program generating under $N(\delta, 1)$ simulated returns $\mathcal{R}_1^*, \ldots, \mathcal{R}_m^*$ of $\mathcal{R} = (R_1 + \cdots + R_J)/J$ with importance weights $w_1^*, \ldots, w_m^*$.

R-*commands*:

```
eps=matrix(rnorm((J+1)*m),m,J+1)+δ;
w=exp(-δ*apply(eps,1,sum)+(J+1)*δ**2/2);
eps=sqrt(ρ)*eps[,1]+sqrt(1-ρ)*eps[,1:J+1];
R=apply(exp(ξ+σ*eps)-1,1,mean).
```

(c) Run the program when $J = 4$, $\xi = 0.05$, $\sigma = 0.20$, $\rho = 0.6$, $\delta = 0.5$ and $m = 10\,000$ and compute the lower $\epsilon = 1\%$ percentile of $\mathcal{R}$ under the importance distribution.

R-*commands*:

```
qϵ=sort(R)[ϵ*m].
```

Exercise 4.18

(a) Use Exercise 4.17 to compute the lower percentile q_ϵ of $\mathcal{R}$ under the correct distribution.

R-*commands*:

Take `R` and `w` from Exercise 4.17 and use `ind=sort.list(R);`
`s=cumsum(w[ind]); ii=length(s[s<m*ϵ]); qϵ=R[ind[ii]].`

(b) Compute q_ϵ under the conditions in Exercise 4.17 when $\delta = -0.5$ and $\delta = 0$ and redo a few times to get a feeling for the simulation uncertainty.

(c) Utilize the R-function `e418c` (or write a program yourself) and compute the simulation mean and standard deviation of the importance estimate of q_ϵ when $\delta = 0, -0.25, -0.5, -0.75$ and -1 and find out which is the best choice.

Exercise 4.19 Let $\mathcal{X} = Z_1 + \cdots + Z_\mathcal{N}$ with $\mathcal{N} \sim$ Poisson(λ) and $Z_1, Z_2, \ldots$ independent and Pareto(α,β). Consider the importance distribution Pareto(α_1,β) with $\alpha_1 < \alpha$.

(a) Look up the Pareto density function and show that the importance weight for the sequence $\mathcal{N}^*$ and $Z_1^*, \ldots, Z_{\mathcal{N}^*}^*$ is

$$w^* = \left(\frac{\alpha}{\alpha_1}\right)^{\mathcal{N}^*} \left(\prod_{i=1}^{\mathcal{N}^*}(1 + Z_i^*/\beta)\right)^{\alpha_1 - \alpha}.$$

(b) Write a program generating m importance simulations of $\mathcal{X}$ and w.

R-*commands*:

```
N=rpois(m,λ); X=1:m*0; w=X; for (i in 1:m)
{Z=(runif(N[i])**(-1/α1)-1)*β; X[i]=sum(Z);
w[i]=(α/α1)**N[i]*prod(1+Z/β)**(α1-α)}.
```

(c) Run the program when $\lambda = 10$, $\alpha = 4$, $\beta = 3$, $\alpha_1 = 3$ and $m = 10\,000$ and compute the upper $\epsilon = 1\%$ percentile of `X` under the importance distribution.

R-*commands*:

```
qϵ=sort(X)[m*(1-ϵ)].
```

Exercise 4.20

(a) Write a program converting the simulations and weights in Exercise 4.19 to an importance estimate of q_ϵ.

R-*commands*:

With `X` and `w` in Exercise 4.19 use `ind=order(X,decreasing=T); s=cumsum(w[ind]); ii=length(s[s<m*`ϵ`]);` q_ϵ`=X[ind[ii]]`.

(b) Compute q_ϵ under the conditions in Exercise 4.19 using $\alpha_1 = 4$ and $\alpha_1 = 3$ and redo a few times to assess the Monte Carlo uncertainty.

(c) Use the R-function `e420c` and vary α_1 among 4, 3.5, 3, 2.5 and 2 and report when the simulation standard deviation is smallest.

Exercise 4.21 With $\mathcal{X}$ as in Exercise 4.19 let $\pi^{\text{re}} = E(\mathcal{X} - a|\mathcal{X} > a)$ for some threshold a.

(a) If $w_1^*, \ldots, w_m^*$ are the importance weights, convince yourself that the Monte Carlo estimate of π^{re} is

$$\pi^{\text{re}*} = \frac{1}{m}\{w_1^* \max(\mathcal{X}_1^* - a, 0) + \cdots + w_m^* \max(\mathcal{X}_m^* - a, 0)\}.$$

(b) How is $\pi^{\text{re}*}$ computed from the output in Exercise 4.19?

R-*commands*:

$\pi^{\text{re}*}$`= mean(w*pmax(X-a,0))`.

(c) Compute $\pi^{\text{re}*}$ when $a = 20$ under the conditions in Exercise 4.20.

(d) Use the R-function `e421d` to run a numerical study parallelling the one in Exercise 4.20 and select the best importance parameter α_1.

Section 4.5

Exercise 4.22 Let $\mathcal{X}^{\text{re}} = \max(\mathcal{X} - a, 0)$ be the reinsurer responsibility under the Poisson/Gamma portfolio in Exercise 4.2.

(a) Write a program computing the reinsurance premium.

R-*commands*:

With $\mathcal{X}$ as in Exercise 4.2(a) use $\mathcal{X}^{\text{re}}$`=pmax(`$\mathcal{X}$`-a,0);` π^{re}`=mean(`$\mathcal{X}^{\text{re}}$`)`.

(b) Run the program when $a = 5$ and $a = 15$ and redo a few times to examine simulation uncertainty or use the R-function `e422b` to evaluate the Monte Carlo standard deviation.

Exercise 4.23

(a) Design and program a control scheme for π^{re} and use it to recompute the reinsurance premia in Exercise 4.22 for $a = 5$ and $a = 15$.

R-*commands*:

Since $E(\mathcal{X}) = \lambda$, take $\mathcal{X}$ and $\mathcal{X}^{\mathrm{re}}$ from Exercise 4.22 and use

```
π^re=λ-mean(X-X^re).
```

(b) Redo (a) and (b) a few times to judge the simulation uncertainty or use the R-function `e423b` to compute the standard deviation more formally.

(c) Compare with the evaluations in Exercise 4.22 and verify that the best method depends on the threshold a.

Exercise 4.24 Consider a put option with payoff $X = \max(r_g - \mathcal{R}, 0)$ where $\mathcal{R} = (R_1 + \cdots + R_J)/J$ is the return of a portfolio of equally weighted investments. Suppose the risk-neutral model is $R_j = e^{r-\sigma^2/2+\sigma\varepsilon_j} - 1$ where $\varepsilon_1, \ldots, \varepsilon_J$ are standard normals with common correlation coefficient ρ.

(a) Deduce from (4.22) that $\tilde{\sigma} = \sigma\sqrt{\rho + (1-\rho)/J}$ and $\tilde{r} = r + (\tilde{\sigma}^2 - \sigma^2)/2$ in the control scheme in Section 4.5.

(b) Compute $\tilde{\sigma}$, $\tilde{r}$ and also the Black–Scholes price $\tilde{\pi}$ when $J = 4$, $\sigma = 0.25$, $\rho = 0.5$, $r_g = 0.04$ and $r = 0.04$.

R-*commands*:

```
σ̃=σ*sqrt(ρ+(1-ρ)/J); r̃=r+(σ̃**2-σ**2)/2;
a=(log(1+r_g)-r̃+σ̃**2/2)/σ̃;
π̃=(1+r_g)*exp(-r̃)*pnorm(a)-pnorm(a-σ̃).
```

Exercise 4.25

(a) Write a program simulating the payoff X of the preceding exercise.

R-*commands*:

```
eps=matrix(rnorm((J+1)*m),m,J+1);
eps=sqrt(ρ)*eps[,1]+sqrt(1-ρ)*eps[,1:J+1];
R=exp(r-σ^2/2+σ*eps)-1; ℛ=apply(R,1,mean); X=pmax(r_g-ℛ,0).
```

(b) Add commands so that the control variable $\tilde{X}$ is simulated too.

R-*commands*:

```
ε̃=σ/σ̃*apply(eps,1,mean); R̃=exp(r̃-σ̃**2/2+σ̃*ε̃)-1;
X̃=pmax(r_g-R̃,0).
```

(c) Use $m = 10\,000$ simulations to compute the option premium under the conditions in Exercise 4.24 and redo a few times to indicate Monte Carlo uncertainty.

R-*commands*:

With $\tilde{r}$ and $\tilde{\pi}$ from Exercise 4.24 use

```
π=exp(r̃-r)*π̃+exp(-r)*mean(X-X̃).
```

Exercise 4.26 Assume once more the model in Exercise 4.24.

(a) How can the simulated matrix `X` in Exercise 4.25(a) be used to approximate the option premium π? Use the R-function `e426a` to evaluate the Monte Carlo uncertainty of this method when $m = 10\,000$ simulations are used.
(b) Redo for the control scheme using the R-function `e426b` and report on how much lower the Monte Carlo uncertainty has become.

Section 4.6

Exercise 4.27
(a) Find out how the seed on your random number generator is controlled.
R-*commands*:
`set.seed(6534234)` with arbitrary input.

(b) Draw $m = 10\,000$ simulations of the log-normal $R = e^{\sigma\varepsilon} - 1$ from a fixed seed for 100 different values of σ between $\sigma_1 = 0.1$ and $\sigma_2 = 0.3$ and plot the Monte Carlo approximations of the upper $\epsilon = 1\%$ percentile against σ.
R-*commands*:
```
σ=σ1+(σ2-σ1)*(1:100-1)/99; qϵ=σ;
for (i in 1:100){set.seed(157894); R=exp(σ[i]*rnorm(m))-1;
qϵ[i]=sort(R)[(1-ϵ)*m]}; plot(σ,qϵ,''l'').
```

(c) Redo (b) with seed control removed and note how the plot changes.

Exercise 4.28 Consider the upper percentile q_ϵ of a Gamma variable with mean 1 and shape α.

(a) Controlling the seed as in Exercise 4.27, use $m = 10\,000$ simulations to compute q_ϵ for $\epsilon = 1\%$ as α varies between $\alpha_1 = 0.5$ and $\alpha_2 = 5$ in 100 equal steps and plot the approximations against α.
R-*commands*:
```
α=α1+(α2-α1)*(1:100-1)/99; qϵ=α;
for (i in 1:100) {set.seed(7465434); X=rgamma(m,α[i])/α[i];
qϵ[i]=sort(X)[(1-ϵ)*m]}; plot(α,qϵ,''l'').
```

(b) Redo (a) without seed control.
(c) Do you understand why there are Monte Carlo bumps in (a)?

Exercise 4.29
(a) Sample $m = 1000$ pairs of independent $N(0, 1)$ variables and scatterplot them.
R-*commands*:
`plot(rnorm(m),rnorm(m))`.

(b) Redo (a) when the pairs are quasi-random and compare.
R-*commands*:
Download `rnorm.sobol` and use `X=rnorm.sobol(m,2);`
`plot(X[,1],X[,2])`.

Exercise 4.30 Redo Exercise 4.29 for log-normal returns $R = e^{\xi+\sigma\varepsilon} - 1$.

(a) Scatterplot $m = 1000$ independent random pairs when $\xi = 0.05$ and $\sigma = 0.25$.

R-*commands*:

```
eps=matrix(rnorm(2*m),m,2)-1; R=exp(ξ+σ*eps)-1;
plot(R[,1],R[,2]).
```

(b) Redo (a) for quasi-random pairs and note the change.

R-*commands*:

`eps=rnorm.sobol(m,2)` with the rest as in (a).

Exercise 4.31

(a) Generate $m_b = 10$ batches of $m = 10\,000$ realizations from the standard normal, convert them to financial returns through the model in Exercise 4.30 and compute $m_b = 10$ Monte Carlo approximations of the lower $\epsilon = 0.01$ percentile.

R-*commands*:

```
eps=rnorm(m*m_b); eps=matrix(eps,m,m_b);
R=exp(ξ+σ*eps)-1; apply(R,2,sort)[ϵ*m,].
```

(b) Redo for quasi-normal numbers.

R-*commands*:

`eps=rnorm.sobol(m,m_b)` and continue as in (a).

(c) Compare the accuracy of the evaluations with the exact value.

R-*commands*:

```
exact=exp(ξ+σ*qnorm(ϵ))-1.
```

Exercise 4.32 Consider log-normal assets $R_j = e^{\xi+\sigma\varepsilon_j} - 1$ with $\mathrm{cor}(\varepsilon_i, \varepsilon_j) = \rho$ for $i \neq j$ and let $\mathcal{R} = (R_1 + \cdots + R_J)/J$.

(a) Write a program converting an $m \times (J+1)$ matrix of independent $N(0, 1)$ variables to an approximation of the lower ϵ-percentile of $\mathcal{R}$.

R-*commands*:

With `eps` the matrix use

```
eps=sqrt(ρ)*eps[,1]+sqrt(1-ρ)*eps[,1:J+1];
R=exp(ξ+σ*eps)-1; 𝓡=apply(R,1,mean); q_ϵ=sort(𝓡)[ϵ*m].
```

(b) Compute q_ϵ when $m = 10\,000$, $J = 4$, $\xi = 0.05$, $\sigma = 0.25$, $\rho = 0.5$, $\epsilon = 0.01$ and repeat a few times.

R-*commands*:

`eps=matrix(rnorm(m*(J+1)),m,J+1)` prior to (a).

(c) Redo (b) using quasi-random numbers.

R-*commands*:

`eps=rnorm.sobol(m,J+1)` and then (a).

(d) Does quasi-random sampling offer an improvement? [*Hint*: The exact value is close to −0.3288.]

Exercise 4.33

(a) Draw $m_b = 10$ batches of $m = 10\,000$ uniform Sobol numbers and convert them to quasi-random Pareto variables when $\alpha = 3$ and $\beta = 1$.

R-*commands*:

Download `runif.sobol` and use `U=runif.sobol(m,`m_b`);`
`Z=(U**(-1/`α`)-1)*`β.

(b) Compare the mean and upper $\epsilon = 0.01$-percentile of each Pareto sample with their exact values 0.5 and 3.6416.

R-*commands*: `Mean=apply(Z,2,mean);` q_ϵ`=apply(Z,2,sort)[m*(1-`ϵ`),]`.

(c) Redo for ordinary Monte Carlo and compare with the results in (b).

R-*commands*:

`U=matrix(runif(`m_b`*m),m,`m_b`)` and the rest as before.

Exercise 4.34 Suppose $\pi = e^{-r}E(X)$ where $X = \max(R - r_g, 0)$ and $R = e^{r-\sigma^2/2+\sigma\varepsilon} - 1$ for $\varepsilon \sim N(0, 1)$.

(a) Write a Monte Carlo program evaluating π m_b times.

R-*commands*:

`eps=matrix(rnorm(`m_b`*m),m,`m_b`); R=exp(r-`σ`**2/2+`σ`*eps)-1;`
`X=pmax(R-`r_g`,0);` π`=exp(-r*)*apply(X,2,mean)`.

(b) Run the program when $r = 0.04$, $\sigma = 0.25$, $r_g = 0.04$, $m_b = 10$ and $m = 10\,000$ and compare with the exact value 0.0990487.

(c) Redo with quasi-random numbers and examine the accuracy now.

R-*commands*:

`eps=rnorm.sobol(m,`m_b`)` and the rest as in (a).

Exercise 4.35 Change the payoff in Exercise 4.34 to $X = \max(\mathcal{R} - r_g, 0)$ where $\mathcal{R} = (R_1 + \cdots + R_J)/J$ with the assets as in Exercise 4.32.

(a) Write a program approximating $\pi = e^{-r}E(X)$ by Monte Carlo.

R-*commands*:

Generate $\mathcal{R}$ as in Exercise 4.32(b) when $\xi = r - \sigma\frac{2}{2}$ and use `X=pmax(`$\mathcal{R}$`-`r_g`,0);`
π`=exp(-r)*mean(X)`.

(b) Run the program a few times when $r = 0.04$, $\sigma = 0.25$, $r_g = 0.04$, $\rho = 0.5$ and $m = 10\,000$ and compare with the exact value close to 0.07839.

(c) Redo with quasi-random numbers and note the outstanding accuracy.

R-*commands*:

Generate $\mathcal{R}$ as in Exercise 4.32(c) when $\xi = r - \sigma\frac{2}{2}$ and use `X=pmax(`$\mathcal{R}$`-`r_g`,0);`
π`=exp(-r)*mean(X)`.

5

Modelling I: Linear dependence

5.1 Introduction

Risk modelling beyond the most elementary requires **stochastically dependent** variables. The non-linear part of the theory, much needed in insurance, is treated in Chapter 6, and the topic here is linear relationships which are the main workhorse for financial risk. Two examples are shown in Figure 5.1. On the left, monthly log-returns on two equity indexes from the New York Stock Exchange (NYSE) are scatterplotted for a period of 25 years. They tend to move in the same direction and by related amounts. This is **cross-sectional** dependence; what happens at the same time influences both simultaneously. The dynamic or **longitudinal** side is indicated on the right. Equity returns $R_{0:k}$ accumulated over k months are plotted against k. They start at zero (by definition) and then climb steadily until the investments in 2001 were 10–15 times more valuable than at the beginning. A downturn (only partly shown) then set in.

The first part of this chapter concerns cross-sectional dependence with random vectors $\boldsymbol{X}= (X_1, \dots, X_J)$. Models for pairs were treated in Section 2.4, and their scatterplots in Figure 2.5 (look them up!) match the real data in Figure 5.1 left fairly well. It is those models that are now being extended to J variables. They play a main role in longitudinal modelling too, where the setup is a random sequence $X_1, X_2, \dots$ with X_k occurring at time $t_k = kh$. The value of the time increment h depends on the application. In long-term finance 1 year is often sufficient, yet much (and important) theoretical modelling applies when $h \to 0$. How models on different time scales are related is discussed at the end of the chapter.

5.2 Descriptions of first and second order

5.2.1 Introduction

Linear dependence among random variables $X_1, \dots, X_J$ is expressed in terms of covariances and correlations, among the first things you learn in statistics courses.

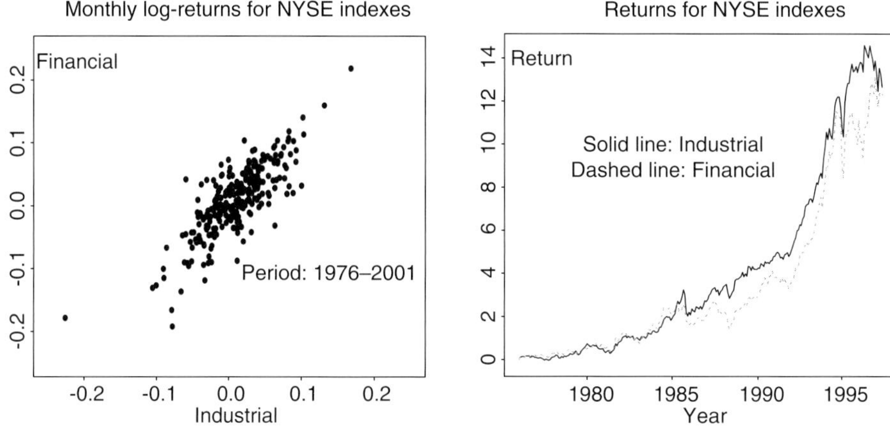

Figure 5.1 Monthly log-returns (*left*) and current returns (*right*) for two New York Stock Exchange indexes.

Write $\sigma_{ij} = \text{cov}(X_i, X_j)$ for covariances which reduce to variances $\sigma_{ii} = \text{var}(X_i)$ if $i = j$, and $\sqrt{\sigma_{ii}}$ (often σ_i earlier) are the standard deviations. Covariances (like variances) are used principally for mathematical derivations, and the real meaning usually resides in the **correlation** coefficients

$$\rho_{ij} = \text{cor}(X_i, X_j) = \frac{\sigma_{ij}}{\sqrt{\sigma_{ii}\sigma_{jj}}},$$

which are dimensionless quantities between -1 and 1. Variables with zero correlation are **uncorrelated**, which is a weak form of independence.

Covariance and correlation are statistical measures of **second order** (volatility too; expectations have order 1). They are intimately connected to linear modelling and pop up in linear relationships like those in Section 2.4. The correlation coefficient is arguably the most important single way of describing dependence, yet it works poorly in relationships that are strongly non-linear. An example is $\text{cor}(X, X^2) = 0$ if $X \sim N(0, 1)$. The correlation is zero despite one variable being fixed by the other! In Chapter 13 we shall be concerned with dependencies among volatilities, and these are not picked up by correlations at all.

5.2.2 What a correlation tells us

If $\text{cor}(X_1, X_2) = 0.6$, what does it mean? The unhelpful answer is that it depends on the situation. One point of view is **prediction**. Knowing $X_1 = x_1$ tells us something about X_2, and indeed the best guess under Gaussian models is

$$\hat{X}_2 = \xi_2 + \rho\sigma_2 \frac{x_1 - \xi_1}{\sigma_1} \quad \text{where} \quad \text{sd}(\hat{X}_2 - X_2) = \sigma_2\sqrt{1 - \rho^2}$$

and we have written ξ_1 and ξ_2 for the means and σ_1 and σ_2 for the volatilities. The underlying mathematics can be found in Section 6.2, and it also has much to do with the theory of **credibility** in Section 10.5. What interests us here is the prediction error $\hat{X}_2 - X_2$, and the fact that its standard deviation depends on ρ^2. Is $\rho = 0.6$ a 'large' correlation? Answer: Not very, since $\sqrt{1 - 0.6^2} = 0.8$ and knowing X_1 reduces the uncertainty of X_2 by no more than 20%.

But there is a second interpretation too. Let $X_1 = R_1$ and $X_2 = R_2$ be returns on financial assets with common volatility σ. An equally weighted portfolio has return $\mathcal{R} = (R_1 + R_2)/2$ with variance similar to (4.3); i.e.,

$$\mathrm{var}(\mathcal{R}) = \frac{\sigma^2}{2}(1+\rho) \quad \text{so that} \quad \frac{\mathrm{sd}(\mathcal{R})}{\mathrm{sd}(R_1)} = \sqrt{(1+\rho)/2},$$

which illustrates the effect of diversifying on two assets. The uncertainty does go down with ρ, but not fast. If $\rho = 0.6$, the portfolio volatility is nearly 90% of what it was with a single asset. An extension of this argument in Section 5.3 will lead to $\sqrt{\rho}$ as a rough measure of how financial risk reacts to changes in asset correlations.

5.2.3 *Many correlated variables*

With J random variables $X_1, \dots, X_J$ there are J variances and $J(J-1)/2$ covariances which are conveniently summarized in matrix form as

$$\boldsymbol{\Sigma} = \begin{pmatrix} \sigma_{11} & \cdots & \sigma_{1J} \\ \cdot & \cdots & \cdot \\ \cdot & \cdots & \cdot \\ \sigma_{J1} & \cdots & \sigma_{JJ} \end{pmatrix}, \tag{5.1}$$

known as the **covariance matrix**, in shorthand notation $\boldsymbol{\Sigma} = (\sigma_{ij})$. There is more to this than mere book-keeping. Consider the sum

$$\mathcal{X} = w_1 X_1 + \cdots + w_J X_J \quad \text{for which} \quad \mathrm{var}(\mathcal{X}) = \sum_{i=1}^{J}\sum_{j=1}^{J} w_i w_j \sigma_{ij}; \tag{5.2}$$

see Table A.2 in Appendix A.3. A first benefit of this identity is a purely mathematical one. Since variances can't be negative,

$$\sum_{i=1}^{J}\sum_{j=1}^{J} w_i w_j \sigma_{ij} \geq 0 \quad \text{for all } w_1, \dots, w_J. \tag{5.3}$$

Matrices $\boldsymbol{\Sigma} = (\sigma_{ij})$ satisfying (5.3) are known as **positive semi-definite**. They are **positive definite** if the inequality is strict everywhere except when $w_1 = \cdots = w_J = 0$.

Most covariance matrices encountered in practice are positive definite, for example the one estimated from historical data below. They can then be operated through the **Cholesky decomposition** from Appendix C.2 (a cornerstone when Gaussian vectors are simulated) and through their inverse $\boldsymbol{\Sigma}^{-1}$ (which is crucial for the portfolio theory in Section 5.3). Positive definiteness is more than just operational convenience. It tells us that there is an inner consistency in covariances and variances; certain combinations are not logically possible. We can't by judgement choose a value for some of them without thinking of the others. Linear algebra for covariance matrices is reviewed in Appendix B.

5.2.4 Estimation using historical data

Means, variances, covariances and correlations are typically estimated through their sample versions. If $x_{1k}, \dots, x_{Jk}$ are historical observations for $k = 1, \dots, n$, let

$$\overline{x}_i = \frac{1}{n}\sum_{k=1}^{n} x_{ik} \quad \text{and} \quad \hat{\sigma}_{ij} = \frac{1}{n-1}\sum_{k=1}^{n}(x_{ik} - \overline{x}_i)(x_{jk} - \overline{x}_j); \tag{5.4}$$

$\overline{x}_i$ and $\hat{\sigma}_{ij}$ are used as estimates of means ξ_i and covariances σ_{ij}. Variances are included as $\hat{\sigma}_{ii}$ and correlation coefficients as

$$\hat{\rho}_{ij} = \frac{\hat{\sigma}_{ij}}{\sqrt{\hat{\sigma}_{ii}\hat{\sigma}_{jj}}}. \tag{5.5}$$

We may organize $\hat{\sigma}_{ij}$ into a covariance matrix $\hat{\boldsymbol{\Sigma}} = (\hat{\sigma}_{ij})$ which is then positive semi-definite. To see this insert for $\hat{\sigma}_{ij}$ from (5.4) right and switch the order of summation so that k is taken first. This yields

$$\begin{aligned}\sum_{i=1}^{J}\sum_{j=1}^{J} w_i w_j \hat{\sigma}_{ij} &= \frac{1}{n-1}\sum_{k=1}^{n}\left(\sum_{i=1}^{J}\sum_{j=1}^{J} w_i w_j (x_{ik} - \overline{x}_i)(x_{jk} - \overline{x}_j)\right)\\ &= \frac{1}{n-1}\sum_{k=1}^{n}\left(\sum_{i=1}^{J} w_i (x_{ik} - \overline{x}_i)\right)^2 \geq 0.\end{aligned}$$

The inequality is strict **almost surely**, which requires mathematical measure theory to be treated rigorously. The practical point is that routine algebraic operations like inversion and Cholesky decomposition are most unlikely *not* to work when applied to estimated covariance matrices. If software crashes, look at your problem again. There are approximate linear relationships among the variables, and the number of them should probably be reduced.

Estimation error was discussed in Section 2.2, where the means $\overline{x}_i$ turned out to be hopelessly inaccurate for financial data. The chances are better with volatilities and correlations; more on that in Section 5.7.

5.3 Financial portfolios and Markowitz theory

5.3.1 *Introduction*

Traditional financial portfolio theory is an exercise in linear dependence and second-order descriptions. One example is the **Sharpe ratio** where financial risk is examined against a **benchmark** portfolio, typically a central index like the Dow Jones. If $\mathcal{R}$ is the return on the portfolio in question and $\mathcal{R}_b$ that on the benchmark, the Sharpe ratio is

$$\text{Sharpe}(\mathcal{R};\mathcal{R}_b) = \frac{E(\mathcal{R}-\mathcal{R}_b)}{\text{sd}(\mathcal{R}-\mathcal{R}_b)} = \frac{E(\mathcal{R}-\mathcal{R}_b)}{(\sigma^2+\sigma_b^2-2\rho\sigma\sigma_b)^{1/2}},$$

where $\sigma = \text{sd}(\mathcal{R})$, $\sigma_b = \text{sd}(\mathcal{R}_b)$ and $\rho = \text{cor}(\mathcal{R},\mathcal{R}_b)$. The criterion is in terms of the *surplus* return $\mathcal{R}-\mathcal{R}_b$ and looks favourably on portfolios highly correlated with the benchmark.

A deeper issue is portfolio *design*, the main topic of the section. Optimal portfolio selection was introduced by Harry Markowitz in the mid-twentieth century (see, e.g., Markowitz, 1952) and has held a prominent place in the theory of financial risk ever since. Deriving the 'best' portfolios tells us how effectively risk can be reduced by spreading investments over many assets, but the underlying parameters are hard to find which leads to much uncertainty if Markowitz portfolios are put to practical use.

5.3.2 *The Markowitz problem*

Consider J risky assets and their returns $R_1,\dots,R_J$ with expectations $\xi_1,\dots,\xi_J$ and covariance matrix $\boldsymbol{\Sigma} = (\sigma_{ij})$. There is also a riskless opportunity (a bank deposit) giving fixed return r. With weights $w_0, w_1,\dots,w_J$ the *portfolio* return is

$$\mathcal{R} = w_0 r + w_1 R_1 + \cdots + w_J R_J \quad \text{where} \quad w_0 + w_1 + \cdots + w_J = 1.$$

Short positions are permitted; i.e., weights may be both positive and negative. If w_0 is negative, money is borrowed in a bank. Portfolios are defined by freely varying weights $w_1,\dots,w_J$, the remaining one w_0 being fixed by the others.

The expected portfolio return is

$$E(\mathcal{R}) = w_0 r + \sum_{j=1}^{J} w_j\xi_j \quad \text{or} \quad E(\mathcal{R}) = r + \sum_{j=1}^{J} w_j(\xi_j - r) \tag{5.6}$$

after inserting $w_0 = 1 - w_1 - \cdots - w_J$, and the portfolio variance coincides with (5.2); i.e.,

$$\mathrm{var}(\mathcal{R}) = \sum_{i=1}^{J}\sum_{j=1}^{J} w_i w_j \sigma_{ij}. \tag{5.7}$$

The problem, as posed by Markowitz, is to obtain a high expected return while keeping the variance low.

5.3.3 Solutions

No specific solution is possible without a price on risk. A jump over that hurdle is to *specify* an expected gain e_g for the portfolio and let the issue be

$$\text{minimize } \mathrm{var}(\mathcal{R}) \quad \text{subject to} \quad E(\mathcal{R}) = e_g, \tag{5.8}$$

which is the minimization of the quadratic form (5.7) under a linear constraint, an exercise in linear algebra carried out in Section 5.8.

We shall deal here with the solution and what it tells us. The central ingredient is the portfolio with weights $\tilde{w}_1, \ldots, \tilde{w}_J$ determined from the linear system of equations

$$\sum_{j=1}^{J} \sigma_{ij}\tilde{w}_j = \xi_i - r, \qquad i = 1, \ldots, J \tag{5.9}$$

which has a unique solution if the covariance matrix $\boldsymbol{\Sigma} = (\sigma_{ij})$ is positive definite. This **Markowitz** portfolio can be intepreted as a market solution (Exercise 5.11), and with $\tilde{w}_0 = 1 - \tilde{w}_1 - \cdots - \tilde{w}_J$ the weight on the risk-free asset, the expected gain becomes $\tilde{e}_g = r + \tilde{w}_1(\xi_1 - r) + \ldots + \tilde{w}_J(\xi_J - r)$ as in (5.6). Numerical software (Appendix C.2) is needed to compute $\tilde{w}_1, \ldots, \tilde{w}_J$.

For the original problem (5.8) the optimal weights are

$$w_j = \gamma\tilde{w}_j, \quad j = 1, \ldots, J \qquad \text{and} \quad w_0 = 1 - w_1 - \cdots - w_J \tag{5.10}$$

with expected gain

$$E(\mathcal{R}) = r + \sum_{j=1}^{J} \gamma\tilde{w}_j(\xi_j - r) = r + \gamma(\tilde{e}_g - r),$$

and $E(\mathcal{R}) = e_g$ if $\gamma = (e_g - r)/(\tilde{e}_g - r)$. Note that the mean excess return $E(\mathcal{R}) - r$ and the volatility $\mathrm{sd}(\mathcal{R})$ are both proportional to γ so that their ratio $(E(\mathcal{R}) - r)/\mathrm{sd}(\mathcal{R})$ is fixed by the model. An investor pursuing a Markowitz strategy will shrink or expand the weights $\tilde{w}_1, \ldots, \tilde{w}_J$ to achieve the right mix of earnings and risk.

5.3.4 Numerical illustration

The optimum Markowitz weights are heavily dependent on the correlations and quite unstable. Here is an illustration with three risky assets. Suppose

$$\underset{\textit{expected gain assets}}{\xi_1 = \xi_2 = \xi_3 = 11\%} \qquad \underset{\textit{risk free}}{r = 4\%} \qquad \underset{\textit{expected portfolio gain}}{e_g = 10\%}$$

and introduce two covariance matrices

$$\mathbf{\Sigma}_1 = 0.25^2 \begin{pmatrix} 1 & 0.4 & 0.4 \\ 0.4 & 1 & 0.4 \\ 0.4 & 0.4 & 1 \end{pmatrix} \quad \text{and} \quad \mathbf{\Sigma}_2 = 0.25^2 \begin{pmatrix} 1 & 0.8 & 0.8 \\ 0.8 & 1 & 0.4 \\ 0.8 & 0.4 & 1 \end{pmatrix},$$

which differ in their correlations, but have the same volatility (25%). When the Markowitz solution $(\tilde{w}_1, \tilde{w}_2, \tilde{w}_3)$ is determined from the linear equations (5.9) and adapted to the desired $e_g = 10\%$, the weights on the three risky assets become

$$\underset{\textit{first covariance matrix } \Sigma_1}{0.2857,\ 0.2857,\ 0.2857} \quad \text{and} \quad \underset{\textit{second covariance matrix } \Sigma_2}{-0.8571,\ 0.8571,\ 0.8571}$$

and the effect of changing the correlations of the first asset from 0.4 to 0.8 is enormous. Yet the portfolio standard deviation turns out to be the same in both cases (the value is 16.60%). Is that counter-intuitive with $\mathbf{\Sigma}_2$ (higher correlations) seemingly more risky? The point is that short positions (negative weights) are allowed, and this absorbs the correlation differences.

5.3.5 Two risky assets

The form of the Markowitz solution for two risky assets signals a warning that applies generally. Let $\sigma_1^2 = \sigma_{11}$ and $\sigma_2^2 = \sigma_{22}$. The covariance is then $\sigma_{12} = \rho\sigma_1\sigma_2$ where ρ is the correlation coefficient. There are now two equations for the weights $\tilde{w}_1$ and $\tilde{w}_2$; i.e., from (5.9)

$$\sigma_1^2\tilde{w}_1 + \rho\sigma_1\sigma_2\tilde{w}_2 = \xi_1 - r \quad \text{and} \quad \rho\sigma_1\sigma_2\tilde{w}_1 + \sigma_2^2\tilde{w}_2 = \xi_2 - r,$$

and the solution when multiplied by γ gives the optimum Markowitz weights

$$w_1 = \frac{\gamma}{\sigma_1(1-\rho^2)}\left(\frac{\xi_1 - r}{\sigma_1} - \rho\frac{\xi_2 - r}{\sigma_2}\right), \quad w_2 = \frac{\gamma}{\sigma_2(1-\rho^2)}\left(-\rho\frac{\xi_1 - r}{\sigma_1} + \frac{\xi_2 - r}{\sigma_2}\right).$$

It is easy to verify that this is the solution. Remove γ and note that the rest is $\tilde{w}_1$ and $\tilde{w}_2$, which satisfy the defining equations when you insert them.

The factor $1 - \rho^2$ in the denominators is an important feature. Highly correlated assets blow the weights up, and their signs become opposite. Let $|\rho| \to 1$ and you'll discover that $w_1 w_2 \leq 0$, which means that one of the investments must be a

Table 5.1 Asset model and optimum portfolio of the LTCM fund

Time scale: Month

	Corporate bond	Treasury bond	Risk free
Mean	0.6107%	0.4670%	0.4361%
Volatility	1.58%	1.90%	
Correlation	0.9654		
Portfolio weights	19.66	−15.59	−3.06

large, short one. Even if the market is liquid enough to sustain such positions, there is something discomforting about it that hints at an inderlying instability. The following example, due to Jorion (2001), shows that this is indeed true. With more than two assets such effects may be even more disturbing; see Litterman (2003).

5.3.6 Example: The crash of a hedge fund

One of the more prominent collapses on Wall Street was that of the so-called LTCM fund (Long Term Capital Management) in 1998; see Ferguson (2008) for an entertaining account. An investment that contributed to the debacle was the use of highly correlated assets. Consider the bonds in Table 5.1. They expired on the same date, and one of them was a corporate bond that had both a higher expected return and a lower volatility than the treasury bond. A portfolio which was long in the former and short in the latter seemed a good bet as the price of the two assets inevitably had to converge when expiry came closer, hence the high correlation.

Does the situation call for an aggressive ('bull') strategy? The Markowitz portfolio is found by inserting the parameters into the expressions for w_1 and w_2 above. With $\gamma = 0.2228$ the weights become those in Table 5.1 (last row). The portfolio value is one money unit (add the three weights), but individual weights are very much higher and the short position is more than 15 times larger than the portfolio value itself! With the values of γ selected *monthly* expected return is a healthy 3.3869%, but the uncertainty is high too. Inserting the parameters from Table 5.1 into (5.7) yields monthly volatilities

$$8.1\% \text{ for } \rho = 0.9654 \quad \text{and} \quad 18.1\% \text{ for } \rho = 0.80;$$

see Exercise 5.7. Why the second calculation for the lower value of ρ? Because that was what the correlation dropped to in August 1998 (due to the so-called Russian liquidity crisis that hit the financial markets at that point). The volatility has suddenly gone up 2.5 times, and the position has become much more exposed. In practice it brought disaster.

Lessons are how unstably 'optimum' solutions perform for highly correlated assets and also that statistical parameters vary over time and the risk with them; more on that in Chapter 13.

5.3.7 Diversification of financial risk I

How far down does the Markowitz portfolio push financial risk when there are many assets available? The issue is nicely illustrated by the equicorrelation model. Suppose

$$E(R_j) = \xi, \quad \mathrm{sd}(R_j) = \sigma \quad \text{and} \quad \mathrm{cor}(R_i, R_j) = \rho$$

for $j = 1, \dots, J$ and $i \neq j$. The perfect symmetry means that Markowitz weights coincide for all the risky assets; i.e., $w_j = w$ for all $j > 0$, and the variance (5.7) adds

$$\underset{J\ terms}{w^2\sigma^2} \quad \text{and} \quad \underset{J(J-1)\ terms}{w^2\rho\sigma^2}$$

so that

$$\mathrm{var}(\mathcal{R}) = w^2\{J\sigma^2 + J(J-1)\rho\sigma^2\}. \tag{5.11}$$

Consider the alternative portfolio of a *single* asset (return $\mathcal{R}_1$). We must invest $w_1 = Jw$ for the same expected return, and the variance becomes

$$\mathrm{var}(\mathcal{R}_1) = J^2w^2\sigma^2.$$

These are optimum portfolios, and the ratio of their standard deviations conveys the effect of diversification; i.e.,

$$\frac{\mathrm{sd}(\mathcal{R})}{\mathrm{sd}(\mathcal{R}_1)} = \{\rho + (1-\rho)/J\}^{1/2} \to \sqrt{\rho} \quad \text{as} \quad J \to \infty.$$

For large J this is approximately $\sqrt{\rho}$, not a huge reduction (try $\rho = 0.5$), but within the model assumed that is the best we can do.

5.3.8 Diversification under CAPM

CAPM (Capitial Asset Pricing Model) is a widely used model with economic arguments in support. Under certain assumptions on the rational investor, the mean return of asset j must be

$$\xi_j = r + \beta_j(\xi_M - r) \tag{5.12}$$

for $j = 1, \dots, J$. Here β_j is a coefficient and $\xi_M = E(\mathcal{R}_M)$ is the expected return on the so-called market portfolio M; see Exercises 5.11 and 5.12. CAPM is the extension

$$R_j = r + \underbrace{\beta_j(R_M - r)}_{\textit{market risk}} + \underbrace{\tau_j\varepsilon_j}_{\textit{specific risk}} \quad \text{where} \quad \text{cor}(R_M, \varepsilon_j) = 0. \qquad (5.13)$$

Now ξ_j and ξ_M in (5.12) have been replaced by returns R_j and R_M and an error term $\tau_j\varepsilon_j$ has been added. The latter, known as the **specific** risk factor for asset j, consists of a volatility $\tau_j > 0$ and a random ε_j with no link to market fluctuations as a whole, so that $\text{cor}(R_M, \varepsilon_j) = 0$.

Standard assumptions are uncorrelated $\varepsilon_1, \dots, \varepsilon_J$ with mean zero and standard deviation one. Variances and covariances of $R_1, \dots, R_J$ then become

$$\sigma_{jj} = \beta_j^2\sigma_M^2 + \tau_j^2 \quad \text{and} \quad \sigma_{ij} = \beta_i\beta_j\sigma_M^2 \qquad (5.14)$$

as in Exercise 5.5. CAPM is of interest in its own right, but here the issue is risk diversification. It is proved in Section 5.8 that if $\mathcal{R}$ is the return of the Markowitz portfolio, then under CAPM

$$\text{sd}(\mathcal{R}) \geq \sigma_M \frac{|e_g - r|}{|\xi_M - r|}, \qquad (5.15)$$

and the best possible solution can do no better than the right-hand side of this inequality. If the expected return is higher than the risk-free one, risk is inevitable no matter how many assets we diversify on. Specific risk can be removed (as in insurance), the market risk not.

5.4 Dependent Gaussian models once more

5.4.1 Introduction

Let $\eta_1, \dots, \eta_J$ be independent and $N(0, 1)$ and define for $j = 1, \dots, J$

$$X_j = \xi_j + \varepsilon_j \quad \text{where} \quad \varepsilon_j = c_{j1}\eta_1 + \cdots + c_{jJ}\eta_J \qquad (5.16)$$

with ξ_j and c_{ji} parameters. There are as many X-variables as there are ηs. This is the general **multivariate Gaussian** model, a tool for much stochastic modelling. It is being developed here slightly differently from in Section 2.4, where the volatilities σ_j were explicit parameters. The review below comes with as little mathematics as possible; for proofs consult Appendix B.2.

5.4.2 Uniqueness

Are all the models in (5.16) different? The answer is no. What goes on follows from

$$E(X_j) = \xi_j \quad \text{and} \quad \sigma_{ij} = \text{cov}(X_i, X_j) = \sum_{k=1}^{J} c_{ik}c_{jk} \tag{5.17}$$

with $\text{var}(X_j) = \text{cov}(X_j, X_j)$ being the variances. The expectation is immediate since all random terms in (5.16) have mean zero whereas the covariances are consquences of rule (A.22) in Appendix A.3. Indeed,

$$\text{cov}(X_i, X_j) = \text{cov}(\varepsilon_i, \varepsilon_j) = \text{cov}\left(\sum_{k=1}^{J} c_{ik}\eta_k, \sum_{l=1}^{J} c_{jl}\eta_l\right) = \sum_{k=1}^{J}\sum_{l=1}^{J} c_{ik}c_{jl}\text{cov}(\eta_k, \eta_l)$$

which reduces to (5.17) right since $\text{cov}(\eta_k, \eta_l) = 0$ for $k \neq l$ and $\text{cov}(\eta_k, \eta_k) = 1$.

Let $\mathbf{C} = (c_{ij})$ be coefficients satisfying (5.17) right for a given covariance matrix $\mathbf{\Sigma} = (\sigma_{ij})$. Clearly $-\mathbf{C} = (-c_{ij})$ would too, and there are countless other possibilities. Which one is picked doesn't matter since all $\mathbf{C} = (c_{ij})$ satisfying (5.17) lead to the same model, not at all difficult to prove by means of linear algebra. What it says is that the Gaussian class is determined by the expectation vector $\boldsymbol{\xi} = (\xi_1, \dots, \xi_J)^{\text{T}}$ and the covariance matrix $\mathbf{\Sigma} = (\sigma_{ij})$.

5.4.3 Properties

The multivariate Gaussian model has a number of useful operational properties, proved in Appendix B.3. If $X_1, \dots, X_J$ are dependent Gaussian variables, then

- subsets are Gaussian,
- subsets are conditionally Gaussian given the rest,
- linear functions are Gaussian.

The first assertion means that single variables X_i, pairs (X_i, X_j), triples (X_i, X_j, X_k) and so on are all Gaussian when the full vector is Gaussian. The next one applies to situations where some of the variables have been observed, say $X_i = x_i$, $X_j = x_j$ and $X_k = x_k$ and so forth, and although the distribution of the rest is changed, they remain Gaussian. Finally, linear operations on $X_1, \dots, X_J$ mean new variables

$$Y_j = a_j + b_{j1}X_1 + \cdots + b_{jJ}X_J, \quad j = 1, 2, \dots$$

where a_j and b_{ji} are fixed coefficients. Any such collection $Y_1, Y_2, \dots$ is Gaussian with mean, variances and covariances determined by the operating rules in Appendix A.

5.4.4 Simulation

Software often has routines for simulating dependent Gaussian vectors, but it *is* a good idea to have an inkling of how they work, especially if the model is to be extended to cover heavy-tailed phenomena as at the end of the section. Typically $\mathbf{\Sigma} = (\sigma_{ij})$ is given, and we need the coefficients $\mathbf{C} = (c_{ij})$. A common approach is to restrict them by imposing $c_{ij} = 0$ whenever $j > i$. The resulting matrix bears the name of the Russian mathematician **Cholesky** and reads

$$\mathbf{C} = \begin{pmatrix} c_{11} & 0 & \cdots & 0 \\ c_{21} & c_{22} & \cdots & 0 \\ \cdot & \cdot & \cdots & \cdot \\ \cdot & \cdot & \cdots & \cdot \\ c_{J1} & c_{J2} & \cdots & c_{JJ} \end{pmatrix}, \tag{5.18}$$

where the elements above the main diagonal are zero. It is always possible to find a solution of (5.17) right in this form if Σ is positive definite and it is not difficult, but a computer is needed; see Appendix C.2 for details. Standard software has procedures for this.

With the Cholesky matrix (or some other solution) in the bag and stored as $\mathbf{C} = (c_{ij})$ you copy the defining equations (5.16) in matrix form. If $\mathbf{X} = (X_1, \ldots, X_J)^{\mathrm{T}}$, $\boldsymbol{\xi} = (\xi_1, \ldots, \xi_J)^{\mathrm{T}}$ and $\boldsymbol{\eta} = (\eta_1, \ldots, \eta_J)^{\mathrm{T}}$, then

$$\mathbf{X} = \boldsymbol{\xi} + \mathbf{C}\boldsymbol{\eta} \quad \text{with Monte Carlo version} \quad \mathbf{X}^* \leftarrow \boldsymbol{\xi} + \mathbf{C}\boldsymbol{\eta}^* \tag{5.19}$$

where the random vector $\boldsymbol{\eta}^*$ consists of J independent $N(0, 1)$ drawings.

5.4.5 Scale for modelling

A powerful way of constructing models for correlated phenomena is to transform the variables of interest, say $Y_1, \ldots, Y_J$ to Gaussian ones $X_1, \ldots, X_J$ through specifications of the form

$$Y_j = H_j(X_j), \quad j = 1, \ldots, J \tag{5.20}$$

where $H_1(x), \ldots, H_J(x)$ are known as **transformations**. Dependence is then taken care of by the Gaussian vector $(X_1, \ldots, X_J)$, whereas many different marginal distributions are possible for Y_j by adjusting $H_j(x)$. Simulation is easy, simply slip the variables of the Monte Carlo vector $\mathbf{X}^*$ in (5.19) into (5.20). Correlations are always diminished in absolute value from $X_1, \ldots, X_J$ to $Y_1, \ldots, Y_J$ (a result due to Lancaster, 1957), but this matters little, and the construction is common in statistics and elsewhere.

The logarithmic scale where $\log(Y_j) = X_j$ is popular, and $Y_1, \ldots, Y_J$ are then

Table 5.2 Percentiles (in %) of returns for portfolios described in the text

Risk-free interest: 4% *expected portfolio gain*: 10% $m = 10^6$ *simulations*

	Normal returns					Normal log-returns				
	1%	25%	50%	75%	99%	1%	25%	50%	75%	99%
Percentiles	–28.9	–1.1	10.0	21.2	48.5	–22.5	–1.8	8.5	20.2	54.7

correlated log-normals. Normal equity log-returns where $\log(1 + R_j) = X_j$ have been met on several occasions. If $\xi_j = E(X_j)$ and $\sigma_{ij} = \text{cov}(X_i, X_j)$, then

$$E(R_j) = e^{\xi_j+\sigma_{jj}/2} - 1 \quad \text{and} \quad \text{cov}(R_i, R_j) = e^{\xi_i+\xi_j+(\sigma_{ii}+\sigma_{jj})/2}(e^{\sigma_{ij}} - 1), \tag{5.21}$$

an extension of the results in Section 2.4. These are among the most important formulae in the entire theory of risk. Variances are included since $\text{var}(R_j) = \text{cov}(R_j, R_j)$. Here ξ_j and σ_{ij} are being used with a meaning different from that in Section 5.3, where they referred to the returns themselves.

5.4.6 Numerical example: Returns or log-returns?

Is the choice between normal and log-normal equity returns an important one? Here is an illustration with three risky assets and a bank account. Expected return and volatility for the former are 11% and 25% and correlations 0.8 between the first and the other two and 0.4 for the remaining pair. The bank rate is 4%. If R_1, R_2, R_3 and r are asset returns and rate of interest, consider the portfolio

$$\mathcal{R} = (1 - w)r + w(-R_1 + R_2 + R_3) \quad \text{where} \quad w = 0.8571$$

which is Markowitz optimal; see Section 5.3. Percentiles of the portfolio return are shown in Table 5.2 for both normal and log-normal asset returns. The comparison requires the parameters underlying the two models to be carefully matched; consult Exercises 5.17 and 5.18 to see how it's done.

Table 5.2 suggests that the choice of modelling scale does matter as the upside is larger under the log-normal model. Simulations were generated as explained above.

5.4.7 Making tails heavier

The most common way of constructing heavy-tailed models from normal vectors is to let a single $Z > 0$ be responsible, so that (5.16) is extended to

$$X_j = \xi_j + \sqrt{Z}\varepsilon_j, \quad j = 1, \ldots, J \tag{5.22}$$

where Z and the vector $(\varepsilon_1, \dots, \varepsilon_J)$ are independent, but nothing prevents a more general design with Z in (5.22) being allowed to depend on j.

By rule (A.14) in Appendix A.2

$$E(\sqrt{Z}\varepsilon_j) = E(\sqrt{Z})E(\varepsilon_j) = 0 \quad \text{and} \quad E(Z\varepsilon_i\varepsilon_j) = E(Z)E(\varepsilon_i\varepsilon_j),$$

and it follows that $E(X_j) = \xi_j$ and $\text{cov}(X_i, X_j) = E(Z)\text{cov}(\varepsilon_i, \varepsilon_j)$. The latter implies

$$\text{cor}(X_i, X_j) = \text{cor}(\varepsilon_i, \varepsilon_j), \quad i \neq j, \tag{5.23}$$

and the new model inherits expectations and correlations from the old one. Standard deviations, which depend on $E(Z)$, may have changed. The standard choice $Z = 1/G$ where $G \sim \text{Gamma}(\alpha)$ yields $E(Z) = \alpha/(\alpha - 1)$ so that $\text{sd}(X_j) = \sqrt{\alpha/(\alpha-1)}\text{sd}(\varepsilon_j)$. This is the multivariate t-distribution with 2α degrees of freedom, a direct extension of the univariate version in Section 2.4.

Simulation is a straightforward extension of the normal case. Simply draw Z^* and replace the right-hand side of (5.19) by $\mathbf{X}^* \leftarrow \boldsymbol{\xi} + \sqrt{Z^*}\mathbf{C}\boldsymbol{\eta}^*$.

5.5 The random walk

5.5.1 Introduction

Financial variables are **stochastic processes**, which means a collection of random variables attached to points in time. They can, from a modelling point of view, be divided into two groups. Some, like equity, have no natural ceiling. They tend to climb indefinitely, with shorter or longer spells of decline in between. Their fluctuations have a **random walk** nature. The equity indexes in Figure 5.1 are examples. Others, like rate of interest and rate of inflation, behave differently. If these move too far out from the centre, there are forces in the economy that pull them back again. They exhibit a **reversion to mean**. Random-walk and reversion-to-mean models are the basic building blocks when the dynamic properties of financial variables are described mathematically. Reversion to mean is discussed in Section 5.6.

5.5.2 Random walk and equity

A series $\{Y_k\}$ is a **random walk** if generated by the recursion

$$Y_k = Y_{k-1} + X_k, \quad k = 1, 2, \dots \tag{5.24}$$

where $X_1, X_2, \dots$ are independent **increments**. The underwriter model of Section 3.6 is an example, but usually a random walk signifies increments that are identically distributed. It is convenient to represent them as

$$X_k = \xi + \sigma\varepsilon_k, \quad k = 1, 2, \dots \tag{5.25}$$

where the random sequence $\varepsilon_1, \varepsilon_2, \dots$ is identically and independently distributed with zero mean and unit variance, but not necessarily Gaussian. Expectation ξ is sometimes called the **drift**.

The random walk is the standard model for equity. A popular form, introduced in Section 1.5, is to apply it on a logarithmic scale. Then $Y_k = \log(S_k)$ in (5.24) and

$$S_k = S_{k-1}e^{X_k} = S_{k-1}e^{\xi+\sigma\varepsilon_k}, \quad k = 1, 2, \dots, \quad \text{starting at} \quad S_0 = s_0 \tag{5.26}$$

which is known as a **geometric** random walk. Note that

$$X_k = \log(S_k/S_{k-1}) = \log(1 + R_k), \tag{5.27}$$

where R_k is the return in period k and increments under the geometric random walk are the log-returns. These are models for phenomena of high risk and uncertain behaviour; consult the simulations in Figure 1.5.

Fitting these models to historical data requires nothing new. Let $y_1, \dots, y_n$ or $s_1, \dots, s_n$ be random walk or geometric random walk data. The increments $x_k = y_k - y_{k-1}$ or $x_k = \log(s_k/s_{k-1})$ are then independent and identically distributed, and the elementary methods in Section 5.2 yield estimates of ξ and σ. Volatility estimates may often be improved by using a smaller time scale; see Section 5.7.

5.5.3 Elementary properties

Much random walk behaviour can be understood almost directly from the definition. From (5.24) and (5.25) it is easily deduced that

$$Y_K = Y_0 + X_1 + \cdots + X_K = Y_0 + K\xi + \sigma(\varepsilon_1 + \cdots + \varepsilon_K)$$

or

$$Y_K = Y_0 + \underset{\textit{drift}}{K\xi} + \underset{\textit{random}}{\sqrt{K}\sigma\eta} \tag{5.28}$$

where

$$\eta = (\varepsilon_1 + \cdots + \varepsilon_K)/\sqrt{K}.$$

Here η is another standardized error term; i.e., $E(\eta) = 0$ and $\text{sd}(\eta) = 1$.

In the long run the drift (proportional to K) dominates the stochastic term (proportional to $\sqrt{K}$), and as $K \to \infty$ random walks are carried to infinity on the same side of the origin as ξ. A geometric random walk is similar. Now

$$S_K = e^{Y_K} = S_0 e^{K\xi + \sqrt{K}\sigma\eta},$$

and if this is a model for equity, the investment eventually exceeds the initial value

S_0 by huge amounts if the drift is positive (however small). In practice it isn't quite that simple!

The case $\xi = 0$ is an exception not covered by the preceding argument. If you simulate (try $K = 100\,000$), the random walk will now wander *very* slowly from one side of the origin to the other (and very far out); see Karlin and Taylor (1975) for the mathematics and Exercise 5.26 for numerical experimentation.

5.5.4 Several processes jointly

It is straightforward (and important) to handle several random walks jointly. With J different series the defining equations are

$$Y_{jk} = Y_{jk-1} + X_{jk} \quad \text{where} \quad X_{jk} = \xi_j + \sigma_j \varepsilon_{jk} \tag{5.29}$$

for $j = 1, \ldots, J$. The error terms are now dependent, *correlated* variables $\varepsilon_{1k}, \ldots, \varepsilon_{Jk}$ that are independent from one point in time to another; i.e.,

$$\underbrace{\varepsilon_{1k}, \ldots, \varepsilon_{Jk}}_{\text{at time } k} \quad \text{independent of} \quad \underbrace{\varepsilon_{1l}, \ldots, \varepsilon_{Jl}}_{\text{at time } l} \quad \text{if } k \neq l.$$

As before, $E(\varepsilon_{jk}) = 0$ and $\text{sd}(\varepsilon_{jk}) = 1$. There are covariances and correlations too, but they raise no new issues over those in Section 5.2, and the estimation methods are now applied to the historical increments $X_{jk} = Y_{jk} - Y_{jk-1}$.

The extension of (5.28) is

$$Y_{jK} = Y_{j0} + K\xi_j + \sqrt{K}\sigma_j \eta_j \quad \text{where} \quad \eta_j = (\varepsilon_{j1} + \cdots + \varepsilon_{jK})/\sqrt{K} \tag{5.30}$$

for $j = 1, \ldots, J$, and the question is the distribution of $\eta_1, \ldots, \eta_J$. By the covariance formula (rule (A.22) of Appendix A.3)

$$\begin{aligned} \text{cov}(\eta_i, \eta_j) &= \frac{1}{K}\text{cov}(\varepsilon_{i1} + \cdots + \varepsilon_{iK}, \varepsilon_{j1} + \cdots + \varepsilon_{jK}) = \frac{1}{K}\sum_{k=1}^{K} \text{cov}(\varepsilon_{ik}, \varepsilon_{jk}) \\ &= \text{cov}(\varepsilon_{ik}, \varepsilon_{jk}), \end{aligned}$$

since $\text{cov}(\varepsilon_{ik}, \varepsilon_{jl}) = 0$ for $k \neq l$. It follows that $\eta_1, \ldots, \eta_J$ have the same variances and covariances as the original error terms (and obviously $E(\eta_j) = 0$).

5.5.5 Simulating the random walk

Random walks are simulated from their definition. Algorithm 5.1 details the steps for an equity portfolio with J log-normal assets which are not rebalanced. The portfolio value $\mathcal{V}_k$ then evolves according to

$$\mathcal{V}_k = S_{1k} + \cdots + S_{Jk} \quad \text{where} \quad S_{jk} = S_{jk-1}e^{\xi_j + \sigma_j \varepsilon_{jk}}, \quad j = 1, \ldots, J, \tag{5.31}$$

simulated in Algorithm 5.1.

Algorithm 5.1 Equity portfolio under a geometric random walk

Input: $s_{10}, \ldots, s_{J0}$, parameters of the increment model
For $j = 1, \ldots, J$
  $S_j^* \leftarrow s_{j0}$ *%The initial portfolio*
For $k = 1, 2, \ldots, K$ do *%The time loop*
  Generate $\varepsilon_1^*, \ldots, \varepsilon_J^*$ *%Use (5.16) with $\sum_i c_{ji}^2 = 1$ which yields unit volatilities*
  $\mathcal{V}_k^* \leftarrow 0$
  For $j = 1, \ldots, J$
    $S_j^* \leftarrow S_j^* \exp(\xi_j + \sigma_j \varepsilon_j^*)$ *%New value for asset j %Stochastic volatility: Replace σ_j by σ_j^**
    $\mathcal{V}_k^* \leftarrow \mathcal{V}_k^* + S_j^*$
Return $\mathcal{V}_1^*, \ldots, \mathcal{V}_K^*$.

The investments are initially worth $S_{10} = s_{10}, \ldots, S_{J0} = s_{J0}$ and the portfolio $\mathcal{V}_0 = s_{10} + \cdots + s_{J0}$. The logic follows (5.31) closely. Note how easy it would be to include **stochastic** volatility. Simply replace $\sigma_1, \ldots, \sigma_J$ by a Monte Carlo version $\sigma_1^*, \ldots, \sigma_J^*$. Such modelling was touched on briefly in Section 5.4, and there is more in Chapter 13.

If only the final portfolio value $\mathcal{V}_K$ is of interest, much computation is saved by omitting the intermediate steps in Algorithm 5.1. You then simulate (5.30) left directly using a Gaussian model for $\eta_1, \ldots, \eta_J$. Simulations are exact if the original model is Gaussian, but only approximate otherwise.

5.5.6 Numerical illustration

The monthly NYSE indexes in Figure 5.1 provide illustrations. Their drift and volatility were about 1% and 5% per month for both assets. These estimates will now be projected 10 years ahead. Drift and volatility over this period are $0.01 \times 120 = 1.20$ and $0.05 \times \sqrt{120} \doteq 0.55$, and if weights 1/2 are placed on both assets originally, the portfolio has after 10 years grown to

$$\mathcal{V}_{120} = \frac{1}{2}e^{1.2+0.55\eta_1} + \frac{1}{2}e^{1.2+0.55\eta_2} \qquad \text{starting at} \qquad \mathcal{V}_0 = 1.$$

The error terms η_1 and η_2 inherit the monthly correlation, which is close to 0.8.

Density functions for the 10-year returns $\mathcal{R}_{120} = \mathcal{V}_{120} - 1$ have been computed in Figure 5.2 from $m = 100\,000$ simulations and plotted with correlation 0.8 to the left and 0 to the right. Investments in only one asset are included for comparison. The most pronounced feature is the enormous uncertainty of the outcome. Nominal *losses* (return below zero) are possible even over such a long time span. There is

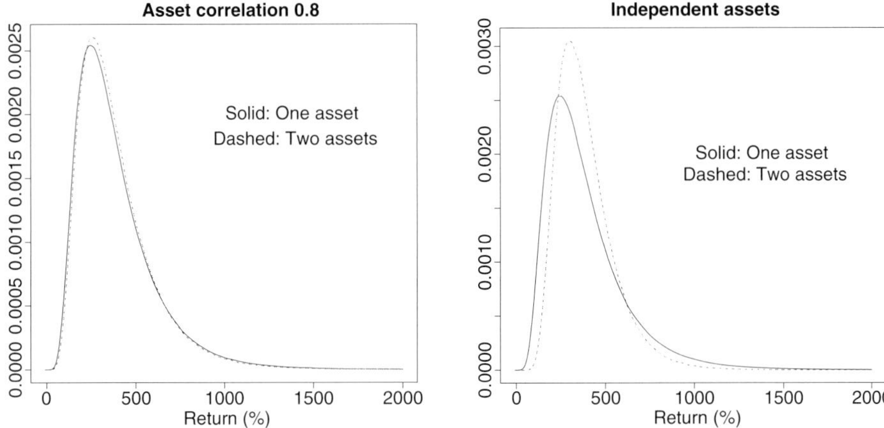

Figure 5.2 Density functions for 10-year returns of equity portfolio with one asset (solid line) or two assets (dashed line) with asset correlations 0.8 (*left*) and 0 (*right*).

not much effect of spreading the investment over two assets when the correlation is 0.8, but an uncorrelated pair is different and would have reduced risk substantially.

5.6 Introducing stationary models

5.6.1 Introduction

Stochastic processes might be **stationary** or they might not be. The random walk belongs to the second category, and the topic of this section is the first. Stationary phenomena are forever attracted towards the average. There is no systematic growth or decline for example, and nor do oscillations become dampened or reinforced. Stationary patterns are irregularly cyclic and may look like those in Figure 1.4. A proper mathematical definition is given below. Another name is **reversion to mean**.

Classes of stationary models are presented in Chapter 13. The single most important among them is arguably the first-order autoregressive process. Its easy mathematics makes it a good vehicle when seeking insight into the behaviour of stationary models in general, and it is also an important contributor to risk-neutral money market modelling (Chapter 14). The simple structure and parsimonious use of parameters make this model attractive for long-term modelling of economic and financial variables.

5.6.2 Autocovariances and autocorrelations

Let $\{Y_k\}$ be a stochastic process and define

$$\xi = E(Y_k) \quad \text{and} \quad \gamma_l = \text{cov}(Y_k, Y_{k-l}), \quad l = 0, 1, \ldots, \tag{5.32}$$

where ξ is expectation and γ_l the covariance for pairs that are l time units apart (or at **lag** l). The covariances are known as the **autocovariances** and the sequence $\gamma_0, \gamma_1, \ldots$ as the autocovariance function. Stationarity means what is implied by the mathematical notation, that neither ξ nor γ_l depend on time k. In particular, the standard deviation $\mathrm{sd}(Y_k) = \sqrt{\gamma_0}$ is the same for all k, which implies that the **autocorrelations** $\rho_l = \mathrm{cor}(Y_k, Y_{k-l})$ are

$$\rho_l = \frac{\gamma_l}{\gamma_0}, \tag{5.33}$$

again not depending on k. The autocorrelation function $\{\rho_l\}$ may exhibit several types of behaviour. Exponential decay, as in Figure 5.3, is common and adjacent variables are then the most correlated ones. A model with this property is constructed below.

Stationarity defined through means, variances and covariances is known as the **weak** form and is enough for this book. Other versions can be found among the references in Section 5.9.

5.6.3 Estimation from historical data

Autocovariances and autocorrelations can be determined from historical data. The average of the observed historical series $y_1, \ldots, y_n$ is then used for the mean, and the covariance and the correlation at lag l are estimated from the sequence

Time	$l+1$	$l+2$	$\cdots$	n
	y_{l+1}	y_{l+2}	$\cdots$	y_n
	y_1	y_2	$\cdots$	y_{n-l}

where the second series is shifted l time units back compared with the first. With ordinary covariance estimation applied to the pairs (y_k, y_{k-l}) for $k = l+1, \ldots, n$ these estimates become

$$\bar{y} = \frac{1}{n}\sum_{k=1}^{n} y_k \quad \text{and} \quad \hat{\gamma}_l = \frac{1}{n}\sum_{k=l+1}^{n} (y_k - \bar{y})(y_{k-l} - \bar{y}), \tag{5.34}$$

where $\hat{\gamma}_0$ is the variance. Let $\hat{\sigma}_{ij} = \hat{\gamma}_{|i-j|}$ be the estimate of $\gamma_{|i-j|} = \mathrm{cov}(Y_i, Y_j)$. The matrix $\hat{\boldsymbol{\Sigma}} = (\hat{\sigma}_{ij})$ is often needed, and it becomes positive definite if we divide by n instead of $n - l$ in (5.34) right (that's why this is done). Autocorrelation estimates are $\hat{\rho}_l = \hat{\gamma}_l / \hat{\gamma}_0$.

An example is shown in Figure 5.3. Simulations of annual interest rates over 25 and 100 years were generated under the Vasiček model introduced below and autocorrelation functions estimated from the simulations. They are plotted against lag l and compared with the true one (solid line in the middle). Errors are large in all 10 replications. Note the oscillations in the estimates themselves. These are caused

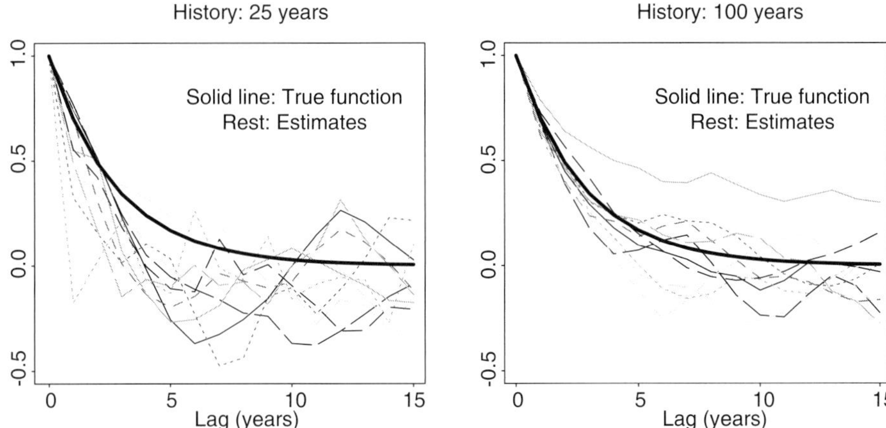

Figure 5.3 True and estimated (10 replications) autocorrelation functions using data simulated from the Vasiček model with parameters $a = 0.7$ and $\sigma = 0.016$.

by estimation error being correlated at neighbouring lags and carry no meaning other than being a random phenomenon.

5.6.4 Autoregression of first order

One of the most popular models for rates of interest $\{r_k\}$ was proposed by Vasiček (1977) and bears his name. Future rates then evolve according to

$$r_k = r_{k-1} + (1-a)(\xi - r_{k-1}) + \sigma\varepsilon_k, \quad \text{for} \quad k = 1, 2, \ldots \tag{5.35}$$

where $\varepsilon_1, \varepsilon_2, \ldots$ are independent and identically distributed with mean 0 and standard deviation 1. The coefficient a defines a mean-reverting second term on the right that pushes r_k towards ξ if $|a| < 1$. Alternatively the model may also be written

$$r_k - \xi = a(r_{k-1} - \xi) + \sigma\varepsilon_k,$$

or, with $Y_k = r_k$ and $X_k = r_k - \xi$,

$$\underbrace{Y_k = \xi + X_k}_{\text{defining the level}} \quad \text{where} \quad \underbrace{X_k = aX_{k-1} + \sigma\varepsilon_k,}_{\text{the dynamics}} \qquad k = 1, 2, \ldots \tag{5.36}$$

This second form is known as an **autoregressive** series of first order (for higher orders, see Section 13.4). It is started at

$$X_0 = y_0 - \xi = x_0 \qquad (y_0 \text{ observed at time } 0). \tag{5.37}$$

You will encounter the Vasiček version in financial economics, whereas the other one is common in statistics.

The relationship on the left in (5.36) simply adapts the fluctuations to an average level ξ without changing anything else, whereas $\{X_k\}$ is a **driver** process that handles the dynamics. Its behaviour follows from (5.36) right, which yields

$$X_k = aX_{k-1} + \sigma\varepsilon_k = a(aX_{k-2} + \sigma\varepsilon_{k-1}) + \sigma\varepsilon_k = \sigma\varepsilon_k + a\sigma\varepsilon_{k-1} + a^2X_{k-2},$$

and we may go on like this. Next $X_{k-2} = aX_{k-3} + \sigma\varepsilon_{k-2}$ is inserted on the right, then X_{k-3} and so on. Going all the way down to $X_0 = x_0$ the end result is

$$X_k = \sigma\varepsilon_k + a\sigma\varepsilon_{k-1} + \cdots + a^{k-1}\sigma\varepsilon_1 + a^k x_0, \tag{5.38}$$

and X_k is a sum of independent, random contributions with the initial value added. All linear stationary processes satisfy this kind of representation (more in Section 13.4). What varies from one model to another are the coefficients. The exponential powers in (5.38) are for the first-order autoregression.

5.6.5 The behaviour of first-order autoregressions

Let $E(X_k|x_0)$, $\text{sd}(X_k|x_0)$ and $\text{var}(X_k|x_0)$ be mean, standard deviation and variance of X_k. They depend on the initial value x_0 in a way that is crucial to understand. The mean is easy since all ε_k in (5.38) have mean zero, which makes $E(X_k|x_0) = a^k x_0$. To calculate the variance recall the ordinary formula for sums of independent variables, which when applied to (5.38) yields

$$\text{var}(X_k|x_0) = \sigma^2 + (a\sigma)^2 + \cdots + (a^{k-1}\sigma)^2 = (1 + a^2 + \cdots + a^{2k-2})\sigma^2 = \frac{1-a^{2k}}{1-a^2}\sigma^2,$$

and in summary

$$E(X_k|x_0) = a^k x_0 \quad \text{and} \quad \text{sd}(X_k|x_0) = \sqrt{\frac{1-a^{2k}}{1-a^2}}\,\sigma. \tag{5.39}$$

Only the restriction $|a| < 1$ interests us. The powers a^k then dwindle towards zero as k grows, and the conditional mean appoaches zero too. By contrast, the standard deviation rises quickly at the beginning and then stabilizes. This was observed in Figure 1.4 if you care to look that up, and it will be encountered repeatedly in later chapters. In the limit as $k \to \infty$

$$E(X_k|x_0) \to 0 \quad \text{and} \quad \text{sd}(X_k|x_0) \longrightarrow \sigma_x = \frac{\sigma}{\sqrt{1-a^2}} \quad \text{if} \quad |a| < 1. \tag{5.40}$$

Similar results for the covariances (verified in Section 5.8) are

$$\text{cov}(X_k, X_{k-l}) = a^l\text{var}(X_{k-l}) \longrightarrow a^l\sigma_x^2 \quad \text{if } l \geq 0. \tag{5.41}$$

Even autocovariances (and autocorrelations) stabilize in the long run when $|a| < 1$.

This kind of behaviour applies to stationary processes in general. There are two separate stages. At the beginning (the **transient** state) the process is pushed towards the middle from where it starts, which is the reversion to mean mentioned earlier. In theory this gradual adaptation goes on for ever, but in practice we may pretend that after a while the second, **stationary** stage is reached. How long that takes depends on the model. By now the value at the beginning has been forgotten, and means, standard deviations and covariances have become

$$E(X_k) = 0, \ \mathrm{sd}(X_k) = \sigma_x = \frac{\sigma}{\sqrt{1-a^2}} \quad \text{and} \quad \mathrm{cor}(X_k, X_{k-l}) = a^l, \tag{5.42}$$

not depending on k. There is no reference to x_0 now, and formally the process started in the infinitely distant past. These properties are inherited by the shifted process $Y_k = \xi + X_k$.

5.6.6 Non-linear change of scale

There are many ways a given driver process X_k can be converted into a model for interest rates r_k or other economic variables. The Vasiček model $r_k = \xi + X_k$ was a simple adaptation to a given average level ξ, but general specifications of the form $r_k = H(X_k)$ are also possible. Here the transformation $H(x)$ is an increasing function depending on ξ. It is still the role of X_k to take care of the dynamic properties, but there is now a second element $H(x)$ which offers interesting modelling opportunities, for example guaranteeing positive interest rates if $H(x) > 0$.

Many of the numerical experiments in later chapters make use of the **Black–Karasinski** model, with the exponential function as transformation. A convenient form is

$$r_k = \xi e^{-\sigma_x^2/2 + X_k} \quad \text{where} \quad \sigma_x = \frac{\sigma}{\sqrt{1-a^2}}, \tag{5.43}$$

and the driver process $\{X_k\}$ starts at

$$x_0 = \log(r_0/\xi) + \frac{1}{2}\sigma_x^2, \tag{5.44}$$

which you obtain by solving (5.43) for X_0 when $k = 0$. The transient stage passes gradually into a steady one as before, and eventually

$$E(r_k) = \xi \quad \text{and} \quad \mathrm{sd}(r_k) = \xi\sqrt{e^{\sigma_x^2} - 1} \tag{5.45}$$

which are the ordinary formulae under log-normal distributions.

One of the advantages of the Black–Karasinski model is that interest rates now fluctuate more strongly at higher levels; see Exercise 5.33. This seems plausible and isn't delivered by the linear Vasiček model under which the effect of the error term $\sigma\varepsilon_k$ is the same at any level.

Algorithm 5.2 Simulating Black–Karasinski

---

0 Input: ξ, a, σ, r_0 and $\sigma_x = \sigma/\sqrt{1-a^2}$
1 $X^* \leftarrow \log(r_0/\xi) + \sigma_x^2/2$, $P^* \leftarrow 1$ %*Alternative:* $X^* \sim N(0, \sigma_x)$
2 For $k = 1, \dots, K$ do
3 Draw $\varepsilon^* \sim N(0, 1)$
4 $X^* \leftarrow aX^* + \sigma\varepsilon^*$ %*Updating the driver process*
5 $r_k^* \leftarrow \xi \exp(-\sigma_x^2/2 + X^*)$, $P^* \leftarrow P^*(1 + r_k^*)$ %*Vasiček:* $r_k^* \leftarrow \xi + X^*$
6 Return $r_1^*, \dots, r_K^*$ and $r_{0:K}^* \leftarrow P^* - 1$.

5.6.7 Monte Carlo implementation

Algorithm 5.2 shows how the driver process is simulated and converted to realizations from the Black–Karasinski model. The logic is based on the stochastic recursion (5.36) right, which is repeated on Line 4 and converted to interest rates on Line 5. We are often interested in the return of an account under floating rates of interest. The mathematical definition in Section 1.4 was

$$r_{0:K} = \prod_{k=1}^{K}(1 + r_k) - 1$$

which yields simulations

$$r_{0:K}^* = \prod_{k=1}^{K}(1 + r_k^*) - 1,$$

and this has been built into the algorithm.

There are several ways to initialize. You start from the current state of the economy by using the expression on Line 1 (Black–Karasinski) or replacing it with $X^* \leftarrow r_0 - \xi$ (Vasiček). Simulations may also be run from the stationary state (see the comment on Line 1) or even from a middle value (now take $X_0^* \leftarrow 0$ on Line 1); for more on the initialization of time series models, consult Section 13.6.

5.6.8 Numerical illustration

How important is dynamic interest rate modelling, and would it lead to very wrong evaluations if rates for each period were redrawn independently of each other? What about the choice of model? Black–Karasinski (B–K) might appear superior to Vasiček (Va) as a description of interest rate fluctuations, but perhaps it doesn't really matter. An illustration is provided in Figure 5.4, where 10-year returns from floating rates of interest have been examined through annual simulations. The average rate was $\xi = 5\%$ and all the scenarios were started at $r_0 = \xi$. Other parameters were:

Autocorrelation ($a = 0.7$)	Independence ($a = 0$)
$\sigma = 0.25$ (B–K), $\sigma = 0.0129$ (Va)	$\sigma = 0.35$(B–K), $\sigma = 0.0181$ (Va),

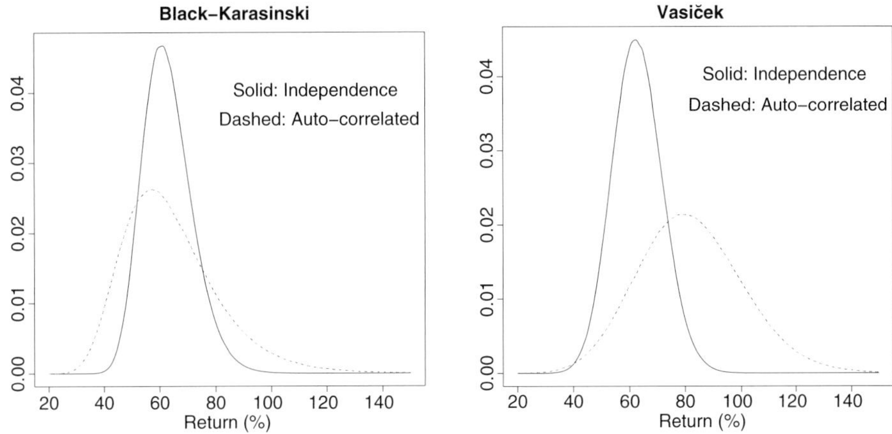

Figure 5.4 Density functions for 10-year returns under independent (solid line) and autocorrelated (dashed line) interest rate models with conditions as in the text, the Black–Karasinski model (*left*) and Vasiček (*right*).

where $a = 0.7$ to the left could well be realistic in practice (see Section 13.5). The values of σ were selected to make $\mathrm{sd}(r_k)$ equal under stationarity in all four cases examined.

Density functions of 10-year returns (obtained from $m = 1000$ simulated scenarios) are plotted in Figure 5.4, the Black–Karasinski model on the left and the Vasiček model on the right. The independent case ($a = 0$) implies a severe underestimation of the uncertainty compared with $a = 0.7$. Disregarding autocorrelations in interest rate movements seems too crude. Model choice is different. The discrepancy between the density functions on the left and on the right isn't that severe, and parameter uncertainty might account for much more; see Chapter 7.

5.7 Changing the time scale

5.7.1 *Introduction*

Modelling is, in many situations, carried out over a time increment shorter than that one used for evaluation, which raises the question of how to switch between time scales. Fix the mathematical notation as

$$\underbrace{t_k = kh}_{\text{original time scale}} \quad \text{and} \quad \underbrace{T_k = kT \quad \text{where} \quad T = Kh.}_{\text{new } K\text{-step scale}} \tag{5.46}$$

Suppose the original series $\{Y_k\}$ ran on t_k while needed as $Y_K, Y_{2K}, \ldots$ only. If we move from days to months and there are 25 days in a *financial* month, then $K = 25$, and $Y_K, Y_{2K}, \ldots$ are end-of-month values. This section is about passing from one time scale to another. An important part is modelling in continuous time where $h \to 0$.

5.7.2 Historical data on short time scales

The first issue is historical data with higher sampling frequency than in the ensuing analysis of risk. Suppose evaluations of equity risk are going to be monthly or annual. Records of equity log-returns are certainly daily. Should that be utilized? Answer: There is no gain with expectations (same estimates), but with volatilities things are different. The argument is simplest for log-returns, but conclusions wouldn't differ much for ordinary returns. Let σ_K be the volatility of log-returns over $T = Kh$. There are n such periods, and we are assuming that data are also available on nK sub-intervals of length h. If σ is the volatility on this smaller time scale, then $\sigma_K = \sqrt{K}\sigma$. There are now two strategies for estimating σ_K:

$$\underbrace{\hat{\sigma}_K}_{\textit{from } n \textit{ log-returns } (K\textit{-step})} \qquad \text{and} \qquad \underbrace{\sqrt{K}\hat{\sigma}.}_{\hat{\sigma} \textit{ from } nK \textit{ log-returns (one-step)}} \tag{5.47}$$

The question is which is the more accurate.

The answer isn't entirely obvious, and a simple calculation is necessary. The result involves the kurtosis κ on time scale h and makes use of (2.3) in Section 2.2, which approximates standard deviations of volatility estimates. In Section 5.8 we verify that

$$\frac{\text{sd}(\hat{\sigma}_K)}{\text{sd}(\sqrt{K}\hat{\sigma})} \doteq \sqrt{\frac{K + \kappa/2}{1 + \kappa/2}} > 1. \tag{5.48}$$

With daily equity returns a realistic value for κ might be 5–6, and if $K = 25$ the ratio in (5.48) is 2.6–2.8, which indicates a worthwile improvement in using daily data for monthly volatilities. As $\kappa \to \infty$ the advantage is wiped out; i.e., for very heavy-tailed distributions there is no gain in drawing on the short time scale. How far down should we go? Should *hourly* equity returns replace daily ones? Answer: Perhaps not; see Exercise 5.40. Covariance estimation is much the same issue and treated in Section 5.8.

5.7.3 The random walk revisited

Let $\{Y_k\}$ be an ordinary random walk and recall (5.28) which connects Y_K at time $T = Kh$ to the initial value Y_0. The relationship was

$$Y_K = Y_0 + K\xi + \sqrt{K}\sigma\eta_1 \quad \text{where} \quad \eta_1 = (\varepsilon_1 + \cdots + \varepsilon_K)/\sqrt{K}.$$

There is a similar connection between Y_K and Y_{2K}, between Y_{2K} and Y_{3K} and so on, leading to a recursion running over every Kth member of the original series. It will be convenient to highlight real time by writing $Y(T_k) = Y_{kK}$. The model on the new time scale is

$$Y(T_k) = Y(T_{k-1}) + \underset{\textit{drift}}{K\xi} + \underset{\textit{random}}{\sqrt{K}\sigma\eta_k}, \qquad k = 1, 2, \ldots \tag{5.49}$$

where $\eta_1, \eta_2, \ldots$ have mean 0 and standard deviation 1 and are identically distributed. They come from non-overlapping periods, which makes them independent as well.

This second series $Y(T_0), Y(T_1), Y(T_2), \ldots$ is *another random walk*! Drift and standard deviation of the increments are now $K\xi$ and $\sqrt{K}\sigma$, and the way η_1 is defined (and hence $\eta_2, \eta_3, \ldots$ too) should convince you (through the central limit theorem) that the model becomes more and more Gaussian as K grows. There are consequences for equity. Under a geometric random walk, monthly and annual log-returns are closer to the normal than daily ones, which is seen in real data.

5.7.4 Continuous time: The Wiener process

One of the most important modelling tricks in insurance and finance is to let $h \to 0$ while $T = Kh$ is kept fixed, so that $K = T/h \to \infty$. Mathematical limit operations of this type (known as **continuous time**) arise under many different circumstances. Here the question is how the process $Y(T_0), Y(T_1), \ldots$ behaves when the number of random contributions per period becomes infinite. We need additional conditions linking the parameters ξ and σ to the time increment h. The only consistent way is

$$\xi = \xi_q h \quad \text{and} \quad \sigma = \sigma_q \sqrt{h}, \tag{5.50}$$

where ξ_q and σ_q are parameters.[3] Why must the mean and variance be proportional to h? Because the formulae for sums of means and variances can't hold otherwise. Now

$$K\xi = \xi_q hK = \xi_q T \quad \text{and} \quad \sqrt{K}\sigma = \sigma_q \sqrt{h}\sqrt{K} = \sigma_q \sqrt{T},$$

and the random walk model (5.49) becomes

$$Y(T_k) = Y(T_{k-1}) + \xi_q T + \sigma_q \sqrt{T}\eta_k, \quad k = 1, 2 \ldots$$

When $h \to 0$, the drift $\xi_q T$ and the standard deviation $\sigma_q \sqrt{T}$ do not change; only the distribution of the error terms η_k do. Eventually the number of random contributions has become infinite, and η_k is now $N(0, 1)$ by the central limit theorem.

[3] The index q is because the model in this book is only used for **risk-neutral** modelling.

The continuous-time random walk is, in the Gaussian case, known as the **Wiener process** or as **Brownian motion**. Take $T = t-s$, and it emerges than *any* increment $Y(t) - Y(s)$ is normal with parameters

$$E\{Y(t) - Y(s)\} = \xi_q(t-s) \quad \text{and} \quad \mathrm{sd}(Y(t) - Y(s)\} = \sigma_q\sqrt{t-s}. \tag{5.51}$$

This opens up an observation that will play a key role in the pricing of options in Chapter 14. It has been noted earlier (Section 5.5) that in the long run, drift in random walk models is sure to overtake uncertainty. *Small* time differentials are the opposite. Now the square root $\sqrt{t-s}$ is much *larger* than $t-s$, and the random term is the dominating one.

5.7.5 First-order autoregression revisited

The time scale is an issue with mean reversion too. Suppose $\{X_k\}$ is an autoregressive process of order one. It was shown in Section 5.6 that

$$X_K = a^K X_0 + \sigma\varepsilon_k + a\sigma\varepsilon_{k-1} + \cdots + a^{K-1}\sigma\varepsilon_1;$$

see (5.38). It is easy to verfy that this may also be written

$$X_K = a^K X_0 + \sigma_K \eta_1 \tag{5.52}$$

where

$$\sigma_K = \sigma\sqrt{\frac{1-a^{2K}}{1-a^2}} \quad \text{and} \quad \eta_1 = \sqrt{\frac{1-a^2}{1-a^{2K}}}(\varepsilon_k + a\varepsilon_{k-1} + \cdots + a^{K-1}\varepsilon_1), \tag{5.53}$$

and η_1 defines the uncertainty over $T = Kh$. Clearly $E(\eta_1) = 0$, and $\mathrm{sd}(\eta_1) = 1$ by (5.39).

Now, follow the line used with the random walk and let X_0 and X_K be the first two terms in a sequence $X_0, X_K, X_{2K}, \ldots$ As before, write $X(T_k) = X_{kK}$ to emphasize real time. The relationship between $X(T_k)$ and $X(T_{k-1})$ is similar to that between $X(T_1) = X_K$ and $X(0)$, and

$$X(T_k) = a^K X(T_{k-1}) + \sigma_K \eta_k \quad \text{for} \quad k = 1, 2 \ldots \tag{5.54}$$

where $\eta_1, \eta_2, \ldots$ are independent since they apply to different periods. They have a common distribution with $E(\eta_k) = 0$ and $\mathrm{sd}(\eta_k) = 1$.

The new time scale doesn't change the basic structure of the model. *This is still a first-order autoregression*, though with different parameters. But the sequence $\eta_1, \eta_2, \ldots$ does *not* now become Gaussian as $K \to \infty$, as was the case with the random walk. The reason is that the first few terms dominate even in the limit, which is contrary to the Lindeberg condition in Appendix A.4.

5.7.6 Continuous-time autoregression

The mathematical limit operations defining continuous-time autoregression are the same as for the Wiener process. Let $h \to 0$ while $T = Kh$ is fixed so that $X(T_1)$, $X(T_2), \ldots$ run on fixed time points $T_1, T_2, \ldots$ The parameters must be specified as

$$a = 1 - a_q h \quad \text{and} \quad \sigma = \sigma_q \sqrt{h},$$

where a_q and σ_q^2 are intensities. On the short time scale the model becomes

$$X_k = (1 - a_q h) X_{k-1} + \sigma_q \sqrt{h}\, \varepsilon_k, \quad k = 1, 2, \ldots$$

or if $r_k = \xi + X_k$,

$$r_k - r_{k-1} = \underset{\textit{foreseeable change}}{a_q(\xi - r_{k-1})h} + \underset{\textit{random change}}{\sigma_q \sqrt{h}\, \varepsilon_k}, \tag{5.55}$$

which has a familiar structure. The expected term (first on the right) is proportional to h and the uncertainty, proportional to $\sqrt{h}$, dominates for small h. Continuous-time autoregression is used for risk-neutral modelling in the money market; see Section 6.4.

We must examine the limits of a^K and σ_K in (5.54). As $h \to 0$, or equivalently as $K = T/h \to \infty$, then

$$a^K = (1 - a_q h)^K = \left(1 - \frac{a_q T}{K}\right)^K \longrightarrow e^{-a_q T} = a_T,$$

whereas after inserting $a = 1 - a_q h$ and $\sigma = \sigma_q \sqrt{h}$ in (5.53) left

$$\sigma_K^2 = \sigma^2 \frac{1 - a^{2K}}{1 - a^2} = \sigma_q^2 \frac{1 - a^{2K}}{2a_q - a_q^2 h} \longrightarrow \sigma_q^2 \frac{1 - a_T^2}{2a_q} = \sigma_T^2.$$

The continuous-time, first-order regression is therefore on time scale T of the form

$$X(T_k) = a_T X(T_{k-1}) + \sigma_T \eta_k \quad \text{where} \quad a_T = e^{-a_q T}, \quad \sigma_T = \sigma_q \sqrt{\frac{1 - a_T^2}{2a_q}}. \tag{5.56}$$

Unlike the case where a and σ are fixed parameters, the sequence $\eta_1, \eta_2, \ldots$ now becomes Gaussian as $K \to \infty$. This can be verified by the Lindeberg condition in Appendix A.4.

The conclusion is similar to that for the random walk. Continuous-time, *Gaussian* first-order autoregressions appear in the limit. The parameters a_q and σ_q may be easier to understand when passing to time scale T. By solving the equation on the right in (5.56)

$$a_q = -\frac{\log(a_T)}{T} \quad \text{and} \quad \sigma_q = \sigma_T \sqrt{\frac{2a_q}{1 - a_T^2}}, \tag{5.57}$$

and a_q and σ_q follows from a ‘position’ on a_T and σ_T.

5.8 Mathematical arguments

5.8.1 Markowitz optimality

Let $\mathbf{w} = (w_1, \ldots, w_J)^{\mathrm{T}}$ be the weights assigned to the risky assets and introduce

$$L(\mathbf{w}) = \sum_{j=1}^{J} w_j(\xi_j - r) \quad \text{and} \quad Q(\mathbf{w}) = \sum_{i=1}^{J}\sum_{j=1}^{J} w_i w_j \sigma_{ij}$$

where $L(\mathbf{w}) = E(\mathcal{R}) - r$. Optimal portfolios in the Markowitz sense mimimize $Q(\mathbf{w})$ subject to $L(\mathbf{w}) = e_g - r$. Note that

$$\frac{\partial Q}{\partial w_i} - 2\frac{\partial L}{\partial w_i} = 2\sum_{j=1}^{J} w_j\sigma_{ij} - 2(\xi_i - r) = 0 \quad \text{if} \quad \sum_{j=1}^{J} w_j\sigma_{ij} = \xi_i - r$$

which applies for $i = 1, \ldots, J$. This is the linear system of equations (5.9) with $\tilde{\mathbf{w}} = (\tilde{w}_1, \ldots, \tilde{w}_J)^{\mathrm{T}}$ as its solution. It follows that $\tilde{\mathbf{w}}$ minimizes the function $Q(\mathbf{w}) - 2L(\mathbf{w})$.

Note that $L(\gamma\mathbf{w}) = \gamma L(\mathbf{w})$ and $Q(\gamma\mathbf{w}) = \gamma^2 Q(\mathbf{w})$ where γ is a real number. Hence, for arbitrary weights $\mathbf{w} = (w_1, \ldots, w_J)^{\mathrm{T}}$

$$\begin{aligned} Q(\gamma\tilde{\mathbf{w}}) - 2\gamma L(\gamma\tilde{\mathbf{w}}) &= \gamma^2\{Q(\tilde{\mathbf{w}}) - 2L(\tilde{\mathbf{w}})\} \\ &\leq \gamma^2\{Q(\mathbf{w}/\gamma) - 2L(\mathbf{w}/\gamma)\} = Q(\mathbf{w}) - 2\gamma L(\mathbf{w}). \end{aligned}$$

But if $\gamma\tilde{\mathbf{w}}$ and $\mathbf{w}$ have the same expected gain so that $L(\gamma\tilde{\mathbf{w}}) = L(\mathbf{w})$, then $Q(\gamma\tilde{\mathbf{w}}) \leq Q(\mathbf{w})$ and portfolios of the form $\gamma\tilde{\mathbf{w}}$ are optimal ones.

5.8.2 Risk bound under CAPM

To prove inequality (5.15) recall that the return of a portfolio based on weights $w_1, \ldots, w_J$ has variance

$$\mathrm{var}(\mathcal{R}) = \sum_{i=1}^{J}\sum_{j=1}^{J} w_i w_j \sigma_{ij} = \sum_{i=1}^{J}\sum_{j=1}^{J} w_i w_j \beta_i \beta_j \sigma_M^2 + \sum_{j=1}^{J} w_j^2 \tau_j^2$$

after inserting the CAPM variances/covariances $\sigma_{jj} = \beta_j^2\sigma_M^2 + \tau_j^2$ and $\sigma_{ij} = \beta_i\beta_j\sigma_M^2$; see (5.14). Hence

$$\mathrm{var}(\mathcal{R}) = \sigma_M^2\left(\sum_{j=1}^{J} w_j\beta_j\right)^2 + \sum_{j=1}^{J} w_j^2\tau_j^2 \geq \sigma_M^2\left(\sum_{j=1}^{J} w_j\beta_j\right)^2.$$

But $\xi_j = r + \beta_j(\xi_M - r)$ for $j = 1, \ldots, J$, and (5.6) right yields

$$E(\mathcal{R}) = r + \sum_{j=1}^{J} w_j(\xi_j - r) = r + (\xi_M - r)\sum_{j=1}^{J} w_j\beta_j$$

so that if $e_g = E(\mathcal{R})$, then

$$\sum_{j=1}^{J} w_j\beta_j = \frac{e_g - r}{\xi_M - r} \quad \text{or} \quad \text{var}(\mathcal{R}) \geq \sigma_M^2 \left(\frac{e_g - r}{\xi_M - r}\right)^2.$$

5.8.3 Covariances of first-order autoregressions

Consider the process $\{X_k\}$ defined in (5.36) right and recall the representation (5.38) which for $k \geq l$ implies that

$$X_k = \sigma\varepsilon_k + a\sigma\varepsilon_{k-1} + \cdots + a^{l-1}\sigma\varepsilon_{k-l+1} + a^l X_{k-l}.$$

All the terms but the last one are uncorrelated with X_{k-l}. Hence by the covariance of sums formula (Table A.2 in Appendix A.3)

$$\text{cov}(X_k, X_{k-l}) = \text{cov}(a^l X_{k-l}, X_{k-l}) = a^l \text{cov}(X_{k-l}, X_{k-l}) = a^l \text{var}(X_{k-l}),$$

as claimed in (5.41).

5.8.4 Volatility estimation and time scale

Let $x_1, \ldots, x_n$ be log-returns accumulated over K periods each and let σ_K and κ_K be their volatility and kurtosis. We may decompose each x_k as the sum $x_k = x_{k1} + \cdots + x_{kK}$ over one-period log-returns. Assume that the entire collection of x_{ki} for $k = 1, \ldots, n$ and $i = 1, \ldots, K$ are independent and identically distributed with standard deviation σ and kurtosis κ, which must relate to those of x_k through

$$\sigma_K = \sqrt{K}\sigma \quad \text{and} \quad \kappa_K = \frac{\kappa}{K};$$

see Appendix A.2. Consider now the usual estimate $\hat{\sigma}_K$ based on $x_1, \ldots, x_n$ and recall the approximate formula for its standard deviation in Section 2.2; see (2.3). Then

$$\text{sd}(\hat{\sigma}_K) \doteq \frac{\sigma_K}{\sqrt{2n}} \sqrt{1 + \kappa_K/2} = \frac{\sigma}{\sqrt{2n}} \sqrt{K + \kappa/2}$$

after replacing σ_K and κ_K. But we may also compute an estimate $\hat{\sigma}$ from the nK observations x_{ki} and use $\sqrt{K}\hat{\sigma}$ instead of $\hat{\sigma}_K$. Now

$$\text{sd}(\hat{\sigma}) \doteq \frac{\sigma}{\sqrt{2nK}} \sqrt{1 + \kappa/2} \quad \text{or} \quad \text{sd}(\sqrt{K}\hat{\sigma}) \doteq \frac{\sigma}{\sqrt{2n}} \sqrt{1 + \kappa/2}.$$

Taking the ratio of $\text{sd}(\hat{\sigma}_K)$ and $\text{sd}(\sqrt{K}\hat{\sigma})$ yields (5.48).

5.8.5 The accuracy of covariance estimates

There is a similar theory for the covariance estimate (5.4). Now

$$\text{sd}(\hat{\sigma}_{ij}) \doteq \frac{\sigma_i\sigma_j}{\sqrt{n}} \sqrt{1 + \rho_{ij}^2 + \kappa_{ij}} \qquad (5.58)$$

where $\rho_{ij} = \text{cor}(X_i, X_j)$ is the ordinary correlation coefficient and κ_{ij} the **cross-kurtosis**

$$\kappa_{ij} = \frac{E(X_i - \xi_i)^2(X_j - \xi_j)^2}{\sigma_i^2\sigma_j^2} - (1 + 2\rho_{ij}^2); \tag{5.59}$$

see Kendall and Stuart (1977), p. 250. The cross-kurtosis vanishes for normal data and reduces to ordinary kurtosis if $i = j$.

Covariances, like standard deviations, are more accurately estimated on a shorter time scale. Suppose the historical data consist of nK one-step returns with $\hat{\sigma}_{ij}$ as the standard covariance estimate. Then $K\hat{\sigma}_{ij}$ is an estimate of the covariance $\sigma_{K;ij}$ of K-step returns, and the approximation (5.58) yields

$$\text{sd}(K\hat{\sigma}_{ij}) \doteq K\frac{\sigma_i\sigma_j}{\sqrt{nK}}\sqrt{1 + \rho_{ij}^2 + \kappa_{ij}} = \sqrt{K}\frac{\sigma_i\sigma_j}{\sqrt{n}}\sqrt{1 + \rho_{ij}^2 + \kappa_{ij}}.$$

Compare this with the estimate $\hat{\sigma}_{K;ij}$ using the K-step returns only. With $\kappa_{ij;K}$ the cross-kurtosis of such returns, then

$$\text{sd}(\hat{\sigma}_{K;ij}) \doteq \frac{(\sqrt{K}\sigma_i)(\sqrt{K}\sigma_j)}{\sqrt{n}}\sqrt{1 + \rho_{ij}^2 + \kappa_{K;ij}}$$

since $\sqrt{K}\sigma_i$ are the volatilities of K-step returns. As with the ordinary kurtosis

$$\kappa_{K;ij} = \frac{\kappa_{ij}}{K} \quad \text{which yields} \quad \text{sd}(\hat{\sigma}_{K;ij}) \doteq \sqrt{K}\frac{\sigma_i\sigma_j}{\sqrt{n}}\sqrt{K(1 + \rho_{ij}^2) + \kappa_{ij}},$$

so that

$$\frac{\text{sd}(\hat{\sigma}_{K;ij})}{\text{sd}(K\hat{\sigma}_{ij})} \doteq \sqrt{\frac{K(1 + \rho_{ij}^2) + \kappa_{ij}}{1 + \rho_{ij}^2 + \kappa_{ij}}} > 1.$$

The gain in a shorter time scale may again be considerable.

5.9 Bibliographical notes

5.9.1 General work

Much of the material in this chapter is covered in more detail in standard textbooks on statistics and financial economics. The portfolio theory in Section 5.3, going back to Markowitz (1952), is outlined in classics like Copeland *et al.* (2005) as is the CAPM of Section 5.4 also. Litterman (2003) and Rachev *et al.* (2008) discuss a possible stabilization of the Markowitz solution along the Bayesian line introduced in Section 7.6. The much-cited book by Mardia *et al.* (1979) on multivariate statistics develops the Gaussian distribution theory (Section 5.4 and Appendix B.3) in much the same way as here. A very readable account of the correlation diminishing property of non-linear transformations when applied to Gaussian models is found in Kendall and Stuart (1979), see p. 600. The time series models (Sections 5.5 and 5.6) only scratch the surface of a huge theory (more in Chapter 13). Priestley (1981) is a thorough and fairly elementary classic; see also Schumway and Stoffer (2006). For an actuarial and financial perspective consult Mikosch (2004) (elementary) and Rolski *et al.* (1999) or Kijima (2003) (more advanced).

5.9.2 Continuous-time processes

The link to continuous time can be understood (as we have seen) without stochastic analysis, but if you want that perspective Neftci (2000) is a good place to start. Random walk models in Section 5.5 were only treated from a Gaussian angle. A more general line is the **Lévy** process. It is now assumed that:

(i) the distribution of the increments $Y(t+h) - Y(t)$ of the process $Y(t)$ in continuous time is the same for all t;
(ii) $Y(t+h_1) - Y(t)$ and $Y(s+h_2) - Y(s)$ are independent whenever the two intervals $(t, t+h_1)$ and $(s, s+h_2)$ are non-overlapping;
(iii) $Y(t+h) - Y(t)$ tends to zero as $h \to 0$ (see Appendix A.2 for definitions of such *stochastic* convergence).

An elementary account of Lévy processes is offered by Benth (2004); see also Applebaum (2004) and Cont and Tankov (2004) for mathematically more advanced reviews.

5.9.3 Historical data and the time scale

It was established in Section 5.7 that volatiltity and covariance estimates are more accurate when computed from shorter time scales than used for analysis. This is well known in financial economics; see De Santis *et al.* (2003). Deeper studies on this issue are appearing in economics and statistics, where new and improved estimation methods have been derived by examining limits when the sampling interval $h \to 0$; see Barndorff-Nielsen and Shepard (2004), Zhang *et al.* (2005) and Gloter (2007).

5.10 Exercises

Section 5.2

Exercise 5.1

(a) Insert $w_i = 1/\sigma_i$ and $\sigma_{ij} = \rho\sigma_i\sigma_j$ into the variance formula (5.2) and verify that this yields $\text{var}(\mathcal{X}) = J + J(J-1)\rho$. [*Hint*: There are $J(J-1)$ pairs (i, j) with $i \neq j$.]

(b) Argue that $\rho > -1/(J-1)$ in equicorrelation models.

Exercise 5.2 Suppose a model for three assets specifies $\rho_{ij} = 0.8$ for $i \neq j$. Somebody claims that the correlation ρ_{23} between assets 2 and 3 is too high and should be reduced to $\rho_{23} = 0.25$ so that now $\rho_{12} = \rho_{13} = 0.8$ and $\rho_{23} = 0.25$. Is such a change possible? [*Hint*: Insert $w_1 = -1.5/\sqrt{\sigma_{11}}$, $w_2 = 1/\sqrt{\sigma_{22}}$ and $w_3 = 1/\sqrt{\sigma_{33}}$ into the variance formula (5.2).]

Exercise 5.3 Let $R_1 = e^{\xi+\sigma\varepsilon_1} - 1$ and $R_2 = e^{\xi+\sigma\varepsilon_2}$ be log-normal returns with $\rho = \mathrm{cor}(\varepsilon_1, \varepsilon_2)$ and let $\mathcal{R} = wR_1 + (1-w)R_2$.

(a) Write a simulation program computing $\mathrm{sd}(\mathcal{R})/\mathrm{sd}(R_1)$.

R-*commands*:

```
eps=matrix(rnorm(2*m),m,2);
eps[,2]=ρ*eps[,1]+sqrt(1-ρ**2)*eps[,2]; R=exp(ξ+σ*eps)-1;
Ratio=sd(w*R[,1]+(1-w)*R[,2])/sd(R[,1]).
```

(b) Use 100 000 simulations to compute this diversification ratio when $\xi = 0.05$, $\sigma = 0.25$, $w = 0.5$ and $\rho = 0.0$, 0.5 and 0.8 and compare with the exact ratio $\sqrt{(1+\rho)/2}$ for *normal* asset returns.

Exercise 5.4 Daily log-returns of the industrial, transport, utility and finance indexes of the New York Stock Exchange for the period 1983 to 2001 are stored as the four columns in `newyork.daily.txt`.

(a) Download the data.

R-*commands*:

```
x=matrix(scan(''newyork.daily.txt''),byrow=T,ncol=4).
```

(b) Compute their means and covariance matrix.

R-*commands*:

```
x̄=apply(x,2,mean); Covx=cov(x).
```

(c) Redo (b) for the returns.

R-*commands*:

```
R=exp(x)-1; R̄=apply(R,2,mean); CovR=cov(R).
```

(d) Compute the volatilities and the correlation matrix of the returns.

R-*commands*:

```
VolR=sqrt(diag(CovR)); CorR=cor(R).
```

Exercise 5.5 If $a_1, \ldots, a_J$ are coefficients satisfying $|a_j| \leq 1$ and $\eta_0, \ldots, \eta_J$ are independent and $N(0,1)$, define

$$\varepsilon_j = a_j\eta_0 + \sqrt{1-a_j^2}\,\eta_j, \quad j = 1, \ldots, J.$$

(a) Show that $\varepsilon_1, \ldots, \varepsilon_J$ are $N(0,1)$ with $\text{cor}(\varepsilon_i, \varepsilon_j) = a_i a_j$ when $i \neq j$. [*Hint*: Evaluate the product $\varepsilon_i \varepsilon_j$ and add the expectations of the four terms.] Let $X_j = \xi_j + \sigma_j \varepsilon_j$ for $j = 1, \ldots, J$ where ξ_j and σ_j are parameters.
(b) Argue that $\text{cor}(X_i, X_j) = a_i a_j$ for $i \neq j$. The popular CAPM in financial economics (Section 5.3) is of this type.

Exercise 5.6 Compute the correlation matrix in Exercise 5.5 when $a_1 = 0.970$, $a_2 = 0.767$, $a_3 = 0.746$ and $a_4 = 0.746$ and compare it with the one in Exercise 5.4(d).
R-*commands*:

```
a=c(a1,a2,a3,a4); Cor=a%o%a; diag(Cor)=1.
```

Section 5.3

Exercise 5.7

(a) Compute the weights and volatilities of a Markowitz portfolio with e_g as expected gain.
R-*commands*:
```
w̃=solve(Σ,ξ-r);
γ=(e_g-r)/w̃%*%(ξ-r); w=γ*w̃; vol=sqrt(w%*%Σ%*%w).
```
(b) Read the LTCM parameters in Table 5.1 into $\boldsymbol{\xi}$, $\boldsymbol{\Sigma}$ and r when $\rho = 0.9654$. Verify that the asset weights become those in Table 5.1 when $e_g = 3.3869\%$ and compute the portfolio volatility.
R-*commands*:
Those in (a) with
```
v=c(1.58**2,ρ*1.58*1.90,ρ*1.58*1.90,1.90**2);
Σ=matrix(v,2,2); ξ=c(0.6107,0.4670); r=0.4361.
```
(c) Redo (b) when $\rho = 0.8$ and $\rho = 0.6$ and examine how much the weights and volatilities change.

Exercise 5.8 Take expectations and covariance matrix from the daily New York Stock Exchange returns in Exercise 5.4 and let $r = 0.00025$.

(a) Compute the Markowitz weights $\tilde{w}_1, \ldots, \tilde{w}_4$ and also the mean ($\tilde{e}_g$) and volatility ($\tilde{\sigma}$) of $\mathcal{R} = r + \tilde{w}_1(R_1 - r) + \cdots + \tilde{w}_4(R_4 - r)$.
R-*commands*:
With $\boldsymbol{\xi}=\overline{R}$ and $\boldsymbol{\Sigma} = \text{Cov}_R$ from Exercise 5.4 and $r = 0.00025$ use
```
w̃=solve(Σ,ξ-r); ẽ_g=r+w̃%*%(ξ-r); σ̃=sqrt(w̃%*%Σ%*%w̃).
```
(b) Tabulate the volatility of the Markowitz portfolios when e_g varies in 10 equal steps between 0.0005 and 0.0015.
R-*commands*:
```
e_g=0.0005+0:10*0.0001; γ=(e_g-r)/(ẽ_g-r); vol=γ*σ̃.
```

Exercise 5.9

(a) Compute the covariance matrix of the New York Stock Exchange data when its correlation matrix is replaced by the approximation in Exercise 5.6 and the volatilities are unchanged.
R-*commands*:
Take `VolR` and `Cor` from Exercises 5.4(d) and 5.6 and use
`D=diag(VolR); Σ=D%*%Cor%*%D`.

(b) Compute for this new covariance matrix weights, expectation and volatility for the portfolio in Exercise 5.8(a) with other conditions as before and compare with the results there.
R-*commands*:
As in Exercise 5.8(a).

Exercise 5.10

(a) If ξ_j and σ_j are expectation and volatility of asset j returns, argue that $(\xi_j - r)/\sigma_j$ is the Sharp ratio with the risk-free investment as benchmark.
(b) Redo the computations in Exercise 5.8 with new expected returns ξ'_j for which $(\xi'_j - r)/\sigma_j$ is the same for all j and coinciding with the average Sharp ratio in the earlier model.
R-*commands*:
With $\overline{R}$ and Vol_R from Exercise 5.4 use `ξ=r+VolR*mean((R̄ -r)/VolR)` and continue as in Exercise 5.8(a).

(c) How much have the weights $\tilde{w}$ changed from Exercise 5.8? The difficulty in estimating expected equity returns was discussed in Section 2.2.

Exercise 5.11 Consider an economy of I investors with wealth $v_1, \ldots, v_I$. There are J assets, and investor i holds V_{ij} in asset j. Total and relative market values are then $V_j = V_{1j} + \cdots + V_{Ij}$ and $w_{Mj} = V_j/(V_1 + \cdots + V_J)$.

(a) Argue that if investors pursue Markowitz strategies, then $V_{ij} = \theta_i \tilde{w}_j v_i$ where $\theta_1, \ldots, \theta_I$ are determined by attitudes towards risk and $\tilde{w}_1, \ldots, \tilde{w}_J$ by (5.9).
(b) Show that $w_{Mj} = \gamma \tilde{w}_j$ for $j = 1, \ldots, J$ where γ is a constant of proportionality. The portfolio $\tilde{w}_1, \ldots, \tilde{w}_J$ is in this sense a **market** portfolio.

Exercise 5.12 Let R_M be the return of the market portfolio in Exercise 5.11 with $\xi_M = E(R_M)$ and $\sigma_M = \text{sd}(R_M)$. Similarly, let $\xi_j = E(R_j)$ and $\sigma_j = \text{sd}(R_j)$ for asset j. Suppose a Markowitz portfolio is set up in terms of M, asset j and cash with w_M and w_j the weights on M and j.

(a) Deduce from (5.9) and (5.10) that w_M and w_j satisfy the equations

$$\sigma_M^2 w_M + \sigma_{Mj} w_j = \gamma(\xi_M - r) \quad \text{and} \quad \sigma_{Mj} w_M + \sigma_j^2 w_j = \gamma(\xi_j - r)$$

where $\sigma_{Mj} = \text{cov}(R_M, R_j)$, r is the risk-free return and γ a constant.

(b) If M is Markowitz efficient itself, argue that the preceding equations hold with $w_j = 0$ so that $\sigma_M^2 w_M = \gamma(\xi_M - r)$ and $\sigma_{Mj} w_M = \gamma(\xi_j - r)$, from which it follows that $\xi_j - r = \beta_j(\xi_M - r)$ where $\beta_j = \sigma_{Mj}/\sigma_M^2$. This is the **CAPM**.

Exercise 5.13 Economists describe investor behaviour by assigning **utility** $U(v)$ to wealth v. Usually $dU(v)/dv > 0$ and $d^2U(v)/dv^2 < 0$ with much wealth being preferred to little, but less strongly as v grows. Common examples are $U(v) = \log(v)$, $U(v) = v^\gamma$ for $0 < \gamma < 1$ and $U(v) = 1 - e^{-\gamma v}$ for $\gamma > 0$. A standard assumption in academic work is investors trying to maximize *expected* utility $u = E\{U(v_0 + \mathcal{R}v_0)\}$ where v_0 is initial wealth and $\mathcal{R}$ portfolio return.

(a) Argue that if $\mathcal{R} \sim N(\xi_p, \sigma_p)$, then $u = u(\xi_p, \sigma_p)$ is

$$u(\xi_p, \sigma_p) = \int_{-\infty}^{\infty} U(v_0 + v_0\xi_p + v_0\sigma_p x)\varphi(x)\,dx \quad \text{where } \varphi(x) = \frac{1}{\sqrt{2\pi}}e^{-x^2/2}$$

so that $u(\xi_p, \sigma_p)$ increases with ξ_p.

(b) Write $U'(v) = dU(v)/dv$ and show that

$$\begin{aligned}\frac{\partial u(\xi_p, \sigma_p)}{\partial \sigma_p} &= v_0 \int_{-\infty}^{\infty} U'(v_0 + v_0\xi_p + v_0\sigma_p x)x\varphi(x)\,dx \\ &= v_0 \int_0^{\infty} \{U'(v_0 + v_0\xi_p + v_0\sigma_p x) - U'(v_0 + v_0\xi_p - v_0\sigma_p x)\}x\varphi(x)\,dx \\ &< 0.\end{aligned}$$

[*Hint*: Utilize the fact that $\varphi(x) = \varphi(-x)$ and $U'(v)$ is decreasing in v.]

(c) Deduce from (a) and (b) that the Markowitz portfolio (5.10) maximizes expected utility for normal returns.

Section 5.4

Exercise 5.14 Verify that the covariance matrices

$$\boldsymbol{\Sigma} = \begin{pmatrix} 1 & \rho \\ \rho & 1 \end{pmatrix} \quad \text{and} \quad \boldsymbol{\Sigma} = \begin{pmatrix} 1 & \rho_{12} & \rho_{13} \\ \rho_{12} & 1 & \rho_{23} \\ \rho_{13} & \rho_{23} & 1 \end{pmatrix}$$

can be factorized as $\boldsymbol{\Sigma} = CC^{\mathrm{T}}$ where

$$\mathbf{C} = \begin{pmatrix} 1 & 0 \\ \rho & \sqrt{1-\rho^2} \end{pmatrix} \quad \text{and} \quad \mathbf{C} = \begin{pmatrix} 1 & 0 & 0 \\ \rho_{12} & \sqrt{1-\rho_{12}^2} & 0 \\ \rho_{13} & (\rho_{23} - \rho_{12}\rho_{13})\big/\sqrt{1-\rho_{12}^2} & c_{33} \end{pmatrix}$$

for $c_{33} = \sqrt{(1 - \rho_{12}^2 - \rho_{13}^2 - \rho_{23}^2 + 2\rho_{12}\rho_{13}\rho_{23})/(1-\rho_{12}^2)}$. Numerical methods are needed above 3×3!

Exercise 5.15

(a) Compute the Cholesky matrix of the covariance matrix of the New York Stock Exchange returns in Exercise 5.4.

R-*commands*:

With `CovR` from Exercise 5.4(c) use `C=t(chol(CovR))`.

(b) Write a program generating m simulations of normal asset returns with means, volatilities and correlations from the New York data.

R-*commands*:

With ξ=$\overline{R}$ from Exercise 5.4(c) use `eta=matrix(rnorm(4*m),4,m); eps=C%*%eta; R=ξ+eps`.

(c) Run the program with $m = 100\,000$ and check it by comparing means, volatilities and correlations computed from the simulations with those in Exercise 5.4.

R-*commands*:

`Mean=apply(R,1,mean); Vol=apply(R,1,sd); Cor=cor(t(R))`.

Exercise 5.16 Let $\mathbf{w} = (w_1, \ldots, w_4)$ be weights on the four assets in Exercise 5.15.

(a) Write a program generating m simulations of the portfolio return $\mathcal{R}$.

R-*commands*:

With R from Exercise 5.15(b) use `𝓡=apply(w*R,2,sum)`.

(b) Run the program when all $w_j = 0.25$ and compare the volatility of the portfolio with those of the individual assets.

R-*commands*:

`Vol=sd(𝓡)`.

Exercise 5.17 Using (5.21), show that means ξ_i and covariances σ_{ij} of normal log-returns yield given means $E(R_i)$ and covariances $\text{cov}(R_i, R_j)$ of returns when

$$\sigma_{ij} = \log\left(1 + \frac{\text{cov}(R_i, R_j)}{\{1 + E(R_i)\}\{1 + E(R_j)\}}\right) \quad \text{and} \quad \xi_i = \log\{1 + E(R_i)\} - \sigma_{ii}/2.$$

Exercise 5.18

(a) Write a program adapting the mean vector $\boldsymbol{\xi}$ and covariance matrix $\boldsymbol{\Sigma}$ for log-returns to given means and covariances for their returns.

R-*commands*:

With $\overline{R}$ and Cov_R the mean vector and covariance matrix for the returns use `D=diag(1/(1+R̄)); Σ=log(1+D%*%CovR%*%D); ξ=log(1+R̄)-diag(Σ)/2`.

(b) If $E(R_i) = 11\%$, $\mathrm{sd}(R_i) = 25\%$ for $i = 1, 2, 3$ and $\mathrm{cor}(R_1, R_2) = \mathrm{cor}(R_1, R_3) = 0.8$ and $\mathrm{cor}(R_2, R_3) = 0.4$, show that for the log-returns $\xi_i = 7.926\%$ and $\sigma_i = 22.24\%$ whereas the correlations only change slightly to 0.804 and 0.406. This was used to compute Table 5.2.

Exercise 5.19 Let $X_1, \ldots, X_J$ be a heavy-tailed random vector of the form $X_j = \xi_j + \sqrt{Z}\,\varepsilon_j$ where $\varepsilon_1, \ldots, \varepsilon_J$ are dependent and Gaussian and independent of $Z = (\alpha - 1)/(\alpha G)$ for $G \sim \text{Gamma}(\alpha)$. Show that the covariance matrix of $X_1, \ldots, X_J$ coincides with that of $\varepsilon_1, \ldots, \varepsilon_J$. [*Hint*: $E(1/G) = \alpha/(\alpha - 1)$.]

Exercise 5.20

(a) Write a program simulating $X_1, \ldots, X_J$ in Exercise 5.19.

R-*commands*:

With $\boldsymbol{\xi}$ and $\boldsymbol{\Sigma}$ the mean vector and covariance matrix use

```
C=t(chol(Σ)); eta=matrix(rnorm(4*m),4,m); eps=t(C%*%eta);
Z=(α-1)/rgamma(m,α); X=ξ+t(sqrt(Z)*eps).
```

(b) Run the program when $m = 100\,000$ and $\alpha = 1.5$ with $\boldsymbol{\xi}$ and $\boldsymbol{\Sigma}$ taken from the New York log-return data and compare the mean vector and covariance matrix with those in Exercise 5.4(b).

R-*commands*:

```
Mean=apply(t(X),2,mean); Cov=cov(t(X)).
```

Exercise 5.21 Let $\mathcal{R} = (R_1 + \cdots + R_4)/4$ be a portfolio return for the log-returns in Exercise 5.20.

(a) Write a program generating m simulations of $\mathcal{R}$.

R-*commands*:

With `X` as in Exercise 5.20(a) use `R=apply(exp(X)-1,2,mean)`.

(b) Compute portfolio percentiles 0.01, 0.10, 0.25, 0.50, 0.75, 0.90 and 0.99 when $m = 100\,000$ and $\alpha = 1.5$.

R-*commands*:

```
ind=c(0.01,0.10,0.25,0.50,0.75,0.90,0.99)*m;
percentile=sort(R)[ind].
```

(c) Redo (b) when $\alpha = 5$ and $\alpha = 500$ to indicate sensitivity towards α.

Section 5.5

Exercise 5.22 Let $R_{0:K} = (S_K - S_0)/S_0$ be the return after K periods when $S_k = S_{k-1}e^{\xi + \sigma\varepsilon_k}$ for $k = 1, \ldots, K$ with $\varepsilon_1, \ldots, \varepsilon_K$ independent and $N(0, 1)$.

(a) Argue that $R_{0:K} = e^{K\xi + \sqrt{K}\sigma\varepsilon} - 1$ where $\varepsilon \sim N(0, 1)$.

(b) Compute the 5%, 25%, 50%, 75% and 95% percentiles for $R_{0:K}$ when $K = 20$, $\xi = 0.05$ and $\sigma = 0.25$ and note the huge variation in such earnings.

R-*commands*:

```
ϵ=c(0.05,0.25,0.50,0.75,0.95);
percentiles=exp(K*ξ+sqrt(K)*σ*qnorm(ϵ))-1.
```

(c) To what extent is the evaluation valid when $\varepsilon_1, \ldots, \varepsilon_K$ isn't Gaussian?

Exercise 5.23

(a) Write a program generating m simulations of $R_{0:1}, \ldots R_{0:K}$ under the model in the preceding exercise.

R-*commands*:

```
eps=matrix(rnorm(m*K),K,m);
R=exp(apply(ξ+σ*eps,2,cumsum))-1.
```

(b) Run the program when $K = 20$, $\xi = 0.05$, $\sigma = 0.25$ and $m = 50$ and plot the accumulated returns against time for all the simulated sequences jointly.

R-*commands*:

```
R=rbind(rep(0:m),R); matplot(0:K,R,''l'').
```

(c) Redo a couple of times to examine the variation.

Exercise 5.24 Introduce stochastic volatilities $\sigma_k = \xi_\sigma / \sqrt{G_k}$ with $G_k \sim \text{Gamma}(\alpha)$ so that the model in Exercise 5.22 becomes $S_k = S_{k-1} e^{\xi + \sigma_k \varepsilon_k}$ with all volatilities independent.

(a) Write a simulation program similar to that in Exercise 5.23.

R-*commands*:

```
eps=matrix(rnorm(m*K),K,m); G=rgamma(m*K,α)/α;
R=exp(apply(ξ+ξσ*eps/sqrt(G),2,cumsum))-1.
```

(b) Run the program when $K = 20$, $\xi = 0.05$, $\xi_\sigma = 0.25$, $\alpha = 5$ and $m = 50$ and plot the accumulated returns as in Exercise 5.23(b).

(c) Is there any sign of the oscillations now having changed?

Exercise 5.25

(a) Redo the simulations in Exercise 5.24(b) when $m = 10\,000$ so that the 5%, 25%, 50%, 75% and 95% percentiles of $R_{0:20}$ can be approximated.

R-*commands*:

With R as in Exercise 5.24 use `ind=c(0.05,0.25,0.50,0.75,0.95)*m;`

```
percentiles=sort(R[20,])[ind].
```

(b) Compare with Exercise 5.22(b) and judge the impact of the quite substantial stochastic volatility.

Exercise 5.26 Investigate Gaussian random walk behaviour when $\xi = 0$ (no drift) and $\sigma = 0.25$. Draw a single realization of the log-returns $X_{0:k} = \log(1 + R_{0:k})$ for k up to $m = 10^6$ years (!) and plot every hundredth of it against k.

R-*commands*:

```
X=σ*cumsum(rnorm(m)); ind=1:(m/100)*100;
plot(ind,X[ind],''l'').
```

Exercise 5.27 Let $S_{ik} = S_{ik-1}e^{\xi+\sigma\varepsilon_{ik}}$ for $i = 1, 2$ be Gaussian random walks similar to those in earlier exercises and correlated through $\rho = \text{cor}(\varepsilon_{1k}, \varepsilon_{2k})$.

(a) Write a program generating, for both assets, simulations of accumulated returns up to time K.

R-*commands*:

```
eps=matrix(rnorm(2*K),K,2);
eps[,2]=ρ*eps[,1]+sqrt(1-ρ**2)*eps[,2];
R=exp(ξ+σ*apply(eps,2,cumsum))-1.
```

(b) Run the program when $K = 50$, $\xi = 0.05$, $\sigma = 0.25$ and $\rho = 0$ and plot the returns jointly against time.

R-*commands*:

```
R=cbind(c(0,0),R); matplot(0:K,R,''l'').
```

(c) Redo the plot in (b) a few times when $\rho = 0$, 0.9 and -0.9 and examine the patterns and how they vary with ρ.

Section 5.6

Exercise 5.28

(a) Download Norwegian interest rates for the period 1990–2008 from `nibornor.txt`.

R-*commands*:

```
r=scan(``nibornor.txt'').
```

(b) Compute and plot the autocorrelation function and argue that a first-order autoregression is a possible model.

R-*commands*:

```
acf(r).
```

Exercise 5.29 A simple way to fit the Vasiček model is to utilize that the sample mean and standard deviation $\bar{r}$ and s tend to ξ and $\sigma/\sqrt{1-a^2}$ and the first-order autocorrelation $\hat{\rho}_1$ to a as the length of the historical data vector $n \to \infty$.

(a) Argue that $\hat{\xi} = \bar{r}$, $\hat{a} = \hat{\rho}_1$ and $\hat{\sigma} = s\sqrt{1-\hat{a}^2}$ are possible estimates.

(b) Compute them for the data in Exercise 5.28.

R-*commands*:

With data `r` use $\hat{\xi}$=`mean(r)`; $\hat{a}$=`acf(r)[[1]][2]`; $\hat{\sigma}$=`sd(r)*sqrt(1-`$\hat{a}^2$`)`.

[*Answer*: $\hat{\xi} = 0.062$, $\hat{\sigma} = 0.018$, $\hat{a} = 0.71$.]

Exercise 5.30

(a) Write a program generating m simulations of $r_0, \ldots, r_K$ under a Gaussian Vasiček model.

R-*commands*:

```
x0 = r0 − ξ; X=matrix(x0,K+1,m);
for (k in 1:K+1) X[k,]=a*X[k-1,]+σ*rnorm(m); r=X+ξ.
```

(b) Run the program when $\xi = 0.062$, $\sigma = 0.018$, $a = 0.71$ as in Exercise 5.29 and $r_0 = 0.04$, $K = 25$ and $m = 25$ and plot the simulations jointly against time.

R-*commands*:

```
matplot(0:K,r,''l'').
```

(c) Redo (b) when $r_0 = 0.10$.

Exercise 5.31

(a) Simulate the model in Exercise 5.30 when $r_0 = 0.04$, $K = 10$ and $m = 100\,000$. Estimate the density function for all r_k and plot them jointly.

R-*commands*:

Use the R-function `e531a`.

(b) Redo when $r_0 = 0.10$.

(c) Interpret the patterns in (a) and (b) and what they tell you about the behaviour of stationary processes.

Exercise 5.32 Suppose the mean level of the Norwegian Nibor for the period 1990–2008 is considered too high for the twenty-first century and that $\xi = 4\%$ is deemed more appropriate.

(a) Redo simulations and plots in Exercise 5.30 under this condition.

R-*commands*:

As in Exercise 5.30.

(b) Use the plots to criticize the model.

Exercise 5.33

(a) Let $\sigma_x = \sigma/\sqrt{1-a^2}$ and insert $X_k = aX_{k-1} + \sigma\varepsilon_k$ and $X_{k-1} = \log(r_{k-1}/\xi) + \sigma_x^2/2$ into (5.43) to show that for the Black–Karasinski model

$$r_k = r_{k-1}^a \xi^{1-a} e^{-\sigma^2/(2+2a)+\sigma\varepsilon_k}.$$

(b) Point out that $\mathrm{sd}(r_k|r_{k-1})$ is proportional to r_{k-1}^a and argue that this means that interest rate oscillations under the Black–Karasinski model are higher at higher levels.

Exercise 5.34

(a) Show that under the Black–Karasinski model (5.43)

$$E(r_k|r_0) \to \xi \quad \text{and} \quad \mathrm{sd}(r_k|r_0) \to \xi\sqrt{e^{\sigma^2/(1-a^2)} - 1} \quad \text{as } k \to \infty.$$

[*Hint*: Use properties of the log-normal distribution.]

(b) If the Black–Karasinski model is calibrated so that its limiting standard deviation coincides with Vasiček's, show that its σ, written σ^{BK}, becomes

$$\sigma^{\mathrm{BK}} = \sqrt{\log\left(1 + \frac{\sigma^2}{(1-a^2)\xi^2}\right)(1-a^2)}.$$

(c) Compute σ^{BK} when $\xi = 0.062$, $\sigma = 0.018$, $a = 0.71$ as in Exercise 5.29. [*Answer*: $\sigma^{\mathrm{BK}} = 0.28$.]

Exercise 5.35

(a) Revise the program in Exercise 5.30 to generate simulations under the Black–Karasinski model.

R-*commands*:

```
σx=σ/sqrt(1-a**2);x0=log(r0/ξ)+σx**2/2; X=matrix(x0,K+1,m);
for (k in 1:K+1)X[k,]=a*X[k-1,]+σ*rnorm(m);
r=ξ*exp(-σx**2/2+X).
```

(b) Run the program when $\xi = 0.062$, $\sigma = 0.28$, $a = 0.71$, $r_0 = 0.04$, $K = 25$ and $m = 25$ and plot the simulations jointly against time.

R-*commands*:

```
matplot(0:K,r,''l'').
```

(c) Compare with Exercise 5.30(b) (redo a few times if necessary) and summarize the differences between the patterns under the two models.

Exercise 5.36

(a) Simulate $r_{0:K} = (1 + r_1)\cdots(1 + r_K) - 1$ under the Vasiček model.

R-*commands*:

With `r` as in Exercise 5.30 use `r0:K=apply(1+r,2,prod)-1`.

(b) Draw $m = 10\,000$ simulations of $r_{0:K}$ when $\xi = 0.062$, $\sigma = 0.018$, $a = 0.71$, $r_0 = 0.04$ and $K = 20$ and estimate/plot its density function.

R-*commands*:

`plot(density(r0:K))`.

(c) Redo (a) and (b) for the Black–Karasinski model in Exercise 5.35 and plot the new density function jointly with the other.

R-*commands*:

With `r` from Exercise 5.35 use

`r0:K=apply(1+r,2,prod)-1; d=density(r0:K); lines(d$x,d$y)`.

(d) What is the difference between the two models?

Section 5.7

Exercise 5.37 Suppose the daily log-returns in Exercise 5.4 are increments in random walks defining log-returns on a larger time scale. Use the covariance matrix to compute volatilities and correlation matrices for weekly, monthly and annual log-returns.

R-*commands*:

With `Covx` the covariance matrix in Exercise 5.4(b) use

`Vol=sqrt(diag(K*Covx)); Cor=(K*Covx)/(Vol%o%Vol)` for

$K = 5$ (week), $K = 25$ (month) and $K = 250$ (year).

Exercise 5.38

(a) Download the New York log-return data from file as in Exercise 5.4 and check for normality by Q–Q plotting.

R-*commands*:

With `x` as in Exercise 5.4 use `qqnorm(x[,j])` for `j` $= 1, \ldots, 4$.

(b) Write a program converting the data to K-day log-returns.

R-*commands*:

```
n=floor(4690/K); x1=matrix(0,n,4);
for (i in 1:n) x1[i,]=apply(x[(1+(i-1)*K):(i*K),],2,sum).
```

(c) Run the program for $K = 5$, 25 and 250 and check each time the normality through Q–Q plotting.

R-*commands*:

As in (a) with `x1` in place of `x`.

(d) Comment on how the fit to the normal depends on K.

Exercise 5.39

(a) Run the program in Exercise 5.38(b) when $K = 5$ and estimate volatilities and correlations for returns on this weekly time scale.

R-*commands*:

With `x₁` as in Exercise 5.38(b) use `Vol=apply(x₁,2,sd); Cor=cor(x₁)`.

(b) Compare with the results in Exercise 5.37, which were obtained by estimating on a daily time scale and then converting to a weekly one.
(c) Redo (a) and (b) when $K = 25$ and $K = 250$.
(d) Is there any sign in the results that the method in this exercise is inferior to the one in Exercise 5.37?

Exercise 5.40 Let σ_K be the volatility of K-day log-returns and $\hat{\sigma}_K$ an estimate using K-day data. Suppose data over periods of length $1/M$ days are available with $\hat{\sigma}_0$ the volatility estimate on this time scale.

(a) Use (5.48) to deduce that

$$\frac{\text{sd}(\hat{\sigma}_K)}{\text{sd}(\sqrt{KM}\hat{\sigma}_0)} \doteq \sqrt{\frac{KM + \kappa_0/2}{1 + \kappa_0/2}}$$

where κ_0 is the kurtosis of $1/M$-data.
(b) If κ is the kurtosis of daily log-returns, argue that $\kappa = \kappa_0/M$. [*Hint*: Use the kurtosis for the mean of independent and identically distributed data in Appendix A.2.]
(c) Show that $\text{sd}(\hat{\sigma}_K)/\text{sd}(\sqrt{KM}\hat{\sigma}_0)$ is approximately $\sqrt{(K + \kappa/2)/(1/M + \kappa/2)}$, which is an increasing function of M.
(d) Argue that the benefit of going from $M = 1$ (daily data) to $M = 24$ (hourly data) isn't so great when $K = 25$ (monthly volatilities) and $\kappa = 6$.

Exercise 5.41 Suppose there are 250 days in a financial year. Determine the parameters of a geometric random walk on a daily time scale corresponding to $\xi = 0.05$ and $\sigma = 0.25$ on an annual one.

Exercise 5.42 Let $X_k = aX_{k-1} + \sigma\varepsilon_k$ for $k = 1, 2, \ldots$ be a first-order autoregressive process on a monthly time scale.

(a) Argue that the process X_{12k} for $k = 1, 2, \ldots$ on an annual time scale is still first-order autoregressive, but now with parameters a^{12} and $\sigma\sqrt{(1 - a^{24})/(1 - a^2)}$. Suppose simulations are needed on an annual time scale. The scheme may then be run on the original monthly scale or directly on the annual one.
(b) Explain that the results are the same if the error process $\varepsilon_1, \varepsilon_2, \ldots$ is Gaussian.
(c) What if the distribution is a different one?

Exercise 5.43 Consider a Black–Karasinski model (5.43) on an annual time scale with parameters $\xi = 0.05$, $a = 0.7$ and $\sigma = 0.25$. Use (5.57) to identify the parameters σ_q and a_q of the corresponding model in continuous time.

6

Modelling II: Conditional and non-linear

6.1 Introduction

Insurance requires modelling tools different from those of the preceding chapter. Pension schemes and life insurance make use of **lifecycle** descriptions. Individuals start as 'active' (paying contributions), at one point they 'retire' (drawing benefits) or become 'disabled' (benefits again) and they may die. Stochastic models are needed to keep track of what happens, but they cannot be constructed by means of linear relationships like those in the preceding chapter. There are no numerical variables to connect! Distributions are used instead.

The central concept is **conditional** probabilities and distributions, expressing mathematically that what has occurred is going to influence (but not determine) what comes next. That idea is the principal topic of the chapter. As elsewhere, mathematical aspects (here going rather deep) are downplayed for the conditional viewpoint as a modelling tool. Sequences of states in lifecycles involve time series (but of a different kind from those in Chapter 5) and are treated in Section 6.6. Actually, time may not be involved at all. Risk heterogeneity in property insurance is a typical (and important) example. Consider a car owner. What he encounters daily in the traffic is influenced by randomness, but so is (from a company point of view) his ability as a driver. These are uncertainties of entirely different origin and define a **hierarchy** (driver comes first). Conditional modelling is the natural way of connecting random effects operating on different levels like this. The same viewpoint is used when errors due to estimation and Monte Carlo are examined in the next chapter, and there are countless other examples.

Conditional arguments will hang over much of this chapter, and we embark on it in the next section. **Copulas** are an additional tool. The idea behind them is very different from conditioning and is a popular approach of fairly recent origin. Yet copulas have without doubt come to stay. Section 6.7 is an introduction.

6.2 Conditional modelling

6.2.1 Introduction

Conditional probabilities are defined in elementary textbooks in statistics. When an event A has occurred, the probability of B changes from $\Pr(B)$ to

$$\Pr(B|A) = \frac{\Pr(A \cap B)}{\Pr(A)} \quad \text{or equivalently} \quad \Pr(B|A) = \frac{\Pr(A|B)}{\Pr(A)}\Pr(B) \tag{6.1}$$

where the right-hand side is known as **Bayes' formula**. New information A leads to new odds for B, and also new prices as we shall see in Section 6.4. Conditional probabilities in this book are above all instruments for modelling and used to express random relationships between random variables. Note the mathematical notation. The condition is always placed to the right of a vertical bar. Similar notation is $Y|x$ (the random variable Y given $X = x$) with conditional density functions and expectations $f(y|x)$ and $E(Y|x)$.

Conditional modelling is **sequential** modelling, first X and then Y given X. The purpose of this section is to demonstrate the power in this line of thinking. It is the natural way to describe countless stochastic phenomena, and simulation is easy. Simply

$$\text{generate } X^* \quad \text{and then} \quad Y^* \text{ given } X^*,$$

the second drawing being dependent on the outcome of the first. The following examples all have major roles to play.

6.2.2 The conditional Gaussian

Bivariate normal models were defined in Chapter 2 through

$$X_1 = \xi_1 + \sigma_1\eta_1 \quad \text{and} \quad X_2 = \xi_2 + \sigma_2(\rho\eta_1 + \sqrt{1-\rho^2}\,\eta_2),$$

where η_1 and η_2 are independent and $N(0, 1)$; see (2.23). Suppose $X_1 = x_1$ is fixed. Then $\eta_1 = (x_1 - \xi_1)/\sigma_1$. Insert this into the representation for X_2, and we have

$$X_2 = \xi_2 + \sigma_2(\rho\frac{x_1 - \xi_1}{\sigma_1} + \sqrt{1-\rho^2}\,\eta_2),$$

or after some reorganizing

$$X_2 = \underbrace{(\xi_2 + \rho\sigma_2\tfrac{x_1-\xi_1}{\sigma_1})}_{\textit{expectation}} + \underbrace{(\sigma_2\sqrt{1-\rho^2})}_{\textit{standard deviation}}\eta_2. \tag{6.2}$$

Now η_2 is the only random term and X_2 is by definition normal with mean and standard deviation

$$E(X_2|x_1) = \xi_2 + \rho\sigma_2\frac{x_1 - \xi_1}{\sigma_1} \quad \text{and} \quad \mathrm{sd}(X_2|x_1) = \sigma_2\sqrt{1-\rho^2} \tag{6.3}$$

which applies when $X_1 = x_1$ is given. We are dealing with a **conditional distribution**. As x_1 is varied, so is the expectation and (for other models) also the standard deviation.

6.2.3 Survival modelling

Central quantities in life insurance are the **survival probabilities**

$$_tp_{y_0} = \Pr(Y > y_0 + t|Y > y_0) \tag{6.4}$$

where Y is how long an individual lives. A person of age y_0 reaches age $y_0 + t$ with probability $_tp_{y_0}$. If $F(y)$ is the distribution function of Y, then from (6.1) left

$$_tp_{y_0} = \frac{\Pr(Y > y_0 + t)}{\Pr(Y > y_0)} = \frac{1 - F(y_0 + t)}{1 - F(y_0)}. \tag{6.5}$$

Survival probabilities are needed on multiples of a given increment T, and both age and time sequences are involved. Let

$$\underbrace{y_l = lT, \quad l = 0, 1, \ldots}_{age} \quad \text{and} \quad \underbrace{T_k = kT, \quad k = 0, 1, \ldots,}_{time}$$

and write $_kp_{l_0} = {}_tp_{y_0}$ when $y_0 = l_0T$ and $t = kT$. The single-period version $p_l = {}_1p_l$ is a building block for the rest. Survival over longer time horizons means living through the coming periods so that

$$_kp_{l_0} = \underbrace{p_{l_0}}_{\text{first period}} \times \underbrace{p_{l_0+1}}_{\text{second period}} \times \cdots \times \underbrace{p_{l_0+k-1}}_{k\text{th period}}. \tag{6.6}$$

There will be more on such modelling in Section 12.3.

6.2.4 Over-threshold modelling

Conditional probabilities of the same type are needed in property insurance too, now in connection with large claims and reinsurance. For a given threshold b we seek the distribution of

$$Z_b = Z - b \quad \text{given} \quad Z > b, \tag{6.7}$$

and it can be written down by replacing t and y_0 by z and b on the right in (6.5). Thus

$$\Pr(Z_b > z|Z > b) = \frac{1 - F(b + z)}{1 - F(b)},$$

where $F(z)$ is the distribution function of Z. When differentiated with respect to z, this leads to

$$f_b(z) = \frac{f(b+z)}{1-F(b)}, \quad z > 0 \tag{6.8}$$

which is the density function for the amount exceeding a threshold b. Such tail distributions possess the remarkable property that, for most models used in practice, they become Pareto or exponential as $b \to \infty$. That story is told in Section 9.5.

6.2.5 Stochastic parameters

Let X be a random variable depending on a parameter ω. It is common, particularly in insurance, for ω to vary between individuals or differ in different periods of time. Such phenomena are expressed mathematically by making ω random. The model for X is now a *conditional* one, and an additional sub-model must be supplied for ω; i.e., first ω and then $X|\omega$. An early example in this book is the stochastic volatilities in Section 2.4.

Another is claim numbers in property insurance, where the model in Section 3.2 was the Poisson distribution with parameters $\lambda = \mu T$ for policies and $\lambda = J\mu T$ for portfolios. The key quantity μ may well vary between policy holders and also between different periods of time. Claim numbers (N for an individual or $\mathcal{N}$ for a portfolio) now become the outcome of two experiments, which may be expressed as

$$\underbrace{\mu = \xi G, \;\; N|\mu \sim \text{Poisson}(\mu T)}_{\textit{policy level}} \quad \text{or} \quad \underbrace{\mu = \xi G, \;\; \mathcal{N}|\mu \sim \text{Poisson}(J\mu T)}_{\textit{portfolio level}}, \tag{6.9}$$

where $E(G) = 1$ to make ξ *mean intensity*. The standard model for G is Gamma(α), one of the distributions introduced in Section 2.5. Now $E(\mu) = \xi$ and $\text{sd}(\mu) = \xi/\sqrt{\alpha}$. The μ-uncertainty is controlled by α and goes away as $\alpha \to \infty$, so that $\mu = \xi$ becomes fixed at the end; see Section 8.3 for more on such models.

6.2.6 Common factors

We may let ω influence more than one random variable. A special case of considerable interest is the **common factor** situation where

$$X_1, \ldots, X_J \quad \text{are } \textbf{conditionally} \text{ independent} \quad \text{given } \omega. \tag{6.10}$$

Claim numbers in general insurance is an example (see below), and the market component of the CAPM of Section 5.3 another. If ω isn't directly observable, factors are **hidden** or **latent**.

Common factors (whether hidden or not) increase risk and can't be diversified

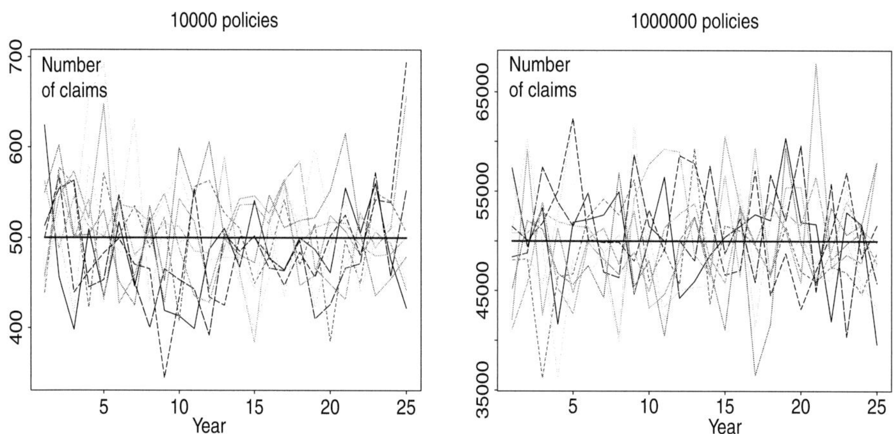

Figure 6.1 Simulated portfolio claim number scenarios ($m = 20$) under common, annual random intensities for $J = 10\,000$ policies (*left*) and $J = 1\,000\,000$ (*right*).

away. As an example, let $N_1, \ldots, N_J$ be annual claim numbers for J individuals. Suppose they are independent and Poisson distributed with parameter μT. Their sum $\mathcal{N} = N_1 + \cdots + N_J$ is Poisson too, with parameter $J\mu T$ as in (6.9); see Section 8.2. A common phenomenon is μ depending om weather conditions. This makes μ random, and the distribution of $N_1, \ldots, N_J$ must now be interpreted conditionally. Make μ Gamma distributed, and the portfolio number of claims is simulated as follows:

$$G^* \sim \text{Gamma}(\alpha), \quad \mu^* \leftarrow \xi G^* \quad \text{and then} \quad \mathcal{N}^* \sim \text{Poisson}(J\mu^* T).$$

Claim numbers for 25 consecutive years were generated independently of each other and plotted against time in Figure 6.1. The parameters used were $\xi = 5\%$, $\alpha = 100$ and $T = 1$. There was one small portfolio (with $J = 10\,000$) and one large one ($J = 1\,000\,000$). Realizations fluctuate around the mean (straight lines), and the relative uncertainty doesn't seem to go down for the large portfolio. This is contrary to what we saw in Section 3.2, and caused by the common factor; see Section 6.3 for the mathematics.

6.2.7 Monte Carlo distributions

Monte Carlo experiments are often generated from parameters that have been estimated from historical data, and their errors influence simulations. To understand what goes on, consider the number of claims $\mathcal{N}$ against a portfolio and assume the ordinary Poisson model with fixed intensity μ. Let $\hat{\mu}$ be its estimate (method in

Section 8.2). The scheme is then

$$\text{historical data} \underset{\textit{estimation}}{\longrightarrow} \hat{\mu} \underset{\textit{Monte Carlo}}{\longrightarrow} \mathcal{N}^*,$$

and the question is the effect of both sources of error. A first step is to note that the model for $\mathcal{N}^*$ is a *conditional* one; i.e.,

$$\Pr(\mathcal{N}^* = n|\hat{\mu}) = \frac{(JT\hat{\mu})^n}{n!}e^{-JT\hat{\mu}}, \quad n = 0, 1, \dots,$$

and we must combine this with statistical errors in the estimation process. Such issues are studied in Section 7.2.

6.3 Uncertainty on different levels

6.3.1 Introduction

Risk variables X influenced by a second random factor ω on a **subordinate** level were introduced above. This kind of uncertainty was examined in Section 5.3 through a specific model (CAPM), but it is also possible to proceed more generally through the conditional mean and standard deviation. Let

$$\xi(\omega) = E(X|\omega) \quad \text{and} \quad \sigma(\omega) = \text{sd}(X|\omega), \tag{6.11}$$

and consider $\mathcal{X} = X_1 + \cdots + X_J$ where $X_1, \dots, X_J$ are realizations of X. The purpose of this section is to study $\mathcal{X}$ under different sampling regimes for ω.

6.3.2 The double rules

Our tool consists of two operational rules that are best introduced generally. Suppose the distribution of Y depends on a random vector $\mathbf{X}$. The conditional mean $\xi(\mathbf{x}) = E(Y|\mathbf{x})$ plays a leading role in pricing and prediction; see Section 6.4. Here the issue is how $\xi(\mathbf{x})$ and $\sigma(\mathbf{x}) = \text{sd}(Y|\mathbf{x})$ influence Y. Much insight is provided by the identities

$$\underset{\textit{double expectation}}{E(Y) = E\{\xi(\mathbf{X})\}} \quad \text{for} \quad \xi(\mathbf{x}) = E(Y|\mathbf{x}) \tag{6.12}$$

and

$$\underset{\textit{double variance}}{\text{var}(Y) = \text{var}\{\xi(\mathbf{X})\} + E\{\sigma^2(\mathbf{X})\}} \quad \text{for} \quad \sigma(\mathbf{x}) = \text{sd}(Y|\mathbf{x}) \tag{6.13}$$

which are proved in Appendix A.3. Both $\xi(\mathbf{X})$ and $\sigma^2(\mathbf{X})$ are random variables, and their mean and variance can be calculated. The double-variance formula decomposes var(Y) into two positive contributions and is one of the most useful results in risk theory. Neither formula requires conditional modelling beyond mean and standard deviation.

6.3.3 Financial risk under CAPM

The CAPM in Section 5.3 used the market component R_M as a common factor for asset returns $R_1, \dots, R_J$ through the specification $R_j = r + \beta_j(R_M - r) + \tau_j\varepsilon_j$ with r, β_j and τ_j fixed parameters and $\varepsilon_1, \dots, \varepsilon_J$ independent with mean 0 and standard deviation 1. Consider the portfolio return $\mathcal{R} = w_1R_1 + \cdots + w_JR_J$ where $w_1 + \cdots + w_J = 1$. Its conditional mean and variance given R_M are

$$E(\mathcal{R}|R_M) = r + \left(\sum_{j=1}^{J} w_j\beta_j\right)(R_M - r) \quad \text{and} \quad \mathrm{var}(\mathcal{R}|R_M) = \sum_{j=1}^{J} w_j^2\tau_j^2,$$

and the double-variance rule with $Y = \mathcal{R}$ and $\mathbf{X} = R_M$ yields

$$\mathrm{var}(\mathcal{R}) = \left(\sum_{j=1}^{J} w_j\beta_j\right)^2 \sigma_M^2 + \sum_{j=1}^{J} w_j^2\tau_j^2$$

where $\sigma_M^2 = \mathrm{var}(R_M)$. The variance is decomposed into a sum of two contributions where the first is due to common market risk which doesn't go away however many assets we diversify on; see Section 5.3.

6.3.4 Insurance risk

As a second example consider portfolio risk in general insurance and its representation in Section 3.2; i.e., $\mathcal{X} = Z_1 + \cdots + Z_{\mathcal{N}}$ where $\mathcal{N}, Z_1, Z_2, \dots$ are stochastically independent. Let $E(Z_i) = \xi_z$ and $\mathrm{sd}(Z_i) = \sigma_z$. Elementary rules for random sums imply

$$E(\mathcal{X}|\mathcal{N}) = \mathcal{N}\xi_z \quad \text{and} \quad \mathrm{var}(\mathcal{X}|\mathcal{N}) = \mathcal{N}\sigma_z^2$$

so that $Y = \mathcal{X}$ and $\mathbf{X} = \mathcal{N}$ in (6.12) and (6.13) yield

$$E(\mathcal{X}) = E(\mathcal{N})\xi_z \quad \text{and} \quad \mathrm{var}(\mathcal{X}) = E(\mathcal{N})\sigma_z^2 + \mathrm{var}(\mathcal{N})\xi_z^2. \tag{6.14}$$

If $\mathcal{N}$ is Poisson distributed so that $E(\mathcal{N}) = \mathrm{var}(\mathcal{N}) = J\mu T$, then

$$E(\mathcal{X}) = J\mu T\xi_z \quad \text{and} \quad \mathrm{var}(\mathcal{X}) = J\mu T(\sigma_z^2 + \xi_z^2), \tag{6.15}$$

which will be used repeatedly.

6.3.5 Impact of subordinate risk

There is a general argument for sums of the form $\mathcal{X} = X_1 + \cdots + X_J$ where each X_j depends on some underlying ω_j. Suppose all pairs (ω_j, X_j) follow the same distribution (*not* essential) and let $X_1, \ldots, X_J$ be conditionally independent given $\omega_1, \ldots, \omega_J$, often a reasonable condition in property insurance, as mentioned. The sampling regimes may be two different ones:

$$\underbrace{\omega_1 = \cdots = \omega_J = \omega}_{\textit{common factor}} \quad \text{and} \quad \underbrace{\omega_1, \ldots, \omega_J \quad \text{independent.}}_{\textit{individual parameters}}$$

On the left, ω is a common background factor affecting the entire portfolio whereas on the right, ω_j is attached to each X_j individually. The effect on $\mathcal{X}$ is widely different.

Consider first the case where ω is common background. We are assuming that $\xi(\omega) = E(X_j|\omega)$ and $\sigma(\omega) = \text{sd}(X_j|\omega)$, the same for all j. When all contributions to $\mathcal{X}$ are added,

$$E(\mathcal{X}|\omega) = J\xi(\omega) \quad \text{and} \quad \text{var}(\mathcal{X}|\omega) = J\sigma^2(\omega)$$

where conditional independence is crucial for the variance formula. Invoke the double rules with $Y = \mathcal{X}$ and $\mathbf{X} = \omega$. Then, by (6.13)

$$\text{var}(\mathcal{X}) = \text{var}\{J\xi(\omega)\} + E\{J\sigma^2(\omega)\} = J^2\text{var}\{\xi(\omega)\} + JE\{\sigma^2(\omega)\}$$

which with (6.12) leads to

$$E(\mathcal{X}) = JE\{\xi(\omega)\} \quad \text{and} \quad \underbrace{\text{sd}(\mathcal{X}) = J\sqrt{\text{var}\{\xi(\omega)\} + E\{\sigma^2(\omega)\}/J}}_{\omega \text{ common}}, \tag{6.16}$$

and the standard deviation is of the same order of magnitude J as the expectation itself. *Such risk cannot be diversified away* by increasing the portfolio size. Indeed,

$$\frac{\text{sd}(\mathcal{X})}{E(\mathcal{X})} \to \frac{\text{sd}\{\xi(\omega)\}}{E\{\xi(\omega)\}} \quad \text{as} \quad J \to \infty$$

which does not vanish when $\text{sd}\{\xi(\omega)\} > 0$.

Things change drastically when each X_j is attached to a separate and independently drawn ω_j. The mean and variance of each X_j are now calculated by inserting $J = 1$ in (6.16) and then added over all j for the mean and variance of $\mathcal{X}$. Hence

$$E(\mathcal{X}) = JE\{\xi(\omega)\} \quad \text{and} \quad \underbrace{\text{sd}(\mathcal{X}) = \sqrt{J[E\{\sigma^2(\omega)\} + \text{var}\{\xi(\omega)\}]}}_{\omega \text{ individual}}. \tag{6.17}$$

The mean is the same as before, but the standard deviation now has the familiar form proportional to $\sqrt{J}$.

6.3.6 Random claim intensity in general insurance

The preceding argument enables us to understand how random intensities $\mu_1, \dots, \mu_J$ in general insurance influence portfolio claim numbers $\mathcal{N} = N_1 + \cdots + N_J$ and payoffs $\mathcal{X} = Z_1 + \cdots + Z_{\mathcal{N}}$. Consider the sampling regimes

$$\underbrace{\mu_1 = \cdots = \mu_J = \mu}_{\textit{common factor}} \quad \text{and} \quad \underbrace{\mu_1, \dots, \mu_J \;\; \text{independent}}_{\textit{individual parameters}}$$

where μ on the left affects all policy holders jointly whereas there is one μ_j for each individual on the right. Claim numbers $N_1, \dots, N_J$ are in either case conditionally independent given $\mu_1, \dots, \mu_J$. To understand how the uncertainty of $\mathcal{N}$ is linked to common or individual sampling we may invoke (6.16) and (6.17). The functions $\xi(\omega)$ and $\sigma(\omega)$ are now $\xi(\mu) = \mu T$ and $\sigma(\mu) = \sqrt{\mu T}$ assuming the usual Poisson model. This implies $E(\mathcal{N}) = JT\xi_\mu$ and

$$\underbrace{\text{sd}(\mathcal{N}) = JT\sqrt{\sigma_\mu^2 + \xi_\mu/(JT)}}_{\mu\ \textit{common}} \quad \text{and} \quad \underbrace{\text{sd}(\mathcal{N}) = T\sqrt{J(\sigma_\mu^2 + \xi_\mu/T)},}_{\mu\ \textit{individual}} \tag{6.18}$$

writing $\xi_\mu = E(\mu)$ and $\sigma_\mu = \text{sd}(\mu)$. The form of the standard deviation on the left (almost proportional to J) explains the simulated patterns in Figure 6.1, where relative uncertainty seemed unaffected by J.

How these results are passed on to $\mathcal{X}$ may be examined by inserting the expressions for $E(\mathcal{N})$ and $\text{sd}(\mathcal{N})$ into (6.14). This leads to $E(\mathcal{X}) = JT\xi_\mu\xi_z$ and some algebra (detailed in Section 6.8) yields

$$\text{sd}(\mathcal{X}) = \underbrace{\sqrt{JT\xi_\mu(\sigma_z^2 + \xi_z^2)}}_{\textit{pure Poisson}} \times \underbrace{\sqrt{1 + \gamma\delta}}_{\textit{due to random } \mu} \tag{6.19}$$

where

$$\delta = T\frac{\sigma_\mu^2}{\xi_\mu}\frac{\xi_z^2}{\sigma_z^2 + \xi_z^2} \quad \text{and} \quad \gamma = \begin{cases} 1 & \text{for } \textbf{individual}\ \mu \\ J & \text{for } \textbf{common}\ \mu. \end{cases} \tag{6.20}$$

There is on the right in (6.19) a pure Poisson factor and a correction caused by μ being random. How important is the latter? In practice, δ is quite small (hardly more than a few percent, see Exercise 6.9) and when $\mu_1, \dots, \mu_J$ are drawn independently of each other (so that $\gamma = 1$), the correction factor becomes $\sqrt{1+\delta} \doteq 1 + \delta/2$, *not* a large increase. A common background factor is different. Now $\gamma = J$ and the correction $\sqrt{1 + J\delta}$ may be huge.

6.4 The role of the conditional mean

6.4.1 Introduction

The conditional mean is much more than a brick in the double rules of the preceding section. Consider

$$\hat{Y} = \xi(\mathbf{X}) = E(Y|\mathbf{X}), \tag{6.21}$$

where $\mathbf{X}$ is one or more observations. In theory, $\hat{Y}$ is the best way to *predict* Y if $\mathbf{X}$ is known; see below. This is a celebrated result in engineering and statistics. It is relevant in actuarial science too, yet not that prominent. When Y belongs to the future, we are less concerned with its actual value than with summaries through its probability distribution.

There is a second issue. If $\mathbf{X}$ is information available, $E(Y|\mathbf{X})$ is what is expected given that knowledge and a natural break-even price for carrying the risk Y. Shouldn't what we charge reflect what we know? Valuation in finance and insurance is based on that view, which is the main topic of this section. Think of $\mathbf{X}$ in this context as present and past information with bearing on Y. The theoretical literature refers to $\mathbf{X}$ as a **sigma-field** (often denoted $\mathcal{F}$).

6.4.2 Optimal prediction and interest rates

The central mathematical properties of the conditional mean are

$$\underbrace{E(\hat{Y} - Y) = 0}_{\textit{expected error}} \quad \text{and} \quad \underbrace{E(\hat{Y} - Y)^2 \leq E(\tilde{Y} - Y)^2}_{\textit{expected squared error}} \quad \text{for all } \tilde{Y} = \tilde{Y}(\mathbf{X}). \tag{6.22}$$

Here the left-hand side is just a rephrasing of the rule of double expectation (6.12) and tells us that $\hat{Y}$ is an **unbiased** prediction. The inequality on the right shows that the conditional mean is on average the most accurate way of utilizing the information $\mathbf{X}$; see Section 6.8 for the proof.

A simple example is interest rate forecasting. Suppose the rates r_k follow the Vasiček model in Section 5.6 with conditional mean and standard deviation

$$E(r_k|r_0) = \xi + a^k(r_0 - \xi) \quad \text{and} \quad \text{sd}(r_k|r_0) = \sigma\sqrt{\frac{1 - a^{2k}}{1 - a^2}},$$

an immediate consequence of (5.39). The best possible prediction of r_k given r_0 today is thus $\hat{r}_k = \xi + a^k(r_0 - \xi)$, and the standard deviation indicates the accuracy. Possible parameters on an annual time scale could be $\sigma = 0.016$ and $a = 0.7$, and for those $\text{sd}(r_k|r_0) = 1.4\%$ after 1 year and 2.2% after 5 years. This signals huge prediction error, up to 3–4% and more. Forecasting interest rates through a simple statistical technique is futile.

6.4.3 The conditional mean as a price

Most theoretical prices in finance and insurance are conditional means. As a first example consider a policy holder in general insurance with claim record $Y_1, \dots, Y_K$. Two possibilities for the break-even price of a *future* claim Y are

$$\pi = E(Y) \quad \text{or} \quad \pi = E(Y|Y_1, \dots, Y_K).$$

Shouldn't we rely on the historical record to tell us *something*? If so, go for the second assessment and the **credibility** methods in Section 10.5.

Another issue in general insurance is risk varying between groups of individuals, larger for some than for others. This is attacked through explanatory variables $x_1, x_2, \dots,$ say age, sex, income, geogaphical location and so on which would be known for each policy holder and which might affect risk. The break-even price is now of the form

$$\pi = E(Y|x_1, x_2, \dots),$$

which can be determined by studying relationships between payoff and explanatory variables in historical data through regression methods; see Sections 8.4 and 10.4.

The conditional mean was also there when equity options were valued in Section 3.5. Consider put options where the payoff was $X = \max(r_g - R, 0)v_0$, writing r_g and R for guaranteed and actual return. Suppose the shares, originally worth $S_0 = v_0$, stand at $S_k = s_k$ at time $t_k = kh$ and at $S_K = (1 + R)v_0$ at expiry $T = Kh$. Then

$$X = \max\{(1 + r_g)v_0 - (1 + R)v_0, 0\} = \max(A - S_K, 0) \quad \text{where} \quad A = (1 + r_g)v_0,$$

and when discounting is added, the conditional means $E_Q(X|v_0)$ and $E_Q(X|s_k)$ under a risk-neutral model define the value of the option at time 0 and k. Such pricing is only plausible when all information on the future uncertainty of the stock resides in the most recent value. This **Markov** condition is followed up in the next section.

6.4.4 Modelling bond prices

Still another application of the conditional mean as a price is to construct mathematical models describing how bonds fluctuate. Consider a unit-faced, zero-coupon bond maturing at time T. What people are willing to pay for it today must depend on the current rate of interest r_0, and in its simplest form a mathematical model would be some expression $P(r_0, T)$. It should match the observed price, denoted $P(0\colon K)$ in Section 1.4 when $T = Kh$, and it's common to calibrate models that way. But why models at all when there are market prices available? Answer: To describe future uncertainty. For example, if r^* is a Monte Carlo rate of interest at a future time t, then $P(r^*, T)$ is the corresponding value of a bond expiring at $t + T$. Such simulations will, in Chapter 15, enable us to examine **fair value** accounting and also the coordination of assets and liabilities in the life insurance industry.

Theoretical bond prices are derived through a mathematical limit process akin to the one in Section 5.7. Follow the market over $t_k = kh$ for $k = 1, \ldots, K$ with $T = Kh$ kept fixed while $h \to 0$ and $K \to \infty$. Suppose interest rates are described as intensities and discounts as $d_k = e^{-r_k h}$. The aggregated discount over $(0, T)$ is then

$$d_{0:K} = d_1 \cdots d_K = e^{-(r_1 + \cdots + r_K)h},$$

and its expectation might be the price today for one money unit delivered at T. In the limit

$$P(r_0, T) = \lim_{K \to \infty} E_Q\{e^{-(r_1 + \cdots + r_K)T/K} | r_0\}, \tag{6.23}$$

where Q signals a **risk-neutral** model as in Section 3.5. Many models for r_k allow closed mathematical expressions; consult Björk (2006).

6.4.5 *Bond price schemes*

The limit (6.23) can be calculated by elementary means if the interest rate intensities r_k follow the Vasiček model. With $\xi_q = \xi$, a_q and σ_q being the parameters of the continuous-time version in Section 5.7, it follows that

$$P(r_0, T) = e^{A(T) - B(T) r_0} \tag{6.24}$$

where

$$B(T) = \frac{1 - e^{-a_q T}}{a_q} \quad \text{and} \quad A(T) = (B(T) - T)\left(\xi_q - \frac{\sigma_q^2}{2a_q^2}\right) - \frac{\sigma_q^2 B(T)^2}{4a_q}; \tag{6.25}$$

see Section 6.8 for the derivation.

Could the first-order autoregression on log-scale have been used instead of the linear Vasiček model? Only if we rely on Monte Carlo and table $P(r_0, T)$ as an approximation on a suitable set of pairs (r_0, T). But that is a perfectly practical approach that does not restrict us to models allowing closed expressions. Implementation with the Black–Karasinski model runs as in Algorithm 6.1.

The algorithm starts by using the transformation formulae (5.57) to convert the continuous-time parameters a_q and σ_q to those (a and σ) on the time scale selected. Future interest rate intensities are then simulated and the stochastic discounts d^* updated as the scheme goes through the *inner* loop over k. Output from the *outer* loop are Monte Carlo approximations $P^*(k)$ to $P(r_0, kh)$. Reruns for many different r_0 are necessary.

Algorithm 6.1 Black–Karasinski bond prices

Input: $\xi_q, a_q, \sigma_q, r_0, T, h, m$ and $a = e^{-a_q h}$,
$\quad\sigma = \sigma_q\sqrt{(1-a^2)/(2a_q)},\ \sigma_x = \sigma/\sqrt{1-a^2},\ x_0 = \log(r_0/\xi) + \sigma_x^2/2$

$P^*(k) \leftarrow 0$ for $k = 1, \dots, K$ %*$P^*(k)$ the theoretical bond price*

Repeat m times

$\quad X^* \leftarrow x_0,\ d^* \leftarrow 1/m$ %*d^* will serve as discount*

$\quad$ For $k = 1, \dots, K$ do

$\quad\quad$ Draw $\varepsilon^* \sim N(0,1)$ and $X^* \leftarrow aX^* + \sigma\varepsilon^*$

$\quad\quad r^* \leftarrow \xi e^{-\sigma_x^2/2 + X^*}$ and $d^* \leftarrow d^* e^{-r^* h}$

$\quad\quad P^*(k) \leftarrow P^*(k) + d^*$ %*The k-step discount summarized*

Return: $P^*(k)$ for $k = 1, \dots, K$.

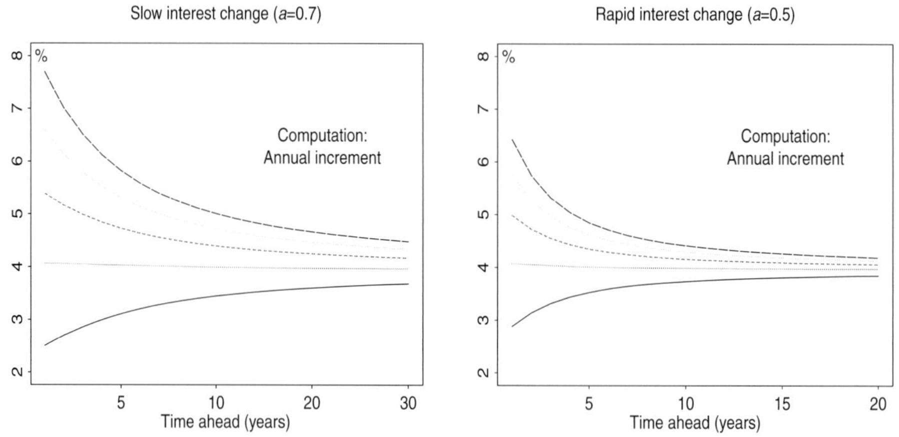

Figure 6.2 Interest rate curves (from $m = 10\,000$ simulations) under the Black–Karasinski model for two values of a when the initial rate of interest is varied.

6.4.6 Interest rate curves

Bond prices are easier to understand when converted to average interest rates (or **yields**) as in Section 1.4. If there are K periods, the yield $\bar{r}_K$ is connected to the bond price $P(0\colon K)$ through

$$P(0\colon k) = \frac{1}{(1+\bar{r}_K)^K} \quad \text{or} \quad \bar{r}_K = P(0\colon K)^{-1/K} - 1. \tag{6.26}$$

An example under the Black–Karasinski model is shown in Figure 6.2 after having used Algorithm 6.1 with $h = 1$ (too crude in practice) for computation. The parameters were $\xi_q = 4\%$, $a_q = 0.356$ and $\sigma_q = 0.211$ on the left and $\xi_q = 4\%$, $a_q = 0.693$ and $\sigma_q = 0.230$ on the right.

The initial interest rate intensity r_0 was varied between $r_0 = 2\%, 4\%, 6\%, 8\%$

and 10% per year, which produced the different shapes in Figure 6.2. In the long run all the curves approach a stationary level at a speed determined by a_q.

Similar concepts of average interest rates can also be constructed when bond prices are model based. Consider the intensity form of the model with $r_k h$ the actual interest in period k. Suppose h is small. Then $1 + r_k h \doteq e^{r_k h}$ so that $(1 + r_1 h) \cdots (1 + r_K h) \doteq e^{(r_1 + \cdots + r_K)h} = e^{\bar{r}T}$ where $\bar{r} = (r_1 + \cdots + r_K)/K$, and in the limit as $h \to 0$ the average interest rate intensity $\bar{r} = \bar{r}(r_0, T)$ is related to the bond price through

$$P(r_0, T) = e^{-\bar{r}(r_0,T)T} \quad \text{or} \quad \bar{r}(r_0, T) = -\log\{P(r_0, T)\}/T, \tag{6.27}$$

which will be illustrated among the exercises.

6.5 Stochastic dependence: General

6.5.1 Introduction

General probabilistic descriptions of dependent random variables $X_1, \ldots, X_n$ are provided by **joint density functions** $f(x_1, \ldots, x_n)$ or **joint distribution functions** $F(x_1, \ldots, x_n)$. The latter are defined as the probabilities

$$F(x_1, \ldots, x_n) = \Pr(X_1 \leq x_1, \ldots, X_n \leq x_n).$$

Its n-fold partial derivative with respect to $x_1, \ldots, x_n$ is (when it exists) the density function $f(x_1, \ldots, x_n)$, which may also be interpreted as the likelihood of the event

$$X_1 = x_1, X_2 = x_2, \ldots, X_n = x_n,$$

though formally (in a strict mathematical sense) such probabilities are zero for continuous variables. Textbooks in probability and statistics often *start* with density functions. Their mathematical expressions are needed for parameter estimation (and for the importance sampling in Section 4.4), but are otherwise not much used in this book where the recursive viewpoint is emphasized. Copulas in Section 6.7 address joint distribution functions directly.

6.5.2 Factorization of density functions

Whether $X_1, \ldots, X_n$ is a series in time or not, we may always envisage them in a certain order. This observation opens up a general simulation technique. Go recursively through the scheme

Sample	X_1^*	$X_2^*\|X_1^*$	$\cdots$	$X_n^*\|X_1^*, \ldots, X_{n-1}^*$
Probabilities	$f(x_1)$	$f(x_2\|X_1^*)$	$\cdots$	$f(x_n\|X_1^*, \ldots, X_{n-1}^*)$,

where each drawing is conditional on what has come up before. We start by generating X_1 and end with X_n given all the others. The order selected does not matter in theory, but in practice there is often a natural sequence to use. If it isn't, look for other ways to do it.

The sampling scheme reflects a factorization of joint density functions. Multiply the conditional ones together, and you get

$$f(x_1,\dots,x_n) = f(x_1)f(x_2|x_1)\cdots f(x_n|x_1,\dots,x_{n-1}) \tag{6.28}$$

general factorization

where density functions (all denoted f) are distinguished through their arguments. A special case is **Bayes**' formula. One version is

$$f(x_1|x_2,\dots,x_n) = \frac{f(x_2,\dots,x_n|x_1)f(x_1)}{f(x_2,\dots,x_n)}, \tag{6.29}$$

where the conditional density function of X_1 given $x_2,\dots,x_n$ is referred back to the opposite form of $X_2,\dots,X_n$ given x_1. This type of identity will be crucial for Bayesian estimation in Section 7.6.

6.5.3 Types of dependence

Several special cases of (6.28) are of interest. The model with a common random factor in Section 6.2 is of the form

$$f(x_1,\dots,x_n) = f(x_1)f(x_2|x_1)\cdots f(x_n|x_1). \tag{6.30}$$

common factor: First variable

Here the conditional densities only depend on the first variable, and all the variables $X_2,\dots,X_n$ are conditionally independent. Full independence means

$$f(x_1,\dots,x_n) = f(x_1)f(x_2)\cdots f(x_n). \tag{6.31}$$

independence

Finally, there is the issue of **Markov dependence**, typically associated with time. If X_k occurs at time k for $k = 1,\dots n$, the factorization now becomes

$$f(x_1,\dots,x_n) = f(x_1)f(x_2|x_1)\cdots f(x_n|x_{n-1}) \tag{6.32}$$

Markov dependence

where X_k depends on the past through X_{k-1} whereas the earlier $X_{k-2}, X_{k-3},\dots$ are irrelevant. Most models in life insurance belong to this class, and the random walk and the first-order autoregression models of Section 5.6 do too; see below. How the general sampling scheme above is adapted is obvious, but the Markov situation is so important that an algorithm of its own is justified; Algorithm 6.2 is a summary.

Algorithm 6.2 Markov sampling

0 Input: Conditional models
1 Generate X_1^*
2 For k=2,...,n do
3   Generate X_k^* given X_{k-1}^* *%Sampling from* $f(x_k|X_{k-1}^*)$
4 Return $X_1^*, \ldots, X_n^*$.

6.5.4 *Linear and normal processes*

We could have introduced all the time series models in Chapter 5 as Markov processes via a recursive sequence of distributions. Consider the Vasiček model (5.35) in the Gaussian case. Now

$$r_k = \xi + a(r_{k-1} - \xi) + \sigma\varepsilon_k \quad \text{or} \quad r_k|r_{k-1} = r \quad \sim \quad N(\xi + a(r - \xi), \sigma),$$

for $k = 1, \ldots, K$, and a model for the series is constructed by iterating over k, first specifying $r_1|r_0$, then $r_2|r_1$ and so on. This brings no particular benefit over the approach in Chapter 5, and indeed the dynamic properties of the model were derived in Section 5.6 without assuming the normal.

The sequence $r_1, \ldots, r_K$ inherits Gaussianity from the errors $\varepsilon_1, \ldots, \varepsilon_K$, and it *is* possible to write down the joint density function. In the general case where $\boldsymbol{\xi} = (\xi_1, \ldots, \xi_K)^{\mathrm{T}}$ is the vector of expectations and $\boldsymbol{\Sigma}$ the covariance matrix, the Gaussian density function reads

$$f(\mathbf{x}) = (|2\pi\boldsymbol{\Sigma}|)^{-1/2} \exp\left(-\frac{1}{2}(\mathbf{x} - \boldsymbol{\xi})^T \boldsymbol{\Sigma}^{-1}(\mathbf{x} - \boldsymbol{\xi})\right) \tag{6.33}$$

where $|2\pi\boldsymbol{\Sigma}|$ is the determinant of the matrix $2\pi\boldsymbol{\Sigma}$. This expression, though famous, plays no role in this book.

6.5.5 *The multinomial situation*

One joint density function that *will* be needed later is the multinomial one; for example in Section 8.5. The situation is multinomial sampling (Section 4.2), where one label among M is selected according to probabilities $p_1, \ldots, p_M$ where $p_1 + \cdots + p_M = 1$. This is repeated n times, each trial being independent of the others. Let $N_i = n_i$ be the number of times label i appears and introduce

$$s_i = n_1 + \cdots + n_i \quad \text{and} \quad p_{i|} = \frac{p_i}{p_i + \cdots + p_M}.$$

From introductory probability courses $N_1 \sim$ binomial(n, p_1), which is the start of the recursion,

$$N_i|n_1, \ldots, n_{i-1} \quad \sim \quad \text{binomial}(n - s_{i-1}, p_{i|}), \quad i = 2, \ldots, M.$$

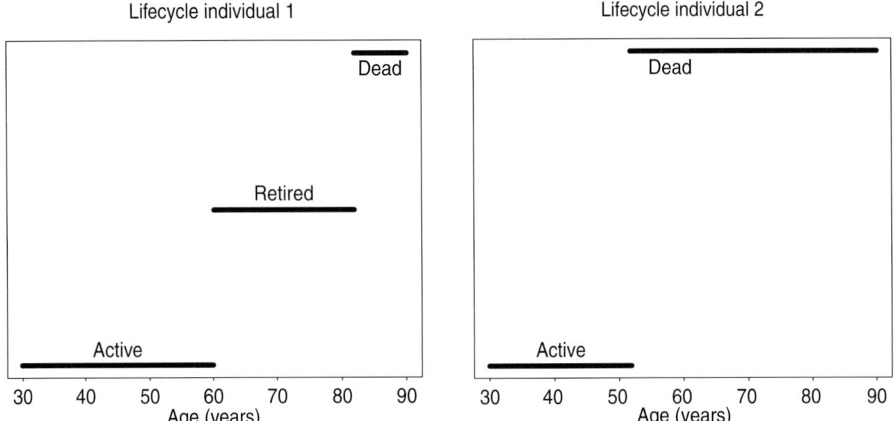

Figure 6.3 The lifecycles of two members of a pension scheme.

Why is that? When the first $i-1$ labels have been counted, there are $n - s_{i-1}$ trials left and the probability of label i among them is precisely $p_{i|}$.

These M conditional density functions may be multiplied together for the density function of $N_1, \dots, N_M$ jointly, which yields the **multinomial** distribution

$$\Pr(N_1 = n_1, \dots, N_M = n_M) = \frac{n!}{n_1! \dots n_M!} p_1^{n_1} \cdots p_M^{n_M} \tag{6.34}$$

where $n_1 + \cdots + n_M = n$. Try to verify it when $M = 3$. There are now $M - 1 = 2$ binomial probabilities. Their product is

$$\frac{n!}{n_1!(n-n_1)!} p_1^{n_1}(1-p_1)^{n-n_1} \times \frac{(n-n_1)!}{n_2!(n-n_1-n_2)!} \left(\frac{p_2}{p_2+p_3}\right)^{n_2} \left(1 - \frac{p_2}{p_2+p_3}\right)^{n-n_1-n_2},$$

where many of the factors cancel so that the expression becomes (6.34) with $M = 3$.

6.6 Markov chains and life insurance

6.6.1 Introduction

Liability risk in life, pension and disability insurance is based on probabilistic descriptions of lifecycles like those in Figure 6.3. The individual on the left dies at 82 having retired 22 years earlier at 60, whereas the other is a premature death at 52. A pension scheme consists of many (perhaps millions) of members like these, each with an individual lifecycle. Disability is a little more complicated, since there might be transitions back and forth; see below. A switch from active to retired is determined by a clause in the contract, whereas death and disability must be described in random terms.

Each of the categories of Figure 6.3 is known as a **state**. A lifecycle is a sequence $\{C_l\}$ of such states with C_l being the category occupied by the individual at age $y_l = lT$. We may envisage $\{C_l\}$ as a step function, jumping occasionally from one state to another. There are three of them in Figure 6.3. The present topic is how such schemes are described mathematically. Do we really have to bother with it since uncertainty due to lifecycle movements turned out to be of minor importance in Section 3.4? However, that does not make the underlying stochastic model irrelevant. It is needed both to compute expected liabilities in Chapter 12 *and* to study parameter error and its effect on portfolio risk in Section 15.2.

6.6.2 Markov modelling

Let $\{C_l\}$ be a random step function jumping between a limited number of states. The most common model by far is the **Markov chain**, which is set in motion by the **transition probabilities**

$$p_l(i|j) = \Pr(C_{l+1} = i|C_l = j). \tag{6.35}$$

There is at each point in time a random experiment which takes the state from its current j to a possibly new i. Note that the probabilities defining the model *do not depend on the track record* of the individual prior to age l, which is the Markov assumption. Monte Carlo is a good way to gain insight into how such models work; consult the exercises.

Transition probabilities are usually different for men and women (not reflected in the mathematical notation). They depend on the age l and on the survival probabilities $p_l = {}_1p_l$ introduced in Section 6.2. For a simple pension scheme, such as in Figure 6.3, the three states 'active', 'retired' and 'dead' replace each other through the following probabilities:

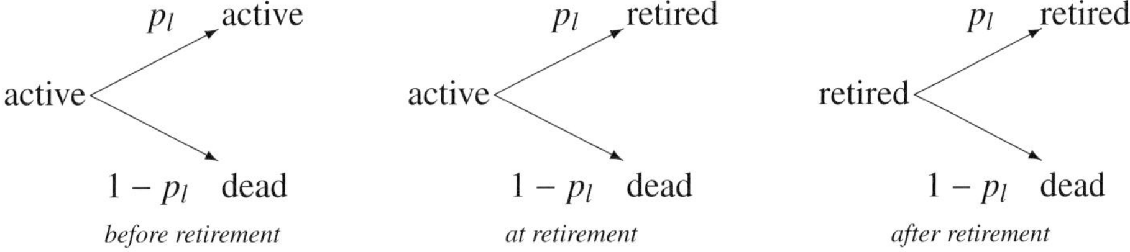

The details differ according to whether we are before, at or after retirement. Note the middle diagram in particular, where the individual from a clause in the contract moves from 'active' to 'retired' if staying alive.

6.6.3 A disability scheme

Disability modelling, with movements back and forth between states, is more complicated. Consider the following scheme:

An individual may become 'disabled' (state i), but there is also a chance of a return to 'active' (state a). Such rehabilitations are not too frequent as this book is being written, but it could be different in the future, and we should certainly be able to handle it mathematically. New probabilities are then needed in addition to those describing survival; i.e., $p_l(i|a)$ (going from 'active' to 'disabled') and $p_l(a|i)$ (the opposite), both depending on age l.

The transition probabilities for the scheme must combine survival and disability/rehabilitation, and the full matrix is as follows:

	To new state			
From	Active	Disabled	Dead	Row sum
Active	$p_l\{1 - p_l(i\|a)\}$	$p_l p(i\|a)$	$1 - p_l$	1
Disabled	$p_l p_l(a\|i)$	$p_l\{1 - p_l(a\|i)\}$	$1 - p_l$	1
Dead	0	0	1	1

Each entry is the product of probabilities. For example, to remain 'active' (upper left corner) the indvidual must survive *and* not become 'disabled', and similarly for the others. Note the row sums. *They are always equal to one* (add them and you will see it is true). *Any* set of transition probabilities for Markov chains must satisfy this restriction, which merely reflects that individuals move somewhere or remain in the state they are.

6.6.4 Numerical example

Figure 6.4 shows a portfolio development that might occur in practice. The survival model was the same as in Section 3.4, i.e.,

$$\log(p_l) = -0.0009 - 0.000044e^{0.09076\times l}.$$

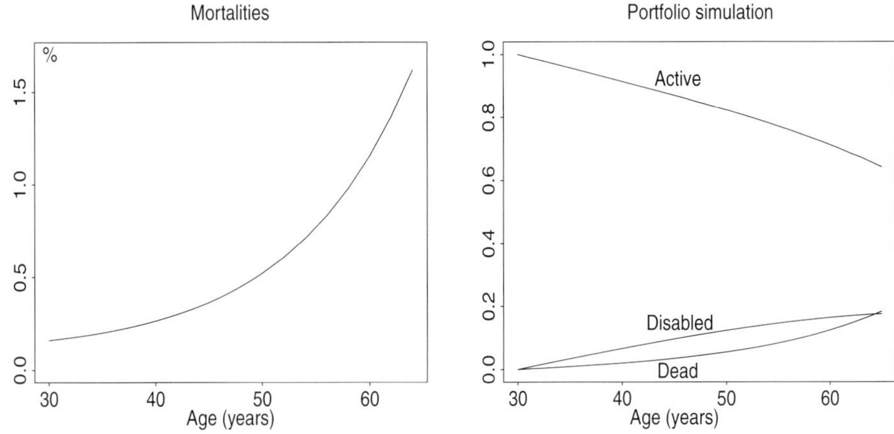

Figure 6.4 A disability scheme in life insurance: Survival model in terms of mortalities (*left*) and one portfolio simulation (*right*).

Their corresponding annual **mortalitites** $q_l = 1 - p_l$ are plotted in Figure 6.4 left. Note the steep increase on the right for the higher age groups, where the likelihood of dying within the coming year has reached 1.5% and more.

This model corresponds to an average life of 75 years. It will be used in Chapter 12 as well and may describe males in a developed country. Disability depends on the current political climate and on economic cycles, and is harder to hang numbers on. The computations in Figure 6.4 are based on $p_l(i|a) = 0.7\%$ and $p_l(a|i) = 0.1\%$, which are invented values. Note the rehabilitation rate, which may be too high. In practice both probabilities are likely to depend on age, as mentioned earlier.

How individuals distribute between the three states is shown in Figure 6.4 right (for a portfolio originally consisting of one million 30-year males). The scenario has been simulated using Algorithm 6.2 (details in Exercise 6.33). There is very little Monte Carlo uncertainty in portfolios this size, and one *single* run is enough. At the start all are active, but with age the number of people in the other two classes grows. At 65 years a little over 80% remain alive (distributed between 'active' and 'disabled'), a realistic figure. What may not be true in practice is the downward curvature in disability, which might be turned around if the disability rate is made age-dependent.

6.7 Introducing copulas

6.7.1 Introduction

For U_1 and U_2 uniform and *dependent* define

$$X_1 = F_1^{-1}(U_1) \quad \text{and} \quad X_2 = F_2^{-1}(U_2), \tag{6.36}$$

where $F_1^{-1}(u_1)$ and $F_2^{-1}(u_2)$ are the percentiles of two distribution functions $F_1(x)$ and $F_2(x)$. This simple setup defines an increasingly popular modelling strategy where dependence and univariate variation are approached as separate issues. The inversion algorithm (Section 2.3) ensures that the distribution functions of X_1 and X_2 become $F_1(x_1)$ and $F_2(x_2)$ no matter how U_1 and U_2 depend on each other. Their joint distribution function $C(u_1, u_2)$ is called a **copula** and a huge number of models have been proposed for it.

The idea goes back to the mid-twentieth century, originating with the work of Sklar (1959). It enables us to tackle situations such as those in Figure 6.5, where correlation depends on the level of the variables. Equity in falling markets is an example (Longin and Solnik, 2001), and such phenomena have drawn interest in insurance too; see Wütrich (2004).

6.7.2 Copula modelling

A bivariate copula $C(u_1, u_2) = \Pr(U_1 \leq u_1, U_2 \leq u_2)$ is a joint distribution function for a uniform and dependent pair (U_1, U_2). Any function that is to play such a role must be increasing in u_1 and u_2 and satisfy

$$C(u_1, 0) = 0, \;\; C(0, u_2) = 0 \quad \text{and} \qquad C(u_1, 1) = u_1, \;\; C(1, u_2) = u_2 \tag{6.37}$$

where the conditions on the right ensure that U_1 and U_2 are uniform. Simple examples are

$$\underbrace{C(u_1, u_2) = u_1 u_2}_{\textit{independent copula}} \qquad \text{and} \qquad \underbrace{C(u_1, u_2) = (u_1^{-\theta} + u_2^{-\theta} - 1)^{-1/\theta}}_{\textit{Clayton copula}}$$

where $\theta > 0$ on the right. You can easily convince yourself that (6.37) is valid for both.

Copula modelling rests on a representation theorem discovered by Sklar (1959). Any joint distribution function $F(x_1, x_2)$ with strictly increasing marginal distribution functions $F_1(x_1)$ and $F_2(x_2)$ may be written

$$\underbrace{F(x_1, x_2) = C(u_1, u_2)}_{\textit{copula modelling}} \qquad \text{where} \qquad \underbrace{u_1 = F_1(x_1), \;\; u_2 = F_2(x_2)}_{\textit{univariate modelling}} \tag{6.38}$$

with a modified version even for counts; see Nelsen (2006). The copula approach

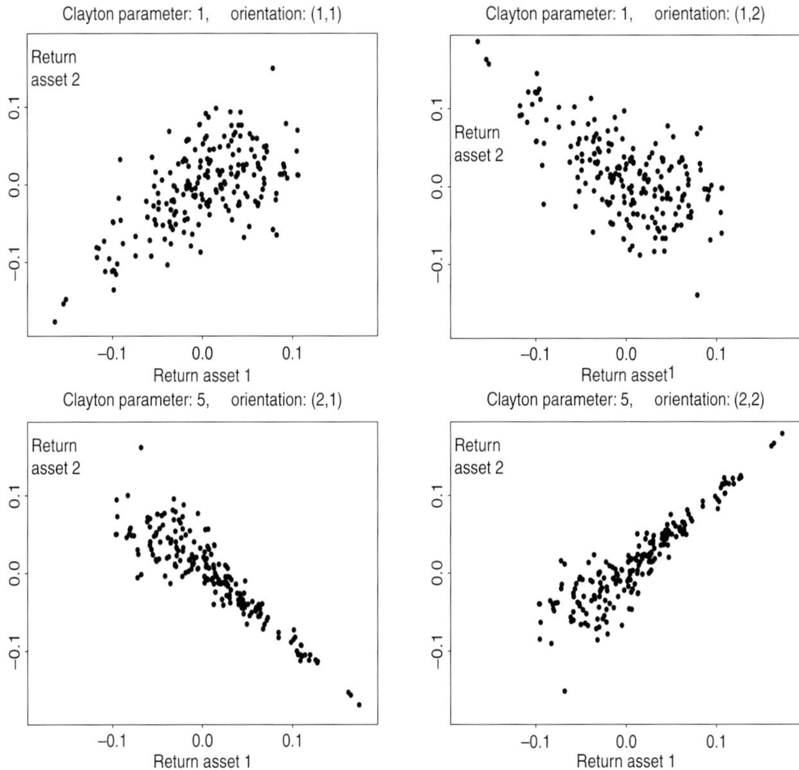

Figure 6.5 Simulated financial returns for Gaussians combined with the Clayton copula.

does not restrict the model at all, and there are additional versions when antithetic twins (Section 4.3) are supplied for the uniforms. Indeed, the copula on the left in (6.38) may be combined with either of

$$\left.\begin{array}{ll} u_1 = F_1(x_1), \quad 1-u_2 = F_2(x_2) & \textit{orientation } (1,2) \\ 1-u_1 = F_1(x_1), \quad u_2 = F_2(x_2) & \textit{orientation } (2,1) \\ 1-u_1 = F_1(x_1), \quad 1-u_2 = F_2(x_2) & \textit{orientation } (2,2) \end{array}\right\} \tag{6.39}$$

and the effect is to rotate the copula patterns 90°, 180° and 270° compared with the orginal one denoted orientation $(1, 1)$; see Figure 6.5.

6.7.3 The Clayton copula

The definition of the Clayton copula can be extended to

$$C(u_1, u_2) = \max\left((u_1^{-\theta} + u_2^{-\theta} - 1)^{-1/\theta}, 0\right), \quad \theta \geq -1 \tag{6.40}$$

where it is again easy to check that the copula requirements (6.37) are satisfied for all $\theta \neq 0$ and ≥ -1. Nor is it difficult to show (see Exercise 6.35) that $C(u_1, u_2) \to u_1 u_2$ as $\theta \to 0$, which means that $\theta = 0$ is the independent case. If $\theta < 0$, then

$$C(u_1, u_2) = 0 \quad \text{if} \quad 0 < u_2 < (1 - u_1^{-\theta})^{-1/\theta},$$

and certain pairs (u_1, u_2) are forbidden territory. Hard restrictions of that kind are often undesirable. Yet when negative θ is included, the family in a sense covers the entire range of dependency that is logically possible; see Exercises 6.34 and 6.35.

Simulated structures under the Clayton copula are shown in Figure 6.5 for normal X_1 and X_2 with mean $\xi = 0.005$ and volatility $\sigma = 0.05$, precisely as in Figure 2.5 (and realistic for monthly equity returns). The cone-shaped patterns signify unequal dependence in unequal parts of the space. Note, for example, the plot in the upper left corner where correlations are much stronger for downside returns. Ordinary Gaussian models don't capture such phenomena, which do appear in real life; see Longin and Solnik (2001). The other plots in Figure 6.5 rotate patterns by changing the orientation of the copula (two of them have become *negatively* correlated), and the degree of dependence is adjusted by varying θ.

6.7.4 Conditional distributions under copulas

Additional insight is gained by examining conditional distributions. Let $c(u_1, u_2)$ and $c(u_2|u_1)$ be the joint and conditional density function. Then

$$c(u_2|u_1) = c(u_1, u_2) = \frac{\partial^2 C(u_1, u_2)}{\partial u_1 u_2},$$

and when this is integrated with respect to u_2,

$$C(u_2|u_1) = \int_0^{u_2} c(v|u_1)\, dv = \int_0^{u_2} \frac{\partial^2 C(u_1, v)}{\partial u_1 \partial v}\, dv = \frac{\partial}{\partial u_1} \int_0^{u_2} \frac{\partial C(u_1, v)}{\partial v}\, dv$$
$$= \frac{\partial C(u_1, u_2)}{\partial u_1}.$$

For the Clayton copula (6.40)

$$C(u_2|u_1) = u_1^{-(1+\theta)} \max\left((u_1^{-\theta} + u_2^{-\theta} - 1)^{-(1+1/\theta)}, 0\right), \tag{6.41}$$

where the expression is zero when $\theta < 0$ and $u_2 < (1 - u_1^{-\theta})^{-1/\theta}$. It has been plotted in Figure 6.6 with θ large and positive on the left and large and negative on the right. Shapes under $u_1 = 0.1$ and $u_2 = 0.9$ differ markedly, a sign of strong dependence, but the most notable feature is a lack of symmetry. On the left U_2 is largely confined to a narrow strip around u_1 when $u_1 = 0.1$, but is much

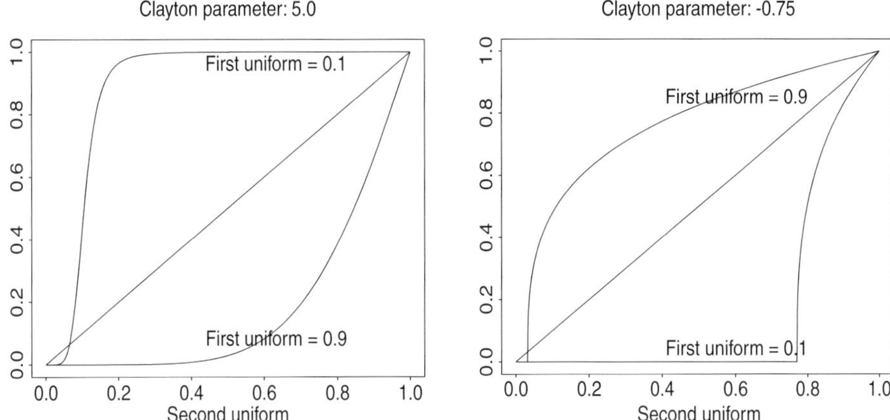

Figure 6.6 Conditional distribution functions for the *second* variable of a Clayton copula; given first variable marked on each curve.

more variable when $u_1 = 0.9$. It is precisely this feature that creates the cones in Figure 6.5.

The preceding argument may be flawed when the **support** of (U_1, U_2) (i.e., the region of positive probability) doesn't cover the entire unit quadrate. Clayton copulas with negative θ is such a case, though for those the argument does go through; see Genest and MacKay (1986) for a simple account of these issues.

6.7.5 *Many variables and the Archimedean class*

Copulas can be extended to any number of variables. A J-dimensional one is the distribution function $C(u_1, \ldots, u_J)$ of J dependent, uniform variables $U_1, \ldots, U_J$ and satisfies consistency requirements similar to those in (6.37). Transformations back to the original variables are now through $X_1 = F_1^{-1}(U_1), \ldots, X_J = F_J^{-1}(U_J)$, and there are 2^J ways of rotating patterns through antithetic twins, not just 4. Copulas of sub-vectors follow from higher-order ones. For example, if $j < J$ then $C(u_1, \ldots, u_j, 1, \ldots, 1)$ is the copula for $U_1, \ldots, U_j$.

Arguably the most convenient copulas are the **Archimedean** ones

$$C(u_1, \ldots, u_J) = \phi^{-1}\{\phi(u_1) + \cdots + \phi(u_J)\}, \tag{6.42}$$

where $\phi(u)$ with inverse $\phi^{-1}(x)$ is known as the **generator**. The Clayton copula is the special case

$$\phi(u) = \frac{1}{\theta}(u^{-\theta} - 1) \quad \text{and} \quad \phi^{-1}(x) = (1 + \theta x)^{-1/\theta},$$

and if $\theta \geq 0$ so that the support is the entire J-dimensional unit quadrate, it readily

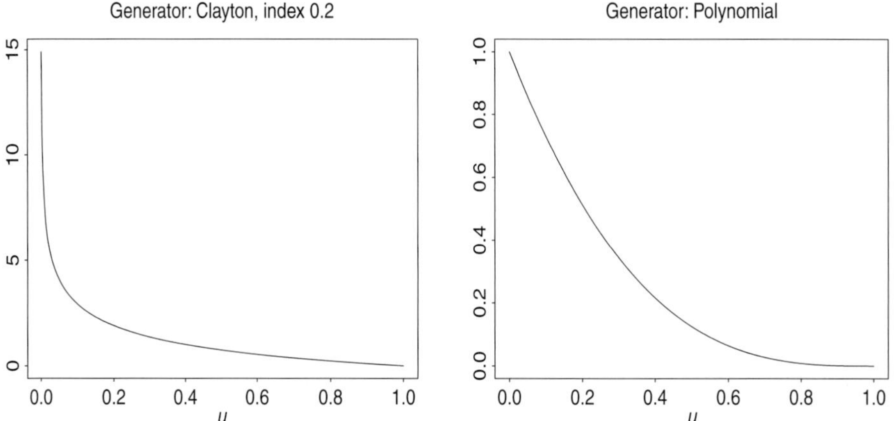

Figure 6.7 Generator functions for Archimedean copulas.

follows that

$$C(u_1, \ldots, u_J) = (u_1^{-\theta} + \cdots + u_J^{-\theta} - J + 1)^{-1/\theta} \tag{6.43}$$

which is an extension of (6.40).

A huge list of generators is compiled in Nelsen (2006). Such functions must in general be monotone with $\phi(1) = 0$, and it is usually desirable that $\phi(0) = \infty$. If not, certain sub-regions are ruled out which we may not want. Thus, generators for practical use are more likely to look like the Clayton example with $\theta = 0.2$ on the left in Figure 6.7 than the other one with $\phi(u) = (1 - u)^3$ on the right. Archimedean copulas go back to Kimberling (1974).

6.7.6 The Marshall–Olkin representation

Some of the most useful Archimedean copulas satisfy a stochastic representation due to Marshall and Olkin (1988). Let Z be a positive random variable with density function $g(z)$. Its moment generating function (or **Laplace transform**) is

$$M(x) = E(e^{-xZ}) = \int_0^\infty e^{-xz} g(z)\, dz; \tag{6.44}$$

see Appendix A.2. Only positive x is of interest in the present context, and $M(x)$ decreases monotonically from one at $x = 0$ to zero at infinity. Define

$$U_j = M\left(-\frac{\log(V_j)}{Z}\right), \quad j = 1, \ldots, J \tag{6.45}$$

where $V_1, \ldots, V_J$ is a sequence of independent and uniform random variables. It turns out that $U_1, \ldots, U_J$ are uniform too (not immediate!), and their joint dis-

Algorithm 6.3 Archimedean copulas

0 Input: $\phi(u)$
1 Draw Z^* *%Z with Laplace transform* $M(x) = \phi^{-1}(x)$
2 For $j = 1, \dots, J$ repeat
3   Draw $V^* \sim$ uniform and $U_j^* \leftarrow M(-\log(V^*)/Z^*)$
4 Return $U_1^*, \dots, U_J^*$.

tribution function is an Archimedean copula with generator $\phi(u) = M^{-1}(u)$; see Section 6.8 for the proof.

The Clayton copula emerges when Z is Gamma distributed with density function

$$g(z) = \frac{\alpha^\alpha}{\Gamma(\alpha)} z^{\alpha-1} e^{-\alpha z} \quad \text{where} \quad \alpha = 1/\theta.$$

Then

$$M(x) = \int_0^\infty e^{-xz} \frac{\alpha^\alpha}{\Gamma(\alpha)} z^{\alpha-1} e^{-\alpha z}\, dz = \left(1 + \frac{x}{\alpha}\right)^{-\alpha} = (1 + \theta x)^{-1/\theta},$$

which is the inverse Clayton generator. Positive distributions with simple moment generating functions and inverses are natural candidates for Z.

6.7.7 Copula sampling

A Monte Carlo simulation $U_1^*, \dots, U_J^*$ of a copula vector is passed on to the original variables through

$$X_1^* \leftarrow F_1^{-1}(U_1^*), \dots, X_J^* \leftarrow F_J^{-1}(U_J^*).$$

This is inversion sampling which does not work for all distributions, but the table look-up algorithm in Section 4.2 (which is an *approximate* inversion) is a satisfactory way around.

What about $U_1^*, \dots, U_J^*$ themselves? A general recursive scheme will be worked out in Section 6.8, but it is far from being universally practical. One class of models that *is* easy to handle is that of Archimedean copulas under the Marshall–Olkin stochastic representation (6.45). Copying this into the computer yields Algorithm 6.3, which returns simulations from the Clayton copula if Z^* is drawn from the standard Gamma distribution with shape $\alpha = 1/\theta$.

For Clayton copulas, there is an alternative (Algorithm 6.4) which is justified by the scheme in Section 6.8. The sample $U_1^*, \dots, U_J^*$ emerging from this second algorithm consists of smooth functions of θ. Why is this useful? Consider the next example.

Algorithm 6.4 The Clayton copula

```
Input: θ > 0
Draw U*_1 ~ uniform and S* ← 0
For j = 2, ..., J do
    S* ← S* + (U*_{j-1})^{-θ} − 1                          %Updating from preceding uniform
    Draw V* ~ uniform
    U*_j ← {(1 + S*)(V*)^{-θ/(1+(j-1)θ)} − S*}^{-1/θ}     %Next uniform
Return U*_1, ..., U*_J.
```

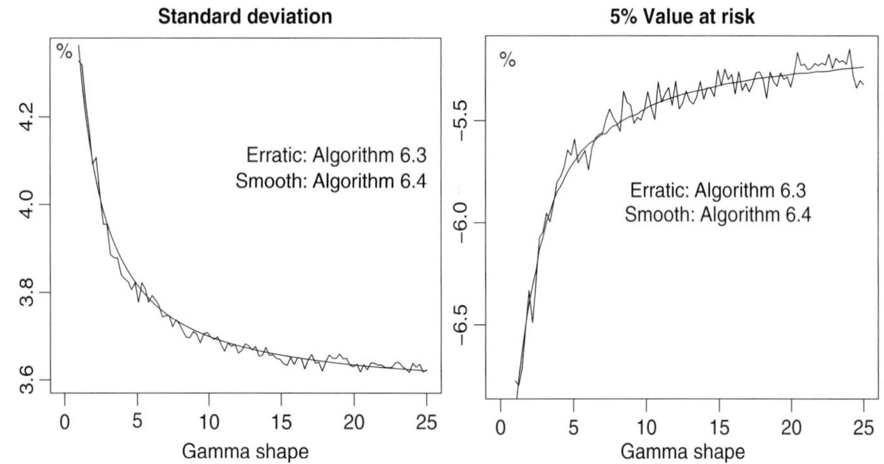

Figure 6.8 Standard deviation (*left*) and lower 5% percentiles (*right*) for the equity portfolio described in the text under variation of the inverse Clayton parameter $\alpha = 1/\theta$.

6.7.8 Example: An equity portfolio

Let $\mathcal{R} = (R_1 + R_2)/2$ be the return of an equally weighted equity portfolio with individual asset returns

$$R_1 = e^{\xi_1 + \sigma_1 \varepsilon_1} - 1 \quad \text{and} \quad R_2 = e^{\xi_2 + \sigma_2 \varepsilon_2} - 1$$

where ε_1 and ε_2 are both $N(0, 1)$. Suppose they are Clayton dependent with parameter θ. The lower 5% percentile and the standard deviation of the portfolio are plotted in Figure 6.8 against the inverse $\alpha = 1/\theta$ when $\xi_1 = \xi_2 = 0.005$ and $\sigma_1 = \sigma_2 = 0.05$, which might be monthly returns for equity. Both downside and variability depend sensitively on α, with low α for strong dependency between asset returns.

There is a more technical side to the display in Figure 6.8. Monte Carlo (m = 10 000 simulations) was used for computation with common random numbers (Section 4.3) to smooth the curves. The random number generator was then run from the same start for each of the 100 values of α plotted; see Section 4.3, where the issue is explained. Yet the picture is smooth *only* when the copulas were sampled by Algorithm 6.4. Why the erratic behaviour when Algorithm 6.3 was used? The reason is the underlying Gamma variables having been generated by Algorithm 2.9, which is a random stopping rule with non-smooth output even when common random numbers are being used.

6.7.9 Example: Copula log-normals against pure log-normals

If the preceding copula log-normal is indeed the true model, how much do results deviate with the traditional log-normal in its place? Comparisons of that kind require careful calibration of models. With $\Phi^{-1}(u)$ Gaussian percentiles the univariate part is defined by $\varepsilon_1 = \Phi^{-1}(U_1)$ and $\varepsilon_2 = \Phi^{-1}(U_2)$ with correlation

$$\rho = E\{\Phi^{-1}(U_1), \Phi^{-1}(U_2)\},$$

and one way to make models comparable is to let the value be the same whether (U_1, U_2) comes from the Clayton copula or corresponds to an ordinary bivariate normal.

The experiments reported in Figure 6.9 were based on the Clayton copula with $\theta = 1$, and the corresponding ρ for the pure Gaussian was determined by Monte Carlo. If (U_{1i}^*, U_{2i}^*) for $i = 1, \ldots, m$ are simulations of (U_1, U_2) under the copula, then ρ is approximated by

$$\rho^* = \frac{1}{m}\sum_{i=1}^{m} \Phi^{-1}(U_{1i}^*)\Phi^{-1}(U_{2i}^*)$$

which gave $\rho^* = 0.498$. The other conditions were those of the preceding example. Density functions of $\mathcal{R}$ are plotted in Figure 6.9 (one million simulations used). There are model discrepancies on the left, but not for the 5-year returns on the right. Why is that? Over such long time horizons equity returns are nearly log-normal (Section 5.5) in this case with parameters almost the same whether the copula is used or not. That is due to the calibration which leads to models for log-returns with coinciding first- and second-order moments, carried to portfolio level *approximately*. Monte Carlo is run through the recursion

$$\mathcal{R}_{0:k}^* = \mathcal{R}_{0:k-1}^*(1 + \mathcal{R}_k^*), \qquad k = 1, \ldots, 60 \quad \text{starting at} \quad \mathcal{R}_{0:0}^* = 1,$$

where $\mathcal{R}_k^*$ is the Monte Carlo return in period k. Long-range asset risk may not be too strongly influenced by subtle copula effects. Other values of θ gave similar results.

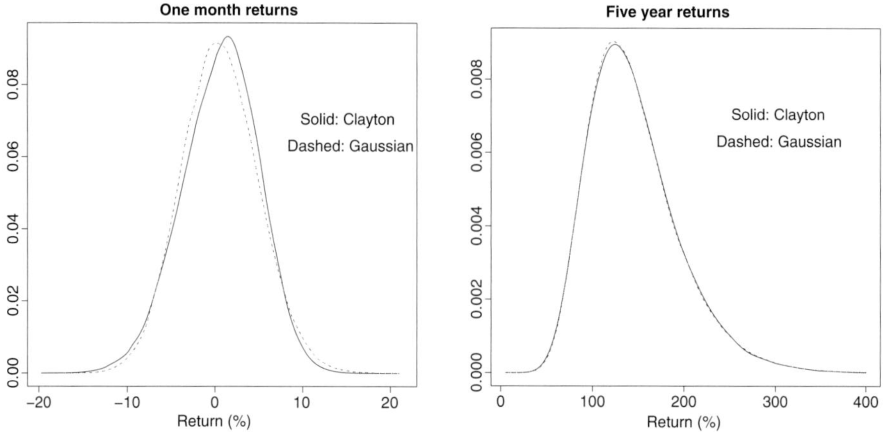

Figure 6.9 Density functions for monthly returns (*left*) and 5-year returns (*right*) under models described in the text.

6.8 Mathematical arguments

6.8.1 Portfolio risk when claim intensities are random

Let $\mathcal{X} = Z_1 + \cdots + Z_{\mathcal{N}}$, where $Z_1, Z_2 \ldots$ are independent and identically distributed with mean ξ_z and standard deviation σ_z and independent of $\mathcal{N}$. The variance of $\mathcal{X}$ is then

$$\text{var}(\mathcal{X}) = \text{var}(\mathcal{N})\xi_z^2 + E(\mathcal{N})\sigma_z^2;$$

see (6.14) right. Suppose $\mathcal{N}$ is Poisson distributed with random claim intensities $\mu_1, \ldots, \mu_J$ for which $\xi_\mu = E(\mu_j)$ and $\sigma_\mu = \text{sd}(\mu_j)$. Then

$$E(\mathcal{N}) = J\xi_\mu T \quad \text{and} \quad \text{var}(\mathcal{N}) = JT^2(\gamma\sigma_\mu^2 + \xi_\mu/T),$$

where γ depends on how the intensities are sampled; i.e., $\gamma = 1$ if they are independent and $\gamma = J$ if they share a common value for all policies; see (6.18). Inserting these expressions into the formula for var($\mathcal{X}$) yields

$$\text{var}(\mathcal{X}) \;=\; JT^2(\gamma\sigma_\mu^2 + \xi_\mu/T)\xi_z^2 + J\xi_\mu T\sigma_z^2 \;=\; J\xi_\mu T(\sigma_z^2 + \xi_z^2) + \gamma JT^2\sigma_\mu^2\xi_z^2$$

or

$$\text{var}(\mathcal{X}) = \left(J\xi_\mu T(\sigma_z^2 + \xi_z^2)\right) \times \left(1 + \gamma T\frac{\sigma_\mu^2}{\xi_\mu}\frac{\xi_z^2}{\sigma_z^2 + \xi_z^2}\right),$$

which is (6.19).

6.8.2 Optimal prediction

To prove that $\hat{Y} = E(Y|\mathbf{X})$ is the optimal predictor for Y note that

$$E(Y-a)^2 = E(Y^2) - 2aE(Y) + a^2, \quad \text{minimized by} \quad a = E(Y)$$

so that $E(Y - EY)^2 \leq E(Y-a)^2$ for all a. This inequality may be applied conditionally given $\mathbf{X}$. If $\tilde{Y} = \tilde{Y}(\mathbf{X})$ is an arbitrary function, then since $\hat{Y} = E(Y|\mathbf{X})$

$$E\{(Y-\hat{Y})^2|\mathbf{X}\} \leq E\{(Y-\tilde{Y})^2|\mathbf{X}\}.$$

Take the expectation with respect to $\mathbf{X}$ over both sides. The rule of double expectation then yields

$$E(Y-\hat{Y})^2 \leq E(Y-\tilde{Y})^2,$$

which is (6.22).

6.8.3 Vasiček bond prices

The Vasiček model for interest rates is $r_k = \xi_q + (1-a_q h)(r_{k-1} - \xi_q) + \sigma_q \sqrt{h}\,\varepsilon_k$ for $k = 1, \dots, K$ where $\varepsilon_1, \dots, \varepsilon_K$ are independent and $N(0,1)$. Consider $E(e^{-hs_K})$ where $s_K = r_1 + \cdots + r_K$. We seek the limit as $h \to 0$ and $K \to \infty$ while $T = Kh$ is kept fixed. Let $a = 1 - a_q h$ and note that $r_k - \xi_q = \sigma_q \sqrt{h}\,\varepsilon_k + a(r_{k-1} - \xi_q) = \sigma_q \sqrt{h}\,\varepsilon_k + a\sigma_q \sqrt{h}\,\varepsilon_{k-1} + a^2(r_{k-2} - \xi_q)$ and so on all the way down to

$$r_k - \xi_q = \sigma_q \sqrt{h}(\varepsilon_k + a\varepsilon_{k-1} + \cdots + a^{k-1}\varepsilon_1) + a^k(r_0 - \xi_q).$$

It follows that

$$s_K = \sum_{k=1}^{K} r_k = K\xi_q + \sum_{k=1}^{K}(r_k - \xi_q) = K\xi_q + \sigma_q \sqrt{h} \sum_{k=1}^{K}\sum_{i=0}^{k-1} a^i \varepsilon_{k-i} + \sum_{k=1}^{K} a^k (r_0 - \xi_q),$$

where the double sum on the right after noting that $1 + a + \cdots + a^{K-i} = (1 - a^{K-i+1})/(1-a)$ can be rewritten

$$\sum_{k=1}^{K}\sum_{i=0}^{k-1} a^i \varepsilon_{k-i} = \sum_{k=1}^{K}\sum_{i=1}^{k} a^{k-i}\varepsilon_i = \sum_{i=1}^{K}\left(\sum_{k=i}^{K} a^{k-i}\right)\varepsilon_i = \sum_{i=1}^{K} \frac{1-a^{K-i+1}}{1-a}\varepsilon_i.$$

This yields

$$s_K = K\xi_q + \frac{\sigma_q \sqrt{h}}{1-a}\sum_{i=1}^{K}(1-a^{K-i+1})\varepsilon_i + a\frac{1-a^K}{1-a}(r_0 - \xi_q),$$

where $a + \cdots + a^K = a(1-a^K)/(1-a)$ has been utilized to simplify the last term on the right. It is now straightforward to calculate $E(hs_K)$ and $\text{var}(hs_K)$. The former is

$$E(hs_K) = K\xi_q h + a(1-a^K)(r_0 - \xi_q)h/(1-a) \quad \text{where} \quad a = 1 - a_q h.$$

Since $h = T/K$, it follows that $a^K = (1 - a_q T/K)^K \rightarrow e^{-a_q T}$ as $K \rightarrow \infty$ so that

$$E(hs_K) \longrightarrow T\xi_q + \frac{1 - e^{-a_q T}}{a_q}(r_0 - \xi_q) = Br_0 - (B - T)\xi_q$$

where $B = (1 - e^{-a_q T})/a_q$. For the variance,

$$\text{var}(hs_K) = \frac{\sigma_q^2 h^3}{(1-a)^2} \sum_{i=1}^{K} (1 - a^{K-i+1})^2 = \frac{\sigma_q^2 h^3}{(1-a)^2}\left(K - 2\frac{a(1-a^K)}{1-a} + \frac{a^2(1-a^{2K})}{1-a^2}\right)$$

after reducing the sum to several geometric series. Inserting $a = 1 - a_q h$ and utilizing $a^K \rightarrow e^{-a_q T}$ yield

$$\text{var}(hs_K) \longrightarrow \frac{\sigma_q^2}{a_q^2}\left(T - 2\frac{1 - e^{-a_q T}}{a_q} + \frac{1 - e^{-2a_q T}}{2a_q}\right) = \frac{\sigma_q^2}{a_q^2}\left(T - B - a_q\frac{B^2}{2}\right)$$

after some algebra. The ordinary formula for the expectation of log-normal variables now implies

$$E(e^{-hs_K}) = E^{-E(hs_K) + \text{var}(hs_K)/2} \longrightarrow e^{-Br_0 + (B-T)\xi_q + (\sigma_q^2/2a_q^2)(T - B - a_q B^2/2)},$$

which is the Vasiček bond price model (6.24) and (6.25).

6.8.4 The Marshall–Olkin representation

Let $V_1, \ldots, V_J, Z$ be independent random variables with $V_1, \ldots, V_J$ uniform and Z positive with density function $g(z)$ and moment generating function $M(x) = \int_0^\infty e^{-xz} g(z)dz$. Define $U_j = M(-\log(V_j)/Z)$ for $j = 1, \ldots, J$. We shall prove that $U_1, \ldots, U_J$ follow an Archimedean copula with generator $\phi(u) = M^{-1}(u)$. First note that $V_j = e^{-M^{-1}(U_j)Z}$. Hence, if $Z = z$ is fixed, then

$$\Pr(U_1 \leq u_1, \ldots, U_J \leq u_J | z) = \Pr(V_1 \leq e^{-M^{-1}(u_1)z}, \ldots, V_J \leq e^{-M^{-1}(u_J)z} | z)$$

since $M^{-1}(u)$ is decreasing in u. But $V_1, \ldots, V_J$ are independent and uniform, and this yields

$$\Pr(U_1 \leq u_1, \ldots, U_J \leq u_J | z) = e^{-M^{-1}(u_1)z - \cdots - M^{-1}(u_J)z}$$

which implies

$$\Pr(U_1 \leq u_1, \ldots, U_J \leq u_J) = \int_0^\infty e^{-\{M^{-1}(u_1) + \cdots + M^{-1}(u_J)\}z} g(z)\, dz.$$

This can also be written

$$\Pr(U_1 \leq u_1, \ldots, U_J \leq u_J) = M\{M^{-1}(u_1) + \cdots + M^{-1}(u_J)\},$$

which is an Archimedean copula with generator $\phi(u) = M^{-1}(u)$.

6.8.5 A general scheme for copula sampling

Some copulas can be sampled through inversion. Start by drawing J uniforms U_1^* and $V_2^*, \dots, V_J^*$ and proceed iteratively through

$$C(U_j^*|U_1^*, \dots, U_{j-1}^*) = V_j^*, \quad j = 2, \dots, J \tag{6.46}$$

where $C(u_j|u_1, \dots, u_{j-1})$ is the conditional distribution function of U_j given $U_1, \dots, U_{j-1}$. This yields the desired vector $U_1^*, \dots, U_J^*$, but whether it is practical hinges on the work needed to solve the equations. We must in any case derive an expression for $C(u_j|u_1, \dots, u_{j-1})$. Let $c(u_j|u_1, \dots, u_{j-1})$ be its density function so that

$$C(u_j|u_1, \dots, u_{j-1}) = \int_0^{u_j} c(v|u_1, \dots, u_{j-1})\, dv.$$

To calculate the integral let $c(u_1, \dots, u_j)$ be the density function of $U_1, \dots, U_j$ and recall that $C(u_1, \dots, u_{j-1}, 1)$ is the distribution function of $U_1, \dots, U_{j-1}$. It follows that

$$c(u_j|u_1, \dots, u_{j-1}) = \frac{c(u_1, \dots, u_j)}{c(u_1, \dots, u_{j-1})} = \frac{\partial^j C(u_1, \dots, u_j)/\partial u_1, \dots, \partial u_j}{\partial^{j-1} C(u_1, \dots, u_{j-1}, 1)/\partial u_1, \dots, \partial u_{j-1}}.$$

If D is the denominator, then

$$\begin{aligned}\int_0^{u_j} c(v|u_1, \dots, u_{j-1})\, dv &= D^{-1} \int_0^{u_j} \frac{\partial^j C(u_1, \dots, u_{j-1}, v)}{\partial u_1 \dots, \partial u_{j-1} \partial v}\, dv \\ &= D^{-1} \frac{\partial^{j-1}}{\partial u_1, \dots, \partial u_{j-1}} \int_0^{u_j} \frac{\partial C(u_1, \dots, u_{j-1}, v)}{\partial v}\, dv \\ &= D^{-1} \frac{\partial^{j-1} C(u_1, \dots, u_j)}{\partial u_1 \dots \partial u_{j-1}},\end{aligned}$$

and it has been established that

$$C(u_j|u_1, \dots, u_{j-1}) = \frac{\partial^{j-1} C(u_1, \dots, u_{j-1}, u_j)/\partial u_1 \dots \partial u_{j-1}}{\partial^{j-1} C(u_1, \dots, u_{j-1}, 1)/\partial u_1 \dots \partial u_{j-1}} \tag{6.47}$$

which is the extension of the bivariate case in Section 6.7. If the equation (6.46) is easy to solve after having calculated the derivatives, we have a sampling method.

6.8.6 Justification of Algorithm 6.4

The preceding recursive technique works for Clayton copulas if $\theta > 0$. Then

$$C(u_1, \dots, u_j) = \left(\sum_{i=1}^{j} u_i^{-\theta} - j + 1 \right)^{-1/\theta},$$

which is easily differentiated with respect to $u_1, \ldots, u_{j-1}$. After a little work

$$\frac{\partial^{j-1} C(u_1, \ldots, u_j)}{\partial u_1 \ldots \partial u_{j-1}} = \left(\sum_{i=1}^{j} u_i^{-\theta} - j + 1\right)^{-1/\theta - j + 1} \times \prod_{i=1}^{j-1} \left(u_i^{-(1+\theta)}\{1 + (i-1)\theta\}\right),$$

and the conditional distribution function of U_j given $u_1, \ldots, u_{j-1}$ now follows from (6.47) as

$$C(u_j | u_1, \ldots, u_{j-1}) = \left(\frac{\sum_{i=1}^{j} u_i^{-\theta} - j + 1}{\sum_{i=1}^{j-1} u_i^{-\theta} - j + 2}\right)^{-1/\theta - j + 1} = \left(\frac{u_j^{-\theta} + s_{j-1}}{1 + s_{j-1}}\right)^{-1/\theta - j + 1}$$

where $s_{j-1} = \sum_{i=1}^{j-1} u_i^{-\theta} - j + 1$. A Monte Carlo simulation of U_j^* given $U_1^*, \ldots, U_{j-1}^*$ is therefore generated by drawing another uniform V^* and solving the equation

$$\left(\frac{(U_j^*)^{-\theta} + S_{j-1}^*}{1 + S_{j-1}^*}\right)^{-1/\theta - j + 1} = V^* \quad \text{where} \quad S_{j-1}^* = \sum_{i=1}^{j-1} (U_i^*)^{-\theta} - j + 1.$$

The expression for U_j^* in Algorithm 6.4 follows from this.

6.9 Bibliographical notes

6.9.1 General work

Markov models and other basic topics in probability can be found in almost any textbook. The classical treatise Feller (1968, 1971) is still a good place to start. Specialist monographs on multivariate distributions are Johnson *et al.* (1997) (discrete ones) and Kotz *et al.* (2000) (continuous ones); see also Balakrishnan (2004a,b) for the actuarial context on this.

6.9.2 Applications

You will encounter the hierarchical risk model of Section 6.3 in most textbooks on general insurance; see Mikosch (2004) for example. The Vasiček bond prices in Section 6.4 are only one among a huge number of possibilities; consult James and Webber (2000), Brigo and Mercurio (2001), Cairns (2004) and others.

6.9.3 Copulas

The interest in copulas exploded around the turn of the century, although Mikosch (2006) raised a sceptical eye. General introductions for insurance and finance are Embrechts *et al.* (2003) and Cherubini *et al.* (2004); see also Nelsen (2006) for a more mathematical treatment or even Joe (1997) for a broader angle on dependence modelling. You will find a good discussion of how Archimedean copulas are simulated in Whelan (2004); see also Frees and Valdez (1998). For applications in insurance consult (among others) Klugman and Parsa (1999), Carriére (2000), Venter (2003), Bäuerle and Grübel (2005) and Escarela and Carriére (2006).

6.10 Exercises

Section 6.2

Exercise 6.1 Let $X|G \sim N(\xi, \xi_\sigma/\sqrt{G})$ where ξ and ξ_σ are parameters and $G \sim$ Gamma(α). Argue that X is t-distributed as in Section 2.4. [*Hint*: The t-model is $X = \xi + (\xi_\sigma/\sqrt{G})\varepsilon$ where $\varepsilon \sim N(0,1)$ with ε and G independent.]

Exercise 6.2 Let $G \sim$ Gamma(α) and $X|G \sim$ normal with $E(X|G) = \xi + \beta(G-1)$ and $\text{sd}(X|G) = \xi_\sigma/\sqrt{G}$, which is an extension of the model in Exercise 6.1. Use the double rules in Section 6.3 and derive $E(X) = \xi$ and $\text{sd}(X) = \sqrt{\beta^2/\alpha + \alpha\xi_\sigma^2/(\alpha-1)}$. [*Hint*: Utilize that $\text{var}(G) = 1/\alpha$ and $E(1/G) = \alpha/(\alpha-1)$.]

Exercise 6.3

(a) Write a program generating m simulations of X in Exercise 6.2.
R-*commands*:
```
G=rgamma(m,α)/α; X=ξ+β*(G-1)+ξσ*rnorm(m)/sqrt(G).
```
(b) Run the program when $m = 100\,000$, $\xi = 0.04$, $\xi_\sigma = 0.01$, $\alpha = 10$ and $\beta = 0.07$, compute their mean and standard deviation, estimate and plot the density function and speculate whether X could be a rate of inflation.
R-*commands*:
```
Mean=mean(X); Sd=sd(X); plot(density(X)).
```
(c) Check that the mean and standard deviation match the theoretical ones in Exercise 6.2.
(d) Redo (b) when $\beta = -0.1$ and note the switch in skewness.

Exercise 6.4 Let $\Pr(C=2) = 1 - \Pr(C=1) = p$ and $X|C \sim N(\xi_C, \sigma_C)$ with two sets of parameters (ξ_1, σ_1) and (ξ_2, σ_2) according to the **regime** C of the economy.

(a) Write a program generating m simulations of $R = e^X - 1$.
R-*commands*:
```
ξ=c(ξ1,ξ2); σ=c(σ1,σ2); C=1+rbinom(m,1,p);
R=rlnorm(m,ξ[C],σ[C])-1.
```
(b) Run the program when $m = 100\,000$, $p = 0.5$, $\xi_1 = 0.02$, $\sigma_1 = 0.12$, $\xi_2 = 0.08$ and $\sigma_2 = 0.25$, compute the average and standard deviation of the simulations of the return R and estimate and plot the density function.
R-*commands*:
```
Mean=mean(R); Sd=sd(R); plot(density(R)).
```

(c) Compute the average *log*-return and argue that it should be close to 0.05.

R-*commands*:

```
Mean=mean(log(1+R)).
```

Exercise 6.5 Let $\mathcal{N}|\mu \sim \text{Poisson}(J\mu T)$ where $\mu = \xi e^{-\sigma^2/2+\sigma\varepsilon}$ for $\varepsilon \sim N(0,1)$ which is an alternative to model (6.9). Use the double rules in Section 6.3 to argue that $E(\mathcal{N}) = J\xi T$ and $\text{var}(\mathcal{N}) = J\xi T + (J\xi T)^2(e^{\sigma^2} - 1)$. [*Hint*: $E(\mu) = \xi$ and $\text{sd}(\mu) = \xi\sqrt{e^{\sigma^2} - 1}$.]

Exercise 6.6

(a) Determine σ in Exercise 6.5 so that $\text{sd}(\mu) = \xi/10$. [*Answer*: $\sigma = 0.09975$ and if $\xi = 0.05$, $\text{sd}(\mu)$ is now the same as in Figure 6.1.]

(b) Write a program generating m simulations of independent realizations $\mathcal{N}_1, \ldots, \mathcal{N}_K$ of $\mathcal{N}$.

R-*commands*:

```
μ=ξ*exp(-σ^2/2+σ*rnorm(m*K));
N=matrix(rpois(m*K,J*μ*T),K,m).
```

(c) Run the program when $m = 20$, $K = 25$, $\xi = 0.05$, $\sigma = 0.09975$, $T = 1$ and $J = 10^4$ and plot the simulations against time as in Figure 6.1.

R-*commands*:

```
matplot(1:K,N,''l'').
```

(d) Redo for $J = 10^6$ and compare with the plot in (c).

Exercise 6.7 Let $\hat{Z} = e^{\hat{\theta}+\hat{\sigma}\varepsilon}$ be the fitted version of the log-normal model $Z = e^{\theta+\sigma\varepsilon}$ with $\hat{\theta}$ and $\hat{\sigma}$ the average and standard deviation of historical data $\log(z_1), \ldots, \log(z_n)$.

(a) Write a program generating m simulations of $\hat{Z}$ with $\hat{\theta}$ and $\hat{\sigma}$ redrawn each time.

R-*commands*:

```
z=matrix(rlnorm(n*m,θ,σ),n,m); θ̂=apply(log(z),2,mean);
σ̂=apply(log(z),2,sd); Ẑ=rlnorm(m,θ̂,σ̂).
```

(b) Run the program when $m = 10\,000$, $n = 20$, $\theta = 0$ and $\sigma = 1$, compute the mean and standard deviation of the simulations and compare with $E(Z) = e^{\theta+\sigma^2/2}$ and $\text{sd}(Z) = E(Z)\sqrt{e^{\sigma^2} - 1}$.

R-*commands*:

```
Mean=mean(Ẑ); Sd=sd(Ẑ).
```

(c) Redo when $n = 100$ and note that the standard deviation is closer to the theoretical one now.

Exercise 6.8 Redo Exercise 6.7 for log-normal equity returns $R = e^{K\xi + \sqrt{K}\sigma\varepsilon} - 1$ with estimates $\hat{\xi}$ and $\hat{\sigma}$ the average and standard deviation of historical log-returns $\log(1 + r_1), \dots, \log(1 + r_n)$.

(a) Write a program generating m simulations of $\hat{R} = e^{K\hat{\xi} + \sqrt{K}\hat{\sigma}\varepsilon} - 1$ with $\hat{\xi}$, $\hat{\sigma}$ redrawn each time.

R-*commands*:

Minor modification of Exercise 6.7(a).

(b) Run the program when $m = 10\,000$, $n = 250$, $\xi = 0.0002$, $\sigma = 0.01$ and $K = 250$, compute the mean and standard deviation and compare with $E(R) = e^{K\xi + K\sigma^2/2} - 1$ and $\text{sd}(R) = \{1 + E(R)\}\sqrt{e^{K\sigma^2} - 1}$.

(c) The discrepancy is considerable, but try 4 years of historical data with $n = 1000$.

Section 6.3

Exercise 6.9 Independent variation in μ among policy holders inflates the standard deviation of portfolio losses by $\sqrt{1 + \delta}$, where $\delta = T(\sigma_\mu^2/\xi_\mu)\xi_z^2/(\sigma_z^2 + \xi_z^2)$; see (6.19) and (6.20).

(a) Deduce that $\delta \le T\sigma_\mu^2/\xi_\mu$.

(b) Argue that this added portfolio uncertainty is likely to be only moderate in practice.

Exercise 6.10 Suppose μ of the preceding exercise is a common parameter for all policy holders. Now the standard deviation of portfolio losses increases by $\sqrt{1 + J\delta}$ with δ as in Exercise 6.9.

(a) Compute $\sqrt{1 + J\delta}$ when $\xi = 5\%$, $\sigma_\mu = 1\%$, $\sigma_z/\xi_z = 0.5$ and $J = 100\,000$ and argue that the impact of common μ-variation is very different from the individual one.

(b) Point out that $\sqrt{1 + J\delta}$ decreases with σ_z/ξ_z and explain what this tells us.

Exercise 6.11 Suppose $X^*|\hat{\xi}, \hat{\sigma} \sim N(\hat{\xi}, \hat{\sigma})$ where $\hat{\xi}$ and $\hat{\sigma}$ are estimates of ξ and σ.

(a) Use the rules of double expectation and double variance to verify that $E(X^*) = E(\hat{\xi})$ and $\text{var}(X^*) = E(\hat{\sigma}^2) + \text{var}(\hat{\xi})$.

(b) If $\text{var}(\hat{\xi}) = \sigma^2/n$ and $E(\hat{\sigma}^2) = \sigma^2$ with n the number of observations, show that $\text{var}(X^*) = \sigma^2(1 + 1/n)$.

Exercise 6.12 Let $\mathcal{N}^*|\hat{\mu}$ be Poisson$(J\hat{\mu}T)$ where $\hat{\mu}$ is an estimate of the true intensity μ.

(a) Use the rules of double expectation and double variance to prove that

$$E(\mathcal{N}^*) = JTE(\hat{\mu}) \quad \text{and} \quad \text{var}(\mathcal{N}^*) = JTE(\hat{\mu}) + (JT)^2\text{var}(\hat{\mu}).$$

(b) Why does this prohibit $\mathcal{N}^*$ from being Poisson distributed when estimation and Monte Carlo uncertainty are both taken into account?

(c) Argue that the impact of estimation error on the distribution of $\mathcal{N}^*$ might well be much larger than it was in Exercise 6.11.

Exercise 6.13 The double rule for covariances is

$$\text{cov}(Y_1, Y_2) = \text{cov}\{\xi_1(\mathbf{X}), \xi_2(\mathbf{X})\} + E\{\sigma_{12}(\mathbf{X})\},$$

where $\xi_1(\mathbf{x}) = E(Y_1|\mathbf{x})$, $\xi_2(\mathbf{x}) = E(Y_2|\mathbf{x})$ and $\sigma_{12}(\mathbf{x}) = \text{cov}(Y_1, Y_2|\mathbf{x})$; see Appendix A.3. Consider financial returns R_1 and R_2 under the stochastic volatility model in Section 2.4; i.e., suppose $R_1 = \xi_1 + \sigma_{\xi_1}\sqrt{Z}\varepsilon_1$ and $R_2 = \xi_2 + \sigma_{\xi_2}\sqrt{Z}\varepsilon_2$ where $\varepsilon_1, \varepsilon_2$ are $N(0,1)$ with $\text{cor}(\varepsilon_1, \varepsilon_2) = \rho$.

(a) If Z is independent of $(\varepsilon_1, \varepsilon_2)$, calculate $\text{cov}(R_1, R_2|z)$ and show that $\text{cov}(R_1, R_2) = \rho\sigma_{\xi_1}\sigma_{\xi_2}E(Z)$.

(b) Write down an expression for the covariance in the t-situation where $Z = 1/G$ for $G \sim \text{Gamma}(\alpha)$. [*Hint*: Recall $E(1/G) = \alpha/(\alpha - 1)$.]

Section 6.4

Exercise 6.14 Let X_1 and X_2 be dependent normal variables with expectations ξ_1 and ξ_2, standard deviations σ_1 and σ_2 and correlation ρ.

(a) Argue that $\hat{X}_2 = \xi_2 + \rho\sigma_2(x_1 - \xi_1)/\sigma_1$ is the most accurate prediction of X_2 given $X_1 = x_1$ and that $\text{sd}(\hat{X}_2|x_1) = \text{sd}(X_2)\sqrt{1-\rho^2}$. [*Hint*: Look up (6.3).]

(b) By how much is the uncertainty in X_2 reduced by knowing X_1 if $\rho = 0.3$, 0.7 and 0.9?

(c) Argue that ρ from this point of view should be interpreted as ρ^2, as claimed in Section 5.2.

Exercise 6.15 With $K = T/h$ let $\bar{r}(r_0, K) = P(r_0, T)^{-1/K} - 1$ be the average yield under the Vasiček bond price model (6.24) and (6.25).

(a) Show that $\bar{r}(r_0, K) \to e^{\{\xi_q - \sigma_q^2/(2a_q^2)\}h} - 1$ as $K \to \infty$.

(b) Also examine the intensity version $\bar{r}(r_0, T) = -\log\{P(r_0, T)\}/T$ as $T \to \infty$.

(c) Argue that these expressions may be negative.

Exercise 6.16

(a) Write a program tabulating the Vasiček bond price model $P(r_0, kh)$ for $k = 1, \ldots, K$ when $K = T/h$.

R-*commands*:

$\texttt{K=T/h; tk=0:K*h; B=(1-exp(-}a_q\texttt{*tk))/}a_q\texttt{;}$
$\texttt{A=(B-tk)*(}\xi_q\texttt{-}\sigma_q\texttt{**2/(2*}a_q\texttt{**2))-}\sigma_q\texttt{**2*}B\texttt{**2/(4*}a_q\texttt{);}$
$\texttt{P=exp(A-B*}r_0\texttt{).}$

(b) Compute/plot these bond prices when $T = 50$, $h = 1$, $r_0 = 0.08$, $\xi_q = 0.04$, $a_q = 0.35$ and $\sigma_q = 0.02$.

R-*commands*:

```
plot(tk,P).
```

(c) Redo (b) when $\sigma_q = 0.05$ and $\sigma_q = 0.08$ and plot the new bond prices jointly with the old ones.

R-*commands*:

For the plot use `lines(tk,P)`.

(d) Argue that high σ_q goes with high bond prices.

Exercise 6.17

(a) Write a program converting the Vasiček bond prices in Exercise 6.16 to interest-rate intensities $\bar{r}(r_0, kh) = -\log\{P(r_0, kh)\}/(kh)$.

R-*commands*:

With `K`, `tk` and `P` as in Exercise 6.16(a) use $\bar{r}$`=-log(P[1:K+1])/tk[1:K+1]`.

(b) Compute and plot the interest-rate curve with the conditions in Exercise 6.16(b).

R-*commands*:

$\texttt{plot(tk[1:K+1],}\bar{r}\texttt{).}$

(c) Redo for $\sigma_q = 0.05$ and $\sigma_q = 0.08$ and plot the three curves jointly.

R-*commands*:

As in Exercise 6.16(c).

(d) Redo (b) for $a_q = 0.2$ and $a_q = 0.5$ and again plot the curves jointly.

R-*commands*:

As before.

Exercise 6.18 How accurate are Monte Carlo bond prices/interest-rate curves under Vasiček conditions?

(a) Generate m simulations of $r_1, \dots, r_K$ and compute approximate bond prices.

R-*commands*:

Apply the R function `vasicek` with $\texttt{K=T/h; a=exp(-}a_q\texttt{*h);}$
$\sigma\texttt{=}\sigma_q\texttt{*sqrt((1-a**2)/(2*}a_q\texttt{));}$
$\texttt{r=vasicek(m,K,}r_0\texttt{,}\xi_q\texttt{,a,}\sigma\texttt{)\$r;s=apply(r[1:K+1,],2,cumsum);}$
`P=apply(exp(-h*s),1,mean).`

(b) Run the program under the conditions in Exercise 6.16(b) with $m = 10\,000$ and $h = 1$ and compare with the exact result.

R-*commands*:

After Exercise 6.16(b) use `lines(1:K*h,P)`.

(c) Redo (b) when $h = 0.1$ and $h = 0.05$.

(d) Redo (b), (c) for the interest-rate curve.

R-*commands*:

After Exercise 6.17(b) use `tk=1:K*h; r̄=-log(P[1:K+1])/tk; lines(tk,r̄)`.

Exercise 6.19

(a) Modify the program in Exercise 6.18(a) so that Black–Karasinski bonds are valued instead.

R-*commands*:

With K, a, σ as in Exercise 6.18 use

```
x0=log(r0/ξq)+0.5*σ**2/(1-a**2);
X=vasicek(m,K,x0,ξ=0,a,σ)$r;
r=ξq*exp(-σ**2/(2*(1-a**2))+X);
s=apply(r[1:K+1,],2,cumsum); P=apply(exp(-h*s),1,mean).
```

(b) Run the program when $m = 10\,000$, $T = 50$, $r_0 = 0.08$, $\xi_q = 0.04$, $a_q = 0.35$, $\sigma_q = 0.46$ and $h = 1$, 0.1 and 0.05 and plot the results jointly against time.

R-*commands*:

First $h = 1$ with `plot(1:K*h,P,''l'')`, then $h = 0.1$ with `lines(1:K*h,P)` and similarly for $h = 0.05$.

Exercise 6.20

(a) Redo Exercise 6.19(b) when $h = 0.1$ with the bond prices converted to the interest-rate curve.

R-*commands*:

With `P` as in Exercise 6.19(b) use `tk=1:K*h, r̄=-log(P[1:K+1])/tk; plot(tk,r̄)`.

(b) Compare the Vasiček interest-rate curve in Exercise 6.16(b) with that of Black–Karasinski with σ_q now being

$$\sigma_q^{\mathrm{BK}} = \sqrt{2a_q \log\left(1 + \frac{\sigma_q^2}{2a_q\xi_q^2}\right)},$$

which yields coinciding values of $\mathrm{var}(r_k)$ for the two models as $h \to 0$.

R-*commands*:

First `plot(tk,`$\bar r$`)` with $\bar r$ from Exercise 6.16(b) and then `lines(tk,`$\bar r$`)` with $\bar r$ taken from the simulations in (a).

Exercise 6.21 The **CIR** model is $r_k = \xi + a(r_{k-1} - \xi) + \sqrt{r_k}\sigma\varepsilon_k$ for $k = 1, 2, \dots$ and is often applied to bond pricing with continuous-time parameters $\xi = \xi_q$, $a = 1 - a_q h$ and $\sigma = \sigma_q\sqrt{h}$. As $h \to 0$ this leads to $P(r_0, T) = e^{A(T) - B(T)r_0}$ where

$$B(T) = \frac{2(1 - e^{-\gamma_q T})}{(\gamma_q + a_q)(1 - e^{-\gamma_q T}) + 2\gamma_q e^{-\gamma_q T}}, \qquad A(T) = \frac{2a_q\xi_q}{\sigma_q^2}\log\left(\frac{\gamma_q e^{(a_q-\gamma_q)T/2}B(T)}{1 - e^{-\gamma_q T}}\right)$$

for $\gamma_q = \sqrt{a_q + 2\sigma_q^2}$; see Cox *et al.* (1985).

(a) With $K = T/h$ and $\bar r(r_0, K) = P(r_0, T)^{-1/K} - 1$ show that

$$\bar r(r_0, K) \to e^{-\{a_q(a_q-\gamma_q)\xi_q/\sigma_q^2\}h} \quad \text{as} \quad K \to \infty.$$

(b) Argue that unlike in Exercise 6.15 there is no possibility of negative values.

Exercise 6.22

(a) Write a program tabulating the CIR interest-rate curve

$$\bar r(r_0, kh) = -\log\{P(r_0, kh)\}/(kh) \quad \text{for } k = 1, \dots, K, \text{ where } K = T/h.$$

R-*commands*:

```
K=T/h; tk=1:K*h; γq=sqrt(aq+2*σq**2); d=1-exp(-γq*tk);
B=2*d/((γq+aq)*d+2*γq*exp(-γq*tk));
f=γq*exp((aq-γq)*tk/2)*B/d;
A=(2*aq*ξq/σq**2)*log(f); r̄=-(A-B*r0)/tk.
```

(b) Run the program under the conditions in Exercise 6.17(b) and plot the intensity curve against time.

R-*commands*:

```
plot(tk,r̄).
```

(c) Add the Vasiček intensity curve in Exercise 6.17(b) to the plot.

R-*commands*:

After computing $\bar r$ as in Exercise 6.17(b) use `lines(tk,`$\bar r$`)`.

Section 6.5

Exercise 6.23 Modify Algorithm 6.2 so that it becomes a skeleton for sampling common factors models.

Exercise 6.24 Let $N_1, \ldots, N_J|\mu$ be independent and Poisson(μT) with

$$\mu = \xi_\mu e^{-\tau^2/2+\tau\varepsilon}$$

where $\varepsilon \sim N(0,1)$ and ξ_μ and τ parameters.

(a) Write a program generating m simulations of $N_1, \ldots, N_J$.
R-*commands*:
```
μ=ξμ*rlnorm(m,-τ**2/2,τ); N=matrix(rpois(J*m,μ*T),m,J).
```
(b) Run the program when $\xi_\mu = 0.05$, $\tau = 0.5$, $T = 1$, $J = 100$ and $m = 10\,000$ and compute the mean and standard deviation of the portfolio counts $\mathcal{N} = N_1 + \cdots + N_J$.
R-*commands*:
```
𝒩=apply(N,1,sum); Mean=mean(𝒩); Sd=sd(𝒩).
```
(c) Redo (b) when $\tau = 1$ and explain why the portfolio mean is stable and the standard deviation not.

Exercise 6.25 Consider a log-normal loss $Z = \theta e^{-\sigma^2/2+\sigma\varepsilon}$ in property insurance and suppose realizations $Z_1, \ldots, Z_n|\theta$ are independent with $\theta = \xi_z G$ where $G \sim$ Gamma(α).

(a) Argue that this is a common factor model with mean loss varying from one period to another.
(b) Write a program generating m simulations of $Z_1, \ldots, Z_n$.
R-*commands*:
```
θ=ξz*rgamma(m,α)/α;
Z=matrix(θ*rlnorm(m*n,-σ**2/2,σ),m,n).
```
(c) Run the program when $\xi_z = 1$, $\sigma = 0.5$, $\alpha = 20$, $n = 100$ and $m = 10\,000$ and compute the mean and standard deviation of $S = Z_1 + \cdots + Z_n$.
R-*commands*:
```
S=apply(Z,1,sum); Mean=mean(S); Sd=sd(S).
```
(d) Redo when $\alpha = 2$ and explain why the mean is stable and the standard deviation not.

Exercise 6.26 Let $\{C_k\}$ be a Markov chain switching between states 1 and 2 according to $\Pr(C_k = 2|C_{k-1} = 1) = 1 - p_1$ and $\Pr(C_k = 1|C_{k-1} = 2) = 1 - p_2$.

(a) Write a program generating m realizations of $C_0, \ldots, C_K$ starting in $C_0 = c_0$.
R-*commands*:
```
p=c(p0,p1); C=matrix(c0,K+1,m);
for (k in 1:K+1) {I=runif(m)>p[C[k-1,]];
C[k,]=C[k-1,]+I*(3-2*C[k-1,])}.
```

(b) Run the program when $m = 100\,000$, $p_1 = 0.8$, $p_2 = 0.6$, $K = 25$ and $C_0 = 1$ and compute/plot $\Pr(C_k = 2|C_0 = 1)$ against k.

R-*commands*:

```
p2k=apply(C==2,1,mean); plot(0:K,p2k).
```

(c) Redo when $C_0 = 2$ and plot the new probabilities jointly with the old ones.

R-*commands*:

```
lines(0:K,p2k).
```

Exercise 6.27 Consider equity returns $R_k = e^{\xi_{C_k}+\sigma_{C_k}\varepsilon_k} - 1$ where C_0, $C_1, \ldots$ are as in Exercise 6.26, so that the parameters oscillate between two sets (ξ_1, σ_1) and (ξ_2, σ_2) and let $R_0, R_1, \ldots$ be independent and log-normal given the **regimes** $C_0, C_1, \ldots$

(a) Argue that the pair (R_k, C_k) is a Markov process.

(b) Write a program generating m simulations of $R_0, \ldots, R_K$.

R-*commands*:

With C as in Exercise 6.26 use
```
ξ=c(ξ1,ξ2); σ=c(σ1,σ2);
R=matrix(rlnorm(m*(K+1),ξ[C],σ[C]),K+1,m)-1.
```

(c) Run the program when $m = 10$, $p_1 = p_2 = 0.9$, $\xi_1 = 0.03$, $\xi_2 = 0.06$, $\sigma_1 = \sigma_2 = 0.01$, $c_0 = 1$ and $K = 25$ and plot the simulations jointly against time.

R-*commands*:

```
matplot(0:K,R,''l'').
```

(d) Redo when $\sigma_1 = 0.12$ and $\sigma_2 = 0.24$ (more appropriate for equity) and try to see the regime switches now.

Exercise 6.28

(a) Redo the simulations in Exercise 6.27(c) with $m = 100\,000$ and $K = 2$, 5 and 25, estimate and plot each time the density function of R_K and interpret the patterns you see.

R-*commands*:

```
plot(density(R[K+1,])).
```

(b) Redo (a) when $\sigma_1 = 0.12$ and $\sigma_2 = 0.24$ and note the difference from (a).

Section 6.6

Exercise 6.29 Let $\{C_l\}$ be a Markov chain for disability insurance with states a, i and d where $p_l(i|a)$ is the probability of passing from a to i at age l whereas $p_l(a|i) = 0$. Mortalities are the same in states a and i and $F(l)$ the probability of living l years or less.

(a) Argue that $\Pr(C_{l_0+k} = d|C_{l_0} = a) = \{F(l_0 + k) - F(l_0)\}/\{1 - F(l_0)\}$.

(b) Show that

$$\Pr(C_{l_0+k} = a|C_{l_0} = a) = \frac{1 - F(l_0 + k)}{1 - F(l_0)}\{1 - p_{l_0}(i|a)\}\cdots\{1 - p_{l_0+k-1}(i|a)\}.$$

(c) How do you determine the third probability $\Pr(C_{l_0+k} = i|C_{l_0} = a)$?

Exercise 6.30 Suppose $F(l) = 1 - e^{-\alpha(e^{\beta l}-1)}$ in Exercise 6.29 with α and β parameters.

(a) Write a program tabulating $F(l)$ up to $l = l_e$.
R-*commands*:
`F=1-exp(-`α`*(exp(`β`*0:`l_e`)-1)).`

(b) Plot these probabilities against l when $l_e = 116$, $\alpha = 0.0003$ and $\beta = 0.10$.
R-*commands*:
`plot(0:`l_e`,F).`

(c) Argue that $q_l = \{F(l + 1) - F(l)\}/\{1 - F(l)\}$ is the probability of dying within the year at age l and plot these quantities against age for the parameters in (b).
R-*commands*:
`ll=1:`l_e`; q=(F[ll+1]-F[ll])/(1-F[ll]); plot(ll-1,q).`

Exercise 6.31 Let $p_l(i|a) = 1-e^{-\psi_0-\psi_1 e^{\psi_2 l}}$ be the probability of becoming disabled at age l. This model with $\psi_0 = 0.0005$, $\psi_1 = 0.0000113$ and $\psi_2 = 0.124$ was for many years used for Norwegian women. Plot $p_l(i|a)$ against l for $l = 20, \ldots, 66$ and comment on the pattern.
R-*commands*:
`ll=20:66; `p_{ia}`=1-exp(-`ψ_0`-`ψ_1`*exp(`ψ_2`*ll)); plot(ll,`p_{ia}`).`

Exercise 6.32 Consider the model in Exercise 6.29 with the sub-models in Exercises 6.30 and 6.31.

(a) Write a program tabulating ${}_kp_{l_0}(c|a) = \Pr(C_{l_0+k} = c|C_{l_0} = a)$ for $c = d$, a and i and $k = 0, \ldots, K$.
R-*commands*:
`kk=0:K; `${}_kp_{da}$`=1-exp(-`α`*exp(`β`*`l_0`)*(exp(`β`*kk)-1));`
p_{ia}`=1-exp(-`ψ_0`-`ψ_1`*exp(`ψ_2`*(`l_0`-1+1:K)));`
${}_kp_{aa}$`=(1-`${}_kp_{da}$`)*c(1,cumprod(1-`p_{ia}`)); `${}_kp_{ia}$`=1-`${}_kp_{da}$`-`${}_kp_{aa}$`.`

(b) Run the program when $\alpha = 0.0003$, $\beta = 0.10$, $\psi_0 = 0.0005$, $\psi_1 = 0.0000113$, $\psi_2 = 0.124$, $l_0 = 25$ and $K = 40$ and plot the three probabilities jointly against time k.
R-*commands*:
`plot(kk,`${}_kp_{da}$`,''l'',ylim=c(0,1)); lines(kk,`${}_kp_{aa}$`);`
`lines(kk,`${}_kp_{ia}$`).`

Exercise 6.33 Consider the disability scheme of the preceding exercises and suppose there are $\mathcal{N}_{l_0}$ individuals in age l_0 and state a in year $k = 0$.

(a) Argue that the total expected cost of their disability in year k is $\mathcal{X}_k = {}_kp_{l_0}(i|a)\mathcal{N}_{l_0}s$ if s is the cost per individual.
(b) Write a program computing $\mathcal{X}_0, \dots, \mathcal{X}_K$.
    R-*commands*:
    With ${}_kp_{ia}$ as in Exercise 6.32 use `X=`${}_kp_{ia}$`*`$\mathcal{N}_{l_0}$`*s`.
(c) Compute and plot $\mathcal{X}_0, \dots, \mathcal{X}_K$ against time under the model in Exercise 6.32 when $l_0 = 25$, $K = 40$ and $\mathcal{N}_{l_0} = 100\,000$.
    R-*commands*:
    `plot(0:K,X,''l'')`.
(d) Redo (c) for $K = 10$ when $l_0 = 25$, $l_0 = 40$ and $l_0 = 55$ and plot the three sets of expenses jointly against time.
    R-*commands*:
    After redoing (c) for $K = 10$ run the program in (b) twice and each time use `lines(0:K,X)`.

Section 6.7

Exercise 6.34 Let U_1 and U_2 be uniform.

(a) If $U_2 = 1 - U_1$, verify that their copula is $C^{\min}(u_1, u_2) = \max(u_1 + u_2 - 1, 0)$ for $0 < u_1, u_2 < 1$.
(b) Also argue that $C^{\max}(u_1, u_2) = \min(u_1, u_2)$ is the copula when $U_2 = U_1$.
(c) Prove the **Frechet–Hoeffding** inequality, which states that for an arbitrary copula $C(u_1, u_2)$,

$$C^{\min}(u_1, u_2) \le C(u_1, u_2) \le C^{\max}(u_1, u_2), \quad 0 \le u_1, u_2 \le 1.$$

[*Hint*: Note that $C(u_1, u_2) \le \Pr(U_i \le u_i)$, which yields the upper inequality. Introduce $H(u_1) = C(u_1, u_2) - (u_1 + u_2 - 1)$ and argue that $H(1) = 0$ and $dH(u_1)/du_1 = \Pr(U_2 \le u_2|u_1) - 1 \le 0$.]

Exercise 6.35 Consider the Clayton copula $C(u_1, u_2) = \max(u_1^{-\theta} + u_2^{-\theta} - 1, 0)^{-1/\theta}$ where $\theta \ge -1$.

(a) Argue that it coincides with the minimum copula $C^{\min}(u_1, u_2)$ in Exercise 6.34 when $\theta = -1$ and converges to the maximum one $C^{\max}(u_1, u_2)$ as $\theta \to \infty$. [*Hint*: Apply l'Hôpital's rule to $\log(u_1^{-\theta} + u_2^{-\theta} - 1)/\theta$.]
(b) Verify that the independent copula u_1u_2 is the limit when $\theta \to 0$. [*Hint*: Same argument.]

Exercise 6.36 A popular model is the **Frank** copula

$$C(u_1,u_2)=\frac{1}{\theta}\log\left(1+\frac{(e^{\theta u_1}-1)(e^{\theta u_2}-1)}{e^{\theta}-1}\right),\qquad 0<u_1,u_2<1$$

where $\theta \neq 0$.

(a) Check that the copula conditions are satisfied for both positive and negative θ.
(b) Show that the independent copula emerges as $\theta \to 0$ [*Hint*: Use the approximation $e^x \doteq 1+x$, valid for small x, to write $C(u_1,u_2) \doteq \log\{1+(\theta u_1)(\theta_2 u_2)/\theta\}/\theta \to u_1 u_2$ as $\theta \to 0$.]

Exercise 6.37

(a) Verify that the Frank copula tends to $C^{\max}(u_1,u_2)$ in Exercise 6.34 as $\theta \to -\infty$. [*Hint*: Utilize that $e^{\theta}-1 \to -1$ as $\theta \to -\infty$ so that $C(u_1,u_2) \doteq \log(-e^{\theta(u_1+u_2)}+e^{\theta u_1}+e^{\theta u_2})/\theta = u_1+\log(-e^{\theta u_2}+1-e^{\theta(u_2-u_1)})/\theta \to u_1$ when $u_1<u_2$.]
(b) Show that $C^{\min}(u_1,u_2)$ is the limit when $\theta \to \infty$. [*Hint*: Argue that $C(u_1,u_2) \doteq \log(1+e^{\theta(u_1+u_2-1)})/\theta \to \max(u_1+u_2-1,0)$.]

Exercise 6.38

(a) Differentiate the Frank copula and show that

$$\frac{\partial C(u_1,u_2)}{\partial u_1}=\frac{e^{\theta u_1}(e^{\theta u_2}-1)}{(e^{\theta}-1)+(e^{\theta u_1}-1)(e^{\theta u_2}-1)}.$$

(b) Use this and the inversion algorithm to derive the Frank sampler

$$U_2^* \leftarrow \frac{1}{\theta}\log\left(1+\frac{V^*(e^{\theta}-1)}{V^*+e^{\theta U_1^*}(1-V^*)}\right)\quad\text{for}\quad U_1^*, V^* \sim \text{uniform}.$$

Exercise 6.39

(a) Write a program generating m simulations of (U_1,U_2) under the Frank copula.
R-*commands*:
```
U1=runif(m); V=runif(m);
Y=V*(exp(θ)-1)/(V+exp(θ*U1)*(1-V));
U2=log(1+Y)/θ.
```
(b) Draw $m = 1000$ simulations of (U_1,U_2) when $\theta=-10$ and $\theta=10$ and scatterplot them.
R-*commands*:
```
plot(U1,U2).
```

Exercise 6.40

(a) For the Archimedean copula with generator $\phi(u) = (1-u)^3$, verify that $C(u_1,u_2)=0$ whenever $u_2 \le 1-\{1-(1-u_1)^3\}^{1/3}$.

(b) Prove a similar result for an Archimedean copula with monotone decreasing generator $\phi(u)$ with finite $\phi(0)$; i.e., show that $C(u_1, u_2) = 0$ whenever $\phi(u_1) + \phi(u_2) \geq \phi(0)$ or equivalently if $u_2 \leq \phi^{-1}\{\phi(0) - \phi(u_1)\}$.

Exercise 6.41 Let $R_1 = e^{\xi+\sigma\varepsilon_1} - 1$ and $R_2 = e^{\xi+\sigma\varepsilon_2} - 1$ where ε_1 and ε_2 are $N(0, 1)$ and Clayton dependent with parameter θ.

(a) Write a program generating m simulations of (R_1, R_2).

R-*commands*:

```
U1=runif(m); S=U1**(-θ)-1;
U2=((1+S)*runif(m)**(-θ/(1+θ))-S)**(-1/θ);
R1=qlnorm(U1,ξ,σ)-1; R2=qlnorm(U2,ξ,σ)-1.
```

(b) Run the program when $m = 1000$, $\xi = 0.05$, $\sigma = 0.25$ and $\theta = 0.1$ and scatterplot.

R-*commands*:

```
plot(R1,R2).
```

(c) Repeat (b) when $\theta = -0.5$, $\theta = 2$ and $\theta = 10$ and note how the pattern changes.

Exercise 6.42

(a) Modify the program in Exercise 6.41 so that it applies to Frank dependence.

R-*commands*:

Generate $(U_1 U_2)$ as in Exercise 6.39 and then (R_1, R_2).

(b) Run the program for $m = 1000$, $\xi = 0.05$, $\sigma = 0.25$ and $\theta = -10, -5, 5$ and 10 and scatterplot the returns.

R-*commands*:

```
plot(R1,R2).
```

(c) Compare the patterns with those in Exercise 6.41.

Exercise 6.43 Let $\mathcal{R} = (R_1 + R_2)/2$ be the portfolio return for two log-normal, Clayton-dependent assets.

(a) Write a program simulating portfolio return.

R-*commands*:

Draw (R_1, R_2) as in Exercise 6.41 and use `R=(R1+R2)/2`.

(b) Run the program when $m = 100\,000$, $\xi = 0.05$, $\sigma = 0.25$ and $\theta = 0.1$ and estimate and plot the density function of the portfolio returns.

R-*commands*:

```
plot(density(R)).
```

(c) Redo (a) for $\theta = 2$ and 10 and comment on how the density function changes.

Exercise 6.44 Let $R_j = e^{\xi+\sigma\varepsilon_j} - 1$ for $j = 1,\dots,J$ where $\varepsilon_1,\dots,\varepsilon_J$ are $N(0,1)$ and Clayton dependent with parameter $\theta > 0$.

(a) Write a program generating m simulations of $R_1,\dots,R_J$ using the Marshall–Olkin representation (6.45).

R-*commands*:

$Z \sim \text{Gamma}(1/\theta)$ and $M(x) = (1+\theta x)^{-1/\theta}$ in Algorithm 6.3, which yields

```
Z=rgamma(m,1/θ)*θ; V=matrix(runif(J*m),m,J);
U=(1-θ*log(V)/Z)**(-1/θ); R=qlnorm(U,ξ,σ)-1.
```

(b) Run the program when $\xi = 0.05$, $\sigma = 0.25$, $\theta = 2$, $J = 4$ and $m = 100\,000$ and estimate/plot the density function of $\mathcal{R} = (R_1 + \cdots + R_J)/J$.

R-*commands*:

```
ℛ=apply(R,1,mean); plot(density(ℛ)).
```

(c) Redo (b) when $\theta = 0.1$ and $\theta = 10$ and comment on how the portfolio risk depends on θ.

7

Historical estimation and error

7.1 Introduction

Assessing risk is assessing uncertainty, but such assessments are also uncertain themselves. The pure premium π in property insurance is a simple example. It depends on claim frequency μT and expected loss ξ per claim, but where do μ and ξ come from? They are not available by themselves! In practice we only have access to a different pair $\hat{\mu}$ and $\hat{\xi}$, and the situation is as follows:

$$\underbrace{\pi = \mu T \xi}_{\textit{real life}} \qquad \text{and} \qquad \underbrace{\hat{\pi} = \hat{\mu} T \hat{\xi}}_{\textit{estimated}}\,. \tag{7.1}$$

Usually, $\hat{\mu}$ and $\hat{\xi}$ are estimated from historical data. The discrepancy between $\hat{\pi}$ and π matters as pricing and business decisions are influenced. With oil rigs, ships or big industrial installations where claims can be large and where the experience to draw on is limited, errors in $\hat{\pi}$ might be huge.

The general case is a vector $\boldsymbol{\theta} = (\theta_1, \dots, \theta_v)$ of unknown quantities and a quantity of interest $\psi = \psi(\boldsymbol{\theta})$. In the example above $\boldsymbol{\theta} = (\mu, \xi)$ and $\psi(\mu, \xi) = \mu T \xi$. Another important case is $\psi(\boldsymbol{\theta}) = q_\epsilon(\boldsymbol{\theta})$, where $q_\epsilon(\boldsymbol{\theta})$ is a percentile of some distribution. The general version of (7.1) is the scheme

$$\underbrace{\psi = \psi(\boldsymbol{\theta})}_{\textit{real life}} \qquad \text{and} \qquad \underbrace{\hat{\psi} = \psi(\hat{\boldsymbol{\theta}})}_{\textit{estimated}}\,, \tag{7.2}$$

where $\hat{\boldsymbol{\theta}}$ is plugged in for the true $\boldsymbol{\theta}$. Many sources of information may be utilized to find the estimate $\hat{\boldsymbol{\theta}}$; see Figure 1.1 in Section 1.1.

The present chapter treats the use of historical data denoted $z_1, \dots, z_n$. This is surely the most important source of all, and certainly the one most amenable to error analysis. Now

$$\hat{\boldsymbol{\theta}} = g(\mathbf{Z}) \quad \text{where} \quad \mathbf{Z} = (z_1, \dots, z_n), \tag{7.3}$$

and there are techniques (coming from statistics) that enable us to evaluate the error in $\hat{\boldsymbol{\theta}}$. In finance and insurance the target is usually some derived quantity $\hat{\psi} = \psi(\hat{\boldsymbol{\theta}})$, and how the error in $\hat{\boldsymbol{\theta}}$ is passed on depends strongly on the circumstances. Not all the parameters in $\boldsymbol{\theta}$ are equally important to get right. A second complicating factor arises when $\psi(\boldsymbol{\theta})$ is computed by Monte Carlo. There are now *two* sources of uncertainty with simulation on top of estimation error. Their relative importance is discussed in the next section.

General estimation techniques such as maximum likelihood and moment matching are treated in introductory statistics courses, and it is assumed that you have seen those before (though they *are* briefly reviewed with a few examples in Section 7.3). Software (free or commercial) makes use of such methods for fitting stochastic models to historical data. Estimates $\hat{\boldsymbol{\theta}}$ and their standard deviations are then provided, but not the uncertainty in $\hat{\psi}$ which is our real target. Monte Carlo is even here the all-purpose tool, now known as the **bootstrap**. There is also a second approach to uncertainty evaluation and indeed to estimation itself. So-called **Bayesian** methods regard $\boldsymbol{\theta}$ as stochastic rather than fixed. Random parameters have already been discussed in earlier chapters, but the rationale is now different. Section 7.6 is a brief introduction.

7.2 Error of different origin

7.2.1 Introduction

Our target is a quantity $\psi = \psi(\boldsymbol{\theta})$ describing some feature of a risk variable X, but in practice we have to be content with its estimated version $\hat{\psi} = \psi(\hat{\boldsymbol{\theta}})$. If Monte Carlo is involved, there are two steps. *First*, the estimate $\hat{\theta}$ is obtained from historical data; and *then*, simulations are run from that estimate. Writing $\psi_m^*(\boldsymbol{\theta})$ for the Monte Carlo approximation of $\psi(\boldsymbol{\theta})$ the final estimate is $\hat{\psi}_m^* = \psi_m^*(\hat{\boldsymbol{\theta}})$, and there are three types of error involved:

$$\begin{array}{rll} \hat{\psi}_m^* - \psi & \text{total error} & \\ \hat{\psi}_m^* - \hat{\psi} & \text{Monte Carlo error} & (m \text{ simulations being used}) \\ \hat{\psi} - \psi & \text{estimation error} & (n \text{ observations, suppressed in the notation}). \end{array}$$

The second line (the discrepancy $\hat{\psi}_m^* - \hat{\psi}$) defines the error due to Monte Carlo only, and the third line $\hat{\psi} - \psi$ is caused by $\hat{\boldsymbol{\theta}}$ deviating from $\boldsymbol{\theta}$. Usually

$$\underbrace{\hat{\psi}_m^* \to \hat{\psi} \quad \text{as } m \to \infty}_{\textit{Monte Carlo}} \qquad \text{and} \qquad \underbrace{\hat{\psi} \to \psi \quad \text{as } n \to \infty}_{\textit{estimation}}.$$

These relationships were illustrated in Chapter 2. Their precise mathematical meaning is not quite the ordinary one; see Appendix A.4.

The dependency of $\hat{\psi}$ on n is not explicitly stated (to avoid cumbersome notation). There is a certain logic in that choice. Monte Carlo experiments are under our control. We may in principle run as many replications as we please and lower simulation uncertainty below any prescribed level. By contrast, the number of observations n is *not* chosen judiciously, but rather something we receive passively, often with limited ability to influence. The error it induces is usually much more severe than Monte Carlo (see below). Model error, a third contributor, will be introduced at the end of the section.

7.2.2 Quantifying error

The first issue is the relative importance of Monte Carlo and estimation error. Such analyses require formal error criteria. The standard choice is the mean-squared error, which has convenient operational properties. Indeed,

$$\hat{\psi}_m^* - \psi = (\hat{\psi} - \psi) + (\hat{\psi}_m^* - \hat{\psi})$$

so that

$$(\hat{\psi}_m^* - \psi)^2 = (\hat{\psi} - \psi)^2 + (\hat{\psi}_m^* - \hat{\psi})^2 + 2(\hat{\psi} - \psi)(\hat{\psi}_m^* - \hat{\psi}).$$

Taking expectations everywhere yields

$$\underset{\textit{total error}}{E(\hat{\psi}_m^* - \psi)^2} \quad = \quad \underset{\textit{estimation error}}{E(\hat{\psi} - \psi)^2} \quad + \quad \underset{\textit{Monte Carlo error}}{E(\hat{\psi}_m^* - \hat{\psi})^2} \quad + \quad \underset{\textit{remainder}}{E(\mathcal{E})}, \tag{7.4}$$

where $\mathcal{E} = 2(\hat{\psi} - \psi)(\hat{\psi}_m^* - \hat{\psi})$. We may treat $E(\mathcal{E})$ as a remainder. It vanishes when ψ is the mean (see below) and is often dominated by the other terms. There is a conditional argument in support of this. Suppose $\mathbf{Z} = \mathbf{z}$ is given. The estimation error $\hat{\psi} - \psi$ is now a constant and

$$E(\mathcal{E} \mid \mathbf{z}) = (\hat{\psi} - \psi)E(\hat{\psi}_m^* - \hat{\psi} \mid \mathbf{z}) = (\hat{\psi} - \psi)\frac{\hat{\beta}}{m} \quad \text{where} \quad \frac{\hat{\beta}}{m} = E(\hat{\psi}_m^* - \hat{\psi} \mid \mathbf{z}).$$

Here $\hat{\beta}$ is bias, which makes the Monte Carlo evaluation $\hat{\psi}_m^*$ deviate from $\hat{\psi}$ on average. Such a discrepancy is usually of order $1/m$, which is reflected in the way it has been written; see Appendix A.4, where the issue is discussed. By the rule of double expectation

$$E(\mathcal{E}) = \frac{1}{m}E\{(\hat{\psi} - \psi)\hat{\beta}\}, \tag{7.5}$$

which is of order $1/(m\sqrt{n})$ against $1/n$ and $1/m$ for the other contributions in (7.4).

7.2.3 Numerical illustration

That the error contributions from estimation and Monte Carlo add on quadratic scale is important, as the following example shows. Suppose (purely hypothetically) that Monte Carlo error is 25% of estimation error. We are then assuming that

$$E(\hat{\psi}-\psi)^2 = \tau^2 \quad \text{and} \quad E(\hat{\psi}^*_m - \hat{\psi})^2 = (0.25\tau)^2.$$

If the remainder in (7.4) is overlooked, the root-mean-squared error becomes

$$\sqrt{E(\hat{\psi}^*_m - \psi)^2} \doteq \sqrt{\tau^2 + (0.25\tau)^2} \doteq 1.03\tau$$

and Monte Carlo raises the *total* error no more than 3%, a much smaller factor than the 25% we started with. The square root scales the error assessment properly.

The inaccuracy in $\hat{\psi}^*_m$ is not necessarily raised greatly, even by a quite substantial Monte Carlo component; see, e.g., Figure 7.1 below. When total error is what counts, a big simulation experiment may not be needed! Obvious examples of this are the evaluation of reserves in insurance and value at risk in finance. The position *could* be different if ψ is a price of some transaction, since most people won't accept much Monte Carlo error in what they pay or receive. Yet the formal valuation is usually only a guideline for what the market offers.

7.2.4 Errors and the mean

One of the most important special cases is the estimation of $\pi = E(X)$ where X depends on some unknown $\boldsymbol{\theta}$. Then $\pi = \pi(\boldsymbol{\theta})$ with the estimate $\hat{\pi} = \pi(\hat{\boldsymbol{\theta}})$. Monte Carlo is often necessary, but there is an important distinction between the simulations we want and those we get. Consider

$$\underbrace{X^*_1, \dots, X^*_m}_{\textit{generated under } \boldsymbol{\theta}} \qquad \text{and} \qquad \underbrace{\hat{X}^*_1, \dots, \hat{X}^*_m}_{\textit{generated under } \hat{\boldsymbol{\theta}}}.$$

The sample on the left isn't available, and the approximation to π has to be computed from the other, i.e., by means of

$$\hat{\pi}^*_m = \frac{1}{m}\sum_{i=1}^m \hat{X}^*_i \quad \text{where} \quad E(\hat{X}^*_i \mid \mathbf{z}) = \hat{\pi} \quad \text{and} \quad \text{sd}(\hat{X}^*_i \mid \mathbf{z}) = \hat{\sigma}. \tag{7.6}$$

Since the simulations are generated as if $\hat{\boldsymbol{\theta}}$ were the true parameter, their expectation becomes $\hat{\pi} = \pi(\hat{\boldsymbol{\theta}})$. The mean has the elementary statistical properties

$$E(\hat{\pi}^*_m - \hat{\pi}|\mathbf{z}\} = 0 \quad \text{and} \quad E\{(\hat{\pi}^*_m - \hat{\pi})^2|\mathbf{z}\} = \frac{\hat{\sigma}^2}{m}$$

where the result on the left means zero bias $\hat{\beta}$ and zero remainder in (7.4). By the rule of double expectation $E(\hat{\pi}_m^* - \hat{\pi})^2 = E\hat{\sigma}^2/m$, and we can establish

$$\underbrace{E(\hat{\pi}_m^* - \pi)^2}_{\textit{total error}} = \underbrace{E(\hat{\pi} - \pi)^2}_{\textit{estimation error}} + \underbrace{\frac{E\hat{\sigma}^2}{m}}_{\textit{Monte Carlo error}} \tag{7.7}$$

which is an *exact* result.

Total error is, in this case, a sum of one estimation and one Monte Carlo component. The simulation experiment should be large enough for the second contribution to be overshadowed by the first. What is meant by that was discussed above.

7.2.5 Example: Option pricing

Consider a guarantee not to lose in the equity market. This is a put option, and a *negative* return R will at expiry T release a payoff $X = \max(-R, 0)v_0$ where v_0 is the original investment. The premium charged is

$$\pi = e^{-rT} E\{\max(-R, 0)\}v_0 \quad \text{where} \quad R = e^{(r-\sigma^2/2)T+\sigma\sqrt{T}\,\varepsilon} - 1, \quad \varepsilon \sim N(0, 1);$$

see Section 3.5. Here r (risk-free rate of interest) is known and σ (volatility) unknown. There is a closed formula for π, but we shall pretend it is not to illustrate Monte Carlo and estimation error jointly.

Let $r_1, \dots, r_n$ be historical returns on equity and $\hat{\sigma}$ the standard deviation of the log-returns $x_1, \dots, x_n$ where $x_i = \log(1 + r_i)$. This is the usual estimate of σ, and the Monte Carlo approximation of π now becomes

$$\hat{\pi}_m^* = \frac{e^{-rT}}{m}\left(\sum_{i=1}^{m} \max(-\hat{R}_i^*, 0)\right) v_0 \text{ where } \hat{R}_i^* = e^{(r-\hat{\sigma}^2/2)T+\hat{\sigma}\sqrt{T}\,\varepsilon_i^*} - 1,\ i = 1, \dots, m.$$

As numerical example, consider a 5-day option ($T = 5$) with daily risk-free rate of interest $r = 0.024\%$ and historical returns over $n = 150$ days. The underlying, true daily volatility was fixed as $\sigma = 1\%$. Historical returns drawn in the computer gave the estimate $\hat{\sigma} = 1.036\%$, from which the Monte Carlo approximation $\hat{\pi}_m^*$ was computed from $m = 10\,000$ simulations. The last step was repeated 1000 times, leading to 1000 different Monte Carlo prices. Their density function, plotted on the left in Figure 7.1, fluctuates around the exact price under $\hat{\sigma}$ and differs from the exact price under σ; consult the plot. Raising *m only* makes the variation smaller around the wrong price!

Contrast this with the total uncertainty on the right in Figure 7.1. The historical material was now redrawn 1000 times, leading to 1000 different estimates $\hat{\sigma}$ with 1000 different Monte Carlo approximations $\hat{\pi}_m^*$ (as before with $m = 10\,000$). There are again 1000 different prices, but the uncertainty is now due to *both* estimation and Monte Carlo, and the variation is much larger than on the left (scales

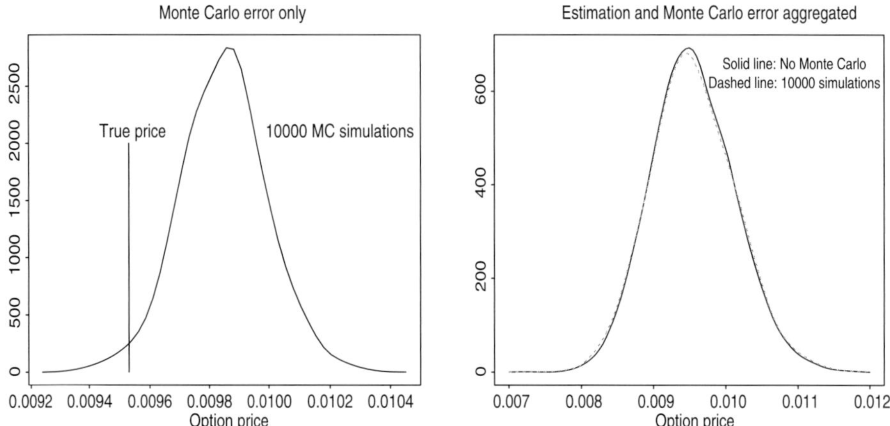

Figure 7.1 Density functions of the estimated option price. *Left*: Common estimate of the volatility. *Right*: Uncertainty due to the volatility estimate. *Note*: Axis scales differ.

on horizontal axes differ). Figure 7.1 right also contains a second version, where the approximation $\hat{\pi}_m^*$ has been replaced by the exact Black–Scholes formula in Section 3.5, but this doesn't change the density function much. Though the extra Monte Carlo uncertainty is far from negligible on its own, it counts for very little compared with the error in $\hat{\sigma}$.

7.2.6 Example: Reserve in property insurance

As a second example consider a portfolo in general insurance with Poisson number of claims $\mathcal{N}$ and log-normal individual losses Z where the Poisson parameter is $J\mu T$ and $Z = e^{\xi+\sigma\varepsilon}$ with $\varepsilon \sim N(0,1)$. The parameters μ, ξ and σ must be estimated from historical data. Suppose there are n claims $z_1, \dots. z_n$. Natural estimates are

$$\hat{\mu} = \frac{n}{A} \quad \text{and} \quad \hat{\xi} = \frac{1}{n}\sum_{i=1}^{n}\log(z_i), \quad \hat{\sigma}^2 = \frac{1}{n-1}\sum_{i=1}^{n}(\log(z_i) - \hat{\xi})^2$$

where A is total **risk exposure**; i.e., the number of policies times their average period under risk; see Section 8.2. Typically, n is the realization of a Poisson variable with parameter $A\mu$. If the aim is to compute the reserve, the entire process becomes

$$\underset{\textit{historical data}}{n \text{ claims } z_1, \dots, z_n} \longrightarrow \underset{\textit{estimates}}{\hat{\mu}, \hat{\xi}, \hat{\sigma}} \longrightarrow \underset{\textit{simulation}}{\hat{\mathcal{X}}_1^*, \dots, \hat{\mathcal{X}}_m^*} \longrightarrow \underset{\textit{estimated reserve}}{\hat{q}_{\epsilon m}^* = \hat{\mathcal{X}}_{(\epsilon m)}^*}$$

where Monte Carlo is run as explained in Section 3.3, but now under the *estimated* parameters $\hat{\mu}, \hat{\xi}$ and $\hat{\sigma}$. If $\hat{\mathcal{X}}_{(1)}^* \geq \dots \geq \hat{\mathcal{X}}_{(m)}^*$ are the simulations in descending order, $\hat{\mathcal{X}}_{(\epsilon m)}^*$ is the estimated reserve.

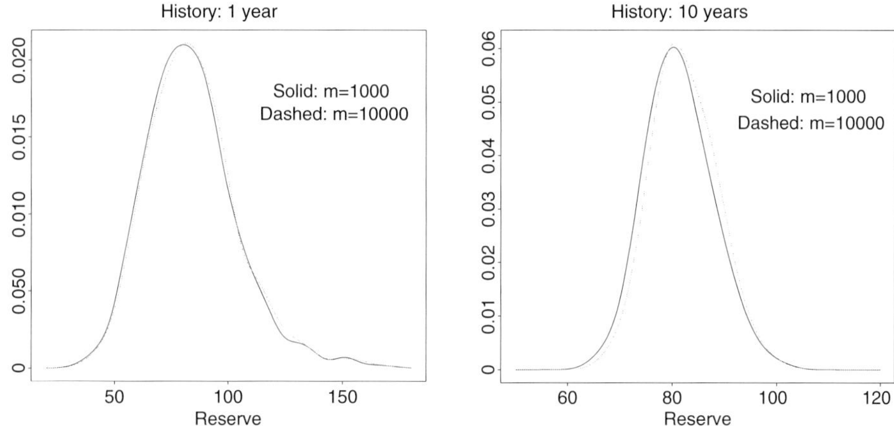

Figure 7.2 Density functions of the estimated 99% reserve in a property insurance portfolio when the historical record is varied. *Note*: Axis scales differ.

A laboratory experiment is reported in Figure 7.2. The true values of the underlying parameters were $\mu = 5\%, \xi = -0.5$ and $\sigma = 1$, and 1000 policies were followed over 1 or 10 years so that exposure to risk in the historical data was $A = 1000$ or 10 000. Estimates $\hat{\mu}, \hat{\xi}$ and $\hat{\sigma}$ were computed as detailed above. This was repeated 1000 times for 1000 different estimates, for which the 99% annual ($T = 1$) reserve was computed for a portfolio of $J = 1000$ policies. Both $m = 1000$ and $m = 10\,000$ simulations were tried for this second round of Monte Carlo. The effect of estimation and Monte Carlo uncertainty together is shown in Figure 7.2, where the uncertainty is much smaller with 10 years of historical data on the right. Note how little the size of the Monte Carlo experiment matters! 1000 or 10 000 simulations is almost inconsequential compared with the estimation error. Look back at Table 3.1 in Section 3.3, and you will see how much uncertainty 1000 simulations leave!

7.2.7 Bias and model error

Estimates $\hat{\psi}$ or $\hat{\psi}^*_m$ are **biased** if they differ from the true ψ on average; i.e., if $E(\hat{\psi}) \neq \psi$ or $E(\hat{\psi}^*_m) \neq \psi$. This is often difficult to avoid and may well occur even if the parameter estimates $\hat{\boldsymbol{\theta}}$ themselves are unbiased. An example is percentiles, and it will emerge in Section 7.4 that the reserve in insurance and value at risk in finance are often underestimated. Bias is one of the basic issues of stochastic modelling and connected to **model error**, a concept that needs some elaboration. The following argument is more abstract than elsewhere.

Our paradigm is that a true stochastic model does exist. Some of its secrets will always remain hidden, and it is best understood as an idealized mechanism M_0. Let $M_{\boldsymbol{\theta}}$ be an assumed model depending on unknown parameters $\boldsymbol{\theta}$. The situation may then be depicted as follows:

$$\underset{\textit{true world}}{M_0 \to \psi_0,} \qquad \underset{\textit{model world}}{M_{\boldsymbol{\theta}} \to \psi = \psi(\boldsymbol{\theta})} \qquad \text{and} \qquad \underset{\textit{Monte Carlo world}}{M_{\hat{\boldsymbol{\theta}}} \to \hat{\psi}^*_m.} \tag{7.8}$$

Here ψ_0 is the quantity sought, for example a reserve or a premium associated with a risk variable X that originates with M_0. Our assumption is that X has been generated by a model of the form $M_{\boldsymbol{\theta}}$, and Monte Carlo is run from an estimated version $M_{\hat{\boldsymbol{\theta}}}$. Usually $\hat{\boldsymbol{\theta}}$ tends to some limit $\boldsymbol{\theta}$ as $n \to \infty$. This is a standard result with likelihood and moment estimation (Section 7.3 below), and you can look it up in textbooks like Lehmann and Casella (1998). Actually, there is typically a limit even if the model is wrong; see Huber (1967) or White (1982). Model error means that this limit $M_{\boldsymbol{\theta}}$ and the corresponding value $\psi = \psi(\theta)$ in the middle of (7.8) deviate from the true M_0 and ψ_0. This is **model bias**, and the concept of total error now becomes

$$\underset{\textit{total error}}{\hat{\psi}^*_m - \psi_0} \quad = \quad \underset{\textit{model bias}}{\psi - \psi_0} \quad + \quad \underset{\textit{under assumed model}}{\hat{\psi}^*_m - \psi,} \tag{7.9}$$

where $\hat{\psi}^*_m - \psi$ on the right consists of estimation and simulation error as explained earlier. It typically goes away if n and m are infinite, but model error remains.

Model bias is hard to quantify, since it isn't known how wrong the model is and it varies with the circumstances. Consider large-claim property insurance with limited amount of historical data. It is hopeless to know whether the claim size distribution belongs to the Pareto or some other family, and yet the uncertainty of the parameters estimated may well account for more than the wrong family of distributions. The detailed structure of an interest-rate model might be less important than getting the parameters right. Model bias is always there when things are changing, and we are unable to correct for it. Longevity in life insurance (Section 15.2) is such an example. Obsolete historical data create bias when a fitted model is used to project risk.

7.3 How parameters are estimated

7.3.1 Introduction

Use of historical data $\mathbf{z} = (z_1, \ldots, z_n)$ is an important part of all modelling. How we go about it depends on the situation, but there are a few general fitting techniques, and the present section is an introduction to these. The oldest method (extending back to the early nineteenth century) is **least squares**. That one is skipped, but not **moment matching**, another ancient idea that will be utilized on several occasions.

Software you rely on often makes use of **likelihoods**. Common experience holds these estimates to be about the best possible. There is a theoretical result in support which applies as $n \to \infty$, but with much historical data everything works so well that it doesn't matter too much how it is done anyhow. Still another way is the **Bayesian** approach, based on a different philosophy discussed in Section 7.6.

7.3.2 The quick way: Moment matching

The idea is to link sample and model versions of lower-order moments such as means and variances. It is possible to use the median too, and with time series even autocovariances (see below). To introduce this line of thought, let $z_1, \dots, z_n$ be independent and identically distributed with mean and standard deviation $\bar{z}$ and s. Suppose there are two unknown parameters θ_1 and θ_2. Then $E(z_i) = \xi(\theta_1, \theta_2)$ and $\mathrm{sd}(z_i) = \sigma(\theta_1, \theta_2)$, which should match $\bar{z}$ and s. This leads to estimates $\hat{\theta}_1$ and $\hat{\theta}_2$ as solutions of the equations

$$\xi(\hat{\theta}_1, \hat{\theta}_2) = \bar{z} \quad \text{and} \quad \sigma(\hat{\theta}_1, \hat{\theta}_2) = s. \tag{7.10}$$

A simple example is the Gamma family of distributions, where the parameters are ξ and α; see Section 2.5. Now $E(z_i) = \xi$ and $\mathrm{sd}(z_i) = \xi/\sqrt{\alpha}$, and moment matching yields

$$\hat{\xi} = \bar{z},\ \hat{\xi}/\sqrt{\hat{\alpha}} = s \quad \text{so that} \quad \hat{\xi} = \bar{z},\ \hat{\alpha} = \left(\frac{\hat{\xi}}{s}\right)^2.$$

There will be more on Gamma fitting in Section 9.3.

The method of moments may work with weaker assumptions than the likelihood method; consult Section 8.3 for an example. There must be as many equations as there are unknown parameters, and if needed, third- and fourth-order moments may be added to those above. Solutions are not necessarily unique and may be cumbersome to find. If you run across such obstacles, pursue a different line. With Pareto models moment matching is unattractive (*infinite* variance is a practical possibility), but you could use other types of quantity. There is an example of this in Section 9.5.

7.3.3 Moment matching and time series

Autocovariances in time series can be used for moment matching, and some fairly advanced models will be fitted in this way in later parts of the book (Sections 11.3 and 13.2). Here is an example with the exponential autoregressive model in Section 5.6. Let $r_1, \dots, r_n$ be historical rates of interest evolving as in (5.43), or for $k = 1, \dots, n$

$$r_k = \xi e^{-\frac{1}{2}\sigma^2/(1-a^2)+X_k} \quad \text{where} \quad X_k = aX_{k-1} + \sigma\varepsilon_k.$$

Pass to logarithms through $y_k = \log(r_k)$ and let $\bar{y}$, s^2 and $\hat{\gamma}_1$ be mean, variance and first-order autocovariance for the y-series. Theoretical expressions for these were derived in Section 5.6. When k is so large that the initial state has been forgotten, then

$$E(y_k) = \log(\xi) - \frac{\sigma^2}{2(1-a^2)}, \quad \text{var}(y_k) = \frac{\sigma^2}{1-a^2} \quad \text{and} \quad \text{cov}(y_k, y_{k+1}) = a\frac{\sigma^2}{1-a^2},$$

which yields the equations

$$\log(\hat{\xi}) - \frac{\hat{\sigma}^2}{2(1-\hat{a}^2)} = \bar{y}, \quad \frac{\hat{\sigma}^2}{1-\hat{a}^2} = s^2 \quad \text{and} \quad \hat{a}\frac{\hat{\sigma}^2}{1-\hat{a}^2} = \hat{\gamma}_1$$

with solution

$$\log(\hat{\xi}) = \bar{y} + \frac{1}{2}s^2, \quad \hat{a} = \frac{\hat{\gamma}_1}{s^2} \quad \text{and} \quad \hat{\sigma} = s\sqrt{1-\hat{a}^2}. \tag{7.11}$$

The method, though useable, has a tendency to underestimate a for short series (Exercises 7.16 and 7.17), and likelihood estimation might be superior.

7.3.4 The usual way: Maximum likelihood

Let $f(z_1, \ldots, z_n|\boldsymbol{\theta})$ be the joint density function of the historical data where the mathematical notation signifies that it depends on parameters $\boldsymbol{\theta}$. A **likelihood** is the same except that now $\boldsymbol{\theta}$ is varied and $z_1, \ldots, z_n$ (the data) kept fixed. The idea is to adjust $\boldsymbol{\theta}$ to make the observed sequence as likely as possible, with the maximizing value $\hat{\boldsymbol{\theta}}$ as the estimate. Both theoretical studies and numerical computations use the logarithmic version

$$\underbrace{\mathcal{L}(\boldsymbol{\theta}) = \log\{f(z_1, \ldots, z_n|\boldsymbol{\theta})\}}_{\textit{general}} \quad \text{and} \quad \underbrace{\mathcal{L}(\theta) = \textstyle\sum_{i=1}^n \log\{f(z_i|\boldsymbol{\theta})\}}_{\textit{independent data}}, \tag{7.12}$$

known as the **log-likelihood**. There is a highly polished theory of error which applies formally when $n \to \infty$. In most models considered in this book, $\hat{\boldsymbol{\theta}}$ then becomes normal with mean $\boldsymbol{\theta}$ and estimated covariance matrix $\hat{\Sigma} = \hat{I}^{-1}$ where

$$\hat{I} = (\hat{I}_{ij}) \quad \text{for} \quad \hat{I}_{ij} = \frac{\partial^2 \log\{f(z_1, \ldots, z_n|\hat{\boldsymbol{\theta}})\}}{\partial\theta_i \partial\theta_j}. \tag{7.13}$$

Here $\hat{I}$ is known as the **information** matrix. Most error assessments in statistical software rely on this technique.

Numerical methods are usually required when likelihood estimates are computed. If you have to do it yourself, consult Appendix C. There are a number of simple numerical procedures among the exercises and in the text.

Table 7.1 Damages (in million NOK) caused by natural disasters in Norway, 1980–1999 (about 8 NOK to 1 euro)

21.1	25.6	25.9	30.3	30.8	30.8	30.8	32.8	51.1	55.6	57.2
65.0	69.5	82.5	103.9	119.3	174.1	175.6	514.8	855.0	1210.6	

7.3.5 Example: Norwegian natural disasters

The data in Table 7.1 shows the payouts in the period 1980–1999 from the fund set up by the insurance companies in Norway to cover property damage due to storms and other natural causes. This is a typical example of large-claim insurance based on limited experience and well suited to illustrate error. It is used several times below. The entries (ordered according to size) are in Norwegian kroner (NOK) (divide by 8 for an indication of value in euros).

It is reasonable to see this as a Poisson/Pareto portfolio, and the first issue is the parameters. With risk exposure $A = 21$ (one policy over 21 years), the Poisson probability of n claims is

$$f(n|\mu) = \frac{(A\mu)^n}{n!}e^{-A\mu}$$

leading to the log-likelihood

$$\mathcal{L}(\mu) = \underbrace{n\log(\mu) - A\mu}_{\text{varying with } \mu} + \underbrace{n\log(A) - \log(n!)}_{\text{constant}}.$$

This is maximized by $\hat{\mu} = n/A$, which was used as estimate in Section 7.2. From the data in Table 7.1, $\hat{\mu} = 21/20 = 1.05$. How the log-likelihood function varies is shown in Figure 7.3 left.

To fit the Pareto model to the losses, recall from Section 2.5 its density function $f(z) = (\alpha/\beta)(1 + z/\beta)^{-(1+\alpha)}$ which yields as log-likelihood

$$\mathcal{L}(\alpha,\beta) = n\log(\alpha/\beta) - (1+\alpha)\sum_{i=1}^{n}\log\left(1 + \frac{z_i}{\beta}\right).$$

The maximizing $\alpha = \hat{\alpha}_\beta$ for given β is easily determined by elementary differentiation, leading to

$$\mathcal{L}(\hat{\alpha}_\beta,\beta) = n\{\log(\hat{\alpha}_\beta/\beta) - (1 + 1/\hat{\alpha}_\beta)\} \quad \text{where} \quad \hat{\alpha}_\beta = \left(\frac{1}{n}\sum_{i=1}^{n}\log(1 + z_i/\beta)\right)^{-1}, \tag{7.14}$$

and the optimization with respect to β must be done numerically. A safe way is through the **bracketing** method in Appendix C.4, but it is also feasible to compute it on a tight grid of points.

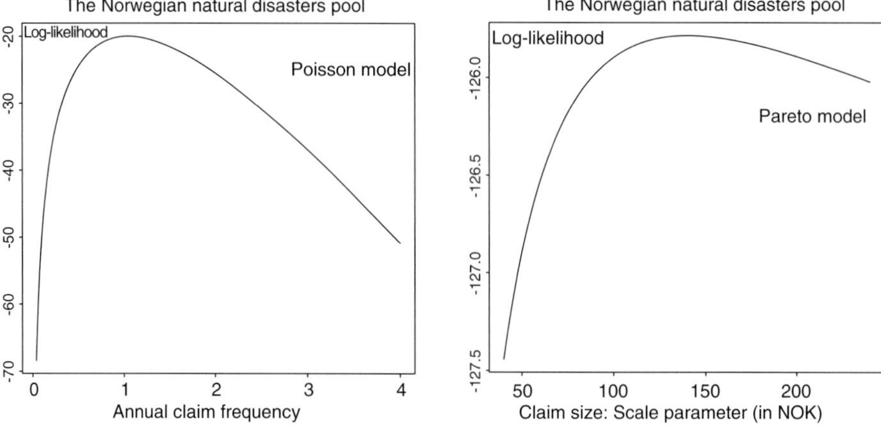

Figure 7.3 Log-likelihood functions for the Norwegian natural disaster data as explained in the text with claim intensity (*left*) and claim size (*right*).

The estimates are $\hat{\beta} = 140$ and $\hat{\alpha} = \hat{\alpha}_{\hat{\beta}} = 1.71$, which come from the log-likelihood function $\mathcal{L}(\hat{\alpha}_\beta, \beta)$ plotted against β in Figure 7.3 right. Take a look at the scale of the vertical axis, and you will discover that the curve is very flat. Many combinations (α, β) are then almost equally likely, which can only mean a large estimation error.

7.4 Evaluating error I

7.4.1 Introduction

Standard software packages fit stochastic models to historical data and provide estimates $\hat{\boldsymbol{\theta}} = (\hat{\theta}_1, \ldots, \hat{\theta}_v)$ of unknown parameters $\boldsymbol{\theta} = (\theta_1, \ldots, \theta_v)$. The error is evaluated too. Let $\sigma_{ij} = \text{cov}(\hat{\theta}_i, \hat{\theta}_j)$ so that $\boldsymbol{\Sigma} = (\sigma_{ij})$ is the covariance matrix of $\hat{\boldsymbol{\theta}}$. There is often access to an *estimated* version $\hat{\boldsymbol{\Sigma}} = (\hat{\sigma}_{ij})$, but that is rarely enough. Our target is some derived quantity $\psi = \psi(\boldsymbol{\theta})$, and what we seek is the uncertainty of $\hat{\psi} = \psi(\hat{\boldsymbol{\theta}})$, not that of $\hat{\boldsymbol{\theta}}$ itself. There are several ways to proceed. The traditional methods reviewed at the end of the section are based on much historical data. A relaxed attitude towards this is certainly in order, yet today priority rests with the more versatile and more accurate **bootstrap**.

The US statistician Bradley Efron proposed, around 1980, a Monte Carlo-based general technique that evaluates all kinds of error due to estimation; see Efron (1979). His bootstrap method swiftly gained momentum in statistics and elsewhere, and theoretical studies and practical experience during the ensuing decades have confirmed its attractive properties; see Efron and Tibshirani (1993) or Davison and

Algorithm 7.1 The bootstrap

0 Input: Model for $\mathbf{Z}$, estimate $\hat{\boldsymbol{\theta}}$
1 Draw $\hat{\mathbf{Z}}^\star$ *%Using assumed model with $\hat{\boldsymbol{\theta}}$ as parameter*
2 $\hat{\boldsymbol{\theta}}^\star \leftarrow g(\hat{\mathbf{Z}}^\star)$ *%**Same** estimation method as for $\hat{\boldsymbol{\theta}}$*
3 $\hat{\psi}^\star \leftarrow \psi(\hat{\boldsymbol{\theta}}^\star)$ *%Simulated risk variable*
4 Return $\hat{\boldsymbol{\theta}}^\star$ and $\hat{\psi}^\star$.

Hinkley (1997). Most of the present section (and the next one) deals with bootstrap estimation of error. Many of the examples come from property insurance. Applications in life insurance are given in Section 15.2.

7.4.2 Introducing the bootstrap

Monte Carlo imitates in the computer what goes on in real life, and bootstrapping is no different. Consider the process that takes you from historical data $\mathbf{Z}$ to a risk estimate $\hat{\psi}$. The bootstrap copies this scheme and defines a dual one as follows:

$$\underset{\textit{the real world}}{\theta \longrightarrow \mathbf{Z},} \quad \underset{\textit{estimation}}{\begin{array}{c}\hat{\boldsymbol{\theta}} = g(\mathbf{Z})\\ \hat{\psi} = \psi(\hat{\boldsymbol{\theta}})\end{array}} \quad \text{and} \quad \underset{\textit{in the computer}}{\hat{\theta} \longrightarrow \hat{\mathbf{Z}}^\star,} \quad \underset{\textit{estimation}}{\begin{array}{c}\hat{\boldsymbol{\theta}}^\star = g(\hat{\mathbf{Z}}^\star)\\ \hat{\psi}^\star = \psi(\hat{\boldsymbol{\theta}}^\star).\end{array}} \tag{7.15}$$

On the left, the historical data $\mathbf{Z}$ yields estimates $\hat{\boldsymbol{\theta}} = g(\mathbf{Z})$ and then $\hat{\psi} = \psi(\hat{\boldsymbol{\theta}})$. The same procedure is run in the computer with one difference. We can't generate the Monte Carlo historical series $\hat{\mathbf{Z}}^\star$[4] in quite the same way as the real data $\mathbf{Z}$ since the true parameter $\boldsymbol{\theta}$ is unknown. What *can* be done is to use the estimate $\hat{\boldsymbol{\theta}}$ and generate $\hat{\mathbf{Z}}^\star$ from $\hat{\boldsymbol{\theta}}$ instead. In summary, the scheme comprises the three main steps in Algorithm 7.1.

When the historical observations are independent and identically distributed, it is also possible to draw bootstrap samples from the empircal distribution function as in Algorithm 4.1 (see the example in Exercise 7.21). How the setup in Algorithm 7.1 is extended when ψ is itself computed by Monte Carlo is discussed in the next section.

The idea is to identify the distribution of $\hat{\psi}^\star$ given $\hat{\theta}$ with that of $\hat{\psi}$ given θ. These distributions are the same only when $\hat{\theta} = \theta$, but discrepancies are small if $\hat{\theta}$ is a good estimate, and we have a tool for the uncertainty of $\hat{\psi}$ itself; i.e., run Algorithm 7.1 m_b times and examine $\hat{\psi}_1^\star, \dots, \hat{\psi}_{m_b}^\star$. One possibility is to compute

[4] Bootstrap simulations (and also posterior ones in Section 7.6) are marked with * to distinguish them from other types of simulation where * is used.

Algorithm 7.2 Poisson bootstrap

---

0 Input: A, $\hat{\mu} = n/A$
1 Draw $\hat{N}^\star \sim \text{Poisson}(A\hat{\mu})$ %*Use Algorithm 2.14*
2 Return $\hat{\mu}^\star \leftarrow \hat{N}^\star/A$.

---

their mean and standard deviation

$$\bar{\hat{\psi}}^\star = \frac{1}{m_b}\sum_{i=1}^{m_b}\hat{\psi}_i^\star \quad \text{and} \quad \hat{s}^\star = \sqrt{\frac{1}{m_b-1}\sum_{i=1}^{m_b}(\hat{\psi}_i^\star - \bar{\hat{\psi}}^\star)^2},$$

and use them as approximations of $E(\hat{\psi})$ and $\text{sd}(\hat{\psi})$. What is the significance of $\bar{\hat{\psi}}^\star$ on the left? Since $\hat{\psi}$ is the ψ-value underlying the bootstrap experiment, we might expect to find it in the middle of the simulated sample $\hat{\psi}_1^\star, \dots, \hat{\psi}_{m_b}^\star$, but if it is not, this suggests a natural tendency of historical estimation to produce ψ-values too small or too large. Suppose the former, so that the bootstrap average $\bar{\hat{\psi}}^\star < \hat{\psi}$. This indicates that ψ is being underestimated; useful to know, and we can correct for it too. Take

$$\hat{\psi}^{\star\text{bc}} = \underbrace{\hat{\psi}}_{\textit{estimate}} - \underbrace{(\bar{\hat{\psi}}^\star - \hat{\psi})}_{\textit{adjustment}} = 2\hat{\psi} - \bar{\hat{\psi}}^\star, \tag{7.16}$$

which is the **bias-corrected** bootstrap estimate of ψ. Such adjustments may sometimes be considerable; see Section 7.5.

7.4.3 Introductory example: The Poisson bootstrap

Consider the estimated intensity $\hat{\mu}$ in property insurance when there are n historical claims with A the underlying risk exposure (number of policies times average period under risk). The real world–computer world analogy is now

$$\underbrace{\mu \longrightarrow n \longrightarrow \hat{\mu} = n/A}_{\textit{real scheme}} \quad \text{and} \quad \underbrace{\hat{\mu} \longrightarrow \hat{N}^\star \longrightarrow \hat{\mu}^\star = N^\star/A}_{\textit{bootstrap scheme}},$$

using the estimation method of the preceding section. If we make the routine assumption that n is a realization of a Poisson variable with parameter $A\mu$, Algorithm 7.1 reduces to Algorithm 7.2.

To see how the method performs, consider the Norwegian natural disaster data for which $A = 21$ and $n = 20$. Then $\hat{\mu} = 21/20 = 1.05$ with $\text{sd}(\hat{\mu}) = \sqrt{\mu/A}$, estimated as $\sqrt{1.05/21} \doteq 0.22$. The mathematical expression for $\text{sd}(\hat{\mu})$ is justified in Section 8.2, but what about the bootstrap which does not depend on such rare results? When run $m_b = 1000$ times from $\hat{\mu} = 1.05$ the standard deviation of the sample $\hat{\mu}_1^\star, \dots, \hat{\mu}_{1000}^\star$ turned out to be $\hat{s}^\star = 0.22$, exactly as before. That is no

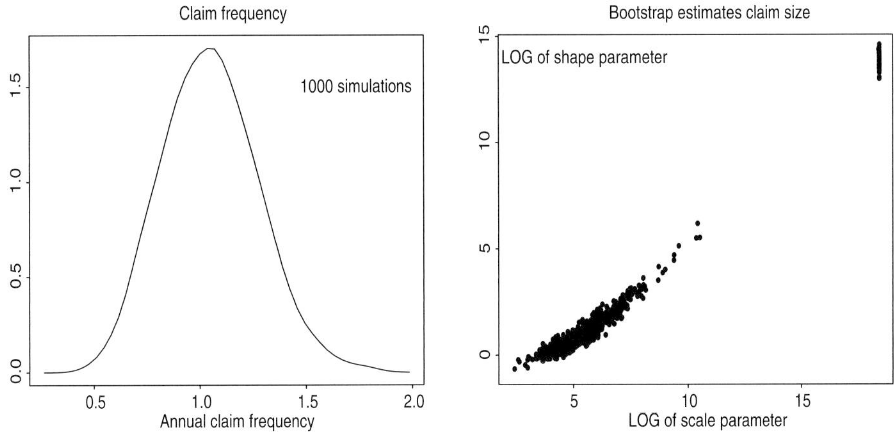

Figure 7.4 Bootstrap calculations for the Norwegian natural disaster data. *Left*: Estimated density function for claim intensity. *Right*: Scatterplot of the bootstrap sample of the Pareto parameters.

Algorithm 7.3 Pareto bootstrap

---

0 Input: $\hat{\alpha}$ and $\hat{\beta}$ *%Likelihood estimates from* $z_1, \ldots, z_n$
1 For $i = 1, \ldots, n$ do
2 Draw $\hat{Z}_i^\star \sim \text{Pareto}(\hat{\alpha}, \hat{\beta})$ *%Algorithm 2.13*
3 Compute $\hat{\alpha}^\star$ and $\hat{\beta}^\star$ *%Likelihood estimation from* $\hat{Z}_1^\star, \ldots, \hat{Z}_n^\star$
4 Return $\hat{\alpha}^\star$ and $\hat{\beta}^\star$.

---

coincidence (it can be verified that it must be so as $m \to \infty$). Even the density function of $\hat{\mu}$ can be estimated from the bootstrap simulations. It is plotted on the left in Figure 7.4. The shape around $\hat{\mu} = 1.05$ resembles a Gaussian one (you will see why in Section 8.2).

7.4.4 Second example: The Pareto bootstrap

The Poisson example only tried to convince you that the bootstrap works, but for a fitted Pareto distribution we actually need it. Experiments are then organized as in Algorithm 7.3.

The method has been tested on the Norwegian natural disaster data. There were $n = 21$ historical incidents, which lead to likelihood estimates $\hat{\alpha} = 1.71$ and $\hat{\beta} = 140$. Bootstrap reconstructions ($m_b = 1000$) of this estimate have been scatterplotted in Figure 7.4 right. The variability is enormous (both axes are logarithmic!).[5]

[5] The points in the upper right corner represent infinite α, which corresponds to the exponential distribution; see Section 2.5.

Algorithm 7.4 Pure premium bootstrap

0 Input: Fitted models for claim frequency and size
1 Draw $\hat{\mu}^\star$ *%Often by means of Algorithm 7.2*
2 Draw $\hat{\xi}^\star$ *%Many possibilities*
3 Return $\hat{\pi}^\star \leftarrow \hat{\mu}^\star T\hat{\xi}^\star$.

One thing learned is that the shape parameter α is almost always *overestimated.* The bootstrap was run from $\hat{\alpha} = 1.71$ or $\log(\hat{\alpha}) = 0.54$, and most bootstrapped $\log(\hat{\alpha}^\star)$ in Figure 7.4 right exceeds 0.54. This means that the extreme right tail is prone to *under*estimation, and very large claims are too. This phenomenon is common in many forms of extreme risk, though rarely in such an overwhelming manner as here.

7.4.5 The pure premium bootstrap

The pure premium $\pi = \mu T\xi$ is estimated as $\hat{\pi} = \hat{\mu}T\hat{\xi}$, where ξ is mean loss per claim. Error is now due to two independent sources, which are combined in Algorithm 7.4.

Implementation requires detailed assumptions regarding ξ. The following example is for the Pareto distribution with an upper limit b on the compensation per claim. Now

$$\xi = \int_0^b zf(z)\,dz + \int_b^\infty bf(z)\,dz \quad \text{where} \quad f(z) = \frac{\alpha/\beta}{(1+z/\beta)^{1+\alpha}}.$$

When the integrals are evaluated, this becomes

$$\xi = \frac{\beta}{\alpha-1}\left(1 - \frac{1}{(1+b/\beta)^{\alpha-1}}\right), \text{ estimated as } \hat{\xi} = \frac{\hat{\beta}}{\hat{\alpha}-1}\left(1 - \frac{1}{(1+b/\hat{\beta})^{\hat{\alpha}-1}}\right);$$

see also Section 10.6. For the Norwegian natural disasters, $\hat{\alpha} = 1.71$ and $\hat{\beta} = 140$, and if $b = 6000$ is the maximum responsibility per claim (in force during the period in question), we obtain $\hat{\xi} = 185$. The pure premium becomes $\hat{\pi} = 1.05 \times 185 = 194$, and the question is the error in that assessment.

Bootstrap experiments were run from $\hat{\mu}$, $\hat{\alpha}$ and $\hat{\beta}$ producing bootstrap estimates $\hat{\mu}^\star$, $\hat{\alpha}^\star$ and $\hat{\beta}^\star$, then $\hat{\xi}^\star$ and $\hat{\pi}^\star$. When this was repeated $m_b = 1000$ times, the density functions of $\hat{\xi}$ and $\hat{\pi}$ could be estimated. They are plotted in Figure 7.5. Their similarity is striking, which suggests that $\hat{\xi}$ means more for the uncertainty in $\hat{\pi}$ than does $\hat{\mu}$. This is confirmed by the percentiles of the two distributions, which are

Percentiles of $\hat{\xi}$				Percentiles of $\hat{\pi}$		
5%	50%	95%	and	5%	50%	95%
83	167	379		78	174	405.

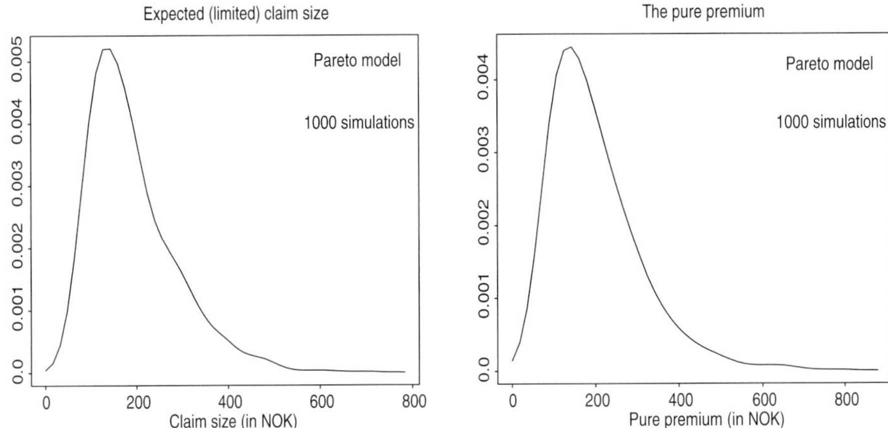

Figure 7.5 Density functions for estimated mean payment per claim $\hat{\xi}$ (*left*) and pure premium $\hat{\pi}$ (*right*) for the Norwegian natural disaster data.

The pure premium can't be determined with much certainty from historical experience this limited. Note that the error distribution of $\hat{\pi}$ is quite skewed towards the right which suggests underestimation; more on that in Section 7.5.

7.4.6 Simplification: The Gaussian bootstrap

What if the historical data is not available? This might be the situation if the model is taken from the literature (the Wilkie model in Chapter 13 is an example). One possibility is to assume that $\hat{\boldsymbol{\theta}}$ is normal, which is a good approximation when there is plenty of historical data and tolerable in general to get a rough idea of the uncertainty involved. The two dual schemes now become

$$\underbrace{\hat{\boldsymbol{\theta}} \sim N(\boldsymbol{\theta}, \boldsymbol{\Sigma})}_{\text{the real world}} \qquad \text{and} \qquad \underbrace{\hat{\boldsymbol{\theta}}^\star \sim N(\hat{\boldsymbol{\theta}}, \hat{\boldsymbol{\Sigma}}),}_{\text{in the computer}} \tag{7.17}$$

where the real world is imitated by replacing the true $\boldsymbol{\theta}$ and $\boldsymbol{\Sigma}$ by their estimates $\hat{\boldsymbol{\theta}}$ and $\hat{\boldsymbol{\Sigma}}$. Computer simulations are run from the latter, and on Line 2 in Algorithm 7.1 $\hat{\boldsymbol{\theta}}^\star$ is generated by Gaussian sampling (Section 5.4). You determine the Cholesky matrix $\hat{\boldsymbol{C}}=(\hat{c}_{ij})$ so that $\hat{\boldsymbol{\Sigma}}=\hat{\boldsymbol{C}}\hat{\boldsymbol{C}}^{\mathrm{T}}$ and enter the scheme

$$\hat{\psi}^\star = \psi(\hat{\boldsymbol{\theta}}^\star) \quad \text{where} \quad \hat{\boldsymbol{\theta}}^\star = \hat{\boldsymbol{\theta}} + \hat{\boldsymbol{C}}\boldsymbol{\epsilon}^\star$$

with $\boldsymbol{\epsilon}^\star=(\varepsilon_1^\star,\dots,\varepsilon_v^\star)^{\mathrm{T}}$ being a vector of independent drawings from $N(0,1)$. This is then repeated m_b times for the Gaussian bootstrap.

7.4.7 The old way: Delta approximations

Before the era of powerful computers, the error in $\hat{\psi} = \psi(\hat{\boldsymbol{\theta}})$ was usually calculated from those in $\hat{\boldsymbol{\theta}}$ through linear approximations; see Lehmann and Casella (1998). The first-order terms of a (multivariate) Taylor series justify the approximation

$$\hat{\psi} - \psi \doteq \sum_{i=1}^{v} \psi_i(\hat{\theta}_i - \theta_i) \quad \text{where} \quad \psi_i = \frac{\partial \psi(\theta_1, \dots, \theta_v)}{\partial \theta_i}.$$

Now $\text{var}(\hat{\psi})$ may be evaluated *approximately* by the ordinary formula for the variance of sums. This leads to

$$\text{sd}(\hat{\psi}) \doteq \left(\sum_{i=1}^{v} \sum_{j=1}^{v} \hat{\psi}_i \hat{\psi}_j \hat{\sigma}_{ij} \right)^{1/2} \quad \text{where} \quad \hat{\psi}_i = \frac{\partial \psi(\hat{\theta}_1, \dots, \hat{\theta}_v)}{\partial \theta_i}. \tag{7.18}$$

If the partial derivatives can be calculated (an obstacle here, see below), we have a method that accumulates parameter uncertainty.

As an example, consider an estimate $\hat{\pi} = \hat{\mu} T \hat{\xi}$ of the pure premium $\pi = \mu T \xi$ in property insurance. Normally $\hat{\mu}$ and $\hat{\xi}$ are stochastically independent. Let $\hat{\sigma}^2_{\hat{\mu}}$ and $\hat{\sigma}^2_{\hat{\xi}}$ be their estimated variances. We need $\pi_\mu = \partial \pi / \partial \mu$ and $\pi_\xi = \partial \pi / \partial \xi$, which are $\pi_\mu = T\xi$ and $\pi_\xi = \mu T$, and since there is no covariance term, (7.18) leads to

$$\text{sd}(\hat{\pi}) \doteq T \sqrt{\hat{\xi}^2 \hat{\sigma}^2_{\hat{\mu}} + \hat{\mu}^2 \hat{\sigma}^2_{\hat{\xi}}}. \tag{7.19}$$

In practice this might be a fair approximation; see Exercise 7.23.

If $\hat{\psi}$ is approximated by Monte Carlo as $\hat{\psi}^*_m$, the standard deviation formula is the same. It may be written

$$\text{sd}(\hat{\psi}^*_m) \doteq \left(\sum_{i=1}^{v} \sum_{j=1}^{v} \hat{\psi}^*_{im} \hat{\psi}^*_{jm} \hat{\sigma}_{ij} \right)^{1/2},$$

where $\hat{\psi}^*_{im}$ is the partial derivative of $\hat{\psi}^*_m$ with respect to θ_i and often hard to compute through ordinary mathematics. To outline how it can be done by numerical methods, let $\mathbf{e}_i = (0, \dots, 0, 1, 0, \dots, 0)$ be the base vector i (zeros everywhere except at position i). Then

$$\hat{\psi}^*_{im} \doteq \frac{1}{2h} \{\psi^*_m(\hat{\boldsymbol{\theta}} + h\mathbf{e}_i) - \psi^*_m(\hat{\boldsymbol{\theta}} - h\mathbf{e}_i)\}, \quad i = 1, \dots, v$$

where h is some small number. This is the standard method of differentiating numerically; see Appendix C.3. Simulations are run from both $\hat{\boldsymbol{\theta}} + h\mathbf{e}_i$ and $\hat{\boldsymbol{\theta}} - h\mathbf{e}_i$, and you should definitely use common random numbers (Section 4.3) to cut down the Monte Carlo error (which is blown up by the small h in the denominator). A reasonable choice of h could be $h = 0.0001$ or $h = 0.001$; see also the comments in Appendix C.3.

Algorithm 7.5 The nested bootstrap

0 Input: Models for $\mathbf{Z}$ and X, estimate $\hat{\theta}$
1 Generate $\hat{\mathbf{Z}}^\star$ from $\hat{\theta}$ %*The bootstrap part; i.e.,*
2 $\hat{\theta}^\star \leftarrow g(\hat{\mathbf{Z}}^\star)$ *the outer layer of simulations*
3 Generate $\hat{X}_1^{\star *}, \dots, \hat{X}_m^{\star *}$ from $\hat{\theta}^\star$ %*The inner loop starts here*
4 $\hat{\psi}_m^{\star *} \leftarrow \hat{X}_1^{\star *}, \dots, \hat{X}_m^{\star *}$ %*Example:* $\hat{\psi}_m^{\star *} = \hat{X}_{(\epsilon m)}^{\star *}$ *for percentiles*
5. Return $\hat{\psi}_m^{\star *}$.

7.5 Evaluating error II: Nested schemes

7.5.1 Introduction

The bootstrap can still be used when $\hat{\psi} = \psi(\hat{\boldsymbol{\theta}})$ is calculated by Monte Carlo; simply repeat the simulations for the bootstrapped parameters $\hat{\boldsymbol{\theta}}^\star$. As an example, consider the upper ϵ-percentile of some risk variable X. Simulations $\hat{X}_1^*, \dots, \hat{X}_m^*$ are then generated under some estimate $\hat{\boldsymbol{\theta}}$ and sorted in descending order as $\hat{X}_{(1)}^* \geq \dots \geq \hat{X}_{(m)}^*$ with $\hat{X}_{(\epsilon m)}^*$ as the approximate percentile. The bootstrap duplicates this sequence from a bootstrap-estimate $\hat{\boldsymbol{\theta}}^\star$ and produces another ordered sample $\hat{X}_{(1)}^{\star *} \geq \dots \geq \hat{X}_{(m)}^{\star *}$, now with percentile $\hat{X}_{(\epsilon m)}^{\star *}$. The notation ${}^{\star *}$ is to emphasize that there is an ordinary bootstrap *and* a second round of Monte Carlo. Carrying out the procedure m_b times yields a sample of m_b percentiles $\hat{X}_{(\epsilon m)}^{\star *}$ to evaluate uncertainty due to estimation. The idea is outlined in more detail below, with examples from property insurance and financial risk.

7.5.2 The nested algorithm

In the general case $\hat{\psi} = \psi(\hat{\boldsymbol{\theta}})$, and we are assuming that the exact function must be replaced by an approximation $\hat{\psi}_m^*$ based on simulations $\hat{X}_1^*, \dots, \hat{X}_m^*$ under $\hat{\boldsymbol{\theta}}$. The bootstrap becomes

$$\underbrace{\hat{\boldsymbol{\theta}} \longrightarrow \mathbf{Z}^\star,}_{\textit{bootstrap data}} \qquad \underbrace{\hat{\boldsymbol{\theta}}^\star = g(\hat{\mathbf{Z}}^\star),}_{\textit{bootstrap estimate}} \qquad \underbrace{\hat{\boldsymbol{\theta}}^\star \longrightarrow \hat{X}_1^{\star *}, \dots, \hat{X}_m^{\star *} \longrightarrow \hat{\psi}_m^{\star *},}_{\textit{Monte Carlo under the bootstrap}}$$

where the second Monte Carlo experiment on the very right is a new feature compared with the scheme in Algorithm 7.1. Instead of $\hat{\psi}^\star = \psi(\hat{\theta}^\star)$ we have to settle for an approximation $\hat{\psi}_m^{\star *}$ based on simulations generated under the bootstrap estimate $\hat{\theta}^\star$. The setup amounts to **nested** simulation. For *each* bootstrap estimate $\hat{\theta}^\star$, m simulations $\hat{X}_1^{\star *}, \dots, \hat{X}_m^{\star *}$ are generated. Repeating this m_b times amounts to a total of $m_b m$ simulations. Modern computers are powerful enough for such schemes to be practical.

How the nested algorithm works is summarized in Algorithm 7.5. Line 3 may be implemented with or without common random numbers (Section 4.3). The total

Algorithm 7.6 The Poisson/Pareto reserve bootstrap

0 Input: Likelihood estimates $\hat{\mu}$, $\hat{\alpha}$, $\hat{\beta}$ and A, J, T
1 Draw $\hat{N}^\star \sim \text{Poisson}(A\hat{\mu})$, $\hat{Z}_1^\star, \dots, \hat{Z}_n^\star \sim \text{Pareto}(\hat{\alpha}, \hat{\beta})$ *%Bootstrap part*
2 $\hat{\mu}^\star \leftarrow \hat{N}^\star / A$, $\hat{\alpha}^\star, \hat{\beta}^\star \overset{\text{likelihood}}{\longleftarrow} \hat{Z}_1^\star, \dots, \hat{Z}_n^\star$ *on these two lines*
3 For $i = 1, \dots, m$ do
4 Draw $\hat{N}^{\star *} \sim \text{Poisson}(J\hat{\mu}^\star T)$, $\hat{\mathcal{X}}_i^{\star *} \leftarrow 0$ *%Draws from*
5 Repeat $\hat{N}^{\star *}$ times *bootstrap*
6 Draw $\hat{Z}^{\star *} \sim \text{Pareto}(\hat{\alpha}^\star, \hat{\beta}^\star)$, $\hat{\mathcal{X}}_i^{\star *} \leftarrow \hat{\mathcal{X}}_i^{\star *} + H(\hat{Z}^{\star *})$ *estimates*
7 Sort $\hat{\mathcal{X}}_1^{\star *}, \dots, \hat{\mathcal{X}}_m^{\star *}$ as $\hat{\mathcal{X}}_{(1)}^{\star *} \geq \cdots \geq \hat{\mathcal{X}}_{(m)}^{\star *}$
8 Return $\hat{q}_\epsilon^{\star *} \leftarrow \hat{\mathcal{X}}_{(\epsilon m)}^{\star *}$. *%The reserve*

number mm_b of simulations is potentially much higher than m or m_b on their own, and we should reflect on how many we need. Scope for high accuracy in error assessments isn't that strong. Several of the earlier examples have been run with $m_b = 1000$, but the specialist bootstrap literature often maintains that it may be lowered to $m_b = 50$ or even less; see Efron and Tibshirani (1993).

7.5.3 Example: The reserve bootstrap

Reserves in property insurance are percentiles and were, in Chapter 3, reported as $\mathcal{X}_{(m\epsilon)}^*$ where $\mathcal{X}_{(1)}^* \geq \cdots \geq \mathcal{X}_{(m)}^*$ are simulated portfolio losses in descending order. There is in practice estimation error in the underlying stochastic models. Suppose the historical material consists of n incidents based on an exposure-to-risk coefficient A. Claim intensity is then estimated as $\hat{\mu} = n/A$, and the model for the losses identified from the observed claims $z_1, \dots, z_n$. The example below assumes the Pareto distribution with parameters α and β fitted by maximum likelihood. The issue is the impact of errors in $\hat{\mu}$, $\hat{\alpha}$ and $\hat{\beta}$ on the projected reserve.

Algorithm 7.6 is a specialization of Algorithm 7.5 that combines the bootstrap part of Algorithms 7.2 and 7.3 with Algorithm 3.1 (simulation of the portfolio loss). The reserve is based on losses from J policies over a period of length T. We start from the original estimates $\hat{\mu}$, $\hat{\alpha}$ and $\hat{\beta}$ (on Line 0) and run experiments on Lines 3–6 leading to the bootstrap estimates $\hat{\mu}^\star$, $\hat{\alpha}^\star$, and $\hat{\beta}^\star$, from which the portfolio losses are simulated. The output on Line 8 is then a realization of the reserve and can be repeated to evaluate the impact of parameter uncertainty. To replace the Pareto distribution with other models, modify Lines 1, 2 and 6.

7.5.4 Numerical illustration

The following example has been constructed from the Norwegian natural disaster data and is meant to imitate a small industrial portfolio of large risks. We are dealing with an annual ($T = 1$) Poisson/Pareto portfolio for which

$$\underbrace{\hat{\mu} = 1.05,\ \hat{\alpha} = 1.71,\ \hat{\beta} = 17.5,}_{\textit{estimated parameters}} \qquad \underbrace{J = 20,}_{\textit{number of policies}} \qquad \underbrace{b = 750.}_{\textit{maximum responsibility per event}}$$

Estimated parameters are the same as in Section 7.3, except that $\hat{\beta}$ and b have been divided by 8 (the currency is thereby changed to million euros). The estimated 99% reserve is around $\hat{q}^*_{0.01m} = 1380$ (there were $m = 10\,000$ simulations).

What is the uncertainty in such assessments? The answer depends mainly on how much historical data there is to go on. With n the number of claims and A the exposure to risk, consider the scenarios

$$\underbrace{A = 20,\ n = 21}_{\textit{'small' historical record}} \qquad \text{and} \qquad \underbrace{A = 200,\ n = 210}_{\textit{'large' historical record}}$$

where $\hat{\mu} = n/A$ has the same value in both cases. Algorithm 7.6 was run $m_b = 1000$ times with $m = 10\,000$ in the inner loop. With $J = 20$ policies under risk, the number of Pareto drawings for the nested scheme is then about $20 \times 1000 \times 10\,000 = 200$ million, but a Fortran program handled it easily, and even the R-programs in the exercises work.

The bootstrap summary in Table 7.2 reveals large standard deviations and much uncertainty, and the same message comes from the plots of the density functions of the estimates in Figure 7.6. Note the much more pronounced skewness for the 'small' historical record on the left. Patterns of that kind suggest underestimation. The mean bootstrap reserve is 1290 in Table 7.2 left, 90 *less* than the estimate at 1380. This means that the simulations came from a model for which the answer is 1380, whereas we obtain 1280 on average. Such underestimation is corrected by the bias-corrected estimate (7.16) which becomes 1380 – (1290 – 1380) = 1470, a not insignificant jump upwards. With more historical data on the right in Table 7.2 the bias has disappeared.

7.5.5 A second example: Interest-rate return

Financial assets are routinely simulated for values at risk and other risk measures. What is the impact of estimation error on such assessments? An answer will now

Table 7.2 Bootstrap statistics of the artificial industrial portfolio

	'Small' historical record					'Large' historical record				
Estimate	mean	sd	5%	50%	95%	mean	sd	5%	50%	95%
1380	1290	710	410	1170	2550	1380	250	1000	1360	1810

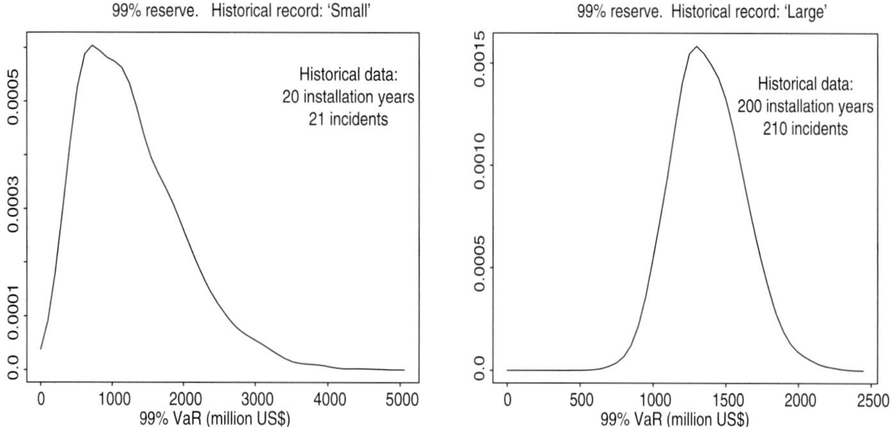

Figure 7.6 Density functions of estimated reserve (99%) for 'small' (*left*) and 'large' (*right*) historical record.

Algorithm 7.7 The floating-rate-return bootstrap

---

0 Input: Estimates $\hat{\xi},\ \hat{\sigma},\ \hat{a}$ — *%From the historic series* $r_1, \dots, r_n$
1 Generate $\hat{r}_1^\star, \dots, \hat{r}_n^\star$ — *%From* $\hat{\xi}, \hat{\sigma}, \hat{a}$ *using Algorithm 5.2*
2 Re-estimate parameters $\hat{\xi}^\star, \hat{\sigma}^\star, \hat{a}^\star$ — *%From* $\hat{r}_1^\star, \dots, \hat{r}_n^\star$*, same method as on Line* 0
3 For $i = 1, \dots, m$ do — *%Entering the inner loop*
4 Generate $\hat{r}_1^{\star *}, \dots, \hat{r}_K^{\star *}$ — *%From* $\hat{\xi}^\star, \hat{\sigma}^\star, \hat{a}^\star$ *using Algorithm 5.2*
5 $r_{0:K,i}^{\star *} \leftarrow (1 + \hat{r}_1^{\star *}) \cdots (1 + r_K^{\star *}) - 1$
6 Return $r_{0:K,1}^{\star *}, \dots, r_{0:K,m}^{\star *}$. — *%K-step returns*

---

be suggested through an account earning the floating rate of interest. The return $r_{0:K}$ over K periods is then

$$r_{0:K} = \left(\prod_{k=1}^{K} (1 + r_k) \right) - 1 \quad \text{with Monte Carlo version} \quad r_{0:K}^* = \left(\prod_{k=1}^{K} (1 + r_k^*) \right) - 1.$$

Here r_k and r_k^* are the real and simulated rates of interest generated under some stochastic mechanism, say the Black–Karasinski model of Section 5.6. If $\varepsilon_1^*, \varepsilon_2^*, \dots$ are independent and $N(0, 1)$, the simulations become

$$r_k^* = \xi e^{-\frac{1}{2}\sigma^2/(1-a^2) + X_k^*} \quad \text{where} \quad X_k^* = aX_{k-1}^* + \sigma \varepsilon_k^*.$$

The issue addressed is the consequence of replacing the three parameters (ξ, σ, a) by estimates $(\hat{\xi}, \hat{\sigma}, \hat{a})$. We can analyse this if an historical series $r_1, \dots, r_n$ has been used to fit the model. The nested bootstrap is a natural tool and can be organized as in Algorithm 7.7.

Table 7.3 Parameter estimates and error assessments for interest-rate models and returns

m_b = 1000 and m = 100 000

	Parameters			5-year returns		
					Percentiles	
	ξ	σ	a	Mean	1%	99%
True	5.0%	0.25	0.70	28.2%	15%	51%
Estimated	5.9%	0.31	0.34	33.0%	20%	54%
Bootstrap mean	6.0%	0.31	0.25	33.3%	21%	53%
Bootstrap sd	0.6%	0.05	0.19	3.2%	3%	8%

Start by simulating the historical data (Line 1) from the estimates $(\hat{\xi}, \hat{\sigma}, \hat{a})$. This generates bootstrap data with bootstrap estimates $(\hat{\xi}^\star, \hat{\sigma}^\star, \hat{a}^\star)$, computed in the same way as the original ones. A second Monte Carlo experiment (Lines 3–5) is then run m times from $(\hat{\xi}^\star, \hat{\sigma}^\star, \hat{a}^\star)$, leading to m simulated K-step returns on Line 6 from which standard deviations, percentiles and other measures of risk can be computed. Their variation due to estimation error is evaluated by repeating Algorithm 7.7 a sufficient number of times.

7.5.6 Numerical illustration

How uncertain are risk measures when applied to interest rates? The following experiment is an example where annual, historical data over 25 years was simulated from the Black–Karasinski model with the parameters in Table 7.3 (first row) and fitted through the method of moments (7.11), which produced the estimates on the second row. We are now able to compare risk under a true and fitted model by simulating from both. That gave the mean returns and percentiles for 5-year returns on the very right, with 28.2% as the expectation under the true model growing to 33.0% under the fitted one with similar changes for the percentiles.

This is in the laboratory with the underlying model known, but could the same conclusions have been reached from the historical data alone? Call for the bootstrap. The experiment in the lower half of Table 7.3 used $m_b = 1000$ bootstrap samples with $m = 100\,000$ simulations for the inner loop. A first observation is that estimates of the parameters are quite uncertain, especially the autoregressive coefficient a, and these errors are passed on to the projections of risk. It seems that the upper percentile is more uncertain than both the lower one and the mean return. Bootstrap averages match the values under the fitted model, and there is no scope for a bias correction.

7.6 The Bayesian approach

7.6.1 Introduction

Parameters $\boldsymbol{\theta}$ are uknown, but arguably there is always *some* knowledge as to which values are likely and which are not. The Bayesian tradition expresses such beliefs through probabilities. Suppose a Gaussian distribution with expectation $\boldsymbol{\theta}_0$ is used. Values of $\boldsymbol{\theta}$ close to $\boldsymbol{\theta}_0$ are then considered plausible and those far away unlikely. Prior views are now formalized and can be combined with information from historical data. This section offers an introduction to such **Bayesian** methods. Parameters are stochastic, but with a basis different from in Section 6.3 where policy holders and background conditions were drawn randomly. Those were mechanisms well rooted in what goes on, and it's the same with stochastic volatility and the theory of credibility in Section 10.5. Belief expressed through probabilities is quite different, and indeed the Bayesian approach has at times been hotly debated. Bernardo and Smith (2009) is a thorough account of such methods in statistics; see also Nordberg (1989) for a presentation from an actuarial point of view.

7.6.2 The posterior view

Whether you like the Bayesian paradigm or not, there is the undeniable fact that it opens up a useful machinery for estimation and evaluation of error. As before, let $\mathbf{z} = (z_1, \dots, z_n)$ be the historical data described by a stochastic model with density function $f(z_1, \dots, z_n|\boldsymbol{\theta})$. This part of the modelling brings nothing new, but then comes prior knowledge about $\boldsymbol{\theta}$ which is formalized through a **prior** density function $p(\boldsymbol{\theta})$ expressing what is considered likely and what is not. Whether that can be done in a realistic way is another matter, but suppose it can. There are now two sources of information and their combined weight could be utilized. This is achieved through Bayes' formula (6.29) in Section 6.5, which yields the **posterior** density function

$$p(\boldsymbol{\theta}|z_1, \dots, z_n) = \frac{f(z_1, \dots, z_n|\boldsymbol{\theta})p(\boldsymbol{\theta})}{f(z_1, \dots, z_n)}.$$

Here $f(z_1, \dots, z_n)$ applies to the historical data when the uncertainty of the underlying $\boldsymbol{\theta}$ has been integrated out[6] and is cumbersome computationally. The setup below doesn't require it, and we shall simply write $1/c = f(z_1, \dots, z_n)$ so that

$$p(\boldsymbol{\theta}|z_1, \dots, z_n) = cf(z_1, \dots, z_n|\boldsymbol{\theta})p(\boldsymbol{\theta}) \tag{7.20}$$

which summarizes what is known about $\boldsymbol{\theta}$ from prior belief *and* historical data.

[6] Its exact mathematical form is $f(z_1, \dots, z_n) = \int_{-\infty}^{\infty} f(z_1, \dots, z_n|\boldsymbol{\theta})p(\boldsymbol{\theta})d\boldsymbol{\theta}$.

The mean of the posterior distribution is often used as an estimate; i.e.,

$$\hat{\boldsymbol{\theta}}_B = E(\boldsymbol{\theta}|z_1, \dots, z_n) \quad \text{and} \quad \hat{\psi}_B = E\{\psi(\boldsymbol{\theta})|z_1, \dots, z_n\} \tag{7.21}$$

with posterior standard deviations $\text{sd}(\boldsymbol{\theta}|z_1, \dots, z_n)$ and $\text{sd}\{\psi(\boldsymbol{\theta})|z_1, \dots, z_n\}$ indicating uncertainty. There is also a posterior view on the risk variable X itself. By elementary probability theory

$$p(x|z_1, \dots, z_n) = \int_{-\infty}^{\infty} p(x|\boldsymbol{\theta})p(\boldsymbol{\theta}|z_1, \dots, z_n)\, d\boldsymbol{\theta}, \tag{7.22}$$

and Monte Carlo simulations of X are generated by drawing $\boldsymbol{\theta}^\star$ from $p(\boldsymbol{\theta}|z_1, \dots, z_n)$, followed by $X^\star$ from $p(x|\boldsymbol{\theta}^\star)$. Parameter uncertainty is now incorporated automatically and nested schemes avoided; see Exercise 7.44. Posterior sampling of $\boldsymbol{\theta}$ is a new issue and discussed below. The following two examples illustrate the main features of the Bayesian approach.

7.6.3 Example: Claim intensities

Suppose the intensity μ is to be estimated from n claims with risk exposure A. The density function is

$$f(n|\mu) = \frac{(A\mu)^n}{n!}e^{-A\mu}, \quad n = 0, 1, \dots,$$

but for a Bayesian approach a prior $p(\mu)$ must be added. One possibility is a so-called **non-informative** one for which $p(\mu) = c$ for all μ. All values are then seen as equally likely. The definition is not strictly mathematically legal since μ extends over the entire positive axis, making $\int p(\mu)\, d\mu$ infinite. In practice this doesn't matter; more below.

With likelihood function and prior woven together through (7.20), the posterior density function becomes

$$p(\mu|n) = c\mu^n e^{-A\mu}, \quad n = 0, 1, \dots$$

where quantities that do not depend on μ have been subsumed into the constant c. This is a Gamma density function with mean $E(\mu|n) = (n + 1)/A$ and shape $\alpha = n + 1$; see Section 2.5. For the Norwegian natural disaster data where $A = 20$ and $n = 21$ we obtain $E(\mu|n) = (21 + 1)/20 \doteq 1.10$ and $\text{sd}(\mu|n) = 1.10/\sqrt{22} \doteq 0.23$, very close to earlier results.

7.6.4 Example: Expected return on equity

We have seen (Section 2.2) that it is virtually impossible to determine the mean return on equity from historical returns $r_1, \dots, r_n$ alone. Expert opinion is another source of information, and it seems sensible to try to use their judgement and historical data together; see Litterman (2003) and Herold and Maurer (2006). It is precisely such pooling of information that the Bayesian methodology is meant for. The following Gaussian approach is about the simplest possible. Suppose

$$\underbrace{r_1,\dots,r_n|\xi \sim N(\xi,\sigma)}_{\textit{model for the data}} \qquad \text{and} \qquad \underbrace{\xi \sim N(\xi_0,\tau)}_{\textit{prior}},$$

where the historical returns $r_1,\dots,r_n$ are independent which here means *conditional* independence given ξ. Also note the prior where ξ_0 is expert advice on ξ. How much this view should be trusted is entered through the standard deviation τ. A large τ means that analyst opinion is useless, a small one that it is very good indeed. Assume that σ is known (relaxed in Exercises 7.41 and 7.42).

We seek the posterior distribution of ξ given $r_1,\dots,r_n$. The two factors in (7.20) are then

$$f(r_1,\dots,r_n|\xi) = \prod_{k=1}^{n}\left(\frac{1}{\sqrt{2\pi}\sigma}e^{-(r_k-\xi)^2/(2\sigma^2)}\right) \quad \text{and} \quad p(\xi) = \frac{1}{\sqrt{2\pi}\tau}e^{-(\xi-\xi_0)^2/(2\tau^2)}.$$

When combined (details in Section 7.7), we are led to still another normal density function

$$p(\xi|r_1,\dots,r_n) = \frac{1}{\sqrt{2\pi}\hat{\sigma}_B}e^{-(\xi-\hat{\xi}_B)^2/(2\hat{\sigma}_B^2)}$$

with parameters

$$\hat{\xi}_B = \underbrace{w\bar{r}}_{\textit{impact of data}} + \underbrace{(1-w)\xi_0}_{\textit{impact of prior}} \quad \text{for} \quad w = \frac{\tau^2}{\tau^2+\sigma^2/n} \tag{7.23}$$

and

$$\hat{\sigma}_B = \underbrace{\frac{\sigma}{\sqrt{n}}}_{\textit{data}} \times \underbrace{\frac{\tau}{\sqrt{\tau^2+\sigma^2/n}}}_{\textit{impact of prior}} < \frac{\sigma}{\sqrt{n}}. \tag{7.24}$$

The expressions for $\hat{\xi}_B$ and $\hat{\sigma}_B$ are full of meaning.

Consider $\hat{\xi}_B$, which is the Bayesian estimate of ξ. It is based on a weight w that balances data and prior; see also Section 10.5 for a method in property insurance closely related to this. The posterior standard deviation $\hat{\sigma}_B$ is an assessment of the accuracy of this Bayesian estimate. It is always lower than the data-only uncertainty $\sigma/\sqrt{n}$ and expert opinion has led to an improvement, but that is only when we know how good or bad they are; i.e., when τ is known. This is not so easy, and if a wrong τ is used, expert opinion can even make matters worse.

7.6.5 Choosing the prior

The preceding examples showed prior distributions in two different roles. With equity the idea was to compensate for the high data uncertainty and contribute substantially to the final estimate of the expected return. But in the other example the prior was there more to provide access to the Bayesian concepts (which some people find very attractive). Initially all values of μ were considered equally likely, seemingly imposing no view at all. And yet that isn't quite true.

The Pareto model (which we shall make use of below) illustrates the issue. Its density function is based on two parameters β and α but many authors (for example Embrechts *et al.*, 1997) work with $\gamma = 1/\alpha$ instead. With likelihood methods that doesn't matter. The fitted distribution is the same anyway. But with non-informative priors it *does* matter. Suppose

$$p(\gamma) = \frac{1}{A} \quad \text{for} \quad 0 < \gamma < A,$$

all values being equally likely. The upper bound A is selected so that it is certain to be much larger than the real γ. With α the same model can be written (Exercise 7.40)

$$p(\alpha) = \frac{1}{A\alpha^2} \quad \text{for} \quad \alpha > \frac{1}{A},$$

no longer a neutral view even if it was with γ. And who can decide which of the two parameters to use? There is more in the specialist literature, such as Bernardo and Smith (2009). The choice of prior distribution is a delicate affair.

7.6.6 Bayesian simulation

Monte Carlo is attractive even for Bayesian methods with simulated samples $\boldsymbol{\theta}_1^\star, \dots, \boldsymbol{\theta}_m^\star$ generated from the posterior distribution (7.20). Their mean can be used as an estimate of $\boldsymbol{\theta}$, their standard deviation reveals uncertainty and they can be combined with ordinary sampling of risk variables given $\boldsymbol{\theta}$ as illustrated in Exercise 7.44. Take $\psi_i^\star = \psi(\boldsymbol{\theta}_i^\star)$, and we have posterior samples $\psi_1^\star, \dots, \psi_m^\star$ that summarize our knowledge about ψ. Posterior sampling is an area under development, with much interest academically in more complex models than those considered here; see Gamerman and Lopes (2006) for a review. As with ordinary sampling there is a myriad of special tricks adapted to specific models.

If the number of parameters is small, table methods is *general* possibilities. Let $\boldsymbol{\theta}_1, \dots, \boldsymbol{\theta}_M$ be a set of points, in some way filling out the $\boldsymbol{\theta}$-space; see below. The posterior probability of $\boldsymbol{\theta}_i$ is

$$p_i = cf(z_1, \dots, z_n|\boldsymbol{\theta}_i)p(\boldsymbol{\theta}_i), \quad i = 1, 2, \dots, M$$

Algorithm 7.8 Bayesian table setup

0 Input: Likelihood $f(z_1, \ldots, z_n|\boldsymbol{\theta})$ and prior $p(\boldsymbol{\theta})$
1 $S \leftarrow 0$ *%Sum for normalizing*
2 For $i = 1, \ldots, M$ do
3 $\quad p_i \leftarrow f(z_1, \ldots, z_n|\boldsymbol{\theta}_i)p(\boldsymbol{\theta}_i), \quad S \leftarrow S + p_i$
4 For $i = 1, \ldots, M$ do *%The normalizing loop*
5 $\quad p_i \leftarrow p_i/S$,
6 Return $p_1, \ldots, p_M$.

where the constant c is not needed since the computation can be organized as in Algorithm 7.8, which sets up a discrete probability distribution with each $\boldsymbol{\theta}_i$ assigned p_i. We may then apply Algorithm 4.2, to lay out a guide table and draw $\boldsymbol{\theta}^\star$ and $\psi^\star = \psi(\boldsymbol{\theta}^\star)$ by means of Algorithm 4.3. Eventually (after a considerable setup phase) an ultra-fast, *approximate* sampling procedure has been obtained. If the original problem is replaced by another one, modify Line 3.

We must address how the points $\boldsymbol{\theta}_1, \ldots, \boldsymbol{\theta}_M$ are selected. This was discussed in Section 4.2, but there are now several parameters. Suppose $\boldsymbol{\theta} = (\beta, \gamma)$ and let $\beta_1, \ldots, \beta_{M_1}$ and $\gamma_1, \ldots, \gamma_{M_2}$ be discretizations as in Section 4.2. A *joint* version is $\boldsymbol{\theta}_i = (\beta_j, \gamma_l)$ where all β_j are paired with all γ_l, a total of $M = M_1 \times M_2$ different combinations. Each $\boldsymbol{\theta}_i = (\beta_j, \gamma_l)$ is then assigned a probability p_i through Algorithm 7.8.

The drawback is that M is going to grow rapidly if joined by a third or fourth parameter. Still, 50 points in four different directions is no more than 50^4 combinations (around six million), and a modern computer is up to it, at least if implemented in software like C or Fortran. Many problems can be solved in this way, but no more than a few parameters are possible unless some of the posteriors are independent as in one of the examples below.

7.6.7 Example: Mean payment

The evaluations in Figure 7.5 for the Norwegian natural disaster data in Table 7.1 have, in Figure 7.7, been redone from a Bayesian point of view. As before, assume a Pareto model so that the joint density function of the historical losses $z_1, \ldots, z_n$ becomes

$$f(z_1, \ldots, z_n \mid \beta, \gamma) = \prod_{k=1}^{n} \frac{\alpha/\beta}{(1 + z_k/\beta)^{1+\alpha}} \quad \text{where} \quad \alpha = 1/\gamma.$$

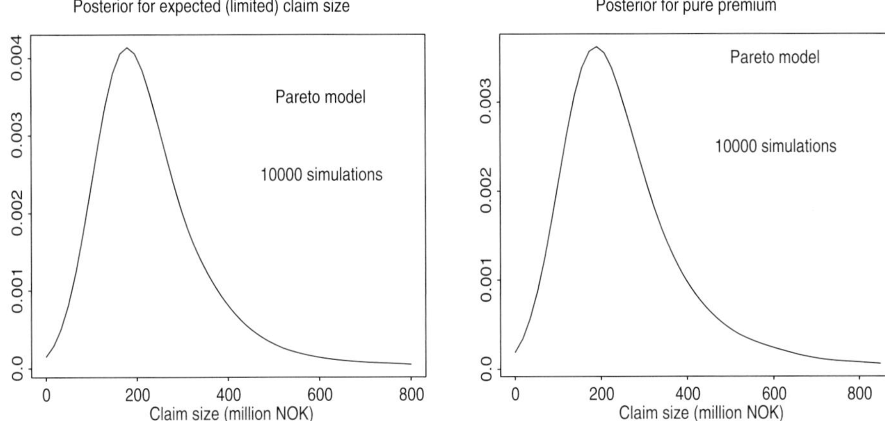

Figure 7.7 Posterior density functions from the Norwegian natural disaster data (using $M = 100$ and $m = 10\,000$ simulations); the mean payment per incident (*left*) and the pure premium (*right*).

Assume a non-informative prior $p(\beta, \gamma) = c$ with β and γ uniform over the intervals $(0, 1000)$ and $(0, 10)$ with discretization schemes

$$\beta_j = \frac{1000}{M_1}(j - 1/2), \quad j = 1, \dots, M_1 \quad \text{and} \quad \gamma_l = \frac{10}{M_1}(l - 1/2), \quad l = 1, \dots, M_1,$$

the same number of points for each. Both upper bounds are comfortably much larger than the actual parameters.

Posterior drawings $(\beta^\star, \gamma^\star)$ can now be generated from the machinery above and converted to simulations of the expected claim per incident ξ when the maximum responsibility per event is b. As in Section 7.4, this yields

$$\xi^\star = \frac{\beta^\star}{\alpha^\star - 1}\left(1 - \frac{1}{(1 + b/\beta^\star)^{\alpha^\star - 1}}\right) \quad \text{where} \quad \alpha^\star = 1/\gamma^\star.$$

Bayes' estimates of ξ when $b = 6000$ were

$M_1 = 25$,	$M_1 = 50$,	$M_1 = 100$	against	Section 7.4
239	233	235		185

using one million simulations. The choice of M_1 is not critical, but the estimate has become much larger than in Section 7.4. Why is that? A principal reason is Bayesian evaluations being summaries over *many* possibilities. In cases like the present one very high values of ξ, though not likely, are attached probabilities large enough to pull the estimate strongly upwards. The same message is transmitted by the posterior density function in Figure 7.7 left. Note the shift to the right compared with the bootstrap solution in Figure 7.5.

7.6.8 Example: Pure premium

Bayesian estimation of the pure premium $\pi = \mu T\xi$ requires an additional model for μ. Its posterior distribution would normally be independent from ξ and a separate issue. Using the earlier solution with a non-informative prior and n historical claims under risk exposure A, the posterior distribution is $\mu|n = G(n+1)/A$ where $G \sim \text{Gamma}(n+1)$ is a standard Gamma with mean one. Sampling from this distribution was discussed in Section 2.5.

If $\xi^\star$ and $\mu^\star$ are posterior simulations of ξ and μ, then $\pi^\star = \mu^\star T\xi^\star$ is one of π, and we may from m_b replications compute the mean and standard deviation as an estimate of π with uncertainty. Its posterior density function has been plotted in Figure 7.7 right. It isn't very different from the one for ξ, which tells us (as it did in Section 7.4 too) that claim intensity has less influence on the uncertainty of π than does claim size.

7.6.9 Summing up: Bayes or not?

Obvious areas for Bayesian methods are design of financial portfolios (expert views on expectations needed) and evaluation of financial risk over decades (models can't be taken from historical data alone). Non-informative priors, though popular in some quarters, might not have been too convincing when tested above and brought up an important point. Bayesian estimates merge many possibilities into single numbers. Does this make conclusions less transparent? It isn't the most plausible assessments that are being reported, but rather compromises over alternatives. That may be attractive when the prior information has a sound basis, but less so when the assumptions on which it rests are obscure. A possible replacement for the mean is the **mode**, which is the value where the posterior density function peaks, and Bayesian estimates with a non-informative prior now coincide with the likelihood ones, but the whole approach may have the most going for it when there is genuine prior information available.

7.7 Mathematical arguments

7.7.1 Bayesian means under Gaussian models

The posterior density function for ξ given $r_1, \dots, r_n$ is

$$p(\xi \mid r_1, \dots, r_n) = c\frac{1}{\sqrt{2\pi}\tau}e^{-(\xi-\xi_0)^2/(2\tau^2)} \times \left(\prod_{k=1}^{n} \frac{1}{\sqrt{2\pi}\sigma}e^{-(r_k-\xi)^2/(2\sigma^2)}\right)$$

which can also be written

$$p(\xi|r_1, \dots, r_n) = c'e^{-Q/2} \quad \text{where} \quad Q = \frac{1}{\tau^2}(\xi-\xi_0)^2 + \frac{1}{\sigma^2}\sum_{k=1}^{n}(r_k-\xi)^2$$

with c' a second constant. Expanding Q as a polynomial in ξ yields

$$Q = \left(\frac{n}{\sigma^2} + \frac{1}{\tau^2}\right)\xi^2 - 2\left(\frac{n\bar{r}}{\sigma^2} + \frac{\xi_0}{\tau^2}\right)\xi + \left(\frac{\xi_0^2}{\tau^2} + \frac{1}{\sigma^2}\sum_{k=1}^{n} r_k^2\right)$$

where $\bar{r} = (r_1 + \cdots + r_n)/n$. Alternatively

$$Q = \frac{(\xi - \hat{\xi}_B)^2}{\hat{\sigma}_B^2} + c'' \quad \text{where} \quad \frac{1}{\hat{\sigma}_B^2} = \frac{n}{\sigma^2} + \frac{1}{\tau^2} \quad \text{and} \quad \hat{\xi}_B = \hat{\sigma}_B^2\left(\frac{n\bar{r}}{\sigma^2} + \frac{\xi_0}{\tau^2}\right)$$

with c'' some expression not involving ξ. Insert this into the posterior density function and deduce that

$$p(\xi|r_1, \ldots, r_n) = c' e^{-c''} e^{-(\xi - \hat{\xi}_B)^2/(2\hat{\sigma}_B^2)}.$$

But this is a normal density function with variance

$$\hat{\sigma}_B^2 = \left(\frac{n}{\sigma^2} + \frac{1}{\tau^2}\right)^{-1} = \frac{\sigma^2}{n} \times \frac{\tau^2}{\tau^2 + \sigma^2/n}$$

and expectation

$$\hat{\xi}_B = \hat{\sigma}_B^2\left(\frac{n\bar{r}}{\sigma^2} + \frac{\xi_0}{\tau^2}\right) = w\bar{r} + (1 - w)\xi_0 \quad \text{where} \quad w = \frac{\tau^2}{\tau^2 + \sigma^2/n},$$

precisely as stated in (7.24) and (7.23).

7.8 Bibliographical notes

7.8.1 Analysis of error

The study in Section 7.2 is believed to be original and confirmed how little Monte Carlo error means compared with parameter and model uncertainty. A fairly limited number of simulations is enough from the perspective of total error. Mature studies of model and parameter uncertainty have, in finance and actuarial science, been long in coming. Cairns (2000a), who takes a Bayesian view, is certainly worth reading, as is Nietert (2003). In finance, Cont (2006) makes use of other sources of information than merely historical data.

7.8.2 The bootstrap

The bootstrap approach was popularized around 1980. Central, general references are Efron and Tibshirani (1993) and Davison and Hinkley (1997). Examples of published applications in actuarial science are Bacro and Brito (1998) and Brito and Freitas (2006) on modelling extremes (see Section 9.5), England and Verrall

(1999) and Taylor and McGuire (2007) on claims reserving (Section 3.3) and Rempala and Szatzschneider (2004) and Koissi *et al.* (2006) on mortality modelling (Section 15.2).

7.8.3 Bayesian techniques

Bayesian methodology enjoys a long history in actuarial science. Monographs reviewing much important work up to the early 1990s are Nordberg (1989) and Klugman (1992); see also Makov (2001). Rachev *et al.* (2008) is a fairly elementary introduction to Bayesian methods in finance and Congdon (2003) in statistics. Strongly improved computational facilities are doubtlessly the reason for the explosive growth in the published applications of Bayesian methods. Specific contributions in risk theory are Dimakos and Frigessi (2002), Schnieper (2004) and Denuit and Lang (2004) (on premium rates), De Alba (2004, 2006), Gisler (2006) and Goméz-Déniz *et al.* (2007) (different aspects of claim reserving), Migon and Moura (2005) and Deb *et al.* 2006) (health insurance), Czado *et al.*(2005) (mortality projections), Hardy (2002) (equity-linked life insurance) and Harel and Harpaz (2007) (fair value calculations). Among contributions in finance are Bhar *et al.* (2002), Karlis and Lillestöl (2004) and Lee *et al.* (2007). Bayesian methods have also found their way into dynamic modelling of time-varying phenomena, where the main thrust in this book are Chapters 11 and 13. West and Harrison (1997) is a classical monograph from a Bayesian point of view, Bauwens *et al.* (1999) tackles the financial context and for specific applications see (for example) Dimakos and Frigessi (2002) and Ntzoufras *et al.* (2005). Simulation algorithms for Bayesian time-series analysis are advanced material and typically rely on Markov chain or recursive Monte Carlo, which were mentioned briefly in Section 4.8.

7.9 Exercises

Section 7.2

Exercise 7.1 Let $\mathcal{X} \sim \text{Poisson}(J\mu T)$ be the portfolio loss in property insurance if claims are always 1. Consider the fitted version $\hat{\mathcal{X}}$ based on an estimate $\hat{\mu} = n/A$ with n a realization of a Poisson variable with parameter $A\mu$. Then $\hat{\mathcal{X}}|\hat{\mu} \sim \text{Poisson}(J\hat{\mu}T)$ with mean $\hat{\pi} = J\hat{\mu}T$, and $\hat{\pi}$ is approximated by $\hat{\pi}^*_m = (\hat{\mathcal{X}}^*_1 + \cdots + \hat{\mathcal{X}}^*_m)/m$ where $\hat{\mathcal{X}}^*_1, \dots, \hat{\mathcal{X}}^*_m$ are simulations of $\hat{\mathcal{X}}$.

(a) Explain that $E(\hat{\pi}^*_m|\hat{\mu}) = J\hat{\mu}T$ and that $\text{var}(\hat{\pi}^*_m|\hat{\mu}) = J\hat{\mu}T/m$.
(b) Use the double-variance rule from Section 6.3 to deduce that

$$\text{var}(\hat{\pi}^*_m) = \mu(J^2T^2/A + JT/m).$$

(c) Link this result to (7.7), which aggregates estimation and Monte Carlo uncertainty.

Exercise 7.2 Nobody would dream of using Monte Carlo in this example either! Let $\varepsilon_1^*, \dots, \varepsilon_m^*$ be $N(0,1)$ and $\hat{R}_i^* = \hat{\xi} + \hat{\sigma}\varepsilon_i^*$ for $i = 1, \dots, m$ with $\hat{\xi}$ and $\hat{\sigma}$ the usual estimates from n historical returns so that $E(\hat{\xi}) = \xi$, $\mathrm{sd}(\hat{\xi}) = \sigma/\sqrt{n}$ and $E(\hat{\sigma}^2) = \sigma^2$. Let $\pi = \xi$ and $\hat{\pi}_m^* = (\hat{R}_1^* + \cdots + \hat{R}_m^*)/m$.

(a) If $\hat{\xi} = \xi$ is known (a situation arising when Monte Carlo is used to calculate option premia; see Section 3.5), use (7.7) to deduce that $\mathrm{var}(\hat{\pi}_m^*) = \sigma^2/m$ with *no* extra effect due to estimation.
(b) If $\hat{\xi}$ is unknown as well, use the same argument and show that $\mathrm{var}(\hat{\pi}_m^*) = \sigma^2(1/n + 1/m)$.

Exercise 7.3 The remainder term (7.5) does not vanish for percentiles; consult David (1981) for the mathematics. Here is a numerical illustration for the $N(0,1)$-distribution.

(a) Write a program generating m_b batches of m such simulations and compute the Monte Carlo estimate of the upper ϵ-percentile for each batch.
R-*commands*:
```
eps=matrix(rnorm(mb*m),m,mb);
q=apply(eps,2,sort)[m*(1-ϵ),].
```
(b) Run the program when $m_b = 100$, $m = 1000$ and $\epsilon = 0.05$ and compute the mean and standard deviation of the estimates.
R-*commands*:
```
Mean=mean(q); Sd=sd(q).
```
(c) Redo a few times, compare with the exact value 1.6449 and note how the standard deviation dominates the difference between the Monte Carlo mean and the exact mean.

Exercise 7.4 Let N and $\hat{N}$ be true and fitted Poisson variables with parameters $J\mu T = 10$ and $J\hat{\mu}T = 8.6$, respectively.

(a) Plot their density function jointly up to $n = 20$.
R-*commands*:
```
n=0:20; f=dpois(n,10); plot(n,f,ylim=c(0,0.14));
f=dpois(n,8.6); lines(n,f).
```
(b) Estimate the density function of $\hat{N}$ from $m = 1000$ simulations and plot it jointly with the two others.
R-*commands*:
```
N̂=rpois(1000,8.6); lines(density(N̂,from=0,bw=1)).
```
(c) Redo (a) and (b) a few times and describe the pattern you see.

Exercise 7.5 Consider a log-normal loss $Z = e^{\xi+\sigma\varepsilon}$ in property insurance and its fitted analogue $\hat{Z} = e^{\hat{\xi}+\hat{\sigma}\varepsilon}$ where $\varepsilon \sim N(0,1)$.

(a) Plot the density functions of Z and $\hat{Z}$ up to $z = 20$ using $\xi = 1$, $\sigma = 1$, $\hat{\xi} = 0.8$ and $\hat{\sigma} = 0.8$.

R-*commands*:

```
z=0:100/5; f=dlnorm(z,1,1); plot(z,f,ylim=c(0,0.3));
f=dlnorm(z,0.8,0.8); lines(z,f).
```

(b) Generate $m = 1000$ simulations of $\hat{Z}$ and add its estimated density function to the plot in (a).

R-*commands*:

```
Ẑ=rlnorm(m,0.8,0.8); lines(density(Ẑ,from=0)).
```

(c) Redo (a) and (b) a few times, try $m = 10\,000$ and verify that the pattern is that of Exercise 7.4.

Exercise 7.6 Let $R = e^{\xi+\sigma\varepsilon} - 1$ and $\hat{R} = e^{\hat{\xi}+\hat{\sigma}\varepsilon} - 1$ with $\xi = 0.05$, $\sigma = 0.25$, $\hat{\xi} = 0.08$ and $\hat{\sigma} = 0.20$ (annual equity return).

(a) Plot the density functions of R and $\hat{R}$ between -0.6 and 1.2.

R-*commands*:

```
r=-0.6+0:100*1.8/100; z=1+r; f=dlnorm(z,0.05,0.25);
plot(r,f,ylim=c(0,2)); f=dlnorm(z,0.08,0.20);
lines(z,f).
```

(b) Add a density function estimated from $m = 1000$ simulations under $\hat{\xi}$ and $\hat{\sigma}$.

R-*commands*:

```
R̂=rlnorm(m,0.08,0.2); lines(density(R̂)).
```

(c) Redo (a) and (b), and you will find the same pattern as in Exercise 7.5.

Exercise 7.7 The upper percentile of the log-normal $Z = e^{\xi+\sigma\varepsilon}$ is $q_\epsilon = e^{\xi+\sigma\Phi^{-1}(1-\epsilon)}$ with estimate $\hat{q}_\epsilon = e^{\hat{\xi}+\hat{\sigma}\Phi^{-1}(1-\epsilon)}$ and when using Monte Carlo $\hat{q}^*_\epsilon = e^{\hat{\xi}+\hat{\sigma}\varepsilon^*_{(\epsilon m)}}$, where $\varepsilon^*_{(1)} \geq \cdots \geq \varepsilon^*_{(m)}$ are simulations from $N(0, 1)$ in descending order.

(a) Write a program drawing m_b sets of historical data $z_1, \ldots, z_n$ and compute m_b estimates $\hat{\xi}$ and $\hat{\sigma}$ as the mean and standard deviation of their logarithms.

R-*commands*:

```
z=matrix(rlnorm(m_b*n),n,m_b); ξ̂=apply(log(z),2,mean);
σ̂=apply(log(z),2,sd).
```

(b) Add commands which generate m_b =1000 estimates $\hat{q}_\epsilon$ and $\hat{q}^*_\epsilon$ when $\xi = 1$, $\sigma = 1$, $n = 100$, $\epsilon = 0.01$ and $m = 10\,000$.

R-*commands*:

```
q̂_ε=exp(ξ̂+σ̂*qnorm(1-ε)); eps=matrix(rnorm(m*m_b),m,m_b);
per=apply(eps,2,sort)[(1-ε)*m,]; q̂*_ε=exp(ξ̂+σ̂*per).
```

(c) Compute the mean and standard deviation of the estimates in (b) and compare with the exact $q_\epsilon = 27.84$.
R-*commands*:
mean($\hat{q}_\epsilon$); sd($\hat{q}_\epsilon$); mean($\hat{q}_\epsilon^*$); sd($\hat{q}_\epsilon^*$).

Section 7.3

Exercise 7.8 Let $z_1, \dots, z_n$ be historical data from the exponential distribution with density function $f(z) = \xi^{-1}e^{-z/\xi}$ for $z > 0$.

(a) Argue that $\hat{\xi} = (z_1 + \cdots + z_n)/n$ is the moment estimate for ξ.
(b) Show that the log-likelihood function is $\mathcal{L}(\xi) = -n\log(\xi) - \xi^{-1}(z_1 + \cdots + z_n)$ and that it is maximized by the moment estimate.

Exercise 7.9

(a) Program minus the log-likelihood function for the Pareto distribution.
R-*commands*:
With z the data vector use
llminus=function(β,z) {$\hat{\alpha}_\beta$=1/mean(log(1+z/β));
-log($\hat{\alpha}_\beta$/β)+(1+1/$\hat{\alpha}_\beta$)}.
(b) Draw $m_b = 10$ random samples of $n = 10\,000$ Pareto-distributed variables when $\alpha = 4$ and $\beta = 1$, fit each time the model and print the estimates.
R-*commands*:
for (i in 1:m_b) {z=β*(runif(n)**(-1/α)-1);
o=optimize(llminus,c(0.001,1000),z=z); $\hat{\beta}$=o[[1]];
$\hat{\alpha}$=1/mean(log(1+z/$\hat{\beta}$)); print(c($\hat{\alpha}$,$\hat{\beta}$))}.
(c) The estimates were fairly close to the true values, but try $n = 1000$ and $n = 100$.

Exercise 7.10 The Weibull distribution (see Section 2.5) has density function

$$f(z) = (\alpha/\beta)(z/\beta)^{\alpha-1}e^{-(z/\beta)^\alpha}. \quad \text{for } z > 0.$$

(a) Show that the likelihood function given observations $z_1, \dots, z_n$ is

$$\mathcal{L}(\alpha,\beta) = n\log(\alpha) + (\alpha-1)\sum_{i=1}^n \log(z_i) - n\alpha\log(\beta) - \frac{1}{\beta^\alpha}\sum_{i=1}^n z_i^\alpha.$$

(b) Verify that

$$\frac{\partial\mathcal{L}(\alpha,\beta)}{\partial\beta} = -\frac{n\alpha}{\beta} + \frac{\alpha}{\beta^{\alpha+1}}\sum_{i=1}^n z_i^\alpha \qquad \text{which is zero at} \quad \hat{\beta}_\alpha = \left(\frac{1}{n}\sum_{i=1}^n z_i^\alpha\right)^{1/\alpha}.$$

(c) Argue that the likelihood estimate $\hat{\alpha}$ maximizes $\mathcal{L}(\alpha,\hat{\beta}_\alpha)$ with respect to α.

Exercise 7.11

(a) Write a program computing minus the log-likelihood function $-\mathcal{L}(\alpha,\hat{\beta}_\alpha)$ in Exercise 7.10.

R-*commands*:

With `z` as the data vector use `llminus=function(`α`,z)` `{`β_α`= mean(z**`α`)**(1/`α`); -sum(dweibull(z,`α`,`β_α`,log=T))}`.

(b) Simulate $n = 500$ Weibull-distributed observations when $\alpha = 0.6$ and $\beta = 1$ and plot the log-likelihood profile as α varies between $\alpha_1 = 0.1$ and $\alpha_2 = 2.1$.

R-*commands*:

`z=rweibull(n,`α`,`β`); a=`α_1`+0:100*(`α_2`-`α_1`)*0.01; lmin=a;`
`for (i in 1:101)lmin[i]=llminus(a[i],z); plot(a,lmin).`

(c) Compute likelihood estimates of α and β for the Monte Carlo data and compare with the true ones.

R-*commands*:

`o=optimize(llminus,c(0.0001,50));` $\hat{\alpha}$`=o[[1]];`
$\hat{\beta}$`=mean(z**`$\hat{\alpha}$`)**(1/`$\hat{\alpha}$`).`

Exercise 7.12 Test the Weibull model on the Belgian fire losses given in Beirlant *et al.* (1996)[7].

(a) Read the data ($n = 60$ observations) from the file `belgianfire.txt` and print the likelihood profile on the screen.

R-*commands*:

`z=scan(''belgianfire.txt'')` and then as in Exercise 7.11(b).

(b) Fit the Weibull model by maximum likelihood.

R-*commands*:

As in Exercise 7.11(c).

Answers: $\hat{\alpha} = 0.934$ and $\hat{\beta} = 20.26$, not far from an exponential distribution.

(c) Verify that $\hat{\alpha}$ matches the profile in (a) and check the fit through a Q–Q plot.

R-*commands*:

`u=(1:60-0.5)/60; q=qweibull(u,`$\hat{\alpha}$`,`$\hat{\beta}$`); plot(sort(z),q).`

Exercise 7.13

(a) Read the log-returns of the New York equity indexes from file as in Exercise 5.4 and compute their means and volatilities.

R-*commands*:

`x=matrix(scan(''newyork.daily.txt''),byrow=T,ncol=4);`
$\hat{\xi}$`=apply(x,2,mean);` $\hat{\sigma}$`=apply(x,2,sd).`

[7] The money unit is 1000 Belgian francs, comparable with 50 euros today; 20 has been subtracted from all losses to simplify the analysis.

(b) Estimate the kurtosis of the variables though a method similar to that in Exercise 2.9.

R-*commands*:

$\widehat{\texttt{kurt}}$`= apply((t(x)-`$\hat{\xi}$`)**4,1,mean)/`$\hat{\sigma}$`**4-3.`

Exercise 7.14 Consider the t-family of distributions $X = \xi + (\xi_\sigma/\sqrt{G})\varepsilon$ where $G \sim \text{Gamma}(\alpha)$, $\varepsilon \sim N(0,1)$ and G and ε independent. There are three parameters ξ, ξ_σ and α, the last two positive.

(a) Formulate a moment-type estimation method for α using sample kurtosis and the fact that $\text{kurt}(X) = 3/(\alpha - 2)$.

(b) Why is the method unusable if $\alpha \le 2$?

Exercise 7.15 The t-model in Exercise 7.14 can be written $X = \xi + \xi_\sigma Y$ where $Y = \varepsilon/\sqrt{G}$ is the standard t-distribution with density function $g(y)$ available in software like R[8].

(a) Argue that the density function of X is $f(x) = \xi_\sigma^{-1} g\{(x-\xi)/\xi_\sigma\}$ and write a program for minus the log-likelihood function when data $x_1, \dots, x_n$ are given.

R-*commands*:

With data vector `x` and $\theta = (\xi, \log(\xi_\sigma), \alpha)$ use

`llminus=function(`θ`,x)`

`length(x)*`θ`[2]-sum(dt((x-`θ`[1])/exp(`θ`[2]),df=2*`θ`[3],log=T)).`

(b) Write a program computing the maximum likelihood estimates.

R-*commands*:

θ`=c(mean(x),log(sd(x)),1); o=optim(`θ`,llminus,x=x);`

$\hat{\xi}$`=o$par[1];` $\hat{\xi}_\sigma$`=exp(o$par[2]);` $\hat{\alpha}$`=o$par[3].`

(c) Fit the model to the four New York indexes in Exercise 7.13.

(d) Compute $\hat{\xi}_\sigma\sqrt{\hat{\alpha}/(\hat{\alpha}-1)}$ for all variables and argue that the results should match the sample volatilities in Exercise 7.13. [*Hint*: $\text{sd}(X) = \xi_\sigma\sqrt{\alpha/(\alpha-1)}$; see Section 2.4.]

Exercise 7.16

(a) Write a program simulating m_b replications of the Gaussian autoregression $X_k = aX_{k-1} + \sigma\varepsilon_k$ for $k = 1, \dots, n$ where $X_0 \sim N(0, \sigma/\sqrt{1-a^2})$.

R-*commands*:

`X=matrix(0,n+1,`m_b`); X[1,]=rnorm(`m_b`)*`σ`/sqrt(1-a**2);`

`for (k in 1:n+1) X[k,]=a*X[k-1,]+`σ`*rnorm(`m_b`).`

[8] Its expression is $g(y) = c\{1 + y^2/(2\alpha)\}^{-(\alpha+1/2)}$ with $c = \Gamma(\alpha+1/2)/(\Gamma(\alpha)\sqrt{2\pi\alpha})$.

(b) Run the program when $m_b = 100$, $n = 25$, $a = 0.7$ and $\sigma = 0.015$, apply moment estimation to each series and compute the mean and standard deviation of the estimates.

R-*commands*:

$\hat{a}$=diag(cor(X[1:n+1,],X[1:n,]));
$\hat{\sigma}$=apply(X,2,sd)*sqrt(1-$\hat{a}$**2);
mean($\hat{a}$); sd($\hat{a}$); mean($\hat{\sigma}$); sd($\hat{\sigma}$).

(c) Redo when $n = 100$ and compare the estimation accuracy with that in (b).

Exercise 7.17

(a) Redo Exercise 7.16(b) and (c) with likelihood instead of moment estimation.

R-*commands*:

With X as in Exercise 7.16 use $\hat{a}$=rep(0,m_b);
$\hat{\sigma}$=$\hat{a}$; for (i in 1:m_b) {o=ar.mle(X[,i],aic=F,order=1);
$\hat{a}$[i]=o[[2]]; $\hat{\sigma}$[i]=sqrt(o[[3]])} and continue as in Exercise 7.16.

(b) Have you been able to see any difference in estimation accuracy from that in Exercise 7.16?

Section 7.4

Exercise 7.18 Let $\hat{\mu} = n/A$ be an estimate of μ with n a realization of Poisson($A\mu$).

(a) Write a program generating m_b bootstrap estimates of $\hat{\mu}$.

R-*commands*:

$\hat{\mu}^\star$=rpois(m_b,A*$\hat{\mu}$)/A.

(b) Run the program when $n = 60$, $A = 1280$ and $m_b = 1000$ and compute the mean and standard deviation of the bootstrap sample.

R-*commands*:

Mean=mean($\hat{\mu}^\star$); Sd=sd($\hat{\mu}^\star$).

(c) What do these computations tell you? Compare with $\sqrt{\hat{\mu}/A}$, the standard method of evaluating sd($\hat{\mu}$).

Exercise 7.19 Consider exponentially distributed insurance claims Z with mean ξ estimated as the average $\hat{\xi}$ of n historical losses $z_1, \dots, z_n$.

(a) Write a program generating m_b bootstrap estimates of $\hat{\xi}$.

R-*commands*:

$\hat{Z}^\star$=matrix(rexp(m_b*n)*$\hat{\xi}$,n,m_b); $\hat{\xi}^\star$=apply($\hat{Z}^\star$,2,mean).

(b) Run the program with $m_b = 1000$ for the Belgian fire data in Exercise 7.12 for which $n = 60$ and $\hat{\xi} = 20.89$ and compute the bootstrap mean and standard deviation.

R-*commands*:

Mean=mean($\hat{\xi}^\star$); Sd=sd($\hat{\xi}^\star$).

(c) What do the computations in (b) tell you?

Exercise 7.20 Suppose Z in the preceding exercise has been reinsured with reinsurance compensation $Z^{\text{re}} = 0$ if $Z < a$, $Z^{\text{re}} = Z - a$ if $a \leq Z \leq a + b$ and $Z^{\text{re}} = b$ if $Z > a + b$. The mean of Z^{re} is then $\xi^{\text{re}} = \xi e^{-a/\xi}(1 - e^{-b/\xi})$ with estimate $\hat{\xi}^{\text{re}} = \hat{\xi} e^{-a/\hat{\xi}}(1 - e^{-b/\hat{\xi}})$.

(a) Write a program generating m_b bootstrap estimates of $\hat{\xi}^{\text{re}}$.

R-*commands*:

With $\hat{\xi}^\star$ as in Exercise 7.19 use

$\hat{\xi}^{\text{re}\star}$=$\hat{\xi}^\star$*exp(-a/$\hat{\xi}^\star$)*(1-exp(-b/$\hat{\xi}^\star$)).

(b) Run the program when $a = 30$ and $b = 60$ with other conditions as in Exercise 7.19 (which yields $\hat{\xi}^{\text{re}} = 4.69$) and compute the mean and standard deviation of the bootstrap sample.

R-*commands*:

Mean=mean($\hat{\xi}^{\text{re}\star}$); Sd=sd($\hat{\xi}^{\text{re}\star}$).

(c) Evaluate the error in the estimate $\hat{\xi}^{\text{re}} = 4.69$.

Exercise 7.21 An alternative method is to convert historical losses $z_1, \dots, z_n$ to historical *reinsurance* losses $z_1^{\text{re}}, \dots, z_n^{\text{re}}$ and use their average as $\hat{\xi}^{\text{re}}$.

(a) Download the data from `belgianfire.txt`, apply this method when $a = 30$ and $b = 60$ and estimate sd($\hat{\xi}^{\text{re}}$).

R-*commands*:

z=scan(''belgianfire.txt''); z^{re}=pmin(pmax(z-a,0),b);

$\hat{\xi}^{\text{re}}$=mean(z^{re}); Sd=sd(z^{re})/sqrt(length(z^{re})).

(b) Sample from $z_1^{\text{re}}, \dots, z_n^{\text{re}}$ with replacement using $m_b = 1000$ and re-evaluate sd($\hat{\xi}^{\text{re}}$).

R-*commands*:

$\hat{Z}^\star$=matrix(sample(z^{re},m_b*n,replace=T),n,m_b);

$\hat{\xi}^{\text{re}\star}$=apply($\hat{Z}^\star$,2,mean); Sd=sd($\hat{\xi}^{\text{re}\star}$).

(c) Compare the standard deviations in (a) and (b) with those in Exercise 7.20 and comment.

Exercise 7.22 Let $\pi^{\text{re}} = JT\mu\xi^{\text{re}}$ be the pure reinsurance premium under a Poisson/exponential portfolio as in Exercises 7.18 and 7.20.

(a) Write a program computing $\hat{\pi}^{\text{re}}$ from estimates $\hat{\mu}$ and $\hat{\xi}$ and also the mean and standard deviation of a bootstrap sample of $\hat{\pi}^{\text{re}}$.

R-*commands*:

With $\hat{\mu}$ and $\hat{\mu}^\star$ as in Exercise 7.18 and $\hat{\xi}^{\text{re}}$ and $\hat{\xi}^{\text{re}\star}$ as in Exercise 7.20, use

```
π̂re=JT*μ̂*ξ̂re; π̂re★=JT*μ̂★*ξ̂re★;
Mean=mean(π̂re★); Sd=sd(π̂re★).
```

(b) Run the program when $JT = 100$ with other conditions as in Exercises 7.18 and 7.20 and estimate the pure reinsurance premium with uncertainty.

Exercise 7.23 Let $\hat{\mu}$ and $\hat{\xi}$ be independent estimates of claim intensity μ and average loss per claim ξ so that $\hat{\pi} = \hat{\mu}T\hat{\xi}$ is an estimate of the pure premium $\pi = \mu T\xi$. Suppose $\hat{\mu}$ and $\hat{\xi}$ are unbiased with standard deviation $\sigma_{\hat{\mu}}$ and $\sigma_{\hat{\xi}}$.

(a) Show that $\hat{\pi}$ is unbiased with standard deviation $\sigma_{\hat{\pi}} = T\sqrt{\sigma_{\hat{\mu}}^2\sigma_{\hat{\xi}}^2 + \mu^2\sigma_{\hat{\xi}}^2 + \xi^2\sigma_{\hat{\mu}}^2}$. [*Hint*: Utilize $E(\hat{\pi}^2) = E(\hat{\mu}^2)T^2E(\hat{\xi}^2)$ with $E(\hat{\mu}^2) = \mu^2 + \sigma_{\hat{\mu}}^2$ and $E(\hat{\xi}^2) = \xi^2 + \sigma_{\hat{\xi}}^2$.]

(b) Compare the delta approximation (7.19) with this result and judge the importance of the term that is missing there.

Exercise 7.24 Consider log-normal claims $Z = e^{\theta+\sigma\varepsilon}$ with the sample mean and standard deviation of the logarithm of historical losses $z_1, \dots, z_n$ as estimates $\hat{\theta}$ and $\hat{\sigma}$.

(a) Write a program generating m_b bootstrap estimates of $\hat{\theta}$ and $\hat{\sigma}$ by sampling from the fitted log-normal.

R-*commands*:

```
Ẑ★=matrix(rlnorm(n*mb,θ̂,σ̂),n,mb);
θ̂★=apply(log(Ẑ★),2,mean);
σ̂★=apply(log(Ẑ★),2,sd).
```

(b) Run the program when $\hat{\theta} = 2.39$, $\hat{\sigma} = 1.39$, $n = 60$ and $m_b = 1000$ and use the bootstrap to evaluate the uncertainty of the estimated upper ϵ-percentile $\hat{q} = e^{\hat{\theta}+\hat{\sigma}\Phi^{-1}(1-\epsilon)}$ when $\epsilon = 0.01$.

R-*commands*:

```
qnorm=qnorm(1-ϵ); q̂=exp(θ̂+σ̂*qnorm); q̂★=exp(θ̂★+σ̂★*qnorm);
Mean=mean(q̂★); Sd=sd(q̂★).
```

Exercise 7.25 Consider an historical interest rate series $r_1, \dots, r_n$ with $\hat{\xi}$, $\hat{\sigma}$, $\hat{a}$ estimates of ξ, σ, a under the Vasiček model.

(a) Write a program generating m_b bootstrap series $r_1^\star, \dots, r_n^\star$ with $r_1^\star$ coming from the stationary distribution.

R-*commands*:

$\texttt{X=matrix(0,}n\texttt{,}m_b\texttt{); X[1,]=rnorm(}m_b\texttt{)*}\hat{\sigma}\texttt{/sqrt(1-}\hat{a}\texttt{**2);}$

$\texttt{for (k in 2:n) X[k,]=}\hat{a}\texttt{*X[k-1,]+}\hat{\sigma}\texttt{*rnorm(}m_b\texttt{); }r^\star\texttt{=X+}\hat{\xi}.$

(b) Compute bootstrap estimates of ξ, a and σ using the estimation method in Exercises 5.29 and 7.16.

R-*commands*:

$\hat{\xi}^\star\texttt{=apply(}r^\star\texttt{,2,mean); }\hat{a}^\star\texttt{=diag(cor(}r^\star\texttt{[2:n,],}r^\star\texttt{[2:n-1,]));}$

$\hat{\sigma}^\star\texttt{=apply(}r^\star\texttt{,2,sd)*sqrt(1-}\hat{a}^\star\texttt{**2).}$

(c) Run the program when $m_b = 1000$ and $\hat{\xi} = 0.062$, $\hat{\sigma} = 0.018$, $\hat{a} = 0.71$ and $n = 19$ as in Exercise 5.29, compute bootstrap means and standard deviations and evaluate the error in $(\hat{\xi}, \hat{\sigma}, \hat{a})$.

R-*commands*:

$\texttt{Mean=mean(}\xi^\star\texttt{); Sd=sd(}\xi^\star\texttt{)}$ and similar for $\sigma^\star$ and $a^\star$.

Exercise 7.26 Let $q_\epsilon = e^{K\xi+\sqrt{K}\sigma\phi_\epsilon} - 1$ be the lower ϵ-percentile for a log-normal return $R_{0:K}$ with estimate $\hat{q}_\epsilon = e^{K\hat{\xi}+\sqrt{K}\hat{\sigma}\phi_\epsilon} - 1$ where $\hat{\xi}$ and $\hat{\sigma}$ are sample mean and standard deviation of historical log-returns $x_1, \dots, x_n$.

(a) Write a program drawing m_b bootstrap series of $x_1, \dots, x_n$ using sampling with replacement.

R-*commands*:

With data vector `x` use `n=length(x);`

$\hat{x}^\star\texttt{=matrix(sample(x,}m_b\texttt{*n,replace=T),n,}m_b\texttt{).}$

(b) Implement a bootstrap analysis of $\hat{q}_\epsilon$.

R-*commands*:

$\hat{\xi}^\star\texttt{=apply(}\hat{x}^\star\texttt{,2,mean); }\hat{\sigma}^\star\texttt{=apply(}\hat{x}^\star\texttt{,2,sd);}$

$\hat{q}_\epsilon^\star\texttt{=exp(K*}\hat{\xi}^\star\texttt{+}\phi_\epsilon\texttt{*sqrt(K)*}\hat{\sigma}^\star\texttt{)-1;}$

$\texttt{Mean=mean(}\hat{\xi}^\star\texttt{); Sd=sd(}\hat{\sigma}^\star\texttt{).}$

(c) Run the program for the New York data in Exercise 7.13 when $m_b = 1000$, $\phi_\epsilon = -2.326$ and $K = 250$ (1 year) and report on the uncertainty.

R-*commands*:

```
x=matrix(scan(‘‘newyork.daily.txt’’),byrow=T,ncol=4)
```

and apply (a) and (b) to each of `x[,1],...,x[,4]`.

Exercise 7.27

(a) Compute the percentile $\hat{q}_\epsilon$ in Exercise 7.26 for each of the four New York indexes and compare with their bootstrap means.

R-*commands*:

With `x` as in Exercise 7.26(c) use $\hat{\xi}\texttt{=apply(x,2,mean);}$

$\hat{\sigma}\texttt{=apply(x,2,sd); }\hat{q}\texttt{=exp(K*}\hat{\xi}\texttt{+}\phi_\epsilon\texttt{*sqrt(K)*}\hat{\sigma}\texttt{)-1.}$

(b) Find out how much the uncertainty in Exercise 7.26(c) goes down if the means ξ had been known.

R-*commands*:

As in Exercise 7.26(b) with $\hat{\xi}$ in place of $\hat{\xi}^\star$.

Section 7.5

Exercise 7.28 Let $\mathcal{X} = Z_1 + \cdots + Z_\mathcal{N}$ with $\mathcal{N} \sim \text{Poisson}(J\mu T)$ and $Z_1, Z_2 \ldots$ exponential with mean ξ and let q_ϵ be the upper ϵ-percentile of $\mathcal{X}$.

(a) With bootstrap simulations of $\hat{\mu}$ and $\hat{\xi}$ available, write a program bootstrapping the estimate $\hat{q}_\epsilon^* = \hat{\mathcal{X}}^*_{(m\epsilon)}$ where $\hat{\mathcal{X}}^*_{(1)} \geq \cdots \geq \hat{\mathcal{X}}^*_{(m)}$ are ordered simulations under $(\hat{\mu}, \hat{\xi})$.

R-*commands*:

Take $\hat{\mu}^\star$, $\hat{\xi}^\star$ from Exercises 7.18, 7.19 and use

```
m1=m*mb; X=1:m1*0; N=rpois(m1,JT*μ̂★);
ind=rep(1:mb,m); for (i in 1:m1){Z=rexp(N[i])*ξ̂★[ind[i]];
X[i]=sum(Z)}; X=matrix(X,byrow=T,m);
q̂ε*★=apply(X,2,sort)[m*(1-ε),].
```

(b) Run the program when $m_b = 100$, $m = 10\,000$, $JT = 100$ and $\epsilon = 0.01$ and compute the mean and standard deviation of the bootstrap sample.

R-*commands*:

```
Mean=mean(q̂ε*★); Sd=sd(q̂ε*★).
```

(c) Compute the estimate $\hat{q}_\epsilon^*$ and report on its uncertainty and the scope for a bias correction.

R-*commands*:

Run the program in (a) with $m_b = 1$ and $\hat{\mu} = 0.0469$ and $\hat{\xi} = 20.89$ in place of $\hat{\mu}^\star$ and $\hat{\xi}^\star$.

Exercise 7.29 There is in property insurance often an upper limit b on individual payments so that $\mathcal{X}$ in Exercise 7.28 becomes $\mathcal{X} = \min(Z_1, b) + \cdots + \min(Z_\mathcal{N}, b)$.

(a) Modify the program in Exercise 7.28(a) to cover this situation.

R-*commands*:

The statement defining `X[i]` becomes

`if (N[i]>0) X[i]=sum(pmin(Z,b))` with the rest as before.

(b) Run the program under the conditions in Exercise 7.28 when $b = 30$ and note how the bootstrap mean and standard deviation have changed.

(c) Also compute $\hat{q}_\epsilon^*$ now and report on its uncertainty.

R-*commands*:

As explained in Exercise 7.28(c).

Exercise 7.30 Change the model for Z in the preceding exercises to the log-normal $Z = e^{\theta+\sigma\varepsilon}$ where θ and σ are estimated from historical data $z_1, \dots, z_n$ as in Exercise 7.24.

(a) Revise the program in Exercise 7.28 accordingly.

R-*commands*:

With $\hat{\mu}^\star$, $\hat{\theta}^\star$ and $\hat{\sigma}^\star$ the bootstrap vectors in Exercises 7.18 and 7.24 use the program in Exercise 7.28(a) with the statement for Z replaced by
`Z=rlnorm(N[i],`$\hat{\theta}^\star$`[ind[i]],`$\hat{\sigma}^\star$`[ind[i]])`.

(b) Repeat Exercise 7.28(b) with this new model for Z.

(c) Also repeat Exercise 7.28(c) when $\hat{\theta} = 2.39$ and $\hat{\sigma} = 1.39$ are the estimates and judge the uncertainty in $\hat{q}^*_\epsilon$.

R-*commands*:

Run the program in (a) with $m_b = 1$ when $\hat{\theta} = 2.39$ and $\hat{\sigma} = 1.39$ replace $\hat{\theta}^\star$ and $\hat{\sigma}^\star$.

Exercise 7.31

(a) Redo (b) and (c) of the preceding exercise a few times and note the huge Monte Carlo uncertainty due to the extremely volatile distribution of Z.

(b) Introduce an upper limit b on each claim Z as in Exercise 7.29 and modify the program in Exercise 7.30(a) accordingly.

R-*commands*:

The program in Exercise 7.28(a) with `X[i]` computed by
`if (N[i]>0){Z=rlnorm(N[i],`$\hat{\theta}^\star$`[ind[i]],`$\hat{\sigma}^\star$`[ind[i]]);`
`X[i]=sum(pmin(Z,b))}`.

(c) Run the program in (b) with $b = 50$ and note how much the uncertainty is reduced.

Exercise 7.32 Let $\hat{R}_{0:K} = (1 + \hat{r}_1)\cdots(1 + \hat{r}_K) - 1$ where $\hat{r}_0 = r_0$ and $\hat{r}_1, \dots, \hat{r}_K$ follow the Vasiček model with estimates $(\hat{\xi}, \hat{\sigma}, \hat{a})$ replacing the true (ξ, σ, a).

(a) Write a program generating m simulations of $\hat{R}_{0:K}$ for each bootstrap simulation in Exercise 7.25.

R-*commands*:

With $\hat{\xi}^\star$, $\hat{\sigma}^\star$, $\hat{a}^\star$ from Exercise 7.25(b) use
m_b`=length(`$\hat{\xi}^\star$`);` $\hat{R}_K$`=matrix(1,`m_b`,m); X=`$\hat{R}_K$`*(`r_0`-`$\hat{\xi}^\star$`);`
`for (k in 1:K){eps=matrix(rnorm(`m_b`*m),`m_b`,m);`
`X=`$\hat{a}^\star$`*X+`$\hat{\sigma}^\star$`*eps;` $\hat{R}_K$`=`$\hat{R}_K$`*(1+`$\hat{\xi}^\star$`+X)};` $\hat{R}_K$`=t(`$\hat{R}_K$`)-1`.

(b) Run the program when $m = 10\,000$, $K = 5$ and $r_0 = 0.03$ with input from Exercise 7.25(b).

(c) Compute the bootstrap mean and standard deviation of $\hat{\xi}_K = E(\hat{R}_K)$.

R-*commands*:

$\hat{\xi}^\star_K$`=apply(`$\hat{R}_K$`,2,mean); Mean=mean(`$\hat{\xi}^\star_K$`); Sd=sd(`$\hat{\xi}^\star_K$`).`

(d) Explain what these computations tell us and compare with the ordinary estimate $\hat{\xi}_K$.

R-*commands*:

To compute $\hat{\xi}_K$ replace $(\hat{\xi}^\star, \hat{\sigma}^\star, \hat{a}^\star)$ with $(\hat{\xi}, \hat{\sigma}, \hat{a})$ in (a).

Exercise 7.33

(a) Redo Exercise 7.32(c) with $\hat{\sigma}_K = \text{sd}(\hat{R}_K)$ instead of $\hat{\xi}_K$.

R-*commands*:

With $\hat{R}_K$ as in Exercise 7.32 use

$\hat{\sigma}^\star_K$`=apply(`$\hat{R}_K$`,2,sd); Mean=mean(`$\hat{\sigma}^\star_K$`); Sd=sd(`$\hat{\sigma}^\star_K$`).`

(b) Compute $\hat{\sigma}_K$ and report on its uncertainty.

R-*commands*:

Similar to Exercise 7.32(d).

Exercise 7.34

(a) Again redo Exercise 7.32(c), but now for the lower ϵ-percentile $q_{\epsilon K}$ when $\epsilon = 0.01$.

R-*commands*:

Take $\hat{R}_K$ from Exercise 7.32 and use

$\hat{q}^\star_{\epsilon K}$`=apply(`$\hat{R}_K$`,2,sort)[m*`$\epsilon$`,]; Mean=mean(`$\hat{q}^\star_{\epsilon K}$`); Sd=sd(`$\hat{q}^\star_{\epsilon K}$`).`

(b) Compute the ordinary estimate $\hat{q}_{\epsilon K}$ and judge its uncertainty.

R-*commands*:

See Exercise 7.32(d).

(c) Estimate/plot the density function of $\hat{q}_{\epsilon K}$.

R-*commands*:

`plot(density(`$\hat{q}^\star_{\epsilon K}$`,bw=0.03)).`

Section 7.6

Exercise 7.35 Consider a Bayesian Poisson model $f(n|\mu) = (A\mu)^n/n!\,e^{-A\mu}$ with Gamma prior $p(\mu) = (\alpha/\xi)^\alpha \mu^{\alpha-1} e^{-\mu\alpha/\xi}/\Gamma(\alpha)$.

(a) With c a normalization constant show that the posterior density function is

$$p(\mu|n) = c\mu^{\alpha+n-1} e^{-(\alpha+n)\mu/\hat{\mu}_B} \quad \text{with} \quad \hat{\mu}_B = \xi \frac{\alpha + n}{\alpha + A\xi}.$$

(b) Identify this as a Gamma distribution and argue that $E(\mu|n) = \hat{\mu}_B$ and that $\mathrm{sd}(\mu|n) = \hat{\mu}_B/\sqrt{\alpha + n}$.
(c) Explain that the prior becomes non-informative as $\alpha \to 0$ and determine the posterior mean and standard deviation in the limit.
(d) What happens as $\alpha \to \infty$? Interpret the limiting expressions of the posterior mean and standard deviation now.

Exercise 7.36 Apply the Bayesian setup of the preceding exercise to the Norwegian natural disaster data for which $A = 20$ and $n = 21$.

(a) Let $\xi = 0.5$ and compute the Bayes' estimate $\hat{\mu}_B = E(\mu|n)$ when $\alpha = 0, 1, 10$ and 100.

R-*commands*:

```
α=c(0,1,10,100); μ̂B=ξ*(α+n)/(α+A*ξ).
```

(b) Redo when $A = 2100$ and $n = 2100$ are 100 times larger and comment on the behaviour of the estimate.

Exercise 7.37

(a) Write a program generating m drawings of μ under the posterior model in Exercise 7.35.

R-*commands*:

```
μ̂B=ξ*(α+n)/(α+A*ξ); μ⋆=μ̂B*rgamma(m,α+n)/(α+n).
```

(b) Run the program when $m = 10\,000$, $\xi = 0.06$, $\alpha = 0$, $n = 60$ and $A = 1280$, plot the posterior density function of μ and note how it fluctuates around $\hat{\mu}_B$.

R-*commands*:

```
plot(density(μ⋆)).
```

(c) Redo (b) when $\alpha = 100$ and explain why the results change.

Exercise 7.38 Consider the Bayesian estimate (7.23) for the normal mean which is $\hat{\xi}_B = w\bar{r} + (1 - w)\xi_0$ where $w = \tau^2/(\tau^2 + \sigma^2/n)$.

(a) Argue that $w \to 1$ as $\tau \to \infty$ and also as $n \to \infty$.
(b) Also show that $w \to 0$ when $\tau \to 0$ and when $n \to 0$.
(c) Interpret these four results. What do they tell us about the Bayesian machinery?

Exercise 7.39 Suppose $\bar{r} = 0.05$, $n = 20$, $\sigma = 0.25$ and $\tau = 0.0025$ in the preceding exercise. Use (7.24) to compute the accuracy gained by using a Bayesian estimate instead of the ordinary mean.

Exercise 7.40 Let α be a positive parameter with prior density function $p_1(x)$ and suppose $\gamma = 1/\alpha$.

(a) Show that $\Pr(\gamma \leq x) = \Pr(\alpha \leq 1/x)$ so that the prior density function of γ becomes $p_2(x) = x^{-2}p_1(x^{-1})$.
(b) Argue that we can't have non-informative priors for both α and γ at the same time.

Exercise 7.41 Let $Z = e^{\theta+\sigma\varepsilon}$ with θ and σ parameters and $\varepsilon \sim N(0,1)$ and let $\mathbf{z} = (z_1, \ldots, z_n)$ be historical data with $\hat{\theta}$ and $\hat{\sigma}$ the sample mean and standard deviation of $\log(z_1), \ldots, \log(z_n)$.

(a) If θ and σ have independent, non-informative priors, show that

$$p(\sigma \mid \mathbf{z}) = (c/\sigma^{n-1})e^{-(n-1)\hat{\sigma}^2/(2\sigma^2)} \quad \text{and} \quad \theta \mid \sigma, \mathbf{z} \sim N(\hat{\theta}, \sigma/\sqrt{n}).$$

[*Hint*: Argue that the posterior of (θ, σ) is

$$c_1(\mathbf{z})e^{-\{(\log(z_1)-\theta)^2+\cdots+(\log(z_n)-\theta)^2\}/(2\sigma^2)}/\sigma^n$$

where the exponent is $-\{n(\hat{\theta}-\theta)^2 + (n-1)\hat{\sigma}^2\}/(2\sigma^2)$ and where $c_1(\mathbf{z})$ doesn't depend on θ and σ.]

(b) If the prior for θ is $N(\theta_0, \tau)$, use results in the text to argue that $\theta \mid \sigma, \mathbf{z}$ is still normal, now with parameters $E(\theta \mid \sigma, \mathbf{z}) = w\hat{\theta} + (1-w)\theta_0$ and $\text{sd}(\theta \mid \sigma, \mathbf{z}) = \sigma\sqrt{w/n}$ where $w = \tau^2/(\tau^2 + \sigma^2/n)$.

Exercise 7.42

(a) Write a program drawing σ in Exercise 7.41(a) from its posterior distribution using the table method.

R-*commands*:

```
s=1:M*b/M; f=exp(-(n-1)*(log(s)+σ̂**2/(2*s**2)));
p=f/sum(f); σ⋆=sample(s,m,replace=T,p).
```

(b) Generate $m = 10\,000$ posterior samples of σ when $n = 60$ and $\hat{\sigma} = 1.39$ using $b = 3$ and $M = 100$, estimate/plot the density function and compute the posterior mean and standard deviation.

R-*commands*:

```
plot(density(σ⋆,bw=0.03)); Mean=mean(σ⋆); Sd=sd(σ⋆).
```

(c) Redo (b) when $M = 50$ and check how much the results change.

Exercise 7.43

(a) Write a program generating posterior simulations of θ under the model in Exercise 7.41(b) when the posterior of σ is as in Exercise 7.41(a).

R-*commands*:

Use the program in Exercise 7.42(a) and add `w=τ**2/(τ**2+σ⋆**2/n);`
`θ⋆=wθ̂+(1-w)*θ0+rnorm(m)*σ⋆*sqrt(w/n).`

(b) Run the program when $\hat{\theta} = 2.39$, $\theta_0 = 1$ and $\tau = 1000$ with the rest of the conditions as in Exercise 7.42(b), estimate/plot the posterior density function of θ and compute the mean and standard deviation.

R-*commands*:

```
plot(density(θ*)); Mean=mean(θ*); Sd=sd(θ*).
```

(c) Redo (b) when $\tau = 0.1$ and explain why the results change.

Exercise 7.44 Let $\mathcal{N} \sim \text{Poisson}(J\mu T)$ and $Z = e^{\theta+\sigma\varepsilon}$ be log-normal and introduce for μ and (θ, σ) the posterior models in Exercises 7.35 and 7.43(a). Consider $\mathcal{X} = Z_1 + \cdots + Z_{\mathcal{N}}$ with $Z_1, Z_2, \dots$ independent realizations of Z.

(a) Recall (7.22) and argue that posterior samples of $\mathcal{X}$ are generated by

$$\mu^\star \sim p(\mu \mid n), \quad (\theta^\star, \sigma^\star) \sim p(\theta, \sigma \mid z_1, \dots, z_n) \quad \text{and} \quad \mathcal{X}^\star \sim p(x \mid \mu^\star, \theta^\star, \sigma^\star)$$

where $p(x \mid \mu, \theta, \sigma)$ is the density function of $\mathcal{X}$ (a complicated one!).

(b) Implement a program drawing posterior samples of $\mathcal{X}$ with posterior samples of μ and (θ, σ) taken from earlier exercises.

R-*commands*:

Take $\mu^\star$, $\sigma^\star$ and $\theta^\star$ from Exercises 7.37, 7.42 and 7.43 and use

```
X=array(0,m); N=rpois(m,JT*μ*);
for (i in 1:m) {Z=rlnorm(N[i],θ*[i],σ*[i]); X[i]=sum(Z)}.
```

(c) Draw $m = 10\,000$ posterior samples of $\mathcal{X}$ under the assumptions in Exercises 7.37, 7.42 and 7.43 when $JT = 100$, compute the 99% reserve and plot the density function.

R-*commands*:

```
qε=sort(X)[0.99*m]; plot(density(X)).
```

PART II

GENERAL INSURANCE

8

Modelling claim frequency

8.1 Introduction

Actuarial modelling in general insurance is usually broken down on claim size (next chapter) and claim frequency (treated here). Section 3.2 introduced the Poisson distribution as a model for claim numbers. The parameter was $\lambda = \mu T$ (for single policies) and $\lambda = J\mu T$ (for portfolios) where J was the number of policies, μ the claim intensity and T the time of exposure. Most models for claim numbers are related to the Poisson distribution in some way, and this line has strong theoretical support through the Poisson point process in Section 8.2.

The intensity μ is a vehicle for model extensions. One viewpoint with a long tradition in actuarial science is to regard it as random, either drawn independently for each customer or once as a common parameter for all. Models of that kind were initiated in Section 6.3, and there will be more below. Then there are situations where variations in μ are linked to explanatory factors, such as young drivers being more risky than older ones or earthquakes or hurricanes be more common in certain parts of the world than in others. Risk may also be growing systematically over time or be influenced by the season of the year, as in Figure 8.2 later. Explanatory variables are best treated through **Poisson regression**, introduced in Section 8.4.

8.2 The world of Poisson

8.2.1 Introduction

The world of Poisson is the world of the accidental where incidents, though rare, do occur and independently of each other. Insurance processes are much like that, which suggests they can be lifted into a Poisson framework. This is what this section is about. The world we encounter is an orderly one where the Poisson distribution pops up under a wide range of circumstances. It *is* of interest to move beyond this (see Section 8.3), and yet most models for claim numbers (and all in this book) start with Poisson.

8.2.2 An elementary look

What is rare can be described mathematically by cutting a given period of time T into K small pieces of equal length $h = T/K$ as in Figure 8.1. On short intervals the chance of more than one incident is remote. If that possibility is ruled out (relaxed below), the number of events per interval is either zero or one, say I_k on the kth, and the count for the entire period is

$$N = I_1 + \cdots + I_K.$$

If $p = \Pr(I_k = 1)$ is equal for all k and events are independent, this is an ordinary Bernoulli series (about the first thing you learn in probability courses), and N becomes **binomially** distributed with density function

$$\Pr(N = n) = \frac{K!}{n!(K-n)!}p^n(1-p)^{K-n}, \quad \text{for} \quad n = 0, 1, \ldots, K.$$

Surely the probability p is proportional to h? If so, $p = \mu h$ with μ an intensity which applies per time unit. Much of this section is concerned with its interpretation. Our model is going to be the distribution of N as $K \to \infty$ and derived by inserting $p = \mu h = \mu T/K$ into the binomial density function. This yields

$$\Pr(N = n) = B_1 \cdot B_2 \cdot B_3 \cdot B_4$$

where

$$B_1 = \frac{(\mu T)^n}{n!}, \qquad B_2 = \frac{K(K-1)\cdots(K-n+1)}{K^n} \longrightarrow 1,$$

$$B_3 = (1-\mu T/K)^K \longrightarrow e^{-\mu T}, \qquad B_4 = \frac{1}{(1-\mu T/K)^n} \longrightarrow 1.$$

Calculate the product of $B_1, \ldots, B_4$ to convince yourself that it equals $\Pr(N = n)$. The limits for B_2, B_3 and B_4 apply as $K \to \infty$, and when they are multiplied together and with B_1, it emerges that

$$\Pr(N = n) \longrightarrow \frac{(\mu T)^n}{n!}e^{-\mu T} \quad \text{as } K \to \infty.$$

In the limit, N is Poisson distributed with parameter $\lambda = \mu T$.

8.2.3 Extending the argument

The limiting construction above was used in Section 5.7, where an economic variable was followed over a finer and finer mesh of partition points $t_k = kh$ and will

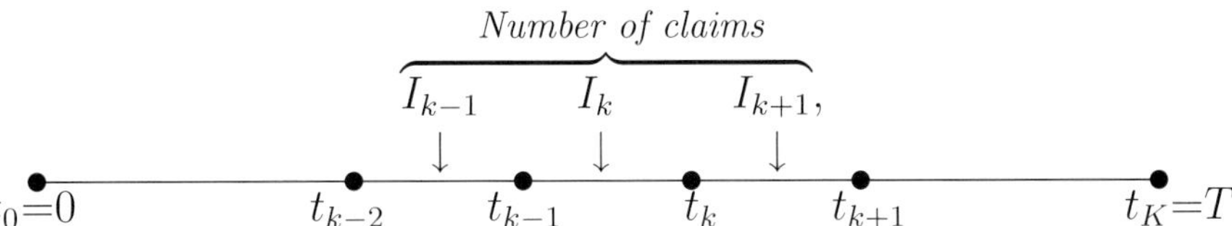

Figure 8.1 The Poisson point process in insurance.

reappear on numerous occasions in Part III. In the present context such a scheme is known as the **Poisson point process**, and we shall be concerned with extensions in several directons. The first one is to remove the zero/one restriction on I_k. A more flexible specification is

$$\Pr(I_k = 0) = 1 - \mu h + o(h), \quad \Pr(I_k = 1) = \mu h + o(h) \quad \text{and} \quad \Pr(I_k > 1) = o(h),$$

where $o(h)$ signifies a mathematical expression for which

$$\frac{o(h)}{h} \to 0 \quad \text{as } h \to 0.$$

It is verified in Section 8.6 that *these small quantities do not count* in the limit. This observation is more than just a mathematical nicety. Consider a portfolio with J policies. There are now J independent processes in parallel and if μ_j is the intensity of policy j and $\mathcal{I}_k$ the total number of claims in period k, then, on ignoring the $o(h)$-terms,

$$\Pr(\mathcal{I}_k = 0) = \underbrace{\prod_{j=1}^{J}(1 - \mu_j h)}_{\textit{no claims}} \quad \text{and} \quad \Pr(\mathcal{I}_k = 1) = \underbrace{\sum_{i=1}^{J}\{\mu_i h \prod_{j \neq i}(1 - \mu_j h)\}}_{\textit{claim policy i only}}.$$

On the left, the probability of no claims is a product over all policies. Exactly one claim is more complicated since the event may affect the first, second, third policy and so on, which leaves J different probabilities to be added for the expression on the right.

Both quantities simplify when the products are calculated and the powers of h identified. Do this for $J = 3$, and the general structure emerges as

$$\Pr(\mathcal{I}_k = 0) = 1 - \left(\sum_{j=1}^{J}\mu_j\right)h + o(h) \quad \text{and} \quad \Pr(\mathcal{I}_k = 1) = \left(\sum_{j=1}^{J}\mu_j\right)h + o(h),$$

where terms of order h^2 and higher have been ignored and lumped into the $o(h)$ contributions. But this means that the portfolio sequence $\mathcal{I}_1, \dots, \mathcal{I}_K$ satisfies the same model as the policy analogue $I_1, \dots, I_K$ with the sum $\mu_1 + \cdots + \mu_J$ taking over

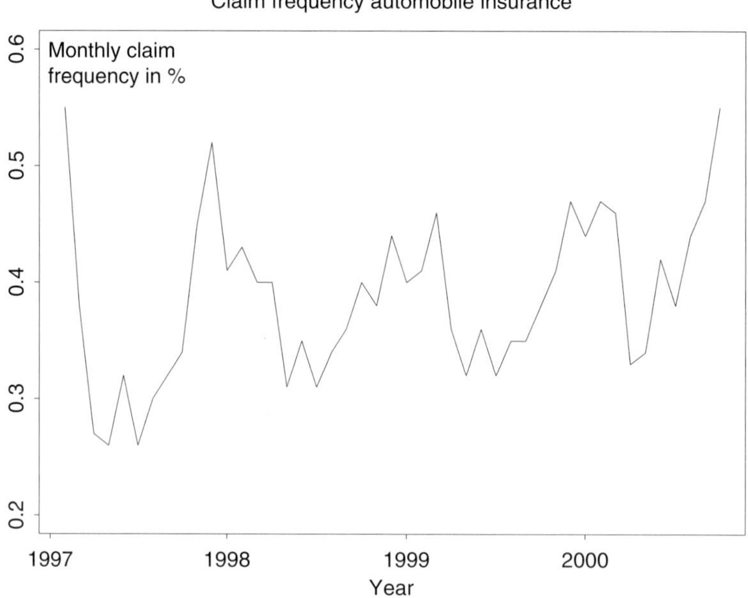

Figure 8.2 Estimated monthly claim intensities for data from a Norwegian insurance company.

from μ. It follows that the portfolio number of claims $\mathcal{N}$ is Poisson distributed with parameter

$$\lambda = (\mu_1 + \cdots + \mu_J)T = J\bar{\mu}T \quad \text{where} \quad \bar{\mu} = (\mu_1 + \cdots + \mu_J)/J.$$

When claim intensities vary over the portfolio, only their average counts.

8.2.4 When the intensity varies over time

Claim intensities do not remain constant over time. One example is shown in Figure 8.2, which comes from a Scandinavian insurance company. Monthly claim numbers have been converted into estimated intensities (method below) and plotted against time. There are significant fluctuations due to the season of the year (slippery roads cause accidents in winter!). Over the period in question, intensities also seem to grow. The data will be examined more closely in Chapter 11. Here they serve as an example of a seasonal variation that is present in many parts of the world (wet season against dry, stormy against calm). What is the impact of such factors on how we evaluate risk? Answer (perhaps surprisingly): Not very significant!

A time-varying function $\mu = \mu(t)$ handles the mathematics. The binary variables $I_1, \ldots, I_K$ are now based on different intensities $\mu_1, \ldots, \mu_K$ where $\mu_k = \mu(t_k)$ for $k = 1, \ldots, K$. When $I_1, \ldots, I_K$ are added to the total count N, this is the same issue as if K different *policies* apply on an interval of length h. In other words, N must still be Poisson, now with parameter

$$\lambda = h \sum_{k=1}^{K} \mu_k \rightarrow \int_0^T \mu(t)\,dt \quad \text{as} \quad h \rightarrow 0$$

where the limit is how integrals are defined. The Poisson parameter for N can also be written

$$\lambda = T\overline{\mu} \quad \text{where} \quad \overline{\mu} = \frac{1}{T}\int_0^T \mu(t)\,dt,$$

and the introduction of a time-varying function $\mu(t)$ doesn't change things much. A *time average* $\overline{\mu}$ takes over from a constant μ.

8.2.5 The Poisson distribution

The world of Poisson, governed by the point process of the same name, is a tidy one where claim numbers, N for policies and $\mathcal{N}$ for portfolios, are Poisson distributed with parameters

$$\underset{\text{policy level}}{\lambda = \mu T} \quad \text{and} \quad \underset{\text{portfolio level}}{\lambda = J\mu T.}$$

The intensity μ, a tool for much extended modelling, is an average over time and policies.

Poisson models have useful operational properties. The mean, standard deviation and skewness are

$$E(N) = \lambda, \quad \text{sd}(N) = \sqrt{\lambda} \quad \text{and} \quad \text{skew}(N) = 1/\sqrt{\lambda}.$$

The earlier argument connecting portfolio and policies also tells us that sums of independent Poisson variables must remain Poisson; i.e., if $N_1, \ldots, N_J$ are independent and Poisson with parameters $\lambda_1, \ldots, \lambda_J$, then

$$\mathcal{N} = N_1 + \cdots + N_J \sim \text{Poisson}(\lambda_1 + \cdots + \lambda_J).$$

A simple consequence of this **convolution property** is that Poisson variables become Gaussian as $\lambda \rightarrow \infty$ (Exercise 8.4). Signs of this are evident in Figure 8.3, where the density function has been plotted for two values of λ. The skewness at $\lambda = 4$ has largely disappeared at $\lambda = 20$.

8.2.6 Using historical data

Claim intensities must be determined from historical data. Let $n_1, \ldots, n_n$ be claim numbers from n policies exposed to risk during $T_1, \ldots, T_n$. The usual estimate of a

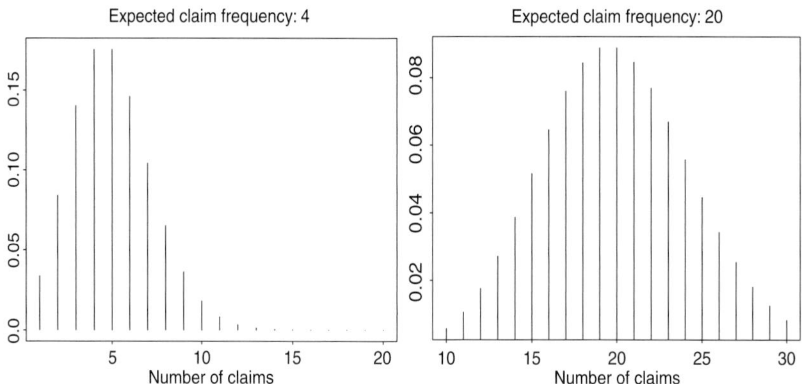

Figure 8.3 Poisson density functions for $\lambda = 4$ (*left*) and $\lambda = 20$ (*right*).

common intensity μ is

$$\hat{\mu} = \frac{n_1 + \cdots + n_n}{A} \quad \text{where} \quad A = T_1 + \cdots + T_n, \tag{8.1}$$

which is the total number of claims divided on total risk exposure A. This is the most accurate method possible (Lehmann and Casella, 1998, p. 121), and

$$E(\hat{\mu}) = \mu \quad \text{and} \quad \text{sd}(\hat{\mu}) = \sqrt{\frac{\mu}{A}}, \tag{8.2}$$

which is verified in Exercise 8.8. The estimate is unbiased with standard deviation determined by A.

A common trick when all T_j are equal is to compute $D = s^2/\bar{n}$ where $\bar{n}$ and s^2 are the sample mean and variance. The ratio D is known as the **coefficient of dispersion** and fluctuates around one for independent and identically distributed Poisson data since s^2 and $\bar{n}$ are equal in expectation. If D deviates strongly from one, it is a sign of the underlying claim intensities being unequal or the distribution being something else. The argument is not valid when $T_1, \ldots, T_n$ are unequal.

8.2.7 Example: A Norwegian automobile portfolio

The automobile portfolio plotted in Figure 8.2 will serve as an example throughout much of this chapter, but the seasonal variation and the apparent increase in μ will be ignored (see Section 11.4 for those). The total number of claims is 6978, and the total risk exposure $T_1 + \cdots + T_n = 123\,069$ automobile years, yielding

$$\hat{\mu} = \frac{6978}{123069} = 5.67\% \qquad \text{with standard deviation} \quad \sqrt{\frac{0.0567}{123\,069}} \doteq 0.07\%.$$

Table 8.1 Estimated annual accident rates of the Norwegian automobile portfolio (standard deviation of estimates in parentheses)

Rates in % annually

	Age groups (years)				
	20–25	26–39	40–55	56–70	71–94
Males	10.5 (0.76)	6.0 (0.27)	5.8 (0.13)	4.7 (0.15)	5.1 (0.22)
Females	8.4 (1.12)	6.3 (0.28)	5.7 (0.23)	5.4 (0.28)	5.8 (0.41)

The estimate is annual, and tells us that about one car in 20 is causing accidents each year.

Considerable variations between groups of individuals are hiding behind this portfolio average. Consider the **cross-classification** in Table 8.1, where the intensities have been broken down on male/female and five age categories. There are now $2 \times 5 = 10$ different sub-groups to which the estimate (8.1) could be applied. What emerged was strong dependence on age. Also note the lower estimate for women in the youngest group, indicating that it might be fair to charge young women 20–25% less than young men[9].

8.3 Random intensities

8.3.1 Introduction

How μ varies over the portfolio will, in the next section, be referred to observables such as the age or sex of the individual, but there are also personal factors a company can't know much about. Take drivers of automobiles. Their ability, caution and power of concentration influence risk and are undoubtedly highly variable, which is uncertainty beyond that coming from the traffic. It is captured by making μ a random variable, redrawn for each driver. Such stochastic intensities have a second rationale too. All insurance processes run against a background that is itself subject to random variation. A striking example is driving conditions during winter months, which may be rainy or icy (and perilous) one year, then safe and dry the next. Such uncertainty affects all policy holders jointly. Much was made of the distinction between individual and collective randomness in Section 6.3. The consequences for risk were widely different, but the mathematics is very much the same. The models are, in either case, conditional ones of the form

$$\underset{\textit{policy level}}{N|\mu \sim \text{Poisson}(\mu T)} \quad \text{and} \quad \underset{\textit{portfolio level}}{N|\mu \sim \text{Poisson}(J\mu T)}.$$

[9] In Norway, with its strict laws on the equality of sexes, such price differentiation is considered illegal! Discrimination according to age is acceptable.

Algorithm 8.1 Poisson mixing

0 Input: T and density function $g(\mu)$ for μ
1 Draw $\mu^* \sim g$ %*Many possibilities*
2 Draw $N^* \sim \text{Poisson}(\mu^* T)$ %*Algorithm 2.14*
3 Return N^*.

Most of this section concentrates on the version on the left. Replace T by JT, and everything applies at the portfolio level too.

8.3.2 A first look

Let $\xi = E(\mu)$ and $\sigma = \text{sd}(\mu)$ and recall that $E(N|\mu) = \text{var}(N|\mu) = \mu T$, which by the double rules in Section 6.3 implies

$$E(N) = E(\mu T) = \xi T \quad \text{and} \quad \text{var}(N) = E(\mu T) + \text{var}(\mu T) = \xi T + \sigma^2 T^2. \tag{8.3}$$

Now $E(N) < \text{var}(N)$, and N is no longer Poisson distributed. A good deal was learned about the behaviour of such models in Section 6.3.

Specific models for μ are handled through the **mixing** relationship

$$\Pr(N = n) = \int_0^\infty \Pr(N = n|\mu) g(\mu)\, d\mu, \tag{8.4}$$

where $g(\mu)$ is the density function of μ. Why is it true? A heuristic argument makes use of a tight grid of points $\mu_i = ih$ for $i = 1, 2, \ldots$ so that the integral is approximately the sum $\sum_i \Pr(N = n|\mu_i)\Pr(\mu = \mu_i)$, which is in turn $\Pr(N = n)$ by elementary probability. Gamma models are traditional choices for $g(\mu)$ and detailed below. Another possibility is the log-normal which doesn't permit a closed formula for the density function of N, but simulation is easy; see Algorithm 8.1.

The algorithm enables you to approximate the density function of N, and it may be applied to individuals and portfolios alike. How the scheme is extended to intensities varying over time is discussed in Section 11.4.

8.3.3 Estimating the mean and variance of μ

Estimates of ξ and σ can be obtained from historical data without specifying $g(\mu)$. Let $n_1, \ldots, n_n$ be claims from n policy holders and $T_1, \ldots, T_n$ their exposure to risk. The intensity μ_j of individual j is then estimated as $\hat{\mu}_j = n_j/T_j$. Uncertainty is huge, but pooling for portfolio estimation is still possible. The issue is similar to the Bühlman–Straub–Sundt method in credibility theory (Section 10.5).

One solution is

$$\hat{\xi} = \sum_{j=1}^{n} w_j \hat{\mu}_j \quad \text{where} \quad w_j = \frac{T_j}{\sum_{i=1}^{n} T_i}, \tag{8.5}$$

and

$$\hat{\sigma}^2 = \frac{\sum_{j=1}^{n} w_j(\hat{\mu}_j - \hat{\xi})^2 - c}{1 - \sum_{j=1}^{n} w_j^2} \quad \text{where} \quad c = \frac{(n-1)\hat{\xi}}{\sum_{j=1}^{n} T_j}, \tag{8.6}$$

which are examined in Section 8.6 where it is verified that both estimates are unbiased with the underlying ξ and σ as limits when $n \to \infty$. The estimated variance does not have to be positive. If a negative value then appears, take the position that the μ-variation over the portfolio is unlikely to be important and let $\hat{\sigma} = 0$.

8.3.4 The negative binomial model

The most commonly applied model for μ is to assume that

$$\mu = \xi G \quad \text{where} \quad G \sim \text{Gamma}(\alpha). \tag{8.7}$$

Here Gamma(α) is the standard Gamma distribution with mean 1, and μ fluctuates around ξ with uncertainty controlled by α. Specifically,

$$E(\mu) = \xi \quad \text{and} \quad \text{sd}(\mu) = \xi/\sqrt{\alpha}. \tag{8.8}$$

Since sd(μ) $\to 0$ as $\alpha \to \infty$, the pure Poisson model with fixed intensity emerges in the limit.

One of the reasons for the popularity of this model is the closed form of the density function of N. It is shown in Section 8.6 that

$$\Pr(N = n) = \frac{\Gamma(n+\alpha)}{\Gamma(n+1)\Gamma(\alpha)} p^{\alpha}(1-p)^n \quad \text{where} \quad p = \frac{\alpha}{\alpha + \xi T} \tag{8.9}$$

for $n = 0, 1, \dots$ This is the **negative binomial** distribution, denoted nbin(ξ, α).

The mean, standard deviation and skewness are

$$E(N) = \xi T, \qquad \text{sd}(N) = \sqrt{\xi T(1 + \xi T/\alpha)} \quad \text{and} \quad \text{skew}(N) = \frac{1 + 2\xi T/\alpha}{\sqrt{\xi T(1 + \xi T/\alpha)}}, \tag{8.10}$$

where $E(N)$ and sd(N) follow from (8.3) when $\sigma = \xi/\sqrt{\alpha}$ is inserted. Skewness requires a fairly long calculation, which is detailed in Section 8.6. There is a convolution property similar to that for Poisson models. If $N_1, \dots, N_J$ are independent with common distribution nbin(ξ, α), then

$$\mathcal{N} = N_1 + \cdots + N_J \sim \text{nbin}(J\xi, J\alpha) \tag{8.11}$$

which is proved in Section 8.6.

8.3.5 Fitting the negative binomial

Moment estimation using (8.5) and (8.6) is the simplest technically. The estimate of ξ is simply $\hat{\xi}$ in (8.5), and for α invoke (8.8) right which yields

$$\hat{\sigma} = \hat{\xi}/\sqrt{\hat{\alpha}} \quad \text{so that} \quad \hat{\alpha} = \hat{\xi}^2/\hat{\sigma}^2.$$

If $\hat{\sigma} = 0$, interpret it as an infinite $\hat{\alpha}$ or a pure Poisson model.

Likelihood estimation (which is what you will find in statistical software) may be a little more accurate in theory. The log-likelihood function follows by inserting n_j for n in (8.9) and adding the logarithm over all j. This leads to the criterion

$$\mathcal{L}(\xi,\alpha) = \sum_{j=1}^{n} \log\{\Gamma(n_j+\alpha)\} - n\{\log\{\Gamma(\alpha)\} - \alpha\log(\alpha)\}$$
$$+ \sum_{j=1}^{n}\{n_j\log(\xi) - (n_j+\alpha)\log(\alpha+\xi T_j)\},$$

where constant factors not depending on ξ and α have been omitted. It takes numerical software to optimize this function. Consult Table 2.3 to see how $\Gamma(x)$ is computed.

8.3.6 Automobile example continued

For the Norwegian automobile portfolio the estimates (8.5) and (8.6) were $\hat{\xi} = 5.60\%$ and $\hat{\sigma} = 2.0\%$, and the μ-variation over the portfolio is huge. The moment estimate of α in a negative binomial model is then $\hat{\alpha} = 0.056^2/0.02^2 = 7.84$. Likelihood estimates are alternative possibilities, and there are now two competing proposals:

$$\underbrace{\hat{\xi} = 5.60\%,\ \hat{\alpha} = 7.84}_{\textit{moment estimates}} \quad \text{and} \quad \underbrace{\hat{\xi} = 5.60\%,\ \hat{\alpha} = 2.94.}_{\textit{likelihood estimates}}$$

For ξ the results are identical to two decimals (they are *not* the same estimate!), but for α the discrepancy is huge with the likelihood estimate implying much more variation. There are more than 100 000 automobile years behind the estimates, so the difference is *not* due to chance. But what lies behind and which one is to be trusted? Answer: In a sense neither! The Gamma model does *not* describe the μ-variation well since the estimates, would have been much closer if it had. The moment estimate is best, because $\sigma = \mathrm{sd}(\mu)$ (determined without the Gamma assumption) is captured correctly. For an example where the Gamma model does work, see Exercise 8.15.

8.4 Intensities with explanatory variables

8.4.1 Introduction

The automobile example in Table 8.1 is a special case of risk linked to **explanatory** variables (or **covariates**). Insurance companies do this to understand which customers are profitable and which are not, and to charge differently in different segments of the portfolio. Whether this accords with the principle of solidarity behind insurance might be a matter of opinion, but individual pricing has in any case become more and more widespread, and we should certainly understand and master the techniques involved.

Credibility theory is a traditional answer, but this historically important method has a scope somewhat different from the present one and is treated in Chapter 10. The issue now is the use of **observable** variables such as the age and sex of the drivers, the geographical location of a house and so forth, which leads to regression and in this chapter **Poisson regression**.

8.4.2 The model

The idea is to attribute variations in μ to variations in a set of observable variables $x_1, \dots, x_v$. Poisson regression makes use of relationships of the form

$$\log(\mu) = b_0 + b_1 x_1 + \cdots + b_v x_v, \tag{8.12}$$

where $b_0, \dots, b_v$ are coefficients determined from historical data. The link between μ and $x_1, \dots, x_v$ discriminates customers according to risk.

Why $\log(\mu)$ in (8.12) and not μ itself? It does lead to a useful interpretation of the model (see below), but the most compelling reason is almost philosophical. Linear functions, such as those on the right, extend over the whole real line whereas μ is always positive. Two quantities differing so widely in range shouldn't be equalized, and arguably a log-transformation makes the scale of the two sides more in line with each other.

8.4.3 Data and likelihood function

Historical data are of the following form:

$$\begin{array}{ccc}
n_1 & T_1 & x_{11} \cdots x_{1v} \\
n_2 & T_2 & x_{21} \cdots x_{2v} \\
\cdot & \cdot & \cdot\cdot\cdot\cdot\cdot \\
\cdot & \cdot & \cdot\cdot\cdot\cdot\cdot \\
n_n & T_n & x_{n1} \cdots x_{nv}. \\
\textit{claims} & \textit{exposure} & \textit{covariates}
\end{array}$$

On row j we have the number of claims n_j, the exposure to risk T_j (sometimes called the **offset**) and the values of the explanatory variables $x_{j1}, \dots, x_{jv}$. This is known as a **data matrix**. General schemes for model fitting work from information stored that way. How specific situations are read into it will be demonstrated below.

The coefficients $b_0, \dots, b_v$ are usually determined by likelihood estimation. It is then assumed that n_j is Poisson distributed with parameter $\lambda_j = \mu_j T_j$, where μ_j are tied to covariates $x_{j1}, \dots, x_{jv}$ as in (8.12). The density function of n_j is then

$$f(n_j) = \frac{(\mu_j T_j)^{n_j}}{n_j!} e^{-\mu_j T_j}$$

or

$$\log\{f(n_j)\} = n_j \log(\mu_j) + n_j \log(T_j) - \log(n_j!) - \mu_j T_j,$$

which is to be added over all j for the likelihood function $\mathcal{L}(b_0, \dots, b_v)$. If the middle terms $n_j T_j$ and $\log(n_j!)$ are dropped (in this context constants), the likelihood criterion becomes

$$\mathcal{L}(b_0, \dots, b_v) = \sum_{j=1}^{n} \{n_j \log(\mu_j) - \mu_j T_j\} \quad \text{where} \quad \log(\mu_j) = b_0 + b_1 x_{j1} + \cdots + b_v x_{jv} \tag{8.13}$$

and there is little point in carrying the mathematics further. Optimization of (8.13) must be done by numerical software. It is rather straightforward, since it can be proved (McCullagh and Nelder, 1989) that $\mathcal{L}(b_0, \dots, b_v)$ is a convex surface with a single maximum.

8.4.4 A first interpretation

Poisson regression is best learned by example, and the rest of this section will use the data underlying the estimates in Table 8.1. There are two explanatory variables, age (x_1) and gender (x_2). The most immediate way of feeding them into the regression model (8.12) is to let them work independently of each other. They are then added on a logarithmic scale, and the model becomes

$$\log(\mu_j) = b_0 + \underbrace{b_1 x_{j1}}_{\text{age effect}} + \underbrace{b_2 x_{j2}}_{\text{male/female}} \tag{8.14}$$

where x_{j1} is the age of the owner of car j and

$$\begin{aligned} x_{j2} &= 0, \quad \text{if } j \text{ is male} \\ &= 1, \quad \text{if } j \text{ is female.} \end{aligned}$$

On the original scale the model is **multiplicative** and reads

$$\mu_j = \underbrace{\mu_0}_{baseline} \cdot \underbrace{e^{b_1 x_{j1}}}_{age} \cdot \underbrace{e^{b_2 x_{j2}}}_{sex}, \quad \text{where} \quad \mu_0 = e^{b_0}. \tag{8.15}$$

Here μ_0 is a baseline intensity, which is driven up or down by the explanatory variables.

As an example consider two drivers i and j of the same age x_1, but of opposite sex. If i is a female and j a male, then

$$\frac{\mu_i}{\mu_j} = \frac{e^{b_0+b_1x_1+b_2}}{e^{b_0+b_1x_1}} = e^{b_2}$$

and if $\hat{b}_2 = 0.037$ (taken from Table 8.2), the estimated intensity ratio is $\hat{\mu}_i/\hat{\mu}_j = e^{0.037} \doteq 1.037$; female drivers on average cause 3.7% more accidents than males. The model offers this evaluation regardless of age, which is questionable; more below.

8.4.5 How variables are entered

The coefficient b_1 in (8.14) is usually negative since the accident rate goes down as drivers become more experienced. But $\log(\mu)$ should not necessarily be a strictly *linear* function of age. For one thing, this doesn't capture very old drivers being less safe than when they were younger. More flexible mathematical formulations are provided by polynomials of higher order, for example by adding a term proportional to x_{j1}^2 in (8.14).

Another possibility is categorization. Age is then divided into, say, g intervals or groups with the exact age x_2 replaced by the group mean. The model (8.14) now becomes

$$\log(\mu_j) = b_0 + b_1(l) + b_2(s) \quad \text{if policy holder } j \text{ is of age } l \text{ and gender } s \tag{8.16}$$

for $l = 1, \ldots, g$ and $s = 1, 2$. Here $b_1(1), \ldots, b_1(g)$, and $b_2(1)$ and $b_2(2)$ are parameters, and they are not unique as the model stands. Add a constant to b_0 and subtract it from $b_1(1), \ldots, b_1(g)$ or from both of $b_2(1)$ and $b_2(2)$, and the model is the same. This **confounding** of parameters is often resolved by zeroing the first category of the explanatory variables so that $b_1(1) = b_2(1) = 0$ as in Table 8.2. With g categories there are now $g - 1$ free parameters, and only a single one for gender. The model is more flexible than it was in (8.14), but with more parameters to estimate. Is it part of the framework (8.12)? A system of zero/one explanantory variables makes it that, but this is typically unnecessary since software like R has special means for entering variables in categorical form; consult the exercises.

An example with five age categories is shown in Table 8.2. This is a much cruder

Table 8.2 Poisson regression fitted on the Norwegian automobile portfolio (standard deviations in parentheses)

Intercept	Male	Female
−2.315 (0.065)	0 (0)	0.037 (0.027)

Age groups (years)				
20–25	26–39	40–55	56–70	71–94
0 (0)	−0.501 (0.068)	−0.541 (0.067)	−0.711 (0.070)	−0.637 (0.073)

subdivision than would be used in practice, but it does convey the usefulness of the approach by showing an increase in accidents for the highest age group where the regression coefficient has started to grow after going consistently down from the youngest drivers onwards. Note the zero coefficients for males and the lowest age group by design. The exercises for this section examine the effect of varying the number of categories.

8.4.6 Interaction and cross-classification

Annual claim rates under the model (8.16) can be computed from the coefficients in Table 8.2 and are shown in Table 8.3. The data are the same as in Table 8.1, and the results are too with the notable exception that the much higher accident rate for men in the youngest age group has disappeared! What lies behind this is the multiplicative form of the model, which *forces* constant ratios of intensities between females and males as age is varied. This washes away the fine structure in Table 8.1, and a feature of some importance has been lost.

There is in this case an **interaction** between age and gender which the multiplicative form of the model doesn't confront. One alternative would be to introduce an additional cross-term of the form x_1x_2 so that $\log(\mu) = b_0 + b_1x_1 + b_2x_2 + b_3x_1x_2$. Alternatively, separate parameters for men/women could be allowed for the youngest age group and the multiplicative model kept for the rest. Details are skipped since the main point is to emphasize the limitation in treating explanatory variables multiplicatively. This is widespread practice and often attractive when there are many covariates. In automobile insurance the annual distance limit on policies (proxy for how much people drive), type of car and zone of residence are all variables that might add to those above.

But why is Poisson regression needed at all? Couldn't we simply **cross-classify** all policy holders into groups as in Table 8.1 and use the elementary estimate (8.1), say one assessment for each combination of age, sex, distance limit, car type and zone of residence? The problem is that there might be too many groups, easily thousands for the five variables mentioned and with individuals unevenly

Table 8.3 Annual claim intensities under Poisson regression

Intensities in % annually

	Age groups (years)				
	20–25	26–39	40–55	56–70	71–94
Male	9.9	5.9	5.8	4.9	5.2
Female	10.3	6.1	6.1	5.1	5.4

distributed. Estimates (at least some of them) would be fraught with random error and unsuitable as a basis for pricing. Regression dampens such randomness; see also Section 10.4.

8.5 Modelling delay

8.5.1 Introduction

Claims are never settled immediately, and for some types of injuries or damages delays are rather long. A typical case is back or neck ailments following a car crash; it may take years before their symptoms arise. Other examples originate with environmental factors like asbestos or radioactivity. Their severe effect on health was not understood at the time, and the repercussions for the insurance industry have been dire indeed. Claims that are only discovered years after the insurable event are called **IBNR** (incurred, but not reported). Companies have to set aside funds to cover them (even though they may not yet have been identified). Claims may also be of **RBNS** status (reported, but not settled), which means that they are in the process of being liquidated, but not finished.

We shall concentrate on IBNR claims which require a longer look than the ordinary period of accountancy T. The situation is portrayed in Figure 8.4. At the end of year 0 (where we are at the moment) there are outstanding claims that will surface later. Companies are responsible. Their balance sheets will be affected up to, say, L periods ahead by claims not yet known, and must look back equally long to include all contributions. A natural approach (though currently not the most popular one) is to see delay as a random phenomenon based on probabilities. This is the way IBNR modelling is developed below; consult Section 8.7 for references to other approaches.

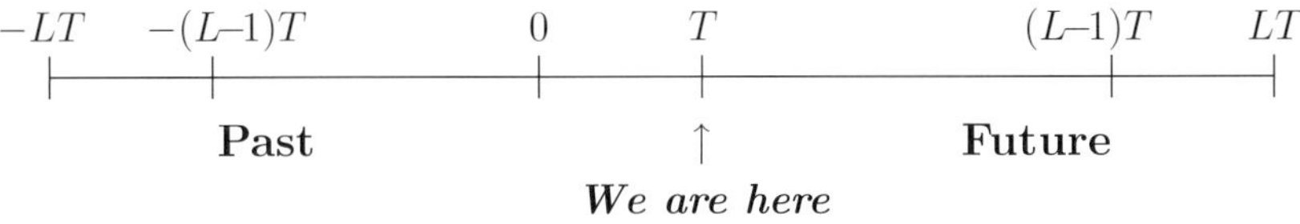

Figure 8.4 The delay scheme looking backwards/forwards from the end of year 0.

8.5.2 Multinomial delay

Let q_l be the probability that a claim is settled l periods after the incident took place, where $q_0+\cdots+q_L = 1$ if L is maximum delay. The process is **multinomial** if different events are independent (as will be assumed). Suppose there are J policies under risk in a period of length T. The number of claims $\mathcal{N}$ is typically Poisson distributed with parameter $\lambda = J\mu T$, but not all are liquidated at once. If $\mathcal{N}_l$ are those settled l periods later, then $\mathcal{N}_0 + \cdots + \mathcal{N}_L = \mathcal{N}$, and the earlier assumptions make the conditional distribution of $\mathcal{N}_0, \dots, \mathcal{N}_L$ given $\mathcal{N}$ multinomial with probabilities $q_0, \dots, q_L$.

This Poisson/multinomial modelling implies

$$\mathcal{N}_l \sim \text{Poisson}(J\mu T q_l), \quad l = 0, \dots, L \tag{8.17}$$

and

$$\mathcal{N}_0, \dots, \mathcal{N}_L \quad \text{stochastically independent.} \tag{8.18}$$

The mathematics is in Section 8.6, but an intuitive point process argument is also possible. Divide the period T under risk into K intervals of length $h = T/K$ as in Figure 8.1. The probability of an incident against the portfolio is $J\mu h$ per interval, which changes to $J\mu h q_l$ for the events delayed l time units, and $\mathcal{N}_l$ has the distribution in (8.17). There is one Poisson process for each l, a total of $L + 1$ of them running in parallel. They are dependent, but only to the order of $o(h)$, which is irrelevant as $h \to 0$, and they become independent in the limit.

8.5.3 IBNR claim numbers

Consider, as in Figure 8.4, the years $0, -1, \dots, -(L-1)$ from year 0 and back from which there are unknown, outstanding claims at the end of year 0. Let J_s be the number of policies at risk in year $-s$, μ_s the average claim intensity during the same year and $\mathcal{N}_{sl}$ the number of claims originating that year and settled l years later. By (8.17) the entire set $\{\mathcal{N}_{sl}\}$ is stochastically independent with

$$\mathcal{N}_{sl} \sim \text{Poisson}(\lambda_{sl}) \quad \text{where} \quad \lambda_{sl} = J_s \mu_s T q_l. \tag{8.19}$$

Our balance sheet k years ahead is affected by the total number of claims disposed of that year; i.e.,

$$\mathcal{N}_k = \sum_{s=0}^{L-k} \mathcal{N}_{s,k+s}, \quad k = 1, \dots, L. \tag{8.20}$$

These are sums of independent Poisson variables and therefore Poisson distributed themselves with parameters

$$\lambda_k = \sum_{s=0}^{L-k} \lambda_{s,k+s} = \sum_{s=0}^{L-k} J_s \mu_s T q_{s+k}, \tag{8.21}$$

and all of $\mathcal{N}_1, \dots, \mathcal{N}_L$ are stochastically independent. These useful results open up for use the same methods for IBNR as elsewhere.

8.5.4 Fitting delay models

Let n_{sl} be the number of claims arising in year $-s$ and settled l years later. These are historical data if $-s+l \leq 0$ (since we are at the end of year 0) and can be used to fit a delay model. Note that the Poisson parameters λ_{sl} in (8.19) are in multiplicative form, so that

$$\log(\lambda_{sl}) = \log(J_s T) + \theta_s + \beta_l \tag{8.22}$$

where

$$\theta_s = \log(\mu_s) \quad \text{and} \quad \beta_l = \log(q_l). \tag{8.23}$$

This is a Poisson log-linear regression of the same type as in Section 8.4.

Note that a constant can be added to all θ_s in (8.22) and subtracted from all β_l without affecting their sum. This ambiguity was present in Section 8.4 too, but it must now be resolved differently by utilizing that $q_0 + \cdots + q_L = 1$. If $\hat{\theta}_s$ and $\hat{\beta}_l$ are estimates obtained by Poisson regression, take

$$\hat{\mu}_s = ce^{\hat{\theta}_s}, \quad \hat{q}_l = e^{\hat{\beta}_l}/c \quad \text{where} \quad c = e^{\hat{\beta}_0} + \cdots + e^{\hat{\beta}_L}; \tag{8.24}$$

consult Exercises 8.29 and 8.30 for details when R-software is used.

8.5.5 Syntetic example: Car crash injury

The example shown in Figures 8.5 and 8.6 is patterned on a real automobile portfolio of a Scandinavian insurance company. We are considering injuries to drivers and passengers following road accidents with claim rates 0.5% annually. Historical data were generated in the computer and based on annual frequencies

$$\mu = \xi G, \quad G \sim \text{Gamma}(\alpha) \qquad \text{where} \quad \xi = 0.5\%, \quad \alpha = 7.84$$

with the underlying, true frequency varying randomly from one year to another in a manner reflecting the automobile portfolio examined earlier in this chapter. The

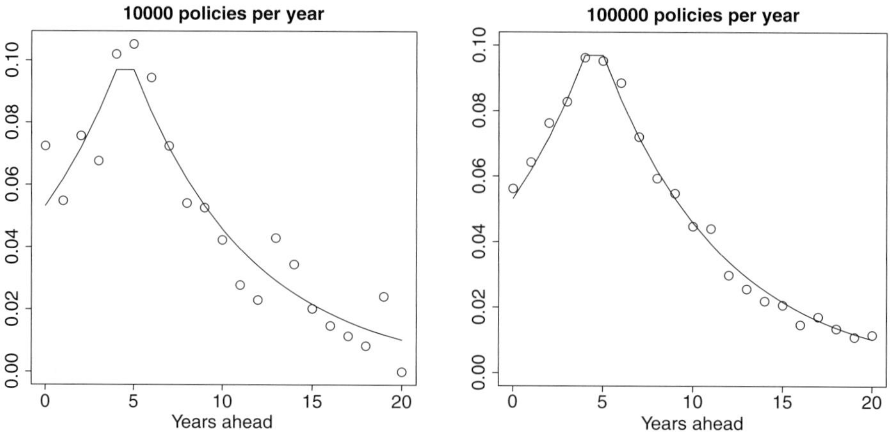

Figure 8.5 True delay probabilities (solid line) with their estimates (points) under the circumstances described in the text.

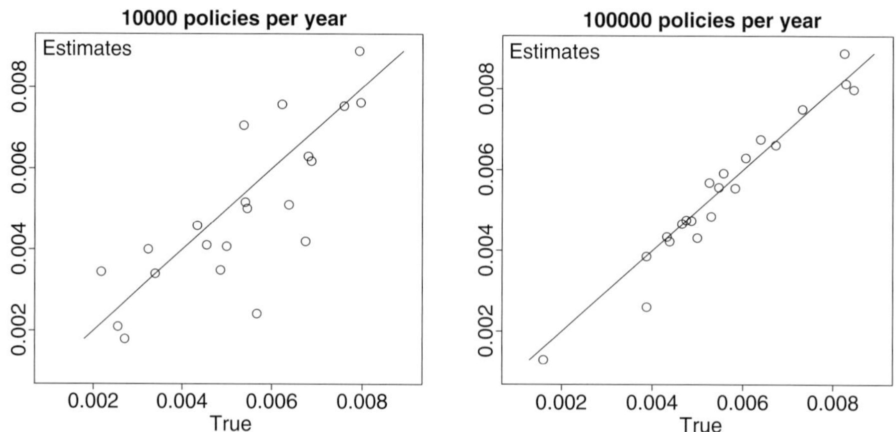

Figure 8.6 Estimates of each claim frequency scatterplotted against the true values under circumstances described in the text.

delay probabilities were

$$q_l = ce^{-\gamma|l-l_m|}, \quad l = 0, \ldots, L,$$

where the constant c ensures $q_0 + \cdots + q_L = 1$. Parameters were $L = 20$, $\gamma = 0.15$ and $l_m = 4.5$, which means that the sequence $q_0, \ldots, q_L$ reaches a peak after 4 and 5 years; see Figure 8.5. All outstanding obligations are assumed settled after 20 years. Historical claims data on a time scale $T = 1$ were simulated by means of Algorithm 8.2.

Algorithm 8.2 Simulating IBNR counts

0 Input: $J, q_0, \dots, q_L, \xi, \alpha$
1 For $s = 0, 1, \dots, L$ do
2 Draw $G^* \sim$ Gamma(α) and $\mu_s^* \leftarrow \xi G^*$
3 For $l = 0, 1, \dots, L$ do
Draw $\mathcal{N}_{sl}^* \sim$ Poisson($J\mu_s^* q_l$)
4 For all s and l return $\mathcal{N}_{sl}^*$.

The algorithm generates complete series of counts $\mathcal{N}_{s0}^*, \dots, \mathcal{N}_{sL}^*$ from each year $-s$ for $s = 0, \dots, L$, and they are known at the end of year 0 if $-s + l \leq 0$. This part was used as historical material with $J = 10\,000$ and $100\,000$ policies per year, which correspond to 50 and 500 new claims on average. Parameter estimates extracted from the simulations are shown in Figures 8.5 and 8.6 and compared with the true ones. Both the delay probabilities (Figure 8.5) and the claim intensities (Figure 8.6) are reconstructed fairly well, though better for the larger portfolio on the right. For other numerical studies, consult the exercises.

8.6 Mathematical arguments

8.6.1 The general Poisson argument

Let $N = I_1 + \cdots + I_K$, where $I_1, \dots, I_K$ are independent and

$$\Pr(I_k = 0) = 1 - \mu h + o(h), \quad \Pr(I_k = 1) = \mu h + o(h) \quad \text{and} \quad \Pr(I_k > 1) = o(h)$$

for $k = 1, \dots, K$. Here $o(h)$ are small quantities for which $o(h)/h \to 0$ as $h \to 0$, or equivalently $Ko(1/K) \to 0$ as $K \to \infty$. We shall prove that these terms don't count. Let A be the event that all $I_1, \dots, I_K$ are 0 or 1 with A^c its complement. Then

$$\Pr(A^c) = \Pr(I_1 > 1 \text{ or } \dots \text{ or } I_K > 1) \leq \sum_{k=1}^{K} \Pr(I_k > 1) = Ko(h) = Ko(1/K) \to 0,$$

and $\Pr(A^c) \to 0$ and also $\Pr(A) \to 1$. Note that

$$\Pr(N = n) = \Pr(N = n|A)\Pr(A) + \Pr(N = n|A^c)\Pr(A^c),$$

from which it follows that $\Pr(N = n) - \Pr(N = n|A) \to 0$. It is therefore sufficient to examine the limit of $\Pr(N = n|A)$, which is a binomial probability with 'success' probability

$$p = \frac{\Pr(I_k = 1)}{\Pr(I_k = 0) + \Pr(I_k = 1)} = \frac{\mu h + o(h)}{1 - \mu h + o(h) + \mu h + o(h)} = \mu h + o(h)$$
$$= \frac{\mu T}{K} + o(1/K).$$

A copy of the argument in Section 8.2 yields

$$\Pr(N = n|A) = B_1 \cdot B_2 \cdot B_3 \cdot B_4,$$

where

$$B_1 = \frac{\{\mu T + Ko(1/K))\}^n}{n!} \longrightarrow \frac{(\mu T)^n}{n!}, \quad B_2 = \frac{K(K-1)\cdots(K-n+1)}{K^n} \longrightarrow 1,$$

$$B_3 = \{1 - \mu T/K - o(1/K)\}^K \longrightarrow e^{-\mu T}, \quad B_4 = \frac{1}{\{1 - \mu T/K - o(1/K)\}^n} \longrightarrow 1,$$

and since $K\,o(1/K) \to 0$, all four limits remain what they were in Section 8.2. Only B_3 requires an argument. Insert $x = -\mu T/K + o(1/K)$ into the Taylor series $\log(1 + x) = x - x^2/2 + \cdots$, which yields

$$\log(B_3) = K \log\{1 - \mu T/K - o(1/K)\} = -\mu T - K\,o(1/K) + \cdots \to -\mu T$$

as asserted. The Poisson probabilities emerge when the limits of B_1, B_2, B_3 and B_4 are multiplied.

8.6.2 Estimating the mean and standard deviation of μ

The estimates proposed for $\xi = E(\mu)$ and $\sigma = \text{sd}(\mu)$ in Section 8.3 were based on $\hat{\mu}_1, \ldots, \hat{\mu}_n$, where $\hat{\mu}_j = N_j/T_j$. Here $N_j|\mu_j \sim \text{Poisson}(\mu_j T_j)$, which implies that $E(\hat{\mu}_j|\mu_j) = \mu_j$ and $\text{var}(\hat{\mu}_j|\mu_j) = \mu_j/T_j$. The rules of double expectation and double variance yield

$$E(\hat{\mu}_j) = E(\mu_j) = \xi \quad \text{and} \quad \text{var}(\hat{\mu}_j) = \text{var}(\mu_j) + E(\mu_j/T_j) = \sigma^2 + \xi/T_j,$$

which will be used repeatedly. The estimate of the mean ξ is

$$\hat{\xi} = w_1\hat{\mu}_1 + \cdots + w_n\hat{\mu}_n \quad \text{where} \quad w_j = \frac{T_j}{T_1 + \cdots + T_n},$$

which is unbiased since $w_1 + \cdots + w_n = 1$ and with variance

$$\text{var}(\hat{\xi}) = \sum_{j=1}^{n} w_j^2 \text{var}(\hat{\mu}_j) = \sum_{j=1}^{n} w_j^2 \left(\sigma^2 + \frac{\xi}{T_j}\right).$$

Consider the estimate (8.6) for σ^2, which is

$$\hat{\sigma}^2 = \frac{Q - c}{1 - \sum_{j=1}^n w_j^2} \quad \text{where} \quad Q = \sum_{j=1}^{n} w_j(\hat{\mu}_j - \hat{\xi})^2 \quad \text{and} \quad c = \frac{(n-1)\hat{\xi}}{\sum_{j=1}^n T_j}.$$

The key quantity Q can be expanded as

$$Q = \sum_{j=1}^{n} w_j(\hat{\mu}_j - \xi)^2 - 2\sum_{j=1}^{n} w_j(\hat{\mu}_j - \xi)(\hat{\xi} - \xi) + \sum_{j=1}^{n} w_j(\hat{\xi} - \xi)^2 = \sum_{j=1}^{n} w_j(\hat{\mu}_j - \xi)^2 - (\hat{\xi} - \xi)^2$$

since $\sum_j w_j(\hat{\mu}_j - \xi) = \hat{\xi} - \xi$ and $w_1 + \cdots + w_n = 1$. It follows that

$$
\begin{aligned}
E(Q) &= \sum_{j=1}^{n} w_j E(\hat{\mu}_j - \xi)^2 - E(\hat{\xi} - \xi)^2 \\
&= \sum_{j=1}^{n} w_j \mathrm{var}(\hat{\mu}_j) - \mathrm{var}(\hat{\xi}) \\
&= \sum_{j=1}^{n} w_j \left(\sigma^2 + \frac{\xi}{T_j}\right) - \sum_{j=1}^{n} w_j^2 \left(\sigma^2 + \frac{\xi}{T_j}\right) \\
&= \sigma^2 \left(1 - \sum_{j=1}^{n} w_j^2\right) + \frac{(n-1)\xi}{\sum_{j=1}^{n} T_j},
\end{aligned}
$$

after some rearrangements. But the last term on the right is $E(c)$, and so

$$
E(\hat{\sigma}^2) = \frac{E(Q) - E(c)}{1 - \sum_{j=1}^{n} w_j^2} = \sigma^2,
$$

and $\hat{\sigma}^2$ is unbiased.

8.6.3 Large-sample properties

The simplest way to verify that the estimates $\hat{\xi}$ and $\hat{\sigma}$ approach ξ and σ as $n \to \infty$ is to regard the exposure times $T_1, \ldots, T_n$ as a random sample of independent and identically distributed variables. As before $E(\hat{\mu}_j | T_j) = \xi$, but the interpretation is now conditional. Moreover, $E(\hat{\mu}_j T_j | T_j) = \xi T_j$, and by the rule of double expectation $E(\hat{\mu}_j T_j) = E(\xi T_j) = \xi E(T_j)$. Hence

$$
\hat{\xi} = \frac{n^{-1} \sum_{j=1}^{n} \hat{\mu}_j T_j}{n^{-1} \sum_{j=1}^{n} T_j} \longrightarrow \frac{E(\hat{\mu}_1 T_1)}{ET_1} = \frac{\xi ET_1}{ET_1} = \xi,
$$

where the limit is due to the weak law of large numbers (Appendix A.4) and $\hat{\xi} \to \xi$. A similar result for $\hat{\sigma}^2$ follows from earlier calculations which showed that

$$
Q = \frac{n^{-1} \sum_{j=1}^{n} T_j (\hat{\mu}_j - \xi)^2}{n^{-1} \sum_{j=1}^{n} T_j} - (\hat{\xi} - \xi)^2 \longrightarrow \frac{ET_1 (\hat{\mu}_1 - \xi)^2}{ET_1} - 0,
$$

again due to the weak law of large numbers. The limit can be simplified by noting that

$$
E(T_1 (\hat{\mu}_1 - \xi)^2 | T_1) = T_1 \mathrm{var}(\hat{\mu}_1 | T_1) = T_1 (\sigma^2 + \xi / T_1) = \sigma^2 T_1 + \xi
$$

so that $ET_1(\hat{\mu}_1 - \xi)^2 = \sigma^2 ET_1 + \xi$. It follows that $Q \to \sigma^2 + \xi/ET_1$ whereas

$$c = \frac{(n-1)\xi}{\sum_{j=1}^n T_j} \longrightarrow \frac{\xi}{ET_1}$$

and

$$n\sum_{j=1}^n w_j^2 = \frac{n^{-1}\sum_{j=1}^n T_j^2}{\left(n^{-1}\sum_{j=1}^n T_j\right)^2} \longrightarrow \frac{ET_1^2}{(ET_1)^2},$$

which means that $\sum_j w_j^2 \to 0$. But then

$$\hat{\sigma}^2 = \frac{Q-c}{1-\sum_{j=1}^n w_j^2} \longrightarrow \frac{\sigma^2 + \xi/ET_1 - \xi/ET_1}{1-0} = \sigma^2.$$

8.6.4 The negative binomial density function

The negative binomial distribution was, in Section 8.3, defined through

$$\Pr(N = n|\mu) = \frac{(\mu T)^n}{n!}e^{-\mu T} \quad \text{and} \quad g(\mu) = \frac{(\alpha/\xi)^\alpha}{\Gamma(\alpha)}\mu^{\alpha-1}e^{-\mu\alpha/\xi}.$$

By the mixing formula (8.4)

$$\Pr(N = n) = \int_0^\infty \frac{(\mu T)^n}{n!}e^{-T\mu} \cdot \frac{(\alpha/\xi)^\alpha}{\Gamma(\alpha)}\mu^{\alpha-1}e^{-\mu\alpha/\xi}\, d\mu,$$

or when reorganized,

$$\Pr(N = n) = \frac{T^n(\alpha/\xi)^\alpha}{n!\Gamma(\alpha)}\int_0^\infty \mu^{n+\alpha-1}e^{-\mu(T+\alpha/\xi)}\, d\mu.$$

Substituting $z = \mu(T + \alpha/\xi)$ in the integrand yields

$$\Pr(N = n) = \frac{T^n(\alpha/\xi)^\alpha}{n!\Gamma(\alpha)(T + \alpha/\xi)^{n+\alpha}}\int_0^\infty z^{n+\alpha-1}e^{-z}\, dz,$$

where the integral is $\Gamma(n+\alpha)$. Hence

$$\Pr(N = n) = \frac{\Gamma(n+\alpha)}{n!\Gamma(\alpha)} \cdot \frac{T^n(\alpha/\xi)^\alpha}{(T + \alpha/\xi)^{n+\alpha}} = \frac{\Gamma(n+\alpha)}{n!\Gamma(\alpha)}p^\alpha(1-p)^n$$

where $p = \alpha/(\alpha + \xi T)$. This is the density function (8.9) since $\Gamma(n+1) = n!$.

8.6.5 Skewness of the negative binomial

Most of the work resides in the third-order moment $\nu_3(N) = E(N - \xi T)^3$ which, can be derived from the stochastic representation of N. Note that $N - \xi T = (N - \mu T) + (\mu - \xi)T$ so that

$$(N - \xi T)^3 = (N - \mu T)^3 + 3(N - \mu T)^2(\mu - \xi)T + 3(N - \mu T)(\mu - \xi)^2T^2 + (\mu - \xi)^3T^3,$$

and we must utilize that $N|\mu \sim \text{Poisson}(\mu T)$. Thus $E(N|\mu) = \text{var}(N|\mu) = \nu_3(N|\mu) = \mu T$, which yields

$$E\{(N - \xi T)^3|\mu\} = \mu T + 3\mu T(\mu - \xi)T + (\mu - \xi)^3T^3.$$

By the rule of double expectation

$$\begin{aligned} E(N - \xi T)^3 &= E(\mu)T + 3E\{\mu(\mu - \xi)\}T^2 + E(\mu - \xi)^3T^3 \\ &= E(\mu)T + 3\text{var}(\mu)T^2 + \nu_3(\mu)T^3, \end{aligned}$$

and inserting $E(\mu) = \xi$, $\text{var}(\mu) = \xi^2/\alpha$ and $\nu_3(\mu) = 2\xi^3/\alpha^2$ for the lower-order moments of μ implies that

$$E(N - \xi T)^3 = \xi T + 3\frac{\xi^2}{\alpha}T^2 + 2\frac{\xi^3}{\alpha^2}T^3 = \xi T\left(1 + \frac{\xi T}{\alpha}\right)\left(1 + 2\frac{\xi T}{\alpha}\right)$$

and the skewness formula (8.10) follows, dividing by $\{\text{var}(N)\}^{3/2}$ where $\text{var}(N) = \xi T(1 + \xi T/\alpha)$.

8.6.6 The convolution property of the negative binomial

Let $\mathcal{N} = N_1 + \cdots + N_J$ where $N_1, \ldots, N_J$ are independent and $\text{nbin}(\xi, \alpha)$. This means that each N_j has the representation

$$N_j|\mu_j \sim \text{Poisson}(\mu_j T) \quad \text{where} \quad \mu_j = \xi G_j, \quad G_j \sim \text{Gamma}(\alpha).$$

The conditional distribution of $\mathcal{N} = N_1 + \cdots + N_J$ given $\mu_1, \ldots, \mu_J$ is then Poisson with parameter

$$\theta = \mu_1 + \cdots + \mu_J = \xi(G_1 + \cdots + G_J) = J\xi\overline{G} \quad \text{where} \quad \overline{G} = (G_1 + \cdots + G_J)/J.$$

Here $\overline{G}$ is the average of J variables that are $\text{Gamma}(\alpha)$, and is therefore Gamma $(J\alpha)$ itself; see Section 9.3. But then

$$\mathcal{N}|\theta \sim \text{Poisson}(\theta T) \quad \text{where} \quad \theta = (J\xi)\overline{G}, \quad \overline{G} \sim \text{Gamma}(J\alpha),$$

and $\mathcal{N}$ is $\text{nbin}(J\xi, J\alpha)$ as claimed in Section 8.3.

8.6.7 IBNR: The delay model

Let $\mathcal{N}$ be the total number of claims during a period T and $\mathcal{N}_l$ those among them settled l periods later for $l = 0, \dots, L$. Clearly $\mathcal{N} = \mathcal{N}_0 + \cdots + \mathcal{N}_L$ and with $n = n_0 + \cdots + n_L$,

$$\Pr(\mathcal{N}_0 = n_0, \dots, \mathcal{N}_L = n_L) = \Pr(\mathcal{N}_0 = n_0, \dots, \mathcal{N}_L = n_L | \mathcal{N} = n)\Pr(\mathcal{N} = n)$$

where by assumption

$$\Pr(\mathcal{N}_0 = n_0, \dots, \mathcal{N}_L = n_L | \mathcal{N} = n) = \frac{n!}{n_0! \cdots n_L!} q_0^{n_0} \cdots q_L^{n_L}$$

and

$$\Pr(\mathcal{N} = n) = \frac{\lambda^n}{n!}e^{-\lambda} = \frac{\lambda^{n_0+\cdots+n_L}}{n!}e^{-\lambda(q_0+\cdots+q_L)} = \frac{1}{n!}\left(\lambda^{n_0}e^{-q_0\lambda}\right)\cdots\left(\lambda^{n_L}e^{-q_L\lambda}\right)$$

since $q_0 + \cdots + q_L = 1$. This yields

$$\Pr(\mathcal{N}_0 = n_0, \dots, \mathcal{N}_L = n_L) = \frac{q_0^{n_0} \cdots q_L^{n_L}}{n_0! \cdots n_L!}\left(\lambda^{n_0}e^{-q_0\lambda}\right)\cdots\left(\lambda^{n_L}e^{-q_L\lambda}\right) = \prod_{l=0}^{L} \frac{(q_l\lambda)^{n_l}}{n_l!}e^{-q_l\lambda}$$

as claimed in (8.17) and (8.18).

8.7 Bibliographical notes

8.7.1 Poisson modelling

Poisson processes with or without random intensities are the usual mathematical description of claim numbers, and there are presentations in all standard textbooks on general insurance, for example Daykin *et al.* (1994) and Mikosch (2004); see also Grandell (2004) and Jacobsen (2006) for treatments with heavier mathematics. Extended modelling with claim intensities as stochastic processes is discussed in Chapter 11.

8.7.2 Generalized linear models

Poisson regression in Section 8.4 is a special case of the class of generalized linear models (**GLM**) which connects expected response to explanatory variables. These methods are available for many of the most common distributions, and they are also relevant for sizes of claims (next chapter) and in life insurance. The classical work on generalized linear models is McCullagh and Nelder (1989), but you may well find Dobson and Barnett (2008) or perhaps Dunteman and Ho (2006) easier to read. Lee *et al.* (2006) allows random coefficients, which is of interest in insurance; see also Wütrich and Merz (2008). An extension in another direction is Wood (2006).

Reviews of GLM in an actuarial context have been provided by Haberman and Renshaw (1996), Antonio and Beirlant (2007) and De Jong and Heller (2008). For specific applications covering a wide range of topics in insurance, consult Yau *et al.* (2003), Butt and Haberman (2004), Hoedemakers *et al.* (2005) and England and Verrall (2006).

8.7.3 Reserving over long

The delay model in Section 8.5 goes back to Kaminsky (1987). It makes reserving for claims that surface long after the incident took place much the same issue as for ordinary claims. Other methods have (perhaps surprisingly) been more popular. Taylor (2000) and Wütrich and Merz (2008) are reviews with much more advanced and complex modelling.

8.8 Exercises

Section 8.2

Exercise 8.1 Let $\mathcal{N}(t)$ be the number of events up to time t in a Poisson point process with constant intensity $J\mu$ and let X be the time the *first* event appears.

(a) Argue that

$$\Pr(X > t) = \Pr(\mathcal{N}(t) = 0) = e^{-J\mu t}.$$

(b) Identify the distribution of X. What is its expectation?

Exercise 8.2 Let $\mathcal{S}_i = X_1 + \cdots + X_i$, where $X_1, X_2, \ldots$ are independent with the same distribution as X in Exercise 8.1.

(a) Argue that $\mathcal{S}_i$ is the time the ith event occurs in the corresponding Poisson process.
(b) Generate $m = 100$ simulations of the pair $(\mathcal{S}_1, \mathcal{S}_2)$ when $J = 100$ and $\mu = 0.01$ per year and visualize the huge uncertainty by scatterplotting the simulations.
R-*commands*:
`S1=rexp(m,J*μ); S2=S1+rexp(m,J*μ); plot(S1,S2).`

Exercise 8.3 Let $\mathcal{N}(t), X_1, X_2, \ldots$ and $\mathcal{S}_1, \mathcal{S}_2, \ldots$ be as in the preceding exercises.

(a) Argue that

$$\Pr(\mathcal{S}_i \leq t < \mathcal{S}_{i+1}) = \Pr(\mathcal{N}(t) = i),$$

provided $\mathcal{S}_0 = 0$.

(b) Explain that this yields Algorithm 2.14 for Poisson sampling; i.e., that $\mathcal{N}(t)$ is the largest integer i for which $X_1 + \cdots + X_i \le t$.

Exercise 8.4 Let $N_1, N_2 \ldots$ be stochastically independent Poisson variables with common parameter μT.

(a) Argue that $Y = N_1 + \cdots + N_J$ is Poisson distributed with parameter $J\mu T$ and tends to the normal distribution as $J \to \infty$.
(b) Justify that if $\mathcal{N} \sim \text{Poisson}(J\mu T)$, then $\mathcal{N}$ becomes normal as either J or $T \to \infty$.

Exercise 8.5 Consider a Poisson point process with claim intensity $J\mu(t)$ and with $\mathcal{N}(t)$ the number of events up to t.

(a) If X is the time of the first incident, copy the argument in Exercise 8.1 and deduce that

$$\Pr(X > t) = \Pr(\mathcal{N}(t) = 0) = \exp\left(-J\int_0^t \mu(s)\,ds\right).$$

(b) Differentiate $\Pr(X > x) = 1 - F(x)$ with respect to x and show that the density function is

$$f(x) = J\mu(x)\exp\left(-J\int_0^x \mu(s)\,ds\right) \quad \text{so that} \quad J\mu(x) = \frac{f(x)}{1 - F(x)},$$

where $f(x) = dF(x)/dx$. This **hazard rate** form of the model is relevant even for mortality modelling in Section 12.3.

Exercise 8.6

(a) Use inversion (Algorithm 2.1) and deduce that X of the preceding exercise can be sampled by solving the equation

$$\int_0^{X^*} \mu(s)\,ds = -\frac{1}{J}\log(U^*), \qquad U^* \sim \text{uniform}.$$

Suppose $\mu(t) = \mu_0 e^{\theta t}$, where $\theta \neq 0$ defines systematic growth or decline.
(b) Argue that

$$X^* = \frac{1}{\theta}\log\left(1 - \frac{\theta}{J\mu_0}\log(U^*)\right).$$

There are closed expressions for the density function of X, but Monte Carlo is just as easy.
(c) Draw $m = 1\,000\,000$ simulations of X when $\mu_0 = 0.005$, $\theta = 0.1$ and $J = 100$ and estimate/plot the density function.

R-*commands*:

```
U=runif(m); a=θ/(J*μ0);
X=log(1-a*log(U))/θ; plot(density(X,from=0)).
```

Exercise 8.7 Suppose insurance incidents for J policies come from J independent Poisson point processes with intensities $\mu(t) = \mu_0 e^{\theta t}$ and let $\mathcal{N}_k$ be the number of incidents between $(k-1)T$ and kT for $k = 1, \dots, K$.

(a) Argue that $\mathcal{N}_k$ is Poisson distributed with parameter $\lambda_k = \lambda_0 e^{\theta kT}$ where $\lambda_0 = J\mu_0(1 - e^{-\theta T})/\theta$.

(b) Generate $m = 100$ simulations of $\mathcal{N}_1, \dots, \mathcal{N}_K$ when $J = 1000$, $\mu_0 = 0.005$, $\theta = 0.1$, $T = 1$ and $K = 20$ and plot them jointly against time.

R-*commands*:

```
λ=J*μ0*(1-exp(-θ*T))/θ*exp(1:K*θ);
N=matrix(rpois(m*K,λ),K,m); matplot(1:K,N,''l'').
```

Exercise 8.8 Let $n_1, \dots, n_n$ be independent Poisson claims with parameters $\mu T_1, \dots, \mu T_n$ and let $A = T_1 + \cdots + T_n$.

(a) Show that $\hat{\mu} = (n_1 + \cdots + n_n)/A$ is an unbiased estimate of μ with standard deviation $\sqrt{\mu/A}$.

(b) Recalculate $E(\hat{\mu})$ when the parameter of n_j is $\lambda_j = \mu_j T_j$ and argue that the estimate has little practical interest when $\mu_1, \dots, \mu_J$ vary between customers.

(c) However, suppose things are arranged so that $T_1 = \cdots = T_n$. Which parameter of practical interest does $\hat{\mu}$ estimate now?

Exercise 8.9 The example in this exercise goes back to Greenwood and Yule (1920). A group of 648 female British munition workers had their accidents counted in a 5-week period during World War I. There were 448, 132, 42, 21, 3 and 2 cases of 0, 1, 2, 3, 4 and 5 accidents; see Stuart and Ord (1987), p. 174.

(a) Compute the mean $\bar{n}$, variance s^2 and dispersion coefficient D of the number of accidents per woman.

R-*commands*:

```
n=c(448,132,42,21,3,2); i=0:5; n̄=sum(i*n)/sum(n);
s²=sum(n*(i-n̄)**2)/(sum(n)-1); D=s²/n̄.
```

(b) Draw $m = 1000$ samples of 648 Poisson variables from $\lambda = \bar{n}$, recompute D for each sample and estimate/plot its density function.

R-*commands*:

```
N=matrix(rpois(sum(n)*m,n̄),sum(n),m);
D=apply(N,2,var)/apply(N,2,mean); plot(density(D)).
```

(c) Is it plausible that the accident data are Poisson distributed? More in Exercise 8.15.

Exercise 8.10 Suppose the premium for an insurance is $\pi = (1+\gamma)\xi\int_0^T \mu(s)\,ds$ where γ is the loading, ξ the mean payment per claim and T the period the contract lasts.

(a) Motivate this expression.
(b) If the premium is paid at the beginning and the customer leaves the contract at T_1 where $T_1 < T$, how much money might it be fair for the company to return?

Section 8.3

Exercise 8.11 Let $\mathcal{N}$ be the number of claims against a portfolio with the same random intensity μ for all policies so that $\mathcal{N}|\mu \sim \text{Poisson}(J\mu T)$.

(a) What is the distribution of $\mathcal{N}$ if $\mu = \xi G$ and $G \sim \text{Gamma}(\alpha)$?
(b) In this case deduce that $E(\mathcal{N}) = J\xi T$ and $\text{var}(\mathcal{N}) = J\xi T(1 + J\xi T/\alpha)$.
(c) Calculate the ratio $\text{sd}(\mathcal{N})/E(\mathcal{N})$ and comment on the behaviour as $J \to \infty$.

Exercise 8.12 The most popular model for random claim intensities might be $\mu = \xi G$ where $G \sim \text{Gamma}(\alpha)$, but another possibility is $\mu = \xi e^{-\tau^2/2+\tau\varepsilon}$ with $\varepsilon \sim N(0,1)$ and τ a parameter.

(a) Argue that $E(\mu) = \xi$ under both models and show that the standard deviations are equal if $\tau = \sqrt{\log(1+1/\alpha)}$. [*Hint*: $\text{sd}(\mu) = \xi\sqrt{e^{\tau^2}-1}$ under the log-normal.]
(b) If $\mathcal{N}|\mu \sim \text{Poisson}(J\mu T)$, argue that $E(\mathcal{N})$ is the same under both models and that $\text{sd}(\mathcal{N})$ is too when τ is selected as in (a).

Exercise 8.13 How discrepant are the two models of the previous exercise?

(a) Draw $m = 10\,000$ simulations of $\mathcal{N}$ under the Gamma model when $JT = 500$, $\xi = 0.05$ and $\alpha = 2$.

   R-*commands*:

   ```
   μ=ξ*rgamma(m,α)/α; Ngamma=rpois(m,JT*μ).
   ```

(b) Redo (a) for the log-normal with $\tau = 0.63676$.

   R-*commands*:

   ```
   μ=ξ*exp(-τ**2/2+τ*rnorm(m)); Nlogn=rpois(m,JT*μ).
   ```

(c) Compute the means and standard deviations of the simulations and compare distributions through a Q–Q plot.

   R-*commands*:

   `mean(Ngamma); sd(Ngamma)` and similarly for `Nlogn` and `plot(sort(Ngamma),sort(Nlogn))`.

Exercise 8.14 Consider a sample of negative binomial observations with risk exposure $T = 1$ for everybody, so that expectations and variances are ξ and $\xi(1 + \xi/\alpha)$.

(a) Show that moment estimates for ξ and α are $\hat{\xi} = \overline{n}$ and $\hat{\alpha} = \overline{n}^2/(s^2 - \overline{n})$, where $\overline{n}$ and s^2 are the ordinary sample mean and variance.
(b) How would you proceed if $\hat{\alpha} \leq 0$? [*Note*: This is a special case of the more general method in the text.]

Exercise 8.15 A possible extension of the Poisson model in Exercise 8.9 is random λ for each woman, for example $\lambda = \xi G$ with $G \sim$ Gamma(α).

(a) Compute estimates $\hat{\xi}$ and $\hat{\alpha}$ using the method in Exercise 8.14.

R-*commands*:

Take $\overline{n}$ and s^2 from Exercise 8.9 and use `ξ̂=n̄; α̂=n̄**2/(s²-n̄)`.

(b) Compute for $i = 0, \dots, 5$ the expected number of workers with i accidents under the present model and under the one in Exercise 8.9, i.e., $648 \times \Pr(N = i)$ and compare with the observed sequence.

R-*commands*:

```
i=0:5; p=α̂/(α̂+ξ̂); Enbin=648*dnbinom(i,α̂,p);
Epois=648*dpois(i,ξ̂).
```

(c) What conclusion do you draw from (b)?

Exercise 8.16 Consider historical claim data $n_1, \dots, n_K$ with risk exposures $A_1, \dots, A_K$ and estimates $\hat{\mu}_k = n_k/A_k$ for the claim intensities; see (8.1). Suppose the underlying μ_k are random with mean ξ and standard deviation σ.

(a) Argue that $\hat{\xi} = w_1\hat{\mu}_1 + \cdots + w_K\hat{\mu}_K$ is an unbiased estimate of ξ when $w_k = A_k/(A_1 + \cdots + A_K)$.
(b) If claim intensities and claims in different periods are independent, show that $\text{var}(\hat{\xi}) = \xi/(A_1 + \cdots + A_K) + \sigma^2(w_1^2 + \cdots + w_K^2)$. [*Hint*: Recall $E(\hat{\mu}_k|\mu_k) = \mu_k$ and $\text{var}(\hat{\mu}_k|\mu_k) = \mu_k/A_k$ and use the rule of double variance.]
(c) Show that $\text{sd}(\hat{\xi}) \geq \sigma/\sqrt{K}$, and there are limits to the accuracy of the estimate however large the portfolio. [*Hint*: Utilize that $K\sum_{k=1}^K A_k^2 \geq (\sum_{k=1}^K A_k)^2$.]

Section 8.4

Exercise 8.17 The estimates in Table 8.4 are an extract of Table 11.2 in Chapter 11 and show the effect of gear type and annual driving limit on claim intensity when estimated from monthly data.

Table 8.4 Regression estimates for Exercises 8.17 and 8.18, standard deviation in parentheses

Intercept			Manual gear	Automatic gear		
−5.407 (0.010)			0	−0.340 (0.005)		
			Annual driving limit of policy (1000 km)			
8	12	16	20	25	30	No limit
0	0.097 (0.006)	0.116 (0.007)	0.198 (0.008)	0.227(0.019)	0.308 (0.012)	0.468 (0.019)

(a) Argue that the model might apply on an annual time scale by changing the intercept parameter.

(b) How much higher is the annual claim intensity for cars with manual gear?

(c) How do you interpret that the driving limit coefficients increase from left to right?

(d) Does the pattern in (c) appear accidental? [*Hint*: If $\hat{b}_1, \ldots, \hat{b}_7$ and $\sigma_1, \ldots, \sigma_7$ are the estimates and their standard deviation, use $|\hat{b}_i - \hat{b}_j|/(\sigma_i + \sigma_j) > 2$ as a formal, *conservative* criterion for significance.]

Exercise 8.18

(a) Use Table 8.4 to compute annual claim intensities broken down on gear type and driving limit in a display similar to that in Table 8.3.

R-*commands*:

```
driv=c(0,0.097,0.116,0.198,0.227,0.308,0.468);
manu=12*exp(-5.407+driv); auto=manu*exp(-0.34);
intensity=cbind(manu,auto).
```

(b) Modify the table by dividing the entries on the corresponding driving limit and argue that this might be a rough measure of claim intensity per 1000 km.

R-*commands*:

```
km=c(8,12,16,20,25,30); intensity[1:6,]/km.
```

(c) Summarize the change in pattern from (a) to (b) and speculate on the reason.

Exercise 8.19 The data stored in `norwegianclaims.txt` come from a Norwegian insurance company and is annual data with four columns, from left to right 'age', 'gender', 'risk exposure' and 'number of claims'. 'Age' has seven categories (20–21, 22–23, 24–25, 26–39, 40–55, 56–70, 71–94 in years), coded 1–7, and 'gender' is 0 for males and 1 for females. Some of the individuals are included more than once (in different years), but this doesn't matter when the data are used as here.

(a) Read the data from file and fit a Poisson regression with 'age' and 'gender' as explanatory variables.

R-*commands*:

```
n=matrix(scan(''norwegianclaims.txt''),byrow=T,ncol=4);
age=factor(n[,1]); gender=factor(n[,2]);
T=n[,3]; o=glm(n[,4]~age+gender+offset(log(T)),poisson).
```

(b) Describe the main features linking claim frequency and age/gender.

R-*commands*:

```
summary(o).
```

Exercise 8.20

(a) Set up a table where annual claim intensity is broken down on age and gender under the model of the preceding exercise.

R-*commands*:

With o as in Exercise 8.20 use $\hat{b}$=o$coefficients;
age=c(0,$\hat{b}$[2:7]); gender=c(0,$\hat{b}$[8]);
intensity= exp($\hat{b}$[1])*exp(gender)%o%exp(age).

(b) Summarize how claim intensity depends on age and gender in this example.

Exercise 8.21 Let T_{ij} and n_{ij} be total risk exposure and total number of claims in gender i and age j for the data in Exercise 8.19.

(a) Write a program computing the matrices $\mathbf{T} = (T_{ij})$ and $\mathbf{n} = (n_{ij})$.

R-*commands*:

```
nn=matrix(0,2,7); T=nn; for (i in 1:2){for (j in 1:7)
{T[i,j]=sum(n[n[,1]==j&n[,2]==i-1,3]);
nn[i,j]=sum(n[n[,1]==j&n[,2]==i-1,4])}}.
```

(b) Compute a table of elementary estimates $\hat{\mu}_{ij} = n_{ij}/T_{ij}$ with their estimated standard deviations.

R-*commands*:

$\hat{\mu}$=nn/T; Sd=sqrt($\hat{\mu}$/T).

(c) Compare with the evaluation in Exercise 8.21 and judge both approaches.

Exercise 8.22 Let $\mu = \alpha e^{\gamma_\mu (x-x_\mu)^2}$ be the annual claim intensity in age x with α, γ_μ and x_μ parameters.

(a) Convince yourself that the model imitates a real situation by plotting μ against x for x between 20 and 89 years when $\alpha = 0.05$, $\gamma_\mu = 0.00025$, $x_\mu = 75$.

R-*commands*:

x=20:89; μ=α*exp(γ_μ*(x-x_μ)**2); plot(x,μ,''l'').

Consider $\mathcal{J} = 10\,000$ individuals between 20 and 89 with J_x in age x.

(b) Compute and plot the age distribution when $J_x = ce^{-\gamma_J (x-x_J)^2}$, where c is a normalizing constant and $\gamma_J = 0.002$, $x_J = 40$.

R-*commands*:

$\texttt{q=exp(-}\gamma_J\texttt{*(x-}x_J\texttt{)**2);}$ $J_x\texttt{=ceiling(q*}\mathcal{J}\texttt{/sum(q));plot(x,}J_x\texttt{).}$

(c) Simulate the annual Poisson counts under this model.

R-*commands*:

$\texttt{n=rpoisson(length(}J_x\texttt{),}J_x\texttt{*}\mu\texttt{).}$

Exercise 8.23

(a) Write a program fitting the model $\log(\mu) = b_0 + b_1 x + b_2 x^2$ to data generated as in Exercise 8.22 and compute the estimated intensities $\hat{\mu} = e^{\hat{b}_0+\hat{b}_1 x+\hat{b}_2 x^2}$.

R-*commands*:

With $\texttt{x,}J_x\texttt{,n}$ as in Exercise 8.22 use $x_2\texttt{=x**2;}$
$\texttt{v=glm(n}\sim\texttt{x+}x_2\texttt{+offset(log(}J_x\texttt{)),poisson);}$ $\hat{b}\texttt{=v[[1]];}$
$\hat{\mu}\texttt{=exp(}\hat{b}\texttt{[1]+}\hat{b}\texttt{[2]*x+}\hat{b}\texttt{[3]*}x_2\texttt{).}$

(b) Simulate data under the conditions in Exercise 8.22, compute the fitted intensities $\hat{\mu}$ and plot them against x jointly with the true intensities μ.

R-*commands*:

With μ from Exercise 8.22 use $\texttt{plot(x,}\mu\texttt{,''l'',ylim=c(0,0.12));}$
$\texttt{points(x,}\hat{\mu}\texttt{).}$

Exercise 8.24 Can the relationship between μ and x in Exercise 8.22 be recovered without the polynomial model (which wouldn't be known in practice)?

(a) Write a program dividing the age axis into n_c equally long categories, fit the model on this categorical form and estimate the intensities for all groups.

R-*commands*:

With $\texttt{x,}J_x\texttt{,n}$ as in Exercise 8.22 use $\texttt{b=(x[length(x)]-x[1]+1)/}n_c\texttt{;}$
$a_c\texttt{=x[1]-(b+1)/2+1:}n_c\texttt{*b;}$ $\texttt{age=factor(floor(1+(x-x[1])/b));}$
$\texttt{v=glm(n}\sim\texttt{age+offset(log(}J_x\texttt{)),poisson);}$
$\hat{b}\texttt{=v[[1]];}$ $\hat{\mu}_c\texttt{=exp(}\hat{b}\texttt{[1]+c(0,}\hat{b}\texttt{[2:}n_c\texttt{])).}$

(b) Apply the program to the simulations in Exercise 8.23 when $n_c = 7$ and plot the true intensities with the estimates per category added.

R-*commands*:

With μ from Exercise 8.22 use
$\texttt{plot(x,}\mu\texttt{,ylim=c(0,0.12));}$ $\texttt{points(}a_c\texttt{,}\hat{\mu}_c\texttt{).}$

(c) Redo (b) when $n_c = 14$ and $n_c = 35$ and comment.

(d) Redo (b), (c) when $\mathcal{J} = 100\,000$.

Exercise 8.25 Add gender to the model in Exercise 8.22 so that $\mu = \alpha e^{\gamma_\mu(x-x_\mu)^2+\theta s}$ where $s = 0$ for males and 1 for females.

(a) Simulate claim numbers under the conditions in Exercise 8.22 when $\theta = 0.05$, assuming equally many males and females.

R-*commands*:

With x as in Exercise 8.22 use
```
s=c(rep(0,length(x)),rep(1,length(x)));
x=c(x,x); μ=α*exp(γ_μ*(x-x_μ)**2+s*θ)
```
and then as in Exercise 8.22(b), (c).

(b) Fit the model and print estimated parameters with their standard deviation.

R-*commands*:
```
x_2=x**2; s=factor(s);
v=glm(n~x+x_2+s+offset(log(J_x)),poisson); summary(v)
```

(c) Redo a few times and judge whether $\mathcal{J} = 10000$ is sufficient to pick up a gender effect.

Section 8.5

Exercise 8.26 Consider an IBNR portfolio where annual claims are Poisson distributed with parameter $J\mu T$ and settled according to the delay probabilities $q_0, \dots, q_L$ and let $\mathcal{N}_k$ be the total number of claims liquidated in year k among those that have occurred in year 0 and earlier.

(a) Argue that $\mathcal{N}_1, \dots, \mathcal{N}_L$ are independent with $\mathcal{N}_k \sim$ Poisson(λ_k), where $\lambda_k = J\mu T(q_k + \cdots + q_L)$.

(b) If $q_l = ce^{-\gamma l}$ where $c = (1 - e^{-\gamma})/(1 - e^{-(L+1)\gamma})$, show that $\lambda_k = J\mu Te^{-k\gamma}(1 - e^{-(L-k+1)\gamma})/(1 - e^{-(L+1)\gamma})$. [*Hint*: Utilize that $1 + x + \cdots + x^n = (1 - x^{n+1})/(1 - x)$ when $x \neq 1$.]

(c) Plot $\lambda_k = E(\mathcal{N}_k)$ against k when $\mu = 0.05$, $JT = 100\,000$, $\gamma = 0.2$ and $L = 20$.

R-*commands*:
```
ll=1:L; a=JT*μ/(1-exp(-(L+1)*γ));
λ=a*exp(-ll*γ)*(1-exp(-γ*(L-ll+1))); plot(ll,λ).
```

Exercise 8.27 Let the situation be as in Exercise 8.26, except for the delay probabilities being $q_l = ce^{-\gamma|l-l_m|}$ for $l = 0, \dots, L$.

(a) Write a program generating m simulations of $\mathcal{N}_1, \dots, \mathcal{N}_L$.

R-*commands*:
```
q=exp(-γ*abs(0:L-l_m)); q=q/sum(q);
λ=JT*μ*(1-cumsum(q[1:L])); N=matrix(rpois(m*L,λ),L,m).
```

(b) Run the program when $m = 50$, $\mu = 0.05$, $JT = 100{,}000$, $\gamma = 0.2$, $l_m = 5$ and $L = 20$ and plot the simulated IBNR counts jointly against time.

R-*commands*:

```
matplot(1:L,N,''l'').
```

Exercise 8.28 Consider historical claims data with $\mathcal{N}_{-s,l}$ the number of claims with origin in year $-s$ and settled in year $-s+l$ for $l = 0,\dots,L$. Introduce $\mu_s = \xi G_s$ as the intensity in year $-s$ where $G_s \sim \text{Gamma}(\alpha)$ and let $\mathcal{N}_{-s,l}|\mu_s \sim \text{Poisson}(J\mu_s T q_l)$. All $\mathcal{N}_{-s,l}$ are conditionally independent given μ_s, and all μ_s are independent.

(a) Write a program simulating such IBNR data for $s = 0,\dots,L$ when $q_l = ce^{-\gamma|l-l_m|}$.

R-*commands*:

```
μ=ξ*rgamma(L+1,α)/α; q=exp(-γ*abs(0:L-l_m)); q=q/sum(q);
λ=JT*q%o%μ; n=matrix(rpois((L+1)*(L+1),λ),L+1,L+1).
```

(b) Run the program when $L = 20$, $\gamma = 0.2$, $l_m = 5$, $\xi = 0.05$, $\alpha = 10$ and $JT = 10\,000$ and plot claim numbers against l for all cohorts s jointly.

R-*commands*:

```
matplot(0:L,n,''l'').
```

Exercise 8.29 Among the counts $\mathcal{N}_{-s,l}$ in Exercise 8.28 only those for which $l \leq s$ are known at the end of year 0.

(a) Generate such historical data and write a program fitting a log-linear model as described in the text.

R-*commands*:

With `n` as in Exercise 8.28 use `z=n[row(n)<=col(n)];`

```
a=factor(rep(1:(L+1),1:(L+1))); b=1;
for (s in 2:(L+1))b=c(b,1:s); b=factor(b);
v=glm(z~a+b+offset(log(rep(JT,length(z)))),poisson).
```

(b) Run the program under the conditions in Exercise 8.28 and try to interpret what you see (which doesn't take you far!).

R-*commands*:

The R-model fitted is of the form $\log(\mu_{sl}) = \zeta + \theta_s + \beta_l$ with two of the parameters zero by design; use $\hat{\zeta}$`=v[[1]][1];`

$\hat{\theta}$`=c(0,v[[1]][1:L+1]);` $\hat{\beta}$`=c(0,v[[1]][1:L+(L+1)]).`

Exercise 8.30 The original model in Exercise 8.29 was $\mu_{sl} = q_l\mu_s$, whereas software works with $\mu_{sl} = e^{\zeta+\theta_s+\beta_l}$.

(a) Argue that q_l is proportional to e^{β_l} so that $q_l = e^{\beta_l}/c$ where $c = e^{\beta_0} + \cdots + e^{\beta_L}$.
(b) Show that $\mu_s = ce^{\zeta+\theta_s}$.
(c) Write a program converting the output of Exercise 8.29(a) to estimates of probabilities and intensities.

R-*commands*:

With $\hat{\zeta}, \hat{\theta}, \hat{\beta}$ as in Exercise 8.29 use

```
c=sum(exp(β̂)); q̂=exp(β̂)/c; μ̂=c*exp(ζ̂+θ̂).
```

(d) Run the program with the estimates from Exercise 8.29 and examine $\hat{q}_l$ and $\hat{\mu}_s$ for $l = 0, \ldots, L$ and $s = 0, \ldots, L$.

Exercise 8.31

(a) Plot the estimates $\hat{q}_l$ against l in Exercise 8.30 jointly with the exact q_l.

R-*commands*:

With q from Exercise 8.28 and $\hat{q}$ from Exercise 8.30 use

```
plot(0:L,q,''l''); lines(0:L;q̂).
```

(b) Plot the estimated intensities against time and explain why the jumps around their mean are not likely to go down much if the insurance portfolio is larger.

R-*commands*:

With $\hat{\mu}$ from Exercise 8.30 use

```
plot(0:L,μ̂).
```

(c) Redo the simulations and plots in (a) and (b) when $JT = 1000$ and examine the estimation errors now.

9

Modelling claim size

9.1 Introduction

Models describing variation in claim size lack the theoretical underpinning provided by the Poisson point process. The traditional approach is to impose a family of probability distributions and estimate their parameters from historical claims $z_1, \ldots, z_n$ (corrected for inflation if necessary). Even the family itself is often determined from experience. An alternative with considerable merit is to throw all prior mathematical conditions overboard and rely solely on the historical data. This is known as a **non-parametric** approach. Much of this chapter is on the use of historical data.

How we proceed is partly dictated by the size of the historical record, and here the variation is enormous. With automobile insurance the number of observations n might be large, providing a good basis for the probability distribution of the claim size Z. By contrast, major incidents in industry (like the collapse of an oil rig) are rare, making the historical material scarce. Such diversity in what there is to go on is reflected in the presentation below. The extreme right tail of the distribution warrants special attention. Lack of historical data where it matters most financially is a challenge. What can be done about it is discussed in Section 9.5.

9.2 Parametric and non-parametric modelling

9.2.1 Introduction

Claim size modelling can be **parametric** through families of distributions such as the Gamma, log-normal or Pareto with parameters tuned to historical data or **non-parametric** where each claim z_i of the past is assigned a probability $1/n$ of reappearing in the future. A new claim is then envisaged as a random variable $\hat{Z}$

for which

$$\Pr(\hat{Z} = z_i) = \frac{1}{n}, \quad i = 1, \dots, n. \tag{9.1}$$

This is an entirely proper probability distribution (the sum over all i is 1). It may appear peculiar, but there are several points in its favour (and one in its disfavour); see below. Note the notation $\hat{Z}$, which is the familiar way of emphasizing that estimation has been involved. The model is known as the **empirical distribution** and will, in Section 9.5, be employed as a brick in an edifice which also involves the Pareto distribution. The purpose of this section is to review parametric and non-parametric modelling at a general level.

9.2.2 Scale families of distributions

All sensible parametric models for claim size are of the form

$$Z = \beta Z_0, \tag{9.2}$$

where $\beta > 0$ is a parameter and Z_0 is a standardized random variable corresponding to $\beta = 1$. This proportionality is inherited by expectations, standard deviations and percentiles; i.e., if ξ_0, σ_0 and $q_{0\epsilon}$ are expectation, standard deviation and ϵ-percentile for Z_0, then the same quantities for Z are

$$\xi = \beta\xi_0, \qquad \sigma = \beta\sigma_0 \qquad \text{and} \qquad q_\epsilon = \beta q_{0\epsilon}. \tag{9.3}$$

To see what β stands for, suppose the currency is changed as part of some international transaction. With c as the exchange rate the claim quoted in foreign currency becomes cZ, and from (9.2) $cZ = (c\beta)Z_0$. The effect of passing from one currency to another is simply that $c\beta$ replaces β, the shape of the density function remaining what it was. Surely anything else makes little sense. It would be contrived to take a view on risk that differed in terms of US\$ from that in £ or €, and this applies to inflation too (Exercise 9.1).

In statistics, β is known as a **parameter of scale** and parametric distributions of claim size should always include them. Superficially the log-normal model $Z = e^{\theta+\sigma\varepsilon}$ where θ and σ are parameters and $\varepsilon \sim N(0, 1)$ does not, but it may be rephrased as

$$Z = \xi Z_0 \qquad \text{where} \quad Z_0 = e^{-\sigma^2/2+\sigma\varepsilon} \quad \text{and} \quad \xi = e^{\theta+\sigma^2/2}.$$

Here $E(Z_0) = 1$, and ξ serves as both expectation and scale parameter. The mean is often the most important of all quantities associated with a distribution, and it is useful to make it visible in the mathematical notation.

9.2.3 Fitting a scale family

Models for scale families satisfy

$$\Pr(Z \leq z) = \Pr(Z_0 \leq z/\beta) \qquad \text{or} \qquad F(z|\beta) = F_0(z/\beta).$$

where $F(z|\beta)$ and $F_0(z)$ are the distribution functions of Z and Z_0. Differentiating with respect to z yields the family of density functions

$$f(z|\beta) = \frac{1}{\beta} f_0\left(\frac{z}{\beta}\right), \quad z > 0 \qquad \text{where} \quad f_0(z) = \frac{dF_0(z)}{dz}. \tag{9.4}$$

Additional parameters describing the shape of the distributions are hiding in $f_0(z)$. Density functions of scale families are always of this form.

The standard method of fitting such models is through likelihood estimation. If $z_1, \ldots, z_n$ are the historical claims, the criterion becomes

$$\mathcal{L}(\beta, f_0) = -n\log(\beta) + \sum_{i=1}^{n} \log\{f_0(z_i/\beta)\}, \tag{9.5}$$

which is to be maximized with respect to β and other parameters. Numerical methods are usually required. A useful extension covers situations with **censoring**. Typical examples are claims only registered as above or below certain limits, known as censoring **to the right** and **left**, respectively. Perhaps the situation where the actual loss is only given as some *lower* bound b is most frequent. The chance of a claim Z exceeding b is $1 - F_0(b/\beta)$, and for n_b such events with lower bounds $b_1, \ldots, b_{n_b}$ the analogous joint probability becomes

$$\{1 - F_0(b_1/\beta)\} \cdots \{1 - F_0(b_{n_b}/\beta)\}.$$

Take the *logarithm* of this product and add it to the log-likelihood (9.5) of the fully observed claims $z_1, \ldots, z_n$. The criterion then becomes

$$\mathcal{L}(\beta, f_0) \;=\; \underbrace{-n\log(\beta) + \textstyle\sum_{i=1}^{n} \log\{f_0(z_i/\beta)\}}_{\textit{complete information}} \;+\; \underbrace{\textstyle\sum_{i=1}^{n_b} \log\{1 - F_0(b_i/\beta)\}}_{\textit{censoring to the right}}, \tag{9.6}$$

which is to be maximized. Censoring to the left is similar and discussed in Exercise 9.3. Details for the Pareto family will be developed in Section 9.4.

9.2.4 Shifted distributions

The distribution of a claim may start at some threshold b instead of at the origin. Obvious examples are deductibles and reinsurance contracts. Models can be constructed by adding b to variables starting at the origin; i.e., $Z = b + \beta Z_0$, where Z_0

is a standardized variable as before. Now

$$\Pr(Z \le z) = \Pr(b + \beta Z_0 \le z) = \Pr\left(Z_0 \le \frac{z-b}{\beta}\right),$$

and differentiation with respect to z yields

$$f(z|\beta) = \frac{1}{\beta} f_0\left(\frac{z-b}{\beta}\right), \qquad z > b \tag{9.7}$$

which is the density function of random variables with b as a lower limit.

It may sometimes be useful to allow an *unknown* threshold b. All historical claims $z_1, \ldots, z_n$ exceed b, and their *minimum* provides an estimate, i.e.,

$$\hat{b} = \min(z_1, \ldots, z_n) - c, \qquad \text{for unbiasedness: } c = \beta \int_0^\infty \{1 - F_0(z)\}^n \, dz; \tag{9.8}$$

see Exercise 9.4 for the unbiasedness adjustment. Typically $\hat{b}$ is a highly accurate estimate even without the correction, and calculating c is rarely worth the trouble (and raises an estimation problem of its own). But it *is* usually a good idea to subtract some small number $c > 0$ from the minimum to make all $z_i - \hat{b}$ strictly positive and avoid software crashes. The estimate $\hat{b}$ is known to be **super-efficient**, which means that its standard deviation for large sample sizes is proportional to $1/n$ rather than the usual $1/\sqrt{n}$; see Lehmann and Casella (1998). Other parameters can be fitted by applying the methods of this section to the sample $z_1 - \hat{b}, \ldots, z_n - \hat{b}$.

9.2.5 Skewness as a simple description of shape

A major issue with claim size modelling is asymmetry and the right tail of the distribution. A simple summary is the **coefficient of skewness**

$$\zeta = \text{skew}(Z) = \frac{\nu_3}{\sigma^3} \qquad \text{where} \quad \nu_3 = E(Z - \xi)^3. \tag{9.9}$$

The numerator is the **third-order moment**. Skewness should *not* depend on currency and doesn't, since

$$\text{skew}(Z) = \frac{E(Z-\xi)^3}{\sigma^3} = \frac{E(\beta Z_0 - \beta\xi_0)^3}{(\beta\sigma_0)^3} = \frac{E(Z_0 - \xi_0)^3}{\sigma_0^3} = \text{skew}(Z_0)$$

after inserting (9.2) and (9.3). Nor is the coefficient changed when Z is shifted by a fixed amount; i.e., $\text{skew}(Z + b) = \text{skew}(Z)$ through the same type of reasoning. These properties confirm skewness as a simplified measure of shape.

The standard estimate of the skewness coefficient ζ from observations $z_1, \ldots, z_n$ is

$$\hat{\zeta} = \frac{\hat{\nu}_3}{s^3} \qquad \text{where} \quad \hat{\nu}_3 = \frac{1}{n - 3 + 2/n} \sum_{i=1}^n (z_i - \bar{z})^3. \tag{9.10}$$

Here $\hat{\nu}_3$ is the natural estimate of the third-order moment (division by $n - 3 + 2/n$ makes it unbiased), and s is the sample standard deviation. In property insurance the estimate is often severely biased downwards; see Exercise 9.5.

9.2.6 Non-parametric estimation

The random variable $\hat{Z}$ that attaches probabilities $1/n$ to all claims z_i of the past is a possible model for *future* claims. Its definition in (9.1) as a discrete set of probabilities may seem at odds with the underlying distribution being continuous, but experience in statistics (see Efron and Tibshirani, 1993) suggests that this matters little. Expectation, standard deviation, skewness and percentiles are all closely related to the ordinary sample versions. For example, by definition

$$E(\hat{Z}) = \sum_{i=1}^{n} \frac{1}{n} z_i = \bar{z} \qquad \text{and} \qquad \text{sd}(\hat{Z}) = \left(\sum_{i=1}^{n} \frac{1}{n} (z_i - \bar{z})^2 \right)^{1/2}, \tag{9.11}$$

where the standard deviation is almost the ordinary sample version. Third-order moment and skewness become

$$\nu_3(\hat{Z}) = \frac{1}{n} \sum_{i=1}^{n} (z_i - \bar{z})^3 \qquad \text{and} \qquad \text{skew}(\hat{Z}) = \frac{\nu_3(\hat{Z})}{\{\text{sd}(\hat{Z})\}^3}, \tag{9.12}$$

whereas upper percentiles are (approximately) the historical claims in descending order; i.e.,

$$\hat{q}_\varepsilon = z_{(\varepsilon n)} \qquad \text{where} \qquad z_{(1)} \geq \cdots \geq z_{(n)}.$$

The empirical distribution function can only be visualized as a **dot plot**, where the observations $z_1, \ldots, z_n$ are recorded on a straight line to make their tightness indicate the underlying distribution. If you want a density function, turn to the kernel estimate in Section 2.2, which is related to $\hat{Z}$ in the following way. Let ε be a random variable with mean 0 and standard deviation 1, and define

$$\hat{Z}_h = \hat{Z} + hs\varepsilon \qquad \text{where} \quad h \geq 0. \tag{9.13}$$

The distribution of $\hat{Z}_h$ coincides with the estimate (2.6) if ε is normal; see Exercise 9.7. Sampling is easy (Exercise 9.8), but there is rarely much point in using a positive h for things other than visualization

The empirical distribution function in finance is often referred to as **historical simulation**. It is ultra-rapidly set up and simulated (use Algorithm 4.1), and there is no worry as to whether a parametric family fits or not. However, skewness tends to be too small (as noted above), and *no simulated claim can be larger than what has been seen in the past*. These are serious drawbacks which imply underestimation of risk, though not severely when economic responsibility per event is sufficiently limited. The method is also usable when there is extensive experience to draw on, such as in the big consumer branches of motors and housing where we might have met much of the worst. It is even possible to call upon specific techniques for tail estimation to button it up; see Section 9.5.

9.3 The log-normal and Gamma families

9.3.1 Introduction

The log-normal and Gamma families of distributions are common models for insurance losses, and one of them is usually in the background when regression methods are used to investigate links between the size of claims and explanatory variables such as those in Section 8.4. A brief review of both models is offered in the following.

9.3.2 The log-normal: A quick summary

A convenient definition of the log-normal model in the present context is as $Z = \xi Z_0$, where $Z_0 = e^{-\sigma^2/2+\sigma\varepsilon}$ for $\varepsilon \sim N(0,1)$. Examples of their density functions were shown in Figure 2.4. The shape depends heavily on σ and is highly skewed when σ is not too close to zero. The mean, standard deviation and skewness are

$$E(Z) = \xi, \qquad \mathrm{sd}(Z) = \xi\sqrt{e^{\sigma^2}-1} \quad \text{and} \qquad \mathrm{skew}(Z) = (e^{\sigma^2}+2)\sqrt{e^{\sigma^2}-1}; \tag{9.14}$$

see Section 2.4. The expression for the skewness coefficient is derived in Exercise 9.11.

Parameter estimation is usually carried out by noting that logarithms are Gaussian. Thus

$$Y = \log(Z) = \underbrace{\log(\xi) - \tfrac{1}{2}\sigma^2}_{mean} + \underbrace{\sigma\varepsilon}_{sd},$$

and when the original log-normal observations $z_1, \dots, z_n$ are transformed to Gaussian ones through $y_1 = \log(z_1), \dots, y_n = \log(z_n)$ with sample mean and standard deviation $\bar{y}$ and s_y, the estimates of ξ and σ become

$$\log(\hat{\xi}) - \frac{1}{2}\hat{\sigma}^2 = \bar{y}, \quad \hat{\sigma} = s_y \qquad \text{or} \qquad \hat{\xi} = e^{s_y^2/2+\bar{y}}, \quad \hat{\sigma} = s_y.$$

Log-normal distributions are used everywhere in this book.

9.3.3 The Gamma model

Good operational qualities and flexible shape make the Gamma model useful in many contexts. It was defined in Section 2.5 as $Z = \xi G$, where $G \sim \mathrm{Gamma}(\alpha)$

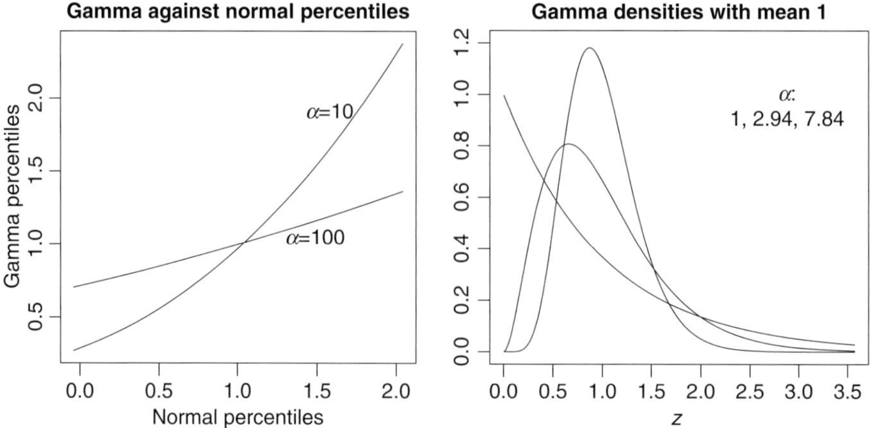

Figure 9.1 *Left*: Q–Q plot of standard Gamma percentiles for $\alpha = 10$ and 100 against the normal. *Right*: Standard Gamma density functions for $\alpha = 1$, 2.94 and 7.84.

is the standard Gamma with mean one and shape α. The mean, standard deviation and skewness are

$$E(Z) = \xi, \qquad \text{sd}(Z) = \xi/\sqrt{\alpha} \qquad \text{and} \qquad \text{skew}(Z) = 2/\sqrt{\alpha}, \tag{9.15}$$

and there is a **convolution** property. Suppose $G_1, \dots, G_n$ are independent with $G_i \sim \text{Gamma}(\alpha_i)$ for $i = 1, \dots, n$. Then

$$\overline{G} \sim \text{Gamma}\,(\alpha_1 + \cdots + \alpha_n) \qquad \text{if} \qquad \overline{G} = \frac{\alpha_1 G_1 + \cdots + \alpha_n G_n}{\alpha_1 + \cdots + \alpha_n},$$

which is proved in elementary textbooks in statistics and probability. In particular, if $\alpha_1 = \cdots = \alpha_n = \alpha$ then $\overline{G} = (G_1 + \cdots + G_n)/n$ and the average of independent, standard Gamma variables is another standard Gamma variable, now with shape $n\alpha$. By the central limit theorem this average also tends to the normal as $n \to \infty$, and this proves that Gamma variables become normal as $\alpha \to \infty$. That is visible in Figure 9.1 left, where percentiles for standard Gamma variables are Q–Q plotted against Gaussian percentiles with mean 1 and standard deviation $1/\sqrt{10}$. The line is much straightened out when $\alpha = 10$ is replaced by $\alpha = 100$. A similar tendency is seen among the density functions in Figure 9.1 right, where two of the distributions were used in Section 8.3 to describe stochastic claim intensities.

9.3.4 Fitting the Gamma familiy

Gamma parameters ξ and α can be determined from historical data $z_1, \dots, z_n$ through the method of moments (Section 7.3), which is the simplest method technically. The sample mean and standard deviation $\bar{z}$ and s are then matched to the theoretical expressions, yielding

$$\bar{z} = \hat{\xi}, \quad s = \hat{\xi}/\sqrt{\alpha} \qquad \text{with solution} \quad \hat{\xi} = \bar{z}, \quad \hat{\alpha} = (\bar{z}/s)^2.$$

Likelihood estimation (a little more accurate) is available in statistical software, but it is not difficult to implement on your own. The logarithm of the density function of the standard Gamma is

$$\log\{f_0(z)\} = \alpha\log(\alpha) - \log\{\Gamma(\alpha)\} + (\alpha-1)\log(z) - \alpha z,$$

which can be inserted into the log-likelihood function (9.5). Then, after some simple manipulations,

$$\mathcal{L}(\xi,\alpha) = n\alpha\log(\alpha/\xi) - n\log\Gamma(\alpha) + (\alpha-1)\sum_{i=1}^{n}\log(z_i) - \frac{\alpha}{\xi}\sum_{i=1}^{n} z_i. \tag{9.16}$$

Note that

$$\frac{\partial\mathcal{L}}{\partial\xi} = -\frac{n\alpha}{\xi} + \frac{\alpha}{\xi^2}\sum_{i=1}^{n} z_i \quad \text{and} \quad \frac{\partial\mathcal{L}}{\partial\xi} = 0 \quad \text{when} \quad \xi = (z_1 + \cdots + z_n)/n = \bar{z}.$$

It follows that $\hat{\xi} = \bar{z}$ is the likelihood estimate and $\mathcal{L}(\bar{z},\alpha)$ can be tracked under variation of α for the maximizing value $\hat{\alpha}$. A better way is by the bracketing method in Appendix C.4. To approximate $\Gamma(\alpha)$, use Table 2.3.

9.3.5 *Regression for claims size*

You may sometimes want to examine whether the claim size tends to be systematically higher with certain customers than with others. In the author's experience the issue is often less important than for claim frequency, but we should certainly know how it's done. The basis is historical data similar to that in Section 8.4, now of the form

$$\begin{array}{cc}
z_1 & x_{11}\cdots x_{1v} \\
z_2 & x_{21}\cdots x_{2v} \\
\vdots & \vdots \\
z_n & x_{n1}\cdots x_{nv}, \\
\textit{losses} & \textit{covariates}
\end{array}$$

and the question is how we use this to understand how a future reported loss Z is connected to the explanatory variables $x_1, \ldots, x_v$. A standard approach is to introduce Z_0 with $E(Z_0) = 1$ and specify

$$Z = \xi Z_0 \qquad \text{where} \quad \log(\xi) = b_0 + b_1x_1 + \cdots + b_vx_v.$$

As the explanatory variables fluctuate, so does the mean loss ξ.

Frequently applied models for Z_0 are log-normal and Gamma. The former simply boils down to ordinary linear regression and least squares with the logarithm of the losses as dependent variable. Gamma regression, a member of the family of generalized linear models (Section 8.7), is available in statistical software and implemented through an extension of (9.16). An example is given in Section 10.4.

9.4 The Pareto families

9.4.1 Introduction

The Pareto distributions, introduced in Section 2.5, are among the most heavy-tailed of all models in practical use and potentially a conservative choice when evaluating risk. Density and distribution functions are

$$f(z) = \frac{\alpha/\beta}{(1+z/\beta)^{1+\alpha}} \quad \text{and} \quad F(z) = 1 - \frac{1}{(1+z/\beta)^{\alpha}}, \qquad z > 0.$$

Simulation is easy (Algorithm 2.13) and the model, which we denote Pareto(α,β), was used for illustration in several earlier chapters. Pareto distributions also play a special role in the mathematical description of the extreme right tail; see Section 9.5. How they were fitted to historical data was explained in Section 7.3 (censoring is added below). A useful generalization to the **extended** Pareto family is covered at the end.

9.4.2 Elementary properties

Pareto models are so heavy tailed that even the mean may fail to exist (that's why another parameter β must be used to represent scale). Formulae for expectation, standard deviation and skewness are

$$\xi = E(Z) = \frac{\beta}{\alpha-1}, \quad \text{sd}(Z) = \xi\left(\frac{\alpha}{\alpha-2}\right)^{1/2} \quad \text{and} \quad \text{skew}(Z) = 2\left(\frac{\alpha-2}{\alpha}\right)^{1/2}\frac{\alpha+1}{\alpha-3}, \tag{9.17}$$

valid for $\alpha > 1$, $\alpha > 2$ and $\alpha > 3$, respectively. It is, in the author's experience, rare in practice that the mean is not finite, but infinite *variances* (values of α between 1 and 2) are not uncommon. We shall also need the median

$$\text{med}(Z) = \beta(2^{1/\alpha} - 1). \tag{9.18}$$

The exponential distribution appears in the limit when the ratio $\xi = \beta/(\alpha - 1)$ is kept fixed and $\alpha \to \infty$; see Section 2.5. There is in this sense an overlap between the Pareto and the Gamma families. The exponential distribution is a *heavy*-tailed Gamma and the most *light*-tailed Pareto, and it is common to regard it as a member of both families.

9.4.3 Likelihood estimation

The Pareto model was used as an illustration in Section 7.3, and likelihood estimation was developed there. **Censored** information is now added. Suppose observations are in two groups, either the ordinary, fully observed claims $z_1, \dots, z_n$ or those (n_b of them) known to have exceeded certain thresholds $b_1, \dots, b_{n_b}$, but not by how much. The log-likelihood function for the first group is, as in Section 7.3,

$$n\log(\alpha/\beta) - (1+\alpha)\sum_{i=1}^{n}\log\left(1+\frac{z_i}{\beta}\right),$$

whereas the censored part adds contributions from knowing that $Z_i > b_i$. The probability is

$$\Pr(Z_i > b_i) = \frac{1}{(1+b_i/\beta)^{\alpha}} \quad \text{or} \quad \log\{\Pr(Z_i > b_i)\} = -\alpha\log\left(1+\frac{b_i}{\beta}\right),$$

and the full log-likelihood becomes

$$\mathcal{L}(\alpha,\beta) = \underbrace{n\log(\alpha/\beta) - (1+\alpha)\textstyle\sum_{i=1}^{n}\log(1+\frac{z_i}{\beta})}_{\textit{complete information}} - \underbrace{\alpha\textstyle\sum_{i=1}^{n_b}\log(1+\frac{b_i}{\beta})}_{\textit{censoring to the right}}. \tag{9.19}$$

This is to be maximized with respect to α and β, a numerical problem very much the same as in Section 7.3; see Exercise 9.20.

9.4.4 Over-threshold under Pareto

One of the most important properties of the Pareto family is its behaviour at the extreme right tail. The issue is defined by the **over-threshold** model, which is the distribution of $Z_b = Z - b$ given $Z > b$. Its density function (derived in Section 6.2) is

$$f_b(z) = \frac{f(b+z)}{1-F(b)}, \qquad z > 0;$$

see (6.8). Over-threshold distributions become particularly simple for Pareto models. Inserting the expressions for $f(z)$ and $F(z)$ yields

$$f_b(z) = \frac{(1+b/\beta)^{\alpha}\alpha/\beta}{(1+(z+b)/\beta)^{1+\alpha}} = \frac{\alpha/(\beta+b)}{\{1+z/(\beta+b)\}^{1+\alpha}},$$

which is another Pareto density function. The shape α is the same as before, but the parameter of scale has now changed to $\beta_b = \beta + b$. Over-threshold distributions preserve the Pareto model and its shape. The mean (if it exists) is known as the **mean excess function**, and becomes

$$E(Z_b|Z > b) = \frac{\beta_b}{\alpha-1} = \frac{\beta+b}{\alpha-1} = \xi + \frac{b}{\alpha-1} \quad \text{(requires } \alpha > 1\text{)}. \tag{9.20}$$

It is larger than the original ξ and increases linearly with b.

These results hold for infinite α as well. Insert $\beta = \xi(\alpha - 1)$ into the expression for $f_b(z)$, and it follows as in Section 2.5 that

$$f_b(z) \to \frac{1}{\xi}e^{-z/\xi} \quad \text{as} \quad \alpha \to \infty.$$

The over-threshold model of an exponential distribution is the same exponential. Now the mean excess function is a constant, which also follows from (9.20) by making α infinite.

9.4.5 The extended Pareto family

Add the numerator $(z/\beta)^\theta$ to the Pareto density function, and you get the **extended** version:

$$f(z) = \frac{\Gamma(\alpha+\theta)}{\Gamma(\alpha)\Gamma(\theta)}\frac{1}{\beta}\frac{(z/\beta)^{\theta-1}}{(1+z/\beta)^{\alpha+\theta}}, \quad z > 0, \tag{9.21}$$

where $\beta, \alpha, \theta > 0$. Shape is now defined by two parameters α and θ, and this creates useful flexibility; see below. The density function is either decreasing over the positive real line (if $\theta \leq 1$) or has a single maximum (if $\theta > 1$). The mean and standard deviation are

$$\xi = E(Z) = \frac{\theta\beta}{\alpha - 1} \quad \text{and} \quad \text{sd}(Z) = \xi\left(\frac{\alpha+\theta-1}{\theta(\alpha-2)}\right)^{1/2}, \tag{9.22}$$

which are valid when $\alpha > 1$ and $\alpha > 2$, respectively, whereas the skewness is

$$\text{skew}(Z) = 2\left(\frac{\alpha-2}{\theta(\alpha+\theta-1)}\right)^{1/2}\frac{\alpha+2\theta-1}{\alpha-3}, \tag{9.23}$$

provided $\alpha > 3$. These results, verified in Section 9.7, reduce to those for the ordinary Pareto distribution when $\theta = 1$.

The distribution function is complicated (unless $\theta = 1$), and it is not convenient to simulate by inversion, but we may utilize that an extended Pareto variable with parameters (α, θ, β) can be written

$$Z = \frac{\theta\beta}{\alpha}\frac{G_1}{G_2} \quad \text{where} \quad G_1 \sim \text{Gamma}(\theta),\ G_2 \sim \text{Gamma}(\alpha). \tag{9.24}$$

Here G_1 and G_2 are two independent Gamma variables with mean 1. The representation, which is proved in Section 9.7, implies that $1/Z$ is extended Pareto distributed as well and leads to Algorithm 9.1. There is an alternative sampling method discussed in Section 9.7.

Algorithm 9.1 The extended Pareto sampler

0 Input: α, θ, β and $\eta = \theta\beta/\alpha$
1 Draw $G_1^* \sim \text{Gamma}(\theta)$ *%Standard Gamma, Algorithms 2.9 and 2.10*
2 Draw $G_2^* \sim \text{Gamma}(\alpha)$ *%Standard Gamma, Algorithms 2.9 and 2.10*
3 Return $Z^* \leftarrow \eta G_1^*/G_2^*$.

The extended Pareto model has an interesting limit when the scale parameter is linked to the mean ξ through

$$\beta = \xi\alpha/\theta, \tag{9.25}$$

which yields $Z = \xi G_1/G_2$ when inserted for β in (9.24). But $G_2 \to 1$ as $\alpha \to \infty$ so that in the limit $Z = \xi G_1$, and Z has become Gamma distributed with mean ξ and shape θ. If you find the argument too light-hearted, there is a second one in Section 9.7. Large values of α make Z approximately Gamma distributed. This generalizes a similar result for the ordinary Pareto distribution, and is testimony to the versatility of the extended family which comprises heavy-tailed Pareto ($\theta = 1$ and α small) *and* light-tailed (almost Gaussian) Gamma (both α and θ large). In practice you let historical experience decide by fitting the model to past claims; see Exercise 9.21.

9.5 Extreme value methods

9.5.1 Introduction

Large claims play a special role because of their importance financially. It is also hard to assess their distribution. They (luckily!) do not occur very often, and historical experience is therefore limited. Insurance companies may even cover claims *larger* than anything that has been seen before. How should such situations be tackled? The simplest method would be to fit a parametric family and extrapolate beyond past experience. That may not be a very good idea. A parametric model such as the Gamma distribution may fit well for small and moderate claims without being reliable at all at the extreme right tail, and such a procedure may easily underestimate big claims severely; more in Section 9.6. The purpose of this section is to enlist help from a theoretical characterization of the extreme right tail of *all* distributions.

9.5.2 Over-threshold distributions in general

It was shown above that Pareto distributions are preserved over thresholds. This is an *exact* result, but there is also an approximate, general version. Let Z be continuous and unbounded and consider its over-threshold model to the right of some lower limit b, which is guaranteed to become Pareto distributed as $b \to \infty$, no matter (essentially) what the original was! There is even a theory when Z is bounded by some finite maximum; for that extension consult Pickands (1975) or Embrechts *et al.* (1997).

Our target is $Z_b = Z - b$ given $Z > b$. Consider its tail distribution function $\overline{F}_b(z) = \Pr(Z_b > z \mid Z > b)$, which can be written

$$\overline{F}_b(z) = \frac{1 - F(b+z)}{1 - F(b)} \quad \text{where} \quad F(z) = \Pr(Z \leq z),$$

and let $Y_b = Z_b/\beta_b$ where β_b is a scale parameter depending on b. We are assuming $Z > b$, and Y_b is then positive with tail distribution $\Pr(Y_b > y) = \overline{F}_b(\beta_b y)$. The general result says that there exists a parameter α (not depending on b and possibly infinite) and some sequence β_b such that

$$\overline{F}_b(\beta_b y) \to \overline{P}(y/\alpha) \text{ as } b \to \infty \quad \text{where} \quad \overline{P}(y/\alpha) = \begin{matrix} (1+y)^{-\alpha}, & 0 < \alpha < \infty \\ e^{-y}, & \alpha = \infty. \end{matrix} \tag{9.26}$$

Here, the limit $\overline{P}(y/\alpha)$ is the tail distribution of the Pareto model, and Z_b becomes Pareto(α, β_b) as $b \to \infty$. Both the shape α and the scale parameter β_b depend on the original model, but only the latter varies with b.

This remarkable result, due to Pickands (1975), holds under mild conditions and for all distributions used in practice. Pickands gave a stronger mathematical statement, but his proof goes beyond the elementary, and we shall be content to examine some of the most common models by simpler means among the exercises. It will then emerge that how large b must be for the approximation to be a good one varies enormously from one case to another.

Whether we get a Pareto proper (with finite α) or an exponential (infinite α) depends on how fast $1 - F(z) \to 0$ as $z \to \infty$. A simple illustration is provided by the Burr model (Exercise 2.33). The tail distribution is $1 - F(z) = \{1 + (z/\beta)^{\alpha_1}\}^{-\alpha_2}$ where α_1 and α_2 are positive. If $\beta_b = \beta + b$ then

$$\overline{F}_b(\beta_b y) = \left(\frac{1 + (b/\beta)^{\alpha_1}}{1 + \{(b + y\beta_b)/\beta\}^{\alpha_1}}\right)^{\alpha_2} = \left(\frac{(\beta/b)^{\alpha_1} + 1}{(\beta/b)^{\alpha_1} + (1 + y + y\beta/b)^{\alpha_1}}\right)^{\alpha_2}$$

and $\overline{F}_b(\beta_b y) \to (1+y)^{-\alpha_1\alpha_2}$ as $b \to \infty$, which is the Pareto distribution with shape $\alpha = \alpha_1\alpha_2$. This is the limiting over-threshold model for the Burr distribution and more generally when the tail $1 - F(z)$ of the original distribution approaches zero at polynomial speed $1/z^\alpha$ as $z \to \infty$. When the decay is faster, the limit is exponential. Examples of the latter are the normal, the log-normal and the Gamma distributions; consult the exercises.

9.5.3 The Hill estimate

The decay rate α can be determined from historical data (though they have to be plenty). One possibility is to select observations exceeding some threshold, impose the Pareto distribution and use likelihood estimation as explained in Section 9.4. This line is tested in the next section. An alternative often promoted by the specialist literature on extremes is the **Hill** estimate. Start by sorting the data in ascending order as $z_{(1)} \leq \cdots \leq z_{(n)}$ and take

$$\hat{\alpha}^{-1} = \frac{1}{n-n_1}\sum_{i=n_1+1}^{n}\log\left(\frac{z_{(i)}}{z_{(n_1)}}\right) \qquad \text{where} \quad n_1 = (1-p)n. \tag{9.27}$$

Here p is some small, user-selected number. The method is non-parametric (no model assumed) and is discussed thoroughly in Embrechts *et al.* (1997), where it is shown to converge to the true value when $np \to \infty$ and $p \to 0$, which requires n huge. The issue is studied among the exercises. A simple justification of the Hill estimate is given in Section 9.7.

We may want to use $\hat{\alpha}$ as an estimate of α in a Pareto distribution imposed over the threshold $b = z_{(n_1)}$ and would then need an estimate of the scale parameter β_b. A possibility that keeps the numerical side simple is

$$\hat{\beta}_b = \frac{z_{(n_2)} - z_{(n_1)}}{2^{1/\hat{\alpha}} - 1} \qquad \text{where} \quad n_2 = \frac{1}{2} + \frac{n_1+n}{2}. \tag{9.28}$$

To justify this estimate suppose n_1 is so large that $z_{(n_1+1)} - z_{(n_1)}, \dots, z_{(n)} - z_{(n_1)}$ is approximately an ordered sample from a Pareto distribution. The median is $z_{(n_2)} - z_{(n_1)}$, which should match the theoretical median (9.18) under the Pareto model. This yields the equation $\hat{\beta}_b(2^{1/\hat{\alpha}} - 1) = z_{(n_2)} - z_{(n_1)}$, which is (9.28).

9.5.4 The entire distribution through mixtures

How can the tail characterization be utilized to model the entire distribution? Historical claims may look like the following:

	Ordinary size		**Large**
Claims:	$z_{(1)}, \dots, z_{(n_1)}$	b	$z_{(n_1+1)}, \dots, z_{(n)}$

There are many values in the small and medium range to the left of the vertical bar and just a few (or none!) large ones to the right of it. What is actually meant by 'large' is not clear-cut, but let us say that 'large' claims are those exceeding some threshold b. Suppose the original claims $z_1, \dots, z_n$ are ranked in ascending order as $z_{(1)} \leq \cdots \leq z_{(n)}$ so that observations from $z_{(n_1)}$ and smaller are below the threshold.

How b is chosen in practice is discussed below; see also Section 9.6 for numerical illustrations.

Modelling may be divided into separate parts defined by the threshold. A claim Z may be written

$$Z = (1 - I_b)Z_{\leq b} + I_b Z_{>b}, \tag{9.29}$$

where

$$\underset{\textit{central region}}{Z_{\leq b} = Z|Z \leq b}, \quad \underset{\textit{extreme right tail}}{Z_{>b} = Z|Z > b} \quad \text{and} \quad I_b = \begin{cases} 0 & \text{if} \quad Z \leq b \\ 1 & \text{if} \quad Z > b. \end{cases} \tag{9.30}$$

The random variable Z coincides with $Z_{\leq b}$ when $Z \leq b$ and with $Z_{>b}$ when $Z > b$. It is easy to check that Z can be represented as in (9.29), but at first sight this merely looks complicated. Why on earth can it help? The point is that we reach out to two different sources of information. To the left of the threshold historical data permits us to identify a model for $Z_{\leq b}$, whereas the result due to Pickands suggests a Pareto distribution on the right. This defines a modelling strategy which will now be developed.

9.5.5 *The empirical distribution mixed with Pareto*

The preceding two-component approach can be implemented in more ways than one. There are many possibilities for $Z_{\leq b}$, but only the empirical distribution function will be detailed. Choose some small probability p and let $n_1 = n(1 - p)$ and $b = z_{(n_1)}$. Then take

$$Z_{\leq b} = \hat{Z} \qquad \text{and} \qquad Z_{>b} = z_{(n_1)} + \text{Pareto}(\alpha, \beta), \tag{9.31}$$

where $\hat{Z}$ is the empirical distribution function over $z_{(1)}, \dots, z_{(n_1)}$; i.e.,

$$\Pr(\hat{Z} = z_{(i)}) = \frac{1}{n_1}, \quad i = 1, \dots, n_1. \tag{9.32}$$

The remaining, delicate part are the parameters α and β of the Pareto distribution and the choice of p. Plenty of historical data would deal with everything. Under such circumstances p can be determined low enough (and hence b high enough) for the Pareto approximation to be a good one, and historical data to the right of b would provide estimates $\hat{\alpha}$ and $\hat{\beta}$.

This rosy picture is not the common one, and limited experience may make a subjective element unavoidable. One of the advantages of dividing modelling into two components is that it clarifies the domain where personal judgement enters. It may not be unreasonable to adopt a conservative view when there is insufficient information for accuracy. If so, that can be achieved by selecting b relatively low and using Pareto modelling to the right of it. Numerical experiments that support

Algorithm 9.2 Claims by mixtures

Input: Sorted claims $z_{(1)} \leq \cdots \leq z_{(n)}$ and p, $n_1 = n(1-p)$, α and β
1 Draw uniforms U_1^*, U_2^*
2 If $U_1^* > p$ then
3 $\quad i^* \leftarrow 1 + [n_1 U_2^*]$ and $Z^* \leftarrow z_{(i^*)}$ *%The empirical distribution, Algorithm 4.1*
else
4 $\quad Z^* \leftarrow z_{(n_1)} + \beta\{(U_2^*)^{-1/\alpha} - 1\}$ *%Pareto, Algorithm 2.13*
5 Return Z^*.

such a strategy are carried out in the next section. Much material on modelling extremes can be found in Embrechts *et al.* (1997).

The mixture model is sampled as in Algorithm 9.2, which operates by testing whether the claim comes from the central part of the distribution or whether it exceeds $b = z_{(n_1)}$. Other distributions could have been used in Line 3. The preceding version is extremely quick to implement.

9.6 Searching for the model

9.6.1 Introduction

How is the final model for claim size selected? There is no single recipe, and it is the kind of issue that can only be learned by example. How to go about it is partly dictated by the amount of historical data. Simple tools are transformations and Q–Q plots. The first example is the so-called Danish fire claims, used by many authors as a test case; see Embrechts *et al.* (1997). These are losses from more than 2000 industrial fires and serve our need for a big example which offers many opportunities for modelling. Several distributions will be fitted and used later in Section 10.3 to calculate reserves.

But what about cases such as the Norwegian fund for natural disasters in Chapter 7, where there were just $n = 21$ historical incidents? It is, from records this size, quite impossible to determine the underlying distribution, and yet we have to come up with a solution. Possible strategies are discussed at the end.

9.6.2 Using transformations

A useful modelling tool is to change data by means of **transformations**. These are monotone, continuous functions, in this book denoted $H(z)$. The situation is as follows:

$$\underset{\textit{original data}}{z_1, \ldots, z_n} \qquad \underset{\textit{new data}}{y_1 = H(z_1), \ldots, y_n = H(z_n),}$$

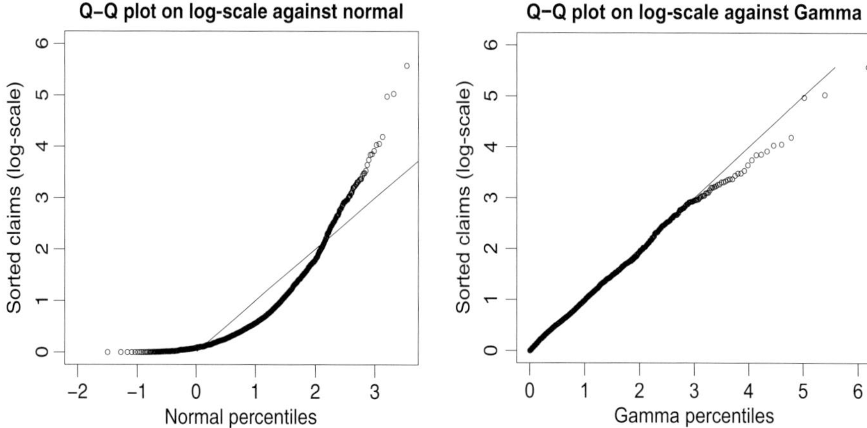

Figure 9.2 Q–Q plots for the Danish fire data on log-scale, the log-normal on the left and the Gamma distribution on the right.

and modelling is attacked through $y_1, \ldots, y_n$. The idea is to make standard families of distributions fit the transformed variable $Y = H(Z)$ better than the orginal Z. At the end, retransform through $Z = H^{-1}(Y)$ with $Z^* \leftarrow H^{-1}(Y^*)$ for the Monte Carlo.

A familiar example is the log-normal. Now $H(z) = \log(z)$ and $H^{-1}(y) = e^y$ with Y normal. General constructions with logarithms are

$$\underbrace{Y = \log(1+Z)}_{Y \text{ positive}} \qquad \text{or} \qquad \underbrace{Y = \log(Z),}_{Y \text{ over the entire real line}}$$

opening up entirely different families of distributions for Y. The logarithm is arguably the most commonly applied transformation. Alternatives are powers $Y = Z^\gamma$, where $\gamma \neq 0$ is some given parameter. This possibility is tested among the exercises.

9.6.3 Example: The Danish fire claims

Many authors have used the Danish fire claims as a testing ground for their methods. There are $n = 2167$ industrial fires with losses starting at one (money unit: million Danish kroner, with around eight kroner to the euro). The largest among them is 263, the average $\bar{z} = 3.39$ and the standard deviation $s = 8.51$. A huge skewness coefficient $\hat{\zeta} = 18.7$ signals that the right tail is heavy, with considerable scope for large losses.

Standard models such as Gamma, log-normal or Pareto do not fit these data (Pareto is attempted below), but matters may be improved by using transformations. The logarithm is often a first choice. Could the log-normal be a possibility?

Table 9.1 Pareto parameters for the over-threshold distribution of the fire claims
Unit: Million Danish kroner

	Part of data fitted			
	All	50% largest	10% largest	5% largest
Threshold (b)	1.00	1.77	5.56	9.88
Shape (α)	1.64	1.43	1.73	2.10
Scale (β_b)	1.53	1.85	7.88	15.18

The construction is then

$$\log(Z) \sim N(\theta, \sigma) \qquad \text{with estimates} \qquad \hat{\theta} = 0.787, \; \hat{\sigma} = 0.717,$$

but this doesn't work. The Q–Q plot on the left in Figure 9.2 does not remotely resemble a straight line. A second attempt with more success is to utilize that the observations exceed one so that the Gamma distribution can be applied to the logarithms. This leads to

$$\log(Z) = \xi G, \quad G \sim \text{Gamma}(\alpha) \quad \text{with estimates} \quad \hat{\xi} = 0.787, \; \hat{\alpha} = 1.102$$

with a fit that is far from hopeless in Figure 9.2 right. The extreme right tail is a bit light, but consequences when the reserve is evaluated in Section 10.3 are not enormous. For a slightly better-fitting model, consult Exercise 9.36.

9.6.4 Pareto mixing

With so much historical data it is tempting to forget all about parametric families and use the strategy advocated in Section 9.5 instead. The central part is then handled by the empirical distribution function and the extreme right tail by Pareto. Table 9.1 shows the results of fitting Pareto distributions over different thresholds (maximum likelihood used). If the parent distribution is Pareto, the shape parameter α is the same for all thresholds b whereas the scale parameter depends on b through $\beta_b = \beta + b$, and there are perhaps slight traces of this in Table 9.1.

But it would be an exaggeration to proclaim the Pareto model for these data. Consider the Q–Q plots in Figure 9.3, where the upper half of the observations have been plotted on the left and the 5% largest on the right. There is a reasonable fit for the latter, and this accords with the theoretical result for large thresholds, but it is different on the left where the Pareto distribution overstates the risk of large claims. Table 9.1 tells us why. The shape parameters 1.42 for the 50% largest observations and 2.05 over the 5% threshold correspond to quite different distributions.

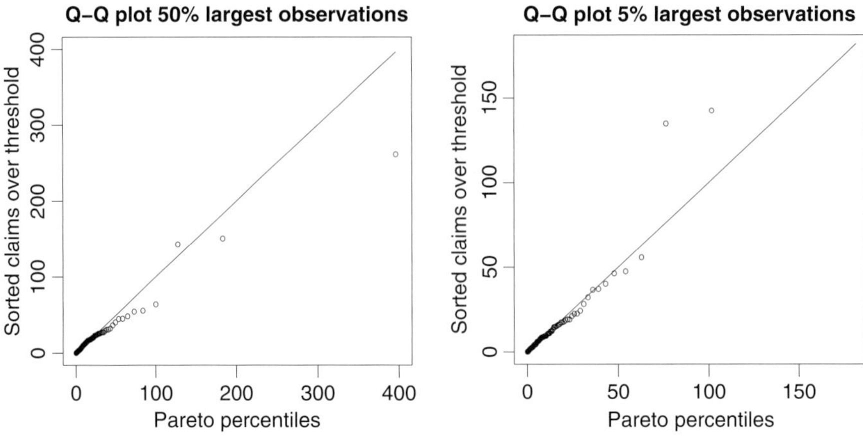

Figure 9.3 Q–Q plots of fitted Pareto distributions against the empirical distribution function, 50% largest observations (*left*) and 5% largest (*right*).

9.6.5 When data are scarce

How should we confront situations like the Norwegian natural disasters in Table 7.1 where there were no more than $n = 21$ claims and where the phenomenon itself is heavy tailed with potential losses much larger than those on record? One possibility is to build physical models of what actually goes on, with destructions and expenses simulated in the computer. That is outside our natural range of topics, and if we stay with the more conventional, nothing prevents us from using Q–Q plots even with small amounts of data. Is it futile to identify parametric families of distributions under these circumstances? Here is an experiment. The entire process of selecting models according to the Q–Q fit must first be formalized. Percentiles $\hat{q}_i$ under some fitted distribution function $\hat{F}(z)$ are then compared with the observations, sorted in ascending order as $z_{(1)} \leq \cdots \leq z_{(n)}$. What is actually done isn't clear-cut (there are different ways for different people), but suppose we try to minimize

$$Q = \sum_{i=1}^{n} |\hat{q}_i - z_{(i)}| \quad \text{where} \quad \hat{q}_i = \hat{F}^{-1}\left(\frac{i - 1/2}{n}\right), \quad i = 1, \ldots, n, \tag{9.33}$$

a criterion that has been proposed as a basis for formal goodness-of-fit tests; see Devroye and Györfi (1985). Competing models are then judged according to their Q-score and the one with the smallest value selected.

The Monte Carlo experiments in Table 9.2 report on this strategy. Simulated historical data were generated under Pareto and Gamma distributions and parametric families of distributions (sometimes different from the true one) fitted. The main

Table 9.2 Probabilities of selecting given models (correct selections in bold)

Shapes in true models: 1.71 *in Pareto,* 0.72 *in Gamma.* 10 000 *repetitions.*

True model	Historical record: $n = 21$ Models found			Historical record: $n = 80$ Models found		
	Pareto	Gamma	log-normal	Pareto	Gamma	log-normal
Pareto	**0.48**	0.29	0.23	**0.70**	0.13	0.17
Gamma	0.48	**0.48**	0.04	0.34	**0.66**	0

steps of the scheme are:

True model Parametric family tried

$$\begin{array}{ccccccc} \text{Pareto} & & & & \textit{fitting}\ \hat{q}_1^* \leq \cdots \leq \hat{q}_n^* & & \\ \text{or} & \longrightarrow & z_1^* \leq \cdots \leq z_n^* & & \longrightarrow & \longrightarrow & Q^* = \sum_i |z_{(i)}^* - \hat{q}_i^*|. \\ \text{Gamma} & & \textit{historical data} & & \textit{sorting}\ z_{(1)}^* \leq \cdots \leq z_{(n)}^* & & \end{array}$$

Three parametric families (Pareto, Gamma, log-normal) were applied to the same historical data, and the one with the smallest Q^*-value picked. How often the right model was found was then counted. Table 9.2 shows the selection statistics. It is impossible to choose between the three models when there are only $n = 21$ claims. Prospects are improved with $n = 80$, and with $n = 400$ (not shown) the success probability was in the range 90–95%.

9.6.6 When data are scarce II

The preceding experiment met (not surprisingly) with mixed success, and when there are merely $n = 21$ observations, statistical methods alone do not take us far. We *might* know something from related phenomena, which would permit an educated guess at the underlying family of distributions. The Bayesian methods in Section 7.6 might also be of assistance if there is a sound basis for quantifying what is known prior to the data. But when there isn't, Bayesian methods only serve to make the final results less transparent since they depend on assumptions that can't be justified.

If high inaccuracy appears inevitable, perhaps our risk strategy should invite overestimation to be on the cautious side? It is tempting to promote Pareto models as such a conservative course, and you are invited to carry out the experiments in Exercises 9.41 and 9.42 where it will emerge that risk does tend to be overestimated when the Pareto family is fitted to Gamma-distributed claims with underestimation in the opposite case when the Gamma model is applied to losses that were in reality generated by Pareto sampling. Huge random variation in the fitted parameters doesn't wipe out such bias. Another side to this issue is how high the responsibility goes. When the Gamma and Pareto models are fitted to the Norwegian natural disaster data (by maximum likelihood), the results look like this:

		percentiles				percentiles	
Shape (α)	Mean	95%	99%	Shape (α)	Mean	95%	99%
0.72	179	603	976	1.71	200	677	1956
Gamma family				*Pareto family*			

These are quite unequal models, yet their discrepancies, though considerable, are not enormous in the central region where mean and upper 95% percentile deviate by 10–12%. This is different for *very* large claims, and the Pareto 99% percentile is twice that of the Gamma. There is a lesson here. Many families may fit reasonably well up to some moderate threshold. *That makes modelling easier when there are strong limits on responsibilities.* When there aren't, the choice between different possibilities becomes more delicate.

9.7 Mathematical arguments

9.7.1 Extended Pareto: Moments

If $f(z)$ is the extended Pareto density (9.21), then

$$E(Z^i) = \int_0^\infty z^i f(z)\,dz = \beta^i \frac{\Gamma(\alpha+\theta)}{\Gamma(\alpha)\Gamma(\theta)} \int_0^\infty \frac{1}{\beta}\frac{(z/\beta)^{\theta+i-1}}{(1+z/\beta)^{\alpha+\theta}}\,dz.$$

The integrand is, except for the normalizing constant, another extended Pareto density function with shape parameters $\alpha - i$ and $\theta + i$. But the integral is then $\Gamma(\alpha-i)\Gamma(\theta+i)/\Gamma(\alpha+\theta)$ so that

$$E(Z^i) = \beta^i \frac{\Gamma(\alpha-i)\Gamma(\theta+i)}{\Gamma(\alpha)\Gamma(\theta)},$$

which can be simplified by utilizing that $\Gamma(x) = (x-1)\Gamma(x-1)$. For $i = 1, 2$ this yields

$$E(Z) = \beta\frac{\theta}{\alpha-1} = \xi \quad \text{and} \quad E(Z^2) = \beta^2 \frac{(\theta+1)\theta}{(\alpha-1)(\alpha-2)},$$

which shows that the expectation is as claimed in (9.22). For the standard deviation use $\mathrm{var}(Z) = E(Z^2) - (EZ)^2$ and simplify. In a similar vein

$$E(Z^3) = \beta^3 \frac{(\theta+2)(\theta+1)\theta}{(\alpha-1)(\alpha-2)(\alpha-3)},$$

which is combined with

$$E(Z-\xi)^3 = E(Z^3 - 3Z^2\xi + 3Z\xi^2 - \xi^3) = E(Z^3) - 3E(Z^2)\xi + 2\xi^3.$$

When the expressions for $E(Z^3)$, $E(Z^2)$ and ξ are inserted, it follows after some tedious calculations that

$$E(Z-\xi)^3 = \beta^3\theta\frac{2\alpha^2+(6\theta-4)\alpha+4\theta^2-6\theta+2}{(\alpha-1)^3(\alpha-2)(\alpha-3)} = 2\beta^3\theta\frac{(\alpha+\theta-1)(\alpha+2\theta-1)}{(\alpha-1)^3(\alpha-2)(\alpha-3)},$$

and the formula (9.23) for skew(Z) emerges by dividing this expression by $\text{sd}(Z)^3$.

9.7.2 Extended Pareto: A limit

To show that extended Pareto models become Gamma distributed as $\alpha \to \infty$, insert $\beta = \xi\alpha/\theta$ into (9.21) which, after some reorganization, may then be written as

$$f(z) = \left(\frac{\theta}{\xi}\right)^{\theta}\frac{z^{\theta-1}}{\Gamma(\theta)} \times \frac{\Gamma(\alpha+\theta)}{\Gamma(\alpha)\alpha^{\theta}} \times \left(1+\frac{\theta z}{\alpha\xi}\right)^{-(\alpha+\theta)}.$$

As the first factor on the right doesn't involve α, the second tends to 1 as $\alpha \to \infty$ (use the expression in the heading of Table 2.3 to see this) and the third becomes $e^{-\theta z/\xi}$ (since $(1+x/a)^{-a} \to e^{-x}$ as $a \to \infty$), it follows that

$$f(z) \to \frac{\theta^{\theta}}{\Gamma(\theta)\xi}(z/\xi)^{\theta-1}e^{-\theta z/\xi} \qquad \text{as} \qquad \alpha \to \infty,$$

which is the Gamma density function claimed in Section 9.4.

9.7.3 Extended Pareto: A representation

Let $Z = X/Y$ where X and Y are independent and positive random variables with density functions $g_1(x)$ and $g_2(y)$, respectively. Then

$$\Pr(Z \le z) = \Pr(X \le zY) = \int_0^{\infty}\Pr(X \le zy)g_2(y)\,dy,$$

and when this is differentiated with respect to z, the density function of Z becomes

$$f(z) = \int_0^{\infty} y g_1(zy)g_2(y)\,dy.$$

Let $X = \theta G_1$ and $Y = \alpha G_2$, where G_1 and G_2 are Gamma variables with mean 1 and shape θ and α, respectively. Then $g_1(x) = x^{\theta-1}e^{-x}/\Gamma(\theta)$ and $g_2(y) = y^{\alpha-1}e^{-y}/\Gamma(\alpha)$, so that

$$f(z) = \frac{z^{\theta-1}}{\Gamma(\theta)\Gamma(\alpha)}\int_0^{\infty} y^{\alpha+\theta-1}e^{-y(1+z)}\,dy = \frac{z^{\theta-1}}{\Gamma(\theta)\Gamma(\alpha)}\frac{1}{(1+z)^{\alpha+\theta}}\int_0^{\infty} x^{\alpha+\theta-1}e^{-x}\,dx$$

after substituting $x = y(1+z)$ in the integral. This is the same as

$$f(z) = \frac{\Gamma(\alpha+\theta)}{\Gamma(\theta)\Gamma(\alpha)}\frac{z^{\theta-1}}{(1+z)^{\alpha+\theta}},$$

Algorithm 9.3 Extended Pareto generator when $\alpha > 1$ and $\theta > 1$

Input: α, θ, β and

$$a = \left(\frac{\theta - 1}{\theta + \alpha}\right)^{(\theta-1)/2} \left(\frac{\alpha + 1}{\theta + \alpha}\right)^{(\alpha+1)/2}, \qquad b = \left(\frac{\theta + 1}{\theta + \alpha}\right)^{(\theta+1)/2} \left(\frac{\alpha - 1}{\theta + \alpha}\right)^{(\alpha-1)/2}$$

Repeat

  Sample $U_1^*, U_2^* \sim$ uniform

  $V^* \leftarrow aU_1^*$ and $Z^* \leftarrow bU_2^*/V^*$

  If $V^* < Z^{*(\theta-1)/2}/(1 + Z^*)^{(\alpha+\theta)/2}$ then **stop** and return $Z^* \leftarrow \beta Z^*$.

which is the extended Pareto density when $\beta = 1$.

9.7.4 Extended Pareto: Additional sampler

The ratio of uniforms method (Algorithm 2.3) delivers a fast and simple extended Pareto sampler. We have to maximize $\sqrt{f(z)}$ and minimize and maximize $z\sqrt{f(z)}$. This leads to $\underline{b} = 0$ and a and $b = \overline{b}$, as stated in Algorithm 9.3. The scheme is very fast when either of θ and α is small, and the efficiency seems to depend on $\min(\alpha, \theta)$.

9.7.5 Justification of the Hill estimate

Start with observations $z_1, \dots, z_n$ exceeding a threshold a which is so large that $z_1 - a, \dots, z_n - a$ are approximately Pareto(α, β) and let $z_{(n_1+1)} - b, \dots, z_{(n)} - b$ be those over an even larger threshold b. This second group is also approximately Pareto distributed, but now with parameters α and $b - a + \beta$; see Section 9.4. Consider the likelihood estimate of α based on $z_{(n_1+1)} - b, \dots, z_{(n)} - b$ which, according to (7.14) right, becomes

$$\hat{\alpha}_\beta^{-1} = \frac{1}{n - n_1} \sum_{i=n_1+1}^{n} \log\left(1 + \frac{z_{(i)} - b}{b - a + \beta}\right) = \frac{1}{n - n_1} \sum_{i=n_1+1}^{n} \log\left(\frac{z_{(i)} + \beta - a}{b + \beta - a}\right).$$

But if b and by consequence all $z_{(i)}$ are much larger than $\beta - a$, then approximately

$$\log\left(\frac{z_{(i)} + \beta - a}{b + \beta - a}\right) \doteq \log\left(\frac{z_{(i)}}{b}\right) = \log\left(\frac{z_{(i)}}{z_{(n_1)}}\right) \quad \text{if} \quad b = z_{(n_1)}.$$

Insert this into the expression for $\hat{\alpha}_\beta$, and it has become the Hill estimate (9.27).

9.8 Bibliographical notes

9.8.1 Families of distributions

Specialist monographs on claim size distributions are Klugman *et al.* (2008) and Kleiber and Kotz (2003), but all textbooks in general insurance include this topic. The literature contains many possibilities that have been neglected here, yet what *has* been presented takes care of much of what is encountered in practice. Curiously, the empirical distribution function often fails to be mentioned at all. Daykin *et al.* (1994) (calling it the **tabular method**) and Mikosch (2004) are exceptions.

9.8.2 Extreme value theory

Large claims and extremes are big topics in actuarial science and elsewhere. If you want to study the mathematical and statistical theory in depth, a good place to start is Embrechts *et al.* (1997). Other reviews at about the same mathematical level are Beirlant *et al.* (2004) and Resnick (2006). You might also try Kotz and Nadarajah (2000), De Haan and Ferreira (2006) or even the short article by Beirlant (2004). Beirlant *et al.* (1996) treats extremes in general insurance only. Extreme value distributions are also reviewed in Falk *et al.* (2010), which is principally preoccupied with the mathematical side. Finkelstädt and Rootzén (2004) and Castillo *et al.* (2005) contain many applications outside insurance and finance.

9.8.3 Over thresholds

The idea of using a Pareto model to the right of a certain boundary (Section 9.5) goes back at least to Pickands (1975). Modelling over thresholds is discussed in Davison and Smith (1990) from a statistical point of view. Automatic methods for threshold selection are developed in Dupuis (1998), Frigessi *et al.* (2002) and Beirlant and Goegebur (2004). This is what you need if asked to design computerized systems where the computer handles a large number of portfolios on its own, but it is unlikely that accuracy is improved much over trial-and-error thresholding. The real problem is usually lack of data, and how you then proceed is rarely mentioned. Section 9.6 (second half) was an attempt to attack model selection when there is little to go on.

9.9 Exercises

Section 9.2

Exercise 9.1 Suppose the cost of settling a claim changes from Z to $Z(1 + I)$ where I is inflation.

(a) If Z follows a Gamma distribution with mean ξ and shape α under the old price system, what are the parameters now?

(b) The same question when the old price is Pareto(α,β).
(c) Again the same question when $Z = e^{\theta+\sigma\varepsilon}$ is log-normal.
(d) What is the general rule for incorporating inflation into parametric models?

Exercise 9.2 Let $z_1, \ldots, z_n$ be historical data with z_k corresponding to the price level $Q_k = 1 + I_k$, with I_k some known inflation index. If z_n is the most recent observation, how do you arrange for the fitted model to correspond to the *current* price level?

Exercise 9.3 Consider an observation z known to be smaller than some threshold a, but not by how much.

(a) Feed on right-censoring in the text and define the contribution to the log-likelihood function of such left-censored information when the distribution function is $F(z) = F_0(z/\beta)$.
(b) If there are n_a such cases with upper thresholds $a_1, \ldots, a_{n_a}$, what is their total contribution to the log-likelihood?

Exercise 9.4 Families of distributions with unknown lower limits b can be defined by taking $Z = b + Y$, where Y starts at the origin. Let $Z_i = b + Y_i$ for $i = 1, \ldots, n$ be an independent sample and introduce $M_z = \min(Z_1, \ldots, Z_n)$ and $M_y = \min(Y_1, \ldots, Y_n)$.

(a) With $F(y)$ the distribution function of Y, show that $\Pr(M_y > y) = \{1 - F(y)\}^n$ and use (A.6) in Table A.1 in Appendix A to prove that

$$E(M_y) = \int_0^\infty \{1 - F(y)\}^n \, dy = \int_0^\infty \{1 - F_0(y/\beta)\}^n \, dy$$

if $F(y) = F_0(y/\beta)$.
(b) Argue that $E(M_z) = b + E(M_y)$ so that

$$E(M_z) = b + \beta \int_0^\infty \{1 - F_0(z)\}^n \, dz,$$

which justifies the bias correction (9.8) when M_z is used as an estimate of b.

Exercise 9.5 How accurate is the skewness estimate (9.10)?

(a) Write a program generating m samples of n independent log-normal losses $Z = e^{\theta+\sigma\varepsilon}$ and compute the skewness coefficient for each sample.

R-*commands*:

```
Z=matrix(rlnorm(m*n,θ,σ),m,n); Z̄=apply(Z,1,mean);
s=apply(Z,1,sd); ν̂3=apply((Z-Z̄)**3,1,sum)/(n-3+2/n);
Skew=ν̂3/s**3.
```

(b) Run the program when $m = 1000$, $n = 50$, $\theta = 0$ and $\sigma = 1$, compute the sample mean and standard deviation of the skewness estimates and estimate/plot their density function.

R-*commands*:

```
mean(Skew); sd(Skew); plot(density(Skew)).
```

(c) Argue that the skewness estimate is biased when you compare with the true value 6.185 taken from Exercise 9.11.

(d) Redo (b) with more data, for example $n = 1000$ and $10\,000$, and check whether the bias disappears.

Exercise 9.6

(a) Rewrite the program in Exercise 9.5(a) when $Z = \xi G$ where $G \sim \text{Gamma}(\alpha)$.

R-*commands*:

`Z=ξ*matrix(rgamma(n*m,α)/α,m,n)` with the rest as in Exercise 9.5(a).

(b) Redo the experiments in Exercise 9.5 when $\alpha = 2$, which corresponds to skewness $2/\sqrt{\alpha} \doteq 1.414$.

(c) Try to extrapolate from these exercises some general view on the accuracy of the skewness estimate.

Exercise 9.7 Let $\hat{Z}$ be the empirical distribution and $\hat{Z}_h = \hat{Z} + hs\varepsilon$, where $\varepsilon \sim N(0,1)$ with s the sample standard deviation.

(a) Argue that

$$\Pr(\hat{Z}_h \le z | \hat{Z} = z_i) = \Phi\left(\frac{z - z_i}{hs}\right) \quad \text{so that} \quad \Pr(\hat{Z}_h \le z) = \frac{1}{n}\sum_{i=1}^{n} \Phi\left(\frac{z - z_i}{hs}\right),$$

where $\Phi(z)$ is the normal integral.

(b) Differentiate and establish that the density function of $\hat{Z}_h$ is the kernel density estimate (2.6) in Section 2.2.

Exercise 9.8 Argue that a Monte Carlo simulation of $\hat{Z}_h$ in the preceding exercise can be generated from two uniform variables U_1^* and U_2^* through

$$i^* \leftarrow [1 + nU_1^*] \quad \text{followed by} \quad \hat{Z}_h^* \leftarrow z_{i^*} + hs\,\Phi^{-1}(U_2^*),$$

where $\Phi^{-1}(u)$ is the percentile function of the standard normal. [*Hint*: Look up Algorithms 2.4 and 4.1.]

(b) Write a program generating m simulations of $\hat{Z}_h$.

R-*commands*:

With z the data vector use `s=sd(z); Ẑh=sample(z,m,T)+h*s*rnorm(m).`

Exercise 9.9 Let $S = Z_1 + \cdots + Z_n$ be the sum n claims under the model $\hat{Z}_h$ in Exercise 9.8.

(a) Generate $m = 10\,0000$ simulations of S when $n = 10$, $h = 0.2$ and the data are the Belgian fires in Exercise 7.12.

R-*commands*:
```
z=scan(‘‘belgianfire.txt’’); s=sd(z);
Ẑh=sample(z,m*n,T)+h*s*rnorm(m*n); Ẑh=matrix(Ẑh,n,m);
S=apply(Ẑh,2,sum); plot(density(S)).
```

(b) Redo (a) when $h = 0$ and plot the density estimate of S jointly with the old one.

R-*commands*:
Repeat (a) with $h = 0$ and use `lines(density(S))`.

(c) Does the choice of h appear important?

Section 9.3

Exercise 9.10 Argue that the fact that sums of normal variables are normal implies product rules for log-normals.

Exercise 9.11 Let $Z = e^{\theta+\sigma\varepsilon}$ where $\varepsilon \sim N(0, 1)$.

(a) Argue that skew(Z) is the same for all θ so that a mathematical expression for it may be determined when $\theta = 0$.
(b) Justify that $(Z - e^{\sigma^2/2})^3 = Z^3 - 3Z^2e^{\sigma^2/2} + 3Ze^{\sigma^2} - e^{3\sigma^2/2}$ and use the identity $E(e^{a\varepsilon}) = e^{a^2/2}$ to deduce that $E(Z - e^{\sigma^2/2})^3 = e^{9\sigma^2/2} - 3e^{5\sigma^2/2} + 2e^{3\sigma^2/2}$ when $\theta = 0$.
(c) Since $\mathrm{sd}(Z) = e^{\sigma^2/2}\sqrt{e^{\sigma^2} - 1}$, argue that

$$\mathrm{skew}(Z) = \frac{e^{3\sigma^2} - 3e^{\sigma^2} + 2}{(e^{\sigma^2} - 1)^{3/2}} = (e^{\sigma^2} + 2)\sqrt{e^{\sigma^2} - 1}.$$

(d) Verify that skew(Z) $\to 0$ as $\sigma \to 0$ and compute it for $\sigma = 0.1, 0.5, 1, 2$.

R-*commands*:
```
σ=c(0.1,0.5,1,2); Skew=(exp(σ**2)+2)*sqrt(exp(σ**2)-1).
```

Exercise 9.12 Is it easier to get skewness right if we (somehow) have selected the right family of distributions?

(a) Write a program generating m replications of n (independent) log-normal losses and compute m skewness estimates through the formula in Exercise 9.11.

R-*commands*:
```
Z=matrix(rlnorm(m*n,θ,σ),n,m); σ̂=apply(log(z),2,sd);
Skew=(exp(σ̂**2)+2)*sqrt(exp(σ̂**2)-1).
```

(b) Run the program when $m = 10\,000$, $n = 50$, $\theta = 0$ and $\sigma = 1$ and estimate/plot the density function of the skewness estimate.

R-*commands*:

`mean(Skew); sd(Skew); plot(density(Skew))`.

(c) Compare with the results in Exercise 9.5.

Exercise 9.13 Consider Gamma data $z_1, \dots, z_n$ with average $\bar{z}$.

(a) Insert $\xi = \bar{z}$ into the log-likelihood (9.16) and verify that with constants removed

$$-\mathcal{L}(\bar{z}, \alpha) = -\alpha(\log(\alpha) - 1) + \log\{\Gamma(\alpha)\} + \alpha\left(\log(\bar{z}) - \frac{1}{n}\sum_{i=1}^{n}\log(z_i)\right).$$

(b) Write a program computing this function.

R-*commands*:

With data `z` use `llminus=function(α,z)-α*(log(α)-1)+lgamma(α)+ α*(log(mean(z))-mean(log(z)))`.

(c) Write a program computing maximum likelihood estimates.

R-*commands*:

```
ξ̂=mean(z);
α̂=optimize(llminus,c(0.001,1000)*ξ̂/sd(z),z=z)[[1]].
```

(d) Check that the program works on $n = 10\,000$ simulated observations when $\alpha = 2.5$ and $\xi = 1$.

R-*commands*:

`z=rgamma(n,α)/α` prior to (c).

Exercise 9.14 Redo Exercise 9.12 for Gamma data.

(a) Write a program generating m samples of n Gamma variables and for each sample compute the skewness after likelihood fitting.

R-*commands*:

With `llminus` from Exercise 9.13 use `α̂=rep(0,m);`

```
for (i in 1:m){z=ξ*rgamma(n,α)/α;
α̂[i]=optimize(llminus,c(0.001,1000*mean(z)/sd(z)),
z=z)[[1]]}; Skew=2/sqrt(α̂).
```

(b) Run the program when $m = 100$, $\xi = 1$, $\alpha = 2$ and $n = 50$, estimate/plot the density function of the skewness estimate with its mean and standard deviation.

R-*commands*:

`mean(Skew); sd(Skew)`.

(c) Compare with the results in Exercise 9.6.

Exercise 9.15 The data in this exercise is insurance losses due to US hurricanes for the period 1949–1980. You will find them as the file `hurricane.txt`. They are in million US$ (and would have been much larger today!); see Beirlant *et al.* (1996).

(a) Read the data from the file and fit the log-normal $Z = e^{\theta+\sigma\varepsilon}$.

R-*commands*:

```
z=scan(''hurricane.txt''); θ̂=mean(log(z)); σ̂=sd(log(z)).
```

(b) Check, through a Q–Q plot, whether the model fits.

R-*commands*:

```
qqnorm(log(z)).
```

Exercise 9.16

(a) Fit the Gamma distribution to the logarithms of the data in the preceding exercise and evaluate through a Q–Q plot.

R-*commands*:

With `llminus` from Exercise 9.13 and `z` as in Exercise 9.15, use

```
ξ̂=mean(log(z));
α̂=optimize(llminus,c(0.001,10 000),z=log(z))[[1]];
n=length(z); p=(1:n-0.5)/n; qgam=ξ̂*qgamma(p,α̂)/α̂;
plot(qgam,sort(log(z))).
```

(b) Apply the moment method instead of maximum likelihood and examine how much the estimates change.

R-*commands*:

```
ξ̂=mean(log(z)); α̂=(ξ̂/sd(log(z)))**2.
```

Exercise 9.17 Both models in Exercises 9.15 and 9.16 seemed to fit the logarithms of the data, but how similar are they on the original scale?

(a) Compute $E(Z)$ and sd(Z) under the fitted log-normal.

R-*commands*:

With $\hat{\theta}$ and $\hat{\sigma}$ as in Exercise 9.15 use

```
Mean=exp(θ̂+σ̂**2/2); Sd=Mean*sqrt(exp(σ̂**2)-1).
```

(b) Redo (b) for the fitted log-Gamma.

R-*commands*:

With $\hat{\xi}$ and $\hat{\alpha}$ taken from Exercise 9.16 and $m = 100\,000$, use

```
Z=exp(ξ̂*rgamma(m,α̂)/α̂); Mean=mean(Z); Sd=sd(Z).
```

(c) Comment on the difficulty of modelling losses with little data.

Section 9.4

Exercise 9.18

(a) What is the conditional distribution of $Z_b = Z - b$ given $Z > b$ if Z is exponential with mean ξ?

(b) How does the result relate to the similar one for Pareto distributions?

Exercise 9.19

(a) Write a program generating m simulations from the extended Pareo distribution.

R-*commands*:

```
Z=β*rgamma(m,θ)/rgamma(m,α).
```

(b) Run the program when $m = 10\,000$, $\alpha = 10$, $\theta = 2$ and $\beta = (\alpha - 1)/\theta$ (so that $E(Z) = 1$) and Q–Q plot the simulations against the Gamma distribution with shape parameter θ.

R-*commands*:

```
p=(1:m-0.5)/m; qgam=qgamma(p,θ)/θ; plot(qgam,sort(Z)).
```

(c) Redo (b) when $\alpha = 20$, 50 and 100 and judge how fast the extended Pareto converges to the Gamma distribution.

Exercise 9.20 Consider fully observed Pareto data $z_1, \dots, z_n$ with additional censored information in terms of lower limits $b_1, \dots, b_{n_b}$ on the actual losses.

(a) Differentiate the log-likelihood function (9.19) with respect to α and show that it is maximized by

$$\hat{\alpha}_\beta = \frac{n}{\sum_{i=1}^{n} \log(1 + z_i/\beta) + \sum_{i=1}^{n_b} \log(1 + b_i/\beta)}.$$

(b) Argue that likelihood estimation with censored Pareto data can be carried out almost as in the uncensored case in Exercise 7.9.

Exercise 9.21

(a) Deduce from (9.21) that the log-likelihood function for the extended Pareto distribution given historical losses $z_1, \dots, z_n$ is

$$\mathcal{L}(\alpha, \theta, \beta) = n[\log\{\Gamma(\alpha + \theta)\} - \log\{\Gamma(\alpha)\} - \log\{\Gamma(\theta)\} - \theta \log(\beta)] \\ +(\theta - 1) \sum_{i=1}^{n} \log(z_i) - (\alpha + \theta) \sum_{i=1}^{n} \log(1 + z_i/\beta).$$

(b) Program minus the log-likelihood function divided by n.

R-*commands*:

With data vector `z` and `s=log(c(α,θ,β))`

use `llminus=function(s,z){t=exp(s);`

l_1=-lgamma(t[1]+t[2])+lgamma(t[1])+lgamma(t[2])+ t[2]*log(t[3]); l_2=-(t[2]-1)*mean(log(z))+ (t[1]+t[2])*mean(log(1+z/t[3])); l_1+l_2}.

(c) Implement likelihood estimation.

R-*commands*:

o=optim(c(1,0.7,log(mean(z))),llminus,z=z);
$\hat{\alpha}$=exp(o$par[1]); $\hat{\theta}$=exp(o$par[2]); $\hat{\beta}$=exp(o$par[3]).

(d) Check that the procedure works on $n = 10\,000$ simulations for $\alpha = 2$, $\theta = 3$ and $\beta = 1$.

R-*commands*:

Use Exercise 9.19(a) to draw the simulations.

Exercise 9.22

(a) Fit the extended Pareto distribution to the Belgian fire data in Exercise 7.12.

R-*commands*:

z=scan(''belgianfire.txt'') prior to the commands in Exercise 9.21.

(b) Argue that the result is consistent with a Gamma distribution and determine its parameters.

Exercise 9.23 The file norwegiancar.txt contains claims originating with a Norwegian company, and holds $n = 6446$ claims in automobile insurance with the deductible subtracted. The money unit is Norwegian kroner (around eight to a euro).

(a) Read the data from the file and compute the mean, standard deviation, minimum and maximum.

R-*commands*:

z=scan(''norwegiancar.txt''); mean(z); sd(z);
min(z); max(z).

(b) Q–Q plot logarithms against the normal.

R-*commands*:

qqnorm(log(z)).

(c) Argue that a log-normal model overestimates small claims and underestimates large ones.

Exercise 9.24

(a) Fit the extended Pareto distribution to the data in Exercise 9.23.

R-*commands*:

With z as in Exercise 9.23, compute estimates $\hat{\alpha}$, $\hat{\theta}$, $\hat{\beta}$ as in Exercise 9.21.

(b) Check that the mean and standard deviation of the fitted model match those of the data.

R-*commands*:

```
ξ̂=θ̂*β̂/(α̂-1); Mean=mean(z); σ̂=ξ̂*sqrt((α̂+θ̂-1)/(θ̂*(α̂-2)));
Sd=sd(z).
```

(c) Check the fit through a Q–Q plot and comment.

R-*commands*:

Determine the extended Pareto percentiles by Monte Carlo. With n the number of observations and $m = 10\,000$, use

```
Z=β̂*rgamma(m*n,θ̂)/rgamma(m*n,α̂);
ind=(1:n-0.5)*m; plot(sort(Z)[ind],sort(z)).
```

Section 9.5

Exercise 9.25 Let $Y_b = (Z - b)/\beta_b$ given $Z > b$, where $\beta_b > 0$, is some parameter.

(a) Show that $\Pr(Y_b > y) = \overline{F}(b + y\beta_b)/\overline{F}(b)$, where $\overline{F}(z) = \Pr(Z \geq z)$.
(b) Use l'Hôpital's rule to argue that the limit of $\Pr(Y_b > y)$ as $b \to \infty$ coincides with the limit of

$$L_b(y) = \frac{f(b + y\beta_b)}{f(b)}(1 + y\frac{d\beta_b}{db})$$

where $f(z)$ is the density function of Z.

Exercise 9.26

(a) Insert $f(z) = cz^{\theta-1}/(1 + z/\beta)^{\alpha+\theta}$ into the function $L_b(y)$ in Exercise 9.25 and show that

$$L_b(y) = \left(1 + \frac{y\beta_b}{b}\right)^{\theta-1}\left(1 + \frac{y\beta_b}{\beta + b}\right)^{-(\alpha+\theta)}\left(1 + y\frac{d\beta_b}{db}\right).$$

(b) If $\beta_b = \beta + b$, show that $L_b(y) \to (1 + y)^{-\alpha}$ as $b \to \infty$, and over-threshold distributions of extended Pareto variables belong to the Pareto family when b is large.

Exercise 9.27 Repeat Exercise 9.26 when $f(z) = cz^{\alpha-1}e^{-\alpha z/\xi}$ and $\beta_b = \xi/\alpha$, and show that

$$L_b(y) = \left(1 + \frac{y\xi}{\alpha b}\right)^{\alpha-1} e^{-y} \longrightarrow e^{-y} \quad \text{as} \quad b \to \infty,$$

and the over-threshold distribution of Gamma variables becomes exponential in the limit.

Exercise 9.28 Show that the exponential is the limiting over-threshold distribution for normal variables too, i.e., when $f(z) = ce^{-(z-\xi)^2/(2\sigma^2)}$ and $\beta_b = \sigma^2/b$ show that

$$L_b(y) = e^{-(1-\xi/b)y-y^2\sigma^2/(2b^2)}(1 - y\sigma^2/b^2) \longrightarrow e^{-y} \quad \text{as} \quad b \to \infty.$$

Exercise 9.29 The density function of log-normal variables $Z = e^{\theta+\sigma\varepsilon}$ is

$$f(z) = \frac{1}{\sqrt{2\pi}\,\sigma z}\exp\left(-\frac{(\log(z)-\theta)^2}{2\sigma^2}\right), \qquad z > 0.$$

(a) Insert $f(z)$ and $\beta_b = \sigma^2 b/\log(b)$ into $L_b(y)$ in Exercise 9.25 and verify that

$$L_b(y) = \left(1 + \frac{y}{b_1}\right)^{-1}\exp\left(-\frac{\{\log(1+y/b_1)\}^2}{2\sigma^2} - (b_1 - \theta/\sigma^2)\log(1+y/b_1)\right)$$
$$\times\left(1 + \frac{y}{b_1} - \frac{y}{\sigma^2 b_1^2}\right),$$

where $b_1 = \log(b)/\sigma^2$.

(b) Show that $L_b(y) \to e^{-y}$ as $b \to \infty$ so that the over-threshold distribution becomes exponential with scale parameter β_b. [*Hint*: Note that $b_1 \to \infty$ and utilize the fact that $n\log(1 + x/n) \to x$ as $n \to \infty$.]

(c) Argue that the convergence is likely to be *very* slow since $L_b(y)$ depends on b through $\log(b)$.

Exercise 9.30 How well does the the Hill estimate (9.27) of the tail index α work?

(a) Generate $m = 10$ simulated Pareto samples of $n = 1000$ observations when $\alpha = 2$ and $\beta = 1$, compute the Hill estimate when $p = 0.1$ and compare with the true $\alpha = 2$.

R-*commands*:
```
U=matrix(runif(m*n),n,m); Z=β*(U**(-1/α)-1);
n1=(1-p)*n; Z=apply(Z,2,sort);
α̂=1/apply(log(Z[(n1+1):n,]/Z[n1,]),2,mean).
```

(b) Redo (a) when $n = 10\,000$ and $n = 100\,000$ and comment on the bias in these estimates.

(c) Experiment with $n = 1\,000\,000$ and $p = 0.001$ and you'll discover that most of the bias has disappeared when $\alpha = 2$ but not when $\alpha = 6$!

Exercise 9.31

(a) Draw $m = 10$ samples of $n = 1000$ simulations from the log-normal $Z = e^{\theta+\sigma\varepsilon}$ when $\theta = 0$ and $\sigma = 0.5$ and compute Hill estimates based on $p = 0.1$.

R-*commands*:

`Z=matrix(rlnorm(m*n,θ,σ),n,m)` and continue as in Exercise 9.30.

(b) Repeat (a) for $n = 10\,000$ and $n = 100\,000$.

(c) Explain the estimation pattern and why the value you are trying to estimate is infinite. [*Hint*: Draw on Exercise 9.29. It doesn't help you much to lower p and increase n.]

Exercise 9.32 Consider historical data $z_{(1)} \leq \cdots \leq z_{(n)}$ in ascending order and let $n_1 = (1-p)n$. Suppose a future claim comes with probability $1-p$ from the empirical distribution of $z_{(1)}, \ldots, z_{(n_1)}$ and with probability p from $z_{(n_1)}$ + Pareto(α, β).

(a) Write a program generating m simulations under this model.

R-*commands*:

With data z use n_1=(1-p)*length(z); z=sort(z); U=runif(m); ind=floor(1+U*n_1); Y=z[n_1]+(U**(-1/α)-1)*β; L=runif(m)<1-p; Z=L*z[ind]+(1-L)*Y.

(b) Run the program when $m = 100\,000$, $z = (1, 2, \ldots, 100)$, $p = 0.25$, $\alpha = 4$ and $\beta = 150$ and check that the average is almost the same as the exact mean 59.75.

R-*commands*:

z=1:100, the program in (a) and then mean(Z).

Exercise 9.33 Suppose β in the Pareto component in Exercise 9.32 is fixed as

$$\beta = (\alpha - 1)\left(\frac{z_{(n_1+1)} + \cdots + z_{(n)}}{n - n_1} - z_{(n_1)}\right).$$

(a) Interpret this condition.

(b) Impose it on the program in Exercise 9.32 when $z_1, \ldots, z_n$ are the hurricane data in Exercise 9.15.

R-*commands*:

z=scan(''hurricane.txt''); n=length(z); n_1=n*(1-p); z=sort(z); β=mean(z[(n_1+1):n]-z[n_1])*(α-1) and then as in Exercise 9.32.

(c) Compute the mean, standard deviation and upper 5% and 1% percentiles from $m = 100\,000$ simulations when $p = 0.05$, $\alpha = 2, 5, 10$ and 50 and comment on how they vary with α.

R-*commands*:

mean(Z); sd(Z); Z=sort(Z); Z[0.95*m]; Z[0.99*m].

Section 9.6

Exercise 9.34 The hurricane data in Exercises 9.15 and 9.16 were fitted through logarithms, but we shall now approach them on their original scale.

(a) Try the ordinary Pareto distribution.

R-*commands*:

Use the R-function `paretofit` (similar to programs in Exercise 7.9) with `z=scan(''hurricane.txt''); paretofit(z)`.

(b) Check the fit through a Q–Q plot.

R-*commands*:

With $\hat{\alpha} = 1.394$ and $\hat{\beta} = 117.255$, use `u=(1:n-0.5)/n;` `q=`$\hat{\beta}$`*((1-u)**(-1/`$\hat{\alpha}$`)-1); plot(q,sort(z))`.

(c) Comments?

Exercise 9.35 Try to improve the fit in Exercise 9.34 by using the extended Pareto model.

(a) Compute likelihood estimates.

R-*commands*:

As in Exercise 9.21 with `z` as in the previous exercise.

(b) Check the fit through a Q–Q plot.

R-*commands*:

As in Exercise 9.24(c).

(c) Judge whether the fitted model is adequate and explain the consequences of $\hat{\alpha}$ being less than 1.

(d) Fit the extended Pareto distribution to the logarithms and argue that this is largely the solution in Exercise 9.16.

R-*commands*:

Use `llminus` from Exercise 9.21(b) with `o=optim(c(1,1,1),llminus, z=log(z))` and then as in Exercise 9.21(c).

Exercise 9.36 The Danish fire data was used as an example in the text.

(a) Read the data from the file and argue that the Gamma model in Figure 9.3 is found when the extended Pareto distribution is fitted to their logarithm.

R-*commands*:

`z=scan(''danishfire.txt'')` and then the program in Exercise 9.21 with `z=log(z)`.

(b) Fit the extended Pareto distribution to $z - 1$ and check the fit by means of a Q–Q plot.

R-*commands*:

With `z-1` in place of `z`, follow the commands in Exercise 9.24(c).

(c) Is the model in (b) a possibility?

Exercise 9.37

(a) Compute the Hill estimate with the corresponding scale estimate (9.28) for the Danish fire data when $p = 0.50$, 0.10 and 0.05.

R-*commands*:

With `z` as in the preceding exercise use, for each p, `n`$_1$`=(1-p)*n;`
`α̂=1/mean(log(z[(n`$_1$`+1):n]/z[n`$_1$`]));` `n`$_2$`=(1+n`$_1$`+n`$_2$`)/2;`
`β̂`$_b$`=(z[n`$_2$`]-z[n`$_1$`])/(2**(1/α̂)-1)`.

(b) Compare with the results in Table 9.1 and point out that the discrepancies are considerable.

Exercise 9.38 The **Box–Cox** family of transformations for positive random variables Z is $Y = \{(1 + Z^\gamma) - 1\}/\gamma$, where $\gamma \neq 0$ is a parameter.

(a) Argue that $Y \rightarrow \log(1 + Z)$ as $\gamma \rightarrow 0$, and $Y = \log(1 + Z)$ is the special case $\gamma = 0$.

(b) Why do you need a positive random variable for Y?

(c) Explain that $Z^* \leftarrow (1 + \gamma Y^*)^{1/\gamma} - 1$ is a simulation of Z when Y^* is a simulation of Y.

Exercise 9.39

(a) Write a program fitting the Gamma distribution to the Box–Cox transformed variables in Exercise 9.38.

R-*commands*:

With `z` the data let `y=((1+z)**γ-1)/γ` and follow the steps in Exercise 9.13 with `y` as the data vector.

(b) Apply the program when $\gamma = 1$, 0.5, 0.3, 0.15 and 0.10 to the Norwegian car data in Exercise 9.23.

R-*commands*:

Download through `z=scan(''norwegiancar.txt'')` and compute for each γ parameter estimates $\hat{\xi}$ and $\hat{\alpha}$ as explained in (a).

(c) Check the fit of the solutions in (b) through Q–Q plotting.

R-*commands*:

`n=length(z); u=(1:n-0.5)/n; q̂`$_y$`=ξ̂*qgamma(u,α̂)/α̂;`
`q̂`$_z$`=(1+γ*q̂`$_y$`)**(1/γ)-1; plot(q̂`$_z$`,sort(z))`.

(d) Which model would you select?

Exercise 9.40

(a) Write a program generating m simulations of Z when its Box–Cox transformation Y follows a Gamma distribution.

R-*commands*:

With ξ and α the mean and shape of Y, use `Y=ξ*rgamma(m,α)/α;`
`Z=(1+γ*Y)**(1/γ)-1`.

(b) Run the program when $m = 10\,000$ and $\gamma = 0.05$, with ξ and α the parameters $\hat{\xi} = 32.44$ and $\hat{\alpha} = 450.12$ obtained for the Norwegian car data in Exercise 9.39, and compare the mean and standard deviation under the model with those of the data.

R-*commands*:

Use `Mean=mean(Z); Sd=sd(Z)` and `Mean=mean(z); Sd=sd(z)` with the data as `z`.

Exercise 9.41 How wrong is it to use the Pareto model when claims are Gamma distributed?

(a) Start by computing the upper ϵ-percentile of the Gamma distribution when $\xi = 1$, $\alpha = 2$ and $\epsilon = 0.75, 0.50, 0.25, 0.05$ and 0.01.

R-*commands*:

```
ϵ=c(0.75,0.50,0.25,0.05,0.01); qϵ=ξ*qgamma(1-ϵ,α)/α.
```

(b) Draw $n = 21$ observations from the model in (a), determine the percentiles of a fitted *Pareto* distribution and report their mean and standard deviation when computed from $m_b = 1000$ replications.

R-*commands*:

With `llminus` as in Exercise 7.9(a) use

```
q̂ϵ=matrix(0,mb,length(ϵ));
for (i in 1:mb){Z=ξ*rgamma(n,α)/α;
β̂=optimize(llminus,c(0.001,1000),z=Z)[[1]];
α̂=1/mean(log(1+Z/β̂)); q̂ϵ[i,]= β̂*(ϵ**(-1/α̂)-1)};
Mean=apply(q̂ϵ,2,mean); Sd=apply(q̂ϵ,2,sd).
```

(c) Argue that the risk of large claims is exaggerated.

Exercise 9.42 Redo Exercise 9.41 with the role of the Gamma and the Pareto model switched.

(a) Compute the same percentiles for the *Pareto* distribution when $\alpha = 3$ and $\beta = 2$.

R-*commands*:

```
ϵ=c(0.75,0.50,0.25,0.05,0.01); qϵ=β*(ϵ**(-1/α)-1).
```

(b) Draw $n = 21$ observations from this model, compute the percentiles of a fitted *Gamma* distribution and report on the mean and standard deviation when it is done $m_b = 1000$ times.

R-*commands*:

With `llminus` as in Exercise 9.13(b) use

```
q̂ϵ=matrix(0,mb,length(ϵ));
for (i in 1:mb){Z=β*(runif(n)**(-1/α)-1); ξ̂=mean(Z);
α̂=optimize(llminus,c(0.001,1000),z=Z)[[1]]; q̂ϵ[i,]=
ξ̂*qgamma(ϵ,α̂)/α̂}; Mean=apply(q̂ϵ,2,mean); Sd=apply(q̂ϵ,2,sd).
```

(c) In what sense is the risk of large claims now *underestimated*?

10

Solvency and pricing

10.1 Introduction

The principal tasks in general insurance are solvency and pricing. Solvency is the financial control of liabilities under nearly worst-case scenarios. The target is the so-called **reserve**; i.e., the upper percentiles q_ϵ of the portfolio liability $\mathcal{X}$. Modelling was reviewed in the preceding chapters, and the issue now is computation. We may need the entire distribution of $\mathcal{X}$, and Monte Carlo is the obvious *general* tool. Some problems can be handled by simpler Gaussian approximations, possibly with a correction for skewness added. Computational methods for solvency are discussed in the next two sections.

The second main topic is the pricing of risk. This has a market side. A company will gladly charge what people are willing to pay! Yet a core is the pure premium $\pi = E(X)$ or $\Pi = E(\mathcal{X})$; i.e., the expected policy or portfolio payout during a certain period of time. Evaluations of these are important not only as a basis for pricing, but also as an aid to decision-making. Not all risks are worth taking! Pricing or **rating** methods follow two main lines. One of them draws on claim histories of individuals. Those with good records are considered lower risk and rewarded (premium reduced), those with bad records are punished (premium raised). The traditional approach is through the theory of **credibility**, a classic presented in Section 10.5. Price differentials can also be administered according to the experience with groups. Credibility is a possible approach even now, but it is often more natural to use regression where risk is allowed to depend on explanatory variables such as age, sex, type of car, location of residence and so on. Section 10.4 summarizes regression methods from earlier chapters.

10.2 Portfolio liabilities by simple approximation

10.2.1 Introduction

The portfolio loss $\mathcal{X}$ for independent risks becomes Gaussian as the number of policies $J \to \infty$. This is a consequence of the central limit theorem and leads to straightforward assessments of the reserve without detailed probabilistic modelling. The method is useful due to its simplicity, but the underlying conditions are restrictive. Normal approximations underestimate risk for small portfolios and in branches with large claims. Some of that is rectified by taking the skewness of $\mathcal{X}$ into account, leading to the so-called **NP** version. The purpose of this section is to review these simple approximation methods, show how they are put to practical use and indicate their accuracy and range of application.

10.2.2 Normal approximations

Let μ be the claim intensity and ξ_z and σ_z the mean and standard deviation of the individual losses. If they are the same for all policy holders, the mean and standard deviation of $\mathcal{X}$ over a period of length T become

$$E(\mathcal{X}) = a_0 J \quad \text{and} \quad \text{sd}(\mathcal{X}) = a_1 \sqrt{J},$$

where

$$a_0 = \mu T \xi_z \quad \text{and} \quad a_1 = (\mu T)^{1/2}(\sigma_z^2 + \xi_z^2)^{1/2}; \tag{10.1}$$

see Section 6.3. This leads to the true percentile q_ϵ being approximated by

$$q_\epsilon^{\text{No}} = a_0 J + a_1 \phi_\epsilon \sqrt{J}, \tag{10.2}$$

where ϕ_ϵ is the (upper) ϵ-percentile of the standard normal distribution. Estimates of μ, ξ_z and σ_z are required, but *not* the entire claim size distribution. Detailed modelling can be avoided by using the sample mean and sample standard deviation as estimates $\hat{\xi}_z$ and $\hat{\sigma}_z$, but they can also be found by fitting a parametric distribution.

The approximation (10.2) is nearly always valid for large portfolios of independent risks, even when $\mu = \mu_j$, $\xi_z = \xi_{zj}$ and $\sigma_z = \sigma_{zj}$ vary with the policy j. This is due to the Lindeberg extension of the central limit theorem; see Appendix A.4. The coefficients a_0 and a_1 now become

$$a_0 = \frac{T}{J}\sum_{j=1}^{J} \mu_j \xi_{zj} \quad \text{and} \quad a_1 = \sqrt{\frac{T}{J}\sum_{j=1}^{J} \mu_j(\sigma_{zj}^2 + \xi_{zj}^2)}, \tag{10.3}$$

which reduce to (10.1) when all parameters are equal. With estimates of μ_j, ξ_{zj} and σ_{zj} available on file this method gives (when applicable) a quick appraisal of the reserve.

Still another version emerges when the underlying parameters are random. The most important special case may be claim frequencies $\mu_1, \dots, \mu_J$ being drawn independently of each other from a distribution with common mean and standard deviation ξ_μ and σ_μ. With the mean and standard deviation ξ_z and σ_z of the claim size distribution fixed as before, the coefficients (10.1) now become

$$a_0 = \xi_\mu T \xi_z \qquad \text{and} \qquad a_1 = T^{1/2}\{\xi_\mu(\sigma_z^2 + \xi_z^2) + T\sigma_\mu^2\xi_z^2\}^{1/2}; \tag{10.4}$$

see (6.19) and (6.20) in Section 6.3. The following example examines the numerical impact of this extension.

10.2.3 Example: Motor insurance

Consider the automobile portfolio in Chapter 8 which comes from a Norwegian company and applies to the years before the turn of the century. Its parameters are

$$\underbrace{\hat{\xi}_\mu = 5.6\%, \quad \hat{\sigma}_\mu = 2.0\%}_{\text{annual parameters}} \qquad \text{and} \qquad \underbrace{\hat{\xi}_z = 23.9, \quad \hat{\sigma}_z = 28.9;}_{\text{unit: 1000 Norwegian kroner}}$$

see Section 8.3 for the claim number part. The loss parameters $\hat{\xi}_z$ and $\hat{\sigma}_z$ exclude personal injuries and were obtained from almost 6500 incidents; see Exercise 9.23. These estimated quantities are all we need for the normal approximation. With $J = 10\,000$ policies (and $T = 1$), the coefficients a_0 and a_1 are obtained from (10.1) and (10.4) and lead to the following assessments:

Fixed claim frequency			*Random claim frequency*	
14 844,	15 449	and	14 846,	15 452.
95% reserve	*99% reserve*		*95% reserve*	*99% reserve*

Note how little heterogeneity among policy holders matters! The message was the same in Section 6.3. Even a quite substantial variation among individuals (as in the present example) is of no more than minor importance for the reserve.

10.2.4 The normal power approximation

Normal approximations are refined by adjusting for skewness in $\mathcal{X}$. This is in actuarial science known as the **normal power** (or **NP**) approximation and is in reality the leading term in a series of corrections to the central limit theorem. Another name is the Cornish–Fisher expansion; see Feller (1971) for a probabilistic introduction and Hall (1992) for one in statistics. The underlying theory is beyond the scope of this book, but a brief sketch of the structure is indicated in Section 10.7. Only the pure Poisson model is considered below. The extension to the negative binomial and other models is treated in Daykin *et al.* (1994). This is a way of including variations in individual risk, but as was seen above, the practical impact is limited.

Let ζ_z be the skewness coefficient of the claim size distribution. The modified approximation then reads

$$q_\epsilon^{\mathrm{NP}} = q_\epsilon^{\mathrm{No}} + a_2(\phi_\epsilon^2 - 1)/6 \quad \text{where} \quad a_2 = \frac{\zeta_z\sigma_z^3 + 3\xi_z\sigma_z^2 + \xi_z^3}{\sigma_z^2 + \xi_z^2}. \tag{10.5}$$

The extra term is due to skewness and is in practice positive; see Section 10.7 for the justification. When (10.1) replaces the normal approximation q_ϵ^{No}, this yields

$$q_\epsilon^{\mathrm{NP}} = \underbrace{a_0 J + a_1\phi_\epsilon\sqrt{J}}_{\text{normal component}} + \underbrace{a_2(\phi_\epsilon^2 - 1)/6}_{\text{NP correction}},$$

which is a series in falling powers of $\sqrt{J}$. The NP correction term is *independent* of portfolio size.

To use the approximation in practice, the skewness ζ_z must be estimated in addition to ξ_z and σ_z (μ as well). There are no new ideas in this. We may fit a parametric family to the historical data or use the sample skewness coefficient introduced in Section 9.2. The situation when parameters vary over the portfolio can be handled too, but the mathematics becomes more cumbersome to write down; see Section 10.7 for the details.

10.2.5 Example: Danish fire claims

Consider a portfolio for which

$$\underbrace{\hat{\mu} = 1\%}_{\text{annual}} \quad \text{and} \quad \underbrace{\hat{\xi}_z = 3.385, \ \hat{\sigma}_z = 8.507, \ \hat{\zeta}_z = 18.74.}_{\text{unit: Million Danish kroner}}$$

The parameters for claim size are those found for the Danish fire data in Section 9.6. With $J = 1000$ and $J = 100\,000$ policies the assessments of the reserve become those in Table 10.1. The NP correction has considerable impact on the small portfolio on the left, raising the 99% reserve by as much as 60%. The principal reason is the losses being strongly skewed towards the right (with skewness exceeding 18). When the number of policies is higher, the relative effect of the adjustment is smaller. With 100 000 policies the difference between the two methods is of minor importance and their almost common assessment can be trusted.

But what about the small portfolio? The huge impact of the NP correction on the left in Table 10.1 is ominous and should make us suspicious. Indeed, the more reliable Monte Carlo assessments in the next section match neither. The approximations of this section are likely to work best when the NP term isn't a dominating one.

Table 10.1 Reserve by the normal and normal power approximations for the Danish fire claims

Money unit: Million Danish kroner

	Portfolio size: J = 1000		Portfolio: J = 100000	
	95% reserve	99% reserve	95% reserve	99% reserve
Normal	81	101	3861	4058
Normal power	123	209	3903	4166

10.3 Portfolio liabilities by simulation

10.3.1 Introduction

Monte Carlo has several advantages over the methods of the preceding section. It is more general (no restriction on use), more versatile (easier to adapt to changing circumstances) and better suited for long time horizons (more on that in Chapter 11). But the method is slow computationally, and doesn't it demand the entire claim size distribution whereas the normal approximation can make do with only mean and variance? The last point is deceptive. If the portfolio is so large that a Gaussian approximation is reasonable, the claim size distribution (apart from the mean and variance) doesn't matter anyhow.

Computational speed is unlikely to be a problem. To give you an idea, suppose there are 1000 policies with average claim frequency $\mu T = 5\%$. A Fortran implementation of Algorithm 10.1 on a T60p processor then produced 1000 portfolio simulations in 0.02 s when the claim size distribution was the empirical one. The Gamma distribution (laborious to sample) required twice as long, still only 0.04 s. R-programs, though slower, are also completed quickly. Computer time is roughly proportional to the mean number of claims, $J\mu T$.

10.3.2 A skeleton algorithm

Portfolio liability is a central issue in general insurance, and its seems worthwhile to sketch a general computational method that collects algorithms spread over several chapters. Suppose claim intensities $\mu_1, \dots, \mu_J$ for J policies are stored on file along with J different claim size distributions and payment functions $H_1(z), \dots, H_J(z)$. If Algorithm 2.14 is used for Poisson sampling, the program can be organized as in Algorithm 10.1. Poisson sampling has been integrated into the code. The algorithm goes through the entire portfolio and for each policy adds the costs of settling incidents until the citerion on Line 4 is *not* satisfied. There are many different algorithms for Line 5. Table 10.2 lists examples from this book.

Often, individual losses take up most of the computer time. If so, there is little

Algorithm 10.1 Portfolio liabilities in the general case

Input: $\lambda_j = \mu_j T$ $(j = 1, \ldots, J)$, claim size models, $H_1(z), \ldots, H_J(z)$
$\mathcal{X}^* \leftarrow 0$
For $j = 1, \ldots, J$ do
  Draw $U^* \sim$ uniform and $S^* \leftarrow -\log(U^*)$
  Repeat while $S^* < \lambda_j$
    Draw claim size Z^* *%Might depend on j*
    $\mathcal{X}^* \leftarrow \mathcal{X}^* + H_j(Z^*)$ *%Add loss*
    Draw $U^* \sim$ uniform and $S^* \leftarrow S^* - \log(U^*)$ *%Update for Poisson*
Return $\mathcal{X}^*$.

Table 10.2 List of claim size algorithms

Distribution		Distribution	
Empirical distribution	Algorithm 4.1	Extended Pareto	Algorithm 9.1
Pareto mixing	Algorithm 9.2	Weibull	Algorithm 2.12
Gamma	Algorithms 2.9, 2.10	Fréchet	Exercise 2.31
Log-normal	Algorithm 2.5	Logistic	Exercise 2.32
Pareto	Algorithm 2.13	Burr	Exercise 2.33

point in faster Poisson samplers such as the guide tables of Section 4.2, which won't bring worthwhile improvements. Nor is speed enhanced much when risks are identical and the algorithm is built around the portfolio number of claims $\mathcal{N}$.

10.3.3 Danish fire data: The impact of the claim size model

The Danish fire data was examined in Section 9.6, and a number of models were tried. Some worked better than others, and Table 10.3 shows how the fit or lack of it is passed on to the reserve. Models considered were the empirical distribution function without or with Pareto mixing for the extremes, pure Pareto, Gamma on log-scale and the log-normal. All were fitted to the historical fire claims as described in Section 9.6. The portfolio size was $J = 1000$ with annual claim rate $\mu = 1\%$, producing no more than 10 claims per year on average. Ten million simulations were used, making Monte Carlo uncertainty very small indeed.

The model scenario is the same as on the left in Table 10.1, and testifies to the difficulty of calculating the reserves for small portfolios. On its own the empirical distribution function underestimates risk, but it seems to work well when mixed with the Pareto distribution, and the results are not overly dependent on where the threshold b is placed. Another reasonably well-fitting model in Section 9.6 was the Gamma distribution on the log-scale, and the reserve calculated under it does not deviate much from Pareto mixing. Other models in Section 9.6 were grossly in error, and produce strongly deviating results here. If you compare with the normal power method in Table 10.1, you will discover that it is on target at 99% and overshoots a bit at 95%.

Reserves at level 99.97% have been added. Luckily, those figures are not in demand! The results are a mess of instability, an example of the extreme difficulty of evaluations very far out into the tails of a distribution where they depend sensitively on modelling details. Percentiles that close to one are rarely needed in insurance, but they are used by rating bureaus in finance.

10.4 Differentiated pricing through regression

10.4.1 Introduction

Very young male drivers or owners of fast cars are groups of clients notoriously more risky than others, and it may not be unfair to charge them more. The technological development which makes it easier to collect and store information with a bearing on risk can only further such practice. A picture of how insurance incidents and their cost are connected to circumstances, conditions and the people causing them must be built up from experience, and a principal tool is regression, typically of log-linear form. The purpose of this section is to indicate how Poisson, Gamma and log-normal regression from the preceding chapters are put to work.

Explanatory variables (observations, registrations, measurements) $x_1 \dots, x_v$ are then linked to claim intensity μ and mean loss per event ξ_z through

$$\log(\mu) = b_{\mu 0}x_0 + \cdots + b_{\mu v}x_v \quad \text{and} \quad \log(\xi_z) = b_{z0}x_0 + \cdots + b_{zv}x_v,$$

where $b_{\mu 0}, \dots, b_{\mu v}$ and $b_{z0}, \dots, b_{zv}$ are coefficients. By default $x_0 = 1$, a convention introduced to make formulae neater. The explanatory variables do not have to be the same for μ and ξ_z, but the mathematics becomes simpler to write down if

Table 10.3 Calculated reserves for the Danish fire data. Money unit: Million Danish kroner (about eight Danish kroner for one euro, or 10 for a dollar)

	EDF[a]	EDF[a] with Pareto above b[b]				Other claim size models		
Reserve		b=10	b=5.6	b=3.0	b=1.8	Pareto	Gamma[c]	Log-normal
95%	72	100	104	105	100	71	85	49
99%	173	200	217	230	225	137	206	61
99.97%	330	590	870	1400	1750	900	2145	84

[a]EDF: The empirical distribution.

[b]Thresholds are 5%, 10%, 25%, 50%.

[c]Log-transformed claims.

they are, and we can always ‘zero’ irrelevant ones away; i.e., take $b_{zi} = 0$ if (for example) x_i isn't included in the regression for ξ_z. In motor insurance (the example below) regression relationships are typically stronger for μ than for ξ_z. Inserting the defining equations for μ and ξ_z into the pure premium $\pi = \mu T \xi_z$ yields

$$\pi = Te^{\theta} \quad \text{where} \quad \theta = (b_{\mu 0} + b_{z0})x_0 + \cdots + (b_{\mu v} + b_{zv})x_v,$$

and estimates of the coefficients must be supplied.

10.4.2 Estimates of pure premia

The pure premium of a policy holder with $x_1, \ldots, x_v$ as explanatory variables is estimated as

$$\hat{\pi} = Te^{\hat{\theta}} \quad \text{where} \quad \hat{\theta} = (\hat{b}_{\mu 0} + \hat{b}_{z0})x_0 + \cdots + (\hat{b}_{\mu v} + \hat{b}_{zv})x_v.$$

Here $\hat{b}_{\mu i}$ and $\hat{b}_{zi}$ are obtained from historical data, usually through statistical software. Assessments of their standard deviations are provided too, and we must learn how they are passed on to $\hat{\pi}$ itself. Bootstrapping (Section 7.4) can be used (as always), but there is also a simpler Gaussian technique. Since the estimated regression coefficients may not be that far from being normally distributed, their sum $\hat{\theta}$ isn't either, and $\hat{\pi}$ becomes approximately log-normal. This is a large-sample result which requires much historical data in principle, but a relaxed attitude is in order. High accuracy in error estimates isn't that important.

There are two sets of estimated coefficients $(\hat{b}_{\mu 0}, \ldots, \hat{b}_{\mu v})$ and $(\hat{b}_{z0}, \ldots, \hat{b}_{zv})$ coming from two different regression analyses. It is usually unproblematic to assume independence *between* sets, so that $(\hat{b}_{\mu i}, \hat{b}_{zj})$ is uncorrelated for all (i, j). If $\sigma_{\mu ij} = \text{cov}(\hat{b}_{\mu_i}, \hat{b}_{\mu_j})$ and $\sigma_{zij} = \text{cov}(\hat{b}_{z_i}, \hat{b}_{z_j})$ are the covariances *within* sets, then

$$E(\hat{\theta}) = \theta \quad \text{and} \quad \text{var}(\hat{\theta}) = \sum_{i=0}^{v}\sum_{j=0}^{v} x_i x_j(\sigma_{\mu ij} + \sigma_{zij}),$$

where the relationship on the right follows from the general variance formula for sums (rule (A.21) in Table A.2). These results are passed on to an approximately log-normal $\hat{\pi}$ through the usual formulae for mean and variance. If $\sigma_\theta^2 = \text{var}(\hat{\theta})$, then

$$E(\hat{\pi}) \doteq \pi e^{\sigma_\theta^2/2} \quad \text{and} \quad \text{sd}(\hat{\pi}) \doteq E(\hat{\pi})\sqrt{e^{\sigma_\theta^2} - 1},$$

and $E(\hat{\pi}) > \pi$ so that $\hat{\pi}$ is biased upwards, but usually not by very much (see below). Bias and standard deviation are estimated by

$$\underbrace{\hat{\pi}(e^{\hat{\sigma}_\theta^2/2} - 1)}_{\textit{bias}}, \qquad \underbrace{\hat{\pi}e^{\hat{\sigma}_\theta^2/2}\sqrt{e^{\hat{\sigma}_\theta^2} - 1}}_{\textit{standard deviation}} \quad \text{where} \quad \hat{\sigma}_\theta^2 = \sum_{i=0}^{v}\sum_{j=0}^{v} x_i x_j(\hat{\sigma}_{\mu ij} + \hat{\sigma}_{zij}).$$

Here $\hat{\sigma}_{\mu ij}$ and $\hat{\sigma}_{zij}$ are estimates of variances/covariances provided by standard software. In the formula for $\hat{\sigma}_\theta^2$ take $\hat{\sigma}_{\mu ij} = 0$ or $\hat{\sigma}_{zij} = 0$ if variable i or j (or both) is absent in the regression.

10.4.3 Pure premia regression in practice

Log-linear regression makes estimated pure premia $\hat{\pi}$ fluctuate around some baseline $\hat{\pi}_0$ depending on the values of $x_1, \dots, x_v$. If $x_0 = 1$ and $\hat{\pi}_0$ corresponds to $x_1 = \cdots = x_v = 0$, the estimate can be rewritten

$$\hat{\pi} = \underbrace{\hat{\pi}_0}_{\textit{baseline}} \cdot \underbrace{e^{(\hat{b}_{\mu 1}+\hat{b}_{z1})x_1}}_{\textit{variable}\,1} \cdots \underbrace{e^{(\hat{b}_{\mu v}+\hat{b}_{zv})x_v}}_{\textit{variable}\,v} \quad \text{where} \quad \hat{\pi}_0 = Te^{\hat{b}_{\mu 0}+\hat{b}_{z0}},$$

and the contributions of the explanatory variables drive $\hat{\pi}$ up and down compared with $\hat{\pi}_0$.

As an example, suppose x_1 represents the sex of the individual, say 0 for males and 1 for females. Then

$$\underbrace{\hat{\pi}_m = \hat{\pi}_0 e^{(\hat{b}_{\mu 2}+\hat{b}_{z2})x_2} \cdots e^{(\hat{b}_{\mu v}+\hat{b}_{zv})x_v}}_{\textit{pure premium for males}} \quad \text{and} \quad \underbrace{\hat{\pi}_f = e^{\hat{b}_{\mu 1}+\hat{b}_{z1}}\hat{\pi}_m}_{\textit{pure premium for females}},$$

and the ratio $\hat{\pi}_f/\hat{\pi}_m$ is *independent of all other covariates*. This is the inevitable consequence of linear specifications on a log-scale. The issue is the same as in Section 8.4, where it was pointed out that female drivers with fewer claims than men when young and slightly more when old is incompatible with this model.

Possible modifications are those mentioned in Section 8.4. One method is crossed categories. The problem with this as a general approach is the rapid growth in the number of parameters. Suppose there are three variables consisting of 2, 6 and 6 categories. The total number of combinations is then $2 \times 6 \times 6 = 72$, and the cross-classification comprises 72 groups. Perhaps this does not appear much when the historical material is more than 100 000 policy years as in the example below. There is then for the average group around, say, 1500 policy years and $1500 \times 0.05 = 75$ events if the claim rate is 5% annually. Even if that is enough for fairly accurate assessments of claim intensities groupwise through the elementary estimate (8.1), it isn't for mean losses. Add to this that historical data are often unevenly divided between groups and their number could easily exceed 72. Simplifications through log-linear regression dampen random error and make estimates of pure premia more stable.

10.4.4 Example: The Norwegian automobile portfolio

The Norwegian automobile portfolio of Chapter 8 is useful for illustration. There are around 100 000 policies extending 2 years back, with much customer turnover.

Table 10.4 Estimated coefficients of claim intensity and claim size for automobile data (standard deviation in parentheses). Methods: Poisson and Gamma regression

	Intercept	Age	
		≤ 26	> 26
Freq.	−2.43 (0.08)	0 (0)	−0.55 (0.07)
Size[a]	8.33 (0.07)	0 (0)	−0.36 (0.06)

	Distance limit on policy (1000 km)					
	8	12	16	20	25-30	No limit
Freq.	0 (0)	0.17 (0.04)	0.28 (0.04)	0.50 (0.04)	0.62 (0.05)	0.82 (0.08)
Size[a]	0 (0)	0.02 (0.04)	0.03 (0.04)	0.09 (0.04)	0.11 (0.05)	0.14 (0.08)

	Geographical regions with traffic density from *high* to *low*					
	Region 1	Region 2	Region 3	Region 4	Region 5	Region 6
Freq.	0 (0)	−0.19 (0.0.4)	−0.24 (0.06)	−0.29 (0.04)	−0.39 (0.05)	−0.36 (0.04)
Size[a]	0 (0)	−0.10 (0.0.4)	−0.03 (0.05)	−0.07 (0.04)	−0.02 (0.05)	0.06 (0.04)

[a]Estimated shape of the Gamma distribution: $\hat{\alpha} = 1.1$.

Almost 6500 claims were registered as a basis for claim size modelling. Explanatory variables used are

- age (two categories ≤ 26 and > 26 years)
- driving limit (six categories)
- geographical region (six categories).

Driving limit is a proxy for how much people drive. Age is simplified drastically compared with what would be done in practice. Consider an individual in category i_1 for variable 1 (age), i_2 for variable 2 (distance limit) and i_3 for variable 3 (region). The regression equation for μ is then

$$\log(\mu) = b_{\mu 0} + \underset{age}{b_{\mu 1}(i_1)} + \underset{distance\ limit}{b_{\mu 2}(i_2)} + \underset{region}{b_{\mu 3}(i_3)},$$

with $b_{\mu 1}(1)$, $b_{\mu 1}(2)$ the age parameters and $b_{\mu 2}(1), \ldots, b_{\mu 2}(6)$ and $b_{\mu 3}(1), \ldots, b_{\mu 3}(6)$ those for distance limit and region. There is a similar relation for ξ_z. Regression methods used were Poisson (claim frequency) and Gamma (claim size).

The estimated parameters in Table 10.4 vary smoothly with the categories. As expected, the more people drive and the heavier the traffic the larger is the risk. Claim frequency fluctuates more strongly than claim size (coefficients larger in absolute value). The accidents of young people appear to be both more frequent and more severe. Table 10.4 enables us to assess pure premia for all the 72 groups along with their standard deviation, as explained above. Those for the region with

Table 10.5 Estimated pure premium (euros) for Region 1 of the Scandinavian automobile portfolio (standard deviation in parentheses)

Age	Distance limit on policy (1000 km)					
	80	120	160	200	250–300	No limit
≤ 26 years	365 (6.3)	442 (6.8)	497 (7.5)	656 (8.3)	750 (9.0)	951 (9.8)
> 26 years	148 (2.9)	179 (3.0)	201 (3.7)	265 (3.7)	303 (4.1)	385 (4.3)

heaviest traffic (Oslo area) are shown in Table 10.5. Estimates are smooth and might be used as a basis for pricing. It was pointed out that there is a bias upwards, but it only varied between 0.2 and 0.5 when estimated by the method above and is negligible compared with the standard deviations.

10.5 Differentiated pricing through credibility

10.5.1 Introduction

The preceding section differentiated premium according to observable attributes such as age, sex, geographical location and so on. Other factors with impact on risk could be personal ones that are not easily measured or observed directly. Drivers of automobiles may be able and concentrated or reckless and inexperienced, which influences driving and accident rate. This raises the question of whether risks can be assessed from the track records of the policy holders themselves with premia tailored to the individual. Related examples are shops robbed repeatedly or buildings and houses frequently damaged, again with potential repercussions for what an insurance company might charge.

Rating risks from experience was, in the preceding section, carried out by regression, but the approach is now different (with much in common with the Bayesian ideas in Section 7.6). Policy holders are assigned randomly drawn pure premia $\pi = \pi^{\text{pu}}$, which are determined as **credibility** estimates. This is a method where prior knowledge of how π varies over the portfolio is combined with individual records. The idea can be applied to groups of policy holders too, and both viewpoints are introduced below. Credibility, a classic in actuarial science, is reviewed in Bühlmann and Gisler (2005).

10.5.2 Credibility: Approach

The basic assumption is that policy holders carry a list of attributes ω with impact on risk. What ω is immaterial; the important thing is that it exists and has been drawn randomly for each individual. Let X be the sum of claims during a certain period of time (say a year) and introduce

$$\underbrace{\pi(\omega) = E(X|\omega)}_{\text{conditional pure premium}} \qquad \text{and} \qquad \sigma(\omega) = \text{sd}(X|\omega), \tag{10.6}$$

where the notation reflects that both quantities depend on the underlying ω. We seek $\pi = \pi(\omega)$, the **conditional** pure premium of the policy holder, as a basis for pricing. At the group or portfolio level there is a common ω that applies to all risks jointly. The target is now $\Pi = E(\mathcal{X}|\omega)$, where $\mathcal{X}$ is the sum of claims from many individuals.

Let $X_1, \dots, X_K$ (policy level) or $\mathcal{X}_1, \dots, \mathcal{X}_K$ (group level) be realizations of X or $\mathcal{X}$ dating K years back. The most accurate estimates of π and Π from such records are (Section 6.4) the conditional means

$$\underbrace{\hat{\pi}_K = E(X|x_1, \dots, x_K)}_{\text{policy level}} \qquad \text{and} \qquad \underbrace{\hat{\Pi}_K = E(\mathcal{X}|x_1, \dots, x_K)}_{\text{group level}} \tag{10.7}$$

where $x_1, \dots, x_K$ are the actual values. Differences between methods at the individual and group level are only minor from a mathematical point of view, and the argument will be written out for the former. A natural framework is the common-factor model from Section 6.3, where $X, X_1, \dots, X_K$ are identically and independently distributed given ω. This won't be true when underlying conditions change systematically; consult some of the references in Section 10.8.

A problem with the estimates (10.7) is that they require a joint model for ω *and* $X, X_1, \dots, X_K$. A more natural framework for such constructions is to break X down on claim numbers N and losses per incident Z. This familiar line is introduced later. Consider first an alternative, linear approach which avoids complicated modelling altogether.

10.5.3 Linear credibility

The standard method in credibility is the linear one, with estimates of π of the form

$$\hat{\pi}_K = b_0 + b_1 X_1 + \cdots + b_K X_K,$$

where $b_0, b_1, \dots, b_K$ are coefficients determined so that the mean-squared error $E(\hat{\pi}_K - \pi)^2$ is as small as possible. The fact that $X_1, \dots, X_K$ are conditionally independent with the same distribution forces $b_1 = \cdots = b_K$, and if w/K is their common value, the estimate becomes

$$\hat{\pi}_K = b_0 + w\overline{X}_K \quad \text{where} \quad \overline{X}_K = (X_1 + \cdots + X_K)/K. \tag{10.8}$$

To proceed we need the so-called **structural parameters**:

$$\overline{\pi} = E\{\pi(\omega)\}, \quad \upsilon^2 = \text{var}\{\pi(\omega)\}, \quad \tau^2 = E\{\sigma^2(\omega)\}, \tag{10.9}$$

where $\overline{\pi}$ is the average pure premium for the entire population. It is also the expectation for individuals, since by the rule of double expectation

$$E(X) = E\{E(X|\omega)\} = E\{\pi(\omega)\} = \overline{\pi}.$$

Both υ and τ represent variation. The former is caused by diversity between individuals and the latter by the physical processes behind the incidents. Their impact on var(X) can be understood through the rule of double variance; i.e.,

$$\text{var}(X) = E\{\text{var}(X|\omega)\} + \text{var}\{E(X|\omega)\} = E\{\sigma^2(\omega)\} + \text{var}\{\pi(\omega)\} = \tau^2 + \upsilon^2,$$

and τ^2 and υ^2 represent uncertainties of different origin that add to var(X).

These structural parameters are parsimonious modelling indeed, and it is demonstrated at the end of the section how they are determined from historical data. The optimal linear credibility estimate now becomes

$$\hat{\pi}_K = (1-w)\overline{\pi} + w\overline{X}_K, \quad \text{where} \quad w = \frac{\upsilon^2}{\upsilon^2 + \tau^2/K}; \tag{10.10}$$

which is proved in Section 10.7 where it is also established that

$$E(\hat{\pi}_K - \pi) = 0 \quad \text{and} \quad \text{sd}(\hat{\pi}_K - \pi) = \frac{\upsilon}{\sqrt{1 + K\upsilon^2/\tau^2}}. \tag{10.11}$$

The estimate is unbiased, and its standard deviation decreases with K. It is closely connected to the Bayes' estimate of the normal mean in Section 7.6. The weight w is a compromise between the average pure premium $\overline{\pi}$ of the population and the track record of the policy holder. Note that $w = 0$ if $K = 0$; i.e., without historical information the best estimate is the population average. Other interpretations are given among the exercises.

10.5.4 How accurate is linear credibility?

A reasonable model for an error study is to let $\xi_z = E(Z)$ and $\sigma_z = \text{sd}(Z)$ be common for all policy holders and to allow μ to vary. If $\xi_\mu = E(\mu)$ and $\sigma_\mu = \text{sd}(\mu)$, then

$$\pi(\mu) = E(X|\mu) = \mu T\xi_z \quad \text{and} \quad \sigma^2(\mu) = \text{var}(X|\mu) = \mu T(\xi_z^2 + \sigma_z^2);$$

see Section 6.3. The structural parameters (10.9) therefore become

$$\overline{\pi} = \xi_\mu T\xi_z, \quad \upsilon^2 = \sigma_\mu^2 T^2 \xi_z^2 \quad \text{and} \quad \tau^2 = \xi_\mu T(\xi_z^2 + \sigma_z^2).$$

Insert these expressions into (10.11) right and let $\theta_z = \xi_z^2/(\xi_z^2 + \sigma_z^2)$. Then

$$\text{sd}(\hat{\pi}_K - \pi) = \frac{\sigma_\mu T\xi_z}{\sqrt{1 + K\theta_z T\sigma_\mu^2/\xi_\mu}} \geq \frac{\sigma_\mu T\xi_z}{\sqrt{1 + KT\sigma_\mu^2/\xi_\mu}} \tag{10.12}$$

since $\theta_z \leq 1$. The ratio σ_μ^2/ξ_μ in the denominator isn't a very large number, which makes the error fairly insensitive to the length K of the historical record.

Insert $T = 1$ and $\xi_z = 10\,000$ with the annual parameters $\xi_\mu = 5.6\%$ and $\sigma_\mu = 2\%$ for the Norwegian automobile portfolio. This yields $\mathrm{sd}(\hat{\pi}_K - \pi) \geq 200$, 193.2 and 187.1 when $K = 0$, 10 and 20, which are huge errors when the mean annual claim is $\overline{\pi} = 10\,000 \times 0.056 = 560$. Even 20 years of experience with the same client hasn't reduced uncertainty more than a trifle.

10.5.5 Credibility at group level

Estimation accuracy is much higher at the portfolio level. Suppose we seek $\Pi(\omega) = E(\mathcal{X}|\omega)$, where $\mathcal{X}$ is the sum of claims from a group of policy holders. Now ω represents uncertainty common to the entire group, and the linear credibility estimate (10.10) is applied to the record $\mathcal{X}_1, \dots, \mathcal{X}_K$ of that group. The structural parameters differ from what they were above. If individual risks are independent given ω, then

$$E(\mathcal{X}|\omega) = J\pi(\omega) \quad \text{and} \quad \mathrm{sd}(\mathcal{X}|\omega) = \sqrt{J}\,\sigma(\omega),$$

and the structural parameters (10.9) become $J\overline{\pi}$, $J^2\upsilon^2$ and $J\tau^2$ instead of $\overline{\pi}$, υ^2 and τ^2. It follows from (10.10) that the best linear estimate is

$$\hat{\Pi}_K = (1-w)J\overline{\pi} + w\overline{\mathcal{X}}_K \quad \text{where} \quad w = \frac{\upsilon^2}{\upsilon^2 + \tau^2/(JK)}. \tag{10.13}$$

Here $\overline{\mathcal{X}}_K = (\mathcal{X}_1 + \cdots + \mathcal{X}_K)/K$ is the average claim at the group level. Its weight is much larger than for individual policies, and increases with the group size J.

The estimation error is, from (10.11),

$$E(\hat{\Pi}_K - \Pi) = 0 \quad \text{and} \quad \mathrm{sd}(\hat{\Pi}_K - \Pi) = \frac{J\upsilon}{\sqrt{(1 + KJ\upsilon^2/\tau^2}}. \tag{10.14}$$

The method is unbiased as before, and the presence of the portfolio size J in the denominator makes the error more sensitive to the length K of the historical record.

10.5.6 Optimal credibility

The above estimates are the best *linear* methods, but the Bayesian estimate (10.7) is optimal among *all* methods and offers an improvement. Break the historical record $x_1, \dots, x_K$ down on annual claim numbers $n_1, \dots, n_K$ and losses $z_1, \dots, z_n$ where $n = n_1 + \cdots + n_K$ and assume independence between N and Z. The Bayes' estimate of $\pi = E(X) = E(N)E(Z)$ now becomes

$$\hat{\pi}_K = E(X|n_1, \dots, n_K, z_1, \dots, z_n) = E(N|n_1, \dots, n_K)E(Z|z_1, \dots, z_n),$$

and there are two parts. Often, the claim intensity μ fluctuates more strongly from one policy holder to another than does the expected loss $\xi_z = E(Z)$. We shall go to the extreme and disregard all such variation in ξ_z. Then $\xi_z = E(Z|z_1, \dots, z_n)$ independently of $z_1, \dots, z_n$, and the Bayesian estimate becomes

$$\hat{\pi}_K = \xi_z E(N|n_1, \dots, n_K). \tag{10.15}$$

Credibility estimation of ξ_z is treated in Bühlmann and Gisler (2005).

A model for past and future claim numbers is needed. The natural one is the common-factor model, where $N, N_1, \dots, N_K$ are conditionally independent and identically distributed given μ with N and all N_k being Poisson(μT). For μ assume the standard representation

$$\mu = \xi_\mu G \quad \text{and} \quad G \sim \text{Gamma}(\alpha),$$

where $E(G) = 1$. It is shown in Section 10.7 that the estimate (10.15) now becomes

$$\hat{\pi}_K = \bar{\pi}\frac{\bar{n} + \alpha/K}{\xi_\mu T + \alpha/K}, \quad \text{where} \quad \bar{\pi} = \xi_\mu T \xi_z \quad \text{and} \quad \bar{n} = (n_1 + \cdots + n_K)/K. \tag{10.16}$$

Note that the population average $\bar{\pi}$ is adjusted up or down according to whether the average claim number $\bar{n}$ is larger or smaller than its expectation $\xi_\mu T$. The error is

$$E(\hat{\pi}_K - \pi) = 0 \quad \text{and} \quad \text{sd}(\hat{\pi}_K - \pi) = \frac{\bar{\pi}}{\sqrt{\alpha + K\xi_\mu T}}, \tag{10.17}$$

which is also proved in Section 10.7.

How much better than the linear method is this? Insert $\xi_\mu T \xi_z = \bar{\pi}$ and $\sigma_\mu = \xi_\mu / \sqrt{\alpha}$ into the lower bound in (10.12), and you will discover that it coincides with $\text{sd}(\hat{\pi}_K - \pi)$ in (10.17)! In other words, the optimal method hasn't improved matters substantially, and credibility estimates for individuals remain highly inaccurate.

10.5.7 Estimating the structural parameters

Credibility estimation is based on parameters that must be determined from historical data. Claim numbers were discussed in Section 8.3, and only linear credibility is treated here. Historical data for J policies that have been in the company for $K_1, \dots, K_J$ years are then of the form

1	x_{11}	$\dots$	x_{1K_1}	$\bar{x}_1$	s_1
.	.	$\dots$	.	.	.
.	.	$\dots$	.	.	.
J	x_{J1}	$\dots$	x_{JK_J}	$\bar{x}_J$	s_J,
Policies		*Annual claims*		*mean*	*sd*

where the jth row $x_{j1}, \ldots, x_{jK_j}$ contains the annual claims from client j and $\bar{x}_j$ with s_j their mean and standard deviation. The following estimates are essentially due to Sundt (1983), with a forerunner in Bühlmann and Straub (1970) and even in the biostatistical literature; see section 9.2 in Sokal and Rohlf (1981).

Let $\mathcal{K} = K_1 + \cdots + K_J$. Unbiased moment estimates of the structural parameters are then

$$\hat{\bar{\pi}} = \frac{1}{\mathcal{K}} \sum_{j=1}^{J} K_j \bar{x}_j, \quad \hat{\tau}^2 = \frac{1}{\mathcal{K} - J} \sum_{j=1}^{J} (K_j - 1) s_j^2 \tag{10.18}$$

and

$$\hat{\upsilon}^2 = \frac{\sum_{j=1}^{J} (K_j/\mathcal{K})(\bar{x}_j - \hat{\bar{\pi}})^2 - \hat{\tau}^2 (J-1)/\mathcal{K}}{1 - \sum_{j=1}^{J} (K_j/\mathcal{K})^2}; \tag{10.19}$$

for verification see Section 10.7. The expression for $\hat{\upsilon}^2$ may be negative. If it is, let $\hat{\upsilon} = 0$ and take the position that the underlying variation is too small to be detected.

10.6 Reinsurance

10.6.1 Introduction

Reinsurance was introduced in Section 3.2. Parts of primary risks placed with a cedent are now passed on to reinsurers who may in turn go to other reinsurers leading to a global network of risk sharers. Reinsurers may provide cover for incidents far away both geographically and in terms of intermediaries, but for the original clients at the bottom of the chain all this is largely irrelevant. For them, reinsurance instruments used higher up are without importance as long as the companies involved are solvent. These arrangements are ways to spread risk and may also enable small or medium-sized companies to take on heavier responsibilities than their capital allows.

Methods don't change much from ordinary insurance. The primary risks rest with cedents, and the stochastic modelling is the same as before. Cash flows differ, but these are merely modifications handled through fixed functions $H(z)$ containing contract clauses and easily taken care of by Monte Carlo (Section 3.3). The economic impact may be huge, the methodological one not. This section outlines some of the most common contracts and indicates consequences for pricing and solvency.

10.6.2 Traditional contracts

Reinsurance contracts may apply to single events or to sums of claims affecting the entire portfolio. These losses (denoted Z and $\mathcal{X}$) are then divided between reinsurer and cedent according to

$$\underbrace{Z^{\text{re}} = H(Z), \quad Z^{\text{ce}} = Z - H(Z)}_{\textit{single events}} \quad \text{and} \quad \underbrace{\mathcal{X}^{\text{re}} = H(\mathcal{X}), \quad \mathcal{X}^{\text{ce}} = \mathcal{X} - H(\mathcal{X}),}_{\textit{at portfolio level}} \tag{10.20}$$

where $0 \leq H(z) \leq 1$ and $0 \leq H(x) \leq 1$. Here Z^{ce} and $\mathcal{X}^{\text{ce}}$ are the *net* cedent responsibility after the reinsurance contributions have been subtracted.

One of the most common contracts is the $a \times b$ type considered in Chapter 3. When drawn up in terms of single events, reinsurer and cedent responsibilities are

$$Z^{\text{re}} = \begin{matrix} 0 & \text{if } Z < a \\ Z - a & \text{if } a \leq Z < a + b \\ b & \text{if } Z \geq a + b \end{matrix} \quad \text{and} \quad Z^{\text{ce}} = \begin{matrix} Z & \text{if } Z < a \\ a & \text{if } a \leq Z < a + b \\ Z - b & \text{if } Z \geq a + b, \end{matrix}$$

where $Z^{\text{re}} + Z^{\text{ce}}$=Z. The lower bound a is the **retention** limit of the cedent who covers all claims below this threshold. Responsibility (i.e., Z^{ce}) appears unlimited, but there is in practice usually a maximum insured sum s that makes $Z \leq s$, and the scheme gives good cedent protection if $b = s - a$. If the upper bound b (the retention limit of the *reinsurer*) is infinite (rare in practice), the contract is known as **excess of loss**. This type of arrangement is also used with $\mathcal{X}$, with $\mathcal{X}^{\text{re}}$ and $\mathcal{X}^{\text{ce}}$ being defined from $\mathcal{X}$ in the same way that Z^{re} and Z^{ce} were defined from Z. If b is infinite, the treaty is now known as **stop loss**.

Another type of contract is the **proportional** one for which

$$\underbrace{Z^{\text{re}} = cZ, \quad Z^{\text{ce}} = c(1 - Z)}_{\textit{single events}} \quad \text{and} \quad \underbrace{\mathcal{X}^{\text{re}} = c\mathcal{X}, \quad \mathcal{X}^{\text{ce}} = (1 - c)\mathcal{X}}_{\textit{at portfolio level}} \tag{10.21}$$

where $0 \leq c \leq 1$. A fixed percentage of all losses is then taken over by the reinsurer. Suppose there are J reinsurance treaties of this kind. Such an arrangement is known as a **quota share** if c is the same for all policies. The opposite case, where $c = c_j$ depends on the contract is common. In **surplus** reinsurance

$$c_j = \max\left(0, 1 - \frac{a}{s_j}\right) \quad \text{so that} \quad Z_j^{\text{re}} = \begin{matrix} 0 & \text{if } a \geq s_j \\ (1 - a/s_j)Z_j & \text{if } a < s_j, \end{matrix} \tag{10.22}$$

where s_j is the maximum insured sum of the jth primary risk. Note that a (the cedent retention limit) does not depend on j. As s_j increases from a, the reinsurer part grows.

10.6.3 Pricing reinsurance

Examples of pure reinsurance premia are

$$\underbrace{\pi^{\text{re}} = \mu T \xi^{\text{re}} \quad \text{with} \quad \xi^{\text{re}} = E\{H(Z)\}}_{\textit{single-event contracts}} \quad \text{and} \quad \underbrace{\Pi^{\text{re}} = E\{H(\mathcal{X})\}}_{\textit{contracts at portfolio level}}$$

with Monte Carlo approximations

$$\underbrace{\pi^{\text{re}*} = \frac{\mu T}{m}\sum_{i=1}^{m} H(Z_i^*)}_{\textit{single-event contracts}} \qquad \text{and} \qquad \underbrace{\Pi^{\text{re}*} = \frac{1}{m}\sum_{i=1}^{m} H(\mathcal{X}_i^*).}_{\textit{contracts at portfolio level}}$$

Simulation is usually the simplest way if you know the ropes, and often takes less time to implement than the exact formulae (and the latter may not be possible at all). For portfolio-level simulations, $\mathcal{X}_i^*$ of the total portfolio loss (obtained from Algorithm 10.1) is inserted into the reinsurance contract $H(x)$.

There is a useful formula for $a \times b$ contracts in terms of *single* events. Let β be a scale parameter and as in Section 9.2 write $F(z) = F_0(z/\beta)$ for the distribution function of Z. Then

$$\pi^{\text{re}} = \mu T \int_a^{a+b} \{1 - F_0(z/\beta)\} dz, \tag{10.23}$$

which is verified in Exercise 10.25. Under the Pareto distribution for which $1 - F_0(z) = (1 + z)^{-\alpha}$ this yields

$$\pi^{\text{re}} = \mu T \frac{\beta}{\alpha - 1}\left(\frac{1}{(1 + a/\beta)^{\alpha-1}} - \frac{1}{(1 + (a + b)/\beta)^{\alpha-1}}\right) \quad \text{for} \quad \alpha \neq 1, \tag{10.24}$$

which is utilized below. The cases $\alpha = 1$ and α infinite (the exponential distribution) require special treatment; consult Exercise 10.26.

10.6.4 The effect of inflation

Inflation drives claims upwards into the regions where reinsurance treaties apply, and contracts will be mispriced if reinsurance premia are not adjusted. The mathematical formulation rests on the rate of inflation I, which changes the parameter of scale from $\beta = \beta_0$ to $\beta_I = (1 + I)\beta_0$ (Section 9.2) with the rest of the model as before. For $a \times b$ contracts in terms of single events, (10.23) shows that the pure premium π_I^{re} under inflation is related to the original one through

$$\frac{\pi_I^{\text{re}}}{\pi_0^{\text{re}}} = \frac{\int_a^{a+b}\{1 - F_0(z/\beta_I)\}dz}{\int_a^{a+b}\{1 - F_0(z/\beta_0)\}dz}.$$

Consider, in particular, the case of infinite b with Pareto-distributed claims. Then

$$\frac{\pi_I^{\text{re}}}{\pi_0^{\text{re}}} = (1 + I)\left(\frac{1 + a\beta_0^{-1}}{1 + a\beta_0^{-1}/(1 + I)}\right)^{\alpha-1},$$

which is not small at all for values of α of some size; try some suitable values if $I = 5\%$. The ratio is also an increasing function of α if $I > 0$, which means that the *lighter* the tail of the Pareto distribution, the *higher* the impact of inflation.

Table 10.6 Relative increase in reinsurance premia for Gamma-distributed claims under 5% inflation

Number of simulations: 1 000 000

Retention limit a	median of Z_0			90% percentile of Z_0		
Gamma shape	$\alpha = 1$	$\alpha = 10$	$\alpha = 100$	$\alpha = 1$	$\alpha = 10$	$\alpha = 100$
Premium increase	9%	23%	76%	17%	46%	170%

That appears to be a general phenomenon. A second example is

$$\underbrace{Z_0 \sim \text{Gamma}(\alpha)}_{\textit{original model}} \qquad \text{and} \qquad \underbrace{Z_I = (1 + I)Z_0,}_{\textit{inflated model}}$$

and the pure premia π_0^{re} and π_I^{re} can be computed by Monte Carlo. The relative change $(\pi_I^{\text{re}} - \pi_0^{\text{re}})/\pi_0^{\text{re}}$ is recorded in Table 10.6, when $I = 5\%$ and b is infinite. There is a huge increase in the effect of inflation as α moves from the heavy-tailed $\alpha = 1$ to the light-tailed, almost normal $\alpha = 100$.

10.6.5 The effect of reinsurance on the reserve

Reinsurance may reduce capital requirements substantially. The cedent company loses money on average, but it can get around on less own capital, and its value per share could be higher. A reinsurance strategy must balance extra cost against capital saved. An illustration is given in Table 10.7. Losses were those of the Norwegian pool of natural disasters in Chapter 7, for which a possible claim size distribution is

$$Z \sim \text{Pareto}(\alpha, \beta) \quad \text{with} \quad \alpha = 1.71 \text{ and } \beta = 140.$$

The reinsurance contract was an $a \times b$ arrangement per event with $a = 200$ and b varied. Maximum cedent responsibility is $s = 10\,200$ for each incident. Monte Carlo was used for computation.

Table 10.7 shows the cedent net reserve against the pure reinsurance premium. On the left, where the claim frequency is 1.05 annually, the 99% reserve is down from 2189 to about a quarter in exchange for the premium paid. Five-doubling claim frequency on the right yields smaller savings as a percentage, but larger in value. How much does the cedent lose by taking out reinsurance? It depends on the deals available in the market. If the premium paid is $(1 + \gamma^{\text{re}})\pi^{\text{re}}$, where π^{re} is pure premium and γ^{re} the loading, the average loss due to reinsurance is

$$\underbrace{(1 + \gamma^{\text{re}})\pi^{\text{re}}}_{\textit{premium paid}} \quad - \quad \underbrace{\pi^{\text{re}}}_{\textit{claims saved}} \quad = \quad \underbrace{\gamma^{\text{re}}\pi^{\text{re}}.}_{\textit{average loss}}$$

In practice, γ^{re} is determined by market conditions and may fluctuate violently.

Table 10.7 Reinsurance premium (exact) and cedent 99% net reserve (m=100 000 simulations) under the conditions in the text

Number of simulations: 1 000 000

	Annual claim frequency: 1.05				Annual claim frequency: 5.25			
Upper limit (b)	0	2200	4200	10200	0	2200	4200	10200
Pure premium	0	84	93	101	0	419	464	503
Cedent reserve	2189	570	510	482	6425	3683	1727	1228

10.7 Mathematical arguments

10.7.1 The normal power approximation

The NP method in Section 10.2 is a special case of the Cornish–Fisher expansion (Feller, 1971) which sets up a series of approximations to the percentile q_ϵ of a random sum $\mathcal{X}$ of independent variables. The first three terms are

$$q_\epsilon \doteq \underbrace{E(\mathcal{X}) + \mathrm{sd}(\mathcal{X})\phi_\epsilon}_{\textit{normal approximation}} + \underbrace{\mathrm{sd}(\mathcal{X})\tfrac{1}{6}(\phi_\epsilon^2 - 1)\mathrm{skew}(\mathcal{X})}_{\textit{skewness correction}}. \tag{10.25}$$

A fourth term on the right would involve the kurtosis, but that one isn't much used in insurance. The error for the normal approximation is proportional to $J^{-1/2}$, which goes down to J^{-1} when skewness is added, a considerable improvement.

Let $\mathcal{X}$ be the portfolio loss when the number of claims is Poisson($J\mu T$) and suppose we are dealing with independently and identically distributed individual claims with mean, standard deviation and skewness ξ_z, σ_z and ζ_z. The mean, variance and third-order moment of $\mathcal{X}$ are then

$$E(\mathcal{X}) = J\mu T\xi_z, \quad \mathrm{var}(\mathcal{X}) = J\mu T(\sigma_z^2 + \xi_z^2), \quad \nu_3(\mathcal{X}) = J\mu T(\zeta_z\sigma_z^3 + 3\sigma_z^2\xi_z + \xi_z^3),$$

where the third-order moment $\nu_3(\mathcal{X})$ is verified below (the other two were derived in Section 6.3). Divide $\nu_3(\mathcal{X})$ by $\mathrm{var}(\mathcal{X})^{3/2}$ for the skewness of $\mathcal{X}$, which becomes

$$\mathrm{skew}(\mathcal{X}) = \frac{1}{(J\mu T)^{1/2}} \frac{\zeta_z\sigma_z^3 + 3\sigma_z^2\xi_z + \xi_z^3}{(\sigma_z^2 + \xi_z^2)^{3/2}}.$$

The NP approximation (10.5) follows when the formulae for $\mathrm{sd}(\mathcal{X})$ and $\mathrm{skew}(\mathcal{X})$ are used in (10.25).

10.7.2 The third-order moment of $\mathcal{X}$

By assumption, $\mathcal{N}$ is Poisson distributed with parameter $\lambda = J\mu T$ and the third-order moment $\nu_3(\mathcal{X})$ is the expectation of

$$(\mathcal{X} - \lambda\xi_z)^3 = \{(\mathcal{X} - \mathcal{N}\xi_z) + (\mathcal{N} - \lambda)\xi_z\}^3 = B_1 + 3B_2 + 3B_3 + B_4$$

where

$$B_1 = (\mathcal{X} - \mathcal{N}\xi_z)^3, \qquad B_2 = (\mathcal{X} - \mathcal{N}\xi_z)^2(\mathcal{N} - \lambda)\xi_z,$$
$$B_3 = (\mathcal{X} - \mathcal{N}\xi_z)(\mathcal{N} - \lambda)^2\xi_z^2, \qquad B_4 = (\mathcal{N} - \lambda)^3\xi_z^3.$$

These quantities may be calculated by utilizing that $\mathcal{X}$ is a sum of $\mathcal{N}$ independent variables with mean, standard deviation and skewness ξ_z, σ_z^2 and ζ_z so that by rules in Table A.1 in Appendix A

$$E(\mathcal{X}|\mathcal{N}) = \mathcal{N}\xi_z, \quad \text{var}(\mathcal{X}|\mathcal{N}) = \mathcal{N}\sigma_z^2 \quad \text{and} \quad \nu_3(\mathcal{X}|\mathcal{N}) = \mathcal{N}\zeta_z\sigma_z^3.$$

Hence

$$E(B_1|\mathcal{N}) = \nu_3(\mathcal{X}|\mathcal{N}) = \mathcal{N}\zeta_z\sigma_z^3,$$
$$E(B_2|\mathcal{N}) = \text{var}(\mathcal{X}|\mathcal{N})(\mathcal{N} - \lambda)\xi_z = \mathcal{N}\sigma_z^2(\mathcal{N} - \lambda)\xi_z,$$
$$E(B_3|\mathcal{N}) = 0,$$
$$E(B_4|\mathcal{N}) = (\mathcal{N} - \lambda)^3\xi_z^3,$$

and this yields

$$E\{(\mathcal{X} - \lambda\xi_z)^3|\mathcal{N}\} = \mathcal{N}\zeta_z\sigma_z^3 + 3\mathcal{N}(\mathcal{N} - \lambda)\sigma_z^2\xi_z + 3\cdot 0 + (\mathcal{N} - \lambda)^3\xi_z^3.$$

But by the rule of double expectation

$$\begin{aligned} E(\mathcal{X} - \lambda\xi_z)^3 &= E(\mathcal{N})\zeta_z\sigma_z^3 + 3E\{\mathcal{N}(\mathcal{N} - \lambda)\}\sigma_z^2\xi_z + E(\mathcal{N} - \lambda)^3\xi_z^3 \\ &= \lambda(\zeta_z\sigma_z^3 + 3\sigma_z^2\xi_z + \xi_z^3) \end{aligned}$$

since $E(\mathcal{N}) = \lambda$, $E\{\mathcal{N}(N - \lambda)\} = \text{var}(\mathcal{N}) = \lambda$ and $E(\mathcal{N} - \lambda)^3 = \lambda$; see Section 8.2. Thus $\nu_3(\mathcal{X}) = \lambda(\zeta_z\sigma_z^3 + 3\sigma_z^2\xi_z + \xi_z^3)$ as asserted.

10.7.3 Normal power under heterogeneity

In practice, the NP method still works with risks varying over the portfolio as long as they are independent. The variance and third-order moment of $\mathcal{X} = X_1 + \cdots + X_J$ are found by adding contributions from individual policies so that

$$\text{skew}(\mathcal{X}) = \frac{\nu_3(\mathcal{X})}{\text{var}(\mathcal{X})^{3/2}} = \frac{\nu_3(X_1) + \cdots + \nu_3(X_J)}{\{\text{var}(X_1) + \cdots + \text{var}(X_J)\}^{3/2}},$$

into which we must insert

$$\text{var}(X_j) = \mu_j T(\sigma_{zj}^2 + \xi_{zj}^2) \quad \text{and} \quad \nu_3(X_j) = \mu_j T(\zeta_{zj}\sigma_{zj}^3 + 3\sigma_{zj}^2\xi_{zj} + \xi_{zj}^3),$$

where μ_j, ξ_{zj}, σ_{zj} and ζ_{zj} apply to policy j. The expression for skew($\mathcal{X}$) is entered in (10.25) as before.

10.7.4 Auxiliary for linear credibility

Let $X_1, \ldots, X_K$ be conditionally independent and identically distributed given ω with conditional mean $\pi(\omega)$ and variance $\sigma^2(\omega)$, and let $\overline{\pi} = E\{\pi(\omega)\}$, $\upsilon^2 = \mathrm{var}\{\pi(\omega)\}$, and $\tau^2 = E\{\sigma^2(\omega)\}$ be the structural parameters in Section 10.5. We shall repeatedly make use of the main statistical properties of $\overline{X}_K = (X_1 + \cdots + X_K)/K$, which are

$$E(\overline{X}_K) = \overline{\pi}, \quad \mathrm{var}(\overline{X_K}) = \upsilon^2 + \tau^2/K \quad \text{and} \quad \mathrm{cov}\{\overline{X_K}, \pi(\omega)\} = \upsilon^2. \tag{10.26}$$

To prove this, first note that

$$E(\overline{X}_K|\omega) = E(X_1|\omega) = \pi(\omega) \quad \text{and} \quad \mathrm{var}(\overline{X}_K|\omega) = \mathrm{var}(X_1|\omega)/K = \sigma^2(\omega)/K,$$

and the rule of double expectation yields $E(\overline{X}_K) = E\{E(\overline{X}_K|\omega)\} = E\{\pi(\omega)\} = \overline{\pi}$ while from the double-variance formula

$$\mathrm{var}(\overline{X}_K) = \mathrm{var}\{E(\overline{X}_K|\omega)\} + E\{\mathrm{var}(\overline{X}_K|\omega)\} = \mathrm{var}\{\pi(\omega)\} + E\{\sigma^2(\omega)/K\} = \upsilon^2 + \tau^2/K,$$

which is the second assertion in (10.26). Finally, for the third assertion

$$E\{(\overline{X}_K - \overline{\pi})(\pi(\omega) - \overline{\pi})|\omega\} = E\{\overline{X}_K - \overline{\pi}|\omega\}\{\pi(\omega) - \overline{\pi}\} = \{\pi(\omega) - \overline{\pi}\}^2,$$

and the rule of double expectation yields

$$E\{(\overline{X}_K - \overline{\pi})(\pi(\omega) - \overline{\pi})\} = E\{\pi(\omega) - \overline{\pi}\}^2 = \upsilon^2,$$

with the left-hand side being $\mathrm{cov}\{\overline{X}_K, \pi(\omega)\}$ by definition.

10.7.5 Linear credibility

Consider $\hat{\pi}_K = b_0 + w\overline{X}_K$ with estimation error $\hat{\pi}_K - \pi(\omega)$. Note that

$$E\{\hat{\pi}_K - \pi(\omega)\} = E\{b_0 + w\overline{X}_K - \pi(\omega)\} = b_0 + wE(\overline{X}_K) - E\{\pi(\omega)\} = b_0 - (1-w)\overline{\pi}$$

so that $E\{\hat{\pi}_K - \pi(\omega)\} = 0$ if $b_0 = (1-w)\overline{\pi}$, and $\hat{\pi}_K = (1-w)\overline{\pi} + w\overline{X}_K$ as claimed in (10.10). Moreover,

$$\begin{aligned}\mathrm{var}\{\hat{\pi}_K - \pi(\omega)\} &= \mathrm{var}\{b_0 + w\overline{X}_K - \pi(\omega)\}\\ &= w^2\mathrm{var}(\overline{X}_K) - 2w\mathrm{cov}\{\overline{X}_K, \pi(\omega)\} + \mathrm{var}\{\pi(\omega)\}\end{aligned}$$

or, using (10.26),

$$\mathrm{var}\{\hat{\pi}_K - \pi(\omega)\} = w^2(\upsilon^2 + \tau^2/K) - 2w\upsilon^2 + \upsilon^2,$$

which is minimized by $w = \upsilon^2/(\upsilon^2 + \tau^2/K)$, again as claimed in (10.10). Inserting for w yields

$$\mathrm{var}\{\hat{\pi}_K - \pi(\omega)\} = \frac{\upsilon^2}{1 + K\upsilon^2/\tau^2},$$

which is (10.11). The estimate $\hat{\pi}_K$ is unbiased and minimizes var$\{\hat{\pi}_K - \pi(\omega)\}$, which is the same as minimizing the mean-squared error $E\{\hat{\pi}_K - \pi(\omega)\}^2$.

10.7.6 Optimal credibility

Let $n_1, \dots, n_K$ be claim numbers for a single individual with $\overline{n} = (n_1 + \cdots + n_K)/K$ their mean. Since they are conditionally independent given μ and Poisson distributed, their joint density function is

$$f(n_1, \dots, n_K|\mu) = \prod_{k=1}^{K}\left(\frac{(\mu T)^{n_k}}{n_k!}e^{-\mu T}\right) = c_1\mu^{n_1+\cdots+n_K}e^{-\mu KT} = c_1\mu^{K\overline{n}}e^{-\mu KT},$$

where c_1 doesn't depend on μ. Suppose $p(\mu) = c_2\mu^{\alpha-1}e^{-\mu\alpha/\xi_\mu}$, with c_2 a constant, is a Gamma prior for μ. It is to be multiplied by $f(n_1, \dots, n_K|\mu)$ for the posterior density function, which yields

$$p(\mu|n_1, \dots, n_K) = c\mu^{\alpha+K\overline{n}-1}e^{-\mu(\alpha/\xi_\mu+KT)}$$

where c is still another constant. This is another Gamma density function with expectation

$$E(\mu|n_1, \dots, n_K) = \frac{\alpha + K\overline{n}}{\alpha/\xi_\mu + KT} = \xi_\mu\frac{\overline{n} + \alpha/K}{\xi_\mu T + \alpha/K}.$$

But since $E(N|n_1, \dots, n_K) = E(\mu T|n_1, \dots, n_K)$, this result yields the optimal credibility estimate for $\pi = \mu T\xi_z$ when multiplied by $T\xi_z$. Hence

$$\hat{\pi}_K = \overline{\pi}\frac{\overline{n} + \alpha/K}{\xi_\mu T + \alpha/K} \quad \text{where} \quad \overline{\pi} = \xi_\mu T\xi_z,$$

which is (10.16).

The error is

$$\hat{\pi}_K - \pi = \overline{\pi}\frac{\overline{n} + \alpha/K}{\xi_\mu T + \alpha/K} - \mu T\xi_z = \overline{\pi}\left(\frac{\overline{n} + \alpha/K}{\xi_\mu T + \alpha/K} - \frac{\mu}{\xi_\mu}\right).$$

Since $E(\overline{n}|\mu) = \mu T$, this implies that

$$E(\hat{\pi}_K - \pi|\mu) = \overline{\pi}\left(\frac{\mu T + \alpha/K}{\xi_\mu T + \alpha/K} - \frac{\mu}{\xi_\mu}\right) = -\overline{\pi}\frac{(\mu - \xi_\mu)\alpha/K}{(\xi_\mu T + \alpha/K)\xi_\mu}$$

and, moreover, var$(\overline{n}|\mu) = \mu T/K$ so that

$$\text{var}(\hat{\pi}_K - \pi|\mu) = \overline{\pi}^2\frac{\mu T/K}{(\xi_\mu T + \alpha/K)^2}.$$

By the rule of double variance,

$$\text{var}(\hat{\pi}_K - \pi) = \overline{\pi}^2 \frac{\sigma_\mu^2(\alpha/K)^2}{(\xi_\mu T + \alpha/K)^2 \xi_\mu^2} + \overline{\pi}^2 \frac{\xi_\mu T/K}{(\xi_\mu T + \alpha/K)^2}.$$

Insert $\sigma_\mu^2 = \xi_\mu^2/\alpha$ (the variance of Gamma variables) and the expression reduces to

$$\text{var}(\hat{\pi}_K - \pi) = \frac{\overline{\pi}^2}{\alpha + K\xi_\mu T},$$

which is (10.17).

10.7.7 Parameter estimation in linear credibility

The estimates (10.18) and (10.19) of the structural parameters $\overline{\pi}$, τ^2 and υ^2 rely on the mean and variance of claim histories, say $\overline{X}_j$ and s_j^2 for individual j where $j = 1, \ldots, J$. Recall from (10.26) that

$$E(\overline{X}_j) = \overline{\pi} \quad \text{and} \quad \text{var}(\overline{X}_j) = \upsilon^2 + \frac{\tau}{K_j},$$

where K_j is the length of the claim record. Since $E(\overline{X}_j) = \overline{\pi}$ and $E(s_j^2|\omega_j) = \sigma^2(\omega_j)$ so that by the rule of double expectation $E(s_j^2) = E\{\sigma_j^2(\omega_j)\} = \tau^2$, any weighted averages of $\overline{X}_1, \ldots, \overline{X}_J$ and $s_1^2, \ldots, s_J^2$ are unbiased estimates of $\overline{\pi}$ and τ^2, in particular $\hat{\overline{\pi}}$ and $\hat{\tau}^2$ defined in (10.18). The estimate of υ^2 can be based on

$$Q_\upsilon = \sum_{j=1}^J \frac{K_j}{\mathcal{K}}(\overline{X}_j - \hat{\overline{\pi}})^2 \quad \text{where} \quad \hat{\overline{\pi}} = \sum_{j=1}^J \frac{K_j}{\mathcal{K}}\overline{X}_j \quad \text{and} \quad \mathcal{K} = \sum_{j=1}^J K_j.$$

It is easily seen that

$$Q_\upsilon = \sum_{j=1}^J \frac{K_j}{\mathcal{K}}(\overline{X}_j - \overline{\pi})^2 - 2\sum_{j=1}^J \frac{K_j}{\mathcal{K}}(\overline{X}_j - \overline{\pi})(\hat{\overline{\pi}} - \overline{\pi}) + \sum_{j=1}^J \frac{K_j}{\mathcal{K}}(\hat{\overline{\pi}} - \overline{\pi})^2,$$

and since

$$\hat{\overline{\pi}} - \overline{\pi} = \sum_{j=1}^J \frac{K_j}{\mathcal{K}}(\overline{X}_j - \overline{\pi}) \quad \text{with} \quad \sum_{j=1}^J \frac{K_j}{\mathcal{K}} = 1$$

it follows that

$$Q_\upsilon = \sum_{j=1}^J \frac{K_j}{\mathcal{K}}(\overline{X}_j - \overline{\pi})^2 - (\hat{\overline{\pi}} - \overline{\pi})^2.$$

We need

$$E(\hat{\bar{\pi}} - \bar{\pi})^2 = \text{var}(\hat{\bar{\pi}}) = \sum_{j=1}^{J} \left(\frac{K_j}{\mathcal{K}}\right)^2 \text{var}(X_j) = \sum_{j=1}^{J} \left(\frac{K_j}{\mathcal{K}}\right)^2 (\upsilon^2 + \frac{\tau^2}{K_j})$$

which, recalling that $K_1 + \cdots + K_J = \mathcal{K}$, yields

$$E(Q_\upsilon) = \sum_{j=1}^{J} \frac{K_j}{\mathcal{K}}(\upsilon^2 + \frac{\tau^2}{K_j}) - \sum_{j=1}^{J} \left(\frac{K_j}{\mathcal{K}}\right)^2 (\upsilon^2 + \frac{\tau^2}{K_j}) = \upsilon^2 - \sum_{j=1}^{J} \left(\frac{K_j}{\mathcal{K}}\right)^2 \upsilon^2 + \frac{J-1}{\mathcal{K}}\tau^2.$$

An unbiased estimate of υ^2 is therefore obtained by solving the equation

$$Q_\upsilon = \hat{\upsilon}^2 - \sum_{j=1}^{J} \left(\frac{K_j}{\mathcal{K}}\right)^2 \hat{\upsilon}^2 + \frac{J-1}{\mathcal{K}}\hat{\tau}^2$$

to give (10.19).

10.8 Bibliographical notes

10.8.1 Computational methods

Monte Carlo is the most versatile method for computing reserves and easy to implement. The normal power method worked fairly well in the examples (and also among the exercises), but it takes as much work as Monte Carlo to implement and isn't always accurate. The Panjer recursion and other recursive methods are reviewed in chapter 4 of Dickson (2005). They may have had their day, but in the future they are likely to be superseded by Monte Carlo.

10.8.2 Credibility

Experience rating (Section 10.5) is an ambitious attempt to assess risk from individual track records. An obvious place to study the method further is Bühlmann and Gisler (2005), but you are also likely to appreciate the review article of Nordberg (2004a), which draws methodological lines to parts of statistics. Still another general reference is Goovaerts and Hoogstad (1987). The simple solution for a Gamma prior with Poisson counts in Section 10.5 goes back to Jewell (1974), with later extensions in Kaas *et al.* (1997) and Ohlsson and Johansson (2006); see also Denuit *et al.* (2007) for a lot of material on credibility and claim number modelling. Credibility is still an area for basic research, in particular with respect to time effects and the use of explanatory variables. Frees (2003), Huang *et al.* (2003), Purcaru and Denuit (2003), Luo *et al.* (2004), Pitselis (2004, 2008); Frees and Wang (2006) Yeo and Valdez (2006) and Lo *et al.* (2006) all present extensions in one of these directions.

10.8.3 Reinsurance

The presentation of reinsurance in Section 10.6 owes something to Daykin *et al.* (1994). Current academic research in this area is concerned with contract design, a topic that hasn't been covered here. A lot of effort has been put into such strategies over time (see the references in Section 11.9). One-period contributions are Dassios and Jang (2003), Gajek and Zagrodny (2004), Kaluszka (2004, 2005), Krvavych and Sherris (2006), Lee and Yu (2007) and Cai and Tan (2007), with many others in the years prior to 2004.

10.9 Exercises

Section 10.2

Exercise 10.1 Consider a portfolio of identical risks with Poisson parameter $J\mu T$ and let $\theta_z = \sigma_z/\xi_z$.

(a) Show that the normal approximation q_ϵ^{No} is related to the mean payout $E(\mathcal{X})$ through

$$q_\epsilon^{\text{No}} = E(\mathcal{X})(1+\gamma_\epsilon^{\text{No}}) \quad \text{where} \quad \gamma_\epsilon^{\text{No}} = \sqrt{\frac{1+\theta_z^2}{J\mu T}}\,\phi_\epsilon,$$

writing ϕ_ϵ for the Gaussian percentile.

(b) Interpret the way $\gamma_\epsilon^{\text{No}}$ depends on $J\mu T$ and θ_z.

Exercise 10.2 Let losses Z be Gamma distributed with shape α so that $\theta_z = 1/\sqrt{\alpha}$ in the previous exercise.

(a) Compute $\gamma_\epsilon^{\text{No}}$ when $J\mu T = 20$, $\alpha = 0.5$ or $\alpha = 20$ and $\phi_\epsilon = 2.33$.

(b) For which of the two values of α is the normal approximation likely to be most reliable?

Exercise 10.3 This is an extension of Exercise 10.1 for the normal power approximation q_ϵ^{NP}.

(a) With $\theta_z = \sigma_z/\xi_z$ and ζ_z the skewness coefficient for the losses, deduce from (10.5) that

$$q_\epsilon^{\text{NP}} = E(\mathcal{X})(1+\gamma_\epsilon^{\text{NP}}) \quad \text{where} \quad \gamma_\epsilon^{\text{NP}} = \sqrt{\frac{1+\theta_z^2}{J\mu T}}\,\phi_\epsilon + \frac{(\zeta_z\theta_z^3 + 3\theta_z^2 + 1)(\phi_\epsilon^2 - 1)}{6(1+\theta_z^2)J\mu T}.$$

(b) If $\zeta_z \geq 0$ (common in practice), show that the second term in $\gamma_\epsilon^{\text{NP}}$ increases with θ_z and interpret this.

(c) Also interpret how $\gamma_\epsilon^{\text{NP}}$ depends on $J\mu T$ and ζ_z.

Exercise 10.4 Suppose losses Z are Gamma distributed as in Exercise 10.2 so that $\theta_z = 1/\sqrt{\alpha}$ and $\zeta_z = 2/\sqrt{\alpha}$.

(a) Verify that $\gamma_\epsilon^{\rm No}$ and $\gamma_\epsilon^{\rm NP}$ in Exercises 10.1 and 10.3 now become

$$\gamma_\epsilon^{\rm No} = \sqrt{\frac{1+1/\alpha}{J\mu T}}\,\phi_\epsilon \quad \text{and} \quad \gamma_\epsilon^{\rm NP} = \gamma_\epsilon^{\rm No} + \left(1+\frac{2}{\alpha}\right)\frac{\phi_\epsilon^2 - 1}{6J\mu T}.$$

(b) Compute their values when $J\mu T = 20$, $\epsilon = 0.01$ and $\alpha = 0.5$ or $\alpha = 20$.

R-*commands*:

ϕ_ϵ=`qnorm(1-`ϵ`);` $\gamma_\epsilon^{\rm No}$=`sqrt((1+1/`α`)/J`μ`T)*`ϕ_ϵ`;`
$\gamma_\epsilon^{\rm NP}$=$\gamma_\epsilon^{\rm No}$`+(1+2/`α`)*(`ϕ_ϵ`**2-1)/(6*J`μ`T).`

Exercise 10.5 Suppose $\xi_z = 20.89$, $\sigma_z = 20.89$ and $\zeta_z = 2$, which corresponds to an exponential distribution and is close to the model identified for the Belgian fire data in Exercise 7.12. Compute the normal and normal power approximations $q_\epsilon^{\rm No}$ and $q_\epsilon^{\rm NP}$ when $J\mu T = 50$ and $\epsilon = 0.05$ and 0.01.

R-*commands*:

ϕ_ϵ=`qnorm(1-`ϵ`);` $q_\epsilon^{\rm No}$=`J`μ`T*`ξ_z`+sqrt(J`μ`T*(`σ_z`**2+`ξ_z`**2))*`ϕ_ϵ`;`
a_2`=(`ζ_z`*`σ_z`**3+3*`ξ_z`*`σ_z`**2+`ξ_z`**3)/(`σ_z`**2+`ξ_z`**2);`
$q_\epsilon^{\rm NP}$=$q_\epsilon^{\rm No}$`+`a_2`*(`ϕ_ϵ`**2-1)/6.`

Section 10.3

Exercise 10.6 Portfolio liabilities $\mathcal{X} = Z_1 + \cdots + Z_\mathcal{N}$ are particularly rapidly sampled when individual losses are Gamma distributed. Suppose $Z_i = \xi_z G_i$ with $G_1, G_2 \ldots$ independent and Gamma(α).

(a) Use the convolution property of the Gamma model in Section 9.3 to argue that $\mathcal{X}|\mathcal{N} = n$ is distributed as $n\xi_z G$ where $G \sim$ Gamma($n\alpha$).

(b) Use this result to write a program generating m simulations of $\mathcal{X}$ when $\mathcal{N} \sim$ Poisson($J\mu T$).

R-*commands*:

`N=rpois(m,`$J\mu T$`); X=(`ξ_z/α`)*rgamma(m,N*`α`).`

Exercise 10.7

(a) Run the program in Exercise 10.6 when $m = 100\,000$, $J\mu T = 50$, $\xi_2 = 20.89$ and $\alpha = 1$ and compute the upper percentiles of $\mathcal{X}$ when $\epsilon = 0.05$ and 0.01.

R-*commands*:

ϵ`=c(0.05,0.01); sort(X)[m*(1-`ϵ`)].`

(b) Note that the conditions are those in Exercise 10.5 and compare with the assessments there. [*Answer*: The NP approximations are close to the Monte Carlo answers, but that is no rule!]

Exercise 10.8 Define γ_ϵ through $q_\epsilon = E(\mathcal{X})(1+\gamma_\epsilon)$ where q_ϵ is the upper percentile of $\mathcal{X}$.

(a) Use the program in Exercise 10.6 with $m = 100\,000$ to compute γ_ϵ for $\epsilon = 0.01$ when $J\mu T = 20$, $\xi_z = 1$ and $\alpha = 0.5$ and 20.

R-*commands*:

For each α generate `X` as in Exercise 10.6 and use
`γε=sort(X)[m*(1-ε)]/(JμT*ξz)-1`.

(b) Compare with the analogies $\gamma_\epsilon^{\text{No}}$ and $\gamma_\epsilon^{\text{NP}}$ in Exercise 10.4 and comment on their accuracy.

Exercise 10.9

(a) For each of $\epsilon = 0.05$ and 0.01 and $m = 100{,}000$ compute the upper ϵ-percentile for $\mathcal{X}$ when $J\mu T = 50$ and losses are Gamma distributed with $\xi_z = 1$ and $\alpha = 0.5$ and 20.

R-*commands*:

For each α generate `X` as in Exercise 10.6 and use `ε=c(0.05,0.01);`
`qε=sort(X)[m*(1-ε)]`.

(b) Redo computations for the log-normal loss distribution $Z = \xi_z e^{-\tau^2/2+\tau\varepsilon}$ calibrated with $\tau = \sqrt{\log(1+1/\alpha)}$ as in Exercise 8.12.

R-*commands*:

With $\tau = 1.0481$ and $\tau = 0.2209$, use `N=rpois(m,JμT); X=array(0,m);`
`for (i in 1:m) X=sum(rlnorm(N[i],0,τ))*ξz*exp(-τ**2/2);`
`qε=sort(X)[m*(1 − ε)]`.

(c) How sensitively do the results depend on the choice between Gamma and the log-normal?

Exercise 10.10 Let q_ϵ^* be a Monte Carlo approximation of q_ϵ based on m simulations and let $\xi_q = E(q_\epsilon^*)$ and $s_q = \text{sd}(q_\epsilon^*)$.

(a) Utilize the approximation $s_q \doteq a/\sqrt{m}$ for some constant a to argue that approximately $m_\delta = \{s_q/(\delta\xi_q)\}^2 m$ simulations keep the Monte Carlo standard deviation below δq_ϵ.

(b) Run the program in Exercise 10.6 mm_b times when $m = 10\,000$, $m_b = 100$, $J\mu T = 50$, $\xi_z = 20.89$ and $\alpha = 1$, and approximate ξ_q and s_q when $\epsilon = 0.01$.

R-*commands*:

```
N=rpois(m*mb,JμT); X=(ξz/α)*rgamma(m*mb,N*α);
X=matrix(X,m,mb); qε=apply(X,2,sort)[m*(1-ε),];
ξq=mean(qε); sq=sd(qε).
```

(c) Compute m_δ for the example in (b) when $\delta = 0.01$ and $\delta = 0.001$.

Exercise 10.11 Alternative, well-fitting models for the logaritms of the US hurricane data in Exercises 9.15 and 9.16 were $\log(Z) \sim N(\theta, \tau)$ with $\theta = 4.333$ and $\tau = 1.448$ and $\log(Z) = \theta\,\text{Gamma}(\alpha)$ with $\theta = 4.333$ and $\alpha = 8.846$.

(a) Compute the upper 0.05 and 0.01 percentiles of $\mathcal{X}$ for the log-normal assuming $J\mu T = 50$.

R-*commands*:

```
N=rpois(m,JμT); X=array(0,m); for (i in 1:m)X=
sum(rlnorm(N[i],θ,τ)); q=sort(X)[(1-c(0.05,0.01))*m].
```

(b) Repeat the computations for the log-Gamma.

R-*commands*:

Those in (a) with the log-normal command replaced by

```
X=sum(exp(θ*rgamma(N[i],α)/α)).
```

(c) Why the huge discrepancies? [*Hint*: Consult Exercise 9.17.]

Exercise 10.12

(a) Compute the upper 5% and 1% percentiles of $\mathcal{X}$ when $J\mu T = 50$ and the model for the losses is the empirical distribution function of the $n = 6446$ Norwegian car losses in Exercise 9.23.

R-*commands*:

```
z=scan(''norwegiancar.txt''); N=rpois(m,JμT); X=array(0,m);
for (i in 1:m){ind=floor(1+runif(N[i])*length(z));
X[i]=sum(z[ind])}; qε=sort(X)[m*(1-c(0.05,0.01))].
```

(b) Redo (a) when the loss model is the fitted log-normal.

R-*commands*:

First estimate parameters by `θ=mean(log(z)); τ=sd(log(z))` and replace the for-loop commands in (a) by `X[i]=sum(rlnorm(N[i];θ,τ))`.

(c) Compare the results when you recall the conclusions on the log-normal fit in Exercise 9.23.

Exercise 10.13 A model which seemed to fit the Norwegian car data was the extended Pareto distribution with parameters $\alpha = 3.380$, $\theta = 2.374$ and $\beta = 23770$; see Exercise 9.24.

(a) Redo the computations in Exercise 10.12 with this loss model.

R-*commands*:

As in Exercise 10.12(a) with

```
X[i]=sum(β*rgamma(N[i],θ)/rgamma(N[i],α))
```

in the for-loop.

(b) Compare with the results in Exercise 10.12.

Section 10.4

Exercise 10.14 Estimates of pure premia in Section 10.4 were of the form $\hat{\pi} = Te^{\hat{\theta}}$ with the approximations $E(\hat{\pi}) \doteq \pi e^{\sigma_\theta^2/2}$ and $\text{sd}(\hat{\pi}) \doteq E(\hat{\pi})\sqrt{e^{\sigma_\theta^2} - 1}$ where $\sigma_\theta = \text{sd}(\hat{\theta})$.

(a) Why are $E(\hat{\pi}) - \pi \doteq \pi\sigma_\theta^2/2$ and $\text{sd}(\hat{\pi}) \doteq \pi\sigma_\theta$ if σ_θ is small? [*Hint*: Use the approximation $e^x \doteq 1 + x$, valid for small x.]
(b) Argue that this suggests that bias in $\hat{\pi}$ would often be dominated by the standard deviation.

Exercise 10.15 Gaussian variables deviate less than ±2 standard deviations from their mean with probability close to 95%, which leads to the **Wald** criterion of pronouncing a parameter θ different from zero if $|\hat{\theta}/\hat{\sigma}_\theta| > 2$.

(a) Apply this method to the regression coefficients for claim frequency in Table 10.4 and argue that all of them are significantly different from zero.
(b) Redo for claim size and point out that things are rather different now.

Exercise 10.16

(a) Consider the relationship between distance limit and claim frequency in Table 10.4 and argue that many of these regression coefficients are significantly different. [*Hint*: Utilize the fact that the estimates are positively correlated so that if σ_i is the standard deviation of estimate i, then the variance of the difference between estimates i and j is less than $\sigma_i^2 + \sigma_j^2$. Then use the Wald criterion of the preceding exercise.]
(b) Redo for claim size and paint a different picture.

Exercise 10.17 Explain how you go about it when you want the tabulation of the pure premium in Table 10.5 to apply to the other regions. [*Hint*: Use the linear model on a log-scale in Section 10.4 and compute simple modification factors by means of Table 10.4.]

Exercise 10.18 Consider the sum of claims $X_1, \dots, X_n$ from n policy holders under risk $T_1, \dots, T_n$ and let $\pi = \mu\xi_z$ be the pure premium for a period of length $T = 1$. Introduce standard assumptions and derive the unbiased estimate

$$\hat{\pi} = \frac{X_1 + \cdots + X_n}{T_1 + \cdots + T_n} \quad \text{with standard deviation} \quad \text{sd}(\hat{\pi}) = \sqrt{\frac{\pi\xi_z(1 + \sigma_z^2/\xi_z^2)}{T_1 + \cdots + T_n}}.$$

[*Hint*: Recall $E(X_i) = \mu T_i \xi_z$ and $\text{var}(X_i) = \mu T_i(\xi_z^2 + \sigma_z^2)$.]

Exercise 10.19 The file `norwegianclaims1.txt` contains annual claim data with more than 200 000 rows. Variables are column-wise from left to right 'age', 'gender', 'risk exposure', 'number of claims' and 'sum of claims'. 'Age' has seven categories (20–21, 22–23, 24–25, 26–39, 40–55, 56–70, 71–94 in years) and 'gender' is 0 for males and 1 for females; see also Exercise 8.19 for the same data without 'sum of claims'.

(a) Read the data and compute $T_1 + \cdots + T_n$ and $\hat{\pi}$ in Exercise 10.18 for all combinations of age and gender.
R-*commands*:
`x=matrix(scan(''norwegianclaims1.txt''),byrow=T,ncol=5)` and for each age j and gender i use `y=x[x[,1]==j,]; T=sum(y[y[,2]==i,3]);` `π̂=sum(y[y[,2]==i,5])/T.`

(b) Estimate $\text{sd}(\hat{\pi})$ too.
R-*commands*:
`z=x[x[,4]==1,5];` `ξ̂z=mean(z);`
`σ̂z=sd(z);sd(π̂)=sqrt(π̂*ξ̂z*(1+(σ̂z/ξ̂z)**2)/T).`

(c) Comment on the results and argue that the error in some of the estimates is so large that they may be of little use.

Section 10.5

Exercise 10.20 Consider linear credibility with the three structural parameters $\bar{\pi} = E\{\pi(\omega)\}$, $\upsilon^2 = \text{var}\{\pi(\omega)\}$ and $\tau^2 = E\{\sigma^2(\omega)\}$ and the estimate $\hat{\pi}_K = (1-w)\bar{\pi} + w\bar{X}_K$ where $w = \upsilon^2/(\upsilon^2 + \tau^2/K)$.

(a) Why is the weight w increasing in K?
(b) Explain and interpret why it increases with υ and decreases with τ.

Exercise 10.21 Let $\hat{\Pi}_K$ be the linear credibility estimate of the pure premium $\Pi(\omega) = J\pi(\omega)$ at group level where ω affects all policies equally.

(a) Use the standard deviation formula (10.14) to verify that

$$\frac{\text{sd}(\hat{\Pi}_K - \Pi)}{E(\Pi)} = \frac{\upsilon/\bar{\pi}}{\sqrt{1 + KJ\upsilon^2/\tau^2}}.$$

(b) What is the limit as $J \to \infty$? Explain what this tells us about the accuracy of credibility estimation at group level.

Exercise 10.22 Let $\xi_\mu = E(\mu)$, $\sigma_\mu = \text{sd}(\mu)$, $\xi_z = E(Z)$ and $\sigma_z = \text{sd}(Z)$ and suppose μ is equal for all policies. The structural parameters with such a random μ are then $\bar{\pi} = \xi_\mu T \xi_z$, $\upsilon^2 = \sigma_\mu^2 T^2 \xi_z^2$ and $\tau^2 = \xi_\mu T(\xi_z^2 + \sigma_z^2)$; see Section 10.5.

(a) Show that the standard deviation/mean ratio in Exercise 10.21 depends on ξ_z and σ_z through σ_z/ξ_z.

(b) If $\xi_\mu = 0.056$, $\sigma_\mu = 0.02$, $T = 1$ and $\sigma_z = \xi_z$, tabulate the ratio for $K = 0, 5, 10$ and 20 and $J = 1$ and $J = 10\,000$.

R-*commands*:

```
π̄=ξμ*T*ξz; υ=σμ*T*ξz; τ=sqrt(ξμ*T*(ξz**2+σz**2));
KJ=c(1,10000)%o%c(0,5,10,20);
ratio=(υ/π̄)/sqrt(1+KJ*υ**2/τ**2).
```

(c) Interpret the results and redo when $\sigma_z = 0.1\xi_z$.

Exercise 10.23 The optimal credibility estimate per policy when μ is random and ξ_z is fixed is $\hat{\pi}_K = \bar{\pi}(\bar{n} + \alpha/K)/(\xi_\mu T + \alpha/K)$, an adjustment of the average, pure premium $\bar{\pi}$. Clearly $\hat{\pi}_K > \bar{\pi}$ if $\bar{n} > \xi_\mu T$ and $\hat{\pi}_K \leq \bar{\pi}$ in the opposite case.

(a) What is the intuition behind this?
(b) Show that the adjustment increases with K and decreases with α and explain the intuition behind it.

Exercise 10.24 Let $\Pi = E(\mathcal{X}|\mu)$ be the average claim against a portfolio when claim intensity $\mu = \xi_\mu G$ with $G \sim$ Gamma(α) and equal for all policies. Suppose $\bar{n}$ is the average number of claims against the portfolio over K years.

(a) Use (10.16) to argue that $\hat{\Pi}_K = J\bar{\pi}(\bar{n} + \alpha/K)/(J\xi_\mu T + \alpha/K)$ is the optimal credibility estimate of Π.
(b) Similarly, utilize the standard deviation formula (10.17) right to deduce that

$$\frac{\mathrm{sd}(\hat{\Pi}_K - \Pi)}{E(\Pi)} = \frac{1}{\sqrt{\alpha + JK\xi_\mu T}}.$$

(c) What is the limit as $J \to \infty$? Comment on the potential of optimal credibility estimation at group level.

Section 10.6

Exercise 10.25 Consider an $a \times b$ reinsurance contract per event.

(a) If $f(z)$ and $F(z)$ are the density and distribution function of a claim Z, show that the expected reinsurance payoff is

$$\xi^{\mathrm{re}} = \int_a^{a+b} (z - a)f(z)\,dz + \int_{a+b}^{\infty} bf(z)\,dz = \int_a^{a+b} \{1 - F(z)\}\,dz.$$

[*Hint*: Use integration by parts.]
(b) If $F(z) = F_0(z/\beta)$, argue that the pure premium for the reinsurance contract becomes $\pi^{\mathrm{re}} = \mu T \int_a^{a+b}\{1 - F_0(z/\beta)\}dz$ as in (10.23).

Exercise 10.26

(a) Calculate π^{re} of the previous exercise when Z is Pareto distributed with shape α so that $1 - F_0(z) = (1+z)^{-\alpha}$. [*Hint*: Verify that you obtain (10.24) when $\alpha \neq 1$; the case $\alpha = 1$ has to be treated separately.]

(b) The same problem when α is infinite so that $1 - F_0(z) = e^{-z}$ is the exponential distribution.

Exercise 10.27

(a) Compute π^{re} for the reinsurance contract in Exercise 10.26 when $\mu T = 0.01$, $a = 50$, $b = 500$, $\alpha = 2$ and $\beta = 100$.

R-*commands*:

```
ξz=(β/(α-1))*((1+a/β)**(-(α-1))-(1+(a+b)/β)**(-(α-1)));
πre=μT*ξz.
```

(b) Approximate π^{re} by Monte Carlo using $m = 100\,000$ simulations and compute the standard deviation of the estimate.

R-*commands*:

```
Z=β*(runif(m)**(-1/α)-1); Zre=pmin(pmax(Z-a,0),b);
πre=μT*mean(Zre); Sd=μT*sd(Zre)/sqrt(m).
```

(c) Compare the results in (a) and (b) and argue that 10 million simulations may be needed to get the first three digits correct.

Exercise 10.28 Consider a reinsurance contract over $(0, T)$ with a re-instatement clause under which the cedent in addition to the initial premium π_0 is charged a second fee if a claim turns up.

(a) If S is the time of this event, argue that a plausible rule could be $\pi^{\text{re}} = \pi_0 + \theta \max(T - S, 0)\pi_0$, where $\theta \geq 0$ is a parameter.

(b) Since the density function of S is $f(s) = \mu e^{-\mu s}$ by Exercise 8.1, show that

$$E(\pi^{\text{re}}) = (1 + \theta T)\pi_0 - \theta\frac{1 - e^{-\mu T}}{\mu}\pi_0.$$

[*Hint*: Utilize that $\int_0^T (T - s)\mu e^{-\mu s} ds = T - (1 - e^{-\mu T})/\mu$.]

(c) Construct a **generalized** pure premium; i.e., determine π_0 so that $E(\pi^{\text{re}}) = \mu T \xi_z^{\text{re}}$.

Exercise 10.29 Denote by $\mathcal{X}_1, \ldots, \mathcal{X}_J$ the losses of J clients of a reinsurer with $\mathcal{X}_1^{\text{re}}, \ldots, \mathcal{X}_J^{\text{re}}$ reinsurer responsibilities where $\mathcal{X}_j^{\text{re}} = c_j \mathcal{X}_j$ for some coefficient c_j. Suppose the original claims are independent and approximately Gaussian with mean and standard deviation ξ_j and σ_j for cedent j.

(a) Argue that the total reinsurance obligation $\mathcal{Y}^{\rm re} = \mathcal{X}_1^{\rm re} + \cdots + \mathcal{X}_J^{\rm re}$ is approximately Gaussian too and identify its mean and standard deviation.
(b) Why may the normal approximation be more accurate for the reinsurer than for the cedents individually?
(c) Argue that the approximate $1-\epsilon$ reserve for the reinsurer is $q_\epsilon^{\rm re} = \sum_j c_j \xi_j + \sqrt{\sum_j (c_j\sigma_j)^2}\,\phi_\epsilon$, where ϕ_ϵ is the upper Gaussian percentile.

Exercise 10.30 Let $\xi_j = \xi$ and $\sigma_j = \sigma$ for all j in the preceding exercise and change the contracts to $\mathcal{X}_j^{\rm re} = 0$ if $\mathcal{X}_j < a$, $\mathcal{X}_j^{\rm re} = \mathcal{X}_j - a$ if $a \leq \mathcal{X}_j < a+b$ and $\mathcal{X}_j^{\rm re} = b$ if $\mathcal{X}_j \geq a+b$.

(a) Write a program generating m simulations of $\mathcal{Y}^{\rm re} = \mathcal{X}_1^{\rm re} + \cdots + \mathcal{X}_J^{\rm re}$.
R-*commands*:
```
X=rnorm(m*J,ξ,σ); X=matrix(X,J,m);
Xre=pmin(pmax(X-a,0),b); Yre=apply(Xre,2,sum).
```
(b) Run the program when $m = 10\,000$, $J = 20$, $\xi = 1$, $\sigma = 0.2$, $a = 0.9$ and $b = 1.2$, estimate/plot the density function of $\mathcal{Y}^{\rm re}$ and compute its 5% and 1% upper percentiles.
R-*commands*:
```
plot(density(Yre)); sort(Yre)[(1-c(0.05,0.01))*m].
```
(c) Repeat (b) when $a = 1.1$ and $b = 1.4$ and explain why less money is involved now.

Exercise 10.31 Consider a portfolio of J identical policies with expected number of claims per policy μT and log-normal losses $Z = e^{\theta+\sigma\varepsilon}$ with clients receiving $\min(Z, b)$.

(a) Write a program using Monte Carlo to compute the pure premium of an $a \times b$ reinsurance contract per event.
R-*commands*:
```
Z=rlnorm(m,θ,σ); Zre=pmin(pmax(Z-a,0),b); πre=JμT*mean(Zre).
```
(b) Run the program and tabulate $\pi^{\rm re}$ for $a = 0, 1, 2, 3, 4$ when $J\mu T = 10$, $\theta = -0.5$, $\sigma = 1$ and $b = 5$.

Exercise 10.32

(a) Argue that $Z^{\rm ce} = \min(Z, a)$ is cedent net responsibility in Exercise 10.31.
(b) Write a program simulating cedent net loss when claim numbers are Poisson distributed with parameter $J\mu T$.
R-*commands*:
```
Xce=array(0,m); N=rpois(m,JμT); for (i in 1:m)
{Z=rlnorm(N[i],θ,σ); if(N[i]>0) Xce[i]=sum(pmin(Z,a))}.
```

(c) Run the program when $m = 10\,000$, $J\mu T = 10$, $\theta = -0.5$, $\sigma = 1$ and $a = 3$, estimate/plot the density function and determine the 5% and 1% percentiles for cedent responsibility.

R-*commands*:

`plot(density(`$\mathcal{X}^{\text{ce}}$`)); sort(`$\mathcal{X}^{\text{ce}}$`)[(1-c(0.05,0.01))*m].`

(d) Redo when $a = 2$ and $a = 1$ and note how the capital requirements go down in exchange for the higher reinsurance premia in Exercise 10.31.

11

Liabilities over long terms

11.1 Introduction

General insurance was, in the preceding chapter, treated on a year-to-year basis, but a longer view is also of interest, for example to determine a level of capital sufficient to cope with adverse circumstances over an extended period of time (the 'ruin' problem) or to understand the accumulated effect of reinsuring parts of the portfolio. Issues like these are attacked through recursions over time. A simple scheme is

$$\mathcal{Y}_k = \mathcal{Y}_{k-1} + \underbrace{r\mathcal{Y}_{k-1}}_{\textit{financial income}} + \underbrace{\Pi_k}_{\textit{premium}} - \underbrace{O_k}_{\textit{overhead}} - \underbrace{\mathcal{X}_k}_{\textit{claims paid}} \tag{11.1}$$

for $k = 1, \ldots, K$. Incomes (financial $r\mathcal{Y}_{k-1}$ and premium Π_k) are added and expenses (overhead costs O_k and claims $\mathcal{X}_k$) subtracted for the net value $\mathcal{Y}_k$ at time k. Reinsurance may hide behind Π_k and $\mathcal{X}_k$, which are then net with reinsurance premia and compensations subtracted. Studies of the investment side have a more natural home among life and pension insurance in Part III, and financial earnings are only included here through a fixed rate of interest r. If $r = 0$, we are dealing with **underwriting** only. Additional terms will be introduced in Section 11.5.

Long-term studies may require **dynamic** modelling; i.e., mathematical descriptions of effects due to time. Delayed claims (Section 8.5) will be added in Section 11.6, but there are many other issues. Examples of time-varying factors influencing the variables in (11.1) are planned growth of the portfolio, inflation, claims oscillating with the business cycle or risk in systematic growth or decline. How such things are modelled is demonstrated in this chapter. There is also a computational side. Section 11.2 develops simple approximations to ruin probabilities and the distribution of $\mathcal{Y}_k$, but as a practical problem solver Monte Carlo is unbeatable. Two of the sections (11.5 and 11.6) are devoted to simulation planning and design.

11.2 Simple situations

11.2.1 Introduction

In the pre-computer age issues like the preceding ones had to be attacked through mathematical formulae. Arguments were clever, but circumstances had to be simplified, and the approximate results did not necessarily permit control over error. The present section indicates what this approach has to offer when $\mathcal{X}_k$ is specified in the usual way as

$$\mathcal{X}_k = \sum_{i=1}^{\mathcal{N}_k} Z_{ik}, \qquad \mathcal{N}_k \sim \text{Poisson}(\lambda_k)$$

with all counts $\mathcal{N}_k$ and losses Z_{ik} independent. All parameters are time varying, but non-random. In addition to λ_k there are means ξ_{zk}, standard deviations σ_{zk} and skewness coefficients ζ_{zk} of the losses Z_{ik}, overhead $\mathcal{O}_k$ and premium Π_k. For more flexible modelling consult later sections.

11.2.2 Lower-order moments

The assumptions above made $\{\mathcal{X}_k\}$ the only random terms, and the mathematics is manageable when they are independent. Then

$$E(\mathcal{Y}_k) = (1+r)E(\mathcal{Y}_{k-1}) + (\Pi_k - \mathcal{O}_k) - E(\mathcal{X}_k), \quad E(\mathcal{X}_k) = \lambda_k \xi_{zk}, \tag{11.2}$$

true *generally* and

$$\text{var}(\mathcal{Y}_k) = (1+r)^2 \text{var}(\mathcal{Y}_{k-1}) + \text{var}(\mathcal{X}_k), \quad \text{var}(\mathcal{X}_k) = \lambda_k(\xi_{zk}^2 + \sigma_{zk}^2) \tag{11.3}$$

$$\nu_3(\mathcal{Y}_k) = (1+r)^3 \nu_3(\mathcal{Y}_{k-1}) - \nu_3(\mathcal{X}_k), \quad \nu_3(\mathcal{X}_k) = \lambda_k(\zeta_{zk}\sigma_{zk}^3 + 3\xi_{zk}\sigma_{zk}^2 + \xi_{zk}^3), \tag{11.4}$$

which are valid because of the independence. These are recursions over $k = 1, 2, \ldots$ and easy to derive. Pass expectation, variance and third-order moment over (11.1) and break the right-hand side down on the individual terms through the rules of Table A.1 in Appendix A. Consult Section 10.7 for the expressions for $E(\mathcal{X}_k)$, $\text{var}(\mathcal{X}_k)$ and $\nu_3(\mathcal{X}_k)$. In the beginning

$$E(\mathcal{Y}_0) = v_0, \quad \text{var}(\mathcal{Y}_0) = 0 \quad \text{and} \quad \nu_3(\mathcal{Y}_0) = 0, \tag{11.5}$$

where v_0 is the initial capital. Skewness is computed through

$$\text{skew}(\mathcal{Y}_k) = \frac{\nu_3(\mathcal{Y}_k)}{\text{var}(\mathcal{Y}_k)^{3/2}}. \tag{11.6}$$

This scheme provides an approximate view of the distribution of any $\mathcal{Y}_k$, and implementation as recursions in the computer is straightforward. Both Gaussian and NP approximations of the percentiles $q_{\epsilon k}$ of $\mathcal{Y}_k$ could be contemplated; i.e., as in Section 10.2

$$\underbrace{q_{\epsilon k}^{\text{No}} = E(\mathcal{Y}_k) + \phi_\epsilon \text{sd}(\mathcal{Y}_k)}_{\textit{normal approximation}} \quad \text{and} \quad \underbrace{q_{\epsilon k}^{\text{NP}} = q_{\epsilon k}^{\text{No}} + \text{sd}(\mathcal{Y}_k)\text{skew}(\mathcal{Y}_k)\tfrac{1}{6}(\phi_\epsilon^2 - 1)}_{\textit{normal power approximation}},$$

and their accuracy might be somewhat improved since there is a higher number of independent terms behind them.

11.2.3 When risk is constant

To see how $\mathcal{Y}_k$ varies with time, suppose the parameters are constants so that

$$\underbrace{\Pi_k = J\pi,\ O_k = Jo}_{\textit{premium and overhead}} \qquad \underbrace{\lambda_k = J\mu T}_{\textit{claim frequency}} \qquad \underbrace{\xi_{zk} = \xi_z,\ \sigma_{zk} = \sigma_z,\ \zeta_{zk} = \zeta_z}_{\textit{losses per event}},$$

where J is portfolio size and π and o premium income and overhead per policy holder. Closed expressions for the lower-order moments of $\mathcal{Y}_k$ are, in Section 11.7, deduced from (11.2) and (11.3). Now

$$E(\mathcal{Y}_k) = v_0(1+r)^k + J(\pi - o - \mu T\xi_z)\frac{(1+r)^k - 1}{r} \tag{11.7}$$

and

$$\text{sd}(\mathcal{Y}_k) = \text{sd}(\mathcal{X})\sqrt{\frac{(1+r)^{2k} - 1}{(1+r)^2 - 1}} \quad \text{where} \quad \text{sd}(\mathcal{X}) = \sqrt{J\mu T(\xi_z^2 + \sigma_z^2)}. \tag{11.8}$$

In the long run both the mean and standard deviation grow as $(1+r)^k$, which is the same as a bank account, and the ratio $\text{sd}(\mathcal{Y}_k)/E(\mathcal{Y}_k)$ tends to a fixed, positive value as $k \to \infty$.

By contrast the skewness coefficient is

$$\text{skew}(\mathcal{Y}_k) = -\text{skew}(\mathcal{X})\left(\frac{(1+r)^2 - 1}{(1+r)^{2k} - 1}\right)^{3/2}\frac{(1+r)^{3k} - 1}{(1+r)^3 - 1}, \tag{11.9}$$

which is quite insensitive to the value of r and doesn't wander too far off from the limiting value $-\text{skew}(\mathcal{X})/\sqrt{k}$ as $r \to 0$ unless k and r are *very* large; see Exercise 11.1.

11.2.4 Underwriter results in the long run

The limiting behaviour of $\mathcal{Y}_k$ as $k \to \infty$ is quite different when $r = 0$. A convenient mathematical form is now

$$\mathcal{Y}_k = \mathcal{Y}_{k-1} - \mathcal{U}_k \quad \text{where} \quad \mathcal{U}_k = \mathcal{X}_k - J(\pi - o). \tag{11.10}$$

Here $\mathcal{U}_k$ is the underwriter result in period k, with mean and standard deviation

$$\xi_u = J\{\mu T\xi_z + o - \pi\} \quad \text{and} \quad \sigma_u = \sqrt{J\mu T(\xi_z^2 + \sigma_z^2)}. \tag{11.11}$$

We are dealing with a random walk, and $\mathcal{Y}_k$ becomes Gaussian eventually. Its mean and standard deviation follow from (11.7) and (11.8) by letting $r \to 0$ or alternatively by adding the contributions from $\mathcal{U}_1, \dots, \mathcal{U}_k$. Either approach yields

$$E(\mathcal{Y}_k) = v_0 - k\xi_u \quad \text{and} \quad \text{sd}(\mathcal{Y}_k) = \sqrt{k}\sigma_u. \tag{11.12}$$

Crucial for long-term behaviour is the fact that $\text{sd}(\mathcal{Y}_k)$ now depends on k through $\sqrt{k}$ and becomes dominated by $E(\mathcal{Y}_k)$ as $k \to \infty$ unless $\xi_u = 0$. If $\xi_u > 0$, then $E(\mathcal{Y}_k) \to -\infty$ which carries $\mathcal{Y}_k$ with it to certain ruin; see Exercise 11.2. The portfolio is destined for the same fate when $\xi_u = 0$ (as remarked in Section 5.5), but the natural situation is $\xi_u < 0$, which means that

$$\pi > \mu T\xi_z + o, \tag{11.13}$$

and the premium is high enough to cover losses and overhead on average. A company has misjudged if things are otherwise. Now $E(\mathcal{Y}_k) \to \infty$, which drags $\mathcal{Y}_k$ with it since $\text{sd}(\mathcal{Y}_k)$ becomes so much smaller, but this doesn't rule out negative $\mathcal{Y}_k$ earlier, which is studied next.

11.2.5 Underwriter ruin by closed mathematics

Look K periods into the future and consider the ruin probability

$$p^{\text{ru}}(v_0) = \Pr\{\min(\mathcal{Y}_1, \dots, \mathcal{Y}_K) < 0 | \mathcal{Y}_0 = v_0\}, \tag{11.14}$$

which was examined by means of Monte Carlo in Section 3.6. We shall now see what pure mathematics can achieve when parameters are constant and $r = 0$. The key tool is the moment-generating function $M_u(s) = E(e^{s\mathcal{U}})$, where $\mathcal{U}$ is one of the variables $\{\mathcal{U}_k\}$. Moment-generating functions are reviewed in Appendix A.2. Clearly $M_u(0) = 1$, and when differentiated

$$\frac{dM_u(s)}{ds} = E(\mathcal{U}e^{s\mathcal{U}}) \quad \text{and} \quad \frac{d^2M_u(s)}{ds^2} = E(\mathcal{U}^2e^{s\mathcal{U}}),$$

so that

$$\frac{dM_u(0)}{ds} = E(\mathcal{U}) = \xi_u \quad \text{and} \quad \frac{d^2M_u(s)}{ds^2} > 0,$$

which implies convex behaviour with one of the two shapes in Figure 11.1 according to whether ξ_u is positive or negative. It is the second case that interests us (ruin is certain otherwise). The derivative of $M_u(s)$ is then negative at the origin, but the curve $M_u(s)$ must eventually rise again since it becomes infinite as $s \to \infty$.

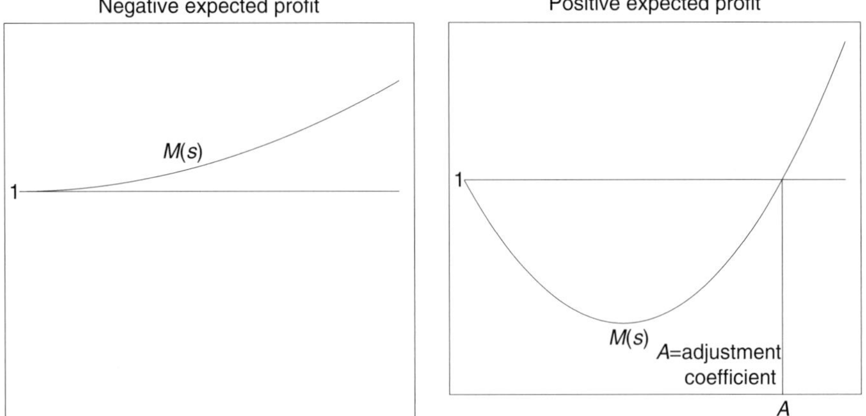

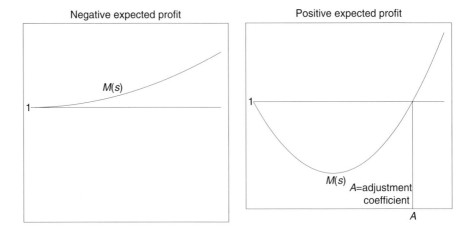

Figure 11.1 The moment-generating function of $\mathcal{U}$ under negative expected profit (*left*) and positive expected profit (*right*).

It follows (Figure 11.1 right) that the equation $M_u(s) = 1$ has a single positive root A. This quantity is known as the **adjustment** coefficient and defines the **Lundberg** bound through

$$p^{\text{ru}}(v_0) \le e^{-Av_0}, \quad \text{condition: } \xi_u < 0, \tag{11.15}$$

which is verified in Section 11.7.

The adjustment coefficient can be calculated. Let $M_z(s) = E(e^{sZ})$ be the moment-generating function of the individual losses Z. Then for a Poisson portfolio

$$M_u(s) = e^{J\mu T\{M_z(s)-1\}-J(\pi-o)s}; \tag{11.16}$$

see Section 11.7 for proof. The adjustment coefficient is the positive root of the equation

$$M_z(A) - 1 = \frac{\pi - o}{\mu T}A, \tag{11.17}$$

and it usually takes numerical methods to solve it. By (11.15) the ruin probability is less than ϵ if the initial capital $v_0 \ge -\log(\epsilon)/A$.

Lundberg's inequality indicates that the ruin probability might tend to zero with an exponential rate as the initial capital v_0 grows. This is true if we let $K \to \infty$ first, so that ruin applies to an infinite time horizon. It can then be proved (Asmussen, 2000, p. 71) that

$$p^{\text{ru}}(v_0) \sim Ce^{-Av_0} \quad \text{where} \quad C = \frac{(\pi - o)/(\mu T) - \xi_z}{A\int_0^\infty ze^{Az}\{1 - F(z)\}dz}, \tag{11.18}$$

with $F(z)$ the distribution function of Z. The mathematical notation signifies that the ratio of the two sides on the left in (11.18) tends to one as $v_0 \to \infty$. How well these approximations work numerically is investigated among the exercises.

11.2.6 Underwriter ruin under heavy-tailed losses

For the preceding results to hold, the right tail of the density function of Z must approach zero at an exponential rate or faster since otherwise $M(s)$ is infinite for $s \neq 0$, and the argument breaks down. These so-called sub-exponential distributions are common in property insurance. Examples are the log-normal and the ordinary and extended Pareto distributions. There is a much more recent theory that covers these. The limit (11.18) is now replaced by

$$p^{\text{ru}}(v_0) \sim C\int_{v_0}^{\infty}\{1 - F(z)\}dz \quad \text{where} \quad C = \frac{\mu T}{(\pi - o) - \mu T \xi_z}; \tag{11.19}$$

see Asmussen (2000), p. 259 where you will find the proof (the result there has been rewritten slightly). If Z follows the Pareto or extended Pareto distribution, the ruin probability approaches zero as $v_0 \to \infty$ at a polynomial rate, much slower than the exponential one in (11.18).

11.3 Time variation through regression

11.3.1 Introduction

The topic in this section is systematic change in risk over time through the Poisson parameters λ_k. Norwegian claim numbers from around 200 000 policies over a period of 45 months are used for illustration. Their summary in Figure 8.2 showed a steady increase in accidents over a 3 to 4 year period, and monthly oscillations linked to the time of the year. Whether we should build risk increases into our projections is a matter of judgement, but the seasonality is no doubt a stable phenomenon and so is random variation in intensities from one period to another. These matters can be examined by Poisson regression, which will be extended at the end of the section to cover random background conditions.

11.3.2 Poisson regression with time effects

Consider historical claim numbers with explanatory variables as in Section 8.4 with time over K periods of length T added. A row of the data matrix then becomes

j	k	n_{jk}	T_{jk}	$x_{j1}, \ldots, x_{jv_x}$
individual	*time*	*claim number*	*exposure*	*ordinary covariates*

where n_{jk} applies to individual j during period k. Note that $T_{jk} = T$ if exposure to risk is the entire period. The link to the covariates $x_{j1}, \dots, x_{jv_x}$ is defined through the intensity μ_{jk}. It will be made random later, and it is convenient to replace it with a second symbol ξ_{jk}, which will serve as $E(\mu_{jk})$ when the setup is extended. The model for the historical claim numbers is then

$$N_{jk} \sim \text{Poisson}(\lambda_{jk}) \quad \text{where} \quad \lambda_{jk} = \xi_{jk} T_{jk}, \tag{11.20}$$

and a regression equation must be imposed on ξ_{jk}. With $x_{j0} = 1$ the natural specification is *multiplicative* as

$$\xi_{jk} = \underbrace{\xi_{j\cdot}}_{\textit{individual}} \times \underbrace{\xi_{\cdot k}}_{\textit{time}} \quad \text{where} \quad \log(\xi_{j\cdot}) = \sum_{i=0}^{v_x} b_i x_{ji},$$

and the individual factor $\xi_{j\cdot}$ with a log-linear relationship to the covariates is joined by the time factor $\xi_{\cdot k}$. The latter requires a second log-linear specification which captures risk in systematic growth or decline, and also seasonal effects that are present in many parts of the world. Seasons could be months, quarters or half-years. With s_k the season at time k and $b_s(s)$ the contribution of season s, a possible model is

$$\log(\xi_{\cdot k}) = \underbrace{b_d kT}_{\textit{drift}} + \underbrace{b_s(s_k)}_{\textit{season}}$$

where $b_d kT$ is a fixed trend. In summary,

$$\log(\xi_{jk}) = \underbrace{\textstyle\sum_{i=0}^{v_x} b_i x_{ji}}_{\textit{covariates}} + \underbrace{b_d kT}_{\textit{drift}} + \underbrace{b_s(s_k)}_{\textit{seasonal}} \tag{11.21}$$

and a side condition on the seasonal parameters $b_s(s)$ is needed, for example $b_s(1) = 0$. The model can be fitted as in Section 8.4.

11.3.3 Example: An automobile portfolio

Consider the monthly claim numbers from the Norwegian car insurance portfolio in Figure 8.2 with oscillations over the year and with systematic change in risk over the observation period. Covariates selected solely for the purpose of demonstration were

- *car type* (two categories, transmission either manual or automatic),
- *driving limit on policy* (seven categories, definitions in Table 11.1 later).

The dynamic part follows (11.21) with systematic drift and 12 seasonal contributions (one for each month). Estimated coefficients are listed in Table 11.2 in Exercise 11.11.

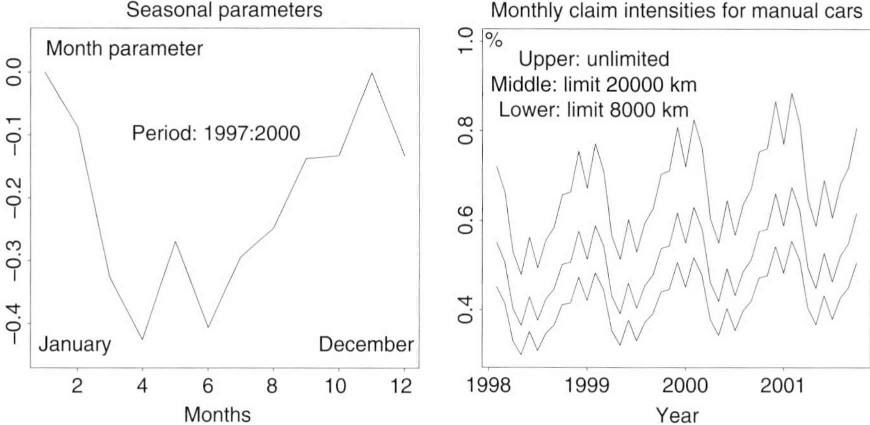

Figure 11.2 *Left*: Regression coefficients for seasonal effects. *Right*: Estimated claim intensities for three groups of policy holders.

The monthly parameters $\hat{b}_s(s)$ have been plotted in Figure 11.2 left with $\hat{b}_s(1) = 0$ (January) by design. The seasonal pattern is a strong one (as expected for a Northern European country), with negative values for the summer months when accidents are less frequent.[10] The fitted model is

$$\hat{\xi}_{jk} \quad = \quad \underbrace{\exp\left(\textstyle\sum_{i=0}^{v_x} \hat{b}_k x_{ji}\right)}_{individuals} \quad \times \quad \underbrace{\exp\left(\hat{b}_d kT + \hat{b}_s(s_k)\right)}_{dynamics},$$

which has been plotted against time in Figure 11.2 right for three different groups of customers. What emerges is an increasing pattern modulated by seasonal effects and pushed up and down in parallel according to the individual risk of the policy holder.

11.3.4 Regression with random background

Insurance claims in branches like automobiles are influenced by weather conditions, with random fluctuations that affect risk. Claim numbers must now be modelled conditionally as $N_{jk}|\lambda_{jk} \sim$ Poisson(λ_{jk}) with a natural specification of λ_{jk} as

$$\lambda_{jk} = \xi_{jk} T_{jk} G_k \quad \text{where} \quad G_k = F_0^{-1}(U_k), \tag{11.22}$$

and G_k is common background uncertainty driving ξ_{jk} up or down for all j. It is, by the inversion algorithm in Section 2.4, assigned a given distribution function $F_0(x)$ when U_k is uniform and $F_0^{-1}(u)$ is the inverse of $F_0(x)$. Let $E(G_k) = 1$. Then

[10] The local top for May is real and inherently Norwegian due to people (for local reasons) driving a lot during that month.

$E(\lambda_{jk}) = \xi_{jk}T_{jk}$, and the regression model (11.21) when applied to ξ_{jk} makes the model an amalgam of those in Sections 8.3 and 8.4. It will be assumed below that the sequence $G_1, G_2, \ldots$ is an independent one, but that restriction is lifted in the next section.

Suppose $G_k \sim \text{Gamma}(\alpha_k)$ as in Section 8.3. This yields **negative binomial regression** with $\alpha_1, \alpha_2, \ldots$, responsible for background uncertainty. We are back to ordinary Poisson regression if all $\alpha_k \to \infty$, since now all $G_k = 1$. Negative binomial regression was introduced in property insurance by Jørgensen and Paes de Souza (1994), with R-software being offered in Faraway (2006); see Chapter 10. If you have to implement it yourself, look up the likelihood function in Section 11.7.

The Gamma parameters can only be determined from historical data, and there shouldn't be too many of them. Possible simplifications are

$$\underbrace{\alpha_k = \alpha}_{\text{constant variability}} \qquad \text{and} \qquad \underbrace{\alpha_k = \alpha(s) \quad \text{for season } s \text{ at time } k.}_{\text{variability depending on season}}$$

Both versions are handled by the likelihood method in Section 11.7. The likelihood function is a lengthy expression (that's why details have been deferred), but its precise form isn't needed to understand what we might get out of it.

11.3.5 The automobile portfolio: A second round

Suppose there are two covariates and two seasonal components ('winter' and 'summer') with separate Gamma parameters $\alpha(1)$ and $\alpha(2)$. The model then becomes

$$\lambda_{jk} = \xi_{jk}T_{jk}G_k \quad \text{where} \quad G_k \sim \text{Gamma}\{\alpha(s_k)\}$$

and

$$\log(\xi_{jk}) = b_0 + b_1x_{1j} + b_2x_{2j} + b_dkT + b_s(s_k).$$

Its parameters are estimated in Table 11.1 and compared with those under the pure Poisson situation when the background uncertainty has been removed.

The differences are not overwhelming from one model to the other, but monthly drift is down from 0.71% with background uncertainty to 0.56%, there without which there would be considerable repercussions for projections over longer time horizons. Background uncertainty is more important in winter than in summer, since α is lower.

Simulated portfolio losses are shown in Figure 11.3 after having used Algorithm 11.2 later. The portfolio contained $J_k = 100\,000$ policies evenly spread on the 14 categories of gear type and distance limits in Table 11.1, and the claim size distribution (the same for all policies) was the empirical one based on 6764 losses on file with mean and standard deviation 3.018 and 3.636, respectively (money

Table 11.1 Estimated (monthly) coefficients when seasonal effects are described by *fixed* and *random* regimes

	Fixed[a]	Random[b]	Car types (according to gear)	Fixed[a]	Random[b]
Intercept	–5.407	–5.407	Manual	0	0
Monthly drift	0.0057	0.0071	Automatic	–0.342	–0.385
Seasonal mean	Fixed[a]	Random[b]	**Distance limits (1000 km)**	Fixed[a]	Random[b]
Summer	0	0	8	0	0
Winter	0.166	0.149	12	0.097	0.111
			16	0.116	0.124
Seasonal α			20	0.198	0.198
Summer	–	20.6	25	0.227	0.224
Winter	–	4.0	30	0.308	0.322
			no limit	0.468	0.483

[a]Model with fixed parameters for season.
[b]Random parameters for season.

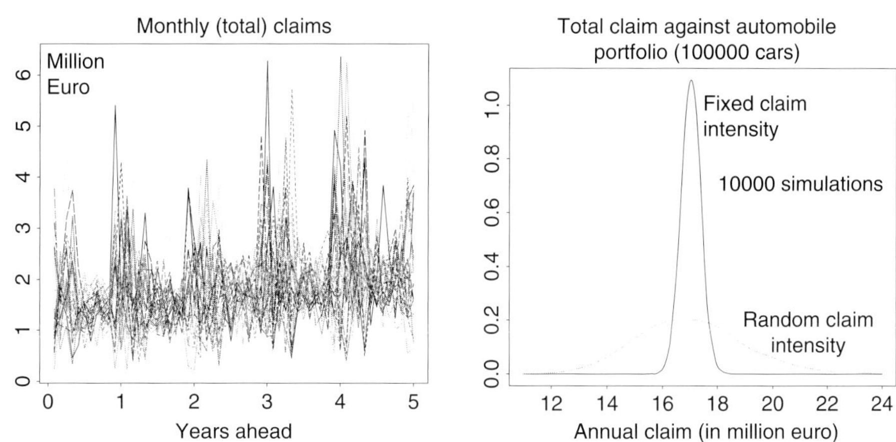

Figure 11.3 *Left*: Monthly portfolio loss (30 replications) for the random regime seasonal model of Table 11.1. *Right*: One-year total loss compared with the fixed regime model.

unit: thousand euros). Monthly liabilities over a period of 5 years have been plotted on the left in Figure 11.3. High background uncertainty makes results highly variable, and much more so in the winter months. The effect of the upward trend in the accident rate is evident. The uncertainty in annual results for the first year is shown on the right in Figure 11.3, which is another example of the importance of random background variation.

11.4 Claims as a stochastic process

11.4.1 Introduction

Background uncertainty was, in the preceding section, treated as an independent sequence, but this is only an approximation. Accidents may be more frequent in times of high economic activity, and weather conditions, with considerable influence on risk, follow cyclic patterns. Features like these make claim intensities a stochastic process. How that is dealt with and what the economic impact might be is the topic of this section. Individuals will be assumed identical risks.

Time series of claims numbers $\mathcal{N}_1, \dots, \mathcal{N}_K$ are now driven by an underlying random series of claim intensities $\mu_1, \dots, \mu_K$. This is **hidden** or **latent** risk, as introduced in Section 6.2. The issue is a challenging one. Our aim is a model for $\mu_1, \dots, \mu_K$ which is only observed indirectly through historical claim numbers. Hierarchies like these are common in many fields of science; consult Section 11.8 for references. Simulation is easy, but model calibration from historical data is not. The log-likelihood function is advanced material computationally, and a simpler criterion is proposed below. Other examples of hidden, dynamic risk in this book are losses per event in Section 11.5 and stochastic volatilities in finance in Chapter 13.

11.4.2 Claim intensity as a stationary process

We seek a way to impose on $\mu_1, \dots, \mu_K$ fluctuations similar to those of business cycles. Such models are stationary, and the tools are those of Section 5.6. The exponential, autoregressive process is a possibility. For $k = 1, \dots, K$ suppose

$$\mu_k = \xi e^{-\tau^2/2+\tau X_k} \quad \text{where} \quad X_k = aX_{k-1} + \sqrt{1-a^2}\,\varepsilon_k, \tag{11.23}$$

with ξ, τ and a parameters and $\varepsilon_1, \dots, \varepsilon_K$ independent and $N(0,1)$. The recursion starts at

$$X_0 = \frac{\tau}{2} + \frac{\log(\mu_0/\xi)}{\tau}; \tag{11.24}$$

solve (11.23) left when $k = 0$ to see this.

Note the specification of the driver process $X_0, \dots, X_K$, which differs slightly from the version in Section 5.6. But if $|a| < 1$, simulated paths of μ_k still separate gradually from a common start until their oscillations stabilize, and at that point $X_k \sim N(0,1)$ due to the special form in (11.23) right. Standard formulae for the log-normal yield

$$E(\mu_k) = \xi \quad \text{and} \quad \text{sd}(\mu_k) = \xi\sqrt{e^{\tau^2}-1} \qquad \text{(initial state forgotten);}$$

look them up in Section 9.3 in case you have forgotten.

11.4.3 A more general viewpoint

Dynamic models for claim intensities can also be constructed by combining autoregression and inversion sampling. This is in reality the copula approach of Section 6.7, which allows the distribution of μ_k to be *selected*. Dynamic copula modelling is discussed in Chen and Fan (2006). The present treatment is elementary. Let

$$\mu_k = \xi G_k \quad \text{where} \quad G_k = F_0^{-1}(U_k), \tag{11.25}$$

where ξ is mean intensity as above and $F_0(x)$ a distribution function with mean one. This is as in Section 11.3, but we now seek a way to make μ_k autocorrelated.

One possibility is to transform the sequence of uniforms $U_1, \dots, U_K$ to Gaussians $X_1, \dots, X_K$ and carry out the modelling there. The approach has been in use in geo-statistics for decades; see Journel and Huijbregts (1978). Let $\Phi(x)$ be the standard normal integral and consider

$$\underbrace{U_k = \Phi(X_k)}_{\text{uniform}} \quad \text{and} \quad \underbrace{X_k = aX_{k-1} + \sqrt{1-a^2}\,\varepsilon_k}_{\text{linear driver}} \tag{11.26}$$

for $k = 1, \dots, K$. Note that $X_1, \dots, X_K$ is the same process as before and $N(0, 1)$ for large k. By the inversion algorithm U_k has now become uniform, and (11.25) implies (inversion again) that the distribution function of μ_k is $F_0(x/\xi)$. The scheme starts at

$$X_0 = \Phi^{-1}\{F_0(\mu_0/\xi)\} \qquad (\mu_0 \text{ initial intensity}), \tag{11.27}$$

which is verified by solving (11.25) and (11.26) for X_0 when $k = 0$.

The exponential version (11.23) is the special case where $F(x)$ is the log-normal distribution with mean one; see Exercise 11.16. Another possibility is to use the standard Gamma distribution with shape α. Now, when the initial state is forgotten, $\xi = E(\mu_k)$ and $\text{sd}(\mu_k) = \xi/\sqrt{\alpha}$ and there are three parameters ξ, α and a.

11.4.4 Model for the claim numbers

The link from $\mu_1, \dots, \mu_K$ to the actual claim numbers $\mathcal{N}_1, \dots, \mathcal{N}_K$ is based on the assumption that the latter are conditionally independent given the former. This is the natural way to express that accidents appear independently of each other, but the realized counts $\mathcal{N}_1, \dots, \mathcal{N}_K$ themselves are now dependent because of the underlying stochastic process. Models of this type go back to Cox (1955), and often bear his name. If J_k is the number of policies at time k, then

$$\mathcal{N}_k|\mu_k \sim \text{Poisson}(\lambda_k) \quad \text{where} \quad \lambda_k = J_k\mu_k T. \tag{11.28}$$

Algorithm 11.1 summarizes how the model is simulated. It has been detailed for log-normal μ_k; see comments on the right for the general form.

Algorithm 11.1 Claim numbers from log-normal intensities

0 Input: ξ, τ, a and $J_1, \dots, J_K$ %*Gamma: α instead of τ*
1 $\mu^* \leftarrow \mu_0$ %*Initial μ_0, comments below*
2 $X^* \leftarrow \tau/2 + \log(\mu^*/\xi)/\tau$ %*General: $X^* \leftarrow \Phi^{-1}\{F_0(\mu^*/\xi)\}$*
3 For $k = 1, \dots, K$ do
4 Draw $\varepsilon^* \sim N(0,1)$, $X^* \leftarrow aX^* + \sqrt{1-a^2}\varepsilon^*$
5 $\mu^* \leftarrow \xi \exp(-\tau^2/2 + \tau X^*)$, $\lambda^* \leftarrow J_k\mu^*$ %*General: $\mu^* \leftarrow \xi F_0^{-1}\{(\Phi(X^*))\}$*
6 Draw $\mathcal{N}_k^* \sim \text{Poisson}(\lambda^*)$
7 Return $\mathcal{N}_1^*, \dots, \mathcal{N}_K^*$.

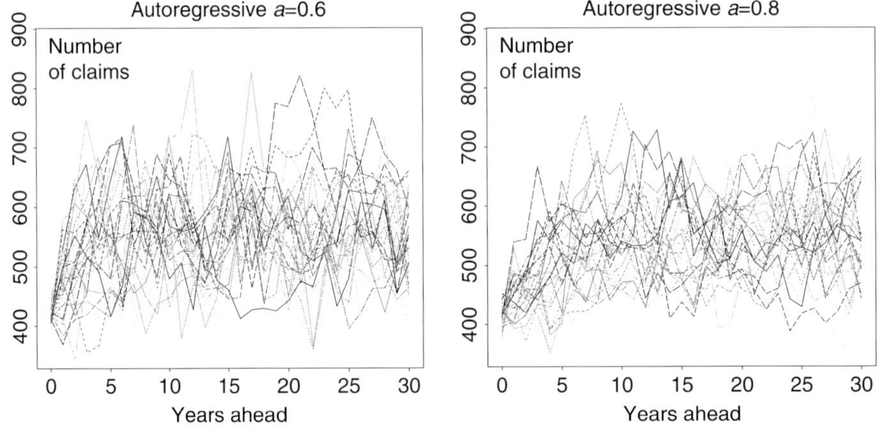

Figure 11.4 Simulated claim numbers (30 replications) for 10 000 policies under log-normal claim intensities for the model described in the text.

The first μ^* may be the current value μ_0. If only available with error (which you may want to take into account), implement the conclusion in Exercise 11.24. Another strategy is to draw the first μ^* from the stationary state of the distribution. Line 1 is then skipped and you take $X^* \sim N(0,1)$ on Line 2. The study of estimation error at the end of the section was run in this manner; see Section 13.6 for more on the initialization issue.

Algorithm 11.1 has, in Figure 11.4, been used to generate Monte Carlo realizations when $K = 30$, $\xi = 0.056$, $\tau = 0.125$, $a = 0.6$ or $a = 0.8$ and $J_k = 10\,000$ for all k. For large k when μ_0 is forgotten, $\text{sd}(\mu_k) = 0.007$. The claim intensity starts low at $\mu_0 = 0.042$, which corresponds to an average count of 420 incidents, and the intensities μ_k^* then grow until the simulated claim numbers fluctuate around the long-term average 560. On the right, the higher value of the autoregressive coefficient leads to slower speed away from the initial condition, and if the oscillations then appear smaller, it is an illusion. The theoretical variation is exactly the same.

11.4.5 Example: The effect on underwriter risk

Random background conditions may bring substantial risk increases (Sections 6.2 and 8.3), but how important is autoregressive dynamics? Here is an illustration under three different log-normal scenarios:

$\tau = 0$	$\tau = 0.125$ and $a = 0$	$\tau = 0.125$ and $a = 0.6$,
fixed μ	*stochastic μ, independence*	*stochastic μ, autocorrelation*

with expectation $\xi = 5.6\%$ and $\mathrm{sd}(\mu_k) = 0.7\%$ at the stationary state as before. Other conditions were

$Z = e^{-\tau_z^2/2+\tau_z\varepsilon}$, $\tau_z = 0.5$	$J_k = 100\,000$	$\pi - o = 0.0612$.
loss distribution per event	*portfolio size*	*net premium per policy*

Note that the net premium exceeds the pure one (0.056) by 10%. Let $\mathcal{Y}_5$ be the net premium income minus payments to the policy holders after 5 years. When this underwriter result was simulated $m = 10\,000$ times using Algorithm 11.3 later, its mean was around 2600 (the same for all scenarios), but standard deviations were far from equal:

$\mathrm{sd}(\mathcal{Y}_5) = 330$	$\mathrm{sd}(\mathcal{Y}_5) = 1600$	$\mathrm{sd}(\mathcal{Y}_5) = 2600$.
fixed μ	*stochastic μ, independence*	*stochastic μ, autoregression*

A positive result from underwriting is in practice guaranteed when μ is fixed, but not under the other two models. Autoregression is not unimportant and should not be ignored.

11.4.6 Utilizing historical data

We have to address how the parameters are determined from historical counts $n_1, \ldots, n_n$ based on $J_1, \ldots, J_n$ policies under risk. Let $\hat{\mu}_k = n_k/(J_kT)$ be the elementary, unbiased estimate of μ_k. One approach is to apply the fitting methods in Section 5.6 to $\hat{\mu}_1, \ldots, \hat{\mu}_n$ and ignore the discrepancies from the underlying series $\mu_1, \ldots, \mu_n$. This works for large portfolios (the two series are close), but perhaps not for smaller ones. The best way (catering for all possibilities) is likelihood estimation, but you won't find that in standard software, and it is too complicated numerically to be included here (see the references in Section 11.8). A simple scheme that will be tested below runs as follows.

Start by estimating ξ and $\sigma = \mathrm{sd}(\mu_k)$ at steady state by (8.5) and (8.6) in

Section 8.3; i.e.,

$$\hat{\xi} = w_1\hat{\mu}_1 + \cdots + w_n\hat{\mu}_n \quad \text{where} \quad w_k = \frac{J_k}{J_1 + \cdots + J_n}, \tag{11.29}$$

$$\hat{\sigma}^2 = \frac{\sum_{k=1}^n w_k(\hat{\mu}_k - \hat{\xi})^2 - c}{1 - \sum_{k=1}^n w_k^2} \quad \text{where} \quad c = \frac{(n-1)\hat{\xi}}{J_1 + \cdots + J_n}. \tag{11.30}$$

Next convert $\hat{\sigma}$ to estimates of the shape of the distributions. Under the log-normal and Gamma models this part becomes

$$\underbrace{\hat{\tau} = \sqrt{\log(1 + (\hat{\sigma}/\hat{\xi})^2)}}_{\textit{log-normal}} \quad \text{or} \quad \underbrace{\hat{\alpha} = (\hat{\xi}/\hat{\sigma})^2}_{\textit{Gamma}}. \tag{11.31}$$

Then reconstruct the process $\{X_k\}$ by taking

$$\underbrace{\hat{X}_k = \hat{\tau}/2 + \log(\hat{\mu}_k/\hat{\xi})/\hat{\tau}}_{\textit{log-normal}} \quad \text{or} \quad \underbrace{\hat{X}_k = \Phi^{-1}\{\hat{F}_0(\hat{\mu}_k/\hat{\xi})\}}_{\textit{Gamma}}, \quad k = 1, \ldots, n, \tag{11.32}$$

where $\hat{F}_0(x)$ is the fitted Gamma distribution with shape $\hat{\alpha}$. Finally take

$$\hat{a} = \frac{n}{n-1} \frac{\sum_{k=2}^n \hat{X}_k \hat{X}_{k-1}}{\sum_{k=1}^n \hat{X}_k^2}, \tag{11.33}$$

which we justify by noting that the estimates $\hat{\tau}$ and $\hat{\alpha}$ follow from the standard deviations of the log-normal and Gamma distributions, $\hat{X}_k$ is similar to (11.24) and (11.27) for general k, and $\hat{a}$ is a routine estimate of the first-order autoregressive coefficient.

11.4.7 Numerical experiment

The preceding argument is so heuristic that we have to check that it works. A possible scenario with annual parameters is $\xi = 0.056$, $\tau = 0.125$ and $a = 0.6$, and there were historical data up to $n = 20$ years with $J_1 = \cdots = J_n = 10\,000$. The log-normal model was run $m = 1000$ times and the parameters reconstructed from the simulations. Averages and standard deviations of the estimates were

mean	sd	mean	sd	mean	sd
0.056	0.003	0.0063	0.0015	0.36	0.21,
for $\xi = 0.056$		*for* σ=0.007		*for* $a = 0.6$	

which suggests that a is the most difficult parameter to estimate [large standard deviation, large bias, with the average estimate (0.36) much smaller than the true one (0.60)]. This state of affairs owes much to the shortness of the time series (20 years), and didn't change much when the number of policies was ten-doubled.

Conclusions were similar when the Gamma distribution replaced the log-normal in other experiments.

11.5 Building simulation models

11.5.1 Introduction

Claims $\mathcal{X}_k$, premium Π_k and overhead cost $\mathcal{O}_k$ were, in Section 11.1, aggregated to net values $\mathcal{Y}_k$. Add taxes $\mathcal{T}_k$ and dividend $\mathcal{D}_k$ to owners and you have the top layer of a simplified insurance system which evolves according to the recursion

$$\mathcal{Y}_k = (1+r)\mathcal{Y}_{k-1} + \Pi_k - \mathcal{O}_k - \mathcal{X}_k - \mathcal{T}_k - \mathcal{D}_k, \quad k = 1, \dots, K \tag{11.34}$$

with financial income treated in the same simplistic way as earlier in this chapter. Monte Carlo is the obvious tool when the uncertainty of such systems is examined. Another term for it in general insurance is dynamic financial analysis (**DFA**); see Blum and Dacorogna (2004) for a review. The enterprise could be a huge one, but the aim here is more to indicate a working process when such programs are being developed than to implement 'big'. General points are implementation step-by-step and through hierarchies. Such things can only be learnt by example. Those below play with the variables in (11.34), but there are many other possibilities. Reinsurance is not included, and financial uncertainty is deferred to Part III where a discussion similar to the present one is offered in Section 15.5. Outstanding claims that are going to be settled in the future are added in Section 11.6.

11.5.2 Under the top level

How do you go about planning a program simulating the system (11.34)? The claims $\mathcal{X}_k$ against the portfolio are central. If broken down on counts $\mathcal{N}_k$ and individual losses Z_k as usual, there was in the preceding section a link further down to intensities μ_k. There might even be time-dependent parameters, say $\boldsymbol{\theta}_k$, driving individual losses Z_k. All of this entails a network of interdependencies, for example

$$\begin{array}{ccccccc} \boldsymbol{\theta}_k & \longrightarrow & Z_k & \searrow & & & \\ \mu_k & \longrightarrow & \mathcal{N}_k & \longrightarrow & \mathcal{X}_k & \longrightarrow & \mathcal{Y}_k \\ & & & \nwarrow & & \nearrow & \\ & & & & J_k & & \end{array}$$

where the accumulations to $\mathcal{Y}_k$ on the right hide such things as premia, taxes and dividends. Note the presence of the number of policies J_k, which is a vehicle

Algorithm 11.2 Claims with seasonal, hidden risk

Input: $A_k = T\sum_j \xi_{jk}$, $\alpha(s)$, v_s, s_0 and model for Z_k *%s_0 season at the beginning*
$s \leftarrow s_0$ *%Enter first season*
For $k = 0, \dots, K$ repeat
  $\alpha \leftarrow \alpha(s)$ and draw $G^* \sim \text{Gamma}(\alpha)$ *%Background from right season*
  $\lambda^* \leftarrow A_k G^*$ and draw $\mathcal{N}^* \sim \text{Poisson}(\lambda^*)$ *%Claim numbers*
  $\mathcal{X}_k^* \leftarrow 0$
  Repeat $\mathcal{N}^*$ times: Draw Z^* and $\mathcal{X}_k^* \leftarrow \mathcal{X}_k^* + Z^*$ *%Liabilities at k*
  $s \leftarrow s + 1$ and if $s > v_s$ then $s \leftarrow 1$ *%Season for next round*
Return $\mathcal{X}_0^*, \dots, \mathcal{X}_K^*$.

for entering planned growth of the portfolio with impact on losses and premium income. Implementation follows the network from left to right.

There are many courses of action when these relationships are detailed. A useful method with premia Π_k and expenses O_k is to break them down on the average for the portfolio through

$$\Pi_k = J_k \pi_k \quad \text{and} \quad O_k = J_k o_k,$$

where π_k and o_k apply per policy. Below, we shall examine a situation where the premium level through π_k interacts with the economic state of the portfolio. Another feature is the future price level (denoted Q_k below), which affects many of the variables. Taxes and dividends to owners $\mathcal{T}_k$ and $\mathcal{D}_k$ depend on the tax code and dividend policy. Simple schemes are introduced at the end. The examples below indicate how complex schemes can be managed and entered in the computer, but there are countless other possibilities!

11.5.3 Hidden, seasonal risk

The first example is the model from Section 11.3, where the claim intensity of individual j at time k was $\mu_{jk} = \xi_{jk} G_k$ with ξ_{jk} fixed and known and G_k random. Let $\mathcal{N}_k$ be the number of claims. Then $\mathcal{N}_k | G_k \sim \text{Poisson}(\lambda_k)$, where $\lambda_k = \sum_j \mu_{jk}$ or in summary

$$\mathcal{N}_k | \lambda_k \sim \text{Poisson}(\lambda_k) \quad \text{where} \quad \lambda_k = A_k G_k \quad \text{with } A_k = T \sum_{j=1}^{J_k} \xi_{jk}.$$

Suppose $G_k \sim \text{Gamma}(\alpha_k)$, where $\alpha_k = \alpha(s_k)$ for v_s different seasonal parameters $\alpha(1), \dots, \alpha(v_s)$. Portfolio losses $\mathcal{X}_0, \dots, \mathcal{X}_K$ can then be simulated as in Algorithm 11.2.

A new feature is claim numbers from time-dependent Poisson parameters. Note the integer s which controls the season and is updated on Line 7. This variable is required for the random part G_k, but even the fixed part A_k may contain seasonal effects buried in the expectations ξ_{jk}. The algorithm was used to generate the plots in Figure 11.3.

11.5.4 Hidden risk with inflation

Many of the central variables in general insurance depend on the price level Q_k, which evolves as

$$Q_k = (1 + I_k)Q_{k-1}, \quad k = 1, \ldots, K \qquad \text{starting at} \quad Q_0 = 1$$

where I_k is the rate of inflation. If claims, premia and expenses all grow with Q_k, then

$$\mathcal{Y}_k = (1 + r)\mathcal{Y}_{k-1} + Q_k\{J_k(\pi_k - o_k) - \mathcal{X}_k\}, \quad k = 1, \ldots, K \tag{11.35}$$

where taxes and dividends to owners have been excluded. Note that π_k, o_k and $\mathcal{X}_k$ are given in prices at time 0 and converted to those at k through Q_k.

Stochastic models for inflation and other financial variables are discussed in Chapter 13. Here is a simple example with claim intensities as in Section 11.4 and inflation. We may hang on to exponential first-order autoregressions, but there must now be two of them and two driver processes $X_{\mu k}$ and X_{ik} with μ and i defining the mother variable (the same convention is used for parameters). The joint model then becomes

$$\mu_k = \xi_\mu e^{-\tau_\mu^2/2 + \tau_\mu X_{\mu k}} \quad \text{and} \quad I_k = \xi_i e^{-\tau_i^2/2 + \tau_i X_{ik}},$$

where

$$X_{\mu k} = a_\mu X_{\mu,k-1} + \sqrt{1 - a_\mu^2}\,\varepsilon_{\mu k} \quad \text{and} \quad X_{ik} = a_i X_{i,k-1} + \sqrt{1 - a_i^2}\,\varepsilon_{ik}.$$

This is a recursion over $k = 1, 2, \ldots,$ starting at

$$X_{\mu 0} = \frac{\tau_\mu}{2} + \frac{\log(\mu_0/\xi_\mu)}{\tau_\mu} \quad \text{and} \quad X_{i0} = \frac{\tau_i}{2} + \frac{\log(i_0/\xi_i)}{\tau_i}.$$

Here μ_0 and i_0 are claim intensity and rate of inflation at the beginning, and ξ_μ, τ_μ, a_μ, ξ_i, τ_i and a_i are parameters similar to those in Section 11.4. *Negative* inflation is not possible under this model, but see Section 13.5.

Suppose $\mathcal{Y}_0 = v_0$ at the beginning. With all error terms $\varepsilon_{\mu k}$ and ε_{ik} independent and $N(0, 1)$, the scheme is implemented in Algorithm 11.3, where the claims $\mathcal{X}^*$ are based on fixed prices (Line 6) as are premia π_k and overhead o_k per policy. All three are adjusted for inflation when entered into the account on Line 8.

Algorithm 11.3 Portfolios with hidden risk and inflation

Input $\xi_\mu, \tau_\mu, a_\mu, \xi_i, \tau_i, a_i,\ v_0, \mu_0, i_0, J_1, \dots, J_K, \pi_1, \dots, \pi_K, o_k, \dots, o_K$
$\mathcal{Y}_0^* \leftarrow v_0,\ \ Q^* \leftarrow 1,\ \ X_\mu^* \leftarrow \tau_\mu/2 + \log(\mu_0/\xi_\mu)/\tau_\mu$
    and $X_i^* \leftarrow \tau_i/2 + \log(i_0/\xi_i)/\tau_i$ *%Starting the recursion*
For $k = 1, 2, \dots, K$ do
  Draw $\varepsilon_\mu^* \sim N(0,1),\ \ \varepsilon_i^* \sim N(0,1)$
  $X_\mu^* \leftarrow a_\mu X_\mu^* + \sqrt{1-a_\mu^2}\,\varepsilon_\mu^*,\ X_i^* \leftarrow a_i X_i^* + \sqrt{1-a_i^2}\,\varepsilon_i^*$ *%The linear processes*
  $\mu^* \leftarrow \xi_\mu \exp(-\tau_\mu^2/2 + \tau_\mu X_\mu^*)$ and $\lambda^* \leftarrow J_k \mu^*$ *%The Poisson parameter*
  Draw $\mathcal{N}^* \sim$ Poisson(λ^*) and then $\mathcal{X}^*$ *%$\mathcal{X}^*$ by usual commands*
  $I^* \leftarrow \xi_i \exp(-\tau_i^2/2 + \tau_i X_i^*)$ and $Q^* \leftarrow (1 + I^*)Q^*$ *%The new price level*
  $\mathcal{Y}_k^* \leftarrow (1+r)\mathcal{Y}_{k-1}^* + Q^*\{J_k(\pi_k - o_k) - \mathcal{X}^*\}$
Return $\mathcal{Y}_0^*, \dots, \mathcal{Y}_K^*$.

11.5.5 Example: Is inflation important?

Suppose the rate of inflation is 3% annually. The corresponding 10-year price increase is $1.03^{10} - 1 \doteq 34\%$, surely significant financially. What about the stochastic part? Random claim intensity has huge impact (as we have seen), but random inflation isn't necessarily equally important. Figure 11.5 is an illustration. The portfolio consists of $J_k = 100\,000$ identical policies with claim size distribution

$$Z_k = \xi_z e^{-\tau_z^2/2 + \tau_z \varepsilon} \quad \text{where } \varepsilon \sim N(0,1) \quad \text{and } \xi_z = 1000,\ \tau_z = 0.5.$$

Claim intensities μ_k and the rate of inflation I_k are exponential autoregressive processes starting at 0.042 and 0.03, respectively and independent. Their parameters are

$$\underbrace{\xi_\mu = 0.056,\ \tau_\mu = 0.125,\ a_\mu = 0.6}_{\text{claim intensity}} \quad \text{and} \quad \underbrace{\xi_i = 0.03,\ \tau_i = 0.5,\ a_i = 0.6,}_{\text{inflation}}$$

which yield $\mathrm{sd}(\mu_k) = 0.007$ and $\mathrm{sd}(I_k) = 0.016$ when k is so large that the initial values have been forgotten. At that point the pure premium per policy has become

$$\pi_k^{\mathrm{pu}} = E(\mu_k)E(Z_k) = \xi_\mu \xi_z = 1000 \times 0.056 = 56.$$

The net premium $\pi_k - o_k$ was selected 5% higher at 58.8. Financial income is not taken into account ($r = 0$ in Algorithm 11.3).

Simulated scenarios (100 replications) are shown in Figure 11.5. The reserve at the beginning was $v_0 = 6$ million. On the left, inflation was fixed at 3% at all times, but the results didn't change much when the stochastic component (not small at all) was added on the right. Is that odd? The reason is the uncertainty of claims dominating the uncertainty of inflation, but there is no rule here (it comes down to

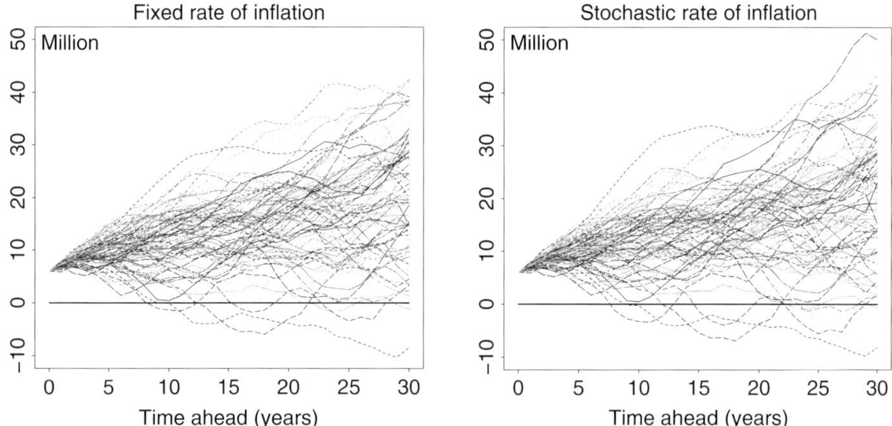

Figure 11.5 Net, nominal underwriter result under hidden risk and inflation (conditions in the text). Fixed inflation (*left*) and stochastic (*right*).

models and parameters), and things won't be the same at all with life insurance in Section 15.6. For the hugely uncertain business of property insurance, probably the very simplest of inflation modelling is good enough.

11.5.6 Market fluctuations

Insurance markets and premia fluctuate; see Daykin *et al.* (1994). Changes in premia affect solvency, but it might work the other way too. If solvency deteriorates, companies are tempted (or even forced) to raise prices, and premium and solvency influence each other mutually. Such mechanisms are known as **feedbacks** and will figure prominently with financial modelling in Chapter 13. A simple premium/solvency scheme will now be set up.

The approach follows that in Daykin *et al.* (1994), though not in detail. A central quantity is the **solvency ratio**, which is surplus over premium; i.e.,

$$y_k = \mathcal{Y}_k/\Pi_k \quad \text{where} \quad \Pi_k = J_k \pi_k.$$

If y_k falls dangerously, the market reacts by setting up prices which might be reduced when the financial situation has again become sound. Nothing of this happens instantly, and we must introduce a delay d that could be 1 or 2 years or more. A primitive imitation of the real mechanism is then

$$\pi_k = (1 + \gamma_k)\pi^{\text{pu}} \quad \text{where} \quad \gamma_k = \xi_\gamma e^{-a_\gamma(y_{k-d}-\xi_y)}. \tag{11.36}$$

Here π^{pu} is the pure premium that exactly covers claims on average, whereas the

Algorithm 11.4 Integrating market fluctuations

0 Input: Earlier parameters, $J_1,\dots,J_K$, $o_1,\dots,o_K$, ξ_γ, a_γ, ξ_y, π_0, π^{pu}, d

1 $\mathcal{Y}_0^* \leftarrow v_0$, $\pi^* \leftarrow \pi_0$ *%Premium at the beginning*

2 For $k = 1, 2, \dots$ do

3 Generate μ^* and $\mathcal{X}^*$ *%μ^* by Algorithm 11.3*

4 If $k \geq d$ then *%After delay d,*
$\gamma^* \leftarrow \xi_\gamma e^{-a_\gamma(y_{k-d}^*-\xi_y)}$ and $\pi^* \leftarrow (1+\gamma^*)\pi^{\mathrm{pu}}$ *update premium*

5 $\mathcal{Y}_k^* \leftarrow (1+r)\mathcal{Y}_{k-1}^* + J_k(\pi^* - o_k) - \mathcal{X}^*$

6 $y_k^* \leftarrow \mathcal{Y}_k^*/(J_k\pi^*)$ *%Solvency ratio for later use*

7 Return $\mathcal{Y}_0^*,\dots,\mathcal{Y}_K^*$.

loading γ_k captures market impact. A solvency ratio y_{k-d} deviating from some typical market value ξ_y pushes the loading towards ξ_γ a couple of years later. The mechanism resembles reversion to mean (Section 5.6) and is controlled by a_γ, which is ≥ 0. There is no market influence on premia if $a_\gamma = 0$.

Suppose a company solvency ratio is identified with the state of the market. This may be a tenable assumption when companies have a herd instinct that shapes their decisions. The preceding model for the loadings can then be applied to a single firm, and the effect on solvency examined through Algorithm 11.4 where the inflation has been removed. The new issue is the command on Line 4, where Monte Carlo loadings follow from the solvency ratio d time units earlier. A given premium level is used at the beginning.

11.5.7 Market fluctuations: Example

How the feedback model behaves has been indicated in Figure 11.6. Many of the underlying conditions are the same as in Figure 11.5. There were $J_k = 100\,000$ policies with the same models for claim intensity and size, but without inflation. Overhead was 20% of the pure premium, and the parameters of the feedback (11.36) were $\xi_\gamma = 0.25$, $a_\gamma = 1$, $\xi_y = 0.6$ and $d = 2$. Financial income was not taken into account.

At the beginning the reserve was $v_0 = 6$ million, the annual claim rate $\mu_0 = 0.042$ and the premium per policy was 25% higher than the pure premium at

$$\pi_0 = \xi_\mu \xi_z (1 + \xi_\gamma) = 0.056 \times 1000 \times 1.250 = 70.$$

The solvency ratio then starts at $y_0 = v_0/(J_0\pi_0) \doteq 0.86$, much *higher* than the typical market value $\xi_y = 0.6$, whereas the claim intensity at $\mu_0 = 0.042$ is *lower* than the long-term average 0.056. Either quantity will gradually be pushed towards the middle. How solvency ratio and premium interact when fed by the huge insurance

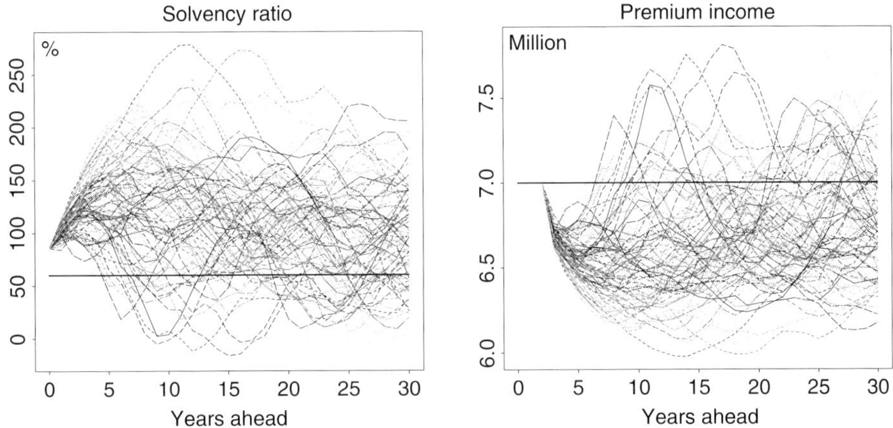

Figure 11.6 Fluctuations (100 scenarios) in the solvency ratio (*left*, %) and premia received (*right*) under the model described in the text.

uncertainty is a complex issue, and fluctuations in Figure 11.6 are wild. On the left there is a tendency for the solvency ratio to overshoot the target marked as the straight line. The premium on the right is pulled down uniformly at the beginning by the high solvency, margin at that point, but later oscillates strongly, influenced by solvency, and is often lower than the initial π_0. Random effects are in this example channelled through a feedback with delay, and it is hard to understand model behaviour without running experiments.

11.5.8 Taxes and dividend

How are taxes $\mathcal{T}_k$ and dividend to owners $\mathcal{D}_k$ worked in? The details depend on the tax code and dividend policy. A simple scheme can be constructed from pre-tax and pre-dividend profit $\mathcal{P}_k$ defined as

$$\mathcal{P}_k = \underbrace{(r\mathcal{Y}_{k-1} + J_k\pi_k)}_{\textit{financial income and premia}} - \underbrace{(J_k o_k + \mathcal{X}_k)}_{\textit{overhead and claims}},$$

which can also be written $\mathcal{P}_k = r\mathcal{Y}_{k-1} - \mathcal{U}_k$ where $\mathcal{U}_k = \mathcal{X}_k - J_k(\pi_k - o_k)$ is the underwriter result. If taxes and dividends are proportional, then

$$\underbrace{\mathcal{T}_k = \theta_t \max(\mathcal{P}_k, 0)}_{\textit{taxes}} \quad \text{and} \quad \underbrace{\mathcal{D}_k = \theta_d \max(\mathcal{P}_k, 0)}_{\textit{dividends}},$$

where θ_t and θ_d are coefficients defining tax code and dividend policy. If there has been a *loss* (i.e., if $\mathcal{P} < 0$), there is neither tax nor dividend under the scheme assumed. When inflation is disregarded, the implementation of taxes and dividends as additions to earlier simulation programs is carried out in Algorithm 11.5.

Algorithm 11.5 Integrating taxes and dividends

Input: Earlier models and θ_t, θ_d
$\mathcal{Y}_0^* \leftarrow v_0$
For $k = 1, 2, \dots, K$ do
  Generate π^* and $\mathcal{X}_k^*$ *%Earlier simulation programs*
  $\mathcal{P}^* \leftarrow r\mathcal{Y}_{k-1}^* + J_k(\pi^* - o_k) - \mathcal{X}^*$ *%Profit prior to tax and dividend*
  $\mathcal{T}^* \leftarrow 0$ and $\mathcal{D}^* \leftarrow 0$
  If $(\mathcal{P}^* > 0)$ then $\mathcal{T}^* \leftarrow \theta_t\mathcal{P}^*$ and $\mathcal{D}^* \leftarrow \theta_d\mathcal{P}^*$ *%Taxes and dividends computed*
  $\mathcal{Y}_k^* \leftarrow \mathcal{Y}_{k-1}^* + \mathcal{P}^* - \mathcal{T}^* - \mathcal{D}^*$
Return $\mathcal{Y}_0^*, \dots, \mathcal{Y}_K^*$.

Many other schemes of taxation and dividend policies can be contemplated, and those used above for illustration are not necessarily the most likely ones.

11.6 Cash flow or book value?

11.6.1 Introduction

Insurance portfolios may contain obligations that will not be liquidated until much later. In life and pension insurance (next chapter) this is the order of the day, but it occurs in property insurance too. One example is the IBNR claims of Section 8.5, which may surface long after the incident took place. Equally common are RBNS claims, which for various reasons take time to settle. Assessing cost may be a slow process, and legal disputes may drag on and on. All future incidents and losses, whose premium has been paid for, are portfolio responsibilities.

These are liabilities with 'long tails', and they must enter our books. How much they are going to cost eventually is not known precisely, yet no statement on the status of the portfolio can be complete without them, and money must be set aside. The purpose of this section is to define relationships between cash and book valuation and indicate how portfolios with outstanding claims can be simulated. A huge number of special methods have been invented for these situations; see Wütrich and Merz (2008).

11.6.2 Mathematical formulation

As before $\mathcal{Y}_k$ stands for cash, but now a second symbol $\mathcal{B}_k$ is needed for bookkeeping. Suppose taxes and dividends to owners are ignored. The scheme then becomes

$$\underbrace{\mathcal{Y}_k = \mathcal{Y}_{k-1} + r\mathcal{Y}_{k-1} + J_k(\pi_k - o_k) - \mathcal{X}_k}_{\text{cash flow}} \quad \text{and} \quad \underbrace{\mathcal{B}_k = \mathcal{Y}_k - \widehat{\mathcal{PV}}_k}_{\text{book value}} \tag{11.37}$$

for $k = 1, \dots, K$, where $\mathcal{Y}_k$ of the left keeps track of the cash flow and is a repetition of (11.1). On the right, the book value $\mathcal{B}_k$ has subtracted an estimate $\widehat{\mathcal{PV}}_k$ of coming losses for which the insurer bears responsibility. The valuation below is based on present values, hence the notation. The exact present value $\mathcal{PV}_k$ is not available, and an estimate must be supplied.

A general mathematical formulation requires portfolio losses $\mathcal{X}_{k+1}, \mathcal{X}_{k+2}, \dots$ to be split into one part which is pending at time k affecting solvency at that point and another part which does not. It is not particularly difficult to do this, but we shall proceed more simply and assume that $\mathcal{B}_k$ is influenced by the entire stream of future liabilities $\mathcal{X}_{k+1}, \mathcal{X}_{k+2}, \dots$ Portfolios in runoff are examples of this; see below. The present value of outstanding claims at k is then

$$\mathcal{PV}_k = d\mathcal{X}_{k+1} + d^2\mathcal{X}_{k+2} + \cdots,$$

where d is the discount. It may be a natural criterion, but future payoffs are not known exactly, and estimates must be supplied. Suppose the rules of book-keeping prescribe expected values. Then

$$\widehat{\mathcal{PV}}_k = de_{k+1|k} + d^2 e_{k+2|k} \dots, \quad \text{where} \quad e_{k+i|k} = E(\mathcal{X}_{k+i}|k) \tag{11.38}$$

and with $E(\mathcal{X}_{k+i}|k)$ being expectation given information upto k. The liability on the right in (11.37) has become a discounted sequence of such expected losses, but the eventual value might deviate substantially. Yet if book-keeping operates in this manner, that's how the system should be simulated.

Note the notation $e_{k+i|k}$, which signifies that the projected losses depend on *when* evaluations are taking place. That is how things are in real life, where new information leads to reassessments so that possibly $e_{k+i|k} \neq e_{k+i|k'}$ if $k \neq k'$. It may not be too easy to formalize such things in order to simulate them. The following example stays clear of this problem.

11.6.3 Adding IBNR claims

A simple model for IBNR accounting was presented in Section 8.5 through Poisson and multinomial modelling. The number of claims settled in year k was then Poisson distributed, and stochastically independent from one year to another. Let λ_k be the Poisson parameter for year k and ξ_{zk} the mean payoff per incident that year. The estimate of the total claim against the portfolio is then $e_{k|0} = \lambda_k \xi_{zk}$. This is the assessment at time 0, but it does not have to be revised later when new information is received, since all claim numbers are independent and it applies right up to time k. The loss projected at k can under these circumstances, be written $e_k = e_{k|0} = \lambda_k \xi_{zk}$ with no reference to the time it is being made.

Algorithm 11.6 Book values with IBNR

```
Input: d, r, v_0 and e_k = λ_k ξ_{zk}, k = 1, ..., K
  Y*_0 ← v_0 and PV^ ← d e_1 + d^2 e_2 + ···           %Expected present value
For k = 1, 2, ..., K do
    Generate X* and possibly π*                          %Earlier algorithms
    Y*_k ← (1 + r)Y*_{k−1} + J_k(π* − o) − X*
    PV^ ← PV^/d − e_k                                    %Present value updated
    B*_k ← Y*_k − PV^
Return B*_1, ..., B*_K.
```

To outline how (11.37) is simulated note that (11.38) yields the recursion

$$\widehat{\mathcal{PV}}_k = de_{k+1} + d\widehat{\mathcal{PV}}_{k+1}, \quad \text{so that} \quad \widehat{\mathcal{PV}}_{k+1} = \frac{\widehat{\mathcal{PV}}_k}{d} - e_{k+1}$$

for $k = 0, 1, \dots$ If Monte Carlo algorithms for $\mathcal{X}_k$ (and possibly π_k) are available, we are led to Algorithm 11.6. The technical interest rate corresponding to the discount d would often differ from the financial return r.

11.6.4 Example: Runoff portfolios

The difference between cash and book-keeping is illustrated by portfolios in **runoff** status. Portfolios are being closed down, and premia are no longer received, but outstanding claims that have been paid for earlier may still come in. With IBNR claims such portfolios may have to be kept alive for several decades after the last contract was drawn up. The situation is covered by Algorithm 11.6 if $\pi^* = 0$ is inserted.

The numerical experiment reported in Figure 11.7 is based on the IBNR delay model in Section 8.5, see Figure 8.5. There were 100 000 policies under risk, and the runoff lasts 20 years. Around 4000 claims can be expected to surface during that period. Poisson parameters λ_k for the claim numbers $\mathcal{N}_k$ are computed by (8.21). Losses per incident imitate personal injuries in automobile insurance through the model

$$Z_k = \xi_z e^{-\tau_z^2/2 + \tau_z \varepsilon_k} \quad \text{where} \quad \xi_z = 100\,000 \quad \text{and} \quad \tau_z = 1.$$

Overhead expenses are each year 20% of the expected losses, and $d = 1/1.02$. Simulations were run with no financial income (Figure 11.7 left) and with $r = 2\%$ (Figure 11.7 right). The initial reserve put up was $v_0 = 500$ million. At the beginning differences between cash and book values are huge, but they are wiped

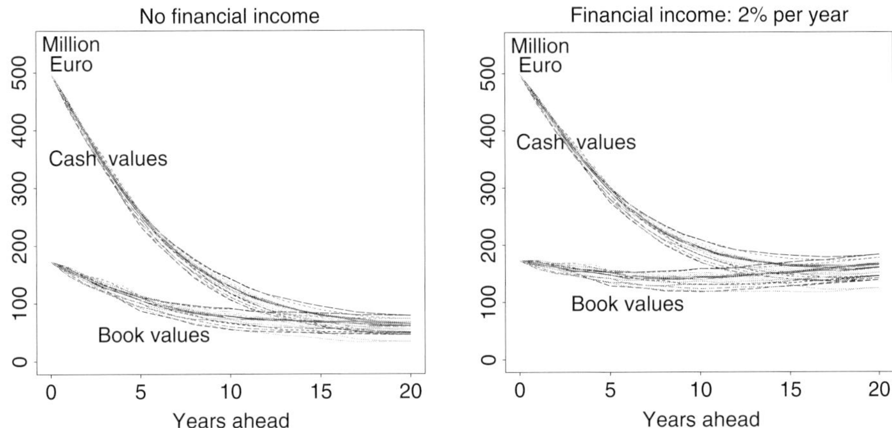

Figure 11.7 Simulated scenarios (20 replications) for runoff portfolio described in the text with both cash and book value recorded. *Left*: No financial income. *Right*: 2% interest annually.

out as obligations are being liquidated. Taking small financial earnings into account lifts the curves appreciatively.

11.7 Mathematical arguments

11.7.1 Lower-order moments of $\mathcal{Y}_k$ under constant risk

Suppose $v_k = av_{k-1} + b$ for $k = 1, 2, \ldots$ and interpret the sequence as an account growing as $a = 1 + r$ and receiving transfers b. After k periods the value is

$$v_k = a^k v_0 + \sum_{i=1}^{k} ba^{k-i} = a^k v_0 + b\sum_{i=0}^{k-1} a^i = a^k v_0 + b\frac{a^k - 1}{a - 1}, \quad a \neq 1.$$

If $a = 1 + r$ and $b = (\Pi_k - \mathcal{O}_k) - E(\mathcal{X}_k) = J(\pi - o - \mu\xi_z)$, then v_k coincides with $E(\mathcal{Y}_k)$ in (11.2), and (11.7) follows. Repeat the argument with $v_0 = 0$, $a = (1 + r)^2$ and $b = \text{var}(\mathcal{X}_k)$, which yields the standard deviation formula (11.8). Finally, take $v_0 = 0$, $a = (1+r)^3$ and $b = -v_3(\mathcal{X}_k)$. The recursion for v_k then coincides with (11.4) for the third-order moment, and this establishes

$$v_3(\mathcal{Y}_k) = -v_3(\mathcal{X}_k)\frac{(1 + r)^{3k} - 1}{(1 + r)^3 - 1}.$$

Divide by the expression for $\{\text{sd}(\mathcal{Y}_k)\}^3$, and skew$(\mathcal{Y}_k)$ emerges as (11.9).

11.7.2 Lundberg's inequality

Consider ruin in infinite time. This is the probability

$$p^{\rm ru}(v_0) = \Pr\{\min(\mathcal{Y}_1, \mathcal{Y}_2, \dots) < 0 \mid \mathcal{Y}_0 = v_0\},$$

which will be studied using an idea in Sundt (1999). Let $g(u)$ be the density function of one of the underwriting losses $\mathcal{U}$ and A the adjustment coefficient. Figure 11.1 then yields

$$M_u(A) = \int_{-\infty}^{\infty} e^{Au} g(u)du = 1, \qquad \frac{dM_u(A)}{dA} = \int_{-\infty}^{\infty} ue^{Au} g(u)du > 0,$$

and $g_A(u) = e^{Au}g(u)$ is a density function with positive mean. Ruin is, under such models, certain.

Suppose the account runs out of money exactly at time k. The probability of this event B_k is the k-dimensional integral

$$\int \cdots \int_{B_k} g(u_1) \cdots g(u_k)du_1 \cdots du_k = \int \cdots \int_{B_k} e^{-A(u_1+\cdots+u_k)} g_A(u_1) \cdots g_A(u_k)du_1 \cdots du_k$$

after inserting $g(u) = e^{-Au}g_A(u)$. But $u_1 + \cdots + u_k \geq v_0$ on B_k, and the second integral is therefore bounded above by

$$e^{-Av_0} \int \cdots \int_{B_k} g_A(u_1) \cdots g_A(u_k)du_1 \cdots du_k = e^{-Av_0}\Pr_A(B_k),$$

where $\Pr_A$ denotes probabilities under $g_A(u)$. Hence $\Pr(B_k) \leq e^{-Av_0} \Pr_A(B_k)$, and since ruin means that exactly one of the disjoint sequence of events $\{B_k\}$ occurs, this yields

$$p^{\rm ru}(v_0) = \sum_{k=1}^{\infty} \Pr(B_k) \leq e^{-Av_0} \sum_{k=1}^{\infty} \Pr_A(B_k) = e^{-Av_0} p_A^{\rm ru}(v_0) = e^{-Av_0},$$

utilizing that ruin under $g_A(u)$ is certain. But the ruin probability in finite time is even smaller, and the Lundberg bound $p^{\rm ru}(v_0) \leq e^{-Av_0}$ follows.

11.7.3 Moment-generating functions for underwriting

Suppose $\mathcal{U} = \mathcal{X} - J(\pi - o)$ where $\mathcal{X} = Z_1 + \cdots + Z_{\mathcal{N}}$ and $\mathcal{N} \sim \text{Poisson}(J\mu T)$. By the rule of double expectation

$$M_x(s) = E(e^{s\mathcal{X}}) = \sum_{n=0}^{\infty} E(e^{s\mathcal{X}}|\mathcal{N} = n)\Pr(\mathcal{N} = n) = \sum_{n=0}^{\infty} E(e^{s(Z_1+\cdots+Z_n)})\Pr(\mathcal{N} = n)$$

$$= \sum_{n=0}^{\infty} M_z(s)^n \frac{(J\mu T)^n}{n!} e^{-J\mu T} = \sum_{n=0}^{\infty} \frac{\{J\mu T M_z(s)\}^n}{n!} e^{-J\mu T} = e^{J\mu T(M_z(s)-1)},$$

and now

$$M_u(s) = E(e^{s\mathcal{U}}) = E(e^{s\mathcal{X}-sJ(\pi-o)}) = M_x(s)e^{-J(\pi-o)s} = e^{J\mu T\{M_z(s)-1\}-J(\pi-o)s}$$

which is (11.16).

11.7.4 Negative binomial regression

The random coefficient regression model in Section 11.3 was specified as

$$N_{jk}|\lambda_{jk} \sim \text{Poisson}(\lambda_{jk}) \quad \text{where} \quad \lambda_{jk} = T_{jk}\xi_{jk}G_k$$

for $j = 1, \ldots, J$ and $k = 1, \ldots, K$. Here T_{jk} is risk exposure, ξ_{jk} expected intensities and G_k random and common for all j. To fit the model the likelihood function for the observed counts n_{jk} is needed. There is a fairly simple expression for the log likelihood of observed counts n_{jk} when $G_k \sim \text{Gamma}(\alpha_k)$. Introduce

$$n_{\cdot k} = \sum_{j=1}^{J} n_{jk}, \quad p_{\cdot k} = \frac{\alpha_k}{\alpha_k + \sum_{j=1}^{J} T_{jk}\xi_{jk}}, \quad q_{jk} = \frac{T_{jk}\xi_{jk}}{\sum_{i=1}^{J} T_{ik}\xi_{ik}}$$

and let $\boldsymbol{\xi}$ and $\boldsymbol{\alpha}$ be the vector of all ξ_{jk} and all α_k, respectively. The log-likelihood function is then, except for constants,

$$\mathcal{L}(\boldsymbol{\xi}, \boldsymbol{\alpha}) = \underbrace{\mathcal{L}_1(\boldsymbol{\xi}, \boldsymbol{\alpha})}_{\textit{negative binomial}} + \underbrace{\mathcal{L}_2(\boldsymbol{\xi})}_{\textit{multinomial}}$$

where

$$\mathcal{L}_1(\boldsymbol{\xi}, \boldsymbol{\alpha}) = \sum_{k=1}^{K} \{\log\{\Gamma(n_{\cdot k} + \alpha_k)\} - \log\{\Gamma(\alpha_k)\} + \alpha_k \log(p_{\cdot k}) - n_{\cdot k} \log(1 - p_{\cdot k})\}$$

and

$$\mathcal{L}_2(\boldsymbol{\xi}) = \sum_{k=1}^{K} \sum_{j=1}^{J} n_{jk} \log(q_{jk}).$$

There is a multinomial and negative binomial part; we will see why shortly. Numerical optimization is required to compute estimates.

To derive this expression recall the independence between periods, which means that logarithms of the joint density function $f(n_{1k}, \ldots, n_{Jk})$ are added over k for the log likelihood. Now

$$f(n_{1k}, \ldots, n_{Jk}) = \underbrace{f(n_{\cdot k})}_{\textit{negative binomial}} \times \underbrace{f(n_{1k}, \ldots, n_{Jk}|n_{\cdot k})}_{\textit{multinomial}},$$

and the two density functions on the right are examined separately. Consider first the total number of claims $n_{\cdot k}$ which is, given G_k, a sum of independent Poisson variables and therefore Poisson itself. Its parameter is

$$\sum_{j=1}^{J}\lambda_{jk}=\left(\sum_{j=1}^{J}T_{jk}\xi_{jk}\right)G_k$$

after inserting for λ_{jk}. But this is exactly how the negative binomial model was defined in Section 8.3, and the negative binomial part $\mathcal{L}_1(\boldsymbol{\xi},\boldsymbol{\alpha})$ of the log-likelihood function becomes the expression above. The second part is similar to the delay model in Section 8.5, and multinomial. The probabilities are

$$q_{jk}=\frac{\lambda_{jk}}{\sum_{i=1}^{J}\lambda_{ik}}=\frac{T_{jk}\xi_{jk}G_k}{\sum_{i=1}^{J}T_{ik}\xi_{ik}G_k}=\frac{T_{jk}\xi_{jk}}{\sum_{i=1}^{J}T_{ik}\xi_{ik}}$$

where G_k has cancelled. Adding the logarithm of this second density function over k yields $\mathcal{L}_2(\boldsymbol{\xi},\boldsymbol{\alpha})$.

11.8 Bibliographical notes

11.8.1 Negative binomial regression

The model in Section 11.3 is a special case of random parameters in generalized linear regression; consult Lee *et al.* (2006) for a general treatment. Lawless (1987) and Hilbe (2007) discuss negative binomial regression specifically. Jørgensen and Paes de Souza (1994) might have been the first to apply the model to claim counts. Actuarial models with random seasonal effects as in Section 11.3 were proposed by Sundt (1979).

11.8.2 Claims as stochastic processes

The model in Section 11.3, where claim numbers $\{\mathcal{N}_k\}$ are conditionally independent given an underlying Markov process $\{\mu_k\}$, arose with Cox (1955). This is an example of a model of the **non-linear state space** type, which has a long history in engineering and statistics. A second example will appear in Section 13.2. Simulation is straightforward, but likelihood estimation is not, and simpler moment estimates were therefore presented in Section 11.4. Suitable, general reviews on state-space modelling are Durbin and Koopman (2001) and Commandeur and Koopman (2007), with Carlin (1992) discussing actuarial applications. All these references develop likelihood procedures for fitting models to historical data. They may be more accurate than moment estimates (see Fuh, 2006), but are also computationally heavy, typically demanding Markov chain Monte Carlo (Section 4.8). The linear sub-class where all relationships are linear and Gaussian is much easier technically and is handled by the Kalman–Bucy filter, well established in actuarial science. Early references are De Jong and Zehnwirth (1983) and Neuhaus (1987). Many dynamic models in insurance are non-linear, but they might be linearized to make Kalman–Bucy filtering applicable; see (for example) Dassios and Jang (2005) and also chapter 11 in Durbin and Koopman (2001). How well this works in actuarial science isn't known, but the related **extended** Kalman–Bucy filter has been popular in engineering for decades; see Gelb (1974).

11.8.3 Ruin

Ruin probabilities have occupied a prominent place in actuarial science for a century. You might enjoy Dickson (2005), a fairly elementary mathematical monograph with insurance applications. Asmussen (2000) has a broader perspective and is more advanced. The field has, since the turn of the century, witnessed an impressive outpour of scientific papers. Much of this research deals with optimal, dynamic strategies with respect to things like reinsurance, dividend policy or investments. Bäuerle (2004) solves an extended Markowitz problem (see Section 5.3), Liang and Guo (2007) and Guerra and Centeno (2008) maximize the adjustment coefficient (a proxy for ruin) and Schäl (2004), Bäuerle (2005), Dickson and Waters (2006), Schmidly (2006), Zhang *et al.* (2007) and Luo *et al.* (2008) minimize the ruin probability directly. Dividend payments are considered in Højgaard and Taksar (2004), Azcue and Muler (2005), Schmidly (2006) and Taksar and Hunderup (2007) and utilities in Irgens and Paulsen (2004), Schäl (2004) and Liang and Guo (2007). All these studies derive exact solutions under simplified models. Numerical optimization of Monte Carlo approximations would lead to much more general techniques, but this possibility is largely untried in property insurance. De Lange *et al.* (2004) is an exception; see also Section 15.8 for related references.

11.9 Exercises

Section 11.2

Exercise 11.1 The expressions (11.8) and (11.9) for the underwriter result $\mathcal{Y}_k$ may be written $\mathrm{sd}(\mathcal{Y}_k) = \mathrm{sd}(\mathcal{X})A_1(r)$ and $\mathrm{skew}(\mathcal{Y}_k) = -\mathrm{skew}(\mathcal{X})A_2(r)$, where

$$A_1(r) = \sqrt{\frac{(1+r)^{2k}-1}{(1+r)^2-1}} \quad \text{and} \quad A_2(r) = \frac{1}{A_1(r)^3}\frac{(1+r)^{3k}-1}{(1+r)^3-1}.$$

(a) Show that $A_1(r) \to \sqrt{k}$ and $A_2(r) \to 1/\sqrt{k}$ as $r \to 0$.

(b) Tabulate the coefficients $A_1(r)$ and $A_2(r)$ when $r = 1\%, 5\%, 10\%$ and when $k = 5, 20$ and judge how sensitively the variation of $\mathcal{Y}_k$ depends on r.

R-*commands*:

```
r=c(0.01,0.05,0.10); k=c(5,20);
A1=sqrt((exp(log(1+r)%o%(2*k))-1)/((1+r)**2-1));
A2=(exp(log(1+r)%o%(3*k))-1)/((1+r)**3-1)/A1**3.
```

Exercise 11.2 Suppose $\mathcal{Y}_k = \mathcal{Y}_{k-1} - \mathcal{U}_k$ where $\mathcal{U}_1, \mathcal{U}_2, \dots$ is an independent and identically distributed underwriter sequence with mean ξ_u and standard deviation σ_u.

(a) If the recursion starts at $\mathcal{Y}_0 = v_0$ and $\Phi(x)$ is the normal integral, argue that

$$\Pr(\mathcal{Y}_k \leq 0|v_0) \doteq \Phi(a_k) \quad \text{where} \quad a_k = \frac{-v_0 + k\xi_u}{\sqrt{k}\sigma_u}.$$

(b) Determine the limit of the probability as $k \to \infty$ when $\xi_u \neq 0$. What are the consequences for underwriting in the long run?

Exercise 11.3 Suppose premium π is paid at the beginning in a financial context where d is the discount per time unit. Let N be the number of claims and $Z_1, Z_2, \dots$ losses settled at random time points $S_1, S_2, \dots$

(a) What is the interpretation of $\text{PV} = \pi - d^{S_1} Z_1 - \cdots - d^{S_N} Z_N$?
(b) If $N \sim \text{Poisson}(\mu T)$ and $\xi_z = E(Z_i)$, show that $E(\text{PV}) = \pi - \mu T \xi_z E(d^S)$ under reasonable additional conditions. [*Hint*: Apply the rule of double expectation after first having calculated $E(\text{PV}|N, S_1, \dots S_N)$.]
(c) Argue that $\pi < \mu T \xi_z$ doesn't rule out $E(\text{PV}) > 0$.

Exercise 11.4 Let N in the preceding exercise be the number of claims in $(0, T)$ with $S_1, \dots, S_N$ *when* they occur, and PV the present value.

(a) Argue that the expected value of the stochastic discounts is $E(d^S|S < T)$, where S has the exponential density function $f(s) = \mu e^{-\mu s}$ in Exercise 8.1.
(b) Show that

$$E(PV) = \pi - \frac{\mu^2 T \xi_z}{\mu - \log(d)} \frac{1 - d^T e^{-\mu T}}{1 - e^{-\mu T}}.$$

[*Hint*: Argue that $E(d^S|S < T) = \int_0^T d^s f(s) ds / \int_0^T f(s) ds$ and evaluate the integrals before calculating $E(PV)$ as in Exercise 11.3.]
(c) Which well-known expression does this reduce to when $d = 1$?

Exercise 11.5 Suppose the number of policies J_k varies with k (as part of a plan for future growth), making the underwriter results $\mathcal{U}_k = \mathcal{X}_k - J_k(o - \pi)$ where $\mathcal{X}_k$ is the sum of claims from J_k policies.

(a) If $\mathcal{Y}_k$ is the *accumulated* underwriter result with $\mathcal{Y}_0 = v_0$ at the beginning, argue that $E(\mathcal{Y}_k) = v_0 - (J_1 + \cdots + J_k)(\mu T \xi_z - \pi + o)$ for $k = 1, 2, \dots$
(b) Let $J_k = J_0(1 + \omega)^k$ and show that

$$E(\mathcal{Y}_k) = v_0 - J_0(\mu T \xi_z - \pi + o) \frac{(1 + \omega)^k - 1}{\omega}(1 + \omega).$$

[*Hint*: Utilize that $1 + x + \cdots + x^{k-1} = (x^k - 1)/(x - 1)$ if $x \neq 1$.]

(c) Determine $E(\mathcal{Y}_k)$ as $\omega \to 0$ and interpret the limit.

Exercise 11.6 Repeat the calculations in Exercise 11.5 for the variances.

(a) Introduce standard assumptions and argue that $\text{var}(\mathcal{Y}_k) = \text{var}(\mathcal{Y}_{k-1}) + J_k\mu T(\xi_z^2 + \sigma_z^2)$ for $k = 1, 2, \ldots$
(b) If $J_k = J_0(1+\omega)^k$, show that

$$\text{var}(\mathcal{Y}_k) = J_0\mu T(\xi_z^2 + \sigma_z^2)\frac{(1+\omega)^k - 1}{\omega}(1+\omega).$$

(c) Compute and interpret the limit of $\text{var}(\mathcal{Y}_k)$ as $\omega \to 0$.

Exercise 11.7 Let Z be exponential with density function $f(z) = \xi_z^{-1}e^{-z/\xi_z}$ for $z > 0$.

(a) Verify that the moment-generating function is $M_z(s) = (1 - \xi_z s)^{-1}$.
(b) Use (11.17) and argue that the adjustment coefficient A satisfies the equation

$$\frac{1}{1 - \xi_z A} - 1 = \frac{\pi - o}{\mu T}A \quad \text{so that} \quad A = \frac{1}{\xi_z} - \frac{\mu T}{\pi - o}.$$

(c) Argue that the Lundberg equation $e^{-A\overline{v}_{0\epsilon}} = \epsilon$ defines an upper bound $\overline{v}_{0\epsilon}$ on capital which keeps the ruin probability below ϵ and compute $\overline{v}_{0\epsilon}$ when $\mu T = 0.05$, $\xi_z = 20$, $\pi - o = 1.1$ and $\epsilon = 1\%$. [*Answers*: $A = 0.0045455$ and $\overline{v}_{0\epsilon} = 1013$.]

Exercise 11.8 How much is the upper bound $\overline{v}_{0\epsilon}$ in Exercise 11.7 improved by the approximation (11.18) with the equation for $\overline{v}_{0\epsilon}$ now being $Ce^{-A\overline{v}_{0\epsilon}} = \epsilon$?

(a) Look up the constant C in (11.18) right and show that it becomes $C = \mu T\xi_z/(\pi - o)$ if Z is exponential.
(b) Compute the competing bound $\overline{v}_{0\epsilon} = \log(C/\epsilon)/A$ under the conditions of the preceding exercise. [*Answer*: $\overline{v}_{0\epsilon} = 992$.]

Exercise 11.9 Consider the ruin probability $p^{\text{ru}}(v_0)$ when Z is Pareto distributed with finite mean.

(a) With $F(z) = 1 - (1 + z/\beta)^{-\alpha}$ the distribution function argues that, by evaluating the integral in (11.19);

$$p^{\text{ru}}(v_0) \sim \frac{\mu T\xi_z}{(\pi - o) - \mu T\xi_z}[1 + v_0/\{(\alpha-1)\xi_z\}]^{-(\alpha-1)} \quad \text{where} \quad \xi_z = \beta/(\alpha - 1).$$

(b) Use this to determine an upper bound $\overline{v}_{0\epsilon}$ on the initial capital.
(c) Compute $\overline{v}_{0\epsilon}$ when $\mu T = 0.05, \beta = 20, \alpha = 2, \pi - o = 1.1$ and $\epsilon = 1\%$ [*Answer*: $\overline{v}_{0\epsilon} = 19\,980$.]

Exercise 11.10 How accurate are the upper bounds of the preceding exercises? This can be checked by means of Monte Carlo, and the method was developed in Section 3.6; see Exercises 3.30 and 3.33 for the implementation.

(a) Assume the situation in Exercises 11.7 and 11.8 and compute v_ϵ for all combinations of $K = 10$ and $K = 20$; $J = 100$, 10 000 and 100 000.

R-*commands*:

Download the R-function `e1110a` from the library and use
$v_{0\epsilon}$`=e1110a(m=10000,K,`μ`T,J,`ξ_z`,`π`-o,`ϵ`)`.

(b) Redo (a) for the Pareto loss distribution in Exercise 11.9.

R-*commands*:

Now use `e1110b` with $v_{0\epsilon}$`=e1110b(m=10000,K,`μ`T,J,`α`,`β`,`π`-o,`ϵ`)`.

Section 11.3

Exercise 11.11 Consider a Poisson regression with gear type and driving limit as covariates and with seasonal variables and a general trend. The model is

$$\log(\xi_{glk}) = \underbrace{b_0}_{\textit{intercept}} + \underbrace{b_g(g)}_{\textit{gear type}} + \underbrace{b_l(l)}_{\textit{driving limit}} + \underbrace{b_d kT}_{\textit{drift}} + \underbrace{b_s(s_k)}_{\textit{seasonal}},$$

which is on a monthly time scale. The parameters are those in Table 11.2, which was obtained from the Norwegian claim data in the text.

(a) Is the monthly drift upwards statistically significant on the Wald criterion in Exercise 10.15?

(b) What about the difference between the two gear types?

(c) Plot $e^{b_l(l)}$ against the driving limits and explain what this tells us.

R-*commands*:

Identify unlimited mileage with 50 and use
`dlim=matrix(scan(‘‘drivinglimit.txt’’),byrow=T,ncol=2);`
a_l`=dlim[,1]; `b_l`=dlim[,2]; plot(`a_l`,exp(`b_l`))`.

(d) Also plot e^{b_l}/a_l against a_l and interpret what you now see.

R-*commands*:

`plot(`a_l`,exp(`b_l`)/`a_l`)`.

Exercise 11.12

(a) What is the meaning of the quantity $\gamma_k = e^{b_d kT} - 1$ where b_d is the monthly drift in Table 11.2?

(b) Compute/plot γ_k with 95% log-normal confidence limit for k up to $K = 48$ when $T = 1$.

Table 11.2 Estimated (monthly) coefficients for the Poisson regression model in Section 11.3 with their standard deviation in parentheses

Intercept	−5.407 (0.010)	Manual gear	0
Monthly drift	0.0057% (0.0002%)	Automatic gear	−0.340 (0.005)
	Seasonal	Driving limits (1000 km)	
January	0	8	0
February	−0.088 (0.010)	12	0.097 (0.006)
Mars	−0.323 (0.011)	16	0.116 (0.007)
April	−0.426 (0.012)	20	0.198 (0.008)
May	−0.270 (0.011)	25	0.227 (0.019)
June	−0.406 (0.012)	30	0.308 (0.012)
July	−0.294 (0.011)	No limit	0.468 (0.019)
August	−0.248 (0.011)		
September	−0.137 (0.011)		
October	−0.133 (0.012)		
November	−0.001 (0.011)		
December	−0.132 (0.012)		

R-*commands*:

With $b_d = 0.000057$, $\sigma_{b_d} = 0.000002$ use `kk=1:K;` γ_k`=exp(kk*T*`b_d`)-1; lower=exp(kk*T*(`b_d`-2*`σ_{b_d}`))-1; upper=exp(kk*(`b_d`+2*`σ_{b_d}`))-1; plot(kk,`γ_k`); lines(kk,lower); lines(kk,upper)`.

Exercise 11.13

(a) What is the meaning of the quantities $e^{b_s(s)}$ where $b_s(s)$ are the seasonal parameters in Exercise 11.11?

(b) Plot $e^{b_s(s)}$ against s and summarize the main features of what you see.

R-*commands*:

b_s`=scan(''season.txt''); plot(1:12,exp(`b_s`),''l'')`.

Exercise 11.14 Suppose the premium for the car insurance in Table 11.2 is paid at the start of the year.

(a) If a customer leaves the company at the end of month s, argue that it is fair to return a part γ_s of the premium where

$$\gamma_s = \frac{e^{b_s(s+1)} + \cdots + e^{b_s(12)}}{e^{b_s(1)} + \cdots + e^{b_s(12)}}.$$

(b) Plot γ_s against s for the parameters in Table 11.2.

R-*commands*:

b_s=scan(''season.txt''); γ_s=1-cumsum(exp(b_s))/sum(exp(b_s)); plot(1:12,γ_s,ylim=c(0,1)).

Exercise 11.15 Consider time-varying, random intensities $\mu_k = \xi_k G_k$ with $G_k \sim$ Gamma(α_k) and $\xi_k = e^{b_0+b_s(s_k)}$ where the seasonal parameters $b_s(s)$ and the intercept b_0 are those in Table 11.2.

(a) Generate and plot $m = 20$ simulations of $\mu_1, \dots, \mu_{12}$ when, as in Table 11.1, $\alpha_k = 4$ for the first and last three months of the year and $\alpha_k = 20.6$ for the rest.

R-*commands*:

With $\alpha_1 = 4$ and $\alpha_2 = 20.6$ use b_s=scan(''season.txt''); α=c(rep(α_1,3),rep(α_2,6),rep(α_1,3)); μ=exp(b_0+b_s)*rgamma(12*m,α)/α; μ=matrix(μ,12,m); matplot(1:12,μ,''l'').

(b) Redo for $\alpha_1 = 1000$ and $\alpha_2 = 1000$ and compare with the plot in Exercise 11.13.

Section 11.4

Exercise 11.16 The dynamic model (11.25) and (11.26) is driven by a Gaussian first-order autoregressive process $\{X_k\}$ converted to intensities through $U_k = \Phi(X_k)$, $G_k = F_0^{-1}(U_k)$ and $\mu_k = \xi G_k$, where $F_0(x)$ has mean 1 and $\Phi(x)$ is the Gaussian integral.

(a) If $\tau > 0$ is a parameter, argue that $F_0^{-1}(u) = e^{-\tau^2/2+\tau\Phi^{-1}(u)}$ is the percentile function of a log-normal variable with mean 1.
(b) Show that $\{\mu_k\}$ with this choice of $F_0^{-1}(u)$ follows the Black–Karasinski model $\mu_k = \xi e^{-\tau^2/2+\tau X_k}$ for $k = 1, 2, \dots$

Exercise 11.17 When $\{X_k\}$ is the autoregressive process in (11.23) right, define

$$\mu_k = \xi[-\log\{1 - \Phi(X_k)\}], \quad k = 1, 2, \dots$$

(a) Show that this is a dynamic model for $\{\mu_k\}$ with exponential marginal distribution. [*Hint*: $F_0^{-1}(u) = -\log(1-u)$ for the exponential distribution with mean 1.]
(b) Why should the recursion for X_k be started at $X_0 = \Phi^{-1}(1 - e^{-\mu_0/\xi})$ where μ_0 is the intensity at the beginning?

Exercise 11.18 The Weibull distribution function with parameter $\alpha > 0$ and mean 1 is $F_0(x) = 1 - e^{-(x/\beta)^\alpha}$ where $\beta = 1/\{1 + \Gamma(\alpha^{-1})\}$; see Section 2.5 and (2.32) in particular.

(a) Show that the Weibull version of the model in the preceding exercises is

$$\mu_k = \frac{\xi}{1+\Gamma(\alpha^{-1})}[-\log\{1-\Phi(X_k)\}]^{1/\alpha}, \quad k=1,2,\ldots$$

(b) Explain why the recursion for X_k should be started at

$$X_0 = \Phi^{-1}(1-e^{-\{\mu_0\{1+\Gamma(\alpha^{-1})\}/\xi\}^\alpha}).$$

Exercise 11.19

(a) Write a program generating m simulations of $\mu_1,\ldots,\mu_K$ when they follow the log-normal model in Exercise 11.16.

R-*commands*:

```
X0=τ/2+log(μ0/ξ)/τ; s=sqrt(1-a*a); X=matrix(X0,K+1,m);
for (k in 1:K+1) X[k,]=a*X[k-1,]+s*rnorm(m);
μ=ξ*exp(-τ**2/2+τ*X[1:K+1,]).
```

(b) Extend the program so that it simulates $\mathcal{N}_1,\ldots,\mathcal{N}_K$ under conditional independence when $\mathcal{N}_k|\mu_k \sim \text{Poisson}(J\mu_k T)$.

R-*commands*:

```
N=matrix(rpois(K*m,JT*μ),K,m).
```

(c) Run the programs in (a) and (b) when $m=20$, $JT=1000$, $K=20$, $\mu_0=0.08$, $\xi=0.05$, $\tau=0.5$ and $a=0.6$ and plot the simulated claim counts jointly against time.

R-*commands*:

```
matplot(1:K,N,''l'').
```

Exercise 11.20

(a) Redo the simulations in Exercise 11.19(c) when $m = 10\,000$ (or preferably $m=100\,000$) and plot approximate evaluations of $E(\mathcal{N}_k)$ against k.

R-*commands*:

With `N` as in the preceding exercise use $\overline{N}$= `apply(N,1,mean);` `plot(1:K,`$\overline{N}$`).`

(b) Redo (a) for the standard deviation.

R-*commands*:

```
sN=apply(N,1,sd); plot(1:K, sN).
```

Theoretical expressions with the initial situation forgotten are $E(\mathcal{N}_k) = J\xi T$ and $\text{var}(\mathcal{N}_k) = J\xi T + (J\xi T)^2(e^{\tau^2}-1)$.

(c) Do the curves in (a) and (b) match their numerical values $E(\mathcal{N}_k) = 50$ and $\text{sd}(\mathcal{N}_k) = 27.6$?

Exercise 11.21

(a) Modify the programs in Exercise 11.19 so that they apply to Gamma-distributed intensities with shape α.

R-*commands*:

Change the first and last command in Exercise 11.19(a) to
X_0=qnorm(pgamma(μ_0/ξ*α,α)) and
μ=ξ*qgamma(pnorm(X[1:K+1,]),α)/α.

(b) Run the programs and plot simulated scenarios against time when $\alpha = 3.521$ with the rest of the conditions as in Exercise 11.19(c).

R-*commands*:

```
matplot(1:K,N,''l'').
```

[*Comment*: You won't see much difference from the plots in Exercise 11.19(c) since the mean and standard deviation are the same under either model; see Exercise 8.12 for the calibration.]

Exercise 11.22 Suppose the dynamic model in Section 11.4 has Gamma-distributed claim intensities.

(a) Write a program computing the parameter estimates (11.29)–(11.33) when m simulated sequences of historical data from J policies have been generated for K years.

R-*commands*:

With the data as the columns of nn, use $\hat{\mu}$=pmax(nn/J,0.0001);
$\hat{\xi}$=apply($\hat{\mu}$,2,mean); Var=pmax(apply($\hat{\mu}$,2,var)-$\hat{\xi}$/J,0.0001);
$\hat{\alpha}$=$\hat{\xi}$**2/Var;$\hat{X}$=qnorm(pgamma($\hat{\mu}/\hat{\xi}$*$\hat{\alpha}$,$\hat{\alpha}$));
$\hat{a}$=apply($\hat{X}$[2:K-1,]*$\hat{X}$[2:K,],2,mean)/apply($\hat{X}$**2,2,mean).

(b) To check the program generate simulations for $m = 10$, $K = 1000$, $JT = 100\,000$, $\mu_0 = 0.08$, $\xi = 0.05$, $\alpha = 3.5$ and $a = 0.6$ and compute/print estimates.

R-*commands*:

Use Exercise 11.21(a) for the Monte Carlo.

Exercise 11.23 Suppose $\mu_0 = 0.08$, $\xi = 0.05$, $\alpha = 3.5$ and $a = 0.6$ as in the preceding exercise, but now with data of realistic length $K = 20$ years.

(a) Draw $m = 1000$ replications of such series when $JT = 1000$ and compute equally many estimates with their mean and standard deviations.

R-*commands*:

After generating simulations and computing vectors $\hat{\xi}$, $\hat{\alpha}$ and $\hat{a}$ as in Exercise 11.22(a), use mean($\hat{\xi}$), sd($\hat{\xi}$) and so on.

(b) Interpret the results.

(c) Redo (a) when $JT = 100\,000$ to see how much the results change when the portfolio is larger.

Exercise 11.24 The initial intensity μ_0 when claim numbers are simulated is only known indirectly through a Poisson variable $\mathcal{N}_0 = n_0$ with parameter $J\mu_0 T$.

(a) If $p(\mu_0)$ is a prior density function for μ_0, argue that the posterior density function becomes $p(\mu_0|n_0) = c\mu_0^{n_0}e^{-J\mu_0 T}p(\mu_0)$ for some constant c.
(b) Insert the Gamma prior $p(\mu_0) = c\mu_0^{\alpha-1}e^{-\alpha\mu_0/\xi}$ and show that the posterior distribution becomes a second Gamma model.
(c) How do we draw from it? [*Reminder*: These calculations were also carried out in Section 10.5.]

Section 11.5

Exercise 11.25 Let $\mathcal{N}_k \sim \text{Poisson}(J_k\mu_k T)$ be the number of claims and $Z_k = \xi_z G_k$ with $G_k \sim \text{Gamma}(\alpha)$ the losses at time k.

(a) Write a program generating m simulations of $\mathcal{X}_1,\dots,\mathcal{X}_K$ with $J_1,\dots,J_K$ and m simulations of $\mu_1,\dots,\mu_K$ as input.

R-*commands*:

If `J=`$(J_1,\dots,J_K)$ and μ is a $K\times m$ matrix of simulations of $\mu_1,\dots,\mu_K$ use `λ=J*μ*T; X=array(0,m*K); N=rpois(m*K,λ); for (i in 1:(m*K)) X[i]=ξz*sum(rgamma(N[i],α)/α; X=matrix(X,K,m)`.

(b) Run the program when $m = 50$, $K = 20$, $J_k = J_0(1+\omega)^k$ with $J_0 = 1000$ and $\omega = 0.10$, $\mu_1 = \dots = \mu_K = 0.05$, $T = 1$, $\xi_z = 20$ and $\alpha = 1$.

R-*commands*:

Use (a) with `J=J0*(1+ω)**(1:K)` and $\mu = 0.05$.

(c) Plot the simulations jointly against time and interpret the pattern.

R-*commands*:

```
matplot(1:K,X,''l'').
```

Exercise 11.26 Suppose the claim intensities in Exercise 11.25 are made random through the log-normal autoregression $\mu_k = \xi_\mu e^{-\tau_\mu^2/2+\tau_\mu X_k}$ with $X_k = a_\mu X_{k-1} + \sqrt{1-a_\mu^2}\varepsilon_k$.

(a) Generate $m = 50$ simulations of $\mathcal{X}_1,\dots,\mathcal{X}_K$ when $K = 20$, $\mu_0 = 0.05$, $\xi_\mu = 0.05$, $\tau_\mu = 0.3$ and $a_\mu = 0.7$ with the rest of the conditions as in Exercise 11.25.

R-*commands*:

Use the program in Exercise 11.19 to generate a $K\times m$ matrix μ of simulated intensities as input to the program in Exercise 11.25.

(b) Plot the simulated scenarios of $\mathcal{X}_1,\dots,\mathcal{X}_K$ against time and compare with Exercise 11.25(c).

R-*commands*:

```
matplot(1:K,X,''l'').
```

(c) Repeat (a) and (b) when $a_\mu = 0$ and $a_\mu = 1$ and interpret the patterns you see.

Exercise 11.27 The net result due to underwriting grows as $\mathcal{Y}_k = \mathcal{Y}_{k-1} - \mathcal{U}_k$, where $\mathcal{U}_k = \mathcal{X}_k - J_k(\pi - o)$,

(a) Write a program simulating $\mathcal{Y}_0, \ldots, \mathcal{Y}_K$ given m realizations of $\mathcal{X}_1, \ldots, \mathcal{X}_K$ when $\mathcal{Y}_0 = v_0$ at the beginning.

R-*commands*:

With `J` and `X` as in the preceding exercises use `U=X-J*(`π`-`o`);` `Y=`v_0`-apply(U,2,cumsum); Y=rbind(rep(`v_0`,m),Y)`.

(b) Run the program with the simulations of $\mathcal{X}_1, \ldots, \mathcal{X}_K$ in Exercise 11.25 and plot $\mathcal{Y}_0, \ldots, \mathcal{Y}_K$ against time when $\pi - o = 1.1$ and $v_0 = 1000$.

R-*commands*:

`matplot(0:K,Y,''l'')`.

(c) Redo (b) for the simulations in Exercise 11.26(b) and comment on the change.

Exercise 11.28 Let $v_{0\epsilon}$ be the capital which with probability $1 - \epsilon$ keeps the underwriter account in Exercise 11.27 positive at all times up to K.

(a) Write a program computing $v_{0\epsilon}$ approximately through Monte Carlo.

R-*commands*:

The method was outlined in Section 3.6. You run the program in Exercise 11.27 with $\mathcal{Y}_0 = 0$ and with the simulations stored as the m columns of `Y` use `Ymin=apply(Y,2,min);` $v_{0\epsilon}$`=-sort(Ymin)[`ϵ`*m]`.

(b) Look $K = 5$ years ahead and compute $v_{0\epsilon}$ under the conditions in Exercise 11.25(b) when $\epsilon = 0.05$ and 0.01.

R-*commands*:

Run the program in Exercise 11.27(a) with $m = 10\,000$ (or if you can afford it $m = 100\,000$) and $K = 5$ prior to the commands in (a).

(c) Redo (b) when $\alpha = 4$ so that the losses are less variable.

(d) Comment on how the results depend on ϵ and α.

Exercise 11.29

(a) Compute the reserve $v_{0\epsilon}$ under the model in Exercise 11.26(a) when $K = 5$ and $\epsilon = 0.05$ and 0.01.

R-*commands*:

Generate $m = 10\,000$ simulations of $\mathcal{Y}_0, \ldots, \mathcal{Y}_K$ with $\mathcal{Y}_0 = 0$ through the program in Exercise 11.27(a) after having drawn $\mathcal{X}_1, \ldots, \mathcal{X}_K$ and follow Exercise 11.28(a).

(b) Redo a few times to get a feeling for the Monte Carlo uncertainty.

(c) Redo (a) when $\alpha = 4$ instead of $\alpha = 1$ to examine the effect of the loss distribution being less variable.

(d) Explain why the results are so insensitive α compared with what they were in Exercise 11.28.

Exercise 11.30 Suppose rising prices affect losses and income equally with the rate of inflation being the log-normal $I_k = \xi_i e^{-\tau_i^2/2+\tau_i X_k}$ where $X_k = a_i X_{k-1} + \sqrt{1-a_i^2}\varepsilon_k$.

(a) Write a program generating m simulations of future price levels $Q_1, \ldots, Q_K$ when $I_0 = \xi_i$ and $Q_0 = 1$.

R-*commands*:

```
X=matrix(0,K+1,m);
for (k in 1:K+1)X[k,]=ai*X[k-1,]+sqrt(1-ai**2)*rnorm(m);
I=ξi*exp(-τi**2/2+τi*X[1:K+1,); Q=apply(1+I,2,cumprod).
```

(b) Redo the computations of $v_{0\epsilon}$ in Exercise 11.28(b) a few times when $\xi_i = 0.03$, $\sigma_i = 0.5$ and $a_i = 0.6$.

R-*commands*:

With Y as in Exercise 11.28 use `QYmin=apply(Q*Y[1:K+1,],2,min);` `v0ϵ=-sort(QYmin)[ϵ*m]`.

(c) Redo (b) a few times when $\sigma_i = 0$ (inflation fixed) and when $\xi_i = 0$ (no inflation) and comment on the impact of inflation in this example.

Exercise 11.31

(a) Write a program computing an approximate solution $v_{0\epsilon}$ of the ruin equation when there is financial income with a fixed rate of interest r.

R-*commands*:

Let X be a matrix of simulated losses and J the vector of portfolio counts as in Exercise 11.25. Draw on (3.27) in Section 3.6 and use `U=X-J*(π-o);` `B=U/(1+r)**(1:K); S=apply(B,2,cumsum);` `Smax=apply(S,2,max); v0ϵ=sort(Smax)[(1-ϵ)*m]`.

(b) Generate $m = 10\,000$ or $m = 100\,000$ simulations of $\mathcal{X}_1, \ldots, \mathcal{X}_K$ up to $K = 5$ under the conditions in Exercise 11.25(b) and compute $v_{0\epsilon}$ for $\epsilon = 0.05$ and 0.01 when $\pi - o = 1.1$ and $r = 0.03$.

R-*commands*:

The program in Exercise 11.25 prior to that in (a).

(c) Redo (b) when $r = 0$ and check that the answer is close to that in Exercise 11.28(b).

(d) Redo (b) and (c) when $K = 20$.

(e) Comment on how much capital requirements are lowered by including future financial earnings.

Exercise 11.32 Introduce into the scheme in Exercise 11.27 financial income with a fixed rate of interest r and taxes of the form $\mathcal{T}_k = \theta \max(\mathcal{P}_k, 0)$ where $\mathcal{P}_k = r\mathcal{Y}_{k-1} - \mathcal{U}_k$ is pre-tax profit.

(a) Write a program generating m simulations of $\mathcal{Y}_0, \dots, \mathcal{Y}_K$ now.

R-*commands*:

With `X` and `J` as in Exercise 11.27 use `U=X-J*(π-o);`
`Y=matrix(v0,K+1,m); for (k in 1:K) {P=r*Y[k,]-U[k,];`
`T=θ*pmax(P,0); Y[k+1,]=(1+r)*Y[k,]-U[k,]-T}.`

(b) Run the program under the conditions in Exercise 11.27(b) when $r = 0.04$ and $\theta = 0.1$ and plot the simulations jointly against time.

R-*commands*:

`matplot(0:K,Y,''l'').`

(c) Redo (b) for the simulations in Exercise 11.27(c).

Section 11.6

Exercise 11.33 Let $\mathcal{X}_1, \dots, \mathcal{X}_K$ be future payoffs in an IBNR situation with independent and Poisson-distributed number of claims with parameters $\lambda_k = Ae^{-\gamma|k-k_m|}$ for $k = 1, \dots, K$.

(a) Write a program generating m simulations of $\mathcal{X}_1, \dots, \mathcal{X}_K$ when the losses are Gamma distributed as in Exercise 11.25.

R-*commands*:

Use the program in Exercise 11.25(a) with `λ=A*exp(-γ*abs(1:K-km)).`

(b) Run the program when $m = 50$, $K = 20$, $A = 100$, $\gamma = 0.25$, $k_m = 5$, $\xi_z = 20$ and $\alpha = 1$ and plot the portfolio losses against time for the simulated scenarios jointly.

R-*commands*:

`matplot(1:K,X,''l'').`

(c) Redo for $A = 1000$ and note how the underlying pattern now emerges more clearly.

Exercise 11.34 Suppose the IBNR scheme of the preceding exercise is in runoff with no premium coming in, so that the underwriter account evolves as $\mathcal{Y}_k = \mathcal{Y}_{k-1} - O_k - \mathcal{X}_k$.

(a) If the expenses $O_k = \theta\lambda_k\xi_z$ are proportional to the expected payment in year k, write a program computing the initial capital $v_{0\epsilon}$ necessary to keep the account positive up to time K with probability $1 - \epsilon$.

R-*commands*:

Utilize that $\mathcal{Y}_K = \min(\mathcal{Y}_1, \ldots, \mathcal{Y}_K)$. With `X` and λ as in Exercise 11.33(a), use `O=`θ`*`λ`*`ξ_z`; Ymin=-apply(X+O,2,sum);`
$v_{0\epsilon}$`=-sort(Ymin)[`ϵ`*m]`.

(b) Assume the conditions in Exercise 11.33(b) and determine $v_{0\epsilon}$ for $\epsilon = 0.01$ and 0.05 when $\theta = 0.1$.

Exercise 11.35 Add financial earnings to the scheme in Exercise 11.34 so that the recursion now reads $\mathcal{Y}_k = (1 + r)\mathcal{Y}_{k-1} - O_k - \mathcal{X}_k$ where r is a fixed rate of interest.

(a) Write a program computing $v_{0\epsilon}$ now.

R-*commands*:

With `X` and λ as before use the commands in Exercise 11.31(a) with `J=1;` π`=0; o=`θ`*`λ`*`ξ_z.

(b) Compute the initial capital $v_{0\epsilon}$ under the conditions in the preceding exercise when $r = 0.03$ and 0.05 and compare with the result in Exercise 11.34.

Exercise 11.36

(a) Write a program generating m simulations of $\mathcal{Y}_0, \ldots, \mathcal{Y}_K$ in the preceding exercise when $\mathcal{Y}_0 = v_0$ at the beginning.

R-*commands*:

With `X` and λ generated as in Exercise 11.33, use

```
O=θ*λ*ξz; Y=matrix(v0,K+1,m);
for (k in 1:K) Y[k+1,]=(1+r)*Y[k,]-O[k]-X[k,].
```

(b) Generate $m = 50$ simulations under the conditions in Exercise 11.35 when $r = 0.03$ and $v_0 = 13\,000$ and plot them jointly against time.

R-*commands*:

```
matplot(0:K,Y,''l'').
```

(c) Redo when $r = 0.05$ and note the effect of higher financial earnings.

Exercise 11.37 Consider once again the scheme of the preceding exercises.

(a) Argue that the book value at time k might be $\mathcal{B}_k = \mathcal{Y}_k - (d\lambda_{k+1} + \cdots + d^{K-k}\lambda_K)\xi_z$ where d is the discount.

(b) Write a program generating m simulations of $\mathcal{B}_0, \ldots, \mathcal{B}_K$ when $\mathcal{Y}_0 = v_0$.

R-*commands*:

Note that $\mathcal{B}_k = \mathcal{Y}_k - d^{-k}(d^{k+1}\lambda_{k+1} + \cdots + d^K\lambda_K)\xi_z$. With X and λ as before and Y generated as in Exercise 11.36, use

```
PV=cumsum(d**(K:1)*λ[K:1])[K:1]/d**(1:K-1); B=Y-c(PV,0).
```

(c) Run the program when $m = 50$, $d = 0.97$ and $r = 0.03$ or $r = 0.05$ with the rest of the conditions as in Exercise 11.36 and plot the simulations of $\mathcal{B}_0, \ldots, \mathcal{B}_K$ jointly against time.

R-*commands*:

```
matplot(0:K,B,''l'').
```

(d) Compare with the simulations of cash values in Exercise 11.36.

Exercise 11.38 As in the preceding exercise, let $\mathcal{B}_k = \mathcal{Y}_k - \mathcal{PV}_k$ where $\mathcal{PV}_k = (d\lambda_{k+1} + \cdots + d^{K-k}\lambda_K)\xi_z$ and suppose we seek the initial capital $v_{0\epsilon}$ keeping all of $\mathcal{B}_0, \ldots, \mathcal{B}_K$ positive with probability $1 - \epsilon$.

(a) If there are no premia, show that

$$\mathcal{B}_k = (1+r)^k\left(v_0 - \mathcal{S}_k - \frac{\mathcal{PV}_k}{(1+r)^k}\right) \quad \text{where} \quad \mathcal{S}_k = \sum_{i=1}^{k} \frac{\mathcal{X}_i + \mathcal{O}_i}{(1+r)^i}.$$

[*Hint*: Utilize the representation $\mathcal{Y}_k = (1+r)^k(v_0 - \mathcal{S}_k)$ which was established in Section 3.6.]

(b) If $\mathcal{A}_1^*, \ldots, \mathcal{A}_m^*$ are Monte Carlo simulations of $\mathcal{A} = \max_k(\mathcal{S}_k + \mathcal{PV}_k/(1+r)^k)$, argue that $\mathcal{A}_{(m\epsilon)}^*$ is an approximation of $v_{0\epsilon}$ where $\mathcal{A}_{(1)}^* \geq \cdots \geq \mathcal{A}_{(m)}^*$ are in descending order.

Exercise 11.39

(a) Write a program computing $v_{0\epsilon}$ defined in the preceding exercise.

R-*commands*:

With X, λ generated in Exercise 11.33 and PV in Exercise 11.37 use

```
kk=1:K; O=θ*λ*ξz; S=apply((X+O)/(1+r)**kk,2,cumsum);
Amax=apply(S+PV/(1+r)**kk,2,max); v0ε=sort(Amax)[(1-ε)*m].
```

(b) Compute $v_{0\epsilon}$ under the conditions in Exercise 11.37 when $\epsilon = 0.05$ and 0.01 using $m = 10\,000$ and compare the values for $r = 0.03$ and $r = 0.05$ with those you found in Exercise 11.35.

(c) How important is the distinction between cash and book value for the capital requirement?

Exercise 11.40 Suppose we want to include rising prices.

(a) Modify the program in Exercise 11.36, so that m simulations of $\mathcal{Y}_0, \ldots, \mathcal{Y}_K$ are generated when $\mathcal{Y}_k = \mathcal{Y}_{k-1} - Q_k(\mathcal{O}_k + \mathcal{X}_k)$ for $k = 1, \ldots, K$.

R-*commands*:

Modify Exercise 11.36(a). With X and λ as in Exercise 11.33 and Q as in Exercise 11.30, use O=θ*λ*ξ_z; Y=matrix(v_0,K+1,m);
for (k in 1:K) Y[k+1,]=(1+r)*Y[k,]-Q[k+1,]*(O[k]+X[k,]).

(b) Redo the plots in Exercise 11.36(b), (c) when the inflation model is that in Exercise 11.30(b) and comment on the change.

R-*commands*:

matplot(0:K,Y,''l'').

Exercise 11.41

(a) Write a program generating, as in Exercise 11.40, m simulations of the book values $\mathcal{B}_k = \mathcal{Y}_k - Q_k(d\lambda_{k+1} + \cdots + d^{K-k}\lambda_K)\xi_z$ for $k = 0, \ldots, K$.

R-*commands*:

An extension of those in Exercise 11.37. With λ from Exercise 11.36 and Q and Y as in Exercise 11.40, use
PV=cumsum(d**(K:1)*λ[K:1])[K:1]/d**(1:K-1); B=Y-Q*c(PV,0).

(b) Redo the simulations in Exercise 11.40 when $d = 0.97$.

Exercise 11.42

(a) Modify the program in Exercise 11.39 so that $v_{0\epsilon}$ is computed with rising prices.

R-*commands*:

With Q as in Exercise 11.30 generate S and Amax as
S=apply(Q[1:k+1,]*(X+O)/(1+r)**kk,2,cumsum);
Amax=apply(S+Q[1:k+1,]*PV/(1+r)**kk,2,max).

(b) Compute $v_{0\epsilon}$ when, under the conditions in Exercise 11.41, $\epsilon = 0, 05$ and 0.01.
(c) Redo when $\xi_i = 0$ (no inflation).
(d) Redo (b) and (c) when $r = 0$ (interest not counted) and comment on the results.

PART III

LIFE INSURANCE AND FINANCIAL RISK

12

Life and state-dependent insurance

12.1 Introduction

Life and pension insurance are arrangements for which payment streams are determined by **states** occupied by individuals, for example active, retired, disabled and so on. These contracts typically last for a long time, up to half a century and more. A simple example is an arrangement where an account is first built up and then harvested after a certain date. At first glance this is only a savings account, but insurance can be put into it by including randomness due to how long people live. When such accounts are managed for many individuals simultaneously, it becomes possible to balance lifecycles against one another so that short lives (for which savings are not used up fully) partially finance long ones. There is much sense in this. In old age benefits do not stop after an agreed date, but may go on until the recipient dies.

Many versions and variants of such contracts exist. Benefits may be one-time settlements upon retirement or death of a policy holder or distribute over time as a succession of payments. Traditional schemes have often been **defined benefit**, where economic rights after retirement determine the contributions that sustain them. **Defined contributions** are the opposite. Now the pension follows from the earlier build-up of the account. Whatever the arrangement, the values created depend on investment policy and interest rate and also on inflation (which determines the real worth of the pension when it is put to use). All of that must be high risk indeed, and who carries it? With defined benefit arrangements it is typically pension schemes or companies that must guarantee the rights of policy holders. Defined contributions are different. Now risk typically resides with the individuals themselves. Such financial issues are deferred until Chapter 15. The target here is the traditional part of the methodology where the so-called **technical** rate of interest r is given and where benefits are not linked to economic variables like inflation or wage level.

This creates an orderly system of pricing and valuation which must be mastered before the complications of the financial side are introduced in Chapter 15.

12.2 The anatomy of state-dependent insurance

12.2.1 Introduction

All payment streams in this chapter run over a fixed time sequence $T_k = kT$ for $k = 0, 1, \dots$, and there are similar age sequences $y_l = lT$ for $l = 1, 2, \dots$, always indexed by l. The interest rate r is fixed and is proportional to T. An important, elementary concept is that of an **annuity**, which is a constant cash flow over $T_0, T_1, T_2, \dots$ Suppose each payment is 1, run over K time steps and is **in arrears** at the end of each period. Its present value is then

$$d + d^2 + \cdots + d^K = d\frac{1 - d^K}{1 - d} \quad \text{where} \quad d = \frac{1}{1 + r}. \tag{12.1}$$

Schemes can also be **in advance** at the beginning of each period. The present value is then the slightly higher

$$1 + d + \cdots + d^{K-1} = \frac{1 - d^K}{1 - d}. \tag{12.2}$$

In life and pension insurance such payment streams are broken off when the individual dies, and valuation must be corrected for it. This is a big issue in traditional life insurance mathematics, with special notation derived; see Section 12.4. Here the main ideas will be introduced from a more general viewpoint.

12.2.2 Cash flows determined by states

Life insurance mathematics deals with cash flows influenced by **lifecycles**. A payment ζ_k at k is then determined by a **state** C_l occupied by the individual at that time. A simple example is $C_l = 1$ if the individual is alive and $C_l = 2$ if he is dead, where l represents age. More complicated schemes will be introduced later. A lifecycle is in general a random sequence $\{C_l\}$, where each C_l is a label among a small number of possibilities; see Section 6.6. Markov chains (also in Section 6.6) are the standard models, and we shan't move beyond these. To this probabilistic description must be added the contracts which specify payments $s_l(i)$ (positive or negative) when the individual is in state i at age l.

A general representation of a life insurance cash flow $\{\zeta_k\}$ must link time k and age l. Suppose the contract was drawn up at time 0 for a policy holder of age l_0. Then

$$\zeta_k = s_l(C_l) \quad \text{where} \quad l = l_0 + k, \tag{12.3}$$

which reflects that the age at time k has become $l = l_0 + k$. As C_l changes so does the payment. Portfolio versions follow by adding over all policies; see below.

As an example, consider pensions of the ordinary defined benefit type. There are now contributions π up to some retirement age l_r, with benefits s being received after that. One way to fit this into the general scheme is to define $C_l = 1$ if the policy holder is alive at age l and $C_l = 2$ if he is dead. There are then the three possibilities

$$\underset{\textit{contributing premium, } l < l_r}{s_l(1) = -\pi} \qquad \underset{\textit{receiving benefit, } l \geq l_r}{s_l(1) = s} \qquad \underset{\textit{dead}}{s_l(2) = 0;}$$

contributions (premia) being counted as *negative* (the usual convention). Although the simple arrangements of pensions and term insurance will be tackled in Section 12.4 without this formalism, it is a useful one in more complex situations.

There is nothing unique in the representation (12.3), and how the sequence $\{C_l\}$ is defined is a matter of convenience with more than one possibility. The present section deals with cash flows $\{\zeta_k\}$ of the form (12.3) and introduces the basic concepts for pricing and control.

12.2.3 Equivalence pricing

The present value of a sequence of payments $\{\zeta_k\}$ is

$$\mathrm{PV}_0 = \sum_{k=0}^{\infty} d^k \zeta_k \quad \text{with expectation} \quad E(\mathrm{PV}_0) = \sum_{k=0}^{\infty} d^k E(\zeta_k). \tag{12.4}$$

Here PV_0 is random since the future states of the individual are unknown. One way to plan the arrangement is to make

$$E(\mathrm{PV}_0) = 0 \qquad \text{(equivalence condition)}. \tag{12.5}$$

This is known as the **principle of equivalence**. All payments into and out of the scheme are then balanced so that their expected present value is zero. There is for the insurer no profit in this (and no expenses are covered), but obviously that comes down to the specification of d (or r). A company would expect surplus returns on the management of assets.

Equivalence adjusts premium (paid early) to match given benefits later. Consider a simple pension scheme, entered at age l_0. If π and s are premium and benefit, then

$$\underset{\textit{while saving}}{E(\zeta_k) = -\pi \, {}_kp_{l_0}} \quad \text{and} \quad \underset{\textit{while drawing benefit}}{E(\zeta_k) = s \, {}_kp_{l_0},}$$

where ${}_kp_{l_0}$ is the probability that an individual of age l_0 is alive at age $l_0 + k$. These quantities were introduced in Section 6.2, and there will be more in Section 12.3

below. Both expressions are intuitive. Surely the expectation must be the payment itself times the probability that it is made? Suppose retirement starts at l_r, lasting until the end of life. With payments in advance the expected present value is

$$E(\mathrm{PV}_0) = -\pi \sum_{k=0}^{l_r-l_0-1} d^k \, {}_kp_{l_0} + s \sum_{k=l_r-l_0}^{\infty} d^k \, {}_kp_{l_0},$$

and the equivalence condition yields an equation that can be solved for π. Arrangements of this kind are discussed in Section 12.4.

12.2.4 The reserve

Consider a contract k time units after it has been set up. The present value of the *remaining* payments is then

$$\mathrm{PV}_k = \sum_{i=0}^{\infty} d^i \zeta_{k+i},$$

with expectation

$$V_k = E(\mathrm{PV}_k | C_{l_0+k}) \quad \text{or} \quad V_k = \sum_{i=0}^{\infty} d^i E(\zeta_{k+i} | C_{l_0+k}), \tag{12.6}$$

where it has been highlighted that V_k is a *conditional* expectation. At the beginning $V_0 = E(\mathrm{PV}_0 | C_0)$, which is zero if the contract is by equivalence.

An individual of age l_0 originally is at time k of age $l_0 + k$ and is now in state C_{l_0+k}. We may regard V_k as the **value** of the contract at k. A client renouncing all future rights in exchange for a lump sum may be paid the amount V_k, and neither party would then lose on average. Note that V_k has become known at time k, but it is uncertain earlier since there are then several possibilities for the state C_{l_0+k}. The way treaties are designed usually makes $V_k > 0$. Simple examples of how the conditional expectations in (12.6) are identified are given later in this chapter and among the exercises.

For (12.6) to be a valid definition of value, $\{C_l\}$ must be a Markov chain. Otherwise the future lifecycle is influenced by the history of the individual prior to k, and we can't condition on the current state C_{l_0+k} alone; see some of the references in Section 12.8. The quantity V_k is also known as the **reserve** and enters the balance sheets of companies. It is interesting to compare it with the savings value V'_k of the preceding payments $\zeta_0, \ldots, \zeta_{k-1}$, which is

$$V'_k = \sum_{i=0}^{k-1} (1+r)^{k-i}(-\zeta_i) \tag{12.7}$$

where payments $-\zeta_i$ enter with interest. The minus sign signifies that the first payments (usually premia) are counted as negative so that V'_k is positive. Savings values exclude all risk, and in arrangements where the company takes over the account when the individual dies early $V'_k < V_k$; more in Section 12.4. There is for equivalence contracts a relationship between the two valuations. Now

$$E(V'_k|C_0) = E(V_k|C_0) \qquad \text{(under equivalence)}, \tag{12.8}$$

which is verified in Section 12.7. At the time an equivalence contract is drawn up the future savings and mortality-adjusted values V'_k and V_k are equal *on average*.

12.2.5 The portfolio viewpoint

In (12.6), V_k is unused surplus for the policy holder and a **liability** for a company or pension scheme. Suppose there are J contracts of this type set up $k_1, \dots, k_J$ time units earlier and valued as $V_{1k_1}, \dots, V_{Jk_J}$. The **portfolio** liability is then the sum $V_{1k_1} + \cdots + V_{Jk_J}$. This is only a book value, but it must be available on the asset side, and although the present value of the actual payments will not be quite this amount, the difference is usually small; see Section 3.4.

An interesting issue is how portfolio liabilities distribute over time. For policy j (12.6) becomes

$$V_{jk_j} = \sum_{k=0}^{\infty} d^k E(\zeta_{jk_j+k}|C_{jk_j}),$$

where all quantities depending on the contract are indexed by j. In particular, C_{jk_j} is the state occupied by individual j at $k = 0$, i.e., k_j periods into the life of the contract. Now

$$\sum_{j=1}^{J} V_{jk_j} = \sum_{j=1}^{J}\left(\sum_{k=0}^{\infty} d^k E(\zeta_{jk_j+k}|C_{jk_j})\right) = \sum_{k=0}^{\infty} d^k \left(\sum_{j=1}^{J} E(\zeta_{jk_j+k}|C_{jk_j})\right)$$

after switching the order of the sums. This defines the portfolio liability

$$\mathcal{PV}_0 = \sum_{k=0}^{\infty} d^k \mathcal{X}_k \quad \text{where} \quad \mathcal{X}_k = \sum_{j=1}^{J} E(\zeta_{jk_j+k}|C_{jk_j}), \tag{12.9}$$

and $\mathcal{X}_k$ is the expected payout at k. The portfolio liability is the present value of the cash flow $\{\mathcal{X}_k\}$. In simulation studies (Chapter 15), $\{\mathcal{X}_k\}$ is simply stored as a fixed sequence since it deviates only slightly from the actual, future payment stream.

A simple example is a pension scheme of identical contracts where cash flows are divided into contributions π prior to the retirement age l_r and benefits s

afterwards. Let $\mathcal{N}_l$ be the number of individuals of age l today and ${}_k\mathcal{N}_l$ those alive k periods later. Clearly

$$E({}_k\mathcal{N}_l) = {}_kp_l\mathcal{N}_l,$$

where ${}_kp_l$ is the probability of survival. It follows from the remarks above that we do not normally distinguish between ${}_k\mathcal{N}_l$ and $E({}_k\mathcal{N}_l)$, and the net portfolio payoff at time k will be

$$\mathcal{X}_k = -\pi \sum_{l<l_r-k} {}_k\mathcal{N}_l + s \sum_{l\geq l_r-k} {}_k\mathcal{N}_l \quad \text{where} \quad \underbrace{{}_k\mathcal{N}_l = {}_kp_l\mathcal{N}_l}_{\text{an expectation}}.$$

The sums are over the age l of the individuals. There are premia π (counted as negative) for those who at time k haven't reached the retirement age l_r and benefits s for the rest. Men and women have different survival probabilities ${}_kp_l$, and separate calculations are needed.

12.3 Survival modelling

12.3.1 Introduction

Stochastic modelling in life insurance starts with how long people live. Actuarial evaluation on a time increment T counts life length as $Y = LT$, where T may be in years, quarters or months and L is an integer. The probability distribution of L is known as a **life table** and is usually specified through the conditional probabilities

$$\underbrace{{}_kp_l = \Pr(L \geq l + k|L \geq l)}_{\text{survival probabilities}} \quad \text{and} \quad \underbrace{{}_kq_l = \Pr(k + l - 1 \leq L < l + k|L \geq l)}_{\text{mortalities}}.$$

On the left the **survival** probability is the likelihood of living k periods longer whereas the **mortality** on the right is the probability that the individual dies during the last period. Both quantities depend on current age l. Survival probabilities were introduced in Section 6.2.

The purpose of this section is to review the main steps when these quantities are modelled. Historical data are involved, but also theoretical arguments, above all continuous time with links to the Poisson point process of Section 8.2. Women live longer than men, and separate models are needed.

12.3.2 Deductions from one-step transitions

The one-step survival probabilities ${}_1p_l = p_l$ and mortalities ${}_1q_l = q_l = 1 - p_l$ play a special role in the sense that the entire life table can be construced from them through the recursion

$${}_{k+1}p_l = (1 - q_{l+k}) \cdot {}_kp_l, \quad k = 0, 1, \ldots \qquad \text{starting at} \quad {}_0p_l = 1, \tag{12.10}$$

and for the mortalities

$$_{k+1}q_l = q_{l+k} \cdot {}_kp_l, \quad k = 0, 1, \ldots \tag{12.11}$$

These relationships are established by noting that if $b > a \geq l + k$, then

$$\Pr(b > L \geq a|L \geq l) = \Pr(b > L \geq a|L \geq l + k)\Pr(L \geq l + k|L \geq l).$$

Insert $b = \infty$ and $a = l+k+1$ for (12.10) and $b = l+k+1$ and $a = l+k$ for (12.11).

12.3.3 Modelling through intensities

Life tables are often constructed through modelling in continuous time. Mortality at age y is now defined through an intensity $\mu(y)$ which specifies the probability of dying within a short time increment h as $\mu(y)h$. This is similar to the time-heterogeneous Poisson process of Section 8.2, although now the incident (death) can only occur once. The main result of Section 8.2 can still be exploited. Consider a time-heterogeneous Poisson process and let N be the number of events in the interval from y_0 to y_1. Then

$$\Pr(N = n) = \frac{\lambda^n}{n!}e^{-\lambda} \quad \text{where} \quad \lambda = \int_{y_0}^{y_1} \mu(y)\,dy.$$

Our interest is in $n = 0$, and with the preceding argument the chance of surviving the period from y_0 to y_1 becomes

$$\Pr(N = 0) = \exp\left(-\int_{y_0}^{y_1} \mu(y)\,dy\right),$$

which is the key to continuous-time survival modelling.

Let Y be how long an individual lives. Then $Y \geq y_0$ for a person of age y_0, and survival up to y_1 means that $Y \geq y_1$. Hence

$$\Pr(Y \geq y_1|Y \geq y_0) = \exp\left(-\int_{y_0}^{y_1} \mu(y)\,dy\right), \quad y_1 \geq y_0.$$

Insert $y_0 = lT$ and $y_1 = (l + k)T$, and it has been established that

$$_kp_l = \exp\left(-\int_{lT}^{(l+k)T} \mu(y)\,dy\right), \quad k = 0, 1, 2, \ldots \tag{12.12}$$

Constructions from intensity functions will be extended to general state processes $\{C_l\}$ in Section 12.5.

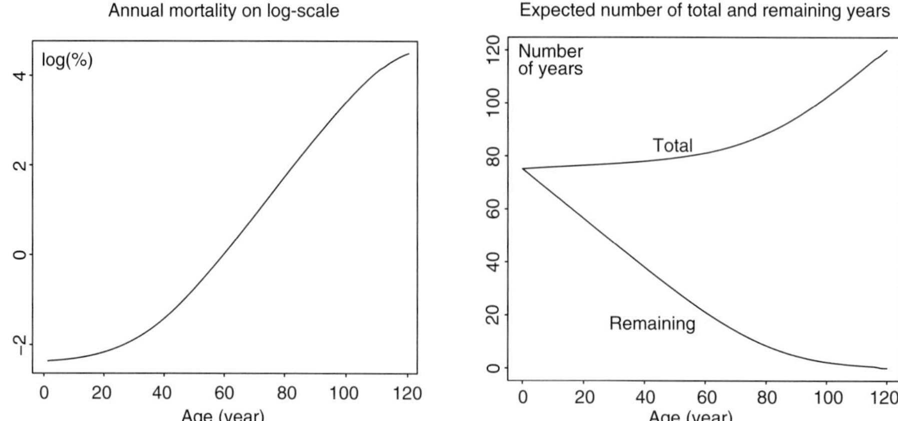

Figure 12.1 A Gomperz–Makeham model (parameters in text). *Left*: Logarithms of annual mortalities (%). *Right*: Expected total and expected remaining number of years.

12.3.4 A standard model: Gomperz–Makeham

The most popular mathematical description of mortality goes back to 1860 and bears the name of Gomperz and Makeham, who made separate contributions. The intensity is now a parametric curve of the form

$$\mu(y) = \theta_0 + \theta_1 e^{\theta_2 y}, \tag{12.13}$$

where θ_0, θ_1 and θ_2 are parameters. Under this model the survival probabilities become

$${}_k p_l = \exp\left(-\theta_0 kT - \frac{\theta_1}{\theta_2}(e^{\theta_2 kT} - 1)e^{\theta_2 lT}\right), \tag{12.14}$$

which you prove by noting that

$$\int_{lT}^{(k+l)T} (\theta_0 + \theta_1 e^{\theta_2 y})\, dy = \theta_0 kT + \frac{\theta_1}{\theta_2}(e^{\theta_2 kT} - 1)e^{\theta_2 lT}$$

and (12.14) follows by replacing the exponent in (12.12) by this expression.

The 1-year mortalities $q_l = 1 - p_l$ have been plotted in Figure 12.1 left when $\theta_0 = 0.0009$, $\theta_1 = 0.000044$ and $\theta_2 = 0.090761$, which corresponds to an average life of about 75 years, plausible for males in developed countries. Note that the vertical axis is logarithmic (the resolution would have been poor otherwise). The curve crosses zero at about 60 years, which signifies a 1% chance of a 60-year-old male dying within a year. Mortalities rise rapidly as people grow older. This model will be used for laboratory experiments later.

Algorithm 12.1 Expected remaining survival

0 Input: $\{p_l\}$, h, $l = y/h$, l_e	%*For example choose* $l_e = 120/h$
1 $P \leftarrow 1$ and $E \leftarrow 1/2$	%*Initial survival probability and expectation*
2 For $k = l, \ldots, l_e$ do	
3 $P \leftarrow Pp_k$ and $E \leftarrow E + P$	%*At this point P is* ${}_{k-l+1}p_l$
4 Return $E \leftarrow Eh$.	%*Expected number of years remaining*

12.3.5 Expected survival

The parameters of a Gomperz–Makeham model are difficult to interpret and tell us little about how long we expect people to live. It takes a bit of work to find out. Of interest is not only the average total life $E(Y)$, but also the average *remaining* life for a person of age y; i.e., the conditional mean $E(Y - y|Y > y)$ which coincides with $E(Y)$ if $y = 0$. An exact expression is

$$E(Y - y|Y > y) = \int_0^\infty \Pr(Y > y + z|Y > y)\, dz;$$

see (A.6) in Table A.1 in Appendix A. Computing this needs numerical methods. The trapezoidal rule in Appendix C.3 yields the approximation

$$E(Y - y|Y > y) \doteq \frac{h}{2} + h \sum_{k=1}^{\infty} \Pr(Y > y + kh|Y > y)$$

where h is small, or for $y = lh$

$$E(Y - y|Y > y) \doteq \frac{h}{2} + h \sum_{k=1}^{\infty} {}_kp_l \tag{12.15}$$

where ${}_kp_l = \Pr(Y > (l + k)h|Y > lh)$ is the life table in (12.14) with $T = h$. Algorithm 12.1 takes one-step transition probabilities $p_l = \mu(lh)h$ as input and generates ${}_kp_l$ from the recursion (12.10) jointly with the rest of the computations.

Output is an approximation of the expected remaining number of years for an individual of age $y = lh$. Add y and you have $E + y$ as the expected total number of years. The results become exact as $h \to 0$, and the procedure can also be used when the model isn't in intensity form with p_l having been estimated directly on the time scale T (now insert $h = T$ in Algorithm 12.1). How the expected remaining and total number of years vary with the age of the individual is indicated in Figure 12.1 right using the model on the left (and $h = 0.01$ years). A male at 60 has, under this model, around 20 years left on average.

12.3.6 Using historical data

Life tables must be fitted to historical data, and this must be done separately for men and women. Suppose a group of people is followed over some period of time, keeping track on those who live and those who die. This leads to counts

$$n_{l_0} \geq n_{l_0+1} \geq \cdots \geq n_{l_e},$$

where n_l is the number of individuals who have survived to age l. Passing from n_l to n_{l+1} is simply a sequence of n_l Bernoulli trials with the survival probability p_l as 'success'.

The elementary textbook method is to estimate p_l by

$$\hat{p}_l = \frac{n_{l+1}}{n_l}. \tag{12.16}$$

An alternative is to fit a parametric function like the Gomperz–Makeham model. With three parameters θ_0, θ_1 and θ_2 the modelling strategy becomes

$$\underbrace{p_l = H_l(\theta_0, \theta_1, \theta_2)}_{\textit{assumed relationship}} \quad \text{and} \quad \underbrace{\hat{p}_l = H_l(\hat{\theta}_0, \hat{\theta}_1, \hat{\theta}_2)}_{\textit{estimated relationship}},$$

with $\hat{\theta}_0$, $\hat{\theta}_1$, $\hat{\theta}_2$ estimates. A maximum likelihood procedure is developed by noting that the sequence $n_{l_0}, n_{l_0+1}, \ldots, n_{l_e}$ is Markov dependent, as in Section 6.5, with conditional density functions

$$f(n_{l+1}|n_l) = \binom{n_l}{n_{l+1}} p_l^{n_{l+1}}(1 - p_l)^{n_l - n_{l+1}}.$$

The log-likelihood function is calculated by taking logarithms and adding over all l. With constant factors removed we are led to the criterion

$$\mathcal{L}(\theta_0, \theta_1, \theta_2) = \sum_{l=l_0}^{l_e} \{n_{l+1} \log(p_l) + (n_l - n_{l+1}) \log(1 - p_l)\}, \tag{12.17}$$

into which $p_l = H_l(\theta_0, \theta_1, \theta_2)$ is inserted and the expression maximized. This takes numerical methods; consult Exercise 12.14.

Is this more complicated procedure superior to the simpler estimate (12.16)? There is bias if the assumed relationship $p_l = H_l(\theta_0, \theta_1, \theta_2)$ is wrong, but there are advantages too. Random errors are smaller, and a plot of $\hat{p}_l$ against l traces out a smooth curve without the random bumps and wriggles you might find with the other estimate; more on this in Section 15.2.

12.4 Single-life arrangements

12.4.1 Introduction

Insurance products for which the mortality risk is the only source of uncertainty are among the most common ones. Cash flows are then influenced by the death of a policy holder and by nothing else that is random. In practice this isn't quite true. There *are* additional sources of uncertainty (and important ones too); see Section 15.2.

Two basic cash flows are those that persist as long as the policy holder is alive and those that are one-time payments upon death. Their expected present values can be written down by means of the survival probabilities ${}_kp_l$ and mortalities ${}_kq_l$ of the preceding section. If s_k is the agreed payment at time k and l_0 the age at the beginning, then

$$\underbrace{E(\mathrm{PV}_0) = \textstyle\sum_{k=0}^{\infty} d^k s_k\, {}_kp_{l_0}}_{\textit{payments while alive}} \quad \text{and} \quad \underbrace{E(\mathrm{PV}_0) = \textstyle\sum_{k=0}^{\infty} d^k s_k\, {}_kq_{l_0}}_{\textit{payment (one-time) upon death}}. \tag{12.18}$$

Are you familiar with such expressions? At time k take the payment agreed and multiply by the probability that it is actually made. When you add over all k (and discount!) the expected present value emerges. We argue like this many times during this chapter.

Many insurance contracts are combinations of these schemes, often with delays, and everything in this section could have been referred back to the pair of expressions in (12.18). However, actuaries often make use of a traditional nomenclature of mortality-adjusted annuities which enable premia and present values to be written in compact form. Much of the present section is a review of this methodology; see Gerber (1997) for more on this.

12.4.2 How mortality risk affects value

The value of an insurance account is usually higher than the savings value. Consider a cash flow $\{s_k\}$ which is stopped when the individual dies. In life insurance there are often contributions (counted as negative) at the beginning and withdrawals (counted as positive) later. The value of an insurance contract was, in Section 12.2, defined as the expected present value of all remaining transactions. This **prospective** version is the left-hand side of (12.19), but there is also, on the right, an additional **retrospective** one involving past savings and they are equal for equivalence contracts. Indeed, if (12.5) is satisfied then

$$\underbrace{\sum_{i=0}^{\infty} d^i s_{k+i}\, {}_i p_{l_0+k}}_{\textit{prospective reserve}} = \underbrace{\sum_{i=0}^{k-1} \frac{(-s_i)(1+r)^{k-i}}{{}_{k-i}p_{l_0+i}}}_{\textit{retrospective reserve}}; \tag{12.19}$$

see Section 12.7 for the proof.

The retrospective reserve on the right adds the payments $-s_0, \ldots, -s_{k-1}$ with interest, but $-s_i$ has at time k been assigned a higher contribution than the ordinary savings value $v = (-s_i)(1+r)^{k-i}$. Why is that? Why should the account be credited with v/p rather than just v where $p = {}_{k-i}p_{l_0+i}$? One explanation is that the *expected* value of $-s_i$ at k now becomes

$$\frac{v}{p} \cdot p + 0 \cdot (1-p) = v,$$

coinciding with the savings value. The extra on the right in (12.19) is compensation for the insurer pocketing the money if the policy holder dies early.

12.4.3 Life insurance notation

Insurance products are often fixed annuities, and their mortality-adjusted valuation is handled by special mathematical notation. Suppose one money unit is received at each of K time periods, but ceases when the individual dies. The expected discounted value of the kth payment is $d^k {}_k p_{l_0}$, and with payment in arrears the expected present value of the entire cash flow is

$$\ddot{a}_{l_0:\,\overline{K}|} = \sum_{k=1}^{K} d^k {}_k p_{l_0} \qquad \text{(in arrears while alive).} \tag{12.20}$$

This is a special case of (12.18) left. The notation signifies that the age is l_0 at the beginning and that payments (up to K of them) take place at the end of periods (none at $k = 0$). There is a similar quantity for payments in advance; i.e.,

$$a_{l_0:\,\overline{K}|} = \sum_{k=0}^{K-1} d^k {}_k p_{l_0} \qquad \text{(in advance while alive).} \tag{12.21}$$

Now there is nothing at $k = K$. The two variants are related to each other through the relationships

$$a_{l_0:\,\overline{K}|} = 1 + \ddot{a}_{l_0:\,\overline{K-1}|} \qquad \text{or} \qquad \ddot{a}_{l_0:\,\overline{K}|} = a_{l_0:\,\overline{K+1}|} - 1,$$

which are obvious once you have deciphered what the definitions mean! Annuities of infinite extensions are denoted

$$\underset{\textit{in arrears}}{\ddot{a}_{l_0} = \ddot{a}_{l_0:\,\overline{\infty}|}} \quad \text{and} \quad \underset{\textit{in advance}}{a_{l_0} = a_{l_0:\,\overline{\infty}|}}, \tag{12.22}$$

where cash flows go on until the recipient dies.

There are **deferred** versions too. Consider an annuity starting k periods from now, but only if the individual is still alive. The present values of such schemes are

$$\underset{\textit{in arrears}}{d^k \cdot {}_kp_{l_0} \cdot \ddot{a}_{l_0+k:\,\overline{K}|}} \quad \text{or} \quad \underset{\textit{in advance}}{d^k \cdot {}_kp_{l_0} \cdot a_{l_0+k:\,\overline{K}|}}, \tag{12.23}$$

where future annuities $a_{l_0+k:\,\overline{K}|}$ and $\ddot{a}_{l_0+k:\,\overline{K}|}$ that apply to individuals of age $l_0 + k$ are discounted back to a value today *and* adjusted for the probability that the individual is alive when payments begin. You will find in specialist literature annuity coefficients (with still more complicated nomenclature!) for deferred versions; see Gerber (1997).

Analogous quantities for one-time payments upon death are needed too. These are by tradition written with a capital A, for example for payment in arrears

$$\ddot{A}_{l_0:\,\overline{K}|} = \sum_{k=1}^{K} d^k {}_kq_{l_0} \quad \text{and} \quad \ddot{A}_{l_0} = \ddot{A}_{l_0:\,\overline{\infty}|}\,, \tag{12.24}$$

which are justified as before. Death at time k occurs with probability ${}_kq_{l_0}$, and if this releases one money unit, the expected value is ${}_kq_{l_0}$ which must be discounted and added over all k for the expected present value. On the left the contract stops after K time units. Deferred versions are defined as above.

12.4.4 Computing mortality-adjusted annuities

The present value of fixed annuities broken off by death is needed in many actuarial computations, and they are easily programmed if you need them; simply enter the commands in Algorithm 12.2. R-programs for $a_{l_0:\,\overline{K}|}$ and $\ddot{a}_{l_0:\,\overline{K}|}$ are given among the exercises, with procedures for some of the other coefficients too.

12.4.5 Common insurance arrangements

The following examples show how the mortality-adjusted annuity coefficients are put to work. It is assumed that premia are calculated through equivalence. Most payments are in advance (but in arrears would be almost the same). Other examples can be found among the exercises.

Algorithm 12.2 The coefficients $a_{l_0:\,\overline{K|}}$ and $\ddot{a}_{l_0:\,\overline{K|}}$

```
Input: l_0, K, d = 1/(1 + r), {q_l}
a ← 0,  b ← 1,    l ← l_0 − 1
For k = 0, ..., K − 1 repeat
    a ← a + b    and    l ← l + 1
    b ← b(1 − q_l)d             %For next round, recall _k p_{l_0} = (1 − q_{l_0+k−1}) _{k−1}p_{l_0}
Return a and ä ← a + b − 1.     %a and ä are a_{l_0: K|} and ä_{l_0: K|}
```

Life annuities. This is conceivably the simplest way of smoothing mortality risk among policy holders. Suppose an individual has savings Π at retirement l_r and purchases an annuity that lasts K time periods with interruption by death. The mortality-adjusted value of a unit annuity is then $a_{l_r:\,\overline{K|}}$, and the pension s received each period is determined from

$$s \cdot a_{l_r:\,\overline{K|}} = \Pi \qquad \text{or} \qquad s = \frac{\Pi}{a_{l_r:\,\overline{K|}}}. \tag{12.25}$$

Note that the amount received goes up by the fact that the company is allowed to take over the remainder of the money in case of an early death (for a company there are losses on long-living clients). The savings Π belong to the individual, but may well have been managed by professional asset managers.

Defined benefit. Pensions were, in the preceding example, a consequence of savings. Defined benefit schemes are the other way around. Now savings are built up to support a given pension. Suppose the individual enters the arrangement at age l_0 and retires at l_r to receive a fixed pension s broken off by death or after K periods. With all payments in advance the present value of the scheme at the time it is drawn up is

$$\underbrace{-\pi \cdot a_{l_0:\,\overline{l_r-l_0|}}}_{\textit{contributing stage}} \quad + \quad \underbrace{s \cdot d^{l_r-l_0} \cdot {}_{l_r-l_0}p_{l_0} \cdot a_{l_r:\,\overline{K|}}}_{\textit{benefit stage}},$$

where the benefit part comes from the deferred annuity (12.23). The equivalence premium becomes

$$\pi = s \cdot d^{l_r-l_0} \cdot {}_{l_r-l_0}p_{l_0} \cdot \frac{a_{l_r:\,\overline{K|}}}{a_{l_0:\,\overline{l_r-l_0|}}}. \tag{12.26}$$

It is implicit that the insurer takes over the surplus in case of an early death, which makes the contribution π smaller than it would have been otherwise.

Pure endowments. These are savings contracts where the policy holder is paid a lump sum at a future date if alive, merely a pension plan with a single benefit. The contribution necessary to sustain such an arrangement is

$$\pi = s \cdot d^{l_r - l_0} \cdot \frac{{}_{l_r - l_0}p_{l_0}}{a_{l_0:\,\overline{l_r - l_0}|}}, \qquad (12.27)$$

which follows from (12.26) by inserting $K = 1$ and noting that $a_{l_r:\,\overline{1}|} = 1$.

Term insurance. Such arrangements are typically used to protect a financially weaker party, for example a household against the main income being lost. Upon the death of the policy holder a single sum is paid to the beneficiary. A contract of that kind lasting K time units with premium in advance and compensation in arrears has, at $k = 0$, the present value

$$\underset{\textit{premium}}{-\pi \cdot a_{l_0:\,\overline{K}|}} \quad + \quad \underset{\textit{term benefit}}{s \cdot \ddot{A}_{l_0:\,\overline{K}|}}$$

where $\ddot{A}_{l_0:\,\overline{K}|}$ was defined in (12.24). This is zero if

$$\pi = s \cdot \frac{\ddot{A}_{l_0:\,\overline{K}|}}{a_{l_0:\,\overline{K}|}}, \qquad (12.28)$$

which is the equivalence premium. In practice such contracts (like pension schemes) carry positive values at any point in time, and if broken off, the insured is entitled to compensation. The reason is that the mortalities are *smaller* at the beginning, which means that the insurer has received a higher premium than the risk carried; see Exercise 12.21.

Endowments. These are combinations of term insurance and pure endowments. There is a one-time payment s_1 following the death of the policy holder and also a final endowment s_2 if she (or he) is alive at the expiry of the contract. The present value at time 0 is now

$$\underset{\textit{premium}}{-\pi \cdot a_{l_0:\,\overline{K}|}} \quad + \quad \underset{\textit{payment upon death}}{s_1 \cdot \ddot{A}_{l_0:\,\overline{K}|}} \quad + \quad \underset{\textit{pure endowment at } K}{s_2 \cdot d^K \cdot {}_K p_{l_0}},$$

where the contributions due to the two types of benefit are added. The premium if determined through equivalence becomes

$$\pi = s_1 \cdot \frac{\ddot{A}_{l_0:\,\overline{K}|}}{a_{l_0:\,\overline{K}|}} + s_2 \cdot d^K \cdot \frac{{}_K p_{l_0}}{a_{l_0:\,\overline{K}|}}, \qquad (12.29)$$

which adds premia for two components.

12.4.6 A numerical example

How reserves and savings values in ordinary pension insurance evolve is illustrated in Figure 12.2. The contract was entered into at the age of 30 years with retirement at 65. After that date a pension of 12 500 (say euros) was received four times a year in advance up to the age of 90. The survival probabilities followed the Gomperz–Makeham model in Section 12.3, and the premium was calculated from the equivalence condition. Contributions (in advance, four times a year) were (in thousands of euros)

Premium (quarterly)	1.634	2.180	2.902
Interest (annual)	4%	3%	2%

where the rate of interest wields considerable influence on the premium charged.

The reserve (at an annual technical rate of 4%) is shown in Figure 12.2 left, where it is assumed that the insured has stayed alive. There is a top at the retirement age (65 years), which decreases to zero at 90 when the scheme terminates. It is interesting to compare this with the savings values V'_k, which summarize the account from the point of view of the insurer. Since premium π is paid before retirement and benefit s withdrawn afterwards, V'_k, develops according to the recursion

$$\underbrace{V'_k = (1+r)(V'_{k-1}+\pi)}_{\textit{before retirement, } k < l_r - l_0} \quad \text{and} \quad \underbrace{V'_k = (1+r)(V'_{k-1}-s)}_{\textit{after retirement, } k \geq l_r - l_0},$$

starting at $V'_0 = 0$. All quantities are *quarterly* (including the rate of interest r, slightly smaller than 1% since it corresponds to an annual rate of 4%). The savings value is, in Figure 12.2, *smaller* than the reserve during the contributing stage, because it fails to adjust for mortality risk. It becomes strongly negative at the end for very long lives, causing a loss for the insurer, but *he* has compensation through the short lives of others where the account is positive.

12.5 Multi-state insurance I: Modelling

12.5.1 Introduction

Multi-state insurance was introduced in Section 12.2, but not much was said about the modelling of the state process $\{C_l\}$ and about the evaluation of premia and liabilities in detail. Much of the literature is in continuous time, as in Haberman and Pitacco (1999). Actually a lot can be achieved by simple means through recursions running in *discrete* time. We then need the transition probabilities

$$p_l(i|j) = \Pr(C_{l+1} = i|C_l = j) \tag{12.30}$$

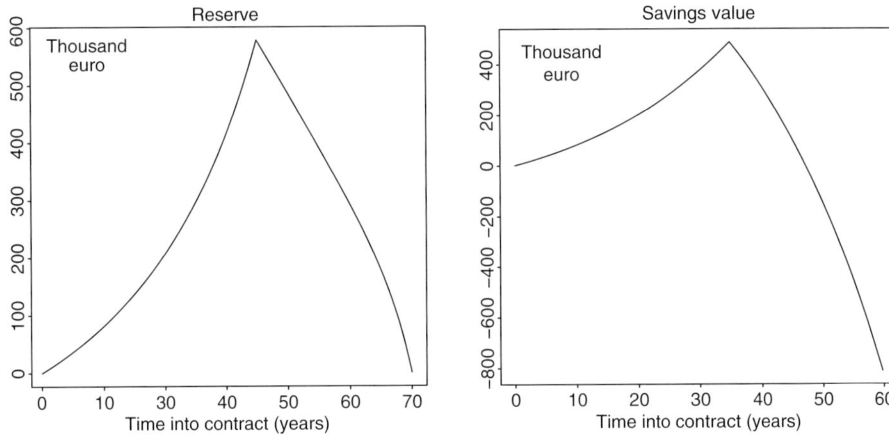

Figure 12.2 Reserve (*left*) and savings value (*right*) of a pension insurance contract (conditions in the text). *Note*: Scales on vertical axes are different.

introduced in Section 6.6 and their k-step extension

$$_kp_l(i|j) = \Pr(C_{l+k} = i|C_l = j). \tag{12.31}$$

As before, l (the subscript) defines age and k (the prefix) the time ahead. All actuarial evaluations will be carried out in terms of these quantities when we get around to it in the next section.

In reality there is a state $C(y)$ attached to *any* age y, not only to the sequence $y_l = lT$, and we may write

$$C_l = C(y_l) \quad \text{with} \quad y_l = lT.$$

This kind of viewpoint was used with survival modelling in Section 12.3 and is equally important here. The process $C(y)$ runs in continuous time and is assumed to be a **Markov process**, which means that all information on the future course of $C(y)$ rests with the current state. This property is passed on to *any* sequence $C_l = C(lT)$ in discrete time, whatever the choice of T. A central theme in this section is how models on different time scales are linked.

12.5.2 From one-step to k-step transitions

As with ordinary survival modelling (Section 12.3), k-step transition probabilities are connected to one-step versions through simple recursions. Consider an individual starting in state j at age l and ending $k + 1$ time units later in state i while occupying state j_1 immediately before the end. The path from j to i is then

$$\begin{array}{lccccc} & & {}_kp_l(j_1|j) & & p_{l+k}(i|j_1) & \\ \textit{state} & j & \longrightarrow & j_1 & \longrightarrow & i \\ \textit{age} & lT & & (l+k)T & & (l+k+1)T \end{array}$$

where the probabilities of the two transitions are those shown. They must be multiplied for the probability of the entire path, and when added over all j_1 in the middle provide the probability of ending in state i. In other words,

$$ {}_{k+1}p_l(i|j) = \sum_{j_1=1}^{v} p_{l+k}(i|j_1)\ {}_kp_l(j_1|j), \quad \text{for} \quad i, j = 1, \ldots, v, \tag{12.32}$$

where v is the number of states. This is a recursion over k, starting at

$$ {}_0p_l(i|j) = \begin{array}{ll} 1, & i = j \\ 0, & i \neq j \end{array} \tag{12.33}$$

and all future states can now be assigned probabilities. Computer implementation is easy (see Algorithm 12.3 later), and the scheme can be run for *any* time or age increment T. This is a useful observation that will connect an underlying stochastic model in continuous time to what is needed for actuarial evaluation. A formal proof of (12.32) draws on the Markov assumption; see Section 12.7.

12.5.3 Intensity modelling

The main issues of continuous-time modelling can be introduced through the disability scheme from Section 6.6. There were three states (here relabelled 1, 2 and 3), and they were connected through a layout of the form

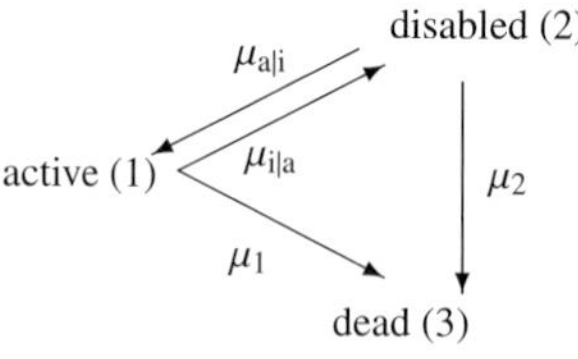

The propensity to move from one state to another is described by intensities. Four different ones are needed. In addition to the mortalities $\mu_1(y)$ and $\mu_2(y)$ in state 1 and 2, there are $\mu_{i|a}(y)$ and $\mu_{a|i}(y)$ which make individuals switch between being active and disabled. In practice, $\mu_1(y)$ and $\mu_2(y)$ are often unequal, typically $\mu_2(y) > \mu_1(y)$. This model is our main example in the present and next section.

The general case makes use of intensities $\mu_{i|j}(y)$ for passing from state j to state

i. For the disability scheme these are, in matrix form,

$$\begin{matrix} & \mu_{2|1}(y) = \mu_{i|a}(y) & \mu_{3|1}(y) = \mu_1(y) \\ \mu_{1|2}(y) = \mu_{a|i}(y) & & \mu_{3|2}(y) = \mu_2(y) \\ \mu_{1|3}(y) = 0 & \mu_{2|3}(y) = 0 & \end{matrix}$$

where diagonal elements $\mu_{ii}(y)$ are not needed. Systems like these with general, age-dependent intensities $\mu_{i|j}(y)$ are a powerful modelling tool. In practice the number of states can easily be higher than three.

Intensities are virtually the same as probabilities on a small time scale h. This viewpoint, familiar from Poisson modelling (Section 8.2) and survival modelling (Section 12.3), is formally valid as $h \to 0$. Since there are many states, the mathematics is now more complex, yet the basic interpretation remains the same. For small h individuals in state j at age y move to a *different* state i at $y+h$ with probability approximately $\mu_{i|j}(y)h$. How transition probabilities are obtained on time scales used for evaluation is discussed below.

12.5.4 Example: A Danish disability model

Disability models for public schemes vary between countries; see Haberman and Pitacco (1999). The old Danish model is one of the very simplest and therefore a useful introductory example. **Rehabilitation** from the disabled state is ignored[11] and active and disabled mortalities are equal. The earlier disability scheme is now simplified through

$$\mu_2(y) = \mu_1(y) \quad \text{and} \quad \mu_{a|i}(y) = 0,$$

which (unusually) leads to closed expressions for the transition probabilities (12.31). To see how, note that both disability and death may cause an individual to leave the active state 1. The probability of this during a small time interval of length h is approximately

$$\underset{\textit{individual dies}}{\mu_1(y)h} \quad + \quad \underset{\textit{becomes disabled}}{\mu_{i|a}(y)h} \quad = \quad \{\mu_1(y) + \mu_{i|a}(y)\}h,$$

which conveys (as was seen in Section 8.2 too) that intensities due to different, independent sources are *added*.[12] Since no one enters state 1 after having left it we may conclude, similar to (12.12), that

$$_kp_l(1|1) = \exp\left(-\int_{lT}^{(l+k)T} \{\mu_1(y) + \mu_{i|a}(y)\}\,dy\right), \qquad (12.34)$$

[11] As this book is being written, rehabilitation is not a very strong possibility in many countries, despite the authorities often being keen on promoting it.

[12] We may ignore the possibility of becoming disabled and dying within the same period since the joint probability is of order h^2. It was seen in Section 8.6 that this is too small to matter as $h \to 0$.

and in the same way

$$ {}_k p_l(2|2) = \exp\left(-\int_{lT}^{(l+k)T} \mu_1(y)\,dy\right) \qquad (12.35)$$

whereas

$$ {}_k p_l(1|2) = 0 \quad \text{and} \quad {}_k p_l(2|1) = {}_k p_l(2|2) - {}_k p_l(1|1) \qquad (12.36)$$

with the one on the right due to

$$ {}_k p_l(2|1) = 1 - {}_k p_l(1|1) - {}_k p_l(3|1) \quad \text{and} \quad {}_k p_l(3|1) = {}_k p_l(3|2) = 1 - {}_k p_l(2|2).$$

12.5.5 Numerical examples

The Danish model makes use of Gomperz–Makeham descriptions for the two remaining intensities, notably

$$\mu_1(y) = \theta_0 + \theta_1 e^{\theta_2 y} \quad \text{and} \quad \mu_{i|a}(y) = \psi_0 + \psi_1 e^{\psi_2 y},$$

with parameters[13] $\theta_0 = 0.0004$, $\theta_1 = 0.00000347$, $\theta_2 = 0.1382$, $\psi_0 = 0.0005$, $\psi_1 = 0.0000759$ and $\psi_2 = 0.08750$, which defines a survival model that differs quite a lot from the one in Section 12.3. An average life is now 71.4 years, more than 3 years less, for example. It is possible to find closed mathematical expressions for the probabilities (12.34)–(12.36); consult Exercise 12.31. Other and more general lines are developed below. The plot in Figure 12.3 left shows how a population gradually splits between the three states when everybody enters the scheme as active at age 20 (the parameter M is explained below).

A simple modification is offered on the right in Figure 12.3. No change is made to $\mu_{\text{i|a}}(y)$ and $\mu_2(y)$, which are as before, but now

$$\mu_1(y) = 0.6 \cdot \mu_2(y) \quad \text{and} \quad \mu_{a|i}(y) = 0.2.$$

The mortalities in the active group are now smaller, and there is strong recovery from disability (20% chance within a year, independent of age). At the time of writing rehabilitation is nowhere near this, but its impact on the distribution among the three states in Figure 12.3 right is interesting. The number of disabled individuals has become much smaller, despite people entering the disabled state equally often. The lower mortality in the active group is evident too.

[13] They are adapted to the present notation; different ones are found in Haberman and Pitacco (1999), p. 100.

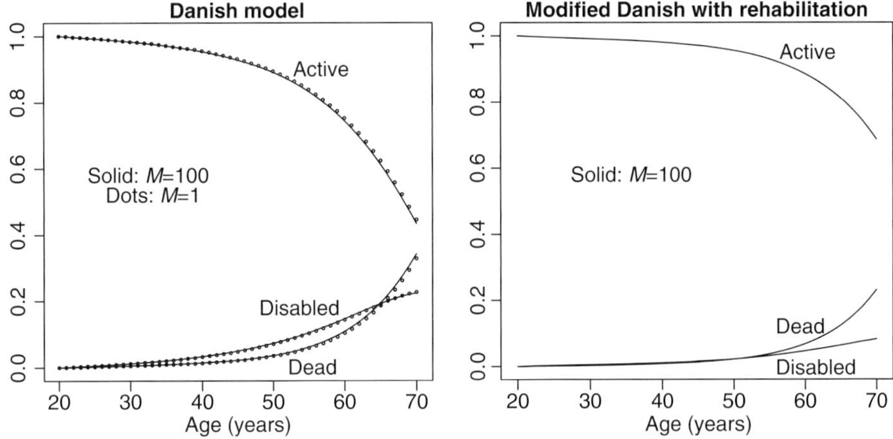

Figure 12.3 Distributions among states in disability schemes under the conditions described in the text.

12.5.6 From intensities to transition probabilities

We need a general procedure that connects models in terms of intensities to models on other time scales. The matrix form is convenient. Let

$$
{}_k\mathbf{p}_l = \begin{pmatrix} {}_kp_l(1|1) & \cdots & {}_kp_l(v|1) \\ \cdot & \cdots & \cdot \\ \cdot & \cdots & \cdot \\ {}_kp_l(1|v) & \cdots & {}_kp_l(v|v) \end{pmatrix} \tag{12.37}
$$

where ${}_kp_l(i|j)$ is the probability of moving from state j at age l to state i at age $l+k$. In particular, write $\mathbf{p}_l = {}_1\mathbf{p}_l$ for the one-step transitions. The recursion (12.32) can now be written more compactly as

$$
{}_{k+1}\mathbf{p}_l = {}_k\mathbf{p}_l\,\mathbf{p}_{l+k}, \quad k = 0, 1, \ldots \quad \text{starting at} \quad {}_0\mathbf{p}_l = \mathbf{I}, \tag{12.38}
$$

where $\mathbf{I}$ is the $v \times v$ identity matrix. This follows immediately when the matrix product is written out element-wise (take a look at Appendix B.2 if you need to). The result is a matrix version of (12.10) in Section 12.2.

But the starting point was a set of intensities $\mu_{i|j}(y)$ for jumps from state j to state i at age y, which must be converted to transition probabilities ${}_kp_l(i|j)$ on the time scale T selected for the evaluation of risk. The traditional method is through the **Chapman–Kolmogorov** differential equations; consult some of the references in Section 12.8. Here is an alternative which you can easily implement on your own. Let $y_0 = lT$, choose some large integer M and define the age sequence

$$
y_k = y_0 + kh, \quad k = 1, 2, \ldots \quad \text{where} \quad h = \frac{T}{M}. \tag{12.39}
$$

Algorithm 12.3 Transition probabilities from intensities

Input: $\{\mu_{i|j}(y)\}$, $\quad l, T, M, K, h = T/M, K_1 = MK$ $\quad$ *%M large, say $M \geq 100$*
$y \leftarrow lh, \quad {}_0\tilde{\mathbf{p}} \leftarrow \mathbf{I}$ $\quad$ *%**I** the identity matrix*
For $k = 1, \ldots, K_1$ do
  Repeat for all i:
    $t(i, i) \leftarrow 1$
    Repeat for all $j \neq i$: $\quad$ *%$t(i, j)$ are element*
      $t(i, j) \leftarrow \mu_{i|j}(y)h\ ,\ t(i, i) \leftarrow t(i, i) - t(i, j)$ $\quad$ *(i, j) of $\mathbf{t} = \tilde{\mathbf{p}}_{l+k}$*
  ${}_{k+1}\tilde{\mathbf{p}} \leftarrow {}_k\tilde{\mathbf{p}} \cdot \mathbf{t}$
  $y \leftarrow y + h$ $\quad$ *%Age updated*
Return ${}_K\mathbf{p}_l \leftarrow {}_{kM}\tilde{\mathbf{p}}$ for $k = 0, \ldots, K$.

Introduce one-step transition probabilities on time scale h through

$$\tilde{p}_l(i|i) = 1 - \sum_{j \neq i} \mu_{j|i}(y_l)h \quad \text{and} \quad \tilde{p}_l(i|j) = \mu_{i|j}(y_l)h \quad i \neq j. \tag{12.40}$$

The corresponding k-step solution ${}_k\tilde{\mathbf{p}}_l$ can be computed by means of (12.38), but we only seek those of the form ${}_{kM}\tilde{\mathbf{p}}_l$ for $k = 1, 2, \ldots$ which apply to the time sequence $kMh = kT$. As $h \to 0$ (or equivalently $M \to \infty$) the model (12.40) tends to the original one, and the exact solution ${}_k\mathbf{p}_l = {}_{kM}\tilde{\mathbf{p}}_l$ is obtained in the limit.

Algorithm 12.3 summarizes the scheme. On output the transition matrices ${}_1\mathbf{p}_l, \ldots, {}_K\mathbf{p}_l$ have been computed on time scale T. The algorithm must be rerun for all l. There isn't really any need to keep M low (since the computations are completed rapidly in any case), but intensity functions are in practice smooth functions of age y, and $M = 100$ is good enough for most purposes. An illustration for the Danish disability model is given in Figure 12.3 left. Even such a crude choice as $M = 1$ (dots) does not seem to deviate too much (though it *is* too inaccurate); consult also the exercises for this section.

12.5.7 Using historical data

Multi-state insurance models are often harder to identify from historical data than ordinary survival distributions. One of the problems is lack of data. Public disability schemes, for example, are vulnerable to political currents (and whims!), and it isn't uncommon for states to be redefined so that they mean different things in different periods. If there is much historical data, a non-parametric approach may be attempted. Consider some period of observation and count the number $n_l(i, j)$ of individuals who at some point are in state j at age l and in state i one time unit later. An estimate of $p_l(i|j)$ is then

$$\hat{p}_l(i|j) = \frac{n_l(i,j)}{n_l(j)} \quad \text{where} \quad n_l(j) = \sum_{i=1}^{v} n_l(i,j) \tag{12.41}$$

or the relative number of transitions to state i from state j at age l.

Lack of sufficient data often makes such estimates vulnerable to random error, and hence unattractive. A likelihood approach based on parametric intensity functions (as in Section 12.3) might do better; see Haberman and Pitacco (1999).

12.6 Multi-state insurance II: Premia and liabilities

12.6.1 Introduction

General multi-state insurance has a *stochastic* part defined by intensities $\mu_{i|j}(y)$ or transition probabilities $p_l(i|j)$ and a *contract* part with payments $s_l(i)$ in state i at age $y = lT$. This powerful setup handles most arrangements found in practice. Add general recipes for premia and liabilities and you have a toolkit for all sorts of insurance obligations. Calculations use the same set of averages as in earlier sections of this chapter, but with many states the mathematics becomes more messy.

12.6.2 Single policies

Consider a contract set up for an individual of age l_0 and state i_0 at the beginning. There is at time k a money transfer $s_{l_0+k}(i)$ depending on the state i at that time. It might be negative (premium paid) or positive (benefit received). Average payments are

$$\underbrace{s_{l_0+k}(i)\,{}_kp_{l_0}(i|i_0)}_{\textit{individual in state i}} \quad \text{and} \quad \underbrace{\textstyle\sum_{i=1}^{v} s_{l_0+k}(i)\,{}_kp_{l_0}(i|i_0)}_{\textit{average over all states}},$$

where ${}_kp_{l_0}(i|i_0)$ is a k-step transition probability as before. Adding the right-hand side over k with appropriate discounting yields the expected present value of the entire cash flow

$$E(\mathrm{PV}_0) = \sum_{k=0}^{\infty} d^k \left(\sum_{i=1}^{v} s_{l_0+k}(i)\,{}_kp_{l_0}(i|i_0) \right) = \sum_{i=1}^{v} \left(\sum_{k=0}^{\infty} d^k s_{l_0+k}(i)\,{}_kp_{l_0}(i|i_0) \right). \tag{12.42}$$

Equivalence premia may be adjusted to make $E(\mathrm{PV}_0) = 0$; how is indicated below.

12.6.3 Example 1: A widow scheme

One of the things we must learn is how contracts and their detailed clauses find their way into this machinery. The first example is a pension with compensation for a widow outliving the policy holder. In detail, the *husband* pays premia until retirement, and following *his* death the *widow* receives a fixed annual pension s_2 during the rest of her life. When he retires, the *couple* benefits from a different sum s_1 which is changed back to s_2 upon his death, but remains s_1 if she dies first. Many other clauses are possible.

The mathematical formulation can be based on the four states

state 1	state 2	state 3	state 4
both alive	*he alive, she dead*	*he dead, she alive*	*both dead*

with identical cash flows in states 1 and 2; i.e.,

$$\begin{array}{ll} s_l(1) = s_l(2) = -\pi, & l < l_r \\ s_l(1) = s_l(2) = s_1, & l \geq l_r \end{array} \qquad s_l(3) = s_2 \quad \text{and} \quad s_l(4) = 0.$$

Premium π is paid until his retirement at l_r or until his early death, and the pension is s_1 when *he* is alive and s_2 when *he* is dead. The transition probabilities between states require life tables, say ${}_kp_{l_0}$ for men and ${}_k\tilde{p}_{\tilde{l}_0}$ for women, and also their initial age l_0 and $\tilde{l}_0$. If the deaths of the spouses are independent events, then

$${}_kp_{l_0,\tilde{l}_0}(1|1) = {}_kp_{l_0}\,{}_k\tilde{p}_{\tilde{l}_0}, \quad {}_kp_{l_0,\tilde{l}_0}(2|1) = {}_kp_{l_0}(1 - {}_k\tilde{p}_{\tilde{l}_0}), \quad {}_kp_{l_0,\tilde{l}_0}(3|1) = (1 - {}_kp_{l_0})\,{}_k\tilde{p}_{\tilde{l}_0},$$

and these probabilities must be combined with the rules laid down by the contract for the expected present value (12.42) of the scheme. The fact that payments are equal in states 1 and 2 offers simplification. Since ${}_kp_{l_0,\tilde{l}_0}(1|1) + {}_kp_{l_0,\tilde{l}_0}(2|1) = {}_kp_{l_0}$, it follows that

$$E(\mathrm{PV}_0) = \underbrace{-\pi \sum_{k=0}^{l_r-l_0-1} d^k\,{}_kp_{l_0}}_{\textit{premium prior to } l_r} + \underbrace{s_1 \sum_{k=l_r-l_0}^{\infty} d^k\,{}_kp_{l_0}}_{\textit{pension he alive}} + \underbrace{s_2 \sum_{k=1}^{\infty} d^k(1 - {}_kp_{l_0})\,{}_k\tilde{p}_{\tilde{l}_0}}_{\textit{widow pension}},$$

and solving the equation $E(\mathrm{PV}_0) = 0$ determines the equivalence premium. The first two sums on the right can be written in terms of the annuity coefficients in Section 12.4, but the third can't. Extended annuity notation can be found among the references in Section 12.8.

12.6.4 Example 2: Disability and retirement in combination

As a second example consider a disability scheme with fixed benefit s_1 for each period of disability. At retirement l_r all individuals (whether disabled ot not) are transferred to an ordinary pension s_2, often different from s_1. A simple mathematical description makes use of

state 1	state 2	state 3
active/retired	*disabled/retired*	*dead*

with payment functions

$$\begin{array}{llll} s_l(1) = -\pi, & l < l_r & s_l(2) = s_1, & l < l_r \\ s_l(1) = s_2, & l \geq l_r & s_l(2) = s_2, & l \geq l_r \end{array} \quad \text{and} \quad s_l(3) = 0.$$

The cash flow in both states 1 and 2 depends on whether the individual is beyond retirement age or not. Possible models for jumps between states are those of the disability scheme in Section 12.5.

Consider an individual entering this arrangement at age l_0 as active. For the expected present value of the future payment stream, multiply the state-dependent money transfers by the transition probabilities ${}_kp_{l_0}(i|1)$ and discount. This yields

$$E(\mathrm{PV}_0) = \underbrace{-\pi \sum_{k=0}^{l_r-l_0-1} d^k \, {}_kp_{l_0}(1|1)}_{\textit{premium stage}} + \underbrace{s_1 \sum_{k=1}^{l_r-l_0-1} d^k \, {}_kp_{l_0}(2|1)}_{\textit{disability stage}}$$

$$+ \underbrace{s_2 \sum_{k=l_r-l_0}^{\infty} d^k \{{}_kp_{l_0}(1|1) + {}_kp_{l_0}(2|1)\}}_{\textit{benefit after retirement}},$$

where the pension after retirement is the same in states 1 and 2. The equivalence premium is determined by solving $E(PV_0) = 0$.

12.6.5 Portfolio liabilities

Portfolio liabilities $\mathcal{X}_k$ depend on many contracts with many different clauses which must be summarized and entered into the computer. In practice, a company or public institution might evaluate the policies one by one and add them. A general mathematical treatment must divide the portfolio into groups (l, j) according to the age l and state j of the individuals when the evaluations are being made, and work from the average contract for each group; see Exercise 12.39. This has to be done separately for men and women. The detailed mathematics though not difficult, is inelegant and we shall proceed more simply through a single average contract with payment $s_l(i)$ for an individual of state i at age l and a single set of transition probabilities ${}_kp_l(i|j)$.

Let $\mathbf{s}_l = \{s_l(1), \ldots, s_l(v)\}^{\mathrm{T}}$ and $\mathcal{N}_l = \{\mathcal{N}_l(1), \ldots, \mathcal{N}_l(v)\}^{\mathrm{T}}$ with $\mathcal{N}_l(j)$ the number of individuals at age l and state j at time 0. The liability at time k is then

$$\mathcal{X}_k = \sum_l \mathcal{N}_l^{\mathrm{T}} \, {}_k\mathbf{p}_l \, \mathbf{s}_{l+k} \tag{12.43}$$

where ${}_k\mathbf{p}_l$ was defined in (12.37). Why is it true? Write out the quadratic form

Algorithm 12.4 Liabilities in state-dependent insurance

```
Input: {_k p_l}, {N_l}, {s_l}, d, K                         %{_k p_l} from Algorithm 12.3
PV_0 <- 0   d_0 <- 1
For k = 0, ..., K do
    X_k <- 0
    Repeat for all l:    X_k <- X_k + N_l^T _k p_l s_{l+k}
    PV_0 <- PV_0 + d_k X_k,    d_{k+1} <- d_k d            %Discount for next round
Return X_0, ..., X_K, PV_0.
```

$\mathcal{N}_l^{\mathrm{T}}\ {}_k\mathbf{p}_l\,\mathbf{s}_{l+k}$ and it emerges that

$$\mathcal{N}_l^{\mathrm{T}}\ {}_k\mathbf{p}_l\,\mathbf{s}_{l+k} = \sum_{i=1}^{v} s_{l+k}(i)\,{}_k\mathcal{N}_l(i) \quad \text{where} \quad {}_k\mathcal{N}_l(i) = \sum_{j=1}^{v} {}_kp_l(i|j)\mathcal{N}_l(j),$$

with ${}_k\mathcal{N}_l(i)$ the number of individuals in state i at time k among those of age l at the beginning. Multiply this by the payment $s_{l+k}(i)$ per policy, and you get the total payment $s_{l+k}(i)\,{}_k\mathcal{N}_l(i)$ for those individuals. Adding over all i and l yields the portfolio value $\mathcal{X}_k$.

The matrices ${}_k\mathbf{p}_l$ were provided by Algorithm 12.3, and (12.43) is a simple recipe for $\mathcal{X}_k$ and their present value. Computations can be organized as in Algorithm 12.4.

12.6.6 Example: A disability scheme

As a simple example consider the standard disability scheme under the Danish or modified Danish model from Section 12.5. It is assumed that $s_1 = 30$, $s_2 = 20$, $l_r = 65$ and $r = 4\%$ with thousand euro or US$ as money unit. Equivalence premia are plotted in Figure 12.4 left against the age of entry l_0. The individual was in the active state at the beginning. When contributions start at 30, the amount is a little over 3000 annually, but it increases rapidly as l_0 is raised.

The portfolio liabilities on the right were calculated from one million individuals between 30 and 89 years of age. Age distributions used were

$$\text{Portfolio I:} \quad \mathcal{N}_l = ce^{-0.05|\,l-40|}, \qquad l = 30, \ldots, 89$$
$$\text{Portfolio II:} \quad \mathcal{N}_l = ce^{-0.05|\,l-50|}, \qquad l = 30, \ldots, 89$$

and at the beginning there were 90% active and 10% disabled in each age group. The constant c ensured that the number of policies was one million exactly. There are $v = 3$ states (active, disabled and dead), and contributions π in the active state are the equivalence premia for people entering the scheme at age 30. The payment

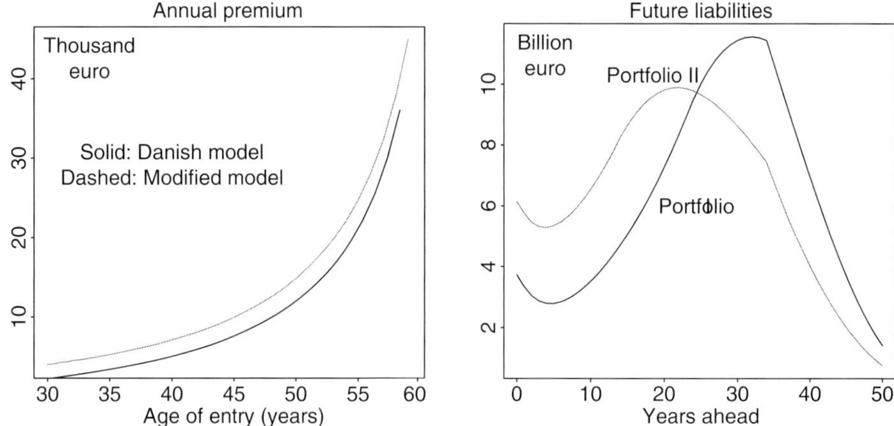

Figure 12.4 The combined disability/pension scheme described in the text. *Left*: Premia against age of entry. *Right*: Distribution of liabilities under the modified Danish model.

vectors that go into (12.43) are then

$$\mathbf{s}_l = \begin{pmatrix} -\pi \\ s_1 \\ 0 \end{pmatrix}, \quad l < l_r - l \quad \text{and} \quad \mathbf{s}_l = \begin{pmatrix} s_2 \\ s_2 \\ 0 \end{pmatrix}, \quad l \geq l_r - l$$

where the pension s_2 received after retirement is the same whether the individual comes from active or disabled. Take $\pi = 0$ if you seek gross liabilities without future premia taken into account.

Net liabilities, including π, are shown on the right of Figure 12.4. The model is the modified Danish one with rehabilitation. There are pronounced differences between the two portfolios due to their different age distributions. The much higher share of young members in Portfolio I shifts the bulk of the payments about one decade into the future. Such information is relevant when planning investments, a topic discussed in Section 15.6.

12.7 Mathematical arguments

12.7.1 Savings and mortality-adjusted value

Consider the savings value V_k' in (12.7) and the mortality-adjusted value V_k in (12.6) and their expectations $E(V_k'|C_0)$ and $E(V_k|C_0)$, which will be written $E(V_k')$ and $E(V_k)$ without reference to C_0. For the savings value

$$E(V_k') = E\left(\sum_{i=0}^{k-1}(1+r)^{k-i}(-\zeta_i)\right) = -(1+r)^k \sum_{i=0}^{k-1} d^i E(\zeta_i) \quad \text{where} \quad d = \frac{1}{1+r},$$

whereas from (12.6) right

$$E(V_k) = E\left(\sum_{i=0}^{\infty} d^i E(\zeta_{k+i}|C_{l_0+k})\right) = \sum_{i=0}^{\infty} d^i E(\zeta_{k+i})$$

using the rule of double expectation. This implies

$$\begin{aligned}
-E(V_k') + E(V_k) &= (1+r)^k \sum_{i=0}^{k-1} d^i E(\zeta_i) + \sum_{i=0}^{\infty} d^i E(\zeta_{k+i}) \\
&= (1+r)^k \left(\sum_{i=0}^{k-1} d^i E(\zeta_i) + \sum_{i=0}^{\infty} d^{k+i} E(\zeta_{k+i})\right) \\
&= (1+r)^k \sum_{i=0}^{\infty} d^i E(\zeta_i) = 0
\end{aligned}$$

by the condition of equivalence (12.5).

12.7.2 The reserve formula (12.19)

The expected present value of a pension plan $\{s_k\}$ is

$$E(\text{PV}_0) = \sum_{i=0}^{\infty} d^i s_i \, {}_ip_{l_0} = \sum_{i=0}^{k-1} d^i s_i \, {}_ip_{l_0} + \sum_{i=0}^{\infty} d^{k+i} s_{k+i} \, {}_{k+i}p_{l_0}$$

where

$$d^{k+i} = d^i \cdot d^k \quad \text{and} \quad {}_{k+i}p_{l_0} = {}_ip_{l_0+k} \cdot {}_kp_{l_0}.$$

The factorization on the right breaks survival to age $l_0 + k + i$ into two stages with $l_0 + k$ as an intermediate, and the probabilities of two events must be multiplied. Inserting into the second part of $E(\text{PV}_0)$ yields

$$E(\text{PV}_0) = \sum_{i=0}^{k-1} d^i s_i \, {}_ip_{l_0} + d^k \, {}_kp_{l_0} \sum_{i=0}^{\infty} d^i s_{k+i} \, {}_ip_{l_0+k},$$

and it is assumed that $E(\text{PV}_0) = 0$. Hence, since $d = 1/(1+r)$,

$$\sum_{i=0}^{\infty} d^i s_{k+i} \, {}_ip_{l_0+k} = -\frac{1}{d^k \, {}_kp_{l_0}} \sum_{i=0}^{k-1} d^i s_i \, {}_ip_{l_0} = -\sum_{i=0}^{k-1} (1+r)^{k-i} s_i \frac{{}_ip_{l_0}}{{}_kp_{l_0}}.$$

But ${}_kp_{l_0} = {}_{k-i}p_{l_0+i} \cdot {}_ip_{l_0}$ if $i < k$, and it follows that

$$\sum_{i=0}^{\infty} d^i s_{k+i} \, {}_ip_{l_0+k} = -\sum_{i=0}^{k-1} (1+r)^{k-i} s_i \frac{1}{{}_{k-i}p_{l_0+i}},$$

which is the link (12.19) between the retrospective and prospective reserve.

12.7.3 The k-step transition probabilities

To prove the recursion (12.32), invoke the elementary formula for sums of probabilities of disjoint events, which yields

$$\Pr(C_{l+k+1} = i|C_l = j) = \sum_{j_1=1}^{v} \Pr(C_{l+k+1} = i, C_{l+k} = j_1|C_l = i).$$

This implies

$$\Pr(C_{l+k+1} = i|C_l = j) = \sum_{j_1=1}^{v} \Pr(C_{l+k+1} = i|C_{l+k} = j_1, C_l = j)\Pr(C_{l+k} = j_1|C_l = j)$$

$$= \sum_{j_1=1}^{v} \Pr(C_{l+k+1} = i|C_{l+k} = j_1)\Pr(C_{l+k} = j_1|C_l = j),$$

where the last identity is due to the Markov assumption. This is the same as

$$_{k+1}p_l(i|j) = \sum_{j_1=1}^{v} p_{l+k}(i|j_1)\ _kp_l(j_1|j),$$

which is (12.32).

12.8 Bibliographical notes

12.8.1 Simple contracts and modelling

Life insurance mathematics goes back to an era long before computers, presumably the reason for the indigenous notation in Section 12.4. Gerber (1997) has much more of this than has been presented here. For an elementary introduction to the liability side of life insurance, you may also consult Promislow (2006). A brief (and eminently readable) introduction to the traditional theory is Nordberg (2004b), which includes continuous-time modelling with continuous payment streams, a viewpoint that has been ignored here. Only the bare necessity of survival modelling was discussed in Section 12.3. A good place to start for more on mathematical mortality concepts may be Wilmoth *et al.* (2007). This is a report outlining how the so-called Human Mortality Database (with historical survival data from all over the world) has been constructed. Other useful references are Forfar (2004) and Pollard (2004). Pitacco (2004) has many alternatives to the Gomperz–Makeham curves used in this book. A monograph from a demographic point of view is Keyfitz and Caswell (2005). In practice, life tables change with time and quite a lot too. Simple dynamic modelling is treated in Section 15.2; see also Section 15.8 for other references.

12.8.2 General work

For a broad, practical perspective on life insurance the book to read might be Booth *et al.* (1999), with an extensive list of references. The interplay with mathematical finance is not covered there, but you can look it up in Panjer (1998); see also Chapter 15 later. A specialist book dealing with multi-state models is Haberman and Pitacco (1999), containing (among other things) transition probability estimates that are much better than the primitive method in Section 12.5.

12.9 Exercises

Section 12.2

Exercise 12.1 Consider a pension with benefits s running from age l_r up to age l_e, broken off when the recipient dies. The scheme is financed through a single payment π_{l_0} at age l_0, known as a **one-time** premium; see also Section 3.4.

(a) If ${}_kp_{l_0}$ is the probability of survival, argue that the expected present value of the payment stream at the time the premium is paid is

$$E(\mathrm{PV}_0) = -\pi_{l_0} + s \sum_{k=l_r-l_0}^{l_e-l_0} d^k\,{}_kp_{l_0},$$

provided $l_0 \leq l_r$.

(b) How must the expression be modified when $l_0 > l_r$?

(c) Argue that under the equivalence condition

$$\pi_{l_0} = s \sum_{k=k_r}^{l_e-l_0} d^k\,{}_kp_{l_0} \quad \text{where} \quad k_r = \max(l_r - l_0, 0).$$

Exercise 12.2 A pension portfolio consists of $\mathcal{N}_l$ individuals of age l, all drawing a pension s from age l_r up to l_e with benefits stopped when a recipient dies.

(a) Argue that the expected present value of all these payments is $\mathcal{PV}_0 = \sum_l \mathcal{N}_l \pi_l$, where π_l is the one-time premium in Exercise 12.1.

(b) In what sense is this expression for $\mathcal{PV}_0$ a gross liability?

Exercise 12.3

(a) Derive an alternative decomposition of $\mathcal{PV}_0$ in the previous exercise; i.e., show that

$$\mathcal{PV}_0 = \sum_{k=0}^{l_e} d^k \mathcal{X}_k \quad \text{where} \quad \mathcal{X}_k = s \sum_{l=l_k}^{l_e-k} {}_kp_l \mathcal{N}_l, \quad l_k = \max(l_r - k, 0).$$

(b) Interpret the expression for $\mathcal{X}_k$.

Exercise 12.4 A policy holder contributes a premium π at the beginning of each of K periods in exchange for a sum s paid to a beneficiary in case of an early death before time K.

(a) Argue that the payment stream $\zeta_0, \dots, \zeta_K$ of the contract has expectations

$$\begin{aligned} E(\zeta_0) &= -\pi \\ E(\zeta_k) &= -\pi\,{}_kp_{l_0} + s\,{}_kq_{l_0}, \quad 0 < k < K \\ E(\zeta_K) &= s\,{}_Kq_{l_0} \end{aligned}$$

where l_0 is the age at the beginning and ${}_kq_{l_0}$ the mortality in Section 12.3.

(b) Find an expression for the expected present value of the contract and determine the equivalence premium.

Exercise 12.5 If the policy holder in Exercise 12.4 is alive after k periods, argue that the value of the contract at that time is

$$V_k = -\pi \sum_{i=0}^{K-k-1} d^i\,{}_ip_{l_0+k} + s \sum_{i=1}^{K-k} d^i\,{}_iq_{l_0+k}.$$

Exercise 12.6 Term insurance as in Exercise 12.4 may be combined with a clause under which the policy holder receives s_1 at the end of period K if alive at that time.

(a) Explain that the expected payments $E(\zeta_k)$ coincide with those in Exercise 12.4 except at time K and determine $E(\zeta_K)$ now.
(b) Modify the expression for the value V_k in Exercise 12.5 so that it still applies.
(c) Determine the equivalence premium by solving the equation $V_0 = 0$.

Exercise 12.7 Consider a widow scheme where premium is paid by *him* at the beginning of each of K periods to set up a pension s for *her* after *his* death (they receive nothing if he stays alive). The entire scheme is abolished if she dies first, and the capital accumulated is then taken over by the insurer. Two survival models are needed, say ${}_kp_{l_0}$ (for him) and ${}_k\tilde{p}_{\tilde{l}_0}$ (for her), where l_0 and $\tilde{l}_0$ are the age at the time the arrangement is set up.

(a) If deaths of spouses are independent events, argue that the expected values of the payment stream $\zeta_0, \zeta_1, \dots$ are

$$\begin{aligned} E(\zeta_0) &= -\pi \\ E(\zeta_k) &= -\pi\,{}_kp_{l_0}\,{}_k\tilde{p}_{\tilde{l}_0} + s(1 - {}_kp_{l_0})\,{}_k\tilde{p}_{\tilde{l}_0}, \quad 0 < k < K \\ E(\zeta_k) &= s(1 - {}_kp_{l_0})\,{}_k\tilde{p}_{\tilde{l}_0}, \quad k \geq K. \end{aligned}$$

(b) Find a mathematical expression for the equivalence premium.

Exercise 12.8

(a) If $k \geq K$ in Exercise 12.7, show that the value of the contract is

$$\underbrace{V_k = s\sum_{i=0}^{\infty} d^i(1 - {}_ip_{l_0+k})\,{}_i\tilde{p}_{\tilde{l}_0+k}}_{\text{both alive at time } k} \quad \text{and} \quad \underbrace{V_k = s\sum_{i=0}^{\infty} d^i\,{}_i\tilde{p}_{\tilde{l}_0+k}}_{\text{he dead, she alive}}.$$

(b) Modify the expressions so that they apply when $k < K$.

Section 12.3

Exercise 12.9 Let $\mu(y)$ be an intensity as in Section 12.3 and $F(y)$ the distribution function of Y.

(a) Argue that

$$\frac{1 - F(y)}{1 - F(y_0)} = \exp\left(-\int_{y_0}^{y} \mu(z)\,dz\right).$$

(b) Differentiate with respect to y and show that

$$\mu(y) = \frac{f(y)}{1 - F(y)} \quad \text{where} \quad f(y) = \frac{dF(y)}{dy}.$$

In this form $\mu(y)$ is known as a **hazard rate**.

Exercise 12.10 The file `japusmale.txt` contains survival data for Japanese males in 2008 (first column) and US ones in 2007 (second column) with $l_e + 1$ lines where $l_e = 110$. On line $l + 1$ is stored n_l survivors up to age l years among $n_0 = 100\,000$ at the beginning[14].

(a) Compute estimates of Japanese and US mortalities using $\hat{q}_l = 1 - n_{l+1}/n_l$.

R-*commands*:

```
nn=matrix(scan(''japusmale.txt''),byrow=T,ncol=2);
q̂=1-nn[1:le+1,]/nn[1:le,].
```

(b) Plot the estimated mortalities jointly against age.

R-*commands*:

`ll=1:le-1; plot(ll,q̂[,1]); lines(ll,q̂[,2])` with dots for the Japanese and a solid line for the US.

(c) Plot logarithms too.

R-*commands*:

```
plot(ll,log(q̂[,1])); lines(ll,log(q̂[,2])).
```

[14] The data are extracts downloaded from the Human Mortality Database (www.mortality.org).

Exercise 12.11 Redo the preceding exercise for Japanese and US women using survival data stored under the same format in `japusfem.txt`.
R-*commands*:

Those in Exercise 12.10 with `japusfem.txt`.

Exercise 12.12

(a) Write a program using (12.10) to tabulate ${}_kp_l$ for $k = 0, \dots, K$ and $l = 0, \dots, l_e$.
R-*commands*:
With `q` a vector of mortalities use `p=c(1-q,rep(0,`l_e`+1));`
${}_kp$`=matrix(1,K+1,`l_e`+1);`
`for (l in 0:`l_e`+1)`${}_kp$`[1:K+1,l]=cumprod(p[l:(l+K-1)])`.

(b) Run the program for the Japanese males in Exercise 12.10 when $K = 50$ and $l_e = 110$ and plot ${}_kp_l$ against k for $l = 10, 30, \dots, 100$ jointly.
R-*commands*:
With $\hat{q}$ from Exercise 12.10 use `q=`$\hat{q}$`[,1]` in (a) and then
`ind=1+1:10*10; matplot(0:K,`${}_kp$`[,ind])`.

(c) Redo for US males.
R-*commands*:
As in (b) with `q=`$\hat{q}$`[,2]`.

Exercise 12.13

(a) Write a program computing the mortalities ${}_kq_l$ in (12.11) for $k = 0, \dots, K$ and $l = 0, \dots, l_e$ under the conditions in Exercise 12.12.
R-*commands*:
With `p` and ${}_kp$ from Exercise 12.12 use ${}_kq$`=matrix(0,K+1,`l_e`+1);`
`for (l in 0:`l_e`+1)`${}_kq$`[1:K+1,l]=`${}_kp$`[1:K,l]*(1-p[1:K+(l-1)])`.

(b) Run the program for the Japanese males in Exercise 12.10 when $K = 100$ and $l_e = 110$ and plot ${}_kq_l$ against k for $l = 10, 30, \dots, 100$ jointly.
R-*commands*:
Given $\hat{q}$ from Exercise 12.10 use `q=`$\hat{q}$`[,1]`, the commands in (a) and then
`ind=1+1:10*10; matplot(0:K,`${}_kq$`[,ind])`.

(c) Redo for US males.
R-*commands*:
As in (b) with `q=`$\hat{q}$`[,2]`.

Exercise 12.14

(a) Fit the Gomperz–Makeham model to the Japanese males in Exercise 12.10 and plot the estimated mortalities jointly with those there.

R-*commands*:

With nn as in Exercise 12.10 and the R-function gompmakfit, use ll=1:l_e-1; plot(ll,$\hat{q}$[,1]); $\hat{\theta}$=gompmakfit(n=nn[,1])\$$\hat{\theta}$; $\hat{q}^{\text{gm}}$= 1-exp(-$\hat{\theta}$[1]-$\hat{\theta}$[2]*(exp($\hat{\theta}$[3])-1)*exp($\hat{\theta}$[3]*ll)/$\hat{\theta}$[3]); lines(ll,$\hat{q}^{\text{gm}}$).

(b) Redo (a) for the US males.

R-*commands*:

As in (a) with n=nn[,2].

(c) Redo (a) for the Japanese females in Exercise 12.11.

R-*commands*:

As in (a) with nn from Exercise 12.11.

(d) Redo (c) for US females.

R-*commands*:

As in (b) with nn from Exercise 12.11.

(e) What is your verdict on the Gomperz–Makeham fit?

Exercise 12.15 The plots of $_kq_l$ under the Japanese and US mortalities in Exercise 12.13 were a bit unsmooth; here is an alternative.

(a) Write a program tabulating $_kq_l$ for $k = 0, \ldots, K$ and $l = 0, \ldots, l_e$ under the Gomperz–Makeham model.

R-*commands*:

ll=0:(2*l_e); hh=exp(θ_2*ll); $_kp$=exp(-θ_0*ll-(θ_1/θ_2)*(hh-1)%o%hh); $_kq$=matrix(0,K+1,l_e+1); for (l in 0:l_e+1) $_kq$[1:K+1,l]=$_kp$[1:K,l]*(1-$_kp$[2,l:(l+K-1)]).

(b) Run the program for the US male parameters $\theta_0 = 0.000780$, $\theta_1 = 0.0000374$, $\theta_2 = 0.0928$ when $l_e = 110$ and $K = 100$ and plot as in Exercise 12.13.

R-*commands*:

ind=1+1:10*10; matplot(0:K,$_kq$[,ind]).

Exercise 12.16 To solve this exercise either implement Algorithm 12.1 yourself or use the R-function gompmakmean.

(a) Let y_0 vary between $l_1 = 18$ and $l_2 = 100$ years and compute/plot the average remaining life under the Gomperz–Makeham model with US 2007 male parameters.

R-*commands*:

θ=c(0.000780,0.0000374,0.0928); E=rep(0,l_2+1);
for (l in l_1:l_2); E[l+1]=gompmakmean(θ,l,h=1);
plot(l_1:l_2,E[l_1:l_2+1],''l'').

(b) Redo when $h = 0.1$ and 0.01 and plot the results jointly with the old ones.

R-*commands*:

As in (a) with h different and lines(l_1:l_2,E[l_1:l_2+1]) instead of plot.

(c) Replace remaining life with total life and redo (a) and (b).

R-*commands*:

Use l_1:l_2+E[l_1:l_2+1] when plotting.

Exercise 12.17 Let Y be how long an individual lives with $F(y)$ its distribution function and y_ϵ its ϵ-percentile.

(a) If $\mu(y)$ is the intensity function, use the results in the text to argue that

$$F(y) = 1 - \exp\left(-\int_0^y \mu(x)\,dx\right)$$

so that

$$-\int_0^{y_\epsilon} \mu(x)\,dx = \log(1-\epsilon).$$

(b) Write down the equation for y_ϵ when $\mu(y) = \theta_0 + \theta_1 e^{\theta_2 y}$.

(c) Implement a program for y_ϵ when $\epsilon = 0.02, 0.06, \ldots, 0.98$.

R-*commands*:

ϵ=1:25*0.04-0.02; y_ϵ=ϵ;
fe=function(y,e) $-\theta_0$*y-θ_1/θ_2*(exp(θ_2*y)-1)-log(1-e);
for (i in 1:25)y_ϵ[i]=uniroot(fe,e=ϵ[i],c(0.01,120))[[1]].

(d) Compute and plot y_ϵ against ϵ for the US male 2007 parameters $\theta_0 = 0.000780$, $\theta_1 = 0.0000374$ and $\theta_2 = 0.0928$.

R-*commands*:

plot(ϵ,y_ϵ,''l'').

Section 12.4

Exercise 12.18 Let $a_{l_r:\overline{K}|}$ be the mortality-adjusted present value (12.21) of an annuity starting at the retirement age l_r. If that is k periods into the future, argue that its value today is $d^k {}_kp_{l_0} a_{l_r:\overline{K}|}$ if l_0 is the age of the individual now.

Exercise 12.19 The sum needed to fund a pension s from a retirement age l_r up to some terminal age l_e (possibly infinite) was, in Exercise 12.1, called a one-time premium, denoted by π_{l_0} where l_0 is the age of the individual. Argue that

$$\pi_{l_0} = \begin{cases} sd^{l_r-l_0}\,{}_{l_r-l_0}p_{l_0}\, a_{l_r:\,\overline{l_e-l_r}|} & \text{if} \quad l_0 < l_r \\ s\, a_{l_0:\,\overline{l_e-l_0}|} & \text{if} \quad l_0 \geq l_r. \end{cases}$$

Exercise 12.20 Suppose a policy holder receives a fixed pension s from age l_r. Payments are in advance and last K periods, and the scheme, set up at age l_0, was financed by fixed contributions π at the beginning of each period until retirement. Argue that the value of the contract at time k is

$$V_k = \begin{cases} -\pi a_{l_0+k:\,\overline{l_r-l_0-k}|} + sd^{l_r-l_0-k}\,{}_{l_r-l_0-k}p_{l_0+k}\, a_{l_r:\,\overline{K}|} & \text{if} \quad k < l_r - l_0 \\ sa_{l_0+k:\,\overline{K-(l_0+k-l_r)}|} & \text{if} \quad k \geq l_r - l_0, \end{cases}$$

where $a_{l:\,\overline{K}|}$ is the coefficient in (12.21).

Exercise 12.21 A policy holder of age l_0 pays the equivalence premium π at the beginning of each of K periods in exchange for beneficiaries receiving a sum s if he dies prior to time K. Suppose the contract is cancelled after k years, where $k < K$.

(a) Why may the policy holder be entitled to compensation?
(b) Use the value concept to argue that a fair amount could be

$$V_k = -\pi a_{l_0+k:\,\overline{K-k}|} + s\ddot{A}_{l_0+k:\,\overline{K-k}|},$$

where $a_{l_0+k:\,\overline{K-k}|}$ and $\ddot{A}_{l_0+k:\,\overline{K-k}|}$ are the coefficients in (12.21) and (12.24).

Exercise 12.22

(a) Write a program computing the coefficient $a_{l:\,\overline{K}|}$ for $l = 0, \ldots, l_e$ and $K = 1, \ldots, K_1$ when ${}_kp_l$ has been tabulated.

R-*commands*:

With ${}_kp$ from Exercise 12.12 use

```
M=d**(0:(K₁ - 1))*ₖp[1:K₁,]; a=apply(M,2,cumsum).
```

(b) Run the program for the US males in Exercise 12.12 when $d = 0.97$, $K_1 = 50$ and plot $a_{l:\,\overline{K}|}$ jointly against K for all l between $l_1 = 25$ and $l_2 = 70$.

R-*commands*:

```
matplot(1:K₁,a[,l₁:l₂+1]).
```

(c) Interpret the fact that some of the curves become horizontal.

Exercise 12.23 A life annuity in advance over K periods purchased at age l_0 yields $\Pi/a_{l_0:\,\overline{K}|}$ per period if the original capital is Π. An alternative strategy may be to withdraw fixed amounts s until nothing is left.

(a) If the interest rate is r, argue that the value of such an account at time $K-1$ is

$$\Pi(1+r)^{K-1} - \sum_{k=0}^{K-1} s(1+r)^{K-1-k} = \Pi(1+r)^{K-1} - s\frac{(1+r)^K - 1}{r}.$$

(b) Show that this is zero if $s = \Pi/a_K$, where $a_K = (1-d^K)/(1-d)$ with $d = 1/(1+r)$.

(c) Compute a_K when $d = 0.97$ and $K = 5, 10, \ldots, 50$.

R-*commands*:

`K = 1:10*5;` a_K`=(1-d**K)/(1-d).`

(d) Compare with the corresponding values of $a_{l:\overline{K}|}$ under the conditions in Exercise 12.22 when $l = 40$.

R-*commands*:

With a from Exercise 12.22 use `print(`a_K`); print(a[K,l+1]).`

(e) Redo (d) for $l = 20$ and $l = 60$ and explain the way the discrepancies between a_K and $a_{l:\overline{K}|}$ depend on l.

Exercise 12.24 An annual pension s, received in advance from l_r to the end of life at $l_e = 110$, is purchased at age l_0 and financed by fixed contributions π at the start of each year until retirement.

(a) Write a program computing the equivalence π for a US male.

R-*commands*:

Take ${}_kp$ and $a_{l:\overline{K}|}$ from the tabulations in Exercises 12.12 and 12.22 and use
π`=s*d**(`l_r`-`l_0`)*`${}_kp[l_r - l_0 + 1, l_0 + 1]$`*a[`$l_e$`,`$l_r$`+1]/a[`$l_r$`-`$l_0$`,`$l_0$`+1].`

(b) Extend the program so that π is computed for all l_r between $l_{r1} = 55$ and $l_{r2} = 75$ and all l_0 between $l_1 = 20$ and $l_2 = 45$ and plot the results jointly against l_r for all l_0 when $s = 1$ and $d = 0.97$.

R-*commands*:

`ll=`l_{r1}`:`l_{r2}`;` π`=s*d**(ll-`l_1`)*`${}_kp[\text{ll}-l_1+1, l_1+1]$`*a[`$l_e$`,ll+1]/a[ll-`$l_1$`,`$l_1$`+1];`
`plot(ll,`π`,''l'',ylim=c(0,1.5)); for (`l_0` in (`l_1+1`):`l_2`){`π`=`
`s*d**(ll-`l_0`)*`${}_kp[\text{ll}-l_0+1, l_0+1]$`*a[`$l_e$`,ll+1]/a[ll-`$l_0$`,`$l_0$`+1];lines(ll,`$\pi$`)}.`

(c) Interpret the plot.

Exercise 12.25 The coefficient $\ddot{A}_{l:\overline{K}|}$ for the mortalities ${}_kq_l$ was defined in (12.24).

(a) Write a program tabulating it when $l = 0, \ldots, l_e$ and $K = 1, \ldots, K_1$.

R-*commands*:

With ${}_kq$ as in Exercise 12.13 use
`M=d**(1:`K_1`)*`${}_kq$`[1:`K_1`+1,]; A=apply(M,2,cumsum).`

(b) Run the program for the mortalities in Exercise 12.13 when $d = 0.97$, $K_1 = 50$ and plot $\ddot{A}_{l:\overline{K}|}$ against K jointly for all l between $l_1 = 25$ and $l_2 = 55$ years.

R-*commands*:

```
matplot(1:K1,A[,l1:l2 + 1],''l'').
```

(c) Interpret the pattern you see.

Exercise 12.26 Suppose the death of a policy holder before time K releases a one-time payment s. Premia π are paid per period in advance, and the discount is d.

(a) Use (12.28) to write a program tabulating the equivalence π when K varies between 1 and K_1 and l_0 between 0 and $l_e = 110$.

R-*commands*:

With a and A as in Exercises 12.22 and 12.25 use

```
π=s*A[1:K1+1,]/a[1:K1,].
```

(b) Run the program for US males as in Exercises 12.22 and 12.25 when $s = 1$, $d = 0.97$, $K_1 = 50$, and plot π against K for all l between $l_1 = 25$ and $l_2 = 55$.

R-*commands*:

```
matplot(1:K1,π[,l1:l2 + 1],''l'').
```

(c) Interpret the pattern.

Exercise 12.27 As in Exercise 12.1 let π_{l_0} be the one-time premium for a pension running from l_r to l_e.

(a) Write a program tabulating it when l_0 varies between 0 and l_e.

R-*commands*:

Take ${}_kp$ from Exercise 12.12 and use

```
I=matrix(0,le+1,le+1);
I[row(I)+col(I)>lr+1]=1; ll=0:le; M=s*d**ll*kp*I;
πl0=apply(M,2,sum).
```

(b) Run the program when $d = 0.97$, $l_r = 60$ and $s = 1$ with ${}_kp$ for the US males in Exercise 12.12 and plot π_{l_0} when l_0 varies between $l_1 = 20$ and $l_2 = 109$.

R-*commands*:

```
plot(l1:l2; πl0[l1:l2+1],''l'').
```

(c) Redo (b) when $d = 0.96$ and compare.

Exercise 12.28 How much does π_{l_0} in Exercise 12.27 change when the Gomperz–Makeham model is assumed?

(a) Write a program tabulating π_{l_0} now.

R-*commands*:

```
ll=0:le; hh=exp(θ2*ll); kp=exp(-θ0*ll-(θ1/θ2)*(hh-1)%o%hh)
```

and then the commands in Exercise 12.27(a).

(b) Run the program under the US male 2007 parameters $\theta_0 = 0.000780$, $\theta_1 = 0.0000374$, $\theta_2 = 0.0928$ with the rest of the assumptions as in Exercise 12.27(b) and redo the plot there.

R-*commands*:

As in Exercise 12.27(b).

(c) How much has the Gomperz–Makeham model changed the evaluations?

Section 12.5

Exercise 12.29 Insurance arrangements involving couples need the four states

$$\underset{\textit{both alive}}{(1,1)} \quad \underset{\textit{he is dead}}{(2,1)} \quad \underset{\textit{she is dead}}{(1,2)} \quad \underset{\textit{both dead}}{(2,2),}$$

where the middle ones mean one spouse is alive. Let ${}_kp_l$ and ${}_k\tilde{p}_{\tilde{l}}$ be the survival probabilities for men and women. Argue that under a plausible assumption

$${}_kp_{l,\tilde{l}}(1,1|1,1) = {}_kp_l\,{}_k\tilde{p}_{\tilde{l}}, \qquad {}_kp_{l,\tilde{l}}(2,1|1,1) = (1 - {}_kp_l)\,{}_k\tilde{p}_{\tilde{l}},$$
$${}_kp_{l,\tilde{l}}(1,2|1,1) = {}_kp_l\,(1 - {}_k\tilde{p}_{\tilde{l}}), \qquad {}_kp_{l,\tilde{l}}(2,2|1,1) = (1 - {}_kp_l)\,(1 - {}_k\tilde{p}_{\tilde{l}}),$$

where l and $\tilde{l}$ are the age at the beginning.

Exercise 12.30 Let ${}_kp_l$ and ${}_k\tilde{p}_{\tilde{l}}$ in Exercise 12.29 be the life tables for US men and women in Exercises 12.10 and 12.11.

(a) Write a program tabulating the k-step transition probabilities for couples when $k = 0, \ldots, K$ and $l = \tilde{l} = 0, \ldots, l_e$.

R-*commands*:

With ${}_kp$ from Exercise 12.12(c) generate ${}_k\tilde{p}$ in the same way from the mortalities in Exercise 12.11 and use `pm=`${}_kp$`[0:K+1,]; pf=`${}_k\tilde{p}$`[0:K+1,];`
`p11=pm*pf; p21=(1-pm)*pf; p12=pm*(1-pf); p22=(1-pm)*(1-pf).`

(b) Run the program when $K = 50$ and plot the four probabilities against k when $l = \tilde{l} = 30$.

R-*commands*:

```
kk=0:K; plot(kk,p11[,l+1],''l''); lines(kk,p21[,l+1]);
lines(kk,p12[,l+1]); lines(kk,p22[,l+1]).
```

(c) Redo when $l = \tilde{l} = 40$.

Exercise 12.31 Consider the Danish disability model (12.34)–(12.36) with the same mortalities in states a and i and with no rehabilitation so that $p_l(1|2) = 0$. If the intensities are $\mu_1(y) = \theta_0 + \theta_1 e^{\theta_2 y}$ and $\mu_{\mathrm{i|a}}(y) = \psi_0 + \psi_1 e^{\psi_2 y}$, show that

$$
\begin{aligned}
{}_kp_l(1|1) &= \exp\left(-k(\theta_0+\psi_0)T - \tfrac{\theta_1}{\theta_2}(e^{\theta_2 kT}-1)e^{\theta_2 lT} - \tfrac{\psi_1}{\psi_2}(e^{\psi_2 kT}-1)e^{\psi_2 lT}\right),\\
{}_kp_l(2|2) &= \exp\left(-k\theta_0 T - \tfrac{\theta_1}{\theta_2}(e^{\theta_2 kT}-1)e^{\theta_2 lT}\right),\\
{}_kp_l(2|1) &= \exp\left(-k\theta_0 T - \tfrac{\theta_1}{\theta_2}(e^{\theta_2 kT}-1)e^{\theta_2 lT}\right)\left(1-\exp\left(-k\psi_0 T - \tfrac{\psi_1}{\psi_2}(e^{\psi_2 kT}-1)e^{\psi_2 lT}\right)\right).
\end{aligned}
$$

Exercise 12.32 Consider a disability model with Gomperz–Makeham intensities with parameters $\boldsymbol{\theta}=(\theta_0,\theta_1,\theta_2)$ for survival, $\boldsymbol{\psi}=(\psi_0,\psi_1,\psi_2)$ for becoming disabled and $\boldsymbol{\zeta}=(\zeta_0,\zeta_1,\zeta_2)$ for going back to active. The R-function `disableprob` tabulates for given l the transition probabilities ${}_kp_l(i|j)$ for $k = 0,\dots,K$ using the recursion (12.38) with time increment $h = 1/M$. Let $\theta_0 = 0.000780$, $\theta_1 = 0.0000374$, $\theta_2 = 0.0928$ (US males), $\psi_0 = 0.0005$, $\psi_1 = 0.0000759$, $\psi_2 = 0.0875$ (apply for Norwegian males) and $\zeta_0 = 0.0005$, $\zeta_1 = 0$, $\zeta_2 = 0$ (invented).

(a) Compute/plot the probabilities ${}_kp_l(i|1)$ against k jointly for $i = 1,2,3$ when $l = 20$ and $K = 40$ using $M = 1$.

R-*commands*:

${}_kp$`=disableprob(`$\boldsymbol{\theta}$`,`$\boldsymbol{\psi}$`,`$\boldsymbol{\zeta}$`,l,K,M)$`${}_kp$`; matplot(0:K,t(`${}_kp$`[,1,]),''l'')`.

(b) Redo when $M = 12$ and plot the new values of the transition probabilities jointly with the old ones.

R-*commands*:

Recompute ${}_kp$ and use `lines(0:K,`${}_kp$`[1,1,]); lines(0:K,`${}_kp$`[2,1,]); lines(0:K,`${}_kp$`[3,1,])`.

(c) Any comments?

Exercise 12.33

(a) Compute the transition probabilities in Exercise 12.32 up to $K = 30$ with l varied between $l_1 = 20$ and $l_2 = 40$ and plot the probabilities ${}_kp_l(1|1)$ against k for all l jointly.

R-*commands*:

With $M = 12$ generate ${}_kp$ for $l = l_1$ as in Exercise 12.32 and use `plot(0:K,`${}_kp$`[1,1,],''l'',ylim=c(0,1))`. Then redo for all $l = l_1+1,\dots,l_2$ with `lines(0:K,`${}_kp$`[1,1,])` added to the plot each time.

(b) Redo (a) for ${}_kp_l(2|1)$.

R-*commands*:

As in (a) except for ${}_kp$`[2,1, ]` being plotted with `ylim=c(0,0.5)`.

Exercise 12.34

(a) First redo Exercise 12.32(b).
(b) Then recompute the transition probabilities (with $M = 12$) without rehabilitation and add these modifications to the plot in (a).

R-*commands*:

Run the program in Exercise 12.32 with ζ=(0, 0, 0) and use
`lines(0:K,`$_kp$`[1,1,]); lines(0:K,`$_kp$`[2,1,]); lines(`$_kp$`[3,1,]).`

(c) Compare the two evaluations.

Section 12.6

Exercise 12.35 Consider a mutual contract where the death of one partner in a couple releases a life-long pension s for the other. Let l_0 and $\tilde{l}_0$ be their age when the contract is drawn up, and $_kp_{l_0}$ and $_k\tilde{p}_{\tilde{l}_0}$ their survival probabilities.

(a) Argue that the amount ζ_k received at time k has expectation

$$E(\zeta_k) = \{(1 - {_kp_{l_0}})_k\tilde{p}_{\tilde{l}_0} + {_kp_{l_0}}(1 - {_k\tilde{p}_{\tilde{l}_0}})\}s.$$

(b) Write down a mathematical expression for the equivalence premium π if the entire pension is paid at once.
(c) Modify π if the pension only starts to run when the surviving partner has reached retirement age l_r.

Exercise 12.36 Mutual term insurance means one partner in a couple receiving a single payment s if the other dies.

(a) Argue that the expected benefit at time k now becomes

$$E(\zeta_k) = \{{_kp_{l_0}}{_k\tilde{q}_{\tilde{l}_0}} + {_kq_{l_0}}{_k\tilde{p}_{\tilde{l}_0}}\}s,$$

where $_kq_{l_0}$ and $_k\tilde{q}_{\tilde{l}_0}$ are the mortalities for men and women in Section 12.3.
(b) What is the equivalence premium π if the contract lasts K periods and is paid for at the beginning?
(c) Modify if the premium is contributed as K equal amounts at the start of each period.

Exercise 12.37 Suppose the couple of the preceding exercise wants to sell the contract after k periods when both are alive.

(a) How much do they get for it when it was financed as a one-time payment at the beginning?
(b) What is the answer when premia are contributed in K equal portions?

Exercise 12.38 Consider the disability/retirement scheme in Example 2 on page 456 where premium π is paid at the beginning of each period up to age $l_r - 1$, but only when the individual is in the active state.

(a) Examine the expression given for $E(\text{PV}_0)$ and modify it so that it defines the value of the contract at time k for individuals in state active.
(b) Redo for disabled individuals.

Exercise 12.39

(a) Argue that a future pension s per period requires an amount ρs to be set aside where ρ is some constant of proportionality.
(b) What factors influence ρ?
(c) If a portfolio is divided into groups with $\rho = \rho_g$ being the same for all individuals in group g, show that the total liability is

$$\mathcal{PV}_0 = \sum_j \rho_j s_j = \sum_g \mathcal{N}_g \rho_g \bar{s}_g$$

where $\mathcal{N}_g$ is the number of individuals in group g and $\bar{s}_g$ the average s-value.
(d) Explain that portfolio liabilities follow from such average contracts and that the argument applies *net* (future premia taken into account) and *gross* (the opposite).

Exercise 12.40 Consider a life insurance portfolio with age distribution $\mathcal{N}_l = ce^{-\gamma|l-l_m|}$ for $l = l_1, \ldots, l_2$ with γ and l_m parameters and c determined so that there is a total of $\mathcal{S}$ individuals.

(a) With the one-time premia π_{l_0} tabulated as in Exercise 12.27, write a program computing the present value of the portfolio liabilities.

R-*commands*:

With π_{l0} from Exercise 12.27 use `N=exp(-`γ`*abs(`l_1`:`l_2`-`l_m`));`
`N=(`$\mathcal{S}$`/sum(N))*N; PV=sum(`π_{l0}`[`l_1`:`l_2`+1]*N).`

(b) Run the program under the conditions in Exercise 12.27 with $l_1 = 20$, $l_2 = 100$, $\mathcal{S} = 10\,000$, $\gamma = 0.10$ and compute the present value when $l_m = 30$, 50 and 70.
(c) Comment on the importance of the age distribution.

Exercise 12.41 Let $\mathcal{X}_k$ be the payoff at time k for the portfolio in Exercise 12.40.

(a) With ${}_kp_l$ the life table tabulated in Exercise 12.12(c), l_r the retirement age and s the pension, write a program computing $\mathcal{X}_k$ for $k = 0, \ldots, l_e$ where l_e is the maximum age.

R-*commands*:

Take ${}_kp$ from Exercise 12.12(c), N from Exercise 12.40 and use `N=c(rep(0,`l_1`),N,rep(0,`l_e`-`l_2`)); I=matrix(0,`l_e`+1,`l_e`+1); I[row(I)+col(I)>`l_r`+1]=1; X=s*(`${}_kp$`*I)%*%N`.

(b) Run the program under the conditions in Exercises 12.27 and 12.40 and plot the liabilities against time up to $K = 80$ for the three age distributions jointly.

R-*commands*:

Use `plot(0:K; X[0:K+1],''l'')` for the first set of liabilities and then `lines(0:K,X[0:K+1])` for the other two.

Exercise 12.42

(a) When $\mathcal{X}_0, \mathcal{X}_1, \ldots$ have been computed as in the preceding exercise, how is the present value of the portfolio obligations determined?

(b) Compute it for the three age distributions in Exercise 12.40 when $d = 0.97$ and check with the results there, which were run under exactly the same conditions.

R-*commands*:

With `X` as in Exercise 12.41 use `PV=sum(d**(0:`l_e`)*X)`.

Exercise 12.43 Suppose all the individuals of the preceding exercises contribute a premium π at the start of each year up to age $l_r - 1$ as long as they are alive and let Π_k be the total premium income in year k.

(a) Write a program computing Π_k for $k = 0, \ldots, l_e$.

R-*commands*:

Almost the same as in Exercise 12.41; change the last two commands to `I[row(I)+col(I)<`l_r`+2]=1; Π=π*(`${}_k$`p*I)%*%N`.

(b) Run the program under the conditions in Exercise 12.40 when $\pi = 0.218$ (the equivalence premium when the contract is entered at $l_0 = 25$ years) and plot the premium income against time up to $K = 40$.

R-*commands*:

`plot(0:K; Π[0:K+1,],''l'')`.

Exercise 12.44 *Net* liabilities subtract future premium income. Compute and plot these quantities against time up to $K = 40$ under the same conditions and age distributions as in the previous exercises.

R-*commands*:

Take `X` and `Π` from Exercises 12.41 and 12.43 and use `plot(0:K,(X-Π)[0:K+1],''l'')` for the first age distribution and then `lines` instead of `plot` for the other two.

Exercise 12.45 Suppose all individuals in the disability scheme in Exercise 12.32 contribute the equivalence premium π in advance when in the active state. This lasts until retirement at age l_r, when the entire scheme stops.

(a) Write a program computing π for an individual of l_0 years and in the active state at time 0 when the arrangement is set up.

R-*commands*:

Take ${}_kp$ from Exercise 12.32 and use K=l_r-l_0-1;
a_1=sum(d**(0:K)*${}_k$p[2,1,]); a_2=sum(d**(0:K)*${}_k$p[1,1,];
π=s*a_1/a_2.

(b) Run the program when $s = 1$, $l_r = 65$, $d = 0.97$ and $l_0 = 25$, 35 or 45 and examine how equivalence premia depend on l_0.

Exercise 12.46 Suppose the age distribution of the disability scheme in Exercise 12.45 is $\mathcal{N}_l = ce^{-\gamma|l-l_m|}$ for $l = l_1, \ldots, l_2$ with c determined so that the total count is $\mathcal{S}$. At the beginning a fraction ω is disabled (the same for all l) and the rest active.

(a) Compute/plot the liabilities $\mathcal{X}_0, \ldots, \mathcal{X}_K$ for $K = l_r - l_1 - 1$ when $s = 1$, $l_r = 65$, $l_1 = 20$, $l_2 = 63$, $\gamma = 0.1$, $\mathcal{S} = 10\,000$, $\omega = 0.1$ and $l_m = 30$.

R-*commands*:

With θ, ψ and ζ the parameters in Exercise 12.32 and the R-function disableport available from the library use
X=disableport(θ,ψ,ζ,s,l_r,$\mathcal{S}$,l_1,l_2,ω,γ,l_m)RX;
plot(1:(l_r-l_1)-1,X,''l'').

(b) Redo (a) when $l_m = 40$ and $l_m = 50$ and plot the three sequences of liabilities jointly against time.

R-*commands*:

After having recomputed X, use lines(1:(l_r-l_1)-1,X,''l'').

(c) Comment on the significance of the age distribution.

Exercise 12.47

(a) Use the computations of the preceding exercise to determine the present value of the expenses for the three age distributions when $d = 0.97$.

R-*commands*:

With X,l_1,l_r as in Exercise 12.46 use, for each age distribution,
PV=sum(d**(1:($l_r - l_1$)-1)*X).

(b) Redo for $d = 0.96$ and comment on how the changes vary with the age distribution.

Exercise 12.48 Consider once again the disability scheme of the preceding exercises and suppose everybody has to contribute $\pi = 0.1134$ per period when they are in the active state (the equivalence premium for somebody entering the arrangement at age 25).

(a) Modify the computations in Exercise 12.46 so that the total premia $\Pi_0, \ldots, \Pi_K$ are computed/plotted instead.

R-*commands*:

With the R-function `disableprem` similar to `disableport` in Exercise 12.46, use Π=`disableprem(`θ,ψ,ζ,π,l_r,S,l_1,l_2,ω,γ,l_m`)`RΠ; `plot(1:(`l_r`-`l_1`)-1,`Π`,''l'')` for $l_m = 30$ and continue for the other age distributions with `lines` replacing `plot`.

(b) Comment on the difference between the age distributions.

Exercise 12.49 Use the programs in Exercises 12.46 and 12.48 to compute/plot the *net* expenses $X_k - \Pi_k$ against k for the same three age distributions and under the same conditions as before.

R-*commands*:

Compute `X` and Π as in Exercises 12.46 and 12.48 and follow the steps in Exercise 12.48 with `X-`Π replacing Π.

13
Stochastic asset models

13.1 Introduction

The liabilities of the preceding chapter extended over decades, and assets covering them should be followed over decades too, which requires models for equities and the interest-rate curve. Inflation is relevant too, since liabilities might depend on the future wage or price level. This chapter is on the joint and dynamic modelling of such variables. This is a cornerstone when financial risk is evaluated and makes use of linear, normal and heavy-tailed models, stochastic volatility, random walks and stationary stochastic processes. The topic is not elementary; above all it is **multivariate**. Economic and financial variables influence each other mutually, some of them heavily.

The central models, reviewed below and extended from the treatment in Part I, are huge classes, and here is the real difficulty: Which models to pick in specific situations and what about their parameters? Sources of information are historical data, implications of market positions and even economic and financial analyses and theory. Much of that is beyond the scope of this book, and unlike elsewhere model building through historical data is touched on only briefly. A specific model to work with will be needed in Chapter 15. The most established in actuarial science may be the Wilkie models, set up in a purely empirical way by examining historical data from the last 70 years of the twentieth century; see Wilkie (1995). A major part of it is presented in Sections 13.5 and 13.6.

13.2 Volatility modelling I

13.2.1 Introduction

Stochastic volatility was introduced in Chapter 2 through models with standard deviations

$$\underset{\text{stochastic volatility}}{\sigma = \xi_\sigma\sqrt{Z},} \qquad \text{below extended to} \qquad \underset{\text{time-varying version}}{\sigma_k = \xi_\sigma\sqrt{Z_k},}$$

where Z and Z_k are positive random variables. These constructions lead to heavy-tailed distributions. Why such extensions from the ordinary normal are needed is indicated in Figure 13.1, where log-returns from the Standard & Poor (SP) financial index have been Q–Q plotted against the normal over the period from 1983 to 2000. Heavier tails than the normal are evident for daily and weekly data, less so for annual data, which is in line with the central limit theorem. There is a dynamic perspective too. Many financial variables exhibit bursts of violent (nervous!) fluctuations followed by periods of relative tranquillity as in Figure 13.2. Volatilities are in reality a stochastic process.

13.2.2 Multivariate stochastic volatility

A simple, general construction is to start with correlated $N(0, 1)$ variables $\varepsilon_1, \ldots, \varepsilon_J$ as in Section 5.4 and assume a single random source Z for all volatilities. The model for a collection of variables $Y_1, \ldots, Y_J$ then becomes

$$Y_j = \xi_{yj} + \sigma_j\varepsilon_j, \quad \sigma_j = \xi_{\sigma j}\sqrt{Z}, \quad j = 1, \ldots, J \tag{13.1}$$

with Z positive and independent of $\varepsilon_1, \ldots, \varepsilon_J$. The parameters are $\xi_{y1}, \ldots, \xi_{y_J}$ and $\xi_{\sigma 1}, \ldots, \xi_{\sigma_J}$. To let volatilities oscillate in perfect synchrony like this has no special justification apart from being the most common model. It is natural to demand (exactly or approximately) that

$$E(\sqrt{Z}) = 1 \quad \text{or} \quad E(Z) = 1,$$

which makes $E(\sigma_j) = \xi_{\sigma j}$ or $E(\sigma_j^2) = \xi_{\sigma j}^2$ with the second version used for the GARCH models in Section 13.3. Note that

$$\text{cov}(Y_i, Y_j) = E(Y - \xi_{yi})(Y_j - \xi_{yj}) = E(\sigma_i\sigma_j\varepsilon_i\varepsilon_j) = E(\sigma_i\sigma_j)E(\varepsilon_i\varepsilon_j)$$

so that

$$\text{cov}(Y_i, Y_j) = \xi_{\sigma i}\xi_{\sigma j}E(Z)\text{cor}(\varepsilon_i, \varepsilon_j) \quad \text{and also} \quad \text{var}(Y_j) = \xi_{\sigma j}^2 E(Z).$$

Hence

$$\text{cor}(Y_i, Y_j) = \text{cor}(\varepsilon_i, \varepsilon_j) \quad i \neq j, \tag{13.2}$$

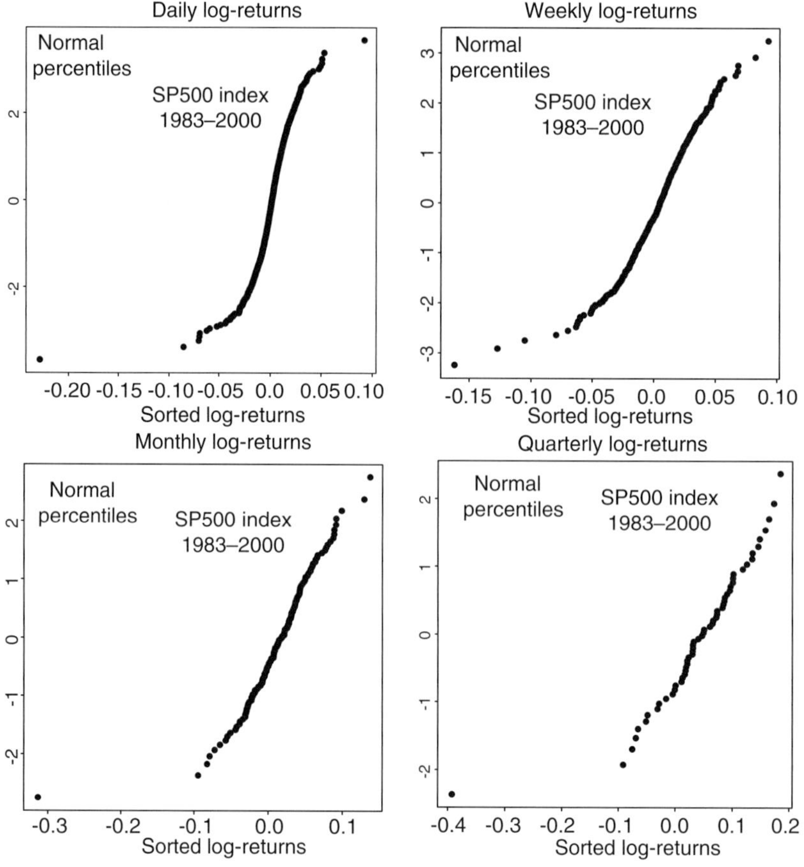

Figure 13.1 Q–Q plots against the normal for the log-returns of the SP 500 index

and the correlations of the defining normals are passed unchanged to $Y_1, \ldots, Y_J$.

13.2.3 The multivariate *t*-distribution

A common specification is $Z = 1/G$, with G a Gamma variable with mean 1. Then

$$Y_j = \xi_{yj} + \xi_{\sigma j} G^{-1/2} \varepsilon_j \quad \text{where} \quad G \sim \text{Gamma}(\alpha), \tag{13.3}$$

and the resulting model for $Y_1, \ldots, Y_J$ is known as the **multivariate** t, an extension of the univariate version from Section 2.4. Recall that $G \to 1$ as $\alpha \to \infty$, which means that the multivariate normal appears in the limit. Small α yield distributions with heavy tails, and mean, standard deviation and kurtosis become infinite when

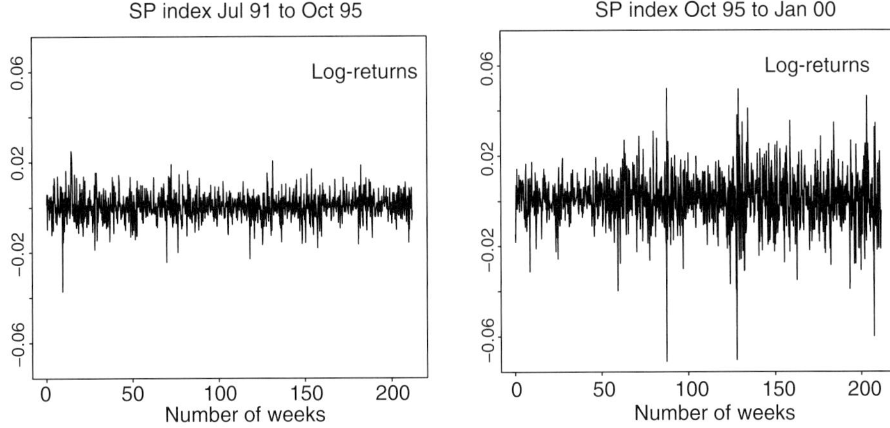

Figure 13.2 Time series plots of the daily log-return of the SP 500 index in two periods.

α is $1/2$, 1 and 2 or smaller. Their formulae (when they exist) are

$$E(Y_j) = \xi_{yj}, \quad \mathrm{sd}(Y_j) = \xi_{\sigma j}\sqrt{\frac{\alpha}{\alpha-1}} \quad \text{and} \quad \mathrm{kurt}(Y_j) = \frac{3}{\alpha-2}, \tag{13.4}$$

whereas $\mathrm{skew}(Y_j) = 0$. Simulation is easy from the definition with G drawn from Algorithms 2.9 and 2.10 and $\varepsilon_1, \dots, \varepsilon_J$ as outlined in Section 5.4.

Likelihood fitting requires numerical procedures, and moment estimation is simpler technically. The correlations of $\varepsilon_1, \dots, \varepsilon_J$ are then taken as the sample correlations of the observations, say $y_{j1}, \dots, y_{jn}$ for variable j whereas the rest of the parameters make use of

$$\overline{y_j} = \frac{1}{n}\sum_{k=1}^{n} y_{jk}, \quad s_j^2 = \frac{1}{n-1}\sum_{k=1}^{n}(y_{jk} - \overline{y}_j)^2, \quad \hat{\kappa}_j = \left(\frac{1}{ns_j^4}\sum_{k=1}^{n}(y_{kj} - \overline{y}_j)^4\right) - 3$$

with $\hat{\kappa}_j$ a kurtosis estimate. Inverting (13.4) yields

$$\hat{\alpha}_j = 3/\hat{\kappa}_j + 2, \quad \hat{\xi}_{\sigma j} = s_j\sqrt{\frac{\hat{\alpha}_j - 1}{\hat{\alpha}_j}} \quad \text{and} \quad \hat{\xi}_{yj} = \overline{y}_j,$$

which allows different $\hat{\alpha}_j$ for different variables. This is a quick way to check whether a common α assumed by the multivariate t is supported by experience, and it could be estimated as $\hat{\alpha} = 3/\overline{\hat{\kappa}}$ where $\overline{\hat{\kappa}} = (\hat{\kappa}_1 + \cdots + \hat{\kappa}_J)/J$. But the method breaks down in case of infinite kurtosis, which is a practical possibility; see Exercise 7.15 for a better method.

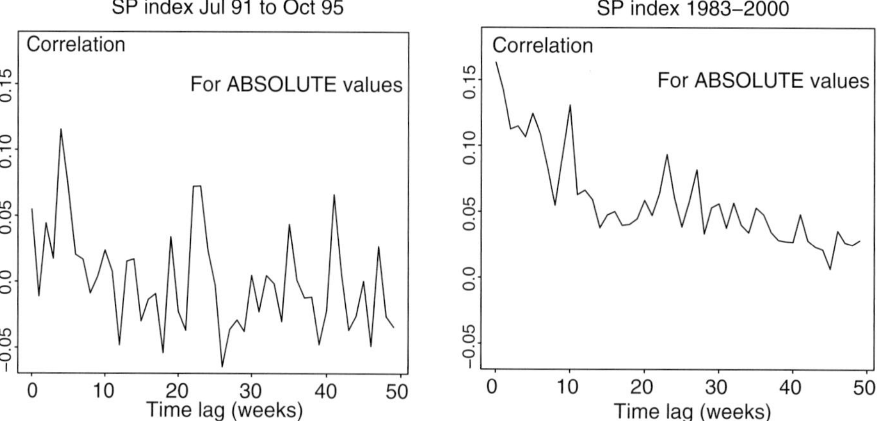

Figure 13.3 Autocorrelation plots of **absolute** deviations from the mean for the SP 500 index.

13.2.4 Dynamic volatility

The example in Figure 13.2 shows daily returns of the SP index for two different periods of about 4 years. Patterns are distinctly unequal, with the calm oscillations on the left replaced by instability on the right. This is an example of time-varying volatilities. A simple mathematical formulation is

$$Y_k = \xi_y + \sigma_k \varepsilon_k \quad \text{where} \quad \sigma_k = \xi_\sigma \sqrt{Z_k}, \tag{13.5}$$

with $\{Z_k\}$ a stochastic process. Standard tools like sample autocorrelations don't detect such phenomena. To understand why, let ε_k be independent of σ_k and everything else from the past. This is satisfied by all models in practical use. Now

$$E(Y_k) = \xi_y + E(\sigma_k \varepsilon_k) = \xi_y + E(\sigma_k)E(\varepsilon_k) = \xi_y,$$

and if $l > 0$,

$$\begin{aligned} \text{cov}(Y_k, Y_{k-l}) &= E\{(Y_k - \xi_y)(Y_{k-l} - \xi_y)\} = E(\sigma_k \varepsilon_k \sigma_{k-l} \varepsilon_{k-l}) \\ &= E(\varepsilon_k)E(\sigma_k \sigma_{k-l} \varepsilon_{k-l}) = 0. \end{aligned}$$

Expectation and autocovariances remain what they were without Z_k, and with equity that is exactly what we want (since the model would otherwise have allowed future stock prices to be prediced), but it also tells us that studies of dynamic volatility require other means. Simple possibilities are autocorrelations of absolute values $|Y_k|$, squares Y_k^2 or absolute deviations $|Y_k - \overline{Y}|$, where $\overline{Y}$ is the ordinary average.

The third of these is shown in Figure 13.3, applied to the data in Figure 13.2. There are on the right positive correlations at all lags, hinting at some underlying phenomenon that surely must be of interest, whereas it seems hardly present at all on the left.

13.2.5 Volatility as driver

One model construction is to let $\{\varepsilon_k\}$ and $\{\sigma_k\}$ in (13.5) be independent processes, which means that the latter acts as a prior **driving** $\{Y_k\}$. There is no influence the other way, and future volatilities are not affected by the market at all. Is that questionable? The approach is less popular than the alternative in the next section, yet it does lead to straightforward models, easy to simulate and the interest may be on its way up; see references in Section 13.8.

Suppose $\{\varepsilon_k\}$ is an independent $N(0, 1)$ series. It is verified in Section 13.7 that

$$E(|Y_k - \xi_y|) = E(\sigma_k)\sqrt{\frac{2}{\pi}} \quad \text{and} \quad \text{var}(|Y_k - \xi_y|) = \text{var}(\sigma_k) + (E\sigma_k)^2\left(1 - \frac{2}{\pi}\right), \tag{13.6}$$

where $\pi \doteq 3.141593$ and also

$$\text{cov}(|Y_k - \xi_y|, |Y_{k-l} - \xi_y|) = \frac{2}{\pi}\text{cov}(\sigma_k, \sigma_{k-l}). \tag{13.7}$$

This holds *approximately* even when $\overline{Y}$ replaces ξ, so that

$$\text{cov}(|Y_k - \overline{Y}|, |Y_{k-l} - \overline{Y}|) \doteq \frac{2}{\pi}\text{cov}(\sigma_k, \sigma_{k-l})$$

and patterns such as those in Figure 13.3 are referred to autocorrelations in the underlying σ_k.

It is reasonable to restrict the models for volatilities to stationary ones. The initial value σ_0 is then forgotten as $k \to \infty$, and

$$E(\sigma_k|\sigma_0) \to \xi_\sigma, \quad \text{sd}(\sigma_k|\sigma_0) \to \sigma_\sigma \quad \text{and} \quad \text{cor}(\sigma_k, \sigma_{k-l}|\sigma_0) \to \rho_{\sigma l}$$

with similar limiting results for the Y-series. Indeed, $\text{cor}(|Y_k - \xi_y|, |Y_{k-l} - \xi_y||\sigma_0) \to \rho_{yl}$ where

$$\rho_{yl} = c\rho_{\sigma l} \quad \text{with} \quad \frac{1}{c} = \pi/2 + (\pi/2 - 1)\left(\frac{\xi_\sigma}{\sigma_\sigma}\right)^2, \tag{13.8}$$

and the autocorrelations of absolute deviations are proportional to those of the volatilities. The result is verified by noting that (13.6) right yields

$$\text{var}(|Y_k - \xi_y||\sigma_0) \to \sigma_\sigma^2 + \xi_\sigma^2\left(1 - \frac{2}{\pi}\right) \quad \text{as} \quad k \to \infty,$$

and (13.8) follows when (13.7) is divided by this.

13.2.6 Log-normal volatility

A simple model for volatilities is the log-normal

$$\sigma_k = \xi_\sigma e^{-\tau^2/2 + \tau X_k} \quad \text{where} \quad X_k = aX_{k-1} + \sqrt{1 - a^2}\,\eta_k, \tag{13.9}$$

for $k = 1, 2, \dots$, which is to be combined with $Y_k = \xi_y + \sigma_k \varepsilon_k$. Two independent $N(0, 1)$ series $\eta_1, \eta_2, \dots$ and $\varepsilon_1, \varepsilon_2, \dots$ of independent terms are driving the system. The recursion on the right in (13.9) starts at $X_0 = \log(\sigma_0/\xi_\sigma)/\tau + \tau/2$.

As $k \to \infty$ the initial σ_0 is forgotten, and the construction ensures $E(\sigma_k|\sigma_0) \to \xi_\sigma$, and after a while the volatilities fluctuate around ξ_σ. Moreover,

$$\mathrm{cor}(|Y_k - \xi_y|, |Y_{k-l} - \xi_y||\sigma_0) \to \frac{e^{\tau^2 a^{|l|}} - 1}{e^{\tau^2} - 1} \quad \text{as} \quad k \to \infty, \tag{13.10}$$

which is verified in Section 13.7. It is possible to use this expression to estimate parameters by fitting it to the sample autocorrelations of the sequence $|Y_1 - \overline{Y}|, |Y_2 - \overline{Y}|, \dots$, but this requires numerical methods. Likelihood estimation is more accurate, but also much more demanding technically; see references in Section 13.8.

13.2.7 Numerical example

How important is dynamic volatility for long-term financial risk? Here is a numerical illustration based on the preceding model with parameters $\xi_y = 0.00068$, $\xi_\sigma = 0.01$, $\tau = 0.63$ and $a = 0.95$, which are likelihood estimates for the 1-day returns from the SP 500 index from 1983 to 2000. Figure 13.4 shows density functions of 5-year returns obtained with $m = 10\,000$ simulations, generated as described below. There are two comparisons. On the left, density functions for returns under the SP 500 parameters are plotted jointly with what we get when σ_k is fixed as the average $\xi_\sigma = 0.01$. Making volatilities stochastic makes uncertainty go up and that is equally so on the right, where the experiment on the left has been repeated with $a = 0$ instead of $a = 0.95$. Volatilities are now independent, but their fluctuations from the mean are as large as on the left, and the resulting density function not very different. In this example the dynamic model didn't change things much, but that isn't a general rule.

The model is daily, and unlike in Section 5.7 it is now not possible to switch to other time scales in a simple manner. Simulations were therefore run for $K = 250 \times 5 = 1250$ days for a 5-year view (250 days in a *financial* year). If $R_{0:k}$ is the return over k time units (here days), it evolves under the log-normal, stochastic volatility model according to the recursion

$$1 + R_{0:k} = (1 + R_{0:k-1})e^{\xi_y + \sigma_k \varepsilon_k}, \quad \sigma_k = \xi_\sigma e^{-\tau^2/2 + \tau X_k}, \quad X_k = a X_{k-1} + \sqrt{1 - a^2}\,\eta_k$$

for $k = 1, 2, \dots$ The scheme was started at $R_{0:0} = 0$, $\sigma_0 = \xi_\sigma$ and $X_0 = \tau/2$. Monte Carlo requires simulated realizations ε_k^* and η_k^* to be inserted for the error terms ε_k and η_k.

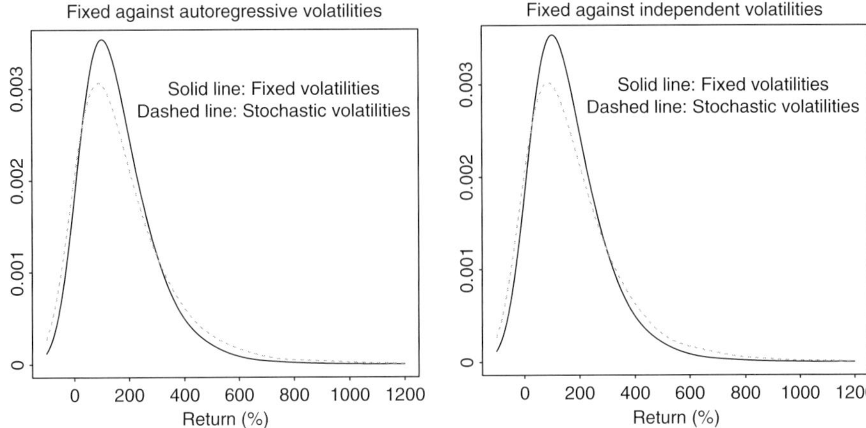

Figure 13.4 *Left*: Density functions of 5-year returns (%) under the model fitted to the SP 500 index with stochastic volatilities (solid line) and fixed volatilities (dashed line). *Right*: The same with independent volatilities.

13.2.8 Several series in parallel

Extensions to several series running in parallel are straightforward, for example

$$Y_{jk} = \xi_{yj} + \sigma_{jk}\varepsilon_{jk} \quad \text{where} \quad \sigma_{jk} = \xi_{\sigma j}\sqrt{Z_k}, \quad j = 1, \ldots, J,$$

for $k = 1, 2, \ldots$, and a single process $\{Z_k\}$ is responsible for the way volatilities are fluctuating. It may be log-normal as in the example above, but we may also take $Z_k = 1/\sqrt{G_k}$ where $\{G_k\}$ are Gamma-distributed variables. The model is now a dynamic version of the multivariate t. Autocorrelated Gamma variables were constructed in Section 11.4.

13.3 Volatility modelling II: The GARCH type

13.3.1 Introduction

The most popular and established method of describing dynamic volatility is through the **GARCH** models, where the processes $\{Y_k\}$ and $\{\sigma_k\}$ influence each other mutually. Such relationships are known as **feedbacks**, and there will be more of them in Section 13.4. The idea that $\{Y_k\}$ acts upon $\{\sigma_k\}$ is attractive. Shouldn't market behaviour influence how the future is perceived? When transactions deviate strongly from what is expected, surely uncertainty might go up? A simple implementation of this idea is the ARCH and GARCH models originating with Engle (1982), where ARCH stands for autoregressive conditional heteroscedasticity with GARCH being generalized ARCH. There has been much development since that time, see Bollerslev (2001), but the so-called first-order GARCH (an early contribution) is still favoured by many users. This is an autoregression of order 1 for *variances*, and like its sister version in Section 5.6 is easy to analyse mathematically. Much of the section is devoted to it.

13.3.2 How GARCH models are constructed

Start out as in Section 13.2 with $Y_k = \xi_y + \sigma_k\varepsilon_k$ where $\{\varepsilon_k\}$ is an independent and $N(0, 1)$ process, but generate volatilities through recursions that involve past observations. A GARCH model of order $(1, 1)$ specifies

$$\sigma_k^2 = (1 - \theta_1 - \theta_2)\xi_\sigma^2 + \theta_1(Y_{k-1} - \xi_y)^2 + \theta_2\sigma_{k-1}^2, \quad k = 1, 2, \ldots \tag{13.11}$$

with ξ_σ, θ_1, θ_2 positive parameters. There are three contributions to the new σ_k^2, with the middle one defining the impact of preceding trading. Initial values $Y_0 = y_0$ and σ_0 are needed to start the recursion. It is often sensible to let σ_0 be an extra parameter along with ξ_y, ξ_σ, θ_1 and θ_2.

The definition only makes sense if $\theta_1 + \theta_2 < 1$ since the first term on the right in (13.11) becomes negative otherwise. Actually, an even stronger condition is needed; see below. Higher-order versions are straightforward by adding extra terms on the right in (13.11), for example $\theta_3(Y_{k-2} - \xi_y)^2$ or $\theta_4\sigma_{k-2}^2$.

13.3.3 Volatilities under first-order GARCH

The variances σ_k^2 can be examined by inserting $Y_{k-1} = \xi_y + \sigma_{k-1}\varepsilon_{k-1}$ into (13.11). This yields, after some reorganization,

$$\sigma_k^2 - \xi_\sigma^2 = (\theta_1 + \theta_2)(\sigma_{k-1}^2 - \xi_\sigma^2) + \theta_1\eta_k \quad \text{where} \quad \eta_k = \sigma_{k-1}^2(\varepsilon_{k-1}^2 - 1). \tag{13.12}$$

It is verified in Section 13.7 that

$$E(\eta_k) = 0, \quad \text{cor}(\eta_k, \eta_{k-l}) = 0, \quad \text{cor}(\eta_k, \sigma_{k-l}^2) = 0 \quad \text{if } l > 0. \tag{13.13}$$

It follows that $\{\eta_k\}$ behaves like an independent series of errors, so that (13.12) defines an autoregressive process of order 1 which can be analysed as in Chapter 5; see Section 13.7.

Central properties of the variance series are

$$E(\sigma_k^2|y_0, \sigma_0) = \xi_\sigma^2 + (\theta_1 + \theta_2)^k(\sigma_0^2 - \xi_\sigma^2) \tag{13.14}$$

and

$$\text{cov}(\sigma_k^2, \sigma_{k-l}^2|y_0, \sigma_0) = (\theta_1 + \theta_2)^l\text{var}(\sigma_{k-l}^2|y_0, \sigma_0) \quad \text{for} \quad l > 0, \tag{13.15}$$

showing that $\theta_1 + \theta_2$ (known as the **persistence** parameter) defines the memory of the process and plays the same role as a in Section 5.6. In the long run, as $k \to \infty$,

$$E(\sigma_k^2|y_0, \sigma_0) \to \xi_\sigma^2 \quad \text{and} \quad \mathrm{sd}(\sigma_k^2|y_0, \sigma_0) \to \xi_\sigma^2 \sqrt{\frac{2\theta_1^2}{1 - 2\theta_1^2 - (\theta_1 + \theta_2)^2}} \tag{13.16}$$

and from (13.15) also

$$\mathrm{cor}(\sigma_k^2, \sigma_{k-l}^2|y_0, \sigma_0) \to (\theta_1 + \theta_2)^l \quad \text{as } k \to \infty. \tag{13.17}$$

Eventually the initial values y_0 and σ_0 are forgotten, and the process enters a stationary state where means, standard deviations and autocorrelations stabilize as values that do not change over time. The prerequisite is that

$$\theta_1 + \theta_2 < \sqrt{1 - 2\theta_1^2} \qquad (\text{and } \theta_1, \theta_2 \geq 0), \tag{13.18}$$

stronger than merely $\theta_1 + \theta_2 < 1$. In (13.16) right the denominator becomes negative if this isn't true.

13.3.4 Properties of the original process

These properties of the volatility series are passed on to the observations $Y_k = \xi_y + \sigma_k \varepsilon_k$ themselves. In Section 13.7 it is verified for their squares Y_k^2 that, as $k \to \infty$,

$$\left.\begin{aligned} E(Y_k^2|y_0, \sigma_0) &\to \xi_y^2 + \xi_\sigma^2 \\ \mathrm{sd}(Y_k^2|y_0, \sigma_0) &\to \xi_\sigma^2 \sqrt{2\frac{1 + \theta_1^2 - (\theta_1 + \theta_2)^2}{1 - 2\theta_1^2 - (\theta_1 + \theta_2)^2} + 4\left(\frac{\xi_y}{\xi_\sigma}\right)^2} \end{aligned}\right\}. \tag{13.19}$$

More useful in practice may be the limiting form of the autocorrelations; i.e.,

$$\frac{\mathrm{cor}(Y_k^2, Y_{k-l}^2|y_0, \sigma_0)}{\mathrm{cor}(Y_k^2, Y_{k-1}^2|y_0, \sigma_0)} \to (\theta_1 + \theta_2)^{l-1}, \quad l > 1 \tag{13.20}$$

and for $l = 1$,

$$\mathrm{cor}(Y_k^2, Y_{k-1}^2|y_0, \sigma_0) \to \frac{\theta_1\{1 - \theta_2(\theta_1 + \theta_2)\}}{\{1 + \theta_1^2 - (\theta_1 + \theta_2)^2\} + 2(\xi_y/\xi_\sigma)^2\{1 - 2\theta_1^2 - (\theta_1^2 + \theta_2)^2\}}.$$

The complicated expression at lag 1 may not be too interesting, but (13.20) tells us that the autocorrelation function of the squares Y_k^2 decays exponentially above lag 1. This may be used diagnostically by computing the sample autocorrelations from squared historical data $y_1^2, \ldots, y_n^2$ and checking it against the theoretical form.

Algorithm 13.1 Simulating first-order GARCH

0 Input: ξ_y ,ξ_σ, θ_1, θ_2, y_0 and $\theta_0 = (1 - \theta_1 - \theta_2)\xi_\sigma^2$
1 $Y_0^* \leftarrow y_0$, $\sigma^* \leftarrow \sigma_0$ *%Initializing, see also comment below*
2 For $k = 1, \dots, K$ do
3 $\quad \sigma^* \leftarrow \sqrt{\theta_0 + \theta_1(Y_{k-1}^* - \xi_y)^2 + \theta_2(\sigma^*)^2}$ *%New volatility, store it as σ_k^* if you want to examine it*
4 $\quad$ Draw $\varepsilon^* \sim$ N (0,1)
5 $\quad Y_k^* \leftarrow \xi + \sigma^*\varepsilon^*$ *%Next log-return*
6 Return $Y_1^*, \dots, Y_K^*$.

13.3.5 Fitting GARCH models

It is possible to determine the persistence parameter $\theta_1 + \theta_2$ of the first-order GARCH from the decay of the sample autocorrelations of $y_1^2, \dots, y_n^2$ and use some of the other relationships above for the other parameters. Likelihood estimation proceeds as follows, with the initial volatility σ_0 among the parameters. If the error terms $\varepsilon_1, \dots, \varepsilon_n$ are Gaussian, the log-likelihood function is

$$\mathcal{L}(\xi_y, \xi_\sigma, \theta_1, \theta_2, \sigma_0) = -\frac{1}{2}\sum_{k=1}^{n}\left(\log(\sigma_k^2) + \frac{(y_k - \xi_y)^2}{\sigma_k^2}\right) \tag{13.21}$$

with $\sigma_1^2, \dots, \sigma_n^2$ obtained from the historical series $y_1, \dots, y_n$ through the defining recursion, say (13.11) for the first-order GARCH. A numerical method is needed to optimize; consult Exercises 13.12 and 13.13. The example below was fitted by this method.

13.3.6 Simulating GARCH

Monte Carlo algorithms are implemented straightforwardly from the definition, with commands organized as in Algorithm 13.1. On output, simulations of the Y-series are returned with the volatilities overwritten. If you want to examine them, store as indicated on Line 3.

The initial $Y_0^* = y_0$ and σ_0 may represent the present state of the economy. A random start when the process has reached stationarity is another possibility. You then use a **warm-up** period and run the algorithm $K = K_1 + K$ steps from somewhere with the first K_1 realizations discarded. If K_1 is large enough, the initial state is forgotten when we come to the last K. How large K_1 must be depends on the parameters of the model; see Exercise 13.11. There is more on initialization in Section 13.6.

Table 13.1 Parameters (daily) for the first-order GARCH for the SP 500 index during four periods

Period	ξ_σ (%)	θ_1	θ_2	Period	ξ_σ (%)	θ_1	θ_2
83 Jan – 87 Mar	0.85	0.017	0.976	87 Apr –91 Jun	1.20	0.156	0.769
91 Jul – 95 Sep	0.56	0.000	0.989	95 Oct – 00 Jan	1.33	0.067	0.917

13.3.7 Example: GARCH and the SP 500 index

GARCH parameters for the daily SP 500 index are shown in Table 13.1 for four different periods between 1983 and 2000. The condition (13.18) for stationarity is satisfied in all four cases, but the models differ a lot in other respects and their behaviour would deviate strongly if simulated. The 1991–1995 model is not far from being an ordinary Gaussian one with fixed volatilities.

There is (unlike in the preceding section) no simple way of switching between time scales, and models are most easily simulated on the scale they have been fitted. In the present case this means that the processes must be run 250 steps for an annual view. To see how this is implemented, suppose the GARCH model applies to log-returns. The recursion for the k-step returns is then

$$1 + R_{0:k} = (1 + R_{0:k-1})e^{\xi_y + \sigma_k \varepsilon_k}, \quad \sigma_k = \sqrt{(1 - \theta_1 - \theta_2)\xi_\sigma^2 + \theta_1 \sigma_k^2 \varepsilon_k^2 + \theta_2 \sigma_{k-1}^2}$$

for $k = 1, 2, \ldots$, starting at $R_{0:0} = 0$ and σ_0.

What is the GARCH impact in the long run? The phenomenon itself is not in doubt, but it doesn't necessarily follow that its contribution is important when risk is examined over many years. An illustration for 5-year equity returns is given in Figure 13.5. On the left, the GARCH parameters are taken from the 1995–2000 period in Table 13.1 and compared with a fixed volatility sequence with $\sigma_k = 1.33\%$. Daily drift upwards is $\xi_y = 0.68\%$. The variability of the returns under the two models is almost the same, with the ordinary uncertainty of equity investments almost wiping out the GARCH effect. This differs from what we saw in Figure 13.4, where the volatility model was from a different period. When the GARCH parameters are changed to $\theta_1 = 0.156$ and $\theta_2 = 0.769$ on the right of Figure 13.5, discrepancies are larger.

13.4 Linear dynamic modelling

13.4.1 Introduction

Linear and stationary processes coupled with suitable non-linear transformations are the most important mathematical approach to asset modelling. The Black–Karasinski model in Section 5.6 is a simple example, but often the number of vari-

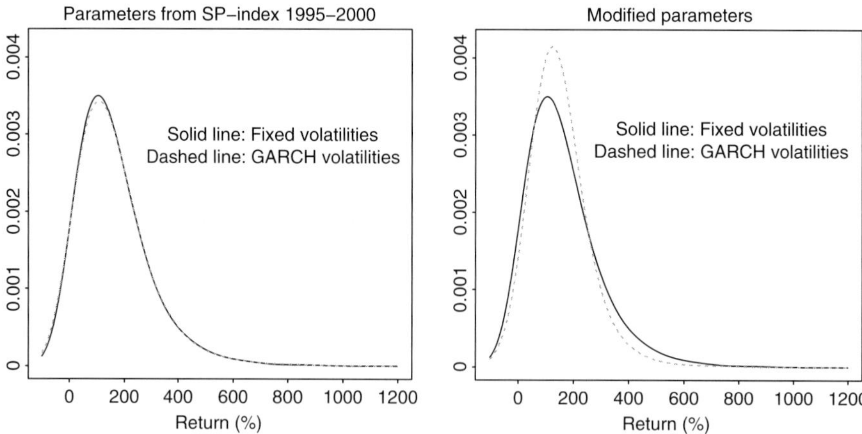

Figure 13.5 *Left*: Density functions of 5-year returns (%) under the GARCH 1995–2000 model in Table 13.1 (dashed lines) and under fixed volatilities (solid lines). *Right*: The same with GARCH 1987–1991.

ables is more than one, and how they influence each other mutually is as important as how they evolve over time. As a simple example, consider share prices S_k and consumer prices Q_k. The two series are driven by equity returns R_k and consumer price inflation I_k through the relationships

$$\underbrace{S_k = (1 + R_k)S_{k-1}}_{\textit{value of equity}} \quad \text{and} \quad \underbrace{Q_k = (1 + I_k)Q_{k-1}}_{\textit{consumer prices}}, \quad k = 1, 2 \ldots$$

with stochastic models for R_k and I_k. These should be stationary, since being in a well-functioning economy limits how far out from the average such variables fluctuate.

The approach throughout the rest of this chapter is basically **linear**. In the equity/consumer price example it boils down to the scheme

$$\underset{\textit{linear driver processes}}{X_k^r, X_k^i} \quad \longrightarrow \quad \underset{\textit{stationary variables}}{R_k, I_k} \quad \longrightarrow \quad \underset{\textit{target variables}}{S_k, Q_k,}$$

where X_k^r and X_k^i are linear stochastic processes acting through non-linear transformations as **drivers** of R_k and I_k, which are in turn driving S_k and Q_k. This is the way the **Wilkie** model is set up in Section 13.5, but the topic is now the linear drivers themselves and their construction mathematically. How these models are fitted to historical data is not addressed, and their detailed behaviour is only examined through Monte Carlo among the exercises. Specialist books have much additional material here, consult Section 13.8. A second issue is how linear drivers are linked to the variables of interest.

13.4.2 ARMA models

Stationary stochastic processes were introduced in Section 5.6, but so far only special cases have been considered. Even the linear ones are in reality huge classes, and it isn't difficult to write them down. Start with the first-order autoregressive model $X_k = aX_{k-1} + \sigma\varepsilon_k$ with $\varepsilon_1, \varepsilon_2, \dots$ a sequence of independent variables with zero means/unit variances. An obvious extension is a recursion of higher order, for example

$$X_k = a_1 X_{k-1} + \cdots + a_p X_{k-p} + \sigma\varepsilon_k, \quad k = 1, 2, \dots \tag{13.22}$$

where $a_1, \dots, a_p$ are coefficients. This is known as an **autoregression** (or **AR**) of order p and run from p initial values $x_0, x_{-1}, \dots, x_{-p+1}$, which are gradually forgotten as $k \to \infty$ if the model is stationary. The case $p = 2$ is known as the **Yule** process (after a British statistician) and has been popular in many scientific areas.

The condition for stationarity comes from the so-called **characteristic polynomial**

$$P(z) = a_p + a_{p-1}z + \cdots + a_1 z^{p-1} - z^p \quad \text{and its roots} \quad P(z_i) = 0, \quad i = 1, \dots, p.$$

Stationarity is guaranteed if all $|z_i| < 1$.[15] As an example, suppose $p = 1$. Then $P(z) = a_1 - z$, and the only root is $z_1 = a_1$. The condition $|z_1| < 1$ is now equivalent to $|a_1| < 1$, which was obtained as a prerequisite for stationarity in Section 5.6. Expressions for variances and covariances are complicated when $p > 1$; consult the references in Section 13.8.

Most stationary models for continuous variables can be approximated by autoregressive ones (see Priestley, 1981), but the order p is not necessarily low and other linear models have their place too. Another type is the **moving average** (or **MA**) process

$$X_k = \sigma(\varepsilon_k + b_1\varepsilon_{k-1} + \cdots + b_q\varepsilon_{k-q}), \quad k = 1, 2, \dots \tag{13.23}$$

where $b_1, \dots, b_q$ are coefficients. Neighbouring values of $\{X_k\}$ depend on the *same* terms from the error series $\{\varepsilon_k\}$, and this creates autocorrelations up to lag q. Indeed, writing $b_0 = 1$, then

$$\text{cov}(X_k, X_{k-l}) = \sigma^2(b_l + b_1 b_{l+1} + \cdots + b_{q-l} b_q), \quad l = 0, 1, \dots, q \tag{13.24}$$

with $\text{cov}(X_k, X_{k-l}) = 0$ for $l > q$. The MA processes are always stationary and, like AR models, approximate given stationary processes if q is high enough.

Combining AR and MA is popular and leads to the **ARMA** version:

$$X_k = a_1 X_{k-1} + \cdots + a_p X_{k-p} + \sigma(\varepsilon_k + b_1\varepsilon_{k-1} + \cdots + b_q\varepsilon_{k-q}), \quad k = 1, 2, \dots, \tag{13.25}$$

usually denoted ARMA(p, q). The rationale in merging AR and MA terms is that

[15] The roots z_i may be real or complex. For complex z_i the absolute value is its modulus.

the number of parameters (now $1 + p + q$) may be smaller than when either type is used alone. Stationarity is ensured by the criterion for pure AR; i.e., the characteristic polynomial $P(z)$ with $a_1, \dots, a_p$ as coefficients must possess roots $z_1, \dots, z_p$ less than 1 in absolute value. Simulation is straightforward, simply copy (13.25). If $\{\varepsilon_k^*\}$ is a Monte Carlo version of $\{\varepsilon_k\}$, then ARMA simulations are

$$X_k^* = a_1 X_{k-1}^* + \cdots + a_p X_{k-p}^* + \sigma(\varepsilon_k^* + b_1\varepsilon_{k-1}^* + \cdots + b_q\varepsilon_{k-q}^*), \quad k = 1, 2, \dots$$

Initial values $x_0, \dots, x_{-p+1}$ adapted to the present state of the economy can be tricky; see Section 13.6.

13.4.3 Linear feedback

How do we go about it when several linear processes are needed? A central idea is the feedback concept introduced in Section 13.3. Equity prices and volatilities were there allowed to influence each other mutually, and that idea works in a linear context too. Let $\{X_{1k}\}$ and $\{X_{2k}\}$ be two linear processes and consider the following two types of relationship:

$$\begin{aligned} X_{1k} &= a_{11}X_{1k-1} + \sigma_1\varepsilon_{1k}, \\ X_{2k} &= a_{21}X_{1k-1} + a_{22}X_{2k-1} + \sigma_2\varepsilon_{2k}, \end{aligned}$$

process 1 **driving** *process 2*

$$\begin{aligned} X_{1k} &= a_{11}X_{1k-1} + a_{12}X_{2k-1} + \sigma_1\varepsilon_{1k}, \\ X_{2k} &= a_{21}X_{1k-1} + a_{22}X_{2k-1} + \sigma_2\varepsilon_{2k}, \end{aligned}$$

process 1 and 2 in **feedback**

where all a_{ij} are coefficients, and σ_1 and σ_2 are fixed volatilities. Each pair $(\varepsilon_{1k}, \varepsilon_{2k})$ is correlated with zero means/unit variances, with independence between pairs. The situation on the left is the **driving** one. Here the first process $\{X_{1k}\}$ influences the second, but is not itself influenced back. In the next section the rate of inflation is used as a driver of all the other variables in this way. The model on the right specifies a full feedback, with either process affecting the other. Many of the relationships in Section 13.5 are of that type.

The feedback case is a *vector* autoregression of order 1. It extends the single-variable version in Section 5.6 and creates very different models. The individual processes $\{X_{1k}\}$ and $\{X_{2k}\}$ are no longer first-order AR, although still members of the ARMA class. The condition for stationarity changes too. Now the characteristic polynomial becomes

$$P(z) = (a_{11} - z)(a_{22} - z) - a_{12}a_{21} \quad \text{with roots} \quad P(z_i) = 0, \quad i = 1, 2.$$

The criterion is again that both $|z_i| < 1$. If $a_{12} = a_{21} = 0$, this is the same as $|a_{11}| < 1$ and $|a_{22}| < 1$.

Many-variable versions are immediate extensions of the preceding bivariate case. Simply fill in a third, fourth variable and so on and use linear schemes of higher order.[16] Simulation is again easy, and as starting values we would often take current observations. For references on multivariate linear processes, consult Section 13.8.

13.4.4 Enter transformations

The preceding X-processes are basic building blocks, but they are never used as they are. A minimum is to adapt them to a general mean. We worked in Section 5.6 with

$$\underbrace{r_k = \xi + X_k}_{\textit{Vasiček}} \quad \text{and} \quad \underbrace{r_k = \xi e^{-\sigma_x^2/2 + X_k}}_{\textit{Black–Karasinski}},$$

where r_k was the rate of interest, ξ its mean and $\mathrm{sd}(X_k|x_0) \to \sigma_x$ as $k \to \infty$. These are examples of **transformations**, fixed functions applied to variables. The Vasiček model is no more than a simple shift, whereas Black–Karasinski changes X_k exponentially. In Section 5.6 $\{X_k\}$ was the first-order autoregression, but both transformations work with any of the linear processes introduced above. The standard deviation σ_x would change, but mathematical expressions could be looked up in standard references. We could go further and introduce *general* transformations $H(x)$ so that $r_k = H(X_k)$, or if the target is inflation $I_k = H(X_k)$. Two possibilities are

$$H(x) = (1 + \xi)e^x - 1 \quad \text{and} \quad H(x) = \xi \frac{\log(1 + e^x)}{\log(2)},$$

where in either case $H(0) = \xi$ which means that ξ is the median of the transformed variable. The example on the left is the **Wilkie** transformation used with inflation in Section 13.5. The other one is rarely mentioned, yet its combination of curvature around zero and linearity (almost) for small and large x is interesting; see Exercise 13.24.

Gaussian models for $\{X_k\}$ are frequently combined in finance with transformations that are increasing and convex with curvature upwards (first- and second-order derivatives positive). This makes the distribution of $H(X_k)$ skewed towards the right (often more realistic than symmetry), and random variation becomes higher at higher level (also plausible); see Exercise 5.33, where this is proved for the Black–Karasinski model. For the linear Vasiček model, $\mathrm{sd}(r_k|r_{k-1}) = \sigma$ (the same for all r_{k-1}).

[16] The characteristic polynomial above can be written as the determinant

$$P(z) = \begin{vmatrix} a_{11} - z & a_{12} \\ a_{21} & a_{22} - z \end{vmatrix} = (a_{11} - z)(a_{22} - z) - a_{12}a_{21},$$

and this is the way the criterion extends to schemes of three variables and more. Simply replace the 2×2 determinant by higher-order analogues. Again we must for stationarity require the roots to be less than 1 in absolute value.

Distributions for r_k and other variables may also be *specified* and $H(x)$ determined accordingly. This is the copula approach of Section 6.7, which was also used in Section 11.4. One possibility is the Gamma distribution. More generally, if $F_0^{-1}(u)$ is the percentile function of a distribution with mean 1, let $\{X_k\}$ be Gaussian and take

$$r_k = \xi F_0^{-1}(U_k) \quad \text{where} \quad U_k = \Phi\left(\frac{X_k}{\sigma_x}\right), \tag{13.26}$$

writing $\Phi(x)$ for the standard normal integral. When X_k has forgotten the initial state, X_k/σ_x is $N(0, 1)$ making U_k uniform (the inversion algorithm of Chapter 2), and $F_0(x)$ is the distribution function of $F_0^{-1}(U_k)$ (inversion again). The construction ensures that r_k (after having reached stationarity) follows a given distribution with mean ξ, while $\{X_k\}$ takes care of the dynamics. The formal transformation is

$$H(x) = \xi F_0^{-1}\{\Phi(x/\sigma_x)\}.$$

Try to plot it, and you will see that it is convex when $F_0(x)$ is a Gamma distribution.

13.5 The Wilkie model I: Twentieth-century financial risk

13.5.1 Introduction

The twentieth-century performance of financial assets should not be used uncritically as a description of the financial risk ahead, but it does represent experience to draw on and provides useful models for laboratory experiments. This section presents the **Wilkie** system of models. The justification in Wilkie (1995) is purely empirical, with little theory in support, and is derived through the use of advanced statistical techniques beyond the scope of this book. Our more modest aim is to write down the model and connect it to the toolkit of the preceding section. The detailed structure, parameters and notation are completely rewritten compared with what you will find in Wilkie's original article, but there is nothing new apart from this. The model is run on an annual time scale. Its main variables are summarized in Table 13.2. For other, competing models consult Lee and Wilkie (2000).

13.5.2 Output variables and their building blocks

The output variables are those on the left in Table 13.2, i.e., at time T_k the price level (Q_k), dividend, price and return of equity (D_k, S_k and R_k^e) and the short and long rate of interest (r_k and $\overline{r}_k(k{:}\ k+K)$). Here $\overline{r}_k(k{:}\ k+K)$ is the yield at T_k for bonds expiring at T_{k+K} and will be written $\overline{r}_k(K)$ for short. In Chapter 15 all these variables will go into practical evaluations of risk. Additional ones not included

Table 13.2 Economic variables of the Wilkie model used in this book with their symbols and defining processes

Output variables		Stationary building blocks			
			Name	Drivers	Errors*
Price index	Q_k	Ordinary inflation	I_k	X_k^i	ε_k^i
Share dividend index	D_k	Share yield	y_k	X_k^y, X_k^i	ε_k^y
Share price index	S_k	Dividend inflation	I_k^d	$X_k^{d\|y}, X_k^{d\|i}$	ε_k^d
Return on equity	R_k^s, R_k^e	Long interest rate	$\overline{r}_k(K)$	$X^{r\|y}$, $X_k^{r\|i}$	ε_k^r
Short interest rate	r_k	Interest rate ratio	F_k	X_k^f	ε_k^f
Long interest rate	$\overline{r}_k(K)$				

*All error terms are independent also for the same k

here are wage and property indexes; consult Wilkie (1995) for these. Many pension schemes have liabilities linked to the wage level. The price level is a possible (though not perfect) proxy and is used in this book instead.

The output variables are linked to five stationary building blocks which are ordinary inflation (I_k), share yield (y_k), share dividend inflation (I_k^d), the long rate of interest ($\overline{r}_k(K)$) and an interest-rate ratio (F_k). Their precise meaning is outlined below. These variables are, in turn, linked to a set of correlated, linear **driver** processes (X_k^i, X_k^y and so forth, see Table 13.2) which define the stochastic part of the system. The second and third layers of the model are dealt with below, and we now concentrate on relationships between the output variables and their stationary generators. There are three groups. The first one is price level and the rate of inflation. Their relationship is

$$Q_k = (1 + I_k)Q_{k-1}, \tag{13.27}$$

as presented earlier. Inflation does not normally grow indefinitely, and so is reasonably taken as a stationary process.

Equity modelling is attacked through **dividend** D (to owners) and **yield** y, which is dividend per unit price of the stock. The defining relationships are

$$D_k = (1 + I_k^d)D_{k-1}, \tag{13.28}$$

$$S_k = \frac{D_k}{y_k}, \tag{13.29}$$

where I_k^d is the dividend rate of inflation and S_k the stock price. The principal building blocks of the model are the processes I_k^d and y_k, both assumed stationary. The return on equity investments is either

$$R_k^s = \frac{S_k}{S_{k-1}} - 1 \quad \text{or} \quad R_k^e = \frac{S_k + D_k}{S_{k-1}} - 1, \tag{13.30}$$

where R_k^s applies to the value of the stock only whereas R_k^e also includes the dividend earned. Useful alternative expressions emerge if (13.28) and (13.29) are used to replace D_k, S_k and S_{k-1} in (13.30). Then

$$R_k^s = (1 + I_k^d)\frac{y_{k-1}}{y_k} - 1 \quad \text{and} \quad R_k^e = (1 + I_k^d)(1 + y_k)\frac{y_{k-1}}{y_k} - 1, \tag{13.31}$$

and both types of return inherit stationarity from dividend inflation and yield. If we want to examine the properties of the model through a single, long simulation, it is therefore better to work with the returns than with the indexes D_k and S_k, which grow indefinitely; consult the exercises, which also investigate how far the Wilkie equity model departs from the earlier assumption of independent returns.

Finally, there are the rates of interest. The Wilkie model is based on the short rate r_k and the long rate $\bar{r}_k(K)$ that applies K periods ahead. Wilkie worked with so-called **consols**; i.e., bonds that never expire (they exist!), their yield being used as an approximation of interest rates over long time horizons. Their stationary building blocks are the long rate of interest (which therefore appears twice in Table 13.2), but (perhaps surprisingly) *not* the short rate, as Wilkie chose to use the ratio

$$F_k = \frac{r_k}{\bar{r}_k(K)}. \tag{13.32}$$

There are, in summary, five stationary variables I_k, y_k, I_k^d, $\bar{r}_k(K)$ and F_k. The next step is to link them to the linear part of the model through the tools of Section 13.4.

13.5.3 Non-linear transformations

Wilkie proposed the following five transformations:

Inflation

$$I_k = (1 + \xi^i)\exp(X_k^i) - 1 \tag{13.33}$$

Equity

$$y_k = \xi^y \exp(X_k^y + \theta^{y|i} X_k^i), \tag{13.34}$$

$$I_k^d = (1 + \xi^d)\exp(X_k^{d|y} + X_k^{d|i}) - 1 \tag{13.35}$$

Interest

$$\bar{r}_k(K) = \xi^r \exp(X_k^{r|y}) + \xi^i + X_k^{r|i}, \tag{13.36}$$

$$F_k = \xi^f \exp(X_k^f) \tag{13.37}$$

where $\{X_k^i\}$, $\{X_k^y\}$ and so on are zero-mean, normal processes. Superscripts are used to indicate the variables to which they belong. *Double* superscripts $X_k^{d|y}$, $X_k^{d|i}$ and so on means correlation with the process to the right of the vertical bar, for example, $X_k^{d|y}$ being correlated with y_k and driving I_k^d. There are many links to inflation at the bottom of the system.

The ξ-parameters are *medians* here (they have mostly been expectations elsewhere). Thus ξ^i, ξ^y, ξ^d and ξ^f are the medians of I_k, y_k, I_k^d and F_k, respectively. The fifth parameter ξ^r is the median of the *real* contribution to the long rate of interest.

13.5.4 The linear and stationary part

There are, in the preceding relationships, a total of seven X-processes which are responsible for all time variation and covariation between variables. Wilkie made use of advanced statistical tools to find them. His end product takes inflation (or its linear driver X_k^i) in a baseline role influencing all the others. The model is driven by the five $N(0,1)$ processes ε_k^i, ε_k^y, ε_k^d, ε_k^r and ε_k^f in Table 13.2. All have in this rewriting been constructed so that they are *uncorrelated both over time and between themselves*. The superscripts again identify to which variable they belong; some of them enter other variables too. In detail, their model reads

Inflation

$$X_k^i = a^i X_{k-1}^i + \sigma^i \varepsilon_k^i \tag{13.38}$$

Equity

$$X_k^y = a^y X_{k-1}^y + \sigma^y \varepsilon_k^y, \tag{13.39}$$

$$X_k^{d|y} = \sigma^d(\varepsilon_k^d + b_1^d \varepsilon_{k-1}^d) + \underbrace{\theta^{d|y}\varepsilon_{k-1}^y}_{\text{due to equity}}, \tag{13.40}$$

$$X_k^{d|i} = a^{d|i} X_{k-1}^{d|i} + \underbrace{(b_0^{d|i} X_k^i + b_1^{d|i} X_{k-1}^i)}_{\text{due to inflation}} \tag{13.41}$$

Interest rates

$$X_k^{r|y} = a^{r|y} X_{k-1}^{r|y} + \sigma^r \varepsilon_k^r + \underbrace{\theta^{r|y}\varepsilon_k^y}_{\text{due to equity}}, \tag{13.42}$$

$$X_k^{r|i} = a^{r|i} X_{k-1}^{r|i} + \underbrace{(1 - a^{r|i}) X_k^i}_{\text{due to inflation}}, \tag{13.43}$$

$$X_k^f = a^f X_{k-1}^f + \sigma^f \varepsilon_k^f. \tag{13.44}$$

Most of the linear models of Section 13.4 are represented one way or another. There are autoregressive terms, moving average terms and feedback terms with a total of 22 parameters.

Table 13.3 Estimated parameters for the Wilkie long-term asset models with standard error in parentheses.

	Inflation (I_k)			
$\hat{\xi}^i = 4.80\%$	$\hat{a}^i = 0.58$	$\hat{\sigma}^i = 0.040$		
(1.2%)	(0.08)	(0.004)		
		Yield(y_k)		
$\hat{\xi}^y = 4.10\%$	$\hat{a}^y = 0.55$	$\hat{\sigma}^y = 0.16$	$\hat{\theta}^{y\|i} = 1.79$	
(0.3%*)	(0.10)	(0.01)	(0.59)	
	Dividend inflation (I_k^d)			
$\hat{\xi}^d = 6.50\%$	$\hat{b}_1^d = 0.57$	$\hat{\theta}^{d\|y} = -0.027$	$\hat{\sigma}^d = 0.067$	
(1.8%*)	(0.13)	(0.007*)	(0.006)	
$\hat{a}^{d\|i} = 0.87$	$\hat{b}_0^{d\|i} = 0.50$	$\hat{b}_1^{d\|i} = -0.36$		
(0.08)	(0.19*)	(0.19*)		
		Long interest rate ($\bar{r}_k(K)$)		
$\hat{\xi}^r = 3.05\%$	$\hat{a}^{r\|y} = 0.90$	$\hat{\theta}^{r\|y} = 0.052$	$\hat{\sigma}^r = 0.19$	$\hat{a}^{r\|i} = 0.955$
(0.65%*)	(0.04)	(0.02*)	(0.02)	(NA)
	Interest ratio (F_k)			
$\hat{\xi}^f = 0.80$	$\hat{a}^f = 0.74$	$\hat{\sigma}^f = 0.18$		
(0.06*)	(0.08)	(0.02*)		

* Standard error: Rough conversion from values in Wilkie (1995).

13.5.5 Parameter estimates

The model was identified from annual data for the period from 1923 to 1994. Parameters estimated (British ones) are shown in Table 13.3, with their standard errors. Some of the parameters have been changed from those in Wilkie (1995). It was therefore necessary to recompute standard errors by a rough approximation technique.[17] These are the ones marked * in Table 13.3. Note the high uncertainty in almost all the ξ-estimates.[18] That is unfortunate since these are the most important parameters, but it is a familiar phenomenon which was encountered when equity was simulated in Section 2.2.

A frequent criticism against the Wilkie model is the way it handles inflation. The mean and standard deviation of the ordinary and dividend rate of inflation are

$$E(I_k) = 4.9\%, \quad \text{sd}(I_k) = 5.1\% \quad \text{and} \quad E(I_k^d) = 6.9\%, \quad \text{sd}(I_k^d) = 9.4\%$$

which were computed by Monte Carlo as explained below. Note the large standard deviations, which make *negative* inflation far from unlikely. That may not be unreasonable for dividend inflation, but it may be more questionable that the price index

[17] It was impossible to do that accurately from the information in Wilkie's paper, since correlations between estimates are not given there. The values obtained are computed by the so-called delta-method as if the original Wilkie estimates were uncorrelated.

[18] The exception is $\hat{\xi}^y$, for which the standard error recorded in Table 13.3 is strikingly low.

Table 13.4 Mean, standard deviation and correlation matrix of annual inflation and returns under the Wilkie model

	Nominal (%)				Inflation-adjusted (%)		
	I_k	R_k^e	$\bar{r}_k(K)$	r_k	R_k^e	$\bar{r}_k(K)$	r_k
Mean	4.9	13.3	8.2	6.8	8.2	3.3	2.0
Sd	5.1	23.0	2.1	2.6	22.8	5.0	5.2

	Correlation matrix				Correlation matrix		
	I_k	R_k^e	$\bar{r}_k(K)$	r_k	R_k^e	$\bar{r}_k(K)$	r_k
I_k	1.0	−0.02	0.23	0.16			
R_k^e	−0.02	1.0	0.14	0.10	1.0	0.29	0.27
$\bar{r}_k(K)$	0.23	0.14	1.0	0.68	0.29	1.0	0.93
r_k	0.16	0.10	0.68	1.0	0.29	0.93	1.0

has a chance of around 17% of going down from one year to the next. Is that realistic for the present century? If you don't think so, it means that you consider the historical data on which the Wilkie model is fitted unrepresentative for the decades ahead.[19] It is not one of the aims of the present book to take a stand on this, and evaluations in the second half of Chapter 15 have been based on the estimates in Table 13.3.

13.5.6 Annual inflation and returns

Mean, standard deviation and correlations under the Wilkie model are summarized in Table 13.4 for inflation and returns from equity and the short and long rates of interest. The assessments were obtained by Monte Carlo and apply when the economy is in a random (or stationary) state; how the detailed computer implementation is carried out to achieve this is explained in the next section. Both **nominal** and **inflation-adjusted** returns are given. To define these concepts, let R and I be return and inflation over a certain period. The nominal value of an investment V_0 has, at the end of the period, grown to

$$V_1 = (1 + R)V_0 \quad \text{or in real terms} \quad \frac{V_1/(1 + I) - V_0}{V_0} = \frac{R - I}{1 + I}$$

after inserting for V_1. Real returns are negative if I exceeds R, which was not uncommon for rates of interest during certain periods of the twentieth century.

There are several interesting features in Table 13.4. Equity has much higher *expected* return than the money market assets in both nominal and real terms, but

[19] The reason for the Wilkie rate of inflation being so volatile is the high inflation (double digit) during the mid-1920s. If the period after the Second World War is used to refit the model, you will find about the same value for a^i, but a much smaller one for σ^i.

the risk is higher with the standard deviation ten times larger when inflation is not corrected for and about four times when it is. If the Wilkie model is to be believed, equity is a better hedge against inflation than the money market (as has often been maintained), though their correlation is close to zero. The two interest rates are by contrast strongly correlated, particularly in real terms, whereas their correlations with equity are again small.

13.6 The Wilkie model II: Implementation issues

13.6.1 Introduction

This section is technical, and details the implementation of the Wilkie model in the computer. Much of it is no more than a summary of equations and recursions above. A problem of its own is how the system is initialized. The price level Q_0 and the equity dividend D_0 are simple; take $Q_0 = 1$ and $D_0 = d_0$ where d_0 is the value observed. The scheme (13.38)–(13.44) of the linear driver processes is more difficult. Before entering it we have to specify

$$x_0^i,\ x_0^y,\ \varepsilon_0^y,\ \varepsilon_0^d,\ x_0^{d|i},\ x_0^{r|y},\ x_0^{r|i},\ x_0^f,$$

where lowercase letters x_0^i, x_0^y and so forth are used for actual values of $X_0^i, X_0^y, \dots$ There are several ways to proceed, depending on what kind of situation we want to imitate.

13.6.2 How simulations are initialized

We may often want to start from the present state of the economy, whereas in Table 13.4 the setup was from an arbitrary, randomly selected beginning. Still another possibility is to proceed from a 'typical' state in some sense. The three alternatives are now presented in reverse order, going from the simple to the complicated.

The median state. A simple solution is to take

$$x_0^i = 0,\ x_0^y = 0,\ \varepsilon_0^y = 0,\ \varepsilon_0^d = 0,\ x_0^{d|i} = 0,\ x_0^{r|y} = 0,\ x_0^{r|i} = 0,\ x_0^f = 0.$$

The five stationary variables I_k, y_k, I_k^d, $\bar{r}_k(K)$ and F_k driving the Wilkie system are then started from the *medians* of their stationary distributions. That is as good a way to define a 'typical spot' of the economy as any, and used in the R-function `Wilkie` which you can download for your own programming; consult also the exercises for Section 13.5.

Table 13.5 How the Wilkie model is adapted to the present state of the economy.

Input quantities from values observed: i_{-k} for $k = 0, -1, -2, \dots, y_0, y_{-1}, y_{-2}, i_0^d, \bar{r}_0(K), f_0$

1	$x_0^i = \log\left(\dfrac{1+i_0}{1+\xi^i}\right)$	$x_{-k}^i = \log\left(\dfrac{1+i_{-k}}{1+\xi^i}\right), \quad k = 1, 2, \dots$
2	$x_0^y = \log\left(\dfrac{y_0}{\xi^y}\right) - \theta^{y\|i} x_0^i$	$x_{-k}^y = \log\left(\dfrac{y_{-k}}{\xi^y}\right) - \theta^{y\|i} x_{-k}^i, \quad k = 1, 2$
3	$\varepsilon_0^y = \dfrac{x_0^y - a^y x_{-1}^y}{\sigma^y}$	
4	$x_0^{d\|i} = \sum_{k=0}^{\infty} (a^{d\|i})^k \{b_0^{d\|i} x_{-k}^i + b_1^{d\|i} x_{-(k+1)}^i\}$	
5	$\varepsilon_0^d = \dfrac{x_0^{d\|y} - \theta^{d\|y}(x_{-1}^y - a^y x_{-2}^y)/\sigma^y}{\sigma^d(1+(b_1^d)^2)}$	
6	$x_0^{r\|i} = \sum_{k=0}^{\infty} (a^{r\|i})^k (1 - a^{r\|i}) x_{-k}^i$	
7	$x_0^{r\|y} = \log(\bar{r}_0(K) - \xi^i - x_0^{r\|i}) - \log(\xi^r)$	
8	$x_0^f = \log\left(\dfrac{f_0}{\xi^f}\right)$	

The stationary state. An alternative is to select the initial state randomly. We may then utilize the fact that inflation I_k, equity yield y_k and the three other stationary drivers eventually forget what they were at the beginning. The mechanism was explained in detail for the first-order autoregression in Section 5.6, and it is the same in general (although the mathematical argument is more complicated). Run each simulation $K_1 + K$ time steps from the median state, but keep only the last K of them. If K_1 is large enough ($K_1 = 20$ is certainly enough for the Wilkie model), virtually all effects of the initial values have gone away and the last K simulations are (approximately) from a random start. The operation can be repeated as many times as desired. Table 13.4 was computed in this way.

The present state. Often, simulations come from the actual situation in the financial market. The eight initial variables $x_0^i, x_0^y, \dots, x_0^f$ must then be adapted to the current value of inflation i_0, equity yield y_0, dividend inflation i_0^d, the long rate of interest $\bar{r}_0(K)$ and the interest-rate ratio f_0. But there are only *five* equations (13.33)–(13.37), and *eight* variables to initialize, and additional information is therefore needed. A reasonably simple solution is available if historical values i_{-k} of inflation for $k = 1, 2, \dots$ are used along with equity yields y_{-1} and y_{-2} 2 years into the past. The resulting method is detailed in Table 13.5 and justified in Section 13.7. Note the 2 infinite sums (rows 4 and 6), which are added until they do not change any more. Such convergence is guaranteed since $a^{d|i}$ and $a^{r|i}$ are less than 1 in absolute value (see Table 13.3). If the rate of inflation isn't available far enough backwards, simply cut the sums accordingly.

Algorithm 13.2 Wilkie inflation

Input: ξ^i, a^i, σ^i

$Q_0^* \leftarrow 1, X_0^{i*} \leftarrow x_0^i$ %x_0^i *user selected*

For $k = 1, \ldots, K$ do

  Draw $\varepsilon_k^{i*} \sim \text{N}(0,1)$

  $X_k^{i*} \leftarrow a^i X_{k-1}^{i*} + \sigma^i \varepsilon_k^{i*}$ %*Equation (13.38)*

  $Q_k^* \leftarrow Q_{k-1}^* \{(1 + \xi^i) \exp(X_k^{i*})\}$ %*Equations (13.27) and (13.33)*

Return $Q_k^*, X_k^{i*}, k = 0, \ldots, K$.

Algorithm 13.3 Wilkie equity

Input: $\xi^y, \theta^{y|i}, \xi^d, a^y, \sigma^y, b_1^d, \theta^{d|y}, \sigma^d, a^{d|i}, b_0^{d|i}, b_1^{d|i}, \{X_k^{i*}\}$

$D_0^* \leftarrow d_0, X_0^{y*} \leftarrow x_0^y, X_0^{d|i*} \leftarrow x_0^{d|i}, \varepsilon_0^{y*}, \varepsilon_0^{d*}$ %*User-selected values*

For $k = 1, \ldots, K$ do

  Draw $\varepsilon_k^{y*}, \varepsilon_k^{d*} \sim \text{N}(0,1)$

  $X_k^{y*} \leftarrow a^y X_{k-1}^{y*} + \sigma^y \varepsilon_k^{y*}$ %*Equation (13.39)*

  $y_k^* \leftarrow \xi^y \exp(X_k^{y*} + \theta^{y|i} X_k^{i*})$ %*Equation (13.34)*

  $X_k^{d|y*} \leftarrow \sigma^d(\varepsilon_k^{d*} + b_1^d \varepsilon_{k-1}^{d*}) + \theta^{d|y} \varepsilon_{k-1}^{y*}$ %*Equation (13.40)*

  $X_k^{d|i*} \leftarrow a^{d|i} X_{k-1}^{d|i*} + (b_0^{d|i} X_k^{i*} + b_1^{d|i} X_{k-1}^{i*})$ %*Equation (13.41)*

  $D_k^* \leftarrow D_{k-1}^*(1 + \xi^d) \exp(X_k^{d|y*} + X_k^{d|i*})$ %*Equations (13.28) and (13.35)*

  $S_k^* = D_k^*/y_k^*$ %*Equation (13.29)*

Return $D_k^*, S_k^*, \varepsilon_k^{y*}, k = 0, \ldots, K$.

13.6.3 Simulation algorithms

The Monte Carlo algorithms have been divided into three parts. Output is not the only process of interest; other certain intermediate processes are needed further down. We start with inflation as the driver of everything else in Algorithm 13.2, where the sequence $\{X_k^{i*}\}$ is stored to be used with the other schemes. For equity the simulations are organized as in Algorithm 13.3, and for interest rates as in Algorithm 13.4. Again this is no more than a condensation of equations given earlier. Note that we have to store the sequence ε_k^{y*}, which is needed with interest rates during the final part of the algorithm.

Running Algorithms 13.2, 13.3 and 13.4 provides the future price level, equity and interest rates that will be used in Chapter 15.

Algorithm 13.4 Wilkie rates of interest

Input: ξ^r, ξ^i, ξ^f, $a^{r|y}$, σ^r, $\theta^{r|y}$, $a^{r|i}$ a^f, σ^f, $\{X_k^{i*}\}$, $\{\varepsilon_k^{y*}\}$

$X_0^{f*} \leftarrow x_0^f$, $X_0^{r|i*} \leftarrow x_0^{r|i}$ % x_0^f, x_0^r *user selected*

For $k = 1, \ldots, K$ do

  Draw ε_k^{f*}, $\varepsilon_k^{r*} \sim$ N(0,1)

  $X_k^{r|y*} \leftarrow a^{r|y} X_{k-1}^{r|y*} + \sigma^r \varepsilon_k^{r*} + \theta^{r|y} \varepsilon_k^{y*}$ *%Equation (13.42)*

  $X_k^{r|i*} \leftarrow a^{r|i} X_{k-1}^{r|i*} + (1 - a^{r|i}) X_k^{i*}$ *%Equation (13.43)*

  $X_k^{f*} \leftarrow a^f X_{k-1}^{f*} + \sigma^f \varepsilon_k^{f*}$ *%Equation (13.44)*

  $F_k^* \leftarrow \xi^f \exp(X_k^{f*})$ *%Equation (13.37)*

  $\overline{r}_k(K)^* \leftarrow \xi^r \exp(X_k^{r|y*}) + \xi^i + X_k^{r|i*}$ *%Equation (13.36)*

  $r_k^* \leftarrow F_k^* \overline{r}_k(K)^*$ *%Equation (13.32)*

Return $\overline{r}_k(K)^*$, r_k^* for $k = 0, \ldots, K$

13.6.4 Interest-rate interpolation

The Wilkie model provides only the long and short rate of interest, whereas the entire interest-rate curve may be needed. Linear interpolation offers the solution

$$\overline{r}_k(j) = \frac{(K-j)r_k + (j-1)\overline{r}_k(K)}{K-1}, \quad j = 1, \ldots, K, \tag{13.45}$$

which is at odds with the curved shape often seen in practice; see Figure 6.2. A rough way around this is to interpolate on a different scale. If $H(x)$ is a strictly increasing or decreasing function with inverse $H^{-1}(x)$, take

$$\overline{r}_k(j) = H^{-1}\{(1 - x_j)H(r_k) + x_j H(\overline{r}_k(K)\} \quad \text{where} \quad x_j = \frac{j-1}{K-1}$$

which is an interpolation since it is exactly r_k and $\overline{r}(K)$, when $j = 1$ and $j = K$. A possible function is $H(r) = e^{\omega r}$, with ω defining the degree of curvature. Try $\omega = 50$ if $r_k < \overline{r}(K)$ and -50 if $r_k > \overline{r}(K)$, and you will find the shape in Figure 6.2.

13.7 Mathematical arguments

13.7.1 Absolute deviations from the mean

We seek the lower-order moments of the stochastic process $|Y_k - \xi_y|$ when $Y_k = \xi_y + \sigma_k \varepsilon_k$ for mutually independent processes $\{\varepsilon_k\}$ and $\{\sigma_k\}$, with the former independent and $N(0, 1)$. Inserting for Y_k yields

$$E(|Y_k - \xi_y|) = E(|\sigma_k \varepsilon_k|) = E(\sigma_k)E(|\varepsilon_k|) = E(\sigma_k)\sqrt{\frac{2}{\pi}}$$

since $E(|\varepsilon_k|) = \sqrt{2/\pi}$. This is (13.6) left, and for the assertion on the right

$$\begin{aligned}\mathrm{var}(|Y_k - \xi_y|) = E(Y_k - \xi_y)^2 - (E|Y_k - \xi_y|)^2 &= E(\sigma_k \varepsilon_k)^2 - (E\sigma_k)^2 \frac{2}{\pi} \\ = E(\sigma_k^2)E(\varepsilon_k^2) - (E\sigma_k)^2\frac{2}{\pi} &= \mathrm{var}(\sigma_k) + (E\sigma_k)^2(1 - 2/\pi)\end{aligned}$$

as claimed. Finally, for $l \neq 0$,

$$\begin{aligned}\mathrm{cov}(|Y_k - \xi_y|, |Y_{k-l} - \xi_y|) &= E(|Y_k - \xi_y||Y_{k-l} - \xi_y|) - E(|Y_k - \xi_y|)E(|Y_{k-l} - \xi_y|) \\ &= E(|\sigma_k\varepsilon_k||\sigma_{k-l}\varepsilon_{k-l}|) - E(\sigma_k)E(\sigma_{k-l})\frac{2}{\pi} \\ &= E(\sigma_k\sigma_{k-l})E(|\varepsilon_k|)E(|\varepsilon_{k-l}|) - E(\sigma_k)E(\sigma_{k-l})\frac{2}{\pi} \\ &= \{E(\sigma_k\sigma_{k-l}) - E(\sigma_k)E(\sigma_{k-l})\}\frac{2}{\pi} \\ &= \mathrm{cov}(\sigma_k, \sigma_{k-l})\frac{2}{\pi},\end{aligned}$$

which is (13.7).

13.7.2 Autocorrelations under log-normal volatilities

We are assuming $\sigma_k = \xi_\sigma e^{-\tau^2/2+\tau X_k}$ where $X_k = aX_{k-1} + \sqrt{1-a^2}\,\varepsilon_k$, so that

$$\sigma_k\sigma_{k-l} = \xi_\sigma^2 e^{-\tau^2+\tau(X_k+X_{k-l})}.$$

Suppose k is so large that the initial value is forgotten. Then $\mathrm{var}(X_k) = \mathrm{var}(X_{k-l}) = 1$ and $\mathrm{cor}(X_k, X_{k-l}) = a^{|l|}$; see Section 5.6. Hence

$$\mathrm{var}(X_k + X_{k-l}) = 2(1 + a^{|l|}) \quad \text{so that} \quad E(e^{\tau(X_k+X_{k-l})}) = e^{\tau^2(1+a^{|l|})}$$

and $E(\sigma_k\sigma_{k-l}) = \xi_\sigma^2 e^{\tau^2 a^{|l|}}$. But then $\mathrm{cov}(\sigma_k, \sigma_{k-l}) = \xi_\sigma^2(e^{\tau^2 a^{|l|}} - 1)$, and

$$\mathrm{cov}(|Y_k - \xi_y|, |Y_{k-l} - \xi_y|) = \frac{2}{\pi}\mathrm{cov}(\sigma_k\sigma_{k-l}) = \frac{2}{\pi}\xi_\sigma^2(e^{\tau^2 a^{|l|}} - 1).$$

Inserting $l = 0$ yields

$$\mathrm{var}(|Y_k - \xi_y|) = \frac{2}{\pi}\xi_\sigma^2(e^{\tau^2} - 1),$$

and when the covariance is divided by this, the autocorrelation function (13.10) follows.

13.7.3 The error series for GARCH variances

The variances under a first-order GARCH model satisfy (13.12), which is the recursion

$$\sigma_k^2 - \xi_\sigma^2 = (\theta_1 + \theta_2)(\sigma_{k-1}^2 - \xi_\sigma^2) + \theta_1\eta_k \quad \text{with} \quad \eta_k = \sigma_{k-1}^2(\varepsilon_{k-1}^2 - 1).$$

Here $\varepsilon_1, \varepsilon_2, \ldots$ are independent and $N(0,1)$ with ε_k independent of σ_k, and all else from the past. Central properties of the η-series are

$$E(\eta_k) = 0, \quad \text{var}(\eta_k) = 2E(\sigma_{k-1}^4) \tag{13.46}$$

and

$$\text{cov}(\eta_k, \eta_{k-l}) = 0, \quad \text{cov}(\eta_k, \sigma_{k-l}^2) = 0 \quad \text{if } l > 0, \tag{13.47}$$

where the reference to y_0 and σ_0 at the beginning has been omitted. To prove (13.46) note that

$$E(\eta_k) = E\{\sigma_{k-1}^2(\varepsilon_{k-1}^2 - 1)\} = E(\sigma_{k-1}^2)E(\varepsilon_{k-1}^2 - 1) = 0,$$

and for the variance

$$\text{var}(\eta_k) = E(\eta_k^2) = E\{\sigma_{k-1}^4(\varepsilon_{k-1}^2 - 1)^2\} = E(\sigma_{k-1}^4)E(\varepsilon_{k-1}^2 - 1)^2 = 2E(\sigma_{k-1}^4)$$

since $E(\varepsilon_{k-1}^2 - 1)^2 = E(\varepsilon_{k-1}^4 - 2\varepsilon_{k-1}^2 + 1) = 3 - 2 + 1 = 2$. If $l > 0$, then

$$\begin{aligned}\text{cov}(\eta_k, \eta_{k-l}) &= E(\eta_k\eta_{k-l}) = E\{\sigma_{k-1}^2(\varepsilon_{k-1}^2 - 1)\sigma_{k-l-1}^2(\varepsilon_{k-l-1}^2 - 1)\}\\ &= E(A_k)E(\varepsilon_{k-1}^2 - 1)\end{aligned}$$

where $A_k = \sigma_{k-1}^2\sigma_{k-l-1}^2(\varepsilon_{k-l-1}^2 - 1)$ and

$$\text{cov}(\eta_k, \sigma_{k-l}^2) = E(\eta_k\sigma_{k-l}^2) = E\left\{\sigma_{k-1}^2(\varepsilon_{k-1}^2 - 1)\sigma_{k-l}^2\right\} = E(\sigma_{k-1}^2\sigma_{k-l}^2)E(\varepsilon_{k-1}^2 - 1).$$

(13.47) follows since $E(\varepsilon_{k-1}^2) = 1$.

13.7.4 Properties of GARCH variances

Note that

$$\sigma_k^2 = \theta_0 + (\theta_1 + \theta_2)\sigma_{k-1}^2 + \theta_1\eta_k \quad \text{where} \quad \theta_0 = (1 - \theta_1 - \theta_2)\xi_\sigma^2.$$

Since $\text{cor}(\eta_k, \sigma_{k-1}^2) = 0$, (13.46) right yields

$$\text{var}(\sigma_k^2) = (\theta_1 + \theta_2)^2\text{var}(\sigma_{k-1}^2) + \theta_1^2\text{var}(\eta_k) = (\theta_1 + \theta_2)^2\text{var}(\sigma_{k-1}^2) + 2\theta_1^2E(\sigma_{k-1}^4).$$

But $E(\sigma_{k-1}^4) = \text{var}(\sigma_{k-1}^2) + \{E(\sigma_{k-1}^2)\}^2$, so that

$$\text{var}(\sigma_k^2) = \{(\theta_1 + \theta_2)^2 + 2\theta_1^2\}\text{var}(\sigma_{k-1}^2) + 2\theta_1^2\{E(\sigma_{k-1}^2)\}^2$$

where $E(\sigma_k^2) \to \xi_\sigma^2$ as $k \to \infty$. A similar limit L for $\text{var}(\sigma_k^2)$ must therefore satisfy

$$L = \{(\theta_1 + \theta_2)^2 + 2\theta_1^2\}L + 2\theta_1^2\xi_\sigma^4 \quad \text{with solution} \quad L = \xi_\sigma^4 \frac{2\theta_1^2}{1 - 2\theta_1^2 - (\theta_1 + \theta_2)^2},$$

which is (13.16) right.

Apply the general formula for covariances of sums to $\sigma_k^2 = \theta_0 + (\theta_1 + \theta_2)\sigma_{k-1}^2 + \theta_1\eta_k$ and σ_{k-l}^2 when $l > 0$. This yields

$$\text{cov}(\sigma_k^2, \sigma_{k-l}^2) = \text{cov}(\theta_0, \sigma_{k-l}^2) + (\theta_1 + \theta_2)\text{cov}(\sigma_{k-1}^2, \sigma_{k-l}^2) + \theta_1\text{cov}(\eta_k, \sigma_{k-l}^2),$$

where the first and third terms on the right are 0. Hence

$$\text{cov}(\sigma_k^2, \sigma_{k-l}^2) = (\theta_1 + \theta_2)\text{cov}(\sigma_{k-1}^2, \sigma_{k-l}^2),$$

which can be repeated for $\text{cov}(\sigma_{k-1}^2, \sigma_{k-l}^2)$ and so on. By iteration we end up with

$$\text{cov}(\sigma_k^2, \sigma_{k-l}^2) = (\theta_1 + \theta_2)^l\text{cov}(\sigma_{k-l}^2, \sigma_{k-l}^2) = (\theta_1 + \theta_2)^l\text{var}(\sigma_{k-l}^2),$$

which is (13.15).

13.7.5 The original process squared

Note that

$$Y_k^2 = (\xi_y + \sigma_k\varepsilon_k)^2 = \xi_y^2 + 2\xi_y\sigma_k\varepsilon_k + \sigma_k^2\varepsilon_k^2,$$

so that

$$E(Y_k^2) = \xi_y^2 + 2\xi_y E(\sigma_k\varepsilon_k) + E(\sigma_k^2\varepsilon_k^2) = \xi_y^2 + 2\xi_y E(\sigma_k)E(\varepsilon_k) + E(\sigma_k^2)E(\varepsilon_k^2)$$

or

$$E(Y_k^2) = \xi_y^2 + E(\sigma_k^2) \to \xi_y^2 + \xi_\sigma^2 \quad \text{as} \quad k \to \infty,$$

as claimed in (13.19) upper line.

To examine the variances, subtract the expression for $E(Y_k^2)$ from that of Y_k^2, which yields

$$Y_k^2 - E(Y_k^2) = 2\xi_y\sigma_k\varepsilon_k + \sigma_k^2\varepsilon_k^2 - E\sigma_k^2 = (\sigma_k^2 - E\sigma_k^2) + 2\xi_y\sigma_k\varepsilon_k + \eta_{k+1}, \quad (13.48)$$

where $\eta_{k+1} = \sigma_k^2(\varepsilon_k^2 - 1)$. The three terms on the right are uncorrelated, for example

$$\text{cov}(\sigma_k\varepsilon_k, \eta_{k+1}) = E(\sigma_k\varepsilon_k\eta_{k+1}) = E\{\varepsilon_k\sigma_k^3(\varepsilon_k^2 - 1)\} = E(\sigma_k^3)\{E(\varepsilon_k^3) - E(\varepsilon_k)\} = 0,$$

and the other two are similar. Hence

$$\text{var}(Y_k^2) = \text{var}(\sigma_k^2) + (2\xi_y)^2\text{var}(\sigma_k\varepsilon_k) + \text{var}(\eta_{k+1}) = \text{var}(\sigma_k^2) + 4\xi_y^2 E(\sigma_k^2) + 2E(\sigma_k^4),$$

using (13.46) right. But $E(\sigma_k^4) = \text{var}(\sigma_k^2) + (E\sigma_k^2)^2$, so that

$$\text{var}(Y_k^2) = 3\text{var}(\sigma_k^2) + 2(E\sigma_k^2)^2 + 4\xi_y^2 E(\sigma_k^2)$$

where $E(\sigma_k^2)$ and $\text{var}(\sigma_k^2)$ have the limits (13.16) as $k \to \infty$. Insert those, and it emerges that $\text{var}(Y_k^2)$ tends to the limit in (13.19).

Finally, to derive $\text{cor}(Y_k^2, Y_{k-l}^2)$, use (13.48) to deduce that

$$\text{cov}(Y_k^2, Y_{k-l}^2)$$
$$= E\{(\sigma_k^2 - E\sigma_k^2 + 2\xi_y\sigma_k\varepsilon_k + \eta_{k+1})(\sigma_{k-l}^2 - E\sigma_{k-l}^2 + 2\xi_y\sigma_{k-l}\varepsilon_{k-l} + \eta_{k-l+1})\}$$

where the product must be multiplied out and the expectations of the cross-products evaluated. All but two are zero, which leaves us with

$$\text{cov}(Y_k^2, Y_{k-l}^2) = E\{(\sigma_k^2 - E\sigma_k^2)(\sigma_{k-l}^2 - E\sigma_{k-l}^2)\} + E\{(\sigma_k^2 - E\sigma_k^2)\eta_{k-l+1}\}$$

with the last term 0 if $l > 1$. Then $\text{cov}(Y_k^2, Y_{k-l}^2) = \text{cov}(\sigma_k^2, \sigma_{k-l}^2)$, and (13.20) follows from (13.17). The extra term when $l = 1$ is, by (13.12) and (13.46),

$$E\{(\sigma_k^2 - E\sigma_k^2)\eta_k\} = E\{((\theta_1 + \theta_2)(\sigma_{k-1}^2 - E\sigma_{k-1}^2) + \theta_1\eta_k)\eta_k\} = \theta_1 E(\eta_k^2) = 2\theta_1 E(\sigma_{k-1}^4)$$

so that

$$\text{cov}(Y_k^2, Y_{k-1}^2) = \text{cov}(\sigma_k^2, \sigma_{k-1}^2) + 2\theta_1 E(\sigma_{k-1}^4),$$

and the complicated limiting expression for $\text{cor}(Y_k^2, Y_{k-1}^2)$ follows after some calculations.

13.7.6 Verification of Table 13.5

How simulations under the Wilkie model are adapted given values of inflation, equity yield, dividend inflation, long rate of interest and interest-rate ratio is a tedious exercise in inverting (13.33)–(13.44). We need (row 1 of Table 13.5) historical values of the linear driving process underlying ordinary inflation; i.e., x_{-k}^i for $k = 0, -1, -2, \ldots$, which is found by inverting (13.33) when $I_{-k} = i_{-i}$. In row 2 of Table 13.5, x_0^y, x_{-1}^y and x_{-2}^y are similar consequences of (13.34). Next, ε_0^y is deduced by inserting $k = 0$, $X_0^y = x_0^y$ and $X_{-1}^y = x_{-1}^y$ into (13.39). In row 4, $x_0^{d|i}$ is found from (13.41) by writing it as a sum of historical values of the linear driver process x_{-k}^i in the same way as an autoregressive process was represented as an exponential sum of random input in Section 5.6. To handle ε_0^d use (13.40) with $k = 0$, which yields

$$x_0^{d|y} = \sigma^d(\varepsilon_0^d + b_1^d\varepsilon_{-1}^d) + \theta^{d|y}\varepsilon_{-1}^y = \sigma^d(\varepsilon_0^d + b_1^d\varepsilon_{-1}^d) + \theta^{d|y}(x_{-1}^y - a^y x_{-2}^y)/\sigma^y$$

after inserting (13.39) for $k = -1$. From this it can be deduced that the conditional expectation of ε_0^d becomes the expression in row 5 of Table 15.5. The sum for $x_0^{r|i}$ in row 6 follows from (13.43) in the same way as $x_0^{d|i}$ was found from (13.41).

Finally, $x_0^{r|y}$ and x_0^f are determined as solutions of (13.36) and (13.37) after simple inversions.

13.8 Bibliographical notes

13.8.1 Linear processes

The literature on stochastic asset modelling has grown to enormous proportions, but a main workhorse will always be linear time series models. The brief review in Section 13.4 is extended in a host of monographs and textbooks, for example Priestley (1981), Schumway and Stoffer (2011) and Brockwell and Davis (2002) in statistics and Taylor (1986), Mills and Markellos (2008), Christoffersen (2003), Wang (2003), Lütkepohl and Krätzig (2004), Franke *et al.* (2004), Lütkepohl (2005) and Tsay (2010) in financial economics. Zivot and Wang (2003) and Carmona (2004) are introductions connected with S-plus/R software, and Fomby and Carter Hill (2003) review the impact of misspecification in econometric models. If you want to study interest-rate modelling specifically, a good place is the very thorough monograph by James and Webber (2000), but you may also try Fabozi (2002). Hughston (2000) is a collection of articles which are heavier on the mathematical side. A special topic not covered here is processes with **long memory**, where the autocorrelaton function decays only very slowly towards zero when the time lag is increased. Such models have attracted much attention in finance, but also criticism. Beran (1994) and Robinson (2003) are introductions, while Mikosch and Stărică (2000) raise a sceptical eye. Nor have we discussed processes with jumps, known as **Lévy** processes. The Poisson process (Section 8.2) is a special case. Schoutens (2003) (fairly elementary) and Cont and Tankov (2004) (more advanced) are introductions to Lévy processes in a financial context.

13.8.2 Heavy tails

Heavy-tailed distributions were introduced in Section 13.2 by making volatilities stochastic. We find t-distributions emerging when the inverse volatility is the square root of a Gamma variable, but there are many other possibilities. The example in Exercise 13.3 is a special case of the **normal inverse Gaussian** (Barndorff-Nielsen, 1997) or, more generally, the **generalized hyperbolic** distributions (Barndorff-Nielsen and Stelzer, 2005). Both classes have proved popular in finance, and neither is straightforward to sample in general. The key is a generator for the **generalized inverse Gaussian**, for which the rejection method in Dagpunar (1989) is reasonably simple to implement. There are multivariate extensions for all of this. The multivariate t introduced in Section 13.2 is reviewed in Kotz and Nadarajah (2004). It is possible to use other models than square roots of Gamma variables as drivers of the volatilities. This leads to the class of **elliptically contoured** distributions; see, for example, Fang *et al.* (1990). Multivariate heavy-tailed models with other properties can be constructed through the copulas in Section 6.7. Heavy tails are never far from the surface in the elegant little book by Embrechts and Maejima (2002) on so-called **self-similar** processes.

13.8.3 Dynamic volatility

A central part of heavy-tailedness is how volatility propagates in time. Engle (1982) pioneered the ARCH model, which started an avalanche of research. The GARCH(1,1) in Section 13.3 has a huge number of extensions. Bollerslev (2001) may be a good place to begin if you want to examine the literature. Other references (with fairly simple mathematics) are Rachev and Mittnik (2000) and Franses and van Dijk (2000); see also the collections of articles in Knight and Satchell (2001, 2002) and Rachev (2003). Modern GARCH constructions certainely allow several variables, but the generalization from the univariate case is not immediate. This is easier with the approach in Section 13.2, where $\{\sigma_k\}$ is a Markov process hidden in the observations $\{Y_k\}$. Such models were proposed by Shepard (1994) and Harvey *et al.* (1994) in the econometric literature and Ball and Torous (2000) in the financial literature; see also Shephard (2005) for a collection of review articles. Likelihood fitting to historical data is technically more demanding than for the GARCH type, and is still not a closed subject. The reason is the same as in Chapter 11. The models are of the non-linear state-space type for which Markov chain Monte Carlo (Section 4.8) is typically needed for the likelihood; see Harvey *et al.* (2004) for a general reference in addition to those in Section 11.9. Later contributions are Bos and Shephard (2006), Chib *et al.* (2006) and Omori *et al.* (2007). The simple moment estimates hinted at in Section 13.2 have a general form in Genon-Catalot *et al.* (2000).

13.9 Exercises

Section 13.2

Exercise 13.1 Consider the stochastic volatility model $Y|Z \sim N(\xi_y, \xi_\sigma\sqrt{Z})$ where $Z = e^{-\tau^2/2+\tau X}$ and $X \sim N(0,1)$ with three parameters ξ_y, ξ_σ and τ.

(a) Write a program generating m simulations of Y.
R-*commands*:
```
Z=rlnorm(m,-τ**2/2,τ); Ylnvol=rnorm(m,ξy,ξσ*sqrt(Z)).
```

(b) Run the program for $\xi_y = 0.01$, $\xi_\sigma = 0.1$ and $\tau = 0.3$ using $m = 10\,000$ and estimate and plot the density function of Y.

R-*commands*:

```
plot(density(Ylnvol)).
```

Exercise 13.2 Replace Z in Exercise 13.1 by $Z = (\alpha - 1)/(\alpha G)$ where $G \sim$ Gamma(α). This leaves $E(Y)$ and sd(Y) unchanged, whereas kurt(Y) becomes $3/(\alpha - 2)$ against $3(e^{\tau^2} - 1)$ before.

(a) Show that $\alpha = (2e^{\tau^2} - 1)/(e^{\tau^2} - 1)$ makes kurt(Y) the same as in Exercise 13.1.
(b) Write a program generating m simulations of Y.

R-*commands*:

```
Z=(α-1)/rgamma(m,α); Yt=rnorm(m,ξy,ξσ*sqrt(Z)).
```

(c) Run the program in (b) under the conditions in Exercise 13.1 with α adapted to τ and Q–Q plot simulations of Y under the two stochastic volatility models.

R-*commands*:

With `Ylnvol` from Exercise 13.1 use `plot(sort(Ylnvol),sort(Yt))`.

Exercise 13.3 Another construction with stochastic volatility is

$$Y|G \sim N(\xi_y + \beta G, \xi_\sigma \sqrt{G}) \quad \text{where} \quad G \sim \text{Gamma}(\alpha),$$

a special case of the **normal inverse gaussian** (or **NIG**) family; see Section 13.8 for references. There are four parameters ξ_y, β, ξ_σ and α.

(a) Argue that $E(Y|G) = \xi_y + \beta G$ and that var$(Y|G) = \xi_\sigma^2 G$, and use the rules of double expectation and variance to prove that $E(Y) = \xi_y + \beta$ and var$(Y) = \xi_\sigma^2 + \beta^2/\alpha$.
(b) Write a program generating m simulations of Y.

R-*commands*:

```
G=rgamma(m,α)/α; Ynig=rnorm(m,ξy+β*G,ξσ*sqrt(G)).
```

(c) Generate $m = 100\,000$ simulations when $\xi_y = 0.01$, $\xi_\sigma = 0.1$, $\alpha = 6$ and compare $\beta = 0$ and $\beta = 1$ by estimating/plotting the density function.

R-*commands*:

```
plot(density(Ynig)).
```

Exercise 13.4 Let $\beta = 0$ in Exercise 13.3 so that $Y = \xi_y + \xi_\sigma \sqrt{G}\,\varepsilon$.

(a) Argue that the mean, standard deviation and kurtosis coincide with those in Exercise 13.1 if $\alpha = 1/(e^{\tau^2} - 1)$. [*Hint*: kurt$(Y)$ is $3/\alpha$ against $3(e^{\tau^2} - 1)$ in Exercise 13.1.]
(b) Run the program in Exercise 13.3 with ξ_y and ξ_σ as in Exercise 13.1, $\beta = 0$ and with α adapted to $\tau = 0.3$ and Q–Q plot against the simulations in Exercise 13.1.

R-*commands*:

With `Ylnvol` from Exercise 13.1 use `plot(sort(Ylnvol),sort(Ynig))`.

(c) Compare with the simulations in Exercise 13.2 instead.

R-*commands*:

Take `Yt` from Exercise 13.2 and use `plot(sort(Yt),sort(Ynig))`.

Exercise 13.5 Let $Y_1, \ldots, Y_J$ be independent and identically NIG distributed as in Exercise 13.3 and let $\overline{Y} = (Y_1 + \cdots + Y_J)/J$.

(a) If $G_1, \ldots, G_J$ are the underlying Gamma variables, show that

$$\overline{Y}|G_1, \ldots, G_J \sim N(\xi_y + \beta\overline{G}, \xi_\sigma\sqrt{\overline{G}/J}),$$

where $\overline{G} = (G_1 + \cdots + G_J)/J$.

(b) Since $\overline{G} \sim \text{Gamma}(J\alpha)$, deduce that $\overline{Y}$ is NIG distributed with $\xi_\sigma/\sqrt{J}$ and $J\alpha$ replacing ξ_σ and α.

Exercise 13.6 Let $X_k = aX_{k-1} + \sqrt{1-a^2}\,\eta_k$ for $k = 1, \ldots, K$ with $\eta_1, \ldots, \eta_K$ independent and $N(0,1)$ and $\sigma_k = \xi_\sigma e^{-\tau^2/2+\tau X_k}$ as in (13.9).

(a) Write a program simulating $\sigma_1, \ldots, \sigma_K$ m times.

R-*commands*:

```
x0=log(σ0/ξσ)/τ+τ/2; X=matrix(x0,K+1,m); b=sqrt(1-a**2);
for (k in 1:K) X[k+1,]=a*X[k,]+b*rnorm(m);
σ=ξσ*exp(-τ**2/2+τ*X[1:K+1,]).
```

(b) Generate m simulations of $Y_1, \ldots, Y_K$ when they are conditionally independent given $\sigma_1, \ldots, \sigma_K$ with $Y_k|\sigma_k \sim N(\xi_y, \sigma_k)$.

R-*commands*:

```
Y=matrix(rnorm(m*K,ξy,σ),K,m).
```

(c) Run the program when $m = 1$, $K = 250$, $\xi_y = 0.00034$, $\xi_\sigma = 0.01$, $\tau = 0.63$, $a = 0.95$ and $\sigma_0 = 0.006$ (1 year on a daily time scale) and plot the simulations against time.

R-*commands*:

```
ts.plot(Y).
```

(d) Redo (c) for $a = 0$ and then for $\tau = 0.00001$ and note the changes.

Exercise 13.7 Pass to annual time scale in Exercise 13.6 and let $\xi_y = 0.08$, $\xi_\sigma = 0.25$, $\tau = 0.3$, $a = 0.5$ and $\sigma_0 = 0.15$.

(a) Draw $m = 100\,000$ simulations of $Y_1, \ldots, Y_K$ with their returns $R_k = e^{Y_k} - 1$ when $K = 10$.

R-*commands*:

Generate `Y` as in Exercise 13.6 and use `R=exp(Y)-1`.

(b) Estimate the density functions of $R_1, \dots, R_K$ and plot them jointly.

R-*commands*:

```
plot(density(R[1,])); for (k in 2:K){d=density(R[k,]);
lines(d$x,d$y)}.
```

(c) Interpret the pattern in (b).

Exercise 13.8 With $\sigma_1, \dots, \sigma_K$ as in Exercise 13.6 let $(Y_{11}, Y_{21}), \dots, (Y_{1K}, Y_{2K})$ be conditionally independent pairs with $Y_{1k} \sim N(\xi_y, \sigma_k)$, $Y_{2k} \sim N(\gamma\xi_y, \gamma\sigma_k)$ and $\rho = \text{cor}(Y_{1k}, Y_{2k}|\sigma_k)$.

(a) Write a program simulating these pairs m times.

R-*commands*:

With σ as in Exercise 13.6(a) use

```
eps=array(rnorm(2*m*K),dim=c(2,K,m));
eps[2,,]=ρ*eps[1,,]+sqrt(1-ρ**2)*eps[2,,];
Y1=ξy+σ*eps[1,,]; Y2=γ*(ξy+σ*eps[2,,]).
```

(b) Run the program when $m = 1$ and plot realizations Y_{1k} and Y_{2k} jointly against time up to $K = 50$ when $\xi_y = 0.08$, $\xi_\sigma = 0.25$, $\tau = 0.3$, $a = 0.5$, $\gamma = 0.7$ and $\rho = 0.5$ with $\sigma_0 = 0.15$ at the beginning.

R-*commands*:

```
kk=1:K; matplot(kk,cbind(Y1,Y2),''l'').
```

(c) Redo (b) when $\rho = 0.9$ and note the change.

(d) Redo (b) when $m = 3$ and examine the three joint plots of (Y_{1k}, Y_{2k}) against k.

Section 13.3

Exercise 13.9 Let $Y_0, \dots, Y_K$ be conditionally independent given a first-order GARCH sequence $\sigma_0, \dots, \sigma_K$ and assume $Y_k|\sigma_k \sim N(\xi_y, \sigma_k)$.

(a) Write a program simulating $Y_0, \dots, Y_K$ m times.

R-*commands*:

With the start on $Y_0 = y_0$ and σ_0, use `Y=matrix(y0,K+1,m);`

```
v=σ0**2*rep(1,m);
for (k in 1:K) {v=(1-θ1-θ2)*ξσ**2+ θ1*(Y[k,]-ξy)**2+θ2*v;
Y[k+1,]=rnorm(m,ξy,sqrt(v))}.
```

(b) Draw a single realization of $Y_0, \dots, Y_K$ on a daily time scale when $K = 1000$, $\xi_y = 0.0006$, $y_0 = 0.0006$, $\xi_\sigma = 0.013$, $\sigma_0 = 0.0065$, $\theta_1 = 0.22$ and $\theta_2 = 0.7$ and plot the simulations against k.

R-*commands*:

```
ts.plot(Y).
```

(c) Redo when $\sigma_0 = 0.026$ and check the impact when σ_0 is smaller.
(d) Try $\theta_1 = \theta_2 = 0$ in (b) and (c) and note the change in patterns.

Exercise 13.10

(a) Compute and plot the autocorrelation function of the simulations in Exercise 13.9(b).

R-*commands*:

```
acf(Y).
```

(b) Use the absolute value instead and explain why the two plots are so different.

R-*commands*:

```
acf(abs(Y)).
```

Exercise 13.11

(a) Run the program in Exercise 13.9 with $m = 100\,000$, $K = 25$, $\xi_y = 0.08$, $y_0 = 0.08$, $\xi_\sigma = 0.25$, $\sigma_0 = 0.10$, $\theta_1 = 0.2$ and $\theta_2 = 0.6$ (annual time scale) and use the simulations to plot sd(Y_k) against k.

R-*commands*:

With `Y` from Exercise 13.9 use `s=apply(Y,1,sd); plot(0:K,s)`.

(b) Compute the density functions of $Y_0, \ldots, Y_K$ and plot them jointly.

R-*commands*:

```
d=density(Y[1,],bw=0.05);
plot(d$x,d$y,''l'',xlim=c(-0.7,0.9));
for (k in 1:K+1){d=density(Y[k,],bw=0.05); lines(d$x,d$y)}.
```

(c) Interpret the pattern and judge how long it takes for the initial value σ_0 to be forgotten.

Exercise 13.12

(a) Simulate 4 years of daily GARCH data under the model in Exercise 13.9(b) and reconstruct the underlying parameters through likelihood fitting.

R-*commands*:

Generate data y by means of the program in Exercise 13.9(a) with $K = 1000$ and use the R-function `garchfit` through the command `garchfit(y)`.

(b) Redo (a) a few times to examine how much the estimates vary.
(c) Redo (a) and (b) when $K = 250$ (1-year data) and judge whether the underlying GARCH model can be determined now.

Exercise 13.13

(a) Read historical, daily log-returns for the Oslo stock exchange (1983 to 2000) and fit the GARCH model.

R-*commands*:
`y=scan(''Oslo83-2000.txt'')` and then `garchfit(y)` as in Exercise 13.13(b).

(b) Compute and plot the autocorrelation function of the abolute values of the data and compare with those in Exercise 13.10, which were computed from a series simulated under the parameters you found in (a).
R-*commands*:
`acf(abs(y))`.

(c) Does the model appear to fit well? [*Answer*: Not clear!]

Exercise 13.14 Suppose the GARCH model of the preceding exercises applies to log-returns so that $R_{0:K} = e^{Y_1+\cdots+Y_K} - 1$ is accumulated return.

(a) Compute the 10%, 25%, 50%, 75% and 90% percentiles of $R_{0:K}$ when $\xi_y = 0.006$, $y_0 = 0.006$, $\xi_\sigma = 0.013$, $\sigma_0 = 0.013$, $\theta_1 = 0.2$, $\theta_2 = 0.7$ and $K = 250$ (1 year on a daily time scale) using $m = 100\,000$ simulations.
R-*commands*:
Generate `Y` as in Exercise 13.9 and use
`R=exp(apply(Y[1:K+1,],2,sum))-1;`
`ind=c(0.1,0.25,0.5,0.75,0.9)*m;` q_ε`=sort(R)[ind]`.

(b) Redo (a) when $\theta_1 = 0$ and $\theta_2 = 0$ and examine the impact of removing the GARCH effect.

(c) Explain why changing σ_0 to $\sigma_0/2$ likely to be of little importance for our 1-year projections (check and see!).

Exercise 13.15 Redo the preceding exercise on an *annual* time scale, i.e., let $\xi_y = 0.08$, $y_0 = 0.08$, $\xi_\sigma = 0.25$, $\sigma_0 = 0.25$, $\theta_1 = 0.2$, $\theta_2 = 0.7$.

(a) Run the program in Exercise 13.14 when $K = 10$ and $m = 100\,000$ and compute the same percentiles for these 10-year returns.
(b) Remove the GARCH effect by taking $\theta_1 = \theta_2 = 0$ and investigate the effect.
(c) Argue that replacing σ_0 by $\sigma_0/2$ might, unlike in Exercise 13.14, have considerable impact and verify that it is so.

Exercise 13.16 How important is the choice between the *driver* model in Section 13.2 and the *feedback* GARCH model? One way to make the them comparable is to make the mean, standard deviation and first-order autocorrelation of σ_k^2 equal under the two models when k is large, which means that in Exercise 13.6

$$\tau = \frac{1}{2}\sqrt{\log\left(1 + \frac{2\theta_1^2}{1 - 2\theta_1^2 - (\theta_1+\theta_2)^2}\right)} \quad \text{and} \quad a = \frac{1}{4\tau^2}\log\{1 + (\theta_1+\theta_2)(e^{4\tau^2} - 1)\}$$

whereas ξ_σ is reduced to $\xi_\sigma e^{-\tau^2/2}$.

(a) Redo the computations of the percentiles in Exercise 13.14 for the driver model with these matching parameters and compare results.
R-*commands*:
Generate `Y` as in Exercise 13.6 and use the commands in Exercise 13.14(a).

(b) Redo (a) on an *annual* time scale and compare with the results in Exercise 13.15.

(c) What conclusions do you draw from the experiments in (a) and (b)?

Section 13.4

Exercise 13.17 Let $X_k = a_1 X_{k-1} + a_2 X_{k-2} + \sigma\varepsilon_k$ for $k = 1, 2, \ldots$ be an autoregression of order two with $\varepsilon_1, \varepsilon_2, \ldots$ independent and $N(0, 1)$.

(a) Write a program generating m realizations of $X_1, \ldots, X_K$ when $X_0 = X_{-1} = 0$.
R-*commands*:
`X=matrix(0,K+2,m); for (k in 1:K) X[k+2,]=`a_1`*X[k+1,]+`a_2`*X[k,] +`σ`*rnorm(m)`. The simulations are column-wise on rows 3 to $K + 2$.

(b) Run the program $m = 5$ times up to $K = 50$ when $a_1 = 0.4$, $a_2 = 0.5$ and $\sigma = 0.3$ and plot the simulations jointly against time.
R-*commands*:
`matplot(-1:K, X, ''l'')`.

(c) Redo (b) when $a_2 = -0.5$ and note the change in behaviour. [*Comment*: See Priestley (1981) for conditions of stationarity.]

Exercise 13.18 Autocorrelation functions of autoregressive processes of order 2 have closed mathematical expressions; see Priestley (1981) or Brockwell and Davis (2011), but they may also be examined through Monte Carlo.

(a) Run the program in Exercise 13.17 a single time up to $K = 10\,000$ when $a_1 = 0.4$, $a_2 = 0.5$ and $\sigma = 0.3$ and compute and plot the autocorrelation function.
R-*commands*:
With `X` as in Exercise 13.17 use `acf(X)`.

(b) Redo when $a_2 = -0.5$ and try to link the autocorrelation function to the simulated patterns in Exercise 13.17.

Exercise 13.19 Consider the ARMA(1,1) model $X_k = aX_{k-1} + \sigma(\varepsilon_k + b\varepsilon_{k-1})$ with $\varepsilon_1, \varepsilon_2, \ldots$ independent and $N(0, 1)$.

(a) Write a program generating m simulations of $X_1, \ldots, X_K$ when $X_0 = x_0$.
R-*commands*:

```
X=matrix(x0,K+1,m); eps=matrix(rnorm(m*(K+1)),K+1,m);
for (k in 1:K) {s=σ*(eps[k+1,]+b*eps[k,]);
X[k+1,]=a*X[k,]+s}.
```

(b) Run the program up to $K = 50$ when $m = 5$, $x_0 = 0$, $\sigma = 1$, $a = 0.7$ and $b = 1$ and plot the simulated series jointly against time.
R-*commands*:
```
matplot(0:K,X,''l'').
```

(c) Generate a single realization when $K = 10\,000$ and compute/plot the autocorrelation function.
R-*commands*:
```
acf(X).
```

(d) Does the autocorrelation pattern differ much from what it was under AR(1)?

Exercise 13.20 Let $(\varepsilon_{1k}, \varepsilon_{2k})$ be $N(0, 1)$ with correlation $\rho = \mathrm{cor}(\varepsilon_{1k}, \varepsilon_{2k})$ and with independence between pairs for $k = 1, 2, \ldots$

(a) Write a program simulating $(\varepsilon_{1k}, \varepsilon_{2k})$ up to time K.
R-*commands*:
```
eps=matrix(rnorm(2*K),K,2);
eps[,2]=ρ*eps[,1]+sqrt(1-ρ**2)*eps[,2].
```

(b) Use (a) as input to a simulation program for the linear feedback model

$$X_{1k} = a_{11}X_{1k-1} + a_{12}X_{2k-1} + \sigma_1\varepsilon_{1k},$$
$$X_{2k} = a_{21}X_{1k-1} + a_{22}X_{2k-1} + \sigma_2\varepsilon_{2k}$$

for $k = 1, \ldots, K$ and $X_{10} = X_{20} = 0$.
R-*commands*:
```
A=matrix(c(a11,a21,a12,a22),2,2); s=c(σ1,σ2);
X=matrix(0,K+1,2); for (k in 1:K) X[k+1,]=
A%*%X[k,]+s*eps[k,].
```

(c) Simulate the processes up to $K = 100$ when $a_{11} = 0.8$, $a_{12} = 0$, $a_{21} = 0.5$, $a_{22} = 0.8$, $\sigma_1 = \sigma_2 = 1$ and $\rho = 0.5$ and plot them jointly against time.
R-*commands*:
```
matplot(0:K,X,''l'').
```

(d) Redo (c) when $a_{12} = -0.4$ and comment on how the relationship between the two variables has changed.

Exercise 13.21 Let $r_k = \xi e^{-\sigma_x^2/2+X_k}$ with X_k the second-order autoregression in Exercise 13.17. The standard deviation of X_k when the initial value is forgotten is then $\sigma_x = \gamma\sigma$, where

$$\gamma = \sqrt{\frac{1 - a_2}{1 - a_1^2 - a_2^2 - a_2 - a_1^2 a_2 + a_2^3}};$$

see Priestley (1981).

(a) Extend the program in Exercise 13.17 so that it simulates r_k as well.

R-*commands*:

With X from Exercise 13.17 use r=ξ*exp(-σ_x^2/2+X).

(b) Use the simulations in Exercise 13.17(c) (for which $\sigma_x = 0.359$) to generate Monte Carlo rates of interest when $\xi = 0.04$, compute their mean and plot them jointly against time.

R-*commands*:

```
Mean=mean(r); matplot(0:K,r,''l'').
```

(c) Check that the mean is close to 0.04.

Exercise 13.22 Let $X_1, X_2, \ldots$ be a stationary stochastic process with mean 0 and standard deviation σ_x when the initial state has been forgotten and consider the transformations

$$\underset{\textit{log-normal}}{r_k = \xi e^{-\sigma_x^2/2+X_k}} \quad \text{and} \quad \underset{\textit{Gamma}}{r_k = \xi G_\alpha^{-1}\{\Phi(X_k/\sigma_x)\}}$$

where, on the right, $G_\alpha^{-1}(u)$ is the percentile function of the standard Gamma distribution with shape α and $\Phi(x)$ the Gaussian integral.

(a) Argue that $E(r_k) = \xi$ for large k.

(b) Show that $\text{sd}(r_k)$ is the same under both models for large k if $\alpha = 1/(e^{\sigma_x^2} - 1)$. [*Hint*: Expressions for $\text{sd}(r_k)$ for large k are $\xi\sqrt{e^{\sigma_x^2} - 1}$ and $\xi/\sqrt{\alpha}$.]

Exercise 13.23

(a) Simulate $r_0, \ldots, r_K$ up to $K = 100$ under the log-normal model in Exercise 13.22 when $\xi = 0.04$, $a = 0.7$, $\sigma = 0.3$ and $r_0 = 0.02$, assuming AR(1) for $\{X_k\}$.

R-*commands*:

```
σx=σ/sqrt(1-a**2); x0=log(r0/ξ)+σx**2/2; X=rep(x0,K+1);
for (k in 1:K) X[k+1]=a*X[k]+σ*rnorm(1);
rln=ξ*exp(-σx**2/2+X).
```

(b) Adapt α as explained in Exercise 13.22 and simulate the Gamma version of the model using the same simulations of $X_1, \ldots, X_K$.

R-*commands*:

```
α=1/(exp(σx**2)-1); U=pnorm(X/σx); rgam=ξ*qgamma(U,α)/α.
```

(c) Plot the two simulated interest-rate series jointly against time and examine their discrepancy.

R-*commands*:

```
matplot(0:K,cbind(rln,rgam),''l'').
```

Exercise 13.24 Let $X_1, X_2, \ldots$ be a stationary Gaussian process with mean 0 and standard deviation σ_x when x_0 has been forgotten and introduce as possible model for the rate of inflation

$$I_k = H(X_k) \quad \text{where} \quad H(x) = \xi\frac{\log(1-\theta+e^x)}{\log(2-\theta)} \quad \text{for} \quad \theta < 1.$$

(a) Argue that ξ is the median of I_k for large k. [*Hint*: The median of X_k is then 0.]

(b) Also argue that $I_k > \xi\log(1-\theta)/\log(2-\theta)$ and that $\Pr(I_k < 0) = \Phi(\log(\theta)/\sigma_x)$ for large k.

Exercise 13.25 Suppose $X_1, X_2, \ldots$ in Exercise 13.24 is a Gaussian first-order autoregression.

(a) Write a program generating m simulations of $I_1, \ldots, I_K$ when $I_0 = i_0$.

R-*commands*:

```
x0=log((2-θ)**(i0/ξ)-1+θ); X=matrix(x0,K+1,m);
for (k in 1:K) X[k+1,]=a*X[k,]+σ*rnorm(m);
I=ξ*log(1-θ+exp(X))/log(2-θ).
```

(b) Run the program when $m = 10$, $K = 50$, $\theta = 0.93$, $i_0 = 0.02$, $\xi = 0.048$, $\sigma = 0.04$ and $a = 0.58$. Estimate how often the simulations go into minus and plot them jointly against time.

R-*commands*:

```
Pr=length(I[I<0])/(m*K); matplot(0:K,I,''l'').
```

Section 13.5

Exercise 13.26 Consider the Wilkie inflation model $I_k = (1+\xi^i)e^{X_k} - 1$ where $X_k = a^i X_{k-1} + \sigma^i\varepsilon_k$ with $\varepsilon_1, \varepsilon_2, \ldots$ independent and $N(0,1)$; see (13.33) and (13.38).

(a) Show that for large k

$$\Pr(I_k < 0) = \Phi\left(\frac{-\log(1+\xi^i)}{\sigma_x}\right) \quad \text{where} \quad \sigma_x = \frac{\sigma^i}{\sqrt{1-(a^i)^2}}.$$

(b) Insert the Wilkie parameters $\xi^i = 0.048$, $\sigma^i = 0.04$ and $a^i = 0.58$ in Table 13.3 and determine the chance of negative inflation. A frequent criticism of this model is that this value is too high for the twenty-first century.

(c) Change σ^i so that the probability of negative inflation is 5%. [*Answer*: $\sigma^i = 0.0232$.]

Exercise 13.27

(a) Argue that the mean and standard deviation of I_k in Exercise 13.26 are, for large k,

$$E(I_k) = (1+\xi^i)e^{\sigma_x^2/2} - 1 \quad \text{and} \quad \text{sd}(I_k) = (1+\xi^i)e^{\sigma_x^2/2}\sqrt{e^{\sigma_x^2} - 1}.$$

[*Hint*: Use the formulae for mean and standard deviation of log-normal variables.]

(b) Argue that rough approximations are $E(I_k) \doteq \xi^i$ and $\text{sd}(I_k) \doteq (1+\xi^i)\sigma_x$.

Exercise 13.28

(a) Write a program simulating Wilkie inflation m times up to time K with $I_0 = \xi^i$ at the beginning.

R-*commands*:

```
X=matrix(0,K+1,m); for (k in 1:K) X[k+1,]=
a^i*X[k,]+σ^i*rnorm(m); I=(1+ξ^i)*exp(X)-1.
```

(b) Generate $m = 10$ realizations under the Wilkie parameters $\xi^i = 0.048$, $\sigma^i = 0.04$ and $a^i = 0.58$ when $K = 50$ and plot them jointly.

R-*commands*:

```
matplot(0:K,I,''l'').
```

(c) Add commands simulating price levels $Q_0, \ldots, Q_K$ with $Q_0 = 1$.

R-*commands*:

```
Q=apply(1+I[1:K+1,],2,cumprod); Q=rbind(rep(1,m),Q).
```

(d) Generate $m = 100$ simulated price sequences up to $K = 50$ and plot them jointly.

R-*commands*:

```
matplot(0:K,Q,''l'').
```

Exercise 13.29 Inflation and prices in Exercise 13.28 reflected the instability of the twentieth century.

(a) Redo the simulations when $\sigma^i = 0.02$ (corresponding to about a 5% chance of negative inflation).

R-*commands*:

As in Exercise 13.28.

(b) Also redo when $\xi^i = 0.024$, $\sigma^i = 0.02$ and when $\xi^i = 0.024$, $\sigma^i = 0.01$.

(c) Try to judge the scope for adapting Wilkie inflation and prices to a more stable future; see also Exercise 13.25.

Exercise 13.30

(a) Generate a single simulation of equity under the Wilkie model up to $K = 10\,000$ years(!) and compute/plot the autocorrelation function of its returns R_e^k.

R-*commands*:

Use the R-function `wilkie` and `o=wilkie(1,K); acf(o$`R_e`)`.

(b) Redo (a) for the returns $R_k = (S_k - S_{k-1})/S_k$ without dividend.

R-*commands*:

`acf(o$`R_s`)`.

(c) Do the autocorrelations deviate much from a random walk?

(d) Compute the mean and standard deviation for both types of return.

R-*commands*:

`Mean=mean(o$`R_e`); Sd=sd(o$`R_e`)` and similar for o\$$R_s$.

Exercise 13.31

(a) Plot $m = 100$ simulations of how the initial value $s_0 = 1$ of equity evolves under the Wilkie model up to $K = 50$ years.

R-*commands*:

Use the R-function `wilkie` with `o=wilkie(m,K);`
`S=apply(1+o$`R_s`,2,cumprod); matplot(0:K,S,''l'')`.

(b) If all dividends are used to buy new stock free of charge, argue that the value now grows according to the return R_e in Section 13.5, and simulate and plot as in (a).

R-*commands*:

`V=apply(1+o$`R_e`,2,cumprod); matplot(0:K,V,''l'')`.

Exercise 13.32

(a) Argue that the real value S_k/Q_k of stock grows as $(1 + R_k^s)/(1 + I_k)$, where I_k is the rate of inflation.

(b) Redo Exercise 13.31(a) with such real values.

R-*commands*:

`o=wilkie(m,K);` S^{real}`=apply((1+o$`R_s`)/(1+o$`I`),2,cumprod);`
`matplot(0:K,`S^{real}`,''l'')`.

(c) Redo Exercise 13.31(b) too.

R-*commands*:

V^{real}`=apply((1+o$`R_e`)/(1+o$`I`),2,cumprod);`
`matplot(0:K,`V^{real}`,''l'')`.

Exercise 13.33

(a) Plot $m = 10$ simulations of the Wilkie ratio between the short and long rate of interest up to $K = 50$ years.

R-*commands*:

```
o=wilkie(m,K); matplot(0:K,o$F,''l'').
```

(b) Redo (a) for the long rate of interest.

R-*commands*:

```
matplot(0:K,o$rK,''l'').
```

(c) Redo (a) for the short rate too.

R-*commands*:

```
matplot(0:K,o$r,''l'').
```

Exercise 13.34

(a) If r is a rate of interest and I the rate of inflation, argue that the real *rate* of interest is $r^{\text{real}} = (r - I)/(1 + I)$. [*Hint*: Examine the growth of the account in real value.]

(b) Simulate/plot $m = 10$ scenarios of the real, long rate of interest under the Wilkie model.

R-*commands*:

```
o=wilkie(m,K); rK^real=apply((o$rK-o$I)/(1+o$I),2,cumprod);
matplot(0:K,rK^real,''l'').
```

(c) Redo (b) for the short, real rate.

R-*commands*:

```
r^real=apply((o$r-o$I)/(1+o$I),2,cumprod);
matplot(0:K,r^real,''l'').
```

(d) Comment on the potential for *negative* real rates judged from the experience of the twentieth century.

Exercise 13.35

(a) Generate a single simulation of the long and short rates of interest under the Wilkie model up to $K = 50$ years and plot them jointly against time.

R-*commands*:

```
o=wilkie(1,K); plot(0:K,o$r); lines(0:K,o$rK).
```

Suppose the long rate of interest is a J-year rate with $J = 10$.

(b) Interpolate on the logarithmic scale and plot j-year rates jointly against time for $j = 1, \ldots, 10$.

R-*commands*:

```
jj=(1:J-1)/(J-1); rj=exp(log(o$r[,1])%o%(1-jj)+
log(o$rK[,1])%o%jj); matplot(0:K,rj,''l'').
```

(c) Redo (a) and (b) a few times to get a feel for the variation.

14
Financial derivatives

14.1 Introduction

Financial derivatives or options are contracts derived from primary, financial assets such as equity, bonds or currency. The risk of an adverse development is then passed on to somebody else. Savings with guaranteed return is an example. A financial institution then reimburses customers when earnings fall below a certain floor. Companies also seek protection themselves. If it is inconvenient to carry the risk of the stock market going down or interest rates dropping, it may pay another company to take over, partially or completely.

The similarity to insurance and reinsurance is striking. What is different is the detailed mathematical models and above all a potential for **hedging** financial risk. To indicate the mechanism at work, consider put options on equity (Section 3.5). The payoff is

$$X = \max(r_g - R, 0)S_0$$

where S_0 is the value of the original stock and R their return. There is a payoff if $R < r_g$. Now, introduce a second operation where $\Delta \cdot S_0$ in equity is sold short. Payment is then received today for shares bought and delivered later. The net earning in this is $-R\Delta S_0$, gaining if the market has fallen, losing otherwise. When the option and the short position are added, the balance sheet becomes

$$\underbrace{-\max(r_g - R, 0)S_0}_{\textit{put option}} \quad - \quad \underbrace{R\Delta S_0}_{\textit{short selling}},$$

and as R changes the two contributions move in opposite directions. The second operation **hedges** the first.

Surely the option price must drop? The payoff (if there is one) is now partially offset by earnings, and there is no reason for $E(X)$ to be a break-even price. But even if this actuarial price isn't the answer (as will be established below), how much lower should it be? There is a neat solution if we are permitted to run repeated risk-reducing operations that fine-tune many times the stock ΔS_0 held on the side. The argument is subtle and works equally well with currency, but interest-rate derivatives are different since the underlying asset is missing. We can't buy interest! What we *can* do is reduce risk through assets that correlate with the derivative, the stronger the better, and the idea remains the same. Derivative prices reflect risk *after* hedging has been taken into account. The money-market derivatives in Section 14.5 are among the most important risk-reducing instruments of all.

This chapter is an informal introduction, sufficient to get the main ideas, and it will enable us to incorporate risk-reducing strategies in Chapter 15. The formalism of stochastic calculus is *not* used. An elementary text supplementing the material in that direction is Neftci (2000). In this chapter, interest rates are mostly quoted as rh or $r_k h$ and compounded continuously.

14.2 Arbitrage and risk neutrality

14.2.1 Introduction

In 1973 American economists Fischer Black, Robert Merton and Myron Scholes started an avalanche of research into the consequences of assuming financial markets to be free from **arbitrage**; see Black and Scholes (1973) or Merton (1973). Riskless financial income is then regarded as impossible. Suppose V_0 is the market value of a financial asset today (at time 0) and V_1 its future value at time T in an environment where an ordinary bank account grows as e^{rT}. No arbitrage means that things *cannot* be arranged so that

$$V_1 \geq e^{rT} V_0 \quad \text{and sometimes} \quad V_1 > e^{rT} V_0,$$

which says that financial investments do not *always* beat riskless bank deposits. A discount formula illustrates the idea. If a zero-coupon bond of face 1 for delivery at T is bought at time 0, surely you should pay e^{-rT}. Otherwise, one of the parties is a sure winner.

Actually there *are* people earning money this way. They are known as **arbitrageurs** and operate in terms of small margins and huge size. It is a fair assumption that their activities wipe out riskless income possibilities, leading to markets free from arbitrage. This innocent-looking condition has wide-reaching consequences and has led to a tidy theory for derivative pricing. Here is a second, less trivial example.

14.2.2 Forward contracts

Contracts where the price of future transactions is traded in advance is known as **forwards**. Consider a financial asset sold at $T = Kh$ for a sum agreed at time 0. This forward price, denoted $V_0(0\colon K)$, might not be the same as the value V_0 of the asset today, but what is it? There exists, perhaps mildly surprisingly, a solution that does not take future market uncertainty into account at all. The argument is based on no arbitrage and runs like this.

Start by buying the asset (which costs V_0) and finance it through the sale of zero-coupon, unit-faced bonds maturing at T. Let $P_0(0\colon K)$ be the price of one such bond. To cover the amount V_0, the number sold is $V_0/P_0(0\colon K)$. At $T = Kh$, when all contracts mature, the agreed $V_0(0\colon K)$ is collected for the asset and the amount $V_0/P_0(0\colon K)$ transferred to the bond holders. The net value of these operations is

$$\underbrace{V_0(0\colon K)}_{\textit{asset sale}} \quad - \quad \underbrace{V_0/P_0(0\colon K)}_{\textit{bond repayments}}.$$

There has been *no* risk at any time. Surely the net value is zero? If so, it follows that

$$V_0 = P_0(0\colon K)V_0(0\colon K), \tag{14.1}$$

as anything else would imply profit from riskless investments (that could be scaled up to enormous proportions!). It is precisely such things that the no-arbitrage assumption rules out. Note that the actual price of the underlying asset at maturity is irrelevant (it could be worth more or less than $V_0(0\colon K)$ at that time). Also note that the argument applies to any liquid asset and that no assumption is made on the future movements of bond prices and interest. The relationship (14.1) will be crucial for pricing interest-rate derivatives in Section 14.5.

14.2.3 Binomial movements

A useful exercise is to analyse the consequences of no arbitrage for assets moving **binomially**. There are now only two possibilities, and the return is either

$$R = e^{x_l T} - 1 \quad \text{or} \quad R = e^{x_u T} - 1 \quad \text{where} \quad x_l < r < x_u. \tag{14.2}$$

Here $x_l T$ and $x_u T$ are log-returns over the period T, and there is a riskfree log-return rT too. We may assume $x_l T < rT < x_u T$ as anything else would be implausible economically. Restricting the movements of the asset in this way may appear highly artificial, yet not only does it illustrate the main idea, but it could also be the first step towards general constructions; see Exercises 14.4 and 14.5. The payoff $X = H(R)$ of a derivative of a binomial asset is either

$$H_l = H(e^{x_l T} - 1) \quad \text{or} \quad H_u = H(e^{x_u T} - 1),$$

and the issue is the value V_0 of such a contract at the time it is drawn up.

Consider an additional portfolio in terms of the risky asset (initial value w_1) and a riskless bank account (value w_2). The portfolio is worth $w_1 + w_2$ at the start and has, by the end of the period, grown to

$$w_1 e^{x_l T} + w_2 e^{rT} \quad \text{or} \quad w_1 e^{x_u T} + w_2 e^{rT}.$$

There are just these two possibilities, and they move with the derivative exactly if w_1 and w_2 are determined from

$$w_1 e^{x_l T} + w_2 e^{rT} = H_d \quad \text{and} \quad w_1 e^{x_u T} + w_2 e^{rT} = H_u. \tag{14.3}$$

The portfolio is known as a **replicating** one. Its balance sheet is as follows:

	start	end of period		
Value of derivative	$-V_0$	$-H_l$	or	$-H_u$
Value of replicate portfolio	$w_1 + w_2$	H_l	or	H_u

Whatever happens, there is no *net* payment at the end of the period. But the net payment must then be zero even at the beginning, as there would be riskless income for someone otherwise. It follows that $V_0 = w_1 + w_2$, which is determined from the equations (14.3). Rewrite them as

$$w_1(e^{x_l T} - e^{rT}) + (w_1 + w_2)e^{rT} = H_l \quad \text{and} \quad w_1(e^{x_u T} - e^{rT}) + (w_1 + w_2)e^{rT} = H_u.$$

Then eliminate w_1 and solve for $V_0 = w_1 + w_2$, which yields

$$V_0 = e^{-rT}\left(\frac{e^{x_u T} - e^{rT}}{e^{x_u T} - e^{x_l T}} H_l + \frac{e^{rT} - e^{x_l T}}{e^{x_u T} - e^{x_l T}} H_u\right). \tag{14.4}$$

The interpretation of this result is next.

14.2.4 Risk neutrality

The value V_0 in (14.4) can be rewritten

$$V_0 = e^{-rT}(q_l H_l + q_u H_u), \tag{14.5}$$

where

$$q_l = \frac{e^{x_u T} - e^{rT}}{e^{x_u T} - e^{x_l T}} \quad \text{and} \quad q_u = \frac{e^{rT} - e^{x_l T}}{e^{x_u T} - e^{x_l T}}. \tag{14.6}$$

Clearly $q_l + q_u = 1$, and condition (14.2) right makes q_l and q_u positive so that (q_l, q_u) is a probability distribution. The second factor on the right in (14.5) is an expectation with respect to this model Q, and the option premium is re-expressed as

$$V_0 = \underbrace{e^{-rT}}_{\textit{discount factor}} \times \underbrace{E_Q\{H(R)\}}_{\textit{expected payoff}}, \tag{14.7}$$

which calls for a number of comments.

Discounting is obvious (a premium is charged today for a payment in the future). The interesting factor is the second one. Since R is either $e^{x_l T}-1$ or $e^{x_u T}-1$, it follows that

$$E_Q(R) = q_l(e^{x_l T}-1) + q_u(e^{x_u T}-1) = e^{rT}-1$$

after inserting (14.6) for q_l and q_u. In other words, the expected return under model Q grows as an ordinary bank account. Why is that? The point is that the option seller carries no risk, and valuation is therefore in terms of a model where risk is free of charge. Note that the original probabilities of R were not mentioned at all. The model Q is called **risk neutral**, and you will often see it referred to as a **measure**.

The binomial situation is artificial. Values of assets change in an infinite number of ways, not just two, but the same type of construction works for more plausible models, and the pricing formula (14.7) is valid generally. It will, in Section 14.4, be derived through a series of replicating portfolios where option sellers hedge and rehedge their positions. A mathematical limit operation not unlike the Poisson point process in Section 8.2 will in the end lead to a risk-neutral valuation model of the form

$$R = e^{(r-\sigma^2/2)T+\sigma\sqrt{T}\varepsilon} - 1 \quad \text{where} \quad \varepsilon \sim N(0,1),$$

which again satisfies $E_Q(R) = e^{rT}-1$ when you recall the formula for log-normal means.

14.3 Equity options I

14.3.1 Introduction

Stock options are often written in terms of so-called **strikes** A_g, which are guaranteed prices. Payoffs under puts and calls are then

$$\underbrace{X_P = \max(A_g - S, 0)}_{\text{put option}} \quad \text{and} \quad \underbrace{X_C = \max(S - A_g, 0)}_{\text{call option}}, \tag{14.8}$$

where S is the value of the shares at expiry. With put options there is a right to *sell* and with calls a right to *buy*. A put is exercised if $S < A_g$ (gaining $A_g - S$) and a call if $S > A_g$ (now the gain is $S - A_g$).

There is a simple link to the version in Section 3.5, which was expressed in terms of the return R. Let S_0 be the original value of the stock. Then $S = (1+R)S_0$ and

$$A_g - S = A_g - (1+R)S_0 = \left(\frac{A_g - S_0}{S_0} - R\right)S_0,$$

which yields for puts

$$X_P = \max(A_g - S, 0) = \max(r_g - R, 0)S_0 \quad \text{where} \quad r_g = \frac{A_g - S_0}{S_0}. \tag{14.9}$$

A guaranteed return r_g and a strike A_g is the same thing, and the argument works for calls too. The discussion below is in terms of strikes.

We need the value S_k of the asset at time $t_k = kh$ for $k = 0, 1, 2, \ldots, K$ where $h = T/K$. Here $S_0 = s_0$ is the current value (and known) whereas $S_1, \ldots, S_K$ belong to the future (and are unknown). The present section introduces some main types of equity options and deduces simple properties of their valuation by means of arbitrage arguments. Hedging and its impact on pricing is treated in the next section.

14.3.2 Types of contract

Derivatives are **European** if they expire at some fixed $T = Kh$. Payoff functions are then of the form

$$X = H(S_K),$$

where K (or $T = Kh$) is the point of **expiry**. Put, call and cliquet options of this type were considered in Section 3.5.

Derivatives that are not European are **path dependent** with payoff influenced by the entire sequence $S_1, \ldots, S_K$. One of the most important types is the **American** one, where the option holder may decide to sell or buy at any point in time. If a call is exercised at t_k, the gain is $S_k - A_g$. Valuation of American-style options may appear difficult, involving decisions when to sell or buy. Yet it will emerge below that the solution for calls is simple (but not for puts). American puts and calls are among the most important equity options of all.

So-called **exotic** versions employ other functions of the path $S_1, \ldots, S_K$. An example is **Asian** options of the form

$$X = H(\bar{S}_K) \quad \text{where} \quad \bar{S}_K = \frac{1}{K - L}(S_{L+1} + \cdots + S_K).$$

Here $\bar{S}_K$ is the average value of the asset over the last $K-L$ readings. By varying the function H we obtain Asian calls, Asian puts and even Asian cliquets. Numerous other forms have been invented, and there is a highly polished pricing theory for all of them.

14.3.3 Valuation: A first look

We shall only be concerned with European options. How they should be valued is a subtle theme and the topic of the next section, but what, exactly, can be said at the outset without detailed assumptions? Suppose the contract is drawn up at $t_0 = 0$. A European option must then be worth

$$\pi = V(s_0, T),$$

where $S_0 = s_0$ is the value of the underlying stock and $V(s,t)$ some function. The prerequisite is that $\{S_k\}$ is a Markov process with all information on future movements residing in s_0. Buyers of the option are charged a premium π upfront, but the focus is now on how values evolve over time.

Suppose the underlying asset S follows a geometric random walk with constant drift and volatility as in (14.14) and with value $S = s$ at time t. Surely the option must now be worth $V(s, T-t)$, since the situation is the same as at the beginning except for s and $T-t$ having taken over from s_0 and T. Let V_k be the value at time $t_k = kh$. Then

$$V_k = V(S_k, T - t_k) \quad \text{and at expiry} \quad V_K = H(S_K). \tag{14.10}$$

On the right the value is the same as the payout, but prior to T the option price is a mystery. What we *can* assume is that the function $V(s,t)$ is smooth; i.e., that small changes in s or t do not lead to more than small changes in V. The precise condition needed is that $V(s,t)$ is one-time differentiable in t and twice in s.

The value of the option also depends on the strike A_g, the risk-free interest intensity r and parameters controlling the movements of the underlying asset, but there is no point in burdening the mathematical notation with these fixed quantities.

14.3.4 The put–call parity

Arbitrage arguments similar to those in the preceding section yield additional introductory insight. One useful deduction is a simple connection between the values of European calls and puts, known as their **parity** relation. To derive this result let $V_P(s,T)$ and $V_C(s,T)$ be prices for a put and call with the same strike A_g. Consider a portfolio where we have purchased a European call and are responsible for a European put. There is also a short position in the underlying stock and an amount of cash. The balance sheet at the beginning and the end is as follows:

	at $t_0 = 0$	at $t_K = T$
European call	$V_C(s_0, T)$	$\max(S_K - A_g, 0)$
European put	$-V_P(s_0, T)$	$-\max(A_g - S_K, 0)$
underlying asset	$-s_0$	$-S_K$
Cash	$\exp(-rT)A_g$	A_g
Portfolio value	?	0

At expiry $T = Kh$ the assets have the values shown, and the portfolio value is zero. This is true regardless of whether $S_K < A_g$ or $\geq A_g$, and easy to verify. But then the value must be zero even at the beginning as there would have been riskless financial income for someone otherwise. Hence

$$V_C(s_0, T) - V_P(s_0, T) = s_0 - e^{-rT} A_g, \tag{14.11}$$

which shows that pricing European puts and calls amounts to the same thing.

14.3.5 A first look at calls and puts

The parity relation leads to lower bounds on the value of European options. Since $V_P(s_0, T) \geq 0$, it follows from (14.11) that

$$V_C(s_0, T) \geq s_0 - e^{-rT} A_g \tag{14.12}$$

and, remarkably, this simple result tells us how *American* call options should be valued. Recall that they differ from European options in that they can be terminated at will. Their value (say $V_C^{\text{am}}(s_0, T)$ for an American call) can't slip below the European counterpart since the freedom to cash in must be worth *something*. Hence, from (14.12),

$$V_C^{\text{am}}(s_0, T) \geq V_C(s_0, T) \geq s_0 - e^{-rT} A_g > s_0 - A_g$$

since $r > 0$. But the right-hand side is the amount we receive by exercising the option at $t_0 = 0$, which can't be advisable since the value of the American option is higher. In other words, American calls will never be liquidated early (there would be an arbitrage opportunity for someone otherwise) and *should be priced as European calls*.

Puts are different. As above $V_C(s_0, T) \geq 0$, and the parity relation (14.11) yields

$$V_P(s_0, T) \geq e^{-rT} A_g - s_0, \tag{14.13}$$

which is similar to (14.12). However, a lower bound on the value of American puts no longer follows the way it did for calls, and the situation has become more complicated. If the prices of the assets are low enough, it *is* profitable to cash in on an American put, but closed pricing formulae, similar to those we shall derive later in this chapter, are not available. Technical complications like these are beyond an elementary introduction; consult the references in Section 14.7.

14.4 Equity options II: Hedging and valuation

14.4.1 Introduction

Valuation of derivatives under the binomial model in Section 14.2 didn't require specific probabilities at all (the risk-neutral model was *derived*). This is a forerunner of what is to come, although more realistic situations do require probabilities. With equity options, pricing is based on the geometric random walk introduced in Section 5.5. It is then assumed that

$$S_{k+1} = S_k e^{\xi h + \sigma\sqrt{h}\,\varepsilon_{k+1}} \quad \text{where} \quad \varepsilon_{k+1} \sim N(0,1), \tag{14.14}$$

for $k = 0, 1, \ldots$ As usual, the sequence $\varepsilon_1, \varepsilon_2, \ldots$ is an independent one. Note the form of the exponent in (14.14), with mean and standard deviation being ξh and $\sigma\sqrt{h}$. Why the model is in that form was explained in Section 5.7. An immediate consequence is that the random term (proportional to $\sqrt{h}$) dominates for small h, and this has a profound influence on option pricing. Below we shall run hedging operations at each $t_k = kh$ and let $h \to 0$. The random effects are then the most important ones and must be analysed more thoroughly than changes due to time. When $h \to 0$, the model is known as **geometrical Brownian motion**.

This section examines hedging and its consequences. It is demonstrated why such opportunites must influence option prices in a liquid market (where there are buyers and sellers for everything), and a simulated hedging process will visualize what happens. Pricing formulae used in practice are derived at the end.

14.4.2 Actuarial and risk-neutral pricing

Consider a future payoff $X = H(S_K)$ and its valuation at time $t_0 = 0$. Two alternative versions are

$$\underset{actuarial}{V_0 = e^{-rT} E\{H(S_K)|s_0\}} \quad \text{and} \quad \underset{Q\text{-model, risk neutral}}{V_0 = e^{-rT} E_Q\{H(S_K)|s_0\}}, \tag{14.15}$$

both depending on the current value s_0 of the underlying asset (hence the *conditional* means). In insurance, ordinary actuarial valuation leads to break-even prices with neither party gaining or losing, but financial options are different since the real risk is reduced through hedging. Indeed, when the entire process is simulated in the computer in Figure 14.1 later, it will emerge that actuarial valuation would have brought huge, virtually riskless profit for the seller.

In a free market a situation like that doesn't last long. Below, we shall arrive at the solution on the right in (14.15) where the evaluation is under the risk-neutral Q-model which differs from the real one in that the real drift parameter ξ is replaced by

$$\xi_q = r - \sigma^2/2 \quad \text{(risk-neutral } \xi\text{)}. \tag{14.16}$$

Otherwise the model remains what it was with the same volatility. Note that *the price does not depend on the real ξ at all.* That is fortunate, since ξ is hard to pin down; see Section 2.2. The actual price is now the question of recalling elementary properties of the random walk; see Section 5.5. Indeed,

$$S_K = s_0 e^{(r-\sigma^2/2)T+\sigma\sqrt{T}\varepsilon} \quad \text{(under the Q-model)}$$

where $\varepsilon \sim N(0,1)$, and the right-hand side of (14.15) may now be calculated. The general case demands simulation (or numerical integration), but for puts and calls there are closed expressions; i.e.,

$$V_P(s_0, T) = e^{-rT} A_g \Phi(a) - s_0 \Phi(a - \sigma\sqrt{T}) \quad \text{(European put)}, \tag{14.17}$$

$$V_C(s_0, T) = s_0 \Phi(-a + \sigma\sqrt{T}) - e^{-rT} A_g \Phi(-a) \quad \text{(European call)}, \tag{14.18}$$

where

$$a = \frac{\log(A_g/s_0) - rT + \sigma^2 T/2}{\sigma\sqrt{T}}. \tag{14.19}$$

The formula for the put can be adapted from (3.16) in Section 3.5, but they are also derived in Exercise 14.12. The volatility σ is typically taken from the market. Prices observed are then entered on the left in (14.17) or (14.18) and the resulting equation solved for σ; see Exercise 14.14 for the details.

14.4.3 The hedge portfolio and its properties

Hedging requires insight into how the values $\{V_k\}$ of an option evolve over time. Suppose $V_k = V(S_k, T - t_k)$, where $V(s, T-t)$ is a smooth function of s and t that can be approximated by an ordinary Taylor series around S_k and t_k. With two terms for s and one for t, this yields

$$V(s, T-t) \doteq V(S_k, T-t_k) + \Delta_k(s - S_k) + \frac{1}{2}\Gamma_k(s - S_k)^2 + \Theta_k(t - t_k),$$

where

$$\Delta_k = \frac{\partial V(S_k, T-t_k)}{\partial s}, \quad \Gamma_k = \frac{\partial^2 V(S_k, T-t_k)}{\partial s^2} \quad \text{and} \quad \Theta_k = \frac{\partial V(S_k, T-t_k)}{\partial t}. \tag{14.20}$$

Insert $s = S_{k+1}$ and $t = t_{k+1}$, and we have the approximation

$$V_{k+1} \doteq V_k + \underbrace{\Delta_k(S_{k+1} - S_k)}_{\text{order } \sqrt{h},} + \underbrace{\tfrac{1}{2}\Gamma_k(S_{k+1} - S_k)^2}_{\text{order } h} + \underbrace{\Theta_k(t_{k+1} - t_k)}_{\text{order } h}, \tag{14.21}$$

where the order of magnitude of the various terms has been indicated. To capture contributions up to order h there are two terms in s and only one in t. The complete Taylor series requires an infinite number of such terms. Those neglected are all of order $h^{3/2}$ and smaller.

Now, consider the hedge portfolio of Section 14.1 where the option seller at time t_k buys $\Delta_k S_k$ of the underlying asset. Values of the portfolio at consecutive points in time are

$$\underbrace{\mathcal{H}_k = -V_k + \Delta_k S_k}_{\text{value at time } t_k} \quad \text{and} \quad \underbrace{\mathcal{H}_{1k} = -V_{k+1} + \Delta_k S_{k+1}}_{\text{value at time } t_{k+1}}, \tag{14.22}$$

and changes from t_k to t_{k+1} are caused by both derivative and asset. Note that

$$\mathcal{H}_{1k} - \mathcal{H}_k = -(V_{k+1} - V_k) + \Delta_k S_{k+1} - \Delta_k S_k,$$

or after inserting (14.21)

$$\mathcal{H}_{1k} - \mathcal{H}_k \doteq -\frac{1}{2}\Gamma_k(S_{k+1} - S_k)^2 - \Theta_k(t_{k+1} - t_k), \tag{14.23}$$

where the dominant $\sqrt{h}$ term in (14.21) has disappeared! That was the idea, and the hedge portfolio has now become much less uncertain than the original option.

We may study this further by inserting (14.14) for S_{k+1}. This yields

$$\mathcal{H}_{1k} - \mathcal{H}_k \doteq -\frac{1}{2}\Gamma_k S_k^2(e^{\xi h + \sigma\sqrt{h}\varepsilon_{k+1}} - 1)^2 - \Theta_k(t_{k+1} - t_k) \doteq -(\frac{1}{2}\Gamma_k S_k^2\sigma^2\varepsilon_{k+1}^2 + \Theta_k)h$$

after using the Taylor approximation $e^{\xi h + \sigma\sqrt{h}\varepsilon_{k+1}} - 1 \doteq \sigma\sqrt{h}\varepsilon_{k+1}$ and removing terms of order h^2. It follows that

$$\mathcal{H}_{1k} - \mathcal{H}_k \doteq -(\frac{1}{2}\Gamma_k S_k^2\sigma^2 + \Theta_k)h + \eta_k h \quad \text{where} \quad \eta_k = -\frac{1}{2}\Gamma_k S_k^2\sigma^2(\varepsilon_{k+1}^2 - 1). \tag{14.24}$$

The random terms η_k resemble those encountered with the GARCH models in Section 13.3. Their cumulative effect has order smaller than h (why is explained in Section 14.6), and they can be ignored as $h \to 0$. But since they are the only sources of uncertainty, the future of the hedge portfolios has now become perfectly foreseeable. The option seller no longer carries any risk, and ξ has disappeared in (14.24)! This means that *the value of the option can't depend on* ξ as there would have been arbitrage opportunities otherwise.

14.4.4 The financial state over time

The aggregated effect of hedging can be analysed by following the financial state of the option seller from beginning to end. In addition to the sequence of values $\{V_k\}$ and $\{\Delta_k S_k\}$ of derivatives and hedges, there are also holdings of cash $\{C_k\}$ which fluctuate as the underlying asset is bought and sold. We are assuming that the seller collects the option premium upfront and uses what's necessary to purchase the underlying stock, borrowing if required. The cash holding develops according to the scheme

$$\underset{\textit{at the start}}{C_0 = V_0 - \Delta_0 S_0,} \qquad \underset{\textit{for } k=1,2,\dots,K-1}{C_k = e^{rh}C_{k-1} + (\Delta_{k-1} - \Delta_k)S_k,} \qquad \underset{\textit{at expiry}}{C_K = e^{rh}C_{K-1},} \tag{14.25}$$

where $(\Delta_{k-1} - \Delta_k)S_k$ is received for equity sold when the hedge for the next period is set up. The sequence of values $\{\mathcal{Y}_k\}$ of the entire portfolio of derivative, asset and cash is then

$$\underset{\textit{at the start}}{\mathcal{Y}_0 = 0,} \qquad \underset{\textit{for } k=1,2,\dots,K-1}{\mathcal{Y}_k = -V_k + \Delta_k S_k + C_k,} \qquad \underset{\textit{at expiry}}{\mathcal{Y}_K = -V_K + \Delta_{K-1} S_K + C_K,} \tag{14.26}$$

written down *after* the underlying asset has been adjusted for the coming period. There is no such sale at expiry, where the values of the option and the payoff $H(S_K)$ coincide.

These relationships are developed further below, but they will first be examined numerically for call options. Key quantities are $V_k = V(S_k, T - t_k)$ defined in (14.18) and its derivative Δ_k with respect to S_k, which defines the hedge. It can be proved (see Exercise 14.16) that

$$\Delta_k = \Phi(-a_k + \sigma\sqrt{T - t_k}),$$

where a_k is the same as a in (14.19) with $T - t_k$ and S_k in place of T and s_0. Since $V_k = S_k\Delta_k - e^{-r(T-t_k)}A_g\Phi(-a_k)$ by (14.18), a simulation of $\mathcal{Y}_0, \mathcal{Y}_1, \dots$ can be organized as in Algorithm 14.1, where the comments on the right outline the logic. Intermediate quantities such as V_k, Δ_k and S_k are not stored in the loop and written without the subscript k. Note that the simulations are run from the real model for equity with the real ξ as drift parameter.

14.4.5 Numerical experiment

A portfolio $\mathcal{Y}_k$ set up to hedge call options has been simulated ten times in Figure 14.1, with monthly rebalancing on the left and four times a day on the right. With 250 days in a financial year the latter corresponds to $K = 1000$ portfolio changes. Detailed conditions were as follows:

Algorithm 14.1 Simulating hedge portfolios for call options

Input: $\xi, \sigma, r, A_g, T, s_0, h$ and $K = T/h$

$\mathcal{Y}_0^* \leftarrow 0,\ \ S^* \leftarrow s_0,\ \ C^* \leftarrow 0\ \ \Delta_{\text{old}}^* \leftarrow 0$ *%Initializing*

For $k = 0, \ldots, K-1$ do

$\quad T_e \leftarrow T - kh,\ a^* \leftarrow (\log(A_g/S^*) - rT_e + \sigma^2 T_e/2)/(\sigma\sqrt{T_e})$

$\quad \Delta_{\text{new}}^* \leftarrow \Phi(-a^* + \sigma\sqrt{T_e})$ *%Hedge*

$\quad V^* \leftarrow S^*\Delta_{\text{new}}^* - e^{-rT_e}A_g\Phi(-a^*)$ *%Option value*

$\quad C^* \leftarrow e^{rh}C^* + (\Delta_{\text{old}}^* - \Delta_{\text{new}}^*)S^*$ *%New cash account*

$\quad \mathcal{Y}_k^* \leftarrow -V^* + \Delta_{\text{new}}^* S^* + C^*$ and $\Delta_{\text{old}}^* \leftarrow \Delta_{\text{new}}^*$ *%Hedge stored*

$\quad$ Draw $\varepsilon^* \sim N(0,1)$ and $S^* \leftarrow S^* e^{\xi h + \sigma\sqrt{h}\varepsilon^*}$ *%For next round*

$\mathcal{Y}_K^* \leftarrow -H(S^*) + \Delta_{\text{old}}^* S^* + e^{rh}C^*$ *%Last value*

Return $\mathcal{Y}_0^*, \ldots, \mathcal{Y}_K^*$.

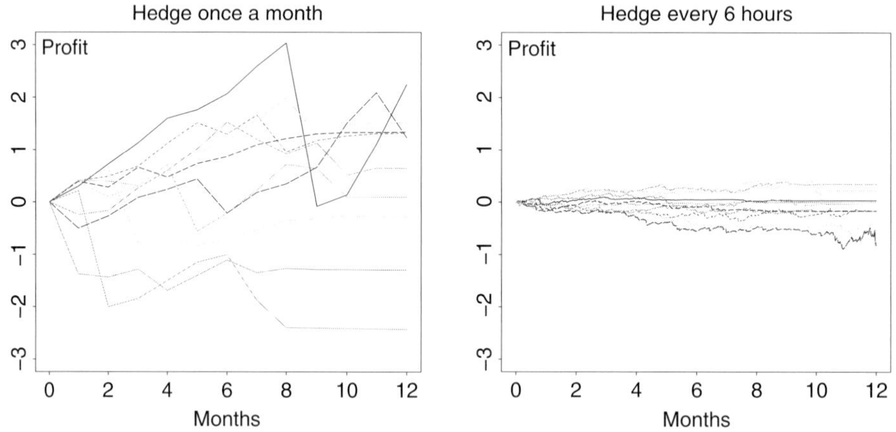

Figure 14.1 Simulated scenarios of a portfolio set up to hedge call options. Rebalancing is monthly (*left*) and four times a day (*right*).

Equity drift:	10% annually	Time to maturity:	1 year
Equity volatility:	25% annually	Option strike:	100
Risk-free interest:	4% annually	Initial value equity:	100

The most striking feature of Figure 14.1 is how much risk is reduced on the right, and it would have vanished completely had the rebalancing been carried out even more frequently.

What would have happened if the market had allowed actuarial pricing of the derivative? An option seller who knew the ropes would have been able to run the same risk-reducing operations, but would now have collected more money upfront.

The actuarial option premium is

$$s_0 e^{T(\xi+\sigma^2/2-r)}\Phi(-a+\sigma\sqrt{T}) - e^{-rT}A_g\Phi(-a) \quad \text{where} \quad a = \frac{\log(A_g/s_0)-\xi T}{\sigma\sqrt{T}};$$

see Exercise 14.12. This reduces to (14.18) if the risk-neutral $\xi_q = r - \sigma^2/2$ is inserted for ξ. Under the conditions above, $\xi_q = 0.04 - \frac{1}{2}\times 0.25^2 = 0.00875$ (much smaller than the original ξ) and the two prices become

$$\underbrace{18.334 \text{ under } \xi = 10\%}_{\textit{actuarial}} \qquad \underbrace{11.837 \text{ under } \xi_q = 0.875\%.}_{\textit{risk neutral}}$$

The actuarial price is more than 50% higher! All simulations in Figure 14.1 would have been lifted that amount (around 6.5) had the market been willing to pay that much. The resulting profit for the option seller would have been very handsome indeed, with little risk attached. Free markets do not permit that kind of (almost) riskless profit. Rebalancing costs (which have been ignored) would not change things much.

14.4.6 The situation at expiry revisited

The option seller has at $t_K = T$ been involved in three types of transaction. Premium V_0 (by now grown to $e^{rT}V_0$) was collected at the beginning, the claim $H(S_K)$ (if any) has to be paid and there are the investments $\Delta_k S_k$ in the underlying stock. The latter may have produced earning or loss, conveniently expressed through

$$G_k = e^{-rh}\Delta_k S_{k+1} - \Delta_k S_k, \tag{14.27}$$

which is the gain from the kth equity position when discounted back to t_k. Adding these operations with interest yields the account of the option seller at expiry; i.e.,

$$\mathcal{Y}_K = \underbrace{V_0 e^{rT}}_{\textit{premium received}} - \underbrace{H(S_K)}_{\textit{payoff}} + \underbrace{\textstyle\sum_{k=0}^{K-1} G_k e^{r(T-t_k)}}_{\textit{accumulated in the stock market}}, \tag{14.28}$$

which is obvious from an economic point of view. That's simply how a sequence of transactions adds up.

In case you remain unconvinced, here is a mathematical proof using (14.25) and (14.26). Consider first the cash account C_K, which is (as always) the sum of all deposits/withdrawals with interest. From (14.25)

$$C_K = (V_0 - \Delta_0 S_0)e^{rT} + \sum_{k=1}^{K-1}(\Delta_{k-1}-\Delta_k)S_k e^{r(T-t_k)},$$

which must be inserted into (14.26) right, i.e., $\mathcal{Y}_K = -H(S_K) + \Delta_{K-1}S_K + C_K$. We get

$$\mathcal{Y}_K = -H(S_K) + \Delta_{K-1}S_K + (V_0 - \Delta_0 S_0)e^{rT} + \sum_{k=1}^{K-1}(\Delta_{k-1} - \Delta_k)S_k e^{r(T-t_k)},$$

where each Δ_k is involved in precisely two terms. When those are identified, the expression for $\mathcal{Y}_K$ can be rewritten

$$\mathcal{Y}_K = V_0 e^{rT} - H(S_K) + \sum_{k=0}^{K-1}\Delta_k(S_{k+1}e^{r(T-t_{k+1})} - S_k e^{r(T-t_k)})$$
$$= V_0 e^{rT} - H(S_K) + \sum_{k=0}^{K-1}\Delta_k(e^{-rh}S_{k+1} - S_k)e^{r(T-t_k)},$$

which is (14.28).

14.4.7 Valuation

No fresh money has been invested. Shouldn't the option premium received adjust to make

$$E(\mathcal{Y}_K|s_0) = 0?$$

This is an ordinary break-even condition, and it *must* hold when the option seller avoids risk through hedging (arbitrage otherwise). The conditional expectation can be calculated through the decomposition formula (14.28), which yields

$$E(\mathcal{Y}_K|s_0) = V_0 e^{rT} - E\{H(S_K)|s_0\} + \sum_{k=0}^{K-1} E(G_k|s_0)e^{r(T-t_k)}$$

where V_0 is a constant fixed by s_0. Demanding $E(\mathcal{Y}_K|s_0) = 0$ leads to

$$V_0 = e^{-rT}E\{H(S_K)|s_0\} - \sum_{k=0}^{K-1} E(G_k|s_0)e^{-rt_k}, \tag{14.29}$$

an interesting identity revealing that the 'fair' option price is its expected *discounted* payoff at expiry *minus* the expected *discounted* result of the stock investments.

To examine the latter, recall (14.27) which yields

$$G_k = \left(e^{-rh}\frac{S_{k+1}}{S_k} - 1\right)\Delta_k S_k = (e^{-rh+\xi h+\sigma\sqrt{h}\varepsilon_{k+1}} - 1)\Delta_k S_k$$

and the conditional mean given $S_k = s_k$ becomes

$$E(G_k|s_k) = \left(E(e^{-rh+\xi h+\sigma\sqrt{h}\varepsilon_{k+1}}|s_k) - 1\right)\Delta_k s_k = \left(e^{(\xi+\sigma^2/2-r)h} - 1\right)\Delta_k s_k$$

since the expectation applies to the mean of a log-normal variable. But then we have $E(G_k|s_k) = 0$ if $\xi = r - \sigma^2/2$, and by the rule of double expectation

$$E(G_k|s_0) = 0 \quad \text{if} \quad \xi = r - \sigma^2/2, \tag{14.30}$$

which is the risk-neutral condition introduced earlier.

It was argued above that the value V_0 of the option does not depend on ξ. We may therefore insert any ξ we want in (14.29), in particular the risk-neutral one which makes the second term on the right go away, and

$$V_0 = e^{-rT} E_Q\{H(S_K|s_0)\},$$

as claimed in (14.15) right.

14.5 Interest-rate derivatives

14.5.1 Introduction

Derivatives are as common with interest rates as they are in the equity market. The duration is longer (up to decades) and there may be many transactions. An example is interest-rate **floors**, which are a series of put agreements (known as **floorlets**) compensating the option holder whenever the floating rate of interest r_k falls below some barrier r_g. If r_k applies during the kth period, there is at $T_k = kT$ the payment

$$X_k = \max(r_g - r_k, 0)v_0 \tag{14.31}$$

with v_0 known as the **principal**. A floor is an interest-rate guarantee, used by individuals and institutions seeking returns above some minimum. Unlike the rest of this chapter, r_g and r_k are now rates and not intensities.

There are a huge number of risk-reducing instruments like these. Caps are call-like opposites of floors providing compensation for borrowers when future rates of interest exceed some threshold. Pricing is again linked to hedging, but the earlier argument for equity no longer works since there is no underlying commodity to be bought or sold. To reduce risk, the option seller must now invest in other money-market products. The theoretical approach doesn't seem quite settled, but there *is* a version justifying the prices used in practice. This is dealt with in the next section, and our concern here is standard contracts and their valuation.

14.5.2 Risk-neutral pricing

Suppose the discount factor e^{-rT} earlier in this chapter is replaced by the bond price $P_0(0\colon K)$. The value of equity options upfront then becomes

$$V_0 = P_0(0\colon K)E_Q\{H(S_K)|s_0\},$$

which *applies to interest-rate derivatives* too if the payoff $H(S_K)$ is replaced by the uncertain future value V_K of the asset. Thus

$$V_0 = P_0(0\colon K)E_Q(V_K|r_0), \tag{14.32}$$

which is justified for the money market in Section 14.6. Information at $T_0 = 0$ (in this case r_0) influences the price, and Q is again a risk-neutral model.

Observations of forward contracts in the market provide information on Q. Suppose a transaction is settled at T_K for a price $V_0(0\colon K)$ agreed at $T_0 = 0$. The value of the contract at that time is

$$V_0 = P_0(0\colon K)V_0(0\colon K);$$

see Section 14.2 and in particular (14.1). But from (14.32) it now emerges that

$$E_Q(V_K|r_0) = V_0(0\colon K), \tag{14.33}$$

and the mean of V_K under Q can be taken from known forward prices $V_0(0\colon K)$. A log-normal V_K must therefore be of the form

$$V_K = V_0(0\colon K)e^{-\sigma_K^2/2+\sigma_K\varepsilon} \quad \text{where} \quad \varepsilon \sim N(0,1), \tag{14.34}$$

as otherwise the mean isn't right, and the evaluation of (14.32) under this model provides formulae similar to those for equity. This is the valuation used in practice. The volatility σ_K is determined by trading observed in the market ('the implied view'); see Exercise 14.14.

14.5.3 Implied mean and forward prices

The preceding argument revealed that risk-neutral expectations and prices of forward contracts are the same thing. To explore the meaning of this, let $V_k = r_k$, where r_k is the uncertain rate of interest for the kth period. Suppose a forward contract agreed at $T_0 = 0$ stipulates $r_0(k-1\colon k)$ for the same rate. Then $V_0(0\colon K) = r_0(k-1\colon k)$, and (14.33) implies that

$$E_Q(r_k|r_0) = r_0(k-1\colon k), \tag{14.35}$$

an important relationship that will be used several times below. There is an analogy for bonds. Consider a zero coupon expiring at $T_L = LT$. The price agreed at T_k for a purchase at $T_J = JT$ will be denoted $P_k(J\colon L)$ where $k \leq J < L$. According to (14.33) the expected bond price at T_k is the same as the forward price today; i.e.,

$$E_Q\{P_k(J\colon L)|r_0\} = P_0(J\colon L), \tag{14.36}$$

and the mean under Q is again pinned down by the market.

If you find the mathematical notation intricate, that can't be helped. We have to emphasize both when deals are struck (through subscripts) and for what periods they apply (placed in parentheses) so that $P_k(J\colon L)$ and $r_k(J\colon L)$, agreed at T_k, are for transactions between T_J and T_L. There are countless relationships among these quantities, for example

$$P_0(0\colon k) = \frac{P_0(0\colon k-1)}{1 + r_0(k-1\colon k)} \quad \text{or} \quad r_0(k-1\colon k) = \frac{P_0(0\colon k-1)}{P_0(0\colon k)} - 1. \tag{14.37}$$

Why are they true? A mathematically equivalent version is

$$\frac{1}{P_0(0\colon k-1)}\{1 + r_0(k-1\colon k)\} = \frac{1}{P_0(0\colon k)},$$

which is easy to interpret. The right-hand side is the number of unit-faced, zero-coupon bonds one money unit gives you at $T_0 = 0$, and the money they release at T_k can be no different from what is received for bonds expiring at T_{k-1} with interest agreed at the beginning added for the last period.

14.5.4 Interest-rate swaps

Swaps are assets switched between two parties. They may be in terms of interest rates, currency, equity, commodities and even volatilities; see Hull (2006). Only interest-rate swaps of the simple **vanilla** form will be considered here. The floating rate r_k is then exchanged for a fixed rate f_0, known as the **swap rate**. Such arrangements are among the most popular ways of managing interest-rate risk. At points in time covered by the contract, one of the parties receives $f_0 v_0$ and pays $r_k v_0$ where v_0 is a principal. The net transfer of money is $X_k = (f_0 - r_k)v_0$.

Suppose this starts at T_J and terminates at T_L, where $0 < J \leq L$. The present value of the net cash flow is then

$$\text{PV} = \sum_{k=J}^{L} P_0(0\colon k)(f_0 - r_k)v_0,$$

and the natural price for the contract is the risk-neutral expectation $E_Q(\text{PV}|r_0)$. Now

$$E_Q(\text{PV}|r_0) = \sum_{k=J}^{L} P_0(0\colon k)\{f_0 - E_Q(r_k|r_0)\}v_0 = \sum_{k=J}^{L} P_0(0\colon k)\{f_0 - r_0(k-1\colon k)\}v_0,$$

where $r_0(k-1\colon k)$ is the forward rate of interest. The design of the contract usually makes $E_Q(\text{PV}|r_0) = 0$ with no premium upfront, which defines the swap rate by solving for $f_0 = f_0(J : L)$. This yields

$$f_0(J : L) = \sum_{k=J}^{L} w_k r_0(k-1\colon k) \quad \text{where} \quad w_k = \frac{P_0(0\colon k)}{P_0(0\colon J) + \cdots + P_0(0\colon L)}, \tag{14.38}$$

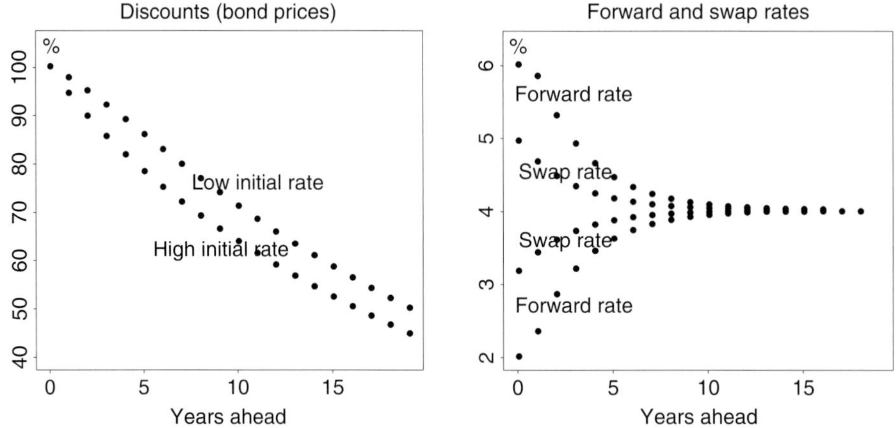

Figure 14.2 Bond prices (*left*) and forward rates of interest with swap rates over 5-year periods (*right*) with high (6%) and low (2%) interest rate originally.

and the swap rate is a weighted sum of forward rates. A second expression of interest follows by inserting $r_0(k-1\colon k) = P_0(0\colon k-1)/P_0(0\colon k)-1$ in the left side of (14.38). After a few rearrangements this yields

$$f_0(J\colon L) = \frac{P_0(0\colon J-1) - P_0(0\colon L)}{P_0(0\colon J) + \cdots + P_0(0\colon L)}, \tag{14.39}$$

and bond prices define swap rates.

A numerical example is shown in Figure 14.2. Bond prices $P_0(0\colon k)$ under the Vasiček model with parameters $\xi_q = 4\%$, $a_q = 0.357$ and $\sigma_q = 0.0137$ are plotted on the left and converted to forward rates $r_0(k-1\colon k)$ and swap rates $f_0(k\colon k+5)$ which are plotted against k on the right; for the explicit formula for the Vasiček term structure, consult Exercise 6.16 and also Section 6.4. There are two initial rates of interest, $r_0 = 2\%$ and $r_0 = 6\%$, which produce curves of different shape. Forward rates of interest and swap rates are two rather different quantities, and the swap rate (looking 5 years ahead) converges faster to the long-term average (4%) than the other one.

14.5.5 Floors and caps

Another popular type of interest-rate derivative is the **floor** and the closely related **cap**. Their payoffs at time T_k, known as **floorlets** and **caplets**, are

$$\underbrace{X_{Fk} = \max(r_g - r_k, 0)v_0}_{\textit{floorlet payment}} \quad \text{and} \quad \underbrace{X_{Ck} = \max(r_k - r_g, 0)v_0}_{\textit{caplet payment}}, \tag{14.40}$$

and a single contract usually includes many of them. Introduce

$$\underbrace{\pi_{Fk}(v_0) = P_0(0\colon k)E_Q(X_{Fk}|r_0)}_{\textit{floorlet price}} \quad \text{and} \quad \underbrace{\pi_{Ck}(v_0) = P_0(0\colon k)E_Q(X_{Ck}|r_0)}_{\textit{caplet price}} \tag{14.41}$$

as the upfront floorlet and caplet prices. The detailed development concentrates on floorlets.

Suppose the risk-neutral model for the floating rate r_k is log-normal as in (14.34). Since the expectation is the forward rate $r_0(k-1\colon k)$, it must be of the form

$$r_k = r_0(k-1\colon k)e^{-\sigma_k^2/2+\sigma_k\varepsilon_k} \quad \text{where} \quad \varepsilon_k \sim N(0,1).$$

The volatility σ_k depends on k, but a complete dynamic model for $\{r_k\}$ is *not* needed. We have to evaluate $E_Q\{\max(r_g - r_k, 0)\}v_0$, which is a calculation of Black–Scholes type; see Exercise 14.21. The floorlet price becomes

$$\pi_{Fk}(v_0) = P_0(0\colon k)\{r_g\Phi(a_k) - r_0(k-1\colon k)\Phi(a_k - \sigma_k)\}v_0, \tag{14.42}$$

where

$$a_k = \frac{\log\{r_g/r_0(k-1\colon k)\} + \sigma_k^2/2}{\sigma_k}, \tag{14.43}$$

and the price of the entire floor is $\pi_F = \sum_k \pi_{Fk}$, adding over all floorlets.

With minor variations the argument takes care of caplets too, but a parity relation is another possibility. Deduce from (14.40) that $X_{Fk} - X_{Ck} = (r_g - r_k)v_0$, which implies that

$$E_Q(X_{Fk}|r_0) - E_Q(X_{Ck}|r_0) = E_Q(X_{Fk} - X_{Ck}|r_0) = E_Q(r_g - r_k|r_0)v_0,$$

or, since $r_0(k-1\colon k) = E_Q(r_k|r_0)$,

$$E_Q(X_{Fk}|r_0) - E_Q(X_{Ck}|r_0) = \{r_g - r_0(k-1\colon k)\}v_0.$$

Floorlet and caplet premia π_{Fk} and π_{Ck} are therefore related through

$$\pi_{Fk}(v_0) - \pi_{Ck}(v_0) = P_0(0\colon k)\{r_g - r_0(k-1\colon k)\}v_0; \tag{14.44}$$

for explicit caplet prices see Exercise 14.22.

14.5.6 Options on bonds

Financial markets offer options on bonds too. In the simplest European case the owner of such an instrument may at T_K sell (or buy) a bond expiring at T_L at a price P_g traded at $T_0 = 0$. Net payoffs are similar to those for puts and calls for equity; i.e.,

$$\underbrace{X_K = \max(P_g - P_K(K\colon L), 0)}_{\textit{payoff put}} \quad \text{and} \quad \underbrace{X_K = \max(P_K(K\colon L) - P_g, 0)}_{\textit{payoff call}}, \tag{14.45}$$

where $P_K(K{:}\ L)$ is the value at T_K of a bond maturing at T_L. Holders of these options take advantage of how the bond market has moved.

The entire pricing theory is similar to that for floorlets and caplets. We need the risk-neutral mean $E_Q\{P_K(K{:}\ L)|r_0\}$ of the future bond price $P_K(K{:}\ L)$. As was seen above, this is simply the forward price $P_0(K{:}\ L)$ and if the volatility is σ_K, the buyer of the put option will be charged

$$\pi_K = P_0(0{:}\ K)\{P_g\Phi(a_K) - P_0(K{:}\ L)\Phi(a_K - \sigma_K)\} \tag{14.46}$$

where

$$a_K = \frac{\log\{P_g/P_0(K{:}\ L)\} + \sigma_K^2/2}{\sigma_K}. \tag{14.47}$$

This is similar to the floorlet price (14.42); for calls consult Exercise 14.22.

14.5.7 Options on interest-rate swaps

Options on swaps, known as **swaptions**, are one of the most common interest-rate derivatives and permit entry into a swap on favourable conditions. A **receiver** swaption expiring at T_K gives the right to receive an agreed swap rate f_g in exchange for paying the floating rate r_k, say when $J \leq k \leq L$. The option will be exercised when $f_g > f_K$, where $f_K = f_K(J : L)$ is the market swap rate at T_K. There is also the opposite **payer** swaption. Now the option holder may choose to pay a fixed rate f_g in exchange for receiving the floating rate if $f_g < f_K$.

Like all other derivatives, swaptions mean the transfer of money if the right it implies is utilized. Only the difference between the floating swap rate f_K and the agreed one f_g counts. Indeed, a swaption entails a *fixed* flow of money from one party to the other during the life of the underlying swap. The amount transferred at T_k is

$$\underbrace{X_k = \max(f_g - f_K, 0)v_0}_{\textit{receiver swaption}} \quad \text{and} \quad \underbrace{X_k = \max(f_K - f_g, 0)v_0}_{\textit{payer swaption}} \tag{14.48}$$

for $k = J, \ldots, L$. We are again dealing with a put (receiver) and a call (payer) option.

Swaption premia are payed at $T_0 = 0$ and are calculated in the familiar way. A risk-neutral, log-normal distribution is introduced for the swap rate $f_K = f_K(J : L)$ with mean taken from market deals. Indeed, as with other quantities in this section,

$$E_Q(f_K|r_0) = f_0 \quad \text{where} \quad f_0 = f_0(J{:}\ L) \quad \text{and} \quad f_K = f_K(J{:}\ L). \tag{14.49}$$

If σ_K is the volatility of f_K, the premium for a receiver swaption becomes

$$\pi(v_0) = \{P_0(0\colon J) + \cdots + P_0(0\colon L)\}\{f_g\Phi(a_K) - f_0\Phi(a_K - \sigma_K)\}v_0 \tag{14.50}$$

where

$$a_K = \frac{\log(f_g/f_0) + \sigma_K^2/2}{\sigma_K}. \tag{14.51}$$

The expression is the same as for floorlets and bond options except for the discounts which are added over the transaction periods. Payer swaptions are discussed in Exercise 14.22.

14.5.8 Numerical experimenting

Numerical experiments in this book use the Gaussian Vasiček model as a risk-neutral description of the money market. Simple mathematical expressions for bond prices $P_0(0\colon k)$, forward rates $r_0(k-1\colon k)$ and swap rates $f_0 = f_0(J\colon L)$ are then available, but there is a logical inconsistency in that pricing formulae assume log-normal rates of interest. This gap is bridged approximately by the following argument detailed for floors. Recall that

$$\underbrace{\mathrm{var}(r_k|r_0) = \frac{\sigma_q^2}{2a_q}(1 - e^{-2ka_q})}_{\textit{Vasiček}} \quad \text{and} \quad \underbrace{\mathrm{var}(r_k|r_0) = r_0(k-1\colon k)^2(e^{\sigma_k^2} - 1)}_{\textit{log-normal}};$$

see Section 5.6 for the Vasiček variance on the left. Equating the variances yields

$$\sigma_k = \sqrt{\log\left(1 + \frac{e^{-2ka_q}\sigma_q^2}{2a_q r_0(k-1\colon k)^2}\right)}, \tag{14.52}$$

which can be used as volatility in the floor price formula (14.42) and (14.43); see also Exercise 14.28 for a similar argument for swaptions.

An example with a 20-year floor agreement is shown in Figure 14.3, with $\xi_q = 0.04$, $\sigma_q = 0.025$ and $a_q = 0.5$ in the Vasiček model and $r_g = 0.03$ as the guarantee. The initial rate of interest r_0 was low (1%), middle (4%) and high (7%) with substantial impact on both the forward rates on the left in Figure 14.2 and the floorlet prices on the right.

Fees charged for the floor strongly reflect the state of the economy. With low interest rates the guarantee must be expensive since the option is likely to be exercised.

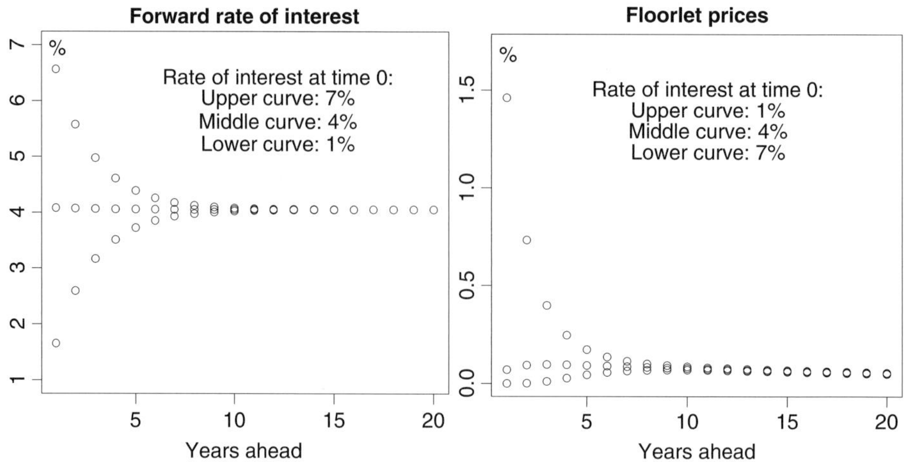

Figure 14.3 Forward rates of interest (*left*) and corresponding floorlet prices without discounting (*right*) under the conditions described in the text.

14.6 Mathematical summing up

14.6.1 Introduction

A main aim of this section is the pricing equation (14.32) for money-market derivatives. Unlike the equity market there isn't any underlying commodity to hang risk reduction on, and hedge portfolios must make use of other money-market products. This doesn't allow unique prices, but they do satisfy a system of consistency requirements defined through the so-called **market price of risk**, a stochastic process characterizing the entire money market. The mathematical limit process is the same as before. All variables are still followed over $t_k = kh$ for $k = 0, \dots, K$, and eventually $h \to 0$ while the time to expiry $T = Kh$ is kept fixed.

It will be assumed that the money market is driven by a single process $\{r_k\}$ which will be the spot interest-rate intensity; for other approaches consult Section 14.7. This simple assumption leads to the prices used in practice. Much of the argument has a bearing on equity as well, and both markets may be considered through the same framework model of the form

$$\underbrace{r_{k+1} = r_k e^{\xi_k h + \sigma_k \sqrt{h}\varepsilon_{k+1}}}_{\textit{interest-rate intensity}} \quad \text{and} \quad \underbrace{S_{k+1} = S_k e^{\xi_k h + \sigma_k \sqrt{h}\varepsilon_{k+1}}}_{\textit{equity}}, \tag{14.53}$$

with $\xi_k = \xi_k(r_k)$ and $\sigma_k = \sigma_k(r_k)$ on the left and $\xi_k = \xi_k(S_k)$ and $\sigma_k = \sigma_k(S_k)$ on the right. These are known functions and in practice widely different for r_k and S_k. The process $\{\varepsilon_k\}$ is independent and $N(0, 1)$ as before. Though a considerable extension of the model for equity in Section 14.4, the argument given there is still valid with minor changes (and would have worked for several assets too).

14.6.2 How values of derivatives evolve

The models in (14.53) are Markovian and imply valuations of the form

$$\underbrace{V_k = V(r_k, T - t_k)}_{\text{money-market derivative}} \quad \text{and} \quad \underbrace{V_k = V(S_k, T - t_k).}_{\text{equity option}} \tag{14.54}$$

Surely both functions $V(s, T - t)$ and $V(r, T - t)$ must be smooth? If they are twice differentiable in s and r and once in t, the model (14.53) is passed on as $h \to 0$ with V_k evolving as

$$V_{k+1} \doteq V_k e^{\xi_{vk}h + \sigma_{vk}\sqrt{h}\,\varepsilon_{k+1}}, \tag{14.55}$$

where ξ_{vk}, σ_{vk} are related to ξ_k and σ_k in (14.53) in a way clarified at the end of the section where the result is proved. Drift and volatility are now time dependent even if $\xi_k = \xi$ and $\sigma_k = \sigma$ were not originally. These results are as valid for equity as in the money market.

There is a second, equivalent version where the exponential form in (14.55) is replaced by a linear one. The model for V_k now becomes

$$V_{k+1} - V_k \doteq V_k(\tilde{\xi}_{vk}h + \sigma_{vk}\sqrt{h}\,\varepsilon_{k+1}) \quad \text{where} \quad \tilde{\xi}_{vk} = \xi_{vk} + \sigma_{vk}^2/2, \tag{14.56}$$

and the drift has changed from ξ_{vk} to $\tilde{\xi}_{vk}$ whereas the volatility σ_{vk} has remained what it was. The derivation of (14.56) from (14.55) makes use of the Taylor approximation $e^x \doteq 1 + x + x^2/2$, and the two versions of the model are equal in the limit as $h \to 0$. Both will be needed below. Again the argument is given at the end of the section.

It is the same for a second derivative V'_k. The exponential and linear form of the model can now be written

$$V'_{k+1} \doteq V'_k e^{\xi_{v'k}h + \sigma_{v'k}\sqrt{h}\,\varepsilon_{k+1}} \quad \text{and} \quad V'_{k+1} - V'_k \doteq V'_k(\tilde{\xi}'_{vk}h + \sigma'_{vk}\sqrt{h}\,\varepsilon_{k+1}), \tag{14.57}$$

with drift and volatility $\xi_{v'k}$ and $\sigma_{v'k}$ differing from those for V_k and with $\tilde{\xi}_{v'k} = \xi_{v'k} + \sigma_{v'k}^2/2$ on the right, but with the error series $\{\varepsilon_k\}$ remaining what it was in (14.53). *There is a single stochastic driver behind all derivatives.* Such unidimensional uncertainty can be removed completely if a second derivative is used to counter the risk of the first, as we shall now see.

14.6.3 Hedging

Consider portfolios of the form

$$\underbrace{\mathcal{H}_k = -V_k + w_k V'_k}_{\text{value at } t_k} \quad \text{and} \quad \underbrace{\mathcal{H}_{1k} = -V_{k+1} + w_k V'_{k+1},}_{\text{value at } t_{k+1}}$$

where V'_k is a second derivative hedging the first and w_k a weight to be determined. The change in value from t_k to t_{k+1} is

$$\mathcal{H}_{1k} - \mathcal{H}_k = -(V_{k+1} - V_k) + w_k(V'_{k+1} - V'_k), \tag{14.58}$$

where the assets must be examined. For equity options $V_k = V_k(S_k)$ and $V'_k = S_k$ if the underlying stock is used as hedge. The argument in Section 14.4 showed that the choice $w_k = \partial V_k/\partial S_k$ worked so beautifully that all risk disappeared as $h \to 0$.

The general case makes use of the linear form of the value processes. If we insert (14.56) and (14.57) right into (14.58) and identify the terms of order $\sqrt{h}$ and h, it emerges that

$$\mathcal{H}_{1k} - \mathcal{H}_k \doteq \underbrace{-(V_k\sigma_{vk} - w_kV'_k\sigma_{v'k})\sqrt{h}\,\varepsilon_{k+1}}_{\textit{random term}} \quad - \quad \underbrace{(V_k\tilde{\xi}_{vk} - w_kV'_k\tilde{\xi}_{v'k})h}_{\textit{fixed term}},$$

and the random part goes away if $w_k = (V_k\sigma_{vk})/(V'_k\sigma_{v'k})$. The value of the hedge portfolio at t_{k+1} is then perfectly known at t_k, though such statements are only true in the limit as $h \to 0$.

14.6.4 The market price of risk

Consider such a riskless portfolio which must earn the spot rate of interest $e^{r_kh} - 1$ (arbitrage otherwise). When the defining weight $w_k = (V_k\sigma_{vk})/(V'_k\sigma_{v'k})$ is inserted into both $\mathcal{H}_{1k} - \mathcal{H}_k$ and $\mathcal{H}_k = -V_k + w_kV'_k$ and the approximation $e^{r_kh} - 1 \doteq r_kh$ utilized, it emerges that

$$\mathcal{H}_{1k} - \mathcal{H}_k \doteq -\left(\tilde{\xi}_{vk} - \frac{\sigma_{vk}}{\sigma_{v'k}}\tilde{\xi}_{v'k}\right)V_kh \quad \text{and} \quad (e^{r_kh} - 1)\mathcal{H}_k \doteq -r_k\left(1 - \frac{\sigma_{vk}}{\sigma_{v'k}}\right)V_kh,$$

and these values coincide as $h \to 0$. Thus, when the common factor V_kh is removed, it follows that

$$\tilde{\xi}_{vk} - \frac{\sigma_{vk}}{\sigma_{v'k}}\tilde{\xi}_{v'k} = r_k\left(1 - \frac{\sigma_{vk}}{\sigma_{v'k}}\right) \quad \text{or} \quad \frac{\tilde{\xi}_{vk} - r_k}{\sigma_{vk}} = \frac{\tilde{\xi}_{v'k} - r_k}{\sigma_{v'k}},$$

which is true for *arbitrary* pairs of derivatives. Hence

$$\frac{\tilde{\xi}_{vk} - r_k}{\sigma_{vk}} = \lambda_k \quad \text{or equivalently} \quad \tilde{\xi}_{vk} = r_k + \lambda_k\sigma_{vk}, \tag{14.59}$$

where $\{\lambda_k\}$ *applies to the entire money market* as a universal process linked to all derivatives. A rational market without arbitrage and with buyers and sellers of everything is organized so that (14.59) holds.

The process $\{\lambda_k\}$ is known as the **market price of risk**. It becomes strikingly simple when derivatives can be hedged through the underlying asset. The entire derivative market is then risk free (Section 14.4) and grows with the spot rate of interest e^{r_kh}. But the only way for (14.55) to accord with that is to make

$\xi_{vk} = r_k - \sigma_{vk}^2/2$, which is the risk-neutral drift denoted ξ_q earlier, and from (14.59) and (14.56) right

$$\lambda_k = \frac{\tilde{\xi}_{vk} - r_k}{\sigma_{vk}} = \frac{\xi_{vk} + \sigma_{vk}^2/2 - r_k}{\sigma_{vk}} = 0.$$

The market price of risk is now zero; i.e., *no risk is a free lunch*. When hedges can only be set up through alternative instruments, the situation becomes different as we shall see next.

14.6.5 Martingale pricing

Fixed rates of interest were tenable with equity options since the underlying stock is much more volatile, but in the money market such an assumption is no longer feasible. How values of derivatives evolve now has much to do with what alternative investments would have brought. Consider the ratio

$$M_k = V_k/V_k', \tag{14.60}$$

where V_k' is the value of a second instrument. From (14.55)

$$M_{k+1} = \frac{V_{k+1}}{V_{k+1}'} \doteq \frac{V_k}{V_k'} e^{(\xi_{vk}-\xi_{v'k})h+(\sigma_{vk}-\sigma_{v'k})\sqrt{h}\,\varepsilon_{k+1}} = M_k e^{(\xi_{vk}-\xi_{v'k})h+(\sigma_{vk}-\sigma_{v'k})\sqrt{h}\,\varepsilon_{k+1}},$$

where ε_{k+1} is $N(0, 1)$ and independent of both V_k and V_k' and hence M_k. The usual expression for the expectation of log-normals then yields

$$E_Q(M_{k+1}|r_k) \doteq e^{\gamma_k h} M_k \quad \text{where} \quad \gamma_k = \xi_{vk} - \xi_{v'k} + (\sigma_{vk} - \sigma_{v'k})^2/2.$$

Moreover, by (14.56) and (14.59), $\xi_{vk} = \tilde{\xi}_{vk} - \sigma_{vk}^2/2 = r_k + \lambda_k\sigma_{vk} - \sigma_{vk}^2/2$ and by analogy also $\xi_{v'k} = r_k + \lambda_k\sigma_{v'k} - \sigma_{v'k}^2/2$. It follows that

$$\begin{aligned}\gamma_k &= (\lambda_k\sigma_{vk} - \sigma_{vk}^2/2) - (\lambda_k\sigma_{v'k} - \sigma_{v'k}^2/2) + (\sigma_{vk} - \sigma_{v'k})^2/2\\ &= (\sigma_{vk} - \sigma_{v'k})(\lambda_k - \sigma_{v'k}),\end{aligned}$$

and $\gamma_k = 0$ if $\lambda_k = \sigma_{v'k}$. Under this assumption

$$E_Q(M_{k+1}|r_k) = M_k, \tag{14.61}$$

which becomes exact as $h \to 0$. A stochastic process $\{M_k\}$ satisfying this identity is known as a **martingale**. Expected future values are then the same as those today. Martingales are much studied in the probabilistic literature (see references in the next section), but not much of that is needed here. The underlying condition $\lambda_k = \sigma_{v'k}$ says that the volatility of the hedging instrument coincides with the market price of risk. This isn't so easy to justify, but it does lead to the system of prices used in practice.

By assumption, $\{M_k\}$ is a Markov process. This means that (14.61) can also be written $E_Q(M_{k+1}|r_k, r_0) = M_k$, where r_0 is the value of r_k at $t_0 = 0$. Pass the expectation of r_k given r_0 over this, and it follows by the rule of double expectation that

$$E_Q(M_{k+1}|r_0) = E_Q(M_k|r_0).$$

This is true for all k, so that $E_Q(M_K|r_0) = E_Q(M_0|r_0) = M_0$ where K is time to expiry. If $M_K = V_K/V'_K$ and $M_0 = V_0/V'_0$, then

$$E_Q\left(\frac{V_K}{V'_K}|r_0\right) = \frac{V_0}{V'_0}. \qquad (14.62)$$

Suppose a unit-faced zero-coupon bond expiring at $T = Kh$ is used as hedge so that $V'_k = P_k(k\colon K)$. Then $V'_K = P_K(K\colon K) = 1$ and $V'_0 = P_0(0\colon K)$, and it follows that

$$P_0(0\colon K)E_Q(V_K|r_0) = V_0,$$

precisely (14.32) which was used to price the derivatives in Section 14.5.

14.6.6 Closing mathematics

It remains to demonstrate how the models (14.55) and (14.56) follow from (14.53) and (14.54). The argument will be written down for the money market (equity is the same). We shall need the same greeks as in Section 14.4; i.e.,

$$\Delta_k = \frac{\partial V(r_k, T - t_k)}{\partial r}, \quad \Gamma_k = \frac{\partial^2 V(r_k, T - t_k)}{\partial r^2}, \quad \Theta_k = \frac{\partial V(r_k, T - t_k)}{\partial t}$$

and also the logarithmic version

$$a_k = \frac{\partial \log V(r_k, T - t_k)}{\partial r}, \quad b_k = \frac{\partial^2 \log V(r_k, T - t_k)}{\partial r^2}, \quad c_k = \frac{\partial \log V(r_k, T - t_k)}{\partial t}$$

which can be linked to the original greeks through elementary differentiation. Indeed,

$$a_k = \frac{\Delta_k}{V_k}, \quad b_k = \frac{\Gamma_k}{V_k} - \left(\frac{\Delta_k}{V_k}\right)^2, \quad c_k = \frac{\Theta_k}{V_k}$$

which are the coefficients when $\log V(r, T - t)$ is Taylor approximated. The usual two terms from r and one from t yield

$$\log V(r, T - t) \doteq \log V(r_k, T - t_k) + a_k(r - r_k) + \frac{1}{2}b_k(r - r_k)^2 + c_k(t - t_k).$$

Insert $r = r_{k+1}$ and $t = t_{k+1}$ and recall $V_k = V(r_k, T - t_k)$ and $V_{k+1} = V(r_{k+1}, T - t_{k+1})$. Then

$$\log V_{k+1} - \log V_k \doteq a_k(r_{k+1} - r_k) + \frac{1}{2}b_k(r_{k+1} - r_k)^2 + c_k(t_{k+1} - t_k) \qquad (14.63)$$

where the difference $r_{k+1} - r_k$ must be examined.

When the approximation $e^x \doteq 1+x+x^2/2$ is applied to the defining model (14.53) for r_k, then

$$r_{k+1} = r_k e^{\xi_k h+\sigma_k \sqrt{h}\,\varepsilon_{k+1}} \doteq r_k\{1 + \xi_k h + \sigma_k \sqrt{h}\,\varepsilon_{k+1} + \frac{1}{2}(\xi_k h + \sigma_k \sqrt{h}\,\varepsilon_{k+1})^2\},$$

or when the terms of order $\sqrt{h}$ and h are identified

$$r_{k+1} - r_k \doteq r_k\{\sigma_k \sqrt{h}\varepsilon_{k+1} + (\xi_k + \sigma_k^2/2)h\} + \eta_{1k}h,$$

where $\eta_{1k} = r_k\sigma_k^2(\varepsilon_{k+1}^2 - 1)/2$. The last term $\eta_{1k}h$ has mean zero and loses all importance as $h \to 0$, despite being of order h. Why this is so is indicated below. When $\eta_{1k}h$ is removed and the rest of $r_{k+1} - r_k$ inserted into (14.63), we obtain after a few simplifications

$$\log V_{k+1} - \log V_k \doteq a_k r_k \sigma_k \sqrt{h}\,\varepsilon_{k+1} + \{a_k r_k(\xi_k + \sigma_k^2/2) + b_k r_k^2\sigma_k^2/2 + c_k\}h + \eta_{2k}h,$$

where $\eta_{2k} = b_k r_k^2\sigma_k^2(\varepsilon_{k+1}^2 - 1)/2$ is a second rest term of the same type as η_{1k}. It can again be ignored (see below), and we have derived a model for V_k of the form (14.55) with $\xi_{vk} = a_k r_k(\xi_k + \sigma_k^2/2) + b_k r_k^2\sigma_k^2/2 + c_k$ and $\sigma_{vk} = a_k r_k \sigma_k$.

The linear version (14.56) follows by a related argument. Now

$$V_{k+1} = V_k e^{\xi_{vk}h+\sigma_{vk} \sqrt{h}\,\varepsilon_{k+1}} \doteq V_k\{1 + \xi_{vk}h + \sigma_{vk} \sqrt{h}\,\varepsilon_{k+1} + \frac{1}{2}(\xi_{vk}h + \sigma_{vk} \sqrt{h}\,\varepsilon_{k+1})^2\},$$

which may be written

$$V_{k+1} - V_k \doteq V_k(\sigma_{vk} \sqrt{h}\,\varepsilon_{k+1} + \tilde{\xi}_{vk}h) + \eta_{3k}h \quad \text{where} \quad \tilde{\xi}_{vk} = \xi_{vk} + \sigma_{vk}^2/2.$$

Here $\eta_{3k} = V_k\sigma_{vk}^2(\varepsilon_{k+1}^2 - 1)/2$ is still another negligible remainder, and (14.56) has been established.

The terms η_{1k}, η_{2k} and η_{3k} must be examined, and there was a similar one in Section 14.4. Why do they count for nothing despite bringing contributions of order h? Here is a heuristic explanation. The basic form of η_k is $\eta_k = Y_k(\varepsilon_{k+1}^2 - 1)$, where Y_k is a random variable which is independent of ε_{k+1} and (as usual) $\varepsilon_1, \dots, \varepsilon_K$ are independent and $N(0, 1)$. Similar quantities were encountered with the GARCH model in Section 13.3, and their properties were elucidated there; see (13.13). In particular, it was shown that

$$E(\eta_k) = 0 \quad \text{and} \quad \text{cor}(\eta_k, \eta_{k'}) = 0 \quad \text{if } k \neq k',$$

and if we consider the aggregated effect of $\eta_1, \dots, \eta_K$ through $\mathcal{E} = (\eta_1 + \cdots + \eta_K)h$, then $E(\mathcal{E}) = 0$ whereas var$(\mathcal{E})$ is h^2 times the sum of K variances which is a quantity of order $h^2K = hT \to 0$. Hence var$(\mathcal{E}) \to 0$ as $h \to 0$, and the same must be true for $\mathcal{E}$. The aggregated effect of $\eta_1, \dots, \eta_K$ disappears in the limit.

14.7 Bibliographical notes

14.7.1 Introductory work

Financial derivatives are priced via continuous-time models, and the theory is usually developed through stochastic calculus. Introductions along that line with emphasis on the economic rather than the mathematical side are Kolb and Overdahl (2003), Rebonato (2004), Hull (2006) and McDonald (2009). Stochastic calculus is used more heavily in Wilmott *et al.* (1995), Capinski and Zastavniak (2003), Benth (2004) and Williams (2006), though without going beyond the most elementary. The flavour in Lin (2006) is similar, and now insurance applications are included as well. Howison *et al.* (1995) is a collection of fairly non-technical articles over a wide range of issues, as is also the style in Tapiero (2004). The binomial example in Section 14.2 is a popular construction in finance, and has drawn wide attention even as a numerical tool. Shreve (2004a) and Van der Hoeck and Elliot (2006) are fairly simple reviews; see also Pliska (1997) (which is harder reading).

14.7.2 Work with heavier mathematics

If stochastic calculus is unknown territory, you might try Neftci (2000) (emphasizing financial applications) or Øksendal (2003) (a general introduction). Reviews of option theory with mathematics at the intermediate level are (for example) Lamberton and Lapeyre (1996), Dana and Jeanblanc-Picqué (2003), Shreve (2004b) and Björk (2006). Heavier in terms of formal mathematics are Fornari and Mele (2000) (on stochastic volatility), Delbaen and Schachermayer (2006) (arbitrage theory) and Carmona and Tehranchi (2006) (money-market theory and options); see also Bingham and Kiesel (2004) and Elliot *et al.* (2005). Books dealing with derivative pricing under stochastic volatility and other deviations from pure Gaussian models are Fouque *et al.* (2000), Boyarchenko and Levendorskiĭ (2002) and Hafner (2004). There is much more to be said about money-market derivatives and their theory than has been included here; see Hughston (2000) and Carmona and Tehranchi (2006).

14.7.3 The numerical side

Often, valuation of derivatives presents numerical challenges. One example is the American type, where the buyer at any time is free to decide whether to exercise his rights. Shaw (1998) (using Mathematica) and Benninga (2000) (Excel) are elementary introductions to the numerical side of option pricing. More advanced texts are Lyuu (2002) and Fries (2007), both Java oriented. Seydel (2009), Glasserman (2004) and Bolia and Juneja (2005) are general reviews, still concerned with the practical side of things.

14.8 Exercises

Section 14.2

Exercise 14.1 Consider a bond which pays B_1 at T_k for $k = J, \dots, L-1$ and a principal B_0 at T_L.

(a) What is the arbitrage-free price for this security at $T_0 = 0$?

(b) What is this price at a future T_K where $K < J$?

Exercise 14.2 Let X_k be liabilities (known) of a pension portfolio at T_k for $k = 1, \dots, K$.

(a) What is the arbitrage-free price when the portfolio is traded from one company to another at $T_0 = 0$? Suppose the two parties agree to transfer the portfolio at T_k for a price fixed at $T_0 = 0$ where $k < K$.

(b) What is the price now when the first company handles all liabilities up to (but not including) T_k?

Exercise 14.3 Let r be fixed interest-rate intensity so that a bank account grows by e^{rT} over a period of length T. Explain why the risk-neutral model for equity returns is of the form $R = e^{(r-\sigma^2/2)T)+\sigma\sqrt{T}\varepsilon} - 1$ where $\varepsilon \sim N(0,1)$.

Exercise 14.4 Consider independent and binomial equity returns $R_1, \dots, R_K$ for which $\Pr(R_k = e^{x_l h} - 1) = q$ and $\Pr(R_k = e^{x_u h} - 1) = 1 - q$ where $x_l < x_u$. Let $X_k = \log(1 + R_k)$ and introduce $X_{0:K} = X_1 + \cdots + X_K$ as the K-step log-return.

(a) Why is $\Pr(X_k = x_l h) = q$ and $\Pr(X_k = x_u h) = 1 - q$?

(b) Show that

$$E(X_{0:K}) = K\{(qx_l + (1-q)x_u\}h \quad \text{and} \quad \mathrm{sd}(X_{0:K}) = \sqrt{Kq(1-q)}\,(x_u - x_l)h.$$

(c) Argue that $X_{0:K}$ becomes approximately Gaussian as $K \to \infty$.

Exercise 14.5 Consider $X_{0:K}$ in Exercise 14.4 and introduce the risk-neutral $q = (e^{rh} - e^{x_l h})/(e^{x_u h} - e^{x_l h})$ where $x_l < r < x_u$; see (14.6).

(a) If $x_l = \xi - \sigma/\sqrt{h}$ and $x_u = \xi + \sigma/\sqrt{h}$, show that $q \to 1/2$ as $h \to 0$.

(b) Verify that $E(X_{0:K}) \to \xi T$ and $\mathrm{sd}(X_{0:K}) \to \sigma\sqrt{T}$ when $h \to 0$ and $T = Kh$ is kept fixed.

(c) Argue that the corresponding model for $R = R_{0:K}$ tends to the risk-neutral one in Exercise 14.3 when $\xi = r - \sigma^2/2$.

Section 14.3

Exercise 14.6

(a) What is the guaranteed return r_g for a call option with strike A_g? Consider a cliquet option with strikes A_g and B_g for which the payoff function is

$$H(S) = \begin{array}{ll} A_g - S, & S \leq A_g \\ 0, & A_g < S < B_g \\ -(S - B_g), & S \geq B_g. \end{array}$$

(b) What is the guaranteed return r_g and what is the maximum return r_c the option holder can receive?

Exercise 14.7

(a) Show that the payoff $X_P = \max(A_g - S, 0)$ under a put and the payoff $X_C = \max(S - A_g, 0)$ under a call satisfy $X_C - X_P = S - A_g$.
(b) Pass expectation E_Q under the risk-neutral model over this identity for an alternative proof of the parity relation (14.11); i.e., show that $V_C(s_0, T) - V_P(s_0, T) = s_0 - e^{-rT} A_g$.

Exercise 14.8 Let $X(A_g, B_g)$ be the payoff under the cliquet option in Exercise 14.6.

(a) Show that $X(A_g, B_g) = X_P(A_g) - X_C(B_g)$ where $X_P(A_g)$ and $X_C(B_g)$ are payoffs of put and call with strikes A_g and B_g, respectively.
(b) Apply the risk-neutral expectation to this identity and explain how the price of a cliquet option follows from those for puts and calls.

Exercise 14.9 Consider an exotic put option maturing at $T_{2K} = 2T$ with payoff $X = \max(A_g - \sqrt{S_K S_{2K}}, 0)$.

(a) If $\{S_k\}$ follows a risk-neutral geometric random walk, argue that

$$S_K = s_0 e^{(r-\sigma^2/2)T+\sigma\sqrt{T}\,\varepsilon_1} \quad \text{and} \quad S_{2K} = s_0 e^{2(r-\sigma^2/2)T+\sigma\sqrt{T}\,(\varepsilon_1+\varepsilon_2)}$$

where ε_1 and ε_2 are independent and $N(0, 1)$.
(b) With ε still another $N(0, 1)$ variable verify that

$$\sqrt{S_K S_{2K}} = s_0 e^{(3/2)(r-\sigma^2/2)T+\sqrt{5/4}\,\sigma\sqrt{T}\,\varepsilon} = s_0' e^{(r-\sigma'^2/2)2T+\sigma'\sqrt{2T}\varepsilon}$$

where $s_0' = s_0 e^{-(r/2+\sigma^2/8)T}$ and $\sigma' = \sqrt{5/8}\,\sigma$.
(c) Write a program for the premium using the ordinary Black–Scholes formula for puts.

R-*commands*:

```
T′=2*T; σ′=sqrt(5/8)*σ; s′0=s0*exp(-(r/2+σ**2/8)*T);
a=(log(Ag/s′0)-r*T′+σ′**2*T′/2)/(σ′*sqrt(T′));
π=exp(-r*T′)*Ag*pnorm(a)-s′0*pnorm(a-σ′*sqrt(T′)).
```

(d) What is the price when $s_0 = 1$, $A_g = 1$, $T = 0.5$, $r = 0.04$ and $\sigma = 0.25$?

Exercise 14.10

(a) Write a program generating m simulations of (S_K, S_{2K}) in Exercise 14.9.

R-*commands*:

```
ξ=(r-σ**2/2)*T; s=σ*sqrt(T);
e1=rnorm(m); e2=rnorm(m); SK=s0*exp(ξ+s*e1);
S2K=s0*exp(2*ξ+s*(e1+e2)).
```

(b) Evaluate the option premium in Exercise 14.9 by simulating $X = \max(A_g - \sqrt{S_K S_{2K}}, 0)$.

R-*commands*:

```
X=pmax(0,Ag-sqrt(SK*S2K)); π=exp(-r*2*T)*mean(X).
```

(c) Compute π under the conditions in Exercise 14.9(d) using $m = 100\,000$ simulations and compare with the exact price.

Exercise 14.11

(a) Modify the program in Exercise 14.10(b) so that it applies when the payoff is $X = \max\{A_g - (S_K + S_{2K})/2, 0\}$ (no closed formula for the option price now!).

R-*commands*:

With S_K and S_{2K} from Exercise 14.10, use `X=pmax(0,Ag-0.5*(SK+S2K));`
`π=exp(-r*2*T)*mean(X).`

(b) Compute π under the conditions in Exercise 14.9 and examine the effect of changing the payoff from geometric to arithmetic average.

Section 14.4

Exercise 14.12 Let $X_P = \max(A_g - S, 0)$ and $X_C = \max(S - A_g, 0)$, where $S = s_0 e^{\xi + \sigma\sqrt{T}\varepsilon}$ and $\varepsilon \sim N(0, 1)$.

(a) With $\Phi(x)$ the standard normal integral verify that

$$E(X_P) = A_g\Phi(a) - s_0 e^{\xi+\sigma^2 T/2}\Phi(a - \sigma\sqrt{T}) \quad \text{where} \quad a = \frac{\log(A_g/s_0) - \xi}{\sigma\sqrt{T}}.$$

(b) Argue that $X_C - X_P = S - A_g$ and that this yields

$$E(X_C) = s_0 e^{\xi+\sigma^2 T/2}\Phi(-a + \sigma\sqrt{T}) - A_g\Phi(-a).$$

[*Hint*: $E(S) = s_0 e^{\xi+\sigma^2 T/2}$ and $\Phi(x) = 1 - \Phi(-x)$.]

(c) Insert $\xi = T(r - \sigma^2/2)$ and establish pricing formulae (14.17) and (14.18) for put and call.
(d) Replace ξ by ξT instead and determine actuarial prices.
(e) Compare the prices in (c) and (d) when $s_0 = 1$, $A_g = 1$, $r = 0.03$, $T = 1$, $\xi = 0.05$ and $\sigma = 0.25$.

R-*commands*:

R-function `e1412e`.

Exercise 14.13

(a) If $\Phi(x)$ in (14.17) is replaced by its density function $\varphi(x) = (2\pi)^{-1/2}e^{-x^2/2}$, show that the resulting expression is 0; i.e., verify that

$$e^{-rT}A_g\varphi(a) - s_0\varphi(a - \sigma\sqrt{T}) = 0 \quad \text{when} \quad a = \frac{\log(A_g/s_0) - rT + \sigma^2T/2}{\sigma\sqrt{T}}.$$

(b) Differentiate (14.17) with respect to σ, simplify by means of (a) and deduce that

$$\upsilon_P = \frac{\partial V_P(s_0, T)}{\partial\sigma} = s_0\varphi(a - \sigma\sqrt{T})\sqrt{T}.$$

(c) Use the parity relation in Exercise 14.7(b) to determine a similar coefficent υ_C for calls.
(d) How does the price of puts and calls react to changes in σ?

Exercise 14.14 Let v_{P0} and v_{C0} be observed prices for put and call and consider the volatility σ determined from one of the equations $V_P(s_0, T) = v_{P0}$ or $V_C(s_0, T) = v_{C0}$.

(a) Use Exercise 14.13 to argue that each equation has a unique solution which must be the same in a rational market.
(b) What does the solution (known as the **implied** volatility) convey? A numerical method such as bisection in Appendix C.4 is needed to find it.

Exercise 14.15 Partial derivatives of option prices with respect to σ, s_0, T and r are known as the **greeks**. In each of the four cases below, prove the formula and comment on what we may learn from it. Use the identity in Exercise 14.13(a) to simplify calculations.

(a) $\Delta_P = \dfrac{\partial V_P(s_0, T)}{\partial s_0} = -\Phi(a - \sigma\sqrt{T}).$

(b) $\Gamma_P = \dfrac{\partial^2 V_P(s_0, T)}{\partial s_0^2} = \dfrac{\varphi(a - \sigma\sqrt{T})}{s_0\sigma\sqrt{T}}.$

(c) $\Theta_P = \dfrac{\partial V_P(s_0, T)}{\partial T} = -re^{-rT}A_g\Phi(a) + \dfrac{s_0\sigma\varphi(a - \sigma\sqrt{T})}{2\sqrt{T}}.$

(d) $\rho_P = \dfrac{\partial V_P(s_0, T)}{\partial r} = -Te^{-rT} A_g \Phi(a).$

Exercise 14.16

(a) Use the parity relation $V_C(s_0, T) - V_P(s_0, T) = s_0 - e^{-rT} A_g$ to find greeks υ_C, Δ_C, Γ_C, Θ_C and ρ_C for the call from those of the put.

(b) In particular, deduce that $\upsilon_C - \upsilon_P = 0$ and $\Delta_C - \Delta_P = 1$ so that $\Delta_C = \Phi(-a + \sigma\sqrt{T})$.

Exercise 14.17 Consider a put option expiring at T with values S_k of the underlying equity at $t_k = kh$ where $h = T/K$.

(a) Write a program simulating $S_0, \ldots, S_K$ under risk-neutrality when $S_0 = s_0$.

R-*commands*:

```
h=T/K; ξ=h*(r-σ**2/2); eps=matrix(rnorm(K*m),K,m);
S=s0*rbind(rep(1,m),exp(ξ*(1:K)+σ*sqrt(h)*
apply(eps,2,cumsum))).
```

(b) Add commands simulating the values $V_0, \ldots, V_K$ of the put option.

R-*commands*:

```
kk=K:0; ak=(log(Ag/S)-ξ*kk)/(σ*sqrt(h*kk));
Delta=-pnorm(ak-σ**sqrt(h*kk));
V=exp(-r*h*kk)*Ag*pnorm(ak)+S*Delta.
```

(c) Generate $m = 50$ replications of $V_0, \ldots, V_K$ when $s_0 = 1$, $A_g = 1$, $\sigma = 0.25$, $r = 0.03$, $T = 1$ and $K = 12$ and plot them jointly against time.

R-*commands*:

```
matplot(0:K,V,''l'').
```

Exercise 14.18

(a) Redo the simulations in Exercise 14.17(c), but now with $m = 100\,000$ and plot average values of the put option against time.

R-*commands*:

With `V` as in Exercise 14.17 use

```
Mean=apply(V,1,mean); plot(0:K,Mean).
```

(b) Add a plot of $V_0 e^{rt_k}$ against k to that in (a).

R-*commands*:

```
lines(0:K,V[1,1]*exp(0:K*r*T/K)).
```

(c) Redo a few times and try to explain why the two plots match approximately; see also Exercise 14.33.

Exercise 14.19 Let $\mathcal{H}_k = -V_k + \Delta_k S_k$ be the hedge portfolio for a put option and $\mathcal{H}_{1k} = -V_{k+1} + \Delta_k S_{k+1}$ its value one time unit later.

(a) Generate, under the conditions in Exercise 14.17, $m = 50$ simulations of $G_k = \mathcal{H}_{1k} - \mathcal{H}_k$ for $k = 0, \ldots, K-1$ with $K = 12$.

R-*commands*:

With `S, Delta, V` from Exercise 14.17 use

```
G=-(V[1:K+1,]-V[1:K,])+Delta[1:K,]*(S[1:K+1,]-S[1:K,]).
```

(b) Plot G_k against k and note how the uncertainty differs from that of the option itself.

R-*commands*:

```
matplot(1:K,G,''l'').
```

(c) Redo when monthly rebalancing $K = 12$ is replaced by weekly $K = 50$ and note the changes.

Exercise 14.20

(a) Write a program simulating the cash holdings (14.25) of a seller of a put option.

R-*commands*:

With `S,Delta,V,h` from Exercise 14.17 use `Delta[K+1,]=Delta[K,];`

```
C=matrix(0,K+1,m); C[1,]=V[1,]-Delta[1,]*S[1,];
for (k in 1:K+1) C[k,]=exp(r*h)*C[k-1,]+(Delta[k-1,]-
Delta[k,])*S[k,].
```

(b) Simulate the portfolio (14.26) too.

R-*commands*:

```
Y=-V+Delta*S+C.
```

(c) Draw $m = 50$ scenarios of cash holding and portfolio under the conditions in Exercise 14.17 and plot them against time.

R-*commands*:

```
matplot(0:K,C,''l''); matplot(0:K,Y,''l'').
```

(d) Redo when $K = 50$ and $K = 1000$ and comment on the uncertainty compared with that in Exercise 14.17.

Section 14.5

Exercise 14.21 Pricing interest-rate derivatives of the put type requires expectations of $X_P = \max(c_g - Y, 0)v_0$ where $Y = \xi e^{-\tau^2/2+\tau\varepsilon}$ and $\varepsilon \sim N(0,1)$.

(a) Show that

$$E_Q(X_P) = \{c_g\Phi(a) - \xi\Phi(a-\tau)\}v_0 \quad \text{where} \quad a = \frac{\log(c_g/\xi) + \tau^2/2}{\tau},$$

with $\Phi(x)$ the standard normal integral.

(b) Insert $c_g = r_g$, $\xi = r_0(k-1\colon k)$ and $\tau = \sigma_k$ and verify the pricing formula (14.42) for a floorlet.
(c) The same question for the price of the bond option; i.e., insert $c_g = P_g$, $\xi = P_0(K\colon L)$, $\tau = \sigma_K$ and $v_0 = 1$ and deduce (14.46).
(d) Finally insert $c_g = f_g$, $\xi = f_0$ and $\tau = \sigma_K$, which yields the expression (14.50) for the price of receiver swaptions.

Exercise 14.22 Write $X_C = \max(Y - c_g, 0)v_0$ for the call-like opposite of X_P of the preceding exercise.

(a) Show that $X_C - X_P = (Y - c_g)v_0$ so that $E_Q(X_C) - E_Q(X_P) = \{E_Q(Y) - c_g\}v_0$.
(b) Deduce from Exercise 14.21 (a) that

$$E_Q(X_C) = \{-c_g\Phi(-a) + \xi\Phi(-a+\tau)\}v_0$$

with a as before. [*Hint*: Utilize $1 - \Phi(x) = \Phi(-x)$.]
(c) Use this result to find a formula for the price of the caplet in (14.41) right.
(d) The same question for a bond option of the call type in (14.45) right.
(e) And finally (through the same argument) the price for the payer swaption in (14.48) right.

Exercise 14.23 An interest-rate **collar** is an instrument similar to cliquet options for equity. There are two levels r_g and r_c with $r_g < r_c$ with negative payoff above r_c. The payoff at time T_k is

$$X_k = \begin{matrix} r_g - r_k, & r_k \le r_g \\ 0, & r_g < r_k < r_c \\ -(r_k - r_c), & r_k \ge r_c, \end{matrix}$$

and the premium for a collar that typically extends over many periods is paid at the beginning.

(a) Show that collars are differences between floors and caps. [*Hint*: Much similarity to Exercise 14.8.]
(b) Determine the premium for collars from those for floors and caps.

Exercise 14.24

(a) Write a program tabulating Vasiček forward rates $r_0(k-1\colon k)$ for $k \le K$.

R-*commands*:

Use the R-function `vasicekP` (copy of program in Exercise 6.16) with
`P=vasicekP(K,`ξ_q`,`σ_q`,`a_q`,`r_0`)$P; rforward=P[1:K]/P[1:K+1]-1.`

(b) Compute/plot the forward rates when $K = 25$, $\xi_q = 0.04$, $\sigma_q = 0.012$, $a_q = 0.357$ and $r_0 = 0.02$.

R-*commands*:

`plot(1:K,rforward)`.

(c) Redo when $a_q = 0.1$ and plot the new forward rates jointly with the old ones.

(d) Look up the continuous-time Vasiček model in Section 5.7 and explain the slower growth in (c).

Exercise 14.25

(a) Using (14.39) tabulate, under Vasiček bond prices, the swap rate $f_0 = f_0(J : L)$ for fixed J and $L = J + 1, \ldots, K$.

R-*commands*:

With the R-function `vasicekP` use `P=vasicekP(K,`ξ_q`,`σ_q`,`a_q`,`r_0`)$P;`
f_0`=(P[J]-P[J:K+1])/cumsum(P[J:K+1])`.

(b) Compute and plot the swap rate against L when $K = 25$, $J = 1$, $\xi_q = 0.04$, $\sigma_q = 0.012$, $a_q = 0.357$ and $r_0 = 0.02$.

R-*commands*:

`plot(J:K,`f_0`)`.

(c) Recompute when $a_q = 0.1$ and plot the new swap rates jointly with the old ones.

R-*commands*:

`lines(1:K,`f_0`)`.

(d) Why is the increase in (c) slower?

Exercise 14.26

(a) Write a program tabulating $f_0 = f_0(J : K)$ in Exercise 14.25 when K is fixed and $J = 0, \ldots, K - 1$.

R-*commands*:

`P=vasicekP(K,`ξ_q`,`σ_q`,`a_q`,`r_0`)$P;`
f_0`=(P[1:K]-P[K+1])/(sum(P)-cumsum(P[1:K]))`.

(b) Compute and plot the swap rate against J under the conditions in Exercise 14.25(b).

R-*commands*:

`plot(1:K-1,`f_0`)`.

(c) Recompute the swap rates when $a_q = 0.1$ and plot them jointly with the old ones.

R-*commands*:

`lines(1:K-1,`f_0`)`.

(d) Why do the curves stabilize much faster than in Exercise 14.25?

Exercise 14.27

(a) Write a program generating m simulations of Vasiček swap rates $f_0, \ldots, f_{J-1}$ for swaps from J to L.

R-*commands*:

With R-functions `vasicekP` and `ar1` use `o=vasicekP(L,`ξ_q`,`σ_q`,`a_q`,`r_0`);` `r=ar1(m,J-1,`ξ_q`,`σ_q`,`a_q`,`r_0`)$r; f=matrix(0,J,m); for (k in 1:J) {P=exp(o$A[0:(L-k+1)+1]-o$B[0:(L-k+1)+1]%o%r[k,]); f[k,]=(P[J-k+1,]-P[L-k+2,])/apply(P[J:L-k+2,],2,sum)}`.

(b) Generate $m = 50$ simulations of $f_0, \ldots, f_{J-1}$ when $J = 10$, $L = 20$, $\xi_q = 0.04$, $\sigma_q = 0.012$, $a_q = 0.357$, $r_0 = 0.02$ and plot them jointly against time.

R-*commands*:

`matplot(1:J-1,f,''l'')`.

(c) Redo (b) when $a_q = 0.1$ and note the change.

Exercise 14.28

(a) If the swap rate f_k follows a log-normal model with volatility σ_K for $\log(f_K)$, copy the argument behind (14.52) in Section 14.5 and argue that

$$\sigma_K = \sqrt{\log\left(1 + \frac{\operatorname{var}(f_K|r_0)}{\{E(f_K|r_0)\}^2}\right)}.$$

(b) Use the program in Exercise 14.27 to calibrate σ_K to Vasiček swap rates when $K = 0, \ldots, J-1$.

R-*commands*:

With `f` as in Exercise 14.27, use `E=apply(f,1,mean); Sd=apply(f,1,sd);` σ_K`=sqrt(log(1+(Sd/E)**2))`.

(c) Plot, under the conditions in Exercise 14.27(b), σ_K against K for $K = 0, \ldots, J-1$ using $m = 10\,000$ simulations.

R-*commands*:

`plot(1:J-1,`σ_K`)`.

(d) Redo under the conditions in Exercise 14.27(c).

Exercise 14.29 Consider a receiver swaption maturing at K with guarantee $f_g = (1+\gamma)f_0$ for a swap from J to L.

(a) Write a program tabulating the premium (14.50) when $K = 1, \ldots, J-1$.

R-*commands*:

Generate P as in Exercise 14.24 with $K = L$, let σ_K be as in Exercise 14.28 and use `S=sum(P[J:L+1]);` f_0`=(P[J]-P[L+1])/S;` f_g`=(1+`γ`)*`f_0`;`
`vol=`σ_K`[2:J]; a=(log(`f_g/f_0`)+vol**2/2)/vol;`
π`=S*(`f_g`*pnorm(a)-`f_0`*pnorm(a-vol))*`v_0.

(b) Compute and print the premia when $\xi_q = 0.04$, $\sigma_q = 0.012$, $a_q = 0.357$, $J = 10$, $L = 20$, $v_0 = 1$ and $\gamma = -0.1, 0, 0.1$ and 0.2.

(c) Why do the swaption premia in some of the examples seem to be independent of the expiry K of the option?

Exercise 14.30

(a) Write a program tabulating floorlet premia for $k = 1, \ldots, K$.

R-*commands*:

With P from Exercise 14.24 and recalling (14.52), use
`rforward=P[1:K]/P[1:K+1]-1;`
σ_K`=sqrt(log(1+(`σ_q`/rforward)**2* exp(-`a_q`*2*1:K)/(2*`a_q`)));`
`a=(log(`r_g`/rforward)+0.5*`σ_K`**2)/`σ_K`;`
π`=P[1:K+1]*(`r_g`*pnorm(a)-rforward*pnorm(a-`σ_K`))*`v_0.

(b) Compute the floorlet prices for $k = 1, \ldots, 20$ when $\xi_q = 0.04$, $\sigma_q = 0.012$, $a_q = 0.357$, $r_0 = 0.02$, $v_0 = 1$ and $r_g = 0.02, 0.04$ and 0.06.

(c) Why are the floorlet prices decreasing functions of K?

Section 14.6

Exercise 14.31 Suppose $M_k = M_k(r_k)$ evolves through the recursion $M_{k+1} = e^{\xi_k h + \sigma_k \sqrt{h}\,\varepsilon_{k+1}} M_k$ for $k = 0, 1, \ldots$ with $\sigma_k = \sigma_k(r_k)$ and $\varepsilon_{k+1}|r_k \sim N(0, 1)$.

(a) Determine ξ_k so that the martingale criterion $E(M_{k+1}1|r_k) = M_k$ is satisfied.

(b) Argue that under this condition $E(M_{k+1}|r_0) = E(M_k|r_0)$ so that $E(M_k|r_0) = M_0$.

Exercise 14.32 Let $V_k = V_k(S_k)$ be the value of an equity option at t_k and suppose the risk-free rate of interest r is constant. Explain why $M_k = V_k e^{-r(T-t_k)}$ is a martingale.

Exercise 14.33 If V_k is the value of a European equity option at t_k, show that $E_Q(V_k|s_0) = V_0 e^{rt_k}$ which means that the average value under risk neutrality evolves as the risk-free rate of interest. [*Hint*: Utilize $V_k = e^{-r(T-t_k)} E_Q\{H(S_K)|S_k\}$ and calculate $E_Q(V_k|s_0)$ using the rule of double expectation.]

Exercise 14.34

(a) Using Exercise 14.15(a) show that Δ_k for a put option evolves according to

$$\Delta_k = -\Phi(a_k - \sigma\sqrt{T - t_k}) \quad \text{where} \quad a_k = \frac{\log(A_g/S_k) - r(T - t_k) + \sigma^2(T - t_k)/2}{\sigma\sqrt{T - t_k}}.$$

(b) Argue that if $S_K \neq A_g$, then $a_k \to -\infty$ or $+\infty$ as $t_k \to T$ so that $\Delta_k \to 0$ or -1.

(c) Also argue that the value of the hedge portfolio close to expiry becomes either $V_k + S_k$ or just V_k, and explain why it must be like that.

Exercise 14.35 The Black–Karasinski interest-rate model is $r_k = \theta e^{X_k}$, where θ is a parameter and $X_{k+1} = (1 - a_q h)X_k + \sigma_q\sqrt{h}\varepsilon_{k+1}$ for $k = 0, 1, \ldots$, with $\varepsilon_1, \varepsilon_2, \ldots$ independent and $N(0, 1)$. Show that $r_{k+1} = r_k e^{\xi_k h + \sigma_k\sqrt{h}\varepsilon_{k+1}}$ where $\xi_k = -a_q \log(r_k/\theta)$ and $\sigma_k = \sigma_q$.

15

Integrating risk of different origin

15.1 Introduction

With risks from many sources, maybe the first thing that comes into mind is that they are added. Consider net assets in the life insurance industry. At time $T_k = kT$ their value might be

$$\mathcal{B}_k = \underset{equity}{V_{1k}} + \underset{cash}{V_{2k}} + \underset{bonds}{V_{3k}} - \underset{liabilities}{\mathcal{PV}_{xk}}, \quad k = 0, 1, \ldots \tag{15.1}$$

where property would be an additional term in practice. The recursion defines the framework of this chapter. Liabilities $\mathcal{PV}_{xk}$ are subtracted from investments in equity, bonds and cash. This is a book value, where a large portion of the liabilities belong to the future. It was demonstrated in Chapter 12 how they are calculated. The accuracy was high (hence no estimation symbol $\widehat{\mathcal{PV}}_{xk}$ as in Section 11.6), but that isn't the whole story; see Sections 15.2 and 15.3. Can simulation programs be developed independently for each component? That would be naive. Not only do financial variables influence each other mutually (Chapter 13), but there may be connections to the liabilities too (Section 15.3). The exercise is a **multivariate** one with many interdependent links.

It is also a **hierarchical** one. If net assets is the target, an entire evaluation and modelling process could be as complicated as

$$\textbf{historical data} \xrightarrow{\text{estimation}} \textbf{model} \xrightarrow{\text{simulations}} \textbf{variables} \longrightarrow \textbf{net asset value}.$$

The variables are those in (15.1) (and perhaps a couple of others), but they could (especially on the investment side) be the sum of many sub-variables. How you cope with that and how you plan an entire analysis can only be learnt by example. We start with life-table risk in the next section, continue with liability risk due to inflation and discounting, then financial risk and finally assets and liabilities together. Computer implementation will be indicated everywhere; i.e., how programs are planned, merged, modified and extended. A number of numerical illustrations are included on the way.

Error in parameters and models is only considered at the beginning. Should projections of risk include uncertainty of that kind? It can be done through the Bayesian approach in Section 7.6. Risk is then seen as an amalgam of liability, asset and model uncertainty, but a full-scale approach along these lines leads to technical complexity and a possible lack of transparency in the final results. A simpler alternative is to vary key input conditions and examine how simulations and evaluations react. The variability is often huge! *Differences* between portfolios are usually more stable. To understand why this is so, let ψ be a measure of financial risk valued as $\hat{\psi}_1$ (for portfolio 1) and $\hat{\psi}_2$ (for portfolio 2), both depending on the same estimated parameters. If $\rho = \text{cor}(\hat{\psi}_1, \hat{\psi}_2)$, then

$$\text{sd}(\hat{\psi}_2 - \hat{\psi}_1) \doteq \text{s}(\hat{\psi}_1)\sqrt{2(1-\rho)} \quad \text{if} \quad \text{sd}(\hat{\psi}_1) \doteq \text{sd}(\hat{\psi}_2),$$

which is the argument behind antithetic sampling in Section 4.3; see (4.4). Here ρ might be approaching 1, and $\hat{\psi}_2 - \hat{\psi}_1$ is much less variable than $\hat{\psi}_1$ and $\hat{\psi}_2$ on their own. One portfolio could be superior to another over a wide range of conditions, despite their level fluctuating strongly.

15.2 Life-table risk

15.2.1 Introduction

The way life and pension insurance was launched in Chapter 12 relegated uncertainty to a subordinate role. There was good reason to concentrate on the average (Section 3.4), yet both discounting and life tables are potential sources of risk. Discounting is dealt with in the next section, and the topic here is errors in life tables. Mortalities are always estimated from historical data. *Random* error is then inevitable in principle, although negligible for large countries. Very small countries and pension schemes are different. Historical data are now more scarce, and life tables for pension schemes may differ substantially from the country average. With disability modelling, the lack of data is felt even more strongly.

Random error and its impact are a main topic of this section, but there is also *systematic* error or bias when the historical material is too old or applies to the wrong social group. An example of the latter is **adverse selection**, which signifies longer lives for life-insurance clients than on average. In a cross-country study, Mitchell and McCarthy (2002) found mortalities to be as much as 25% lower for this group, with obvious effects on pension cost. Future increases in longevity pull in the same direction. Life expectancy in the Western world went up by around 5 years (the same for women and men) during the second half of the twentieth century, and consequences for pensions will be considerable if the trend continues.

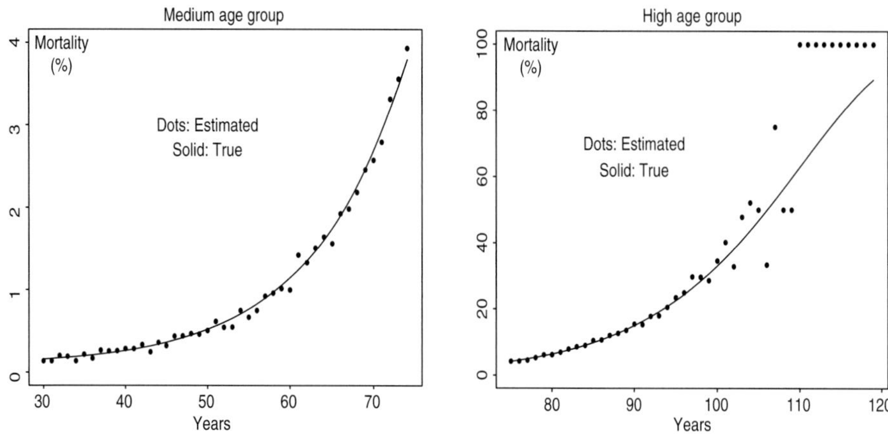

Figure 15.1 Estimated and true mortalities $q_l = 1 - p_l$ plotted against age l with the high age groups to the right.

15.2.2 Numerical example

How large are random errors in life tables? The illustration in Figure 15.1 is a numerical experiment. A portfolio of $\mathcal{J} = 100\,000$ individuals was followed over $K = 6$ years with death and survival drawn in the computer and with the number n_l of individuals reaching l years at some point counted. Let p_l be the probability of living to age $l+1$ when at age l, with $q_l = 1-p_l$ the corresponding mortality. Simple estimates are $\hat{p}_l = n_{l+1}/n_l$ and $\hat{q}_l = 1-\hat{p}_l$; see Section 12.3. Figure 15.1 shows plots of the true mortalities (solid line) and the estimated ones (dots) against l. Errors go up on the right for the higher age groups, but the economic consequences are not necessarily serious since there are so few people involved.

This was a laboratory experiment with the true mortalities known. Errors may not have seemed too severe, but the real test is their impact on the actuarial evaluations; see below. The conditions behind the experiment are detailed in Table 15.1, and define a portfolio which will be used for numerical illustrations throughout the entire chapter. There are $\mathcal{J} = 100\,000$ individuals between $l_0 = 30$ and $l_e = 120$ years, with the number at age l being

$$J_l = \frac{\mathcal{J}}{c}\,{}_{l-l_0}p_{l_0}, \quad l = l_0, \ldots, l_e \qquad \text{where} \quad c = \sum_{k=0}^{l_e-l_0} {}_kp_{l_0}. \tag{15.2}$$

The construction ensures $J_{l_0} + \cdots + J_{l_e} = \mathcal{J}$ and makes use of the k-step survival probabilities ${}_kp_{l_0}$, calculated as in Section 12.3. The portfolio is a young one, as its age distribution in Figure 15.2 later illustrates[20].

[20] There is a simple probabilistic mechanism behind the design. Suppose N individuals enter at age l_0 and remain

Table 15.1 Demography of the pension portfolio in Chapter 15

Quantity	Symbol	Assumption
Portfolio size	$\mathcal{J}$	$\mathcal{J} = 100\,000$
Time increment		Annual
Survival probabilities (annual)	p_l	$\log(p_l) = -0.0009 - 0.000044e^{0.090761\times l}$
Recruitment age	l_0	30 years
Maximum age	l_e	120 years

Algorithm 15.1 Monte Carlo survival data

0 Input: n_l and p_l for all l
1 For all l do
2 $\quad Z_l^\star \sim \text{binomial}(n_l, p_l)$
3 Return $Z_l^\star$ for all l.

15.2.3 The life-table bootstrap

Random errors in life tables *can* be examined by means of theoretical results from statistics, but the effect on actuarial projections is more easily studied by Monte Carlo. How are random mortality data generated in the computer? *Real* data are obtained as in the experiment by following individuals over a certain period of time and counting the number n_l reaching age l, at some point. Then $n_{l+1}|n_l \sim \text{binomial}(n_l, p_l)$ for all l, which was utilized to fit survival models in Section 12.3. Exact imitation in the computer is not too difficult, but there is a simpler alternative which is good enough in practice. Keep the historical counts n_l fixed and draw the number of survivors Z_l among them as in Algorithm 15.1. In practice, the counts are drawn from some estimate $\hat{p}_l$ rather than from the true p_l itself.

The algorithm is used below to investigate consequences of error in life tables. The survival model is then fitted to the Monte Carlo data $(n_l, Z_l^\star)$ in the same way as it was fitted to the real data, and if $\hat{p}_l = n_{l+1}/n_l$ is the real estimate then $\hat{p}_l^\star = Z_l^\star/n_l$ is the Monte Carlo analogue. Log-likelihoods become

$$\underbrace{\textstyle\sum_l \{n_{l+1}\log(p_l) + (n_l - n_{l+1})\log(1-p_l)\}}_{\text{real data}}, \quad \underbrace{\textstyle\sum_l \{Z_l^\star \log(p_l) + (n_l - Z_l^\star)\log(1-p_l)\}}_{\text{bootstrap data}},$$

and a parametric model is inserted for p_l for estimation under models such as Gomperz–Makeham.

until they die. After k years their expected count is ${}_kp_{l_0}N$, and if this pattern of recruiting new members solely at age l_0 goes on long enough, the expected relative number of individuals at age l will eventually become ${}_{l-l_0}p_{l_0}$ as in (15.2).

15.2.4 The bootstrap in life insurance

Our interest is the equivalence premium π and the liabilities $\mathcal{X}_0, \mathcal{X}_1, \ldots$ with present value $\mathcal{PV}_0$. Their original estimates involve the following operations:

$$\{p_l\} \longrightarrow \underset{\substack{\textit{history,}\\ \textit{survival data}}}{\mathbf{Z}} \quad \underset{\textit{fitting}}{\longrightarrow} \quad \{\hat{p}_l\} \longrightarrow \{{}_k\hat{p}_l\} \begin{array}{l} \nearrow \hat{\pi} \\ \searrow \{\hat{\mathcal{X}}_k\},\ \widehat{\mathcal{PV}}_0. \end{array}$$

actuarial calculations

On the left, the historical survival data (designated $\mathbf{Z}$) have been generated from the true survival probabilities $\{p_l\}$. Our estimates $\{\hat{p}_l\}$, obtained from one of the methods in Section 12.3, are converted to estimated k-step probabilities $\{{}_k\hat{p}_l\}$ and then to estimates $\hat{\pi}$, $\{\hat{\mathcal{X}}_k\}$ and $\widehat{\mathcal{PV}}_0$ of equivalence premia and liabilities.

The entire procedure can be repeated from simulated historical data that have been generated from the estimated survival probabilities $\{\hat{p}_l\}$. This is the bootstrap trick, the true probabilities $\{p_l\}$ being unavailable. The scheme now becomes

$$\{\hat{p}_l\} \longrightarrow \underset{\substack{\textit{history,}\\ \textit{survival data}}}{\mathbf{Z}^\star,} \quad \underset{\textit{fitting}}{\longrightarrow} \quad \{\hat{p}_l^\star\} \longrightarrow \{{}_k\hat{p}_l^\star\} \begin{array}{l} \nearrow \hat{\pi}^\star \\ \searrow \{\hat{\mathcal{X}}_k^\star\},\ \widehat{\mathcal{PV}_0^\star} \end{array},$$

actuarial calculations

where all bootstrap analogies have been *-marked. When this is repeated, m_b times, we obtain replications $\hat{\pi}_1^\star, \ldots, \hat{\pi}_{m_b}^\star$ of $\hat{\pi}$ and similarly for the other quantities, and their variability may be examined as in Section 7.4. The detailed implementation is to generate bootstrap historical data $\mathbf{Z}^\star$ by Algorithm 15.1 and run the original sequence of operations with $\mathbf{Z}^\star$ in place of $\mathbf{Z}$. Published examples on the use of the life-table bootstrap are Karlis and Kostaki (2002), Brouhns *et al.* (2005), Koissi *et al.* (2006) and Rempala and Szatzschneider (2006).

15.2.5 Random error and pension evaluations

Consider an ordinary pension insurance portfolio where all individuals enter the scheme at age l_0, retire at l_r on a pension s (the same for all) and draw benefit until l_e if they stay alive. The estimated equivalence premium $\hat{\pi}$ is then the solution of

$$\hat{\pi} \sum_{k=0}^{l_r-l_0-1} d^k\,{}_k\hat{p}_{l_0} = s \sum_{k=l_r-l_0}^{l_e-l_0} d^k\,{}_k\hat{p}_{l_0}$$

Table 15.2 Conditions and clauses for the pension portfolio in Chapter 15

Quantity	Symbol	Assumption	Quantity	Symbol	Assumption
Time step	T	Annual	Interest rate	r	3% annually
Retirement	l_r	65 years	Maximum age	l_e	120 years
Benefit	s	20 000 annually	Payment details		In advance
Premium	π	Equivalence			

with $d = 1/(1+r)$ the discount, and the estimated present value of net liabilities becomes

$$\widehat{\mathcal{PV}}_0 = \sum_{k=0}^{l_e-l_0} d^k \hat{\mathcal{X}}_k$$

where

$$\hat{\mathcal{X}}_k = -\hat{\pi} \sum_{l=l_0}^{l_r-k-1} \mathcal{J}_l \cdot {}_k\hat{p}_l \; + \; s \sum_{l=l_r-k}^{l_e-k} \mathcal{J}_l \cdot {}_k\hat{p}_l;$$

see also Section 12.4. This is to be copied for Monte Carlo survival data, which are generated by Algorithm 15.1 under the fitted model. The life table is then re-estimated, and the new values ${}_k\hat{p}^\star_{l_0}$ instead of ${}_k\hat{p}_{l_0}$ yield new equivalence premia and reserve through

$$\hat{\pi}^\star \sum_{k=0}^{l_r-l_0-1} d^k {}_k\hat{p}^\star_{l_0} = s \sum_{k=l_r-l_0}^{l_e-l_0} d^k {}_k\hat{p}^\star_{l_0}$$

and

$$\widehat{\mathcal{PV}_0}^\star = \sum_{k=0}^{l_e-l_0} d^k \hat{\mathcal{X}}^\star_k,$$

where

$$\hat{\mathcal{X}}^\star_k = -\hat{\pi}^\star \sum_{l=l_0}^{l_r-k-1} \mathcal{J}_l \cdot {}_k\hat{p}^\star_l \; + \; s \sum_{l=l_r-k}^{l_e-k} \mathcal{J}_l \cdot {}_k\hat{p}^\star_l.$$

If it is repeated m_b times, m_b bootstrap assessments are obtained from which standard deviations and density functions can be computed.

For a numerical illustration, suppose the estimated survival probabilities $\hat{p}_l$ are those in Table 15.1 with other conditions and payment clauses as in Table 15.2. The premium and present value of the liabilities are then estimated as

$$\hat{\pi} = 9.162 \text{ (unit: thousand)} \quad \text{and} \quad \widehat{\mathcal{PV}}_0 = 30.691 \text{ (unit: billion)}.$$

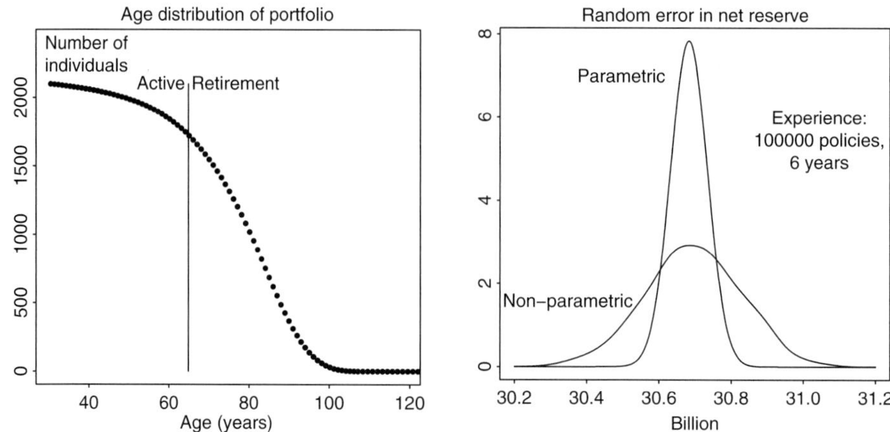

Figure 15.2 The age distribution of the pension portfolio (*left*) and the density function of the net reserve (*right*) due to random errors in the life table (detailed conditions in text).

What is their uncertainty when the historical data come from a portfolio of 100 000 individuals observed for 6 years? This is the numerical experiment in Figure 15.1, but the uncertainty also depends on the method with which the life table is fitted. Possibilities (Section 12.3) are the simple non-parametric estimate and the Gomperz–Makeham model. Both methods were tried, leading to estimated standard deviations

$$\underset{\textit{non-parametric}}{\mathrm{sd}(\hat{\pi}) = 0.050}, \; \underset{\textit{Gomperz–Makeham}}{\mathrm{sd}(\hat{\pi}) = 0.011} \quad \text{and} \quad \underset{\textit{non-parametric}}{\mathrm{sd}(\widehat{\mathcal{PV}_0}) = 0.13}, \underset{\textit{Gomperz–Makeham}}{\mathrm{sd}(\widehat{\mathcal{PV}_0}) = 0.03.}$$

Gomperz–Makeham fittings are more than four times as accurate! Discrepancies are similar in Figure 15.2 right, where the density functions of the estimated reserve have been plotted.

15.2.6 Bias against random error

Random error in the preceding example was around 0.1% of the true value under Gomperz–Makeham fitting, and four or five times more when the non-parametric method was used. That is not very much, and for entire countries such errors may be very small indeed. Small or medium-sized pension schemes with limited amounts of historical data are different. Consider the case of 2000 individuals, 500 times smaller than in the preceding example. A rough rule of thumb is that random error is now around $\sqrt{500} \doteq 22$ times larger than in the preceding example. This would correspond to an error of 2% if the Gomperz–Makeham model is used; substantial, but why is it of interest when accurate country mortalities are available? The answer has already been given. Mortalities of people who are insured or members of pension schemes are often much lower than the average, and liabilities are under-estimated if this is ignored. Bias of that kind could be much larger than 2%.

Here there is a typical dilemma between the correct population (no bias, *large* random error) and a larger one (bias, *small* random error). How that is resolved depends on the situation (and on personal judgement), and there is also the choice of estimation method. Random error for entire countries may be close to zero, however the estimation is carried out, and the non-parametric approach with no bias is attractive. The Gomperz–Makeham model is wrong (like all models) and introduces bias, but it dampens random error, as we saw above. Parametric modelling is the way small and medium-sized populations should be handled.

15.2.7 Dealing with longer lives

Systematic error also arises when people are living longer and longer, a cause for financial concern since future benefits last longer. Such issues can be analysed by introducing a default sequence q_{l0} of mortalities, say those we are presently making use of, and extending them to time-dependent versions. One approach is **cohort** dependence, where the mortality q_l at age l depends on the year of birth. The group of people (or cohort) born at $T_{-i} = -iT$ in the past is then assigned mortalities $q_l = q_l(i)$. An alternative is to increase longevity gradually so that the mortalities $q_l = q_{lk}$ depend on the time T_k they apply to, for example becoming smaller in the future than they are today. Steadily improving health care has this effect.

Simple models along these lines are

$$\underbrace{q_l(i) = q_{l0}e^{-\gamma(i)}}_{\textit{cohort version}} \quad \text{and} \quad \underbrace{q_{lk} = q_{l0}e^{-\gamma_k},}_{\textit{time-dynamic version}} \tag{15.3}$$

where $\gamma(i)$ and γ_k are parameters that make the mortalities deviate from the default sequence q_{l0}. Positive $\gamma(i)$ means that people from cohort i tend to live longer than presently assumed, and positive γ_k that mortalities will go down in the future. In practice, $\gamma(i) = \gamma_l(i)$ or $\gamma_k = \gamma_{lk}$ are likely to depend on age l as well, as in the **Lee–Carter** model in Exercise 15.9.

It is, in either case, easy to derive the k-step survival probabilities required for actuarial calculations through a small revision of the method in Section 12.3. Indeed, the recursion (12.10) now becomes

$$\underbrace{{}_{k+1}p_l = \{1 - q_{l+k}(l)\} \cdot {}_kp_l}_{\textit{cohort version}} \quad \text{and} \quad \underbrace{{}_{k+1}p_l = (1 - q_{l+k,k}) \cdot {}_kp_l}_{\textit{time-dynamic version}} \tag{15.4}$$

for $k = 0, 1, 2 \ldots$, starting for both schemes at ${}_0p_l = 1$. Justification: We are at time $T_0 = 0$, and people of age l were born at $-l$ (and belong to cohort l). The

Table 15.3 Net reserve and parameter γ when people (on average) live longer than we are aware of

	Added average life (years)					
	0	1	2	3	4	5
Mortality parameter	$\gamma = 0$	$\gamma = 0.077$	$\gamma = 0.155$	$\gamma = 0.233$	$\gamma = 0.312$	$\gamma = 0.391$
Net reserve (billion)	30.7	32.1	33.5	34.9	36.3	37.8

probability that they survive the period from k to $k+1$ is then $1 - q_{l+k}(l)$, which yields the scheme on the left. On the right, $1 - q_{l+k,k}$ plays the same role with $q_{l+k,k}$ being the mortality at time k for an individual at age l today. Inserting the simple models (15.3) into (15.4) yields

$$\underbrace{{}_{k+1}p_l = (1 - q_{l0}e^{-\gamma(l)}) \cdot {}_kp_l}_{\textit{cohort version}} \quad \text{and} \quad \underbrace{{}_{k+1}p_l = (1 - q_{l0}e^{-\gamma_k}) \cdot {}_kp_l}_{\textit{time-dynamic version}}$$

for $k = 0, 1, \ldots,$ and the entire table ${}_kp_l$ has been computed. The machinery of Chapter 12 has now become available; see Section 12.4 in particular.

15.2.8 Longevity bias: Numerical examples

Suppose the default mortalities $\{q_{l0}\}$ in (15.3) are those of Table 15.1, and that unknown to us the real world differs. As a first model let

$$\gamma(i) = \gamma \quad \text{(the same for all cohorts)},$$

with no change over time. On average, people live equally long regardless of birth, but if $\gamma > 0$, they live longer than we are aware of. *How much* longer is shown in Table 15.3, where the parameter γ is adapted to a given increase in longevity. For example, when $\gamma = 0.077$, each individual lives 1 year extra on average. Note the regular, almost proportional relationship between γ and the added average life (but this is only an approximation).

The effect on the net reserve is shown in the last row of Table 15.3. Recall that we are (by ignorance!) using the wrong model. *Premia* have therefore been calculated under the default mortalities $\{q_{l0}\}$ (which we believe in), whereas *payments* are due to the probabilities $\{q_l(i)\}$ actually at work. All other conditions are as in Tables 15.1 and 15.2. One year longer life on average corresponds to 1.3–1.4 billion in added net expenses, a striking increase. The computations emphasize the seriousness of adverse selection when mortalities for the insured population are smaller than the country average. If the reduction is 25%, as suggested in Mitchell and McCarthy (2002), the corresponding γ would be $-\log(0.75) \doteq 0.29$, and by Table 15.3 net liabilities would go up by around 5 billion, or 16–17% of the original assessment.

As a second example, suppose future mortalities drop gradually. The dynamic model on the right of (15.3) permits us to analyse the impact of this. Let

$$\gamma_k = bk \quad \text{where} \quad b = \frac{0.194}{50} = 0.00380 \quad \text{or} \quad b = \frac{0.391}{50} = 0.00742,$$

where the two values of b make people live 2.5 and 5 years longer on average after half a century (see Table 15.3). If the dynamic effect is allowed to influence premia (see Exercise 15.11), then net reserves become

Added longevity (years)	0	2.5	5
Net reserve (billion)	30.7	32.0	33.4

The assessment on the very right reflects the development seen in many developed countries during the second half of the twentieth century. Such phenomena bring substantial underestimation (here 8–9%) if ignored.

15.3 Risk due to discounting and inflation

15.3.1 Introduction

Let $\mathcal{X}_0, \ldots, \mathcal{X}_K$ be fixed liabilities and $\mathcal{PV}_0 = d_0\mathcal{X}_0 + \cdots + d_1\mathcal{X}_K$ their present value with several possible specifications for the discounts d_k, for example

$$\underset{\text{technical rate}}{d_k = \frac{1}{(1+r)^k}}, \qquad \underset{\text{fair value discounting}}{d_k = P_0(0\colon k)}, \qquad \underset{\text{inflation included}}{d_k = \frac{Q_k}{(1+r)^k}}. \tag{15.5}$$

The traditional method is the version on the left in terms of the **technical rate** r, which is determined administratively. It may be vulnerable to bias or pressure towards high values to keep liabilities low, but that weakness is avoided with the **fair value** method in the middle. Discounts are now the market bond prices $P_0(0\colon k)$ or equivalently $d_k = 1/\{1 + \bar{r}_0(k)\}^k$ with $\bar{r}_0(k)$ the market interest-rate curve. Does the idea appear attractive? There is a drawback. Bond prices and interest-rate curves fluctuate, and market-based present valuation with them even if the liabilities $\mathcal{X}_k$ themselves are fixed.

The coefficients d_k may be used for more than discounting. Suppose liabilities depend on inflation, common in traditional defined benefit schemes where pension rights and contributions are linked to some price or wage index Q_k. A simple approach is to quote $\mathcal{X}_k$ in fixed prices (using the methods of Chapter 12) with the actual payments being $Q_k\mathcal{X}_k$. Inflation is now entered through $d_k = Q_k/(1+r)^k$ in (15.5) right or $d_k = P_0(0\colon k)Q_k$ if fair value accounting is being used.

Algorithm 15.2 Fair value accounting through Black–Karasinski

0 Input: $\mathcal{X}_0, \dots, \mathcal{X}_K, T, P(r, T), r_0, \quad a, \sigma, \xi, \sigma_x = \sigma/\sqrt{1-a^2}$ %*a, σ, ξ for $\{r_k\}$*
1 $X^* \leftarrow \log(r_0/\xi) + \sigma_x^2/2$ %*Initial for $\{X_k\}$*
2 For $k = 0, 1, \dots, K$ do
3 $\quad \mathcal{PV}_k^* \leftarrow 0$ and $r^* \leftarrow \xi \exp(-\sigma_x^2/2 + X^*)$ %*r^* new floating rate*
4 $\quad$ For $i = 0, \dots, K - k$ do $\mathcal{PV}_k^* \leftarrow \mathcal{PV}_k^* + \mathcal{X}_{k+i} P(r^*, iT)$
5 $\quad$ Draw $\varepsilon^* \leftarrow N(0, 1)$ and $X^* \leftarrow aX^* + \sigma\varepsilon^*$ %*X^* for next round*
6 Return $\mathcal{PV}_0^*, \dots, \mathcal{PV}_K^*$. % *$\mathcal{PV}_0^* = \mathcal{PV}_0$ is fixed*

15.3.2 Market-based valuation

What fair value discounts will be in the future is not known, and this induces uncertainty in valuation. It may be examined by looking at historical bond prices, but another way is through mathematical models like those in Section 6.4. Let $P(r, T)$ be the price of a bond maturing at T when r is the current rate of interest. If $\mathcal{X}_0, \dots, \mathcal{X}_K$ is a given liability stream, $\mathcal{X}_k, \dots, \mathcal{X}_K$ is still pending at $T_k = kT$ with present value at that time

$$\mathcal{PV}_k = \sum_{i=0}^{K-k} P(r_k, T_i)\mathcal{X}_{k+i}, \quad k = 0, 1, \dots \tag{15.6}$$

where $P(r_k, T_i)$ was written $P_k(k\colon k + i)$ in the preceding chapter.

A model for the driver process $r_0, r_1, \dots$ is needed to examine the distribution of $\mathcal{PV}_k$. With the Black–Karasinski model from Section 5.6, a simulation can be organized as in Algorithm 15.2. The recursion starts at r_0 on Line 1 with the liability cash flow stopping at time K. Two money-market models are involved. A risk-neutral one leads to the bond prices $P(r, T)$, and there is a second one for the floating rate r_k. There is a link between them through the market price of risk; see Section 14.6.

15.3.3 Numerical example

Fair values of the pension portfolio in Section 15.2 have been simulated in Figure 15.3 under the conditions in Table 15.4. There is one low and one medium-level interest-rate scenario with the same initial rate $r_0 = 2\%$. Since the main point is to visualize uncertainty due to discounting, the liability sequence $\mathcal{X}_0, \mathcal{X}_1, \dots$ at time 0 was kept unchanged at all times k with recruitment compensating exactly for claims that had been liquidated. Algorithm 15.2 must be modified; on Line 4 extend the loop to K and replace $\mathcal{X}_{k+i}$ with $\mathcal{X}_i$.

Fluctuations in Figure 15.3 are considerable. The medium interest-rate scenario

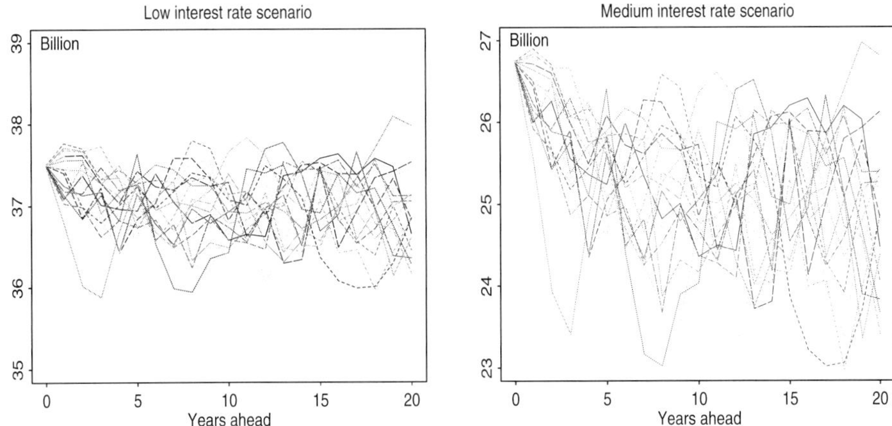

Figure 15.3 Simulated fair value accounting (20 replications) for the pension portfolio defined in Tables 15.1 and 15.2. *Note*: Scale on vertical axes is different.

Table 15.4 Interest-rate models for the experiments in Sections 15.3 and 15.4

	Black-Karasinski real rate	Vasiček bond prices[a]
	$r_k = \xi e^{-\sigma_x^2/2+X_k}, \quad \sigma_x = \frac{\sigma}{\sqrt{1-a^2}}$	$P(r,T) = e^{A-Br}, \quad B = \frac{1-e^{-a_q T}}{a_q},$
	$X_k = aX_{k-1} + \sigma\varepsilon_k$	$A = (B-T)\left(\xi_q - \frac{\sigma_q^2}{2a_q^2}\right) - \frac{\sigma_q^2 B(t)^2}{4a_q}$
Low level	$\xi = 2.5\%$ $a = 0.7$ $\sigma = 0.15$	$\xi_q = 2\%$ $a_q = 0.357$ $\sigma_q = 0.0045$
Medium level	$\xi = 4.5\%$ $a = 0.7$ $\sigma = 0.25$	$\xi_q = 4\%$ $a_q = 0.357$ $\sigma_q = 0.0137$

[a]The standard deviation of r_k is the same under both models, namely $\sigma_q = \xi\sqrt{2(e^{\sigma_x^2} - 1)a_q}$.

on the right produces *stronger* oscillations at a *lower* level than on the left, but there is random variation up to a couple of billion even in the latter case. The low interest-rate level at the beginning is easily discernible, and after a few years both Monte Carlo patterns stabilize as a stationary one in a familiar manner.

15.3.4 Inflation: A first look

Inflation has an impact so severe that a good deal can be gauged through a fixed rate ξ. The price level at time T_k is then $Q_k = (1+\xi)^k$, and the present value of the entire *inflated* payment stream is now

$$\mathcal{PV}_0 = \sum_{k=0}^{K} \frac{Q_k \mathcal{X}_k}{(1+r)^k} = \sum_{k=0}^{\infty} \frac{(1+\xi)^k}{(1+r)^k} \mathcal{X}_k.$$

Define r_ξ as the solution of the equation $1 + r_\xi = (1 + r)/(1 + \xi)$. Then

$$\mathcal{PV}_0 = \sum_{k=0}^{K} \frac{\mathcal{X}_k}{(1 + r_\xi)^k} \quad \text{where} \quad r_\xi = \frac{r - \xi}{1 + \xi}, \tag{15.7}$$

and a fixed rate of inflation changes the technical rate of interest from r to an inflation-adjusted one r_ξ which could even be *negative*.

The expression for r_ξ tells us that inflation is important. If, for example, $r = 3\%$ and $\xi = 2\%$, then $r_\xi = 0.98\%$, much smaller than r. If contributions and benefits under the scheme in Section 15.2 both grow with the price level Q_k, the net reserve under non-inflationary and inflationary scenarios becomes

$$\underset{\xi = 0}{\mathcal{PV}_0 = 30.7} \quad \text{and} \quad \underset{\xi = 2\%}{\mathcal{PV}_0 = 39.0},$$

a huge increase due to inflation, despite all contributions being adjusted too. Inflation is not an issue to be taken lightly!

15.3.5 Simulating present values under stochastic discounts

Had the rate of inflation been fixed and known, it would have been easy to foresee and plan for, but there is, of course, much uncertainty. The following illustration makes use of the Wilkie inflation model from Chapter 13. Recall the form of the model as

$$\underset{\text{linear driver process}}{X_k = aX_{k-1} + \sigma\varepsilon_k}, \qquad \underset{\text{rate of inflation}}{I_k = (1 + \xi)e^{X_k} - 1}, \qquad \underset{\text{price index}}{Q_k = Q_{k-1}(1 + I_k)}$$

with ξ, a and σ parameters and $\varepsilon_1, \varepsilon_2, \dots$ independent and $N(0, 1)$. The fluctuations in X_k around zero yield oscillations in I_k around the median ξ. It is easy to calculate $d_k = Q_k/(1+r)^k$ in (15.5) right and then arrive at inflation-dependent present values. Indeed,

$$d_k = \frac{Q_k}{(1 + r)^k} = \frac{1 + I_k}{1 + r}\frac{Q_{k-1}}{(1 + r)^{k-1}} = \frac{(1 + \xi)e^{X_k}}{1 + r}d_{k-1} = \frac{e^{X_k}}{1 + r_\xi}d_{k-1}$$

where r_ξ is the inflation-adjusted rate of interest in (15.7). This leads to the recursion

$$\underset{\text{linear driver process}}{X_k = aX_{k-1} + \sigma\varepsilon_k} \quad \text{and} \quad \underset{\text{discount}}{d_k = d_{k-1}e^{X_k}/(1 + r_\xi)}, \tag{15.8}$$

which runs over $k = 1, 2, \dots$, starting at

$$X_0 = \log\left(\frac{1 + I_0}{1 + \xi}\right) \quad \text{and} \quad d_0 = 1.$$

Algorithm 15.3 Present values under Wilkie inflation

0 Input: $\{\mathcal{X}_k\}$, K, r, I_0 and a, σ, ξ, $r_\xi = (r - \xi)/(1 + \xi)$ %*a, σ, ξ in* $\{I_k\}$
1 $X^* \leftarrow \log\{(1 + I_0)/(1 + \xi)\}$, $d^* \leftarrow 1$, $\mathcal{PV}^* \leftarrow \mathcal{X}_0$ %*Initializing*
2 For $k = 1, \ldots, K$ do
3 Draw $\varepsilon^* \leftarrow N(0, 1)$ and $X^* \leftarrow aX^* + \sigma\varepsilon^*$ %*Updating* X^*
4 $d^* \leftarrow d^* \exp(X^*)/(1 + r_\xi)$ and $\mathcal{PV}^* \leftarrow \mathcal{PV}^* + d^*\mathcal{X}_k$ %*Discount and* $\mathcal{PV}$
5 Return $\mathcal{PV}^*$.

A simulation is organized through Algorithm 15.3.

With minor changes the program also works for stochastic rates of interest. Now write $d_k = d_{k-1}/(1 + r_k)$, where r_k applies between T_{k-1} and T_k. Under the Black–Karasinski model in Table 15.4 the analogy of the scheme (15.8) is

$$\underbrace{X_k = aX_{k-1} + \sigma\varepsilon_k}_{\text{linear driver process}} \quad \text{and} \quad \underbrace{d_k = d_{k-1}/(1 + \xi e^{-\sigma_x^2/2 + X_k})}_{\text{discount}}, \tag{15.9}$$

where $\sigma_x = \sigma/\sqrt{1 - a^2}$. In Algorithm 15.3 modify the discount updating on Line 4 and the initialization of X^* on Line 1.

15.3.6 Numerical examples

Uncertainty generated by stochastic discounts is illustrated in Figure 15.4 using the pension portfolio in Section 15.2. The inflation scenarios on the left are

$$\underbrace{\xi = 2\%,\ \sigma = 2\%,\ a = 0.58}_{\textit{Scenario I}} \quad \text{and} \quad \underbrace{\xi = 2\%,\ \sigma = 1\%,\ a = 0.58}_{\textit{Scenario II}},$$

where the parameters have been changed from those given by Wilkie for the twentieth century; see Table 13.3. Median inflation was cut down from 4.8% to 2% and the volatility was reduced too. Scenario I has the same flavour as the original Wilkie model in that it allows a high chance of *negative* inflation (this model would have critics!).

It is evident from Figure 15.4 left that inflation brings much uncertainty, but there is an additional effect. The mean has been pushed upwards! It was 39 billion when inflation was fixed and much higher now. That expectations go up when fixed effects are made random is a common phenomenon (due to the Jensen inequality (A.5) in Appendix A). In both examples inflation represents a calm and stable economy, with much lower price increases than under the Wilkie model based on twentieth century experience. The impact is still huge!

What is the effect on present values when discounts correspond to the future rates of interest? Figure 15.4 right provides an illustration using the Black–Karasinski

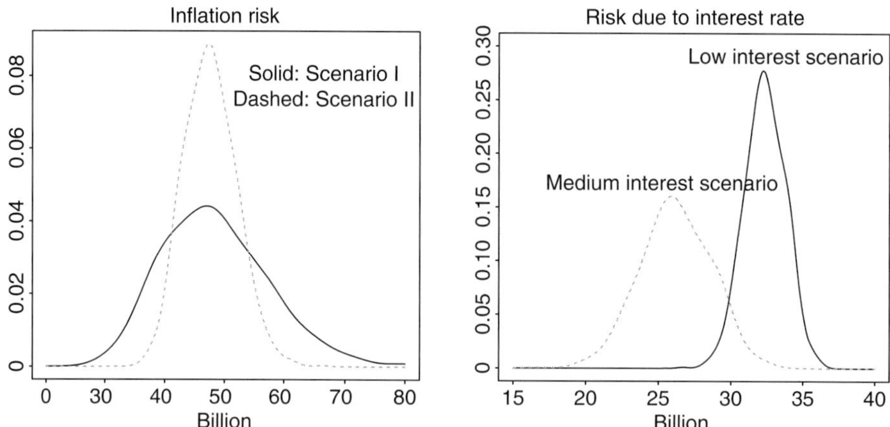

Figure 15.4 Estimated density function (10 000 simulations) for the portfolio described in the text, inflation risk (*left*) and interest rate risk (*right*).

model with parameters

$$\underbrace{\xi = 3\%,\ \sigma = 0.15,\ a = 0.7}_{\textit{low-interest-rate scenario}} \quad \text{and} \quad \underbrace{\xi = 5\%,\ \sigma = 0.25,\ a = 0.7.}_{\textit{medium-interest-rate scenario}}$$

Note that the mean of 3% in the scenario on the left coincides with the technical rate used earlier. That assumption led to 30.6 billion as present value, but the most likely values in Figure 15.4 right have now become several billion higher. This is another case of randomness bringing higher expectation. The example also demonstrates that lower interest-rate regimes might lead to higher present values with less uncertainty.

15.4 Simulating assets protected by derivatives

15.4.1 Introduction

The rest of this chapter is devoted to the asset part, with the present section dealing with financial derivatives and how they are built into simulation programs. Risk-neutral models and prices from Chapter 14 are needed, and we shall examine how returns are influenced by option strategies where premium is siphoned off at the beginning in exchange for higher earnings and less uncertainty later. Suppose these initial fees come from selling parts of the underlying asset. If v_0 is the value *before* and v_0' *after* that transaction has taken place, then

$$v_0' = \underbrace{v_0}_{\textit{original value}} - \underbrace{\pi v_0',}_{\textit{option premium}}$$

where $\pi = \pi(1)$ is the option price per unit capital and $\pi v_0'$ the total premium. Solving the equation yields $v_0' = v_0/(1+\pi)$, an investment that will perform better from a lower level than the original one.

15.4.2 Equity returns with options

Investments in equity protected by derivatives can be studied through **net** returns. Let $V_0 = v_0$ and $V_1 = (1+R)v_0$ be the value of the stock at the beginning and at the end of the period (V is now used instead of the earlier S). Buying the derivative reduces the value of the original asset to $v_0' = v_0/(1+\pi)$, but there is an extra compensating payoff $H(R)v_0'$. At expiry, strategies without and with derivatives yield

$$\underbrace{V_1 = (1+R)v_0}_{\text{without derivatives}} \quad \text{and} \quad \underbrace{V_1 = \{1+R+H(R)\}\frac{v_0}{1+\pi}}_{\text{with derivatives}}.$$

Let R_H be the return of the original investment with derivatives. Then $V_1 = (1 + R_H)v_0$, and from the expression on the right

$$R_H = \frac{R + H(R) - \pi}{1+\pi}, \tag{15.10}$$

which reduces to the ordinary return R when $H(R)$ (and hence π) is zero.

As an example, consider a put option with guarantee r_g. Then $H(R) = \max(r_g - R, 0)$ and $R + H(R) = \max(R, r_g)$, so that

$$R_H = \frac{\max(R, r_g) - \pi}{1+\pi} \quad \text{with minimum} \quad R_H \geq \frac{r_g - \pi}{1+\pi}$$

where the premium π is given by (14.17) in Section 14.4. The exact distribution of R_H is available under the standard log-normal model (Exercise 15.18), but Monte Carlo is just as easy, and we need to learn how it's done in any case to handle more complex problems later; see Algorithm 15.4. Density functions for R and R_H are compared on the left of Figure 15.5 when $r_g = 7\%$, $r = 3\%$, $\xi = 7\%$ and $\sigma = 0.25$, which yields $\pi = 12.17\%$. The downside can't be worse than $R_H \geq (0.07 - 0.1217)/(1 + 0.1217) = -4.6\%$, but the upside is lower, and so was the average return. Only in about one-third of the simulated scenarios did the option strategy come out on top; see also Exercise 15.19.

15.4.3 Equity options over longer time horizons

Simulating equity backed by derivatives for more than 1 year raises new issues. Stock options are rarely longer than annual, and **rollover** strategies where the contracts are renewed periodically must therefore be used. Yet it is easy enough to

Algorithm 15.4 Equity protected by puts

0 Input: $K, \xi, \sigma, r_g, r, \pi$ %*π option price (14.17)*
1 $V^* \leftarrow 1$, %*Initial value immaterial*
2 For $k = 1, \ldots, K$ do
3 Draw $\varepsilon^* \leftarrow N(0,1)$ and $R^* \leftarrow \exp(\xi + \sigma\varepsilon^*) - 1$ %*Ordinary return*
4 If $(R^* < r_g)$ then $H^* \leftarrow r_g - R^*$ else $H^* \leftarrow 0$ %*Option payment*
5 $R_H^* \leftarrow (R^* + H^* - \pi)/(1 + \pi)$ and $V^* \leftarrow V^*(1 + R_H^*)$ %*The asset evolves*
6 Return $R_{0:K}^* \leftarrow V^* - 1$. %*K-step return*

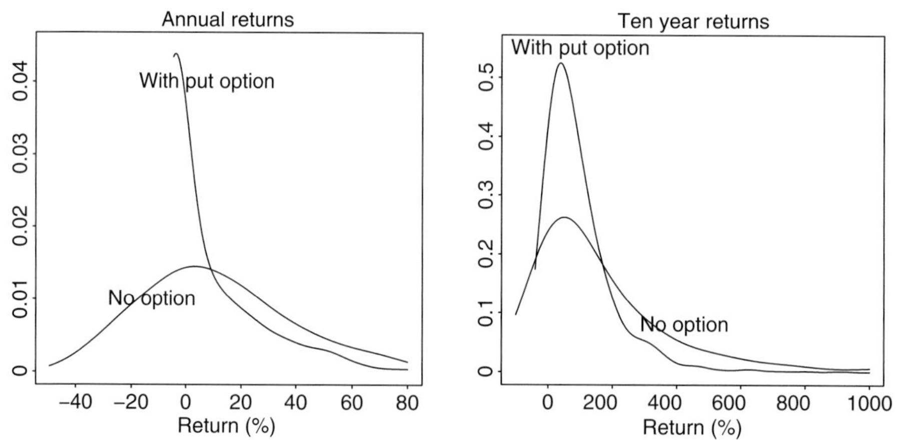

Figure 15.5 Density functions of equity returns from 10 000 simulations with and without put options under conditions in the text, annual case (*left*) and the 10-year one (*right*).

accumulate the effective returns R_H. Algorithm 15.4 is for put options and generates K-step returns $R_{0:K}$. A general derivative may be handled by modifying the premium π and the payoff on Line 4. The algorithm assumes that money received for the options is reinvested in stock free of charge. In practice, both interest rates $r = r_k$ and volatilities $\sigma = \sigma_k$ fluctuate over time and option premia $\pi = \pi_k$ with them. It isn't difficult to introduce this into the algorithm if suitable models are available.

Ten-year returns with and without put options are shown in Figure 15.5 right under the same conditions as on the left. Computations are annual, and the derivatives are rolled over 10 times. The results have the same flavour as on the left. Put options provide more stable returns in exchange for reduced upside and lower average. Use of derivatives wasn't profitable in more than one out of three simulated scenarios.

15.4.4 Money-market investments with floors and caps

Floors protect against low rates of interest. These are multi-period contracts, and Monte Carlo is no longer conveniently organized through one-period returns. Suppose an interest-rate derivative over K periods pays $H(r_k)$ per unit capital at the end of period k. The original premium lowers the initial investment from v_0 to $v_0/(1+\pi)$ as above, and the account V_k now evolves according to

$$V_k = (1 + r_k)V_{k-1} + H(r_k)\frac{v_0}{1+\pi} \quad \text{starting at} \quad V_0 = \frac{v_0}{1+\pi} \tag{15.11}$$

for $k = 1, \dots, K$. If a floor is used, then $H(r_k) = \max(r_g - r_k, 0)$ where r_g is the guarantee, and compensation is provided whenever the floating rate r_k falls below r_g. Monte Carlo implementation is easy. Simulate the floating rate and insert the interest-rate scenarios r_k^* into the recursion (15.11). Caps are almost the same.

How should the option premium π be selected for numerical experimentation? In this chapter we are assuming the Vasiček bond prices of Table 15.4, which are inconsistent with the log-normal distribution on which the floorlet prices in Section 14.5 were based. An approximate way to bridge the gap is to let the standard deviation σ_k under the log-normal match the Vasiček ones; see (14.52) in Section 14.5. This trick has been used with the experiments in Figure 15.6, where 10-year returns from the floating rate of interest are compared with and without a floor strategy. Interest rates follow the models in Table 15.4 with $r_0 = 3\%$ at the beginning. The floor guarantee $r_g = 3\%$ leads to option premia $\pi = 6.40\%$ when interest rates are low and $\pi = 2.01\%$ when they are medium, a higher fee when options are more likely to be used. It emerges from Figure 15.6 that floors protect the downside, but upside is lost, and they were profitable in no more than one out of six cases. The higher rates of interest on the right yield higher uncertainty at a higher level.

15.4.5 Money-market investments with swaps and swaptions

Interest-rate swaps are agreements where floating rates r_k are traded for a fixed swap rate f. The receiver type cedes r_k and collects f, and the payer type is the opposite. There is no fee upfront. Consider a receiver swap with principal V_K traded at T_K for the period between T_J and T_L where $K < J \leq L$. The account then evolves according to

$$\begin{aligned} V_k &= (1 + r_k)V_{k-1} & \text{if} \quad k < J \\ &= (1 + r_k)V_{k-1} + (f_K - r_k)V_K & \text{if} \quad J \leq k \leq L, \end{aligned} \tag{15.12}$$

where $f_K = f_K(J\colon L)$ is the swap rate at T_K and determined by the forward bond prices at that point; see (14.39) and also Line 5 in Algorithm 15.5 later. A payer swap replaces $f_K - r_k$ by $r_k - f_K$ and is apart from this the same.

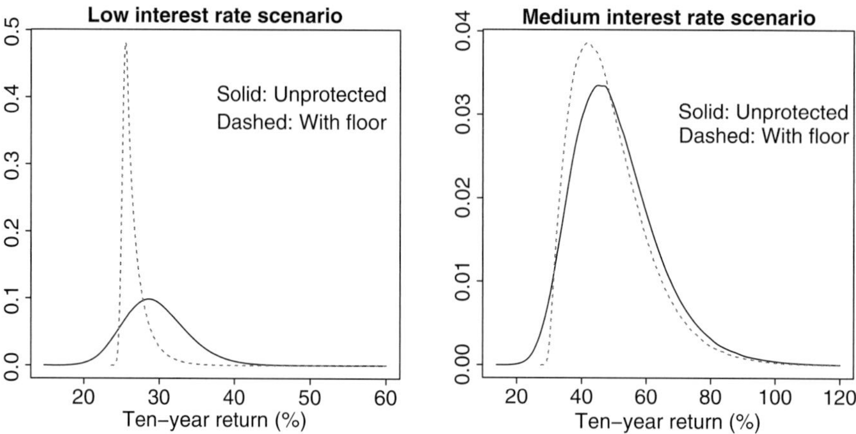

Figure 15.6 The density functions (10 000 simulations) of 10-year returns from the floating rate of interest with and without floor contracts, low interest rate (*left*) and medium (*right*).

Swaptions are options on swaps. Buyers of such instruments may swap interest rates on favourable conditions with a receiver swaption giving the holder the right (but not the obligation) to receive a fixed, agreed swap rate f_g in exchange for paying the floating rate r_k. Such an option expiring at T_K will be exercised if the market swap rate $f_K < f_g$. Suppose the swaption is set up at $T_0 = 0$ with principal $v_0/(1+\pi)$ equal to the remaining capital when the premium has been subtracted. The option holder obtains the better of the rates f_g and f_K, and if the underlying swap lasts from T_J to T_L, the account evolves as

$$\begin{aligned} V_k &= (1+r_k)V_{k-1} & \text{if} \quad k < J \\ &= (1+r_k)V_{k-1} + \{\max(f_K, f_g) - r_k\}\frac{v_0}{1+\pi} & \text{if} \quad J \le k \le L, \end{aligned} \qquad (15.13)$$

starting at $V_0 = v_0/(1+\pi)$.

Programming swap and swaption strategies has much in common with fair value accounting in Algorithm 15.2. A model for the floating rate is needed (Black–Karasinski below) and also a theoretical expression $P(r, T)$ for the bond prices. Commands under a receiver swaption are as in Algorithm 15.5, where the logic is much like the simulation of an ordinary cash account except for a swap rate being generated at T_K and used from T_J onwards. If you want a swap instead, insert $f_g = 0$ and $\pi = 0$ and use the same commands. Simple variations provide payer versions.

Numerical experimentation runs into the same problem as with floors. The premium π is based on a risk-neutral, log-normal model $f_K = f_0 e^{-\sigma_K^2/2+\sigma_K\varepsilon}$ where f_0 is the forward rate for f_K at $T_0 = 0$ and given by the bond prices at the beginning. This

Algorithm 15.5 Receiver swaptions using Black–Karasinski

0 Input: v_0, r_0, $K \leq J < L$, $P(r, T)$, f_g, π and $a, \sigma, \xi, \sigma_x = \sigma/\sqrt{1-a^2}$

1 $V_0^* \leftarrow v_0$ and $X^* \leftarrow \log(r_0/\xi) + \sigma_x^2/2$ *%Initialization*

2 For $k = 1, \ldots, L$ do

3 Draw $\varepsilon^* \leftarrow N(0, 1)$ and $X^* \leftarrow aX^* + \sigma\varepsilon^*$

4 $r^* \leftarrow \xi \exp(-\sigma_x^2/2 + X^*)$ and $V_k^* \leftarrow (1 + r^*)V_{k-1}^*$ *%r^* new floating rate*

5 If $k = K$ then

$$f^* \leftarrow \frac{P(r^*, T_{J-1} - T_K) - P(r^*, T_L - T_K)}{P(r^*, T_J - T_K) + \cdots + P(r^*, T_L - T_K)}$$ *%f^* swap rate*

and if $f^* < f_g$ then $f^* \leftarrow f_g$ *%Switch to f_g if larger*

6 If $k \geq J$ then $V_k^* \leftarrow V_k^* + (f^* - r^*)V_K^*$ *%Receiver swap,* **subtract** *last term for payer swap*

7 Return $V_0^*, \ldots, V_L^*$.

is inconsistent with Vasiček bond prices, but it can be overcome approximately by the method in Exercise 14.28. Consider a receiver swaption expiring at $K = 5$ with guaranteed rate $f_g = 4\%$ for a swap between $J = 6$ and $L = 10$. Let $r_0 = 3\%$ be the initial floating rate and assume the interest-rate models in Table 15.4. Then

$$\underbrace{f_0 = 2.09\%,\ \sigma_K = 0.115,\ \pi = 7.92\%}_{\textit{low-interest-rate scenario}} \qquad \underbrace{f_0 = 3.93\%,\ \sigma_K = 0.201,\ \pi = 1.32\%}_{\textit{medium-interest-rate scenario}}$$

and the swaption is much more costly under the low-interest-rate scenario on the left. Density functions of 10-year returns under floating rate, swap and swaption are shown in Figure 15.7. The picture is the familiar one of the option reducing the downside at the expense of a smaller upside. Swaptions offered improvements in only one out of four cases.

15.5 Simulating asset portfolios

15.5.1 Introduction

Long-term financial risk is influenced by a myriad of details regarding investment tools, options, strategies and portfolio readjustments. The purpose of this section is to indicate how such arrangements and rearrangements find their way into the computer. There are J assets or asset classes valued $V_1, \ldots, V_J$ and followed over K periods of time. These are components of a computer program that should be developed to allow local changes in the code without affecting the rest. The first part of the section defines the top level of a hierarchical scheme of that kind. Applications are lifted into it during the second part. Specific strategies and clauses must then be entered, and there is an asset model. The Wilkie model is used below,

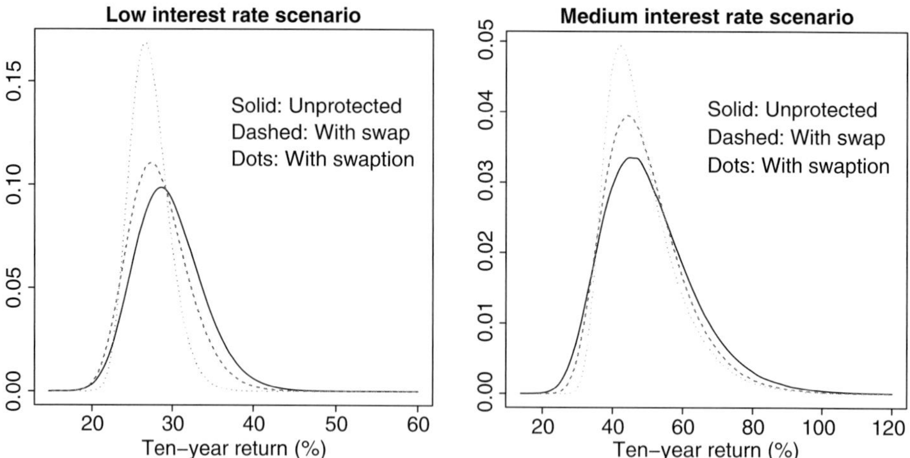

Figure 15.7 Density functions (10 000 simulations) of 10-year interest-rate returns with and without swaps and swaptions, low interest rate (*left*) and medium (*right*). *Note*: Scales on the axes differ.

and the detailed implementation reflects its idiosyncracies. Simulations are always annual and run from a 'typical spot' of the economy (see Section 13.6). When interpreting the numerical examples, bear in mind that inflation and rates of interest in the Wilkie model are higher than some critics find reasonable for the twenty-first century.

15.5.2 Defining the strategy

Financial portfolios were introduced in Section 1.4 through weights $w_1, \ldots, w_J$ which define the relative value of the assets. In mathematical terms

$$w_j = \frac{V_j}{\mathcal{V}} \quad \text{where} \quad \mathcal{V} = V_1 + \cdots + V_J, \tag{15.14}$$

and as $V_1, \ldots, V_J$ fluctuate over time, so do $w_1, \ldots, w_J$. An investment strategy is a rule that specifies the weights. One possibility is weights $w_{10}, \ldots, w_{J0}$ selected in advance, known as the **fixed mix** strategy. Then

$$w_1 = w_{10}, \ldots, w_J = w_{J0} \quad \text{with} \quad w_{10} + \cdots + w_{J0} = 1,$$

and as the relative values of the investments vary, buying and selling is undertaken to achieve the right asset mix. Such **rebalancing** of the portfolio is not free of charge; see below.

The opposite strategy is **buy-and-hold**. Now the weights $w_1, \ldots, w_J$ are allowed to oscillate freely without intervention. There are no trading expenses, but the risk becomes high in cases where the equity share of the portfolio grows. An intermediate position is to require

$$a_j \leq w_j \leq b_j, \quad j = 1, \ldots, J,$$

where $a_j \leq b_j$ define lower and upper limits. Now the portfolio is rebalanced only when weights are outside the admissible interval. Still another strategy (and a popular one too) is constant proportional portfolio insurance (or **CPPI**). The weight on equity (say the first one) is now of the form

$$w_1 = \alpha\left(1 - \frac{F}{\mathcal{V}}\right),$$

where F is a floor (under which $\mathcal{V}$ is not supposed to fall) and α a multiplier. Both F and α are fixed by the design. CPPI assigns progessively higher weight to equity when the portfolio value rises above the floor. This strategy is examined in Exercise 15.33.

Simulations under restrictions such as $a_j \leq w_j \leq b_j$ require rules for what's going to happen when weights are inadmissible. As a simple example, suppose there is a ceiling on asset 1 (still equity) so that $w_1 > b_1$ is not allowed. When that occurs, the equity holding must be trimmed down with all other weights being affected too. If $V_1, \ldots, V_J$ and $\mathcal{V} = V_1 + \cdots + V_J$ are asset and portfolio values *prior* to the rebalance, a possible procedure could be

$$\begin{aligned} &w_j = \frac{V_j}{\mathcal{V}}, \quad j = 1, \ldots, J \quad \text{if} \quad V_1 \leq b_1\mathcal{V} \\ &w_1 = b_1, \quad w_j = \frac{1 - b_1}{\mathcal{V} - V_1}V_j, \quad j = 2, \ldots, J \quad \text{if} \quad V_1 > b_1\mathcal{V} \end{aligned} \tag{15.15}$$

with equity being assigned the maximum weight when forced down. If $V_1 > b_1\mathcal{V}$, then

$$w_1 + \cdots + w_J = b_1 + \frac{1 - b_1}{\mathcal{V} - V_1}(V_2 + \cdots + V_J) = b_1 + (1 - b_1) = 1,$$

and the new set of weights add to one as before. Other rules can easily be constructed.

15.5.3 Expenses due to rebalancing

Purchasing and liquidating assets are not free of charge, and we should be able to build such expenses into the simulations. A possible cost function when changing V_j into Y_j is the proportional one where

$$C_j = \gamma_j|Y_j - V_j|, \quad j = 1, \ldots, J \tag{15.16}$$

with $\gamma_1, \dots, \gamma_J$ coefficients. Suppose $w_1, \dots, w_J$ are the desired weights. Then $Y_j = w_j\mathcal{Y}$ where $\mathcal{Y}$ is the value of the portfolio *after* the rebalance expenses have been subtracted. But if $\mathcal{V} = V_1 + \cdots + V_J$ is the value *prior* to these operations, then

$$\mathcal{Y} = \mathcal{V} - \sum_{j=1}^{J} C_j = \mathcal{V} - \sum_{j=1}^{J} \gamma_j|Y_j - V_j| = \mathcal{V} - \sum_{j=1}^{J} \gamma_j|w_j\mathcal{Y} - V_j|$$

and $\mathcal{Y}$ is determined from the equation

$$\mathcal{Y} + \sum_{j=1}^{J} \gamma_j|w_j\mathcal{Y} - V_j| = \mathcal{V}. \tag{15.17}$$

Although pathological examples with several solutions $\mathcal{Y} < \mathcal{V}$ *can* be constructed, there is in practice a single one and guaranteed if short positions are ruled out. Indeed, let

$$g(y) = y + \sum_{j=1}^{J} \gamma_j|w_j y - V_j|,$$

and if all $w_j \geq 0$ and $0 \leq \gamma_j < 1$, then

$$g'(y) \geq 1 - \sum_{j=1}^{J} \gamma_j w_j > 1 - \sum_{j=1}^{J} w_j = 0$$

except at the singular points $V_1/w_1, \dots, V_J/w_J$. It follows that the function $g(y)$ is strictly increasing, and (15.17) has a single solution. A numerical method is needed to find it; see Section C.4.

15.5.4 A skeleton algorithm

Let $V_{1k}, \dots, V_{Jk}$ be the value of the assets at $T_k = kT$ with $\mathcal{V}_k = V_{1k} + \cdots + V_{Jk}$ the portfolio value at that time. The skeleton Algorithm 15.6 outlines how a simulation experiment is planned. On Line 3 an asset model (such as Wilkie's) is needed and possibly some of the schemes in Section 15.4 if derivatives are being used. The weights on Line 4 are random. They depend on success or failure of the investments and also on the strategy adopted, for example (15.15) if there is a ceiling on the first asset. If cost due to rebalancing is ignored, take $\mathcal{Y}^* = V^*_{1k} + \cdots + V^*_{Jk}$ on Line 5.

Portfolio values may be wanted in real terms. The price level Q_k must then be simulated jointly with the assets as in Section 13.6. Monte Carlo nominal and real portfolio returns at T_k become

$$\mathcal{R}^*_{0:k} = \frac{\mathcal{V}^*_k}{\mathcal{V}^*_0} - 1 \quad \text{and} \quad \frac{\mathcal{V}^*_k/Q^*_k}{\mathcal{V}^*_0} - 1 = \frac{1 + \mathcal{R}^*_{0:k}}{Q^*_k} - 1, \tag{15.18}$$

Algorithm 15.6 Dynamic asset portfolio

Input: Initial portfolio $(v_{10}, \dots, v_{J0})$, rebalancing cost $(\gamma_1, \dots, \gamma_J)$, asset model

$V^*_{j0} \leftarrow v_{j0} \quad (j = 1, \dots, J)$ *%Initialization*

Repeat for $k = 1, 2, \dots, K$

%Asset development next

Generate $V^*_{1k}, \dots, V^*_{Jk}$ from $V^*_{1k-1}, \dots, V^*_{Jk-1}$ *%Model needed here*

%If rebalancing is carried out:

Desired weights $w^*_1, \dots, w^*_J$ from $V^*_{1k}, \dots, V^*_{Jk}$ *%Depends on strategy*

%If rebalancing costs are ignored, take $\mathcal{Y}^* \leftarrow V^*_{1k} + \cdots + V^*_{Jk}$, *skip next line*

Determine $\mathcal{Y}^*$ from $\mathcal{Y}^* + \sum_{j=1}^J \gamma_j |w^*_j \mathcal{Y}^* - V^*_{jk}| = \sum_{j=1}^J V^*_{jk}$

%Numerical method

$V^*_{jk} \leftarrow w^*_j \mathcal{Y}^* \ (j = 1, \dots, J)$ *%Rebalance completed*

$\mathcal{V}^*_k \leftarrow V^*_{1k} + \cdots + V^*_{Jk}$

Return $\mathcal{V}^*_1, \dots, \mathcal{V}^*_K$.

where $\mathcal{V}^*_k = (1 + \mathcal{R}^*_{0:k})\mathcal{V}^*_0$ has been inserted on the right.

15.5.5 Example 1: Equity and cash

As a first example consider a portfolio of equity V_{1k} and cash V_{2k} under the Wilkie model. The equity and money market are then driven by

- dividend inflation I^d_k
- equity yield y_k
- long rate of interest $\bar{r}_k(K)$
- interest ratio F_k;

see (13.34)–(13.37) and also (13.28) and (13.29) which yield the recursions

$$V_{1k} = \frac{D_k}{y_k} \quad \text{where} \quad D_k = (1 + I^d_k) y_{k-1} V_{1k-1} \tag{15.19}$$

and

$$V_{2k} = (1 + r_k) V_{2k-1} + D_k \qquad \text{where } r_k = F_k \bar{r}_k(K). \tag{15.20}$$

Here D_k is the dividend and $r_k = F_k \bar{r}_k(K)$ the short rate of interest. The time increment $T = 1$, and the recursion starts at

$$V_{10} = w_0 \mathcal{V}_0 \quad \text{and} \quad V_{20} = (1 - w_0) \mathcal{V}_0, \tag{15.21}$$

where w_0 is the initial weight on equity and $\mathcal{V}_0 = v_0$ the initial investment. To see how simulations are implemented, consult Algorithm 15.7 later.

Table 15.5 Distribution of the 10-year returns of the equity–cash portfolio (see text)

100 000 simulations used

	No derivative used					Annual guarantee 3% on equity				
Percentiles	5%	25%	50%	75%	95%	5%	25%	50%	75%	95%
Free oscillation	0.65	0.91	1.15	1.43	1.96	0.70	0.94	1.15	1,41	1.81
At most 30%	0.67	0.92	1.15	1.41	1.87	0.70	0.93	1.13	1.37	1.80
Fixed at 30%	0.69	0.98	1.23	1.51	2.00	0.73	0.96	1.21	1.47	1.96

The experiments reported in Table 15.5 left compare three strategies with $w_0 =$ 30% invested in stock originally. Equity weights are either allowed to vary freely (first strategy), float below a ceiling at 30% (second strategy) or fixed at 30% (third strategy). The second strategy forces the portfolio manager to sell equity whenever the threshold of 30% is exceeded, and the third one implies selling or buying at the end of each period. Rebalancing costs for equity were 0.1%. Distributions under the three strategies are shown as percentiles in Table 15.5 left (discrepancies would hardly be visible at all in the density plots used elsewhere). The fixed-weight strategy (where stock is sold high and bought low) has an edge over the other two.

15.5.6 Example 2: Options added

Derivatives require changes in the programs. Floors, swaps and swaptions that affect the cash account V_{2k} are handled by the algorithms in Section 15.4. We shall now consider equity options written on the value of the stock with premia and payoffs drawn from and entered into the cash account. The value V_{1k} of the shares evolves according to (15.19) as before, but the recursion for V_{2k} contains additional terms. Under a put option

$$V_{2k} = \underbrace{(1+r_k)V_{2k-1} + D_k}_{\text{as before}} + \underbrace{\min(r_g - R_k, 0)V_{1k-1}}_{\text{received from the put}} - \underbrace{\pi_k V_{1k}}_{\text{fee for the put}} \tag{15.22}$$

where

$$\begin{aligned} R_k &= \frac{V_{1k}}{V_{1k-1}} - 1, \\ \pi_k &= (1+r_g)e^{-r_k}\Phi(a_k) - \Phi(a_k - \sigma_k), \\ a_k &= \frac{\log(1+r_g) - r_k + \sigma_k^2/2}{\sigma_k}; \end{aligned} \tag{15.23}$$

see (3.16) and (3.17) in Section 3.5. How the various features are put together is shown by Algorithm 15.7.

The algorithm has been written with equity volatility fixed as σ, but the option price π still fluctuates because of the interest rate. If the option isn't in use, remove

Algorithm 15.7 Single time step of equity portfolio

0 Input: σ, r_g, I^{d*}_{k-1}, y^*_{k-1}, $\overline{r}_{k-1}(K)^*$, F^*_{k-1}, V^*_{1k-1}, V^*_{2k-1}
1 Generate I^{d*}_k, y^*_k, $\overline{r}_k(K)^*$, F^*_k *%Through Algorithms 13.3 and 13.4*
2 $D^*_k \leftarrow (1+I^{d*}_k)y^*_{k-1}V^*_{1k-1}$, $r^* \leftarrow F^*_k\overline{r}_k(K)^*$ *%Dividend and the short rate*
3 $V^*_{1k} = D^*_k/y^*_k$, $R^* \leftarrow V^*_{1k}/V^*_{1k-1} - 1$ *%Equity and equity return*
4 $a^* \leftarrow (\log(1+r_g) - r^* + \sigma^2/2)/\sigma$
5 $\pi^* = (1+r_g)e^{-r^*}\Phi(a^*) - \Phi(a^* - \sigma)$ *%Option premium*
6 $X^* \leftarrow \max(r_g - R^*, 0)$ *%Option payoff*
7 $V^*_{2k} \leftarrow (1+r^*)V^*_{2k-1} + D^* + X^* - \pi^* V^*_{1k}$
8 Return V^*_{1k} and V^*_{2k}.

Lines 4–6 (replace π^* and X^* with zeros) or fix r_g close to -1, say $r_g = -0.999999$. The output is inserted on Line 3 in Algorithm 15.6.

Experiments were run with $\sigma = 20.5\%$ and $r_g = 3\%$ (the volatility is representative for the Wilkie model when approximated by the geometric random walk). The rest of the conditions were as in Example 1 above, which gave the results in Table 15.5 right. Returns now have (predictably!) a higher downside and a lower upside than on the left, where options were not used.

15.5.7 Example 3: Bond portfolio and inflation

The third example is a bond portfolio which will, in Section 15.6, be used to match liabilities. At $T_k = k$ the investor holds B_{jk} unit-faced, zero-coupon bonds maturing at $T_{k+j} = k + j$ for $j = 1, \ldots, J$. The value of the portfolio is then

$$V_{3k} = \sum_{j=1}^{J} \frac{B_{jk}}{\{1 + \overline{r}_k(j)\}^j}, \tag{15.24}$$

where $\overline{r}_k(j)$ is the forward rate of interest at T_k. We must take a position on what is done with cash that is released. Suppose it is used to purchase new bonds of duration J. The portfolio at T_k is then a mix of assets maturing at $T_{k+1}, \ldots, T_{k+J}$.

Our target is both nominal and real return, and a joint model for the rate of inflation I_k and the interest-rate curve $\overline{r}_k(j)$ is needed. As elsewhere, the detailed implementation makes use of the Wilkie model. Since it only describes the short rate r_k and a very long one $\overline{r}_k(K)$, we must resort to interpolation to find the intermediate rates (see Section 13.6). Algorithm 15.8 defines a skeleton of a program, where the key computations are those on Line 2. The interest-rate curve and the rate of inflation are then generated from a joint model such as Wilkie's; consult Section 13.6 for details. Note the way the portfolio is revised on Lines 3 and 4. Nominal and real return is determined from the output through (15.18).

Algorithm 15.8 Rolling bond portfolio with inflation

Input: Interest rate/inflation model, initial portfolio $B_{01}, \dots, B_{0J}$
$B_j^* \leftarrow B_{0j},\ j = 1, \dots, J$
For $k = 1, \dots, K$ do
  Generate Q_k^* and $\bar{r}_k(j)^*$ for $j = 1, \dots, J$ *%Algorithms 13.2–13.4 with interpolation for $\bar{r}_k(j)^*$*
  $B_j^* \leftarrow B_{j+1}^*$ for $j = 0, \dots, J-1$ *%Time to expiry shorter*
  $B_J^* \leftarrow B_0^*/\{1 + \bar{r}_k^*(J)\}^J$ *%Buying new bonds*
  $V_{3k}^* \leftarrow \dfrac{B_1^*}{\{1+\bar{r}_k(1)^*\}^1} + \cdots + \dfrac{B_J^*}{\{1+\bar{r}_k(J)^*\}^J}$ *%Valuation here*
  Return $V_{31}^*, \dots, V_{3K}^*$ and $Q_1^*, \dots, Q_K^*$.

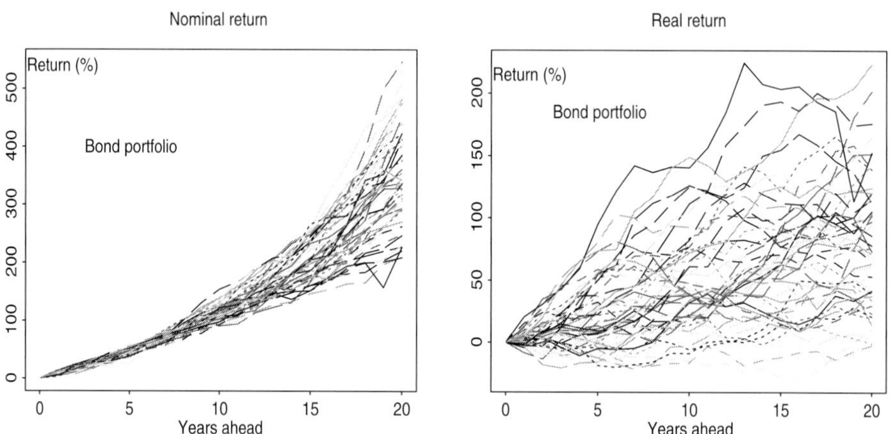

Figure 15.8 Simulated k-step returns (50 scenarios) for the bond portfolio described in the text, nominal values (*left*) and real ones (*right*).

The experiments reported in Figure 15.8 started from a portfolio of $J = 10$ different bonds expiring $j = 1, 2, \dots, 10$ years into the future. Bonds were initially weighted equally. Inflation has a striking impact, and real return on the right in Section 15.8 has a larger *relative* variability than the nominal one on the left. Real return may even be *negative*, a phenomenon that wasn't unknown in the twentieth century.

15.5.8 Example 4: Equity, cash and bonds

Monte Carlo programs when bonds are mixed with equity and cash can be referred back to the previous examples. All we have to do is add the values (say V_{3k}) of

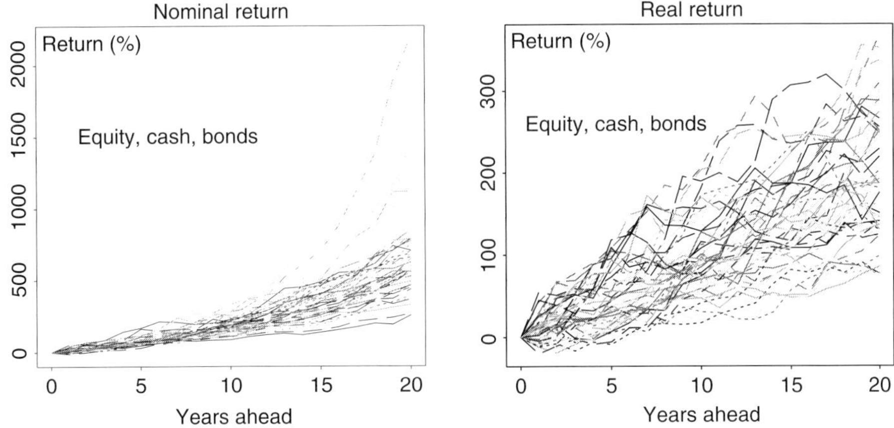

Figure 15.9 Simulated k-step returns (50 scenarios) under a buy-and-hold strategy for the equity, cash and bond portfolio described in the text, nominal (*left*) and real (*right*).

the bond portfolio to equity (V_{1k}) and cash (V_{2k}). The detailed implementations are as before, whether equity options are in use or not. We simply lump all of it into Algorithm 15.6 (through Line 3) and run the Wilkie (or some other) model. Of course, all economic and financial variables are mutually correlated, but that is precisely what the Wilkie model (and the others) provide. Actual simulations are shown in Figure 15.9, based on a buy-and-hold strategy. The original weights were

$$\underset{\textit{equity}}{w_1 = 0.5} \qquad \underset{\textit{cash}}{w_2 = 0.1} \qquad \underset{\textit{bonds}}{w_3 = 0.4}$$

with strong emphasis on equity. In the long run, returns are now consistently higher than for the bond portfolio in Figure 15.8, and real returns on the right rise markedly more steeply. Equity offers better protection against inflation if we can rely on the Wilkie summary of the twentieth century.

15.6 Assets and liabilities

15.6.1 Introduction

Assets of insurance companies were once managed insulated from the rest, but the advantage of coordination has long since been realized. An extreme example is fixed liabilities $\{\mathcal{X}_k\}$, replicated exactly by a bond portfolio that releases $\mathcal{X}_k$ at time T_k. *All* risk is then removed! That would be a dull way to run the business (and not very profitable). Nor could it be carried out in practice. There may be a shortage of long bonds, and life-table risk and inflation make $\{\mathcal{X}_k\}$ uncertain rather than fixed.

Yet the example does convey that tailoring investments to liabilities might be an idea worth pursuing.

The issue is known as asset liability management (or **ALM**) and is the topic of this section. One thing that matters is the timing of the liabilities and in particular their **duration**, which is the time average of the cash flow; see Section 1.4. Liabilities of long duration may make it attractive to bet on a long-term potential of the stock market. Equity, if performing as robustly with respect to inflation as indicated by the Wilkie model, could even be an answer to future price increases blowing liabilities up as in Section 15.3. Inflation-linked bonds are a second tool here if available in sufficient numbers. Another concern is interest-rate movements. If they go down, the value put on future liabilities goes up, and modern fair-value accounting leads to the uncomfortable cyclic fluctuations in Figure 15.3. Perhaps clever investment strategies may alleviate such interest-rate risk? It is this kind of issue that is addressed below.

15.6.2 Auxiliary: Duration and spread of liabilities

The present value of a liability stream $\mathcal{X}_0, \dots, \mathcal{X}_K$ is

$$\mathcal{PV}_x(r) = \sum_{k=0}^{K} \frac{\mathcal{X}_k}{(1+r)^k} \tag{15.25}$$

with duration

$$\mathcal{D}_x(r) = \sum_{k=0}^{K} T_k q_{xk}(r) \quad \text{where} \quad q_{xk}(r) = \frac{\mathcal{X}_k(1+r)^{-k}}{\sum_{i=0}^{K} \mathcal{X}_i(1+r)^{-i}}; \tag{15.26}$$

see (1.20). There is a simple relationship between these quantities. If $T_k = kT$, then

$$\frac{\partial \log\{\mathcal{PV}_x(r)\}}{\partial r} = -\frac{1+r}{T}\mathcal{D}_x(r) \tag{15.27}$$

which is verified in Section 15.7. When $T = 1$, the duration is not far from the slope of the log present value and would have been exactly that had the discounts been $d_k = e^{-kr}$; see Exercise 15.39.

From (15.26) right

$$\sum_{k=0}^{K} q_{xk}(r) = 1 \quad \text{(all } r\text{)},$$

formally a probability distribution, and the duration becomes (also formally) an expectation which may be interpreted as a time average of a cash flow. A notion of

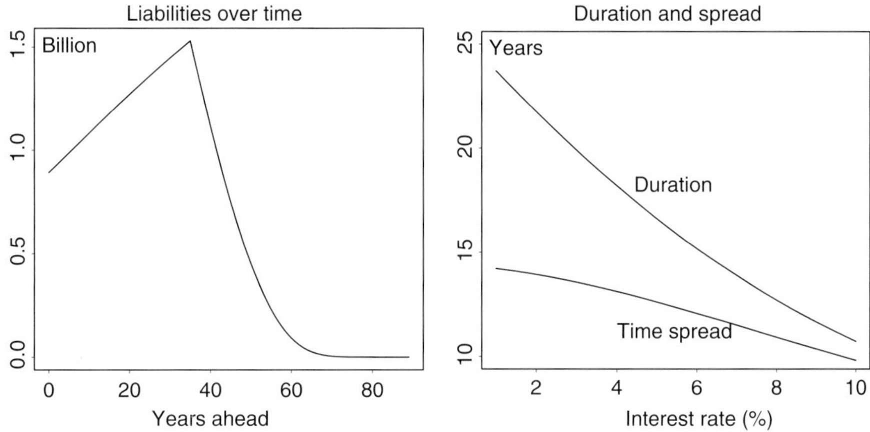

Figure 15.10 How net liabilities of the portfolio in Section 15.2 distribute over time (*left*) and duration and time spread (*right*).

spread will be needed too. Define

$$C_x(r) = \sum_{k=0}^{K} T_k^2 q_{xk}(r) \quad \text{and} \quad \tau_x(r) = \sqrt{C_x(r) - \mathcal{D}_x^2(r)}, \tag{15.28}$$

where $C_x(r)$ is the *coefficient of convexity*. It is also (once again formally) a second-order moment and the spread $\tau_x(r)$ a standard deviation. Duration and spread have been plotted in Figure 15.10 right for the pension insurance portfolio in Section 15.2 with the liability cash flow on the left. As r is raised long payments are reduced in importance, and the duration must go down.

15.6.3 Classical immunization

The British actuary Frank Reddington pointed out long ago that the way assets are invested may protect liabilities against interest-rate movements; see, e.g., Reddington (1952). His idea, presented in an era when the investment arm of companies was run independently from the rest, was based on matching the duration of assets to that of liabilities, known today as **immunization**. Reddington sought an investment strategy that worked whichever way the money market was moving. Let $\mathcal{X}_0, \dots, \mathcal{X}_K$ be given liabilities, r_0 the current rate of interest and suppose assets, placed as bonds, produce a cash flow $\mathcal{V}_0, \dots, \mathcal{V}_K$. The latter has duration $\mathcal{D}_v(r)$ and spread $\tau_v(r)$ similar to $\mathcal{D}_x(r)$ and $\tau_x(r)$ for the liabilities (insert $\mathcal{V}_0, \dots, \mathcal{V}_K$ in the definitions above).

The first step is to plan the bond portfolio so that

$$\mathcal{D}_v(r_0) = \mathcal{D}_x(r_0), \tag{15.29}$$

which makes asset and liability cash flows equally long under the current rate of interest r_0. Consider the present values $\mathcal{PV}_v(r)$ and $\mathcal{PV}_x(r)$ under other rates. It is shown in Section 15.7 that their ratio is approximately

$$\frac{\mathcal{PV}_v(r)}{\mathcal{PV}_x(r)} \doteq \frac{\mathcal{PV}_v(r_0)}{\mathcal{PV}_x(r_0)} e^{\gamma(r_0)(1+r_0)^2(r-r_0)^2/(2T^2)} \tag{15.30}$$

where $\gamma(r) = \tau_v^2(r) - \tau_x^2(r)$, and this becomes an equality as $r \to r_0$. The result is, from a mathematical point of view, simply a Taylor series around r_0 where the linear term vanishes due to (15.29).

The key quantity is the coefficient $\gamma(r)$, which is the difference in the cash flow variances. Suppose it is possible to plan investments so that

$$\tau_v(r_0) \geq \tau_x(r_0). \tag{15.31}$$

Then $\gamma(r_0) \geq 0$ in (15.30), and for *all* r not too far from r_0

$$\frac{\mathcal{PV}_v(r)}{\mathcal{PV}_x(r)} \geq \frac{\mathcal{PV}_v(r_0)}{\mathcal{PV}_x(r_0)},$$

which makes the present technical rate r_0 *a worst-case scenario*. In theory, *any* interest-rate movement away from r_0 is an improvement that makes us financially more secure. Such a glorious situation is created through a portfolio with a suitable mix of long and short bonds, so that its spread is larger than for the liabilities, with duration the same. A prerequisite is enough long bonds, which is a problem in practice. For more on classical immunization, consult chapter 3 in Panjer (1998).

15.6.4 Net asset values

New problems (and opportunities!) arise when fair-value discounting replaces the technical rate of interest. The value put on liabilities will then oscillate, and we may try to counter through investments. Consider assets (market valued) minus liabilities (also market valued). Such net assets, a complex affair in practice, are simplified here as

$$\mathcal{B}_k = \underbrace{V_{1k}}_{\textit{equity}} + \underbrace{V_{2k}}_{\textit{cash}} + \underbrace{V_{3k}}_{\textit{bonds}} - \underbrace{\mathcal{PV}_{xk}}_{\textit{liabilities}}$$

with equity, cash and bonds as asset classes. *Future* liabilities are valued through

$$\mathcal{PV}_{xk} = \sum_{i=0}^{K-k} \frac{\mathcal{X}_{k+i}}{\{1+\bar{r}_k(i)\}^i},$$

where $\bar{r}_k(i)$ is the interest-rate curve. Inflation will be added later.

The scheme is detailed for the Wilkie model. Equity is now driven by the stationary processes $\{y_k\}$ (share yield) and $\{I_k^d\}$ (dividend inflation), which are connected to the share values $\{V_{1k}\}$ through

$$V_{1k} = \frac{D_k}{y_k}, \quad D_k = (1 + I_k^d) y_{k-1} V_{1k-1} \tag{15.32}$$

where D_k is the dividend. Let B_k be the number of zero-coupon, unit-faced bonds maturing at T_k and C_k the cost of purchasing new bonds. The recursion for the cash account is then

$$V_{2k} = (1 + r_k)V_{2k-1} + \underbrace{D_k}_{\textit{dividend}} + \underbrace{B_k}_{\textit{bonds repaid}} - \underbrace{C_k}_{\textit{bonds bought}} - \underbrace{\mathcal{X}_k}_{\textit{liability liquidated}} \tag{15.33}$$

where overhead has been excluded. Suppose the bond portfolio is as in Example 3 above. At T_k there are now bonds $B_{k+1}, \ldots, B_{k+J}$ maturing at $T_{k+1}, \ldots, T_{k+J}$, and their total value is

$$V_{3k} = \sum_{i=0}^{J} \frac{B_{k+i}}{\{1 + \bar{r}_k(i)\}^i}, \tag{15.34}$$

using the same discounts as for the liabilities.

15.6.5 Immunization through bonds

There is in real life often a shortage of long bonds. Such situations can be imitated by exluding bonds of long duration, say those exceeding J years. To define an immunization scheme start at time $T_0 = 0$ by purchasing

$$B_i = \mathcal{X}_i \quad \text{for} \quad i = 1, \ldots, J.$$

During the first J years money released at T_i matches the obligation $\mathcal{X}_i$ exactly, and this pattern can be maintained. At T_k buy bonds maturing at T_{k+J}; i.e.,

$$B_{k+J} = \mathcal{X}_{k+J} \quad \text{which costs} \quad C_k = \frac{B_{k+J}}{\{1 + \bar{r}_k(J)\}^J} \tag{15.35}$$

where the forward rate of interest $\bar{r}_k(J)$ determines the price C_k of the purchase. In (15.33) $B_k = \mathcal{X}_k$ and $C_k = \mathcal{X}_{k+J}/\{1 + \bar{r}_k(J)\}^J$, so that

$$V_{2k} = (1 + r_k)V_{2k-1} + D_k - \frac{\mathcal{X}_{k+J}}{\{1 + \bar{r}_k(J)\}^J}$$

and the design ensures that

$$\mathcal{PV}_{xk} - V_{3k} = \sum_{i=0}^{K-k} \frac{\mathcal{X}_{k+i}}{\{1 + \bar{r}_k(i)\}^i} - \sum_{i=0}^{J} \frac{B_{k+i}}{\{1 + \bar{r}_k(i)\}^i} = \sum_{i=J+1}^{K-k} \frac{\mathcal{X}_{k+i}}{\{1 + \bar{r}_k(i)\}^i}.$$

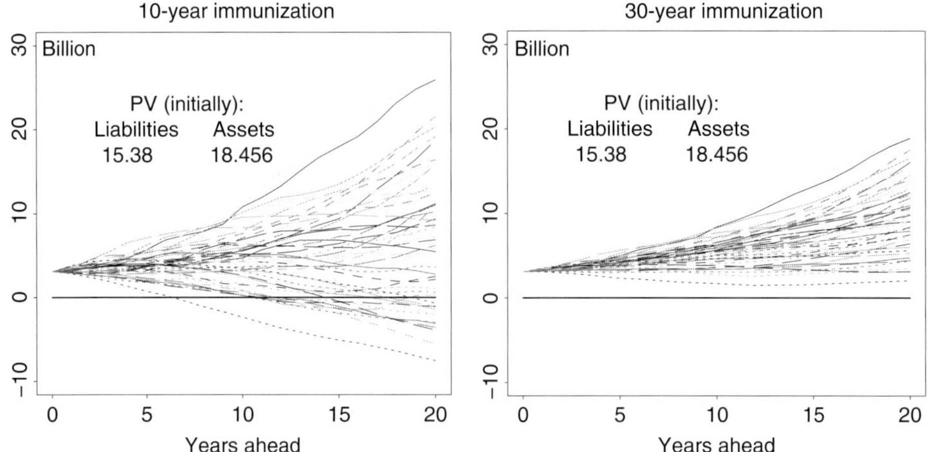

Figure 15.11 Simulated net asset value scenarios (50) with bond investments, up to 10-year bonds available (*left*) and up to 30-year ones (*right*).

The sum on the right starts at $J + 1$, and the uncertainty in $\mathcal{PV}_{xk} - V_{3k}$ might be much smaller than in $\mathcal{PV}_{xk}$ alone. How simulation programs can be organized is demonstrated in Algorithm 15.9 later. At the start

$$V_{10} = v_0 w_{10}, \; V_{20} = v_0(1 - w_{10}) - V_{30}, \; V_{30} = \sum_{i=0}^{J} \frac{\mathcal{X}_i}{\{1 + \bar{r}_0(i)\}^i} \tag{15.36}$$

where v_0 is the initial capital and w_{10} the weight placed on equity.

Examples are shown in Figure 15.11 for the pension portfolio of Section 15.2. The Wilkie model is used for the rate of interest, and the liabilities are then initially valued at 15.38 billion, lower than the valuations earlier in this chapter since the Wilkie model represents high-interest-rate scenarios. An amount 20% higher (18.456) was put up to support the scheme. Equity isn't used at all (i.e., $w_{10} = 0$), and assets other than bonds are held in cash. On the left of Figure 15.11 the maximum duration of bonds was 10 years, and the capital is not sufficient to support the scheme, but that changes on the right where bonds up to 30 years were available. Note that the *sole* difference between the two scenarios is the duration of the bonds.

15.6.6 Enter inflation

Immunization through ordinary bonds, as above, is less effective when the liabilities depend on inflation. Now the nominal net payments at T_k become $Q_k\mathcal{X}_k$, where Q_k is the price level. The profile of the liability cash flow is changed and with it

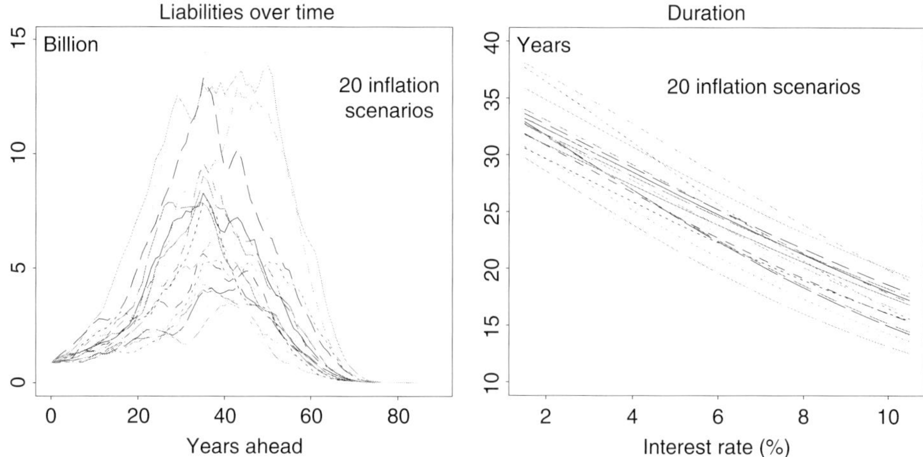

Figure 15.12 Monte Carlo time distributions of liabilities influenced by inflation (*left*) and Monte Carlo durations coming from the same liability sequences (*right*).

duration. One way to examine this is to generate Monte Carlo simulations Q_k^* of future price levels which yield realizations $Q_k^* \mathcal{X}_k$ of the cash flow itself. The corresponding Monte Carlo durations are then

$$\mathcal{D}_x^*(r) = \sum_{k=0}^{K} T_k q_{xk}^*(r) \qquad \text{where} \qquad q_{xk}^*(r) = \frac{Q_k^* \mathcal{X}_k (1+r)^{-k}}{\sum_{i=0}^{K} Q_i^* \mathcal{X}_i (1+r)^{-i}}.$$

An example where the price level Q_k follows the Wilkie model is shown in Figure 15.12 with the cash flow on the left and duration on the right. Inflation is important (that was seen in Figure 15.4 too). Here duration is shifted upwards up to 15 years compared with the curve in Figure 15.10.

When liabilities are influenced by inflation, the future cash flow $Q_{k+1}\mathcal{X}_{k+1}$, $Q_{k+2}\mathcal{X}_{k+2}, \dots$ is no longer known at T_k even if $\mathcal{X}_{k+1}, \mathcal{X}_{k+2}, \dots$ still are, and to define the status of the portfolio we are forced (as in Section 11.6) to take a stand on accounting. One solution is to use the current *known* price level Q_k instead of the future *unknown* $Q_{k+1}, Q_{k+2}, \dots$. The net asset value at T_k is then

$$\underset{}{\mathcal{B}_k} = \underset{\text{equity}}{V_{1k}} + \underset{\text{cash}}{V_{2k}} + \underset{\text{bonds}}{V_{3k}} - \underset{\text{liabilities}}{Q_k \mathcal{PV}_{xk}}$$

where $\mathcal{PV}_{xk}$ is calculated as above. The new issue is whether it is possible to force assets to follow growth and uncertainty in future price levels *and* fluctuations in discounting schemes. Simulation experiments can be implemented as in Algorithm 15.9. If you do not want inflation included, insert $Q_k^* = 1$ everywhere.

The example in Figure 15.11 right is redone in Figure 15.13 with liabilities

Algorithm 15.9 Net asset values with inflation

Input: v_0, w_{10}, $\mathcal{X}_0, \dots, \mathcal{X}_K$, Wilkie asset model
For $k = 1, \dots, K$ do
  Generate I_k^*, I_k^{d*}, y_k^*, $\bar{r}_k(K)^*$, F_k^* *%Through Algorithms 13.2–13.4*
  $Q_k^* \leftarrow (1 + I_k^*)Q_{k-1}^*$, $D^* \leftarrow (1 + I_k^{d*})D^*$ *%Price level, dividend*
  $V_{1k}^* \leftarrow D_k^*/y_k^*$, $r^* \leftarrow F_k^*\bar{r}_k(K)^*$ *%Value of equity and the short rate*
  Compute $\bar{r}_k(j)^*$, $j = 1, \dots, J$ *%By interpolation between r_k^* and $r_k(K)^*$*
  $C^* \leftarrow \mathcal{X}_{k+J}/\{1 + \bar{r}_k(J)^*\}^J$ *%$\mathcal{X}_k = 0$ if $k > K$*
  $V_{2k}^* \leftarrow (1 + r_k^*)V_{2k-1}^* + D^* - C^*$ *%The cash account*
  $S^* \leftarrow 0$ *%Liabilities minus bonds*
  For $j > J$ do $S^* \leftarrow S^* + \mathcal{X}_{k+j}/\{1 + \bar{r}_k(j)^*\}^j$ *when inflation is ignored*
    $\mathcal{B}_k^* \leftarrow V_{1k}^* + V_{2k}^* - Q_k^* S^*$ *%Net assets*
Return $\mathcal{B}_1^*, \dots, \mathcal{B}_K^*$.

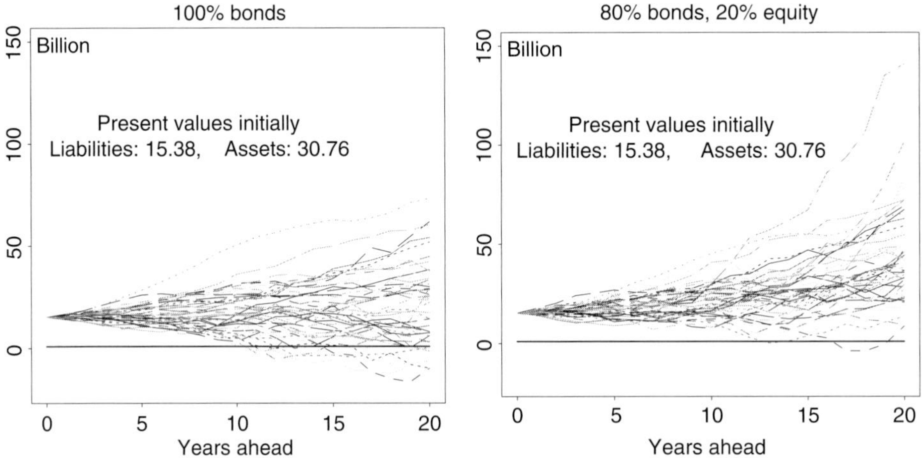

Figure 15.13 Simulated net asset value scenarios (50) with liabilities influenced by inflation using bonds only (*left*) and 20% equity (*right*). Bonds available: Up to 30 years.

linked to the price level. Bonds up to 30 years were assumed available in sufficient quantity. The initial capital to fund the scheme was raised more than 60%, but this is not enough to avoid negative numbers in some scenarios in Figure 15.13. Switching to equity must provide better protection against inflation if the Wilkie model is to be believed. Using a fixed 20% weight on shares (no rebalance cost) leads to the simulated scenarios in Figure 15.13 right, where negative net assets have now become rarer.

15.7 Mathematical arguments

15.7.1 Present values and duration

Elementary differentiation of (15.25) yields

$$\frac{\partial \mathcal{PV}_x(r)}{\partial r} = -\sum_{k=0}^{K} k \frac{\mathcal{X}_k}{(1+r)^{k-1}} = -\frac{1+r}{T}\sum_{k=0}^{K} T_k \frac{\mathcal{X}_k}{(1+r)^k}$$

since $T_k = kT$. Dividing by $\mathcal{PV}_x(r)$ on both sides implies that

$$\frac{\partial \log\{\mathcal{PV}_x(r)\}}{\partial r} = -\frac{1+r}{T}\sum_{k=0}^{K} T_k q_{xk}(r)$$

where

$$q_{xk}(r) = \frac{\mathcal{X}_k(1+r)^{-k}}{\sum_{i=0}^{K}\mathcal{X}_i(1+r)^{-i}}.$$

The probabilities $q_{xk}(r)$ are those in (15.26) and

$$\frac{\partial \log(\mathcal{PV}_x(r))}{\partial r} = -\frac{1+r}{T}\mathcal{D}_x(r),$$

as claimed in (15.27).

15.7.2 Reddington immunization

The argument rests on the Taylor series of the function

$$\log\left(\frac{\mathcal{PV}_v(r)}{\mathcal{PV}_x(r)}\right) = \log\{\mathcal{PV}_v(r)\} - \log\{\mathcal{PV}_x(r)\}$$

which is approximated through

$$\log\left(\frac{\mathcal{PV}_v(r)}{\mathcal{PV}_x(r)}\right) \doteq \log\left(\frac{\mathcal{PV}_v(r_0)}{\mathcal{PV}_x(r_0)}\right) + a_1(r-r_0) + \frac{1}{2}a_2(r-r_0)^2$$

where a_1 and a_2 are derivatives of the log-ratio at $r = r_0$. Since the durations were assumed equal,

$$a_1 = \frac{\partial \log\{\mathcal{PV}_v(r_0)\}}{\partial r} - \frac{\partial \log\{\mathcal{PV}_x(r_0)\}}{\partial r} = -\frac{1+r}{T}\mathcal{D}_v(r) + \frac{1+r}{T}\mathcal{D}_x(r) = 0$$

and the linear term disappears. To calculate a_2 note that

$$\frac{\partial \log\{\mathcal{PV}_v(r)\}}{\partial r} = \frac{\partial \mathcal{PV}_v(r)}{\partial r}\frac{1}{\mathcal{PV}_v(r)},$$

and when differentiated a second time

$$\frac{\partial^2 \log\{\mathcal{PV}_v(r_0)\}}{\partial r^2} = \frac{\partial^2 \mathcal{PV}_v(r_0)}{\partial r^2}\frac{1}{\mathcal{PV}_v(r_0)} - \left(\frac{\partial \log\{\mathcal{PV}_v(r_0)\}}{\partial r}\right)^2.$$

Here

$$\frac{\partial^2 \mathcal{PV}_v(r_0)}{\partial r^2} = \sum_{k=0}^{K} k(k-1)\frac{\mathcal{V}_k}{(1+r_0)^{k-2}} = \sum_{k=0}^{K} k^2\frac{\mathcal{V}_k}{(1+r_0)^{k-2}} - \sum_{k=0}^{K} k\frac{\mathcal{V}_k}{(1+r_0)^{k-2}}$$

after splitting the sum in two parts. This can be written in terms of duration and convexity. A small calculation shows that

$$\frac{\partial^2 \mathcal{PV}_v(r_0)}{\partial r^2} = \frac{(1+r_0)^2}{T^2}\{C_v(r_0) - T\mathcal{D}_v(r_0)\}\mathcal{PV}_v(r_0)$$

where

$$C_v(r_0) = \sum_{k=0}^{K} q_{vk}(r_0)T_k^2.$$

Hence

$$\frac{\partial^2 \log\{\mathcal{PV}_v(r_0)\}}{\partial r^2} = \frac{(1+r_0)^2}{T^2}\{C_v(r_0) - T\mathcal{D}_v(r_0) - \mathcal{D}_v(r_0)^2\}$$

and by analogy

$$\frac{\partial^2 \log\{\mathcal{PV}_x(r_0)\}}{\partial r^2} = \frac{(1+r_0)^2}{T^2}\{C_x(r_0) - T\mathcal{D}_x(r_0) - \mathcal{D}_x(r_0)^2\}.$$

Their difference is the coefficient a_2, and since the durations cancel

$$a_2 = \frac{\partial^2 \log\{\mathcal{PV}_v(r_0)\}}{\partial r^2} - \frac{\partial^2 \log\{\mathcal{PV}_x(r_0)\}}{\partial r^2} = \frac{(1+r_0)^2}{T^2}\{C_v(r_0) - C_x(r_0)\},$$

or by (15.28) right

$$a_2 = \frac{(1+r_0)^2}{T^2}\{\tau_v^2(r_0) + \mathcal{D}_v^2(r_0) - \tau_x^2(r_0) - \mathcal{D}_x^2(r_0\} = \frac{(1+r_0)^2}{T^2}\{\tau_v^2(r_0) - \tau_x^2(r_0)\}$$

so that

$$\log\left(\frac{\mathcal{PV}_v(r)}{\mathcal{PV}_x(r)}\right) \doteq \log\left(\frac{\mathcal{PV}_v(r_0)}{\mathcal{PV}_x(r_0)}\right) + \frac{(1+r_0)^2}{2T^2}\{\tau_v^2(r_0) - \tau_x^2(r_0)\}(r-r_0)^2$$

which yields (15.30).

15.8 Bibliographical notes

15.8.1 Survival modelling

Adverse selection lowers mortalities in pension portfolios compared with the average. Quantitative assessments are offered in Mitchell and McCarthy (2002) and Finkelstein and Poterba (2002); see also De Jong and Ferris (2006) and Valdez *et al.* (2006) for contributions to actuarial method. Pension obligations might be underestimated by future decline in mortalities. An improvement of the simplistic treatment in Section 15.2 was proposed by Lee and Carter (1992). The mortality in age l at a future time k is now

$$q_{lk} = q_{l0}\omega_l^{Y_k},$$

with ω_l fixed, age-dependent factors and $\{Y_k\}$ a stochastic process for which $Y_0 = 0$, often a random walk; see, for example, Tuljapurkar *et al.* (2000). The Lee–Carter model is used for mortality projections in Wang and Lu (2005) and Renshaw and Haberman (2003a,b). For extensions of the original version, consult Renshaw and Haberman (2003a), Koissi *et al.* (2006) and De Jong and Tickle (2006). Other dynamic models for mortalities are presented in Pitacco (2004), Schrager (2006) and Cairns *et al.* (2011). Valuation and hedging within such models (in the manner of Chapter 14) is discussed in Milevsky and Promislow (2001), Dahl (2004) and Cairns *et al.* (2006).

15.8.2 Fair values

Section 15.3 demonstrated how financial issues like inflation and market valuation are entered into present value calculations through extended discount sequences $\{d_k\}$. The first to suggest market discounts in insurance may have been Brennan and Schwartz (1976). Other references are Babbel *et al.* (2002) and Ballotta *et al.* (2006) which offer a discussion of the consequences for reserving and solvency; see also Wütrich *et al.* (2010).

15.8.3 Financial risk and ALM

The last three sections dealt with simulation of asset portfolios over a long time, with liabilities added in Section 15.6. Monte Carlo algorithms connect basic procedures from earlier parts of the book and are fairly straightforward to develop. A more challenging issue is planning and strategy. An early contribution in insurance is Reddington (1952), who pointed out that liability risk may be immunized through portfolios of bonds. A simple version of that idea was presented in Section 15.6, but there is more in chapter 3 of Panjer (1998); see also Hürlimann

(2002) and Gajek (2005). Many optimal investment plans have also been conceived through simplified models allowing exact mathematical solutions. Owadally and Haberman (1999), Owadally (2003) and Leippold *et al.* (2004), as well as Djehiche and Hörfelt (2005), make use of discrete-time modelling, but the main thrust is currently through diffusions and stochastic differential equations. Papers in insurance or finance are Nordberg (1999), Cairns (2000b), Sbaraglia *et al.* (2003), Gerber and Shiu (2003), Rudolf and Ziemba (2004), Josa-Fombellida and Rincón-Zapatero (2006) and Chiu and Li (2006), but even operations research journals contain contributions, for example Papi and Sbaraglia (2006) and Josa-Fombellida and Rincón-Zapatero (2008).

15.8.4 Stochastic dynamic optimization

Finally, there is a growing literature on optimal investments in models where asset and liability cash flows are *not* being simplified through models of the diffusion type. Much of this is found in operations research. Asset and liability scenarios are now laid out by Monte Carlo. This is a guarantee for high generality, but it also takes us into the realm of stochastic, dynamic optimization, computationally much more demanding than ordinary dynamic optimization used in several of the preceding papers. A good way to start may be to read the elegant paper by Hilli *et al.* (2007). Other principally applied studies are Kouwenberg (2001), Fleten *et al.* (2002), Konthoghiorges *et al.* (2002) and Krokhmal *et al.* (2002). For more algorithmic contributions consult Rockafeller and Uryasev (2000), Gondzio and Kouwenberg (2001), Berkelaar *et al.* (2002), Butenko *et al.* (2005) and Krokhmal and Uryasev (2007). Stochastic dynamic optimization is an area in computational infancy, and its promise is untested, although Hilli *et al.* (2007) reports good performance compared with more conventional investment plans.

15.9 Exercises

Section 15.2

Exercise 15.1 Consider mortality data with z_l the number of dead within 1 year among n_l individuals at age l for $l = l_1, \ldots, l_2$ and suppose $n_l = c/(1 + e^{\gamma|l-l_m|})$ with c determined so that $n_{l_1} + \cdots + n_{l_2} = N$.

(a) Write a program generating m_b replications of such data when the true mortalities are $q_l = 1 - \exp(-\theta_0 - \theta_1 e^{\theta_2 l})$.

R-*commands*:

```
ll=l1:l2; n=1/(1+exp(γ*abs(ll-lm))); c=N/sum(n);
n=ceiling(c*n);
```

q=1-exp(- θ_0 - θ_1 *exp(θ_2 *ll));
Z=matrix(rbinom(m_b *(l_2 - l_1 +1),n,q), l_2 - l_1 +1, m_b).

(b) Compute the non-parametric estimates $\hat{q}_l = z_l/n_l$.

R-*commands*:

$\hat{q}$=Z/n.

(c) Run the programs when $\theta_0 = 0.00031$, $\theta_1 = 0.000022$, $\theta_2 = 0.10$, $m_b = 20$, $N = 100\,000$, $l_1 = 20$, $l_2 = 100$, $\gamma = 0.14$ and $l_m = 50$ and plot $\hat{q}_l$ against l for all the estimates jointly with the true probabilities added.

R-*commands*:

matplot(ll, $\hat{q}$,''l''); lines(ll,q,lwd=4).

(d) Redo (c) when $N = 10\,000$ and $1\,000\,000$.

Exercise 15.2

(a) Fit the Gomperz–Makeham model to the historical data in Exercise 15.1.

R-*commands*:

With n and Z given, use the R-function gompmakfit1 and
$\hat{q}$=matrix(0, l_2 - l_1 +1, m_b) for (i in 1: m_b)
{ $\hat{\theta}$ =gompmakfit1($l_1 : l_2$,n,Z[,i])\$ θ ;
$\hat{q}$ [,i]=1-exp(- $\hat{\theta}$ [1]- $\hat{\theta}$ [2]*exp($\hat{\theta}$ [3]*(l_1 : l_2)))}.

(b) Run the program under the conditions in Exercise 15.1(c) and plot the fitted Gomperz–Makeham probabilities against age with the true values added.

R-*commands*:

As in Exercise 15.1(c).

(c) Redo when $N = 10\,000$ and $1\,000\,000$ and summarize the changes from Exercise 15.1.

Exercise 15.3

(a) Write a program converting the estimated mortalities in Exercise 15.1 to estimates of the life tables ${}_kp_{l_0}$ for $k = 0, 1, \ldots, l_2 - l_0 + 1$ with l_0 given.

R-*commands*:

Take $\hat{q}$ from Exercise 15.1 and use
${}_k\hat{p}$ =apply(1- $\hat{q}$ [l_0 : l_2 - l_1 +1,],2,cumprod); ${}_k\hat{p}$ =rbind(rep(1, m_b), ${}_k\hat{p}$).

(b) Run the program under the conditions in Exercise 15.1(c) when $l_0 = 30$ and plot the estimated life tables jointly with the true one.

R-*commands*:

matplot(0:(l_2 - l_0 +1), ${}_k\hat{p}$,''l''); q=1-exp(- θ_0 - θ_1 *exp(θ_2 *(l_0 : l_2)));
${}_kp$ =c(1,cumprod(1-q)); lines(0:(l_2 - l_0 +1), ${}_kp$,lwd=4).

(c) Redo when there are $N = 10\,000$ and $1\,000\,000$ individuals.

Exercise 15.4

(a) Write a program computing the estimated life tables for the Gomperz–Makeham fit in Exercise 15.2.

R-*commands*:

As in Exercise 15.3(a) with the input vector $\hat{q}$ from Exercise 15.2.

(b) Plot as in Exercise 15.3(b).

R-*commands*:

Those in Exercise 15.3(b).

(c) Redo (b) with $N = 10\,000$ and $1\,000\,000$ and compare estimation errors with those in the preceding exercise.

Exercise 15.5 One-time premia π_{l_0} are the cost of a pension for an individual at age l_0; see Exercise 12.1.

(a) Write a program computing estimates $\hat{\pi}_{l_0}$ under the estimated mortalities in Exercise 15.1 when l_0 varies between l_1 and l_2.

R-*commands*:

With $\hat{q}$ as in Exercise 15.1(b), use the R-function `onetimeprem` (identical to `e1227a` in Chapter 12) and

```
π̂=matrix(0,l2-l1+2,mb);
for (i in 1:mb) π̂[,i]=onetimeprem(q̂[,i],s,lr-l1,d)$π.
```

(b) Run the program under the conditions in Exercise 15.1(c) when $s = 1$, $l_r = 65$ and $d = 0.97$, and plot the estimated one-time premia against l_0 with those under the true model added.

R-*commands*:

```
matplot(l1:(l2+1),π̂,''l''); q=1-exp(-θ0-θ1*exp(θ2*(l1:l2)));
π=onetimeprem(q,s,lr-l1,d)$π; lines(l1:(l2+1),π,lwd=4).
```

(c) Redo (b) when $N = 10\,000$ and $1\,000\,000$.

Exercise 15.6

(a) Write a program computing one-time premia under the Gomperz–Makeham mortality estimates in Exercise 15.2.

R-*commands*:

As in Exercise 15.5(a) with $\hat{q}$ from Exercise 15.2(b).

(b) Plot the estimated one-time premia now.

R-*commands*:

Those in Exercise 15.5(b).

(c) Redo (b) when $N = 10\,000$ and $1\,000\,000$ and compare with the errors in Exercise 15.5.

Exercise 15.7 Let $q'_l = \zeta_l q_l$ be mortalities differing from a country average q_l through $\zeta_l = (1 + e^{-g_l})^{-1}$ where $g_l = \beta_0 + \beta_1(l - 20) + \beta_2(l - 20)^2$ with estimates $\beta_0 = 1.340, \beta_1 = -0.099$ and $\beta_2 = 0.00235$ for a European company.

(a) Plot the fitted $\hat{\zeta}_l$ for l between $l_1 = 20$ and $l_2 = 105$ and notice the shape.

R-*commands*:

```
ll=l₁:l₂; g=β₀+β₁*(ll-20)+β₂*(ll-20)**2;
ζ=1/(1+exp(-g)); plot(ll,ζ).
```

(b) Let $s = 1$, $d = 0.97$, $l_r = 65$ and q_l as in Exercise 15.1 and compare the one-time premia π_{l_0} under q_l and q'_l by plotting the evaluations jointly for l_0 between $l_1 = 20$ and $l_2 = 105$.

R-*commands*:

Take `q` from Exercise 15.1(b) and the R-function `onetimeprem` and use

```
π=onetimeprem(q,s,lr-l₁,d)$π; π'=onetimeprem(q*ζ,s,lr-l₁,d)$π;
matplot(l₁:(l₂+1),cbind(π,π'),''l'').
```

Exercise 15.8 Stress tests on mortalities typically impose flat cuts independent of l.

(a) Redo Exercise 15.7(b) when $\zeta_l = 0.85$ for all l.

R-*commands*:

As in Exercise 15.7(b).

(b) What about the difference between the two evaluations now, compared with what it was in Exercise 15.7?

Exercise 15.9 The model due to Lee and Carter (1992) describes dynamic changes in how long people live. A simplified version takes the mortality of an individual at age l in year k as

$$q_{lk} = \omega_l^k q_{l0},$$

where

$$\log(\omega_l) = -\alpha \frac{e^{g_l}}{(1 + e^{g_l})^2} \quad \text{and} \quad g_l = \beta_0 + \beta_1 l + \beta_2 l^2$$

with parameter estimates for Norway for the last part of the twentieth century being $\alpha = 0.0505, \beta_0 = 5.192, \beta_1 = -0.202$ and $\beta_2 = 0.0018$.

(a) Write a program tabulating ω_l when l varies between l_1 and l_2.

R-*commands*:

```
ll=l₁:l₂; g=β₀+β₁*ll+β₂*ll**2;
ω=exp(-α*exp(g)/(1+exp(g))**2).
```

(b) Run the program for the Norwegian parameters when $l_1 = 20$, $l_2 = 110$ and plot the reduction factors ω_l^k against l when $k = 5$, 10 and 50.

R-*commands*:

```
k=c(5,10,50); fac=cbind(ω**k[1], ω**k[2], ω**k[3]);
matplot(l1:l2,fac,''l'').
```

Exercise 15.10 Let q_{l0} in Exercise 15.9 be the Gomperz–Makeham probabilities in Exercise 15.1.

(a) Write a program tabulating q_{lk} for $0 \leq l \leq l_2$ and $0 \leq k \leq K$.

R-*commands*:

With ω from Exercise 15.9, use `q0=1-exp(-θ0-θ1*exp(θ2*(0:l2)));`
`qk=exp(log(ω)%o%(0:K))*q0.`

(b) Run the program with $\theta_0, \theta_1, \theta_2$ and $\alpha;\beta_0,\beta_1,\beta_2$ in Exercises 15.1 and 15.9, $l_2 = 110$ and $K = 50$ and compute/plot the expected length of life E_k under q_{lk}.

R-*commands*:

Draw on Algorithm 12.1 and use `kpk=apply(1-qk,2,cumprod);`
`Ek=0.5+apply(kpk,2,sum); plot(0:K,Ek).`

Exercise 15.11

(a) Write a program evaluating one-time premia π_{l_0} for $l_1 \leq l_0 \leq l_2$ with Lee–Carter reduction in mortalities taken into account when the pension stops at l_2.

R-*commands*:

With qk from Exercise 15.10 and l_r and d retirement age and discount, use

```
π=rep(0,l2-l1+1); for (l0 in l1:l2){K=l2-l0;
q=diag(qk[l0+1+0:K,1+0:K]); kp=c(1,cumprod(1-q));
kr=max(lr-l0,0); π[l0-l1+1]=sum(d**(kr:K)*kp[kr:K+1])}.
```

(b) Run the program under the conditions in Exercise 15.10 when $l_1 = 20$ and $l_2 = 110$ and plot π_{l_0} against l_0.

R-*commands*:

```
plot(l1:l2,π,''l'').
```

(c) Rerun (b) when $\alpha = 0$ (so that $q_{lk} = q_{l0}$ for all k) and plot the one-time premia jointly with (b).

R-*commands*:

```
lines(l1:l2,π,''l'').
```

(d) Interpret the difference between (b) and (c).

Section 15.3

Exercise 15.12 Let $d_k = P(r_0, T_k)$ where $P(r_0, T_k)$ is the Vasiček bond price in Table 15.4.

(a) Write a program generating m Monte Carlo scenarios of $d_0, \ldots, d_K$ when $r_0 = \xi e^{-\sigma_x^2/2+X}$ with $X \sim N(0, \sigma_x)$.

R-*commands*:

Use the R-function `vasicekP` (similar to `e616a` in Chapter 6) with `X=rnorm(m); `r_0`=`ξ`*exp(-`σ_x`**2/2+`σ_x`*X);` `d=vasicekP(K,`ξ_q`,`σ_q`,`a_q`,`r_0`)$P`.

(b) Run the program when $m = 50$, $K = 50$, $\xi_q = 0.04$, $\sigma_q = 0.012$, $a_q = 0.5$, $\xi = 0.04$ and $\sigma = 0.5$ and plot the discounts jointly against k.

R-*commands*:

`matplot(0:K,d,''l'')`.

Exercise 15.13 Introduce liabilities $\mathcal{X}_k = ce^{-\gamma|k-k_m|}$ for $k = 0, \ldots, K$ with c determined by $\mathcal{X}_0 + \cdots + \mathcal{X}_K = \mathcal{S}$ for $\mathcal{S}$ given.

(a) Write a program storing the liabilities.

R-*commands*:

`X=exp(-`γ`*abs(0:K-`k_m`)); X=X*`$\mathcal{S}$`/sum(X)`.

(b) Simulate their present value for the discounts in Exercise 15.12.

R-*commands*:

With `d` from Exercise 15.12(a) use `PV=apply(X*d,2,sum)`.

(c) Generate $m = 10\,000$ simulations of the present value when $K = 50$, $\mathcal{S} = 1000$, $\gamma = 0.1$ and $k_m = 10$ with other conditions as in Exercise 15.12, compute the mean and standard deviation and plot the density function.

R-*commands*:

`Mean=mean(PV); Sd=sd(PV); plot(density(PV))`.

(d) Redo when $k_m = 20$ to see what happens when the liabilities are longer into the future.

Exercise 15.14 Consider the liabilities in Exercise 15.13 and let $\mathcal{PV}_{xk}$ be the present value of $\mathcal{X}_k, \ldots, \mathcal{X}_K$.

(a) Write a program generating m simulations of $\mathcal{PV}_{x0}, \ldots, \mathcal{PV}_{xK}$ under Vasiček discounts with the Black–Karasinski model for $r_0, \ldots, r_K$.

R-*commands*:

With `X` from Exercise 15.13 and R-function `blackkar` (same as `e535a` in Chapter 5), use `r=blackkar(m,K,`ξ`,`σ`,a,`r_0`)$r; PV=matrix(0,K+1,m); for (k in 0:K){d=vasicekP(K-k,`ξ_q`,`σ_q`,`a_q`,r[k+1,])$P; PV[k+1,]=apply(X[k:K+1]*d,2,sum)}`.

(b) Draw $m = 50$ simulations of the present values when $K = 50$, $\mathcal{S} = 1000$, $\gamma = 0.1$, $k_m = 10$, $\xi_q = 0.04$, $\sigma_q = 0.012$, $a_q = 0.5$ with $\xi = 0.04$, $\sigma = 0.5$, $a = 0.5$ and $r_0 = 0.03$ in the Black–Karasinski model and plot the simulated present values jointly against time.

R-*commands*:

```
matplot(0:K,PV,''l'')
```

(c) Redo when $k_m = 20$ and note the change.

Exercise 15.15 Suppose what's actually paid in Exercise 15.14 is $Q_0\mathcal{X}_0, \dots, Q_K\mathcal{X}_K$ with Q_k the price level.

(a) Write a program generating m simulations of these inflated liabilities under the Wilkie inflation model in Exercise 13.28.

R-*commands*:

With `X` from Exercise 15.13 and R-function `wilkieinflation`, use

```
I=wilkieinflation(m,K,ξ^i,σ^i,a^i)$I;
Q=apply(1+I[1:K+1,],2,cumprod);
Q=rbind(rep(1,m),Q); X=X*Q.
```

(b) Let $\xi^i = 0.03$, $\sigma^i = 0.015$ and $a^i = 0.58$ in the inflation model and draw $m = 50$ simulated sequences of these payments under the conditions in Exercise 15.14 and plot them against time.

R-*commands*:

```
matplot(0:K;X;''l'').
```

(c) Redo (b) for the Wilkie parameters $\xi^i = 0.048$ and $\sigma^i = 0.04$.

Exercise 15.16

(a) Write a program simulating present values under the inflation model in Exercise 15.15 when using the discounts in Exercise 15.12.

R-*commands*:

With `d` and `X` in Exercises 15.12 and 15.15 use `PV=apply(d*X,2,sum)`.

(b) Run the program when $m = 10\,000$ under the conditions in earlier exercises, compute the mean and standard deviation of the present value and plot its density function.

R-*commands*:

```
Mean=mean(PV); Sd=sd(PV); plot(density(PV)).
```

Exercise 15.17

(a) Reprogram the present value simulations in Exercise 15.16 under a fixed discount d.

R-*commands*:

With `X` as before use `PV=apply(d**(0:K)*X,2,sum)`.

(b) Let $d = 0.96$ (close to the average discount in Exercise 15.16), compute the mean and standard deviation of the present value and plot its density function.

R-*commands*:

```
Mean=mean(PV); Sd=sd(PV);
plot(density(PV)).
```

(c) Why do the results vary so little from those in Exercise 15.16?

Section 15.4

Exercise 15.18 Let $R = e^{\xi+\sigma\varepsilon} - 1$ be a log-normal equity return and $R_H = (\max(R, r_g) - \pi)/(1+\pi)$ the net return when a put option is used.

(a) If $r'_g = (r_g - \pi)/(1+\pi)$ and $\Phi(x)$ the standard normal integral, show that

$$\Pr(R_H = r'_g) = \Phi\left(\frac{\log(1+r_g) - \xi}{\sigma}\right) \quad \text{and}$$

$$\Pr(R_H > r) = 1 - \Phi\left(\frac{\log\{(1+r)(1+\pi)\} - \xi}{\sigma}\right), \quad r > r'_g.$$

(b) Determine the density function of R_H by differentiating the second expression.

Exercise 15.19

(a) Argue that $R_H > R$ in the preceding exercise if and only if $R < r'_g$, where $r'_g = (r_g - \pi)/(1+\pi)$.

(b) Tabulate the probability that the option improves the result when $\xi = 0.06$, $\sigma = 0.25$, $r = 0.03$ and $r_g = 0, 0.04, 0.08$ and 0.12.

R-*commands*:

Use R-function `putprem` (copy of `e323a`) with r_g`=c(0,0.04,0.08,0.12);`
π`=putprem(`σ`,`r_g`,r,T=1,`v_0`=1)$`π`;` r'_g`=(`r_g`-`π`)/(1+`π`);`
`Pr=pnorm((log(1+`r'_g`)-`ξ`)/`σ`).`

(c) Redo (b) when $\xi = 0$; why are the probabilities higher now?

Exercise 15.20 Let $R_1, \dots, R_K$ be ordinary returns on equity and $R_{H1}, \dots, R_{HK}$ returns under a put option so that $R_{Hk} = (\max(R_k, r_g) - \pi)/(1+\pi)$.

(a) Write a program generating m realizations of $R_{H1}, \dots, R_{HK}$ when ξ, σ, r_g, r and π are fixed and $T = 1$.

R-*commands*:

With R-function `putprem`, use π=`putprem(`σ`,`r_g`,r,T=1,`v_0`=1)$`π`;`
`R=matrix(rlnorm(m*K,`ξ`,`σ`),K,m)-1;` R_H`=(pmax(R,`r_g`)-`π`)/(1+`π`).`

(b) Simulate accumulated returns $R_{0:0},\dots,R_{0:K}$ under the put option.

R-*commands*:

`R0K=apply(1+`R_H`,2,cumprod)-1; R0K=rbind(rep(0,m),R0K).`

(c) Run the program when $m = 100$, $K = 20$, $\xi = 0.06$, $\sigma = 0.25$, $r_g = 0.04$ and $r = 0.03$ and plot the accumulated returns jointly.

R-*commands*:

`matplot(0:K,R0K,''l'').`

(d) Redo (c) when $r_g = -0.99999$ (removing the option) and examine the change.

Exercise 15.21

(a) Redo Exercise 15.20(c) when $m = 10\,000$ and $K = 5$, compute the mean and standard deviation of $R_{0:K}$ and plot its density function.

R-*commands*:

With `R0K` from Exercise 15.20 use $R_{0:K}$`=R0K[K+1,]; Mean=mean(`$R_{0:K}$`);`
`Sd=sd(`$R_{0:K}$`); plot(density(`$R_{0:K}$`),''l'').`

(b) Redo (a) when $r_g = -0.99999$ and summarize how the option strategy has influenced the risk.

(c) Redo (a) and (b) when $\xi = 0.02$ and compare with the earlier results.

Exercise 15.22 Let V_k^{sw} be the value at time k of a cash account under a receiver swap with the initial value $V_0^{\text{sw}} = v_0$ as notational, so that $V_k^{\text{sw}} = (1 + r_k)V_{k-1}^{\text{sw}} + (f_0 - r_k)v_0$ for $k = 1,\dots,K$.

(a) Write a program generating m simulations of $V_0^{\text{sw}},\dots,V_K^{\text{sw}}$ and also of an ordinary account $V_1,\dots,V_K$ when $r_0,\dots,r_K$ follow the Black–Karasinski model.

R-*commands*:

With R-function `blackkar`, use `r=blackkar(m,K,`ξ`,`σ`,a,`r_0`)$r;`
`V=matrix(`v_0`,K+1,m);` V^{sw}`=V;`
`for (k in 1:K+1){V[k,]=(1+r[k,])*V[k-1,];`
V^{sw}`[k,]=(1+r[k,])*`V^{sw}`[k-1,]+(`f_0`-r[k,])*`v_0`}.`

(b) Run the program when $m = 100$, $K = 20$, $\xi = 0.03$, $\sigma = 0.25$, $a = 0.7$, $r_0 = 0.03$, $f_0 = 0.03$ and $v_0 = 1$ and plot the ratios V_k^{sw}/V_k against k for all the simulated scenarios jointly.

R-*commands*:

`matplot(0:K,`V^{sw}`/V,''l'').`

Exercise 15.23

(a) Redo Exercise 15.22 when $m = 10\,000$ and $K = 10$, compute the mean and standard deviation of $V_K^{\rm sw}/V_K$, and plot its density function.

R-*commands*:

With $V^{\rm sw}$ and V as in Exercise 15.22, use `ratio=`$V^{\rm sw}$`[K+1,]/V[K+1,];` `Mean=mean(ratio); Sd=sd(ratio); plot(density(ratio),''l'')`.

(b) Redo (a) when $f_0 = 0.035$ (higher than ξ) and $f_0 = 0.025$ (lower than ξ) and examine the impact on the ratio.

Exercise 15.24 Let $V_k^{\rm fl}$ be the value at time k of a cash account protected by a floor agreement paid for at the beginning. Then $V_k^{\rm fl} = (1 + r_k)V_{k-1}^{\rm fl} + \max(r_g - r_k, 0)v_0/(1 + \pi)$ for $k = 1, \dots, K$ with $V_0^{\rm fl} = v_0/(1 + \pi)$.

(a) Write a program generating m simulations of $V_0^{\rm fl}, \dots, V_K^{\rm fl}$ and of an ordinary account $V_1, \dots, V_K$ when $r_0, \dots, r_K$ follow the Black–Karasinski model.

R-*commands*:

Let `r=blackkar(m,K,`ξ`,`σ`,a,`r_0`)$r` as in Exercise 15.22 and use
`V=matrix(`v_0`,K+1,m);` $V^{\rm fl}$`=V/(1+`π`);`
`for (k in 1:K+1){V[k,]=(1+r[k,])*V[k-1,];`
$V_k^{\rm fl}$`[k,]=(1+r[k,])*`$V_k^{\rm fl}$`[k-1,]+pmax(`r_g`-r[k,],0)*`v_0`/(1+`π`)}`.

(b) Run the program when $m = 100$, $K = 10$, $\xi = 0.04$, $\sigma = 0.25$, $a = 0.7$, $r_0 = 0.04$, $r_g = 0.04$, $\pi = 0.0378$ and $v_0 = 1$ and plot the ratios $V^{\rm fl}/V$ against k for all the simulated scenarios jointly.

R-*commands*:

`matplot(0:K,`$V^{\rm fl}$`/V,''l'')`.

Exercise 15.25

(a) Redo Exercise 15.24 with $m = 10\,000$ simulations, compute the mean and standard deviation of $V_K^{\rm fl}/V_K$, plot its density function and find out how often the floor strategy is superior.

R-*commands*:

With $V^{\rm fl}$, V as in Exercise 15.24 use `ratio=`$V^{\rm fl}$`[K+1,]/V[K+1,];`
`Mean=mean(ratio);Sd=sd(ratio);plot(density(ratio),''l'');`
`Gain=length(ratio[ratio> 1])/m`.

(b) The premium $\pi = 0.0378$ in Exercise 15.24 was computed by the program in Exercise 14.30, but redo (a) when the market demands the higher premium $\pi = 0.045$ or is content with the lower one $\pi = 0.035$.

Section 15.5

Exercise 15.26 Let $R_1, \ldots, R_K$ be independent equity returns with $E(R_k) = \xi$ and $\text{sd}(R_k) = \sigma$ and consider portfolio returns $\mathcal{R}_k = wR_k + (1-w)r$ with r and w fixed.

(a) Show that the mean of the K-step return $\mathcal{R}_{0:K} = (1+\mathcal{R}_1)\cdots(1+\mathcal{R}_K) - 1$ is

$$E(\mathcal{R}_{0:K}) = (1+e_w)^K - 1 \quad \text{where} \quad e_w = w\xi + (1-w)r.$$

(c) Also show that

$$\text{sd}(\mathcal{R}_{0:K}) = \sqrt{\{w^2\sigma^2 + (1+e_w)^2\}^K - (1+e_w)^{2K}}.$$

[*Hint*: Utilize that $\text{var}(X_1 \cdots X_K) = (\tau^2+\theta^2)^K - \theta^{2K}$ if $X_1 \cdots X_K$ are independent with mean and standard deviation θ and τ.]

Exercise 15.27 Suppose the investment strategy in Exercise 15.26 is changed to buy-and-hold with w the initial weight on equity.

(a) Why is $\mathcal{R}_{0:K} = w(1+R_1)\cdots(1+R_K) + (1-w)(1+r)^K - 1$?
(b) Show that

$$E(\mathcal{R}_{0:K}) = w(1+\xi)^K + (1-w)(1+r)^K - 1.$$

(c) Use an argument resembling that in Exercise 15.27(c) to deduce that

$$\text{sd}(\mathcal{R}_{0:K}) = w\sqrt{\{\sigma^2 + (1+\xi)^2\}^K - (1+\xi)^{2K}}.$$

Exercise 15.28

(a) Prove, under the conditions in the preceding exercises, that expected K-step returns are smaller under a fixed-mix than under buy-and-hold when $0 \le w \le 1$. [*Hint*: Show that $d^2E(\mathcal{R}_{0:K})/dw^2 > 0$ for a fixed-mix and $d^2E(\mathcal{R}_{0:K})/dw^2 = 0$ for buy-and-hold with expected returns equal when $w = 0$ and $w = 1$.]
(b) Establish the same result for volatilities numerically when $\xi \ge r$ by running R-function `e1528b` when $K = 10$, $\sigma = 0.2$, $r = 0.03$ and $\xi = 0.03, 0.05$ and 0.08.

Exercise 15.29 Let $\xi = 0.08$, $\sigma = 0.25$, $r = 0.03$ and $K = 10$ in the preceding exercises.

(a) Plot $E(\mathcal{R}_{0:K})$ against $\text{sd}(\mathcal{R}_{0:K})$ for the fixed-mix strategy when w varies between 0 and 1.

R-*commands*:

```
w=0:100/100; e_w=w*ξ+(1-w)*r; e_fm=(1+e_w)**K-1;
s_fm =(1+e_w)**K*sqrt(((w*σ/(1+e_w))**2+1)**K-1);
plot(e_fm,s_fm,''l'').
```

(b) Redo (a) for buy-and-hold and compare the two strategies through a joint plot.

R-*commands*:

$e_{\rm bh}$=w*(1+ξ)**K+(1-w)*(1+r)**K-1;
$s_{\rm bh}$=w*(1+ξ)**K*sqrt(((σ/(1+ξ))**2+1)**K-1); lines($e_{\rm bh}$,$s_{\rm bh}$).

Exercise 15.30 The R-function equityint returns m simulated sequences of $R_1, \ldots, R_K$ and $r_1, \ldots, r_K$ when $R_k = e^{\xi_1+\sigma_1\varepsilon_{1k}} - 1$ and $r_k = \xi_2 e^{-\sigma_2^2/2+\sigma_2 X_k}$, where $X_k = aX_{k-1} + \sqrt{1-a^2}\varepsilon_{2k}$ and $X_0 = \log(r_0/\xi_2)/\sigma_2 + \sigma_2/2$. Error terms are $N(0,1)$ and independent except for $\rho = \text{cor}(\varepsilon_{1k}, \varepsilon_{2k})$.

(a) Write a program generating m simulations of the accumulated portfolio returns $\mathcal{R}_{0:1}, \ldots, \mathcal{R}_{0:K}$ under the fixed-mix strategy.

R-*commands*:

o=equityint(m,K,ξ_1,σ_1,ξ_2,σ_2,a,ρ,r_0);
$\mathcal{R}$=apply(1+w*o\$R+(1-w)*o\$r,2,cumprod)-1.

(b) Run the program when $m = 100$, $K = 10$, $\xi_1 = 0.05$, $\sigma_1 = 0.25$, $\xi_2 = 0.04$, $\sigma_2 = 0.25$, $a = 0.6$, $\rho = 0.5$, $r_0 = 0.02$ and $w = 0.5$ and plot the portfolio returns jointly.

R-*commands*:

matplot(1:K,$\mathcal{R}$,''l'').

(c) Rerun the program with $m = 10\,000$ and compute 1, 5, 25, 50, 75, 95, 99% percentiles of $\mathcal{R}_{0:K}$.

R-*commands*:

ind=c(0.01,0.05,0.25,0.50,0.75,0.95,0.99)*m;
q_ϵ=sort($\mathcal{R}$[K,])[ind].

Exercise 15.31

(a) Rewrite the program in Exercise 15.30(a) when the strategy is buy-and-hold.

R-*commands*:

With o\$R and o\$r as in Exercise 15.30 use
R=apply(1+o\$R,2,cumprod)-1; r=apply(1+o\$r,2,cumprod)-1;
$\mathcal{R}$=w*R+(1-w)*r.

(b) Plot $m = 100$ simulated scenarios jointly under the conditions in Exercise 15.30(b).

R-*commands*:

Exercise 15.30(b).

(c) Compute the percentiles of $\mathcal{R}_{0:K}$ for $K = 10$.

R-*commands*:

Those in Exercise 15.30(c).

(d) Compare fixed-mix and buy-and-hold performance.

Exercise 15.32 Assume the model in Exercises 15.30 and 15.31.

(a) Write a program computing $E(\mathcal{R}_{0:K})$ and $\mathrm{sd}(\mathcal{R}_{0:K})$ when w varies between 0 and 1 in a fixed-mix strategy.
R-*commands*:
With o$R and o$r as in Exercise 15.30, use e_{fm}=rep(0,101); s_{fm}=e_{fm}; for (i in 0:100){w=i/100; $\mathcal{R}_{0:K}$=apply(1+w*o$R+(1-w)*o$r,2,prod)-1; e_{fm}[i+1]=mean($\mathcal{R}_{0:K}$); s_{fm}[i+1]=sd($\mathcal{R}_{0:K}$)}.

(b) Rewrite the program for buy-and-hold.
R-*commands*:
w=(0:100)/100; R_{0K}=apply(1+o$R,2,prod)-1; r_{0K}=apply(1+o$r,2,prod)-1; $\mathcal{R}_{0:K}$=w%o%R_{0K}+(1-w)%o%r_{0K}; e_{bh}=apply($\mathcal{R}_{0:K}$,1,mean); s_{bh}=apply($\mathcal{R}_{0:K}$,1,sd).

(c) Run the programs in (a) and (b) under the conditions in Exercise 15.30 and plot $E(\mathcal{R}_{0:K})$ against $\mathrm{sd}(\mathcal{R}_{0:K})$ for both strategies jointly.
R-*commands*:
plot(e_{fm},s_{fm},''l''); lines(e_{bh},s_{bh}).

Exercise 15.33 The CPPI strategy in Section 15.5 was based on a multiplier α and a floor F.

(a) If shorting equity is not allowed, argue that the values $\mathcal{V}_k$ of a cash/equity portfolio under CPPI evolve as

$$w_k = \max(\alpha(1 - F/\mathcal{V}_{k-1}), 0) \quad \text{and} \quad \mathcal{V}_k = \{1 + w_k R_k + (1 - w_k) r_k\}\mathcal{V}_{k-1}$$

for $k = 1, \ldots, K$.

(b) Write a program generating m simulations of $\mathcal{V}_0, \ldots, \mathcal{V}_K$ when $\mathcal{V}_0 = v_0$.
R-*commands*:
With o$R and o$r as in Exercise 15.30 use
V=matrix(v_0,K+1,m); for (k in 1:K){w=pmax(α*(1-F/V[k,]),0); V[k+1,]=(1+w*o$R[k,]+(1-w)*o$r[k,])*V[k,]}.

(c) Run the program under the conditions in Exercise 15.30 when $m = 100$, $v_0 = 1$, $\alpha = 2$ and $F = 0.9$ and plot the portfolio returns jointly against time.
R-*commands*:
$\mathcal{R}$=(V-v_0)/v_0; matplot(0:K,$\mathcal{R}$,''l'').

Exercise 15.34

(a) Run the CPPI program as in Exercise 15.33(c) and scatterplot the portfolio and equity returns $\mathcal{R}_{0:K}$ and $R_{0:K}$ accumulated up to $K = 10$.

R-*commands*:

With v_0, `o$R` and `V` as in Exercise 15.33, use $\mathcal{R}_{0:K}$`=(V[K+1,]-`v_0`)/`v_0`;` $R_{0:K}$`=apply(1+o$R,2,prod)-1; plot(`$\mathcal{R}_{0:K}$`,`$R_{0:K}$`)`.

(b) Interpret the plot.

(c) Run the program when $m = 10\,000$, compute the same percentiles of the portfolio return $\mathcal{R}_{0:K}$ as in Exercises 15.30(c) and 15.31(c) and compare.

R-*commands*:

See Exercise 15.30(c).

Exercise 15.35 Suppose the weight on equity in an equity/cash portfolio is changed from w' to w. If buying/selling stock costs η per money unit, show that the value of the portfolio is reduced by the factor

$$\gamma = \frac{1-\eta w'}{1-\eta w} \text{ if } w \le w' \quad \text{and} \quad \gamma = \frac{1+\eta w'}{1+\eta w} \text{ if } w > w'.$$

[*Hint*: Let V' and $V = \gamma V'$ be the portfolio value before and after the transaction. Argue that the cost is $\eta|w'V' - wV|$, which when added to V yields the equation $\gamma + \eta|w' - w\gamma| = 1$.]

Exercise 15.36 Let $\mathcal{V}_0, \dots, \mathcal{V}_K$ be the values of a fixed-mix equity/cash portfolio after the transaction cost in Exercise 15.35 has been subtracted. If $\mathcal{R}_k = wR_k + (1-w)r_k$ is the portfolio return, argue that $\mathcal{V}_{k-1}$ and $\mathcal{V}_k$ are related through

$$\mathcal{V}_k = \gamma_k(1+\mathcal{R}_k)\mathcal{V}_{k-1}$$

where

$$\gamma_k = \min\left(\frac{1-\eta w_k}{1-\eta w}, \frac{1+\eta w_k}{1+\eta w}\right) \quad \text{and} \quad w_k = \frac{1+R_k}{1+\mathcal{R}_k} w.$$

Exercise 15.37

(a) Write a program generating m simulations of $\mathcal{V}_0, \dots, \mathcal{V}_K$ in Exercise 15.36 when $\mathcal{V}_0 = v_0$.

R-*commands*:

With `o$R` and `o$r` as in Exercise 15.30, use `V=matrix(`v_0`,K+1,m);`
`for (k in 1:K){`$\mathcal{R}_k$`=w*o$R[k,]+(1-w)*o$r[k,];`
w_k`=w*(1+o$R[k,])/(1+`$\mathcal{R}_k$`);`
γ_k`=pmin((1-`η`*`w_k`)/(1-`η`*w),(1+`η`*`w_k`)/(1+`η`*w));`
`V[k+1,]=`γ_k`*(1+`$\mathcal{R}_k$`)*V[k,]}`.

(b) Run the program under the conditions in Exercise 15.30 when $\eta = 0.01$ and $v_0 = 1$ and plot the simulations of the accumulated returns $\mathcal{R}_{0:0}, \dots, \mathcal{R}_{0:K}$ jointly against time.

R-*commands*:

```
R=(V-v0)/v0; matplot(0:K, R,''l'').
```

(c) Any difference from Exercise 15.30?

Exercise 15.38

(a) Write a program generating m simulations of the portfolio value $\mathcal{V}_K$ in Exercise 15.37 for values of w between 0 and 1.

R-*commands*:

With o$R and o$r as before use

```
w=(0:100)/100; VK=matrix(v0,101,m);
for (k in 1:K){Rk=w%o%o$R[k,]+(1-w)%o%o$r[k,];
wk=w%o%(1+o$R[k,])/(1+Rk);
γk=pmin((1-η*wk)/(1-η*w),(1+η*wk)/(1+η*w));
VK=γk*(1+Rk)*VK}.
```

(b) Run the program under the conditions in Exercise 15.30 when $m = 10\,000$, $\eta = 0.01$ and $v_0 = 1$, compute $E(\mathcal{R}_{0:K})$ and $\text{sd}(\mathcal{R}_{0:K})$ for all values of w and plot them against each other.

R-*commands*:

```
efm=apply(VK-1,1,mean); sfm=apply(VK-1,1,sd);
plot(sfm,efm,''l'').
```

(c) Redo when $\eta = 0$ and plot the new curve jointly with the old one.

R-*commands*:

Use `lines(sfm,efm)`.

(d) Any comments?

Section 15.6

Exercise 15.39 Let $\mathcal{PV}_x(r) = \sum_k e^{-rk}\mathcal{X}_k$ be the present value of $\mathcal{X}_0, \dots, \mathcal{X}_K$ under exponential discounts. Calculate $\mathcal{D}_x = -T\partial \log\{\mathcal{PV}_x(r)\}/\partial r$ and argue that it is a duration similar to (15.26).

Exercise 15.40 Consider a portfolio consisting of B_j unit-faced, zero-coupon bonds maturing at $T_j = jT$ for $j = 0, \dots, J$.

(a) Define its duration $\mathcal{D}$.

(b) Show that $\mathcal{D} = JT/2$ if $B_0 = \cdots = B_J$ and $r = 0$.

Exercise 15.41 Let $\mathcal{X}_k = \mathcal{X}_0/(1+\gamma)^k$ for $k = 0, 1, \dots$ be liabilities of infinite time span.

(a) Show

$$\mathcal{PV}_x(r) = \frac{\mathcal{X}_0(1+r)(1+\gamma)}{(1+\gamma)r+\gamma} \quad \text{and} \quad \mathcal{D}_x(r) = \frac{T/(1+r)^2}{(1+\gamma)r+\gamma}.$$

[*Hint*: Use (15.25) and (15.27) and utilize the fact that $1+y+y^2+\cdots = 1/(1-y)$ if $|y| < 1$.]

(b) Why does duration go down with γ?

(c) If a fixed rate of inflation changes the liabilities to $(1+\xi)^k \mathcal{X}_k$, argue that γ must be replaced by $\gamma_\xi = (1+\gamma)/(1+\xi) - 1$ and that duration increases with ξ.

Exercise 15.42 As in Exercise 15.13 let $\mathcal{X}_k = ce^{-\gamma|k-k_m|}$ for $k = 0, \ldots, K$ with c determined so that $\mathcal{X}_0 + \cdots + \mathcal{X}_K = \mathcal{S}$.

(a) Write a program computing the present value of these liabilities under Vasiček discounting.

R-*commands*:

With the R-function vasicekP and X as in Exercise 15.13, use d=vasicekP(K,ξ_q,σ_q,a_q,r_0)\$P; PV=apply(X*d,2,sum).

(b) Run the program when $K = 50$, $\mathcal{S} = 1000$, $\gamma = 0.1$, $k_m = 25$, $\xi_q = 0.04$, $\sigma_q = 0.012$, $a_q = 0.5$ with r_0 varying between 0.005 and 0.25 in steps of 0.005 and plot the present value against r_0.

R-*commands*:

r_0=0.005+(0:49)*0.005; the program in (a); plot(r_0,PV,''l'').

Exercise 15.43 Consider a receiver swaption with expiry at K on a swap from J to L with premium π depending on the guarantee f_g and the volatility σ_K of the swap rate.

(a) Compute π by means of the R-function vasicekP as in Exercise 15.42.

R-*commands*:

d=vasicekP(L,ξ_q,σ_q,a_q,r_0)\$P; S=apply(d[J:L+1,],2,sum);
f_0=(d[J,]-d[L+1,])/S; a_K=(log(f_g/f_0)+σ_K**2/2)/σ_K;
π=S*(f_g*pnorm(a_K)-f_0*pnorm(a_K-σ_K)).

(b) Run the program when $K = 10$, $J = 11$, $L = 20$, $f_g = 0.035$ and $\sigma_K = 0.02$ with r_0 and the rest of the conditions as in Exercise 15.42 and plot π against r_0.

R-*commands*:

plot(r_0,π,''l'').

(c) Redo (b) when $f_g = 0.03$ and $f_g = 0.04$.

(d) Compare with Exercise 15.42 and argue that receiver swaptions may hedge interest-rate risk.

Exercise 15.44 Let $\mathcal{Y}_k = (1 + \mathcal{R}_k)\mathcal{Y}_{k-1} - \mathcal{X}_k$ for $k = 1, \ldots, K$ where $\mathcal{X}_1, \ldots, \mathcal{X}_K$ are the liabilities in Exercise 15.42.

(a) Write a program generating m simulations of $\mathcal{Y}_0, \ldots, \mathcal{Y}_K$ when $\mathcal{R}_1, \ldots, \mathcal{R}_K$ are returns for a fixed-mix strategy in an equity/cash portfolio.

R-*commands*:

With `X` as in Exercise 15.13 and the R-function `equitysim`, use

```
o=equityint(m,K,ξ1,σ1,ξ2,σ2,a,ρ,r0);
R=w*o$R+(1-w)*o$r; Y=matrix(v0,K+1,m);
for (k in 1:K) Y[k+1,]=(1+R[k,])*Y[k,]-X[k+1].
```

(b) Run the program and plot the cash holdings jointly against time when $m = 100$, $K = 50$, $\mathcal{S} = 1000$, $\gamma = 0.1$, $k_m = 10$, $\xi_1 = 0.05$, $\sigma_1 = 0.25$, $\xi_2 = 0.04$, $\sigma_2 = 0.25$, $a = 0.6$, $\rho = 0.5$, $r_0 = 0.02$, $w = 0.2$, $v_0 = 800$.

R-*commands*:

```
matplot(0:K,Y,''l'').
```

(c) Redo a few times and also let $w = 0.4$ so that more equity is used.

Exercise 15.45

(a) Argue that the program in Exercise 15.44 is, with minor modifications, available for any fixed sequence of liabilities.

(b) Explain how future fixed-premium income and overhead expenses can be built into the scheme.

Exercise 15.46 Let $\mathcal{B}_k = \mathcal{Y}_k - \mathcal{PV}_{xk}$ be the balance sheet of the insurer in Exercise 15.44 where $\mathcal{PV}_{xk} = d\mathcal{X}_{k+1} + \cdots + d^{K-k}\mathcal{X}_K$ is the present value of future liabilities.

(a) Write a program computing $\mathcal{PV}_{x0}, \ldots, \mathcal{PV}_{xK}$ given $\mathcal{X}_1, \ldots, \mathcal{X}_K$.

R-*commands*:

With `X` as in Exercise 15.13, use

```
dx=d**(1:K)*X[1:K+1];
PV=cumsum(dx[K:1])[K:1]/d**(1:K); PV=c(PV,0).
```

(b) Also compute $\mathcal{B}_0, \ldots, \mathcal{B}_K$.

R-*commands*:

With `Y` from Exercise 15.44 use `B=Y-PV`.

(c) Run the program when $d = 0.97$ with the rest of the conditions as in Exercise 15.44(b) and plot the Monte Carlo realizations of $\mathcal{B}_0, \ldots, \mathcal{B}_K$ jointly against time.

R-*commands*:

```
matplot(0:K,B,''l'').
```

(d) Comment on the discrepancies from Exercise 15.44(b).

Exercise 15.47 Recall from Section 3.6 that $\mathcal{Y}_k$ in Exercise 15.44 satisfies $\mathcal{Y}_k = (1+\mathcal{R}_{0:K})(v_0 - \mathcal{S}_k)$ where

$$\mathcal{S}_k = \frac{\mathcal{X}_1}{1+\mathcal{R}_{0:1}} + \cdots + \frac{\mathcal{X}_k}{1+\mathcal{R}_{0:k}}.$$

(a) Argue that the initial capital $v_{0\epsilon}$ ensuring $\mathcal{Y}_1, \dots, \mathcal{Y}_K > 0$ with probability $1-\epsilon$ is the upper ϵ-percentile of $\max(\mathcal{S}_1, \dots, \mathcal{S}_K)$.

(b) Show that when positive *book* values $\mathcal{B}_1, \dots, \mathcal{B}_K$ are sought instead, then $v_{0\epsilon}$ is the upper ϵ-percentile of $\max(\mathcal{A}_1, \dots, \mathcal{A}_K)$ where $\mathcal{A}_k = \mathcal{S}_k + \mathcal{PV}_{xk}/(1+\mathcal{R}_{0:k})$. [*Hint*: $\mathcal{B}_k = (1+\mathcal{R}_{0:k})(v_0 - \mathcal{A}_k)$.]

Exercise 15.48

(a) Write a program generating m simulations of $\mathcal{S}_1, \dots, \mathcal{S}_K$ in Exercise 15.47 when the liabilities are those in Exercise 15.42 and when the returns come from the fixed-mix equity/cash portfolio in Exercise 15.30.

R-*commands*:

Take `X` and $\mathcal{R}$ from Exercises 15.13 and 15.30 and use `S=apply(X[1:K+1]/(1+`$\mathcal{R}$`),2,cumsum)`.

(b) Add commands computing $v_{0\epsilon}$.

R-*commands*:

`Smax=apply(S,2,max);` $v_{0\epsilon}$`=sort(Smax)[m*(1-`ϵ`)]`.

(c) Compute $v_{0\epsilon}$ under the conditions in Exercise 15.44 when $\epsilon = 0.05$ and 0.01 using $m = 10\,000$ simulations.

(d) Redo when the equity weight is increased from $w = 0.2$ to $w = 0.4$.

Exercise 15.49

(a) Continue Exercise 15.48 by writing a program which computes the initial capital $v_{0\epsilon}$ necessary to keep the book values $\mathcal{B}_1, \dots, \mathcal{B}_K$ positive with probability $1-\epsilon$.

R-*commands*:

With `X`, $\mathcal{R}$ and $\mathcal{S}$ as in Exercise 15.48 compute `PV` from `X` as in Exercise 15.46(a) and use `A=S+PV[1:K+1]/(1+`$\mathcal{R}$`);`
`Amax=apply(A,2,max);` $v_{0\epsilon}$`=sort(Amax)[m*(1-`ϵ`)]`.

(b) Compute $v_{0\epsilon}$ under the assumptions in Exercise 15.48(c) when $d = 0.97$.

(c) Redo when w is increased from 0.2 to 0.4 and compare both assessments with the corresponding ones in Exercise 15.48.

Appendix A
Random variables: Principal tools

A.1 Introduction

The following brief review is geared to the needs of this book. Many of the arguments in the main text draw on the operating rules for means, variances, covariances and lower-order moments which are listed in tables below. Single random variables are treated first and then random vectors with laws of large numbers at the end. Random variables are designated by letters such as X and Y (often indexed) and real numbers by a, b, c and d.

A.2 Single random variables

A.2.1 Introduction

Random variables are real functions on basic elements assigned probabilities, but this is for theoretical puposes, and a more relaxed way is to see them as uncertain quantities ruled by density functions which define how likely different outcomes are. Binomial or Poisson random variables are counts and always integers, while normal variables are real numbers. These are examples of the two main types in practice. **Discrete** random variables vary over some countable set $x_1, x_2, \ldots$ and **continuous** ones over the real line or some part of it. The mathematical formalism is almost the same.

A.2.2 Probability distributions

Random variables X carry probability **distributions**. The most immediate mathematical definition is through

$$\underbrace{\Pr(X = x_i) = f(x_i),\ i = 1, 2, \ldots}_{\text{discrete set of values}} \quad \text{or} \quad \underbrace{\Pr(x < X \leq x + h) = \int_x^{x+h} f(y)\, dy}_{\text{continuous set of values}}$$

where the **density function** $f(x_i)$ on the left assigns probabilities to all outcomes. On the right the integral is for small h approximately $hf(x)$, and again we may (loosely) think of $f(x)$ as representing $\Pr(X = x)$ though formally this probability is zero. All non-negative functions $f(x_i)$ or $f(x)$ are legitimate density functions if

$$\sum_{i=1}^{\infty} f(x_i) = 1 \quad \text{or} \quad \int_{-\infty}^{\infty} f(x)\,dx = 1.$$

There *are* other types of random variables (some are met in this book), but their probabilistic formalism need not concern us. The presentation below is in terms of continuous random variables.

Probability distributions can be represented in many forms. Transforms will be introduced at the end of this section, and four other ways are

$$\underset{\textit{density function}}{f(x),} \qquad \underset{\textit{distribution function}}{F(x) = \int_{-\infty}^{x} f(y)\,dy,} \qquad \underset{\textit{lower percentile}}{q_\epsilon = F^{-1}(\epsilon),} \qquad \underset{\textit{upper percentile}}{q_\epsilon = 1 - F^{-1}(\epsilon)}$$

where $F^{-1}(\epsilon)$ is the solution of the equation $F(q_\epsilon) = \varepsilon$. These quantities can be deduced from each other. For example, the distribution function $F(x)$ has the density function $f(x) = dF(x)/dx$ as its derivative, and the percentile functions are its inverses. Discrete random variables are treated similarly.

All density functions $f(x) \to 0$ as $x \to \pm\infty$ (its integral isn't finite otherwise), and the speed with which this occurs designates the tails of the distribution as **heavy** or **fat** when convergence is slow. The Gaussian density function is often a point of reference, and $f(x)$ is heavy tailed if for all $a > 0$

$$\frac{e^{-x^2/2}}{f(ax)} \to 0 \quad \text{as} \quad \underset{\textit{left tail}}{x \to -\infty} \quad \text{or} \quad \underset{\textit{right tail}}{x \to \infty.}$$

There are countless examples of such models in the main text.

A.2.3 Simplified description of distributions

Modelling and reporting are often concerned with simple measures of centre and spread. Two possibilities based on the percentile function $q_\epsilon = F^{-1}(\epsilon)$ are

$$\underset{\textit{median}}{\text{med}(X) = q_{0.5}} \quad \text{and} \quad \underset{\textit{quartile difference}}{qd(X) = q_{0.75} - q_{0.25},}$$

where median represents the centre of a distribution in the sense that there is a 50:50 chance of exceeding it. The quartile difference on the right contains 50% of all realizations and is an assessment of spread.

These quantities are always well defined mathematically, and yet in risk contexts other ways are often preferred. The following measures are not finite for certain members of the Pareto families of distributions, but this does not matter greatly. Define

$$\underset{\textit{expectation or mean}}{\xi = E(X) = \int_{-\infty}^{\infty} xf(x)\,dx}, \qquad \underset{\textit{variance}}{\sigma^2 = \text{var}(X) = E(X-\xi)^2}, \qquad \underset{\textit{moments of order } j}{\nu_j(X) = E(X-\xi)^j}$$

where only $E(X)$ is interpreted as it is. The others are converted to standard deviation, skewness and kurtosis through

$$\underset{\textit{standard deviation}}{\sigma = \sqrt{\text{var}(X)}}, \qquad \underset{\textit{skewness}}{\text{skew}(X) = \frac{\nu_3(X)}{\sigma^3}}, \qquad \underset{\textit{kurtosis}}{\text{kurt}(X) = \frac{\nu_4(X)}{\sigma^4} - 3},$$

and the scaling should be noted. Though standard deviation and variance are mathematically equivalent, the latter is on a quadratic scale (the wrong one). A useful (though rough) rule of thumb is that a random variable is located within $\pm\sigma$ from its mean in two-thirds of all cases and within $\pm 2\sigma$ 19 times out of 20, for Gaussian distributions almost exact statements.

Skewness and kurtosis are dimensionless coefficients satisfying

$$\text{skew}(a + bX) = \text{sign}(b)\text{skew}(X) \quad \text{and} \quad \text{kurt}(a + bX) = \text{kurt}(X),$$

and neither the centre of the distribution nor the measurement unit (i.e., currency) matter. What skewness and kurtosis convey is **shape**. Both are zero for normal distributions, and skewness is zero for all symmetric distributions too. Positive skewness with heavy tails on the right is common in property insurance, and positive kurtosis with heavy tails on both sides occurs frequently in finance.

A.2.4 Operating rules

Means, variances and other moments are operated through a number of useful rules. The most important ones are listed in Table A.1 with $X_1, \dots, X_n$ random variables and a, b real numbers. Theoretical arguments in this book have made frequent use of these identities, especially those involving sums. Note that while (A.10) holds in general, (A.11)–(A.15) require $X_1, \dots, X_n$ to be independent.

A.2.5 Transforms and cumulants

Probability distributions can be represented by transforms. This book doesn't make too much of that, but it *does* utilize the **moment-generating function** or **Laplace** transform

$$M(s) = E(e^{sX}),$$

Table A.1 Operating rules for moments of random variables

	Condition	Label
$E(a+bX) = a + bE(X)$		(A.1)
$\text{var}(a+bX) = b^2\text{var}(X)$		(A.2)
$E(X-a)^2 = (EX-a)^2 + \text{var}(X)$		(A.3)
$E\{H(x)\} = \int_{-\infty}^{\infty} H(x)f(x)dx$		(A.4)
$H\{E(X)\} \le E\{H(X)\}$	$H(x)$ convex	(A.5)
$E(X) = \int_0^{\infty}\{1-F(x)\}\,dx$	$\Pr(X>0)=1$	(A.6)
$\nu_j(a+bX) = b^j\nu_j(X)$	$j>1$	(A.7)
$E(X-a)^2 \ge \text{var}(X)$		(A.8)
$\Pr(\lvert X-EX\rvert > a) \le \text{var}(X)/a^2$		(A.9)
$E(X_1+\cdots+X_n) = E(X_1)+\cdots+E(X_n)$		(A.10)
$\text{var}(X_1+\cdots+X_n) = \text{var}(X_1)+\cdots+\text{var}(X_n)$	independence	(A.11)
$\nu_3(X_1+\cdots+X_n) = \nu_3(X_1)+\cdots+\nu_3(X_n)$	independence	(A.12)
$\nu_4(X_1+\cdots+X_n) = \sum_i \nu_4(X_i) + 3\sum_{i\ne j}\text{var}(X_i)\text{var}(X_j)$	independence	(A.13)
$E(X_1\cdots X_n) = E(X_1)\cdots E(X_n)$	independence	(A.14)
$\text{var}(X_1\cdots X_n) = \prod_i\{\text{var}(X_i)+(EX_i)^2\} - \prod_i(EX_i)^2$	independence	(A.15)

which is useful concept whenever it is finite in some neighbourhood around the origin, however small. That is far from being true for all distributions; it isn't for the Pareto families, for example. But if it does hold, then $d^jM(s)/ds^j = E(X^je^{sX})$ by differentiating under the expectation operator, and $E(X^j)$ becomes the jth-order derivative at $s=0$. In such cases the Laplace transform admits a Taylor series

$$M(s) = \sum_{j=0}^{\infty}\frac{E(X^j)}{j!}s^j \quad \text{with} \quad \frac{d^jM(0)}{ds^j} = E(X^j).$$

If a closed expression for $M(s)$ is available, differentiation is usually the fastest route to the moments of a distribution. If you seek the centralized moments $\nu_j(X)$, apply the moment-generating function to the variable $X-\xi$.

Let X and Y be independent random variables with moment-generating functions $M_x(s)$ and $M_y(s)$. Using rule (A.14) in Table A.1, this yields for the sum $X+Y$

$$M_{x+y}(s) = E(e^{s(X+Y)}) = E(e^{sX}e^{sY}) = E(e^{sX})E(e^{sY}) = M_x(s)M_y(s)$$

so that

$$\log\{M_{x+y}(s)\} = \log\{M_x(s)\} + \log\{M_y(s)\},$$

which motivates an interest in the logarithms of Laplace transforms, known as **cumulant-generating functions**. If X has finite Laplace transform $M(s)$ with a

Taylor series, then there is one for the logarithm too; i.e.,

$$\log\{M(s)\} = \sum_{j=1}^{\infty} \frac{\tilde{\nu}_j}{j!} s^j,$$

with the coefficients $\tilde{\nu}_j = \tilde{\nu}_j(X)$ known as **cumulants**. They are complicated in general, but not the first four which relate to the ordinary central moments through

$$\tilde{\nu}_1 = \xi, \quad \tilde{\nu}_2 = \sigma^2, \quad \tilde{\nu}_3 = \nu_3 \quad \text{and} \quad \tilde{\nu}_4 = \nu_4 - 3\sigma^4.$$

Consider $\tilde{\nu}_j(X+Y)$ when X and Y are independent. Since the cumulant-generating function of $X+Y$ is the sum of those for X and Y, the same must be true for the coefficients of the Taylor series so that $\tilde{\nu}_j(X+Y) = \tilde{\nu}_j(X) + \tilde{\nu}_j(Y)$, or more generally, if $X_1, \ldots, X_n$ are independent, then

$$\tilde{\nu}_j(X_1 + \cdots + X_n) = \tilde{\nu}_j(X_1) + \cdots + \nu_j(X_n), \quad j = 1, 2, \ldots$$

Rules (A.11), (A.12) and (A.13) in Table A.1 are all consequences of this result.

A.2.6 Example: The mean

An important special case is the mean $\bar{X} = (X_1 + \cdots + X_n)/n$ of identically and independently distributed variables $X_1, \ldots, X_n$. Let

$$\xi = E(X_i), \quad \sigma = \text{sd}(X_i), \quad \zeta = \text{skew}(X_i) \quad \text{and} \quad \kappa = \text{kurt}(X_i).$$

Then

$$E(\bar{X}) = \xi, \quad \text{sd}(\bar{X}) = \frac{\sigma}{\sqrt{n}}, \quad \text{skew}(\bar{X}) = \frac{\zeta}{\sqrt{n}} \quad \text{and} \quad \text{kurt}(\bar{X}) = \frac{\kappa}{n}$$

with interesting consequences as $n \to \infty$, a topic addressed in Section A.4 below. Skewness and kurtosis may not be as familiar as the other two, but they follow from the sum formulae for cumulants since $\text{skew}(X) = \tilde{\nu}_3(X)/\sigma^3$ and $\text{kurt}(X) = \tilde{\nu}_4(X)/\sigma^4$.

A.3 Several random variables jointly

A.3.1 Introduction

Random vectors introduce **stochastic dependence** between individual variables, a new and complex issue. There is for random pairs X and Y a joint density function $f(x, y)$ and for $X_1, \ldots, X_n$ an n-dimensional one $f(x_1, \ldots, x_n)$. These are non-negative functions with integrals satisfying

$$\int_{-\infty}^{\infty}\int_{-\infty}^{\infty} f(x,y)\,dx\,dy = 1 \quad \text{or} \quad \underbrace{\int_{-\infty}^{\infty}\cdots\int_{-\infty}^{\infty}}_{n \text{ integrals}} f(x,\ldots,x_n)\,dx_1\cdots dx_n = 1$$

and with the density functions of individual variables buried inside through

$$f(y) = \int_{-\infty}^{\infty} f(x,y)\,dx \quad \text{or} \quad f(x_n) = \underbrace{\int_{-\infty}^{\infty}\cdots\int_{-\infty}^{\infty}}_{n-1 \text{ integrals}} f(x,\ldots,x_n)\,dx_1\cdots dx_{n-1}.$$

There are similar links to density functions for pairs or triples, for example

$$f(x_{n-1},x_n) = \underbrace{\int_{-\infty}^{\infty}\cdots\int_{-\infty}^{\infty}}_{n-2 \text{ integrals}} f(x_1,\ldots,x_n)\,dx_1\cdots dx_{n-2}.$$

A.3.2 Covariance and correlation

None of the simplifying measures of stochastic dependence that have been proposed over the years compete in popularity (and importance) with **covariance** and **correlation**. They apply to pairs of random variables, which is their strength (easy to adapt to any number of variables) but also their weakness (higher-order dependence is left out). Let $\xi_x = E(X)$ and $\xi_y = E(Y)$ be the expectations of X and Y. Covariance and correlation are then

$$\text{cov}(X,Y) = E\{(X-\xi_x)(Y-\xi_y)\} \quad \text{and} \quad \text{cor}(X,Y) = \frac{\text{cov}(X,Y)}{\text{sd}(X)\text{sd}(Y)},$$

with covariance a nebelous mixture of dependence and variation and lacking useful interpretation. But it is important for calculations and enters many of the rules in Table A.2 below. By contrast, correlation coefficients satisfy

$$\text{cor}(a+bX, c+dY) = \text{cor}(X,Y) \quad \text{and} \quad -1 \leq \text{cor}(X,Y) \leq 1,$$

which shows that centres and measurement units are immaterial. Correlation is a real measures of dependence, with impact discussed in Section 6.2. Independent pairs of random variables have zero correlation.

The extension to many variables is simple in principle, with covariance and correlation calculated for all pairs and arranged as matrices as detailed in Section 5.4. Their operations are intimately connected to linear algebra and treated in Section B.2.

Table A.2 Operating rules involving covariance and correlation

	Condition	Label
$\mathrm{cov}(X, Y) = E(XY) - E(X)E(Y)$		(A.16)
$\mathrm{cov}(X, X) = \mathrm{var}(X)$		(A.17)
$\mathrm{cov}(a + bX, c + dY) = bd\mathrm{cov}(X, Y)$		(A.18)
$\mathrm{cor(X,X)=1},\ \mathrm{cor}(X, -X) = -1$		(A.19)
$\mathrm{cor}X, Y) = \mathrm{cov}(X, Y) = 0$	X and Y independent	(A.20)
$\mathrm{var}\left(\sum_{i=1}^{n} a_i X_i\right) = \sum_{i=1}^{n} a_i^2 \mathrm{var}(X_i) + \sum_{i \neq j} a_i a_j \mathrm{cov}(X_i, X_j)$		(A.21)
$\mathrm{cov}\left(\sum_{i=1}^{n} a_i X_i, \sum_{j=1}^{n} b_j Y_j\right) = \sum_{i=1}^{n} \sum_{j=1}^{n} a_i b_j \mathrm{cov}(X_i, Y_j)$		(A.22)
$\mathrm{cov}\left(\sum_{i=1}^{n} a_i X_i, \sum_{j=1}^{n} b_j Y_j\right) = \sum_{i=1}^{n} a_i b_i \mathrm{cov}(X_i, Y_i)$	$(X_1, Y_1), \ldots, (X_n, Y_n)$ independent pairs	(A.23)

A.3.3 Operating rules

The main operating rules involving covariance and correlation are summarized in Table A.2. Note in particular rule (A.21) which gives the variance of a sum of random variables in the general case, and (A.23) which is a covariance version of (A.11) in Table A.1.

A.3.4 The conditional viewpoint

Conditional distributions, used extensively in the main text as a modelling tool, are defined through conditional density functions, say $f(y|x)$ of a random variable Y given $X = x$ or more generally $f(y_1, \ldots, y_m|x_1, \ldots, x_n)$ for $Y_1, \ldots, Y_m$ given $X_1 = x_1, \ldots, X_n = x_n$. Mathematical definitions are

$$f(y|x) = \frac{f(x, y)}{f(x)} \quad \text{and} \quad f(y_1, \ldots, y_m|x_1, \ldots, x_n) = \frac{f(x_1, \ldots, x_n, y_1, \ldots, y_m)}{f(x_1, \ldots, x_n)},$$

and these are ordinary density functions in terms of y and $y_1, \ldots, y_m$. Their integrals are one, and they have ordinary means and variances (depending on x and $x_1, \ldots, x_n$).

Note that $f(x, y) = f(x)f(y|x)$. This simple factorization is extended in Table A.3, and the relationships there have many applications in this book. An important special case is the conditional density function coinciding with the non-conditional one; i.e., $f(y|x) = f(y)$ for all x and y. This is **stochastic independence**, which is generalized to n variables through the last entry in Table A.3.

Conditional distributions have expectations, variances and covariances which depend on the condition itself,say $\mathbf{X} = \mathbf{x}$ if $\mathbf{X} = (X_1, \ldots, X_n)$ and $\mathbf{x} = (x_1, \ldots, x_n)$.

Table A.3 Factorization of joint distributions according to type of dependence

	Type of dependence
$f(x_1,\dots,x_n) = f(x_1)f(x_2\|x_1)\cdots f(x_n\|x_1,\dots x_{n-1})$	General
$f(x_1,\dots,x_n) = f(x_1)f(x_2\|x_1)\cdots f(x_n\|x_{n-1})$	Markov
$f(x_1,\dots,x_n) = f(x_1)f(x_2\|x_1)\cdots f(x_n\|x_1)$	Conditional independence
$f(x_1,\dots,x_n) = f(x_1)f(x_2)\cdots f(x_n)$	Independence

Table A.4 The double rules for conditional moments

	Name	Label
$E(Y) = E\{\xi(\mathbf{X})\}$	Double expectation	(A.24)
$\text{var}(Y) = \text{var}\{\xi(\mathbf{X})\} + E\{\sigma^2(\mathbf{X})\}$	Double variance	(A.25)
$\text{cov}(Y_1, Y_2) = \text{cov}\{\xi_1(\mathbf{X}), \xi_2(\mathbf{X})\} + E(\sigma_{12}(\mathbf{X})\}$	Double covariance	(A.26)

For another variable Y, define

$$\xi(\mathbf{x}) = E(Y|\mathbf{X} = \mathbf{x}) \quad \text{and} \quad \sigma^2(\mathbf{x}) = \text{var}(Y|\mathbf{X} = \mathbf{x})$$

and similarly for Y_1 and Y_2,

$$\xi_1(\mathbf{x}) = E(Y_1|\mathbf{X} = \mathbf{x}), \quad \xi_2(\mathbf{x}) = E(Y_2|\mathbf{X} = \mathbf{x}) \quad \text{and} \quad \sigma_{12}(\mathbf{x}) = \text{cov}(Y_1, Y_2|\mathbf{X} = \mathbf{x}).$$

These quantities when averaged over $\mathbf{X}$ lead to the operating rules in Table A.4, which are widely used in this book, and they will now be verified.

Let $f(\boldsymbol{x}, y)$ be the joint density function of $(\boldsymbol{X}, Y)$. It can be factorized as $f(\boldsymbol{x}, y) = f(\boldsymbol{x})f(y|\boldsymbol{x})$ so that

$$E(Y) = \int_{-\infty}^{\infty}\int_{-\infty}^{\infty} yf(\mathbf{x}, y)\,dy\,d\mathbf{x} = \int_{-\infty}^{\infty}\left(\int_{-\infty}^{\infty} yf(y|\mathbf{x})\,dy\right)f(\mathbf{x})\,d\mathbf{x} = \int_{-\infty}^{\infty} \xi(\mathbf{x})f(\mathbf{x})\,d\mathbf{x},$$

where the expression on the very right is $E\{\xi(\boldsymbol{x})\}$ as in (A.24). For the double variance formula let $\xi_y = E(Y)$ and note that

$$Y - \xi_y = \{Y - \xi(\boldsymbol{x})\} + \{\xi(\boldsymbol{x}) - \xi_y\},$$

which leads to

$$(Y - \xi_y)^2 = \{Y - \xi(\boldsymbol{x})\}^2 + \{\xi(\boldsymbol{x}) - \xi_y\}^2 + 2\{Y - \xi(\boldsymbol{x})\}\{\xi(\boldsymbol{x}) - \xi_y\}.$$

Take the conditional expectation given $\boldsymbol{x}$ over both sides. This yields

$$E\{(Y - \xi_y)^2|\boldsymbol{x}\} = \sigma^2(\boldsymbol{x}) + \{\xi(\boldsymbol{x}) - \xi_y\}^2,$$

where the last term has vanished. Now, multiply this identity by $f(\mathbf{x})$ and integrate over x. Since $\xi_y = E\{\xi(\boldsymbol{x})\}$, it follows that

$$E(Y - \xi_y)^2 = E\{\sigma^2(\boldsymbol{X})\} + \text{var}\{\xi(\boldsymbol{X})\},$$

which is rule (A.25). The double covariance formula (A.26) is proved similarly.

A.4 Laws of large numbers

A.4.1 Introduction

Let $X_1, \dots, X_n$ be independent and identically distributed with mean $\bar{X}_n = (X_1 + \cdots + X_n)/n$. Recall that

$$E(\bar{X}_n - \xi)^2 = \text{var}(\bar{X}_n) = \frac{\sigma^2}{n} \to 0 \quad \text{as} \quad n \to \infty,$$

and $\bar{X}$ converges towards ξ through a stochastic limit known as convergence in **quadratic mean**, often written $\bar{X}_n \overset{\text{qm}}{\to} \xi$. A second stochastic limit will be introduced below, and there are additional types in probabilistic literature. These limits were cited in the main text without explicit reference to their stochastic nature.

Asymptotic results of this type are relevant for historical estimation (n the number of observations) and for Monte Carlo experiments ($n = m$ the number of simulations). Monte Carlo assessments do provide the right answer eventually, but there is error when m is finite, an issue even more important for historical estimation; see Chapter 7. Insight is provided by probabilistic large-sample theory, leading to approximations which almost always work well for Monte Carlo (m typically large) and are useful, though a good deal less accurate, for historical estimation.

A.4.2 The weak law of large numbers

A second stochastic limit is convergence **in probability** $\overset{\text{P}}{\to}$. A sequence $\hat{\psi}_n \overset{\text{P}}{\to} \psi$ if for all $\epsilon > 0$

$$\Pr(|\hat{\psi}_n - \psi| > \epsilon) \to 0 \quad \text{as} \quad n \to \infty,$$

which means that any discrepancy $\hat{\psi}_n \neq \psi$ has for large n negligible probability, and $\hat{\psi}_n$ approaches ψ. It is easy to prove this for the mean. Invoke rule (A.9) in Table A.1 (known as **Chebyshev's** inequality), which yields

$$\Pr(|\bar{X}_n - \xi| > \epsilon) \leq \frac{\text{var}(\bar{X}_n)}{\epsilon^2} = \frac{\sigma^2}{n\epsilon^2} \to 0 \quad \text{as} \quad n \to \infty,$$

and $\bar{X}_n \stackrel{\text{P}}{\rightarrow} \xi$. This is known as the **weak law of large numbers** and is true (by a different argument) even when the variance is infinite!

Similar results are available in a great many situations and virtually all stochastic quantities encountered in this book converge in probability as n or m becomes infinite, for example sample standard deviation s_n, percentile estimates $\hat{q}_{\epsilon n}$ and moment or likelihood estimates $\hat{\theta}_n$. For all these

$$s_n \stackrel{\text{P}}{\rightarrow} \sigma, \quad \hat{q}_{\epsilon n} \stackrel{\text{P}}{\rightarrow} q_\epsilon \quad \text{and} \quad \hat{\theta}_n \stackrel{\text{P}}{\rightarrow} \theta \quad \text{as} \quad n \rightarrow \infty.$$

Why are such results so prevalent? In short, because many quantities resemble the mean probabilistically when n is large! Two rather general examples of this are examined below.

A.4.3 Central limit theorem

Weak laws such as $\bar{X}_n \stackrel{\text{P}}{\rightarrow} \xi$ are one thing, but what about the discrepancy $\bar{X}_n - \xi$? The **central limit** theorem tells us that it becomes Gaussian as n grows. If divided by the standard deviation, then

$$\sqrt{n}\frac{\bar{X}_n - \xi}{\sigma} \stackrel{\text{D}}{\rightarrow} N(0,1) \quad \text{as} \quad n \rightarrow \infty$$

where $\stackrel{\text{D}}{\rightarrow}$ stands for **convergence in distribution**, with the precise mathematical meaning that the distribution function of $\sqrt{n}(\bar{X}_n - \xi)/\sigma$ converges to the standard normal integral. This is in essence the explanation for Monte Carlo error nearly always being Gaussian.

The main condition for the central limit theorem is independence, but $X_1, \dots, X_n$ do *not* have to be identically distributed. Indeed, $\bar{X}_n$ is for large n still approximately normal provided *a handful of variables do not dominate the rest*. The precise assumption is known as the **Lindeberg** condition. Let $f_i(x)$ be the density function of X_i, with mean ξ_i, and standard deviation σ_i, and define $\tau_n^2 = \sigma_1^2 + \cdots + \sigma_n^2$. A necessary and sufficient condition for the central limit theorem to hold for independent variables is

$$\frac{1}{\tau_n^2}\sum_{i=1}^{n}\int_{|x-\xi_i|>\epsilon\tau_n}(x-\xi_i)^2 f_i(x)\,dx \rightarrow 0 \quad \text{as} \quad n \rightarrow \infty$$

for all $\epsilon > 0$, which is very often satisfied. One example is the pension portfolio in Section 15.2, where uncertainty due to estimation error turned out to be Gaussian.

Normality under large samples is common for the same reason as for the weak law. Many quantities $\hat{\psi}_n$ behave probabilistically like means, for example sample standard deviation s_n and percentiles and parameter estimates $\hat{q}_{\epsilon n}$ and $\hat{\theta}_n$, which all typically become Gaussian as $n \to \infty$, as does Monte Carlo uncertainty in most forms. The quality of these Gaussian approximations varies. It has to do with the type of quantity and above all with the distribution of the individual observations. Try to simulate the mean of exponential variables and you will discover that n must be much larger for approximate normality than for uniforms. The determining factor is skewness (large for the exponential and zero for uniforms). Estimated percentiles for small ϵ become Gaussian much more slowly than means and standard deviations.

A.4.4 Functions of averages

Let $(X_1, Y_1), \ldots, (X_n, Y_n)$ be independently distributed pairs of observations with dependence within pairs. Introduce

$$V_n = g(\bar{X}_n, \bar{Y}_n)$$

where $\bar{X}_n$ and $\bar{Y}_n$ are the averages of $X_1, \ldots, X_n$ and $Y_1, \ldots, Y_n$ and $g(x, y)$ some function. We know that $\bar{X}_n$ and $\bar{Y}_n$ become Gaussian as $n \to \infty$, and it will now be demonstrated that V_n does too if $g(x, y)$ is a smooth function. The precise assumption is that $g(x, y)$ is differentiable with continuous derivatives at (ξ_x, ξ_y), where ξ_x and ξ_y are expectations of X_i and Y_i, respectively.

The argument is based on the linear Taylor approximation, which yields

$$V_n \doteq g(\xi_x, \xi_y) + a(\bar{X}_n - \xi_x) + b(\bar{Y}_n - \xi_y)$$

where

$$a = \frac{\partial g(\xi_x, \xi_y)}{\partial x} \quad \text{and} \quad b = \frac{\partial g(\xi_x, \xi_y)}{\partial y}.$$

Introduce

$$Z_i = a(X_i - \xi_x) + b(Y_i - \xi_y), \quad i = 1, \ldots, n$$

and note that

$$V_n \doteq g(\xi_x, \xi_y) + \bar{Z}_n \quad \text{where} \quad \bar{Z}_n = (Z_1 + \cdots + Z_n)/n,$$

which tells us that V_n behaves probabilistically like a mean if the linear approximation is accurate. When is that? Answer: When n is large so that $\bar{X}_n$ and $\bar{Y}_n$ are concentrated around ξ_x and ξ_y. Note that $E(Z_i) = 0$ for all i, so that $\bar{Z}_n$ tends to 0 in probability and its distribution function to a Gaussian with mean 0, and it is almost the same for V_n. Indeed, $V_n \xrightarrow{\text{P}} g(\xi_x, \xi_y)$ and V_n is approximately Gaussian around $g(\xi_x, \xi_y)$.

The preceding argument can be repeated in situations where the number of means is arbitrary (not just two), and the story is a general one. Smooth functions of averages of independent vectors of random variables are usually Gaussian. Sample variances and sample standard deviations are covered by this example.

A.4.5 Bias and standard deviation of estimates

Many statistical estimates $\hat{\theta}_n$ are either exact or approximate functions of means of independent random variables. Suppose $\hat{\theta}_n = g(\bar{X}_n, \bar{Y}_n)$ is an estimate of $\theta = g(\xi_x, \xi_y)$. Then, approximately,

$$\underbrace{E(\hat{\theta}_n - \theta) \doteq \beta/n}_{\textit{bias}} \quad \text{and} \quad \underbrace{\mathrm{sd}(\hat{\theta}_n) \doteq \tau/\sqrt{n}}_{\textit{random error}},$$

where β and τ are constants. The conclusions are valid as $n \to \infty$, and show that estimation bias then become *smaller* (order $1/n$) than random error (order $1/\sqrt{n}$). These results are used in Section 7.2.

The bias assertion on the left requires a second-order Taylor approximation. Suppose $g(x, y)$ is twice continuously differentiable at (ξ_x, ξ_y). Then

$$\hat{\theta}_n \doteq \theta + a(\bar{X}_n - \xi_x) + b(\bar{Y}_n - \xi_y) + \frac{c}{2}(\bar{X}_n - \xi_x)^2 + \frac{d}{2}(\bar{X}_n - \xi_x)(\bar{Y}_n - \xi_y) + \frac{e}{2}(\bar{Y}_n - \xi_y)^2,$$

where

$$a = \frac{\partial g(\xi_x, \xi_y)}{\partial x}, \quad b = \frac{\partial g(\xi_x, \xi_y)}{\partial y}, \quad c = \frac{\partial^2 g(\xi_x, \xi_y)}{\partial x^2}, \quad d = \frac{\partial^2 g(\xi_x, \xi_y)}{\partial x \partial y}, \quad e = \frac{\partial^2 g(\xi_x, \xi_y)}{\partial y^2}$$

are the partial derivatives. It follows that

$$E(\hat{\theta}_n) - \theta \doteq \frac{c}{2}\mathrm{var}(\bar{X}_n) + \frac{d}{2}\mathrm{cov}(\bar{X}_n, \bar{Y}_n) + \frac{e}{2}\mathrm{var}(\bar{Y}_n),$$

and the ordinary formulae for variances and covariances of sums of independent random variables (rules (A.11) and (A.23) of Tables A.1 and A.2) lead to

$$E(\hat{\theta}_n) - \theta \doteq \frac{\beta}{n} \quad \text{where} \quad \beta = \{c\,\mathrm{var}(X_1) + d\,\mathrm{cov}(X_1, Y_1) + e\,\mathrm{var}(Y_1)\}/2.$$

The argument behind the approximation for $\mathrm{sd}(\hat{\theta}_n)$ is similar, only simpler as the quadratic terms are not needed.

A.4.6 Likelihood estimates

Even likelihood estimates resembles means for large samples and become approximately normal. Suppose for simplicity that the model contains a single parameter

θ (the multi-parameter case is the same). Let $X_1, \dots, X_n$ be independent and identically distributed observations with density function $f(x;\theta)$. The log-likelihood function is

$$\mathcal{L}(\theta) = \sum_{i=1}^{n} \log\{f(X_i;\theta)\}$$

with first and second order derivatives

$$\frac{d\mathcal{L}(\theta)}{d\theta} = \sum_{i=1}^{n} \frac{\partial \log\{f(X_i;\theta)\}}{\partial\theta} = \sum_{i=1}^{n} Y_i \quad\text{and}\quad \frac{d^2\mathcal{L}(\theta)}{d\theta^2} = \sum_{i=1}^{n} \frac{\partial^2 \log\{f(X_i;\theta)\}}{\partial\theta^2} = \sum_{i=1}^{n} Z_i.$$

The likelihood estimate $\hat{\theta}_n$ maximizes $\mathcal{L}(\theta)$ and satisfies $d\mathcal{L}(\hat{\theta}_n)/d\theta = 0$. Hence

$$0 = \frac{d\mathcal{L}(\hat{\theta}_n)}{d\theta} \doteq \frac{d\mathcal{L}(\theta)}{d\theta} + \frac{d^2\mathcal{L}(\theta)}{d\theta^2}(\hat{\theta}_n - \theta),$$

once again a Taylor approximation. Let $\bar{Y}_n = (Y_1 + \cdots + Y_n)/n$ and $\bar{Z}_n = (Z_1 + \cdots + Z_n)/n$. Then

$$0 \doteq n\bar{Y}_n + n\bar{Z}_n(\hat{\theta}_n - \theta) \quad \text{so that} \quad \sqrt{n}(\hat{\theta}_n - \theta) \doteq -\frac{\sqrt{n}\,\bar{Y}_n}{\bar{Z}_n},$$

with means in both numerator and denominator. Since $\int_{-\infty}^{\infty} f(x;\theta)dx = 1$ for all θ, we may differentiate to obtain

$$0 = \int_{-\infty}^{\infty} \frac{\partial f(x;\theta)}{\partial\theta}\,dx = \int_{-\infty}^{\infty} \frac{\partial \log\{f(x;\theta)\}}{\partial\theta} f(x;\theta)\,dx = E\left(\frac{\partial \log\{f(X_1;\theta)\}}{\partial\theta}\right) = E(Y_1),$$

and the numerator $\sqrt{n}\bar{Y}_n$ in $\sqrt{n}(\hat{\theta}_n - \theta)$ converges in distribution to a normal with mean zero. This suggests that the same must be true for $\sqrt{n}(\hat{\theta}_n - \theta)$, since the denominator $\bar{Z}_n \xrightarrow{P} E(Z_1)$. A new round of differentiation under the integral reveals that

$$E(Z_1) = -E\left(\frac{\partial \log(f(X_1;\theta))}{\partial\theta}\right)^2 < 0.$$

Appendix B
Linear algebra and stochastic vectors

B.1 Introduction

Matrices are rectangular arrangements such as

$$\mathbf{A} = \begin{pmatrix} a_{11} & \cdots & a_{1n} \\ \cdot & \cdots & \cdot \\ \cdot & \cdots & \cdot \\ a_{m1} & \cdots & a_{mn} \end{pmatrix} \quad \text{or its transpose} \quad \mathbf{A}^{\mathrm{T}} = \begin{pmatrix} a_{11} & \cdots & a_{m1} \\ \cdot & \cdots & \cdot \\ \cdot & \cdots & \cdot \\ a_{1n} & \cdots & a_{mn} \end{pmatrix},$$

where the difference between the original version on the left and its **transpose** on the right is that elements (i, j) and (j, i) are swapped. In shorthand notation $\mathbf{A} = (a_{ij})$ and $\mathbf{A}^{\mathrm{T}} = (a_{ji})$. The numbers of rows and columns define the **shape** of the matrices, $m \times n$ for $\mathbf{A}$ and $n \times m$ for $\mathbf{A}^{\mathrm{T}}$. Note the use of bold face to distinguish $\mathbf{A}$ and $\mathbf{A}^{\mathrm{T}}$ from ordinary real numbers (also called **scalars**).

Vectors are special cases of matrices, for example

$$\mathbf{v} = \begin{pmatrix} v_1 \\ \cdot \\ \cdot \\ v_m \end{pmatrix} \quad \text{or} \quad \mathbf{w} = (w_1, \ldots, w_n)$$

for **column** vectors $\mathbf{v}$ and **row** vectors $\mathbf{w}$. The transpose of a row vector is a column vector and vica versa, but typographically the former is most convenient, for example $\mathbf{v}^{\mathrm{T}} = (v_1, \ldots, v_m)$. Bold face, lowercase letters are used for vectors. Operations on matrices and vectors are known as **matrix algebra**, and the summary in Section B.2 covers the bare necessities for this book. The general Gaussian model is developed in Section B.3.

B.2 Operations on matrices and vectors

B.2.1 Introduction

This section is a brief summary of fixed and stochastic vectors and matrices with their rules of operation. Computational issues are deferred to Section C.2. No mathematical prerequisites beyond the very simplest are needed.

B.2.2 Addition and multiplication

Matrices $\mathbf{A} = (a_{ij})$ and $\mathbf{B} = (b_{ij})$ can be added and multiplied if their shapes match. If both are $m \times n$, then their sum $\mathbf{C} = \mathbf{A} + \mathbf{B}$ is another $m \times n$ matrix for which

$$\mathbf{C} = (c_{ij}) \quad \text{and} \quad c_{ij} = a_{ij} + b_{ij}.$$

The difference $\mathbf{C} = \mathbf{A} - \mathbf{B}$ is similar with $c_{ij} = a_{ij} - b_{ij}$. Then there is the ordinary matrix product $\mathbf{C} = \mathbf{AB}$, which requires the number of *columns* of $\mathbf{A}$ to be the same as the number of *rows* of $\mathbf{B}$. Thus, if $\mathbf{A}$ is $m \times s$ and $\mathbf{B}$ is $s \times n$, then

$$\mathbf{C} = (c_{ij}) \quad \text{with} \quad c_{ij} = \sum_{k=1}^{s} a_{ik} b_{kj},$$

and the shape of $\mathbf{C}$ is $m \times n$. Normally $\mathbf{AB} \neq \mathbf{BA}$ even if both products are defined. Mathematicians have invented several other matrix products, for example the **Hadamard** product $\mathbf{C} = \mathbf{A} \cdot \mathbf{B}$ where $c_{ij} = a_{ij} b_{ij}$, used with the R-programs. If $\mathbf{A}$ is a matrix and b a scalar, then $\mathbf{C} = \mathbf{A} + b$ is the matrix for which $c_{ij} = a_{ij} + b$, and $\mathbf{C} = b\mathbf{A}$ means $c_{ij} = ba_{ij}$.

Important special cases of general matrix multiplication are products between matrices and vectors and between two vectors, for example if $\mathbf{A} = (a_{ij})$ is $m \times n$ and $\mathbf{v} = (v_1, \ldots, v_n)^{\mathrm{T}}$ and $\mathbf{w} = (w_1, \ldots, w_n)^{\mathrm{T}}$ are column vectors, then

$$\mathbf{Av} = \begin{pmatrix} \sum_{j=1}^{n} a_{1j} v_j \\ \vdots \\ \sum_{j=1}^{n} a_{mj} v_j \end{pmatrix} \quad \text{and} \quad \mathbf{v}^{\mathrm{T}}\mathbf{w} = \sum_{j=1}^{n} v_j w_j.$$

The sum on the right is known as the **scalar** product between $\mathbf{v}$ and $\mathbf{w}$. Combining the two operations yields the **quadratic forms** $\mathbf{v}^{\mathrm{T}}\mathbf{Av} = \sum_{i,j} v_i a_{ij} v_j$ if A is $n \times n$.

B.2.3 Quadratic matrices

A matrix $\mathbf{A}$ is **symmetric** if $\mathbf{A} = \mathbf{A}^{\mathrm{T}}$, which means that $a_{ij} = a_{ji}$ for all (i, j). Such matrices must be **quadratic** or **square**, with the same number of rows and columns.

Covariance matrices are important examples of symmetric matrices. A special case is the **identity** matrix

$$\mathbf{I} = \begin{pmatrix} 1 & 0 & \cdots & 0 \\ 0 & 1 & \cdots & 0 \\ \cdot & \cdot & \cdots & \cdot \\ 0 & 0 & \cdots & 1 \end{pmatrix},$$

with ones on the main diagonal (from the top left-hand corner) and zeros elsewhere. In matrix algebra $\mathbf{I}$ plays the same role as the number 1 in the ordinary real number system. A matrix is unchanged when multiplied by $\mathbf{I}$ of the right shape; i.e., $\mathbf{A} = \mathbf{AI} = \mathbf{IA}$.

A square matrix A is **non-singular** if there is a matrix $\mathbf{A}^{-1}$ (known as the **inverse**) for which

$$\mathbf{AA}^{-1} = \mathbf{I} \quad \text{or equivalently} \quad \mathbf{A}^{-1}\mathbf{A} = \mathbf{I}.$$

It usually takes a computer to determine $\mathbf{A}^{-1}$; see Section C.2. Matrices $\mathbf{O}$ for which $\mathbf{O}^{-1} = \mathbf{O}^{\mathrm{T}}$ with the transpose as inverse are called **orthonormal**; more on these below.

Any square matrix $\mathbf{A}$ is assigned a real number $|\mathbf{A}|$ known as its **determinant**. The formal definition is horrendeously complicated, i.e.,

$$|\mathbf{A}| = \sum_{i_1,\dots,i_n} (-1)^{s_{i_1,\dots,i_n}} a_{1i_1} \cdots a_{ni_n}$$

where $i_1, \dots, i_n$ are the integers $1, \dots, n$ in a different order, and the sum is over all these **permutations**. The exponents $s_{i_1,\dots,i_n}$ are -1 if $i_1, \dots, i_n$ can be reordered to $1, \dots, n$ by swapping positions an uneven number of times and $+1$ otherwise. To compute $|\mathbf{A}|$ by this sum you have to add $n!$ different products of the elements a_{ij}. For n of some size not even a computer can do that.

Square matrices are **positive semi-definite** if $\mathbf{v}^{\mathrm{T}}\mathbf{A}\mathbf{v} \geq 0$ for all vectors $\mathbf{v}$ of the right length and **positive definite** if the inequality is strict whenever $\mathbf{v} \neq \mathbf{0}$. Positive definite matrices are non-singular with positive determinants.

B.2.4 The geometric view

Orthonormal matrices hold the key to the theory of Gaussian models in Section B.3. The 2×2 version can be written

$$\mathbf{O} = \begin{pmatrix} \sin\omega & \cos\omega \\ -\cos\omega & \sin\omega \end{pmatrix}$$

where ω is an angle. It is easy from the definition to check that $\mathbf{O}^{\mathrm{T}} = \mathbf{O}^{-1}$. If $\mathbf{v} = (v_1, v_2)^{\mathrm{T}}$, then $\mathbf{w} = \mathbf{Ov}$ is a rotation of it, and this interpretation is valid for any

Table B.1 Rules of operation for vectors and matrices

	Condition	Label
$\mathbf{A}+\mathbf{B}=\mathbf{B}+\mathbf{A}$	$\mathbf{A}, \mathbf{B}$ same shape	(B.1)
$(\mathbf{A}+\mathbf{B})+\mathbf{C}=\mathbf{A}+(\mathbf{B}+\mathbf{C})$	$\mathbf{A}, \mathbf{B}, \mathbf{C}$ same shape	(B.2)
$(\mathbf{AB})\mathbf{C}=\mathbf{A}(\mathbf{BC})$	Multiplication allowed	(B.3)
$\mathbf{A}=\mathbf{AI}=\mathbf{IA}$	$\mathbf{I}$ the identity, multiplication allowed	(B.4)
$(\mathbf{A}^{\mathrm{T}})^{\mathrm{T}}=\mathbf{A}$		(B.5)
$(\mathbf{AB})^{\mathrm{T}}=\mathbf{B}^{\mathrm{T}}\mathbf{A}^{\mathrm{T}}$	Multiplication allowed	(B.6)
$(\mathbf{AB})^{-1}=\mathbf{B}^{-1}\mathbf{A}^{-1}$	$\mathbf{A}, \mathbf{B}$ non-singular, same quadratic shape	(B.7)
$(\mathbf{A}^{\mathrm{T}})^{-1}=(\mathbf{A}^{-1})^{\mathrm{T}}$	$\mathbf{A}$ quadratic, non-singular	(B.8)
$\mathbf{A}$ non-singular	$\mathbf{A}$ quadratic and $\lvert\mathbf{A}\rvert \neq 0$	(B.9)
$\mathbf{v}^{\mathrm{T}}\mathbf{A}\mathbf{v}>0$ if $\mathbf{v}\neq\mathbf{0}$	$\mathbf{A}$ quadratic and $\lvert\mathbf{A}\rvert > 0$	(B.10)
$\lvert\mathbf{AB}\rvert=\lvert\mathbf{A}\rvert\lvert\mathbf{B}\rvert$	$\mathbf{A}, \mathbf{B}$ same quadratic shape	(B.11)
$\lvert\mathbf{A}^{-1}\rvert=1/\lvert\mathbf{A}\rvert$	$\mathbf{A}$ non-singular	(B.12)
$\lvert\mathbf{Av}\rvert=\lvert\mathbf{v}\rvert$	$\mathbf{A}^{-1}=\mathbf{A}^{\mathrm{T}}$ ($\mathbf{A}$ orthonormal)	(B.13)
$\lvert\mathbf{v}^{\mathrm{T}}\mathbf{w}\rvert \leq \sqrt{(\mathbf{v}^{\mathrm{T}}\mathbf{v})(\mathbf{w}^{\mathrm{T}}\mathbf{w})}$	$\mathbf{v}, \mathbf{w}$ same dimension	(B.14)

n. Let $|\mathbf{v}| = \sqrt{v_1^2+\cdots+v_n^2}$ and $|\mathbf{w}| = \sqrt{w_1^2+\cdots+w_n^2}$ be the **length** of the vectors $\mathbf{v}$ and $\mathbf{w}$. Then

$$|\mathbf{w}| = |\mathbf{v}| \quad \text{if} \quad \mathbf{w} = \mathbf{O}\mathbf{v},$$

and operating $\mathbf{O}$ on $\mathbf{v}$ preserves length, which is the same as a rotation.

B.2.5 Algebraic rules

Table B.1 summarizes the main operational rules for matrices and vectors. They are proved in any text on linear algebra, and most of them are easily verified from their definitions.

B.2.6 Stochastic vectors

Random variables $X_1, \ldots, X_n$ define random vectors $\mathbf{X} = (X_1, \ldots, X_n)^{\mathrm{T}}$, and this opens up convenient manipulations through linear algebra. Means, variances and covariances of the individual variables are then displayed as vectors and matrices. Let

$$\xi_i = E(X_i), \quad \sigma_{ii} = \mathrm{var}(X_i, X_i) \quad \text{and} \quad \sigma_{ij} = \mathrm{cov}(X_i, X_j),$$

yielding

$$E(\mathbf{X}) = \boldsymbol{\xi} = (\xi_1, \ldots, \xi_n)^{\mathrm{T}} \quad \text{and} \quad \mathrm{VAR}(\mathbf{X}) = \boldsymbol{\Sigma} = \begin{pmatrix} \sigma_{11} & \cdots & \sigma_{1n} \\ \vdots & \vdots & \vdots \\ \sigma_{n1} & \cdots & \sigma_{nn} \end{pmatrix}$$

with $\boldsymbol{\xi}$ the mean vector and $\boldsymbol{\Sigma}$ the covariance matrix. When it is suitable to emphasize the underlying $\mathbf{X}$, notation like $E(\mathbf{X})$ and $\mathrm{VAR}(\mathbf{X})$ can be used. If $\boldsymbol{\varepsilon} = (\varepsilon_1, \ldots, \varepsilon_n)^{\mathrm{T}}$ is a vector of independent variables with mean zero and variance one, then $E(\boldsymbol{\varepsilon}) = \mathbf{0}$ and $\mathrm{VAR}(\boldsymbol{\varepsilon}) = \mathbf{I}$ with $\mathbf{0} = (0, \ldots, 0)^{\mathrm{T}}$ the zero vector and $\mathbf{I}$ the identity matrix.

B.2.7 Linear operations on stochastic vectors

Let $\mathbf{X} = (X_1, \ldots, X_n)^{\mathrm{T}}$ be a stochastic vector with mean vector $\boldsymbol{\xi}$ and covariance matrix $\boldsymbol{\Sigma}$ and consider

$$Y = a + b_1 X_1 + \cdots + b_n X_n = a + \mathbf{b}^{\mathrm{T}}\mathbf{X} \quad \text{where} \quad \mathbf{b} = (b_1, \ldots, b_n)^{\mathrm{T}}.$$

The mean and variance of Y can then be calculated by the rules from Appendix A, for example

$$E(Y) = a + b_1\xi_1 + \cdots + b_n\xi_n = a + \mathbf{b}^{\mathrm{T}}\boldsymbol{\xi}$$

and by (A.21) of Table A.2

$$\mathrm{var}(Y) = \sum_{i=1}^{n}\sum_{j=1}^{n} b_i b_j \sigma_{ij} = \mathbf{b}^{\mathrm{T}}\boldsymbol{\Sigma}\mathbf{b},$$

the double sum being written more compactly through the use of matrix algebra. Such mathematical formalism is even more useful with several linear functions of $\mathbf{X}$. Let $\mathbf{a} = (a_1, \ldots, a_m)^{\mathrm{T}}$ be a vector and $\mathbf{B} = (b_{ij})$ a $m \times n$ matrix and define

$$\mathbf{Y} = \mathbf{a} + \mathbf{B}\mathbf{X} \quad \text{where} \quad \mathbf{Y} = (Y_1, \ldots, Y_m)^{\mathrm{T}}.$$

Each Y_i is then a sum similar to Y above, and its expectation and variance can be written down as before, and even covariances are similar. Indeed, if

$$Y_i = a_i + b_{i1}X_1 + \cdots + b_{in}X_n \quad \text{and} \quad Y_j = a_j + b_{j1}X_1 + \cdots + b_{jn}X_n,$$

then by (A.22) in Table A.2

$$\mathrm{cov}(Y_i, Y_j) = \sum_{k=1}^{n}\sum_{l=1}^{n} \sigma_{kl} b_{ik} b_{jl},$$

and in matrix notation the mean vector and covariance matrix of **Y** relate to those of **X** through

$$E(\mathbf{Y}) = \mathbf{a} + \mathbf{B}\boldsymbol{\xi} \quad \text{and} \quad \text{VAR}(\mathbf{Y}) = \mathbf{B}\boldsymbol{\Sigma}\mathbf{B}^{\mathrm{T}}, \tag{B.1}$$

much more elegant and compact than through sums.

B.2.8 Covariance matrices and Cholesky factors

Variances cannot be negative, which means

$$\mathbf{b}^{\mathrm{T}}\boldsymbol{\Sigma}\mathbf{b} \geq 0 \quad \text{for all} \quad \mathbf{b} = (b_1, \ldots, b_n)^{\mathrm{T}},$$

and covariance matrices are positive semi-definite. Those in this book have also been positive definite (strict inequality for all $\mathbf{b} \neq \mathbf{0}$) and therefore non-singular with inverses computed as explained in Section C.2. *Non*-positive definite covariance matrices correspond to situations where one or more of the variables $X_1, \ldots, X_n$ are determined through *exact* relationships to others, for example $X_4 = 2X_3 - 5X_7$. If encountered in practice, the problem might well be reformulated.

Non-singular covariance matrices have square roots which may be defined in more ways than one. This book has made use of upper-triangular **Cholesky** matrices of the form

$$\mathbf{C} = \begin{pmatrix} c_{11} & 0 & \cdots & 0 \\ c_{21} & c_{22} & \cdots & 0 \\ \cdot & \cdot & \cdots & \cdot \\ \cdot & \cdot & \cdots & \cdot \\ c_{n1} & c_{n2} & \cdots & c_{nn} \end{pmatrix}$$

with zeros above the main diagonal. *Any* positive definite covariance matrix $\boldsymbol{\Sigma}$ is the product of a Cholesky matrix and its transpose through

$$\boldsymbol{\Sigma} = \mathbf{C}\mathbf{C}^{\mathrm{T}},$$

and **C** is non-singular with inverse $\mathbf{C}^{-1}$. The proof of the factorization and how it is computed is largely the same issue; see Section C.2.

B.3 The Gaussian model: Simple theory

B.3.1 Introduction

Gaussian models hold a central position in many areas of risk analysis and were defined in Section 5.4 as a matrix operation on a random vector $\boldsymbol{\varepsilon} = (\varepsilon_1, \ldots, \varepsilon_n)^{\mathrm{T}}$ of independent $N(0, 1)$ variables. A Gaussian vector is of the form

$$\mathbf{X} = \boldsymbol{\xi} + \mathbf{C}\boldsymbol{\varepsilon} \tag{B.2}$$

where $\mathbf{C} = (c_{ij})$ is a non-singular matrix (that will eventually be restricted to the Cholesky type). The main properties of Gaussian models are:

- *Parameters* are the mean vector $\boldsymbol{\xi}$ and the covariance matrix $\boldsymbol{\Sigma} = \mathbf{C}\mathbf{C}^{\mathrm{T}}$.
- *Linear operations* on Gaussian vectors lead to new Gaussian vectors.
- *Sub-vectors* of Gaussian vectors are Gaussian.
- The *conditional distribution* of one Gaussian sub-vector given another is Gaussian.

The covariance matrix $\boldsymbol{\Sigma} = \mathbf{C}\mathbf{C}^{\mathrm{T}}$ follows from (B.1) right, but there is an issue of uniqueness that must be clarified first. It will be shown below that the entire Gaussian family is generated if $\mathbf{C}$ in (B.2) is a Cholesky matrix.

B.3.2 Orthonormal operations

The Gaussian model is developed by orthonormal operations on independent and $N(0,1)$ variables $\varepsilon_1, \dots, \varepsilon_n$. Let $\mathbf{O} = (o_{ij})$ be an orthonormal matrix and define

$$\boldsymbol{\eta} = \mathbf{O}\boldsymbol{\varepsilon}$$

where

$$\boldsymbol{\varepsilon} = (\varepsilon_1, \dots, \varepsilon_n)^{\mathrm{T}} \quad \text{and} \quad \boldsymbol{\eta} = (\eta_1, \dots, \eta_n)^{\mathrm{T}}.$$

The fact that $\mathbf{O}^{\mathrm{T}}\mathbf{O} = \mathbf{I}$ implies $\boldsymbol{\eta}^{\mathrm{T}}\boldsymbol{\eta} = (\mathbf{O}\boldsymbol{\varepsilon})^{\mathrm{T}}\mathbf{O}\boldsymbol{\varepsilon} = \boldsymbol{\varepsilon}^{\mathrm{T}}\mathbf{O}^{\mathrm{T}}\mathbf{O}\boldsymbol{\varepsilon} = \boldsymbol{\varepsilon}^{\mathrm{T}}\mathbf{I}\boldsymbol{\varepsilon} = \boldsymbol{\varepsilon}^{\mathrm{T}}\boldsymbol{\varepsilon}$ or

$$\eta_1^2 + \cdots + \eta_n^2 = \varepsilon_1^2 + \cdots + \varepsilon_n^2.$$

The second vector $\boldsymbol{\eta}$ is a rotation of the first and has the same length.

The preceding result means that $\eta_1, \dots, \eta_n$ *are independent and* $N(0,1)$ just as the original sample $\varepsilon_1, \dots, \varepsilon_n$ was. To prove this we need transformation theory for random vectors. A heuristic argument runs as follows. The joint density function of $\varepsilon_1, \dots, \varepsilon_n$ is

$$\left(\frac{1}{\sqrt{2\pi}}e^{-\varepsilon_1^2/2}\right) \times \cdots \times \left(\frac{1}{\sqrt{2\pi}}e^{-\varepsilon_n^2/2}\right) = (2\pi)^{-n/2}e^{-(\varepsilon_1^2+\cdots+\varepsilon_n^2)/2} = (2\pi)^{-n/2}e^{-(\eta_1^2+\cdots+\eta_n^2)/2},$$

suggesting that the density function of the second set $\eta_1, \dots, \eta_n$ is the same as the first! This isn't quite rigorous, but we get away with it precisely because we are working with orthonormal transformations $\mathbf{O}$ for which $|\mathbf{O}| = 1$. The specific mathematical form of the normal distribution is crucial.

B.3.3 Uniqueness

If **C** and **B** are matrices so that

$$\mathbf{C}\mathbf{C}^{\mathrm{T}} = \mathbf{B}\mathbf{B}^{\mathrm{T}} = \mathbf{\Sigma},$$

then $\mathbf{X} = \boldsymbol{\xi} + \mathbf{C}\boldsymbol{\varepsilon}$ and $\mathbf{Y} = \boldsymbol{\xi} + \mathbf{B}\boldsymbol{\varepsilon}$ have the same distribution. In particular, the entire Gaussian family is defined when **C** is restricted to Cholesky matrices.

The proof is by matrix algebra. First note that

$$\mathbf{Y} = \boldsymbol{\xi} + \mathbf{C}(\mathbf{C}^{-1}\mathbf{B}\boldsymbol{\varepsilon}) = \boldsymbol{\xi} + \mathbf{C}\boldsymbol{\eta} \quad \text{where} \quad \boldsymbol{\eta} = \mathbf{C}^{-1}\mathbf{B}\boldsymbol{\varepsilon} = \mathbf{O}\boldsymbol{\varepsilon}.$$

The matrix $\mathbf{O} = \mathbf{C}^{-1}\mathbf{B}$ is ortonormal since

$$\mathbf{O}\mathbf{O}^{\mathrm{T}} = (\mathbf{C}^{-1}\mathbf{B})(\mathbf{C}^{-1}\mathbf{B})^{\mathrm{T}} = \mathbf{C}^{-1}\mathbf{B}\mathbf{B}^{\mathrm{T}}(\mathbf{C}^{-1})^{T} = \mathbf{C}^{-1}\mathbf{C}\mathbf{C}^{\mathrm{T}}(\mathbf{C}^{\mathrm{T}})^{-1} = \mathbf{I},$$

and $\boldsymbol{\eta}$ consists of independent $N(0, 1)$ variables since $\boldsymbol{\varepsilon}$ did. But then $\mathbf{X} = \boldsymbol{\xi} + \mathbf{C}\boldsymbol{\varepsilon}$ and $\mathbf{Y} = \boldsymbol{\xi} + \mathbf{C}\boldsymbol{\eta}$ must possess the same distribution.

B.3.4 Linear transformations

Let $\mathbf{Y} = \mathbf{a} + \mathbf{B}\mathbf{X}$, where **a** is a vector and **B** a matrix. Inserting $\mathbf{X} = \boldsymbol{\xi} + \boldsymbol{C}\boldsymbol{\varepsilon}$ yields

$$\mathbf{Y} = \mathbf{a} + \mathbf{B}(\boldsymbol{\xi} + \mathbf{C}\boldsymbol{\varepsilon}) = (\boldsymbol{a} + \mathbf{B}\boldsymbol{\xi}) + (\mathbf{B}\mathbf{C})\boldsymbol{\varepsilon},$$

and **Y** has the same type of representation as **X**. It is therefore normal with mean vector and covariance matrix

$$E(\mathbf{Y}) = \mathbf{a} + \mathbf{B}\boldsymbol{\xi}$$

and

$$\mathrm{VAR}(\mathbf{Y}) = (\mathbf{B}\mathbf{C})(\mathbf{B}\mathbf{C})^{\mathrm{T}} = \mathbf{B}\mathbf{C}\mathbf{C}^{\mathrm{T}}\mathbf{B}^{\mathrm{T}} = \mathbf{B}\mathbf{\Sigma}\mathbf{B}^{\mathrm{T}}.$$

B.3.5 Block representation

Let $\mathbf{X} = \boldsymbol{\xi} + \boldsymbol{C}\boldsymbol{\varepsilon}$ with **C** a Cholesky matrix and divide **X** into upper and lower subvectors through

$$\mathbf{X} = \begin{pmatrix} \mathbf{X}_1 \\ \mathbf{X}_2 \end{pmatrix} \quad \text{with similar partitions} \quad \boldsymbol{\xi} = \begin{pmatrix} \boldsymbol{\xi}_1 \\ \boldsymbol{\xi}_2 \end{pmatrix} \quad \text{and} \quad \boldsymbol{\varepsilon} = \begin{pmatrix} \boldsymbol{\varepsilon}_1 \\ \boldsymbol{\varepsilon}_2 \end{pmatrix}.$$

There is a congruent block structure even for **C**; i.e,

$$\mathbf{C} = \begin{pmatrix} \mathbf{C}_{11} & \mathbf{0} \\ \mathbf{C}_{21} & \mathbf{C}_{22} \end{pmatrix},$$

where the Cholesky matrices $\mathbf{C}_{11}$ (upper left) and $\mathbf{C}_{22}$ (lower right) are of the same dimension as $\mathbf{X}_1$ and $\mathbf{X}_2$. The original specification of $\mathbf{X}$ can now be rewritten

$$\begin{aligned} \mathbf{X}_1 &= \boldsymbol{\xi}_1 + \mathbf{C}_{11}\boldsymbol{\varepsilon}_1, \\ \mathbf{X}_2 &= \boldsymbol{\xi}_2 + \mathbf{C}_{21}\boldsymbol{\varepsilon}_1 + \mathbf{C}_{22}\boldsymbol{\varepsilon}_2, \end{aligned} \tag{B.3}$$

with the first line revealing that sub-vectors of normal vectors are normal themselves.

B.3.6 Conditional distributions

The block construction also clarifies the issue of conditional distributions through an argument that is a direct extension of a simpler one in Section 6.2. Fix $\mathbf{X}_1 = \mathbf{x}_1$ in (B.3) and solve for $\boldsymbol{\varepsilon}_1$. The unique solution is

$$\boldsymbol{\varepsilon}_1 = \mathbf{C}_{11}^{-1}(\mathbf{x}_1 - \boldsymbol{\xi}_1),$$

where $\mathbf{C}_{11}^{-1}$ is the inverse of $\mathbf{C}_{11}$. Insert this into the equation for $\mathbf{X}_2$. Then

$$\mathbf{X}_2 = \{\boldsymbol{\xi}_2 + \mathbf{C}_{21}\mathbf{C}_{11}^{-1}(\mathbf{x}_1 - \boldsymbol{\xi}_1)\} + \mathbf{C}_{22}\boldsymbol{\varepsilon}_2,$$

which is a representation of a Gaussian vector, and we may conclude that the conditional distribution of $\mathbf{X}_2$ given $\mathbf{X} = \mathbf{x}_1$ is normal with mean vector and covariance matrix

$$E(\mathbf{X}_2|\mathbf{x}_1) = \boldsymbol{\xi}_2 + \mathbf{C}_{21}\mathbf{C}_{11}^{-1}(\mathbf{x}_1 - \boldsymbol{\xi}_1) \quad \text{and} \quad \mathrm{VAR}(\mathbf{X}_2|\mathbf{x}_1) = \mathbf{C}_{22}\mathbf{C}_{22}^{\mathrm{T}}.$$

For practical work this is a perfectly feasible solution, but there is also an alternative form. Let

$$\boldsymbol{\Sigma} = \begin{pmatrix} \boldsymbol{\Sigma}_{11} & \boldsymbol{\Sigma}_{12} \\ \boldsymbol{\Sigma}_{21} & \boldsymbol{\Sigma}_{22} \end{pmatrix},$$

with $\boldsymbol{\Sigma}_{11}, \boldsymbol{\Sigma}_{12}, \boldsymbol{\Sigma}_{21}, \boldsymbol{\Sigma}_{22}$ congruent with the blocks of C. Then

$$E(\mathbf{X}_2|\mathbf{x}_1) = \boldsymbol{\xi}_2 + \boldsymbol{\Sigma}_{21}\boldsymbol{\Sigma}_{11}^{-1}(\mathbf{x}_1 - \boldsymbol{\xi}_1) \quad \text{and} \quad \mathrm{VAR}(\mathbf{X}_2|\mathbf{x}_1) = \boldsymbol{\Sigma}_{22} - \boldsymbol{\Sigma}_{21}\boldsymbol{\Sigma}_{11}^{-1}\boldsymbol{\Sigma}_{12},$$

which is the form you will encounter in most texts.

B.3.7 Verfication

To prove that the two versions of the conditional distribution are equal, utilize $\mathbf{C}\mathbf{C}^{\mathrm{T}} = \boldsymbol{\Sigma}$ so that

$$\begin{pmatrix} \mathbf{C}_{11} & \mathbf{0} \\ \mathbf{C}_{21} & \mathbf{C}_{22} \end{pmatrix}\begin{pmatrix} \mathbf{C}_{11}^{\mathrm{T}} & \mathbf{C}_{21}^{\mathrm{T}} \\ \mathbf{0} & \mathbf{C}_{22}^{\mathrm{T}} \end{pmatrix} = \begin{pmatrix} \boldsymbol{\Sigma}_{11} & \boldsymbol{\Sigma}_{12} \\ \boldsymbol{\Sigma}_{21} & \boldsymbol{\Sigma}_{22} \end{pmatrix},$$

which yields

$$\mathbf{C}_{11}\mathbf{C}_{11}^{\mathrm{T}} = \mathbf{\Sigma}_{11}, \quad \mathbf{C}_{21}\mathbf{C}_{11}^{\mathrm{T}} = \mathbf{\Sigma}_{21} \quad \text{and} \quad \mathbf{C}_{21}\mathbf{C}_{21}^{\mathrm{T}} + \mathbf{C}_{22}\mathbf{C}_{22}^{\mathrm{T}} = \mathbf{\Sigma}_{22}.$$

Apply the middle identity and the one on the left afterwards. Then

$$\mathbf{C}_{21}\mathbf{C}_{11}^{-1} = \mathbf{\Sigma}_{21}(\mathbf{C}_{11}^{\mathrm{T}})^{-1}\mathbf{C}_{11}^{-1} = \mathbf{\Sigma}_{21}(\mathbf{C}_{11}\mathbf{C}_{11}^{\mathrm{T}})^{-1} = \mathbf{\Sigma}_{21}\mathbf{\Sigma}_{11}^{-1},$$

and the two forms of the conditional mean $E(\mathbf{X}_2|\mathbf{x_1})$ are equal. This identity also tells us that $\mathbf{C}_{21} = \mathbf{\Sigma}_{21}\mathbf{\Sigma}_{11}^{-1}\mathbf{C}_{11}$. Hence

$$\mathbf{C}_{21}\mathbf{C}_{21}^{\mathrm{T}} = (\mathbf{\Sigma}_{21}\mathbf{\Sigma}_{11}^{-1}\mathbf{C}_{11})(\mathbf{\Sigma}_{21}\mathbf{\Sigma}_{11}^{-1}\mathbf{C}_{11})^{\mathrm{T}} = \mathbf{\Sigma}_{21}\mathbf{\Sigma}_{11}^{-1}(\mathbf{C}_{11}\mathbf{C}_{11}^{\mathrm{T}})\mathbf{\Sigma}_{11}^{-1}\mathbf{\Sigma}_{21}^{\mathrm{T}} = \mathbf{\Sigma}_{21}\mathbf{\Sigma}_{11}^{-1}\mathbf{\Sigma}_{12}$$

so that

$$\mathbf{C}_{22}\mathbf{C}_{22}^{\mathrm{T}} = \mathbf{\Sigma}_{22} - \mathbf{C}_{21}\mathbf{C}_{21}^{\mathrm{T}} = \mathbf{\Sigma}_{22} - \mathbf{\Sigma}_{21}\mathbf{\Sigma}_{11}^{-1}\mathbf{\Sigma}_{12},$$

and $\mathrm{VAR}(\mathbf{X}_2|\mathbf{x}_1)$ has been assigned the second form above.

Appendix C
Numerical algorithms: A third tool

C.1 Introduction

Can't we simply rely on the available software and avoid what is behind numerical methods altogether? A lot of work *can* be completed that way with numerical algorithms as black boxes, but if things go wrong you are stuck without knowledge of what's on the inside, and should you become involved in software development, numerical tools play a leading role. For a broad and practically oriented text try *Numerical Recipes in C* (Press *et al.*, 2007), with sister volumes in C++, Fortran and Pascal, which comes with hundreds of implemented procedures that can be downloaded and used for your own programming.

The purpose of this appendix is the much more modest one of reviewing numerical methods for *this book* in a relaxed manner which doesn't require prior knowledge of numerical mathematics. A lot can actually be achieved with a handful of elementary methods, and some of them are up to 200 years old! Minimizing or maximizing functions is an exception deserving special mention. Since the days of Newton–Raphson the world has moved far, and optimization software may work magnificently even when differentiation is carried out numerically. Why is it advantageous to avoid exact calculation of derivatives? Because implementation is often time consuming, and when the function to be optimized is a Monte Carlo simulation it may be impossible. Don't differentiate the function to be optimized to solve equations instead. This is still advocated in some textbooks, but after considerable effort the original problem has been replaced by a more difficult one! Non-linear equations in one variable are easy (Section C.4). Several of them are best avoided (if possible).

C.2 Cholesky computing

C.2.1 Introduction

Numerical linear algebra is a huge field, with applications everywhere from production planning to partial differential equations. Yet we have only met symmetric

---

Algorithm C.1 The Cholesky factor

---

0 Input: $\mathbf{A} = (a_{ij})$

1 $c_{11} \leftarrow \sqrt{a_{11}}, \quad c_{1j} \leftarrow 0 \;\text{ for }\; j = 2, \ldots, n$ *%Initialization*

2 For $i = 2, \ldots, n$ do *%Recursion here*

3 $\quad c_{ij} \leftarrow (a_{ij} - \sum_{k=1}^{j-1} c_{ik}c_{jk})/c_{jj} \;\text{ for }\; j = 1, \ldots, i-1$

4 $\quad c_{ii} \leftarrow (a_{ii} - \sum_{k=1}^{i-1} c_{ik}^2)^{1/2}$

5 $\quad c_{ij} \leftarrow 0 \;\text{ for }\; j = i+1, \ldots, n$

6 Return $\mathbf{C} = (c_{ij})$.

---

and positive definite matrices, and computational issues arising with these can be developed from the Cholesky decomposistion. How that is done is outlined below, but there are many other ways that inverses $\mathbf{A}^{-1}$ of a postive definite $\mathbf{A}$ can be found or linear equations $\mathbf{Ax} = \mathbf{b}$ solved, for example in R by commands `solve(A)` and `solve(A,b)`.

C.2.2 The Cholesky decomposition

A symmetric and positive definite $n \times n$ matrix $\mathbf{A} = (a_{ij})$ can be factorized as $\mathbf{A} = \mathbf{CC}^{\mathrm{T}}$ where the Cholesky matrix $\mathbf{C} = (c_{ij})$ has zeros over the main diagonal so that $c_{ij} = 0$ for $j > i$. We need $\mathbf{C}$ to simulate Gaussian vectors, and Algorithm C.1 shows how it is computed.

Start by filling out the first row of $\mathbf{C}$ and then enter a recursion over the remaining rows, completing one row after the other until the last one. The scheme is organized so that c_{ij} is always precomputed when needed. Direct multiplication verifies that the coefficients c_{ij} do indeed satisfy the defining relationship.

It is a safe algorithm, despite the presence of c_{jj} in the denominators on Line 3. Positive definitness yields $c_{jj} > 0$, and should some of them be so close to zero that the algorithm crashes, take another look at your problem. It may need reformulation since some of the variables that produced $\mathbf{A}$ are so strongly related that their number might be reduced.

C.2.3 Linear equations

Linear least squares, the Markowitz problem of Section 5.3 and many others are solved by linear equations $\mathbf{Ax} = \mathbf{b}$ where $\mathbf{A}$ is positive definite and symmetric and $\mathbf{b} = (b_1, \ldots, b_n)^{\mathrm{T}}$. One of the simplest and fastest solutions is through the Cholesky factorization of $\mathbf{A}$ with the two equations

$$\mathbf{Cy} = \mathbf{b} \quad \text{and} \quad \mathbf{C}^{\mathrm{T}}\mathbf{x} = \mathbf{y}, \tag{C.1}$$

Algorithm C.2 Linear equations with positive definite matrices

0 Input: $\mathbf{A}$ factorized as $\mathbf{CC}^{\mathrm{T}}$ and $\mathbf{b}$
1 For $i = 1, \dots, n$ do *%First loop for* $y_1, \dots, y_n$
2 $\quad s \leftarrow b_i$ and repeat for $j = 1, \dots, i-1$ $\quad s \leftarrow s - c_{ij}y_j$
3 $\quad y_i \leftarrow s/c_{ii}$
4 For $i = n, \dots, 1$ do *%Second loop for* $x_1, \dots, x_n$
5 $\quad s \leftarrow y_i$ and repeat for $j = n, \dots, i+1$ $\quad s \leftarrow s - c_{ji}x_j$
6 $\quad x_i \leftarrow s/c_{ii}$
7 Return $x_1, \dots, x_n$.

which provides the right $\mathbf{x}$ since $\mathbf{Ax} = \mathbf{CC}^{\mathrm{T}}\mathbf{x} = \mathbf{Cy} = \mathbf{b}$. Why is it easier to solve *two* linear equations instead of one? Because $\mathbf{C}$ and $\mathbf{C}^{\mathrm{T}}$ are both in triangular form with zeros above or below the main diagonal. Solutions of such equations are quickly found by back-substitution. If $\mathbf{x} = (x_1, \dots, x_n)^{\mathrm{T}}$ and $\mathbf{y} = (y_1, \dots, y_n)^{\mathrm{T}}$, then (C.1) yields

$$y_i = \frac{1}{c_{ii}}\left(b_i - \sum_{j=1}^{i-1} c_{ij}y_j\right), \quad i = 1, \dots, n$$

and

$$x_i = \frac{1}{c_{ii}}\left(y_i - \sum_{j=i+1}^{n} c_{ji}x_j\right), \quad i = n, \dots, 1$$

where the second recursion is run backwards. The method is a special case of the general **LU** factorization, which applies to all non-singular matrices.

Computer commands is organized as in Algorithm C.2. The sequence $y_1, \dots, y_n$ is first computed (and stored) in Lines 1–3 and then used to generate the solution (Lines 4–6).

C.2.4 Matrix inversion

The inverse $\mathbf{D} = \mathbf{A}^{-1}$ can also be computed in this way since its columns $\mathbf{d}_1, \dots, \mathbf{d}_n$ are solutions of the linear equations $\mathbf{Ad}_j = \mathbf{e}_j$, where $\mathbf{e}_j$ is the vector with one at position j and zeros everywhere else. We must Cholsky-factorize $\mathbf{A}$ first and then apply Algorithm C.2 with $\mathbf{b} = \mathbf{e}_j$ for $j = 1, \dots, n$.

C.3 Interpolation, integration, differentiation

C.3.1 Introduction

A function is often sought where it has not been tabulated, and not many integrals are available in closed form. General (and very efficient) numerical methods solve such problems. Some of them are very old (much of the material of the present section goes back to the first half of the nineteenth century!). We shall only be dealing with functions $F(x)$ of *single variables* (that's why the history is so long). Problems in higher dimensions are much more difficult, though there *are* modern methods, see Evans and Schwarz (2000) on numerical integration and Buhmann (2003) on high-dimensional interpolation. Numerical differentiation (the third topic of this section) differs in that the issue is the same whatever the number of variables.

C.3.2 Numerical interpolation

Suppose a function $F(x)$ is known at $x_1, \ldots, x_n$ and is demanded at x. Numerical methods provide an *approximate* answer. The most accurate one is more than 150 years old and due to the French mathematician **Lagrange**. Let $y_i = F(x_i)$ for $i = 1, \ldots, n$. The Lagrange interpolating polynomial is then

$$P_n(x) = \sum_{i=1}^{n} c_i(x) y_i \quad \text{where} \quad c_i(x) = \prod_{j \neq i} \frac{x - x_j}{x_i - x_j}. \tag{C.2}$$

Clearly $c_i(x_i) = 1$ and $c_i(x_j) = 0$ for $j \neq i$, so that $P_n(x_i) = y_i = F(x_i)$ for all i. The function $P_n(x)$ **interpolates** $F(x)$ at all x_i. Note that $c_1(x), \ldots, c_n(x)$ are polynomials of degree $n - 1$, and $P_n(x)$ is too. The special case $n = 2$ is the linear interpolation formula

$$P_2(x) = \frac{y_1(x_2 - x) + y_2(x - x_1)}{x_2 - x_1},$$

often used to extend a table beyond the values tabulated. Higher-order versions such as $P_3(x)$ or $P_4(x)$ are usually much more accurate. Recursive forms of the method are presented in Hämerlin and Hoffmann (1991).

Does agreement on n points force approximate agreement elsewhere? It does if $F(x)$ is a smooth function and x located inside the set $x_1, \ldots, x_n$. It can then be proved that the discrepancy is bounded by

$$|P_n(x) - F(x)| \leq \frac{C}{(n + 1)!},$$

where C is a constant depending on the $(n + 1)$th-order derivative of $F(x)$; see Hämerlin and Hoffmann (1991) for details. The denominator $(n + 1)!$ quickly

Algorithm C.3 Lagrange interpolation

```
Input: x_1, ..., x_n, y_1, ..., y_n and x
P ← 0
For i = 1, ..., n do
    c ← 1
    For j = 1, ..., n do
        If j ≠ i then c ← c(x − x_j)/(x_i − x_j)
    P ← P + c y_i
Return P.
```

becomes huge as n is raised, and the error may be very small indeed (the Lagrange answer is often accurate to many decimals). However, the method is hopeless *outside* the given set $x_1, \dots, x_n$ with huge inaccuracies starting on the inside. There are several other forms of interpolation, such as splines (Press *et al.*, 2007) and radial bases (Buhmann, 2003). The popular spline approach can't compete with traditional Lagrange in accuracy when the latter is applicable.

Implementation can be carried out very cleverly through **Neville**'s algorithm (Press *et al.*, 2007), but it also works to proceed more stolidly from Algorithm C.3. On output, P holds the value of the interpolating polynomial at x.

C.3.3 Numerical integration

Most integrals do not permit nice, closed solutions (unlike in mathematics courses!), but there are highly satisfactory and simple numerical ones. The most obvious method is to divide the integration interval (a, b) into equidistant subintervals. Introduce

$$h = \frac{b-a}{n} \quad \text{and} \quad x_i = a + ih, \quad F_i = F(x_i), \quad i = 0, 1, \dots n$$

where $x_0 = a$ and $x_n = b$. The integral and its approximation are then

$$\underbrace{I = \int_a^b F(x)\, dx}_{\text{exact}} \quad \text{and} \quad \underbrace{\tilde{I}_n = h(c_0 F_0 + c_1 F_1 + \cdots + c_n F_n)}_{\text{numerical approximation}}, \tag{C.3}$$

where $c_0, \dots, c_n$ are coefficients. Simple examples with $n = 2$ and $n = 3$ are

$$\underbrace{\tilde{I}_1 = h\left(\tfrac{1}{2}F_0 + \tfrac{1}{2}F_1\right)}_{\text{trapezoidal rule}} \quad \text{and} \quad \underbrace{\tilde{I}_2 = h\left(\tfrac{1}{3}F_0 + \tfrac{4}{3}F_1 + \tfrac{1}{3}F_2\right)}_{\text{Simpson's rule}}.$$

The trapezoidal rule is exact when the integrand is a straight line, but the Simpson method does better and is exact for polynomials up to degree two. Although of little interest in themselves, both procedures can be refined by applying them to sub-intervals and adding the results.

Suppose first that the original integral over (a, b) is split into sub-integrals over (x_0, x_1), (x_1, x_2), and so forth up to (x_{n-1}, x_n), with the trapezoidal rule applied to each sub-integral. Adding the results leads to the approximation

$$\tilde{I}_n = h\left(\frac{1}{2}F_0 + F_1 + \cdots + F_{n-1} + \frac{1}{2}F_n\right), \quad h = \frac{b-a}{n}, \tag{C.4}$$

known as the **extended** trapezoidal. There is an analogous extended Simpson method based on the $2n$ points $x_0, \ldots, x_{2n}$ with $a = x_0$ and $b = x_{2n}$. When elementary Simpson is applied to the integrals over (x_{2i-2}, x_{2i}) for $i = 1, \ldots, n$, we obtain

$$\tilde{I}_{2n} = h\left(\frac{1}{3}F_0 + \frac{4}{3}F_1 + \frac{2}{3}F_2 + \cdots + \frac{2}{3}F_{2n-2} + \frac{4}{3}F_{2n-1} + \frac{1}{3}F_{2n}\right), \quad h = \frac{b-a}{2n} \tag{C.5}$$

which is more accurate than the trapeziodal rule. Errors of these methods are bounded by

$$\underbrace{|\tilde{I}_n - I| \leq Ch^2}_{\textit{extended trapeziodal}} \quad \text{and} \quad \underbrace{|\tilde{I}_{2n} - I| \leq Ch^4}_{\textit{extended Simpson}},$$

with C a constant which is bounded if the integrand has finite second-order derivative (trapeziodal) and fourth-order (Simpson) over the integration interval; see Hämerlin and Hoffmann (1991). Integrands with isolated discontinuities in the function itself or its derivatives are best handled by splitting the integration into sub-intervals with these singularities as end points.

C.3.4 Numerical integration II: Gaussian quadrature

Is it obvious that the points x_i on which the integrand is evaluated should be equally spaced? Nineteenth-century mathematicians were able to do much better through a different strategy! The approximation is now

$$\tilde{I}_n = w_1 F(x_1) + \cdots + w_n F(x_n), \tag{C.6}$$

where the **abscissas** x_i and the **weights** w_i are carefully selected. Remarkably, they can be found so that the sum evaluates integrals of all polynomials up to degree $2n - 1$ exactly! This suggests high accuracy for general integrands, which is indeed true. The method is known as **Gauss–Legendre** quadrature and is supported by a neat mathematical theory. This is beyond our scope, but its conclusion is easy. For integration between 0 and 1, insert abscissas and weights from Table C.1 into (C.6).

Table C.1 Abscissas (x_i) and coefficients (w_i) for Gauss–Legendre quadrature between 0 and 1. For $i > n/2$ take $x_i = 1 - x_{n+1-i}$ and $w_i = w_{n+1-i}$

	$n = 3$		$n = 4$		$n = 5$		$n = 6$	
i	x	w	x	w	x	w	x	w
1	0.112702	0.277778	0.069432	0.173927	0.046910	0.118463	0.033765	0.085662
2	0.500000	0.444444	0.330009	0.326073	0.230765	0.239314	0.169395	0.180381
3					0.500000	0.284444	0.380690	0.233957

	$n = 7$		$n = 8$		$n = 9$		$n = 10$	
i	x	w	x	w	x	w	x	w
1	0.025446	0.064742	0.019855	0.050614	0.015920	0.040637	0.013047	0.033336
2	0.129234	0.139853	0.101667	0.111191	0.081984	0.090324	0.067468	0.074726
3	0.297077	0.190915	0.237234	0.156853	0.193314	0.130305	0.160295	0.109543
4	0.500000	0.208980	0.408283	0.181342	0.337873	0.156174	0.283302	0.134633
5					0.500000	0.165120	0.425563	0.147762

General intervals (a, b) are handled by noting that

$$I = \int_a^b F(z)\,dz = (b-a)\int_0^1 F\{a + x(b-a)\}\,dx,$$

and the Gauss–Legendre approximation becomes

$$\tilde{I}_n = (b-a)\{w_1 F(z_1) + \cdots + w_n F(z_n)\} \quad \text{for} \quad z_i = a + (b-a)x_i$$

with $x_1, \ldots, x_n$ and $w_1, \ldots, w_n$ from Table C.1.

Do you find the values of n in Table C.1 conspiciously small? Good results are often obtained with n as small as 5 or 6 (try a simple function like the exponential and compare the exact result with that provided by quadrature). Behind such accuracy is an error bound of the form

$$|\tilde{I}_n - I| \leq \frac{C}{(2n)!},$$

where C is finite if the derivative of order $2n$ is finite over the integration interval; see Allen and Isaacson (1998). The denominator grows extremely rapidly with n making the error small, but the caveat is that derivatives up to order $2n$ must exist everywhere within (a, b). Otherwise the delicate logic behind the method is destroyed, and it becomes useless. Many other quadrature rules can be found in Press *et al.* (2007).

C.3.5 Numerical differentiation

A lot of implementation work may be saved with numerical optimization (Section C.5) if exact derivatives can be replaced by numerical approximations. The issue is the same whatever the number of variables, and there is no need to go beyond functions $F(x)$ of a single variable x. Its derivative $F'(x)$ may be computed from either of the approximations

$$\frac{F(x+h)-F(x)}{h} \doteq F'(x) \quad \text{or} \quad \frac{F(x+h)-F(x-h)}{2h} \doteq F'(x), \tag{C.7}$$

where $h > 0$ is some small number. The symmetric version on the right is a good deal more accurate. If you think h should be as small as possible, you are wrong since that would blow round-off error sky high. The optimum depends on the accuracy ϵ_m with which real numbers are represented in the computer. Good choices in (C.7) are $h = \epsilon_m^{1/2}$ on the left and $h = \epsilon_m^{1/3}$ on the right; see below. Are these recommendations surprisingly large? They suggest $h = 0.003$ for the second formula in (C.7) in a computer with 32-bit word length and perhaps $h = 0.000001$ if double-precision arithmetic is being used.

Numerical inaccuracies are of two kinds. First there is discretization or truncation error due to the formulae in (C.7) being approximations. The ordinary Taylor series

$$F(x+h) \doteq F(x) + hF'(x) + \frac{1}{2}h^2F''(x)$$

immediately tells us that the discrepancy between the two sides on the left of (C.7) is proportional to h. If you subtract the analogous formula for $F(x-h)$, you will quickly discover that the error in the symmetric version on the right is proportional to h^2, much better accuracy. Additional terms in the numerator will do even better. Take

$$\frac{-F(x+2h)+8F(x+h)-8F(x-h)+F(x-2h)}{12h} \doteq F'(x),$$

and a longer Taylor argument reveals that truncation error is now down to h^4.

But there is not much point in such sophistication when round-off error is taken into account. Here is a neat argument taken from Press *et al.* (2007). Round-off error for numerical differentiation at x is approximately $\epsilon_m a(x)/h$ and truncation error $b(x)h^\gamma$ with ϵ_m machine precision, and γ defined by the method. Total error is close to

$$\frac{\epsilon_m a(x)}{h} + b(x)h^\gamma \quad \text{with minimum} \quad C\epsilon_m^{\gamma/(1+\gamma)} \quad \text{at} \quad h = \left(\frac{a(x)\epsilon_m}{b(x)\gamma}\right)^{1/(1+\gamma)},$$

where C depends on $a(x)$, $b(x)$ and γ, but not on ϵ_m. But then $h = \epsilon_m^{1/(1+\gamma)}$ is close to the optimum and total error proportional to $\epsilon_m^{\gamma/(1+\gamma)}$, which justifies the earlier recommendations on h. There is a useful gain in switching from the one-sided to the two-sided approximation in (C.7), which changes γ from 1 to 2 and the error from $\epsilon_m^{1/2}$ to $\epsilon_m^{2/3}$, but it is less effective to increase γ further.

C.4 Bracketing and bisection: Easy and safe

C.4.1 Introduction

You may have met **Newtons's** method in mathematics courses. Suppose x_0 approximates the solution s of the equation $F(s) = 0$. It can be enhanced by utilizing that

$$F(s) \doteq F(x_0) + F'(x_0)(s - x_0),$$

where $F'(x)$ is the derivative. This is the start of the Taylor series for $F(s)$ and nearly exact if x_0 is close to s. If the right-hand side is equated with zero and solved for s, the solution (now called x_1) becomes

$$x_1 = x_0 - \frac{F(x_0)}{F'(x_0)}, \tag{C.8}$$

which is another approximation and conceivably more accurate than x_0 was. The argument can be repeated, and this sets up a sequence $x_0, x_1, x_2, \ldots$ hopefully approaching s. The algorithm is ultra-fast when it works.

But one thing is disconcerting. Changes permitted are unlimited (small absolute values of $F'(x_0)$ in (C.8) might imply huge jumps), and couldn't that lead the method astray? Divergence towards infinity is certainly possible! Try the equation $e^x/(1 + e^x) - 1/2 = 0$ for which (C.8) becomes $x_1 = x_0 - (e^{x_0} - e^{-x_0})/2$. It will oscillate further and further from the root $s = 0$ if you start at $x_0 > 2.1773$. The remedy is to work with **brackets** which are finite regions with the solution inside. In the present case brackets are finite intervals (a, b) for which $a < s < b$. Numerical mathematicians value brackets as a way of creating **globally** convergent algorithms which reach the solution from any reasonable starting point. When the Newton theme is pursued with many variables in the next section, brackets will be there. With only one variable it is possible to discard Newton and use brackets only! For simple problems that is actually a very good method.

C.4.2 Bisection: Bracketing as iteration

Suppose we seek the solution of the equation $F(s) = 0$ and know that $F(a)F(b) < 0$ for $a < b$. If $F(x)$ is a continuous function, it is bound to possess a root s between a and b which is then a bracket. The idea is to shorten it iteratively. To be specific, suppose

$$F(a) < 0 < F(b) \quad \text{and take} \quad x = (a + b)/2.$$

Algorithm C.4 Bisection

0 Input: $F(x)$, $a < b$, n and either $F(a) < 0 < F(b)$ or $F(a) > 0 > F(b)$
1 Repeat n times.
2 $\quad x \leftarrow (a+b)/2$
3 $\quad$ If $F(x) < 0$ then $a \leftarrow x$ else $b \leftarrow x$ *%Assumes $F(a) < 0 < F(b)$, in the opposite case replace if-condition with $F(x) > 0$*
4 Return $\tilde{s} \leftarrow (a+b)/2$. *%$\tilde{s}$ is the approximation of s*

A little thought tells you that $a < s < x$ if $F(x) > 0$ and $x < s < b$ in the opposite case, so that

$$\text{new bracket} = \begin{matrix} (a,x) & \text{if } F(x) > 0 \\ (x,b) & \text{if } F(x) \leq 0 \end{matrix}$$

and the old bracket has been halved. The idea may be repeated, leading to Algorithm C.4.

The algorithm reduces the bracket to one-half per iteration and is known as **bisection**. It can't fail and doesn't require the derivative. The error is, after n iterations, bounded by

$$|\tilde{s} - s| \leq (b-a)/2^n. \tag{C.9}$$

Use $n = 20$ and the error is less than 10^{-6} times the length of the original bracket $b - a$. If there are several solutions, one of them will be found. Before entering the algorithm we need the initial bracket, which could be determined by trial and error.

C.4.3 Golden section: Bracketing for extrema

The same idea works when you seek maxima or minima. If a convenient expression for the derivative is available, you may solve the equation $F'(s) = 0$ through Algorithm C.4, but a more subtle version of the preceding argument avoids differentiation alltogether. Suppose three points a, b, c are known, for which

$$a < c < b \quad \text{and} \quad F(c) < \min\{F(a), F(b)\}. \tag{C.10}$$

Then $F(x)$ has a (local) minimum s inside the bracket (a, b) (the function doesn't even have to be continuous!). The algorithm proceeds iteratively by constructing new triplets (a, b, c) satisfying (C.10) which dwindle in size towards a single point and must then be a local minimum.

Such schemes switch between raising a and lowering b and work alternately with the intervals (a, c) and (c, b). To be specific consider the former, suppose $a < x < c$

Algorithm C.5 Golden-section search

```
Input: Function F(x), a < c < b with F(c) < min{F(a), F(b)}
F_min ← F(c)     and     γ ← 0.38197
Repeat n times
                                   %The lower of the two intervals if the longest
   If (c − a > b − c) then x ← c − γ(c − a) and
      If (F(x) < F_min) then F_min ← F(x), b ← c, c ← x else a ← x
                                   %The higher of the two intervals if the longest
   If (c − a ≤ b − c) then x ← c + γ(b − c) and
      If (F(x) < F_min) then F_min ← F(x), a ← c, c ← x else b ← x
Return s̃ ← c and F_min.            %s̃ is minimum with function value F_min
```

and define

$$\text{new triplet} = \begin{array}{ll} (a, x, c) & \text{if } F(x) < F(c) \\ (x, c, b) & \text{if } F(x) \geq F(c). \end{array}$$

The *second* point of the new triplet has the smallest F-value and (C.10) is satisfied. Since both $c - a$ and $b - x$ are less than the original $b - a$, the bracket has been shortened. The strategy has maximum efficiency if x is selected in the *largest* of the two intervals (a, c) and (c, b) with $x = c - \gamma(c - a)$ or $x = c + \gamma(b - c)$, where $\gamma = 0.38197$. The detailed implementation in Algorithm C.5 yields on output an approximation, $\tilde{s}$, of the exact solution. If we start at an exact golden-section triple (a, c, b), the error is

$$|\tilde{s} - s| \leq (b - a) \times 0.61803^n \tag{C.11}$$

which is verified below, and it is almost as good in general. When concerned with maximization, find the minimum of $-F(x)$ instead.

C.4.4 Golden section: Justification

The value of $\gamma = (3 - \sqrt{5})/2 \doteq 0.38197$ is the smallest root of the second-order equation $\gamma^2 - 3\gamma + 1 = 0$! A point that divides an interval in pieces of fractions 0.38197 and 0.61803 of the original is known as a **golden section** (and enjoys an ancient history). That is how the new point x is defined in Algorithm C.5. If a triplet (a, c, b) is a golden section, then all sub-triples are too. We shall now prove this along with the error statement above.

Suppose (for example) that $c - a = (1 - \gamma)(b - a)$. Then (a, c) is longer than the other interval (c, b) and $x = c - \gamma(c - a)$. Hence

$$b - x = b - c + \gamma(c - a) = b - a - (1 - \gamma)(c - a) = (1 - (1 - \gamma)^2)(b - a) = (1 - \gamma)(b - a)$$

because of the equation satisfied by γ. This tells us that the width of the new triplet (either $c - a$ or $b - x$) is exactly $1 - \gamma$ times the old one, which proves (C.11). Moreover

$$\frac{x-a}{c-a} = \frac{c-\gamma(c-a)-a}{c-a} = 1-\gamma \quad \text{and} \quad \frac{b-c}{b-x} = \frac{b-c}{(1-\gamma)(b-a)} = \frac{\gamma}{1-\gamma} = 1-\gamma$$

where the last identity on the right is due to the definition of γ. Whether the new triplet is (a, x, c) or (x, c, b) it is still a golden section. When working from the second interval (c, b), the conclusion is the same (by symmetry). The original triplet does not have to be a golden section, but the iteration will leave us with one after the inner point x is chosen as the new c.

C.5 Optimization: Advanced and useful

C.5.1 Introduction

The Newton–Raphson method (Newton extended to several variables) solves non-linear equations and minimizes and maximizes functions. Though often cited in textbooks in actuarial science and statistics, huge improvements have been available for decades. Among these post-Newton methods folklore holds that the **variable metric** type (also known as **quasi-Newton**) is the best. We concentrate on these below. For mathematical proofs you must consult specialist books in numerical mathematics. The present exposition only concerns how such methods work. As with many good things in life they don't perform when used wrongly. Common reasons are suggested at the end.

C.5.2 The Newton–Raphson method

Consider the quadratic form

$$F + \mathbf{x}^{\mathrm{T}}\mathbf{g} + \mathbf{x}^{\mathrm{T}}\mathbf{H}\mathbf{x}$$

with $\mathbf{x} = (x_1, \dots, x_n)^{\mathrm{T}}$ a vector, F and $\mathbf{g} = (g_1, \dots, g_n)^{\mathrm{T}}$ a fixed coefficient and vector and $\mathbf{H} = (h_{ij})$ some matrix. Finding the minimum under variation of $\mathbf{x}$ when $\mathbf{H}$ is positive definite solved the Markowitz problem in Section 5.3. Linear equations were then obtained by differentiation (Section 5.8). The same course here yields the solution $\mathbf{s} = -\mathbf{H}^{-1}\mathbf{g}$, which is the unique minimum of the quadratic form when H is positive definit.

This result provides much of what is needed for the Newton–Raphson method through an argument that is a direct extension of the one used at the start of

Section C.4. Suppose $\mathbf{x}_k$ is an approximation to a (local) mimimum $\mathbf{s}$ of a smooth function $F(\mathbf{x})$ (twice differentiable). Such functions are nearly quadratic forms locally around $\mathbf{x}_k$. Indeed, the multivariate Taylor series yields the approximation

$$F(\mathbf{s}) \doteq F(\mathbf{x}_k) + \mathbf{g}_k^{\mathrm{T}}(\mathbf{s} - \mathbf{x}_k) + \frac{1}{2}(\mathbf{s} - \mathbf{x}_k)^{\mathrm{T}}\mathbf{H}_k(\mathbf{s} - \mathbf{x}_k), \tag{C.12}$$

where $\mathbf{g}_k$ is the **gradient** of $F(\mathbf{x})$ at $\mathbf{x} = \mathbf{x}_k$ and $\mathbf{H}_k$ its **Hessian** at the same point. This means that $\mathbf{g}_k = (g_{k1}, \ldots, g_{kn})^{\mathrm{T}}$ is the column vector and $\mathbf{H}_k = (h_{kij})$ the matrix for which

$$g_{ki} = \frac{\partial F(\mathbf{x}_k)}{\partial x_i} \quad \text{and} \quad h_{kij} = \frac{\partial^2 F(\mathbf{x}_k)}{\partial x_i \partial x_j}.$$

Finding an approximation that improves on $\mathbf{x}_k$ has now become a question of minimizing the quadratic form with respect to $\mathbf{s}$. If $\mathbf{H}_k$ is positive definit, the minimum of the right-hand side of (C.12) occurs at $\mathbf{s} = \mathbf{x}_{k+1}$ where

$$\mathbf{x}_{k+1} - \mathbf{x}_k = -\mathbf{H}_k^{-1}\mathbf{g}_k, \tag{C.13}$$

and $\mathbf{x}_{k+1}$ is the new approximation. This is a recursion which is run until it stabilizes. That doesn't take long when the initial point $\mathbf{x}_0$ is close to the eventual minimum $\mathbf{s}$, but where to start is no trivial matter.

C.5.3 Variable metric methods

The natural-looking Newton–Raphson method has several weaknesses. Hessian matrices do become postive definite (and hence possess inverses) close to the optimum $\mathbf{s}$, but this property may not be true further out, and the method falls apart. Modifications *have* been attempted (see Fletcher, 1987), but in reality other ways are superior. Quasi-Newton (or variable metric) methods replace the Hessian $\mathbf{H}_k$ by positive-definite *approximations* which converge to the exact one at the end, and instead of $\mathbf{H}_k$ itself we now work with its inverse $\mathbf{H}_k^{-1}$. *No* matrix inversion is therefore needed, and nor do we have to supply second-order derivatives (which often takes much effort).

Suppose $\mathbf{x}_k$ has been stored in the computer along with the gradient $\mathbf{g}_k$ and the approximation $\mathbf{A}_k$ to the inverse Hessian $\mathbf{H}_k^{-1}$. The new approximation $\mathbf{x}_{k+1}$ is then

$$\mathbf{x}_{k+1} - \mathbf{x}_k = -\gamma\mathbf{d_k} \quad \text{where} \quad \mathbf{d}_k = \mathbf{A}_k\mathbf{g}_k, \tag{C.14}$$

which feeds on (C.13). A new issue is γ which controls the movement away from $\mathbf{x}_k$, and a typical implementation minimizes $F(\mathbf{x}_k - \gamma\mathbf{d_k})$ with respect to γ before making the jump to $\mathbf{x}_{k+1}$. This one-dimensional problem can be solved by golden search or more sophisticated procedures.

Algorithm C.6 Quasi-Newton minimization

0	Input: $F(\mathbf{x})$, $\mathbf{x}_0$, $F_0 = F(\mathbf{x}_0)$, $\mathbf{A}_0$, tol	*%tol=small value. Often* $\mathbf{A}_0 =$ *identity*
1	For $k = 0, 1, 2, \ldots$ repeat	
2	Compute gradient $\mathbf{g}_k$ at x_k	*%Partial derivatives at* $\mathbf{x}_k$
3	$\mathbf{d} \leftarrow \mathbf{A}_k\mathbf{g}_k$ and let γ minimize $F(\mathbf{x}_k - \gamma\mathbf{d})$ with F_{k+1} as minimum	*%Minimization w.r.t. one variable, Algorithm C.5 or more sophisticated*
4	$\mathbf{x}_{k+1} \leftarrow \mathbf{x}_k - \gamma\mathbf{d}$	
5	If $\lvert F_{k+1} - F_k \rvert <$ tol, then **stop** and return $\mathbf{x}_{k+1}$ as solution	*%Finished now*
6	Compute $\mathbf{A}_{k+1}$	*%For the next round: Using* (C.15) *with* (C.16) *or* (C.17)

What remains is the update of $\mathbf{A}_k$. Let

$$\mathbf{u}_k = \mathbf{x}_{k+1} - \mathbf{x}_k \quad \text{and} \quad \mathbf{v}_k = \mathbf{g}_{k+1} - \mathbf{g}_k. \tag{C.15}$$

One scheme is then

$$\mathbf{A}_{k+1} = \mathbf{A}_k + \frac{\mathbf{u}_k\mathbf{u}_k^{\mathrm{T}}}{\mathbf{u}_k^{\mathrm{T}}\mathbf{v}_k} - \frac{(\mathbf{A}_k\mathbf{v}_k)(\mathbf{A}_k\mathbf{v}_k)^{\mathrm{T}}}{\mathbf{v}_k^{\mathrm{T}}\mathbf{A}_k\mathbf{v}_k}, \tag{C.16}$$

which originated around 1960 through work by Davidon, Fletcher and Powell (hence known as **DFP**). Many experts (see Fletcher, 1987) prefer a version that was proposed 10 years later by Boyden, Fletcher, Goldfarb and Shanno simultaneously. This so-called **BFGS** update reads

$$\mathbf{A}_{k+1} = \mathbf{A}_k + \left(1 + \frac{\mathbf{v}_k^{\mathrm{T}}\mathbf{A}_k\mathbf{v}_k}{\mathbf{u}_k^{\mathrm{T}}\mathbf{v}_k}\right)\frac{\mathbf{u}_k\mathbf{u}_k^{\mathrm{T}}}{\mathbf{u}_k^{\mathrm{T}}\mathbf{v}_k} - \left(\frac{\mathbf{u}_k\mathbf{v}_k^{\mathrm{T}}\mathbf{A}_k + \mathbf{A}_k\mathbf{v}_k\mathbf{u}_k^{\mathrm{T}}}{\mathbf{u}_k^{\mathrm{T}}\mathbf{v}_k}\right). \tag{C.17}$$

It isn't possible with either scheme to gauge that a sequence of positive-definite matrices are produced which tend to the inverse Hessian at the optimum. Fletcher (1987) gives the proof.

In summary, the method proceeds as in Algorithm C.6. In Line 6 all the necessary input to $\mathbf{A}_{k+1}$ has become available. When the tolerance criterion is satisfied (Line 5), $\mathbf{x}_{k+1}$ is returned as an approximation to the minimum. There are in practice additional details concerning the bracketing of the minimum. Good implementations compute bounds on γ prior to entering Line 3, and this makes makes the procedure robust (see Section C.4). It has often been maintained (as is the experience of this author too) that the partial derivatives (Line 2) may be determined numerically (Section C.3 outlined how this is done). That is a great practical advantage since exact differentiation often takes much effort and may be downright impossible if $F(\mathbf{x})$ is the output of a simulation program.

The algorithm constructs a monotone sequence $F_0 \geq F_1 \geq F_2 \ldots$ that forces $\mathbf{x}_0, \mathbf{x}_1, \ldots$ towards a local minimum. In practice, round-off errors might still make the procedure crash. If you start very far away from the optimum, the derivatives could be so huge that they are not properly represented in the computer (if so, try to start elsewhere). Another point is the scaling of the variables. Derivatives depend on the measurement units used and may vary enormously from one variable to another. Again round-off error might bring the method down, but there is a remedy: Rescale to make the derivatives more equal (don't express economic capital in cents!). Bracketing that limits the solution to a bounded region is still another important practical point. Little theory is available here, and the issue is typically tackled problem-dependent.

C.6 Bibliographical notes

C.6.1 General numerical methods

The outstanding monograph on practical computing is Press *et al.* (2007), the latest edition in C of a classic (there are versions in C++, Fortran and Pascal too). A more recent alternative is Salleh *et al.* (2007). There are hosts of introductory books on numerical analysis. You might find Allen and Isaacson (1998) suitable, or Hämerlin and Hoffman (1991) with a little more theory. Gentle (2002) and Lange (1999) are directed towards applications in statistics.

C.6.2 Optimization

Excellent introductory books on numerical optimization are still Fletcher (1987) and Gill *et al.* (1981), with Lange (2004) a more recent alternative.

References

Abramowitz, M. and Stegun, I. (1965). *Handbook of Mathematical Functions.* New York: Dover.

Adelson, R. M. (1966). Compound Poisson distributions. *Operational Research Quarterly*, **17**, 73–75.

Ahrens, J. and Dieter, U. (1974). Computer methods for sampling from Gamma, Beta, Poisson and binomial distributions. *Computing*, **12**, 223–246.

Allen, M. B. and Isaacson, E. L. (1998). *Numerical Analysis for Applied Science.* New York: John Wiley & Sons.

Antonio, K. and Beirlant, J. (2007). Actuarial statistics with generalized linear mixed models. *Insurance: Mathematics and Economics*, **40**, 58–76.

Applebaum. D. (2004). *Lévy Processes and Stochastic Calculus.* Cambridge: Cambridge University Press.

Asmussen, P. and Glynn, P. W. (2007). *Stochastic Simulation. Algorithms and Analysis.* New York: Springer-Verlag.

Asmussen, S. (2000). *Ruin Probabilities.* Singapore: World Scientific.

Asmussen, S. and Kroese, D. P. (2006). Improved algorithms for rare event simulation with heavy tails. *Advances in Applied Probability*, **38**, 545–558.

Atkinson, A. C. (1979). The computer generation of poisson random variables. *Applied Statistics*, **28**, 29–35.

Azcue, P. and Muler, N. (2005). Optimal reinsurance and dividend distribution policies in the Cramér–Lundberg model. *Mathematical Finance*, **15**, 261–308.

Babbel, D., Gold, J. and Merrill, C. B. (2002). Fair value of liabilities: The financial economics perspective. *North American Actuarial Journal*, **6**, 12–27.

Bacro, J. N. and Brito, M. (1998). A tail bootstrap procedure for estimating the tail Pareto-index. *Journal of Statistical Planning and Inference*, **71**, 245–260.

Baier, C. and Katoen, J. -P. (2008). *Principles of Model Checking.* Cambridge, MA: MIT Press.

Balakrishnan, N. (2004a). Continuous multivariate distributions. In Teugels, J. and Sundt, B. (eds), *Encyclopedia of Actuarial Science*. Chichester: John Wiley & Sons; pp. 330–357.

Balakrishnan, N. (2004b). Discrete multivariate distributions. In Teugels, J. and Sundt, B. (eds), *Encyclopedia of Actuarial Science*. Chichester: John Wiley & Sons; pp. 549–571.

Balakrishnan, N. and Nevzorov, V. B. (2003). *A Primer on Statistical Distributions*. Hoboken, NJ: John Wiley & Sons.

Ball, C. A. and Torous, W. N. (2000). Stochastic correlation across international stock markets. *Journal of Empirical Finance*, **7**, 373–388.

Ballotta, L., Esposito, G. and Haberman, S. (2006). The IASB insurance project for life insurance contracts: Impact on reserving methods and solvency. *Insurance: Mathematics and Economics*, **39**, 356–375.

Barndorff-Nielsen, O. (1997). Normal inverse Gaussian distributions and stochastic volatility modelling. *Scandinavian Journal of Statistics*, **24**, 1–13.

Barndorff-Nielsen, O. and Shepard, N. (2004). Econometric analysis of realized covariation: High frequency based covariation, regression and correlation in financial economics. *Econometrica*, **72**, 885–925.

Barndorff-Nielsen, O. and Stelzer, R. (2005). Absolute moments of generalized hyperbolic distributions and approximate scaling of normal inverse Gaussian Lévy processes. *Scandinavian Journal of Statistics*, **32**, 617–637.

Bäuerle, N. (2004). Traditional versus non-traditional reinsurance in a dynamic setting. *Scandinavian Actuarial Journal*, **5**, 355–371.

Bäuerle, N. (2005). Benchmark and mean-variance problems for insurers. *Mathematical Methods of Operations Research*, **62**, 159–165.

Bäuerle, N. and Grübel, R. (2005). Multivariate counting processes. Copulas and Beyond. *Astin Bulletin*, **35**, 379–408.

Bauwens, L., Lubrano, M. and Richard, J.-F. (1999). *Bayesian Inference in Dynamic Econometric Models*. Oxford: Oxford University Press.

Beirlant, J. (2004). Extremes. In Teugels, J. and Sundt, B. (eds), *Encyclopedia of Actuarial Science*. Chichester: John Wiley & Sons: pp. 654–661.

Beirlant, J. and Goegebeur, Y. (2004). Local polynomial maximum likelihood estimation for pareto type distributions. *Journal of Multivariate Analysis*, **89**, 97–118.

Beirlant, J., Teugels, J. L. and Vynckier, P. (1996). *Practical Analysis of Extreme Values*. Leuven: Leuven University Press.

Beirlant, J., Goegebeur, Y., Segers, J. and Teugels, J. (2004). *Statistics of Extremes: Theory and Applications*. Chichester: John Wiley & Sons.

Benninga, S. (2008). *Financial Modelling*, 3rd edn. Cambridge, MA: MIT Press.

Benth, F. (2004). *Option Theory with Stochastic Analysis. An Introduction to Mathematical Finance.* Berlin: Springer-Verlag.

Beran, J. (1994). *Statistics for Long-Memory Processes.* New York: Chapman & Hall.

Berkelaar, A., Dert, C., Oldenkamp, B. and Zhang, S. (2002). A primal–dual decomposition-based interior point approach to two-stage stochastic linear programming. *Operations Research*, **50**, 904–915.

Bernardo, J. M. and Smith, A. F. M. (2009). *Bayesian Theory*. Chichester: John Wiley & Sons.

Best, P. J. (1978). Letter to the Editor. *Applied Statistics*, **28**, 181.

Bhar, R, Chiarella, C. and Runggaldier, W. J. (2002). Estimation in models of the instantaneous short term interest rate by use of a dynamic Bayesian algorithm. In Sandmann, K. and Schönbucher, P. J. (eds), *Advances in Finance and Stochastics*. Berlin: Springer-Verlag; pp. 177–195.

Bingham, N. H. and Kiesel, R. (2004). *Risk-neutral Valuation, Pricing and Hedging of Financial Derivatives*, 2nd edn. London: Springer-Verlag.

Björk, T. (2006). *Arbitrage Theory in Continuous Time*, 2nd edn. Oxford: Oxford University Press.

Black, F. and Scholes, M. (1973). The pricing of options and corporate liabilities. *Journal of Political Economy*, **81**, 637–654.

Blum, P. and Dacorogna, M. (2004). DFA – dynamic financial analysis. In Teugels, J. and Sundt, B. (eds), *Encyclopedia of Actuarial Science*. Chichester: John Wiley & Sons; pp. 505–519.

Bodie, Z. and Davis, E. P. (eds) (2000). *The Foundation of Pension Finance*, Vols I and II. Cheltenham: Edward Elgar Publishing.

Boland, P. J. (2007). *Statistical and Probabilistic Methods in Actuarial Science.* Boca Raton, Fl: Chapman & Hall/CRC.

Bolia, N. and Juneja, S. (2005). Monte Carlo methods for pricing financial options. *Sādhanā*, **30**, 347–385.

Bollerslev, T. (2001). Financial econometrics: past developments and future challenges. *Journal of Econometrics*, **100**, 41–51.

Bølviken, E. (2004) Stochastic simulation. In Teugels, J. and Sundt, B. (eds), *Encyclopedia of Actuarial Science*. Chichester: John Wiley & Sons; pp. 1613–1615.

Booth, P., Chadburn, R., Cooper, D., Haberman, S. and James, D. (1999). *Modern Actuarial Theory and Practice.* London: Chapman & Hall/CRC.

Bos, C. S. and Shephard, N. (2006). Inference for adaptive time series models: Stochastic volatility and conditionally gaussian state space form. *Econometric Reviews*, **25**, 219–244.

Box, G. E. P. and Muller, M. E. (1958). A note on the generation of random normal deviates. *Annals of Mathematical Statistics*, **29**, 610–611.

Boyarchenko, S. I. and Levendorskiĭ, Z. (2002) *Non-Gaussian Merton–Black–Scholes Theory*. River Edge, NJ: World Scientific.

Brennan, M. J. and Schwartz, E. S. (1976). The pricing of equity-linked insurance policies with an asset value guarantee. *Journal of Financial Economics*, **3**, 195–213.

Brigo, D. and Mercurio, F. (2001). *Interest Rate Models. Theory and Practice*. Berlin: Springer-Verlag.

Brito, M. and Freitas, A. C. M. (2006). Weak convergence of bootstrap geometric-type estimator with applications to risk theory. *Insurance: Mathematics and Economics*, **38**, 571–584.

Brockwell, P. J. and Davis, R. A. (2011). *Introduction to Time Series and Forecasting*. New York: Springer-Verlag.

Brouhns, N., Denuit, M. and van Keilegom, I. (2005). Bootstrapping the Poisson log-linear model for forecasting. *Scandinavian Actuarial Journal*, **3**, 212–224.

Bühlmann, H. and Gisler, A. (2005). *A Course in Credibility Theory and its Applications*. Berlin: Springer-Verlag.

Bühlmann, H. and Straub, E. (1970). Glaubwüdigkeit für Schadebsätze. *Mitteleiungen der Vereinigung Scweizerischer Versicherungsmatematiker*, **70**, 111–133.

Buhmann, M. D. (2003). *Radial Basis Functions: Theory and Implementations*. Cambridge: Cambridge University Press.

Butenko, S., Golodnikov, A. and Uryasev, S. (2005). Optimal security liquidation algorithms. *Computational Optimization and Applications*, **32**, 9–27.

Butt, Z. and Haberman, S. (2004). Application of frailty-based mortality models using generalized linear models. *Astin Bulletin*, **34**, 175–197.

Cai, J. and Tan, K. S. (2007). Optimal retention for a stop-loss reinsurance under the VaR and CTE risk measure. *Astin Bulletin*, **37**, 93–112.

Cairns, A. (2000a). A discussion of parameter and model uncertainty in insurance. *Insurance: Mathematics and Economics*, **27**, 313–330.

Cairns, A. (2000b). Some notes on the dynamics and optimal control of stochastic pension fund models in continuous Time. *Astin Bulletin*, **30**, 19–55.

Cairns, A. (2004). *Interest Rate Models: An Introduction*. Princeton, NJ: Princeton University Press.

Cairns, A., Blake, D. and Dowd, K. (2006). Pricing death: Frameworks for the valuation and securization of mortality risk. *Astin Bulletin*, **36**, 79–120.

Cairns, A., Blake, D., Dowd, K, Couglan, G. D., Epstein, D. and Khalaf-Allah, M. (2011). Mortality density forecasts. An analysis of six stochastic mortality models. *Insurance: Mathematics and Economics*, **48**, 355–367.

Capinski, M. and Zastavniak, T. (2003). *Mathematics for Finance. An Introduction to Financial Engineering*. London: Springer-Verlag.

Carlin, B. P. (1992). State space modelling of nonstandard actuarial time series. *Insurance: Mathematics and Economics*, **11**, 209–222.

Carmona, R. A. (2004). *Statistical Analysis of Financial Data in S-plus.* New York: Springer-Verlag.

Carmona, R. A. and Tehranchi, M. R. (2006). *Interest Rate Models. An Infinite Dimensional Stochastic Analysis Perspective.* Berlin: Springer-Verlag.

Carriére, J. F. (2000). Bivariate survival models for coupled lives. *Scandinavian Actuarial Journal*, **1**, 17–32.

Casti, J. (1997). *Would-be World: How Simulation is Changing Frontiers of Science.* New York: John Wiley & Sons.

Castillo, E., Hadi, A. S., Balakrishnan, N. and Sarabia, J.-M. (2005). *Extreme Value and Related Models with Applications in Engineering and Science.* Hoboken, NJ: John Wiley & Sons.

Chan, N. H. and Wong, H. Y. (2006). *Simulation Techniques in Financial Risk Management.* Hoboken, NJ: John Wiley & Sons.

Chen, H. C. and Asau, Y. (1974). On generating random variates from an empirical distribution. *AIEE Transactions*, **6**, 163–166.

Chen, X. and Fan, Y. (2006). Estimation of copula-based semi-parametric time series models. *Journal of Econometrics*, **130**, 307–335.

Cheng, R. C. H. and Feast, G. M. (1979). Some simple gamma variable generators. *Applied Statistics*, **28**, 290–295.

Cherubini, U., Luciano, E. and Vecchiato, W. (2004). *Copula Methods in Finance.* Chichester: John Wiley & Sons.

Chib, S. (2004). Markov Chain Monte Carlo technology. In Gentle, J. E., Härdle, W. and Mori, Y. (eds), *Handbook of Computational Statistics. Concepts and Methods.* New York: Springer-Verlag; pp. 71–102.

Chib. S, Nardari, F. and Shepard, N. (2006). Analysis of high dimensional stochastic volatility models. *Journal of Econometrics*, **134**, 341–371.

Chiu, M. C. and Li, D. (2006). Asset and liability management under a continuous-time mean-variance optimization framework. *Insurance: Mathematics and Economics*, **39**, 330–355.

Chivers, I. and Sleightholme, J. (2006). *Introduction to Programming with Fortran.* London: Springer-Verlag.

Christoffersen, P. (2003). *Elements of Financial Risk Management.* San Diego, CA: Academic Press.

Commandeur, J. J. F. and Koopman, S. J. (2007). *An Introduction to State Space Time Series Analyis.* Oxford: Oxford University Press.

Congdon, P. (2003). *Applied Bayesian Modelling.* Chichester: John Wiley & Sons.

Cont, R. (2006). Model uncertainty and its impact on the pricing of derivative instruments. *Mathematical Finance*, **16**, 519–547.

Cont, R. and Tankov, P. (2004). *Financial Modelling with Jump Processes.* Boca Raton, FL: Chapman & Hall/CRC.

Cook, R. D. and Weisberg, S. (1982). *Residuals and Influence in Regression*. London: Chapman & Hall.

Copeland, T. E., Weston, J. F. and Shastri, K. (2005). *Financial Theory and Corporate Policy*, 4th edn. Upper Saddle River, NJ: Prentice Hall.

Cornil, J.-M. and Testud, P. (2000). *Introduction to Maple V.* Berlin: Springer-Verlag.

Cox, D. R. (1955). Some statistical methods connected with series of events. *Journal of the Royal Statistical Society, Series B*, **17**, 129–164.

Cox, J., Ingersoll, J. and Ross, S. (1985). A theory of the term structure of interest rates. *Econometrica*, **53**, 385–407.

Czado, C., Delwarde, A. and Denuit, M. (2005). Bayesian Poisson log-bilinear mortality projections. *Insurance: Mathematics and Economics*, **36**, 260–284.

Dagpunar, J. S. (1989). An easily implemented generalised inverse Gaussian generator. *Communications in Statistics. Simulation and Computation*, **18**, 703–710.

Dagpunar, J. S. (2007). *Simulation and Monte Carlo with Applications in Finance and MCMC*. Chichester: John Wiley & Sons.

Dahl, M. (2004). Stochastic mortality in life insurance: Market reserves and mortality-linked insurance contracts. *Insurance: Mathematics and Economics*, **35**, 113–136.

Dana, R.-A. and Jeanblanc-Picqué, M. (2003). *Financial Markets in Continuous Time*. Berlin: Springer-Verlag.

Danthine, J.-P. and Donaldson, J. B. (2005). *Intermediate Financial Theory.* San Diego, CA: Academic Press.

Dassios, A. and Jang, J.-W. (2003). Pricing of catastrophe reinsurance and derivatives using the cox process with shot noise intensity. *Finance and Stochastics*, **7**, 73–95.

Dassios, A. and Jang, J.-W. (2005). Kalman–Bucy filtering for linear systems driven by the cox process with shot noise intensity and its Application to the pricing of reinsurance contracts. *Journal of Applied Probability*, **42**, 93–107.

David, H. A. (1981) *Order Statistics*, 2nd edn. New York: John Wiley & Sons.

Davison, A. C. and Hinkley, D. V. (1997). *Bootstrap Methods and their Application.* Cambridge: Cambridge University Press.

Davison, A. C. and Smith, R. L. (1990). Models for exceedances over high thresholds. *Journal of the Royal Statistical Society, Series B*, **5**, 393–442.

Daykin, C. D., Pentikäinen, T. and Pesonen, M. (1994). *Practical Risk Theory for Actuaries.* London: Chapman & Hall/CRC.

De Alba, E. (2004). Bayesian claims reserving. In Teugels, J. and Sundt, B. (eds), *Encyclopedia of Actuarial Science*. Chichester: John Wiley & Sons; pp. 146–153.

De Alba, E. (2006). Claims reserving when there are negative values in the runoff triangle: Bayesian analysis the three-parameter log-normal distribution. *North American Actuarial Journal*, **10**, 45–59.

Deb, P., Munkin, M. K. and Trivedi, P. K. (2006). Private insurance, selection and health care use: A Bayesian analysis of a Roy-type model. *Journal of Business & Economic Statistics*, **24**, 403–415.

De Haan, L. and Ferreira, F. (2006). *Extreme Value Theory: An Introduction*. New York: Springer-Verlag.

De Jong, P. and Ferris, S. (2006). Adverse selection spirals. *Astin Bulletin*, **36**, 589–628.

De Jong, P. and Heller, G. Z. (2008). *Generalized Linear Models for Insurance Data*. Cambridge: Cambridge University Press.

De Jong, P. and Tickle, L. (2006). Extending Lee–Carter mortality forecasting. *Mathematical Population Studies*, **13**, 1–18.

De Jong, P. and Zehnwirth, B. (1983). Credibility theory and the Kalman filter. *Insurance: Mathematics and Economics*, **2**, 281–286.

De Lange, P. E., Fleten, S.-E. and Gaivorinsky, A. A. (2004). Modeling financial reinsurance in the casualty insurance business via stochastic programming. *Journal of Economic Dynamics and Control*, **28**, 991–1012.

Delbaen, F. and Schachermayer, W. (2006). *The Mathematics of Arbitrage*. Berlin: Springer-Verlag.

Denuit, M. and Lang, S. (2004). Non-life rate making with Bayesian GAMs. *Insurance: Mathematics and Economics*, **35**, 627–647.

Denuit, M., Maréchal, X., Pitrebois, S. and Wahlin, J.-F. (2007). *Actuarial Modelling of Claim Counts: Risk Classification, Credibility and Bonus–Malus Systems*. Chichester: John Wiley & Sons.

De Santis, G., Litterman, B., Vesval, A. and Winkelman, K. (2003). Covariance matrix estimation. In Litterman, B. (ed.), *Modern Investment Management: An Equilibrium Approach*. Hoboken, NJ: John Wiley & Sons; pp. 224–248.

Devroye, L. (1986). *Non-uniform Random Variate Generation*. New York: Springer-Verlag.

Devroye, L. and Györfi, L. (1985). *Nonparametric Density Estimation: The L_1 View*. New York: John Wiley & Sons.

Dickson, D. C. M. (2005). *Insurance Risk and Ruin*. Cambridge: Cambridge University Press.

Dickson, D. C. M. and Waters, H. (2006). Optimal dynamic reinsurance. *Astin Bulletin*, **36**, 415–432.

Dimakos, X. K. and Frigessi, A. (2002). Bayesian premium rating with latent structure. *Scandinavian Actuarial Journal*, **3**, 162–184.

Djehiche, B. and Hörfelt, P. (2005). Standard approaches to asset & liability risk. *Scandinavian Actuarial Journal*, **5**, 377–400.

Dobson, A. J. and Barnett, A. G. (2008). *An Introduction to Generalized Linear Models*, 3rd edn. Boca Raton, FL: CRC Press.

Doucet, A., de Freitas, N. and Gordon, N. (eds) (2001). *Sequential Monte Carlo in Practice*. New York: Springer-Verlag.

Dunteman, G. H. and Ho, M. -H. R. (2006). *An Introduction to Generalized Linear Models*. Thousand Oaks, CA: Sage Publications.

Dupuis, D. J. (1998). Exceedances over high thresholds: A guide to threshold selection. *Extremes*, **1**, 251–261.

Durbin, J. and Koopman, S. J. (2001). *Time Series Analysis by State Space Methods*. Oxford: Oxford University Press.

Efron, B. (1979). Bootstrap methods: Another look at the jacknife. *Annals of Statistics*, **7**, 1–26.

Efron, B. and Tibshirani, R. J. (1993). *An Introduction to the Bootstrap*. New York: Chapman & Hall.

Elliott, R. J. and Kopp, P. E. (2005). *Mathematics of Financial Markets*, 2nd edn. New York: Springer-Verlag.

Ellis, T. M. R., Philips, I. R. and Lahey, T. M. (1994). *Fortran 90 Programming*. Harlow: Addison-Wesley.

Embrechts, P. and Maejima, M. (2002). *Selfsimilar Processes*. Princeton, NJ: Princeton University Press.

Embrechts, P., Klüppelberg, C. and Mikosch, T. (1997). *Modelling Extremal Events for Insurance and Finance*. Berlin: Springer-Verlag.

Embrechts, P., Lindskog, F. and Mcneil, A. (2003). Modelling dependence with copulas and applications to risk management. In Rachev, S. T. (ed.), *Handbook of Heavy Tailed Distributions in Finance*. Amsterdam: Elsevier; pp. 329–384.

England, P. and Verrall, R. (1999). Analytic and bootstrap estimates of prediction errors in claim reserving. *Insurance: Mathematics and Economics*, **25**, 281–293.

England, P. D. and Verrall, R. J. (2006). Predictive distributions of outstanding liabilities in general insurance. *Annals of Actuarial Science*, **1**, 221–270.

Engle, R. F. (1982). Autoregressive conditional heteroscedasticity with estimates of the variance of united kingdom inflation. *Econometrica*, **50**, 987–1007.

Escarela, G. and Carriére, J. F. (2006). A bivariate model of claim frequencies and severities. *Journal of Applied Statistics*, **33**, 867–883.

Evans, J. R. and Olson, D. L. (2002). *Introduction to Simulation and Risk Analysis*. Upper Saddle River, NJ: Prentice Hall.

Evans, M. and Schwarz, T. (2000). *Approximating Integrals via Monte Carlo and Deterministic Methods*. Oxford: Oxford University Press.

Fabozzi, F. J. (ed.) (2002). *Interest Rate, Term Structure and Valuation Modeling*. Hoboken, NJ: John Wiley & Sons.

Falk, M., Hüsler, J. and Reiss, R. -D. (2010). *Laws of Small Numbers: Extremes and Rare Events*. 3rd edn. Basel: Birkhauser-Verlag.

Fang, K. T., Kotz, S. and Ng, K. W. (1990). *Symmetric Multivariate and Related Distributions*. London: Chapman & Hall.

Faraway, J. J. (2006). *Extending the Linear Model with R, generalized, mixed effects and non-parametric regression models*. Boca Raton, FL: Chapman & Hall/CRC.

Feller, W. (1968). *An Introduction to Probability Theory and its Applications*, New York: Vol. I. John Wiley & Sons.

Feller, W. (1971). *An Introduction to Probability Theory and its Applications*, Vol. II. New York: John Wiley & Sons.

Ferguson, N. (2008). *The Ascent of Money. A Financial History of the World*. London: Penguin Press.

Fieller, E. C. and Hartley, H. O. (1954). Sampling with control variables. *Biometrika*, **41**, 494–501.

Finkelstädt, B. and Rootzén, H. (eds) (2004). *Extreme Values in Finance, Telecommunications and the Environment*. Boca Raton, FL: Chapman & Hall/CRC.

Finkelstein, A. and Poterba, J. (2002). Selection effects in the United Kingdom Individual annuities market. *The Economic Journal*, **112**, 28–50.

Fishman, G. S. (2001). *Discrete-Event Simulation, Modeling, Programming and Analysis*. New York: Springer-Verlag.

Fishman, G. S. (2006). *A First Course in Monte Carlo*. Belmont, CA: Thomson Brooks/Cole.

Fletcher, R. (1987). *Practical Methods of Optimization*. Chichester: John Wiley & Sons.

Fleten, S. -E., Høyland, K. and Wallace, S. W. (2002). The performance of stochastic dynamic and fixed mix portfolios models. *European Journal of Operational Research*, **140**, 37–49.

Fomby, T. B. and Carter Hill, R. (eds) (2003). *Maximum Likelihood of Misspecified Models. Twenty Years Later*. Amsterdam: Elsevier.

Forfar, D. O. (2004). Life table. In , Teugels, J. and Sundt, B. (eds), *Encyclopedia of Actuarial Science* Chichester: John Wiley & Sons; pp. 1005–1009.

Fornari, F. and Mele, A. (2000). *Stochastic Volatility in Financial Markets. Crossing the Bridge to Continuous Time*. Dordrecht: Kluwer.

Fouque, J. -P., Papanicolaou, G. and Sircar, K. R. (2000). *Derivatives in Financial Markets with Stochastic Volatility*. Cambridge: Cambridge University Press.

Franke, J., Härdle, W. and Hafner, C. (2004). *Statistics of Financial Markets.* Berlin: Springer-Verlag.

Franses, P. H. and van Dijk, D. (2000). *Non-linear Time Series Models in Empirical Finance.* Cambridge: Cambridge University Press.

Frees, E. (2003). Multivariate credibility for aggregate loss models. *North American Actuarial Journal*, **7**, 13–37.

Frees, E. W. and Valdez, E. A. (1998). Understanding relationships using copulas. *North American Actuarial Journal*, **2**, 1–25.

Frees, E. and Wang, P. (2006). Copula credibility for aggregate loss models. *Insurance: Mathematics and Economics*, **38**, 360–373.

Fries, C. (2007). *Mathematical Finance. Theory, Modelling, Implementation.* Hoboken, NJ: John Wiley & Sons.

Frigessi, A., Haug, O. and Rue, H. (2002). A dynamic mixture model for unsupervised tail estimation without threshold selection. *Extremes*, **5**, 219–235.

Fu, M. and Hu, J. -Q. (1997). *Conditional Monte Carlo. Gradient Estimation and Optimization Applications.* Boston, MA: Kluwer.

Fuh, C. -D. (2006). Efficient likelihood estimation in state space models. *Annals of Statistics*, **34**, 2026–2068.

Gajek, L. (2005). Axiom of solvency and portfolio immunization under random interest rates. *Insurance: Mathematics and Economics*, **36**, 317–328.

Gajek, L. and Zagrodny, D. (2004). Optimal reinsurance under general risk measures. *Insurance: Mathematics and Economics*, **34**, 227–240.

Gamerman, D. and Lopes, H. F. (2006). *Markov Chain Monte Carlo. Stochastic Simulation for Bayesian Inference.* Boca Raton, FL: Chapman & Hall/CRC.

Gelb, A. (ed.) (1974). *Applied Optimal Estimation.* Cambridge, MA: MIT Press.

Genest, C. and MacKay, J. (1986). The joy of copulas: Bivariate distributions with uniform marginals. *The American Statistician*, **40**, 280–283.

Genon-Catalot, V., Jeantheau, T. and Larédo, C. (2000). Stochastic volatility models as hidden markov models and statistical applications. *Bernoulli*, **6**, 1051–1079.

Gentle, J. E. (1998). *Numerical Linear Algebra for Applications in Statistics.* New York: Springer-Verlag.

Gentle, J. E. (2002). *Elements of Computational Statistics.* New York: Springer-Verlag.

Gentle, J. E. (2003). *Random Number Generation and Monte Carlo Methods*, 2nd edn. New York: Springer-Verlag.

Gentle, J. E., Härdle, W. and Mori, Y. (eds) (2004). *Handbook of Computational Statistics. Concepts and Methods.* New York: Springer-Verlag.

Gerber, H. U. (1997). *Life Insurance Mathematics*, 3rd edn. Berlin: Springer-Verlag.

Gerber, H. U. and Shiu, E. S. W. (2003). Geometric brownian motion models for assets and liabilities: From pension funding to optimal dividends. *North American Actuarial Journal*, **7**, 37–51.

Gilks, W. R., Richardson, S. and Spiegelhalter, D. J. (eds) (1996). *Markov Chain Monte Carlo in Practice.* London: Chapman & Hall.

Gill, P. E., Murray, W. and Wright, M. H. (1981). *Practical Optimization.* London: Academic Press.

Gisler, A. (2006). The estimation error in the chain ladder reserving method: A bayesian approach. *Astin Bulletin*, **36**, 554–565.

Glasserman, P. (2004). *Monte Carlo Methods in Financial Engineering.* New York: Springer-Verlag.

Gloter, A. (2007). Efficient estimation of drift parameters in stochastic volatility models. *Finance and Stochastics*, **11**, 495–519.

Góméz-Déniz, E., Vázquez-Polo, F. and Pérez, J. (2006). A note on computing bonus-malus insurance premiums using a hierarchical bayesian framework. *Sociedad de Estadística e Investigación Operativa*, **15**, 345–359.

Gondzio, J. and Kouwenberg, R. (2001). High-performance computing for asset-liability management. *Operations Research*, **49**, 879–891.

Goovaerts, M. J. and Hoogstad, W. J. (1987). *Credibility Theory*. Surveys of Actuarial Studies, Vol. **4**, Rotterdam: Nationale-Nederlanden N.V.

Grama, A., Gupta, A., Karypis, G. and Kumar, V. (2003). *Introduction to Parallel Computing*, 2nd edn. Harlow: Pearson/Addison-Wesley.

Grandell, J. (2004). Poisson processes. In Teugels, J. and Sundt, B. (eds), *Encyclopedia of Actuarial Science*. Chichester: John Wiley & Sons, pp. 1296–1301.

Greenwood, M. and Yule, G. U. (1920). An inquiry into the nature of frequency-distributions of multiple happenings, with particular reference to the occurrence of multiple attacks of disease or repeated accidents. *Journal of Royal Statistical Society*, **83**, 255–279.

Guerra, M. and Centeno, M. (2008). Optimal reinsurance policy: The adjustment coefficient and the expected utility criteria. *Insurance: Mathematics and Economics*, **42**, 529–539.

Haberman, S. and Pitacco, E. (1999). *Actuarial Models for Disability Insurance.* Boca Raton, FL: Chapman & Hall/CRC.

Haberman, S. and Renshaw, A. E. (1996). Generalized linear models and actuarial science. *The Statistician*, **45**, 407–436.

Haberman, S. and Sibbett, T. A. (eds) (1995). *History of Actuarial Science.* London: Pickering and Chatto.

Hafner, R. (2004). *Stochastic Implied Volatility. A Factor-Based Model.* Berlin: Springer-Verlag.

Hall, P. (1992). *The Bootstrap and Edgeworth Expansion.* New York: Springer-Verlag.

Hämmerlin, G. and Hoffmann, K.-H. (1991). *Numerical Mathematics.* Berlin: Springer-Verlag.

Hammersley, J. M. and Handscomb, D. C. (1964). *Monte Carlo Methods.* London: Methuen.

Hammersley, J. M. and Morton, K. W. (1956). A new Monte Carlo technique: Antithetic variates. *Proceedings of the Cambridge Philosophical Society*, **52**, 449–475.

Hanson, D. R. (1997). *C Interfaces and Implementations: Techniques for Creating Reusable Software.* Reading, MA: Addison-Wesley.

Harbison, S. P. and Steele, G. L. (2002). *C: A Reference Manual*, 5th edn. Englewood Cliffs, NJ: Prentice-Hall.

Hardy, M. (2002). Bayesian risk management for equity-linked insurance. *Scandinavian Actuarial Journal*, **3**, 185–211.

Hardy, M. (2003). *Investment Guarantees. Modeling and Risk Management for Equity-Linked Insurance.* Hoboken, NJ: John Wiley & Sons.

Harel, A. and Harpaz, G. (2007). Fair actuarial values for deductible insurance policies in the presence of parameter uncertainty. *International Journal of Theoretical and Applied Finance*, **10**, 389–397.

Harvey, A., Ruiz, E. and Shephard, N. (1994). Multivariate stochastic variance models. *Review of Economic Studies*, **61**, 247–264.

Harvey, A., Koopman, S. J. and Shephard, N. (eds) (2004). *State Space and Unobserved Components Models: Theory and Applications.* Cambridge: Cambridge University Press.

Hastings, W. K. (1970). Monte Carlo sampling methods using Markov chains and their applications. *Biometrika*, **57**, 97–109.

Herold, U. and Maurer, R. (2006). Portfolio choice and estimation risk: A comparison of bayesian to heuristic approaches. *Astin Bulletin*, **36**, 135–160.

Hilbe, J. M. (2007). *Negative Binomial Regression.* Cambridge: Cambridge University Press.

Hilli, P., Koivu, M., Pennanen, T. and Ranne, A. (2007). A stochastic programming model for asset liability management of a finnish pension company. *Annals of Operations Research*, **152**, 115–139.

Hoedemakers, T., Beirlant, J., Goovaerts, M. J. and Dhaene, J. (2005). On the distribution of discounted loss reserves using generalized linear models. *Scandinavian Actuarial Journal*, **1**, 25–45.

Højgaard, B. and Taksar, M. (2004). Optimal dynamic portfolio selection for a corporation with controllable risk and dividend distribution policy. *Quantitative Finance*, **4**, 315–327.

Hörmann, W., Leydold, J. and Derflinger, G. (2004). *Automatic Non-Uniform Random Variate Generation.* Berlin: Springer-Verlag.

Howison, S. D., Kelly, F. P. and Wilmott, P. (eds) (1995). *Mathematical Models in Finance.* London: Chapman & Hall.

Huang, X., Song, L. and Liang, Y. (2003). Semiparametric credibility ratemaking using a piecewise linear prior. *Insurance: Mathematics and Economics*, **33**, 585–593.

Huber, P. (1967). The behaviour of maximum likelihood estimates under nonstandard conditions. *Proceedings of the Fifth Berkeley Symposium on Mathematical Statistics and Probability*, Berkeley, CA: University of California Press; pp. 221–233.

Hughston, L. (ed.) (2000). *The New Interest Rate Models*. London: RISK Books.

Hull, J. C. (2006). *Options, Futures and Other Derivatives*, 6th edn. Upper Saddle River, NJ: Prentice Hall, New Jersey.

Hunt, B. R., Lipsman, R. L. and Rosenberg, J. (2001). *A Guide to MATLAB: for Beginners and Experienced Users*. Cambridge: Cambridge University Press.

Hürlimann, W. (2002). On immunization, stop-loss order and the maximum shiu measure. *Insurance: Mathematics and Economics*, **31**, 315–325.

Irgens, C. and Paulsen, J. (2004). Optimal control of risk exposure, reinsurance and investments for insurance portfolios. *Insurance: Mathematics and Economics*, **35**, 21–51.

Jäckel, P. (2002). *Monte Carlo Methods in Finance*. Chichester: John Wiley & Sons.

Jacobsen, M. (2006). *Point Process Theory and Applications. Marked Point and Piecewise Deterministic Processes*. Boston, MA: Birkhäuser.

James, J. and Webber, N. (2000). *Interest Rate Modelling.* Chichester: John Wiley & Sons.

Jensen, J. L. (1995). *Saddlepoint Approximations*. New York: Oxford University Press.

Jewell, W. S. (1974). Credible means are exact Bayesian for exponential families. *Astin Bulletin*, **8**, 77–90.

Joe, H. (1997). *Multivariate Models and Dependence Concepts.* London: Chapman & Hall.

Johnson, N. L., Kotz, S. and Balakrishnan, N. (1994). *Continuous Univariate Distributions.* New York: John Wiley & Sons.

Johnson, N. L., Kotz, S. and Balakrishnan, N. (1997). *Discrete Multivariate Distributions.* New York: John Wiley & Sons.

Johnson, N. L., Kemp, A. W. and Kotz, S. (2005). *Univariate Discrete Distributions*, 3rd edn. Hoboken, NJ: John Wiley & Sons.

Jørgensen, B. and Paes de Souza, M. C. (1994). Fitting Tweedie's compound poisson model to insurance claims data. *Scandinavian Actuarial Journal*, **1**, 69–93.

Jorion, P. (2001). *Value at Risk: The New Benchmark for Managing Financial Risk*, 2nd edn. New York: McGraw-Hill.

Josa-Fombellida, R. and Rincón-Zapatero, J. P. (2006). Optimal investment decisions with a liability: The case of defined benefit pension plans. *Insurance: Mathematics and Economics*, **39**, 81–98.

Josa-Fombellida, R. and Rincón-Zapatero, J. P. (2008). Mean-variance portfolio and contribution selection in stochastic pension funding. *European Journal of Operational Research*, **187**, 120–137.

Journel, A. G. and Huijbregts, C. J. (1978). *Mining Geostatistics*. New York: Academic Press.

Kaas, R. Dannenburg, D. and Goovaerts, M. (1997). Exact credibility for weighted observations. *Astin Bulletin*, **27**, 287–295.

Kaluszka, M. (2004). Mean-variance optimal reinsurance arrangements. *Scandinavian Actuarial Journal*, **1**, 28–41.

Kaluszka, M. (2005). Truncated stop loss as optimal reinsurance agreement in One-period Models. *Astin Bulletin*, **35**, 337–349.

Kaminsky, K. (1987). Prediction of IBNR claim counts by modeling the distribution of report lags. *Insurance: Mathematics and Economics*, **6**, 151–159.

Kaner, C., Falk, J. and Ngyuen, H. (1999). *Testing Computer Software,* 2nd edn. Hoboken, NJ: John Wiley & Sons.

Karlin, S. and Taylor, H. M. (1975). *A First Course in Stochastic Processes.* New York: Academic Press.

Karlis, D. and Kostaki, A. (2002). Bootstrap techniques for mortality models. *Biometrical Journal*, **44**, 850–866.

Karlis, D. and Lillestöl, J. (2004). Bayesian estimation of NIG models via Markov chain Monte Carlo methods. *Applied Stochastic Models in Business and Industry*, **20**, 323–338.

Kendall, M. G. and Stuart, A. (1977). *The Advanced Theory of Statistics. Volume 1. Distribution Theory*, 4th edn. London: Edward Arnold.

Kendall, M. G. and Stuart, A. (1979). *The Advanced Theory of Statistics. Volume 2. Inference and Relationship*, 4th edn. London: Edward Arnold.

Keyfitz, N. and Caswell, H. (2005). *Applied Mathematical Demography*, 3rd edn. New York: Springer-Verlag.

Kijima, M. (2003). *Stochastic Processes with Applications to Finance.* Boca Raton, FL: Chapman & Hall/CRC.

Kimberling, C. H. (1974). A probabilistic interpretation of complete monotonicity. *Aequationes Mathematicae*, **10**, 152–164.

Kinderman, A. J. and Monahan, J. F. (1977). Computer generation of random variables using ratio of uniform deviates. *ACM Transactions of Mathematical Software*, **3**, 257–260.

Kinderman, A. J. and Monahan, J. F. (1980). New methods for generating Student's *t* and Gamma variables. *Computing*, **25**, 369–377.

Kleiber, C. and Kotz, S. (2003). *Statistical Size Distributions in Economic and Actuarial Sciences.* Hoboken, NJ: John Wiley & Sons.

Klugman, S. A (1992). *Bayesian Statistics in Actuarial Science: with Emphasis on Credibility*. Dordrecht: Kluwer.

Klugman, S. A. (2004). Continuous parametric distributions. In Teugels, J. and Sundt, B. (eds), *Encyclopedia of Actuarial Science*. Chichester: John Wiley & Sons, pp. 357–362.

Klugman, S. A. and Parsa, R. (1999). Fitting bivariate loss distributions with copulas. *Insurance: Mathematics and Economics*, **24**, 139–148.

Klugman, S. A., Panjer, H. H. and Willmot, G. E. (2008). *Loss Models: From Data to Decisions*, 3rd edn. New York: John Wiley & Sons.

Knight, J. and Satchell, S. (eds) (2001). *Return Distributions in Finance.* Oxford: Butterworth-Heinemann.

Knight, J. and Satchell, S. (eds) (2002). *Forecasting Volatility in the Financial Markets*, 2nd edn. Oxford: Butterworth–Heinemann.

Koissi, M. -C., Shapiro, A. F. and Högnäs, G. (2006). Evaluating and extending the Lee–Carter model for mortality forecasting: Bootstrap confidence interval. *Insurance: Mathematics and Economics*, **38**, 1–20.

Kolb, R. W. and Overdahl, J. A. (2003). *Financial Derivatives*, 3rd edn. Hoboken, NJ: John Wiley & Sons.

Kontoghiorges, E. J., Rustem, B and Siokos, S. (eds) (2002). *Computational Methods in Decision-Making, Economics and Finance.* Dordrecht: Kluwer.

Kotz, S. and Nadarajah, S. (2000). *Extreme Value Distributions: Theory and Applications.* London: Imperial College Press.

Kotz, S. and Nadarajah, S. (2004). *Multivariate t Distributions and their Applications.* Cambridge: Cambridge University Press.

Kotz, S., Balakrishnan, N. and Johnson, N. L. (2000). *Continuous, Multivariate, Distributions. Volume 1. Models and Applications*, 2nd edn. New York: John Wiley & Sons.

Kouwenberg, R. (2001). Scenario generation and stochastic programming models for asset liability management. *European Journal of Operational Research*, **134**, 279–292.

Krause, A. and Olson, M. (2005). *The Basics of S-plus,* 4th edn. New York: Springer-Verlag.

Krokhmal, P. and Uryasev, S. (2007). A sample-path approach to optimal position liquidation. *Annals of Operations Research*, **152**, 193–225.

Krokhmal, P., Uryasev, S. and Palmquist, J. (2002). Portfolio optimization with conditional value-at-risk objective and constraints. *Journal of Risk*, **4**, 43–68.

Krvavych, Y. and Sherris, M. (2006). Enhancing reinsurer value through reinsurance optimization. *Insurance: Mathematics and Economics*, **38**, 495–517.

Lamberton, D. and Lapeyre, B. (1996). *Introduction to Stochastic Calculus Applied to Finance.* Boca Raton, FL: Chapman & Hall/CRC.

Lancaster, H. O. (1957). Some properties of the bivariate normal distribution considered in the form of a contingency table. *Biometrika*, **44**, 289–292.

Landau, R. H. (ed.) (2005). *A First Course in Scientific Computing: Symbolic, Graphic, and Numerical Modeling Using Maple, Java, Mathematica and Fortran 90.* Princeton, NJ: Princeton University Press.

Lange, K. (1999). *Numerical Analysis for Statisticians.* New York: Springer-Verlag.

Lange, K. (2004). *Optimization.* New York: Springer-Verlag.

Langtangen, H. P. (2003). *Computational Partial Differential Equations: Numerical Methods and Diffpack Programming*, 2nd edn. Berlin: Springer-Verlag.

Lawless, J. F. (1987). Negative binomial and mixed poisson regression. *Canadian Journal of Statistics*, **15**, 209–225.

Lee, R. D. and Carter, L. W. (1992). Modeling and forecasting US mortality (with discussion). *Journal of the American Statistical Association*, **87**, 659–675.

Lee, J. -P. and Yu, M -T. (2007). Valuation of catastrophe reinsurance with catastrophe bonds. *Insurance: Mathematics and Economics*, **41**, 264–278.

Lee, P. J. and Wilkie, A. D. (2000). A comparison of stochastic asset models. Proceedings of AFIR 2000, Tromsø, Norway.

Lee, S. -Y., Poon, W. -Y. and Song, X. -Y. (2007). Bayesian analysis of the factor model with finance applications. *Quantitative Finance*, **7**, 343–356.

Lee, Y., Nelder, J. A. and Pawitan, Y. (2006). *Generalized Linear Models with Random Effects: Unified Analysis via H-Likelihood.* Boca Raton, FL: Chapman & Hall/CRC.

Lehmann, E. and Casella, G. (1998). *Theory of Point Estimation*, 2nd edn. New York: Springer-Verlag.

Leippold, M., Trojani, F. and Vanini, P. (2004). A geometric approach to multiperiod mean variance optimization of assets and liabilities. *Journal of Economic Dynamics and Control*, **28**, 1079–1113.

Levy, G. (2004). *Computational Finance. Numerical Methods for Pricing Financial Instruments*. Oxford: Butterworth-Heinemann.

Levy, M., Levy, H. and Solomon, S. (2000). *Microscopic Simulation of Financial Markets. From Investor Behaviour to Market Phenomena.* London: Academic Press.

Liang, Z. and Guo, J. (2007). Optimal proportional reinsurance and ruin probability. *Stochastic Models*, **23**, 333–350.

Lin, X. S. (2006). *Introductory Stochastic Analysis for Finance and Insurance.* Hoboken, NJ: John Wiley & Sons.

Litterman, B. (2003). Beyond Equilibrium, the Black–Litterman approach. In Litterman, B. (ed.), *Modern Investment Management: An Equilibrium Approach.* Hoboken, NJ: John Wiley & Sons; pp. 76–88.

Liu, J. S. (2001). *Monte Carlo Strategies in Scientific Computing*. New York: Springer-Verlag.

Lo, C.H., Fung, W.K. and Zhu, Z.Y. (2006). Generalized estimating equations for variance and covariance parameters in regression credibility models. *Insurance: Mathematics and Economics*, **39**, 99–113.

Longin, F. and Solnik, B. (2001). Extreme correlation of international equity markets. *Journal of Finance*, **56**, 649–676.

Luenberger, D. G. (1998). *Investment Science.* Oxford: Oxford University, Press.

Luo, Y., Young, V.R and Frees, E. W. (2004). Credibility ratemaking using collateral information. *Scandinavian Actuarial Journal*, 448–461.

Luo, S., Taksar, M. and Tsoi, A. (2008). On reinsurance and investment for large insurance portfolios. *Insurance: Mathematics and Economics*, **42**, 434–444.

Lütkepohl, H. and Krätzig, M. (eds) (2004). *Applied Time Series Econometrics.* Cambridge: Cambridge University Press.

Lütkepohl, H. (2005). *New Introduction to Multiple Time Series Analysis.* Springer-Verlag, Berlin.

Lyuu, Y. D. (2002). *Financial Engineering and Computation. Principles, Mathematics, Algorithms.* Cambridge: Cambridge University Press.

Maddala, G. S. and Rao, C. R. (1996). *Statistical Methods in Finance, Handbook of Statistics 14.* Amsterdam: Elsevier.

Makov, U. (2001). Principal applications of Bayesian methods in actuarial science: A perspective. *North American Actuarial Journal*, **5**, 53–57.

Mardia, K. V., Kent, J. T. and Bibby, J. M. (1979). *Multivariate Analysis.* New York: Academic Press.

Markowitz, H. (1952). Portfolio selection. *Journal of Finance*, **7**, 77–91.

Marsaglia, G.(1980). Generating random variables with a *t*-distribution. *Mathematics of Computation*, **34**, 235–236.

Marshall, A. and Olkin, I. (1988). Families of multivariate distributions. *Journal of American Statistical Association*, **83**, 834–841.

McCullagh, P. and Nelder, J. A. (1989). *Generalized Linear Models*, 2nd edn. London: Chapman & Hall.

McDonald, R. L. (2009). *Derivatives Markets.* Boston, MA: Addison-Wesley.

McLeish, D. L. (2005). *Monte Carlo Simulation and Finance.* Hoboken, NJ: John Wiley & Sons.

McMahon, D. and Topa, D. M. (2006). *A Beginner's Guide to Mathematica.* Boca Raton, FL: Chapman & Hall/CRC.

Merton, R.C. (1973). Theory of rational option pricing. *Bell Journal of Economics and Management Science*, **4**, 141–183.

Metropolis, N., Rosenbluth, A. W., Rosenbluth, M. N., Teller, A. H. and Teller, E. (1953). Equation of state calculations by fast computing machines. *Journal of Chemical Physics*, **21**, 1087–1092. [Reprinted in Kotz, S. and Johnson, N.L. (eds) (1997). *Breakthroughs in Statistics, Volume III.* New York: Springer-Verlag; pp. 127–139].

Migon, H. S. and Moura, F. A. S. (2005). Hierarchical Bayesian collective risk model: An application to health insurance. *Insurance: Mathematics and Economics*, **36**, 119–135.

Mikosch, T. (2004). *Non-Life Insurance Mathematics: An Introduction with Stochastic Processes*. Berlin: Springer-Verlag.

Mikosch, T. (2006). Copulas: Facts and tales. *Extremes*, **9**, 3–20.

Mikosch, T. and Stărică, C. (2000). Is it really long memory we see in financial returns? In Embrechts, P. (ed), *Extremes and Risk Management.* London: RISK Books, pp. 149–168.

Milevsky, M. A. and Promislow, D. (2001). Mortality derivatives and the Option to Annuitise. *Insurance: Mathematics and Economics*, **29**, 299–318.

Mills, T. C. and Markellos, R. N. (2008). *The Econometric Modelling of Financial Time Series*, 3rd edn. Cambridge: Cambridge University Press.

Mitchell, O. S. and McCarthy, D. (2002). Estimating international adverse selection in annuities. *North American Actuarial Journal*, **6**, 38–54.

Nakano, J. (2004). Parallel computing techniques. In Gentle, J. E., Härdle, W. and Mori, Y. (eds), *Handbook of Computational Statistics. Concepts and Methods.* New York: Springer-Verlag; pp. 237–266.

Nelsen, R. B. (2006). *An Introduction to Copulas*, 2nd edn. New York: Springer-Verlag.

Neftci, S. N. (2000). *An Introduction to the Mathematics of Financial Derivatives*, Second Edition. San Diego, CA: Academic Press.

Neuhaus, W. (1987). Early warning. *Scandinavian Actuarial Journal*, 128–156.

Niederreiter, H. (1992). *Random Number Generation and Quasi-Monte Carlo Methods.* Philadelphia, PA: SIAM.

Nietert, B. (2003). Portfolio Insurance and model uncertainty. *OR Spectrum*, **25**, 295–316.

Nordberg, R. (1989). Empirical Bayes in the unbalanced case: Basic theory and applications to insurance. Doctoral Thesis, Department of Mathematics, University of Oslo.

Nordberg, R. (1999). Ruin problems with assets and liabilities of Diffusion Type. *Stochastic Processes and their Applications*, **81**, 255–269.

Nordberg, R. (2004a). Credibility theory. In Teugels, J. and Sundt, B. (eds), *Encyclopedia of Actuarial Science*, Chichester: John Wiley & Sons, pp. 398–406.

Nordberg, R. (2004b). Life insurance mathematics. In Teugels, J. and Sundt, B. (eds), *Encyclopedia of Actuarial Science*, Chichester: John Wiley & Sons, pp. 986–997.

Ntzoufras, I, Katsis, A. and Karlis, D. (2005). Bayesian assessment of the distribution of insurance claim counts using reversible jump MCMC. *North American Actuarial Journal*, **9**, 90–108.

Odeh, R. E. and Evans, J.O. (1974). Algorithm A570: The percentage points of the normal distribution. *Applied Statistics*, **23**, 96–97.

Ohlsson, E. and Johansson, B. (2006). Exact credibility and Tweedie models. *Astin Bulletin*, **36**, 121–133.

Øksendal, B. (2003). *Stochastic Differential Equations: An Introduction with Applications*, 6th edn. Berlin: Springer-Verlag.

Omori, Y., Chib, S., Shephard, N. and Nakajima, J. (2007). Stochastic volatility with leverage: Fast and efficient likelihood inference. *Journal of Econometrics*, **140**, 425–449.

Otto, S. R. and Denier, J. P. (2005). *An Introduction to Programming and Numerical Methods in MATLAB.* London: Springer-Verlag.

Owadally, M. I. (2003). Pension funding and the actuarial assumption concerning investment returns. *Astin Bulletin*, **33**, 289–312.

Owadally, M. I. and Haberman, S. (1999). Pension fund dynamics and gains/losses due to random Rates of investment returns. *North American Actuarial Journal*, **3**, 105–117.

Panjer, H. (1981). Recursive evaluation of a family of compound distributions. *Astin Bulletin*, **12**, 22–26.

Panjer, H. (ed.) (1998). *Financial Economics: with Applications to Investments, Insurance and Pensions*. Schaumburg, IL: The Actuarial Foundation.

Panjer, H. and Willmot, G. E. (1992). *Insurance Risk Models*. Schaumburg, IL: Society of Actuaries.

Papi, M. and Sbaraglia, S. (2006). Optimal asset-liability management with constraints: A dynamic programming approach. *Applied Mathematics and Computation*, **173**, 306–349.

Pickands, J. III (1975). Statistical inference using extreme order statistics. *Annals of Statistics*, **3**, 119–131.

Pitacco, E. (2004). Survival models in a dynamic context: A survey. *Insurance: Mathematics and Economics*, **35**, 279–298.

Pitselis, G. (2004). A seemingly unrelated regression model in a credibility framework. *Insurance: Mathematics and Economics*, **34**, 37–54.

Pitselis, G. (2008). Robust regression credibility. The Influence Function Approach. *Insurance: Mathematics and Economics*, **42**, 288–300.

Pliska, S. (1997). *Introduction to Mathematical Finance. Discrete Time Models*. Oxford: Blackwell.

Pollard, J. (2004). Decrement analysis. In Teugels, J. and Sundt, B. (eds), *Encyclopedia of Actuarial Science*, Chichester: John Wiley & Sons; pp. 436–445.

Press, W. H., Teukolsky, S. A, Vetterling, W. T and Flannery, B. P. (2007). *Numerical Recipes in C*, 3rd edn. Cambridge: Cambridge University Press.

Priestley, M. B. (1981). *Spectral Analysis and Time Series*. San Diego, CA: Academic Press.

Promislow, S. D. (2006). *Fundamentals of Actuarial Mathematics*. Chichester: John Wiley & Sons.

Purcaru, O. and Denuit, M. (2003). Dependence in dynamic claim frequency credibility models. *Astin Bulletin*, **33**, 23–40.

Rachev, S. T. (ed.) (2003). *Handbook of Heavy Tailed Distributions in Finance*. Amsterdam: Elsevier.

Rachev, S. T and Mittnik, S. (2000). *Stable Paretian Models in Finance*, Chichester: John Wiley & Sons.

Rachev, S. T., Hsu, J. S. J, Bagasheva, B. S. and Fabozzi, F. J. (2008). *Bayesian Methods in Finance*. Hoboken, NJ: John Wiley & Sons.

Rebonato, R. (2004). *Volatility and Correlation. The Perfect Hedger and the Fox*, 2nd edn. Chichester: John Wiley & Sons.

Reddington, F. M. (1952). Review of the principles of life office valuations. *Journal of the Institute of Actuaries*, **78**, 286–340.

Rempala, G. A. and Szatzschneider, K. (2004). Bootstrapping parametric models of mortality. *Scandinavian Actuarial Journal*, 53–78.

Renshaw, A. E. and Haberman, S. (2003a). Lee–Carter mortality forecasting with age-specific enhancement. *Insurance: Mathematics and Economics*, **33**, 255–272.

Renshaw, A. E. and Haberman, S. (2003b). Lee–Carter mortality forecasting: A parallel generalized linear modelling approach for england and wales mortality projections. *Journal of the Royal Statistical Society, C*, **52**, 119–137.

Resnick, S. I. (2006). *Heavy-Tail Phenomena. Probabilistic and Statistical Modeling*. New York: Springer-Verlag.

Ripley, B. (2006). *Stochastic Simulation*, 2nd edn. Hoboken, NJ: John Wiley & Sons.

Robert, C. P. and Casella, G. (2004). *Monte Carlo Statistical Methods,* 2nd edn. Berlin: Springer-Verlag.

Robinson, P. M. (ed.) (2003). *Time Series with Long Memory.* Oxford: Oxford University Press.

Rockafeller, R. T. and Uryasev, S. (2000). Optimization of conditional value at risk. *Journal of Risk*, **2**, 21–41.

Rolski, T., Schmidli, H., Schmidt, V. and Teugels, J. (1999). *Stochastic Processes for Insurance and Finance.* Chichester: John Wiley & Sons.

Roman, S. (2004). *Introduction to the Mathematics of Finance.* New York: Springer-Verlag.

Rose, C. and Smith, M. D. (2001). *Mathematical Statistics with Mathematica.* New York: Springer-Verlag.

Ross, S. M. (2002). *Simulation*, 3rd edn. New York: Academic Press.

Rubinstein, R. Y. and Melamed, B. (1998). *Modern Simulation and Modelling.* New York: John Wiley & Sons.

Rudolf, M. and Ziemba, W. T. (2004). Intertemporal surplus management. *Journal of Economic Dynamics and Control*, **28**, 975–990.

Ruppert, D. (2004). *Statistics and Finance: An Introduction.* New York: Springer-Verlag.

Salleh, S., Zomaya, A. Y. and Bakar, S. A. (2008). *Computing for Numerical Methods Using Visual C++.* Hoboken, NJ: John Wiley & Sons.

Savitch, W. (1995). *Pascal: An Introduction to the Art and Science of Programming.* Redwood City, CA: Benjamin Cummings.

Sbaraglia, S., Papi. M., Briani, M., Bernaschi, M. and Gozzi, F. (2003). A model for optimal asset-liability management for insurance companies. *International Journal of Theoretical and Applied Finance*, **6**, 277–299.

Schäl, M. (2004). On discrete-time dynamic programming in insurance: exponential utility and minimising the ruin probability. *Scandinavian Actuarial Journal*, **1**, 189–210.

Schmidly, H. (2006). Optimisation in non-life insurance. *Stochastic Models*, **22**, 689–722.

Schneider, D. I. (2006). *An Introduction to Programming Using Visual Basic 2005.* Upper Saddle River, NJ: Pearson/Prentice Hall.

Schnieper, R. (2004). Robust Bayesian experience rating. *Astin Bulletin*, **34**, 125–150.

Schoutens, W. (2003). *Lévy Processes in Finance: Pricing Financial Derivatives.* Chichester: John Wiley & Sons.

Schrager, D. F. (2006). Affine stochastic mortality. *Insurance: Mathematics and Economics*, **38**, 81–97.

Schumway, R. H. and Stoffer, R. S. (2006). *Time Series Analysis and its Applications with R Examples*. New York: Springer-Verlag.

Scott, P. W. (1992). *Multivariate Density Estimation: Theory, Practice and Visualization*, 2nd edn. New York: John Wiley & Sons.

Seydel, R. (2009). *Tools for Computational Finance*, 2nd edn. Berlin: Springer-Verlag.

Shaw, W. (1998). *Modelling Financial Derivatives with Mathematica.* Cambridge: Cambridge University Press.

Shephard, N. (1994). Local scale models: State space alternative to integrated GARCH processes. *Journal of Econometrics*, **60**, 181–202.

Shephard, N. (ed), (2005). *Stochastic Volatility. Selected Readings.* Oxford: Oxford University Press.

Shreve, S. E. (2004a). *Stochastic Calculus for Finance I. The Binomial Asset Pricing Model.* New York: Springer-Verlag.

Shreve, S. E. (2004b). *Stochastic Calculus for Finance II. Continuous Time Models.* New York: Springer-Verlag.

Sklar, A. (1959). Fonctions de répartition à *n* dimensions et leur marges. *Publications de l'Institut de Statistique de l'Université de Paris*, **8**, 229–231.

Sokal, R. S. and Rohlf, F. J., (1981). *Biometry*, 2nd edn. New York: W.H. Freeman.

Stoustrup, B. (2013). *The C++ Programming Language*, 4th edn. Reading, MA: Addison-Wesley.

Straub, E. (1997). *Non-life Insurance Mathematics.* Berlin: Springer-Verlag.

Stuart, A. (1962). Gamma-distributed products of independent random variables. *Biometrika*, **49**, 564–565.

Stuart, A. and Ord, K. (1987). *Kendall's Advanced Theory of Statistics. Volume 1. Distribution Theory*, 5th edn. London: Edward Arnold.

Sundt, B. (1979). An insurance model with collective seasonal random factors. *Mitteilungen der Vereinigung Schweizericher Versicherungsmatemathematiker*, **79**, 57–64.

Sundt, B. (1983). Parameter estimation in some credibility models. *Scandinavian Actuarial Journal*, 239–255.

Sundt, B. (1999). *An Introduction to Non-Life Insurance Mathematics.* Karlsruhe: Verlag-Versicherungswirtschaft.

Sundt, B. and Vernic, R. (2009). *Recursions for Convolutions and Compound Distributions with Insurance Applications.* Berlin: Springer-Verlag.

Szabo, F. E. (2004). *Actuaries' Survival Guide. How to Succeed in One of the Most Desirable Professions.* San Diego, CA: Elsevier Academic Press.

Taksar, M. and Hunderup, C. L. (2007). The influence of bankruptcy value on optimal risk control for diffusion models with proportional reinsurance. *Insurance: Mathematics and Economics*, **40**, 311–321.

Tapiero, C. (2004). *Risk and Financial Management. Mathematical and Computational Methods*. Chichester: John Wiley & Sons.

Taylor, G. (2000). *Loss Reserving: An Actuarial Perspective*. Boston, MA: Kluwer.

Taylor, G. and McGuire, G. (2007). A synchronous bootstrap to account for dependencies between lines of business in the estimation of loss reserve prediction error. *North American Actuarial Journal*, **3**, 70–88.

Taylor, S. (1986). *Modelling Financial Time Series.* Chichester: John Wiley & Sons.

Teugels, J. and Sundt, B. (eds) (2004). *Encyclopedia of Actuarial Science*. Chichester: John Wiley & Sons.

Tsay, R. (2010). *Analysis of Financial Time series*, 3rd edn. Hoboken, NJ: John Wiley & Sons.

Tuljapurkar, S., Li, N. and Boe, C. (2000). A universal pattern of decline in the G7 countries. *Nature*, **405**, 789–792.

Valdez, E., Piggott, J. and Wang, L. (2006). Demand and adverse selection in a pooled annuity fund. *Insurance: Mathematics and Economics*, **39**, 251–266.

Van der Hoeck, J. and Elliot, R. J. (2006). *Binomial Models in Finance*. New York: Springer-Verlag.

Vasiček, O. (1977). An equilibrium characterization of the term structure. *Journal of Financial Economics*, **5**, 177–188.

Venables, W. N. and Ripley, B. (2002). *Modern Applied Statistics with S-plus*, 4th edn. New York: Springer-Verlag.

Venables, W. N. and Smith, D. M. (2010). *An Introduction to R.* Version 2.11.1, at `http://www.r-project.org`.

Venter, C. G. (2003). Quantifying correlated reinsurance exposures with copulas. In Casualty Actuarial Society Forum, Spring, 215–229.

Vose, D. (2008). *Risk Analysis. A Quantitative Guide*, 3rd edn. Chichester: John Wiley & Sons.

Wand, M. P. and Jones, M. C. (1995). *Kernel Smoothing*. Boca Raton, FL: Chapman & Hall/CRC.

Wang, P. (2003). *Financial Econometrics: Methods and Models.* London: Routledge.

Wang, D. and Lu, P. (2005). Modelling and forecasting mortality distributions in england and wales using the Lee–Carter model. *Journal of Applied Statistics*, **32**, 873–885.

Wasserman, L. (2006). *All of Nonparametric Statistics.* New York: Springer-Verlag.

West, M. and Harrison, J. (1997). *Bayesian Forecasting and Dynamic Models*, 2nd edn. New York: Springer-Verlag.

Whelan, N. (2004). Sampling from Archimedean copulas. *Quantitative Finance*, **4**, 339–352.

White, H. (1982). Maximum likelihood estimation of misspecified models. *Econometrica*, **50**, 1–25.

Wilkie, A. D. (1995). More on a stochastic asset model for actuarial use (with discussion). *British Actuarial Journal*, **1**, 777–964.

Williams, C. A., Smith, M. L. and Young, P. C. (1998). *Risk Management and Insurance*, 8th edn. Boston MA: Irwin/McGraw-Hill.

Williams, R. J. (2006). *Introduction to the Mathematics of Finance*. Providence, RI: American Mathematical Society.

Wilmoth, J. R., Andreev, K., Jdanov, D. and Glei, D. A. (2007). Methods Protocol for the Human Mortality Database. Available at `http://www.mortality.org`.

Wilmott, P., Howison, S. and Dewynne, J. (1995). *The Mathematics of Financial Derivatives*. Cambridge: Cambridge University Press.

Wolfram, S. (2003). *The Mathematica Book*, 5th edn. Champaign, IL: Wolfram Media.

Wood, S. N. (2006). *Generalized Additive Models: An Introduction with R*. Boca Raton, FL: Chapman & Hall.

Wütrich, M. V. (2004). Extreme value theory and archimedean copulas. *Scandinavian Actuarial Journal*, 211–228.

Wütrich, M. V. and Merz, M. (2008). *Stochastic Claim Reserving Methods in Insurance*. Chichester: John Wiley & Sons.

Wütrich, M. V., Bühlmann, H. and Furrer, H. (2010). *Market-Consistent Actuarial Valuation*, 2nd edn. Berlin: Springer-Verlag.

Yau, K., Yip, K. and Yuen, H. K. (2003). Modelling repeated insurance claim frequency data using the generalized linear mixed model. *Journal of Applied Statistics*, **30**, 857–865.

Yeo, K. L. and Valdez, E. A. (2006). Claim dependence with common effects in credibility models. *Insurance: Mathematics and Economics*, **38**, 609–623.

Young, V. R. (2004). Premium principles. In Teugels, J, and Sundt, B. (eds), *Encyclopedia of Actuarial Science*, Chichester: John Wiley & Sons; pp. 1322–1331.

Zhang, L, Mykland, P. A. and Aït-Sahalia, Y. (2005). A tale of two time scales: Determining integrated volatility with noisy high-frequency data. *Journal of American Statistical Association*, **100**, 1394–1411.

Zhang, X., Zhou, M. and Guo, J. (2007). Optimal combination of quota-share and excess-of-loss reinurance policies in a dynamic setting: Research articles. *Applied Stochastic Models in Business and Industry*, **23**, 63–71.

Zivot, E. and Wang, J. (2003). *Modelling Financial Time Series with S-plus*. New York: Springer-Verlag.

Index